Economic Loss

Second edition

To my wife, Janice,

our children, Aaron and Zoë,

and to my father and my late mother

Economic Loss

Second edition

Robby Bernstein

B Com LLB BCL
Solicitor (England and Wales),
Barrister and Solicitor (Ontario)

Sweet & Maxwell

Published by
Sweet & Maxwell Limited of
100 Avenue Road
London NW3 3PF
Set by Servis Filmsetting Ltd, Manchester
Printed in Great Britain by MPG Books Ltd

A CIP catalogue record for this book
is available from the British Library

ISBN 0752 004247

No natural forests were destroyed to make this product,
only naturally farmed timber was used and re-planted

Contents

Foreword to the first edition

By The Right Honourable Lord Justice Steyn

The subject-matter of this book is the recovery of damages for economic loss in the tort of negligence. It is undoubtedly the most controversial area of our law of tort. That is underlined by the fact that in the last fifteen years the House of Lords has had occasion to consider such problems on at least twelve different occasions. A central feature of the problems confronting the courts has been the perceived difficulty of recovering damages for economic loss in tort actions in contractual situations. For the practising lawyer the potential overlap of contract and tort is a matter that will constantly give rise to difficult problems.

Some may have thought that the decision of the House of Lords in *Murphy v Brentwood District Council* [1991] AC 398 finally disposed of all the problems in this corner of the law. This decision will clearly exercise great influence on the development of our law. On the other hand, it does not spell the end of the capacity of our law to develop as the problems of the recovery of economic loss in tort are examined in new factual situations. The general observations of their Lordships in *Murphy v Brentwood District Council* will also no doubt be critically explained in the course of future experience.

The author states frankly that 'the sense of concern which I felt as a practising lawyer, on reading the speeches of the Law Lords in *Murphy v Brentwood District Council*' was the genesis of this book. In criticising this decision in strong terms the author is not alone. By and large academic comment on the decision has been hostile to the approach enunciated by their Lordships. The author proceeds to examine the subject in a careful and methodical way which will place all those who in future dabble in this field—be they academic lawyers, practising lawyers or judges—in his debt. The book contains an exhaustive examination of the relevant case law. Equally important is the fact that the substantive arguments, and countervailing policy considerations, are carefully considered in the different factual situations which arise.

There is already a substantial volume of academic literature on *Murphy v Brentwood District Council*. To a considerable extent such academic writing is contained in legal journals, not all of which are readily available to practitioners. This is the first full length book which deals comprehensively with the subject.

I recommend this book as an important aid to the examination of problems of recovery of economic loss in tort actions.

Johan Steyn
Norfolk
August 1993

Preface to the second edition

In 1932 in *Donoghue v Stevenson* [1932] AC 562, Lord Atkin said that he did not think that a more important problem had ever come before the House of Lords than the question in that case. He articulated the problem as being whether the manufacturer of an article of drink sold by the manufacturer to a distributor, in circumstances which prevent the distributor or the ultimate purchaser or consumer from discovering by inspection any defect, was under a legal duty to the ultimate purchaser or consumer to take reasonable care to ensure that the article was free from defect likely to cause injury to health. Lord Atkin said that the question was important both because of its bearing on public health and because of the 'practical test which it applies to the system under which it arises'.

The law has, of course, moved on since *Donoghue v Stevenson*, and there have been a number of notable milestones along the way, but the legal and practical problems which have arisen from the 'lifting of the lid' in *Donoghue* still abound.

In 1997 in *Reeman v The Department of Transport* (26 March 1997, unreported) Phillips LJ observed this continuing process when he said:

> The formulation of the circumstances in which a tortious duty arises to exercise reasonable care not to cause harm to another is currently a constant preoccupation of the courts both in this country and throughout the common law world. The difficulties that can be inherent in this task are reflected by the fact that we have been referred to no less than five decisions on the topic in the House of Lords in the last two years, in three of which there were dissenting opinions.

Not only has there been a profusion of important decisions since the first edition of this book was published in October 1993, but there has also been a distinct shift in the overall policy of the courts towards claims for pure economic loss. This new 'judicial mood' is exemplified by the way in which the majority (of 3:2) rejected the 'indeterminate class concern' which has usually been the inhibiting factor in economic loss cases, by saying (*per* Lord Goff):

> The ordinary case is one in which the intended beneficiaries are a small number of identified people. If by any chance a more complicated case should arise to test the precise boundaries of the principle in cases of this kind, that problem can await solution when such a case comes forward for decision.

Another example of this new 'openness' is the way in which in *Spring v Guardian Assurance Plc* [1995] 2 AC 296 their Lordships dismissed the argument that employers would be deterred from giving frank references if they knew that they could face liability, when they said (*per* Lord Lowry):

> I am inclined to view this possibility as a spectre conjured up by the defendants to frighten your Lordships into submission. I also believe that the courts in general and your Lordships' House in particular ought to think very carefully before resorting to public policy considerations which will defeat a claim that *ex hypothesi* is a perfectly good cause of action. It has been said that public policy should be invoked only in clear cases in which the potential harm to the public is incontestable, that whether the anticipated harm to the public will be likely to occur must be determined on tangible grounds instead of on mere generalities and that the burden of proof lies on those who assert that the court should not enforce a liability which *prima facie* exists. Even if one should put the matter in a more neutral way, I would say that public policy ought not to be invoked if the arguments are evenly balanced. In such a situation the ordinary rule of law, once established, should prevail.

Another interesting feature of *Spring v Guardian* is the way in which, in upholding the employee's tortious claim against his ex-employer resulting from the negligent reference supplied by the ex-employer to a prospective employer, the majority of 4:1 paid little heed to the warning sounded by Lord Templeman in *Downsview Nominees Ltd v First City Corporation Ltd* [1993] AC 316 'against the danger of extending the ambit of negligence so as to supplant or supplement other torts, contractual obligations, statutory duties or equitable rules in relation to every kind of damage including economic loss'. In similar circumstances the Court of Appeal of New Zealand in *Bell-Booth Group Ltd v Attorney-General* [1989] 3 NZLR 148 had dismissed an employee's claim because to uphold it would have undermined the established defence of qualified privilege in an action for defamation based on an inaccurate reference.

The statements in these cases and the approach they embody would have been unthinkable in the early part of this decade after the House of Lords' milestone decision in *Murphy v Brentwood District Council* [1991] 1 AC 398. In the category of cases with which *Murphy* was concerned (ie claims in tort by purchasers of houses against the builder and professional people involved in the design or construction of the houses for the diminution in value resulting from defects which were covered up in the course of construction and were not discoverable on a pre-purchase inspection), the restrictive approach taken by the House of Lords in *Murphy* still prevails in England. In this type of case English law is out of line with the position in identical cases in New Zealand, Australia and, to a certain extent, Canada. The evil which the House of Lords feels it necessary to guard against is the creation of a transmissable warranty of quality in tort. In this book it is observed that in *Linden Gardens v Lenesta Sludge Disposals Ltd* [1994] 1 AC 85 the House of Lords, by applying the principle in *The Albazero* [1977] AC 774, did in fact create a transmissable warranty of quality in a case of this type (and in relation to a commercial building, not just a house); and that, in the circumstances, there is an inconsistency in English law at the highest level which needs to be resolved.

Another notable change in the last four years has been the ascendancy of the concept of 'voluntary assumption of responsibility'. Previously it was treated as being just one of the possible components in the proximity analysis, and some of the Law Lords were openly dismissive of its utility as a 'helpful or realistic test for liability' (*per* Lord Griffiths in *Smith v Eric S Bush* [1990] 1 AC 831). Now, however, the concept is being treated as a principle in its own right and has become the preferred test for determining whether a duty of care should be imposed in a range of different circumstances. In this book, the comment is made that there is nothing fundamentally wrong with this approach because the concept of assumption of responsibility can be envisaged more vividly and might appear to have a more tangible feel than many of the other concepts that have been suggested. But it is pointed out that this is not the complete analysis because the court still has to be satisfied that in all of the circumstances it would be 'fair, just and reasonable' to impose a duty of care on the defendant of the scope contended for, in accordance with the approach articulated by the House of Lords in *Caparo Industries Plc v Dickman* [1990] 2 AC 605.

The comment is also made that caution should be exercised in applying Lord Goff's *dicta* in *Henderson v Merrett Syndicates Ltd* [1995] 2 AC 145, that:

> If a person assumes responsibility to another in respect of certain services, there is no reason why he should not be liable in damages to that other in respect of economic loss which flows from the negligent performance of those services.

and

> Once the case is identified as falling within the *Hedley Byrne* principle [which Lord Goff described earlier as being voluntary assumption of responsibility by the defendant coupled with reasonable reliance by the plaintiff], there should be no need to embark upon any further enquiry whether it is fair, just and reasonable to impose liability for economic loss.

It is pointed out that Lord Goff intended these *dicta* to be confined to a particular type of case, namely cases where the parties were already in a contractual relationship with each other or, if they were not, where the situation was almost equivalent to a contract on account of their direct dealings with each other because, in such situations, there is no concern about the indeterminacy of the class of potential plaintiffs. He did not mean that there should be a wholesale abandonment of the 'fair, just and reasonable' approach.

Another major development in the last four years has been the unequivocal acceptance by the House of Lords of the principle of concurrent liability in contract and tort. Indeed, the Court of Appeal has now taken the lead over other jurisdictions in holding that (in the absence of any term in the parties' contract which precludes or restricts the duty of care in tort) there is no doctrinal bar against a court holding that the defendant's duty of care in tort is more extensive than his concurrent duties in contract.

These issues (and more) are explored in this second edition of *Economic*

Loss. Both I and my publishers received very positive feedback on the first edition. I hope that practitioners and other readers (who really will constitute an indeterminate class) will find this second edition to be helpful and, dare I say it, enjoyable!

Robby Bernstein
London
10 February 1998

Addendum

In *Williams v Natural Life Health Foods Ltd* [1998] 1 WLR 830, the facts of which are set out in Chapter 10, para 10.2.1, the House of Lords (the panel of which included Lord Goff) overruled the decisions in this case of both the Court of Appeal and the trial judge. In agreeing with the dissenting judgment of Sir Patrick Russell in the Court of Appeal, Lord Steyn, delivering the House's unanimous judgment, said (at p 838):

> In the present case there were no personal dealings between Mr Mistlin and the plaintiffs. There were no exchanges or conduct crossing the line which could have conveyed to the plaintiffs that Mr Mistlin was willing to assume personal responsibility to them. Contrary to the submissions of counsel for the plaintiffs, I am also satisfied that there was not even evidence that the plaintiffs believed that Mr Mistlin was undertaking personal responsibility to them.

It is submitted that, on the facts, this is the correct conclusion in this case; as also is Lord Steyn's dismissal of the significance placed by Hirst LJ on the fact that the knowledge and experience of Mr Mistlin, which was trumpeted in the company's brochure, was derived by Mr Mistlin in his personal capacity when he owned and ran the first shop personally, and had nothing to do with his position as a director of the company. In this regard Lord Steyn said (at p 838):

> The point will simply not bear the weight put on it. Postulate a food expert who over ten years gains experience in advising customers on his own account. Then he incorporates his business as a company and he so advises his customers. Surely, it cannot be right to say that in the new situation his earlier experience on his own account is indicative of an assumption of personal responsibility towards his customers.

This decision has implications in a wider context. As Lord Steyn said (at p 835):

> ... [T]he issue in this case is not peculiar to companies. Whether the principal is a company or a natural person, someone acting on his behalf may incur personal liability in tort as well as imposing vicarious or attributed liability upon his principal. But in order to establish personal liability under the principle of *Hedley Byrne*, which requires the existence of a special relationship between plaintiff and tortfeasor, it is not sufficient that there should have been a special relationship with the principal. There must have been an assumption of responsibility so as to create a special relationship with the director or employee himself.

Lord Steyn referred to this assumption of responsibility as the "extended *Hedley Byrne* principle", which, he said, derives from Lord Goff's speech in *Henderson v Merrett Syndicates Ltd* [1995] 2 AC 145 (see Chapter 3, para 3.5.2). Thus, Lord Steyn said (at p 834):

> In this case the identification of the applicable principles is straightforward. It is clear, and accepted by counsel on both sides, that the governing principles are stated in the leading speech of Lord Goff of Chieveley in *Henderson v Merrett Syndicates Ltd* [1995] 2 AC 145. First, in *Henderson's* case it was settled that the assumption of responsibility principle enunciated in *Hedley Byrne & Co Ltd v Heller & Partners Ltd* [1964] AC 465 is not confined to statements but may apply to any assumption of responsibility for the provision of services. The extended *Hedley Byrne* principle is the rationalisation or technique adopted by English law to provide a remedy for the recovery of damages in respect of economic loss caused by the negligent performance of services. Secondly, it was established that once a case is identified as falling within the extended *Hedley Byrne* principle, there is no need to embark on any further inquiry whether it is 'fair, just and reasonable' to impose liability for economic loss: p 181. Thirdly, and applying *Hedley Byrne*, it was made clear that

> "reliance upon [the assumption of responsibility] by the other party will be necessary to establish a cause of action (because otherwise the negligence will have no causative effect) . . ." (p 180).

> Fourthly, it was held that the existence of a contractual duty of care between the parties does not preclude the concurrence of a tort duty in the same respect.

It is submitted that the second of the "governing principles" stated by Lord Steyn has been expressed too widely because in *Henderson* Lord Goff only meant to say that there is no need to embark on any further inquiry whether it is fair, just and reasonable to impose liability for economic loss in cases where there is no concern about the indeterminacy of the class of potential plaintiffs (see Chapter 3, para 3.2.1).

In discussing the practical application "the extended *Hedley Byrne* principle", Lord Steyn said that two matters require consideration. He said (at p 835) that, first, "there is the approach to be adopted as to what may in law amount to an assumption of risk." He then referred to the fact that in *Henderson* Lord Goff had said that "especially in a context concerned with a liability which may arise under a contract or in a situation 'equivalent to contract', it must be expected that an objective test will be applied when asking the question whether, in a particular case, responsibility should be held to have been assumed by the defendant to the plaintiff . . ."; and then he (Lord Steyn) continued (at p 835):

> The touchstone of liability is not the state of mind of the defendant. An objective test means that the primary focus must be on things said or done by the defendant or on his behalf in dealings with the plaintiff. Obviously, the impact of what a defendant says or does must be judged in the light of the relevant contextual scene. Subject to this qualification the primary focus must be on exchanges (in which term I include statements and conduct) which cross the line between the defendant and the plantiff. Sometimes such an issue arises in a simple bilateral relationship. In the present case a triangular position is under consideration: the prospective franchisees, the franchisor company, and the director. In such a case where the personal liability of the director is in question the internal arrangements between a director and his company cannot be the

foundation of a director's personal liability in tort. The inquiry must be whether the director, or anybody on his behalf, conveyed directly or indirectly to the prospective franchisees that the director assumed personal responsibility towards the prospective franchisees. An example of such a case being established is *Fairline Shipping Corporation v Adamson* [1975] QB 180 [see Chapter 10, para 10.2.1] . . . A case on the other side of the line is *Trevor Ivory Ltd v Anderson* [1992] 2 NZLR 517 [also see Chapter 10, para 10.2.1].

Secondly, Lord Steyn dealt with the aspect of reliance by the plantiff upon the assumption of personal responsibility by the defendant. Lord Steyn said (at p 936): "If reliance is not proved, it is not established that the assumption of personal responsibility had causative effect." In this context Lord Steyn referred to, and approved of, the distinction drawn by LaForest J in the Supreme Court of Canada in *London Drugs Ltd v Kuehne & Nagel International Ltd* (1992) 97 DLR (4th) 261 and in *Edgeworth Construction Ltd v ND Lea & Associates Ltd* (1993) 107 DLR (4th) 169 (see Chapter 10, para 10.2.1) between "mere reliance in fact and reasonable reliance on the employee's pocket-book." With reference to the *dicta* of La Forest J in these two Canadian cases, Lord Steyn said (at p 837):

> The test is not simply reliance in fact. The test is whether the plaintiff could *reasonably* rely on an assumption of personal responsibility by the individual who performed the services on behalf of the company. To that extent I regard what La Forest J said in *Edgeworth's* case [see Chapter 10, para 10.2.1] as consistent with English law.

Finally, Lord Steyn (at p 837) referred to the fact that "distinguished academic writers have criticised the principle of assumption of responsibility as often resting on a fiction used to justify a conclusion that a duty of care exists." In response, Lord Steyn said (at p 837):

> In my view, the general criticism is overstated. Coherence must sometimes yield to practical justice. In any event, the restricted conception of contract in English law, resulting from the combined effect of the principles of consideration and privity of contract, was the backcloth against which *Hedley Byrne* was decided and the principle developed in *Henderson's* case. In *The Pioneer Container* [1994] 2 AC 324, 335, Lord Goff of Chieveley (giving the judgment of the Privy Council in a Hong Kong appeal) said that it was open to question how long the principles of consideration and privity of contract will continue to be maintained. It may become necessary for the House of Lords to re-examine the principles of consideration and privity of contract. But while the present structure of English contract law remains intact the law of tort, as the general law, has to fulfil an essential gap-filling role. In these circumstances there was, and is, no better rationalisation for the relevant head of tort liability than assumption of responsibility. Returning to the particular question before the House it is important to make clear that a director of a contracting company may only be held liable where there was the necessary reliance. There is nothing fictional about this species of liability in tort.

It is submitted that these comments do not answer the criticisms which have been made of the formulation and the application of the concept of (voluntary) assumption of responsibility. This point is discussed further in Chapter 3, para 3.5.2.

Table of Cases

Star Village Tavern v Nield (1976) 71 DLR (3d) 439...17, 183
State of Louisiana, *ex rel* Guste v Motor Vessel *Testbank* (1985) 752 F (2d) 1019 (US CA
   5th Cir)..144, 189, 190, 200, 231
Stennett v Hancock & Peters [1939] 2 All ER 578; (1939) 83 SJ 379................................275
Stevens v Brodribb Sawmilling Co Pty Ltd (1986) 160 CLR 16; [1985–1986] 160 CLR
   16, High Ct. of Australia..50, 54, 55
Stieller v Porirua City Council [1986] 1 NZLR 84; (1987) 3 Const LJ 312 (NZ CA) 382
Storey v Charles Church Developements Ltd [1996] 12 Const LJ 206 ....308, 339–341
Stovin v Wise and Norfolk County Council [1996] AC 923, HL; [1994] 1 WLR 1124;
   [1994] 3 All ER 467; [1994] RTR 225, CA 54, 99, 105, 415, 417, 418, 421, 426,
                          429–431, 433, 436, 438, 461, 500, 532
Sucarseco, The, see Aktielselskabet Cuzo v *The Sucarseco*
Sumitomo Bank v Banque Bruxelles [1997] 1 Lloyd's Rep 487 ....124, 684, 791
Surrey Credit Union v Willson (1990) 73 DLR (4th) 207 698
Swinney v Chief Constable of the Northumbria Police Force [1997] QB 464 494
T (A Minor) v Surrey County Council [1994] 4 All ER 577; [1994] 2 FCR 1269; (1994)
   144 NLJ Rep 319...451
Tai Hing Cotton Mill Ltd v Liu Chong Hing Bank Ltd [1986] AC 80; [1986] 3 WLR 317;
   [1985] 2 All ER 947, PC..778, 779, 797, 800–804
Takaro Properties Ltd v Rowling *see* Rowling v Takaro Properties Ltd
Targett v Torfaen Borough Council [1992] 3 All ER 27; [1991] NLJR 1698, CA.......269–273,
                           350–352
Tate & Lyle Industries Ltd v Greater London Council [1983] 2 AC 509; [1983] 2 WLR
   649; [1983] 1 All ER 1159, HL 168, 290
Tee v Lautro Ltd (1996) (unreported)..449
Tesco Stores Ltd v The Norman Hitchcox Partnership (1997) (unreported)......313, 330, 334,
                          340, 791
Thake v Maurice [1986] QB 644; [1986] 2 WLR 337; [1986] 1 All ER 479, CA 683, 797
Thomas v Winchester (1852) 6 NY 397...250
Thompson (Miles Charles) v Clive Alexander and Partners (A Firm) (1992) CILL 753;
   (1992) 8 Const LJ 199; 59 BLR 77..336
Thorne v MacGregor (1973) 35 DLR (3d) 687..172
Three Rivers District Council v Bank of England (No 3) [1997] 3 All ER 558 448
Tidman v Reading Borough Council [1994] 3 PLR 72; [1994] EGCS 180; [1994] NPC
   136...120, 462, 681
Topp v London County Bus (South West) Ltd [1993] 3 All ER 448; [1993] 1 WLR 976;
   (1993) 137 SJ LB 59; [1993] RTR 279, CA...490
Trans World Airlines v Curtiss-Wright Corp (1955) 148 NYS (2d) 284 ....374, 406, 408
Transcontainer Express Ltd v Custodian Security Ltd [1988] 1 Lloyd's Rep 128; [1988]
   1 FTLR 54, CA..173, 174
Trevor Ivory v Anderson [1992] 2 NZLR 517 ....729, 737
Trusted v Clifford Chance (1996) (unreported)..657, 772
Trustee of the Property of PAF Foster v Crusts [1986] BCLC 307 558
Twomax v Dickson McFarlane & Robinson 1983 SLT 98 558
Ultramares Corporation v Touche Niven & Company (1931) 255 NY 170....13, 28, 200, 362,
            544–546, 557, 617, 638, 705, 714
Union Oil Co v Oppen (1974) 501 F(2d) 588...27, 188, 231
University of Regina v Pettick (1991) 6 CCLT (2d) 1; (1991) 77 DLR (4th) 615 302–304,
                316, 317, 365, 534
Van Oppen v Clerk to the Bedford Charity Trustees [1990] 1 WLR 234; [1989] 3 All ER
   389; (1989) 139 NLJ 900, CA..109, 506, 508
Verderame v Commercial Union Assurance Co plc and Another [1992] BCLC 793, CA....667
Voli v Inglewood Shire Council and Lockwood (1963) 56 QLR 256; (1963) 110 CLR
   74 ....651, 764, 769, 770
W and Others v Essex County Council (1997) *The Times*, 16 July.....................................459
W v The Home Office (1997) (unreported) 472
Weir v National Westminster Bank plc [7 August 1992, Court of Session, Outer House]....506
Weller & Co v Foot and Mouth Disease Research Institute [1966] 1 QB 569; [1965] 3 All
   ER 560; [1965] 3 WLR 1082; (1965) 109 SJ 702; [1965] 2 Lloyd's Rep 414.....14, 17, 23, 28,
                150, 202, 230

Table of Statutes

Table of Statutory Instruments

Chapter 1

Introduction

It is one thing to owe a duty of care to avoid causing injury to the person or property of others. It is quite another to cause others to suffer purely economic loss.
(Lord Bridge in *Caparo Industries plc v Dickman* [1990] 2 AC 605)

The infliction of physical injury to the person or property of another universally requires to be justified. The causing of economic loss does not. **(Lord Oliver in *Murphy v Brentwood District Council* [1991] 1 AC 398)**

Anglo-Australian law has never accepted the proposition that a person owes a duty of care to another person merely because the first person knows that his careless act may cause economic loss to the latter person. Social and commercial life would be very different if it did. Indeed, leaving aside the intentional tort cases, a person will generally owe no duty to prevent economic loss to another person even though the first person intends to cause economic loss to another person. **(McHugh J, dissenting, in *Hill v Van Erp* (1997) 142 ALR 687)**

1.1 Context and scope

This book deals with various situations in which one person's negligent conduct causes another person to suffer an injury which is not to his person or his property. This is called economic loss. In the case where the parties were involved in a contractual relationship with each other, such economic loss is, and always has been, recoverable. However, where this 'relationship' is non-contractual, then, in general, the law says that the defendant does not owe the plaintiff a duty of care in respect of the economic loss which his negligent conduct has caused the plaintiff to suffer. The book examines the legal rules which the courts have developed in relation to the various categories of cases in which questions of economic loss have arisen in the tort of negligence. It also offers an analysis of the social, economic and practical policy considerations which underlie these rules, and contains commentary and suggestions for change.

As will be seen in the pages that follow, there is a principle in English law to the effect that pure economic loss in the tort of negligence is generally not recoverable unless that loss was consequential upon physical injury to the plaintiff or damage to the plaintiff's property, or resulted from the plaintiff having relied upon a negligent misstatement, advice or service made or provided by the defendant. In practice, this can only be regarded as a very restricted basis for allowing such recovery. In other areas of the law of tort, such as defamation and passing off, there is no problem about awarding damages for pure economic loss; and, of course, damages for infringement of copyright or breach of trust are effectively damages for pure economic loss, as are damages for breach of contract.

By way of further contrast, and perhaps more importantly for the purposes of this book, the courts' restrictive attitude towards compensating pure economic loss in the tort of negligence does not extend to physical injury to the plaintiff or damage to his property, albeit that the circumstances in which such injury or damage arose might have been identical to those in which the plaintiff's pure economic loss arose.

1.2   Definition of economic loss

1.2.1   General

Most people would think that a good definition of pure economic loss is financial loss other than payment of money to compensate for physical injury to person or physical damage to property. The example which readily springs to mind is loss of profit in a business. In fact, however, in the tort of negligence, the courts have refined the definition of economic loss in ways which do not always accord with common perceptions.

1.2.2   Different types of pure economic loss

Directly inflicted pure economic loss

In this type of situation the whole of the plaintiff's loss is purely financial, and no questions arise at all as to any physical injury of the plaintiff, or any other person, or as to damage to any property belonging to the plaintiff or to any other person. This type of loss could arise in two distinct categories of cases. The first is where the plaintiff's loss is purely accidental. A typical example would be where the defendant has negligently cut off the electricity supply to the plaintiff's factory, thereby causing the plaintiff to suffer pure economic loss during the period that the electricity is cut off. This type of claim is considered in Chapter 4, para 4.4, where it is noted that, in general, the law does not afford recovery to such a plaintiff for this type of pure economic loss.

Secondly, this type of loss could arise where, for example, the plaintiff has relied on a deficient reference given by a bank about the creditworthiness of one of its customers to whom the plaintiff then extended credit in reliance on that reference. This type of claim is considered in Chapter 9, para 9.7, where it is noted that recovery of this type of loss will be possible if the defendant ought to have realised that his statement would most probably have been relied upon by the plaintiff for the very purpose for which the statement had been made.

Consequential economic loss

This type of economic loss arises where the plaintiff's property has been damaged and he has suffered economic loss in consequence. Here, a distinction is drawn between the plaintiff's direct, or immediate economic losses, consequent upon the physical damage to his property, and his indirect, or non-immediate losses. An example would be where the defendant negligently cuts off the power supply to the plaintiff's factory, thereby causing physical damage to the plaintiff's machinery which was then in use, as well as economic loss (consisting of loss of profits) to the plaintiff on the actual contracts which were then being processed through the plaintiff's machinery, as well as loss of profit on other contracts which the plaintiff would have fulfilled during the period that the power supply was cut off. Here, only the second type of economic loss suffered by the plaintiff (ie loss of profit on other contracts) is regarded as pure economic loss. As was held by the Court of Appeal in *Spartan Steel & Alloys Ltd v Martin & Co (Contractors) Ltd* [1973] QB 27, which is considered in Chapter 4, para 4.3, that loss is irrecoverable, whereas the plaintiff's other economic loss (ie loss of profits from the actual contracts which were being processed when the electricity was cut off) is fully recoverable.

Relational economic loss

This type of economic loss arises where the defendant injures a third party or damages the property of a third party and the plaintiff suffers economic loss in consequence. A typical example would be where the defendant damages a third party's bridge over a river, which the plaintiff has been using to transport goods to his customers, which he can now only do at greater expense as a result of the bridge's closure. Here, all of the plaintiff's losses are regarded as being purely economic. This type of claim is discussed in Chapter 5, para 5.3.2, where it is noted that, in English law, there is a strict exclusionary rule against the recovery of such losses.

Diminished value of defective product or building

Where the plaintiff has acquired a defective chattel or a defective building, any damage to such chattel or building resulting from a defect in it is regarded as pure economic loss vis-à-vis the person who was tortiously responsible for causing that defect. A good example would be where the walls of the plaintiff's house developed bad cracks as a result of inadequate foundations due to inadequate design on the part of the architect and/or the structural engineer, or due to bad workmanship on the part of the builder. If the plaintiff did not have a direct contractual relationship with any of these parties, for example because he was not the original owner for whom the house was constructed, then he would have to sue the architect, engineer or builder in tort to recover damages for this loss. In such an action, this would be regarded as pure economic loss, as would an action by the plaintiff against the local authority if it had negligently passed the inadequate foundations. These claims are considered respectively in Chapters 7 and 8, paras 7.3 and 8.2, where it is noted that there is a general rule of exclusion against awarding recovery for this type of loss.

By way of further example, the exact same legal position as described above (ie the application of the general exclusionary rule) would pertain if the plaintiff's television set were to explode and destroy itself due to a defect in its manufacture, in circumstances where the plaintiff did not have a direct relationship with the manufacturer, because he had purchased the set from a retailer. If the plaintiff were to sue the manufacturer for his loss, he would have to do so in tort, for which purpose this loss would be classified as being purely economic; and, as mentioned *above*, it would not, in general, be recoverable.

In practice, in situations where the defendant's negligent conduct has rendered a building or a chattel less valuable, it is not always easy to determine whether the damage should be categorised as pure economic loss in accordance with the above-mentioned approach, or whether it should be treated as physical damage. In view of the general exclusionary rule that exists in English law in cases of this type, the answer to the question (ie economic loss or physical damage) could be critical to the success of the plaintiff's claim. Some recent cases that have considered this issue are mentioned in Chapter 7, para 7.1.4.

Although judges invented the term 'economic loss' to describe the damage sustained by a defectively constructed building or a defectively manufactured article where the plaintiff and the defendant did not have a contractual relationship with each other, some judges have doubted whether this terminology is in fact apt. For example, Lord Lloyd, in *Invercargill City Council v Hamlin* [1996] AC 624 (speaking for the full panel of the Privy Council in that case) after noting certain New Zealand decisions in this category of cases, said (at p 636):

> Whether it is right to describe such cases as instances of 'pure' economic loss may not matter very much. They do not depend on pure economic loss in the sense of *White v Jones* [1995] 2 AC 207 [see Chapter 9, para 9.7.5] or *Henderson v Merrett Syndicates Ltd* [1995] 2 AC 145 [see para 9.7.6]; for in the building cases, the economic loss is suffered by reason of a defect in a physical object.

Another example is the following statement from the main majority judgment in the High Court of Australia in *Bryan v Maloney* (1995) 69 ALJR 375, which is considered fully in Chapter 7, para 7.6.4. After noting that the significance of the distinction between a relationship of proximity with respect to physical injury differs from such a relationship with respect to pure economic loss 'according to the particular kind of economic loss which is involved in the relevant category of case' (see para 1.3.3, *below*), Mason CJ said (at p 380):

> Here, the distinction is between ordinary physical damage to a house by some external cause and mere economic loss in the form of diminution in value of a house when the inadequacy of its footings first becomes manifest by consequent damage to its fabric. Obviously, that distinction is an essentially technical one. Indeed, it is arguably inapplicable in circumstances where a latent defect in the work of one builder or contractor causes damage to a part of the building constructed by a different builder or contractor.

Thus, the term 'economic loss' is probably a bit of a misnomer in this type of case. However, it continues to be used in the cases, and it is used in this book to describe tortious loss claims for defects caused by the negligence of a builder or a manufacturer in the actual building or article that the defendant constructed or manufactured.

Loss inflicted by a third party

Sometimes the plaintiff's loss can be inflicted by one party, but the plaintiff will seek instead to make another party (the defendant) liable to compensate him. An example would be where the plaintiff has suffered economic loss through having relied upon a misrepresentation made to him by a third party in circumstances where the defendant knew that the third party was acting fraudulently towards the plaintiff, but did nothing to warn the plaintiff about this. This type of claim is considered in Chapter 8, para 8.3, where it will be noted that, in general, recovery of this type of loss is not permitted. This sort of case does not really involve a different type of pure economic loss, but is mentioned here for the sake of completeness. In fact, it could involve any of the four types of pure economic loss defined *above*.

1.3 The categorisation approach

1.3.1 General

The justification for affording different treatment for claims of physical injury and claims for pure economic loss is said to be based on various grounds of policy, such as the need to guard against the imposition of 'indeterminate' liability on the defendant, which is more apt to occur in cases of pure economic loss than in cases of physical injury. However, it is important to realise that it is not simply the fact that the plaintiff's injury is purely economic that creates this difference, but, rather, the circumstances in which that loss arose. In Chapters 4, 5, 7, 8 and 9 the division of similar types of cases into different categories has been made on this basis. This has not been done simply for the convenience of discussing similar cases together. Rather, it has been done for the purpose of highlighting the fact that different policy considerations apply to different categories of cases. Many generalised statements have been made by judges as to the rationale for treating economic loss differently from physical injury (see para 1.4.3). However, unless such comments are related specifically to cases within a particular category, they can be misleading.

In the sub-sections which now follow, the various categories considered in the above-mentioned chapters are briefly described. It will be noted that these categories largely correlate with the definitions of the different types of pure economic loss mentioned above. In the broadest terms, the division of cases made in this book is between those where the defendant's conduct was wholly accidental, and those where the defendant negligently created something which previously did not exist. In the 'accidental sphere' a distinction is drawn between cases of direct infliction of pure economic loss and indirect infliction of it. In the 'indirect infliction sphere' a distinction is drawn between economic loss consequent upon damage to the plaintiff's own property or consequent upon damage to a third party's property. In the 'negligent creation sphere' a distinction is drawn between cases where the defendant has negligently created a defective tangible item, and those where he has made a statement or has provided a service.

1.3.2   The actual categories

Accidental direct economic loss

This type of case involves pure economic loss suffered by the plaintiff in circumstances where the defendant's negligent act or omission did not consist of a statement or the provision of a service and did not injure any person or damage any person's property. An example would be where the defendant negligently cut off the electricity supply to the plaintiff's factory. This type of claim is considered in Chapter 4, para 4.4, where it will be noted that, in general, pure economic loss suffered by a plaintiff in this type of situation is not recoverable.

Consequential economic loss

Here, the plaintiff's economic loss will have arisen as a result of the defendant's accidental negligent act or omission which caused direct physical injury to the plaintiff or direct physical damage to the plaintiff's property. An example would be where the defendant accidentally cut off the supply of electricity to the plaintiff's factory thereby damaging the plaintiff's machinery, and the plaintiff suffered a loss of profits in consequence. This type of claim is also considered in Chapter 4, para 4.3, where it is noted that the plaintiff will only be able to recover his consequential economic losses in this type of situation if, and to the extent that, they are 'truly consequential' upon physical damage to his property.

Relational economic loss

Here, the plaintiff's pure economic loss will have been caused by the defendant's negligent act or omission having injured a third person or damaged a third person's property, thereby preventing the plaintiff from obtaining an economic benefit which he would otherwise have obtained from that third party or from the use of that third party's property. An example would be where the defendant negligently damaged a third party's bridge over a river, thereby rendering it more expensive for the plaintiff to transport his goods from one point to another. This type of claim is considered in Chapter 5, para 5.3.2, where it will be noted that there is a strict rule of exclusion in English law against affording recovery to a plaintiff in these circumstances.

Diminished value of a defective product or building

Here, the plaintiff will have suffered pure economic loss as a result of being the owner of a defective product or building in circumstances where the plaintiff did not have a direct contractual relationship with the defendant, who was the party responsible for the negligent manufacture, construction, design or certification of the defective product or building. An example would be where the plaintiff was the second purchaser of a house which, during the limitation period, exhibited signs of cracking due to the foundations being inadequately constructed or designed. The plaintiff's loss, consisting of the diminution in value of the house, is classified as pure economic loss. This type of claim is considered in Chapter 7, para 8.2 and, to a certain extent, in Chapter 8 (see para 7.3—so far as concerns the negligent acts or omissions of statutory authorities), where it is noted that, in general, recovery of the plaintiff's loss in this type of situation is denied.

Nonfeasance

Here, the plaintiff's loss will have arisen through the failure of the defendant to have acted in circumstances where the defendant owed the plaintiff a duty of care to safeguard the plaintiff's economic interest. This type of claim is considered in Chapter 8, paras 8.2 and 8.3, and embraces two types of situation. First, it includes cases where the plaintiff suffered pure economic loss in consequence of someone failing to perform properly a statutory duty which existed for the protection of the plaintiff, either as a member of a determinable class, or as a member of the public generally. An example would be where a local authority failed to repair the wall of a dam, thereby facilitating the flooding of the plaintiff's farming land and his consequent loss of profits. Secondly, this category embraces pure economic loss suffered by the plaintiff which was caused by a third party for whom the defendant was not vicariously responsible. An example would be where the defendant knew that a third party was acting fraudulently towards the plaintiff, but failed to warn the plaintiff about this.

Negligent misstatements and services

Here, the plaintiff's pure economic loss will have arisen through the plaintiff having been adversely affected by a statement which the defendant made negligently or a service which the defendant provided negligently. These claims are considered in Chapter 9, where it is noted that, in general, the plaintiff's loss will have resulted through his having relied upon the defendant not to provide inaccurate information or to be negligent in the provision of the service in question, and the defendant will be held liable if, in the circumstances, he ought to have foreseen that the plaintiff, or a member of the same class as the plaintiff, would have relied on his skill and judgment for the purpose for which the statement was made or the service was rendered. However, there are also some circumstances where liability will be imposed, even though there was no reliance by the plaintiff on the defendant. The most important of this type of case is those concerned with solicitors who make mistakes relating to the drafting of wills for their clients (see Chapter 9, para 9.7.5).

1.3.3 Recognition by judges

General

Occasionally some judges have made general comments in some of the cases considered in this book which show that they accept the method of categorisation of cases adopted above, and the reason for it. These *dicta* must be distinguished from *dicta* in which judges have embraced the 'incremental approach' expounded by Brennan J in the High Court of Australia in *The Council of the Shire of Sutherland v Heyman* (1985) 157 CLR towards the development of new categories of negligence (see Chapter 3, para 3.4.4).

Dicta in cases

The following *dicta*, albeit isolated, demonstrate the understanding of some of the judges towards the categorisation approach described above.

Caltex Oil (Australia) Pty Ltd v The Dredge Willemstad (1976) 136 CLR 529: Stephen J said (at p 575): "It is the articulation, in the different categories of cases, of circumstances which denote sufficient proximity with respect to mere economic loss, including policy considerations, which will gradually provide a body of precedent productive of the necessary certainty".

Jaensch v Coffey (1985) 155 CLR 549: Brennan J said (at p 575): "It is erroneous to treat all cases of negligence causing economic loss as a subspecies of a general tort of negligence, the elements of which are common to all torts involving negligence. The elements of the several categories of negligence are not identical. What will suffice to establish a duty of care in one category of negligence is not necessarily enough in another. Lord Atkin's general conception of relations giving rise to a duty of care [in *Donoghue v Stevenson* [1932] AC 562], the neighbour principle, cannot be taken as a universal statement of the criterion of duties of care in the several categories of negligence where different kinds of damage are in issue. In *Anns v Merton London Borough Council* [1978] AC 728, Lord Wilberforce's approach 'in two stages' to the establishment of a duty of care [see Chapter 3, para 3.2.2] takes, as its first stage, Lord Atkin's general conception. The second stage takes those further elements which are appropriate to the particular category of negligence".

In this same case, Deane J said (at p 585): "The requirement of a 'relationship of proximity' [see para 2.3, *below*] is a touchstone and a control of the categories of case in which the common law will admit the existence of a duty of care". He repeated this remark in *Sutherland* and added (at p 498): "Both the identity and the relative importance of the factors which are determinative of an issue of proximity are likely to vary in different categories of case".

Leigh and Sillivan Ltd v Aliakmon Ltd [1985] 1 QB 350: In the Court of Appeal Oliver LJ said (at p 377): "The circumstances in which foreseeable 'economic damage' may be suffered are so various that it ought not, perhaps, necessarily to be assumed that there is, or could be, any common principle uniting them. What is, however, possible is to identify five broad categories of case and to discern, even if it is not always possible to justify logically, the policy that the law has adopted in relation to each". He then proceeded to describe five different categories of case in terms similar to those defined *above*. As Lord Oliver, he returned to this theme in *Caparo Industries plc v Dickman* [1990] 2 AC 605 when, after saying that, in his view, it is impossible to express a general principle of liability which will cover all cases, he said (at p 635): "Perhaps, therefore, the most that can be attempted is a broad categorisation of the decided cases according to the type of situation in which liability has been established in the past in order to found an argument by analogy". Lord Bridge expressed a similar sentiment when he said (at p 618): "Whilst recognising the importance of the underlying general principles common to the whole field of negligence, I think the law has now moved in the direction of attaching greater significance to the more traditional categorisation of distinct and recognisable situations as guides to the existence, scope and limits of the varied duties of care which the law imposes".

Reid v Rush & Tompkins plc [1990] 1 WLR 212: Ralph Gibson LJ recognised the fact that different considerations can operate in different categories of case when he said (at p 225): "I take Lord Oliver's statement [in *D & F Estates Ltd v Church Commissioners for England* [1989] AC 177] that damages for pure economic loss cannot be recovered unless the case can be brought within the principle of reliance established via the *Hedley Byrne* case [see Chapter 7, para 7.5.2] to apply only to the sort of case under consideration in *D & F*".

Canadian National Railway Co v Norsk Pacific Steamship Co (1992) 91 DLR (4th) 289: La Forest J, writing for the minority judges, recognised the existence of five different categories of economic loss cases similar to the categories set out *above*, and observed that different policy considerations arise in each category. He said (at p 300): "The present case fits into the category of relational economic loss [see further, Chapter 5]. In my view, both policy and precedent justify narrowing the focus in the present to cases of the kind described in that category".

Bryan v Maloney (1995) 69 ALJR 375: Mason CJ, delivering the main majority judgment (for himself, Deane and Gaudron JJ) said (at p 377): "The field of liability for mere economic loss is a comparatively new and developing area of the law of negligence. In that area, the question whether the requisite relationship of proximity exists in a particular category of case is more likely to be unresolved by previous binding authority, with the consequence that the notion of proximity is of vital importance"; and at p 380: "While the relationship between Mr. Bryan [the defendant—see Chapter 7, para 7.6.4] and Mrs. Manion [the original owner] with respect to physical injury to Mrs. Manion's person or property must be distinguished from the relationship between them with respect to mere economic loss, the significance of such a distinction varies according to the particular kind of economic loss which is involved in the relevant category of case. Thus, there is no basis for thinking that recognition of a relationship of proximity between the builder and the first owner with respect to that particular kind of economic loss would give rise to the type of liability 'in an indeterminate amount for an indeterminate time to an indeterminate class' which the Courts are reluctant to recognise".

Winnipeg Condominium Corporation No 36 v Bird Construction Co (1995) 121 DLR (4th) 193: La Forest J, writing for the unanimous bench of the Supreme Court of Canada, said (at p 199): "I stressed in *Norsk* that the question of recoverability for economic loss must be approached with reference to the unique and distinct policy issues raised in each of these categories [ie the five categories referred to above]. That is because ultimately the issues concerning recovery for economic loss are concerned with determining the proper ambit of the law of tort, an exercise that must take account of the various situations where that question may arise. This case raises issues different from that in *Norsk*, which fell within the fifth category [relational economic loss]. The present case, which involves the negligent construction of a building, falls partially within the fourth category [which La Forest J referred to as "negligent supply of shoddy goods or structures", and which is referred to in this book as "diminution in value of a defective product or building"]".

1.4   Rationale for different treatment

1.4.1   Introduction

In *Murphy v Brentwood District Council* [1991] 1 AC 398 Lord Oliver said (at p 487): "The infliction of physical injury to the person or property of another universally requires to be justified. The causing of economic loss does not". What this means in practice is that, if a defendant negligently causes physical injury to the plaintiff or damage to his property, the law will hold the defendant to be *prima facie* accountable to the plaintiff for his losses; whereas if the defendant's negligent act causes only pure economic loss to the plaintiff, no such presumption of liability will arise. Lord Oliver made it clear that this is also what he had in mind, when he continued with the words quoted above by saying: "If it [the infliction of loss by the defendant on the plaintiff] is to be categorised as wrongful, it is necessary to find some factor beyond the mere occurrence of the loss and the fact that its occurrence could be foreseen. The categorisation of damage as economic serves at least the useful purpose of indicating that something more is required". He made this point again (but slightly differently) when he said (at p 486): "I doubt whether, in searching for such limits [ie the limits which the law needs to place on reasonable foreseeability of loss], the categorisation of the damage as 'physical' or 'economic' provides a particularly useful contribution. Where it does, I think, serve a useful purpose is in identifying those cases in which it is necessary to search for and find something more than the mere reasonable foreseeability of damage which has occurred as providing the degree of 'proximity' necessary to support the action".

Whilst these *dicta* clearly demonstrate that, where the plaintiff's loss is purely economic, a different level of enquiry, or legal analysis, needs to be conducted before a duty of care can be imposed on the defendant, they do not explain why this should be so. The answer will, hopefully, be provided in the *dicta* from other cases considered below.

1.4.2 Historical accident

The first enunciation of any justification for an exclusionary rule occurred in the sphere of relational economic loss, which is discussed in Chapter 5. In *Cattle v Stockton Waterworks Co* (1875) LR 10 QB 453 Blackburn J expressed the rationale for this rule when he said (at p 458): "It may be said that it is just that all such persons [ie people who suffer a loss in consequence of a third party's property being damaged] should have compensation for such a loss, and that, if the law does not give them redress, it is imperfect. Perhaps it may be so. But courts of justice should not allow themselves, in the pursuit of perfectly complete remedies for all wrongful acts, to transgress the bounds which our law, in a wise consciousness of its limited powers, has imposed on itself, of redressing only the approximate and direct consequences of wrongful acts".

Two years later, in *Simpson & Co v Thompson* (1877) 3 App Cas 279 Lord Penzance endorsed this reasoning when he said (at p 290): "Such instances [ie claims by different people who have suffered a loss in consequence of a third party's property being damaged] might be indefinitely multiplied, giving rise to rights of action which in modern communities, where every complexity of mutual relation is daily created by contract, might be both numerous and novel".

Referring to these two cases, Lord Fraser, in *Candlewood Navigation Corporation Ltd v Mitsui OSK Lines Ltd* [1986] AC 1 said (at p 17): "These two cases show, in their Lordships' opinion, that the justification for denying a right of action to a person who has suffered economic damage through injury to the property of another is that, for reasons of practical policy, it is considered to be inexpedient to admit his claim. The rule is a pragmatic one, dictated by necessity".

Whilst all of the above-quoted remarks are unexceptionable, it must be recognised that when the exclusionary rule was formulated in the early cases, it had nothing to do with the fact that the plaintiff's loss was economic. Rather, it was based on the pure impracticality of countenancing a potential multitude of diverse, and sometimes doubtful claims from a wide range of plaintiffs who might claim to have been adversely affected in consequence of the defendant having damaged a third party's property. In the Court of Appeal in *Leigh and Sillivan Ltd v The Aliakmon Shipping Co Ltd* [1985] 1 QB 350 Oliver LJ recognised this point when he said (at p 375): "The premise appears to be that the reason why, in the older authorities, the plaintiff failed to recover damages was that the damage that he suffered was 'economic'. Speaking for myself, I have not felt able to accept that premise, for as I read those cases it was not the 'economic quality' of the damage which prevented recovery, but the reason why that damage had occurred".

Unfortunately, not all of the judges who have been concerned with economic loss claims have absorbed this point. Consequently, the existence of the relational economic loss exclusionary rule has come to be considered by many judges as the justification for saying that economic loss claims should be excluded in all categories of cases. An example of this occurring is the following quote from Lord Bridge in *Caparo Industries plc v Dickman* [1990] 2 AC 605. He said (at p 618):

> One of the most important distinctions always to be observed lies in the law's essentially different approach to the different kinds of damage which one party may have suffered in consequence of the acts or omissions of another. It is one thing to owe a duty of care to avoid causing injury to the person or property of others. It is quite another to cause others to suffer purely economic loss. A graphic illustration of the distinction is embodied in the proposition which derives from *Cattle v Stockton Waterworks Co* [see Chapter 5] that, in the case of a wrong done to a chattel, the common law does not recognise a person whose only rights are a contractual right to have the use or services of that chattel for the purpose of making profits without possession of, or property in the chattel. Such a person cannot claim for injury done to his contractual right.

Lord Bridge then referred to some of the other leading relational economic loss cases and then, by way of further support of this view that economic loss cases are 'essentially different' from cases of physical damage, he cited the *dictum* of Lord Fraser in *Candlewood* (at p 25) that: "Their Lordships consider that some limit or control mechanism has to be imposed upon the liability of a wrongdoer towards those who have suffered economic damage in consequence of his negligence".

This approach fails totally to recognise that the cases which are being relied upon in support of the claimed distinction were cases of relational economic loss, where the reason for excluding the plaintiff's claim was not merely that his loss was economic, but, rather, that it was relational. The rationale behind those cases does not therefore mean that it is right to exclude, or even to treat differently, economic loss claims in all other categories of case.

1.4.3 Specific remarks

General

From time to time one finds judges in cases making comments as to the reason for affording different treatment to economic loss claims for physical injury or damage to property. Some of these *dicta* are set out below. Many of these comments were made in the context of relational economic loss cases, where the need for 'some limit or control mechanism' (see para 1.4.2, *above*) on the multitude of indeterminate and sometimes spurious claims of potential plaintiffs is particularly acute. It will also be noted that none of these comments have been made in the context of economic loss claims consisting of the diminution in value of a defectively manufactured product or building. These claims are considered in Chapter 7, para 7.3, where it is pointed out that the type of concerns just mentioned, which arise in relational economic loss cases, simply do not exist. This is part of the reason for the criticism in Chapter 7, para 7.5 of the exclusionary rule which the courts have developed in product liability cases.

Dicta in cases

The following quotations from judges in a variety of cases will provide a fair cross-section of the reasons which have motivated the courts in a variety of situations to apply a different approach where the plaintiff's loss is purely economic.

Ultramares Corporation v Touche Niven & Company (1931) 255 NY 170: One of the most influential and most often quoted reasons for treating economic loss differently from physical injury is Cardozo J's statement that, if a duty of care for negligence existed in that type of case (ie negligent misstatement by an auditor in the certification of a company's accounts—see Chapter 9, para 9.7.2) then ". . . the defendant would be exposed to a liability in an indeterminate amount for an indeterminate time to an indeterminate class". Although the plaintiff's loss in that case was, of necessity, pure economic loss, it seems that Cardozo J made this comment more in the context of not wishing to impose a liability on the accountants which might be disproportionate to the degree of their negligent conduct, rather than being based on any dangers inherent in the fact that the plaintiff's loss was economic. This can be seen by citing in full the passage from which Cardozo J's celebrated words have been taken. He said: "If liability for negligence exists, a thoughtless slip or blunder, the failure to detect a theft or forgery beneath the cover of deceptive entries, may expose accountants to a liability in an indeterminate amount for an indeterminate time to an indeterminate class. The hazards of a business conducted on these terms are so extreme as to enkindle doubt where a flaw may not exist in the implication of a duty that exposes to these consequences".

Hedley Byrne & Co Ltd v Heller & Partners Ltd [1964] AC 465: Lord Pearce said (at p 536): "How wide the sphere of the duty of care in negligence is to be laid depends ultimately on the courts' assessment of the demands of society for protection from the carelessness of others. Economic protection has lagged behind the protection in physical matters where there is injury to person and property. It may be that the size and the width of the range of possible claims has acted as a deterrent to extension of economic protection". He then proceeded to quote Cardozo J's *dictum* in *Ultramares*. However, Lord Pearce (and all of the other members of the House of Lords) nevertheless upheld the plaintiff's claim in theory (see Chapter 9), albeit that it was a claim for pure economic loss and was in the same category (negligent misstatement) as *Ultramares*. They did this by enunciating and applying certain necessary rules which serve to limit the potentially indeterminate liability to which the defendant in this category of case might otherwise be exposed if foreseeability of loss were the only criterion of liability.

In some cases, particularly those concerned with relational economic loss, it has been argued that the House of Lords' approval of the recovery of pure economic loss in this case meant that the relational economic loss exclusionary rule could be relaxed. An example of this is *Konstantinides v World Tankers Corporation (The World Harmony)* [1967] P 341, which is summarised in para 5.8.1 of the cases at the end of Chapter 5. Hewson J rejected this argument, saying (at p 362): "The facts [of *Hedley Byrne*] are so entirely different from the present case, and the line of cases to which I have been referred in this action [ie the relational economic loss cases] was not quoted in the House of Lords in the *Hedley Byrne* case, that I would hesitate long before I would apply anything that was said by the Lordships in that case to this one".

Weller & Co v Foot and Mouth Disease Research Institute [1966] 1 QB 569: This was a relational economic loss case where the submission was made that "the plaintiff's ultimate success in the House of Lords in *Hedley Byrne* has swept away any notion that direct injury to the person or property of the plaintiff is necessary to support an action in negligence, and that the door is now open for the plaintiffs in the present action to recover the indirect or consequential loss which they have suffered". In rejecting this submission Widgery J said (at p 585):

> I think it is important to remember that in the cases to which I have referred, the act or omission relied upon as constituting a breach of the duty to take care was an act or omission which might foreseeably have caused direct injury to the person or property of another. The world of commerce would come to a halt and ordinary life would become intolerable if the law imposed a duty on all persons at all times to refrain from any conduct which might foreseeably cause detriment to another; but where an absence of reasonable care may foreseeably cause direct injury to the person or property of another, a duty to take such care exists.

This quote is often invoked as a justification for treating economic loss differently from physical injury. However, it seems that Widgery J was, in fact, doing no more than distinguishing between cases where the plaintiff himself was injured, or his property was damaged, and cases where the plaintiff's loss arose through a third party being injured or a third party's property being damaged. Ultimately, he seems to have decided the case on the basis of remoteness of damage. He said that the explanation of the plaintiff's failure in the relational economic loss cases was not that the courts "mistakenly thought that economic damage should not be accepted as sufficient injury to the plaintiff to support an action in negligence", but, rather, was "because the plaintiff was regarded as being outside the scope of the defendant's duty to take care. The duty of care arose only because a lack of care might cause direct injury to the person or property of someone, and the duty was owed only to those whose person or property were foreseeably at risk".

Home Office v Dorset Yacht Co Ltd [1970] AC 1004: Lord Reid said (at p 1027): "I think that the time has come when we can and should say that the well-known passage in Lord Atkin's speech in *Donoghue v Stevenson* [see para 3.2.1] ought to apply unless there is some justification or valid explanation for its exclusion. For example, causing economic loss is a different matter". This remark, too, has been influential in motivating for a different approach to economic loss cases. However, it would seem, from what Lord Reid said next, that he did not have in mind the type of economic loss cases which are considered in this book, but, rather, was concerned with the fact that, in some situations, a person can deliberately cause economic loss to another without being held liable in law. He continued: "For one thing, economic loss is often caused by deliberate action. Competition involves traders being entitled to damage their rivals' interests by promoting their own, and there is a long chapter of the law determining in what circumstances owners of land can, and in what circumstances they may not, use their proprietary rights so as to injure their neighbours".

SCM (United Kingdom) Ltd v W J Whittall & Son Ltd [1971] 1 QB 337 (see Chapter 4, para 4.3.2): The defendants submitted that if the court held them liable for the material damage which they had done to the plaintiff factory owner when they negligently cut off his electricity, and for any loss of profit consequent thereon, then the court would logically have to hold another defendant in their position liable in a subsequent case if only pure economic loss, and no material damage, was caused. In rejecting this submission Lord Denning MR said (at p 344):

> There may be no difference in logic [between economic loss and physical damage], but I think there is a great deal of difference in common sense. In actions of negligence, when the plaintiff has suffered no damage to his person or property, but has only sustained economic loss, the law does not usually permit him to recover that loss. The reason lies in public policy. It was first stated by Blackburn J in *Cattle v Stockton Waterworks Co* [see para 1.4.2] and has been repeated many times since. He gave this illustration: When a mine is flooded by negligence, thousands of men may be thrown out of work. None of them is injured, but each of them loses wages. Has each of them a cause of action? He thought not. So, here I would ask: When an electric cable is damaged, many factories may be stopped from working. Can each of them claim for their loss of profit? I think not. It is not sensible to saddle losses on this scale onto one sole contractor. Very often such losses occur without anyone's fault. A mine may be flooded, or a power failure may occur by mischance as well as by negligence. Where it is only mischance, everyone grumbles, but puts up with it. No one dreams of bringing an action for damages. So, also, when it occurs by negligence. The risk should be borne by the whole community who suffer the losses rather than rest on one pair of shoulders, namely, one contractor who may, or may not, be insured against the risk. There is not much logic in this, but it is still the law. In other words, the economic loss is regarded as too remote to be recoverable as damages.

Lord Denning continued: "Thus far, I have spoken only of accidents which affect a whole community, but the principle has been applied to cases where only one or two persons suffer economic loss". He then referred to some of the relational economic loss cases and then continued (at p 345): "If you refuse to allow the plaintiff in such cases to recover for economic loss, it is not because there is no duty owed to him, nor because it was not caused by the negligence of the defendant, but simply because it is too remote to be a head of damage. I must not be taken, however, as saying that economic loss is always too remote. There are some exceptional cases when it is the immediate consequence of the negligence and is recoverable accordingly". He then referred to *Hedley Byrne* and to *Morrison Steamship Co Ltd v Greystoke Castle (Cargo Owners)* [1947] AC 465 (see Chapter 5) and then said (at p 346): "Seeing these exceptional cases, you may well ask: How are we to say when economic loss is too remote or not? Where is the line to be drawn? Lawyers are continually asking that question. But the judges are never defeated by it. We may not be able to draw the line with precision, but we can always say on which side of it any particular case falls".

In this same case (ie *SCM*) Winn LJ said (at p 352): "Liability for pure economic loss negligently caused without foresight of any physical injury or damage to property from which such loss might consequentially arise would logically involve, *inter alia*, liability to all persons dependent on the survival of a particular individual whose death is caused by a negligent act or omission, and to all consumers of electrical power or water etc, within a wide geographical area. It seems to me that it is far more satisfactory in a sociological sense to say that, apart from the special case of imposition of liability for negligently uttered false statements, there is no liability for unintentional negligent infliction of any form of economic loss which is not itself consequential upon foreseeable physical injury or damage to property".

Spartan Steel & Alloys Ltd v Martin & Co (Contractors) Ltd [1973] QB 27 (see para 4.3.2): In response to a submission by the plaintiff's counsel that "if there was to be any limitation upon the recovery of economic loss, it was to be found by restricting the sphere of the duty, and not by limiting the type of damages recoverable", Lord Denning MR said (at p 36):

> At bottom, I think that the question of recovering economic loss is one of policy. Whenever the courts draw a line to mark out the bounds of duty, they do it as a matter of policy so as to limit the responsibility of the defendant. Whenever the courts set bounds to the damages recoverable—saying that they are, or are not, too remote, they do it as a matter of policy so as to limit the liability of the defendant. In many of the cases where economic loss has been held not to be recoverable, it has been put on the ground that the defendant was under no duty to the plaintiff. In other cases, however, the defendant seems clearly to have been under a duty to the plaintiff, but the economic loss has not been recovered because it was too remote. The more I think about these cases, the more difficult I find it to put each into its proper pigeon-hole. Sometimes I say: 'There was no duty'. In others I say: 'The damage was too remote'; so much so, that I think the time has come to discard those tests which have proved to be so elusive. It seems to me better to consider the particular relationship in hand, and see whether or not, as a matter of policy, economic loss should be recovered or not.

This case is analysed in detail in Chapter 4, para 4.5.5, where it is noted that Lord Denning then went on to identify five 'policy' factors which, in his view, justified the court in denying the plaintiff's claims for economic loss except, and to the extent, that they were 'truly consequential' on the physical damage sustained by the plaintiff's property.

Caltex Oil (Australia) Pty Ltd v The Dredge Willemstad (1976) 136 CLR 529 (An important relational loss case, see Chapter 5, para 5.5.4): Stephen J said (at p 573): "If economic loss is to be compensated, its inherent capacity to manifest itself at several removes from the direct detriment inflicted by the defendant's carelessness makes reasonable foreseeability an inadequate control mechanism". Gibbs J said (at p 551): "If a person committing an act of negligence were liable for all economic loss foreseeably resulting therefrom, an act of careless inadvertence might expose the person guilty of it to claims unlimited in number and crippling in amount". He then posed the example of a ship which collided with a bridge and said that "to require the wrongdoer to compensate for those who had suffered pecuniary loss [when the bridge was out of use] would impose upon him a burden out of all proportion to his wrong. It is true that, under modern conditions, some claims arising from physical injury or material damage can be very large in amount, for example if a passenger train were derailed. Nevertheless, the extent of claims for loss that is purely economic is likely to be very much wider than that of claims arising out of physical injury and material damage. Furthermore, a law which imposes a general duty to take care to avoid causing foreseeable pecuniary loss to others would, as Widgery J suggested [in *Weller*—see *above*], interfere greatly with the ordinary affairs of life. There are sound reasons of policy why economic loss should not be treated in exactly the same way as material loss".

Star Village Tavern v Nield (1976) 71 DLR (3d) 439: This was a relational economic loss case involving damage to a bridge. Hamilton J said that in a case like this:

> the judge should say to himself, if I were the defendant, being a reasonable man, freed from the prejudice of self-interest, would I in these circumstances feel a financial obligation to this plaintiff as a result of my negligence? In answering that question in this case, I would have to say that, while I regret any inconvenience that might have been caused, I could hardly assume the loss. To do so, I would equally have to assume loss to all other users of the bridge who had been put to some expense. If I caused a bridge to be closed, I could imagine that everyone who used the bridge might suffer economic loss by having to drive a further distance to their normal destination. While I accept the 'neighbour' principle with respect to liability in tort, there are also normal risks of living and doing business which one assumes. Every loss or inconvenience in life cannot give rise to a cause of action.

Bethlehem Steel Corp v St Lawrence Seaway Authority (1977) 79 DLR (3d) 522 (Another relational economic loss case involving the closure of a bridge): Addy J made similar comments when he said (at p 525):

The question of whether pure economic loss is recoverable where there has been no damage to the person of the claimant or to property in which he might have a proprietary interest is not one of the areas where the law excels by its clarity or where its various approaches are consistent. Our modern society bestows upon us many advantages and innumerable benefits, most of which result directly from, or depend upon a multitude of very intricate and intimate relationships which exist between its various members, groups and services. There is, however, a price to be paid for these benefits. We must frequently forego the redress of certain wrongs even where the recognition of a right of redress might appeal to one's instinctive thirst for perfect justice or satisfy some theoretically desirable entitlement to compensation. The redress of what might appear to be a real wrong will not be recognised where its enforcement would greatly impede the proper functioning of our society. Such problems must frequently be solved pragmatically and it matters little whether we declare that the limits which must be imposed are dictated by policy, common sense or by the more philosophically acceptable concepts of social justice or of legal theory. The important thing is that the law, in this necessarily hazy area of human relations, must lay down rules which define limits which can be recognised by all members of our society in order that they may be aware of their respective rights, duties and responsibilities, and govern themselves accordingly.

Leigh and Sillivan Ltd v Aliakmon Shipping Co Ltd [1985] 1 QB 350: In the Court of Appeal Robert Goff LJ said (at p 393): "In the case of liability in negligence for economic loss, the line of thought that limits must be imposed upon a generalised liability is based on good sense. It is to the effect that the philosophy of the marketplace presumes that it is lawful to gain profit by causing others economic loss, and that recognised wrongs involving interference with others' contracts are limited to specific intentional wrongs, such as inducing a breach of contract or conspiracy. Certainly there seems to have developed an understanding that economic loss at the hands of others is something we have to accept without legal redress, unless caused by some specifically outlawed conduct such as fraud or duress; although how far this is the outcome of our reasoning, or the product of our law, is not altogether clear".

In the House of Lords in this case ([1986] AC 785) Lord Brandon said (at p 816): "The policy reason for excluding a duty of care in cases like this [ie relational economic loss cases] is to avoid the opening of the floodgates, so as to expose a person guilty of want of care to unlimited liability to an indefinite number of other persons whose contractual rights have been adversely affected by such want of care".

Jaensch v Coffey (1985) 155 CLR 549: Deane J said (at p 578): "In a society where material success is accepted as a legitimate objective, the law must be restrained [ie it must not impose liability to afford damage caused unless there be 'some particular relationship'] if it is to be attuned to social standards and reality. If material success were to be accompanied by legal liability to all who have suffered emotional chagrin or physical or material damage as a consequence, it would be largely self-destructive. In that regard, the common law has neither recognised fault in the conduct of the feasting Dives nor embraced the embarrassing moral perception that he who has failed to feed the man dying from hunger has truly killed him".

The Council of the Shire of Sutherland v Heyman (1985) 157 CLR 424: Deane J continued with this theme by saying (at p 503): "In a competitive society the infliction of pure economic loss upon another will commonly be a concomitant of the successful pursuit of personal advantage by way of lawful conduct, in that there can be discerned, in many commercial transactions, a correlation between the attainment of personal gain for one's self and the sustainment of economic loss by another".

Mason J said (at p 465): "The proposition that, in general, damages are not recoverable for economic loss unless it is consequential upon injury to the plaintiff's person or property is a reflection of the law's concern about endless, indeterminate liability. In the absence of any such concern in a particular class of case, there is no necessity to give effect to the proposition".

Caparo Industries plc v Dickman [1990] 2 AC 605: Lord Oliver said (at p 632): "The opportunities for the infliction of pecuniary loss from the imperfect performance of everyday tasks upon the proper performance of which people rely for regulating their affairs are illimitable and the effects are far reaching. A defective bottle of ginger beer may injure a single consumer, but the damage stops there. A single statement may be repeated endlessly with or without the permission of its author, and may be relied upon in a different way by many different people".

In this case, Lord Bridge also made comments on the difference between economic loss and physical damage. These are noted (and commented upon) in para 1.4.2.

London Drugs Ltd v Kuehne and Nagel International Ltd (1992) 97 DLR (4th) 261: In the Supreme Court of Canada La Forest J opined on the difference between economic loss and property damage cases by saying (at p 271):

> Comparisons between economic loss and property damage in tort cases operate on at least two planes. On one plane there is the question of the relative social importance of the two types of loss. In *Canadian National Railway Co v Norsk Pacific Steamship Co* (1992) 91 DLR (4th) 289 Stevenson J considered that there was no distinction to be made on this plane. He said that, although he was prepared to recognise that a human being is more important than property and lost expectations of profit, he failed to see how property and economic losses could be distinguished. McLachlin J noted that, even if pure economic loss were to be considered less deserving, that should not preclude recovery of such loss where justice so requires. In my view, it is unlikely that any broad comparison is possible. Property damage is more likely to occur in contexts that raise concerns other than compensation, such as safety and the desire to deter dangerous activity. However, where the loss is suffered by a corporation, as in this case [see Chapter 10, para 10.2.1], I can see little reason to distinguish in social importance between the two types of loss from the perspective of compensation. Thus, for London Drugs [the plaintiff] it is of little consequence that their loss of $33,000

occurred as a result of damage to a transformer rather than, say, the late delivery of an envelope, as in *BDC Ltd v Hofstrand Farms Ltd* (1986) 26 DLR (4th) 1 [see Chapter 9, para 9.9.3].

The second plane on which economic loss and property damage are compared in tort law is with respect to the policy concerns they raise in the context of allowing recovery for them in courts of law based on tort principles. The institutional limitations of courts are such that even those who adopt the position that there is no difference in social importance between the two types of damage recognise that many if not all economic loss cases pose policy problems, such as the problem of indeterminacy, not present with the same acuity in the vast majority of property damage cases. Certain of the policy concerns most evidenced in some economic loss cases may not really have much to do with the specific nature of the economic loss. It may just be that the concern is present with particular force in such cases and less often in cases involving physical damage to property.

With reference to the fact that many economic loss cases arise in a contractual context, La Forest J said (at p 272):

> Courts must be sensitive to the impact that an imposition of tort liability would have on the contractual allocation of risk, whether the damage incurred is economic loss or property damage. Tort liability, however, may be less likely to disrupt contractual arrangements in property damage cases. One reason why property damage cases are generally unproblematic from a policy perspective is that they are much less likely than economic loss cases to be associated with planned transactions and contractual expectations. Physical damage to person or property can result from being run down in the street, from fire destroying your house or from a street-cleaning machine bumping your car. Economic loss, on the other hand, very often occurs in a contractual context.

Bryan v Maloney (1995) 69 ALJR 375: Mason CJ (for himself, Deane and Gaudron JJ) reinforced the *dicta* cited *above* from *Jaensch v Coffey* and *Sutherland v Heyman* by saying (at p 377):

> One policy consideration which may militate against recognition of a relationship of proximity in a category of case involving mere economic loss is the law's concern to avoid the imposition of liability 'in an indeterminate amount for an indeterminate time to an indeterminate class'. Another consideration is the perception that, in a competitive world where one person's economic gain is commonly another's loss, a duty to take reasonable care to avoid causing mere economic loss to another, as distinct from physical injury to another's person or property, may be inconsistent with community standards in relation to what is ordinarily legitimate in the pursuit of personal advantage. The combined effect of these two distinct policy considerations is that the categories of case in which the requisite relationship of proximity with respect to mere economic loss is to be found are properly to be seen as special. Commonly, but not necessarily, they will involve an identified element of known reliance (or dependence) or the assumption of responsibility, or a combination of the two.

Brennan J, dissenting, expressed a similar view when he said (at p 385):

> The tort of negligence imposes liability on a defendant for doing something which causes loss to another even though the thing done is otherwise lawful. If

liability were to be imposed for the doing of anything which caused pure economic loss that was foreseeable, the tort of negligence would destroy commercial competition, sterilise many contracts and, in the well-known dictum of Cardozo CJ, expose defendants to potential liability 'in an indeterminate amount for an indeterminate time to an indeterminate class'.

Comment

Thus, a variety of reasons have been advanced as to why claims for economic loss should be treated differently from claims for personal injury or damage to property. It is important to note that it is not anything inherent ᐧ in the nature of the loss itself that necessitates a different approach. Rather, it is the circumstances in which the economic loss has arisen which sound an alarm that something more is required to warrant the imposition of a duty of care on the defendant for the plaintiff's loss than the mere fact that it was reasonably foreseeable that the defendant's negligent act or omission would cause that loss to the plaintiff. Lord Oliver (and those judges who have concurred with him) recognised this point in some of the passages quoted above; in particular the passage in *Murphy* where Lord Oliver said (at p 485): "It is far from clear from these decisions [ie the various relational economic loss cases which he had just referred to] that the reason for the plaintiff's failure was simply that the only loss sustained was 'economic'. Rather, they seem to have been based either upon the remoteness of the damage as a matter of direct causation or, more probably, upon the 'floodgates' argument of the impossibility of containing liability within any acceptable bounds if the law were to permit such claims to succeed".

Unfortunately, Lord Oliver and his fellow Lords in *Murphy* failed to comprehend the corollary of this proposition, namely that if, in any particular category of cases, this concern does not in fact exist, then there is no need for the law to adopt an unduly restrictive approach towards the imposition of duties of care for economic loss. One such category is the category of case which was actually involved in *Murphy*, namely economic loss consisting of the diminution in value of a chattel or a building which is defective due to the negligence of the defendant in its manufacture, construction or design. As there can be only one plaintiff in respect of each defective item, and as the diminution in value (ie the plaintiff's economic loss) will be limited to the replacement cost of the item, and as the maximum period of time for which the defendant could be exposed to such a claim is regulated by the Limitation Act 1980, there is no danger here of the defendant manufacturer, builder, architect etc being exposed to "a liability in an indeterminate amount for an indeterminate time to an indeterminate class". One of the ironies of *Murphy* is that, whilst their Lordships expressed great enthusiasm for the approach of the High Court of Australia in *The Council of the Shire of Sutherland v Heyman* (1985) 157 CLR 424, they failed to notice that this point was wholly appreciated and, indeed, applied in *Sutherland*. Thus, Mason J said (at p 465): "The proposition that, in general, damages are not recoverable for economic loss unless it is consequential upon injury to the plaintiff's personal property is by no means absolute or inflexible; it is a reflection of the law's concern about endless indeterminate liability. In the absence of any such concern in a particular class of case, there is no necessity to give effect to the proposition".

This point was recognised and given effect to by the High Court of Australia in its decision in *Bryan v Maloney* (1995) 69 ALJR 375. Mason CJ, delivering the main majority judgment, said (at p 380):

> The policy considerations underlying the reluctance of the courts to recognise a relationship of proximity and a consequent duty of care in cases of mere economic loss are inapplicable to a relationship of the kind which existed between Mr. Bryan and Mrs. Manion [see Chapter 7, para 7.6.4] as regards to the kind of economic loss sustained by Mrs. Maloney [ie diminution in the value of her house]. Thus, there is no basis for thinking that recognition of a relationship of proximity between the builder and the first owner with respect to that particular kind of economic loss would give rise to the type of liability 'in an indeterminate amount for an indeterminate time to an indeterminate class' which the courts are reluctant to recognise.

1.5 Contrary views

1.5.1 Introduction

From time to time certain judges have said that they cannot see any reason for treating economic loss claims differently from physical injury claims. Their *dicta* are considered and commented upon below.

1.5.2 *Dicta* in cases

Hedley Byrne & Co Ltd v Heller & Partners Ltd [1964] AC 465: Lord Hodson said (at p 509): "It is difficult to see why liability as such should depend on the nature of the damage"; and Lord Devlin, in response to the defendant's counsel's submission that a distinction should be drawn between financial loss which is consequent upon physical injury and financial loss which is caused directly, said (at p 517): "The interposition of the physical injury is said to make a difference in principle. I can find neither logic nor common sense in this". He then posed the example of a doctor who negligently advises a patient that he can safely pursue his occupation, and the patient's health suffers by following that advice, as contrasted with a doctor who negligently advises a patient that he cannot safely pursue his occupation, and the patient follows that advice, but only suffers financial loss thereby. He said that to hold the doctor liable in the first case but not in the latter would, in his view, be "nonsense".

It must be noted that Lord Devlin made these remarks specifically in the context of the old rule against the recovery of damages in tort for negligent misstatement (see Chapter 9, para 9.2), and in response to the defendant's submission that no liability for economic loss could exist unless it was consequential upon physical injury. This is borne out by what he said next, namely: "The line [ie the supposed distinction between economic loss consequential upon physical injury and direct economic loss] is not drawn on any intelligible principle. It just happens to be the line which those who have been driven from the extreme assertion that negligent statements, in the absence of contractual or fiduciary duty, give no cause of action, have in the course of their retreat so far reached".

Ministry of Housing and Local Government v Sharp [1970] 2 QB 223: (See Chapter 9, para 9.7.4.) Salmon LJ said (at p 278): "So far as the law of negligence in relation to civil actions is concerned, the existence of a duty to take reasonable care no longer [ie after *Hedley Byrne*] depends on whether it is physical injury or financial loss which can reasonably be foreseen as a result of a failure to take such care". This is not a correct interpretation of *Hedley Byrne*. The true purport of *Hedley Byrne* was stated by Widgery J in *Weller v The Foot and Mouth Disease Research Institute* [1966] 1 QB 569, when he said (at p 587): "The decision in *Hedley Byrne* recognises that a duty of care may arise in the giving of advice, even though no contract or fiduciary relationship exists between the giver of the advice and the person who may act upon it; and, having recognised the existence of the duty, it goes on to recognise that indirect or economic loss will suffice to support the plaintiff's claim. What the case does not decide is that an ability to foresee indirect or economic loss to another as a result of one's conduct automatically imposes a duty to take care to avoid that loss".

Spartan Steel & Alloys Ltd v Martin & Co (Contractors) Ltd [1973] QB 27: Edmund Davies LJ, dissenting in part (see Chapter 4, para 4.6.3) said (at p 45): "My conclusion is that an action lies in negligence for damages in respect of purely economic loss, provided that it was a reasonably foreseeable and direct consequence of failure in a duty of care. The application of such a rule can undoubtedly give rise to difficulties in certain sets of circumstances, but so can the suggested rule that economic loss may be recovered, provided that it is directly consequential upon physical damage".

This view was expressed in the context of a case of consequential economic loss, but was also intended to be applicable to cases of relational economic loss. It has not found acceptance with other judges, except for Murphy J (in a minority of one against four) in *Caltex Oil (Australia) Pty Ltd v The Dredge Willemstad* (1976) 136 CLR 539 (see Chapter 5, para 5.6.1) when he said (at p 606): "The plaintiff's loss was economic. I do not accept the contention that economic loss not connected with physical damage to the plaintiff's property is not recoverable. I find no reason for limiting recovery".

Chapter 2

The elements of liability

The critical question is not the nature of the damage in itself, whether physical or pecuniary, but whether the scope of the duty of care in the circumstances of the case is such as to embrace damage of the kind which the plaintiff claims to have sustained. **(Lord Oliver in *Murphy v Brentwood District Council* [1991] 1 AC 398)**

It is never sufficient to ask simply whether A owes B a duty of care. It is always necessary to determine the scope of the duty by reference to the kind of damage from which A must take care to save B harmless. The question is always whether the defendant was under a duty to avoid or prevent that damage. **(Lord Bridge in *Caparo Industries plc v Dickman* [1990] 2 AC 605)**

It has to be borne in mind that the duty of care is inseparable from the damage which the plaintiff claims to have suffered from its breach. It is not a duty to take care in the abstract, but a duty to avoid causing to the particular plaintiff damage of the particular kind which he has in fact sustained. **(Lord Oliver in *Caparo Industries plc v Dickman* [1990] 2 AC 605)**

Even if there is sufficient proximity between an adviser and an advisee, that does not expose the adviser to liability for all damage which can be shown to flow from the breach of duty. **(Laddie J, in *BCCI (Overseas) Ltd v Price Waterhouse & Another* (*The Times*, 30 October 1997))**

2.1   Introduction

2.1.1   General

It is trite law that, in order for a court to be able to hold that a defendant is liable in the tort of negligence for the plaintiff's loss, the situation must have been such that the defendant owed a duty of care to the plaintiff for the plaintiff's loss, the defendant must have breached that duty and that breach must have caused the plaintiff's loss. In addition, the plaintiff's loss must not be 'too remote' and the plaintiff must not have voluntarily submitted himself to the risk of injury. Of the above-mentioned components of liability, this book is concerned primarily with questions relating to the imposition of duty of care, because it is in this area that special problems have arisen where the plaintiff's loss is purely economic.

2.1.2   Remoteness of damage

Although the relevant rules are the same whether the plaintiff's loss is physical or economic, it is worthwhile saying a few words about these prin-

24

ciples, because of the similarity of some of the terminology, and because, as noted in Chapter 1, para 1.4.3, the courts' justification for many of the early relational economic loss cases was that the plaintiff's loss was too remote.

It is well known, on the authority of the Privy Council in *Overseas Tankship (UK) Ltd v Morts Dock & Engineering Co Ltd (The Wagon Mound No 1)* [1961] AC 388 that

(a) the only damage for which a defendant can be held liable in the tort of negligence is damage which is of such a 'kind' as a reasonable man should have foreseen;

(b) where damage of a particular kind is suffered, then damage of that kind, and not of another kind, must have been foreseeable;

(c) where damage of a particular kind is foreseeable, then it does not matter that the precise manner in which such damage was caused by the defendant's negligent act is not foreseeable;

(d) where the damage which occurred is of a kind which a reasonable man would have foreseen, then (all other things being equal) the defendant will be liable for the full extent of the plaintiff's loss, even if a reasonable man could not have foreseen the extent of that loss.

For this purpose, the term 'kind of loss' refers not to the distinction between economic loss and physical damage, but to the distinction between physical damage caused by one means (say, by direct impact) rather than by another (say, by fire). Thus, in *The Wagon Mound No 1*, the fact that the trial judge found that a reasonable man in the defendant's position ought reasonably only to have foreseen that the oil spillage would most probably have congealed upon, and interfered with, the use of the plaintiff's slipways, led the Privy Council to hold that this was not sufficient to make the defendant liable for the fire damage which subsequently ensued when (which was not foreseeable) some sparks from welding being carried out on the plaintiff's wharf ignited some cotton waste which was floating on some of the oil upon the water beneath it. A modern application of this principle is the holding of the court in *M/S Aswan Engineering Establishment Co v Lupdine* [1987] 1 WLR 1 (see Chapter 7, para 7.4.4) that, even if the damage sustained by the plaintiff's property was not to be regarded as pure economic loss, it was not recoverable, because it consisted of a type of damage which was outside the range of what was reasonably foreseeable.

This principle was also considered, and correctly applied, by the Court of Appeal in *Muirhead v Industrial Tank Specialities Ltd* [1986] 1 QB 507 (see Chapter 7, para 7.3.6). Robert Goff LJ said (at p 532): "The true question to which the judge should have addressed his mind was simply whether damage of the relevant 'type' was reasonably foreseeable by the first defendant [the manufacturer of the electric motors], ie, physical harm to fish stored in a tank at a fish farm by reason of failure of the circulation and oxygenation pumps through the cutting out of the electric motors driving those pumps. If he had found that damage of that type was reasonably foreseeable, then the fact that, by reason of the full stocking of the tank, the fish died more quickly or in greater quantities was of no relevance, unless it could be said that over-stocking of the tank constituted the sole, or a contributory cause of, the disaster which took place".

In economic loss cases the phrase 'kind of damage' is also used, but it refers to the distinction between economic loss and physical damage, and is used in the context of determining the 'scope' of the defendant's duty of care in that particular category of case. Thus, for example, in *Caparo Industries plc v Dickman* [1990] 2 AC 605, Lord Bridge said (at p 627): "It is never sufficient to ask simply whether A owes B a duty of care. It is always necessary to determine the scope of the duty by reference to the kind of damage from which A must take care to save B harmless". He then quoted the following words of Brennan J in *The Council of the Shire of Sutherland v Heyman* (1985) 157 CLR 424 (at p 487): "The question is always whether the defendant was under a duty to avoid or prevent that damage, but the actual nature of the damage suffered is relevant to the existence and extent of any duty to avoid or prevent it". Brennan J further stressed the importance of identifying the type of damage suffered by the plaintiff—physical or economic—when he said: "It is impermissible to postulate a duty of care to avoid one kind of damage—say, personal injury—and finding the defendant guilty of failing to discharge that duty, to hold him liable for the damage actually suffered that is of another and independent kind—say, economic loss".

2.1.3   The essential ingredients

In *Caparo* Lord Bridge said (at p 617): "In addition to the foreseeability of damage, the necessary ingredients in any situation giving rise to a duty of care are that there should exist between the party owing the duty and the party to whom it is owed a relationship characterised by the law as one of 'proximity' or 'neighbourhood' and that the situation should be one in which the court considers it fair, just and reasonable that the law should impose a duty of a given scope upon the one party for the benefit of the other".

Each of these components is considered separately below by reference to the *dicta* of certain judges in some of the decided cases. In Chapter 3 it is noted that, although the House of Lords did not intend that, in any particular case, each of these components should be considered in isolation of the other, and should be 'ticked off' separately, this is precisely what is happening in practice. Rather, the House intended that these factors should all be treated as being inter-dependent, and that their existence or non-existence in any particular case should be treated as part of a composite question, namely whether, in all the circumstances, the aims of justice and practicality would be better served by imposing a duty of care on the defendant for the plaintiff's loss, than by not doing so.

2.1.4   The composite approach

As just noted, although Lord Bridge in *Caparo* identified three separate 'necessary ingredients' in any situation giving rise to a duty of care, both he and his fellow Law Lords were not in favour of this resulting in the application of a rigid tripartite test, but preferred for each of these separate ingredients to be considered as factors to be weighed in the balance when considering, from the point of view of justice and practicality, whether it is right to impose a duty of care on the defendant in any particular case for the plaintiff's actual loss. Thus, Lord Bridge carried on in the passage quoted above by saying (at p 618): "But it is implicit . . . that the concepts of proximity and fairness embodied in these additional ingredients are not susceptible of any such precise definition as would be necessary to give them utility as practical tests, but amount in effect to little more than convenient labels to attach to the features of different specific situations which, on a detailed examination of all the circumstances, the law recognises pragmatically as giving rise to a duty of care of a given scope".

Lord Oliver expressed the same sentiments when he said (at p 633): "The postulate of a simple duty to avoid any harm that is, with hindsight, reasonably capable of being foreseen, becomes untenable without the imposition of some intelligible limits to keep the law of negligence within the bounds of common sense and practicality. Those limits have been found by the requirement of a 'relationship of proximity' between the plaintiff and the defendant, and by the imposition of a further requirement, namely, that the attachment of liability for harm which has occurred must be 'just and reasonable'. Although the cases in which the courts have imposed or withheld liability are capable of an approximate categorisation, one looks in vain for some common denominator by which the existence of the essential relationship can be tested. Indeed, it is difficult to resist a conclusion that what have been treated as three separate requirements are, at least in most cases, merely facets of the same thing; for, in some cases, the degree of foreseeability is such that it is from that alone that the requisite proximity can be deduced, whilst in others, the absence of that essential relationship can most rationally be attributable simply to the court's view that it would not be fair and reasonable to hold the defendant responsible. 'Proximity' is, no doubt, a convenient expression, so long as it is realised that it is no more than a label which embraces not a definable concept, but merely a description of circumstances, from which, pragmatically, the courts conclude that a duty of care exists".

The nature of the exercise which the court should effectively be conducting in every case was stated succinctly by Weintraub CJ in the Supreme Court of New Jersey in *Goldberg v Housing Authority of the City of Newark* (1962) 186 A(2d) 291 when he said: "Whether a duty exists is ultimately a question of fairness. The enquiry involves a weighing of the relationship of the parties, the nature of the risk and the public interest in the proposed solution". In *Union Oil Co v Oppen* (1974) 501 F(2d) 588 (see Chapter 5, para 5.4.3), Snead CJ expressed a similar view when he said: "The determination whether, in a specific case, the defendant will be held liable to a third person not in privity is a matter of policy, and involves the balancing of various factors, among which are the extent to which the transaction was intended to affect the plaintiff, the foreseeability of harm to him, the degree of certainty that the plaintiff would suffer injury, the closeness of the connection between the defendant's conduct and the injury suffered, the moral blame attached to the defendant's conduct, and the policy of preventing future harm".

2.1.5 The scope of the duty

Introduction

One of the most important concepts to comprehend when considering whether a duty of care is appropriate in any particular category of case is that, although the first two of the 'essential ingredients' (ie foreseeability and proximity) might be satisfied, and although it might in a general sense seem just and reasonable to impose a duty of care, the courts will refuse to do so if this would result in a duty of care being imposed which is of a wider 'scope', ambit or extent, or in respect of damage of a different kind than the judges believe is warranted in the interests of 'fairness', 'justice' or 'pragmatism'. One of the earliest manifestations of this principle was the statement of Blackburn J in *Cattle v Stockton Waterworks Co* (1875) LR 10 QB (a relational economic loss case—see Chapter 5, para 5.8.1):

> It may be said that it is just that all such persons [ie all of the workmen who would lose wages if their employer's mine was flooded by the defendant's negligence] should have compensation for such a loss, and that, if the law does not give them redress, it is imperfect. Perhaps it may be so, but . . . Courts of justice should not allow themselves, in the pursuit of perfectly complete remedies for all wrongful acts, to transgress the bounds which our law, in a wise consciousness . . . of its limited powers, has imposed upon itself, of redressing only the proximate and direct consequences of wrongful acts.

In *Weller & Co v Foot and Mouth Diseases Research Institute* [1966] 1 QB 589, Widgery J, after referring to *Cattle* and other important relational economic loss cases, said (at p 586):

> What is the explanation of the plaintiff's failure in these earlier cases? Is it that the courts mistakenly thought that 'indirect' or 'consequential' or 'economic' damage, as it has variously been called, should not be accepted as sufficient injury to the plaintiff to support an action in negligence, or is it that in the particular circumstances of the case, no duty of care was owed to the plaintiff at all? Economic or consequential damage may be as real to the plaintiff as direct physical injury, and Lord Devlin demonstrated the illogicality of a distinction upon those lines in *Hedley Byrne* [see Chapter 1, para 1.5.1]. In my judgment the plaintiff's failure in these earlier cases was not because this truth to which Lord Devlin has referred, had escaped the eminent judges who decided those cases, but because the plaintiff was regarded as being outside the scope of the defendant's duty to take care.

On a broad level

On a broad level, the desire, if not the need, to limit the possible ambit of any potential duty of care is well articulated in Cardozo J's celebrated *dictum* in *Ultramares Corporation v Touche Niven and Company* (1931) 255

NY 170 that a flaw would exist in the implication of a duty of care in tort which exposes the person on whom the duty is imposed to "liability in an indeterminate amount for an indeterminate time to an indeterminate class" (see Chapter 1, para 1.4.3). Cardozo J said quite rightly that business could not be conducted if businessmen were to be exposed to such potentially far-reaching consequences whenever they did an act or made a statement which they could reasonably foresee would be relied upon by third parties with whom they did not have a contractual relationship. Therefore, to make business (and life in general) workable, the general principle has arisen, inspired by Cardozo J's *dictum*, that any particular duty of care in tort must be limited to the amount of loss that the defendant's breach of the duty caused within a reasonable time after the duty arose, if the person who suffered the loss was within a class of persons whose existence was ascertainable at the time when the duty arose.

On a broad level, too, the rules that the courts have developed for ensuring that a negligent defendant is not liable to compensate a plaintiff for loss that is 'too remote' are another manifestation of the law's pragmatic desire to limit the scope of a defendant's duty of care (see para 2.1.2, *above*). Lord Denning MR was aware of this point when he said in *Spartan Steel and Alloys Ltd v Martin and Co (Contractors) Ltd* [1973] QB 27: "The more I think about these cases, the more difficult I find it to put each case into its proper pigeon-hole. Sometimes I say: 'There was no duty'. In others I say: 'The damage was too remote'; so much so, that I think the time has come to discard those tests which have proved to be so elusive. It seems to me better to consider the particular relationship in hand, and see whether or not, as a matter of policy, economic loss should be recovered or not".

Overlap with remoteness

This overlap between the rules governing remoteness of damage and the application of the principle of limiting the scope of the defendant's duty of care was also noted by the House of Lords in *South Australia Asset Management Corporation v York Montague Ltd* [1997] AC 191 (also indexed as *Banque Bruxelles SA v Eagle Star*). Lord Hoffmann, in commenting on the fact that the House of Lords in *Banque Keyser Ullmann SA v Skandia (UK) Insurance Co Ltd* [1991] 2 AC 249 dismissed the banks' appeal on the ground that the loss that they were seeking to recover from the insurers was too remote because that loss was not foreseeable (see Chapter 8, para 8.3.3), said that this was no different from the way that the House in *South Australia* has now held that the scope of a duty of care should be determined in negligent misstatement cases (see *below*). Lord Hoffmann also observed that, in cases where it is true to say that the plaintiff's loss was not foreseeable in accordance with the remoteness of damage principle, "it shows that the rule that damages are limited to what was within the reasonable contemplation of the parties can sometimes make arguments over the scope of the duty academic".

As noted in para 2.1.2, *above*, the rules governing remoteness of damage provide that where the damage that occurred is of a kind which was reasonably foreseeable, then the defendant will be liable for the full extent of the plaintiff's loss—even if the full extent of that loss was not reasonably foreseeable. However, the application of this principle in any particular case is always subject to the overriding principle that the defendant will only be liable to compensate the plaintiff for such loss as the court deems to be within the scope of the defendant's duty of care in all of the circumstances of the case. A good example of the inter-relationship of these two principles, and the dominance of the 'scope principle', is the House of Lords' decision in the *South Australia* case, the facts of which are set out below. It was common ground that the loss sustained by the valuers through the fall in value of properties in the property market generally was foreseeable, but the House nevertheless held that the valuers were not liable to compensate the lenders for that loss because it was not the *kind* of loss in respect of which their duty of care was owed. The scope of the valuers' duty of care for having made negligent valuations upon which the lenders relied in lending money to the borrower was restricted to such losses as were attributable to the consequences of the information being inaccurate.

On a narrower level

On a narrower level, the task of determining the scope of the defendant's duty of care in any particular case will involve more of a microscopic examination of the exact nature and origin of the plaintiff's loss and the precise position of the plaintiff within an identifiable class, which then has to be viewed against the precise purpose of the rule or principle that empowers the court to impose a duty of care on the defendant in that category of case. A good example of the operation of this exercise in practice is the court's decision in *Woodward v Wolferstans* (20 March 1997, unreported). The plaintiff was a twenty-two-year-old student who had signed a mortgage at her father's behest without any understanding of its implications. The building society repossessed the flat after her father had ceased making the monthly mortgage repayments and sued the plaintiff for the shortfall that resulted on the sale (see Chapter 9, para 9.7.5). The plaintiff then sued the solicitors whom her father had engaged to do the conveyancing work. She alleged that the solicitors owed her a duty of care, which they breached in allowing her to execute the mortgage without first advising her as to its legal effect and, in particular, as to her exposure to personal liability in the event that the building society might have to resort to its security if the mortgage were to fall into default and that security proved to be inadequate to cover the full amount then outstanding under the mortgage. This, the plaintiff alleged, would have afforded her the opportunity, of which she maintained in this action she would have availed herself, either to decline to proceed at all with the purchase, or to decline to proceed except on a basis which would not have exposed her to the risks of a mortgagor.

The judge, Martin Mann QC, sitting as a deputy judge of the High Court, held that in these circumstances a duty of care did exist from the solicitors to the plaintiff, notwithstanding that only her father, and not the plaintiff, was the solicitors' client. However, the plaintiff's claim did not succeed because the alleged breach of the solicitors' duty of care upon which the plaintiff's claim was founded was not within the scope of the duty that they owed to the plaintiff. Thus, his Honour said:

> But it is not enough for the plaintiff to succeed that she was owed a duty of care. She must show that the content of the duty included explaining the transactional details and the implications of the mortgage. The defendant's contract with Mr. Smith [the plaintiff's father] required it to exercise reasonable skill and care in securing a good marketable title to, and the plaintiff's registration as proprietor of, the flat. It did not entail taking the plaintiff on as a client for the purpose of giving her advice, and the Court cannot re-write the contract to bring advising the plaintiff within its ambit. It is *a fortiori* that it should not do so by the back door. Accordingly, I hold that, while the defendant owed the plaintiff a duty of care, it was restricted to the exercise of reasonable skill and care in carrying the transaction into effect according to Mr. Smith's instructions.

Different approaches

Some judges approach the matter by determining first whether there is a sufficiently high degree of proximity between the defendant and the plaintiff so as to give rise, *prima facie*, to a duty of care and then, if that is their preliminary conclusion, they go on to consider the scope of that duty in the particular circumstances of the case at hand. An example is the second stage of the two-stage test for determining duties of care suggested by Lord Wilberforce in *Anns v Merton London Borough Council* [1978] AC 728. In this regard, Lord Wilberforce said: "Secondly, if the first question [ie the existence of a *prima facie* duty of care based on a 'sufficient relationship of proximity'] is answered affirmatively, it is necessary to consider whether there are any considerations which ought to negative, reduce or limit the scope of the duty or the class of person to whom it is owed or the damages to which a breach of it may give rise".

Some other judges have deprecated this approach. Their view is that it is wrong to divorce the consideration of a duty of care from the scope of that duty, and that, therefore, only one composite question must be asked. Thus, in *Caparo Industries plc v Dickman* [1990] 2 AC 605, Lord Bridge said: "It is never sufficient to ask simply whether A owes B a duty of care. It is always necessary to determine the scope of the duty by reference to the kind of damage from which A must take care to save B harmless"; and Lord Oliver said: "The duty of care is inseparable from the damage which the plaintiff claims to have suffered from its breach. It is not a duty to take care in the abstract, but a duty to avoid causing to the particular plaintiff damage of the particular kind which he has in fact sustained"; and in *Council of the Shire of Sutherland v Heyman* (1985) 157 CLR 424, Brennan J, in the High Court of Australia, said: "A postulated duty of care must be stated in reference to the kind of damage that the plaintiff has suffered and in reference to the plaintiff or a class of which the plaintiff is a member. There is no actionable negligence unless duty, breach and consequential damage coincide. For the purposes of determining liability in a given case, each element can be defined only in terms of the others. The question is always whether the defendant was under a duty to prevent that damage [ie damage of the kind that the plaintiff has suffered—see below for the full quotation], but the actual nature of the damage suffered is relevant to the existence and the extent of any duty to avoid or prevent it".

In practice, it does not matter which approach is used, so long as all of the factors that could bear on the determination of the proper scope of the defendant's duty of care for the plaintiff's actual loss in all of the circumstances of the case are taken into account. Indeed, despite the above-cited *dicta* of Lord Bridge and Lord Oliver in favour of a composite test, some judges, even at the highest level, still approach the question in two stages. Thus, in *Deloitte Haskins and Sells v National Mutual Life Nominees Ltd* [1993] AC 774, Lord Jauncey, delivering the unanimous advice of the Privy Council (whose panel included Lord Bridge on this occasion), approached the question of the scope of the defendant's duty of care in two stages, when he said (at p 786): "There is no doubt that, by reason of the provisions of Section 50 of the *Act* of 1978, there was created a relationship of proximity between the auditor and the trustee. The issue in this appeal, however, is not whether there was such a relationship of proximity, but how far any duty arising out of that relationship extended". Similarly, in *HIT Finance Ltd v Cohen Arnold and Co* (24 September 1997, unreported) Mantell J said: "Having decided that, in writing the letter of May 18, 1989, Cohen Arnold did owe a duty of care to HIT [see Chapter 9, para 9.7.2], it is necessary to consider its scope".

General guidance

In *South Australia Asset Management Corporation v York Montague Ltd* [1997] AC 191 (which is also indexed as *Banque Bruxelles SA v Eagle Star*), Lord Hoffmann provided some useful guidance in general terms on the approach to be followed in determining the scope of a duty of care. After noting that, in the present case, there was no dispute that, as an implied term of the valuers' contracts with the lenders, the valuers owed the lenders a duty of care with regard to their valuations of the properties whose value was to form the benchmark for the amount of the loans that the lenders were prepared to advance to the borrower and that "the real question in this case is the *kind* of loss in respect of which the duty was owed", Lord Hoffmann said (at p 212):

> How is the scope of the duty determined? In the case of a statutory duty, the question is answered by deducing the purpose of the duty from the language and context of the statute. In the case of a tort, it will similarly depend upon the purpose of the rule imposing the duty. Most of the judgments in the *Caparo* case are occupied in examining *The Companies Act 1985* to ascertain the purpose of the auditor's duty to take care that the statutory accounts comply with the *Act* [see Chapter 9, para 9.7.2].
>
> Rules which make the wrongdoer liable for all of the consequences of his wrongful conduct are exceptional and need to be justified by some special policy.

Normally, the law limits liability to those consequences which are attributable to that which made the act wrongful. In the case of liability for providing inaccurate information, this would mean liability for the consequences of the information being inaccurate.

In the case of an implied contractual duty, the nature and extent of the liability is defined by the term which the law implies. As in the case of any implied term, the process is one of construction of the agreement as a whole in its contractual setting. The contractual duty to provide a valuation and the known purpose of that valuation compel the conclusion that the contract includes a duty of care. The scope of the duty, in the sense of the consequences for which the valuer is responsible, is that which the law regards as best giving effect to the express obligations assumed by the valuer: neither cutting them down so that the lender obtains less than he was reasonably entitled to expect, nor extending them so as to impose on the valuer a liability greater than he could reasonably have thought he was undertaking.

Kind of loss

In the context of determining the scope of a duty of care, the phrases that one often sees in the cases, namely, the '*type of damage*' or '*kind of loss*', do not necessarily refer to the distinction between economic loss and physical injury or property damage. These phrases could just as well apply to situations where all of the damage is, by its nature, economic (as in the *South Australia* case itself), but the circumstances in which the particular damage occurred, or the fact that the plaintiff is not a person whom the duty of care was designed to protect, will take that damage and that plaintiff out of the scope of the duty of care that the court believes in the circumstances of the case should be imposed on the defendant.

Negligent misstatement cases

The emphasis that will be laid on any of these factors will vary according to the circumstances of each case and will also, in general terms, vary between the different categories of case. The category of negligence that was relevant in the *South Australia* case was negligent misstatement. Here, the defendants, as valuers, had been required by the plaintiffs to value properties on the security of which the plaintiffs were considering advancing money on mortgage. The defendants negligently overvalued the properties. In reliance on the defendants' valuations, the plaintiffs lent vast sums of money to third parties, which they would not have done if they had known the true values of the properties. The borrowers subsequently defaulted, and in the meantime the property market had fallen substantially, thereby greatly increasing the losses eventually suffered by the plaintiffs. The question for determination by the House of Lords was whether the valuers were responsible for the full amount of the lenders' losses, including the effect of the general fall in the property market (which was held to be a foreseeable event), or only the difference between the value put on each property by the defendants and its true value at that time.

In holding that the second of these possibilities provided the correct answer in this type of case, Lord Hoffmann (with whose speech all of the other Law Lords agreed) said (at p 213):

> Normally the law limits liability to those consequences which are attributable to that which made the act wrongful. In the case of liability in negligence for providing inaccurate information, this would mean liability for the consequences of the information being inaccurate.

Lord Hoffmann illustrated the difference between the two possible solutions mentioned above by providing the following example:

> A mountaineer about to undertake a difficult climb is concerned about the fitness of his knee. He goes to a doctor who negligently makes a superficial examination and pronounces the knee fit. The climber goes on the expedition, which he would not have undertaken if the doctor had told him the true state of his knee. He suffers an injury which is an entirely foreseeable consequence of mountaineering, but has nothing to do with his knee.

Lord Hoffmann then contrasted the consequences of applying each of the above-mentioned possible solutions to this example. He said (at p 213):

> On the Court of Appeal's principle [ie adopting the first of these possible solutions], the doctor would be responsible for the injury suffered by the mountaineer because it is damage which would not have occurred if he had been given correct information about his knee: he would not have gone on the expedition and would have suffered no injury. On what I have suggested is the more usual principle, the doctor is not liable. The injury has not been caused by the doctor's bad advice because the injury would have occurred even if the advice had been correct.
>
> Your Lordships might, I would suggest, think that there was something wrong with a principle which, in the example which I have given, produced the result that the doctor was liable. What is the reason for this feeling? I think that the Court of Appeal's principle offends common sense because it makes the doctor responsible for consequences which, though in general terms foreseeable, do not appear to have a sufficient cause or connection with the subject matter of the duty. The doctor was asked for information on only one of the considerations which might affect the safety of the mountaineer on the expedition. There seems to be no reason of policy which requires that the negligence of the doctor should require the transfer to him of all the foreseeable risks of the expedition.

Lord Hoffmann then provided some further general guidance for determining the scope of a duty of care of a defendant who has made a negligent misstatement. He said (at p 214):

> I think that one can to some extent generalise the principle upon which this response depends. It is that a person under a duty to take reasonable care to provide information on which someone else will decide on a course of action is, if negligent, not generally regarded as responsible for all of the consequences of that course of action. He is responsible only for the consequences of the information being wrong. A duty of care which imposes upon the informant responsibility for losses which would have occurred even if the information which he gave had been correct is not in my view fair and reasonable as between

the parties. It is therefore inappropriate either as an implied term of a contract or as a tortious duty arising from the relationship between them.

The principle thus stated distinguishes between a duty to *provide information* for the purpose of enabling *someone else to decide* upon a course of action, and a duty to *advise someone* as to what *course of action he should take.* If the duty is to advise whether or not a course of action should be taken, the adviser must take reasonable care to consider all of the potential consequences of that course of action. If he is negligent, he will be responsible for all the foreseeable loss which is a consequence of that course of action having been taken. If his duty is only to supply information, he must take reasonable care to ensure that the information is correct and, if he is negligent, he will be responsible for all the foreseeable consequences of the information being wrong.

Lord Hoffmann said (correctly) that he thought that this principle is implicit in the House of Lords' decision in *Banque Keyser Ullmann SA v Skandia (UK) Insurance Co Ltd* [1991] 2 AC 249. He said (at p 215):

> Lord Templeman (with whom all the other members of the House agreed) dealt with the matter in terms of causation. He said that, assuming a duty to disclose the information existed, the breach of that duty did not cause the loss. The failure to inform the lenders of the brokers' fraud induced them to think that valid policies were in place. But even if this had been true, the loss would still have happened. The insurers would still have been entitled to repudiate the policies under the fraud exception.
>
> Lord Templeman's speech puts the matter firmly on the ground of causation, and the analysis makes sense only on the footing that he was concerned with the consequences to the lenders of having lent without knowing the true facts, rather than with what would have been the consequences of disclosure.

Warranty vs misstatement

Finally, Lord Hoffmann contrasted the scope of a duty to take reasonable care to ensure that a statement is accurate with the scope of a warranty that the information provided is accurate. He said (at p 216):

> The measure of damages [and, hence, the scope of the defendant's duty of care] in an action for breach of a duty to take care to provide accurate information must also be distinguished from the measure of damages for breach of a warranty that the information is accurate. In the case of breach of a duty of care, the measure of damages [and, hence, the scope of the defendant's duty] is the loss attributable to the inaccuracy of the information which the plaintiff has suffered by reason of having entered into the transaction on the assumption that the information was correct. One therefore compares the loss he has actually suffered with what his position would have been if he had not entered into the transaction, and one asks what element of this loss is attributable to the inaccuracy of the information.
>
> In the case of a warranty, one compares the plaintiff's position as a result of entering into the transaction with what it would have been if the information had been accurate. Both measures are concerned with the consequences of the inaccuracy of the information [or with the scope of the defendant's duty], but the tort measure is the extent to which the plaintiff is worse off because the information was wrong, whereas the warranty measure is the extent to which he would have been better off if the information had been right.

2.1.5   The elements of liability

Application in Caparo

In *Caparo Industries plc v Dickman* [1990] 2 AC 605, another negligent misstatement case, the main issue in the House of Lords, in relation to the plaintiff's claim that, as an existing shareholder, the auditors owed the plaintiff a duty of care when the plaintiff purchased further shares of the target company in reliance on the auditors' report, was also the scope of the defendant's duty of care. Their Lordships held that, even if there was a 'proximate' relationship between the auditors and the shareholders, resulting in some sort of a *prima facie* duty of care, it was negated by the fact that any loss that the plaintiff, as a shareholder, might have incurred in its capacity as an investor, as opposed to its capacity as a shareholder exerting shareholders' rights in a general meeting, was outside the scope of the duty of care that arises when auditors of a public company certify that, in their opinion, the company's accounts represent a true and fair view of the company's financial position (see Chapter 9, para 9.7.2). Thus, Lord Bridge said (at p 626):

> The crucial question concerns the extent [or the 'scope'] of the shareholder's interest which the auditor has a duty to protect. The shareholders of a company have a collective interest in the company's proper management and, in so far as a negligent failure of the auditor to report accurately on the state of the company's finances deprives the shareholders of the opportunity to exercise their powers in general meeting to call the directors to book, and to ensure that errors in management are corrected, the shareholders ought to be entitled to a remedy. But in practice no problem arises in this regard since the interest of the shareholders in the proper management of the company's affairs is indistinguishable from the interest of the company itself, and any loss suffered by the shareholders (eg by the negligent failure of the auditor to discover and expose a misappropriation of funds by a director of the company) will be recouped by a claim against the auditors in the name of the company, not by individual shareholders.

BCCI v Price Waterhouse

Another example of the part played by the scope of the defendant's duty of care in a negligent misstatement case is *BCCI (Overseas) Limited (In Liquidation) v Price Waterhouse and Another* (1997) *The Times*, 10 February, the facts of which are set out in Chapter 9, para 9.7.2. In holding that, even if EW had owed Overseas a duty of care, the loss which Overseas claimed to have suffered in consequence of EW's alleged breach of that duty was outside the scope of that duty, Laddie J said:

> As pointed out in *Caparo*, it is not sufficient to ask simply whether EW owed Overseas a duty of care. It is necessary to determine the scope of the duty by reference to the kind of damage from which the defendants had to take care to save Overseas harmless. Nowhere in the Statement of Claim is it alleged that these defendants knew and intended that the 1985 and 1986 audits of Holdings and SA would be used by Overseas as a basis upon which to decide whether to make loans, pay dividends and tax, make charitable donations, or carry on a variety of other activities which proved to be loss-making. Overseas' case is that, had the audit been carried out correctly, Overseas would have been closed down

or its operation would have been overhauled, and the various frauds and imprudences in operation would not have continued. This is no more than an assertion that Overseas has made losses which it would not have made had Holdings' and SA's audits been carried out properly, and therefore EW is liable. I agree with EW's counsel that this is simply another version of the fallacious equation: Negligence by A + loss by B = liability of A to B.

Relational economic loss cases

In the relational economic loss cases, the phrase, 'the scope of the duty', is used as a means of referring to the need to place 'some limit or control mechanism' on the damages to which the defendant might otherwise be exposed if foreseeability of loss was the only criterion of liability (see Chapter 1, para 1.4.3 and Chapter 5, para 5.5). This need arises, not so much from the nature of the plaintiff's loss (ie usually pure economic loss), but, rather, from the circumstances from which it arose, namely damage to a third party's property. In *Candlewood Navigation Corporation Ltd v Mitsui OSK Lines Ltd* [1986] AC 1, Lord Fraser (at p 16) described the relational economic loss exclusionary rule as "a pragmatic one dictated by necessity". In other words, in order to avoid the creation of a rule of law whereby a person who damages another person's property can be held liable, not only to that person, but also to all third parties for all of the consequences of that damage, the common law developed an exclusionary rule to limit the scope of the defendant's duty of care in this type of case to the person or property directly injured (see Chapter 5).

Diminution in value cases

In some of the defective products and defective buildings cases (such as *Junior Books, Murphy* and *Nitrigen Eireann—below*, and Chapter 7), the 'scope' of the duty seems to refer to the distinction between physical damage and economic loss. However, it is submitted that this is not really what the courts in these cases were trying to convey because, as Lord Oliver said in *Murphy* (at p 485): "The critical question is not the nature of the damage in itself, whether physical or pecuniary, but whether the scope of the duty of care in the circumstances of the case is such as to embrace damage of the kind which the plaintiff claims to have sustained".

The basis for limiting the scope of the duty in *Murphy* was found by their Lordships to vest, first, in what their Lordships believed was the scope and intent of the Defective Premises Act 1972 (see Chapter 7, para 7.5.5) and secondly, and more importantly, in the fact that if a duty of care was imposed on the defendant for the plaintiff's loss consisting of the diminution in value of his house, the defendant would be providing a warranty in tort to a person with whom he did not have a contract that the building (or that goods manufactured by the defendant) were as fit for its/their contemplated purpose as the exercise of reasonable care could make it/them. Not only did their Lordships regard the possibility of the imposition of such a non-contractual warranty of quality as being contrary to principle, but, also, they envisaged serious problems in determining the standards by which the defectiveness of the building or the goods would fall to be decided (see Chapter 7, para 7.5.7). Their view was that the scope of transmissible warranties of quality is properly limited to contractual claims, with the consequence that the scope of any duty of care to be imposed in tort should correspondingly exclude such claims.

Dicta in cases

The following *dicta* of judges in some of the leading cases are instructive on the question of the scope of a duty of care:

Overseas Tankship (UK) Ltd v Morts Dock and Engineering Co Ltd ('The Wagon Mound No 1') [1961] AC 388: The main concern when this case reached the Privy Council was the question of "remoteness of damage" (see para 2.1.2, *above*). But the comments that their Lordships made in this regard are apt in the context of describing what is envisaged when one says that the defendant in any particular case is only liable for the plaintiff's loss if that plaintiff, and the loss that he suffered, were within the 'scope' of the duty which the court is prepared to impose on the defendant.

Thus, Viscount Simonds, delivering the judgment of the Judicial Committee, said (at p 425): "It is no doubt proper, when considering tortious liability for negligence, to analyse its elements, and to say that the plaintiff must prove a duty owed to him by the defendant, a breach of that duty by the defendant, and consequent damage. But there can be no liability until the damage has been done. It is not the act, but the consequences, on which tortious liability is founded. It is vain to isolate the liability from its context, and to say that B is or is not liable, and then to ask for what damage he is liable; for his liability is in respect of that damage and no other. If B's liability depends on the reasonable foreseeability of the consequent damage, how is that to be determined except by the foreseeability of the damage which in fact happened—the damage in suit".

Anns v Merton London Borough Council [1978] AC 728: Lord Wilberforce said (at p 752): "Secondly, if the first question [ie the existence of a prima facie duty of care based on a 'sufficient relationship of proximity'] is answered affirmatively, it is necessary to consider whether there are any considerations which ought to negative, reduce or limit the scope of the duty or the class of person to whom it is owed or the damages to which a breach of it may give rise". Although Lord Wilberforce's 'two-stage test' has been decisively rejected (see Chapter 3, para 3.3.1) and *Anns* has been overruled (see Chapter 7, para 7.3.1), it still remains valid to say that, under the approach which has replaced this test, if and when all of the other factors have been established, it is still necessary for the court to go on and consider whether it is necessary, in the interests of 'fairness, justice or necessity' to limit the scope of the defendant's duty.

Junior Books Ltd v Veitchi Co Ltd [1983] AC 520: Lord Brandon, dissenting, but whose judgment has subsequently been held to be preferable to that of the other Law Lords (see Chapter 7, para 7.3.6) said (at p 548): "The dispute between the parties is not whether the defendant owed a duty of care to the plaintiff in connection with the laying of the flooring. The existence of some duty arising from the proximity of the parties is, rightly in my view, admitted by the defendant. The dispute is rather concerned with the scope of that admitted duty of care".

Governors of the Peabody Donation Fund v Sir Lindsay Parkinson & Co Ltd [1985] 1 AC 210: Lord Keith said (at p 240):

> The true question in each case is whether the particular defendant owed to the particular plaintiff a duty of care having the scope which is contended for, and whether he was in breach of that duty with consequent loss to the plaintiff. A relationship of proximity in Lord Atkin's sense [in *Donoghue v Stevenson*] must exist before any duty of care can arise, but the scope of the duty must depend on all the circumstances of the case. So, in determining whether or not a duty of care of a particular scope was incumbent upon a defendant, it is material to take into consideration whether it is just and reasonable that it should be so.

Council of the Shire of Sutherland v Heyman (1985) 157 CLR 424: Brennan J, in the High Court of Australia, said (at p 487): "A postulated duty of care must be stated in reference to the kind of damage that the plaintiff has suffered and in reference to the plaintiff or a class of which the plaintiff is a member. A duty of care is a thing written on the wind unless damage is caused by the breach of that duty. There is no actionable negligence unless duty, breach and consequential damage coincide. For the purposes of determining liability in a given case, each element can be defined only in terms of the others. It is impermissible to postulate a duty of care to avoid one kind of damage—say, personal injury—and, finding the defendant guilty of failing to discharge that duty, to hold him liable for the damage actually suffered that is of another and independent kind—say, economic loss. Not only may the respective duties differ in what is required to discharge them: the duties may be owed to different persons or classes of persons. That is not to say that a plaintiff who suffers damage of some kind will succeed or fail in an action to recover damages according to the classification of the damage he suffered. The question is always whether the defendant was under a duty to prevent that damage, but the actual nature of the damage suffered is relevant to the existence and the extent of any duty to avoid or prevent it".

Caparo Industries plc v Dickman [1990] 2 AC 605: This case is discussed in detail in Chapter 9, para 9.7.2. Although much of the discussion in the speeches of their Lordships is devoted to determining whether a duty of care existed between the auditors and the take-over bidder when, as an existing shareholder, it bought further shares of the target company whose accounts the auditors had recently audited, in essence the case was concerned with determining whether the scope of any duty of care which the auditors owed to shareholders in carrying out their audit function extended to the plaintiff, as an existing shareholder, buying further shares of the company in reliance on the audit report. Four of their Lordships delivered speeches, and all of them made reference to the importance of determining the scope of any relevant duty of care.

Thus, Lord Bridge said (at p627): "It is never sufficient to ask simply whether A owes B a duty of care. It is always necessary to determine the scope of the duty by reference to the kind of damage which A must take care to save B harmless";

Lord Roskill said (at p628): "Phrases such as 'foreseeability', 'proximity', 'just and reasonable', or 'voluntary assumption of responsibility' will be found from time to time in the different cases. Such phrases are not precise definitions. At best, they are but labels or phrases descriptive of the very different factual situations which can exist in particular cases and which must be carefully examined in each case before it can be pragmatically determined whether a duty of care exists and, if so, what is the scope and extent of that duty";

Lord Oliver said (at p651): "In cases like this, 'proximity' is an expression used, not necessarily as indicating literally 'closeness' in a physical or metaphorical sense, but merely as a convenient label to describe circumstances from which the law will attribute a duty of care. It has to be borne in mind that the duty of care is inseparable from the damage which the plaintiff claims to have suffered from its breach. It is not a duty to take care in the abstract, but a duty to avoid causing to the particular plaintiff damage of the particular kind which he has in fact sustained"; and

Lord Jauncey said (at p655): "If, in any given circumstances, a relationship of proximity is found to exist, consideration must still be given to the scope of the duty which arises therefrom. In the case of physical proximity, few problems will arise, but where there exists a duty of care in relation to the making of statements, problems may arise if those statements are capable of being used for more than one purpose. It is not disputed in the present case that economic loss to the plaintiff as a shareholder was foreseeable by the auditors as a result of any failure on their part to exercise reasonable care in the conduct of the audit. What is disputed is whether the auditors owed any duty to individual shareholders and, if so, what was the scope of that duty"; and (at p661): "Reliance, even if probable, thereby establishing proximity, does not establish a duty of care of unlimited scope. Regard must be had to the transaction or transactions for the purpose of which the statement was made. It is loss arising from such transaction or transactions, rather than 'any loss' to which the duty of care extends".

Murphy v Brentwood District Council [1991] 1 AC 398: Lord Keith said (at p463): "The present problem is concerned with the scope of the duty. The question is whether the defendant council owed the plaintiff a duty to take reasonable care to safeguard him against the particular kind of damage which he had in fact suffered"; and (at p468): "It being recognised that the nature of the loss held to be recoverable in *Anns* was pure economic loss, the next point for examination [in that case] was whether the avoidance of loss of that nature fell within the scope of any duty of care owed to the plaintiffs by the local authority"; and Lord Oliver said (at p 485): "The critical question is not the nature of the damage in itself, whether physical or pecuniary, but whether the scope of the duty of care in the circumstances of the case is such as to embrace damage of the kind which the plaintiff claimed to have sustained".

James McNaughton Paper Group Ltd v Hicks Anderson & Co [1991] 2 QB 113 (see Chapter 9, para 9.7.2.): Neill LJ said (at p 124): "It is sufficient to underline that in every case the court must not only consider the foreseeability of the damage and whether the relationship between the parties is sufficiently proximate, but must also pose and answer the question: In this situation, is it fair, just and reasonable that the law should impose on the defendant a duty of the scope suggested, for the benefit of the plaintiff?".

Nitrigen Eireann Teoranta v Inco Alloys Ltd [1992] 1 WLR 498 (see Chapter 7, para 7.3.6): May J said (at p 501): "To succeed in a claim in negligence, a plaintiff has to establish that the defendant owes him a duty of care and that there has been a breach of that duty causing actionable damage. The critical question is whether the scope of the duty in the circumstances of the case is such as to embrace damage of the kind which the plaintiff claims to have suffered".

South Australia Asset Management Corporation v York Montague Ltd [1997] AC 191 (also indexed as *Banque Bruxelles SA v Eagle Star*): In this case, the plaintiff had lent money on the basis of a surveyor's negligent valuation which the surveyor had made pursuant to a contract with the plaintiff. The question for determination in the House of Lords related to the scope of the valuer's liability for the plaintiff's losses. Lord Hoffmann said (at p 211): "A duty of care such as the valuer owes in this case does not however exist in the abstract. A plaintiff who sues for breach of a duty imposed by the law (whether in contract or in tort or under statute) must do more than prove that the defendant has failed to comply. He must show that the duty was owed to him, and that it was a duty in respect of the kind of loss which he has suffered. Both of these requirements are illustrated by *Caparo Industries plc v Dickman* [1990] 2 AC 605. The auditors' failure to use reasonable care in auditing the company's statutory accounts was a breach of their duty of care. But they were not liable to an outside take-over bidder because the duty was not owed to them. Nor were they liable to shareholders who had bought more shares in reliance on the accounts because, although they were owed a duty of care, it was in their capacity as members of the company and not in the capacity of potential buyers of its shares. Accordingly, the duty which they were owed was not in respect of loss which they might suffer by buying its shares. As Lord Bridge said in *Caparo*, it is never sufficient to ask simply whether A owes B a duty of care. It is always necessary to determine the scope of the duty by reference to the kind of damage from which A must take care to save B harmless. In the present case, there is no dispute that the duty was owed to the lenders. The real question in this case is the kind of loss in respect of which the duty was owed".

BCCI (Overseas) Limited (In Liquidation) v Price Waterhouse and Another (*The Times*, 10 February 1997): Laddie J said: "Even if there is sufficient proximity between the adviser and the advisee, that does not expose the adviser to liability for all damage which can be shown to flow from the breach of duty. As pointed out in *Caparo*, it is not sufficient to ask simply whether [the defendant] owed [the plaintiff] a duty of care. It is necessary to determine the scope of the duty by reference to the kind of damage from which the defendant had to take care to save [the plaintiff] harmless".

2.2   Foreseeability

2.2.1   Introduction

Nowadays it is universally accepted that, whilst foreseeability of loss is a necessary pre-condition for the establishment of a duty of care, it is never, on its own, a sufficient and determinative criterion, at least in cases of pure economic loss. There is still some debate as to whether foreseeability of loss is a sufficient determinant where the plaintiff has suffered personal injury or physical damage. This is discussed below.

In recent times there has been much discussion about the role of foreseeability in economic loss cases. The debate arose from the fact that the first part of Lord Wilberforce's 'two-stage test' in *Anns v Merton London Borough Council* [1978] AC 728 suggested to some judges that Lord Wilberforce, with whom all of the other Lords in that case agreed, intended the test of reasonable foreseeability of loss to be the sole determinant of the existence of the duty of care. Although, in *McLoughlin v O'Brian* [1983] AC 410, Lord Wilberforce made it clear that that was not what he had meant, when he said (at p 420): "That foreseeability does not of itself, and automatically, lead to a duty of care, is, I think, clear", the debate still raged on. Although this is no longer a live issue, a consideration of some of the relevant *dicta* in various leading cases, as set out below, is nevertheless believed to be conducive towards a full understanding of the role of foreseeability in the duty of care process. It is also worth noting, at this point, that the actual words of Lord Wilberforce which gave rise to this controversy were (at p 751): "First one has to ask, whether, as between the alleged wrongdoer and the person who has suffered damage, there is a sufficient relationship of proximity or neighbourhood such that, in the reasonable contemplation of the former, carelessness on his part may be likely to cause damage to the latter—in which case a prima facie duty of care arises".

2.2.2   *Dicta* in cases

The following *dicta* serve to illustrate the role of foreseeability in the duty of care process, particularly in the context of the tendency of some judges to have regarded the first stage of Lord Wilberforce's test as indicating that reasonable foreseeability of loss was the sole determinant of the existence of a duty of care.

Jaensch v Coffey (1984) 155 CLR 549: Deane J said (at p 579): "Lord Atkin [in *Donoghue v Stevenson*] was at pains to stress that the formulation of a duty of care merely in the general terms of reasonable foreseeability would be too wide unless it were limited by 'the notion of proximity' which was embodied in the restriction of the duty of care to one's 'neighbour'"; and (at p 583): "It is not, and has never been the common law that the reasonable foreseeability of risk of injury to another automatically means that there is a duty to take reasonable care with regard to that risk of injury".

The Council of the Shire of Sutherland v Heyman (1985) 157 CLR 424: Brennan J said (at p 477): "The test of foreseeability of injury has never been applied as an exhaustive test for determining whether there is a prima facie duty to act to prevent injury caused by the acts of another or by circumstances for which the alleged wrongdoer is not responsible. [This is the category of cases considered in Chapter 8.] A man on the beach is not legally bound to plunge into the sea when he can foresee that a swimmer might drown. If foreseeability of injury were the exhaustive criterion of a duty to act to prevent the occurrence of that injury, legal duty would be coterminous with moral obligation". Deane J said (at p 495): "The common law imposes no general duty to avoid loss or injury to another merely because it is reasonably foreseeable that one's actions or omissions are likely to cause it".

Yuen Kun Yeu v The Attorney General of Hong Kong [1988] 1 AC 175: Lord Keith, speaking for the Privy Council, accepted that Lord Wilberforce had not "meant to test the sufficiency of proximity simply by the reasonable contemplation of likely harm". He then said (at p 192): "Foreseeability of harm is a necessary ingredient of a relationship giving rise to a duty of care, but it is not the only one. Otherwise there would be a liability in negligence on the part of one who sees another about to walk over a cliff with his head in the air, and forebears to shout a warning".

Hill v The Chief Constable of West Yorkshire [1989] 1 AC 53: Lord Keith said at p 60: "It has been said almost too frequently to require repetition, that foreseeability of likely harm is not in itself a sufficient test of liability in negligence".

2.2.3 Physical damage cases

There are suggestions in some cases that, if the plaintiff's loss is characterised as physical injury or damage to property, then foreseeability of that loss is the only pre-condition for the imposition of a duty of care.

2.2.3 *The elements of liability*

Caparo Industries plc v Dickman [1990] 2 AC 605: Lord Oliver said (at p 635): "Mere foreseeability is not of itself sufficient to ground liability unless, by reason of the circumstances, it itself constitutes the element of proximity, as in the case of direct physical damage";

Murphy v Brentwood District Council [1991] 1 AC 398: Lord Oliver said (at p 486): "In the straightforward case of the direct infliction of physical injury by the act of the defendant, there is no need to look beyond the foreseeability by the defendant of the result in order to establish that he is in a 'proximate relationship' with the plaintiff";

Mariola Marine Corporation v Lloyd's Register of Shipping (The Morning Watch) [1990] 1 Lloyd's Rep 547 (see Chapter 9, para 9.7.4): Phillips J said (at p 557): "Foreseeability alone (without proximity) would be enough to give rise to a duty of care where the harm foreseen is physical damage";

The Hua Lien [1991] 1 Lloyd's Rep 309: Lord Brandon said (at p 328): "The essential feature of the present case is that the damage sued for is not purely economic loss, but ordinary physical damage to property. It follows that the decisions relating to claims for purely economic loss to which their Lordships have referred have no relevance to the present case";

Alcock v Chief Constable of South Yorkshire Police [1991] 3 WLR 1057: Lord Oliver said (at p 1117): "There is in many cases, as for instance direct physical injury in a highway accident, an almost necessary coalescence of the twin elements of foreseeability and proximity, the one flowing from the other. But where such convergence is not self-evident, the question of proximity requires separate consideration".

London Drugs Ltd v Kuehne and Nagel International Ltd (1992) 97 DLR (4th) (see Chapter 10, para 10.2.1): La Forest J, in the Supreme Court of Canada, said (at p 271): "This case involves a claim for property damage. Undoubtedly, if the case involved economic loss, the court would undertake a searching inquiry into policy concerns under the second branch of *Anns* before concluding as to the existence of a duty of care. Since this case concerns property damage, however, the venerable authority of *Donoghue* is invoked in support of the simple and straightforward application of the foreseeability test established in that great case".

Hercules Managements Ltd v Ernst & Young (1997) 146 DLR (4th) 577: La Forest J, speaking for the unanimous panel in the Supreme Court of Canada, said (at p 589): "In the context of actions based on negligence causing physical damage, determining whether harm to the plaintiff was reasonably foreseeable to the defendant is alone a sufficient criterion for deciding proximity or neighbourhood under the first branch of the *Anns/Kamloops* test because the law has come to recognise (even if only implicitly) that, absent a voluntary assumption of risk by a plaintiff, it is always reasonable for a plaintiff to expect that a defendant will take reasonable care of the plaintiff's person and property".

Comment

It is submitted that these *dicta* are misleading. In cases of direct physical injury or property damage sustained by a plaintiff in a road accident or other similar incident, there is little doubt that the defendant will be liable for the plaintiff's injuries if the accident was entirely his fault. An established body of case law has built up in which this result has been confirmed over and over again, albeit that the circumstances of each case might have been unique in its own way, so much so that, in most cases of this type, the courts have dispensed with any separate enquiry as to whether the latter two 'essential elements', ie proximity and justice and fairness, have been satisfied. However, this does not mean that, in these cases, foreseeability of the plaintiff's injuries has been elevated to a higher plane and that the other requirements have been abandoned. All that it means is that, in this category of case, the other requirements are taken as being satisfied because the law, based on numerous similar cases, is so well established that it is pointless to try to argue that, in the circumstances, there was not a sufficient relationship of proximity or that it would not be just and reasonable to impose a duty of care on the defendant for the plaintiff's injuries.

Lord Wilberforce made this point succinctly in *McLoughlin v O'Brian* [1983] AC 410, when he said (at p 420):

> When foreseeability is said to result in a duty of care being owed to a person or class, the statement that there is a duty of care denotes a conclusion into the forming of which considerations of policy have entered.

This point was also recognised by Deane J in *Jaensch v Coffey* (1985) 155 CLR 549, when he said (at p 581):

> In cases falling within some closely settled areas of the law of negligence, such as cases involving ordinary physical injury to an employee in an accident at his place of work or to one user of a public road involved in a collision with another, it will have been established in previous cases that the relationship between the parties necessarily possesses the requisite degree of proximity. The result is that, in cases involving direct physical damage to person or property, separate reference to any notion of proximity has come to be commonly regarded as either unnecessary or as being appropriately formulated in terms of being satisfied if the physical injury sustained was of a kind which was reasonably foreseeable. The fact that, as a practical matter, any separate requirement of proximity is commonly disregarded in cases where no issue is raised about it does not establish that it has been discarded as a matter of principle. All that that fact establishes is that, in such cases, the requirement of proximity is not a subject of dispute.

This is not simply an academic argument. In *Marc Rich & Co AG v The Bishop Rock Marine Co Ltd* (*The Nicholas H*) [1996] 1 AC 211 (see Chapter 9, para 9.7.4), where the plaintiff's loss of cargo, which had sunk at sea, was classified as physical damage, the plaintiff argued that it was sufficient to hold the defendant classification society liable for this loss simply because it was foreseeable. The plaintiff contended that, as its loss was physical, it did not need to establish, in addition, that a relationship of proximity existed between itself and the defendant, or that it was just and reasonable to hold the defendant liable. The defendant argued that, even though the plaintiff's loss was physical, it was still necessary for the plaintiff to establish the existence of these other two factors.

In all three levels of court, all of the judges held in the defendant's favour on this point. In the High Court ([1992] 2 Lloyd's Rep 48) Hirst J said:

> In most claims in respect of physical damage to property, the question of the existence of a duty of care does not give rise to any problem, because it is self-evident that such a duty exists, and the contrary view is unarguable. Typical examples are claims in respect of physical damage to property arising out of the driving of a motor vehicle on a road or the navigation of a ship in a river. With regard to the driving of a motor vehicle on a road, for example, it is self-evident that the driver owes a duty of care to the owners of other vehicles using the road to avoid damage to such vehicles, and a like duty to the owners of property adjacent to the road to avoid damage to such property.

He then considered several *dicta* in a variety of cases, and then concluded: "It seems to me clear that proximity is a relevant criterion in physical damage cases, particularly where [as in this case] there is no direct physical contact between the plaintiff and the defendant, or between vehicles and equipment under their control".

The Court of Appeal ([1994] 1 WLR 1071) was just as emphatic in its rejection of the plaintiff's counsel's submission that foreseeability of loss was sufficient to found liability because the plaintiff's loss consisted of physical damage. Saville LJ said (at p 1076):

> In the light of the whole of the speech of Lord Atkin [in *Donoghue v Stevenson* [1932] AC 562] and the speeches of the others forming the majority, it seems to me to be clear that *Donoghue v Stevenson* is no authority for the proposition advanced by the plaintiff's Counsel; and that, in all cases, more is required than mere foreseeability of loss or damage. Indeed, it seems to me that in Lord Atkin's speech, the element of foreseeability, the relationship between the parties and considerations of fairness, justice and reasonableness are clearly to be seen. That this must be the law is to my mind self-evident, as it was to Lord Diplock in *Dorset Yacht Co Ltd v Home Office* [1970] AC 1004 [see Chapter 8, para 8.3.3].
>
> In my judgment, there is no authority binding on this Court to support the plaintiff's Counsel's submission. On the contrary, it seems to me that the authorities point to the conclusion that, whatever the nature of the harm sustained by the plaintiff, it is necessary to consider the matter not only by inquiring about foreseeability, but also by considering the nature of the relationship between the parties; and to be satisfied that in all the circumstances, it is fair, just and reasonable to impose a duty of care.

In the House of Lords ([1996] 1 AC 235) Lord Steyn, for the majority of 4:1, endorsed this *dictum* and added (at p 235):

Since the decision in *Dorset Yacht Co Ltd v Home Office* [1970] AC 1004 it has been settled law that the elements of foreseeability and proximity, as well as considerations of fairness, justice and reasonableness are relevant to all cases whatever the nature of the harm sustained by the plaintiff.

2.3 Proximity

2.3.1 Introduction

A duty of care in the tort of negligence is imposed by the law without the agreement of the defendant. As noted above, the mere fact that the defendant ought reasonably to have foreseen that his negligent act or omission would most probably cause injury to other persons will not be sufficient to warrant the imposition of a duty of care. In addition, the court must be satisfied that, in all the circumstances, the conduct of both the defendant and the plaintiff was such as to have given rise to the existence of a relationship between them and that that relationship was so close, or 'proximate', as to enable the court to conclude that it would be just and reasonable to impose a duty of care on the defendant in respect of the plaintiff's loss. The term 'proximity' is sometimes used to describe both the existence and the degree of closeness of the relationship which is required in any particular category of case. At other times it is used only to describe the existence of the relationship, and the overall question of 'justice and fairness' is treated separately. Numerous judges in a wide variety of cases have commented on the meaning and the role played by 'the requirement of proximity'. These are considered below. It is submitted that it does not really matter whether one treats the existence and the moral content of the requisite degree of proximity as two questions or one question, so long as one appreciates that these are not simply questions of fact to be decided on an ad hoc basis on the facts of any particular case alone, but are questions of law which are constrained by the category of case which is being considered. Both the existence and the requisite degree of the relationship of proximity which will justify the imposition of a duty of care in any particular case will differ according to the category of case (see Chapter 1, para 1.3.2 for a summary of the relevant categories) in question.

The point made above, that the relevant questions are questions of law, was recognised by Lord Devlin in *Hedley Byrne & Co Ltd v Heller & Partners Ltd* [1964] AC 465, when he said (at p 524):

> It is not, in my opinion, a sensible application of what Lord Atkin was saying [in *Donoghue v Stevenson*—see *below*] for a judge to be invited on the facts of any particular case to say whether or not there was 'proximity' between the plaintiff and the defendant. That would be a misuse of a general conception, and it is not the way in which English law develops. What Lord Atkin did was to use his general conception to open up a category of cases giving rise to a special duty. The real value of *Donoghue v Stevenson* to the argument in this case [see Chapter 9, para 9.4] is that it shows how the law can be developed to solve particular problems. Is the relationship between the parties in this case such that it can be brought within a category giving rise to a special duty?

2.3.2   *Dicta* in cases

An understanding of the part played by 'proximity' in the duty of care process can best be gained by considering the *dicta* of judges in decided cases.

Donoghue v Stevenson [1932] AC 526: Lord Atkin formulated his famous 'neighbour' principle (which is set out in paras 3.2.1 and 9.2.3) for determining the 'range of complainants' and also a definition of 'the notion of proximity' for determining the circumstances in which a duty of care will be owed to those persons who satisfy the 'neighbour test'. As discussed in paras 3.2.1 and 9.2.3, these are separate tests, and they must not be confused. The 'neighbour test' is based on reasonable foreseeability of harm to those persons whom it could reasonably be foreseen would be injured by the defendant's negligent act or omission. Lord Atkin said (at p 581) that this test needs to be "limited by the notion of proximity" introduced by Lord Esher in *Heaven v Pender* (1883) 11 QBD 503 (see para 6.2.5). Lord Esher had formulated his view of proximity in terms of the actual physical closeness between the defendant and the plaintiff when the defendant committed his negligent act which caused the plaintiff's damage. Lord Atkin said (at p 581) that it is wrong to confine proximity "to mere physical proximity". Rather, he said, it extends "to such close and direct relations that the act complained of directly affects a person whom the person alleged to be bound to take care would know would be directly affected by his careless act".

It is worth noting here that Lord Atkin treated the third requirement (fairness) as a separate question and not as part of the content of the relationship which he held to be sufficiently proximate in that case. He said (at p 582): "If this [ie a denial of the plaintiff's case] were the result of the authorities, I should consider the result a grave defect in the law"; and (at p 599): "It will be an advantage to make it clear that the law in this matter, as in most others, is in accordance with sound common sense".

Grant v Australian Knitting Mills Limited [1936] AC 85 (see Chapter 6, para 6.3.5): Lord Wright said that the word 'proximity' in the context of duties of care "is apt to mislead, because of the suggestion of some overt relationship like that in contract. If the term 'proximity' is to be applied at all, it can only be in the sense that want of care [on the part of the defendant] and injury [suffered by the plaintiff] are in essence directly and intimately connected. Although there may be intervening transactions of sale and purchase, the events are themselves unaffected by what happened between them; 'proximity' can only properly be used to exclude any element of remoteness, or of some interfering complication between the want of care and the injury".

Caltex Oil (Australia) Pty Ltd v The Dredge Willemstad (1975) 136 CLR 529: Stephen J distinguished the categories of negligent misstatement and product liability cases from cases of economic loss resulting from accidents and then said (at p 575):

> In the general realm of negligent conduct [ie the residual category of economic loss which he identified] it may be that no more specific proposition can be formulated than a need for insistence upon 'sufficient' proximity between tortious act and compensable detriment. The articulation, through the cases, of situations which denote sufficient proximity will provide a body of precedent productive of the necessary certainty. Some guidance in the determination of the requisite degree of proximity will be derived from the broad principle which underlies liability in negligence, namely 'a general public sentiment of moral wrongdoing for which the offender must pay' (*per* Lord Atkin in *Donoghue v Stevenson*). Such a sentiment will only be present when there exists a degree of proximity between the tortious act and the injury, such that the community will recognise the tortfeasor as being in justice obliged to make good his moral wrongdoing by compensating the victims of his negligence. As Lord Morris said in the *Dorset Yacht* case, courts may have recourse to a consideration of what is 'fair and reasonable' in determining whether, in particular circumstances, a duty of care arises. So, too, I would suggest in determining the requisite degree of proximity before there may be recovery for purely economic loss. As the body of precedent accumulates some general area of demarcation between what is, and is not a sufficient degree of proximity in any particular class [ie category of case] of economic loss will no doubt emerge.

Jaensch v Coffey (1984) 155 CLR 549: Deane J said (at p 580) that Lord Atkin's test of 'proximity' in *Donoghue v Stevenson* "differed in nature from the test of reasonable foreseeability, in that it involved both an evaluation of the closeness of the relationship and a judgment of the legal consequences of that evaluation"; and (at p 584):

> Lord Atkin did not seek to identify the precise content of the requirement of the relationship of 'proximity' which he identified as a limitation upon the test of reasonable foreseeability. It was left as a broad and flexible touchstone of the circumstances in which the common law would admit the existence of a relevant duty of care to avoid causing reasonably foreseeable injury to another. It is directed to the relationship between the parties insofar as it is relevant to the allegedly negligent act of one person, and the resulting injury sustained by the other. It involves the notion of nearness or closeness, and embraces physical proximity (in the sense of space and time) between the person and the property of the plaintiff and the person or property of the defendant, circumstantial proximity, such as an overriding relationship of employer and employee or of professional man and his client, and causal proximity, in the sense of the closeness or directness of the relationship between the particular act and the injury sustained. The identity and relative importance of the considerations relevant to an issue of proximity will vary in different classes of case, and the question whether the relationship is 'so' close 'that' the common law should recognise a duty of care in a new area or class of case may involve value judgments in matters of policy and degree.

Then, in conformity with the point made above about the role of proximity in different categories of case, Deane J said (at p 585): "This does not mean that it is a proper or sensible approach to the requirement of proximity for it to be treated as a question of fact to be resolved merely by reference to the particular relationship between a plaintiff and a defendant in the circumstances of a particular case. The requirement of a 'relationship of proximity' is a touchstone and a control of categories of cases in which the common law will admit the existence of the duty of care. The question whether the relationship between the plaintiff and the defendant with reference to the allegedly negligent act possessed the requisite degree of proximity is a question of law to be resolved by the processes of legal reasoning by induction and deduction".

The Council of the Shire of Sutherland v Heyman (1985) 157 CLR 424: Deane J repeated the passage quoted above about the types of proximity which the requirement of proximity embraces and then added (at p 498): "Proximity may [also] reflect an assumption by one party of a responsibility to take care to avoid loss to the person or property of another, or reliance by one party upon such care being taken by the other in circumstances where the other party knew, or ought to have known of that reliance. Both the identity and the relative importance of the factors which are determinative of an issue of proximity are likely to vary in different categories of case".

Stevens v Brodribb Sawmilling Co Pty Ltd (1986) 160 CLR 16: Deane J said (at p 53): "Proximity remains the general conceptual determinant and the unifying theme of the categories of case in which the common law of negligence recognises the existence of a duty to take reasonable care to avoid a reasonably foreseeable risk of injury to another".

Ernst & Whinney v Willard Engineering (Dagenham) Ltd [1987] Const LJ 292: The judge said (at p 298): "The concept of proximity is both relative and elastic. It expands or contracts in accordance with the circumstances of the case, notably according to whether the likelihood of damage is to the person or to property, the magnitude of the risk created by the conduct in question, the seriousness of its consequences and the foreseeable possibility of the risk or its consequences being eliminated either physically or financially by intermediate examination or financial adjustment along the line from the actor to the person who alleges that he was adversely affected by the actor's negligent act".

Huxford v Stoy Hayward & Co (1989) 5 BCC 421: Popplewell J said (at p 432): "The content of the requirement of proximity is not capable of precise definition. The approach will vary according to the particular facts of the case, but the focus of the enquiry is on the closeness and directness of the relationship between the parties".

Caparo Industries plc v Dickman [1990] 2 AC 605: Lord Bridge said (at p 618): "The concepts of proximity and fairness embodied in these additional ingredients [ie in addition to foreseeability] are not susceptible of any such precise definition as would be necessary to give them utility as practical tests, but amount in effect to little more than convenient labels to attach to features of different specific situations which, on a detailed examination of all the circumstances, the law recognises pragmatically as giving rise to a duty of care of a given scope". Then Lord Roskill said (at p 628): "Phrases such as 'foreseeability', 'proximity', 'voluntary assumptions of responsibility' and 'just and reasonable' are not precise definitions. At best they are but labels or phrases descriptive of the very different factual situations which can exist in particular cases and which must be carefully examined in each case before it can be pragmatically determined whether a duty of care exists and, if so, what is its scope and extent".

Lord Oliver endorsed this view when he said (at p 633): "Proximity is, no doubt, a convenient expression, so long as it is realised that it is no more than a label which embraces not a definable concept, but merely a description of circumstances from which, pragmatically, the courts conclude that a duty of care exists". He goes on to say (at p 651): "Proximity is an expression used not necessarily as indicating literally 'closeness' in a physical or metaphorical sense, but merely as a convenient label to describe circumstances from which the law will attribute a duty of care". Then Lord Jauncey said (at p 655): "The concept of proximity is somewhat elusive, extending as it does beyond mere physical proximity. It might be described as the circumstances in which the law considers it proper that a duty of care should be imposed on one person towards another".

Murphy v Brentwood District Council [1991] 1 AC 398: Lord Oliver said (at p 486): "The essential question which has to be asked in every case, given that damage, which is the essential ingredient of the action, has occurred, is whether the relationship between the plaintiff and the defendant is such—or, to use the favoured expression, whether it is of sufficient 'proximity'—that it imposes upon the latter a duty of care to avoid or prevent that loss which has in fact been sustained".

Beaumont v Humberts (1990) 49 EG 46: Staughton LJ said (at p 48): "Proximity has replaced 'neighbour', the concept of Lord Atkin in *Donoghue v Stevenson*, where it was no doubt derived from the twentieth chapter of Exodus. It describes not physical closeness, but a degree of connection between the conduct of one person and that of another".

This *dictum* is not quite correct, because, as noted above (and in Chapter 9), Lord Atkin's 'neighbour principle' was a test of reasonable foreseeability for determining the class of persons to whom a duty of care might be owed, and his test of proximity was a separate test, based on the relationship between the parties, for determining when such a duty might exist. Also, it is not correct to state that proximity does not describe physical closeness, because sometimes, depending on the category of case in question, it might well do so, as it did in *Home Office v Dorset Yacht Co Ltd* [1970] AC 1004 (see Chapter 8).

2.3.2 *The elements of liability*

Alcock v Chief Constable of South Yorkshire [1991] 3 WLR 1057 (A 'nervous shock' case): Lord Oliver said (at p 1113): "The answer has to be found in the existence of a combination of circumstances from which the necessary degree of 'proximity' between the plaintiff and the defendant can be deduced. And, in the end, it has to be accepted that the concept of 'proximity' is an artificial one which depends more upon the court's perception of what is the reasonable area for the imposition of liability, than upon any logical process of analogical deduction".

Gala v Preston (1991) 172 CLR 243: Mason CJ, speaking for the majority in the High Court of Australia, said (at p 252):

> A relevant duty of care will arise under the common law of negligence only in a case where the requirement of a relationship of proximity between the plaintiff and the defendant has been satisfied. The requirement of proximity constitutes the general determinant of the categories of case in which the common law of negligence recognises the existence of a duty to take reasonable care to avoid a reasonably foreseeable and real risk of injury. In determining whether the requirement is satisfied in a particular category of case in a developing area of the law of negligence, the relevant factors will include policy considerations.

Canadian National Railway Co v Norsk Pacific Steamship Co Ltd (1992) 91 DLR (4th) 289: McLachlin J, speaking for herself and two of the other judges, said (at p 368): "Proximity may be usefully viewed, not so much as a test in itself, but as a broad concept which is capable of subsuming different categories of cases involving different factors".

McLachlin J then referred with approval to the *dicta* of Deane J cited *above* in *Jaensch v Coffey* and *The Council of the Shire of Sutherland v Heyman* and continued (at p 369):

> The matter may be put thus: before the law will impose liability, there must be a connection between the defendant's conduct and the plaintiff's loss which makes it just for the defendant to indemnify the plaintiff. In contract, the contractual relationship provides this link. In trust, it is the fiduciary obligation which establishes the necessary connection. In tort, the equivalent notion is proximity. Proximity may consist of various forms of closeness—physical, circumstantial, causal or assumed—which serve to identify the categories of cases in which liability lies.
>
> Viewed thus, the concept of proximity may be seen as an umbrella, covering a number of disparate circumstances in which the relationship between the parties is so close that it is just and reasonable to permit recovery in tort. The complexity and diversity of the circumstances in which tort liability may arise defy identification of a single criterion capable of serving as the universal hallmark of liability. The meaning of 'proximity' is to be found rather in viewing the circumstances in which it has been found to exist and determining whether the case at issue is similar enough to justify a similar finding.
>
> In summary, it is my view that the authorities suggest that pure economic loss is *prima facie* recoverable where, in addition to negligence and foreseeable loss, there is sufficient proximity between the negligent act and the loss. Proximity is the controlling concept which avoids the spectre of unlimited liability. Proximity

may be established by a variety of factors, depending on the nature of the case. To date, sufficient proximity has been found in the case of negligent misstatements where there is an undertaking and correlative reliance (*Hedley Byrne*); where there is a duty to warn (*Rivtow*), and where a statute imposes a responsibility on a municipality towards the owners and occupiers of land (*Kamloops*). But the categories are not closed. As more cases are decided, we can expect further definition on what factors give rise to liability for pure economic loss in particular categories of cases. In determining whether liability should be extended to a new situation, Courts will have regard to the factors traditionally relevant to proximity, such as the relationship between the parties, physical propinquity, assumed or imposed obligations and close causal connection. And they will insist on sufficient special factors to avoid the imposition of indeterminate and unreasonable liability. The result will be a principled, yet flexible, approach to tort liability for pure economic loss.

The absolute exclusionary rule adopted in *Cattle v Stockton* and affirmed in *Murphy* (subject to *Hedley Byrne*) can itself be seen as an indicator of proximity. Where there is physical injury or damage, one posits proximity on the ground that if one is close enough to someone or something to do physical damage to him or it, one is close enough to be held legally responsible for the consequences. Physical injury has the advantage of being a clear and simple indicator of proximity. The problem arises when it is taken as the *only* indicator of proximity.

Viewed in this way, proximity may be seen as paralleling the requirement in civil law that damages must be direct and certain. Proximity, like the requirement of directness, posits a close link between the negligent act and the resultant loss. Distant losses which arise from collateral relationships do not qualify for recovery.

A comprehensive consideration of proximity requires that the court review all of the factors connecting the negligent act with the loss. This includes not only the relationship between the parties, but all forms of proximity—physical, circumstantial, causal or assumed indicators of closeness. While it is impossible to define comprehensively what will satisfy the requirement of proximity or directness, precision may be found as types of relationships or situations are defined in which the necessary closeness between negligence and loss exists.

While proximity is critical to establishing the right to recover pure economic loss in tort, it does not always indicate liability. It is a necessary but not necessarily sufficient condition of liability. Recognising that proximity is itself concerned with policy, the approach adopted in *Kamloops* (paralleled by the second branch of *Anns*) requires the court to consider the purposes served by permitting recovery as well as whether there are any residual policy considerations which call for a limitation of liability. This permits courts to reject liability for pure economic loss where indicated by policy reasons not taken into account in the proximity analysis.

This case is considered in detail in Chapter 5, where it is noted that McLachlin and two of the other six judges decided the case in the plaintiff's favour on the basis that there was sufficient proximity, three of the judges decided the case against the plaintiff on the basis that the relational economic loss exclusionary rule is absolute, whilst the seventh judge, Stevenson J, rejected both the proximity analysis and the exclusionary rule and decided the case in the plaintiff's favour on the 'known plaintiff exception', which was in turn rejected by all of the other six judges. In rejecting the proximity analysis, Stevenson J said (at p 387):

> I express my reservations about the use of 'proximity' as a test. In my view, proximity expresses a conclusion, a judgment, a result, rather than a principle. If a loss is not proximate, it may be said to be too remote. The concept of proximity is incapable of providing a principled basis for drawing the line on the issue of liability.

La Forest J, speaking for the three judges who rejected the plaintiff's claim, agreed with Stevenson J's views on proximity. Thus, La Forest J said (at p 344): "I agree with Stevenson J that the concept of proximity is incapable of providing a principled basis for drawing the line on the issue of liability. As he notes, it expresses a result, rather than a principle".

Burnie Port Authority v General Jones Pty Ltd (1994) 179 CLR 520: In the High Court of Australia, Mason CJ, after referring to Deane J's above-cited *dictum* in *Stevens v Brodribb Sawmilling Co* that proximity is the unifying theme of the categories of case in which a duty of care is recognised, said (at p 543):

> Without proximity, the tort of negligence would be reduced to a miscellany of disparate categories, among which reasoning by the legal processes of induction and deduction would rest on questionable foundations since the validity of such reasoning essentially depends upon the assumption of underlying unity or consistency.
>
> It is true that the requirement of proximity was neither formulated by Lord Atkin [in *Donoghue v Stevenson*] nor propounded and developed in cases in this Court as a logical definition or a complete criterion which could be directly applied as part of a syllogism of formal logic to the particular circumstances of a particular case. As a general conception deduced from decided cases, its practical utility lies essentially in understanding and identifying the categories of case in which a duty of care arises under the common law of negligence, rather than as a test for determining whether the circumstances of a particular case bring it within such a category, either established or developing. That is, however, the basic function performed by general principles or conceptions in the ascertainment and development of the common law.

Stovin v Wise [1996] AC 923: Lord Nicholls said (at p 932):

> The *Caparo* tripartite test elevates proximity to the dignity of a separate heading. This formulation tends to suggest that proximity is a separate ingredient, distinct from fairness and reasonableness, and capable of being identified by some other criteria. This is not so. Proximity is a slippery word. Proximity is not legal shorthand for a concept with its own, objectively identifiable characteristics. Proximity is convenient shorthand for a relationship between two parties which makes it fair and reasonable that one should owe the other a duty of care. This is only another way of saying that, when assessing the requirement of fairness and reasonableness, regard must be had to the relationship of the parties.

White v Jones [1993] 3 WLR 730: In the Court of Appeal, under the heading: 'a special relationship', Sir Donald Nicholls V-C said:

I turn next to consider whether there is between a solicitor and an intended beneficiary a relationship of proximity and whether it is fair, just and reasonable that liability should be imposed on the solicitor to compensate the intended beneficiary. I shall consider these two headings together, because there is no real demarcation line between them. They shade into each other. Both involve value judgments. Under the latter heading the court makes its assessment of the requirements of justice and reasonableness. Likewise, although less obviously, built into the concept of proximity or neighbourhood is an assessment by the court that, in a given relationship, there 'ought' to be liability for negligence. These two headings are no more than labels under which the court examines the pros and cons of imposing liability in negligence in a particular type of case. This is well illustrated in the present case where some of the points which call for consideration could happily be considered under either heading.

Hercules Managements Ltd v Ernst & Young (1997) 146 DLR (4th) 577: La Forest J, speaking for the unanimous panel of the Supreme Court of Canada, adopting the words of Stevenson J in *CNR v Norsk* (see above), said (at p 588): "The term 'proximity' is nothing more than a label expressing a result, judgment or conclusion; it does not in and of itself provide a principled basis on which to make a legal determination".

Interestingly, the panel of judges in this case, on whose behalf this *dictum* was rendered, included McLachlin J, who, in *CNR v Norsk*, made very extensive comments in favour of the proximity concept (see above).

Hill v Van Erp (1997) 142 ALR 687: Dawson J, in the High Court of Australia, retracted some of the views previously expressed by the High Court on the utility of the concept of proximity. He said:

> The notion of proximity was advanced by Deane J [see above] to describe in general terms the element in a relationship which would give rise to a duty of care where mere foreseeability of harm was insufficient for that purpose, and to provide a unifying conceptual determinant to assist in ascertaining what the content of that element was in any given category of case. Perhaps the attempt was an ambitious one, because the assumption would seem to be that there is a common element in each such relationship, and that it can adequately be described as proximity.
>
> In *Jaensch v Coffey*, Deane J suggested that the concept involves the notion of nearness or closeness [see above], but the features of a relationship which give rise to a duty of care do not always answer the description of nearness or closeness. Likewise, some relationships which would as a matter of language be thought proximate nevertheless do not constitute relationships of proximity. That is because the identification of the particular requirements of proximity in developing areas of the law is not divorced from the considerations of public policy which underlie and enlighten the concept. But if considerations of policy underlie and enlighten the concept of proximity, and if nearness and closeness are neither sufficient or necessary to establish a relationship of proximity in all cases, then it cannot be said that any unifying common element has emerged which can adequately be described as proximity. That is why Deane J went too far in *Stevens v Brodribb Sawmilling Co* when he said that the notion of proximity is a unifying theme explaining why a duty of care has been recognised as arising in particular categories of case [see above]. To the extent that the joint

judgment in *Burnie Port Authority v General Jones* [see above] to which I was a party proceeds along similar lines, it would seem to go too far.

Reasoning by analogy from decided cases by the processes of induction and deduction, informed by, rather than divorced from, policy considerations, is not, in my view, dependent for its validity on those cases sharing an underlying conceptual consistency. It is really only dependent upon the fact that something more than reasonable foreseeability is required to establish a duty of care, and that what is sufficient or necessary in one case is a guide to what is sufficient or necessary in another.

Nevertheless, and notwithstanding the criticism of the concept by Brennan J [see below], I retain the view that the requirement of proximity is at least a useful means of expressing the proposition that, in the law of negligence, reasonable foreseeability of harm may not be enough to establish a duty of care. Something more is required and it is described as proximity. Proximity in that sense expresses the result of a process of reasoning, rather than the process itself, but it remains a useful term because it signifies that the process of reasoning must be undertaken. But to hope that proximity can describe a common element underlying all those categories of case in which a duty of care is recognised is to expect more of the term than it can provide.

Another majority judge, Toohey J, did not have difficulty with the idea that proximity is the unifying theme of the categories of case in which a duty of care has been held to exist, so long as this statement is taken at its face value, and not too much more is read into it. Thus, he said:

To say that proximity represents the general conceptual determinant, and the unifying theme, focuses attention on the categories of cases in which proximity has been held to exist. It is the category of cases with which proximity is concerned, rather than whether a relationship of proximity exists on the facts of a particular case.

[Toohey J then referred to the *dictum* of Lord Devlin in *Hedley Byrne* cited in para 2.3.1, *above*, and continued:]

Used in that way, there is no difficulty in treating proximity as the general conceptual determinant and the unifying theme. That does not mean that proximity of itself identifies with any precision a common element underlying all those cases in which liability in negligence has been held to exist. But the general conception does operate as a limitation on any notion that liability in negligence arises simply from a duty to avoid harm that is reasonably capable of being foreseen.

Gummow J, concurring, criticised the concept of proximity. He said:

Proximity may be no more than the currently fashionable touchstone of duty. My own view is that, in the field of liability for pure economic loss, as elsewhere, the concept of proximity is of limited use in the determination of individual disputes. It may provide a broad conceptual umbrella beneath which the concerns of particular or discrete categories of cases can be discussed. To my mind, there is real difficulty in treating the requirement of the relationship of proximity as an overriding requirement which provides the conceptual determinant (or a determinant) for the recognition of an existence of a duty to take reasonable care to avoid reasonably foreseeable risk of injury. It may well be that the notion of proximity provides a unifying theme for various categories of cases, the genus of which they are species. Each species displays a particular manifestation of the notion of a relationship of proximity. But, by itself, the notion of proximity, used as a legal norm, has the uncertainties and perils of a category of inter-determinate reference, used with shifting meanings to mask no more than policy preferences. To speak of proximity is to invite a series of questions which spring from the particular circumstances of the case in question. Put another way, as it was in the Supreme Court of Canada (by La Forest J in *Canadian National Railway Co v Norsk Pacific Steamship Co* (1992) 91 DLR (4th) 289), proximity expresses a result, rather than a principle.

Comment

Some of the *dicta* cited above require explanation. On the one hand, there are *dicta* which give the impression that the existence of a sufficiently prox-imate relationship between the parties is completely at large; see, for example, Lord Jauncey's statement in *Caparo* that proximity might be described as the circumstances in which the law considers it proper that a duty of care should be imposed on one person towards another. In fact, however, when one looks at the decided cases in any particular category of cases, one finds that the courts have very consciously tried to define the cri-teria which, in general terms, need to exist in that particular category of cases for a sufficiently proximate relationship to exist between the defen-dant and the plaintiff so as to enable the court to consider, either separately or as part of the same question (see para 2.3.1, *above*), whether in all of the circumstances of the case it is fair, just and reasonable to impose a duty of care on that defendant for that plaintiff's loss. Indeed, in *Caparo* itself, both Lord Bridge and Lord Oliver enunciated lists of quite specific criteria to guide judges in negligent misstatement cases generally, and not just to answer the question in the *Caparo* case itself, for determining what Lord Oliver called "the necessary relationship between the maker of a statement and the recipient who acts in reliance upon it" (see Chapter 9, para 9.6.2).

Secondly, there is the group of cases in which judges have criticised the concept of proximity. These criticisms are twofold. One of the most vocal and consistent critics has been Brennan J in the High Court of Australia. His criticism is that the concept of proximity is too uncertain or amorphous to be of assistance to judges. For example, in *San Sebastian Proprietary Ltd v The Minister* (1986) 162 CLR 340, Brennan J said (at p 367):

> Both the *Anns* approach and the proximity approach have been espoused because it was perceived that foreseeability of loss is not the only criterion for imposing a duty of care in some classes of case. Neither the *Anns* approach nor the proximity approach defines the legal rules which apply in those classes of case where foreseeability of loss alone does not suffice to give rise to a duty of care. Yet legal rules are required to determine whether a duty of care exists in a particular case. By a legal rule, I mean a rule that prescribes an issue of fact on which a legal consequence depends. It is necessary to appreciate that neither approach expresses a legal rule. Each approach postulates a framework within which the Courts can develop legal rules which limit the occasions when the law would otherwise impose a duty of care.
>
> [His Honour then referred to Deane J's description of proximity in *The Council for the Shire of Sutherland v Heyman* (see above) and continued:]

The variable content proposed for the notion denies its applicability as a particular proposition of law. True, some legal rules import broad community standards, but proximity is not a community standard by reference to which issues of fact can be determined, nor is it a particular proposition of law excluding a right to relief otherwise open on the facts of a case. If proximity were misunderstood as being a particular proposition of law expressing a touchstone for resolving a *particular* case, the Judge would be required to define its legal content according to some notion of whether it was appropriate to impose a duty of care in that case. A rule without specific content confers a discretion. Damages in tort are not granted or refused in the exercise of a judicial discretion.

In *Gala v Preston* (1991) 172 CLR 243, Brennan J continued with this theme by saying:

The amorphous character of the extended notion of proximity [ie as embracing more than foreseeability—see below] was perceived by Lord Bridge in *Caparo Industries Plc v Dickman* [1990] 2 AC 605.

[Brennan J then referred to the *dictum* of Lord Bridge that is set out above and continued by saying:]

If the term be used as a description of a relationship out of which a duty of care does arise, it would be a sophism to invoke the term as a criterion to determine whether a duty of care arises. If proximity in the extended sense be invoked primarily as a criterion of the existence of a duty of care, it is too amorphous a concept to serve the purpose.

More recently, in *Bryan v Maloney* (1995) 69 ALJR 375, the facts of which are set out in Chapter 7, para 7.6.4, Brennan J, dissenting, said (at p 396):

I am unable to see how the question whether Mr. Bryan owed Mrs. Maloney a duty of care can be resolved by reference to the notion of proximity in what has been called 'its broader sense', that is, embracing more than foreseeability.

I have elsewhere stated my opinion that to treat proximity as a criterion of liability without an *a priori* definition of the elements it contains is to create a judicial discretion. If the elements be not defined, the question whether proximity exists in cases out of the mainstream can be answered confidentially only by the judgment of a court, perhaps involving value judgments on matters of policy and degree. But the law of negligence should be capable of application in solicitors' offices. It should not have to await definition in litigation.

If proximity in the broader sense can be invoked as a criterion of liability in particular cases without *a priori* definition of its content, the certainty which analysis of the different elements of tortious liability in different categories of case can produce will be lost, and the definition of elements which might constitute and distinguish a new category of case will give way to a mere evaluation of the circumstances favouring, or not favouring, recovery. Such a notion of proximity would be a juristic black hole into which particular criteria and rules would collapse, and from which no illumination of principle would emerge.

Another Australian critic of the concept of proximity is McHugh J, who is now a member of the High Court. Writing extra-judicially before this appointment, McHugh J complained that, whilst proximity can consist of one or more of a host of different elements, the doctrine provides no guide as to which one or more of these elements is determinative of the duty issue in a particular case. In *Hill v Van Erp* (1997) 142 ALR 687, McHugh J returned to these criticisms, when he said:

> The use of the concept or principle of proximity as the criterion of duty has not increased the predictability of judicial decisions or given a real explanation of the grounds upon which a duty of care is imposed in many economic losses. In a paper written before I joined this Court, I expressed my scepticism about the usefulness of proximity as a principle or a guide for determining the existence of a duty of care. In *Gala v Preston*, however, I was party to a joint judgment which held that a plaintiff's action failed because there was no proximity between the plaintiff and the defendant. But the present case [the facts of which are set out in Chapter 9, para 9.9.2] has reinforced my scepticism as to whether the concept of proximity provides any real guidance in determining the existence of a duty of care in difficult and novel cases. In cases concerning economic loss where the plaintiff has not relied on the defendant's conduct, the concept of proximity provides no assistance in distinguishing between the cases (if any) where a duty of care is owed and those where it is not owed.
>
> In the field of liability for pure economic loss, as elsewhere, the concept of proximity is of limited use in the determination of individual disputes. It may provide a broad conceptual 'umbrella' beneath which the concerns particular to discrete categories of case can be discussed. To my mind, there is a real difficulty in treating the requirement of a relationship of proximity as an overriding requirement which provides the conceptual determinant for the recognition of the existence of a duty to take reasonable care to avoid reasonably foreseeable risk of injury. It may well be that the notion of proximity provides a unifying theme for various categories of case, the genus of which they are species. Each species displays a particular manifestation of the notion of a relationship of proximity. But, by itself, the notion of proximity, used as a legal norm, has the uncertainties and perils of a category of indeterminate reference, used with shifting meanings to mask no more than policy preferences.

These *dicta* have been set out in detail because they need to be addressed. It is submitted that, whilst there is undoubted truth in these *dicta*, they do not derogate from the use of the proximity analysis in individual cases because the more that that analysis is, in fact, employed in individual cases, the more likelihood there will be of a reasonably certain body of authority emerging in cases that have similar characteristics. As Stephen J said in the passage that is cited above from the *Caltex Oil (Australia)* case: "The articulation, through the cases, of situations which denote sufficient proximity will provide a body of precedent productive of the necessary certainty".

Furthermore, it is submitted that the very fact that the concept is slightly amorphous is a desirable characteristic reflecting the flexibility and adaptability to changing times and circumstances that the common law needs to possess in order to make it acceptable as the legal foundation for the resolution of disputes in tort. In this regard, it is also worth noting the following observation of Gaudron J in *Hill v Van Erp* (1997) 142 ALR 687:

> There has been some criticism of proximity as a criterion of liability, it having been said, for example, by Brennan J that it lacks the specificity of a precise proposition of law. The same may be said of the proposition that the law should

develop incrementally and by analogy [this being the alternative test suggested by Brennan J—see Chapter 3, para 3.4.4]. Inevitably, there will be imprecision in any developing area of the common law.

The other area of criticism of the concept of proximity noted above is that it expresses a conclusion or a result, rather than a principle or a test. This is, of course, true, but it is submitted that the revelation of this fact is semantic and pedantic, because the proximity analysis that judges do carry out in practice is, in any event, only designed to reach a conclusion, namely whether a sufficient relationship of proximity exists in the particular case to warrant the imposition of a duty of care. Although some judges might inadvertently refer to proximity as being a principle or a test, in reality it is clear that they have in fact been treating it as a conclusion or a result, or as a goal to be achieved, before a duty of care can be imposed in any particular case.

Indeed, this is exactly what the Supreme Court of Canada itself did in *Hercules Managements Ltd v Ernst and Young* (1997) 146 DLR (4th) 577. After the passage cited above in which La Forest J, speaking for the whole panel, said that the term 'proximity' is nothing more than a label expressing a result and does not provide a principled basis on which to make a legal determination, La Forest J proceeded to apply a traditional proximity analysis to determine the result in the case. He said (at p 588):

> In order to render 'proximity' a useful tool in defining when a duty of care exists in negligent misrepresentation cases, therefore, it is necessary to infuse that term with some meaning. In other words, it is necessary to set out the basis upon which one may properly reach the conclusion that proximity inheres between a representor and a representee. This can be done most clearly as follows. The label 'proximity', as it was used by Lord Wilberforce in *Anns*, was clearly intended to connote that the circumstances of the relationship in inhering between the plaintiff and the defendant are of such a nature that the defendant may be said to be under an obligation to be mindful of the plaintiff's legitimate interests in conducting his affairs. Indeed, this idea lies at the very heart of the concept of a duty of care, as articulated by Lord Atkin in *Donoghue v Stevenson*.
>
> In cases of negligent misrepresentation, the relationship between the plaintiff and the defendant arises through reliance by the plaintiff on the defendant's words. Thus, if 'proximity' is meant to distinguish the cases where the defendant has a responsibility to take reasonable care of the plaintiff from those where he has no such responsibility, then, in negligent misrepresentation cases, it must pertain to some aspect of the relationship of reliance. To my mind, proximity can be seen to inhere between a defendant/representor and a plaintiff/representee where two criteria relating to reliance may be said to exist on the facts: (a) the defendant ought reasonably to foresee that the plaintiff will rely on his representations; and (b) reliance by the plaintiff would, in the particular circumstances of the case, be reasonable. The plaintiff and the defendant can be said to be in a 'special relationship' whenever these two factors inhere.

It is submitted that, despite the Court's dismissiveness of the concept of proximity, the technique of analysis employed by it in discerning the necessary characteristics of a relationship that would be sufficient to enable the Court to impose a duty of care in this case was the same as the traditional proximity analysis that was enunciated and employed by the House of Lords in *Caparo* (see Chapter 9, para 9.6.2).

2.3.3 Reliance

The concept of 'reasonable reliance' is considered in detail in Chapters 7, 8 and 9. This concept poses the question whether or not liability can be imposed on a defendant for having caused pure economic loss to a plaintiff where this principle is not applicable. The following *dicta* are relevant to this discussion:

Junior Books v Veitchi Co Ltd [1983] AC 520: Lord Roskill said (at p 546): "The concept of proximity must always involve, at least in most cases, some degree of reliance".

The Council of the Shire of Sutherland v Heyman (1985) 157 CLR 424: Mason J said (at p 461): "Reliance has always been an important element in establishing the existence of a duty of care. It has been suggested that liability in negligence is largely, if not exclusively, based on the plaintiff's reliance on the defendant's taking care in circumstances where the defendant is aware, or ought to be aware of that reliance. The concept of proximity involves in most cases a degree of reliance. Reliance has been an influential factor in setting limits to the far-ranging effects of the foreseeability doctrine, and in confining the class of persons to whom a duty of care may be owed".

Banque Keyser Ullmann SA v Skandia (UK) Insurance Co Ltd [1990] 1 QB 665, a 'nonfeasance case': Ralph Gibson LJ said (at p 797): "We are prepared to accept, for the purposes of this judgment, that in some cases (if rare) of pure economic loss, the court may be willing to find the existence of a duty of care owed by a defendant to a plaintiff even in the absence of evidence of any actual voluntary assumption by the defendant of such duty and/or any reliance on such assumption". The 'voluntary assumption' part of this *dictum* was subsequently criticised by the House of Lords in *Smith v Eric S Bush* [1990] 1 AC 831 (see Chapter 9, para 9.5.2).

Murphy v Brentwood District Council [1991] 1 AC 398: Lord Keith, in criticising the House of Lords' decision in *Anns* in 1977, said (at p 468): "The right to recover for pure economic loss not flowing from physical injury did not then [ie in 1977] extend beyond the situation where the loss had been sustained through reliance on negligent misstatements, as in *Hedley Byrne*". In overruling *Anns* he and the other six Law Lords involved in this case effectively held that the principle of 'reasonable reliance' is a pre-condition towards the establishment of a sufficiently proximate relationship to justify the imposition of a duty of care on a defendant who has caused direct economic loss to the plaintiff and that any decisions which did not apply this principle must be regarded as limited and aberrant exceptions.

Thus, Lord Keith continued: "There is room for the view that an exception is to be found in *Morrison Steamship Co Ltd v Greystoke Castle (Cargo Owners)* [1947] AC 265 [see Chapter 5, para 5.4.2]. That case, which was decided by a narrow majority may, however, be regarded as turning on specialities of maritime law or concerned in the relationship of joint adventurers at sea".

On the other hand, Lord Oliver was a bit more broad-minded. He said (at p 486): "It is not necessarily to be assumed that the reliance cases form the only possible category of cases in which a duty to take reasonable care to avoid or prevent pecuniary loss can arise. *Morrison Steamship*, for instance, clearly was not a reliance case. Nor, indeed, was *Ross v Caunters* [see Chapter 9, para 9.7.5] so far as the disappointed beneficiary was concerned. Another example may be *Ministry of Housing and Local Government v Sharp* [see Chapter 9, para 9.7.4], although this may, on analysis, properly be categorised as a reliance case". It is also worth noting that in *Banque Keyser* the Court of Appeal noted that *American Express International Banking Corporation v Hurley* [1985] 3 All ER 564 (see Chapter 9, para 9.7.8) is the only other case in which the plaintiff has succeeded in recovering pure economic loss without having relied on the defendant's skill or judgment.

White v Jones [1993] 3 WLR 730 (CA) (see Chapter 9, para 9.7.5): The Court of Appeal rejected the submission that "there is no liability for damages in negligence, unless there is actual and foreseeable reliance by the plaintiff on the defendant". Sir Donald Nicholls V-C said: "I do not agree that reliance is a prerequisite to the existence of the necessary close and direct relationship. As I read the speeches in the recent House of Lords' decisions, their Lordships have emphasised the importance of reliance in pure economic loss cases, but I do not find in those speeches any indication, still less express statement, that in all cases, reliance is a prerequisite to the existence of liability. Indeed, the thrust of the speeches in *Caparo v Dickman* and *Murphy v Brentwood* is against any attempt to lay down hard-and-fast boundary lines". He and the other members of the court held that it was right to impose a duty of care on the defendant solicitor in that case towards the two beneficiaries who had suffered economic loss through the solicitor not having followed his client's instructions to prepare his will, notwithstanding that the beneficiaries had not relied on the solicitor. They felt that there were compelling reasons of 'justice and fairness' which overrode the constraints of adhering to strict doctrine.

Wessex Regional Health Authority v HLM Design Ltd (1994) 40 Con LR 1: One of the problems in this construction dispute was whether the plaintiff's statement of claim was defective because there was no specific allegation that the plaintiff had relied on the defendants' skill and expertise. The plaintiff had merely pleaded that the defendants, who were respectively the architects and the consulting engineers, "owed a tortious duty to take reasonable care to prevent or avoid economic loss". The judge, Judge Fox-

Andrews QC, sitting as an Official Referee, held that the plaintiff's pleading was not defective. He said:

> Underlying the existence of a duty in respect of negligent advice, statement or information is reliance. But reliance can take many forms. A person may make a purchase in reliance on a structural engineer's report commissioned by him. In such a case it might be thought that if reliance on the report was not pleaded, the action might fail. Again, a person such as a prospective mortgagee may fall into a category of persons who will probably rely on a valuation made by a prospective mortgagee's surveyor to whom, therefore, a duty is owed.
>
> But reliance may be of a quite different nature. A person may enter into a contract with another person professing a special skill or expertise in reliance on that person exercising care in the performance of that skill and expertise including, as will almost always be the case with professional men, care to avoid or prevent economic loss. In circumstances of a case such as the present, either the professional man owes a duty in tort to his client to take reasonable care to prevent economic loss in respect of all aspects of his work or he owes no such duty at all. If this is not to be so, the uncertainty of the law might be significant. Much might depend on the skill of the pleader. Difficult questions would arise as to whether matters had been communicated to the client or whether the client could be shown to have acted upon these matters. I have reached the conclusion that, if it can be shown that it is fair and reasonable, then in respect of all of their work, HLM [the architects] and Webb [the engineers] owed a duty to take reasonable care to avoid economic loss.
>
> But that still leaves open the question as to whether the case as pleaded in the statement of claim can support a case where the client says: 'I entered into a contract in reliance that the architects/engineers would take reasonable care to avoid or prevent economic loss.' A number of decisions at first instance suggest that the pleading is not adequate. But the question arises as to whether it is necessary to plead the obvious. I have reached the conclusion that it is not. It is sufficient to plead facts showing that, in respect of a major project, the clients engaged the services of professional architects/engineers for the purposes of the project. That is the actual matrix supporting the tortious cause of action to avoid or prevent economic loss.

White v Jones [1995] 2 AC 207 (see Chapter 9, para 9.7.5): After considering the House of Lords' decisions in *Hedley Byrne and Co Ltd v Heller and Partners Ltd* [1964] AC 465 and *Nocton v Lord Ashburton* [1914] AC 932 (see Chapter 9), Lord Browne-Wilkinson said (at p 272):

> Since this House was concerned with cases of negligent misstatement or advice, it was inevitable that any test laid down required both that the plaintiff should rely on the statement or advice and that the defendant could reasonably foresee that he would do so. In the case of claims based on negligent statements (as opposed to negligent actions) the plaintiff will have no cause of action at all unless he can show damage and he can only have suffered damage if he has relied on the negligent statement. Nor will a defendant be shown to have satisfied the requirement that he should foresee damage to the plaintiff unless he foresees such reliance by the plaintiff as to give rise to the damage. Therefore, although reliance by the plaintiff is an essential ingredient in a case based on negligent misstatement or advice, it does not follow that in all cases based on negligent action

or inaction by the defendant it is necessary in order to demonstrate a special relationship that the plaintiff has in fact relied on the defendant or the defendant has
foreseen such reliance. If in such a case careless conduct can be foreseen as likely
to cause, and does in fact cause, damage to the plaintiff, that should be sufficient
to found liability.

Esanda Finance Corporation Ltd v Peat Marwick Hungerfords (1997) 142
ALR 750 (see Chapter 9, para 9.9.2): With reference to the High Court of
Australia's earlier decision in *San Sebastian Proprietary Ltd v The Minister*
(1987) 68 ALR 161 (see Chapter 9, para 9.9.2), in which one of the reasons
for the failure of the plaintiff's claim was that the plaintiff was not able to
establish that the defendant made the representation with the intention of
inducing members of the class of developers to act in reliance on it,
Dawson J said:

> The majority pointed out [*San Sebastian*] that there is no convincing reason for
> confining liability for negligent misstatement to cases where there is a request for
> information or advice. The existence of an antecedent request for information
> or advice may assist in demonstrating reasonable reliance on the part of the
> person making the request. However, a request is not a necessary prerequisite for
> reasonable reliance. Reliance was said in *San Sebastian* to be a cornerstone of
> liability for negligent misstatement. Of course, the person acting or refraining
> from acting on the information or advice must demonstrate reliance in order to
> prove that any loss which flows therefrom was caused by the negligent misstate-
> ment. But that reliance must also be reasonable in all the circumstances, and this
> may be demonstrated in a number of ways. An intention to induce a person to
> whom information or advice is given to act in a particular way is merely one of
> the various means by which it may be shown that the reliance by that person
> upon the information or advice is reasonable so that, in combination with other
> relevant circumstances, it may serve to establish a relationship of proximity
> which will support a duty of care.
>
> Brennan J pointed out in *San Sebastian* that it is always necessary in cases of
> negligent misstatement to establish that the statement in question operated as an
> inducement to the person to whom it was made to act upon it. As I have said,
> that is just another way of saying that it is necessary to prove reliance in order
> to show that any loss was caused by reason of the negligence of the maker of the
> statement, and for that purpose it does not matter whether the inducement was
> intentional or not.

Gummow J, concurring, added:

> In a case of auditors' negligence, the alleged damage flows not immediately from
> the making of the statement by the auditor, but from the reliance by the plaintiff
> upon it and from the action or inaction of the plaintiff which produces conse-
> quential loss. Hence the submissions by the auditors that in such a case reliance
> is an essential link between the defendant's conduct and the plaintiff's injury, and
> is a cornerstone of liability in negligence so that, in the present case, it is neces-
> sary for the plaintiff to plead and establish reliance. What is involved is foresee-
> ability of reliance. Moreover, the auditors further contend that even this of itself
> is not sufficient to found a duty of care in a case such as the present. More is
> required. The auditors illustrate this point by citation of the stipulation by Lord
> Goff in *Spring v Guardian Assurance Plc* [1995] 2 AC 296, with reference to

Hedley Byrne, that there must be an assumption or undertaking of responsibility by the defendant towards the plaintiff coupled with reliance by the plaintiff on the exercise by the defendant of due care and skill [see Chapter 3, para 3.5.2].

In Chapter 3, para 3.5.3, it is noted that in *Hill v Van Erp* (1997) 12 ALR 687, Gaudron J introduced the concept of 'control' as being an important factor in the determination of duties of care in tort cases involving an allegation of negligence on the part of the defendant. She returned to this theme in the present case in the judgment she delivered jointly with Toohey J. Their Honours first referred to Mason J's statement in *Kondis v State Transport Authority* (1984) 154 CLR 672 that the relationship which gives rise to a non-delegable duty "arises because the person on whom it is imposed has undertaken the control of the person or property of another or is so placed in relation to that person or his property as to assume a particular responsibility for his or its safety in circumstances where the person affected might reasonably expect that due care will be exercised".

With reference to this *dictum*, Toohey and Gaudron JJ said:

> It is convenient, at this stage, to say something of assumption of responsibility and reliance as indicators of a special relationship of proximity giving rise to a duty to take reasonable care in the provision of information and advice. In that context, neither notion is free from difficulty. It is necessary to distinguish between reliance as an indicator of proximity and reliance as an element of a cause of action for the negligent provision of information or advice. As Lord Browne-Wilkinson pointed out in *White v Jones* [1995] 2 AC 207, "in the case of claims based on negligent statements, the plaintiff will have no cause of action at all unless he can show damage, and he can only have suffered damage if he has relied on the negligent statement". For the purposes of proximity, reliance clearly involves something over and above the fact that the plaintiff relied on the statement in question as the basis for his acting or not acting in a particular way.
>
> In the context of liability for negligent statements, it seems to us that reliance is better expressed in terms similar to those used by Mason J in *Kondis* [see *above*]. Thus, reliance is to be understood in the context of the provision of information or advice, as an expectation, which is reasonable in the circumstances, that due care will be exercised in relation to that provision.

Kripps v Touche Ross and Co (1997) 35 CCLT (2d) 60 (BCCA, leave to appeal to the SCC refused): One of the issues in this case, the facts of which are set out in Chapter 9, para 9.9.3, was whether, in a case where there was more than one possible inducement to the plaintiff's conduct, the plaintiff has the burden of proving that the misrepresentation relied upon was 'fundamental' to its decision. In answering this question in the negative, Finch JA, speaking for the majority of 2:1, said (at p 90):

> It is sufficient for the plaintiff in an action for negligent misrepresentation to prove that the misrepresentation was at least one factor which induced the plaintiff to act to his detriment. I am also of the view that where the misrepresentation is one which was calculated or which would naturally tend to induce the plaintiff to act upon it, the plaintiff's reliance may be inferred. The inference of reliance is one which may be rebutted, but the onus of doing so rests on the representor.

His Honour was in any event sceptical about asking the plaintiff in auditors' negligence cases (and similar cases) whether he did actually rely on the auditors' statement before making an investment in the audited company. Thus Finch JA said (at p 89):

> Whether a representation was made negligently or fraudulently, reliance upon that representation is an issue of fact as to the representee's state of mind. There are cases where the representee may be able to give direct evidence as to what, in fact, induced him to act as he did. Where such evidence is available, its weight is a question for the trier of fact. In many such cases, however, it would be unreasonable to expect such evidence to be given, and if it were, it might well be suspect as being self-serving.

2.3.4 Relationship with foreseeability

Although foreseeability and proximity are distinct concepts, they are not totally unrelated to each other. In *Jaensch v Coffey* (1984) 155 CLR 549 Deane J explained the relationship between them when he said (at p 579): "The fact that an act of one person can be reasonably foreseen as 'likely to injure' another is an indication, and sometimes an adequate indication, that the requirement of proximity is satisfied. At the same time, the overall proximity of the relationship between the person or property of the plaintiff and that of the defendant, or between the allegedly negligent act and its effect, may be relevant to the question whether injury to the plaintiff was reasonably foreseeable".

In *Huxford v Stoy Hayward & Co* (1989) 5 BBC 421 Popplewell J also made this point, when he said (at p 432): "The content of the requirement of proximity is not capable of precise definition. The approach will vary according to the particular facts of the case, but the focus of the inquiry is on the closeness and directness of the relationship between the parties. In determining this, foreseeability must, I think, play an important part; the more obvious it is that A's act or omission will cause harm to B, the less likely a court will be to hold that the relationship of A and B is insufficiently proximate to give rise to a duty of care".

These remarks serve to stress the fact that the exercise which a court has to carry out in any particular case involves a large degree of common sense and practicality.

2.4 Justice and reasonableness

2.4.1 Introduction

Even if the plaintiff's loss caused by the defendant's negligent act was foreseeable, and even if the relationship between them was proximate, in accordance with the principles discussed above, the court will not impose a duty of care on the defendant for the plaintiff's loss unless the court is satisfied that, in all the circumstances, the interests of justice and fairness, or what is sometimes simply called 'policy', would be better served by doing so than by not doing so. An example is *Rondel v Worsley* [1969] 1 AC 191 in which the House of Lords held that a barrister was immune from an action for economic loss suffered by his client as a result of his negligent conduct of a case in court, notwithstanding the obvious foreseeability of the client's loss and the high degree of proximity between the parties. The court stressed that this immunity was not based on the absence of a contract between the barrister and his client, but on the 'public policy' grounds that the administration of justice requires that a barrister should be able to carry out his duty to the court fearlessly and independently, and that actions for negligence against barristers would make the retrying of the original action inevitable, thereby prolonging litigation, contrary to the public interest. Similarly, in *Hill v Chief Constable of West Yorkshire* [1989] 1 AC 53 (see Chapter 8, para 8.3.3) public policy was invoked as a separate and independent ground for holding that no duty of care should be imposed on the police for negligence in respect of their activities in the investigation and suppression of crime.

In defining the limits of duties of care in different categories of cases, different judges use different language. Sometimes they say that they are doing so as a matter of 'policy'; alternatively, they justify their approach by applying 'logic', 'common sense', 'pragmatism' or 'justice and reasonableness'. Whatever language is used, the court is essentially involved in a delicate balancing exercise in which consideration is given to all of the conflicting claims of the defendant and the plaintiff as viewed in the wider context of the demands of society as perceived by the judges themselves. In *Goldberg v Housing Authority of Newark* (1962) 186 A 2d 291 Weintraub CJ described the process when he said (at p 293): "Whether a duty exists is ultimately a question of fairness. The inquiry involves a weighing of the relationship of the parties, the nature of the risk and the public interest in the proposed solution". Another way of thinking of the process is to regard it as an equation, in which the underlying policy considerations applicable to the category of case in question are on the one side, and have to be matched by the requirements on the other side, namely foreseeability and proximity. The question is not simply whether the plaintiff's loss was foreseeable and whether the relationship between the parties was 'proximate'. Rather, the question is whether, given that the plaintiff's loss was foreseeable, the relationship between the parties was 'so' proximate 'that' it would be 'fair, just and reasonable' in all the circumstances to impose a duty of care on the defendant for the plaintiff's loss.

However, this 'equation' approach should not be applied too literally, because sometimes it is simply not possible, for reasons of 'policy', to balance the equation. The example of a barrister's immunity for his negligent acts or omissions in court has been cited above. Another example is most of the cases which fall into the category of relational economic loss (see Chapter 5, para 5.8.1). Even though the requirements of foreseeability and proximity might be satisfied, the plaintiff will still not generally succeed because the policy considerations which underlie the exclusionary rule in this type of case outweigh any other considerations of fairness which might arise in any particular case by virtue of the high degree of foreseeability of the plaintiff's loss or the closeness of the relationship between him and the defendant.

The problem for legal advisers is that it is very difficult to predict in advance how any particular judge will decide a 'policy issue' in an area of law where the precise question for consideration has not arisen before. Although precedent and analogy with similar cases will, of course, play a major part, each judge will have his own particular approach and prejudices and will be able to formulate cogent reasons for ascribing to different philosophies from his fellow judges. A good example of this divergence of approach occurring in practice are the cases considered in Chapter 5 (see para 5.6), of *Caltex Oil (Australia) Pty Ltd v The Dredge Willemstad* (1976) 136 CLR 529, in which each of the five judges of the High Court of Australia decided the case (in the plaintiff's favour) on a different basis, and of *Canadian National Railway Co v Norsk Pacific Steamship Co* (1992) 91 DLR 4th 489, in which three of the majority judges of the Supreme Court of Canada decided the case (in the plaintiff's favour) on one basis and the fourth majority judge decided it on another basis, but each group totally rejected the approach of the other, and (almost by definition) the three minority judges totally rejected the approach of all of the majority judges. Another example is the differing views of various judges in England on the threat posed by the 'floodgates' argument (ie the 'spectre of indeterminate liability') which can arise in certain categories of economic loss cases, particularly relational economic loss (see Chapter 5, para 5.5).

The position is further complicated by virtue of the fact that some judges believe that it is not their role to pronounce on 'policy' issues. Thus, for example, in *Home Office v Dorset Yacht Co Ltd* [1970] AC 1004, Viscount Dilhorne (dissenting) said (at p 1051): "We have not to decide what the law should be, and then alter the existing law. That is the function of parliament"; while Lord Scarman in *McLoughlin v O'Brian* [1983] AC 410, although concurring, said (at p 431): "The policy issue as to where to draw the line is not justiciable. The problem is one of social, economic, and financial policy. The considerations relevant to a decision are not such as to be capable of being handled within the limits of the forensic process".

2.4.2 *Dicta* in cases

The following *dicta* are pertinent to the question of justice and reasonableness.

Donoghue v Stevenson [1932] AC 562 (see Chapter 6, para 6.2): Lord Atkin said (at p 583): "I do not think so ill of our jurisprudence as to suppose that its principles are so remote from the ordinary needs of civilised society as to deny a legal remedy where there is so obviously a social wrong" and (at p 599): "It will be an advantage to make it clear that the law in this matter, as in most others, is in accordance with sound common sense".

Hedley Byrne & Co Ltd v Heller & Partners Ltd [1964] AC 464 (see Chapter 9, para 9.4): Lord Pearce said (at p 536): "How wide the sphere of the duty of care in negligence is to be laid depends ultimately on the courts' assessment of the demands of society for protection from the carelessness of others".

Home Office v Dorset Yacht Co Ltd [1970] AC 1004 (see Chapter 8, para 8.3.3): Lord Morris said (at p 1034): "The decision of a court as to whether a duty of care exists is in reality a policy decision" and (at p 1039): "In the situation stipulated in the present case, it would not only be fair and reasonable that a duty of care should exist, but it would be contrary to the fitness of things were it not so. I doubt whether it is necessary to say, in cases where the court is asked whether in a particular situation a duty existed, that the court is called upon to make a decision as to policy. Policy need not be invoked where reason and good sense will at once point the way. If the test as to whether in some particular situation a duty of care arises may, in some cases, have to be whether it is fair and reasonable that it should so arise, the court must not shrink from being the arbiter. As Lord Radcliffe said in *Davis Contractors v Fareham Urban District Council* [1956] AC 696, 'the court is the spokesman and reasonable man'".

Spartan Steel and Alloys v Martin & Co (Contractors) Ltd [1973] QB 27 (see Chapter 4, para 4.3.2): Lord Denning MR said (at p 36): "At bottom, I think the question of recovering economic loss is one of policy. Whenever the courts draw a line to mark out the bounds of duty, they do it as a matter of policy, so as to limit the responsibility of the defendant".

Caltex Oil (Australia) Pty Ltd v The Dredge Willemstad (1976) 136 CLR 529 (see Chapter 5, para 5.8.2): Stephen J said (at p 575): "Some guidance in the determination of the requisite degree of proximity will be derived from the broad principle which underlies liability in negligence. As Lord Atkin put it in *Donoghue v Stevenson* [at p 580], liability for negligence is 'based upon a general public sentiment of moral wrongdoing for which the offender must pay'. Such a sentiment will only be present when there exists a degree of proximity between the tortious act and the injury, such that the community will recognise the tortfeasor as being in justice obliged to make good his moral wrongdoing by compensating the victims of his negligence".

Dutton v Bognor Regis Urban District Council [1972] 1 QB 373 (see Chapter 7, para 7.2.1): Lord Denning MR said (at p 397):

> This case is entirely novel. It seems to me that it is a question of policy which we, as judges, have to decide. The time has come when, in cases of new import, we should decide them according to the reason of the thing. In previous times, when faced with a new problem, judges have not openly asked themselves: what is the best policy for the law to adopt? But the question has always been there in the background. It has been concealed behind such questions as: was the defendant

under any duty to the plaintiff? Was the relationship between them sufficiently proximate? Was it too remote? And so forth. Nowadays we direct ourselves to considerations of policy. In short, we look at the relationship of the parties: and then say, as matter of policy, on whom should the loss fall.

Lamb v Camden London Borough Council [1981] 1 QB 625 (see Chapter 8, para 8.3.3): Lord Denning MR said (at p 636): "The law has to draw a line somewhere. Sometimes it is done by limiting the range of the persons to whom a duty is owed. Sometimes it is done by saying that there is a break in the chain of causation. At other times it is done by saying that the consequence is too remote to be a head of damage. All these devices are useful in their way. But ultimately it is a question of policy for the judges to decide".

Junior Books v Vietchi Co Ltd [1983] AC 520 (see Chapter 7, para 7.3.6): Lord Fraser said (at p 532): "The concern which has been repeatedly expressed is that the effect of relaxing strict limitations would be to introduce 'liability in an indeterminate amount to an indeterminate class'. This is the 'floodgates' argument. It appears to me to be unattractive, especially if it leads, as I think it would in this case, to drawing an arbitrary and illogical line just because a line has to be drawn somewhere".
Lord Roskill said (at p 539):

> Although it cannot be denied that policy considerations have from time to time been allowed to play their part in the tort of negligence, today I think its scope is best determined by considerations of principle rather than of policy. The floodgates argument is very familiar. It may still on occasion have its proper place, but its principle suggests that the law should develop along a particular route, and if the adoption of that particular route will accord a remedy where that remedy has hitherto been denied, I see no reason why, if it be just that the law should henceforth accord that remedy, that remedy should be denied simply because it will, in consequence of this particular development, become available to many rather than to few.

and (at p 545) he stated: "The history of the development of the law in the last 50 years shows that fears aroused by the floodgates argument have been unfounded".

Governors of the Peabody Donations Fund v Sir Lindsay Parkinson & Co Ltd [1985] 1 AC 210 (see Chapter 8, para 8.2.5): Lord Keith said (at p 241) in a passage which is now often quoted: "In determining whether or not a duty of care of a particular scope was incumbent upon a defendant, it is material to take into consideration whether it is just and reasonable that it should be so".

McLoughlin v O'Brian [1983] AC 410 (A 'nervous shock' case): Lord Wilberforce said (at p 420):

> At the margin, the boundaries of a man's responsibility for acts of negligence have to be fixed as a matter of policy. It does not make any essential difference

whether one says that there is a duty, but as a matter of policy the consequences of a breach of it ought to be limited at a certain point, or whether one says that the fact that the consequences may be foreseeable does not automatically impose a duty of care, does not do so in fact where policy indicates to the contrary. When foreseeability is said to result in a duty of care being owed to a person or a class, the statement that there is 'a duty of care' denotes a conclusion into the forming of which considerations of policy have entered.

Lord Edmund-Davies, after referring to Lord Scarman's views (see para 2.4.1, *above*) said (at p 427): "The proposition [of Lord Scarman] that the 'policy issue is not justiciable' is as novel as it is startling. So novel is it in relation to this appeal that it was never mentioned during the hearing before your Lordships. And it is startling because it runs counter to well established and wholly acceptable law". Quoting from a Canadian case [*Nova Mink Ltd v Trans-Canada Airlines* (1951) 2 DLR 241] he said (at p 246): "There is always a large element of judicial policy and social expediency involved in the determination of the duty problem however it may be obscured by the use of traditional formulae". Lord Russell said (at p 429): "In the last analysis, any policy consideration seems to be rooted in a fear of floodgates opening—the tacit question: 'What next?' I am not impressed by that fear—certainly not sufficiently to deprive this plaintiff of just compensation for the reasonably foreseeable damage done to her. I do not consider that such deprivation is justified by trying to answer in advance the question posed, 'What next?' by a consideration of other circumstances. To attempt in advance solutions, or even guidelines, in hypothetical cases may well, it seems to me, in this field, do more harm than good".

Leigh & Sillivan Ltd v Aliakmon Shipping Co Ltd [1985] 1 QB 350 (see Chapter 5, para 5.8.1): In the Court of Appeal, Oliver LJ in referring to Lord Wilberforce's 'two-stage test' in *Anns v Merton London Borough Council* (see Chapter 3, para 3.2.2) said (at p 373): "Whether one tests the existence of the duty by a one-stage or a two-stage process is immaterial. Either way the policy of the law—and that includes the policy as it has already been exemplified in past decisions—has to be brought into the equation". Robert Goff LJ referred to Lord Roskill's criticism of the floodgates argument in *Junior Books* (see *above*) and said (at p 393): "There are some of us who prefer a controlled opening of the gates, permitting the flooding of a reasonably foreseeable area, rather than a wholesale inundation of unforeseeable and uncontrolled proportions. It is also necessary to consider whether the floodgates argument is, in the particular circumstances, founded upon blind conservatism or has a rational basis".

Candlewood Navigation Corporation Ltd v Mitsui OSK Lines Ltd [1986] AC 1 (see Chapter 5, para 5.8.1): Lord Fraser said (at p 25) in a passage which is often quoted: "Their Lordships consider that some limit or control mechanism has to be imposed upon the liability of a wrongdoer towards those who have suffered economic damage in consequence of his negligence" and (at p 17) he said: "The justification for denying a right of action to a person who has suffered economic damage through injury to the property of another [ie relational economic loss] is that, for reasons of practical policy, it is considered to be inexpedient to admit his claim".

Yuen Kun Yeu v The Attorney General of Hong Kong [1988] 1 AC 175: Lord Keith said (at p 179): "Proximity is a necessary requirement, although by itself it is not sufficient. There is an overall consideration, namely whether it is just and reasonable to hold in the particular factual situation that there is a duty of care".

Caparo Industries plc v Dickman [1990] 2 AC 605 (see Chapter 9, para 9.7.2): Lord Oliver said (at p 633) in a passage which also is being frequently quoted: "Proximity is, no doubt, a convenient expression, so long as it is realised that it is no more than a label which embraces, not a definable concept, but merely a description of circumstances from which, pragmatically, the courts conclude that a duty of care exists" and Lord Bridge, in a similarly familiar passage, said (at p 618): "The concepts embodied in these additional ingredients [ie proximity and fairness, justice and reasonableness] are not susceptible of any such precise definition as would be necessary to give them utility as practical tests, but amount in effect to little more than convenient labels to attach to the features of different specific situations [ie categories of cases] which, on a detailed examination of all the circumstances, the law recognises pragmatically as giving rise to a duty of care of a given scope".

Murphy v Brentwood District Council [1991] 1 AC 398 (see Chapter 7, para 7.3): Lord Oliver said (at p 486): "The solution to borderline cases has so far been achieved pragmatically, not by the application of logic, but by the perceived necessity as a matter of policy to place some limits—perhaps arbitrary limits—to what would otherwise be an endless, cumulative chain bounded only by theoretical foreseeability".

James McNaughton Paper Group Ltd v Hicks Anderson & Co [1991] 2 QB 113 (see Chapter 9, para 9.7.2): Neill LJ said (at p 123): "In the absence of some general principle, it becomes necessary to examine each individual case in the light of the concepts of foreseeability, proximity and fairness. The last of these concepts is elusive and may indeed be no more than one of the criteria by which proximity is to be judged".

Alcock v The Chief Constable of South Yorkshire Police [1991] 3 WLR 1057 (a 'nervous shock' case): Lord Oliver said (at p 1113): "The failure of the law in general to compensate for injuries sustained by persons unconnected with the event precipitated by a defendant's negligence cannot be attributable to some arbitrary but unenunciated rule of 'policy' which draws a line as to the outer boundary of the area of duty, nor can it be made rationally to rest upon such injury being outside the area of reasonable foreseeability.

It must, as it seems to me, be attributable simply to the fact that such persons are not in a relationship of sufficient proximity with the tortfeasor as to give rise to a duty of care; though no doubt 'policy', if that is the right word, or, perhaps, more properly, the impracticability or unreasonableness of entertaining claims to the ultimate limits of the consequences of human activity, necessarily plays a part in the court's perception of what is necessarily proximate".

2.4.3 Indeterminate liability

It has been noted above how the 'spectre of indeterminate liability' can play an important part in the formulation of the policy considerations which underlie the relevant rules which the courts have devised in different categories of economic loss cases. In *Huxford v Stoy Hayward & Co* (1989) 5 BCC 421 Popplewell J, in discussing the requirement of justice and reasonableness, said (at p 432): "If the imposition of a duty on a defendant would for any reason be oppressive, or would expose him 'to a liability in an indeterminate amount to an indeterminate class', that will weigh heavily, probably conclusively, against the imposition of a duty (if it has not already shown a fatal lack of proximity)".

It is important to appreciate that 'indeterminate' in this context is not the same as 'infinite' or 'very large'. The evil against which the court is seeking to guard is not of the actual potentially infinite size in monetary terms of any particular claim, or of the fact that there might be a large number of claims, but of the inability to determine in advance the existence of the number of those claims, or the size of the class of possible claimants. In *Donoghue v Stevenson* [1932] AC 526 Lord Atkin expressed this point when he said (at p 580): "Acts or omissions which any moral code would censure cannot in a practical world be treated so as to give a right to every person injured by them to demand relief. In this way, rules of law arise which limit the range of complainants and the extent of their remedy".

Lord Atkin's statement that these limitations are governed by 'rules of law' indicates that the court's task is to define criteria which can be considered in advance of any particular course of action being embarked upon and not simply by way of *ex post facto* reasoning on an ad hoc basis after the event, when the extent of the actual damage, both as regards its quantum and as regards the number of persons adversely affected, is known. The 'indeterminate time' concern is met by statutory rules of limitation. The 'indeterminate amount' concern is not really dealt with adequately by any of the limiting factors which the courts have devised. The common law does not impose any restrictions on the amount of money in respect of which a defendant might be held liable for the consequences of his negligent act or omission. Those that exist arise chiefly by virtue of the incorporation into domestic law of certain international transport conventions which deal with the transportation of passengers and goods. Examples are the Warsaw Convention 1929, as amended by The Hague Protocol 1955, which has been incorporated into English law by the

Carriage by Air Act 1961, and the Athens Convention on the Carriage of Passengers and their Luggage 1974, which has been adopted as part of English law by the Carriage of Passengers and their Luggage by Sea (Interim Provisions) Order 1980, SI 1980/92, made under s 16 of the Merchant Shipping Act 1979. Both of these Acts impose maximum limits on the amount of damages which a defendant can be ordered to pay to a plaintiff who has been killed, or has suffered personal injury or property loss when travelling as a passenger on certain aeroplanes or ships. These limits are not the amount of damages which the plaintiff will definitely receive, but simply the maximum limit of the plaintiff's proven damages which the defendant will have to pay if the court, on ordinary principles, is prepared to impose a duty of care on the defendant for the plaintiff's loss.

The 'indeterminate class' concern is, however, well suited for adjudication by the courts. The rules which the courts have devised, or should be seeking to devise, should be directed towards determining in advance the class of possible plaintiffs to whom the defendant can anticipate being held liable when he embarks on certain activities which can have repercussions for persons other than himself, such as driving his car on a public road, manufacturing and selling products, erecting a building or making a statement in relation to a company's set of accounts. These rules are considered in Chapters 4, 5, 7, 8 and 9 in relation to the different categories of economic loss cases which have arisen in practice (Chapter 6 is concerned with a physical damage category). In relation to all of these categories, except for the one which is considered in Chapter 7 (ie diminution in value of a defectively manufactured chattel or building), it is considered that the rules which the courts have devised are satisfactory in terms of the admitted policy reasons which underlie the judges' stated aims and anxieties.

In *Reeman v The Department of Transport* (26 March 1997, unreported) the Court of Appeal was aware of the nuances inherent in the concept of a 'determinate class'. Under the heading: "The class of persons to whom the advice is given", Phillips LJ said:

> In *Caparo* both Lord Bridge and Lord Oliver commented on the importance of the advice being given to an identifiable class if the necessary proximity is to exist. Those who, foreseeably, would read the audit and rely on it when making investment decisions did not form such a class. In the present case the judge considered that future potential purchasers of a certified vessel form such a class. The plaintiffs' counsel argued that he was right to do so; that there could be only a handful of potential purchasers and there was no difficulty in identifying these.
>
> I find that the judge and the submissions of the plaintiffs' counsel fail to appreciate the nature of the exercise required by *Caparo*. When Lord Bridge and Lord Oliver spoke of the need for the advice to be given in the knowledge that it would be communicated to an ascertainable or identifiable class of person, I believe that they were probably speaking of a class of persons the membership of which was capable of ascertainment at the time that the advice was given, eg shareholders who could be identified by consultation of the share register. I am certain that they were speaking of a class, in existence at the time of giving the advice, whose identifiable characteristics necessarily limited the number of its members. When a British Fishing Vessel Certificate is issued, those who may in

the future place reliance on that certificate when deciding whether to purchase the vessel do not form part of a class that is capable of definition and delimitation by identifiable characteristics. The vessel may be sold during the currency of the certificate to a buyer from anywhere in the United Kingdom or an even wider geographical area. When Mr Jones re-issued the vessel's certificate, the Reemans had only just moved to Brixham. Mr Reeman was there running a building business. He had no experience of the fishing industry. There is no test which would then have indicated that he was a member of a limited class of future purchasers of the vessel, and the same is probably true of some of the other purchasers in the chain of no less than seven, down which the title to the vessel passed before it reached the Reemans.

Peter Gibson LJ, concurring, said:

> I do not accept that the plaintiffs were members of 'an identifiable class' (to use Lord Bridge's words in *Caparo* [see Chapter 9, para 9.6.2]) to whom the Department knew that its statement in the certificate would be communicated. In my judgment the members of the identifiable class must be capable of identification at the time of the making of the negligent misstatement. It is not sufficient that the plaintiffs should be members of a generic class capable of description at that time, whether as potential purchasers or successors in title of the owner who asks for the certificate. That would be to create a potential liability to an open ended class. I observe that in *Smith v Eric S Bush* [1990] 1 AC 831 [see Chapter 9, para 9.7.3] Lord Griffiths, in finding that a duty of care was owed by a prospective mortgagee's valuer to the prospective mortgagor, limited to that prospective mortgagor the extent of the liability and was not prepared to extend liability to protect subsequent purchasers.

Chapter 3

Alternative theories

There is no escape from the truth that, whatever formula be used, the outcome in a grey area has to be determined by judicial judgment. Formulae can help to organise thinking, but they cannot provide answers. Basically the decision on a duty of care issue depends on a judgment, not a formula. **(Cooke P in** *South Pacific Manufacturing Co Ltd v NZ Security Consultants & Investigations Ltd* **[1992] 2 NZLR 282)**

Acceptance of the incremental approach does not of itself provide an answer to the question of liability in the present case. Indeed the term 'incremental' invites inquiry because what is incremental is to an extent in the eye of the beholder. **(Toohey J in** *Bryan v Maloney* **(1995) 182 CLR 609)**

What to one lawyer may seem a comparatively small and logical step may seem to another a dangerous leap. Thus it is no exaggeration to say that opinions differ as to whether Donoghue v Stevenson [1932] AC 562 and Dutton v Bognor Regis Urban District Council [1972] 1 QB 373 were incremental. **(Cooke P in** *Connell v Odlum* **[1993] 2 NZLR 257)**

3.1 Introduction

This chapter is concerned with the differences that have emerged at different times and in different courts as to the approach which should be adopted by a court in considering whether a duty of care of a particular scope should be imposed on the defendant for the plaintiff's loss. The question of approach arises in two distinct, but interrelated situations.

First, the question of different approaches to the duty of care question can arise in relation to the broad issue as to whether it is possible to state a unifying test or formula applicable to all categories of cases, or whether each category should be treated as being idiosyncratic and having its own test or formula. This point will be considered first.

Secondly, the question of different approaches arises in relation to novel situations, or 'new categories of cases', which are not covered by previous authority. This question will also be considered in this chapter, but, as will be seen below, it overlaps with the first question.

3.2 General formulations

3.2.1 Lord Atkin in *Donoghue*

Historical background

In Chapter 6 the significance of the House of Lords' decision in *Donoghue v Stevenson* [1932] AC 562 is considered in the context of the general exclusionary rule (see Chapter 6, para 6.2.2) which prevented the plaintiff from suing the defendant in tort in this type of case if the defendant had initially supplied the defective product to a third party under contract. In addition, their Lordships' decision, in particular Lord Atkin's speech, broke another mould, namely the traditional approach towards the formulation of duties of care which then existed. Under that approach, the essential requirements necessary to found a duty of care were treated as being distinct in different specific situations, each of which was regarded as exhibiting its own particular characteristics. No attempt was made to formulate a single unifying principle which might be said to underlie all the different situations in which the law had adjudged that the defendant should be liable in the tort of negligence to the plaintiff for the plaintiff's injuries sustained by the defendant's negligent act or omission.

In *Donoghue* Lord Atkin recognised this position, when he said (at p 579):

> It is remarkable how difficult it is to find in the English authorities statements of general application defining the relations between parties that give rise to the duty. The courts are concerned with the particular relations which come before them in actual litigation, and it is sufficient to say whether the duty exists in those circumstances. The result is that the courts have been engaged upon an elaborate classification of duties as they exist in respect of property, whether real or personal, with further divisions as to ownership, occupation or control, and distinctions based on the particular relations of the one side or the other, whether manufacturer, salesman or landlord, customer, tenant, stranger, and so on. In this way, it can be ascertained at any time whether the law recognises a duty, but only where the case can be referred to some particular species which has been examined and classified.

The 'general conception'

Lord Atkin was concerned to discern a common thread running through all of the different types of duty situation referred to above. He said (at p 580):

> The duty which is common to all the cases where liability is established must logically be based upon some element common to the cases where it is found to exist. In English law there must be, and is, some general conception of relations giving rise to a duty of care, of which the particular cases found in the books are but instances. Liability for negligence, whether you style it such or treat it as in other systems as a species of '*culpa*', is no doubt based upon a general public sentiment of moral wrongdoing for which the offender must pay. But acts or omissions which any moral code would censure cannot in a practical world be treated so as to give a right to every person injured by them to demand relief. In this way, rules of law arise which limit the range of complainants and the extent of their remedy.

The 'neighbour principle'

Lord Atkin then proceeded to formulate a principle for regulating the first factor which he said needed to be limited, namely the 'range of complainants'. He said (at p 580): "The rule that you are to love your neighbour becomes, in law, you must not injure your neighbour; and the lawyer's question, Who is my neighbour? receives a restricted reply. You must take reasonable care to avoid acts or omissions which you can reasonably foresee would be likely to injure your neighbour. Who, then, in law is my neighbour? The answer seems to be—persons who are so closely and directly affected by my act that I ought reasonably to have them in contemplation as being so affected when I am directing my mind to the acts or omissions which are called in question".

This is a test for determining the class of plaintiffs to whom a duty of care might be owed. It is not a test for determining the existence of that duty. What is needed in addition, and what Lord Atkin had in mind, is rules of law which limit the extent of the 'neighbour's' remedy. This is clear from the fact that he continued in the passage just quoted by saying that the 'neighbour principle' needed to be limited by "the notion of proximity", which he defined (at p 581) as "such close and direct relations that the act complained of directly affects a person whom the person alleged to be bound to take care would know would be directly affected by his careless act" (see Chapter 2, para 2.3.2). In addition, Lord Atkin made it clear that the court would have to be satisfied that it would be just and reasonable or, as he put it (at p 599), "in accordance with sound common sense" to impose a duty of care on the defendant for the plaintiff's injuries.

Misinterpreting the 'neighbour principle'

In some subsequent cases, some judges treated Lord Atkin's 'neighbour principle' as synonymous with the notion of proximity. Thus, in *Hedley Byrne and Co Ltd v Heller and Partners Ltd* [1964] AC 465, Lord Devlin said (at p 524): "What Lord Atkin called a 'general conception of relations giving rise to a duty of care' is now often referred to as the principle of proximity. You must take reasonable care to avoid acts or omissions which you can reasonably foresee would be likely to injure your neighbour. In the eyes of the law, your neighbour is a person who is so closely and directly affected by your act that you ought reasonably to have him in contemplation as being so affected when you are directing your mind to the acts or omissions which are called into question"; and in *Anns v Merton London Borough Council* [1978] AC 728, Lord Wilberforce said (at p 753): "Although a situation of proximity existed between the council [the defendant] and owners and occupiers of the houses [the plaintiffs], I do not think that a description of the council's duty can be based upon the 'neighbourhood' principle alone".

This equation of the 'neighbour principle' with the notion of proximity is not correct. Lord Atkin's 'neighbour principle' is only a test for determining the class of plaintiffs or, as Lord Atkin put it, "the range of complainants" to whom a duty of care, if it exists, is owed. It does not, however, serve as a test for determining whether such a duty does, in fact, exist. In *Home Office v Dorset Yacht Co Ltd* [1970] AC 1004 Viscount Dilhorne recognised this point when he said (at p 1043): "Lord Atkin's answer to the question, 'Who, then, in law is my neighbour?', while very relevant to determine to whom a duty of care is owed, cannot determine the question whether a duty of care exists".

The fault does not lie with Lord Atkin. He recognised this limitation on his 'neighbour principle' when he formulated the 'notion of proximity' and said that it was a necessary limiting factor on the 'neighbour principle'. This point is discussed further in Chapter 9, para 9.2.3, in relation to the rejection of Lord Atkin's 'neighbour principle' in negligent misstatement cases.

Misapplying the 'neighbour principle'

Apart from the misinterpretation of the ambit of the 'neighbour principle', some judges have treated it as if it is a general statement of principle applicable to all duty of care situations. Thus, in *Home Office v Dorset Yacht Co Ltd* [1970] AC 1004, Lord Reid said (at p 1027):

> *Donoghue v Stevenson* may be regarded as a milestone, and the well-known passage in Lord Atkin's speech [by which he meant Lord Atkin's enunciation of the 'neighbour principle'] should, I think, be regarded as a statement of principle. It is not to be treated as if it were a statutory definition. It will require qualification in new circumstances. But I think that the time has come when we can, and should say that it ought to apply unless there is some justification or valid explanation for its exclusion.

The last-quoted sentence is self-evidently contradictory. Nevertheless, the first part of it goes further than Lord Atkin intended, because he said in *Donoghue* (at p 580): "To seek a complete logical definition of the general principle is probably to go beyond the function of the judge, for the more general the definition, the more likely it is to omit essentials or to introduce non-essentials"; and (at p 583): ". . . in the branch of the law which deals with civil wrongs, dependent in England at any rate entirely upon the application by judges of general principles, also formulated by judges, it is of particular importance to guard against the danger of stating propositions of law in wider terms than is necessary, lest essential factors be omitted in the wider survey and the inherent adaptability of English law be unduly restricted. For this reason it is very necessary in considering reported cases in the law of torts that the actual decision alone should carry authority, proper weight, of course, being given to the dicta of the judges".

The following *dictum* of Lord Morris in *Dorset Yacht* demonstrates, on the one hand, an understanding of the correct application of the 'neighbour principle' and, on the other, an incorrect interpretation of it. Lord Morris said (at p 1034): "It has been generally recognised that Lord Atkin's statement of principle cannot be applied as though his words were contained in a positive and precise legislative enactment. It cannot be, therefore, that in all circumstances where certain consequences can reasonably be foreseen, a duty of care arises". The second sentence in this *dictum* involves the incorrect assumption (see *above*) that Lord Atkin regarded the reasonable foreseeability of harm test inherent in his 'neighbour principle' as being sufficient to establish a duty of care.

On the other hand, Lord Diplock recognised the limitations of Lord Atkin's 'neighbour principle'. He said in *Dorset Yacht* (at p 1060): "Used as a guide to characteristics which will be found to exist in conduct and relationships which give rise to a legal duty of care, this aphorism marks a milestone in the modern development of the law of negligence. But misused as a universal, it is manifestly false".

3.2.2 *Alternative theories*

3.2.2   Lord Wilberforce in *Anns*

Introduction

The most comprehensive and conscious attempt to formulate a single general test, applicable to all cases, appears in the speech of Lord Wilberforce in *Anns v Merton London Borough Council* [1978] AC 728. It is often referred to as Lord Wilberforce's 'two-stage test'. This test has been subjected to the most severe criticism by the Law Lords in certain subsequent decisions, and it is now no longer used at all by judges in the United Kingdom. The impression is given in their Lordships' criticisms that Lord Wilberforce was alone in formulating his 'two-stage test', but it should be noted that Lord Wilberforce's speech was expressly approved and adopted in *Anns* by Lords Diplock, Simon and Russell, and that although Lord Salmon delivered a separate, concurring speech, he did not make any adverse comments on Lord Wilberforce's speech.

The 'two-stage test'

Lord Wilberforce introduced his two-stage formulation by saying (at p 751): "Through the trilogy of cases in this House—*Donoghue v Stevenson* [1932] AC 562, *Hedley Byrne and Co Ltd v Heller and Partners Ltd* [1964] AC 465, and *Dorset Yacht Co Ltd v Home Office* [1970] AC 1004, the position has now been reached that, in order to establish that a duty of care arises in a particular situation, it is not necessary to bring the facts of that situation within those of previous situations in which a duty of care has been held to exist. Rather, the question has to be approached in two stages".

    Lord Wilberforce then continued: "First, one has to ask whether, as between the alleged wrongdoer and the person who has suffered damage, there is a sufficient relationship of proximity or neighbourhood such that, in the reasonable contemplation of the former, carelessness on his part may be likely to cause damage to the latter—in which case a *prima facie* duty of care arises. Secondly, if the first question is answered affirmatively, it is necessary to consider whether there are any considerations which ought to negative, reduce or limit the scope of the duty or the class of person to whom it is owed or the damages to which a breach of it may give rise".

General observations

Two general observations can be made on this formulation. First, Lord Wilberforce regarded the duty of care question as being one of pure principle, divorced from established authority. This aspect of his speech is considered below in para 3.4 on novel categories.

    Secondly, it is not clear whether the "sufficient relationship of proximity" which gives rise to a *prima facie* duty of care, in Lord Wilberforce's first stage, is tested purely by reasonable foreseeability of harm, or whether it also depends on the type of additional factors discussed in Chapter 2, para 2.1.3 as constituting the requisite relationship between the defendant and the plaintiff. As will be seen below, different judges have given different answers to this question.

Dicta in cases

Some judges have had difficulty in applying the 'two-stage test', although these difficulties are to some extent self-inflicted and illusory. Before setting out the *dicta* from various cases, it is worth noting that in *McLoughlin v O'Brian* [1983] AC 410 Lord Wilberforce made it clear that he did not equate foreseeability with proximity when he said (at p 420): "That foreseeability does not of itself, and automatically, lead to a duty of care is, I think, clear. I gave some examples in *Anns v Merton London Borough Council, Anns* itself being one".

The following *dicta* are pertinent to this question.

Governors of the Peabody Donation Fund v Sir Lindsay Parkinson & Co Ltd [1985] 1 AC 210: Lord Keith, after citing Lord Reid's above-quoted *dictum* in *Dorset Yacht* (that Lord Atkin's 'neighbour principle' should be regarded as a statement of principle) and Lord Wilberforce's 'two-stage test', said (at p 240): "There has been a tendency in some recent cases to treat these passages as being themselves of a definitive character. This is a temptation which should be resisted. The true question in each case is whether the particular defendant owed to the particular plaintiff a duty of care, having the scope which is contended for [see Chapter 2, para 2.1.5], and whether he was in breach of that duty with consequent loss to the plaintiff. A relationship of proximity in Lord Atkin's sense must exist before any duty of care can arise, but the scope of the duty must depend on all the circumstances of the case".

The Council of the Shire of Sutherland v Heyman (1985) 157 CLR 424: In the High Court of Australia Gibbs CJ said (at p 440): "There is some difference of opinion as to what Lord Wilberforce intended when he said that one first has to ask 'whether . . . there is a sufficient relationship of proximity such that . . .'. One view is that this passage means that the relationship of proximity exists if it is reasonably foreseeable that carelessness on the defendant's part will cause damage to the plaintiff. I reject this view. It is quite clear that foreseeability does not 'of itself, and automatically' lead to a duty of care, as Lord Wilberforce himself said in *McLoughlin v O'Brian* [see *above*]; and, in my opinion, he did not mean to say in *Anns* that foreseeability alone is sufficient to establish proximity, and consequently to establish the existence of a duty of care, subject to any considerations which might negative the duty at the second stage of the enquiry. I rather think that he meant the expression 'proximity or neighbourhood' to be a composite one, and to refer to the relationship described by Lord Atkin in *Donoghue v Stevenson*".

By way of contrast, Brennan J regarded the first stage of Lord Wilberforce's test as being a test based on foreseeability of harm alone. He said (at p 477): "The first stage is based, of course, on Lord Atkin's seminal phrases in *Donoghue v Stevenson* [ie Lord Atkin's 'neighbour principle', which Brennan J then set out]. However, if Lord Wilberforce's first stage is intended to be applied in cases of non-feasance [see Chapter 8, para 8.1] as well as in cases of misfeasance, it elides the distinction between acts and omissions which appears in Lord Atkin's language. I am unable to see how the first stage, importing Lord Atkin's statement of principle, can be applied to determine whether a failure to act in exercise of a statutory power is negligent. The test of foreseeability of injury never has been applied as an exhaustive test for determining whether there is a *prima facie* duty to act to prevent injury caused by the acts of another, or by circumstances for which the alleged wrongdoer is not responsible".

Brennan J also commented on the second stage of the test. He said (at p 191): "The proper role of the second stage embraces no more than those further elements, in addition to the neighbour principle, which are appropriate to the particular category of negligence, and which confine the duty of care within narrower limits than those which would be defined by an unqualified application of the neighbour principle".

Yuen Kun Yeu v Attorney General of Hong Kong [1988] 1 AC 175 (PC): Lord Keith said (at p 191): "Their Lordships venture to think that the two-stage test formulated by Lord Wilberforce for determining the existence of a duty of care in negligence has been elevated to a degree of importance greater than it merits, and greater perhaps than its author intended. Further, the expression of the first stage of the test carries with it a risk of misinterpretation. There are two possible views of what Lord Wilberforce meant. The first view is that he meant to test the sufficiency of proximity simply by the reasonable contemplation of likely harm. The second view is that Lord Wilberforce meant the expression 'proximity or neighbourhood' to be a composite one, importing the whole concept of necessary relationship between plaintiff and defendant described by Lord Atkin in *Donoghue v Stevenson*. In their Lordships' opinion, the second view is the correct one. As Lord Wilberforce himself observed in *McLoughlin v O'Brian*, it is clear that foreseeability does not, of itself, and automatically, lead to a duty of care".

With regard to the second stage of the test, Lord Keith said (at p 193): "The second stage of Lord Wilberforce's test in *Anns* will rarely have to be applied. It can arise only in a limited category of cases where, notwithstanding that a case of negligence is made out on the proximity basis, public policy requires that there should be no liability. One of the rare cases where that has been held to be so is *Rondel v Worsley* [1969] 1 AC 191 [see Chapter 2, para 2.4.1], dealing with the liability of a barrister for negligence in the conduct of proceedings in court. Such a policy consideration was also invoked in *Hill v Chief Constable of West Yorkshire* [1988] QB 60 (CA) [which was subsequently approved by the House of Lords—see Chapter 8, para 8.3.3, and see *below*]. In view of the direction in which the law has since been developing, their Lordships consider that for the future it should be recognised that the two-stage test in *Anns* is not to be regarded as in all circumstances a suitable guide to the existence of a duty of care".

Rowling v Takaro Properties Ltd [1988] 1 AC 473 (PC) (see Chapter 8, para 8.2.5): Lord Keith said (at p 501): "It is necessary, before concluding that a duty of care should be imposed, to consider all the relevant circumstances. One of the considerations underlying a certain recent decision of the House of Lords (in *Governors of the Peabody Donation Fund v Sir Lindsay Parkinson*) and of the Privy Council (in *Yuen Kun Yeu v Attorney General of Hong Kong*) is the fear that a too literal application of the well-known observation of Lord Wilberforce in *Anns* may be productive of a failure to have regard to, and to analyse and weigh, all the relevant considerations in considering whether it is appropriate that a duty of care should be imposed. Their Lordships consider that question to be of an intensely pragmatic character, well suited for gradual development, but requiring most careful analysis".

Hill v Chief Constable of West Yorkshire [1989] 1 AC 53 (see Chapter 8, para 8.3.3): Lord Keith said (at p 60): "The foundation of the duty of care [in this case] was said to be reasonable foreseeability of harm to potential future victims if Sutcliffe were not promptly apprehended. Lord Atkin's classic propositions in *Donoghue v Stevenson* were prayed in aid, as was Lord Wilberforce's well-known two-stage test of liability in the *Anns* case. It has been said almost too frequently to require repetition that foreseeability of likely harm is not in itself a sufficient test of liability in negligence. Some further ingredient is invariably needed to establish the requisite proximity of relationship between plaintiff and defendant, and all the circumstances of the case must be carefully considered and analysed in order to ascertain whether such an ingredient is present. The nature of the ingredient will be found to vary in a number of different categories of decided cases [see Chapter 1, para 1.3]".

With regard to the second stage of the test, Lord Keith said (at p 63): "In *Yuen Kun Yeu v Attorney General of Hong Kong*, I expressed the view that the category of cases where the second stage of Lord Wilberforce's two-stage test in *Anns* might fall to be applied was a limited one. Application of that second stage is, however, capable of constituting a separate and independent ground for holding that the existence of liability in negligence should not be entertained".

Caparo Industries plc v Dickman [1990] 2 AC 605: Lord Bridge, after setting out Lord Wilberforce's above-quoted *dictum*, said (at p 617): "But, since the *Anns* case, a series of decisions of the Privy Council and of your Lordships' House, notably in judgments delivered by Lord Keith [see *above*], have emphasised the inability of any single general principle to provide a practical test which can be applied to every situation to determine whether a duty of care is owed and, if so, what is its scope".

Lord Oliver, with reference to the plaintiff's counsel's submission that the defendant's knowledge that potential bidders might rely on the accounts to buy shares in the market established a sufficient relationship of proximity, said (at p 643): "This submission appears to equate proximity with mere foreseeability and to rely upon the very misinterpretation of the effect of the decision of this House in *Anns*, which was decisively rejected in *Peabody* and in *Yuen Kun Yeu*".

Murphy v Brentwood District Council [1991] 1 AC 398: The House of Lords overruled its decision in *Anns* (see Chapter 7). The attack of the defendant in *Murphy* on *Anns* was, and the thrust of their Lordships' speeches is, on the actual decision itself in *Anns*, rather than upon the route by which that decision was reached. Lord Oliver did, however, indirectly make some comments on the first stage of the test. Despite the conclusion of the Privy Council in *Yuen Kun Yeu*, of which Lord Oliver was in fact a member of the panel, that the first stage of the test is not to be interpreted as having equated foreseeability with proximity, Lord Oliver did so regard it (and criticised it for this) in *Murphy*. He said (at p 487): "The infliction of physical injury to the person or property of another universally requires to be justified. The causing of economic loss does not. [The wider significance of this *dictum* is discussed in Chapter 1, para 1.4.1.] If it is to be categorised as wrongful, it is necessary to find some factor beyond the mere occurrence of the loss and the fact that its occurrence could be foreseen. Thus, the categorisation of damage as economic serves at least the useful purpose of indicating that something more is required, and it is one of the unfortunate features of *Anns* that it resulted initially in this essential distinction being lost sight of. A series of decisions in this House and in the Privy Council since *Anns* have made it clear beyond argument that in cases other than cases of direct physical injury, reasonable foreseeability of damage is not of itself sufficient, and that there has to be sought, in addition in the relationship between the parties, that elusive element comprehended in the expression 'proximity'".

Comment

Given that their Lordships accepted that the test for establishing a *prima facie* duty of care in the first stage of Lord Wilberforce's test did not equate foreseeability with proximity, and given that the second stage expressly directs the judge to take stock of the situation and consider whether there are "any considerations" which ought to negative, reduce or limit the scope of the duty or the class of person to whom it is owed or the damages to which a breach of it may give rise, it is surprising that their Lordships concluded in subsequent cases that (*per* Lord Keith in *Rowling v Takaro Properties Ltd*, see *above*) "a too literal interpretation of the test may be productive of a failure to have regard to, and to analyse and weigh, all the relevant considerations in considering whether it is appropriate that a duty of care should be imposed". The Supreme Court of Canada and the Court of Appeal of New Zealand have not found any difficulty in applying the two-stage test. Indeed, despite the criticisms which have been made of the test in English and Australian courts, they still adhere to it. Their views are considered in para 3.6, *below*.

3.3   The current approach

3.3.1   Rejection of formulae

For reasons which are impossible to discern, their Lordships in certain cases have determined that an application of Lord Wilberforce's two-stage test might lead to a court not taking into account all the relevant considerations in deciding whether it is appropriate that a duty of care should be imposed in any particular case. The current vogue is to eschew all attempts to try to formulate a general approach which will apply to several categories of case, and to reject all attempts to define the individual concepts, or elements, which might need to be weighed in the balance in determining the duty of care question in any particular case. Instead, the emphasis is laid on ensuring that, relative to the particular category of case in question, the court is satisfied that, 'pragmatically', it is 'just and reasonable' to impose a duty of care on the defendant for the plaintiff's loss.

This change of emphasis, and rejection of definable concepts, has arisen from the perception by some judges, albeit unfounded (see *above*), that the test for determining a *prima facie* duty of care in the first stage of Lord Wilberforce's test equates foreseeability with proximity and therefore leads to a much wider scope of duty being imposed than their Lordships would currently like to see. In this regard, Lord Keith's above-quoted *dictum* in *Rowling v Takaro Properties Ltd* [1988] 1 AC 473 merits repetition. He said (at p 501) that a too literal application of Lord Wilberforce's test "may be productive of a failure to have regard to, and to analyse and weigh, all the relevant considerations in considering whether it is appropriate that a duty of care should be imposed. Their Lordships consider that question to be of an intensely pragmatic character, well suited for gradual development, but requiring most careful analysis". In *Caparo Industries plc v Dickman* [1990] 2 AC 605 Lord Oliver followed through this theme (and the misconception as to the true meaning of the first stage of Lord Wilberforce's test), when he said (at p 633): "To search for any single formula which will serve as a general test of liability is to pursue a will-o'-the-wisp. The fact is that once one discards, as it is now clear that one must, the concept of foreseeability of harm as the single exclusive test—even a *prima facie* test—of the existence of the duty of care, the attempt to state some general principle which will determine liability in an infinite variety of circumstances serves not to clarify the law, but merely to bedevil its development in a way which corresponds with practicality and common sense".

3.3.2 The categorisation approach

In *Caparo* Lords Bridge, Roskill and Oliver delivered major speeches in which they considered the approach which should now be applied towards duties of care. They all rejected the idea of an overall test, or formula, which will be applicable to every category of case. Instead, they have opted for a reversion to the traditional approach which existed before *Donoghue v Stevenson* [1932] AC 562 in which, as noted *above* (see para 3.2.1), Lord Atkin observed (at p 580): "In this way it can be ascertained at any time whether the law recognises a duty, but only where the case can be referred to some particular species which has been examined and classified".

Lord Roskill

The speech which expresses this concept most succinctly is that of Lord Roskill. He said (at p 628):

3.3.2   *Alternative theories*

There is no simple formula or touchstone to which recourse can be had in order to provide in every case a ready answer to the questions whether, given certain facts, the law will or will not impose liability for negligence. Phrases such as 'foreseeability', 'proximity', 'neighbourhood', 'just and reasonable', 'fairness' or 'voluntary assumption of responsibility' will be found used from time to time in the different cases. But such phrases are not precise definitions. At best they are but labels or phrases descriptive of the very different factual situations which can exist in particular cases and which must be carefully examined in each case before it can be pragmatically determined whether a duty of care exists and, if so, what is the scope and extent of that duty. If this conclusion involves a return to the traditional categorisation of cases as pointing to the existence and scope of any duty of care, I think this is infinitely preferable to recourse to somewhat wide generalisations which leave their practical application as matters of difficulty and uncertainty. This conclusion finds strong support from the judgment of Brennan J in *The Council of the Shire of Sutherland v Heyman* (1985) 157 CLR 424 in the High Court of Australia in the passage cited by my noble and learned friends [see 'Lord Bridge', *below*].

Lord Bridge

Lord Bridge's speech arrives at the same conclusion, but along the way he expressed himself in terms which, contrary to his intention, are leading to the emergence of a 'three-stage test'. He said (at p 617):

> Since the *Anns* case, a series of decisions [see para 3.2.2, *above*] have emphasised the inability of any single general principle to provide a practical test which can be applied to every situation to determine whether a duty of care is owed and, if so, what is its scope. What emerges is that, in addition to the foreseeability of damage, necessary ingredients in any situation giving rise to a duty of care are that there should exist between the party owing the duty and the party to whom it is owed a relationship characterised by the law as one of 'proximity' or 'neighbourhood', and that the situation should be one in which the court considers it fair, just and reasonable that the law should impose a duty of a given scope upon the one party for the benefit of the other.

Having thus described these three "necessary ingredients" in "any situation giving rise to a duty of care", Lord Bridge then proceeded to say that these concepts should not, in fact, be applied individually in practice. He continued with the passage just cited by saying (at p 618):

> But it is implicit that the concepts of proximity and fairness embodied in these additional ingredients are not susceptible of any such precise definition as would be necessary to give them utility as practical tests, but amount in effect to little more than convenient labels to attach to the features of different specific situations which, on a detailed examination of all the circumstances, the law recognises pragmatically as giving rise to a duty of care of a given scope. Whilst recognising, of course, the importance of the underlying general principles common to the whole field of negligence, I think the law has now moved in the direction of attaching greater significance to the more traditional categorisation of distinct and recognisable situations as guides to the existence, the scope and the limits of the varied duties of care which the law imposes. We must now, I think, recognise the wisdom of the words of Brennan J in the High Court of Australia in *The Council of the Shire of Sutherland v Heyman* (1985) 157 CLR 424, when he said (at p 481): 'It is preferable, in my view, that the law should

develop novel categories of negligence, incrementally and by analogy with established categories, rather than by a massive extension of a *prima facie* duty of care, restrained only by indefinable consideration which ought to negative, reduce or limit the scope of the duty or the class or person to whom it is owed'.

By way of applying this approach, Lord Bridge then referred to certain cases similar to *Caparo* and said (at p 619): "Consistently with the traditional approach, it is to these authorities and to subsequent decisions directly relevant to this relatively narrow corner of the field that we should look to determine the essential characteristics of a situation giving rise, independently of any contractual or fiduciary relationship, to a duty of care owed by one party to another to ensure the accuracy of any statement which the one party makes and on which the other party may foreseeably rely to his economic detriment".

Lord Oliver

Lord Oliver's speech is very similar, both in its construction and in its conclusion. He said (at p 633): "The postulate of a simple duty to avoid any harm that is, with hindsight, reasonably capable of being foreseen, becomes untenable without the imposition of some intelligible limits to keep the law of negligence within the bounds of common sense and practicality. Those limits have been found by the requirement of what has been called a 'relationship of proximity' between the plaintiff and the defendant, and by the imposition of a further requirement that the attachment of liability for harm which has occurred must be 'just and reasonable'".

Having thus just enunciated three requirements for liability, Lord Oliver, like Lord Bridge, said that these requirements must not be separately identified, defined and applied in any particular case. He continued by saying:

> But, although the cases in which the courts have imposed or withheld liability are capable of an approximate categorisation, one looks in vain for some common denominator by which the existence of the essential relationship can be tested. Indeed, it is difficult to resist a conclusion that what have been treated as three separate requirements are, at least in most cases, in fact merely facets of the same thing; for, in some cases, the degree of foreseeability is such that it is from that alone that the requisite proximity can be deduced [see Chapter 2, para 2.2.3], whilst in others the absence of that essential relationship can most rationally be attributed simply to the court's view that it would not be fair and reasonable to hold the defendant responsible. 'Proximity' is, no doubt, a convenient expression, so long as it is realised that it is no more than a label which embraces not a definable concept, but merely a description of circumstances from which, pragmatically, the courts conclude that a duty of care exists.

Lord Oliver then said, as noted above, that it is futile to attempt to state any general principles which will apply to all categories of case. He then cited Brennan J's above-quoted *dictum* that the law should develop novel categories of negligence incrementally and by analogy with established categories, and then concluded (at p 635): "Perhaps, therefore, the most that can be attempted is a broad categorisation of the decided cases according to the type of situation in which liability has been established in the past in order to found an argument by analogy".

3.3.3 Summary

The approach which the House of Lords would like courts to follow is a composite approach in which all of the relevant considerations relating to the actual facts of the case and the wider implications of imposing or not imposing a duty of care on the defendant for the plaintiff's economic loss are considered. While such well-known concepts as foreseeability and proximity may be invoked as guides to the answer in any particular case, they are not to be applied as steps in a rigid formula in which the answer will self-evidently appear if certain questions are answered one way or the other. Rather, judges are exhorted to bear in mind that they are involved in a delicate balancing exercise of all of the circumstances of the case, with a view to achieving a 'just and reasonable' result. In conducting this exercise, judges are to pay especial regard to settled decisions relating to the same category of case as the individual case calling for their decision, and are to move slowly and, by way of analogy, in small incremental steps in enlarging established duties of care, if at all.

Lord Keith summed up the position pithily when he said, first, in *Governors of the Peabody Donation Fund v Sir Lindsay Parkinson and Co Ltd* [1985] 1 AC 210 (at p 240): "A relationship of proximity in Lord Atkin's sense [in *Donoghue v Stevenson*, see para 3.2, *above*] must exist before any duty of care can arise, but the scope of the duty must depend on all the circumstances of the case" and (at p 241): "In determining whether or not a duty of care of a particular scope was incumbent upon a defendant, it is material to take into consideration whether it is just and reasonable that it should be so"; and, secondly, in *Rowling v Takaro Properties Ltd* [1988] 1 AC 473 when, after saying that a too literal application of Lord Wilberforce's 'two-stage test' may be productive of a failure to have regard to, and to analyse and weigh, all the relevant considerations in deciding whether it is appropriate that a duty of care should be imposed, he said: "Their Lordships consider that question to be of an intensely pragmatic character, well suited for gradual development, but requiring most careful analysis".

In the United States, the English law approach that is currently favoured was also succinctly stated by Weintraub J in the Supreme Court of New Jersey in *Goldberg v Housing Authority of the City of Newark* (1962) 186 A (2d) 291, when he said: "Whether a duty exists is ultimately a question of fairness. The enquiry involves a weighing of the relationship of the parties, the nature of the risk, and the public interest in the proposed solution"; and by Gibson CJ in the Supreme Court of California in *Biakanja v Irving* (1958) 320 P (2d) 16 (see Chapter 9, para 9.9.5) when he said: "The determination whether, in a specific case, the defendant will be held liable to a third person not in privity with him is a matter of policy, and involves the balancing of various factors, among which are the extent to which the transaction was intended to affect the plaintiff, the foreseeability of harm to him, the degree of certainty that the plaintiff suffered injury, the closeness of the connection between the defendant's conduct and the injury suffered, the moral blame attached to the defendant's conduct and the policy of preventing future harm".

3.3.4 Comment

While it is all well and good to say that there is no single formula which will provide the answer in every case, and that there are no particular signposts or concepts, such as foreseeability or proximity, which, if satisfied or not satisfied, will necessarily be decisive in any particular type of case, the fact remains that lawyers and judges do like to have rules, or checklists, against which to evaluate the facts of any particular case in which they have to advise or provide a decision. Lord Bridge himself did this in *Caparo*, when he formulated the three "necessary ingredients in any situation giving rise to a duty of care" (see para 3.3.2, *above*, and Chapter 2, para 2.1.3), despite professing not to. As will be seen *below*, what is emerging now is a 'three-stage test', which is being applied by some judges in a formulaic fashion.

The real mischief of Lord Wilberforce's formulation was the introductory words to it, namely that "in order to establish that a duty of care arises in a particular situation, it is not necessary to bring the facts of that situation within those of previous situations in which a duty of care has been held to exist". The lengths to which their Lordships have gone to dispel this misconception are so extensive and extreme that their emphasis on the method of approach sometimes overshadows the importance of emphasising that the courts should try to discern the policy considerations which underlie the particular category of case in question, rather than simply identifying the fact that the case falls into the same category as other decided cases, and then deciding whether an increment to that category is warranted.

In *South Pacific Manufacturing Co Ltd v New Zealand Security Consultants and Investigations Ltd* [1992] 2 NZLR 282 (see para 3.6.3, *below*), Hardie Boys J, in the Court of Appeal of New Zealand, recognised this point when he said (at p 315):

> Counsel for the defendants presented their argument as if the court were required to declare where its loyalties lie: whether it holds to the two-stage test enunciated by Lord Wilberforce in *Anns*; or whether it will now adopt the incremental approach favoured by the House of Lords in its more recent decisions. There is, I suspect, a danger here of the method of approach becoming more important than the objective. The objective is to ascertain whether it is appropriate that there be a duty of care in the particular case. So long as that objective is realised, I cannot think that it is of great moment whether it is attained by a two-stage test, an incremental approach, or some combination of the two. What matters is that there is an identification, an analysis and a weighing of all the competing considerations, as Lord Keith put it in *Caparo*. It is, in the end, a matter of careful judicial judgment.

Lastly, it should be noted that, by bringing Brennan J's 'incremental approach *dictum*' into their speeches in *Caparo*, their Lordships have effectively altered the meaning of the 'novel categories' of negligence cases, which had been employed previously.

3.4 Novel categories

3.4.1 Introduction

As noted above, the House of Lords has said that the approach of courts in considering whether a duty of care should be imposed in any particular case should, by reference to other cases, be analogical and incremental. This suggestion derives from Brennan J's above-quoted *dictum* in *The Council of the Shire of Sutherland v Heyman* (1985) 157 CLR 424 that "the law should develop novel categories of negligence incrementally and by analogy with established categories". By bringing this *dictum* into their speeches in *Caparo*, their Lordships have blurred the distinction which previously existed between the creation of new categories of cases of negligence and established categories in which the facts of the case in hand differed from other cases in the same category.

This is resulting in a tendency to regard nearly every case which differs from other decided cases as falling into a new category. While, theoretically, there is nothing wrong with this, in practice it might lead to a rigid classification of cases in very narrow bands, with the exclusion of other cases which do not fall precisely within those bands. The underlying policy considerations which have motivated the formulation of the various rules in the larger categories of cases considered in the division of categories employed in this book could in this process be lost sight of. The technique of approach could become more important than the aim of ensuring a just and reasonable result. In the cases discussed in para 3.5, *below*, there is some evidence of this occurring.

3.4.2 The traditional approach

Traditionally, the categorisation of cases has been in accordance with the broad basis adopted in Chapter 5 (relational economic loss cases), Chapter 7 (diminution in value of defective products cases) and Chapter 9 (negligent misstatements and services), with the concepts discussed in Chapter 4 (accidental direct economic loss and consequential economic loss) and in Chapter 8 (non-feasance economic loss cases) being capable of spanning the other categories. Within each category, the technique of approach has been to start off by considering whether the case in hand falls within an established category. If so, then decided cases within that category are considered to see whether the case in hand is sufficiently similar to any of the decided cases within that category as to justify the same decision being reached. This is an approach with which all lawyers will be familiar. However, it also recognises that the creation of a new category of case is a decision of great importance, requiring the most careful consideration of the underlying social and economic policy considerations which might motivate the existence or denial of a particular general rule of law. The creation of a new category, as opposed to a decision relating to a different case within an established category, is not simply a matter of 'increment' or 'analogy'.

This process, and the distinction just described, were recognised by Lord Devlin in *Hedley Byrne and Co Ltd v Heller and Partners Ltd* [1964] AC 465, when he said (at p 525) that the question to be asked is: "Is the relationship between the parties in this case [see Chapter 9, para 9.4.2] such that it can be brought within a category giving rise to a special duty? As always, in English law, the first step in such an enquiry is to see how far the authorities have gone, for new categories in the law do not spring into existence overnight". As is noted in Chapter 9, para 9.4, the facts which called for decision in *Hedley Byrne* did give rise to a new category of case. Their Lordships fully recognised this, and accordingly gave due consideration to the various competing factors motivating for and against the imposition of a duty of care in this category of case.

In *Caltex Oil (Australia) Pty Ltd v The Dredge Willemstad* (1976) 136 CLR 529 (see Chapter 5, paras 5.6 and 5.8), Stephen J recognised the importance of the role of policy considerations when a court is considering a new category of case. He said (at p 567): "Policy considerations must no doubt play a very significant part in any judicial definition of liability and entitlement in new areas of the law; the policy considerations to which their Lordships paid regard in *Hedley Byrne* are an instance of just such a process, and to seek to conceal those considerations may be undesirable". Stephen J was also concerned about every different case being considered as if it gave rise to a new category. He continued in the passage just quoted by saying: "That process should, however, result in some definition of rights and duties, which can then be applied to the case in hand, and to subsequent cases, with relative certainty. To apply generalised policy considerations directly in each case, instead of formulating principles from policy and applying those principles, derived from policy, to the case in hand is, in my view, to invite uncertainty and judicial diversity".

Under the traditional approach, a new category of case would arise only where it was clear that the facts of a new case raised policy considerations which could not be brought within the policy considerations of cases within an existing category. Lord Devlin described this process in *Hedley Byrne* when he said (at p 524):

> What Lord Atkin did [in *Donoghue v Stevenson*] was to use his general conception [see para 3.2, *above*] to open up a category of cases giving rise to a special duty. It was already clear that the law recognised the existence of such a duty in the category of articles that were dangerous in themselves. What *Donoghue v Stevenson* did may be described either as the widening of an old category or as the creation of a new and similar one. The general conception can be used to produce other categories in the same way. An existing category grows as instances of its application multiply, until the time comes when the cell divides.

3.4.3 Comment

The traditional approach, as described here, is both sensible and workable. It accords with the way in which the common law has traditionally developed and operated. It is important for legal advisers, in every case, to be aware of the policy considerations which underlie the rules which the courts have devised for each particular category of case (using the term 'category' in its broad sense, as discussed *above*), because this will serve as a good guide of the 'general direction' in which the court's thinking will go when it considers the facts of the case in hand. While it will be a question of fact in each case whether the limiting rules of the particular category have been satisfied, those limiting rules, once established, will not generally vary from case to case; unless, of course, the case in hand is regarded as being of such importance that, as happened in *Murphy v Brentwood District Council* [1991] 1 AC 398 (see Chapter 7, para 7.3.1), or in *Canadian National Railway Co v Norsk Pacific Steamship Co* (1992) 91 DLR (4th) 289 (see Chapter 5, paras 5.6.2, 5.6.4 and 5.8), the court felt it necessary, and had the authority, to depart from the limiting factors which had previously been held to exist in relation to that particular category of case; or where, as in *Hedley Byrne* (see Chapter 9, para 9.4) and in *Home Office v Dorset Yacht Co Ltd* [1970] AC 1004 (see Chapter 8, para 8.3.3), the House of Lords felt that it was appropriate to open new categories of case, and to define the limiting factors applicable to it.

Thankfully, the vast majority of cases are not of such great moment. The approach of legal advisers in the less radical, 'run of the mill' situation should be to concentrate upon and work within the confines of the particular established category within which the case in hand falls, but always bearing in mind that the underlying policy considerations which led to the initial formulation of the governing rules in that particular category of case will provide a general indication of the way in which the case is likely to be decided. The importance of the role played by policy in the formulation of general rules of guidance for courts by the House of Lords in new categories of cases was recognised by Lord Pearce in *Hedley Byrne* when he said (at p 536): "How wide the sphere of the duty of care in negligence is to be laid depends ultimately on the court's assessment of the demands of society for protection from the carelessness of others"; and by Lord Diplock in *Dorset Yacht* when he said (at p 1058): "What we are concerned with in this appeal is, at bottom, a matter of public policy which we, as judges, must resolve". In both of these cases the House of Lords was concerned with, and opened up, a new category of negligence cases in English law.

3.4.4   The incremental approach

Brennan J's dictum

In the High Court of Australia, in *The Council of the Shire of Sutherland v Heyman* (1985) 157 CLR 424, in a passage which is now cited as a matter of course in English decisions (see para 3.5.1, *below*), Brennan J said (at p 481): "It is preferable, in my view, that the law should develop novel categories of negligence incrementally and by analogy with established categories, rather than by a massive extension of a *prima facie* duty of care restrained only by indefinable 'considerations which ought to negative, or to reduce or limit the scope of the duty or the class of person to whom it is owed'".

Confusion of concepts

It has been noted above that the House of Lords has incorporated this *dictum* into the approach which it wishes to be adopted by courts in deciding duty of care questions in all cases, not just those which involve 'novel categories'. While it is fully in accordance with the development of the common law that cases are decided by way of analogy with other decided cases of the same kind, and that the pace of development is usually done in small, incremental steps within an existing category, it does not follow that, when a completely novel category of case arises for decision, it will succeed only if it can be justified by analogy with cases in an established but different category. If this were so, then the House of Lords in *Hedley Byrne and Co Ltd v Heller and Partners Ltd* [1964] AC 465 would have been prevented from holding in the plaintiff's favour because the issues which arose in that case were not analogous to cases in any other established category of negligence (see Chapter 9, para 9.4).

It would seem that Brennan J's *dictum*, and the way in which it has been interpreted by the House of Lords, involves a confusion of concepts. It is clear from the whole of the paragraph in which Brennan J's *dictum* was included that he was not, in fact, talking about the development of novel categories of negligence in the traditional and proper sense, but rather was concerned with the technique for ruling upon new cases within established categories. His *dictum* was made in the context of his criticism of Lord Wilberforce's 'two-stage' test (see para 3.2.2, *above*), in particular his view that the *prima facie* duty test provided for in the first stage was based purely on foreseeability of harm. Thus, Brennan J preceded his *dictum* by saying (at p 481): "If foreseeability of injury to another were the exhaustive criterion of a *prima facie* duty to act to prevent the occurrence of that injury, it would be essential to introduce some kind of restrictive qualification—perhaps a qualification of the kind stated in the second stage of the general proposition in *Anns* [see para 3.2.2, *above*]. I am unable to accept that approach". Brennan J was thus critical of what he saw as the open-ended nature of the second stage of Lord Wilberforce's test. (See, further, the 'Comment' section in Chapter 2, para 2.3.2, where Brennan J's views on this topic are set out in detail.) Instead of applying that open-ended or 'amorphous' approach, he said that he would prefer for new cases to be considered incrementally and by analogy with established cases.

Unfortunately, in saying this, Brennan J used the word 'categories' (in the first part of his *dictum*) rather than the word 'cases'. However, it is clear from what he said immediately after his *dictum* that he in fact intended to say that, within established categories, the law should develop new cases incrementally and by analogy, and was not trying to say that new categories themselves would have to be so restricted. Thus, he continued (at p 481) (emphasis added): "The proper role of the second stage embraces no more than those further elements in addition to the neighbourhood principle which are appropriate *to the particular category of negligence*, and which confine the duty of care within narrower limits than those which would be defined by an unqualified application of the neighbour principle".

A question of degree

To say, simply, that the development of the law is better served by treading carefully and only allowing small, incremental enlargements of established duty situations within a particular category of cases is slightly meaningless, because an increment is to be made only if it is "justifiable". Whether, in any particular case, an increment is, or is not, justifiable will be a question of judicial judgment. This task will not be made any easier by the judge knowing that he must extend the law only in a way which can be said to be "incremental".

Different judges will be capable of arriving at different conclusions as to whether an extension of liability in a particular new situation is "incremental" and is "justified". An example is the differences in opinion which have emerged between the Court of Appeal in *Dutton v Bognor Regis Urban District Council* [1972] 1 QB 373 and the House of Lords in *Murphy v Brentwood District Council* [1991] 1 AC 398, in relation to the liability in tort of a builder of a house to a remote purchaser for the purchaser's economic loss consisting of the diminution in value of the house when it subsequently sustains structural damage which is attributable to the negligence of the builder during the course of construction. If such a house were to collapse and injure any person or damage any property other than the fabric of the house itself, then all of the judges in both of these cases would agree that the defendant would be liable in damages to the plaintiff. However, if only the fabric of the defectively constructed house itself is damaged, then there is a difference of opinion between the judges in these two cases. This topic is discussed in detail in Chapter 7, para 7.2. For the moment, the point to note is that in *Dutton* the majority regarded this as "an impossible distinction" and saw the imposition of liability on the defendant for the plaintiff's economic loss in this situation as being almost self-evidently a justifiable increment from the personal injury cases in this type of situation. Thus, Lord Denning MR said in *Dutton* (at p 396): "If Mr Tapp's [the defendant's counsel] submission were right, it would mean that if the inspector negligently passes the house as properly built and it collapses and injures a person, the council are liable, but if the owner discovers the defect in time to repair it—and he does repair it—the council are not liable. That is an impossible distinction. They are liable in either case".

In *Murphy* the House of Lords came to exactly the opposite conclusion. With reference to Lord Denning's above-quoted *dictum*, Lord Keith said (at p 465): "The jump which is here made from liability under the *Donoghue v Stevenson* principle for damage to person or property caused by a latent defect in a carelessly manufactured article [see Chapter 6, para 6.2.1], to liability for the cost of rectifying a defect in such an article which is *ex-hypothesi* no longer latent, is difficult to accept".

Another case in which there might be differences of opinion as to whether the result can be justified on an incremental approach is *White v Jones* [1995] 2 AC 207 (see Chapter 9, para 9.7.5), in which a solicitor was held to be liable in tort to a prospective beneficiary who would have inherited half of the testator's estate if the solicitor had drafted the will for the deceased testator within a reasonable period of time after receiving the testator's instructions. Farquharson LJ said: "The incremental approach to the establishment of further categories of negligence, as described by Brennan J in *Sutherland Shire Council v Heyman*, which was approved by the House of Lords in *Caparo Industries v Dickman*, is apt to *Ross v*

Caunters and the present case. To find a duty of care in these circumstances involves no very dramatic extension of the law".

If Farquharson LJ thereby intended simply to say that his decision was just a small increment on the court's decision in *Ross v Caunters* (where the solicitor's negligence consisted of giving the testator incorrect instructions as to the formalities required for the execution of his will), then his *dictum* is acceptable. But if he intended to say that the whole category of cases, of which *Ross v Caunters* and *White v Jones* were both similar but slightly different examples, could be justified on an incremental basis, this would be questionable. It is not clear which of these meanings he intended, but it is possible that he did indeed intend the latter, by virtue of the initial words of his *dictum*, namely (emphasis added): "The incremental approach to the establishment of further *categories* of negligence . . ." and by virtue of his further *dictum* that, in this type of case, "the solicitor is in a unique category".

The recognition of liability by solicitors in this category of case is justifiable, not because it is an increment to a different, established category, but because the policy considerations which are relevant to this particular type of solicitor's negligence (see Chapter 9, para 9.7.5) are so compelling as to warrant the imposition of a duty of care on solicitors for disappointed beneficiaries' pure economic losses, notwithstanding that this might run counter to the other established categories of negligent misstatements or services. In those other categories the defendant does not attract liability unless the plaintiff has placed reliance on him not to act negligently (see Chapter 9, para 9.1.1). This element of reliance is not present in the disappointed beneficiaries' cases.

This is not to say that the decision in *White v Jones* is wrong, or to criticise the court's approach. It is simply to make the point that, if it is being suggested that the category of liability of solicitors for economic loss suffered by disappointed beneficiaries with whom the solicitor had no contractual relationship is to be justified on an incremental basis by reference to any other established category, opinions will differ.

The above-mentioned limitations of the incremental approach were recognised by the Court of Appeal of New Zealand in *South Pacific Manufacturing Co Ltd v New Zealand Security Consultants and Investigations Ltd* [1992] 2 NZLR 282, when Cooke J said (at p 301): "I do not find the 'incremental' test particularly helpful, as so much has to turn on assessments of degree"; and by the High Court of Australia in *Bryan v Maloney* (1995) 182 CLR 609, when Toohey J said (at p 401): "Acceptance of the incremental approach does not of itself provide an answer in the present case. Indeed, the very term 'incremental' invites inquiry because what is incremental is to an extent in the eye of the beholder".

In *Alcock v Chief Constable of South Yorkshire Police* [1991] 3 WLR 1057, Lord Oliver also recognised the limitations of the incremental approach when (together with the other Law Lords) he refused to extend the type of situation in which a duty of care can be imposed on a defendant for mental illness suffered by a plaintiff in consequence of a third person having been injured by the defendant, even though this situation was analogous with other situations in which such a duty has been imposed and would have involved only a small increment. In the earlier cases, defendants had been held liable to plaintiffs who had suffered mental illness through the shock of seeing their injured relatives in hospital. In *Alcock*, which arose out of the disaster at the Hillsborough Stadium when football fans were crushed, the plaintiffs' shock process, which led to their mental illness, occurred more gradually than in the earlier cases. The House of Lords refused to uphold their claims. Lord Oliver said (at p 1119): "To extend the notion of proximity in cases of immediately created nervous shock to this more elongated and, to some extent, retrospective process may seem a logical analogical development. But the law in this area is not wholly logical. I cannot see any pressing reason of policy for taking this further step along a road which must ultimately lead to virtually limitless liability", and (at p 1113): "The concept of proximity is an artificial one which depends more on the court's perception of what is the reasonable area of the imposition of liability than upon any logical process of analogical deduction".

Specific applications

Elgozouli-Daf v The Commissioner of Police of the Metropolis [1995] QB 335 (see Chapter 8, para 8.2.10): Recognising that the issue which arose for decision was not covered by previous authority, Steyn LJ said (at p 345):

> The question before us is a novel one. The authority of a series of decisions in the House of Lords, and notably *Caparo Industries Plc v Dickman* [1990] 2 AC 605, require us to consider the critical question not from the point of view of high principle but pragmatically and by analogy with established categories of liability. And in so approaching the question, we must consider the ultimate question from three perspectives, namely: (a) the foreseeability of the harm that ensued, (b) the nature of the relationship between the parties, usually called the element of proximity, and (c) the question whether it is fair, just and reasonable that the law should impose a duty of care.

It is submitted that this is a correct statement of the approach that should be followed in novel cases.

Skinner v The Secretary of State for Transport (*The Times*, 3 January 1994) (see Chapter 8, para 8.2.10): Having noted that no action had ever before, so far as was known, been instituted against the Coast Guard, Judge Gareth Edwards QC, sitting as a High Court Judge, said:

> The question is no longer to be approached simply on general principles. In *Caparo Industries Plc v Dickman* [1990] 2 AC 605, the majority of their Lordships were of the view that the tort of negligence has now developed to the point where further extensions of it should be made only by analogy with existing categories in which the law already recognises a duty of care, breach of which would be actionable. In short, the approach is in future to be an 'incremental' one.

His Honour then considered numerous cases involving the police, the Home Office and local authorities (see Chapter 8) and concluded: "Accordingly it seems to me that the incremental approach yields a definite and negative answer to the question whether the Coast Guard owes a duty of care to mariners in respect of its watching, search and rescue functions. There is no way to arrive at a duty of care by analogy with the position of other emergency services or by analogy with the position of public bodies exercising statutory functions".

Bryan v Maloney (1995) 69 ALJR 375 (see Chapter 7, para 7.6.4): So far as Australian law was concerned, the issue in this case was novel. One of the judges in the High Court, Toohey J, felt that the incremental approach was of no use in this situation. He said (at p 401):

> Acceptance of the incremental approach does not of itself provide an answer to the question of liability in the present case. Indeed, the very term 'incremental' invites inquiry because what is incremental is to an extent in the eye of the beholder. To answer the question, it is necessary to look more closely at the circumstances in which the appellant was held liable to the respondent [in the courts below].

X (Minors) v Bedfordshire County Council [1995] 2 AC 633 (see Chapter 8, para 8.2.10): In this case, the House of Lords found the incremental approach useful in determining some of the questions in these appeals which had not arisen before. Thus, Lord Browne-Wilkinson said (at p 750):

> Your Lordships' decision in the *Caparo* case lays down that, in deciding whether to develop novel categories of negligence, the court should proceed incrementally and by analogy with decided cases. We were not referred to any category of case in which a duty of care has been held to exist which is in any way analogous to the present cases.

Hill v Van Erp (1997) 142 ALR 687 (see Chapter 9, para 9.7.5): Gaudron J criticised the incremental approach when she said:

> There has been some criticism of proximity as a criterion of liability, it having been said that it lacks the specificity of a precise proposition of law. The same may be said of the proposition that the law should develop incrementally and by analogy. Inevitably, there will be imprecision in any developing area of the common law.

Esanda Finance Corporation Ltd v Peat Marwick Hungerfords (1997) 142 ALR 750 (see Chapter 9, para 9.7.2): Toohey and Gaudron JJ, in their joint judgment, said:

> The question whether the pleaded facts are capable of giving rise to a duty of care falls to be decided in light of the law's insistence that a plaintiff who sues in negligence to recover pure economic loss must establish more than the foreseeability of loss. In this country, the question whether there is a duty of care to take reasonable steps to avoid another's loss depends on whether there is a relationship of proximity. In the United Kingdom, the question is to be answered on the basis that the law will develop novel categories of negligence incrementally and by analogy with established categories.

To the extent that this was intended to be a criticism of the English law approach, it is submitted that these remarks were misguided. First, their Honours were not comparing like with like here. Their first statement makes it clear that the test or approach to which they were referring is that which should be applied in established categories of negligence. They then leap to the approach which English law applies in novel categories. Secondly, in any event, their statement of the approach of the English courts in novel categories is too simplistic. The correct approach is that which was stated by the Court of Appeal in the *Elgozouli-Daf* case, *above*.

Bank of Credit and Commerce International (Overseas) Limited (in liquidation) v Price Waterhouse and Ernst & Whinney (1998) unreported, 13 February: Sir Brian Neill, speaking for the Court of Appeal said:

> The incremental approach has been the subject of criticism, but in the absence of some guiding principle of universal application, this approach ensures that developments in the law will take place in measured steps.

Reconciliation of approaches

In *Hill v Van Erp* (1997) 142 ALR 687, there was a conscious effort by some of the judges in the High Court of Australia to reconcile the application of the proximity analysis in new areas of the law with Brennan J's (now Brennan CJ's) view that the law should develop novel categories of negligence incrementally and by analogy with established cases, rather than by trying to apply any type of general formulation, such as proximity. Thus, Dawson J said:

> Both the approach suggested by Deane J based on proximity [see Chapter 2, para 2.3.2], and that suggested by Brennan J, namely 'that the law should develop novel categories of negligence incrementally and by analogy with established categories', posit an overall framework, but are not specific propositions of law. When the content of proximity falls to be ascertained in a novel case, then one proceeds in accordance with accepted modes of legal reasoning, particularly reasoning by analogy from decided cases. Indeed, although this Court has adopted the approach suggested by Deane J, the reasoning it has employed in formulating the particular requirements of proximity in a novel category is, in my view, similar to that suggested by Brennan J and does not reflect a unifying theme.
>
> Brennan J himself had those similarities in mind when he said in *San Sebastian Proprietary Ltd v The Minister* (1987) 68 ALR 161 that:
>
>> The proposition of law which expresses the appropriate limitations for each class will be devised having regard, no doubt, to factors of the kind to which Deane J referred in *Council of the Shire of Sutherland v Heyman* (1985) 157 CLR 424 [see Chapter 2, para 2.3.2].
>
> Thus, the difference between the approach based on proximity and that suggested by Brennan J is, in my view, far less than the protracted debate on the subject would suggest, and is, perhaps, more a difference of labelling than one of substance;

and Toohey J, in discussing how the proximity analysis is applied in deciding novel cases, said:

> Attention is focused on established categories in which a duty of care has been held to exist; analogies are then drawn and policy considerations examined in order to determine whether the law should recognise a further category, whether

that be seen as a new one or an extension of an old one. Seen in this way, I doubt whether the difference between an approach based on proximity and the incremental approach favoured by Brennan J in *Sutherland Shire Council v Heyman* is as stark as is sometimes suggested.

In *Stovin v Wise* [1996] AC 923, Lord Nicholls proposed a reconciliation of the 'two-stage test' emanating from *Anns*' and the 'three-stage test' emanating from *Caparo*, when he said (at p 931):

> In *Anns v Merton London Borough Council* [1978] AC 728 Lord Wilberforce propounded a two-stage test for the existence of a duty. This test is now generally regarded with less favour than the familiar tripartite formulation subsequently espoused in *Caparo Industries Plc v Dickman* [1990] 2 AC 605: (1) foreseeability of loss, (2) proximity and (3) fairness, justice and reasonableness. The difference is perhaps more a difference of presentation and emphasis than substance. Clearly, foreseeability of loss is by itself an insufficient foundation for a duty to take positive action. Close attention to the language of Lord Wilberforce, with its reference to a sufficient relationship of proximity or neighbourhood, shows that he regarded proximity as an integral requirement: see also *McLoughlin v O'Brian* [1983] 1 AC 410 *per* Lord Wilberforce.

Lord Hoffmann also noted that the two tests are essentially the same if they are properly applied. He said (at p 949):

> Lord Wilberforce, who gave the leading speech in *Anns*, first stated the well known two-stage test for the existence of a duty of care. This involves starting with a *prima facie* assumption that a duty of care exists if it is reasonably foreseeable that carelessness may cause damage and then asking whether there are any considerations which ought to 'negative, or to reduce or limit the scope of the duty or the class of person to whom it is owed or the damages to which a breach of it may arise'. Subsequent decisions in this House and the Privy Council have preferred to approach the question the other way round, starting with situations in which a duty has been held to exist and then asking whether there are considerations of analogy, policy, fairness and justice for extending it to cover a new situation: see for example Lord Bridge in *Caparo Industries Plc v Dickman* [1990] 2 AC 605. It can be said that, provided that the considerations of policy etc are properly analysed, it should not matter whether one starts from one end or the other.

In *Bank of Credit and Commerce International (Overseas) Limited (in liquidation) v Price Waterhouse and Ernst & Whinney* (1998) unreported, 13 February, Sir Brian Neill, speaking for the Court of Appeal, made the same point when he said: "If the facts are properly analysed and the policy considerations are correctly evaluated, the several approaches will yield the same result."

3.4.5 The inductive and deductive approach

Lord Diplock's formulation

It has been noted *above* that the incremental approach does not provide any guidance as to the technique of analysis which should be applied in determining whether any particular increment is 'justified' or not. It has also been noted that this is inevitable, given that ultimately the question in every case is one of judicial judgment, which is an indefinable concept in respect of which opinions will differ. Nevertheless, in *Home Office v Dorset Yacht Co Ltd* [1970] AC 1004, Lord Diplock formulated a technique of analysis which can be very useful in comparing similar cases and deciding whether the differences and the similarities between them are more apparent than real. He said (at p 1058): "The judicial development of the law of negligence proceeds by seeking first to identify the relevant characteristics that are common to the kinds of conduct and relationship between the parties which are involved in the case for decision, and the kind of conduct and relationships which have been held in previous decisions of the courts to give rise to a duty of care".

Lord Diplock then continued: "The method adopted at this stage of the process is analytical and inductive. It starts with an analysis of the characteristics of conduct and relationship involved in each of the decided cases. But the analyst must know what he is looking for, and this involves his approaching his analysis with some general conception of conduct and relationships which ought to give rise to a duty of care. This analysis leads to a proposition which can be stated in the form: 'In all the decisions that have been analysed, a duty of care has been held to exist wherever the conduct and the relationship possessed each of the characteristics A, B, C, D, etc, and has not so far been found to exist when any of these characteristics was absent'".

Lord Diplock then continued: "For the second stage, which is deductive and analytical, that proposition is converted to: 'In all cases where the conduct and relationship possesses each of the characteristics A, B, C, D, etc, a duty of care arises.' The conduct and relationship involved in the case for decision is then analysed to ascertain whether they possess each of those characteristics. If they do, the conclusion follows that a duty of care does arise in the case for decision".

Lord Diplock nevertheless realised that, even under this logical approach, the question is ultimately one of 'policy', or judicial judgment, for he continued by saying:

> But, since *ex hypothesi* the kind of case which we are now considering [which involved a novel category of case so far as English law was concerned, see Chapter 8, para 8.3.3] offers a choice whether or not to extend the kind of conduct or relationship which gives rise to a duty of care, the conduct or relationship which is involved in it will lack at least one of the characteristics A, B, C or D, etc, and the choice is exercised by making a policy decision as to whether or not a duty of care ought to exist if the characteristic which is lacking was absent or was redefined in terms broad enough to include the case under consideration. The policy decision will be influenced by the same general conception of what ought to give rise to a duty of care [ie Lord Atkin's 'general conception' in *Donoghue v Stevenson*, see *above*] as was used in approaching the analysis. The choice to extend is given effect to by redefining the characteristics in more general terms, so as to exclude the necessity to conform to limitations imposed by the former definition which are considered to be inessential.

In *Hill v Van Erp* (1997) 142 ALR 687, Dawson J commented on this approach by saying:

Reasoning by analogy from decided cases by the processes of induction and deduction, informed by, rather than divorced from policy considerations is not in my view dependent for its validity on those cases sharing an underlying conceptual consistency. It really only depends upon the fact that something more than reasonable foreseeability is required to establish a duty of care and that what is sufficient or necessary in one case is a guide to what is sufficient or necessary in another.

Application in Hill

In *Hill v Chief Constable of West Yorkshire* [1989] 1 AC 53 (see Chapter 8, para 8.3.3) Lord Diplock's approach was applied by the House of Lords in determining that the defendant police force did not owe any duty of care to the plaintiff whose daughter had been murdered by a serial killer ('the Yorkshire Ripper') whom the plaintiff alleged the defendants had been negligent in apprehending. In applying Lord Diplock's approach, Lord Keith said (at p 62): "The *Dorset Yacht* case was concerned with the special characteristics or ingredients beyond reasonable foreseeability of likely harm which may result in civil liability for failure to control another man to prevent his doing harm to a third person. The present case falls broadly into the same category. It is plain that vital characteristics which were present in *Dorset Yacht* and which led to the imposition of liability there are here lacking".

Lord Keith then proceeded to identify, compare and isolate the relevant characteristics of the two cases in the manner advocated by Lord Diplock, and concluded that no duty of care was owed by the police to the plaintiff in respect of the death of her daughter.

Comment

As with the incremental approach, it must be appreciated that this approach is no more than a technique of analysis, or a framework to help the court to identify the really important issues. It cannot answer the question whether, in any particular case, it would be just and reasonable for the court to impose a duty of care on the defendant for the plaintiff's loss. As noted above, that is a question of judicial judgment, which is too intangible to be confined within the boundaries of a particular formula or technique of analysis.

This point was recognised by Cooke P in *South Pacific Manufacturing Co Ltd v New Zealand Security Consultants and Investigations Ltd* [1992] 2 NZLR 282, when he said (at p 294): "A broad two-stage approach [see para 3.2.2, *above*] or any other approach is only a framework, a more or less methodical way of tackling a problem. How it is formulated should not matter in the end. Ultimately, the exercise can only be a balancing one, and the important object is that all the relevant factors be weighed. There is no escape from the truth that, whatever formula be used, the outcome in a grey area case has to be determined by judicial judgment. Formulae can help to organise thinking, but they cannot provide answers".

3.5   Post-*Caparo* decisions and new theories

3.5.1   Applying the *Caparo* formulation

Introduction

It has been noted *above* that, in *Caparo Industries plc v Dickman* [1990] 2 AC 605, the House of Lords rejected Lord Wilberforce's two-stage test for determining the existence of a duty of care and, in fact, strongly rejected the idea of any general test, framework or formula applicable to all cases. As noted *above*, Lord Oliver said in *Caparo* (at p 633): "To search for any single formula which will serve as a general test of liability is to pursue a will-o'-the-wisp. The fact is, that once one discards, as it is now clear that one must, the concept of foreseeability of harm as the single exclusive test—even a *prima facie* test—of the existence of the duty of care, the attempt to state some general principle which will determine liability in an infinite variety of circumstances serves not to clarify the law, but merely to bedevil its development in a way which corresponds with practicality and common sense".

Lord Bridge and Lord Roskill made similar remarks. Ironically, however, their speeches, and that of Lord Oliver, have given rise in subsequent cases to the courts applying, as a matter of course, a *three-part test*. Some examples are provided below. While there is clearly a greater awareness in these cases of the need to weigh up all of the competing considerations which might impact on the court's decision, the courts are nevertheless doing exactly what the House of Lords exhorted them not to do, namely applying a single general principle, albeit in three parts, to try to determine the existence of a duty of care in every situation.

Specific instances

Examples of recent cases in which, despite the House of Lords' admonition to the contrary in *Caparo*, the courts have applied a single (tripartite) test are provided below, together with other comments by judges on the three-part/stage approach.

Mariola Marine Corporation v Lloyd's Register of Shipping (The Morning Watch) [1990] 1 Lloyd's Rep 547 (see Chapter 9, para 9.7.4), in which Phillips J said (at p 556): "A duty of care will only arise where (i) it is reasonably foreseeable to the defendant that the plaintiff is liable to rely upon his statement; (ii) there is the necessary proximity between the plaintiff and the defendant; (iii) it is just and reasonable in all the circumstances to impose a duty of care on the part of the defendant to the plaintiff".

Beaumont v Humberts (1990) 49 EG 46 (see Chapter 9, para 9.7.3): Staughton LJ said (at p 48) (emphasis added): "The parties are agreed, on the basis of *Smith*'s case [ie *Smith v Bush*, which was approved by the House of Lords in *Caparo*] that, for a duty of care to be established—(i) there must be sufficient proximity between the task of the surveyor and the affairs of the mortgagor, (ii) it must be foreseeable that the mortgagor is likely to suffer damage if the surveyor is negligent, and *possibly* (iii) it must be just and reasonable to impose liability".

Hiron v Pynford South Ltd (1992) 28 EG 112: In the Official Referee's court, judge John Newey QC concluded that there are in fact two formulations, depending on whether the plaintiff has suffered physical damage or pure economic loss. He said (at p 113): "The requirements for the existence of a duty of care in a '*Donoghue v Stevenson* case' are: first, that the defendant foresaw or ought reasonably to have foreseen when he acted or omitted to act, that if he failed to exercise reasonable care, the plaintiff would be likely to suffer personal injury or damage to his property; second, that there was at the time a sufficient relationship of proximity, not necessarily in a physical sense, between the parties; and, third, that it was just and reasonable that a duty should exist. The requisites for a *Donoghue v Stevenson* duty of care are also required for a *Hedley Byrne* one, but in addition the defendant must, or should have known that the plaintiff would rely upon him, and the plaintiff must have so relied".

Marc Rich and Co AG v Bishop Rock Marine Co Ltd [1994] 1 WLR 1071 (CA) (see Chapter 9, para 9.7.4): Saville LJ recognised how the House of Lords in *Caparo* intended the test should be applied, when he said (at p 1077):

> Whatever the nature of the harm sustained by the plaintiff, it is necessary to consider the matter not only by enquiring about foreseeability, but also by considering the nature of the relationship between the parties; and to be satisfied that in all the circumstances it is fair, just and reasonable to impose a duty of care. Of course, as Lord Oliver pointed out in *Caparo Industries Plc v Dickman* [1990] 2 AC 605, these three matters overlap with each other and are really facets of the same thing. Thus, the three so-called requirements for a duty of care are not to be treated as wholly separate and distinct requirements, but rather as convenient and helpful approaches to the pragmatic question whether a duty should be imposed in any given case. In the end, whether the law does impose a duty in any particular circumstances depends upon those circumstances, though of course under our doctrine of precedent, categories of cases where a duty has been held to exist or not to exist will build up as time goes by.
>
> Taking this approach resolves all or virtually all that might otherwise be regarded as conflicts among the authorities. In some cases the question whether the relationship is one where the plaintiff has relied upon the defendant to exercise care has been regarded as of paramount importance (as in *Simaan General Contracting Co v Pilkington Glass Ltd (No 2)* [1988] QB 758), whereas in other cases (such as *White v Jones* [1993] 3 WLR 730) the absence of reliance has not precluded the existence of a duty. In some cases the existence of contractual rights, obligations and exclusions or limitations of liability have been regarded as militating against the existence of an extra-contractual duty (as in *Pacific Associates Inc v Baxter* [1990] 1 QB 993 and *Norwich City Council v Harvey* [1989] 1 WLR 828), while in other cases such matters have been regarded as irrelevant or immaterial, as in *Grant v Australian Knitting Mills Ltd* [1936] AC 85. In some cases the fact that the claimant would have no other remedy is regarded as an important pointer towards the existence of a duty (as in *White v Jones*), while again in other cases (*Grant*'s case again being a good example) the existence of contractual remedies against others is considered to be of little or no relevance.

3.5.1 *Alternative theories*

These cases are not irreconcilable. What they do is to demonstrate that in differing circumstances the same or similar factors may take on a different significance. To my mind it is this fact that has led the law to draw back from trying to develop the tort of negligence on other than an incremental basis.

Balcombe LJ, concurring, added (at p 1088): "I doubt whether the words 'fair, just and reasonable' impose a test additional to that of 'proximity'; in my judgment, these are the criteria to be adopted in considering whether the necessary degree of proximity exists".

Marc Rich and Co AG v Bishop Rock Marine Co Ltd ('The Nicholas H') [1996] 1 AC 211 (HL) (see Chapter 9, para 9.7.4): Lord Steyn, speaking for the majority of 4:1, treated proximity and 'fairness' as separate tests. He said (at p 241): "I am willing to assume that there was a sufficient degree of proximity in this case to fill that requirement for the existence of a duty of care. The critical question is therefore whether it would be fair, just and reasonable to impose such a duty".

Baker v Kaye (12 June 1996, unreported) (see Chapter 9, para 9.7.7): R Owen QC, sitting as a deputy judge of the High Court, also treated proximity and fairness as being separate tests. He said (at para 59):

> The features that I have identified point clearly to a relationship of sufficient proximity to give rise to a duty of care. What is the nature and extent of that duty? In my judgment, the defendant was under a duty to the plaintiff to take reasonable care in carrying out the medical assessment and in making his judgment as to the plaintiff's suitability for employment by NBC. I turn then to consider the overriding question of whether in all the circumstances it is fair, just and reasonable for such a duty to be imposed.

Stovin v Wise [1996] AC 923 (see Chapter 8, para 8.2.3): Lord Nicholls was dismissive of the way in which, as he saw it, the tripartite test gives undue prominence to the concept of proximity. However, he did not reject the tripartite test itself. He said (at p 932):

> The *Caparo* tripartite test elevates proximity to the dignity of a separate heading. This formulation tends to suggest that proximity is a separate ingredient, distinct from fairness and reasonableness and capable of being identified by some other criteria. This is not so. Proximity is a slippery word. Proximity is not legal shorthand for a concept with its own, objectively identifiable characteristics. Proximity is convenient shorthand for a relationship between two parties which makes it fair and reasonable that one should owe the other a duty of care. This is only another way of saying that, when assessing the requirements of fairness and reasonableness, regard must be had to the relationship of the parties.
>
> Despite this, the pithy, tripartite formulation has advantages. The relationship between the parties is an important ingredient in the overall assessment. The tripartite test is useful in focusing attention specifically on this feature and also in clearly separating this feature from foreseeability of damage. The basic test of fair and reasonable is itself open to criticism for vagueness. Indeed, it is an uncomfortably loose test for the existence of a legal duty. But no better or more precise formulation has emerged so far, and a body of case law is begin-

ning to give the necessary further guidance as courts identify the factors indicative of the presence or absence of a duty.

Bank of Credit and Commerce International (Overseas) Limited (in liquidation) v Price Waterhouse and Ernst & Whinney (1998) unreported, 13 February (see Chapter 9, para 9.7.2): Sir Brian Neill, speaking for the Court of Appeal, after referring to Lord Oliver's and Lord Bridge's above-mentioned caution against searching for any single formula which will serve as a general test of liability, said:

> Notwithstanding these reservations, however, the threefold test has retained its value because it focuses attention on three essential questions:
> (a) Was it reasonably foreseeable that the plaintiff would suffer the kind of damage which occurred?
> (b) Was there sufficient proximity between the parties?
> (c) Was it just and reasonable that the defendant should owe a duty of care of the scope asserted by the plaintiff?

Moreover, it is to be noted that the test was used in *Spring v Guardian Assurance Plc* [1995] 2 AC 296 [see Chapter 9, para 9.7.7] and in *Marc Rich and Co AG v Bishop Rock Marine Co Ltd* [1996] 1 AC 211 [see Chapter 9, para 9.7.4]. I have not overlooked the fact, however, that in *Marc Rich*, Lord Steyn approved the following passage in the judgment of Saville LJ in the court below:

> 'The three so-called requirements for a duty of care are not to be treated as wholly separate and distinct requirements, but rather as convenient and helpful approaches to the pragmatic question whether a duty should be imposed in any given case. In the end, whether the law does impose a duty in any particular circumstances depends on those circumstances . . .' [see above for the rest of this citation].

Sir Brian Neill also noted that the incremental approach and the voluntary assumption of responsibility 'test' have been applied by the House of Lords in other cases and commented thereon:

> The fact that all of these approaches have been used and approved by the House of Lords in recent years suggests:
> (a) that it may be useful to look at any new set of facts by using each of three approaches in turn, though it may be noted that in some cases, such as *Henderson v Merrett Syndicates Ltd* [1995] 2 AC 145, the use of the incremental approach may be sufficient to show that responsibility has been undertaken; and
> (b) that if the facts are properly analysed and the policy considerations are correctly evaluated, the several approaches will yield the same result.

Comment

It is submitted that, whilst both of these statements are correct, it should not be necessary to go through the exercise of applying all three tests to 'any new set of facts'. It is submitted that such an exercise would become too formulaic and would be too cumbersome. Instead, it is submitted that the three-stage test should suffice so long as it is applied flexibly by taking into account and weighing all of the relevant competing considerations which might impact on the question whether a duty of care should be imposed in any particular case. The concept of voluntary assumption of responsibility should be included in this approach as one of the relevant factors, rather than being seen as an alternative test (*see* para 3.5.2, *below*).

Comment

More cases could have been cited, but this is not necessary. The message is clear: judges are working within the framework of a three-stage test to determine whether a duty of care should be imposed in any particular situation. The question then arises as to whether the House of Lords, when the opportunity arises, should put a stop to this. It is submitted that this would be misfounded. The true question to ask is not whether the courts, contrary to what the House of Lords has directed, are purporting to apply any single general principle as a test to determine the existence of a duty of care in every situation, but rather whether, within the framework of the new three-stage test, judges are in fact taking into account and weighing all of the relevant competing considerations which might impact on their decision in any particular case. Indeed, it would have been far more fruitful to the development of the law if the House of Lords had asked this question in relation to Lord Wilberforce's two-stage test, and had given guidance as to how it should have been applied, rather than having spent so much time and effort in discrediting it, purely and simply because of the fact that it was an attempt to state a general framework or test within which courts should operate in considering duty of care questions.

Given that their Lordships concluded in *Yuen Kun Yeu v Attorney General of Hong Kong* [1988] 1 AC 175 that the test for determining the existence of a *prima facie* duty of care in the first stage of Lord Wilberforce's test does not depend on foreseeability of harm alone, but (*per* Lord Keith at p 191) "imports the whole concept of necessary relationships between plaintiff and defendant described by Lord Atkin in *Donoghue v Stevenson*" (para 3.2.2), and given that the second stage of this test requires the court to consider whether there are "any considerations" which ought to negative, reduce or limit the scope of the *prima facie* duty or the class of person to whom it is owed, or the damages to which a breach of it may give rise, it is difficult to discern any real distinction between that test and the new three-part test which has emerged from their Lordships' speeches in *Caparo*. The only real difference is that the courts have now been given some guidance as to how to apply the new approach (ie incrementally and by analogy with other similar decided cases, and to remember to take into account all the relevant considerations), but this could easily have been achieved without jettisoning the two-stage test altogether. As will be seen *below*, the courts of Canada and New Zealand have not had any difficulty in applying it.

3.5.2 Voluntary assumption of responsibility

Introduction

When the first edition of this book was written in 1993, the concept of 'voluntary assumption of responsibility', as used in some of the cases, was not considered to be an especially important element of any of the established criteria for determining whether a duty of care should be imposed in any of the various categories of cases. There were four major reasons for this (see *below*). Since the mid-1990s, however, the concept of voluntary assumption of responsibility has assumed a new centre-stage role, at least in the eyes of some of the judges (see *below*), but it is not always properly understood.

Reasons for rejection

Despite the wide use of the phrase 'voluntary assumption of responsibility' in *Hedley Byrne and Co Ltd v Heller and Partners Ltd* [1964] AC 465, it was not treated as a concept of any special importance until its 'revival' in three major economic loss cases in the House of Lords in the mid-1990s. There were essentially four major reasons for the rejection of a central role for the concept. In the eyes of some judges, these reasons have not been dissipated by the more recent pronouncements in favour of the concept.

First, in cases where it could be said that the defendant voluntarily assumed responsibility to undertake a certain task, this was but one component amongst many in determining whether, in all the circumstances, it could be pragmatically determined whether the relationship between the defendant and the plaintiff was sufficiently close to enable the court to hold that it was fair, just and reasonable to impose a duty of care on the defendant for the plaintiff's loss. This position was well stated by Lord Roskill in *Caparo Industries Plc v Dickman* [1990] 2 AC 605, when he said (at p 628) (emphasis added):

> There is no simple formula or touchstone to which recourse can be had in order to provide in every case a ready answer to the questions whether, given certain facts, the law will or will not impose liability for negligence or, in cases where such liability can be shown to exist, determine the extent [or scope] of that liability. Phrases such as 'foreseeability', 'proximity', 'neighbourhood', 'just and reasonable', 'fairness', '*voluntary acceptance of risk*', or '*voluntary assumption of responsibility*' will be found from time to time in the different cases. But such phrases are not precise definitions. At best they are but labels or phrases descriptive of the very different factual situations which can exist in particular cases and which must be carefully examined in each case before it can be pragmatically determined whether a duty of care exists and, if so, what is the scope and extent of that duty.

Similarly, in Canada, where the two-stage '*Anns* approach' is still followed and proximity is treated separately from the policy and pragmatic considerations that courts in Canada take into account, the voluntary assumption of responsibility by the defendant for a particular task is regarded as just one component of the proximity analysis. Thus, McLachlin J said in *Canadian National Railway Co v Norsk Pacific Steamship Co Ltd* (1992) 91 DLR (4th) 289 (at p 371): "A comprehensive consideration of proximity requires that the Court review all of the factors connecting the negligent act with the loss. This includes not only the relationship between the parties, but all forms of proximity—physical, circumstantial, causal or *assumed* indicators of closeness".

Secondly, the word 'voluntary' in the phrase was regarded as a misnomer because it is a pure legal fiction in most cases to say that a defendant has 'voluntarily' assumed responsibility for the consequences of his negligent act or omission in circumstances where (as will usually be the case in non-contractual tort actions) he, as a matter of fact, did not voluntarily, consciously or intentionally assume such responsibility. Thus, in *Smith v Eric S Bush* [1990] 1 AC 831, Lord Griffiths said (at p 862):

> If an adviser expressly assumes responsibility for his advice, a duty of care will arise, but such is extremely unlikely in the ordinary course of events. The House of Lords in *Hedley Byrne* approved a duty of care being imposed on the facts in *Cann v Willson* (1888) 39 ChD 39 and in *Candler v Crane, Christmas & Co* [1951] 2 KB 164. But if the surveyor in *Cann* or the accountant in *Candler* had actually been asked if he was voluntarily assuming responsibility for his advice to the mortgagee or the purchaser of the shares, I have little doubt he would have replied: 'Certainly not. My responsibility is limited to the person who employs me.' The phrase 'assumption of responsibility' can only have any real meaning if it is understood as referring to the circumstances in which the law will *deem* the maker of the statement to have assumed responsibility to the person who acts upon the advice.

Lord Roskill in *Caparo v Dickman*, echoing these sentiments, said (at p 628):

> Like Lord Griffiths in *Smith v Eric S Bush* [1990] 1 AC 831, 862, I find considerable difficulty in phrases such as 'voluntary assumption of responsibility' unless they are to be explained as meaning no more than the existence of circumstances in which the law will *impose* a liability upon a person making the allegedly negligent statement to the person to whom that statement is made; in which case the phrase does not help to determine in what circumstances the law will impose that liability or, indeed, its scope.

Thirdly, there was some doubt as to whether, in any event, the concept of voluntary assumption of responsibility was a sound legal principle or even a useful tool of analysis in cases of this kind. Thus, Lord Denning MR said in *Ministry of Housing and Local Government v Sharp* [1970] 2 QB 222 (at p 268):

> I think that Lord Devlin used those words in *Hedley Byrne* because of the special circumstances of that case [where the bank disclaimed responsibility]. But he did not in any way mean to limit the general principle. In my opinion the duty to use due care in a statement arises, not from any voluntary assumption of responsibility, but from the fact that the person making it knows, or ought to know, that others, being his neighbours in this regard, would act on the faith of the statement being accurate. That is enough to bring the duty into being. It is owed, of course, to the person to whom the certificate is issued and whom he knows is going to act on it: see the judgment of Cardozo J in *Glanzer v Shepard* [see Chapter 9, para 9.3.3].

Lord Oliver in *Caparo* said (at p 637):

> Voluntary assumption of responsibility is a convenient phrase but it is clear that it was not intended to be a test for the existence of the duty for, on analysis, it means no more than that the act of the defendant in making the statement or tendering the advice was voluntary and that the law attributes to it an assumption of responsibility if the statement or advice is inaccurate and is acted upon. It tells us nothing about the circumstances from which such attribution arises.

Fourthly, the quite extensive use of the phrase in the speeches in *Hedley Byrne and Co Ltd v Heller and Partners Ltd* [1964] AC 465 was regarded as having been made in the context of pronouncing that the disclaimer of liability by the defendants meant that no duty of care was to be imposed on them, whatever else might be said about the appropriate test in a case like *Hedley Byrne*. This view can be seen in the *dictum* cited above from Lord Denning MR's judgment in *Ministry of Housing v Sharp*, and from the following *dictum* of Lord Griffiths in *Smith v Bush*, when he said (at p 862):

> I do not think that voluntary assumption of responsibility is a helpful or realistic test for liability. It is true that reference is made in a number of the speeches in *Hedley Byrne* to the assumption of responsibility as a test of liability but it must be remembered that those speeches were made in the context of a case in which the central issue was whether a duty of care could arise when there had been an express disclaimer of responsibility for the accuracy of the advice.

New central role

In three important cases in the early 1990s dealing with a defendant's possible liability in tort for the negligent *omission* to provide information or make a statement—*Reid v Rush and Tompkins Group plc* [1990] 1 WLR 212, *Van Oppen v Clerk to the Bedford Charity Trustees* [1990] 1 WLR 234 and *Banque Keyser Ullmann SA v Skandia (UK) Insurance Co Ltd* [1990] 1 QB 665 (all of which are discussed in Chapter 8, para 8.3.3)—the Court of Appeal gave the impression that, at least in that category of cases, the foundation of a duty of care is the voluntary assumption of responsibility by the defendant to the plaintiff for the plaintiff's loss.

This idea has been embraced and expanded by certain of their Lordships in the House of Lords, particularly by Lord Goff in some of the major duty of care cases that came before the House of Lords in the mid-1990s, namely *Spring v Guardian Assurance plc* [1995] 2 AC 296, *Henderson v Merrett Syndicates Ltd* [1995] 2 AC 145 and *White v Jones* [1995] 2 AC 207 (this being the order in which these cases were decided, although not the order in which they were reported). In certain *dicta* in these cases, the concept of voluntary assumption of responsibility has been elevated, in the eyes of some of the judges, to being in and of itself the primary determinant of liability in cases of negligent misstatement. The foundation for this elevation is said to derive from certain of the speeches in *Hedley Byrne*.

Hedley Byrne v Heller

The expression 'voluntary assumption of responsibility' (or words similar to it) was used quite extensively in the speeches in *Hedley Byrne & Partners Ltd v Heller & Partners Ltd* [1964] AC 465. Lord Reid said (at p 486):

> A responsible man, knowing that he was being trusted, or that his skill and judgment were being relied on, would, I think, have three courses open to him. He could keep silent or decline to give the information or advice sought; or he could give an answer with clear qualification that he accepted no responsibility for it; or he could simply answer without any such qualification. If he chooses to adopt the last course, he must, I think, be held to have accepted some responsibility for

his answer being given carefully, or to have accepted a relationship with the enquirer which requires him to exercise such care as the circumstances require.

Lord Morris said (at p 502): "If someone possessed of a special skill undertakes, quite irrespective of contract, to apply that skill for the assistance of another person who relies upon such skill, a duty of care will arise". Lord Morris, in a passage repeated by Lord Hodson, also said (at p 503):

If, in a sphere in which a person is so placed that others could reasonably rely upon his judgment or his skill or upon his ability to make careful enquiry, a person takes it upon himself to give information or advice to, or allows his information or advice to be passed on to another person who, as he knows, or should know, will place reliance upon it, a duty of care will arise.

Lord Devlin said (at p 528):

The categories of special relationships which may give rise to a duty to take care in word as well as in deed are not limited to contractual relationships or to relationships of fiduciary duty, but include also relationships which, in the words of Lord Shaw in *Nocton v Lord Ashburton*, are 'equivalent to contract', that is, where there is an assumption of responsibility in circumstances in which, but for the absence of consideration, there would be a contract. Where there is an express undertaking, there can be little difficulty. The difficulty arises in discerning those cases in which the undertaking is to be implied. In this respect, the absence of consideration is not irrelevant. Payment for information or advice is very good evidence that it is being relied upon, and that the informer or adviser knows that it is.

Lord Devlin continued by saying:

The sort of relationship which gives rise to a responsibility towards those who act upon information or advice and so creates a duty of care towards them is a responsibility that is voluntarily accepted or undertaken, either generally, where a general relationship, such as that of solicitor and client or banker and customer, is created, or specifically in relation to a particular transaction. In the present case, the plaintiffs were not the customers of the bank. Responsibility can only attach to the single act, that is, the giving of the reference, and only if the doing of that act implied a voluntary undertaking to assume responsibility. This is a point of great importance because it is, as I understand it, the foundation for the ground for which in the end this House dismisses the appeal. I do not think it possible to formulate with exactitude all the conditions under which the law will in a specific case imply a voluntary undertaking, any more than it is possible to formulate those in which the law will imply a contract.

Lord Devlin concluded by saying (at p 530):

I content myself with the proposition that, wherever there is a relationship equivalent to contract, there is a duty of care. Such a relationship may be either general or particular. Examples of a general relationship are those of solicitor and client and of banker and customer. Where there is a general relationship of this sort, it is unnecessary to do more than prove its existence, and the duty follows. Where, as in the present case, what is relied on is a particular relationship created *ad hoc*, it will be necessary to examine the particular facts to see whether there is an express or implied undertaking of responsibility. I regard this proposition as an application of the general conception of proximity.

Comment

Although Lord Devlin stated that an implied voluntary undertaking to assume responsibility was "the foundation for the ground" on which the House of Lords decided the case, he did not say that it was in and of itself the *principle* upon which the decision was founded. Indeed, Lord Devlin made it clear that the legal principle that would have to be applied to arrive at the *conclusion* that it was justifiable to imply that the defendants in *Hedley Byrne* had impliedly voluntarily undertaken to assume responsibility to the plaintiffs was to be found elsewhere. After the passage cited above, in which Lord Devlin said that an implied voluntary undertaking to assume responsibility was the foundation for the ground on which the House dismissed the appeal, he continued (at p 530):

> But, in so far as your Lordships *describe the circumstances* in which an implication will ordinarily be drawn, I am prepared to adopt any one of your Lordships' statements as showing the general rule; and I pay the same respect to the statement by Denning LJ in his dissenting judgment in *Candler v Crane, Christmas and Co* [see Chapter 9, para 9.6.2] about the circumstances in which he says a duty to use care in making a statement exists.

Thus, it is submitted that, in *Hedley Byrne*, the use of the expression 'voluntary assumption of responsibility' was not meant to state a legal principle as such, but merely a conclusion which it was justifiable to reach by the application of other legal principles. This point is important in view of the manner in which Lord Goff and certain other Law Lords have analysed and explained *Hedley Byrne* in certain more recent cases, which are now discussed below.

Spring v Guardian Assurance Plc

In *Spring v Guardian Assurance Plc* [1995] 2 AC 296 (discussed further in Chapter 9, para 9.7.7), Lord Goff said (at p 316):

> As will appear hereafter, I have come to the conclusion that, on the facts of the present case, the defendants owed a duty of care to the plaintiff in respect of the preparation of the reference in question. In my opinion, the source of the duty of care lies in the principle derived from *Hedley Byrne v Heller, viz.* an assumption of responsibility by the defendants to the plaintiff in respect of the reference, and reliance by the plaintiff upon the exercise by them of due care and skill in respect of its preparation.

Further on, in discussing why he concluded that "the *Hedley Byrne* principle" applied in this case, Lord Goff quoted the passages cited above from certain of the speeches in *Hedley Byrne* and then continued (at p 318):

> All the members of the Appellate Committee in the case spoke in terms of the principle resting upon an assumption or undertaking of responsibility by the defendant towards the plaintiff, coupled with reliance by the plaintiff on the exercise by the defendant of due care and skill. Lord Devlin, in particular, stressed that the principle rested upon an assumption of responsibility when he said that 'the essence of the matter in the present case and in others of the same type is the acceptance of responsibility'. For the purpose of the case now before your Lordships, it is, I consider, legitimate to proceed on the same basis.

111

In applying these *principles* to the facts of the case, Lord Goff concluded (at p 319):

> When the employer provides a reference to a third party in respect of his employee, he does so, not only for the assistance of the third party, but also for the assistance of the employee. Indeed, nowadays, it must often be very difficult for an employee to obtain fresh employment without the benefit of a reference from his previous employer. Indeed, references are part of the currency of the modern employment market. When such a reference is provided by an employer, it is plain that the employee relies upon him to exercise due skill and care in the preparation of the reference before making it available to the third party. In these circumstances, it seems to me that all the elements requisite for the application of the *Hedley Byrne* principle are present. I need only add that, in the context under consideration, there is no question of the circumstances in which the reference is provided being, for example, so informal as to negative an assumption of responsibility by the employer.

The decision in *Spring* was given by a majority of 4:1. Five speeches were delivered. Of the remaining three majority speeches, only Lord Lowry agreed with Lord Goff's interpretation of *Hedley Byrne*. Lord Slynn said (at p 333) that "the proper approach" is to be found in *Caparo Industries Plc v Dickman* [1990] 2 AC 605, in particular in that part of Lord Bridge's speech in which Lord Bridge said that "the necessary ingredients" for the existence of a duty of care are foreseeability, proximity and that in all the circumstances it is fair, just and reasonable to impose a duty of care (see Chapter 2, para 2.1.3) and that the concepts of proximity and fairness are merely "convenient labels to attach to the features of different specific situations which, on a detailed examination of all the circumstances, the law recognises pragmatically, as giving rise to a duty of care of a given scope" (see Chapter 2, para 2.3.2, *above*). Lord Woolf, too, also did not mention assumption of responsibility in his speech. He applied the same approach as Lord Slynn and said (at p 342):

> The claim here is in respect of economic loss. Before there can be a duty owed in respect of economic loss, it is now clearly established that it is important to be able to show foreseeability of that loss, coupled with the necessary degree of proximity between the parties. It is also necessary to establish that in all the circumstances it is fair, just and reasonable for a duty to be imposed in respect of the economic loss.

Henderson v Merrett

In *Henderson v Merrett Syndicates Ltd* [1995] 2 AC 145 (discussed further in Chapter 9, para 9.7.6), Lord Goff, with whose speech the other Law Lords concurred, under the heading "The Governing Principle", said (at p 180): "The principle underlying *Hedley Byrne* rests upon a relationship between the parties, which may be general or specific to the particular transaction, and which may or may not be contractual in nature. All of their Lordships spoke in terms of one party having assumed or undertaken responsibility to the other". Lord Goff then referred to some of the criticisms that have been made against the idea that the expression 'assumption of responsibility' is a (realistic) test for liability (see *above*) and concluded (at p 180):

In subsequent cases concerned with liability under the *Hedley Byrne* principle in respect of negligent misstatements, the question has frequently arisen whether the plaintiff falls within a category of persons to whom the maker of the statement owes a duty of care. In seeking to contain the category of persons within reasonable bounds, there has been some tendency on the part of the courts to criticise the concept of 'assumption of responsibility' as being 'unlikely to be a helpful or realistic test in most cases' (see *Smith v Eric S Bush*, [1990] 1 AC 831, 864–865, *per* Lord Griffiths and *Caparo Industries Plc v Dickman*, [1990] 2 AC 605, 628, *per* Lord Roskill). However, at least in cases such as the present, in which the same problem does not arise, there seems to be no reason why recourse should not be had to the concept, which appears to have been adopted, in one form or another, by all of their Lordships in *Hedley Byrne*.

Furthermore, especially in a context concerned with a liability which may arise under a contract or in a situation 'equivalent to contract', it must be expected that an objective test will be applied when asking the question whether, in a particular case, responsibility should be held to have been assumed by the defendant to the plaintiff: see *Caparo Industries Plc v Dickman, per* Lord Oliver.

In addition, the concept provides its own explanation why there is no problem in cases *of this kind* about liability for pure economic loss; for, if a person assumes responsibility to another in respect of certain services, there is no reason why he should not be liable in damages to that other in respect of economic loss which flows from the negligent performance of those services. It follows that, once the case is identified as falling within the *Hedley Byrne* principle, there should be no need to embark upon any further enquiry whether it is fair, just and reasonable to impose liability for economic loss—a point which is, I consider, of some importance in the present case. The concept indicates too that in some circumstances, for example, where the undertaking to furnish the relevant service is given on an informal occasion, there may be no assumption of responsibility; and likewise an assumption of responsibility may be negatived by an appropriate disclaimer.

White v Jones

In *White v Jones* [1995] 2 AC 207 (discussed further in Chapter 9, para 9.7.5), it was assumed, without discussion, by two of the majority Law Lords (Lords Goff and Nolan) that assumption of responsibility is a legal principle, as opposed to a conclusion reached by applying other principles; and that assumption of responsibility was the correct starting point as a principle in the analysis of the factual situation in the case. The problem was that the principle did not quite fit (see para 9.7.5), so their Lordships 'extended it' to make it fit. Lord Goff said (at p 268):

> The *Hedley Byrne* principle cannot give rise on ordinary principles to an assumption of responsibility by the testator's solicitor towards an intended beneficiary. Even so, it seems to me that it is open to your Lordships' House to fashion a remedy to fill a lacuna in the law and so prevent the injustice which would otherwise occur on the facts of cases such as the present. In my opinion, therefore, your Lordships' House should in cases such as these extend to the intended beneficiary a remedy under the *Hedley Byrne* principle by holding that the assumption of responsibility by the solicitor towards his client should be held in law to extend to the intended beneficiary.

The third majority Law Lord, Lord Browne-Wilkinson, went out of his way "to attempt an analysis of what is meant by assumption of responsibility in the law of negligence". First, he said that the concept was not invented in *Hedley Byrne*, but derives its genesis from *Nocton v Lord Ashburton* [1914] AC 932 (see Chapter 9, para 9.2.2). In support of this assertion, Lord Browne-Wilkinson cited the passage from the speech of Viscount Haldane LC (at p 948) that is quoted in para 9.2.2, in which Viscount Haldane LC said, *inter alia*: "Whether such a duty has been assumed must depend on the relationship of the parties". Lord Browne-Wilkinson said (at p 271) that it can therefore be gathered from *Nocton* that (emphasis added): "There can be special relationships between the parties which give rise to the law *treating the defendant* as having assumed a duty to be careful in circumstances where, apart from such relationship, no duty of care would exist".

Lord Browne-Wilkinson continued by saying that if we can understand the nature of one "special relationship" it may cast light on when, by analogy, it is appropriate for the law to treat other relationships as being "special". He noted that the special relationship in *Nocton* was a fiduciary relationship and he said (at p 271):

> The special relationship (ie, a fiduciary relationship) giving rise to the assumption of responsibility held to exist in *Nocton*'s case does not depend on any mutual dealing between A and B, let alone on any relationship akin to contract. Although such factors may be present, equity imposes the obligation because A has assumed to act in B's affair.

Lord Browne-Wilkinson then said (at p 272) that, in *Hedley Byrne*, the basis on which Lords Reid, Morris and Hodson would have held the defendant liable for negligently giving the reference was that, were it not for the disclaimer, the bank would have assumed responsibility for such reference. He said (at p 272): "The crucial element was that, by choosing to answer the enquiry, the bank had assumed to act, and thereby created the special relationship on which the necessary duty of care was founded".

Lord Browne-Wilkinson continued with this train of thought by seeking to identify exactly what it is that the defendant in these cases assumes. He said (at p 273):

> Just as in the case of fiduciary duties, the assumption of responsibility referred to is the defendant's assumption of responsibility for the *task*, not the assumption of legal liability. Even in cases of *ad hoc* relationships, it is the undertaking to answer the question posed which creates the relationship. If the responsibility for the task is assumed by the defendant, he thereby creates a special relationship between himself and the plaintiff to which the law (not the defendant) attaches a duty to carry out carefully the tasks so assumed.

Lord Browne-Wilkinson drew this distinction with particular reference to the unease that he felt about the criticisms that have been made about the concept of assumption of responsibility (see *above*). He clearly thought that the distinction between assumption of responsibility "for the task" and the assumption of legal liability answered these criticisms. He continued in the passage cited above by saying (at p 273):

> If this be the right view, it does much to allay the doubts about the utility of the concept of assumption of responsibility voiced by Lord Griffiths in *Smith v Eric*

S Bush and by Lord Roskill in *Caparo Industries Plc v Dickman* [see Chapter 9, para 9.5.2]. As I read those judicial criticisms, they proceed on the footing that the phrase 'assumption of responsibility' refers to the defendant having assumed *legal responsibility*. I doubt whether the same criticisms would have been directed at the phrase if the words had been understood, as I think they should be, as referring to a conscious assumption of responsibility for the task, rather than a conscientious assumption of legal liability to the plaintiff for its careful performance.

Lastly, Lord Browne-Wilkinson made clear the very high degree of importance which he attached to the concept of 'voluntary assumption of responsibility' when he said (at p 274):

> The law of England does not impose any general duty of care to avoid negligent misstatements or to avoid causing pure economic loss even if economic damage to the plaintiff was foreseeable. However, such a duty of care will arise if there is a special relationship between the parties. Although the categories of cases in which such special relationship can be held to exist are not closed, as yet only two categories have been identified, *viz*. (1) where there is a fiduciary relationship and (2) where the defendant has voluntarily answered a question or tenders skilled advice or services in circumstances where he knows or ought to know that an identified plaintiff will rely on his answers or advice.
>
> In both these categories the special relationship is created by the defendant voluntarily assuming to act in the matter by involving himself in the plaintiff's affairs or by choosing to speak. If he does so assume to act or speak he is said to have assumed responsibility for carrying through the matter he has entered upon. In the words of Lord Reid in *Hedley Byrne* [1964] AC 465, 486 he has "accepted a relationship . . . which requires him to exercise such care as the circumstances require", ie, although the extent of the duty will vary from category to category, *some* duty of care arises from the special relationship.

Comment

The first comment that arises from the *dicta* cited above is that it is not clear what Lord Goff meant when he said that, if one person assumes responsibility to another in respect of certain services, "there is no reason why" he should not be liable for that other person's consequential economic loss and that, once a case "is identified as falling within the *Hedley Byrne* principle", it is not necessary to ask in addition whether it is fair, just and reasonable to impose liability for economic loss. If Lord Goff meant to treat the concept of assumption of responsibility as being a *conclusion* wherein the maker of the statement or the giver of the advice is *deemed* to have assumed a responsibility to the plaintiff for the plaintiff's economic losses in all of the circumstances of the case, then it is submitted that this statement of Lord Goff is acceptable.

Another possibility, which is considered more fully *below*, is that Lord Goff meant to limit the application of this principle to cases where there is no concern about the indeterminacy of the class of potential plaintiffs because the parties were already in a contractual relationship with each other or, if they were not, the situation was almost equivalent to a contract because of their direct dealings with each other.

If, on the other hand, the concept of voluntary assumption of responsibility is treated as a stand-alone concept in its own right, so that, once the court has concluded that, as a fact, the defendant did assume a responsibility to provide information or a service to the plaintiff with due care and attention, the defendant is *ipso facto* responsible for the economic losses suffered by the plaintiff in relying on that information or service, then these *dicta* of Lord Goff are too simplistic. If they are treated in this fashion, they overlook the fact that important questions of policy and pragmatism are also involved, such as the spectre of indeterminate liability, the reasonableness of the plaintiff's reliance (including the often all-important question of whether it was reasonable for the defendant to assume that the plaintiff would carry out an independent examination before relying blindly on what the defendant had said or done) and whether the scope of the duty of care that the defendant voluntarily assumed extends to the actual loss sustained by the plaintiff (and this last-mentioned factor can include the consideration of a host of different issues, such as the capacity in which the plaintiff incurred the loss and the cause of the loss—see Chapter 2, para 2.1.5).

These factors arise in every case, although they are not usually mentioned in cases where liability in very similar circumstances has already been established in any particular category of cases and the case in hand represents but a small variation on an established theme. However, in relatively novel cases like *Caparo Industries Plc v Dickman* [1990] 2 AC 605 (see para 9.7.2, *below*) and *Marc Rich and Co v Bishop Rock Marine Co Ltd* ('*The Nicholas H*') [1996] 1 AC 211 (see para 9.7.4, *below*), it is impossible to say whether the defendant did or did not assume (or, more accurately, must be deemed to have assumed) responsibility to the plaintiff without *first* embarking upon an enquiry as to whether it is fair, just and reasonable in all the circumstances so to hold. The conduct of that enquiry involves a detailed consideration of the relevant policy and pragmatic considerations applicable to the category of case in question and of the all-important question which loomed large in *Caparo*, as to whether the plaintiff's loss was within the scope of the duty of care which the defendant had voluntarily assumed for the accuracy of the defendant's negligent misstatement (which, in *Caparo*, was contained in the defendant's audit report). This is how the duty of care question was approached in both *Caparo* and *The Nicholas H*. In *Caparo*, Lord Oliver expressed this point clearly when he said (at p 637):

> The nearest that one gets to the establishment of a criterion for the creation of a duty in the case of a negligent statement is the emphasis to be found in all the speeches [in *Hedley Byrne*] upon 'the voluntary assumption of responsibility' by the defendant. This is a convenient phrase but it is clear that it was not intended to be a test for the existence of the duty for, on analysis, it means no more than that the act of the defendant in making the statement or tendering the advice was voluntary and that the law attributes to it an assumption of responsibility if the statement or advice is inaccurate and is acted upon. It tells us nothing about the circumstances from which such attribution arises.

The facts of *The Nicholas H* seemed almost tailor-made for holding that the third defendant (the classification society) had assumed responsibility for the loss of the cargo on board the ship (see para 9.7.4, *below*). Nevertheless, Lord Steyn, speaking for the 4:1 majority, after expanding in detail on the policy considerations that, in his view, rendered it not fair, just and reasonable to impose a duty of care on the classification society for the risk of loss to the cargo, rejected the application of "the doctrine" of voluntary assumption of responsibility quite tersely by saying (at p 242):

> Given that the cargo owners were not even aware of NKK's examination of the ship, and that the cargo owners simply relied on the undertakings of the shipowners, it is in my view impossible to force the present set of facts into even the most expansive view of the doctrine of voluntary assumption of responsibility.

It is interesting to contrast this statement with the way in which the absence of awareness and reliance were not regarded by the House of Lords in *White v Jones* [1995] 2 AC 207 as being impediments to the imposition of a duty of care on the negligent solicitor based on an assumption of responsibility by him for the beneficiaries' losses (see *below*, and para 9.7.5, *below*).

Secondly, it is not clear what Lord Goff meant when he said that the criticism of the concept of assumption of responsibility by Lord Griffiths in *Smith v Bush* and by Lord Roskill in *Caparo* as being "unlikely to be a helpful or realistic test in most cases" (see *above*) did not arise in *Henderson* because in *Smith* and *Caparo* the courts were "seeking to contain the category of person within reasonable bounds". It would seem that Lord Goff is suggesting that, for the purposes of the application of the principle of voluntary assumption of responsibility, a distinction should be drawn between cases in which there is a real concern as to the indeterminacy of the possible members of the class of potential plaintiffs—in which event he seems to accept that the concept is unlikely to be of assistance as a realistic test—and cases in which the category of potential plaintiffs is clear and limited, and possibly also where, as in *Henderson*, there was an already existing contract between the defendant and the plaintiff/s or there had been prior contact between the defendant and the plaintiff/s such that their relationship was "equivalent to contract". In this event the concept of voluntary assumption of responsibility is indeed likely to be of great assistance and, according to Lord Goff, should be invoked and applied in the manner suggested by him in *Henderson* (ie to the exclusion of all other factors once it is found that the defendant did voluntarily undertake to furnish the information or provide the service in question to the plaintiff).

If Lord Goff did intend to draw this distinction—and it is submitted that it is plausible to suggest that he did—then:

(1) it is surprising that Lord Goff went to so much trouble to formulate a principle which:

   (a) was expressly stated by him to be of limited application;

   (b) has the clear potential to cause confusion in future cases; and

   (c) was not necessary because the established approach, formulated by the House of Lords in *Caparo* (ie foreseeability, proximity and "fair, just and reasonable"—see Chapter 3, para 3.3), is a perfectly adequate tool for analysing the fact situation in *Henderson* (and also the fact situations in *Spring* and in *White v Jones*); and

(2) the distinction that Lord Goff has drawn is not valid because the 'indeterminacy of class' problem was not present in *Smith v Bush*,

nor in *Caparo* so far as concerned the plaintiff's claim (which was its main claim) in its capacity as an existing shareholder.

Thirdly, it is also not clear what Lord Browne-Wilkinson meant when he said that he thought that the criticisms that have been made of the phrase 'assumption of responsibility' would not have been made if these words had been understood as referring to an assumption of responsibility by the defendant "for the task", rather than to an assumption of legal liability. It seems clear that in *Hedley Byrne* itself the House of Lords viewed the expression as referring to an assumption of legal liability. Lord Devlin, after stating (at p 530) that he regarded the implication of an undertaking of responsibility as "an application of the general conception of proximity" (see *above*), said that he did not wish to place any doctrinal restrictions on the concept. He then provided the example of a defendant who offers to do something for a plaintiff and expressly tells the plaintiff that he can rely on him. Lord Devlin said that such a defendant could not escape liability simply because he belonged to no profession and had no qualifications or special skills. Then, as if to illustrate the point being made here, Lord Devlin commented on this example by saying (at p 531): "The relevance of these factors is to show the unlikelihood of a defendant in such circumstances assuming a *legal* responsibility".

Lord Mustill, dissenting in *White v Jones*, recognised that their Lordships in *Hedley Byrne* used the phrase as meaning that, in the circumstances, the defendant must be deemed to have assumed legal liability. After citing all of the passages from the speeches in *Hedley Byrne* that are set out *above*, Lord Mustill said (at p 288):

> There is a degree of ambiguity about the use of the word 'undertaking' [in *Hedley Byrne*]. In context, however, I think it is clear that the word was not used in the sense of taking on or tackling a job [*cf.* Lord Browne-Wilkinson, *above*]. The passages quoted [from *Hedley Byrne*] show that the defendants were held liable because the relationship was such as to show that they took upon themselves a *legal* duty to give with reasonable care, whatever reference they chose to furnish.

Fourthly, to the extent that the criticisms of the concept mentioned *above* did proceed on the footing that the phrase 'assumption of responsibility' refers to the defendant having assumed legal responsibility, those criticisms were directed towards demonstrating that the phrase was used in *Hedley Byrne* to explain the effect of the defendants' disclaimer; ie because the defendants had expressly disclaimed any voluntary assumption of legal responsibility, they could not be held liable to the plaintiff even if, on all other grounds, the court would have been justified in imposing a duty of care on them for the plaintiff's loss.

Fifthly, Lord Browne-Wilkinson's suggested rationalisation of the criticisms of the concept fails to appreciate the main thrust of those criticisms, namely that in most cases it is a legal fiction to say that the defendant voluntarily assumed liability to the plaintiff for the plaintiff's loss because, in most cases, the defendant will *not* have voluntarily, consciously or intentionally assumed responsibility for his information, advice or services to a person with whom he did not have a contract. Therefore, liability will be imposed by the court and it will only be possible to say that the defendant is *deemed* to have assumed a responsibility for his words or actions. Lord Griffiths expressed this point succinctly in *Smith v Eric S Bush* [1990] 1 AC 831, when he said (at p 862): "The phrase 'assumption of responsibility' can only have any real meaning if it is understood as referring to the circumstances in which the law will deem the maker of the statement to have assumed responsibility to the person who acts upon the advice".

The utility of the concept of 'voluntary assumption of responsibility' as a legal concept is thus more by way of it being a conclusion that might be able to be reached in particular circumstances, ie that in all the circumstances it is justifiable to impose the same consequences on the defendant as would be imposed on a person who had indeed voluntarily accepted legal responsibility for his acts or omissions, rather than as a test or a principle which has legal meaning in its own right. The process of deeming the defendant to have voluntarily assumed responsibility for his acts or omissions involves the application of other principles, and is not answered simply by saying that the defendant voluntarily undertook responsibility for the task. Ironically, it seems that this point was recognised by Lord Browne-Wilkinson himself in *White v Jones* [1995] 2 AC 207, when he said (at p 273): "If the responsibility for the task is assumed by the defendant, he thereby creates a special relationship between himself and the plaintiff to which the law (not the defendant) attaches a duty to carry out carefully the tasks so assumed".

Proper use

It is submitted that the following observations and conclusions are apt:

(1) The proper use of the phrase or concept 'voluntary assumption of responsibility' is to regard it as being one component amongst many in the proximity analysis or in the overall general pragmatic test for determining liability, in the application of which all the relevant factors are taken into account and are accorded their appropriate weight according to all of the circumstances of the case. As Lord Oliver said in *Caparo Industries Plc v Dickman* [1990] 2 AC 605 (at p 635): "One must be careful about seeking to find any general principle which will serve as a touchstone for all cases, for, even within the limited category of negligent misstatement cases, circumstances may differ infinitely and, in a swiftly developing field of law, there can be no necessary assumption that those features which have served in one case to create the relationship between the plaintiff and the defendant on which liability depends will necessarily be determinative of liability in the different circumstances of another case".

(2) The range of cases in which it is proper to say that, because the defendant voluntarily assumed responsibility to the plaintiff in respect of the provision of certain information or services, there is no need to embark upon any further enquiry whether it is "fair, just and reasonable" to impose liability on the defendant for the plaintiff's economic loss is so narrow (ie it is confined to cases where the parties are already in a contractual relationship or where there has been direct contact between them and their relationship can be regarded as being

'equivalent to contract') that the law would be better served if this application of the concept was abandoned, given the potential for confusion that this idea engenders and given that principles already exist which are equally applicable to resolve these cases.

(3) The concept of 'voluntary assumption of responsibility' is useful, but not necessary, as a conclusion or as a goal to be achieved, or as a benchmark against which to measure different situations. In other words, if one wants to use the concept in this fashion, its utility will be found in asking whether, in all of the circumstances of the case— including whether, as a fact, the defendant voluntarily assumed responsibility for the task whose negligent performance can be regarded as being the origin of the plaintiff's claim—the defendant's acts or omissions were such that it is fair, just and reasonable to regard (or *deem*) the defendant in law to be subject to the same consequences, so far as the plaintiff's actual loss is concerned, as a person who had voluntarily, intentionally or consciously accepted legal liability for such acts or omissions without attaching a valid disclaimer thereto.

(4) When used in the sense described in paragraph (3) *above*, voluntary assumption of responsibility is not a different test from the established test of foreseeability, proximity and "fair, just and reasonable" but is an equal alternative to it. Some judges and practitioners might find it easier to reason in terms of the deemed voluntary assumption of responsibility approach because it can be envisaged more vividly and might appear to have a more tangible feel than the other approach.

Application in subsequent cases

It is instructive to observe how judges in cases since *Spring, Henderson* and *hite v Jones* have interpreted their Lordships' *dicta* on the importance of the concept of 'voluntary assumption of responsibility'.

Tidman v Reading Borough Council

In *Tidman v Reading Borough Council* [1994] 3 PLR 72, the facts of which are set out in para 9.7.8, *below*, Buxton J said:

> It is now recognised in the law of negligence generally that the overall question for the Court in deciding whether a duty of care exists is as stated by Lord Bridge in *Caparo Industries Plc v Dickman* [1990] 2 AC 605 at 617, namely, that "the situation should be one in which the Court considers it fair, just and reasonable that the law should impose a duty of a given scope upon one party for the benefit of the other".
>
> Considering this aspect of the law of negligence in *Henderson v Merrett Syndicates Ltd*, Lord Goff, addressing the problem of liability for economic loss, said that it followed that, once a case is identified as falling within the *Hedley Byrne* principle, there should be no need to embark upon any further inquiry whether it is fair, just and reasonable to impose liability for economic loss.
>
> It follows from this that the overriding question whether the imposition of a duty is fair, just and reasonable is taken up in, and must be referred to in, the preliminary question of whether the situation is not merely one of reliance, but one of reliance such as properly falls within the law of negligence.
>
> It is clear that the nature of the responsibility, or, more precisely, the nature

of the circumstances from which the law will *infer* an assumption of responsibility, is a matter of judgment to be assessed according to the guidance provided in the whole of their Lordships' speeches [in *Hedley Byrne*].

It is interesting to note that, in referring to Lord Goff's *dictum* in *Henderson* that "once a case is identified as falling within the *Hedley Byrne* principle, there should be no need to embark upon any further inquiry whether it is fair, just and reasonable to impose liability for economic loss", Buxton J:

(1) did not take note of the context in which Lord Goff had made this remark, namely that this principle should be confined to cases where no question arises as to whether the plaintiff falls within the category of persons to whom the maker of the statement owes a duty of care (see *above*);

(2) regarded Lord Goff as having made this statement in connection with "the overall question" whether the court considers it fair, just and reasonable to impose a duty of care on the defendant in all of the circumstances of the case. It would seem, however, that this is not what Lord Goff had in mind, but that, as noted *above*, he made this statement in relation to cases in which the 'indeterminate class' concern does not arise; and

(3) nevertheless still regarded the "fair, just and reasonable" test as being overriding, with the result that, in order to comply with Lord Goff's *fiat* of not asking this question at the end of the enquiry if the case in question is identified as falling "within the *Hedley Byrne* principle", Buxton J said that this question must be considered in the preliminary stages of deciding whether the situation is not merely one of reliance, but one of reliance "such as properly falls within the law of negligence". In other words, despite the literal meaning of Lord Goff's *dictum*, Buxton J was not going to leave out of consideration the "fair, just and reasonable" question in deciding the case before him.

It is also interesting to note that Buxton J regarded the concept of assumption of responsibility as being a concept which would be *inferred* by the law, rather than simply being a question of fact as to whether the defendant did or did not assume responsibility for the task that he performed and upon which the plaintiff placed reliance.

Rothschild v Berenson

In the original High Court hearing in *Rothschild and Sons Ltd v Berenson* (22 June 1995, unreported), the facts of which are set out in para 9.7.5, *below*, Knox J recognised the restricted nature of Lord Goff's *dictum* (see *above*) when he said:

> There is an apparent contrast in approach between cases where the problem essentially resides in containing within proper bounds the scope of a tortious duty of care so as not to give rise to excessively wide liability to an undefined class of potential plaintiffs on the one hand, and cases where that particular problem does not arise because the category of potential plaintiffs is clear and limited, but difficulties arise in connection with whether a delictual liability as well as a contractual one should be imposed.

3.5.2 *Alternative theories*

Knox J then commented that in the first category of cases the test for liability is foreseeability, proximity and that the situation should be one in which the court considers it fair, just and reasonable to impose a duty of a given scope upon the defendant for the plaintiff's loss; whereas in the second category of cases, the test is whether the defendant assumed or undertook a responsibility to the plaintiff and that, once that fact is established, there is no reason why the defendant should not be liable for the plaintiff's economic loss sustained through having relied on the defendant's negligent misstatement and there is no need, in such a case, to embark on any further inquiry whether it is fair, just and reasonable to impose liability for economic loss.

Having noted this distinction, and having noted that the present case fell into the latter category in the sense that there was no question of a duty of care arising to any person beyond the plaintiffs, Knox J did not, however, mention the phrase 'voluntary assumption of liability' again in his judgment. Instead, he proceeded to apply a fairly traditional proximity analysis, in which he considered all of the factors that might impinge on the closeness of the relationship between the defendant and the plaintiffs. He did not, however, say whether he was consciously applying or not applying the "fair, just and reasonable" criterion because he held that the defendant had not breached its duty of care to the plaintiffs. On this latter point, Knox J was overruled by the Court of Appeal (7 February 1997, unreported—see para 9.7.5).

ADT Ltd v Binder Hamlyn

In *ADT Ltd v BDO Binder Hamlyn* (6 December 1995, unreported), the facts of which are set out in para 9.7.2, May J seems to have regarded the two approaches as being interchangeable, and he expressed a preference for looking at the question from the point of view of whether, in all of the circumstances, he should *deem* the defendant to have assumed responsibility to the plaintiff for the plaintiff's losses sustained through having relied on the defendant's statement that the accounts that the defendant had prepared did indeed present a true and fair view of the state of affairs of the target company. Thus, after considering all of the relevant facts and circumstances, May J said: "The ingredients of a duty of care are therefore all present in this case, and I have to consider whether objectively, and in fairness, *Binders*, through Mr Bishop, are *to be taken* to have assumed responsibility to *ADT* for the reliability of the advice or information which he gave".

Young v Clifford Chance

In *Young v Clifford Chance* (21 December 1995, unreported), the facts of which are set out in para 9.7.5, Popplewell J applied the established foreseeability, proximity and fairness test, and treated voluntary assumption of responsibility as being just one of the factors to be taken into account in determining proximity. Thus, he said:

> It is not in dispute that the defendants foresaw, or ought reasonably to have foreseen damage suffered by the plaintiff as being a likely result of negligence on their part in failing to complete the transaction by the deadline of February 26, 1990.

I turn to the second element, which is proximity between the plaintiff and the defendants. This seems to embrace a 'special relationship', 'reliance' and an 'assumption of responsibility'.

McCullagh v Lane Fox

In *McCullagh v Lane Fox and Partners Ltd* (1996) 49 Con LR 124, the facts of which are set out in para 9.7.3, it was almost taken for granted by all three Lord Justices of Appeal that what they were trying to ascertain was whether, in all of the circumstances of the case, they could conclude that the defendant had voluntarily assumed responsibility to the plaintiff for the truth of a particular negligent misrepresentation that the defendant had made to the plaintiff. In other words, they regarded the concept of voluntary assumption of responsibility as being a concept of prime importance, and as being the benchmark by which to decide whether a duty of care existed in the circumstances of that case.

Welton v North Cornwall District Council

In *Welton v North Cornwall District Council* [1997] 1 WLR 570, the facts of which are set out in para 8.2.10, Rose LJ regarded the test of voluntary assumption of responsibility as being the same as the 'fair, just and reasonable' test. He said (at p 580):

> There was, within *Hedley Byrne* as subsequently analysed, an assumption of responsibility by Mr Evans and hence a duty of care owed by him. Some of the authorities, of which *Caparo Industries Plc v Dickman* [1990] 2 AC 605 is the obvious example, are expressed in terms of which is fair, just and reasonable and some, notably the police cases, but also *X (Minors) v Bedfordshire County Council* [1995] 2 AC 633, in terms of policy considerations. But I confess that I am unable to discern in the authorities any material difference attributable to that difference in language, either in the route charted or in the ultimate destination, when the existence of a duty of care is recognised or denied. That said, where there is no statutory duty and a case of economic loss falls within the *Hedley Byrne* principle, no further inquiry is necessary as to whether it is fair and reasonable to impose liability: see *per* Lord Goff in *Henderson v Merrett Syndicates Ltd* [1995] 2 AC 145.

It is interesting to note that Rose LJ ended off this statement by saying that, where a case of economic loss falls within the *Hedley Byrne* principle (ie voluntary assumption of responsibility coupled with reasonable reliance), no further inquiry is necessary as to whether it is fair and reasonable to impose liability. He justified this statement by reference to Lord Goff's above-discussed *dicta* in *Henderson v Merrett Syndicates Ltd* [1995] 2 AC 145. As discussed *above* and as mentioned further *below*, it is submitted that Lord Goff did not intend this principle to apply to all cases of voluntary assumption of responsibility and reasonable reliance, but only to those in which no problems arise about the indeterminacy of the class of possible plaintiffs. This will occur where the defendant's statement was made or his services were rendered to the plaintiff in circumstances in which the relationship between them was contractual or was almost equivalent to a contract.

3.5.2 *Alternative theories*

Brostoff v Clark Kenneth Leventhal

In *Brostoff v Clark Kenneth Leventhal* (1996, unreported), the facts of which are set out in Chapter 10, para 10.2.1, it is submitted that Dyson J misapplied Lord Goff's above-discussed *dicta* in *Henderson v Merrett Syndicates Ltd* [1995] 2 AC 145. After referring to the plaintiffs' counsel's submission that it would be just and reasonable that the plaintiffs should be owed a duty of care by CKL, who knew or ought to have known that their employee, Mr Young, was conducting investment business from their premises during ordinary office hours and was using his position of authority at CKL to lend credibility to what he was doing, Dyson J said:

> I am far from persuaded that on the facts of this case it would be just and reasonable to impose such a duty on the defendants, but I do not have to decide this. This is because, as Lord Goff pointed out in *Henderson v Merrett*, in cases concerning pure economic loss, the only question is whether the *Hedley Byrne* requirements have been satisfied, and it is unnecessary to embark on any further inquiry whether it is fair, just and reasonable to impose liability for economic loss.

As noted above, this is not quite what Lord Goff said or intended. He restricted this view to cases where there is no concern about the indeterminacy of the class of potential plaintiffs where "a person assumes responsibility *to another* in respect of certain services". The reason why Lord Goff felt that, in cases of this type, it is not necessary to embark on any further inquiry whether it is fair, just and reasonable to impose liability for economic loss is because the relationship between the parties in such a situation would be almost equivalent to contract on account of their direct dealings with each other. By way of contrast, this was not the situation in the present case (*Brostoff*), with the consequence that it was indeed necessary for the judge to go on and consider specifically whether, in all of the circumstances of the case, it would have been fair, just and reasonable to impose a duty of care on CKL to the indeterminate group of investors to whom Mr Young had provided his investment services.

Sumitomo Bank v Banque Bruxelles

In *Sumitomo Bank v Banque Bruxelles* [1997] 1 Lloyd's Rep 487, the facts of which are set out in para 9.7.2, Langley J regarded voluntary assumption of responsibility as being an entirely separate test from the established three-part test. Thus, he said:

> Two basic approaches to the question whether in a given case a duty of care arises can be discerned from the leading authorities. The first can be summarised in the familiar rubric of foreseeability, proximity, and whether the imposition of a duty of care would be fair, just and reasonable. The second can be summarised in the words 'voluntary assumption of responsibility'. In this case, I do not think it matters which approach is taken, as in my judgment the result is the same on either basis.

Langley J then set out what he believed to be the major statements of principle supporting each of the two approaches, analysed the facts of the case separately under each approach and concluded: "For these reasons, in my judgment, and whether one approaches the matter by way of *Caparo* or *Henderson v Merrett*, the answer is the same".

Reeman v Department of Transport

In *Reeman v The Department of Transport* (26 March 1997, unreported), the facts of which are set out in Chapter 8, para 8.2.10, Phillips LJ doubted the application of the 'test' of assumption of responsibility in a case where there was no contract between the parties and the situation was not equivalent to contract. He said:

> In determining whether a duty of care arose, the judge applied the three criteria suggested in cases such as *Caparo*, of foreseeability, proximity and fairness. However, the plaintiffs' counsel also argues that the alternative test of assumption of responsibility, which was applied in cases such as *Henderson v Merrett Syndicates Ltd* [1995] 2 AC 145, was also satisfied. For my part, I have some difficulty in seeing how that can be the appropriate test in a case such as the present where there is no contract between the plaintiffs and the Department, nor a situation the equivalent of contract, particularly if the adjective 'voluntary' is applied to 'assumption' as it sometimes is, given that the Department was acting under a statutory duty imposed upon it. The circumstances of the present case are wholly different from those, for example, of the managing agents providing services for the identified names in the *Henderson* case or the solicitor drafting a will under which identified beneficiaries were intended to take in *White v Jones* [1995] 2 AC 207, in which cases the defendants were found to have assumed responsibility to the plaintiffs.

Red Sea Tankers v Papachristidis

In *Red Sea Tankers v Papachristidis* (30 April 1997, unreported), Mance J recognised that the test for the imposition of a duty of care is objective and that the concept of assumption of responsibility is no more than a "convenient shorthand" for that test. Thus, he said (at para 188):

> Did Mr Papachristidis, Mr Dunn and Mr Anderson owe any, and if so what, duties in tort when acting on behalf of PL and/or PSML?
>
> The answer to this question depends in each case upon whether the relevant individual owed personally a duty of care in respect of his acts or omissions about which the plaintiffs complain in this action. In the light of *Henderson v Merrett* [1995] 2 AC 145, the plaintiffs do not quarrel greatly with the use as a 'convenient shorthand' of the concept of assumption of responsibility whilst emphasising that the test whether the responsibility should be regarded as having been assumed is objective. It is also common ground that the application of the test is fact-intensive; it requires close attention to all the circumstances and features of the particular case.

Machin v Adams

In *Machin v Adams* (7 May 1997, unreported), the facts of which are set out in para 9.7.4, the Court of Appeal seems to have taken it for granted that the relevant approach was to try to determine whether the defendant had voluntarily undertaken a responsibility towards the plaintiff "in the sense

3.5.2 *Alternative theories*

in which that phrase was used by Lord Goff in *Henderson v Merrett Syndicates Ltd*" (*per* Sir Brian Neill). In the course of applying this approach, Sir Brian Neill said:

> The words 'assumption of responsibility' must be understood in the sense of a conscious assumption of responsibility for the test, rather than a conscious assumption of legal liability to the plaintiff for the careful performance of the task: see Lord Browne-Wilkinson in *White v Jones* [see *above*]. The Court must therefore examine all of the circumstances of the case. Thus, in my judgment, in order to establish liability against the adviser in a case such as the present, the advisee must show some connecting thread between the task the adviser has undertaken to perform, and the course of action upon which the advisee can be foreseen likely to embark.

BCCI v Price Waterhouse

In *Bank of Credit and Commerce International (Overseas) Limited (in liquidation) v Price Waterhouse* (30 January 1997, unreported and 13 February 1998, unreported, CA), the facts of which are set out in para 9.7.2, Laddie J recognised that the two approaches are in fact the same. Thus, he said:

> Although the expression 'assumption of responsibility' is to be found in some of the recent cases, it does not appear to signify any different approach to the imposition of liability to that set out in *Caparo*. It is, as Lord Roskill pointed out in *Caparo*, simply another imprecise phrase used to cover situations in which a duty of care has been held to exist. It does little to define why, or the circumstances in which, liability arises.

In the Court of Appeal, Sir Brian Neill (formerly Neill LJ) delivering the judgment of the Court, regarded assumption of responsibility as a separate, but 'parallel' test. After referring to the way in which this 'test' has been defined in some of the cases, and after referring to the two other 'tests', namely the 'threefold test' and the 'incremental approach', Sir Brian Neill said:

> The fact that all of these approaches have been used and approved by the House of Lords in recent years suggests:
>   (a) that it may be useful to look at any new set of facts by using each of the three approaches in turn, though it may be noted that in some cases, such as *Henderson v Merrett Syndicates Ltd* [1995] 2 AC 145, the use of the incremental approach may be sufficient to show that responsibility has been undertaken; and
>   (b) that if the facts are properly analysed and the policy considerations are correctly evaluated, the several approaches will yield the same result.

Secured Residential Funding v Nationwide Building Society

In *Secured Residential Funding Ltd v Nationwide Building Society* (21 October 1997, unreported), the facts of which are set out in para 9.7.3, Daniel Brennan QC, sitting as a deputy High Court judge, treated assumption of responsibility as being merely an aid to the inquiry into proximity. After setting out at great length the leading *dicta* on voluntary assumption of responsibility, he said: "Thus it is clear that, depending on the circum-

126

stances, the assumption of responsibility by the defendant (whether judged objectively or subjectively) may greatly assist the inquiry into proximity".

Peach Publishing v Slater

In *Peach Publishing Ltd v Slater and Co* (13 February 1997, unreported), the facts of which are set out in para 9.7.2, the Court of Appeal regarded 'assumption of responsibility' as being the *touchstone* of liability. Thus, Morritt LJ, with whose judgment the other Lord Justices of Appeal concurred, said: "The touchstone of liability formerly described as 'a voluntary assumption of responsibility' found to be unhelpful by Lord Griffiths in *Smith v Bush* and by Lord Roskill in *Caparo Industries Plc v Dickman*, has been restored to favour, but without the adjective 'voluntary'".

In applying the principles from the *dicta* on voluntary assumption of responsibility in the leading cases, Morritt LJ made it clear that the decision whether the defendant did (voluntarily) assume responsibility to the plaintiff in any particular case is still a legal question and not just a factual one. Thus, he said:

> The judge placed great weight on the fact that a direct statement had been voluntarily made. But it does not, and this is where I part company from the judge, follow from the fact that a statement was made both voluntarily and directly by A to B, that A is assuming responsibility to B. The circumstances in which the statement was made must also be considered in order to evaluate the significance of the facts that the statement was both voluntary and direct.

It seems apparent from Morritt LJ's judgment that he did not think that there is any difference between the two approaches. Thus, he said:

> I do not think that Mr Slater did assume responsibility for the accuracy of the Management Accounts to Mrs Land and Peach. In so far as there may be a separate point, I do not think that it would be fair, just or reasonable in all of the circumstances of the case that a duty of care should be imposed on Mr Slater in respect of the statement relied on by Peach.

Hill v Van Erp

In *Hill v Van Erp* (1997) 142 ALR 687, the facts of which are set out in para 9.9.2, McHugh J, dissenting in the High Court of Australia, said: "Lord Browne-Wilkinson's use of the term 'assumption of responsibility' [in *White v Jones*] was most unconventional. Prior to *White*, that term had been taken to mean an assumption of legal liability. His Lordship's reasoning therefore departed from the law as previously understood".

Gummow J, although part of the majority, also criticised this aspect of Lord Browne-Wilkinson's use of the concept. He said:

> In *White v Jones*, Lord Browne-Wilkinson sought to meet criticism of the use of the phrase 'assumption of responsibility'. His Lordship said that it should be understood as referring to a conscious assumption of responsibility for the task, rather than a conscious assumption of legal liability to the plaintiff for its careful performance. Any such general notion of 'assumption of responsibility' by reference to the performance of services and without identification of those to whom, or for whose benefit, they are to be performed has attracted criticism, with which I agree.

127

3.5.3 *Alternative theories*

Another of the majority judges, Brennan CJ, also criticised the idea of saying that the defendant in these cases assumed liability only for the task. Thus, he said:

> I would not regard the principle underlying recovery against the solicitor as being an extension of the *Hedley Byrne* assumption of responsibility. The *Hedley Byrne* category of case depends upon an assumption of a duty of care as a factual element in the relationship between the plaintiff and the defendant. In cases of the present kind [which was like *Ross v Caunters*—see para 9.7.5], there is no anterior relationship between the solicitor and the intended beneficiary, and the duty of care is imposed by the law.

3.5.3 Control

In the High Court of Australia, in *Hill v Van Erp* (1997) 142 ALR 687, the facts of which are set out in Chapter 9, para 9.9.3, the feeling by some of the judges that the proximity analysis would not provide the answer in this case led them to introduce a new concept, namely, 'control'. Thus, Gaudron J said:

> The nature of the loss involved when a legal right is defeated or its enjoyment is impaired and the particular nature of the relationship involved when one person is in a position to control the enjoyment of another's legal right, including a right which, but for the first person's act or omission, would have come into existence, lead me to conclude that, subject to one qualification, it should be held that a person in such a position owes a duty of care to the other to take reasonable steps to prevent any reasonably foreseeable loss or impairment of that right. The qualification which I would make is that the duty of care will not arise if it is inconsistent with some overriding duty, as for example occurred in *Smolinski v Mitchell* [1995] 10 WWR 68, where a duty to see to the expeditious execution of a will was inconsistent with the duty which arose in the circumstances of that case, for the solicitor engaged by the testator to refer his client for independent legal advice.
>
> The relationship in this case between Mrs Hill and Mrs Van Erp is not one that is characterised either by the assumption of responsibility or reliance. Rather, what is significant is that Mrs Hill was in a position of control over the testamentary wishes of her client and, thus, in a position to control whether Mrs Van Erp would have the right which the testatrix clearly intended her to have, namely, the right to have her estate properly administered in accordance with the terms of her Will.
>
> The importance of control as a factor in proximity, and also as a factor governing the content of the duty of care, is apparent in *Burnie Port Authority v General Jones Pty Ltd* (1994) 179 CLR 520 [see *below*]. And although Deane J rested his judgment in *Hawkins v Clayton* [see *above*] on the assumption of responsibility and reliance, it seems to me that that case is more easily explained in terms of control. Moreover, control is in some respects a more stringent test than assumption of responsibility. Certainly, neither law nor logic excludes it from consideration as a determinant of proximity in cases of pure economic loss.
>
> I am of the view that, by reason of her position of control, in particular her position to control whether Mrs Van Erp would acquire the right to have the testatrix's estate properly administered in accordance with the terms of her Will, there was a relationship of proximity between Mrs Hill and Mrs Van Erp such

that Mrs Hill was under a duty of care to take reasonable steps to ensure that Mrs Van Erp's testamentary intentions were not defeated by s 15 of the Act [ie the Succession Act 1981 of Queensland, pursuant to which the bequest to the plaintiff was rendered invalid by virtue of the plaintiff's husband having been an attesting witness].

The case of *Burnie Port Authority v General Jones Pty Ltd* (1994) 179 CLR 520, which Gaudron J referred to, involved the possible liability of a building owner for the loss by fire of the goods of a tenant of the building caused by the negligence of an independent contractor engaged by the building owner. The legal issues were concerned with the possibility of the *Rylands v Fletcher* (1866) LR 1 Ex 279 strict liability principle applying to owners of land and with the circumstances in which a person with a duty to take reasonable care to avoid a foreseeable risk of injury to another will be discharged from that duty merely by the employment of a qualified and ostensibly competent independent contractor. Mason CJ, speaking for the majority of 5:2, said that the characteristics of the type of relationship where such a duty cannot be delegated to an independent contractor are that:

> The person on whom the duty is imposed has undertaken the care, supervision or control of the person or property of another, or is so placed in relation to that person or his property as to assume a particular responsibility for his or its safety, in circumstances where the person affected might reasonably expect that due care will be exercised

and he then continued:

> It will be convenient to refer to that common element as 'the central element of control'. Viewed from the perspective of the person to whom the duty is owed, the relationship of proximity giving rise to the non-delegable duty of care in such cases is marked by special dependence or vulnerability on the part of that person.
> The relationship of proximity which exists, for the purposes of ordinary negligence, between a plaintiff and a defendant in circumstances which would *prima facie* attract the rules in *Rylands v Fletcher* is characterised by such a central element of control and by such special dependence and vulnerability. One party to that relationship is a person who is in control of premises, and who has taken advantage of that control to introduce thereon or to retain therein a dangerous substance or to undertake thereon a dangerous activity or to allow another person to do one of those things. The other party to that relationship is a person outside the premises and without control over what occurs therein, whose person or property is thereby exposed to a foreseeable risk of danger which he knows to be mischievous if it gets on his neighbour's property.
> In such a case, the person outside the premises is obviously in a position of special vulnerability and dependence. He is specially vulnerable to danger if reasonable precautions are not taken in relation to what is done on the premises. He is specially dependent upon the person in control of the premises to ensure that reasonable precautions are in fact taken. Commonly, he will have neither the right nor the opportunity to exercise control over, or even to have foreknowledge of, what is done or allowed by the other party within the premises. Conversely, the person who introduces the dangerous substance or undertakes

the dangerous activity on premises which he controls is so placed in relation to the other person or his property as to assume a particular responsibility for his or its safety.

It follows that the relationship of proximity which exists in the category of case into which *Rylands v Fletcher* falls contains the central element of control which generates, in other categories of case, a special 'personal' or 'non-delegable' duty of care under the ordinary law of negligence.

As noted above, the concept of control as enunciated by certain of the judges in the High Court of Australia has been put forward as an alternative approach to the resolution of the duty of care question in economic loss cases where the defendant has provided information or rendered a service to a third party in circumstances where, as the defendant knows or ought reasonably to know, the statement or the service will be relied on or made use of by the plaintiff, being a person with whom the defendant did not have a contractual relationship. In these circumstances, these judges believe that it is instructive to consider the degree of 'control' that the defendant actually had over the provision of the information, advice or service and, correspondingly, the degree of the plaintiff's 'vulnerability' to the defendant's exclusive ability to take steps to ensure that the provision of the information, advice or service to the third party was not negligent.

This approach seems to incorporate some of the ideas that are usually associated with fiduciary relationships, rather than with the tort of negligence. Their Honours recognised this when they said that the control test which they were applying is stricter than the assumption of responsibility approach discussed *above*. It remains to be seen whether, to what extent, and in which jurisdictions this idea will be adopted by judges in future cases.

Lastly, it is interesting to note how Gaudron J in *Hill v Van Erp* saw her concept of 'control' as being more precise than any of the other tests that have been put forward. She said:

Inevitably, there will be imprecision in any developing area of the common law. However, the quest must be for precision whenever possible. It is in the interests of precision that I have attempted to show that the loss involved in this case is not sufficiently described as 'pure economic loss'. Rather, it is the loss of a precise legal right which, in turn, has resulted in economic loss. And it is a loss which occurred by reason of the negligence of a person who was in a position to control the enjoyment of that right. Again, as I have pointed out, control is a stricter requirement than assumption of responsibility.

3.6 Overseas cases

3.6.1 Introduction

It has been noted above (see para 3.3.2) that the High Court of Australia in *The Council of the Shire of Sutherland v Heyman* (1985) 157 CLR 424 rejected Lord Wilberforce's two-stage test for determining the existence of duties of care, and that Brennan J's *dictum* in that case has been strongly influential in the English law approach which has been formulated by the

House of Lords in *Caparo Industries plc v Dickman* [1990] 2 AC 605. Accordingly, no further comment will be made here on the position in Australia.

3.6.2 Canada

The approach of the Supreme Court of Canada is typified by the following *dictum* of Cory J in *Rothfield v Manolakos* (1989) 63 DLR (4th) p 449 (see Chapter 8, para 8.4.3) who said (at p 468):

> I recognise that some critical comments have been made with regard to the *Anns* case; see, for instance, *Governors of the Peabody Donation Fund v Sir Lindsay Parkinson & Co Ltd*, *Sutherland Shire Council v Heyman* and *Yuen Kun Yeu v Attorney General of Hong Kong*. Nevertheless, the approach set forward in *Anns*, which has been confirmed and approved by this court in *City of Kamloops v Nielsen* (1984) 10 DLR (4th) 641 [see Chapter 8, para 8.4.3], is sound. It can be applied effectively and should be applied in any case where negligence or misconduct has been alleged against a government agency.

It is interesting to note that in *Just v British Columbia* (1989) 64 DLR (4th) 689 (see Chapter 8, para 8.4.3), in which judgment was delivered on the same day as in *Rothfield*, Cory J, in terms which are slightly contradictory to his above-quoted *dictum*, said (at p 701):

> It may be that the two-step approach as suggested by Lord Wilberforce should not always be slavishly followed: see *Yuen Kun Yeu v Attorney General of Hong Kong*. Nevertheless, it is a sound approach to first determine if there is a duty of care owed by a defendant to the plaintiff in any case where negligent misconduct has been alleged against a government agency.

The two-stage test deriving from Lord Wilberforce's speech in *Anns* is now firmly established as the favoured test in Canadian cases. Thus, in *Hercules Managements Ltd v Ernst & Young* (1997) 146 DLR (4th) 577 (see Chapter 9, para 9.9.3) LaForest J, speaking for the unanimous panel of the Supreme Court of Canada said (at p 586):

> It is now well established in Canadian law that the existence of a duty of care in tort is to be determined through an application of the two-part test first enunciated by Lord Wilberforce in *Anns v Merton London Borough Council* [1978] AC 728. [He then set out this test and then continued:]

> While the House of Lords rejected the *Anns* test in *Murphy v Brentwood District Council* [1991] 1 AC 398 and in *Caparo Industries plc v Dickman* [1990] 2 AC 605, the basic approach that that test embodies has repeatedly been accepted and endorsed by this court; see eg, *Kamloops (City of) v Nielsen* (1984) 10 DLR (4th) 641 [see Chapter 8, para 8.4.3], *BDC Ltd v Hofstrand Farms Ltd* (1986) 26 DLR (4th) 1 [see Chapter 9, para 9.9.3], *Canadian National Railway Co v Norsk Pacific Steamship Co* (1992) 91 DLR (4th) 289 [see Chapter 5, para 5.8.2], *London Drugs Ltd v Kuehne and Nagel International Ltd* (1992) 97 DLR (4th) 261 [see Chapter 10, para 10.3.3] and *Winnipeg Condominium Corp No 36 v Bird Construction Co* (1995) 121 DLR (4th) 193 [see Chapter 7, para 7.6.3].

In *Kamloops* Wilson J restated Lord Wilberforce's test in the following terms:

3.6.3 *Alternative theories*

(1) Is there a sufficiently close relationship between the parties (the defendant and the person who has suffered the damage) so that, in the reasonable contemplation of the defendant, carelessness on its part might cause damage to that person? If so,

(2) Are there any considerations which ought to negative or limit:
   (a) the scope of the duty; and
   (b) the class of persons to whom it is owed; or
   (c) the damages to which a breach of it might give rise?

A further endorsement of the two-stage test was provided by the Supreme Court of Canada in *Bow Valley Husky (Bermuda) Ltd v Saint John Shipbuilding Ltd* (1998) 153 DLR (4th) 385 (see Chapter 5, para 5.6.8).

3.6.3 New Zealand

Despite the criticisms levelled at Lord Wilberforce's two-stage test in England, the New Zealand courts have steadfastly adhered to it. In applying it, however, they have consciously applied the approach suggested by the House of Lords, namely of ensuring that all of the material facts are considered in combination and that due regard is paid to cases in which duties have already been established within a particular category. This can be seen from a consideration of the following *dicta*.

Meates v Attorney General [1983] NZLR 308 (see Chapter 9, para 9.9.4): Woodhouse P said (at p 334): "In conformity with the clear statement of principle of Lord Wilberforce in *Anns v Merton London Borough Council*, the correct question to ask is whether there is *prima facie* a sufficient relationship of proximity or neighbourhood which indicates the presence of a duty of care; and, if there is, then, whether there are any considerations which ought to negative it or limit its scope", and (at p 335): "The second stage of enquiry indicated in the *Anns* case is whether there are considerations which, in some way, should restrict or even negative the duty which will become apparent on a *prima facie* basis at stage one".

Brown v Heathcote County Council [1986] 1 NZLR 76 (see Chapter 8, para 8.4.2): Cooke P said: "Without necessarily subscribing to everything said by Lord Wilberforce in his well-known opinions in *Anns v Merton London Borough Council* and *McLoughlin v O'Brian*, we have found it helpful to think in a broad way on the lines of his twofold approach. That is to say, we have considered, first, the degree of proximity and foreseeability of harm as between the parties. I would put it as whether these factors are strong enough to point *prima facie* to a duty of care. Second, if necessary, we have considered whether there are other particular factors pointing against a duty. It is also conceivable that other factors could strengthen the case for a duty. In terms of the opinion of Lord Keith in *Peabody*, we have found this kind of analysis helpful in determining whether it is just and reasonable that a duty of care of particular scope was incumbent upon the defendant".

This is a reference to Lord Keith's *dictum* in *Governors of the Peabody*

Donation Fund v Sir Lindsay Parkinson and Co Ltd [1985] 1 AC 210 (at p 241) that: "In determining whether or not a duty of care of particular scope was incumbent upon a defendant, it is material to take into consideration whether it is just and reasonable that it should be so". In other words, the Court of Appeal of New Zealand is satisfied that it is achieving the same result by applying Lord Wilberforce's two-stage test as the courts in England are reaching by rejecting that test and, instead, reaching their decisions as to the justness and reasonableness of any particular case by reference to "all of the circumstances".

First City Corporation Ltd v Downsview Nominees Ltd [1990] 3 NZLR 265: Richardson J said (at p 275): "We have taken the view that the two broad fields of enquiry are (1) the degree of proximity or relationship between the alleged wrongdoer and the person who has suffered damage—which is not of course a simple question of foreseeability of harm as between the parties, and involves the degree of analogy with cases in which duties are already established—and (2) whether there are other policy considerations tending to negative or restrict the duty in that class of case. And, like Lord Keith [in *Rowling v Takaro Properties Ltd*, see para 3.3.2, *above*], we have warned against laying down hard and fast rules as to when a duty of care arises, and have stressed the importance of a step by step application to the facts of particular cases".

South Pacific Manufacturing Co Ltd v New Zealand Security Consultants and Investigations Ltd [1992] 2 NZLR 282: Cooke P reiterated the court's approach in *First City Corporation* and (at p 294) added this caveat: "A broad two-stage approach, or any other approach, is only a framework, a more or less methodical way of tackling a problem. How it is formulated should not matter in the end. Ultimately the exercise can only be a balancing one, and the important object is that all relevant factors be weighed. There is no escape from the truth that, whatever formula be used, the outcome in a grey area case has to be determined by judicial judgment. Formulae can help to organise thinking, but they cannot provide answers", and (at p 295): "Basically, the decision on a duty of care issue depends on a judgment, not a formula".

Richardson J made similar remarks. After setting out the New Zealand approach in *First City Corporation*, he said (at p 306): "Mr Green [counsel for one of the defendants] submitted that, in the light of recent decisions of the House of Lords, particularly *Murphy* and *Caparo*, we should abandon the New Zealand approach to the consideration of common law duties of care in novel situations, and adopt an incremental approach. I consider that we should not do so, for two reasons. First, as all counsel recognised, there are no considerations on an incremental approach which would not be taken into account in the New Zealand focus on the two broad fields of enquiry. That is not surprising, given that the ultimate question is whether it is just and reasonable that a particular duty of care to the particular plaintiff should rest on the particular defendant. In *Rowling v Takaro Properties Ltd*, their Lordships expressed the fear that a too literal

3.6.3 *Alternative theories*

application of Lord Wilberforce's test in *Anns* might be productive of a failure to have regard to, and to analyse and weigh, all the relevant considerations in determining whether it is appropriate that a duty of care should be imposed [see para 3.3.2, *above*]. So long as that crucial point is kept firmly in mind, the precise road to be followed in arriving at the answer to the ultimate question would not seem to be of critical significance. The second reason for not changing course is that, over the last 14 years since the decision in *Anns*, the New Zealand courts have taken the same general approach to duty of care issues without any apparent dissatisfaction. It has not been suggested in any of the cases in this court that the method of approach has caused difficulty or concern to the Bar or to the wider community".

Lastly, Hardie Boys J, in rejecting the defendants' counsel's submission that the court had to choose between the two-stage test and the incremental approach, said (at p 316): "There is a danger here of the method of approach becoming more important than the objective. The objective is to ascertain whether it is appropriate that there be a duty of care in the particular case. So long as that objective is realised, I cannot think that it is of great moment whether it is attained by a two-stage test, an incremental approach, or some combination of the two. What matters is that there is an identification, an analysis and a weighing of all of the competing considerations. It is, in the end, a matter of careful judicial judgment. That said, the courts in this country have found the two-stage approach a helpful way of focusing attention on these various considerations. But we have sought to avoid the danger that a too literal application of Lord Wilberforce's words in *Anns* might be productive of a failure properly to deal with all the relevant considerations".

Invercargill City Council v Hamlin [1994] 3 NZLR 513: Cooke P, after considering the position in this type of case in other jurisdictions (see Chapter 7, para 7.6.2), including the House of Lords' decision in *Murphy v Brentwood District Council* [1991] 1 AC 398, which he and the other judges in the New Zealand Court of Appeal rejected, said (at p 523): "Formulae and doctrine do not provide the answers to new duty of care questions. In the end it is a matter of judicial judgment, formed after looking at established signposts and analogies".

Chapter 4

Consequential loss and accidental pure economic loss

Since Anns v Merton London Borough Council *[1978] AC 728 put the flood-gates on the jar, a fashionable plaintiff alleges negligence. The pleading assumes that we are all neighbours now, Pharisees and Samaritans alike, that foreseeability is a reflection of hindsight and that for every mischance in an accident-prone world, someone solvent must be liable in damages.* **(Lord Templeman in *CBS Songs Ltd v Amstrad Plc* [1988] 1 AC 1013)**

There seems to be a growing belief that every misfortune must, in pecuniary terms at any rate, be laid at someone else's door, and that after every mishap, every tragedy, the cupped palms are outstretched for the solace of monetary compensation. Claims which would have been unheard of 30 years ago are now being entertained, and public money provided for pursuing them. **(Rougier J in *John Monroe (Acrylics) Ltd v London Fire and Civil Defence Authority* [1996] 4 All ER 318)**

4.1 Context

4.1.1 General

This chapter deals with economic losses suffered by a plaintiff in consequence of an accident caused by the defendant. Sometimes property which the plaintiff owns, or in which he has a proprietary or a possessory interest, will be damaged, and the plaintiff will suffer economic loss in consequence of such damage; at other times the defendant might not have damaged the property of any person, but the plaintiff will have suffered economic loss as a direct result of the accident.

4.1.2 Some important distinctions

Accidental damage versus inherent defect

If the property damage suffered by the plaintiff was not truly accidental, in the sense, for example, of the defendant negligently crashing into the plaintiff's car on a highway, but arose because the defendant had voluntarily but negligently created a defective article or building for a third party which subsequently came to be owned by the plaintiff, then the case will fall into another category (namely 'diminished value'), which is dealt with in Chapter 7 (para 7.3). It will be noted that the difference is that if the plaintiff's car is damaged or destroyed by the defendant in an accident, then the plaintiff can recover both the replacement cost of the car and any economic loss which is 'truly consequential' on the material damage; but if the plaintiff's car explodes and is totally destroyed through a defect in its manufacture, and if the plaintiff bought the car from someone other than the manufacturer, the plaintiff will not be able to recover from the manufacturer either the replacement cost of the car or any consequential economic losses. The plaintiff's claim will be restricted to any physical injuries he might suffer in the explosion, or to damage to any other property of his caused by it.

Third party's property damaged

If the situation is such that, although no property of the plaintiff was damaged, but the accident did damage a third party's property, then the case is dealt with under the exclusionary rule discussed in Chapter 5, para 5.2, where it is noted that if a defendant negligently damages property, no person can sue for consequential economic loss unless he owns that property or has a 'proprietary or a possessory interest' in it. As that exclusionary rule is dependent on the defendant having damaged a third party's property, it does not, strictly speaking, cover the situation where no property at all was injured in the accident. This type of situation is considered in this chapter.

Reliance on a statement

Where no person or property was injured, but the plaintiff's pure economic loss arose through having relied on words negligently written or spoken by the defendant, then the case falls in the category of cases considered in Chapter 9 dealing with negligent misstatements.

4.2 The historical context

4.2.1 No appreciation of difference

Direct impact cases

It is well established in law that if a plaintiff suffers personal injury or if his property is damaged in a direct or 'impact' accident, he can recover compensation from the defendant who negligently caused the accident for both his physical injuries/property damage and for his consequential economic loss. In the case of a personal injury this would include the plaintiff's loss of earnings, both actual and prospective. In the case of damage to property, this would include compensation for the loss of use of the item in question and for loss of profits if it had been used in a business. The idea is to put the plaintiff in the same position as if the accident had not taken place. Initially, the only limitation on the consequential damages which a plaintiff could recover was the rules of remoteness of damage which are discussed in Chapter 2 (para 2.1.2). In the early cases no consideration was given to the fact that the plaintiff was often being compensated for pure economic loss.

An example of this is the rule which the courts developed in *The Winkfield* [1902] P 42 to the effect that a bailee in possession can recover the full value of the goods bailed to him if they are destroyed by the negligence of the defendant, even though part of the damage suffered (ie the value of the bailor's interest) is, so far as the bailee is concerned, pure economic loss. The point is further borne out by the fact that the bailee's right of recovery is not dependent on his obligation, if any, to account to the bailor for the amount of the bailor's interest. This point is discussed in more detail in para 4.8.2.

Origin of the exclusionary rule

Before the early 1950s none of the judges had really spoken of any distinction between compensation for physical injury and for economic loss until Denning LJ mentioned the point in *Candler v Crane, Christmas & Co* [1951] 2 KB 164 (see Chapter 9, para 9.2.2). Even in *Morrison Steamship Company Ltd v Greystoke Castle (Cargo Owners)* [1947] AC 265 (HL), in which the House of Lords upheld the plaintiff's claim for pure economic loss (see Chapter 5, para 5.4.3), this was not recognised as a separate point. Similarly, in numerous earlier cases which establish the exclusionary rule in the relational economic loss cases (which are discussed in Chapter 5, para 5.3.2), the basis was not that the plaintiff was seeking compensation for pure economic loss, but, rather, the danger of opening the floodgates to a multitude of claims from the potentially large number of persons who could suffer losses in consequence of the defendant damaging a third person's property. It was not the 'economic nature' of the plaintiff's loss that led to the formulation of this rule, but the circumstances in which the loss arose.

Comment in Murphy

This point was recognised by Lord Oliver in *Murphy v Brentwood District Council* [1991] 1 AC 398. After referring to several of the relational economic loss cases, and to the fact that the plaintiffs' claims were rejected in all of them, he said (at p 485): "It is far from clear from these decisions that the reason for the plaintiff's failure was simply that the only loss sustained was 'economic'. Rather they seem to have been based either upon the remoteness of the damage as a matter of direct causation or, more probably, upon the 'floodgates' argument of the impossibility of containing liability within any acceptable bounds if the law were to permit such claims to succeed".

4.2.2 Recognition of different categories

Hedley Byrne

To the extent that any of the earlier cases did consider the question of recovery of damages for pure economic loss, the judges and counsel involved laboured generally under the impression that such recovery was firmly precluded by the relational loss exclusionary rule, which was thought to apply to all categories of economic loss. This myth was exploded by the House of Lords' decision in *Hedley Byrne & Co Ltd v Heller & Partners Ltd*

[1964] AC 465, in which the House of Lords upheld in principle the plaintiff's claim for damages for the pure economic loss which it had suffered through relying on a business reference which the defendant had negligently given to a third party. Although only three of their Lordships (Lords Hodson, Devlin and Pearce) specifically considered the significance of the fact that the plaintiff's claim was for pure economic loss, the court's decision had the effect of creating an awareness that there are different categories of economic loss to which different policy considerations apply. This awareness is evident in the following extract from a subsequent case.

The World Harmony

In *Konstantinidis v World Tankers Corporation (The World Harmony)* [1967] P 341 (a relational economic loss case which is discussed in Chapter 5, para 5.8.1) the plaintiff's counsel contended that the exclusionary rule had been abolished by the fact that the House of Lords in *Hedley Byrne* had approved the recovery of pure economic loss. Hewson J rejected this argument by saying (at p 362): "The facts are so entirely different from the present case, and, as the line of cases to which I have been referred in this action [ie the relational economic loss cases] was not quoted in the House of Lords in the *Hedley Byrne* case, I would hesitate long before I would apply anything that was said by their Lordships in that case to this one".

4.2.3 Remoteness of damage

General

It was this sort of comment that led judges to become aware that 'an economic loss issue' is sometimes involved when the plaintiff seeks to recover losses which are consequential upon damage to his property and that these cases are different from relational economic loss cases and from cases of pure economic loss where no property at all has been damaged. Sometimes, however, the problem was treated more as a question of remoteness of damage than as a question of whether the defendant's duty of care ought to extend to that type of loss. An example of this is *British Celanese v Hunt*.

British Celanese v Hunt

In *British Celanese Limited v A H Hunt (Capacitors) Ltd* [1969] 1 WLR 959 the question was whether a company (the defendant) on an industrial estate which so conducted its business that the electricity supplied to its neighbours was interrupted was liable to them for any injury to their property and for the consequential loss of production which they might suffer thereby. The defendant, for the purposes of its business of manufacturing electrical components, kept strips of metal foil on its site. These strips were light enough to be blown away in the kind of winds which were experienced in that area. The defendant knew that if any of these strips should come into contact with the bus-bars of the neighbouring electricity supply sub-station, there was likely to be a power failure which would affect neighbouring factories.

Such an accident did occur. The plaintiff, whose synthetic yarn factory was on the same industrial estate, suffered various losses as a result. Its machinery was brought to a stop, material in certain machines became solidified, these machines had to be cleaned out before production could be started again, materials and time were wasted and production was lost. The plaintiff sued the defendant for its estimated loss of profit as a result of this power cut. One of the bases of the plaintiff's claim was strict liability under the rule in *Rylands v Fletcher* 1868 Law Rep 3 HL 330. This argument failed because the defendant had been making a natural use of the site. The defendant had counter-argued that this head of claim was not available because the plaintiff's claim, being for lost profit, was a claim for pure economic loss, which the defendant contended was not recoverable on the basis of strict liability. Lawton J, however, said (at p 965) that the plaintiff's claim was not for pure economic loss, but was for "physical injury with consequential loss of profits".

Having categorised the case as being a case of property damage with consequential loss of profits, Lawton J then considered the defendant's liability in negligence. He said (at p 965): "Under this head of claim the important questions are, first, whether the defendant did owe a duty to the plaintiff to take reasonable care to prevent these strips of metal foil being blown about in such a way as to foul the bus-bars, and, secondly, whether the damage claimed is too remote". He held that the plaintiff's loss was not too remote, and that the defendant was therefore liable for all of it.

4.3   Consequential loss

4.3.1   Confusion with remoteness

In *British Celanese* Lawton J refused to categorise the plaintiff's claim for loss of profit as pure economic loss, but saw it, rather, as a case of property damage with consequential loss of profit (see para 4.2.3). However, he did not consider whether any of that consequential loss of profit itself might have consisted of pure economic loss. Instead, he treated the whole question as being one of remoteness of damage. In fact, however, if there is to be a separate doctrine to the effect that pure economic loss in accident cases is not recoverable (in certain circumstances), then the question should be asked in these 'consequential cases' whether the plaintiff's economic loss was actually caused by the physical damage which the defendant caused to the plaintiff's property, or whether the plaintiff is seeking to take advantage of the occurrence of that physical damage to add on a claim for economic loss which is not the actual consequence of that physical damage.

4.3.2   Identifying 'truly consequential' loss

SCM v Whittall

The above-mentioned question was asked, and made a difference to the result in *SCM (United Kingdom) Ltd v WJ Whittall & Son Ltd* [1971] 1 QB

337, in which the defendant building contractors were working in a road when a workman damaged an electric cable owned by the electricity board, thereby causing a power failure which lasted for seven hours. This cable supplied electricity to several factories, including the plaintiff's typewriter factory, which was brought to a halt. At the time, the plaintiff's machines had molten materials in them, which solidified due to the lack of electric heat. The plaintiff had to strip the machines down, chip away the solidified material and reassemble the machines. Some parts of the machines were damaged beyond recovery. The plaintiff lost the value of those items as well as the profit from one full day's production. The plaintiff claimed damages from the defendant for all that loss.

The court said that it must be accepted that the defendant was negligent in damaging the cable and that it ought reasonably to have foreseen that, if it damaged the cable, the supply of current to factories would be likely to be interfered with and that the occupiers, such as the plaintiff, would be likely to suffer loss and damage, including injury to their property. During the course of the hearing, the question arose as to whether the loss of production was due to the shutting down of the works or whether it was due to the physical damage to the machines which had to be repaired. The plaintiff's counsel assured the court that he confined the plaintiff's claim to the material damage done to the machines plus the loss of production consequent on that damage.

With regard to this point, Lord Denning MR said (at p 341) (emphasis added): "This was an important assurance. It is well settled that when a defendant by his negligence causes physical damage to the person or property of the plaintiff, in such circumstances that the plaintiff is entitled to compensation for the physical damage, then he can claim, in addition, for economic loss consequent on it. Thus a plaintiff who suffers personal injuries recovers his loss of earnings, and a ship owner, whose ship is sunk or damaged, recovers for his loss of freight. If and insofar as the plaintiff is entitled to claim for the material damage, then it can claim for the loss of production which was *truly consequential* on the material damage. But if the loss of production was really due to the cutting off of the electricity for 7 hours and 17 minutes—and the plaintiff took the opportunity during that time of remedying the physical damage—then the claim for loss of production would depend on whether, in this type of case, economic loss is recoverable".

Spartan Steel v Martin

The same distinction was made by the Court of Appeal (or, at least, by the two Lord Justices who formed the majority) in *Spartan Steel and Alloys Ltd v Martin & Co (Contractors) Ltd* [1973] 1 QB 27, in which the defendant contractors, while digging up a road, negligently damaged a cable belonging to the electricity board, thereby causing a power failure which lasted for 14 hours. The plaintiff's business was the manufacture of stainless steel alloys. It operated 24 hours a day, and it drew its electricity from the cable which the defendant's workman severed. The plaintiff claimed damages from the defendant under three heads, namely:

(a) £368 for the reduction in value of the metal in the furnace at the time the electricity supply failed;

(b) £400 for the profit which the plaintiff would have made if that particular melt had been properly completed; and

(c) £1,767 for loss of profit on four further melts which could have been put through the furnace during the period when the power was cut off.

The plaintiff succeeded under the first two of these heads of claim, but not under the third. There was no argument over the first head of claim, as it consisted of physical damage to the plaintiff's property. The second head of claim succeeded on the basis that it was economic loss which (*per* Lord Denning MR at p 39) was "truly consequential" on, or (*per* Lawton LJ at p 47) was the "immediate consequence" of, the material damage. The third head of claim was rejected because it consisted of economic loss independent of the physical damage (ie pure economic loss). This is discussed separately in para 4.4.

Londonwaste v Amec

In *Londonwaste Ltd v Amec Civil Engineering Ltd* (1997) 53 Con LR 66, the defendant (Amec) was the main contractor for works of improvement to the North Circular Road in London. Part of those works comprised sheet piling which was carried out by Amec's sub-contractor. In the course of that work some $33kv$ electricity cables belonging to Eastern Electricity plc were severed. The plaintiff (Londonwaste) owned an electricity generating station about 600 metres from the point of severance, and the severed cables served almost exclusively to feed electricity from the plaintiff's generating plant into Eastern Electricity's electricity grid.

The plaintiff's generating station was operated with waste which was brought in from several North London boroughs and was incinerated as the source of heat for steam turbines. As a result of the cables being severed, the plaintiff's power station was out of operation for two and a half days. The plaintiff claimed damages from the defendant under three heads: namely, (1) physical damage to the plant; (2) loss of income from the sale of electricity; and (3) the cost of transporting and disposing of excess waste which could not be incinerated on site.

The defendant's counsel conceded that the defendant was liable for the cost of repairing physical damage caused to the plaintiff's plant and equipment by the defendant's sub-contractor's negligence. The next question was whether the plaintiff's loss of income was "truly consequential" on any physical damage caused by the defendant to the plaintiff's property. The judge, John Hicks QC, sitting as an Official Referee, answered this question in the negative because there was no overt damage to the plaintiff's plant which required repair or imminent replacement. The only damage to the plaintiff's plant and equipment was latent fatigue damage to the turbines which diminished their value by reducing their useful working life. The only physical damage which could be said to have directly caused the plaintiff's loss of income was the damage caused to the electricity cables, which were not owned by the plaintiff.

The judge considered and approved of all of the decisions considered *above* in this section, as well as the Canadian decision in *Seaway Hotels Ltd v Gragg (Canada) Ltd* (1959) 17 DLR (2d) 292 (see para 4.6.2, *below*), and then concluded on this point:

> There is therefore a clearly established, but limited, head of recoverable economic loss consisting of that which is consequential upon any physical damage caused to the plaintiff's property. The difficulty for the present plaintiff is that although there was physical damage to its turbines, the nature of that damage (as summarised above) is such that it could not cause, and is not alleged to have caused, the loss of income claimed. The cause of that loss was, and is pleaded as being, the severance of the cables. In my view the plaintiff has not surmounted this difficulty, which is fatal, and cannot recover loss of income by this route.

The judge then dealt with the plaintiff's claim for the cost of transporting and disposing of excess waste which could not be incinerated on site. In rejecting the plaintiff's counsel's submission that this loss was analogous to physical damage, in that it was incurred to mitigate physical damage to the power station from the accumulation of unincinerated waste, his Honour said:

> The analogy argument (even if I could see the analogy, which I cannot) is simply an attempt to blur or shift a boundary which is as clear and distinct as can reasonably be expected in this imperfect world, and on the irrecoverable side of which expenses of this kind unarguably lie.
>
> The mitigation basis is not pleaded and must in any event postulate that, had this expense not been incurred, there would have been (1) actual physical damage to the premises, (2) caused by the severance of the cables and (3) not too remote to be recoverable as damages from the defendant. I am very dubious about (1) and do not accept (2) or (3). What seems to me to be conclusive against this argument is that, if sound, it would nullify the accepted classification as economic loss of the cost of remedial work to premises to cure defects discovered before they cause injury or damage.

In rejecting the plaintiff's counsel's submission that this loss was analogous to the clean-up costs allowed in *Spartan Steel and Alloys Ltd v Martin and Co (Contractors) Ltd* [1973] QB 27 (see *above*), his Honour said:

> The clean-up costs in *Spartan Steel* were recovered precisely because they were attributable to the damage to the plaintiff's property, whereas the disposal of the excess waste here was a consequence of the damage to Eastern Electricity's cable, and had nothing to do with the alleged damage to the plaintiff's turbines.

4.3.3 Statement of the rule

General

Thus, the rule would appear to be that, where a defendant causes physical damage to the plaintiff's property (or to property in which the plaintiff has a proprietary or a possessory interest) and, in addition, the plaintiff suffers consequential economic loss, whether that loss will be recoverable will depend on whether it was 'truly consequential' on (or the 'immediate consequence' of) the physical damage or whether it was independent of it. The first part of this principle (ie recovery for consequential as opposed to independent economic loss) has been widely accepted. An example is *Wimpey v Black*.

Wimpey v Martin Black

In *Wimpey Construction (UK) Limited (and others) v Martin Black & Co (Wire Ropes) Limited* 1982 SLT 239 (which is also discussed in para 4.8.3, *below*) the plaintiffs had been engaged in a joint venture for the construction of a tanker terminal, for which purpose they made use of a crane which belonged to the second plaintiff. When this was negligently damaged by the defendant, and the project was delayed for 86 days, both plaintiffs suffered substantial losses. The defendant did not dispute the second plaintiff's claim (for £400,000) for economic loss caused by the 86-day delay because it was consequent upon damage to property of the second plaintiff, but did dispute such a claim by the first plaintiff (for £395,000) because no property of the first plaintiff had been damaged in the accident for which the defendant was responsible. The court upheld the second plaintiff's claims for the cost of reinstating the crane and for its consequential increased costs due to the delay, but rejected the first plaintiff's similar economic loss claims because no property of the first plaintiff had been damaged.

4.3.4 The dividing line

Easy cases

Whilst this rule might be quite easy to define, it is not so easy to decide where to draw the line in any particular case. In a case like *Wimpey* the answer is quite easy, both as regards the distinction between the position of the first plaintiff and the second plaintiff and as regards the whole of the consequential losses claimed by the second plaintiff. It took 86 days for the crane to be repaired and put back into operation. Therefore the whole of the wasted costs suffered by the second plaintiff during this period can properly be said to be 'truly consequential' on the property damage.

Difficult cases

However, in cases like *Spartan Steel* or *SCM* the answer is not so obvious. If the property damage could have been repaired well within the time that the electricity supply was cut off (say, three hours in *Spartan Steel*) and the machines were ready to operate during the remainder of the time (11 hours in *Spartan Steel*), then it might be possible to say that the factory's loss of profits during the three hours was 'truly consequential' on the damage to its machines but that its lost profits during the remaining 11 hours did not result from the property damage, but, rather, from the fact that the supply of electricity was not available during that time. As the loss of one's electricity supply by itself is not property damage, a loss of profits which flows directly from it is therefore classified as pure economic loss. It is not clear if this was the reason for the different awards which were made in *Spartan Steel* in respect of heads two and three, but this reasoning does seem to be borne out by the passage quoted above from Lord Denning MR's judgment in *SCM*, and it does seem to be a logical dividing line, to the extent that logic has got anything to do with this matter.

No property damage

As a slight gloss on the above-suggested theory, it will be noted that in *Spartan Steel* the plaintiff's machines were not actually damaged. However, when the power failed, there was a danger that the metal which was being melted in the furnace at the time might solidify and do damage to the lining of the furnace. The plaintiff therefore used oxygen to melt that metal and poured it from a tap out of the furnace. This meant that the melted metal was of much less value; £368 less, in fact, and this constituted the plaintiff's first head of claim, as mentioned above. In a situation like this, the above-suggested theory would divide the relevant periods of time for claiming economic loss between the amount of time that it took to clear the metal out of the furnace and make it ready to receive further melts, and the time that remained after that until the electricity was re-connected.

4.4   Pure economic loss

4.4.1   Context

This section is concerned with pure economic loss which is suffered by a plaintiff in consequence of an accident caused by the defendant where no property at all is damaged. It thus differs from the type of case considered above, where the defendant has caused some damage to the plaintiff's property, and from the relational economic loss cases considered in Chapter 5, where the defendant has caused damage to a third party's property.

4.4.2   Dearth of authority

Strangely, there do not appear to be any reported decisions of accident cases in which the plaintiff has suffered economic loss without any property damage having been caused at all, unless one so regards a pollution of the sea case like *State of Louisiana, ex rel Guste v M/V Testbank* (1985) 752 F 2d 1019 (US CA 5th Cir), which is discussed in Chapter 5 at para 5.4.4. Nevertheless, all the indications from the relational economic loss cases, and from the consequential loss cases considered above (which, coincidentally, were also relational economic loss cases in the sense that a third party's electricity supply cable had been damaged) are that such a loss would not be recoverable in English law. In Australia and Canada, as discussed in Chapter 5 at para 5.6.1, the position is different.

4.4.3   Probably no duty of care

No recognition of categories

The strict exclusion in the English law relational economic loss cases of any right of recovery to the plaintiff for his economic losses unless he had a proprietary or a possessory interest in the third party's property which the defendant damaged suggests that the courts would come to the same conclusion if no property at all had been damaged by the defendant. This observation is further borne out by the fact that practically all of the English relational economic loss cases proceed on the assumption that there is only one exclusionary rule, which applies to all cases of pure economic loss other than negligent misstatement, without appreciating that there are several different categories of economic loss, in relation to which different policy considerations, and therefore different results, are appropriate.

Perpetuating the misconception

In one of the 'consequential loss' cases mentioned above, *SCM (United Kingdom) Ltd v WJ Whittall & Son Ltd* [1971] QB 337, Lord Denning MR perpetuated this misconception when he said (at p 344): "In actions of negligence, when the plaintiff has suffered no damage to his person or property, but has only sustained economic loss, the law does not usually permit him to recover that loss". The cases which he cited in support of this statement are all relational economic loss cases, where a third party's property had been damaged. However, subject to one exception, Lord Denning's discussion of these cases, and his above-quoted statement, suggests that he would have held that accidental pure economic loss was not recoverable.

Lord Denning said (at p 345) that the reason the plaintiff did not recover his economic loss in these earlier (relational economic loss) cases was that it was "too remote to be a head of damage". The exception to Lord Denning's above-quoted statement of the general rule where the plaintiff has suffered no damage to his person or property arises from what he said next, namely (at p 345–6) (emphasis added):

> I must not be taken, however, as saying that economic loss is always too remote. There are some exceptional cases when it is the *immediate consequence* of the negligence and is recoverable accordingly. Such is the case when a banker negligently gives a good reference on which a man extends credit, and loses the money. The plaintiff suffers economic loss only, but it is the immediate—almost, I might say, the intended—consequence of the negligent reference and is recoverable accordingly: see *Hedley Byrne & Co Ltd v Heller & Partners Ltd* [1964] AC 465. Another is when the defendant by his negligence damages a lorry which is carrying the plaintiff's goods. The goods themselves are not damaged but the lorry is so badly damaged that the goods have to be unloaded and carried forward in some other vehicle. The goods owner suffers economic loss only, namely, the cost of unloading and carriage, but he can recover it from the defendant because it is immediate and not too remote. It is analogous to physical damage: because the goods themselves had to be unloaded. Such was the illustration given by Lord Roche in *Morrison Steamship Co Ltd v Greystoke*

Castle (Cargo Owners) [1947] AC 265 [which is discussed in detail in Chapter 5, para 5.4.6]. Likewise, when the cargo owners have to pay a general average contribution. It is not too remote and is recoverable.

Confusion of concepts

It seems that Lord Denning felt it necessary to make this statement in order to try to reconcile the relational economic loss cases which upheld the exclusionary rule with the two House of Lords' decisions which did grant relief to the plaintiff for his pure economic losses, namely *Greystoke* and *Hedley Byrne*. Although there might well be some sense in Lord Denning's analysis of the position, there also seems to be a manifest air of artificiality about it, which could have been avoided altogether if he had recognised that *Hedley Byrne* is in a completely different category to the relational economic loss cases (including *Greystoke*) and that different policy considerations, or underlying rationales, are applicable.

Inconsistent result

Furthermore, by attempting to reconcile these different types of cases, Lord Denning seems to have forced himself into enunciating a principle to which, it seems, he did not himself ascribe, namely that economic loss is recoverable when it is 'the immediate consequence' of the defendant's negligence. This appears from his discussion in the subsequent case of *Spartan Steel* (see para 4.3.2) of the policy considerations which, in his view, militate against the recovery of pure economic loss when an accident such as the cutting off of the plaintiff's electricity supply occurs. In *Spartan Steel* he said (at p 38): "If claims for economic loss were permitted for this particular hazard, there would be no end of claims. Some might be genuine, but many might be inflated, or even false. Rather than expose claimants to such temptation and defendants to such hard labour—on comparatively small claims—it is better to disallow economic loss altogether, at any rate when it stands alone, independent of any physical damage". Such losses would be 'the immediate consequence' of the defendant's negligence, yet Lord Denning would exclude them when no physical damage had occurred.

4.5   Policy considerations

4.5.1   Context

Chapter 5, para 5.5 contains a discussion of the policy considerations which underlie the exclusionary rule that, where a third person's property is damaged, the plaintiff cannot recover his consequential, or 'relational', economic losses unless he had a proprietary or a possessory interest in the third party's property. Here, we are concerned with the policy considerations which underlie the two rules discussed above, namely, that where an accident occurs then:

(a) If the plaintiff is injured or his property (or property in which he has a proprietary or a possessory interest) is damaged, he can recover damages for his physical injury or property damage as well as for any consequential economic loss that is 'truly consequential' on such physical injury, but not otherwise; and

(b) if no person is injured or if no property at all is damaged, the plaintiff cannot recover damages for the economic losses which he might suffer as a result of the accident.

4.5.2   Consequential losses

General

In the electricity interruption cases considered *above*, not only the plaintiff's property was damaged, but also that of a third party, namely the electricity board whose cable had been severed. Thus, although the plaintiff suffered property damage, this loss was relational, and not direct. In addition to being able to recover damages for this physical damage, the plaintiff was held entitled to recover such economic losses as were 'truly consequential' on the physical damage. If, however, none of the plaintiff's property had been damaged, and his losses were all only economic, then he would not have been entitled to recover anything (see Chapter 5, para 5.2).

Electrochrome v Welsh Plastics

The last-made point is illustrated by *Electrochrome Ltd v Welsh Plastics Ltd* [1968] 2 All ER 205, in which the defendant's lorry driver had negligently collided with a fire hydrant near to the plaintiff's factory on an industrial estate. As a result, the plaintiff's factory had its water supply cut off, and this caused the loss of a day's work, for which the plaintiff sued the defendant. The court rejected the plaintiff's claim because the plaintiff had no proprietary or possessory rights in any property which the defendant had damaged, namely the hydrant, which was the property of the industrial estate.

Two questions

It is therefore necessary to ask two questions:

(a) Why, in these cases, does it make such a crucial difference whether the plaintiff suffered personal injury or property damage?;

(b) Why are economic losses which are 'truly consequential' on physical damage recoverable, but not other economic losses?

4.5.3   Physical damage

False logic—I

In cases like *SCM* and *Spartan Steel*, where the plaintiff's loss is partly physical and partly economic, it could be said that part of the rationale for upholding the plaintiff's claims, and for denying them in a case like *Electrochrome* where the plaintiff's claims are all purely economic, derives from the policy considerations underlying the relational economic loss exclusionary rule: namely, the need to guard against the exposure of the defendant to claims from an indeterminate class of claimants. However, this only needs to be stated to see that it is devoid of logic, because, where an accident has the capacity to cause damage to more than one person (such as the outbreak of a fire in a crowded station, the collapse of a spectators' stand at a football match or the cutting off of the electricity supply on an industrial estate), the indeterminacy problem could be said to loom just as large with regard to personal injury and property damage as to pure economic loss.

Common sense difference

Furthermore, the economic loss suffered by the plaintiff could be just as real in a case like *Electrochrome* as in a case like *SCM*. This was recognised by Lord Denning MR himself in *SCM (United Kingdom) Ltd v WJ Whittall & Son Ltd* [1971] QB 337 when he said (at p 342): "Either all who suffered loss of profit should get damages for it, or none of them should. It should not depend on the chance whether material damage was done as well". This is contradictory to what he said subsequently in this same judgment. He referred to Lord Devlin's statement in *Hedley Byrne* (at p 517) that he could find "neither logic nor common sense" in the defendant's submission that, whilst there could be liability for physical injury caused by negligent misstatements, the law was different when the loss was purely pecuniary, and said (at p 344): "There may be no difference in logic, but I think there is a great deal of difference in common sense".

Illusory answer

What, then, is the difference? The 'answer' which Lord Denning gave in *SCM* is not really an answer at all. He said (at p 344): "When an electric cable is damaged, many factories may be stopped from working. Can each of them claim for their loss of profit? I think not. It is not sensible to saddle losses on this scale on to one sole contractor. The risk should be borne by the whole community who suffer the losses rather than rest on one pair of shoulders, that is, on one contractor who may, or may not, be insured against the risk. There is not much logic in this, but still it is the law".

The 'real' answer: three motivations

This does not answer the question why damage to the plaintiff's property should make a difference to the recovery of his economic losses in accident cases. It is submitted that the true answer lies in three separate motivations, of which it is submitted only the third will be able to stand up to long-term scrutiny. The first of these motivations is founded not in logic or in common sense, but in the historical development of the English common law in the field of negligence. There has always been a noticeable tendency to afford greater protection to, and greater recognition of, the rights of individuals not to be interfered with physically in their person or property, rather than purely financially. The accepted wisdom of the English courts seems to be that it is right to accord greater sanctity to personal injuries and property damage than to pure economic losses. Lord Oliver expressed this sentiment succinctly in *Murphy v Brentwood District Council* [1991] 1 AC 398 when he said (at p 487): "The infliction of physical injury to the person or property of another universally requires to be justified. The causing of economic loss does not". Lord Denning MR made a similar point in *Spartan Steel* when, in enunciating the considerations which, in his view, militated against allowing recovery for pure economic loss when electricity (or any similar utility service) is negligently cut off, he said (at p 39): "The fifth consideration is that the law provides for deserving cases. If the defendant is guilty of negligence which cuts off the electricity supply and causes actual physical damage to person or property, that damage can be recovered".

False logic—II

Whilst it might well be true to say that, in some circumstances, the infliction of pure economic loss does not need to be 'justified' in the same way as the infliction of physical injury or property damage, for example where a bridge is rendered unusable by the defendant's negligence and a wide range of people who have been accustomed to using it claim for their resultant economic losses, it is difficult to see why it should therefore follow that the plaintiff has to suffer some physical damage to himself or his property before he can recover the economic losses which he has sustained as a result of the accident. Again, one only has to compare the fact situations in *SCM* and *Electrochrome* to see the illogicality of the argument. On the other hand, if one accepts the reasoning for the dividing line drawn in *SCM* and *Spartan Steel* between different types of consequential economic loss (which is discussed both in para 4.3.4 and para 4.5.4), then it will not necessarily follow that the plaintiff in a case like *Electrochrome* would recover the whole of a lost day's production simply because he had suffered 'some' property damage. It would depend on how long it took to repair that property damage: he would be entitled to recover for the loss of production during that period, but not during the remainder of the period that the (water) supply was cut off, because that additional loss of production would not have been caused by, or be 'truly consequential' on, the property damage. In reality, this might therefore be a distinction without a practical difference.

The floodgates fear: Gibbs J and Widgery J

The second motivation derives from the courts' perception that, if they were to allow claims for pure economic loss in accident cases, this would open the floodgates to a multitude of claims. Gibbs J expressed this fear in *Caltex Oil (Australia) Pty Limited v The Dredge Willemstad* (1976) 136 CLR 529 when he said (at p 552):

> It is true that under modern conditions some claims arising from physical injury or material damage can be very large in amount —for example if a passenger train were derailed. Nevertheless, the extent of claims for loss that is purely economic is likely to be very much wider than that of claims arising out of physical injury and material damage. Further, a law which imposed a general duty to take care to avoid causing foreseeable pecuniary loss to others would, as Widgery J

149

suggested, interfere greatly with the ordinary affairs of life. There are sound reasons of policy why economic loss should not be treated in exactly the same way as material loss.

Gibbs J's reference to Widgery J is a reference to Widgery J's judgment in *Weller & Co v Foot and Mouth Disease Research Institute* [1966] 1 QB 569 (which is set out in para 5.8.1 of Chapter 5) when he said (at p 585): "The world of commerce would come to a halt and ordinary life would become intolerable if the law imposed a duty on all persons at all times to refrain from any conduct which might foreseeably cause detriment to another". Whilst this is no doubt true, it must be remembered that *Weller* and all of the cases referred to in it were cases of relational economic loss suffered by a plaintiff in consequence of an accident caused by the defendant in which a third party's property was damaged, not cases of direct economic loss suffered by the plaintiff.

Unsatisfactory justification

The importance of this distinction is that, as mentioned above in para 4.2.1, in the early relational economic loss cases, where the exclusionary rule was formulated, it was not the 'economic quality' of the plaintiff's loss that prevented recovery, but the reason why that loss had occurred, namely that the plaintiff was not the primary (ie direct) victim, but the secondary victim of the defendant's negligent act or omission. This rationale for the existence of the relational economic loss exclusionary rule is discussed in detail in Chapter 5, para 5.5. For the moment, the point to note is that it is submitted that this rationale is not a justification for saying that, where the plaintiff is the primary (ie direct) victim of the defendant's negligence in an accident case, he should not be able to recover his economic losses unless he has also suffered physical injury or property damage. In *Caltex* Stephen J expressed this point trenchantly when he said (at p 568):

> To counter the spectre of indeterminate liability by rejecting all recovery for economic loss unless accompanied by, and directly consequential upon, physical injury is Draconic. It operates to confer upon such physical injury a special status unexplained either by logic or by common experience. No reason exists for according to it such special status, other than its character of tending to ensure a reassuringly proximate nexus between tortious act and recoverable damage. In addition to the arbitrary nature of such a rule, it also possesses the unattractive quality of being quite unresponsive to the grossness of the wrongdoer's want of care in its exclusion of non-consequential economic loss.

Pure pragmatism

The third motivation is essentially pragmatic. The feeling of judges in considering claims of pure economic loss unassociated with any physical damage is that such claims are difficult to evaluate, not only from the courts' point of view, but also from the point of view of plaintiffs, who might be tempted to inflate their claims and take advantage of the situation. This point is dealt with more fully below (see para 4.6.1). For the moment, the point to note is that, from a practical point of view, this feeling of unease on the part of judges does not generally extend to economic loss which is consequential on material damage. Lord Denning MR made this point in *Spartan Steel and Alloys Ltd v Martin & Co (Contractors) Ltd* [1973] 1 QB 27 when he rejected the plaintiff's claim for economic loss suffered independently of the physical damage, but allowed it for economic loss which was 'truly consequential' on the material damage. He said (at p 39): "Such cases will be comparatively few. They will be readily capable of proof and will be easily checked. They should be and are admitted".

In other words, the reason for drawing a line between pure economic loss and property damage in this type of case is that, from a practical point of view, it is easier to identify, verify and evaluate property damage than claims of pure economic loss. Whilst this reasoning might well be sound in relation to the accidental cutting off of a utility service which is used by an indeterminate class of consumers, it will not have the same attractiveness where the nature of the hazard is not so widespread and the foresight of the defendant is more narrowly focused. This, too, is discussed *below*.

4.5.4 Truly consequential loss

The applicable principle

It has been noted *above* (para 4.3.2) that the Court of Appeal in *Spartan Steel* held that the plaintiff could recover such part of its consequential economic loss as was 'truly consequential' on (*per* Lord Denning MR) or which was 'the immediate consequence' of (*per* Lawton LJ) the physical damage caused by the defendant's negligent act or omission. This meant that the defendant was liable to compensate the plaintiff for the £400 loss of profit on the first melt which was actually in progress when the electricity was cut off, but not for the £1,767 loss of profit claimed in respect of the further four melts which could also have been put through the furnace during the 14 hours that the power was cut off.

Logical dividing line

The point has been made *above* (para 4.3.4) that this would be a logical dividing line (to the extent that logic has got anything to do with this matter) if it was linked to the length of time that it took to repair the property damage to the plaintiff's machine or, as in this case, to clear the material out of the furnace (which had to be done with oxygen) and to make it ready for use again. It could thus be said that the loss of profit which the plaintiff suffered on the first melt was indeed 'truly consequential' on the property damage caused by the defendant and the inability to use the furnace while the problems associated with that property damage were being rectified, and that the loss of profits on the further four melts which could have been done in the period of time between the furnace being ready to accept further melts and the re-connection of the electricity was only 'truly consequential' on the fact that the electricity had been cut off, irrespective of any physical damage caused as well. This is borne out by Lord Denning's statement (at p 39) that the plaintiff could not recover its loss of profit on the additional four melts "because that was economic loss independent of the physical damage".

Dependence on untested principle

Whilst this reasoning might be logical, it is dependent on an acceptance of the principle that pure economic loss sustained as a result of an accident, without the property of anyone (not even a third party) being damaged, is not recoverable. This is discussed in para 4.5.5 *below*.

4.5.5 Pure economic loss

Context

It must be remembered that we are concerned here only with pure economic loss suffered by a plaintiff as a result of an accident in which no property (not even of a third party) has been damaged. This situation obviously differs from economic loss in the sphere of negligent misstatements, but it also differs from pure economic loss suffered where a product or a building proves to be defective (because those are not accident cases) and, importantly, from relational economic loss cases (because there a third party's property has been damaged).

Different policy considerations

It is therefore wrong to try to argue that because the relational economic loss cases effectively exclude claims by plaintiffs who do not have proprietary or possessory rights in the property that has been damaged, this means that where the defendant has not damaged any property at all, no one should be entitled to recover their pure economic losses suffered in consequence of the defendant's wrongful act or omission. Such an argument would fail to appreciate that the policy considerations which underlie the relational economic loss exclusionary rule are, as mentioned *above* (para 4.2.1), not based on the 'economic quality' of the plaintiff's loss but on the reason why that loss occurred. The voluntary use by the plaintiff of the third party's property, and the indeterminacy of the existence of the plaintiff and others like him when the third party's property is damaged, which are important factors in the relational loss sphere, will not be present in the direct loss sphere as a matter of course; although, depending on the nature of the hazard created by the defendant's negligent act or omission (for example, cutting off an electricity supply), the problem of indeterminacy of the class of possible claimants might arise. Another difference is that the deterrent effect of tort law, which is satisfied in the relational loss sphere because of the defendant's liability to the third party whose property he has damaged, will not be satisfied in the direct loss sphere if the defendant is not liable to anyone.

Consideration in Spartan Steel

In *Spartan Steel* Lord Denning MR considered what the position would have been if the plaintiff had suffered pure economic loss without any property damage as well. Although his comments are *obiter*, it was necessary for him to conduct this exercise in order to be able to justify the dividing line which he drew between recoverable and irrecoverable consequential economic loss.

A question of policy

Lord Denning said (at p 36): "At bottom I think the question of recovering economic loss is one of policy. Whenever the courts draw a line to mark out the bounds of duty, they do it as a matter of policy so as to limit the responsibility of the defendant". He said (at p 37) that, rather than trying to "put each case into its proper pigeonhole", so as to say "there was no duty" or that "the damage was too remote": "It seems to me better to consider the particular relationship in hand, and see whether or not, as a matter of policy, economic loss should be recoverable, or not".

Five policy factors

Lord Denning then considered 'the relationship' in *Spartan Steel*. In so doing, he considered five separate factors, namely that:

    (a) the electricity board, by statute, would not have been liable for such pure economic losses suffered by consumers if it, rather than an independent contractor, had negligently cut off their electricity;

    (b) the nature of the hazard, namely the cutting off of the supply of electricity (or any other utility service), "is a hazard which we all run". He said that this could occur for a variety of reasons, including acts of God, and that, when it happens, it affects a multitude of persons. He said (at p 38): "Such a hazard is regarded by most people as a thing they must put up with—without seeking compensation from anyone. Some install a stand-by system. Others take out insurance. But most people are content to take the risk on themselves. When the supply is cut off, they do not go running round to their solicitor. They just put up with it. They try to make up the economic loss by doing more work the next day. This is a healthy attitude which the law should encourage.";

    (c) if claims for economic loss were permitted for this particular hazard, "there would be no end of claims. Some might be genuine, but many might be inflated, or even false. A machine might not have been in use anyway, but it would be easy to put it down to the cut in supply. It would be well-nigh impossible to check the claims. Rather than expose claimants to such temptation and defendants to such hard labour—on comparatively small claims—it is better to disallow economic loss altogether, at any rate where it stands alone, independent of any physical damage.";

    (d) in such a hazard as this, the risk of economic loss should be suffered by the whole community rather than fall on the one pair of shoulders, namely the contractor, on whom all the claims, added together, might be very heavy; and

    (e) the law provides for 'deserving cases', namely physical injury to person or property.

Limited application

Whilst there is no doubt a good deal of sense in all of these considerations (apart, possibly, from the first, because there might well be good reasons for treating a statutory undertaker (which the relevant electricity board was in *Spartan Steel*) differently from an independent contractor, and the last, because it cannot be correct to generalise that physical injury is more deserving than economic loss), they are tailored very closely to the nature of the hazard in that case, namely the cutting off of the supply of electricity, or any other utility service. Lord Denning recognised this and emphasised it in his judgment. Therefore this case must not be taken as an authority that direct, accidental economic loss is necessarily irrecoverable in English law. Circumstances may well arise where the relationship of the parties, and the nature of the hazard, is so different from those which arose in *Spartan Steel* that the court feels able to discard the type of considerations which Lord Denning took into account in sub-paragraphs (b), (c) and (d) *above*.

4.6 Dissentient voices

4.6.1 Introduction

The judgment of the Ontario Court of Appeal in *Seaway Hotels v Cragg* (1960) (see *below*) and the dissenting judgment of Edmund Davies LJ in *Spartan Steel* (see *below*) are against the trend of the decisions discussed above. So, too, are the decisions of the High Court of Australia in *Caltex Oil (Australia) Pty Limited v The Dredge Willemstad* (1976) 136 CLR 529 and of the Supreme Court of Canada in *Canadian National Railway Co v Norsk Pacific Steamship Co* (1992) 91 DLR (4th) 489. These latter two cases are cases of relational economic loss and are, accordingly, discussed in Chapter 5. *Seaway* is also a relational case in one sense, because the electricity feeder line which the defendant broke belonged to a third party, but it is discussed in this section because the plaintiff's property was also damaged.

4.6.2 Very few decisions

Seaway Hotels v Cragg

In *Seaway Hotels Ltd v Cragg (Canada) Ltd and Consumers Gas Co* (1960) 21 DLR (2d) 264, an underground feeder line supplying electric power to a hotel was broken by the first defendant contractors in the course of installing a gas pipe for the second defendant, who was aware before the work began of the presence of the feeder line. As a result of the power being cut off, the hotel's refrigerators and stoves were rendered inoperative. As a result of this, food which had cost C$1,300 went off and had to be thrown away and the dining room and the bar had to be closed early, at an estimated loss of C$1,500.

The court held that the plaintiff was entitled to recover all of these losses from the defendant. Laidlaw JA said (at p 266): "It is quite certain that the injury for which claim is made in this case was injury that was likely to follow from the interference with the electric duct. It was injury which ought reasonably to have been foreseen by the defendants. Upon that finding, the judgment against the defendants is correct".

The judgment which the Court of Appeal thus upheld was the judgment of McLennan J in *Seaway Hotels Ltd v Gragg (Canada) Ltd* (1959) 17 DLR (2d) 292. In holding that the defendant was liable for all of the plaintiff's losses, McLennan J distinguished the cases which have upheld and applied the exclusionary rule discussed in Chapter 5. He said (at p 297):

These cases undoubtedly establish the proposition that negligence which interferes with contractual rights *only* does not impose liability on the wrongdoer [see Chapter 5]. Different reasons are given for the rule in the cases which I have mentioned, but I do not think it is necessary to discuss those reasons in view of the conclusion to which I have come, which is that the principle established by those cases does not apply to this case. In none of those cases was there any damage to the property or person of the plaintiff, and the loss for which compensation was sought arose solely by reason of interference with contractual relationships. In this case there was direct damage to the plaintiff's property in the food which was spoiled by reason of the refrigeration equipment failing to operate. It may be, and it is unnecessary to decide, that the other items of damage considered alone might fall within the principle established in those cases. But if an actionable wrong has been done to the plaintiff, he is entitled to recover all the damage resulting from it even if some part of the damage considered by itself would not be recoverable.

In *Londonwaste Ltd v Amec Civil Engineering Ltd* (1997) 53 Con LR 66, the facts of which are set out in para 4.3.2, *above*, the judge, despite noting the disapproving remarks of Lord Denning MR and Buckley LJ referred to *below*, nevertheless cited this passage with approval.

Rejection of Seaway

Seaway was relied on by the plaintiff in *SCM*. Both Lord Denning MR and Buckley LJ said that they thought that *Seaway* was correctly decided only so far as damage to the food was concerned. In *Caltex*, Gibbs J also disapproved of the award in *Seaway*, but said that it might be explained because the electricity feeder line which the defendant damaged supplied only the plaintiff's hotel. Perhaps it is this fact, coupled with the second defendant's knowledge of the presence of the feeder line, that serves justifiably to take this case out of the ordinary. It could thus be treated as an example of a case where the relationship between the parties and the nature of the hazard were such as to allow the court to relax the concerns expressed by Lord Denning MR in *Spartan Steel* (which are set out in para 4.5.5, *above*).

Edmund Davies LJ's dissent

In *Spartan Steel* Edmund Davies LJ, dissenting, held that the plaintiff was entitled to recover the entirety of its economic loss. He stressed (at p 46) the fact that the question of recovery of pure economic loss raised in *Spartan Steel*, namely that this economic loss was "a direct consequence of the defendant's negligent act", was different from the question raised in the relational economic loss cases (where the plaintiff is only a secondary loss sufferer). He thus appreciated that each type of case was in a different category and that different policy considerations would therefore be applicable.

Edmund Davies LJ said that he could not see why the £400 loss of profit sustained by the plaintiff should be recoverable, but not the £1,767. He said (at p 41): "It is common ground that both types of loss were equally foreseeable and equally direct consequences of the defendant's admitted negligence, and the only distinction drawn is that the former figure represents the profit lost as a result of the physical damage done to the material in the furnace at the time when the power was cut off. But what has that purely fortuitous fact to do with legal principle? In my judgment, nothing".

Edmund Davies LJ thus concluded (at p 45) that, in a case like this, "an action lies in negligence for damages in respect of purely economic loss, provided that it was a reasonably foreseeable and direct consequence of failure in a duty of care". He recognised that the application of such a rule "can undoubtedly give rise to difficulties in certain sets of circumstances", but said that this applied equally to the majority judges' ruling that economic loss can be recovered provided it is directly consequential upon physical damage. He also referred to some of the "alarming situations" which it was suggested might arise if his view were followed, such as the risk of fictitious claims, expensive litigation and the difficulty of disproving the alleged cause and effect, and said (at p 45): "But I suspect that they (like the illustrations furnished by Lord Penzance in *Simpson & Co v Thomson* (1877) 3 App Cas 279, HL (Sc) [which is set out in para 5.8 of the cases at the end of Chapter 5]) would for the most part be resolved, either on the ground that no duty of care was owed to the injured party or that the damages sued for were irrecoverable, not because they were simply financial, but because they were too remote".

4.6.3 Very limited acceptance

Edmund Davies LJ's approach has not found much favour with his fellow judges. Exceptions are Jacobs J in *Caltex*, who said (at p 602): "I respectfully agree with the dissenting conclusion of Edmund Davies LJ", and Lord Roskill in *Junior Books Ltd v Veitchi Co Ltd* [1983] 1 AC 520, when he said (at p 547) that if his conclusion in that case was correct (as to which, see para 7.3.6), the decision of the majority of the Court of Appeal in *Spartan Steel* might not be correct and the reasoning of Edmund Davies LJ in his dissenting judgment might be preferred.

4.7 Alternative theories

4.7.1 No separation of categories

In Chapter 5, para 5.6 various alternative theories to the relational economic loss exclusionary rule are canvassed. Although those theories derive from *dicta* of judges in various relational economic loss cases, only the three dissenting judges in *Canadian National Railway Co v Norsk Pacific Steamship Co* (1992) 91 DLR (4th) 489 specifically limited their suggested alternative solution (ie the circumstances in which they would be prepared to relax the exclusionary rule) to cases of relational economic loss. All of the other judges in that case and in the other cases considered in Chapter 5, para 5.6 advanced their individual proposed alternative tests for establishing liability on the basis that they were simply concerned with the question whether damages are, or are not, recoverable for economic loss which is not consequential upon injury to the plaintiff's person or property (as opposed to injury to a third person or damage to his property).

4.7.2   Transference of arguments

Accordingly, in any case where the plaintiff suffers direct, accidental economic loss, it will be just as appropriate for legal advisers acting for plaintiffs to try to advance one or more of these alternative theories as if they were acting for a plaintiff in a relational economic loss situation.

4.8   Bailee in possession

4.8.1   Introduction

Context

Chapter 5 deals with claims for economic loss suffered by a plaintiff in consequence of damage to a third party's property. The general rule is that the plaintiff will not be entitled to claim any part of such a loss from the defendant who has negligently damaged the third party's property, unless the plaintiff had a proprietary or a possessory interest in the third party's property at the time when the damage was inflicted upon it. If the plaintiff does have such an interest, his cause of action will not be prohibited by this exclusionary rule, and his right to recover damages for consequential economic loss should be the same as that of an owner of the damaged property, as discussed in this chapter.

More extensive recovery

In fact, however, sometimes the plaintiff with only a possessory interest has been able to recover more extensive consequential economic loss than if his case had been considered simply on the basis of the principles discussed in this chapter in relation to the rights of the owner of the damaged property. Conceptually, this difference should not exist, and, indeed, it has—at least in theory—been abrogated by statute in most parts of the United Kingdom (see para 4.8.5). The reason for the existence of a different rule in these circumstances, at least where the plaintiff is a bailee, is historical. It seems that, sometimes, in these cases, the court has not realised that it is in fact awarding damages for pure economic loss at all, let alone on a more extensive basis than might otherwise be the case.

4.8.2   The rule in *The Winkfield*

The actual decision

This other rule derives from the decision of the Court of Appeal in *The Winkfield* [1902] P 42, in which the Postmaster General of the Cape was assumed for the purposes of the case to be a bailee in possession of letters and parcels which were being transported on a ship which had been sunk by the negligence of the persons in control of *The Winkfield*. The Postmaster General claimed a certain sum of money, as being the estimated value of the contents of those letters and parcels. No claims had been made against him by the senders or the addressees, although he undertook voluntarily to try to distribute amongst them the damages which he was claiming from the tortfeasor.

The Postmaster General's claim was thus for pure economic loss, because no property of the Post Office had been lost or damaged. Nevertheless, the court allowed him to recover the full amount of his claim. The Court of Appeal laid down the principle that, in an action against a defendant for damages for the loss of goods caused by his negligence, the bailee in possession can recover the full value of the goods, even though they were not his goods, and even though he is not obliged to account to the bailor (usually the owner) for their loss. Collins MR, after considering the authorities, said (at p 55): "Against a wrongdoer, possession is title. Therefore it is not open to the defendant to enquire into the nature or limitation of the possessor's right. The question of the possessor's relation to, or liability towards, the true owner cannot come into the discussion at all. Therefore, as between the possessor and the wrongdoer, full damages have to be paid without any further enquiry".

Wider application

This principle, which has become known as 'the rule in *The Winkfield*', has been applied in numerous cases, without question. These include *Glenwood Lumber Co Ltd v Phillips* [1904] AC 405 (PC), *Morrison Steamship Co Ltd v SS Greystoke* [1947] AC 265, and *The Jag Shakti* [1986] AC 337, all of which are discussed in Chapter 5 (paras 5.2.3, 5.4.1 and 5.2.4). It has been stated *above* that the application of this principle sometimes leads to an award of damages for economic loss which might not have been available if the duty of care principle in cases like *Spartan Steel* had been taken into consideration. An example of this occurring is the Canadian case of *Courtenay v Knutson*.

Courtenay v Knutson

In *Courtenay v Knutson* (1961) 26 DLR (2d) 768 the plaintiff was a fish buyer who operated fish camps from barges which were moored at various locations in a bay. The plaintiff was in possession of one such barge under a charter from its owner. The defendant negligently sank that barge. The plaintiff was able to replace it by bringing in his own barge from one of his other fish camps. He was not, however, able to replace that barge. He therefore suffered a loss of business profits at that location. The court held that he was entitled to recover this loss from the defendant because he was a bailee in possession of the barge that sank. However, if the principle of *Spartan Steel* had been applied this loss would not have been recoverable.

HL Motorworks v Alwahbi

Another example is *HL Motorworks (Willesden) Ltd v Alwahbi* [1977] RTR 276, in which the plaintiff was a bailee in possession of a Rolls Royce car which had been left by its owner for repairs at the plaintiff's garage. The car was negligently damaged by the defendant. This delayed the plaintiff in returning it to its owner for 11 days. During that time the owner hired another Rolls Royce, and asked the plaintiff to reimburse him for the cost. The plaintiff did this, and sought to recover that expenditure from the defendant. The Court of Appeal upheld the plaintiff's claim on the simple basis "that they were bailees of their customer's car and it had been damaged while it was in their possession. If it was reasonable for them to meet [their customer's claim for the cost of hiring a substitute Rolls Royce] then it was reasonable for them to claim reimbursement from the defendant" (*per* Cairns LJ at p 280–281). The court said that it was indeed reasonable for the plaintiff to pay the owner's substitute Rolls Royce hire charges, because otherwise the plaintiff might have impaired his goodwill with his customer. Again, these damages would not have been recoverable if the principle of *Spartan Steel* had been applied.

4.8.3 The suggested approach

Introduction

It is submitted that the proper analysis which should have been carried out in these cases involves a synthesis of the rule in *The Winkfield* and the rule in *Spartan Steel*. The former serves to establish that the plaintiff, as a bailee in possession of someone else's goods, has the right to sue for the full replacement cost of those goods, even if his interest in the goods was only partial, and for his consequential losses. The latter establishes the extent of the type of consequential losses for which he can recover.

Example: Wimpey v Martin Black

A case where the suggested approach seems to have been applied is *Wimpey Construction (UK) Ltd v Martin Black & Co (Wire Ropes) Ltd* [1982] SLR 239. Three companies, 'W', 'H' and 'C' were engaged in a joint venture for the construction of a tanker terminal, in the course of which work a wire rope sling, supplied to H by the defendant, failed. A pile which was being carried on the sling, which had been supplied by W, dropped into the river. The accident caused serious damage to the jackup barge and its crane. It took 86 days to repair that damage and bring the barge back into operation. During that period the whole of the works had to be suspended. The barge and the crane were in the possession of H under a hire agreement with a third party.

H claimed damages for the cost of repairing the barge and the crane, as well as damages for the economic loss suffered by it by reason of the 86-day delay. The court upheld all of these claims on the ground that H was a bailee in possession of the barge and the crane. The court did not need to say very much about the basis for this decision, because the defendant did not dispute these claims in principle (see para 4.3.3, *above*). However, it seems that the court was very much alive to 'the *Spartan Steel* principle', and would therefore have made some adverse comment on the defendant's concession in respect of these claims if it had thought that this was wrong, because the court took *Spartan Steel* into consideration in rejecting W's claim for the economic loss which it had suffered by virtue of the delay. Although this was a joint venture contract, only H had an interest in the property which the defendant had damaged, which meant that W's claim failed.

Millar v Candy

The suggested approach was followed in the Australian case of *Millar v Candy* (1982) 38 ALR 299, where a car in the plaintiff's possession under a hire purchase agreement had been damaged beyond repair as a result of the defendant's negligence. The court held, first, that as a bailee in possession, there was no doubt that the plaintiff was entitled to the market value of the car which the defendant had wrongfully destroyed. The court then went on to consider the plaintiff's claims for his additional losses, namely A$200 for loss of use of the car and A$1,704 for the additional amount he was required to pay the owner upon the early termination of the hire purchase agreement.

The court had no difficulty in allowing the plaintiff to recover the A$200, on the basis of authorities which have established that damages can be recovered for loss of use of a non-profit earning chattel. However, the court held that the A$1,704 was not recoverable by the plaintiff. This conclusion was reached by applying the principles which the court believed were established for the recovery of damages for pure economic loss in Australia in *Caltex Oil (Australia) Pty Ltd v The Dredge Willemstad* (1976) 136 CLR 529. The actual reasoning involved in this conclusion is considered in Chapter 5, para 5.6.4. For the moment, the point to note is that the court was not prepared to grant all of the plaintiff's consequential economic losses to him simply because he was a bailee in possession.

O'Sullivan v Williams

In *O'Sullivan and Another v Williams* [1992] 3 All ER 385 (the facts of which are set out in Chapter 5, para 5.2.3) the Court of Appeal was also alive to the fact that the bailee in possession's (ie the second plaintiff's) claim for loss of use of the first plaintiff's car consisted of pure economic loss. However, the court did not need to analyse this claim separately because it took the view that the settlement by the first plaintiff of his claim against the defendant ruled out the second plaintiff's claim altogether. Fox LJ said (at p 388): "Once the first plaintiff's claim for damages for the cost of repairs to, and loss of use of his car was satisfied, no separate cause of action subsisted which the second plaintiff could pursue as a separate claim for loss of use (which incidentally was purely for economic loss)".

4.8.4 Settlement of claims

O'Sullivan v Williams

In any case where a bailee in possession has the right to sue for damages to the bailor's property, the bailor will also have this right. In *O'Sullivan*, where the first plaintiff's car had been damaged whilst it was in the second plaintiff 's possession, the first plaintiff claimed £1,300 as the value of the car and damages of £25 per week for loss of its use, and the second plaintiff claimed damages for inconvenience in not having the use of the car to get to work and for social purposes. The first plaintiff settled his claim without prejudice to the second plaintiff's claim. The Court of Appeal dismissed the second plaintiff's claim, not because it consisted of pure economic loss, but because, as noted above, in its view the settlement by the first plaintiff of his claims against the defendant precluded a claim by the second plaintiff, as bailee. The Court of Appeal said that this conclusion followed as the natural corollary of the rule in *The Winkfield*: "The bailee having recovered damages against the wrongdoer in respect of the tortious damage to the chattel, the wrongdoer has an answer to any action by the bailor" (see *The Winkfield* [1902] P 42 at 60 *per* Collins MR). "The same principle must apply to the bailee if the bailor has sued and recovered damages" (*per* Fox LJ at p 387).

Questionable decision

This judgment must be approached with caution. Whilst the actual decision might possibly be correct on the facts if (which is not clear from the judgment) the damages claimed by the first plaintiff for loss of use of the car were effectively the same as the damages claimed by the second plaintiff, this case should not be taken as being authority that, in every case, a settlement by one of the potential plaintiffs, ie the bailor or the bailee, will necessarily extinguish the other's claim. It will all depend on whether (and the extent to which) these are separate claims or the same claim being brought by two different people. Indeed, it seems that the Court of Appeal, in fact, also intended this, because Fox LJ said (at p 388), in relation to the second plaintiff's claim for damages for nervous shock and other distress, which the trial judge had dismissed: "So far as the second plaintiff's claim for personal injuries is concerned, she was obviously entitled to proceed with that".

The correct approach: Courtenay v Knutson

The point also arose, and, it is submitted, was properly dealt with, in *Courtenay v Knutson* (1961) 26 DLR (2d) 768. It has been noted in para 4.8.3, *above* that the court awarded extensive damages to the bailee in possession in this case. Before the case started the defendant had paid a certain sum of money to the bailor (the owner) of the barge in full settlement of its claim against him for damage to the barge. One of the defendant's arguments against the plaintiff was that this settlement had the effect of extinguishing the plaintiff's separate right of action. The court rejected this, saying that, under the rule in *The Winkfield*, the bailee's right to sue for loss of use of the property damaged was a separate right of action based on the bailee's possession of the bailed property, and was not dependent on the existence of the bailor's rights as owner.

4.8.5   The Torts (Interference with Goods) Act 1977

Introduction

It has been noted that, under the rule in *The Winkfield*, the plaintiff's claim is based purely and simply on his possession of the damaged property, and the defendant is thus prevented from being able to plead that a third party has a better title than the plaintiff. For example, if the plaintiff in possession has only a 1 per cent interest in the damaged goods, or if he is in possession but would owe no liability to the owner (as was the case in *The Winkfield* itself), he is entitled to recover the full market value of the goods if they are negligently destroyed by the defendant. Whilst the plaintiff is obliged to account to the owner for his share if the owner so requests, in cases where the plaintiff is not under any such obligation the plaintiff will have been compensated for more than his actual loss.

Section 8 of the Act

This manifest injustice has been corrected in the United Kingdom (except Scotland) by s 8 of the Torts (Interference with Goods) Act 1977. The definition of 'wrongful interference' in s 1 specifically includes negligence "so far as it results in damage to goods or to an interest in goods". Section 8(1) provides that the defendant, in an action for wrongful interference, shall be entitled to show, in accordance with Rules of Court, that a third party has a better right than the plaintiff as respects all, or any part, of the interest claimed by the plaintiff, and any rule of law to the contrary is abolished.

Ease of application

This section applies to all parts of the United Kingdom except Scotland. This means that the defendant, when sued by a bailee in possession, can, by following the procedure laid down in the Rules of the Supreme Court (O.15, r 10A), resist the bailee's claim for the full market value of the property by showing that the bailee's interest in that property was less than 100 per cent.

Chapter 5

Relational economic loss

The question of whether pure economic loss is recoverable where there has been no damage to the person of the claimant or to the property in which he might have a proprietary interest is not one of the areas where the law excels by its clarity or where its various approaches are consistent. (**Addy J in** *Bethlehem Steel Corp v St Lawrence Seaway Authority* **(1977) 79 DLR (3d) 522)**

A plaintiff who has had the opportunity under his primary contract to obtain full contractual protection against that kind of loss [ie economic loss] cannot expect society to provide further protection through tort law. (**Richardson J in** *South Pacific Manufacturing Co Ltd v NZ Security Consultants & Investigations Ltd* **[1992] 2 NZLR 282)**

5.1 Definition

5.1.1 General

This chapter is concerned with pure economic loss suffered by a plaintiff in consequence of a physical injury to a third party or damage to the third party's property. This 'primary damage' will have been caused by the negligent act or omission of a person (the defendant), who will be liable to compensate the third party in damages for the third party's personal injury or property damage. In a modern commercial society, there will be countless situations in which one or more person(s) will have based his/their actions, or made plans which are dependent on the continued well-being of the third party or the continued existence of the third party's property. When the third person is injured or when his property is damaged, that person(s) (ie the plaintiff) will suffer a consequential economic loss. The question in the cases in this chapter is whether the plaintiff is entitled to recover this loss from the person (ie the defendant) who injured the third party or damaged the third party's property.

5.1.2 Terminology

The term 'relational loss' thus describes a loss which does not arise directly from an injury to the plaintiff or damage to the plaintiff's property, but rather from an interference with the plaintiff's relationship with a third party who has been directly injured, or whose property has been directly damaged by the defendant. Sometimes this situation is described as 'negligent interference with contractual relations'. However, it is felt that the term 'relational economic loss' is more appropriate because the plaintiff's losses need not necessarily arise from the interference of a contract between himself and the injured third party. For example, if a bridge over a river is damaged by a negligent boat owner, the nature of the economic losses suffered by different businessmen who use the bridge to transport goods will be the same whether or not each of them has a contract with the owner of the bridge.

5.2 The exclusionary rule

5.2.1 Introduction

Statement of the rule

In English law, and in New Zealand and the USA but not Australia and Canada, there is a strict rule of exclusion, subject to a few minor exceptions. The exclusionary rule dictates that economic loss suffered by a plaintiff consequential upon a personal injury to a third party or damage to a third party's property by a negligent defendant will not be recoverable from that defendant unless the plaintiff had a proprietary or a possessory interest in the third party or his property.

Extreme application of the rule—I

A strict application of the exclusionary rule can preclude a claim by the actual owner of the damaged property if his loss was sustained in some lesser capacity. This occurred in *Candlewood Navigation Corporation Ltd v Mitsui OSK Lines Ltd (The Mineral Transporter)* [1986] AC 1 (PC) (see para 5.8, *below*). Although the plaintiff was the actual reversionary owner of the ship, at the time of the collision the plaintiff was also a time charterer, but not by demise, having previously let the ship to a third party under a charter by demise. The economic loss which the plaintiff sought to recover from the defendant was suffered by the plaintiff in its capacity as time charterer. As this was not a time charter by demise, this was not a proprietary or possessory interest, and the plaintiff's claim was therefore debarred.

5.2.2 Proprietary interest

Equivalent to ownership

A proprietary interest is absolute ownership or an interest which allows the holder of it to exercise rights equivalent to rights of ownership. An example would be an easement over someone else's land. In *Gypsum Carrier Inc v The Queen* (1977) 78 DLR (3d) 175, three railway companies had agreements with the Crown permitting them, for prescribed tolls, to use a certain bridge. A ship negligently collided with the bridge, causing all railway traffic to be suspended for eight days. The three railway companies incurred expenses in rerouting their trains during the bridge closure. The owners of the bridge were not obliged under their contracts to indemnify the railway companies for these losses. Therefore they sued the owners of the ship in tort. They raised the exclusionary rule as a defence. The railway companies, however, argued that they had a right of way over the bridge in the nature of an easement. The court accepted that, if this were correct, the railway companies would succeed. However, on the facts, the court held that the railway companies did not have any rights annexed to land, or any interest in land. At the most, they had a licence in respect of land. This was not enough to bring them within the confines of the exclusionary rule. Their claims were accordingly rejected.

In *Londonwaste Ltd v Amec Civil Engineering Ltd* (1997) 53 Con LR 66, the facts of which are set out in Chapter 4, para 4.3.2, in referring to this decision the judge said:

> That decision [*Gypsum Carrier Inc v R* (1977) 78 DLR (3d) 175] is not a binding authority for my purposes, but it is consistent both with the familiar rule of English law that wrongful interference with an easement is a tort and with the English authorities to the effect that contractual rights over property are insufficient to justify attaching economic loss claims to the damage of that property.
>
> Turning to the facts, Eastern Electricity plc was the owner of the cables. No proprietary interest or easement vested in the plaintiff is pleaded [this was a striking-out application], nor that the plaintiff was in possession of the cables. The only relevant allegation is that the cables were used exclusively for the export of electricity produced at the plaintiff's power station. Such rights as the plaintiff has in relation to the cables must be derived from the agreements between the plaintiff and Eastern Electricity.

His Honour then considered the terms of these agreements to see whether the plaintiff thereby acquired any proprietary or possessory rights in the cables. Having ascertained that the plaintiff did not, his Honour continued by saying: "On these facts the plaintiff *prima facie* has no sufficient interest in the cables for the purposes of the rule. It has no right of action for the damage to the cables as owner, lessee, possessor or easement-holder".

Equitable interest

A person who has only an equitable interest in land or goods will not have a sufficient proprietary interest for the purposes of the exclusionary rule. In order to have title to sue, he will need, in addition, to have possession:

> There may be cases where a person who is the equitable owner of certain goods has also a possessory title to them. In such a case he is entitled, by virtue of his possessory title rather than his equitable ownership, to sue in tort for negligence anyone whose want of care has caused loss of, or damage to the goods, without joining the legal owner as a party to the action: see for instance *Healey v Healey* [1915] 1 KB 938. If, however, the person is the equitable owner of the goods and no more, then he must join the legal owner as a party to the action, either as co-plaintiff if he is willing or as co-defendant if he is not. This has always been the law in the field of equitable ownership of land and I see no reason why it should not also be so in the field of equitable ownership of goods.

per Lord Brandon in *Leigh and Sillivan Ltd v Aliakmon Ltd (The Aliakmon)* [1986] AC 785 (HL) (at p 812).

5.2.3   *Relational economic Loss*

Third party in possession

On the other hand, if the plaintiff is the full legal owner of property which the defendant has negligently damaged, he will not be prevented from suing the defendant if the property was in the possession of a third party at the time the damage occurred. The plaintiff in this arrangement will be the bailor of his goods and the third party will have been his bailee. In *O'Sullivan and Another v Williams* [1992] 3 All ER 385 (see para 4.8.3), the first plaintiff had allowed his girlfriend, the second plaintiff, to use his car while he was away on holiday. While the car was parked outside her house, it was irreparably damaged when an excavator, which was on a trailer being towed by the defendant, toppled off onto it. The first plaintiff claimed from the defendant the replacement value of the car and damages for its loss of use at a certain sum per week. The second plaintiff, as bailee, also sued the defendant. Her claim is considered below (para 5.2.3). The point to note here is that no objection was taken to the *locus standi* of the first plaintiff to sue for his losses, notwithstanding that the car was not in his possession at the time of the accident.

Another example is *Marc Rich and Co AG v Bishop Rock Marine Co Ltd ('The Nicholas H')* [1996] 1 AC 211, in which the plaintiff was the owner of a cargo on board the vessel *Nicholas H* which sank at sea, resulting in the total loss of the cargo. The cause of the sinking was the unseaworthiness of the vessel. Shortly before the ship had sailed, it had been inspected by the third defendant classification society at the request of its owner. The surveyor had recommended that, subject to certain specified repairs being carried out, the vessel could proceed on its intended voyage (the cargo was already loaded), but that it should be further examined and dealt with as necessary after discharging its cargo at the port of destination prior to loading any other cargo.

A trial of a preliminary issue was held as to whether, on the facts pleaded, the classification society owed a duty of care to the plaintiff in respect of the plaintiff's loss. The first question was whether the plaintiff had the right to sue the classification society, given that the cargo had not actually been damaged and that the plaintiff's claim was therefore parasitic upon, or relational to, the damage that the defendant had caused to the vessel, which belonged to someone else. The fact that the plaintiff actually owned the cargo meant that this question was answered in the plaintiff's favour. As Lord Steyn said, in delivering the majority judgment (at p 234): "First, it was agreed that by reason of their proprietary interest in the cargo, the plaintiffs had title to sue if the classification society otherwise owed them a duty of care".

5.2.3   Possessory interest

Licence not sufficient

It is not possible to provide an all-embracing definition of a possessory interest for the purpose of the exclusionary rule. So far as concerns land, only a lease will suffice, a licence will not. In *East Lothian Angling Association v Haddington Town Council* 1980 SLT 213, the plaintiff angling association had exclusive written permission from the defendant to fish for trout in a certain river and to sell fishing permits to members of the public. As a result of the discharge of sewage into the river by the defendant, the fishing deteriorated and the plaintiff's sale of permits diminished. The plaintiff sought to recover this loss of revenue from the defendant. The court rejected the plaintiff's claim, saying that, although the plaintiff had the exclusive right to fish for trout in this river, this was only a personal right belonging to the plaintiff, which did not confer a proprietary or a possessory interest on the plaintiff in the property damaged (presumably, the water in the river, or the trout in it). Therefore the exclusionary rule applied and the plaintiff had no claim.

Contractual rights not sufficient

So far as concerns chattels, the contest, in the words of Scrutton LJ in *Elliott Steam Tug Co Ltd v Shipping Controller* [1922] 1 KB 127 (at p 139), is between "a person whose only rights are a contractual right to have the use of services of the chattel for purposes of making profits or gains" and a person who has "possession or property in the chattel"; or, as Lord Brandon put it in *Leigh and Sillivan Ltd v Aliakmon Ltd (The Aliakmon)* [1986] AC 785 (HL) (at p 809), the distinction is between a person who "only had contractual rights in relation to the property, which have been adversely affected by the loss of or damage to it" and a person who "had either the legal ownership of or a possessory title to the property concerned at the time when the loss or damage occurred".

Exclusive use not sufficient

It has been noted in para 5.2.2 that in *Londonwaste Ltd v Amec Civil Engineering Ltd* (1997) 53 Con LR 66, the plaintiff did not have a sufficient interest in the damaged electricity cables for the purposes of the exclusionary rule because the plaintiff had no right of action in respect of the damage caused to the cables as owner, lessee, possessor or easement-holder. The plaintiff's counsel submitted that the plaintiff nevertheless had the necessary *locus standi* because the plaintiff had made substantial payments for the installation of the cables and that it had exclusive use of the cables. The judge held, however, that this made no difference. He said:

> The submission based on exclusive use is hopeless. It merely restates in more colloquial terminology one aspect of the fact that the plaintiff has the contractual rights and duties under the connection agreement and the power purchase agreement. Those rights and duties do not on the authorities suffice to give the plaintiff a right of action for economic loss caused by the damage to the cables. It is to be noted that the plaintiff in the *Spartan Steel* case [see Chapter 4, paras 4.3.2 and 4.5.5] also was the exclusive user of the electricity passing through the damaged cable.

Possession per se not sufficient

Thus, the bare fact of possession will not be sufficient: the intention with which that possession is being exercised needs to be considered as well.

5.2.3 *Relational economic Loss*

Where the chattel in question is a ship, and where the plaintiff is in possession under a charterparty (ie a contract by which a ship is let to a merchant for the conveyance of goods on a determined voyage or until the expiration of a specified period) he will not have a 'possessory interest' unless it was a charter by demise. This is a matter for agreement between the owner and the charterer, but, generally, the distinguishing characteristic of a charter by demise is that the master and the crew will, during the period of the charterparty, become the employees of the charterer and, through them, the possession of the ship will pass to him. A charterer not by demise will not have a sufficient possessory interest (see *Candlewood Navigation Corporation Ltd v Mitsui OSK Lines Ltd (The Mineral Transporter)* [1986] AC 1 (PC), discussed above in para 5.2.1).

'Possession' of an intangible right

In *Tate & Lyle Industries Ltd v Greater London Council* [1983] 2 AC 509, the plaintiff's claim was for the amount of money which it had had to spend to dredge a portion of the Thames. The need to do this arose from the build-up of siltation caused by the altered flow of the river after the defendant had built two terminals higher upstream from the plaintiff's jetty. Although the plaintiff's loss was purely economic, the court seems to have treated it as damage to property, which it seems would have been recoverable if the court had felt that the plaintiff had a right in the property which had actually been damaged, namely the plaintiff's right to use that part of the river. Thus, Lord Templeman said (at p 530):

> Tate & Lyle assert that they have suffered damage to their property caused by interference with their right to use their jetties for the benefit of their sugar refining business. But this assertion assumes that Tate & Lyle possess the right to use their jetties in the sense that they are entitled to the maintenance of a depth of water in the relevant parts of the Thames sufficient to enable vessels of the requisite size to load and unload at the jetties. The question is whether Tate & Lyle possess any right to any particular depth of water. If they have any such right then they will have a remedy for interference with that right. But if they have no such right then interference with the depth of water causing damage to Tate & Lyle's business constitutes an injury for which Tate & Lyle have no remedy. The L.C.C. caused siltation to the bed of the river which is owned by the P.L.A. Tate & Lyle can only succeed if they establish that they were obstructed by the L.C.C. in the exercise by Tate & Lyle of rights over the river bed vested in Tate & Lyle.

Although the plaintiff's claim failed in negligence (and in private nuisance), it did succeed in public nuisance. The court ordered the defendant to pay three-quarters of the plaintiff's dredging costs.

Bailee in possession: The Winkfield

A person can, of course, be in possession of a ship which does not belong to him, or of goods on it, otherwise than by way of a charterparty. In *The Winkfield* [1902] P 42, the plaintiff was the Postmaster General of the Cape, suing the owners of *The Winkfield* for the estimated value of the contents

168

of letters and parcels which were being transported on another ship which *The Winkfield* had negligently sunk. The case was dealt with by all parties on the basis that the mail was in the custody of the Postmaster General as bailee at the time of the accident. This was a concession which the defendant's counsel should not have made, but which he probably thought he was safe in making because an earlier case, *Claridge v South Staffordshire Tramway Co* [1892] 1 QB 422, was strongly in his favour. However, in the present case, the Court of Appeal overruled *Claridge* and upheld the Postmaster General's claim. Neither of these cases was concerned directly with what will constitute a sufficient possessory interest; rather, they were concerned with the extent of the right of recovery of a bailee in possession. The importance of *The Winkfield* for the present discussion is the influence which it has had in subsequent relational economic loss cases, namely that a bailee will have a sufficient possessory interest for the purposes of the exclusionary rule. If the plaintiff has such an interest, he will be able to claim from the negligent defendant the full market value of the property destroyed, or the full repair costs if it is capable of repair, together with his consequential economic losses. This is often referred to as 'the rule in *The Winkfield*', and is discussed in Chapter 4 (para 4.8.2).

The Okehampton

If, however, the plaintiff is not able to establish 'a possessory interest' or a proprietary interest, then not only will the plaintiff not be able to claim '*Winkfield* damages', but the defendant will not owe him a duty of care at all, and he will not be able to recover anything from the defendant. This is really just another way of stating the exclusionary rule, but it is mentioned again here for the purpose of underlining how important it can be in these cases to establish a proprietary or a possessory interest in the damaged property. It has been noted *above* that a charterer of a ship under a charter not by demise does not have a sufficient possessory interest. In *The Okehampton* [1913] P 173, the plaintiff, a sub-charterer, was in this position. Nevertheless, he succeeded in his claim to recover from the owners of *The Okehampton*, which had sunk the ship which he had chartered, the bill of lading freight charges which he would have earned at the port of discharge if the voyage had been completed. This was because, unusually, when the plaintiff signed the bill of lading when the cargo was loaded, he did so in his own right, and not as the agent of the shipowner, as is more usual. Vaugham Williams LJ said (at p 179): "The moment you come to the conclusion that the bill of lading was signed by the charterer not on account of the ship, but on his own account, it follows necessarily that he had a sufficient interest—really sufficient possession—to enable him to bring this action"; and Hamilton LJ (who subsequently became Lord Sumner) said (at p 179): "The plaintiffs' claim is not merely for the loss of contractual advantages which have been defeated by the collision; it is a claim for damage suffered by the loss of cargo bailed to them in regard to which they had such rights of possession as entitled them to bring this action".

5.2.3 Relational economic Loss

La Société Anonyme v Bennetts

Two years earlier, in *La Société Anonyme de Remorquage à Hélice v Bennetts* [1911] 1 KB 243, which is regarded as one of the leading cases on relational economic loss, Hamilton J rejected the claim of the plaintiff for lost towing charges against the defendant who negligently collided with and sank a ship which the plaintiff was in the course of towing under a towage contract with a third party who owned the ship. He said (at p 248):

> All that has occurred is that, in the course of performing a profitable contract, an event happened which rendered the contract not further performable, and therefore less profitable to the plaintiff. That appears to me to bring the case within the authority of *Cattle v Stockton Waterworks Co* (1875) LR 10 QB 453 and within the general statement of the law by Lord Penzance in his judgment in *Simpson v Thomson* (1877) 3 App Cas 279, HL (Sc).

However, there is no discussion as to whether or, if not, why the plaintiff did not have a sufficient possessory interest in the ship which it was towing, nor are the terms of the towage contract set out in the case report. Unless those terms expressly or impliedly excluded such possession, it is difficult to see why the plaintiff should not have had it (eg if the master and the crew of the ship being towed remained in possession of it).

Simpson and Cattle

The two cases referred to by Hamilton J are seminal in the field of relational economic loss. They are summarised in para 5.8, *below*. In the second of these, there was no need to consider whether the plaintiff had a possessory interest, because the plaintiff was an insurance company which never had possession of any type at all. In the first of these cases (*Cattle v Stockton*), the plaintiff was held to be disentitled from claiming for its losses on a tunnelling contract on a third party's land which had been negligently flooded by the defendant. Although the plaintiff was thus in possession of the property which had been damaged, again there is no discussion as to whether he might have had a possessory interest. In this case, however, this omission is understandable because the property was land, so that it is unlikely that the owner would have conferred anything other than a licence on the plaintiff.

Nacap v Moffat

A modern-day application of this principle can be seen in the Scottish case of *Nacap Ltd v Moffat Plant Ltd* 1987 SLT 221. The plaintiff was a specialist in the construction and laying of pipelines. It entered into a contract with British Gas (BG) to lay a pipeline on BG's land, for which purpose the plaintiff was given possession of so much of the site as might be required to enable it to commence and proceed with the construction of the works. BG supplied and owned the pipeline, but the contract provided that the plaintiff would be liable for any damage to it. During this period the defendant negligently damaged the pipeline. The court held that the plaintiff was not entitled to recover from the defendant the costs incurred by the plaintiff in making good the damage to the pipeline. Relying on Scrutton LJ's above-quoted *dictum* in *Elliott*, the court said (at p 224) that, although the plaintiff no doubt had physical possession of the pipeline, this was only for the limited purpose of proceeding with the construction of the works and was therefore "not a possessory right or title as recognised by the law".

The Zelo

This approach can be contrasted with *The Zelo* [1922] P 9, in which a ship, 'M', had been sunk, and the plaintiff, a salvage company, had contracted with the owner's underwriters to salve 'M' on a basis of 'no cure, no pay'. After salvage operations had been carried on for some time, the point was reached where 'M' was lying marked and lighted by means of a buoy with a flashing light. In that condition 'M' was run into by *The Zelo*, and was resunk, thereby rending further salvage impossible. The court held that the plaintiff was entitled to sue the owners of *The Zelo* for damage to 'M'. Hill J said that, although the plaintiff was not in actual physical possession of 'M' at the time of the collision, it did have 'possession' because it alone exercised complete control over 'M'.

Courtenay v Knutson

In similar vein is the decision of the British Columbia Supreme Court in *Courtenay v Knutson* (1961) 26 DLR (2d) 768 (see para 4.8.2), in which it was held that the plaintiff in possession of a barge which he had chartered from the owner did have a sufficient possessory interest in it to maintain an action against the defendant who had negligently sunk it for his loss of profits in the business which he ran from the barge. This was a purely oral charter, with practically no defined terms, apart from the duration (one year), and the fact that the plaintiff took the barge away and used it without any control from the owner. Clyne J held that this case was distinguishable from *La Société Anonyme de Remorquage à Hélice v Bennetts* [1911] 1 KB 243. He said (at p 775) that, although nothing is said in that case as to who was in possession of the ship being towed at the time it was sunk, since the towage was from Antwerp to Port Talbot, South Wales, he thought it was "fair to assume" that the ship was manned throughout the voyage by its master and crew; so that, while the plaintiff tug owner might have had temporary control for the purpose of towage, possession of the ship remained in the owners through the agency of the master.

Substance, not form

The various differing decisions discussed above demonstrate how difficult it is to lay down any hard and fast rules on this question. Perhaps the most that can be said is that, in each case, the substance and not merely the form of the relationship between the plaintiff and the third party whose property has been damaged must be closely scrutinised. In *Glenwood Lumber Co Ltd v Phillips* [1904] AC 405 (PC) the plaintiff was the holder of a governmental licence to cut timber on Crown land. The defendant had applied for the same licence and, in the expectation that it would be granted, cut down and removed some timber. The plaintiff, upon being granted the licence itself, sued the defendant for the value of that timber. The defendant argued that the plaintiff, being only a licensee, did not have a sufficient interest in that timber to enable it to sue. The Privy Council rejected this claim. Lord Davey said (at p 408): "It is not a question of words, but of substance. If the effect of the instrument is to give the holder an exclusive right of occupation of the land, though subject to certain reservations or to a restriction of the purposes for which it may be used, it is in law a demise of the land itself".

Hirer has sufficient interest

Having said this, it is worth noting, although one must look carefully at the terms of the agreement in every case, that the hirer of a car from a car rental company and the hirer of industrial machinery have been held (in the Ontario High Court case of *Thorne v MacGregor* (1973) 35 DLR (3d) 687 and in the Scottish case of *Wimpey Construction (UK) Ltd v Martin Black & Co (Wire Ropes) Ltd* 1982 SLT 239, respectively) to have a sufficient possessory interest. In the Federal Court of Australia in *Millar v Candy* (1981) 38 ALR 299 it was taken for granted that the plaintiff had such an interest when he was in possession of a car under a hire purchase agreement. In *HL Motorworks (Willesden) Ltd v Alwahbi* [1977] RTR 276 it was simply assumed that the plaintiff garage owner with whom a third party's car had been left for repair had a sufficient possessory interest when it was negligently damaged by the defendant. These cases are discussed further in Chapter 4, para 4.8.2.

O'Sullivan v Williams

In *O'Sullivan v Williams* [1992] 3 All ER 385, referred to *above* (para 5.2.2), although the court did not need to, and did not, decide that the second plaintiff, being the first plaintiff's girlfriend, who was in possession of the car at the time it was damaged, had a sufficient possessory interest, the indications are that the Court of Appeal would have so held if this point was actually in issue. Fox LJ said (at p 387): "The second plaintiff never had legal ownership of the car. At the time of the accident, however, she was authorised by the first plaintiff to use the car and had control of it. I will assume that she had a possessory title at the material time". The second plaintiff's claim was for damages for the inconvenience which she personally suffered by not being able to continue using the first plaintiff's car. The first plaintiff's claim was for the value of the car (£1,300) and for damages for loss of its use, at the rate of £25 per week. The first plaintiff settled his claims with the defendant. The Court of Appeal held that this had the effect of debarring the plaintiff's separate claim for the damages which she personally had suffered. This aspect of the case is discussed along with the cases dealing with consequential economic loss (in Chapter 4, para 4.8.3), because, although this is a true case of relational economic loss, once the plaintiff has a sufficient possessory interest in the property which the defendant has damaged, the exclusionary rule does not apply, and the plaintiff will not be prohibited from suing for his economic losses.

Transcontainer v Custodian Security—I

In *Transcontainer Express Ltd v Custodian Security Ltd* [1988] 1 Lloyd's Rep 128 (para 5.2.4), the plaintiff, a carrier of bonded goods, had contracted with a third party to transport 400 cases of brandy from France to an address in England. The plaintiff sub-contracted the English leg of the carriage to Crossland Haulage Ltd ('C'), who duly collected the container from the docks and proceeded to try to deliver it to the addressee. This was a Friday afternoon, and the addressee was unable to take delivery until the following Monday. C therefore took the container to the defendant's security park, where the defendant provided a 24-hour security service. The following day the container was stolen from the defendant's premises.

The plaintiff was liable under its contract to pay the seller the value of the lost brandy, and also had to pay the customs duty on it. The plaintiff sought to recover these sums from the defendant. The defendant admitted negligence, but argued that it owed no duty of care to the plaintiff because the plaintiff did not have a possessory or a proprietary interest in the goods at the time of its default. Only the first of these was relevant. The plaintiff contended that it had possession through its sub-contractor, C. The Court of Appeal accepted that it is possible for a person to acquire possession of goods even without having physical control of them: the possession of the agent may be attributed to the principal. However, the court said that the same cannot be said of possession acquired merely by an independent contractor employed by that person. Slade LJ said (at p 133): "Any suggestion that the mere existence of a bailment *ipso facto* confers on the bailee possessory rights against a third party would be misconceived. Much must depend on the particular contractual arrangements between bailor and bailee".

5.2.4   The 'right to possession'

The problem stated

What if the plaintiff was not in actual physical possession of the third party's property at the time it was damaged, but he could have been if he had wanted to? Will such a plaintiff have a sufficient possessory interest to enable him to sue the defendant? The answer would appear to be in the affirmative.

The Jag Shakti

In *Chabbra Corporation Pte Ltd v Jag Shakti (Owners) (The Jag Shakti)* [1986] AC 337 (PC), the plaintiff was the purchaser for value (by way of endorsement) from a pledgee of a bill of lading in respect of certain goods which had been transported on the defendant's ship. This did not give the plaintiff a proprietary interest in the goods, but it did give the plaintiff an immediate right to possession of the goods upon presentation of the bill of lading at the port of discharge. On the ship's arrival at that port, the buyer persuaded the shipowner (in consideration for an indemnity) to release the goods to him without presentation of the bill of lading.

5.2.4 *Relational economic Loss*

The plaintiff sued the shipowner for damages in contract and in the tort of conversion. The question for the court was whether the plaintiff was entitled to the full market value of the goods, or whether it was restricted to the lesser sum which it had paid for the bill of lading. *The Winkfield* [1902] P 42, mentioned *above* (para 5.2.3), is authority that the former of these two measures of damages is available to a bailee in possession. The Privy Council held that this principle also applied to the plaintiff in the present case. Lord Brandon said (at p 345) (emphasis added): "Where a person who has, or *is entitled to have* the possession of goods, is deprived of such possession by the tortious conduct of another person, the proper measure of damages is the full market value of the goods. For this purpose it is irrelevant whether the first person has the general property in the goods as the outright owner of them, or only a special property in them as pledgee, or only possession or *a right to possession* of them as bailee".

Extension too far

It is questionable whether the authorities on bailment do go this far. Indeed, in *The Winkfield* itself, Collins MR, for the whole Court of Appeal, said (at p 60) (emphasis added): "The root principle of the whole discussion is that, as against a wrongdoer, *possession* is title". *The Winkfield*, and cases which have applied its principle, have really been concerned with the measure of damages available to a bailee in possession. Very often the courts have not made the connection between that principle and the relational economic loss cases, where it is also often important to decide whether the plaintiff has a possessory interest. For example, in *The Jag Shakti*, none of those cases was referred to. However, in one of those cases, *Magarine Union GmbH v Cambay Prince Steamship Co Ltd (The Wear Breeze)* [1969] 1 QB 219 Roskill J said (at p 250): "The law of this country is and always has been that an action for negligence in respect of loss or damage to goods cannot succeed unless the plaintiff is, at the time of the tort complained of, the owner of the goods or the person *entitled to possession* of them".

Although the decision in *The Wear Breeze* was expressly approved by the House of Lords in *Leigh and Sillivan Ltd v Aliakmon Ltd (The Aliakmon)* [1986] AC 785, neither it nor *The Aliakmon* should be regarded as definitive of the question whether a 'right to possession' will suffice for the purpose of the exclusionary rule, because in both of these cases the question was whether the plaintiff had a sufficient proprietary interest at the time the goods were damaged, and no question arose as to whether he had 'possession' or 'the right to possession' as, on the facts, both of these possibilities were ruled out.

Transcontainer v Custodian Security—II

The question did, however, arise squarely in the Court of Appeal case of *Transcontainer Express Ltd v Custodian Security Ltd* [1988] 1 Lloyd's Rep 128. The facts are set out *above* (para 5.2.3), and it has been noted that the plaintiff failed to establish that it was in possession of the stolen goods because its sub-bailee was its independent sub-contractor and not its agent. In the alternative, the plaintiff argued that, if it did not have actual possession, the fact that it had the immediate right to possession of the goods gave it 'a possessory title'. This point had not been raised at the trial. The defendant objected to it being raised at this late stage, on appeal. The Court of Appeal upheld the defendant's objection. This means that everything said by the Court of Appeal on the 'right to possession point' is *obiter*. However, the court said that, on authority and in principle, it would be right to say that it is possible for a right to possession to suffice as a sufficient possessory interest. The Court of Appeal was impressed by Roskill J's above-quoted *dictum* in *The Wear Breeze*, and the approval of that decision by the House of Lords in *The Aliakmon*.

In principle the Court of Appeal said that it is quite possible for a person to create a relationship of bailor and bailee or, as in this case, sub-bailor and sub-bailee between himself and another party such as to confer on the bailee or the sub-bailee possession of the goods and on himself the immediate right to possession of them, even though he himself has at no time had physical control of the goods. Whether this situation exists in any case will depend on the contractual arrangements between the bailor or sub-bailor, on the one hand, and the bailee or sub-bailee on the other. They said that if the contractual arrangements between the plaintiff and C did give the plaintiff the right to take, or retake, possession of the goods at any time, they would be reluctant to hold that the law is such that the plaintiff could have no rights to recover its damages in this case from the defendant or, it would seem, from anyone else.

Comment

By way of comment, it could be said that, while this makes good sense from the point of view of justice, it really does no more than beg the question as to whether liability should or should not be imposed on the negligent defendant, and it does not answer the question whether the plaintiff had a sufficient possessory interest for the purposes of the exclusionary rule. After all, in *The Aliakmon* itself, the plaintiff was left without a remedy against anyone (see para 5.8), but the House of Lords was unmoved. At the time when the damage occurred to the goods at sea, the plaintiff, by contract, bore the risk, but did not have title. The seller had title at that time, but he had no interest in suing, because he suffered no loss. Normally the buyer would have had title to the goods while they were being shipped, by being named in the bill of lading. In this case, due to a series of complicated changes to the contractual arrangements, this was not the case. The House of Lords was urged to cure the manifest injustice which would otherwise be caused to the plaintiff by applying "the theory of transferred loss" (which is discussed *below* in para 5.6.2), whereby the defendant shipowner would simply be held liable to the buyer in damages for the loss of which the shipowner would ordinarily be held liable to the goods owner. The House of Lords refused to do this, thereby leaving the plaintiff without a claim against anyone, notwithstanding that, on delivery by the shipowner of the goods which the shipowner had damaged in transit, the plaintiff acquired title to them. The rule is that such title must exist at the date when the damage is caused, and not subsequently.

Scottish Helicopter v United Technologies

The question of 'a right to possession' also arose in *North Scottish Helicopters Ltd v United Technologies Corporation Inc* 1988 SLT 77. The plaintiff had leased a helicopter from a finance company. The plaintiff had the unrestricted use of the helicopter, but was bound to indemnify the finance company against destruction or damage to it. The plaintiff allowed the helicopter to be used by its subsidiary company, during which time the helicopter was damaged by the defendant's negligence. The court held that the subsidiary company had a sufficient possessory interest as bailee, but the point that interests us here is whether the plaintiff also had such an interest. The plaintiff was not in possession, but it had the right to call for possession, and to use the helicopter at any time, because its subsidiary company was wholly under its control. The court relied on the *dictum* of Lord Brandon in *The Jag Shakti*, quoted *above*, and held that the plaintiff did have a sufficient interest.

The role of control

These cases demonstrate that, in appropriate cases, ie where the terms of the relationship of the plaintiff, as bailee, and the person in actual possession, as sub-bailee, are such that the plaintiff still retains control over the property which a third party had bailed to the plaintiff, the plaintiff will most probably be able to establish a sufficient possessory interest for the purposes of the exclusionary rule, notwithstanding that he did not have actual possession of the goods at the time they were damaged. To this extent, it can be said that there has been an extension to the ambit of the qualifying condition, namely "possession" (see the quotation from Collins MR, *above*), required to bring the principle of *The Winkfield* into play and that the concept of "a possessory interest" for the purposes of the exclusionary rule in relational economic loss has been extended accordingly.

Relationship with sub-bailee

On a practical level, it should be noted that, in approaching the 'right to possession' question, it is the relationship between the plaintiff and his sub-bailee that is crucial, not the relationship between the plaintiff and the third party whose property has been damaged. In *North Scottish Helicopters* the court seems to have attributed too much significance to the fact that the plaintiff originally obtained possession of the helicopter from the finance company under a lease, the terms of which were such as to make the plaintiff's position (at p 81) "analogous to that of a charterer of a vessel by demise". The only significance of this fact should be to see whether the plaintiff could have had a sufficient proprietary interest in the helicopter to give him title to sue the defendant. However, with the plaintiff being out of actual physical possession, this fact should not have impacted on the question whether the plaintiff's right to possession of the helicopter *vis-à-vis* its subsidiary company amounted to a sufficient "possessory interest" for the purposes of the exclusionary rule. Only the terms of the contract between the plaintiff and his sub-bailee are relevant to that question.

5.2.5 Not displaced by the 'threefold test'

In *Londonwaste Ltd v Amec Civil Engineering Ltd* (1997) 53 Con LR 66, the facts of which are set out in Chapter 4, para 4.3.2, the plaintiff's counsel argued that the 'threefold test' enunciated by the House of Lords in such cases as *Caparo Industries plc v Dickman* [1990] 2 AC 605 (see Chapter 3, para 3.3.2), while not displacing the relational economic loss exclusionary rule altogether, was the overriding test; and that if it were applied, the plaintiff in *Londonwaste* would have succeeded. First, the plaintiff's counsel placed reliance on Lord Oliver's statement in *Murphy v Brentwood District Council* [1991] 1 AC 398 (at p 485), that ". . . it is far from clear from these decisions [ie some of the leading relational economic loss cases] that the reason for the plaintiff's failure was simply that the only loss sustained was 'economic'. Rather they seem to have been based either on the remoteness of the damage as a matter of direct causation or, more probably, on the 'floodgates' argument of the impossibility of containing liability within any acceptable bounds if the law were to permit such claims to succeed. . . . The essential question which has to be asked in every case . . . is whether the relationship between the plaintiff and the defendant is . . . of sufficient 'proximity' that it imposes on the [defendant] a duty to take care to avoid or prevent the loss which has in fact been sustained".

The judge, John Hicks QC, sitting as an Official Referee, responded to this submission by saying:

> I am by no means persuaded that this passage was intended to promulgate a general test which would override the rule [in relational economic loss cases], and I am clear that it cannot do so. First, and most simply, Lord Oliver cited the rule itself and the authorities for it without any suggestion that they are no longer the law. Secondly, a panel of seven members had assembled in order to consider whether the House should depart from one of its own previous decisions (ie *Anns v Merton London Borough Council* [1978] AC 728), as it unanimously did [see Chapter 7, para 7.3.1]. It cannot be supposed that another case (*Leigh and Sillivan Ltd v Aliakmon Ltd* [1986] AC 785), entirely consistent with the decision in *Murphy*'s case itself, was deprived of its standing in such an oblique way by a passage in one speech. Thirdly, *Murphy* was the culmination of a series of House of Lords decisions of which the thrust was entirely inimical to the supposition that the development of the law of negligence can be shaped simply by the application of broad propositions, rather than arising 'incrementally and by analogy with established categories'. Fourthly, even if the question of proximity is 'the essential question to be asked in every case', a judge is not free to respond by the light of nature if the answer is determined by authority governing the relationship in issue. The 'threefold test', of which proximity is the second limb, is for use in grappling with new questions, not a justification for altering the answers to old ones.

Secondly, the plaintiff's counsel submitted that the plaintiff in the present case was owed a duty of care "on the *Marc Rich* approach". He placed reliance on the passage in Lord Steyn's speech in *Marc Rich and Co AG v Bishop Rock Marine Co Ltd* [1996] 1 AC 211, in which Lord Steyn approved the statement by Saville LJ in the Court of Appeal that "whatever the nature of the harm sustained by the plaintiff, it is necessary to consider the matter not only by inquiring about foreseeability, but also by considering the nature of the relationship between the parties; and to be satisfied that in all of the circumstances it is fair, just and reasonable to impose a duty of care".

In rejecting the plaintiff's counsel's submission that a duty of care was owed to the plaintiff in the present case "on the *Marc Rich* approach", Judge Hicks said:

> I do not agree that any such conclusion can be drawn. In *Marc Rich* the courts were addressing the question whether a duty of care existed in what, so far as authority or its absence went, was a novel situation. As pointed out above, those are the circumstances in which the 'threefold test' is potentially of assistance. The House of Lords was not concerned with, and did not advert to, situations covered by established authority. Nor do Lord Steyn's words in any way encourage the supposition that the distinction between physical damage and economic loss is no longer relevant. When using the words 'whatever the nature of the harm sustained' he was considering and rejecting an argument that proximity and reasonableness were irrelevant to the existence of a duty of care not to cause physical damage—that foreseeability alone was not enough. He was not holding that when proximity or reasonableness were under consideration, the nature of the harm made no difference to the outcome. On the contrary, he said that the materiality of the distinction between direct physical damage and indirect loss was plain.

Comment

While it is submitted that in general terms the judge was right to conclude that the relational economic loss exclusionary rule has not been displaced by the 'threefold test', it is submitted that the whole discussion which his Honour conducted to reach this conclusion was misfounded because the judge was not comparing like with like. The relational economic loss exclusionary *rule* is a rule, principle or concept of law. The 'threefold *test*' is an approach or test which is applicable to ascertain relevant rules, principles or concepts in different circumstances.

Accordingly, it is submitted that the real answer to the plaintiff's counsel's submission should have been that the rules, concepts or principles of law which the House of Lords devised and applied in *Murphy* and *Marc Rich* had no effect on the relational economic loss exclusionary rule which has been applied in such cases as *The Aliakmon*, because each of these cases was concerned with a fact situation in a different category. Furthermore, as noted in Chapter 3, the adoption of a particular test or approach should not dictate the result. If properly applied, the result in any particular case should be the same no matter which of the various tests is applied. Thus, if the threefold test were to be applied in a case like

Londonwaste, the same result could be justified as in all of the preceding relational economic loss cases on the basis that the policy of the law (at least in England) dictates that, where the plaintiff's pure economic loss is parasitic upon or relational to physical damage caused by the defendant to a third person's property in which the plaintiff does not have a proprietary or a possessory interest, it cannot be said that there is a sufficiently close relationship of proximity between the plaintiff and the defendant so as to allow the court to conclude that it is fair, just and reasonable to impose a duty of care on the defendant by way of an application of the threefold test.

5.3 Applications of the exclusionary rule

5.3.1 Personal injury

As it is not possible (at least since the time that slavery was abolished) to have a proprietary or a possessory interest in a person, the existence of the exclusionary rule means that a person cannot recover damages for economic loss suffered by him by the death of, or injury to, a third person, unless recovery of that kind of loss is permitted by a statute. Examples of cases where this has been tried, but where the plaintiff failed, are as follows.

A-G v Perpetual Trustee

In *Attorney-General for New South Wales v Perpetual Trustee Co* [1955] AC 457 (PC) a policeman who was travelling on a tram was badly injured when a car negligently crashed into it. The defendant was the executor of the deceased car driver. The plaintiff was the policeman's employer, suing for the salary and other disability benefits which it had to pay to the plaintiff in consequence of the accident. The court rejected the plaintiff's claim. Viscount Simonds said (at p 484): "It is fundamental that the mere fact that an injury to A prevents a third party from getting from A a benefit which he would otherwise have obtained does not invest the third party with a right of action against the wrongdoer".

Kirkham v Boughey

In *Kirkham v Boughey* [1958] 2 QB 338 the plaintiff worked in Africa, but his wife and children remained in England. While on a home leave visit, he and his wife were injured in a motor accident. He was not injured seriously, but his wife was, and he therefore decided not to return to Africa but to stay in England with his family. He managed to obtain other employment, but at a substantially lower wage. He sued the defendant, who was responsible for the motor accident, for the difference in his wages. The court rejected this claim, relying on *dicta* in the House of Lords in *Best v Samuel Fox & Co Ltd* [1952] AC 716 to the effect that if an employee loses lucrative employment because his employer has been injured in an accident, he cannot recover damages from the person whose negligence caused the employer's injuries.

5.3.1 Relational economic Loss

IRC v Hambrook

In *Inland Revenue Commissioners v Hambrook* [1956] 2 QB 641 the plaintiff's employee, while off duty and riding his own motor cycle, was injured in a collision which was the defendant's fault. The plaintiff paid the officer while he was off work for nearly 10 months. The court held that the plaintiff was not entitled to recover this expenditure from the defendant. The plaintiff's case was based on the ancient right of a master to be compensated for the loss of his servant's services. Denning LJ said (at p 666):

> In my opinion, the action does not lie whenever the relationship of master and servant exists. It only lies when the servant can properly be regarded as a member of the master's household, that is, as part of the family. A servant has long since ceased to be regarded as a slave. It is time he ceased to be looked upon as a chattel. He should be looked upon as a free human being, and not less so when he is a civil servant.

Fifield v Finston

In *Fifield Manor v Sidney S Finston* (1960) 354 P (2d) 1073 (SC of Cal), the plaintiff was a non-profit organisation which had entered into a 'life-care contract' with a Mr Ross, whereby it had agreed to provide to him, in return for an annual premium, all essential medical care which he might require. The defendant negligently injured Ross with his car. Pursuant to its contract, the plaintiff provided essential medical care services for Ross at great expense to the plaintiff. The contract did not contain a subrogation clause. The plaintiff therefore had to bring the action in its own right. The court rejected this claim, saying that it refused to recognise a cause of action based on negligent conduct which rendered the performance of a contract between the plaintiff and a third party more expensive. It will be noted that this case corresponds with the second of the examples given by Lord Penzance in *Simpson & Co v Thomson* (1877) 3 App Cas 279, which is included in para 5.8, *below*.

D'Amato v Badger

In *D'Amato v Badger* (1996) 137 DLR (4th) 129, the plaintiff, Mr D'Amato, owned 50 per cent of Arbor Autobody Repair Shop (1980) Ltd ('Arbor'). The plaintiff also performed physical repairs on vehicles that were brought into the repair shop. One day Mr D'Amato was injured by a car owned by the defendant, Mr Badger. Liability was admitted.

In the accident Mr D'Amato suffered certain injuries, as a result of which he could no longer perform the physical labour required for auto-body repair. He continued to manage, supervise and prepare estimates, but his employer, Arbor, had to engage replacement labour to perform the repair work which Mr D'Amato would otherwise have carried out. In consequence, Arbor suffered a loss of profits of $73,299.

In the Supreme Court of Canada the question was whether the defendant was liable to compensate Arbor for the above-mentioned $73,299. The full complement of all nine judges unanimously answered this question in the negative. Major J, delivering the judgment of the court, said (at p 138):

The facts of this case place it in the category of relational economic loss. Arbor's pure economic loss arises solely because of its relationship with Mr D'Amato. While the two approaches from *Canadian National Railway Co v Norsk Pacific Steamship Co* (1992) 91 DLR (4th) 289 [see para 5.8.2, *below*] differ in principle, they will most often achieve the same result. This is the case in the present appeal as, in my opinion, Arbor cannot succeed under either of the two approaches in *Norsk*.

Arbor cannot succeed in its claim for pure economic loss under the La Forest J approach [see para 5.8.2]. This is a case of contractual relational economic loss. Arbor's loss arises solely because of the contractual relationship between the company and its employee/shareholder, Mr D'Amato. Secondly, there do not appear to be any good policy reasons to depart from this exclusionary rule, if such a rule is to be adopted. La Forest J's analysis calls for a general exclusionary rule, subject to any policy concerns which militate in favour of recovery of relational economic loss. If anything, policy reasons would tend to militate against recovery for this type of loss. If an injury to a key shareholder in a small corporation was held to be sufficient to warrant recovery of pure economic loss, then the indeterminate possibilities with larger corporations are obvious.

A party may have better prospects of recovering pure economic loss under the somewhat broader McLachlin J approach [see para 5.8.2]. However, even using that analysis, Arbor cannot succeed. McLachlin J's theory is based on the *Anns* two-stage test. Arbor must show that the loss was within the reasonable contemplation of the defendant so as to raise a duty of care, and, in addition, that there are no considerations which should limit the scope of the duty, the class of persons to whom it is owed or the damages arising from the breach of the duty. There must also be sufficient proximity between the negligent act and the damage to ground liability.

In *Norsk* McLachlin J listed several factors which are relevant to proximity, namely, the relationship between the parties, physical propinquity, assumed or imposed obligations, and close causal connection. Of these factors, only the last has any relevance in this case. There was no relationship between the defendant and Arbor, nor was there physical propinquity or assumed or imposed obligations. The most that can be said is that the negligence of the defendant caused Arbor's loss. This connection is not direct. In my opinion, there is insufficient proximity in this case to warrant recovery of pure economic loss. In my opinion, the loss was neither foreseeable nor sufficiently proximate to the act of negligence to warrant recovery.

Finally, even if one can say that defendants in the position of the respondent [in this appeal] should have reasonably contemplated persons in the position of Arbor, the second stage of the *Anns* test, dealing with policy reasons to limit recovery, would deny recovery to Arbor. If a company is allowed to recover pure economic loss arising from the loss of a key shareholder and employee, the problem of indeterminacy arises. An injury to one person obviously has a ripple effect, causing economic loss in various forms to a large number of people, both individuals and corporations. To allow recovery in these circumstances would invite similar claims by multi-membered plaintiffs. It would remove the incentive for contracting parties to negotiate on who will bear risk of loss, and for corporations to plan for events such as this, through insurance or otherwise.

Comment

While this decision is in line with authority, it is submitted that in the type of situation which it involved, the Court's statement that "An injury to one person *obviously* has a ripple effect, causing economic loss in various forms to a large number of people, both individuals and corporations", is questionable. The indeterminacy concern requires that the defendant must be able to predict in advance the number of possible claims to which he will be exposed. Where a defendant negligently causes physical injury to a person, and is then sued by that person's employer for the employer's losses through not having been able to benefit from that person's services, it is submitted that it would be unusual to find that, in addition to the employer, there would be a multitude of other contractual relational economic loss claimants also making claims for such losses. While there could clearly be such cases, it is submitted that the answer to the question is not "obvious", as the Supreme Court of Canada has stated in this case. On the other hand, if the answer is "obvious" in this case, then it is submitted that the Supreme Court's judgment should be seen as an affirmation of the exclusionary rule. This point is discussed further in para 5.6.8, *below*.

5.3.2 Property damage

Introduction and leading cases

The variety of circumstances in which one person (the plaintiff) can suffer economic loss in consequence of damage to another person's property by the negligence of another person (the defendant) is practically unlimited. In the first part of the case discussions at the end of this chapter (para 5.8.1), examples are given of some of the leading cases in which the exclusionary rule has been applied, thereby preventing an innocent plaintiff from recovering the economic losses which he suffered when the defendant negligently damaged the property of a third party in circumstances where the plaintiff was depending on the continued existence of that third party's property for the conduct of the plaintiff's affairs.

Other cases

In addition, it is worth noting in brief that the exclusionary rule prevented the plaintiff from recovering its losses in the following cases: *Anglo-Algerian Steamship Co Ltd v The Houlder Line Ltd* [1908] 1 KB 659, where the plaintiff suffered losses through a delay in entering a dock and loading its ship because the defendant had negligently damaged the dock's gates, causing the dock to be closed for several days for repairs; *Chargeurs Réunis Compagnie Française de Navigation à Vapeur v English and American Shipping Co* (1929) 9 LlL Rep 464, where the French Government, which had requisitioned a ship under a charterparty which was not by demise, suffered losses through having to continue paying the hire charges to the owner while the ship was being repaired after being negligently damaged by the defendant; *Electrochrome Ltd v Welsh Plastics Ltd* [1968] 2 All ER 205 (see para 4.5.2), where the plaintiff, whose plating business used copious quantities of water, suffered a loss of profit when the defendant negligently collided with a nearby fire hydrant, which led to the water supply being cut off; *Dynamco Ltd v Holland and Hannen &*

Cubitts (Scotland) Ltd 1972 SLT 38, where the plaintiff suffered loss of profits when the electricity supply cable to their factory was negligently damaged by the defendant building contractors who were working nearby; *Star Village Tavern v Nield* (1976) 71 DLR (3d) 439 (see also para 1.4.3), where the plaintiff suffered a loss of profit at its tavern when business dropped off as a result of the defendant damaging a bridge which linked the tavern with a nearby town; *Gypsum Carrier Inc v The Queen* (1977) 78 DLR (3d) 175, another 'bridge case', which has been noted *above* (para 5.2.2); and *Bethlehem Steel Corp v St Lawrence Seaway Authority* (1977) 79 DLR (3d) 522 (para 1.4.3) where, as a result of a ship running into a lift bridge over a canal, thereby obstructing the canal for some time, one claimant suffered loss of profits on two of its ships which were held up for two weeks and another claimant incurred extra expenditure by transporting its goods overland instead of through the canal, as it had been accustomed to do.

A more recent example is *Londonwaste Ltd v Amec Civil Engineering Ltd* (1997) 53 Con LR 66, the facts of which are set out in Chapter 4, para 4.3.2. The plaintiff—who was the owner of the power station which was put out of operation for two and a half days when the defendant negligently severed the 33*kv* cables which took the electricity away from the power station to the plaintiff's customers—was not able to recover its loss of income during the shut-down period from the defendant because the plaintiff did not own the cables. They were owned by a third party, Eastern Electricity plc, the plaintiff's main customer, and the plaintiff did not have a proprietary interest or an easement in the cables, nor was the plaintiff in possession of the cables: the plaintiff's right to use the cables was purely contractual, under the various agreements which the plaintiff had with Eastern Electricity. It made no difference that the plaintiff had paid a substantial proportion of the cost of the installation of the cables, or that the plaintiff was the exclusive user of the cables (see para 5.2.3, *above*).

Wide ambit of exclusionary rule

In all of these cases, and in the cases in para 5.8.1 at the end of this chapter, the court has held that the defendant owed no duty of care at all to the plaintiff because the plaintiff did not have a proprietary or a possessory interest in the property which the defendant had negligently damaged. It made no difference in these cases that the plaintiff's loss was foreseeable and that the plaintiff was 'proximate' to the defendant or, at least, to the property which the defendant had damaged, or that the plaintiff's losses were suffered in direct consequence of the property damage.

Extreme application of the rule—II

The full rigours of the exclusionary rule can be seen from the case of *Candlewood Navigation Corporation Ltd v Mitsui OSK Lines Ltd (The Mineral Transporter)* [1986] AC 1 (PC), where the plaintiff was actually the owner of the damaged ship and was in possession of it, but was unable to claim for its economic losses resulting from its damage because, at the time of the accident, it was only the time charterer of the ship, having previously let it out to a third party under a bareboat charter; and from *Leigh and Sillivan Ltd v Aliakmon Ltd (The Aliakmon)* [1986] AC 785 (HL), where the application of the exclusionary rule meant that the defendant was not liable to compensate anyone for the property damage which it had caused to goods which were being transported in the third party's ship. At the time the damage was caused, the plaintiff (the buyer) bore the risk, but did not yet have the legal property in the goods. This meant that the plaintiff was unable to sue because of the exclusionary rule and that the seller, whose goods these were, had no interest in suing, because it had suffered no loss. These cases are summarised in para 5.8.1.

Contractual indemnity or insurance

From a contractual point of view, and 'before the event', legal advisers should be astute to advise clients who enter into contracts which are dependent on the continued existence of a third party's property to try to obtain a contractual indemnity from the third party. This is because, where the exclusionary rule is applied, the court simply looks at the terms of the contract between the third party and the plaintiff. If that contract contains such an indemnity, then the third party will be able to recover the plaintiff's economic losses from the defendant and pass them on to the plaintiff. If such an indemnity is not going to be possible, then clients should be counselled on the desirability of obtaining insurance to indemnify them against the possible relational losses which they might suffer in the event of the third party's property being damaged through someone else's negligence.

Conclusion (tort considerations)

From a tort point of view, ie 'after the event', legal advisers acting for the plaintiff in these circumstances should be astute to see whether the plaintiff's case can be brought within one of the established exceptions. If not, consideration should be given to the possibility of trying to push back the frontiers of the exclusionary rule by advancing one or more of the alternative theories which have succeeded in Australia and Canada. These are considered in para 5.6, *below*. It must be said, however, that, at least in English law, the chances of the plaintiff succeeding with such an argument are very faint indeed.

5.3.3 Damage to a financial interest

Sometimes it can happen that the negligent act or omission of the defendant has caused direct economic loss in tort to a corporation and that this, in turn, has caused indirect economic loss to the shareholders, employees and/or creditors of the company. In such circumstances the operation of the exclusionary rule discussed in this chapter, or a rule based on it, should have the effect of the defendant being relieved from owing an independent duty of care in tort to the shareholder, employee or creditor.

Rowling v Takaro

In *Rowling v Takaro Properties Ltd* [1988] AC 473 (see Chapter 8, para 8.2.5), the negligence of the defendant, Mr Rowling, a governmental Minister, in exercising his statutory powers had caused the collapse of a company, Takaro Properties Ltd, in which a Mr Rush had invested a lot of money and, together with his family, held 90 per cent of the shares. After the company's collapse, a receiver appointed by one of the company's creditors took possession of and sold the company's tangible assets.

When it was subsequently established that Mr Rowling had exercised his statutory authority incorrectly, the company and Mr Rush instituted a proceeding against him for their economic losses occasioned through his negligence. The New Zealand Court of Appeal, in *Takaro Properties Ltd v Rowling* [1986] 1 NZLR 22, upheld the company's claim (but the House of Lords reversed it—see para 8.2.5), but rejected Mr Rush's claim because it offended against the exclusionary rule or, more accurately, a rule that the Court devised and applied by analogy with the exclusionary rule. Thus, Cooke P said (at p 70):

> While the *Candlewood* case [ie *Candlewood Navigation Corporation Ltd v Mitsui OSK Lines Ltd* [1986] AC 1—see para 5.8.1] is remote from the present case on the facts, it is right to heed the general statement of Lord Fraser that some limit or control mechanism has to be imposed on the liability of a wrongdoer towards those who have suffered economic damage in consequence of his negligence [see para 1.4.2]. In the kind of situation with which that case was concerned their Lordships limited the scope of the duty at the second stage of Lord Wilberforce's *Anns'* stages [ie the stage of the inquiry where policy considerations are taken into account—see para 3.2.2]. So too here, I think that as a matter of policy it would take the law of negligence unacceptably far to impose on a Minister [Mr Rowling] a duty of care, not merely to the company whose application he was considering, but also to persons interested in the company in various ways, as by shareholding or employment or as creditors.
>
> So wide a vista of liabilities would be opened by such an extension of the law that I cannot think that the legal system is ready for that step. Certainly, harm to persons interested in the company was foreseeable and there was some degree of proximity to them; but, at least at this stage of the evolution of the law, the relationship is not close and direct enough to overcome the indeterminacy fear.

South Pacific Manufacturing v New Zealand Security Consultants

In *South Pacific Manufacturing Co Ltd v New Zealand Security Consultants and Investigations Ltd* [1992] 2 NZLR 282, an insurance company had denied liability under an insurance policy that had been taken out by a limited company because the defendant, a private investigator engaged by the insurer, had reported to the insurer that his investigation revealed that the fire had been started deliberately by someone associated with the insured company. In due course it was established that the fire had not been started deliberately by that person and that the investigator had been negligent in carrying out his investigations and making his report to the insurer.

The insurer's refusal to make payment under the policy caused the insured company to go out of business, and a receiver was appointed by a debenture holder. The receiver sued the insurer. On the first day of that trial the insurer reached a settlement and paid a substantial sum of money to the receiver. That sum was not, however, sufficient to restore the insured company to solvency, or to allow a payment to be made to unsecured creditors or to shareholders.

In the present proceedings the first plaintiff, South Pacific Manufacturing Co Ltd, was a creditor of the insured company. It sued the defendant private investigator for its economic losses consisting of the amount owed to it by the insured company, which sum it could not now recover due to the insured company's demise, which had been caused by the insurer having refused to make payment under the policy by placing reliance on the investigator's report. The second plaintiff, whose cause of action was essentially the same, was a shareholder of the insured company.

The New Zealand Court of Appeal rejected these plaintiffs' cases *in limine* because they offended against the exclusionary rule set out in this chapter or, more correctly, against a similar rule fashioned by analogy. Thus, Cooke P said (at p 299):

> To dispose of what is probably the easiest question first, I think that the claims in the *South Pacific* case, being claims made by a creditor and a shareholder of the insured, fail because, even if the investigators owed a duty of care to the insured, such a duty would not extend to persons financially interested in the insured. The claims are analogous to that made by Mr Rush personally in *Takaro Properties Ltd v Rowling* [see *above*];

and Hardie Boys J said (at p 317):

> In this case [ie the *South Pacific* appeal, as opposed to the *Laing v Mortensen* appeal—see Chapter 7, para 7.6.2], the plaintiffs are not the insured. Even were a duty of care owed to the insured, to extend it to persons having a financial or other interest in the insured would tend to open up an undesirably wide field of liability for which I can see no justification.

5.4 The established exceptions

5.4.1 General average

Bills of lading usually require cargo owners to contribute in general average with the owner of the ship in which the goods have been transported for the cost of repairs to the ship. Sometimes those repairs are necessitated in circumstances where the ship has been damaged, but not the plaintiff's cargo.

The Sucarseco

In 1935 in *The Sucarseco* (1935) 51 LlL Rep 238, the US Supreme Court upheld the plaintiff's claim to recover its general average contribution from the person who had damaged the ship in which the plaintiff's goods were being transported, even though no damage had been done to the plaintiff's goods. This case is summarised in the second part of the cases at the end of this chapter (para 5.8.2). Hughes CJ said (at p 241):

> This is not a case of an attempt to make the tortfeasor liable to another merely because the injured person was under a contract with that other. Here, cargo as well as ship was placed in jeopardy. The claim of the cargo owner [ie the plaintiff] for its general average contribution is not in any sense a derivative claim. It accrues to the cargo owner in its own right because of the cargo owner's participation in the common adventure and the action taken on behalf of the cargo owner to avert a peril with which that adventure was threatened.

Greystoke

This case was followed and applied by the House of Lords on almost identical facts in *Morrison Steamship Co Ltd v Greystoke Castle (Cargo Owners)* [1947] AC 265, which is summarised in para 5.8.2, *below*. This exception is firmly established, but its applicability is obviously limited. The more interesting question for lawyers is whether certain *dicta* in this decision can be used as a springboard for the formulation of a wider principle of recovery of relational economic loss. This is discussed in para 5.4.6, *below*.

The Nicholas H

In *Marc Rich and Co AG v Bishop Rock Marine Co Ltd ('The Nicholas H')* [1996] AC 211, the facts of which are set out in Chapter 9, para 9.7.4 (and, more briefly, in para 5.4.1, *above*), Lord Lloyd, dissenting, argued persuasively that the plaintiffs' claim in tort for the loss of their cargo when the ship sank due to the negligence of a surveyor employed by the defendant classification society in certifying the ship as seaworthy was sustainable on the *"Greystoke principle"*. After noting that the defendant's counsel accepted that the defendant owed a duty of care to the crew of the ship, Lord Lloyd said (at p 226):

> What about the cargo? In some ways the relationship between Mr Ducat [the classification society's surveyor] and the cargo was even closer. For it is a universal rule of maritime law—certainly it is the law of England—that ship and cargo are regarded as taking part in a joint venture. This is the basis on which the whole law of general average rests. This is why, if the temporary repairs at San Juan had been successful, and if the voyage had been completed in safety, the cargo would have had to contribute to the cost of the temporary repairs under Rule XIV of the York Antwerp Rules.

This point is discussed further in para 5.4.6, *below*.

5.4.2 Share fishermen

In *Main v Leask* [1910] SC 772, the plaintiffs were the crew of a fishing boat which had been sunk due to the defendant's negligence. The plaintiffs' remuneration consisted of a one-third share of the profits of the fishing. The Scottish Court of Session held that they were entitled to recover this loss from the defendant.

5.4.3 *Relational economic Loss*

The court's reasoning should be approached with caution because none of the cases on the exclusionary rule was cited and the decision was based almost purely on questions of remoteness of damage. Nevertheless, the decision may well be sustainable, because of the "joint adventure" between the plaintiff and the owner of the boat. Lord Ardwall said (at p 369):

> The members of the crew each suffered a direct and immediate loss through the sinking of the *Gratitude*, that loss being the share of the profits of the joint adventure in which they were engaged, and which was directly caused by the fault of the defenders. I am accordingly unable to hold that the claim of the crew is barred by reason of its remoteness or consequential nature.

5.4.3 Commercial fishermen

If a major oil spill or other form of pollution to the sea should occur, the group of people most likely to suffer economic loss in consequence will be commercial fishermen. In the United States their claims in tort have been upheld against the person who has negligently caused this pollution. In one sense, it could be said that these are not cases of relational economic loss because no third party's property has been damaged, as no one actually owns the sea, but in another sense this is not quite true because, unless the accident occurs in totally open waters, far out at sea, the defendant will usually be accountable to one or more governmental authorities for the costs of cleaning up the pollution it has caused. In practice, these cases are regarded by the courts as falling into the relational economic loss category.

Union Oil v Oppen

This exception was first enunciated in *Union Oil Co v Oppen* (1974) 501 F (2d) 558 (US CA 9th Cir). The plaintiffs were commercial fishermen who used to fish in the waters surrounding the Santa Barbara Channel. The defendant, while drilling for oil in those waters, negligently caused a large spill of crude oil, thereby putting a halt to the plaintiffs' fishing operations. The court upheld the plaintiffs' claims for the losses of profits which they thereby suffered. The court referred with approval to *Main v Leask* and said (at p 567):

> This long recognised rule (the right of fishermen to recover their share of the prospective catch) is no doubt a manifestation of the familiar principle that seamen are the favourites of admiralty and their economic interests are entitled to have fullest possible legal protection. These considerations have given rise to a special right.

The court expressly limited the ambit of this exception by saying (at p 570):

> Our holding in this case does not open the door to claims that may be asserted by those, other than commercial fishermen, whose economic or personal affairs were discommoded by this oil spill. The plaintiffs in the present action lawfully and directly make use of a resource of the sea, *viz* its fish, in the ordinary course of their business. This type of use is entitled to protection from negligent conduct by the defendants in their drilling operations.

This principle was approved in *State of Louisiana, ex rel Guste v M/V Testbank* (1985) 752 F (2d) 1019 (US CA 5th Cir), when the court said (at p 1027): "A substantial argument can be made that commercial fishermen possess a proprietary interest in fish in waters they normally harvest sufficient to allow recovery for their loss".

5.4.4 Other pollution victims

Common law

At common law people other than commercial fishermen who might suffer pure economic loss in consequence of an oil spill or other large-scale act of pollution would not have a claim against the polluter. *State of Louisiana, ex rel Guste v M/V Testbank* (1985) 752 F (2d) 1019 (US CA 5th Cir), which is summarised in para 5.8.1, *below*, provides an example of this principle in practice.

The Merchant Shipping Acts

The Merchant Shipping (Oil Pollution) Act 1971 was enacted to provide for civil liability for oil pollution by merchant ships. It was brought into being pursuant to the International Convention of Civil Liability for Oil Pollution Damage 1969. This Act imposes strict liability on the owner of a ship carrying a cargo of "persistent oil" in bulk (subject to certain limited defences and subject to an overall limit on liability) for damage done by the escape or discharge of any such oil carried by the ship. The Merchant Shipping Act 1974 was passed pursuant to the International Convention on the Establishment of an International Fund for Compensation for Oil Pollution Damage 1971. It provides for the establishment of a fund to provide compensation for those victims of oil pollution damage who have been unable to obtain a complete remedy from the wrongdoing shipowner under the 1971 Act, either because he has been able to set up a statutory defence or because he or his insurers are insolvent. The relevant provisions of both of these Acts have been amended and superseded by s 34 of the Merchant Shipping Act 1988, pursuant to two further International Conventions in 1984 bearing the same names as the two conventions just mentioned. At the time of writing this section had not yet been brought into force.

Although "persistent oil" is not defined, it is accepted as referring only to heavier types of oil, such as crude oil, fuel oil, heavy diesel oil and lubricating oil, as opposed to non-persistent oils, such as gasoline, light diesel oil and kerosene.

Economic loss excluded

Although the 1971 Act (as amended) would (*per* s 1(1)) render the shipowner liable "for any damage caused by contamination resulting from the discharge or escape of oil from the ship" and "for the cost of any measures reasonably taken after the discharge or escape for the purpose of minimising any damage so caused by contamination resulting from the discharge or escape", and although s 3(3) provides that a shipowner's liability under s 1 "for any impairment of the environment [which term does not appear in s 1] shall be taken to be a liability only in respect of any resulting loss of profits and the cost of any reasonable measures of reinstatement actually taken or to be taken", pure economic loss of the type suffered by the unsuccessful claimants in *Testbank* is not covered.

Voluntary compensation schemes

This type of pure economic loss is, however, covered by two voluntary compensation schemes, namely the Tanker Owners Voluntary Agreement concerning Liability for Oil Pollution (TOVALOP) and the Contract Regarding a Supplement to Tanker Liability for Oil Pollution (CRISTAL). Although these are described as voluntary agreements, it is only the decision on whether or not to participate that is voluntary. Having become a party, a shipowner is under a contractual obligation to meet all the terms and conditions of the applicable agreement, including compensating third parties for the pure economic losses suffered in consequence of the shipowner's oil pollution at sea. In practice the TOVALOP Scheme will be more relevant in this type of claim because the CRISTAL Scheme is only a top-up scheme.

Virtually all tankers in the world are entered in the TOVALOP Scheme. As it does not apply where liability is imposed under the Merchant Shipping Act 1971 (as amended), it is the scheme to which a pure economic loss sufferer would look for compensation.

Making a claim against the TOVALOP fund is straightforward. It is not necessary to demonstrate that the tanker owner or charterer was at fault, and there are only a few very limited defences (such as if the incident resulted from an act of war or terrorism). Consequently, compensation can be obtained by claimants without recourse to legal proceedings. The TOVALOP party thereby held liable will not, however, have waived or lost any rights of recovery from any third party whose fault may have caused or contributed to the incident which actually caused the pollution, as the House of Lords' decision in *Esso Petroleum Co Ltd v Hall Russell & Co Ltd* [1989] 1 AC 643 demonstrates.

5.4.5   Integrated unit

In *Domar Ocean Transportation Ltd v M/V Andrew Martin* (1985) 754 F (2d) 616 (US CA 5th Cir), the plaintiff was the charterer of a tug which the plaintiff used to pull certain barges which it owned. One such barge, 'D7', was negligently damaged by the defendant while it was being towed by the tug. The plaintiff was able to deploy the tug elsewhere in its business, but not as profitably as when it was pulling 'D7'. Indeed, the plaintiff had specifically chartered the tug for the purpose of towing 'D7' and the plaintiff had spent US$370,000 of its own money to upgrade the tug for this purpose.

The court upheld the plaintiff's claim for this loss of profit, notwithstanding that, in its capacity as a charterer suing for economic loss, the plaintiff did not have a proprietary interest in the property which the defendant had damaged (ie 'D7'). The court said (at p 619): "Even if the two vessels were not so uniquely designed to work with each other as to exclude other use, they were indisputably so operated that they functioned as an integrated unit. The plaintiff offered its customers the use of 'D7' and the tug as a unit, and not as individual vessels. We are persuaded that the plaintiff had the requisite proprietary interest in the combination".

5.4.6 Common adventure

The 'general average' exception, referred to *above* (para 5.4.1), is based on the fact that the plaintiff and the third party whose property was damaged were engaged in "a common adventure". Hughes CJ used this phrase in *The Sucarseco*, as did Lord Roche in *Greystoke*, and Lord Porter used the expression "a joint adventure". The question arises as to whether this exception is to be restricted to general average contributions, as in *The Sucarseco* and in *Greystoke*, or whether it is of wider application and could, for example, apply in the case of a tug towing a barge. In English law the answer would almost certainly be firmly in the negative. The American case of *Domar Ocean Transportation Ltd v M/V Andrew Martin* (1985) 754 F (2d) 616, mentioned *above*, falls halfway in between. Although the term 'common adventure' was not used, it is clear that the principle involved is very similar. In view of the English courts' strict adherence to the exclusionary rule, it is doubtful whether they would have arrived at the same result.

Ambit of Greystoke and observations in Hedley Byrne

There is practically no discussion in subsequent English decisions as to the ambit of the '*Greystoke* doctrine' of "a common adventure". *Greystoke* is usually only mentioned in the context of referring to the comments made on it by the House of Lords in *Hedley Byrne & Co Ltd v Heller & Partners Ltd* [1964] AC 465. Although the decision in *Hedley Byrne* was unanimous, only three of their Lordships dealt with the significance of the fact that the damage sought to be recovered was purely economic (see para 9.4.4). Lord Hodson (at p 509) said that he found it difficult to see why liability as such should depend on the nature of the damage, and referred to *Greystoke* and, specifically, to Lord Roche's 'lorry example', which is set out in the cases in para 5.8.2, *below*. Lord Pearce (at p 536) referred to *Greystoke* as a decision that economic loss alone, without physical or material damage to support it, can afford a cause of action in negligence by act. Lord Devlin said (at p 518) that *Greystoke* "makes it impossible to argue that there is any general rule showing that financial loss without physical injury to the plaintiff's property is of its nature irrecoverable".

Comments in Candlewood and The Aliakmon

In the light of these observations, and in view of the fact that in *Greystoke* the successful plaintiff's goods had not been physically damaged, the following comment of Lord Fraser in *Candlewood Navigation Corporation Ltd v Mitsui OSK Lines Ltd (The Mineral Transporter)* [1986] AC 1 (PC) is surprising. He said (at p 20) (emphasis added): "That limit [by which he meant the general rule] against recovery of economic loss in tort, and not just the relational economic loss exclusionary rule, was breached by *Hedley Byrne* and *arguably* in the earlier case of *Greystoke*". This is probably indicative that if and when the question comes up again, *Greystoke* will be interpreted very restrictively. It is interesting to note that *Greystoke* is not referred to at all in the subsequent House of Lords' decision in *Leigh and Sillivan Ltd v Aliakmon Ltd (The Aliakmon)* [1986] AC 785. In the Court of Appeal in that case ([1985] 1 QB 350) Oliver LJ (as he then was) said (at p 378) that *Greystoke* is a case which is not easy to classify, and "where it appears that liability rested on the concept of a joint venture". Robert Goff LJ (at p 394) said that he saw *Greystoke* as being a case, not of a generalised right of recovery in negligence for economic loss, but of recovery in a specific instance, namely that there was "a common venture between the shipowners (whose ship was damaged) and the cargo owners (whose cargo was not)". He also said (at p 394) that *Greystoke* "has never been easy to explain".

Comments in Murphy

In *Murphy v Brentwood District Council* [1991] 1 AC 398 Lord Keith, after noting (at p 468) that at the time of *Anns* (1977) the right to recover pure economic loss "did not extend beyond the situation where the loss had been sustained through reliance on negligent misstatements as in *Hedley Byrne*", said: "There is no room for the view that an exception is to be found in *Greystoke*. That case, which was decided on a narrow majority, may, however, be regarded as turning on specialities of maritime law concerned in the relationship of joint adventurers at sea".

Lord Oliver, in contrast to his restrictive view of *Greystoke* in the Court of Appeal in *The Aliakmon* (see *above*), seemed to see *Greystoke* as an illustration of a general point rather than as an obscure exception. After saying (at p 485) that the mere fact that the plaintiff's loss is purely economic does not mean that his claim is bound to fail, he said: "The decision of this House in *Greystoke* demonstrates that the mere fact that the primary damage suffered by a plaintiff is pecuniary is not necessarily a bar to an action in negligence given the proper circumstances, in that case a 'joint venture' interest of shipowners and the owners of cargo carried on board— and if the matter remained in doubt, that doubt was conclusively resolved by the decision of this House in *Hedley Byrne* where Lord Devlin convincingly demonstrated the illogicality of a distinction between financial loss caused directly and financial loss resulting from physical injury to personal property".

Limits of Greystoke

If Lord Roche's 'lorry example', set out in para 5.8.2, *below*, or any variation of it (such as oil being carried in a third party's pipeline which is damaged by the defendant) is to be upheld in English law on the ground that the plaintiff and the lorry owner (or the pipeline owner) were engaged in "a common adventure", the plaintiff's recoverable economic loss will probably be limited to any additional expenses which he personally might have incurred in the transportation of those particular goods to their original ultimate destination; but he will not be entitled to recover any losses which he might have suffered through the resultant delay, nor any losses which he might have suffered through the non-availability of the third party's lorry (or the third party's pipeline) for future transportation of the plaintiff's goods during the period of repair. In Australia and Canada the position is different. The leading cases there are respectively *Caltex Oil (Australia) Pty Limited v The Dredge Willemstad* (1976) 136 CLR 529 and *Canadian National Railway Co v Norsk Pacific Steamship Co* (1992) 91 DLR (4th) 289. As there is not a majority ratio in either of these cases, they are discussed below in section 5.6, Alternative theories.

The Nicholas H

In *Marc Rich and Co AG v Bishop Rock Marine Co Ltd ('The Nicholas H')* [1996] 1 AC 211, the facts of which are considered in Chapter 9, para 9.7.4 (and, more briefly, in para 5.4.1, *above*), Lord Lloyd, dissenting, argued persuasively that the plaintiff's claim in tort for the loss of its cargo on board a ship which had sunk due to the negligence of a surveyor employed by the third defendant ship classification society in incorrectly certifying the ship as seaworthy was recoverable on the 'joint adventure' exception considered in this section. After noting that the defendant's counsel accepted that the defendant owed a duty of care to the crew of the vessel, Lord Lloyd said (at p 226):

> What about the cargo? In some ways the relationship between Mr Ducat [the classification society's surveyor] and the cargo was even closer. For it is a universal rule of maritime law—certainly it is the law of England—that ship and cargo are regarded as taking part in a joint venture. This is the basis on which the whole law of general average rests. This is why, if the temporary repairs at San Juan had been successful, and if the voyage had been completed in safety, the cargo would have had to contribute to the cost of the temporary repairs under Rule XIV of the York Antwerp Rules.

Lord Lloyd then referred in detail to the speeches in *Greystoke*, and continued (at p 227):

> The principle established in the *Greystoke Castle* case is thus directly relevant to the present case. When the Master called in Mr Ducat and thereafter incurred expenditure for the common safety, he was acting as much in the interests and on behalf of the cargo, as of the ship. It seems almost impossible to say, therefore, that, while Mr Ducat owed a duty of care to the ship, he owed no duty of care to the cargo on the ground that the relationship between the parties was insufficiently close. . . . To my mind, the necessary element of proximity was not only present, but established beyond any peradventure. . . . if concern is felt that a decision in favour of the cargo owners would open a wide field of liability, I would reply: 'Not so'. There is an obvious, sensible and

readily defensible line between the surveyor in the present case, where the cargo was on board, and the joint venture was in peril, and a surveyor called in to carry out a periodic survey.

Londonwaste v Amec

In *Londonwaste Ltd v Amec Civil Engineering Ltd* (1997) 53 Con LR 66, the facts of which are set out in Chapter 4, para 4.3.2, the plaintiff's counsel argued that, even if the plaintiff did not have a proprietary or a possessory right in the electricity cables which the defendant negligently severed, the plaintiff should be entitled to sue the defendant for its loss of profits while the plaintiff's power station was out of commission on the ground that the plaintiff and the owner of the cables were involved in a "common adventure" by virtue of the plaintiff being the exclusive user of the cables. In rejecting this argument, the judge, John Hicks QC, sitting as an Official Referee, said:

> I am satisfied that there is no exception to the rule of the nature contended for by the plaintiff's counsel, capable of assisting the plaintiff in this case. In the first place, the ratio decidendi of the decision in the *Greystoke Castle* case was quite plainly confined to the law as to the carriage of goods by sea, and the words of Lord Roche relied upon were obiter. Secondly, Lord Roche himself did not intend his imaginary 'lorry load' illustration to have an application beyond its own immediate field of expenses incurred in the course of carriage of goods by land and exactly analogous to general average expenses, such as the unloading of cargo during repairs. That is the only explanation, as I see it, of his repeated assertion that there is no authority to the contrary.
>
> Thirdly, Lord Denning MR, although prepared to take Lord Roche's words at face value in *SCM (UK) Ltd v WJ Whittall and Son Ltd* [1971] 1 QB 337, did not regard him in *Spartan Steel and Alloys Ltd v Martin and Co (Contractors) Ltd* [1973] QB 27 as justifying the recovery of economic loss not directly consequential upon damage to the plaintiff's property [see Chapter 4, para 4.3.2]. Fourthly, McLachlin J in *Canadian National Railway Co v Norsk Pacific Steamship Co* (1992) 91 DLR (4th) 289 accepted the *Greystoke Castle* exception as being confined in English (and American) law to maritime cases [see para 5.6.3, *below*]. Her extension of it to the case before her was part of the open-ended investigation of proximity which she considered that Canadian law permitted and, indeed, required, but which is not open to me.

5.5 Rationale of the exclusionary rule

5.5.1 Introduction

Fundamental distinction

The exclusionary rule with which we are concerned in this chapter is not simply an exclusion of claims for economic loss *per se*. It is a rule which excludes 'relational' economic loss suffered by a plaintiff in consequence of injury to a third party or damage to a third party's property. This distinction is fundamental towards understanding the rationale of, or the policy considerations underlying, the existence of this exclusionary rule, both in its own right and as compared to other exclusionary rules which apply in other economic loss situations.

Distinct from the rule in 'The Albazero'

The appreciation of the importance of the fact that the exclusionary rule in this category of case derives from the plaintiff's loss being related to, parasitic upon or having occurred in consequence of injury to a third party or damage to a third party's property is enhanced by comparing this exclusionary rule with an 'inclusionary' rule, which is often referred to as 'the rule in *The Albazero*'.

In *Albacruz (Cargo Owners) v Albazero (Owners) ('The Albazero')* [1977] AC 774, the *Albacruz* had been chartered by a charterer (the plaintiff) from its owners (the defendants) under a time charter. On one voyage a charter of crude oil was shipped on the *Albacruz* under a bill of lading naming the plaintiff as consignee, so that the goods were deliverable to the plaintiff's order. The plaintiff thereafter endorsed the bill of lading to the actual purchaser (the cargo owners), so that, from that time onwards, the property in the cargo no longer vested in the plaintiff but in the cargo owners.

In the course of the voyage, the *Albacruz* and its cargo became a total loss owing to breaches of the charterparty by the defendant (the shipowner). The plaintiff brought the present action against the defendant for breach of the time charter, and sought to make the defendant liable for the full value of the cargo that had been lost. The plaintiff's claim suffered from the defect that, at the time the goods were lost, the plaintiff was no longer the owner of the cargo, and therefore suffered no loss itself by reason of the non-delivery of the cargo at its destination. Consequently, although the plaintiff technically had a right of action against the defendant under the bill of lading, the practical effect of that right was worthless because, having suffered no loss, the plaintiff was not entitled to recover damages from the defendant for the defendant's breach of the contract.

Ultimately the plaintiff's claim failed for technical reasons concerned with bills of lading. However, the House of Lords went out of its way to endorse the fact that, in appropriate circumstances, English law does recognise exceptions to the general rule that a plaintiff suing a defendant in an action for breach of contract can recover only the actual loss that he has himself sustained. One such example that their Lordships recognised is the right, which was given effect to in *The Winkfield* [1902] P 42 (see para 5.2.3 and Chapter 4, para 4.8.2), to sue for loss or damage to his bailor's goods even though he cannot be compelled by his bailor to do so and is not himself liable to the bailor for the loss or damage. Recognition was also afforded to the so-called rule in *Dunlop v Lambert* (1839) 6 Cl&F 600, in which the House of Lords held (at a time before the passing of the Bills of Lading Act 1855) that a consignor of goods by ship could recover the full loss of goods lost at sea through the shipowner's negligence, even if the consignor was not the owner of the goods at the time of their loss, so long as the goods were being carried for the consignor under a contract between the consignor and the shipowner; and that the consignor would thereafter be accountable to the true owner for the proceeds of the judgment.

Although their Lordships recognised that the rule in *Dunlop v Lambert* was an anomaly, which could not be explained as being part of the law of trusts, because it has never been suggested that the consignor's right of action against the carrier for breach of contract constitutes trust property, or that he could be compelled by a Court of Equity to exercise his right of action for the benefit of those persons who had in fact suffered actual loss as if they were beneficiaries under a trust because their rights arise only when the consignor has recovered judgment, Lord Diplock, delivering the unanimous decision of the House, said (at p 847):

> ... the rule extends to all forms of carriage including carriage by sea itself where no bill of lading has been issued; and there may still be occasional cases in which the rule would provide a remedy where no other remedy would be available to a person sustaining loss which, under a rational legal system, ought to be compensated by the person who caused it.

Thus, it would appear that, despite the general rule that a plaintiff can recover in an action only the actual loss that he himself has sustained, a plaintiff may exceptionally sue in his own name to recover a loss which he has not suffered, but thereafter he will be personally accountable for any damages so recovered to the person who has in fact suffered the loss. The type of situation in which it might be appropriate to make the exception applicable would be a case in which the plaintiff, as the party who has undoubtedly been wronged (eg because the defendant has breached a contract with the plaintiff), has suffered no loss, but the person who has suffered the damage caused by the defendant's wrongful act did not have a contract with the defendant. In these circumstances, if the party with the contractual right to sue the defendant is prevented from doing so simply because he did not suffer a loss, the defendant, as a wrongdoer in law, would escape scot-free, thereby undermining the law's policy of general deterrence towards contract-breakers and tortfeasors.

This situation needs to be contrasted with the scenario in any relational economic loss claim, where the defendant will, in the first instance, have caused a direct physical injury to a third party or damage to that third party's property and will therefore not get off scot-free because he will have had to compensate that third party for his personal loss before being concerned with the claim of the more remote relational economic loss plaintiff. In this type of situation the courts do not feel the same need to fill a gap in the law as Lord Diplock expressed in the passage cited *above* in his speech in *The Albazero*.

Linden Gardens v Lenesta Sludge

A more recent example of the application of '*The Albazero* principle' is the House of Lords' decision in *Linden Gardens Trust Ltd v Lenesta Sludge Disposals Ltd* [1994] 1 AC 85. This decision was concerned with two separate appeals. In the second of these, *St Martins Property Corporation Ltd v*

Sir Robert McAlpine Ltd, the first plaintiff, St Martins Property Corporation Ltd ('Corporation'), was the developer of a large multi-use commercial and residential property complex. It entered into a building contract with the defendant building contractors (McAlpine) pursuant to a contract which contained a clause prohibiting the employer (the first plaintiff) from assigning the (benefit of the) building contract without the contractor's (the defendant's) consent. During the course of construction the plaintiff assigned the benefit of the building contract to a sister company, St Martins Holdings Limited, the second plaintiff ('Investment').

A few years later, after the building works had been completed, part of the development was found to be leaking. It was repaired at great cost. This cost was borne entirely by Investment. In the present action, both Corporation and Investment sued McAlpine for breach of contract, alleging that the leaks in the building were caused by breaches of contract by McAlpine occurring after the date of assignment of the contract to Investment. The loss claimed was the cost of the repair work.

The House of Lords held, first, that Investment had no cause of action against the defendant because the assignment to Investment had taken place in contravention of the prohibition against assignment without the consent of McAlpine, which had never been sought or given. It was common ground that, if the attempted assignment by Corporation of its rights under the contract to Investment was ineffective, Corporation retained those rights and was entitled to judgment against McAlpine for McAlpine's breach of the contract. The problem here was that Corporation had suffered no loss because all of the repair costs had been borne by Investment, and the general rule in English law is that a plaintiff can recover damages only for his own loss.

Their Lordships said that, while they appreciated the logic of this argument, they were not going to let it render Corporation's claim nugatory. Thus, Lord Browne-Wilkinson said (at p 112): "On any view, the facts of this case bring it within the class of exceptions to the general rule to which Lord Diplock referred in *The Albazero*". Lord Browne-Wilkinson then referred extensively to Lord Diplock's speech in *The Albazero* and continued (on p 114):

> In my judgment the present case falls within the rationale of the exceptions to the general rule that a plaintiff can only recover damages for his own loss. The contract was for a large development of property which, to the knowledge of both Corporation and McAlpine [the defendant], was going to be occupied, and possibly purchased, by third parties and not by Corporation itself. Therefore it could be foreseen that damage caused by a breach [of the contract] would cause loss to a later owner, and not merely to the original contracting party, Corporation. . . . McAlpine had specifically contracted that the rights of action under the building contract *could* not without McAlpine's consent be transferred to third parties who became owners or occupiers and might suffer loss. In such a case, it seems to me proper, as in the case of the carriage of goods by land, to treat the parties as having entered into the contract on the footing that

Corporation would be entitled to enforce contractual rights for the benefit of those who suffered from defective performance but who, under the terms of the contract, could not acquire any right to hold McAlpine liable for breach. It is truly a case in which the rule provides 'a remedy where no other would be available to a person sustaining loss which under a rational legal system ought to be compensated by the person who has caused it' [*per* Lord Diplock in *The Albazero*].

White v Jones

In *White v Jones* [1995] 2 AC 207, Lord Goff noted the obvious similarity between the type of situation in which the principle in *The Albazero* is applicable and the situation in *White v Jones*, where the intended beneficiary was the third party seeking to recover damages for a loss which the contracting party, the testator, would not himself have suffered. Lord Goff rejected the application of *The Albazero* principle as the solution to the problem in *White v Jones*, because the main limitation of *The Albazero* principle is that the third party who has suffered the loss is not able to compel the contracting party to sue for his benefit if the contracting party refuses to do so, or to transfer the contracting party's right of action to him. This fact led Lord Goff to conclude that the extension of *The Albazero* principle to cases like *White v Jones* would be of limited value because the family relationship might be such that the executors might be unwilling to assist the disappointed beneficiary by pursuing a claim against the solicitors for his benefit.

5.5.2 Three policy considerations

The formulation of any rule in the tort of negligence needs to take into account three major policy considerations, namely the need to do justice to innocent plaintiffs, the practicality of trying to do justice to all potential claimants and the need to deter potential defendants from behaving negligently in particular situations. These considerations will always be interrelated and the court will, essentially, be carrying out a delicate balancing exercise in which it has to be recognised that it will not always be possible to satisfy everyone. Sometimes, one or more legitimate aims of the law has to be discarded in order to achieve another aim which, in the circumstances, is considered to be more beneficial overall. For example, in *Leigh and Sillivan Ltd v Aliakmon Ltd (The Aliakmon)* [1986] AC 785 (HL), in refusing to make an exception to the exclusionary rule to cover the peculiar type of contract which the plaintiff buyer had made with the seller of goods which the defendant shipper had damaged at sea, Lord Brandon said (at p 816): "If such detraction were to be permitted in one particular case, it would lead to attempts to have it permitted in a variety of cases, and the result would be that the certainty which the application of the general rule provides would be seriously undermined. Yet certainty of the law is of the utmost importance, especially, but by no means only, in commercial matters. I therefore think that the general rule ought to apply to a case like the present one".

5.5.3   Justice

Plaintiff only a secondary victim

So far as justice to the plaintiff is concerned, one obviously feels that a person who has suffered loss by being the innocent victim of another person's negligence ought to have the right to recover compensation from the wrongdoer. However, in this type of case the plaintiff will not be the primary victim, but only a secondary victim. A pre-condition of the plaintiff's claim is that a third party has been injured or that a third party's property has been damaged by the defendant's negligent act. The plaintiff's loss will thus result primarily, or directly, from his relationship with that third party, and only secondarily, or indirectly, from the defendant's negligent conduct. The 'no injustice argument' therefore dictates that, as the plaintiff voluntarily entered into that relationship with the third party, knowing that there was always a risk that the third party could be injured or that the third party's property could be damaged by someone else, he cannot complain if and when this occurs and he has not taken adequate steps to protect himself against his losses.

Voluntarily assuming a risk

In the Court of Appeal in *The Aliakmon* [1985] 1 QB 350, Oliver LJ, in commenting on the decision in the early leading case of *Simpson & Co v Thomson* (1877) 3 App Cas 279, HL (Sc), took up this theme by saying (at p 380): "There was, in that case, a very good policy reason for denying direct liability to the underwriter. The insurer of goods, by his contract, puts himself consciously and deliberately in the way of the risk. He brings himself within the ambit of foreseeable risk only by a contract which is designed to have that very effect. What causes his loss is not the damage to the goods, but the contractual obligation which he has assumed and the insistence by his insured on the performance of that obligation". He continued (at p 381): "Is there any reason why a different principle should be applicable to the person who, although not an insurer, suffers loss because, by some other contract, he assumes the risk of damage to goods? For my part, I see none. His loss, if the goods are damaged, stems from that contractual obligation, just as the insurer's obligation stems from the contract into which he has entered".

Contractual allocation of risk

Similar comments were made by the House of Lords in this case. Lord Brandon said (at p 818): "English law does, in all normal cases, provide a fair and adequate remedy for loss of, or damage to goods, the subject matter of c.i.f. or c. and f. contract. The buyers in this case could easily, if properly advised at the time when they agreed to the variation of the original c. and f. contract, have secured to themselves the benefit of such a remedy". This was also the view of the minority judges in the Supreme Court of Canada in *Canadian National Railway Co v Norsk Steamship Co* (1992) 91 DLR (4th) 289 in relation to the facts of that case. Notwithstanding that the plaintiff was, to the defendant's knowledge, the primary user of the third party's bridge which the defendant damaged, and notwithstanding that the plaintiff owned track on both sides of the bridge, the minority did not think that it was unjust to reject the plaintiff's claim for its relational economic losses suffered through the bridge's closure, because the licence agreement between the plaintiff and the bridge owner did not confer any right on the plaintiff to recover such losses from the bridge owner. La Forest J said (at p 296): "The contract indicates that the parties either did, or ought to have considered the issue of allocating the risk of the bridge's closing as a result of a ship collision. Indeed, the licence agreement between them did just that".

5.5.4   Practicality

The indeterminacy problem

Reference has been made in para 1.4.3, *above* (and again in para 9.3.3) to the oft-quoted *dictum* of Cardozo CJ in *Ultramares Corporation v Touche* (1931) 255 NY 170, in which he said that it would have been wrong to hold the defendant accountants in that case liable to creditors and investors to whom the trading company (their client) chose to show the accounts prepared by them, because this would have exposed the defendant to "a liability in an indeterminate amount for an indeterminate time to an indeterminate class". What this means in practice is that the courts must avoid devising rules of law which could have this effect. It will not be sufficient if, after the event, it is apparent that there is no indeterminacy problem on the facts of the particular case. 'Determinate' in this context means being able to determine the scope of the defendant's exposure to liability in advance of the event which causes the plaintiff's loss. Where that event is an accident, this question is practically difficult to answer. Nowhere is this difficulty more apparent than in the field of relational economic loss, because, in a modern market economy, relational losses are apt to occur as a result of practically every accident causing property damage in the commercial sphere.

Examples of indeterminacy

For example, in *State of Louisiana, ex rel Guste v M/V Testbank* (1985) 752 F (2d) 1019 (US CA 5th Cir) (summarised in para 8.1), when two ships collided in the Mississippi River, and caused pollution to the water, 41 law suits were filed against the owners of the ships by such diverse plaintiffs as commercial fishermen, shipowners suffering losses from delays or rerouting, wholesale and retail seafood enterprises not actually engaged in fishing, seafood restaurants and bait shops; and in *Bethlehem Steel Corp v St Lawrence Seaway Authority* (1977) 79 DLR (3d) 522 (see paras 1.4.3 and 5.3.2, *above*), nine separate claimants apart from the bridge owner filed claims against the owners of the ship which damaged the bridge and thereby obstructed the canal for some time. All of these claimants were users of the canal who suffered financial loss when it was closed. On the other hand, in *Canadian National Railway Co v Norsk Pacific Steamship Co* (1992) 91 DLR (4th) 489, there were only four plaintiffs besides the bridge owner, because this was purely a rail bridge, and they were the only four users of it; and in *Caltex Oil (Australia) Pty Ltd v The Dredge Willemstad* (1976) 136 CLR 529 there was only one plaintiff in addition to the owner of the damaged pipeline.

Devising a rule

The problem in devising a rule of law in this field is that it will nearly always be a question of pure fortuity as to whether there will be a large or a small number of secondary loss sufferers when the defendant negligently damages a third party's property. In other words, the size of the class of possible secondary claimants will be indeterminate before the accident occurs. It is not sufficient that the size of this class will be known after the accident has occurred, because that would rob the rule of the predictive value, or the certainty, which a rule of law needs to have in order to enable all parties who might be affected by it to take legal advice in advance of basing their proposed actions in reliance on it.

Inability to predict

It is the manifest inability of being able to predict, or determine in advance, how many relational economic loss claims a defendant might face when he injures a third party's property that has led to the imposition of the exclusionary rule. This difficulty has been recognised from the very earliest cases. For example, in the first leading case, *Cattle v The Stockton Waterworks Company* (1875) LR 10 QB 453 (summarised in para 5.8.1), the court said (at p 457) that if it were to uphold the plaintiff's claim for loss suffered by him when his tunnelling contract on a third party's land became less valuable after the defendant flooded that land, this would "establish an authority for saying that, in such a case as *Fletcher v Rylands* (1868 Law Rep 3 HL 330), the defendant would be liable, not only to an action by the owner of the drowned mine, but also to an action by every workman and person employed in the mine who, in consequence of its stoppage, made less wages than he would otherwise have done". The court recognised that it could be unjust to deny a remedy to all such persons, but said: "Courts of Justice should not allow themselves, in the pursuit of perfectly complete remedies for all wrongful acts, to transgress the bounds which our law, in a wise consciousness of its limited powers, has imposed on itself, of redressing only the proximate and direct consequences of wrongful acts".

Practicality

Thus, the rationale of the rule, when it was first formulated, was not logic, but common sense or practicality. This is further borne out by the examples given by Lord Penzance in the House of Lords in *Simpson & Co v Thomson* (1877) 3 App Cas 279, HL (Sc), which is summarised in para 5.8.1, *below*; and by Scrutton LJ's comment in *Elliott Steam Tug Co Ltd v Shipping Controller* [1922] 1 KB 127 (at p 140): "The charterer in collision cases does not recover profits, not because the loss of profits during repairs is not the direct consequence of the wrong, but because the common law 'rightly or wrongly' does not recognise him as able to sue for such an injury to his merely contractual rights".

In *Weller & Co v Foot and Mouth Disease Research Institute* [1966] 1 QB 569 Widgery J expressed the practicality of the exclusionary rule by saying (at p 585): "The world of commerce would come to a halt and ordinary life would become intolerable if the law imposed a duty on all persons at all times to refrain from any conduct which might foreseeably cause detriment to another", as did Lord Fraser in *Candlewood Navigation Corporation Ltd v Mitsui OSK Lines Ltd (The Mineral Transporter)* [1986] AC 1 (PC) when he said, of the passages quoted above from *Cattle*: "It is apparent from that citation that the court regarded the rule as a pragmatic one dictated by necessity". He then referred to Lord Penzance's examples in *Simpson* and said (at p 17): "These two cases show that the justification for denying a right of action to a person who has suffered economic damage through injury to the property of another is that, for reasons of practical policy, it is considered to be inexpedient to admit his claim". These cases are summarised in para 5.8.1, *below*.

The 'floodgates' fear

The policy consideration which Lord Fraser had in mind is variously known as the 'floodgates' argument, or the 'spectre of indeterminate liability' argument. He said (at p 19): "The plaintiff's argument, if accepted, would have far-reaching consequences, which would run counter to the accepted policy of the law. If claims for economic loss by sub-charterers are to be admitted, why not also claims by any person with a contractual interest in any goods being carried in the damaged vessel, and by any passenger in her who suffers economic loss by reason of the delay attributable to the collision? An exceedingly wide, new range of liability would be opened up. Their Lordships accordingly reject this submission". In *Electrochrome Ltd v Welsh Plastics Ltd* [1968] 2 All ER 205 (see also para 4.5.2), Geoffrey Lane J made similar remarks in relation to the plaintiff's claim for loss of profits when it had to shut its factory after the defendant negligently collided with a fire hydrant belonging to a third party, thereby causing the plaintiff's supply of water to be cut off, when he said (at p 208): "It is perfectly true that it may seem inequitable that a person who has undoubtedly suffered loss in this manner should have no right of action against the person who started off the train of events, but one only has to consider the possible results if such an action were to succeed to realise that this is one of the cases where public convenience and interest demand that the right of action must stop short. One can imagine a whole series, maybe hundreds, of actions being brought against the defendants based on this type of negligence".

A total ban

In the light of these considerations, the proponents of the exclusionary rule thus prefer to deny relief to all relational economic loss sufferers rather than to make exceptions in those cases where, as it so turns out, the class of plaintiffs is small, or where to deny relief would seem to be particularly unjust. The High Court of Australia, in *Caltex Oil (Australia) Pty Ltd v The Dredge Willemstad* (1976) 136 CLR 529, and the Supreme Court of Canada, in *Canadian National Railway Co v Norsk Pacific Steamship Co* (1992) 91 DLR (4th) 489, have, however, abandoned this rigidity (see para 5.6, *below*).

5.5.5 Deterrence

Moral wrongdoing

In *Donoghue v Stevenson* [1932] AC 562 Lord Atkin said (at p 580) that liability for negligence is based upon "a general public sentiment of moral wrongdoing for which the offender must pay". It would be wrong, therefore, for rules of law to exist under which defendants could behave negligently with impunity. The law of negligence should, accordingly, have as one of its aims a corrective, or a deterrent, effect with regard to the liability which can befall persons who behave negligently.

Adequate deterrent

It may legitimately be questioned whether the relational loss exclusionary rule defeats this aim. It is submitted that it does not. It must be remembered that the claims which the relational loss exclusionary rule excludes are, by definition, claims of persons who have only suffered a loss because the defendant has negligently injured a third party or damaged a third party's property. While the defendant might not be liable to compensate the secondary victim, he will, subject to any defences which he might be able to raise in the particular circumstances, be liable to compensate a third party whom he has injured, or whose property he has damaged.

The defendant's potential liability to the third party, or the primary victim, of the defendant's negligence should serve as a sufficient incentive to the defendant to take care with respect to his acts or omissions which could injure other persons or their property. In the 'bridge cases', for example, the defendant will have had to pay substantial damages to the bridge owner for the physical damage which he caused. Of course, in addition, there will usually be other people, maybe a large number of them, who have suffered relational economic losses in consequence of the property owner's primary damage, but the defendant's exposure to a substantial damages claim from the bridge owner should put him on his guard to take care.

Comparison with other exclusionary rules

While the deterrent effect on the defendant's behaviour might be greater if the defendant knew that he could be liable to compensate those secondary victims as well, the existence of the defendant's liability to compensate the primary victim for the damage to his person or property means that it is fair to say that the rule which excludes relational economic loss claims does not ignore the deterrent effect of tort law. This is an important difference between the justification for this exclusionary rule and the exclusionary rule which the House of Lords so roundly endorsed in *Murphy v Brentwood District Council* [1991] 1 AC 398 in relation to an economic loss claim in tort by a purchaser of a defective product against its manufacturer.

5.6   Alternative theories

5.6.1   Introduction

General

It has been noted *above* that the exclusionary rule has been departed from in the High Court case of *Caltex Oil (Australia) Pty Ltd v The Dredge Willemstad* (1976) 136 CLR 529 and in the High Court of Canada in *Canadian National Railway Co v Norsk Pacific Steamship Co* (1992) 91 DLR (4th) 289. From time to time, some English judges have also made adverse comments on the exclusionary rule, but there has never been a wholesale rejection of it.

Arguments for relaxation

Apart from Murphy J in *Caltex* (who simply said (at p 606): "I do not accept the contention that economic loss not connected with physical damage to the plaintiff's property is not recoverable"), all of the judges in these cases were agreed that a general exclusionary rule is required in the field of relational economic loss. The debate is as to the circumstances in which that general rule can be relaxed to meet the demands of justice in any particular case. Two types of argument are advanced.

The alternative interests argument

The first of these focuses on the relationship between the plaintiff and the property owner, and may be termed 'the alternative interests argument'. Here, the plaintiff will argue that, although it did not have a proprietary or possessory interest in the third party's property, either it suffered from 'a transferred loss of use' when that property was damaged, or it was involved in 'a common adventure' with the property owner, and therefore it should be treated differently from a normal plaintiff with a mere contractual interest in the third party's property.

The special relationship argument

The second line of argument focuses on the relationship between the plaintiff and the defendant tortfeasor. Here, the plaintiff will argue that, even if its interest in the third party's property was merely contractual, the existence of a high degree of foreseeability of the existence of the plaintiff and its loss, and/or other factors pointing towards a high degree of proximity between the plaintiff and the defendant, are sufficient to justify a deviation from the strict rigours of the exclusionary rule.

5.6.2 Transferred loss

Robert Goff LJ

This was the basis on which Robert Goff LJ (now Lord Goff) would have decided the case in principle in the plaintiff's favour in *The Aliakmon* [1985] QB 350 in the Court of Appeal. He said (at p 399) that the principle of transferred loss is a "recognisable principle underlying the imposition of liability". He said that it applies where a defendent negligently damages a third party's property, but the third party does not suffer a loss because he has transferred the risk of that loss (but not the title to his property) to the plaintiff. In that case, goods which the plaintiff had contracted to buy were damaged at sea due to the negligence of the shipowner. The plaintiff had made an unusual form of contract with the seller, whereunder the seller retained title, but the plaintiff bore the risk of damage to the goods during the voyage. This meant that the seller suffered no loss when the goods were damaged, and that, if the exclusionary rule were applied rigidly, the negligent defendant would not be liable to anyone. Robert Goff LJ said (at p 399):

> It seems to me that the policy reasons pointing towards a direct action by the buyer against the shipowner in a case of this kind outweigh the policy reasons which generally preclude recovery for purely economic loss. There is here no question of any wide or indeterminate liability being imposed on wrongdoers; on the contrary, the shipowner is simply held liable to the buyer in damages for loss which he would ordinarily be liable to the goods owner.
>
> There is a recognisable principle underlying the imposition of liability, which can be called the principle of transferred loss. . . . For the purposes of the present case, I would formulate it in the following deliberately narrow terms, while recognising that it may require modification in the light of experience. Where A owes a duty of care in tort not to cause physical damage to B's property, and commits a breach of that duty in circumstances in which the loss of, or physical damage to the property will ordinarily fall on B but (as is reasonably foreseeable by A) such loss or damage, by reason of a contractual relationship between B and C, falls on C, then C will be entitled, subject to the terms of any contract restricting A's liability to B, to bring an action in tort against A in respect of such loss or damage to the extent that it falls on him, C.

Rejection in the House of Lords

The House of Lords, on appeal ([1986] AC 785), rejected this principle as being inconsistent with authority. Their Lordships also did not think that this was unjust, because (at p 819) "the buyers, when they agreed to the variation to the original contract of sale, did not take the steps to protect themselves which, if properly advised, they should have done". By way of comment, it could be said that the House of Lords' rejection of this principle is a little harsh, because it does mean that the defendant who negligently damaged a third party's property and who would normally be liable to compensate its owner, or someone with a possessory or a proprietary interest in it for that physical damage, escapes liability altogether. To make a limited exception to the exclusionary rule here would be both sensible and 'safe', in that it would not open the floodgates to other claims. *Cf.* the House of Lords' decision in *Linden Gardens Trust Ltd v Lenesta Sludge Disposals Ltd* [1994] 1 AC 85, which is discussed *below* and in para 5.5.1, *above*.

Rejection in CNR v Norsk

This argument was also advanced by the plaintiff in *Norsk*, but it was rejected because that was not a true transferred loss case, as the bridge owner was fully compensated by the defendant for the property damage caused by the defendant to the bridge. The plaintiff's loss was therefore not transferred loss at all in the sense of Robert Goff LJ's above-cited formulation, but a case of loss that was parasitic or consequential on loss suffered by another person who had a direct claim against the defendant in contract or tort for that loss. To allow the plaintiff's claim on that basis would mean disregarding the exclusionary rule altogether in all cases.

Possible revival in Linden Gardens

In *Linden Gardens Ltd v Lenesta Sludge Disposals Ltd* [1994] 1 AC 85, the facts of which are set out in para 5.5.1, *above*, the first plaintiff ('Corporation') had entered into a building contract with the defendant ('McAlpine') which contained a restriction against assignment without the defendant's consent. In breach of that condition Corporation assigned the (benefit of the) building contract to a sister company, the second plaintiff ('Investment'). Subsequently, certain defects materialised in the building, which were due to the defendant's breach of the building contract. These defects were cured at great expense to Investment.

Both Corporation and Investment then brought an action against the defendant to recover the amount expended on the repair work. The House of Lords held, first, that, notwithstanding that Investment was the company that had suffered the loss, Investment had no right to sue the defendant for breach of the building contract because the assignment, having taken place in breach of the prohibition in the contract, conferred no rights under the contract on Investment.

The fact that the assignment conferred no rights under the contract on Investment because the assignment had been ineffective meant that such rights as Corporation originally had under the contract before the assignment remained vested in Corporation. The problem, however, was that Corporation had suffered no loss, because all of the repair costs had been borne by Investment, and the general rule in English law is that a plaintiff can recover damages only for his own loss. The House of Lords nevertheless allowed Corporation to sue the defendant for the full amount of the repair costs, on condition that any damages recovered by Corporation from the defendant would thereafter be paid by Corporation to Investment. Thus, Lord Browne-Wilkinson, with whose speech all of the other Law Lords agreed, said (at p 114):

> In my judgment the present case falls within the rationale of the exceptions to the general rule that a plaintiff can only recover damages for his own loss. The

contract was for a large development of property which, to the knowledge of both Corporation and McAlpine [the defendant], was going to be occupied, and possibly purchased, by third parties, and not by Corporation itself. Therefore it could be foreseen that damage caused by a breach [of the building contract] would cause loss to a later owner and not merely to the original contracting party, Corporation. . . . McAlpine had specifically contracted that the rights of action under the building contract *could* not without McAlpine's consent be transferred to third parties who became owners or occupiers and might suffer loss. In such a case, it seems to me to be proper, as in the case of the carriage of goods by land, to treat the parties as having entered into the contract on the footing that Corporation would be entitled to enforce contractual rights for the benefit of those who suffered from defective performance but who, under the terms of the contract, could not acquire any right to hold McAlpine liable for breach. This is truly a case in which the rule provides 'a remedy where no other would be available to a person sustaining loss which under a rational legal system ought to be compensated by the person who has caused it' [*per* Lord Diplock in *The Albazero*].

Comment

The principle that the House of Lords invoked in *Linden Gardens* to reach the above-mentioned just result was not called 'the principle of transferred loss', but rather was what can be referred to as 'the principle in *The Albazero*', pursuant to which a plaintiff may exceptionally be entitled to sue in his own name to recover a loss which he has not in fact suffered on condition that he will be accountable for any damages so recovered to the person who has in fact suffered the loss (see para 5.5.1, *above*).

However, the discussion of the rule in *The Albazero*, *above*, reveals that the cases in which the rule has been applied have been cases which fall within the description of cases of transferred loss by Robert Goff LJ in the Court of Appeal in *The Aliakmon* (see *above*). Indeed, it is submitted that *Linden Gardens* was itself a case of transferred loss and that the House of Lords, by allowing Corporation to sue the defendant for the full amount of the loss incurred by Investment so long as Corporation thereafter paid that sum to Investment, effectively did uphold and apply the transferred loss principle. The only difference between the way in which the principle has been formulated and the way in which it was applied in *Linden Gardens* is that, as formulated, the person who should have been entitled to bring the action should have been Investment (ie the party who had suffered the loss, or 'C' in Goff LJ's formulation—see para 5.5.1, *above*), instead of, as actually happened, allowing the action to be brought by Corporation (being the party who did not suffer the loss, but who had the contractual right to sue, corresponding to 'B' in Goff LJ's formulation). So long as 'B' is prepared, as Corporation was in *Linden Gardens*, to bring the action on behalf of 'C', it is submitted that this is a distinction without a difference and does amount to authority for the principle of transferred loss, contrary to the House of Lords' rejection of that theory in the appeal in *The Aliakmon* [1986] AC 785 (see *above*).

Lord Goff, previously Robert Goff LJ, was not a member of the panel in the House of Lords in *Linden Gardens*. However, in *White v Jones* [1995]

2 AC 207 he referred to the House's decision in *Linden Gardens*, and to Lord Diplock's *dictum* in *The Albazero* that, in certain exceptional cases, the law should provide a remedy where no other remedy would be available to a person sustaining loss "which, under a rational legal system, ought to be compensated by the person who has caused it" (see para 5.5.1, *above*), and said (at p 267):

> The decision [in *Linden Gardens*] is noteworthy in a number of respects. First, this was a case of transferred loss; and Lord Diplock's dictum, as applied by your Lordships' House, reflects a clear need for the law to find a remedy in cases of this kind. Second, your Lordships' House felt able to do so in a case in which there was a contractual bar against assignment without consent; and, as a result, unlike Lord Diplock, did not find it necessary to look for a common intention that the contract was entered into for the benefit of persons such as the second plaintiffs [ie Investment] which, in this case, having regard to the prohibition against assignment, it plainly was not. Third, the consequence was that your Lordships' House simply made the remedy available as a matter of law in order to solve the problem of transferred loss in the case before them.

White v Jones

In *White v Jones* [1995] 2 AC 207, Lord Goff, in searching for a doctrinal solution to the problem in that case, referred to the principle of transferred loss. He said (at p 265):

> Here there is a lacuna in the law, in the sense that practical justice requires that the disappointed beneficiary should have a remedy against the testator's solicitor in circumstances in which neither the testator nor his estate has in law suffered a loss. Professor Lorenz (*Essays in Memory of Professor FH Lawson*, p 90) has said that 'This is a situation which comes very close to cases of "transferred loss", the only difference being that the damage due to the solicitor's negligence could never have been caused to the testator or to his executor'. In the case of the testator, he suffers no loss because (in contrast to a gift by an inter vivos settlor) a gift under a will cannot take effect until after the testator's death, and it follows that there can be no depletion of the testator's assets in his lifetime if the relevant asset is, through the solicitor's negligence, directed to a person other than the intended beneficiary. The situation is therefore not one in which events have subsequently occurred which have resulted in the loss falling on another. It is one in which the relevant loss could never fall on the testator to whom the solicitor owed a duty, but only on another; and the loss which is suffered by that other . . . is of a character which in any event could never have been suffered by the testator. Strictly speaking, therefore, this is not a case of transferred loss.

Although Lord Goff concluded (correctly) that *White v Jones* was not a true case of transferred loss, the fact that it was closely analogous militated in favour of the court going out of its way to fashion a remedy for the plaintiff. Thus, Lord Goff said (at p 265):

> . . . the analogy is very close. In practical terms, part or all of the testator's estate has been lost because it has been dispatched to a destination unintended by the testator. Moreover, had a gift been similarly misdirected during the testator's lifetime, he would either have been able to recover it from the recipient or, if not,

he could have recovered the full amount from the negligent solicitor as damages. In a case such as the present, no such remedies are available to the testator or his estate. The will cannot normally be rectified: the testator has no remedy: and his estate has suffered no loss because it has been distributed under the terms of a valid will. In these circumstances, there can be no injustice if the intended beneficiary has a remedy against the solicitor for the full amount which he should have received under the will, this being no greater than the damage for which the solicitor could have been liable to the donor if the loss had occurred in his lifetime.

5.6.3 Common adventure

Introduction

It has been noted *above* (para 5.4.6) that the established, 'general average exception' is based on the fact that the plaintiff and the third party whose property was damaged were engaged in "a common adventure". Strictly speaking, what this means is that the arrangements between the plaintiff and the property owner were such that the plaintiff was obliged to contribute to the property owner's loss. In the two cases which established this exception, namely *Aktieselskabet Cuzo v The Sucarseco* (1935) 294 US 394 in the USA, and *Morrison Steamship Company Ltd v Greystoke Castle (Cargo Owners)* [1947] AC 265 (HL) in England, the courts allowed the plaintiff to recover the amount of its contribution from the wrongdoer. The essential feature of such liability is that the contract between the plaintiff and the property owner created joint responsibility between them to reinstate that property if it should be damaged by a third party. In *Norsk* the bridge was owned, operated and maintained by Public Works Canada, and the plaintiff was not obliged to contribute towards the cost of reinstating it.

Partial application in CNR v Norsk

Nevertheless, three of the majority judges held (at p 376) that the plaintiff and the bridge owner were involved in "a joint or common venture". McLachlin J said (at p 376) (emphasis added):

> Where the plaintiff's operations are 'so closely allied' to the operations of the party suffering physical damage and to its property (which—as damaged—causes the plaintiff's loss) that it can be considered a joint venturer with the owner of the property, the plaintiff can recover its economic loss, even though the plaintiff has suffered no physical damage to its own property. To deny recovery in such circumstances would be to deny it to a person who 'for practical purposes is in the same position' as if he or she owned the property physically damaged.

McLachlin J said that there was sufficient proximity to satisfy this test because the plaintiff owned property on either side of the bridge, which property could not be enjoyed without the link of the bridge, and because the plaintiff supplied materials, inspection and consulting services for the bridge, was its preponderant user and was consulted in periodic negotiations surrounding the bridge's closure.

Doctrinally unsound

Although McLachlin J said that this test is based on the courts' reasoning in *Greystoke* and *Amoco Transport* (a 1986 US case which endorses *The Sucarseco* and is summarised in para 5.8.2, *below*), an examination of those cases will reveal that they did not go this far. A doctrinal criticism of this new principle could be that, contrary to what McLauchlin J has said, the real cause of the plaintiff's loss is not the physical damage inflicted to the third party's property, but rather the fact that the plaintiff's contract with the bridge owner did not oblige the bridge owner to indemnify the plaintiff for the relational economic losses which the plaintiff might suffer if the bridge was closed for a period of time. In this respect the plaintiff in *Norsk* was really in no different a position from any other plaintiff in a case of this kind. Indeed, in this case, although the plaintiff was the preponderant user of the bridge, three other railway companies also used it, and it had been agreed with the defendant that their cases would stand or fall with that of the plaintiff. However, McLachlin J's test would only uphold the plaintiff's claim, but would exclude the other three railways' claims.

Contradictory logic

This criticism is borne out by what McLachlin J said next. In addition to the plaintiff needing to have a very close relationship with the property owner, she said (at p 376):

> The second question is whether extension of recovery to this type of loss is desirable from a practical point of view. Recovery serves the purpose of permitting a plaintiff whose position for practical purposes, *vis-à-vis* the tortfeasor, is indistinguishable from that of the owner of the damaged property, to recover what the actual owner could have recovered. This is fair and avoids an anomalous result. Nor does the recovery of economic loss in this case open the floodgates to unlimited liability. The category is a limited one. It does not embrace casual users of the property or those secondarily and incidentally affected by the damage done to the property.

Unjust result

Again, one can ask what is fair about a result which effectively bases recovery on the plaintiff's status as the property owner's principal client, but denies recovery to all other relational economic loss sufferers. Furthermore, it is highly questionable whether the plaintiff's position in *Norsk* was truly "indistinguishable from that of the owner of the damaged property", because of the fact, mentioned *above*, that the plaintiff did not have to contribute towards the reinstatement cost of the property which the defendant had damaged (ie the bridge).

In *Londonwaste Ltd v Amec Civil Engineering Ltd*, the facts of which are set out in Chapter 4, para 4.3.2, the fact that the plaintiff was the exclusive user of the electricity cables which the defendant had negligently damaged did not make any difference to the fact that the plaintiff's right to use the electricity cables was purely contractual (see para 5.2.3, *above*). The judge also expressly rejected the plaintiff's counsel's submission that the plaintiff's case fell within the 'common adventure' exception to the exclusionary rule (see para 5.4.6, *above*).

5.6.4 Known plaintiff

The spectre of indeterminate liability

In *Caltex*, Gibbs J and Mason J accepted the policy consideration underlying the exclusionary rule (ie the 'spectre of indeterminate liability') but held that the exclusionary rule will not apply in cases where this fear does not actually arise. They said that this would be the case where the defendant could have foreseen the actual plaintiff and the fact that he would suffer economic loss in consequence of the defendant's negligent act or omission.

Gibbs J in Caltex

Thus Gibbs J said (at p 551): "If a person committing an act of negligence were liable for all economic loss foreseeably resulting therefrom, an act of careless inadvertence might expose the person guilty of it to claims unlimited in number and crippling in amount", and (at p 555):

> In my opinion it is still right to say that as a general rule damages are not recoverable for economic loss which is not consequential upon injury to the plaintiff's person or property. The fact that the loss was foreseeable is not enough to make it recoverable. However, there are exceptional cases in which the defendant has knowledge, or means of knowledge, that the plaintiff individually, and not merely as a member of an unascertained class, will be likely to suffer economic loss as a consequence of his negligence, and owes the plaintiff a duty to take care not to cause him such damage by his negligent act. All the facts of the particular case will have to be considered. It will be material, but not in my opinion sufficient, that some property of the plaintiff was in physical proximity to the damaged property, or that the plaintiff and the person whose property was injured were engaged in a common adventure.

Mason J in Caltex

And Mason J (at p 592) said: "It is preferable that the delimitation of the duty of care in relation to economic damage through negligent conduct be expressed in terms which are related more closely to the principal factor inhibiting the acceptance of a more generalised duty of care in relation to economic loss, that is, the apprehension of indeterminate liability. A defendant will then be liable for economic damage due to his negligent conduct when he can reasonably foresee that a specific individual, as distinct from a general class of persons, will suffer financial loss as a consequence of his conduct. This approach eliminates or diminishes the prospect that there will come into existence liability to an indeterminate class of persons".

Rejection in England

This principle, which is referred to as 'the known plaintiff test', has been criticised by judges in England. In the Court of Appeal in *The Aliakmon*

5.6.4 *Relational economic Loss*

[1985] 1 QB 350 Robert Goff LJ (at p 395) said that he thought that it is arbitrary to try to distinguish between foreseeability of economic loss to the plaintiff as a particular individual, rather than as a member of an ascertained class. He said: "Is the single company which uses a bridge for the purposes of its business to recover damages when the bridge is damaged and rendered unusable, but not a number of companies which use another bridge similarly damaged?" Similarly, in *Candlewood Navigation Corporation Ltd v Mitsui OSK Lines Ltd (The Mineral Transporter)* [1986] AC 1 (PC) Lord Fraser said (at p 24): "Their Lordships have difficulty in seeing how to distinguish between a plaintiff as an individual and a plaintiff as a member of an unascertained class. The test can hardly be whether the plaintiff is known by name to the wrongdoer. Nor does it seem logical for the test to depend upon the plaintiff being a single individual".

Lord Fraser's criticism

Lord Fraser enlarged the scope of this test, and consolidated his criticism of it by adding:

> Further, why should there be a distinction for this purpose between a case where the wrongdoer knows (or has the means of knowing) that the persons likely to be affected by his negligence consist of a definite number of persons whom he can identify either by name or in some other way (for example as being the owners of particular factories or hotels) and who may therefore be regarded as an ascertained class, and a case where the wrongdoer knows only that there are several persons, the exact number being to him unknown, and some or all of whom he could not identify or otherwise, and who may therefore be regarded as an unascertained class? Moreover, much of the argument in favour of an ascertained class seems to depend upon the view that the class would normally consist of only a few individuals. But would it be different if the class, though ascertained, was large? Suppose for instance that the class consisted of all the pupils in a particular school. If it was a kindergarten school with only six pupils they might be regarded as constituting an ascertained class, even if their names were unknown to the wrongdoer. If the school was a large one with over a thousand pupils it might be suggested that they were not an ascertained class. But it is not easy to see a distinction in principle merely because the number of possible claimants is larger in one case than in the other. Apart from cases of negligent misstatement, with which their Lordships are not here concerned, they do not consider that it is practicable by reference to an ascertained class to find a satisfactory control mechanism which could be applied in such a way as to give reasonable certainty in its results.

Partial application in Millar v Candy

These are sound words in so far as relational economic loss claims are concerned. Indeed, the illogicality of the 'known plaintiff test' can be seen from Franki J's judgment in *Millar v Candy* [1982] 3 All ER 299, which is discussed in Chapter 4 (para 4.8.3) in the section dealing with consequential losses of bailees. Although Franki J was in the minority, it is worth noting how he decided the case. The issue was whether the

212

plaintiff, whose hire purchase car had been damaged beyond repair in an accident which was the defendant's fault, could recover, in addition to the market value of the car, the additional amount which he was required to pay to the owner upon the early termination of the hire purchase agreement. By pure coincidence the plaintiff and the defendant worked together and had had a prior conversation in which the plaintiff had told the defendant that he had acquired the car from a certain finance company under a hire purchase agreement. Franki J, who said that the 'known plaintiff test' is the applicable test, therefore held that the plaintiff could recover this loss from the defendant; but otherwise (ie if the plaintiff and the defendant had not known each other) he would have rejected this claim. It is submitted that this is an unsatisfactory basis for reaching such a decision.

Stevenson J in CNR v Norsk

The fourth majority judge in *Norsk*, Stevenson J, favoured this test. He said (at p 387–8):

> The line must be drawn by considering the policy concerns which underlie the need to limit the recovery of relational losses. The policy rationale which precludes recovery for most relational losses does not exist if there is no danger of indeterminate liability. There is no danger of indeterminate liability, and thus no policy reason to deny recoverability, when the defendant actually knows or ought to know of a specific individual or individuals, as opposed to a general or unascertained class of the public, who is or are likely to suffer a foreseeable kind of loss as a result of negligence by that defendant. With a known plaintiff, the scope of liability cannot become indeterminate. Liability is kept within a limited and determinate scope.

Rejection by six judges

Stevenson J's judgment was rejected by all six of the other judges in this case. For the three minority judges, La Forest J (at p 341) said that, as this case concerns an accident (as contrasted with negligent misrepresentation cases, in which the defendant makes the representation voluntarily), the plaintiff cannot be said to contemplate a particular plaintiff or a particular loss in the same sense as a bank manager who provides financial information. La Forest J said:

> Knowledge of the individual plaintiff operates arbitrarily both in terms of singling out defendants and in terms of singling out plaintiffs. Surely no one is suggesting that tort law should strive to protect bridges with high profile users more than bridges used by anonymous users, or that defendants who damage bridges with high profile users are more guilty than others. This test has the effect of singling out the wrong parties for relief. It would offer a premium to notoriety, a premium for which I can find no legal or social justification, particularly since such persons are most likely to advert to the matter and to contract out or insure against the harm.

McLachlin J, for the other three majority judges, concurred in these sentiments.

5.6.5   *Relational economic Loss*

Rejection in Londonwaste

In *Londonwaste Ltd v Amec Civil Engineering Ltd* (1997) 53 Con LR 66, the facts of which are set out in Chapter 4, para 4.3.2, in rejecting the 'specific individual' argument the judge, John Hicks QC, sitting as an Official Referee, said that the partial acceptance of this argument in the High Court of Australia in *Caltex* did not assist the plaintiff in the present case because this argument was expressly disapproved by the Privy Council in *Candlewood* (see *above*). He also said that Stevenson J's acceptance of the 'known plaintiff' approach in *Norsk* was of no assistance to the plaintiff because Stevenson J's reasons were disclaimed by all six of the other judges. His Honour then said:

> There is thus no extant authority, even in the persuasive category, for this exception, and there is the disapproval of the Privy Council against it. Moreover *Spartan Steel and Alloys Ltd v Martin and Co (Contractors) Ltd* [1973] QB 27 [see Chapter 4, paras 4.3.2 and 4.5.5] is direct and binding authority on the point, for it is there stated that the defendants knew that the cable which they damaged was the direct supply to the plaintiff's factory.

5.6.5   **Proximity**

Imprecise concept

This was the basis of Stephen J's judgment in *Caltex*. He rejected the exclusionary rule and said that it should be replaced by "proximity", but he did not attempt to define its content. He said (at p 575): "It may be that no more specific proposition can be formulated than a need for insistence upon 'sufficient' proximity between tortious act and compensable detriment. The articulation, through the cases, of circumstances which denote sufficient proximity will provide a body of precedent productive of the necessary certainty; the gradual accumulation of decided cases and the impact of evolving policy considerations will reflect the courts' assessment of the demands of society for protection from the carelessness of others".

Stephen J in Caltex

Stephen J continued: "Some guidance in the determination of the requisite degree of proximity will be derived from the broad principle which underlies liability in negligence, namely, *per* Lord Atkin in *Donoghue v Stevenson*, 'a general public sentiment of moral wrongdoing for which the offender must pay'. Such a sentiment will only be present when there exists a degree of proximity between the tortious act and the injury, such that the community will recognise the tortfeasor as being in justice obliged to make good his moral wrongdoing by compensating the victims of his negligence". Stephen J held that this was such a case with regard to the plaintiff's economic losses, which consisted of extra transport costs incurred when the defendant negligently damaged a third party's pipeline through which the third party used to transport refined oil to the plaintiff's terminal at the other side of a bay. He reached this conclusion by way of an accumulation of what he saw (at p 576) as "the salient features" of this case, namely:

The defendant's knowledge that the property damaged was of a kind inherently likely to be productive of consequential economic loss to those who rely directly on its use; the nature of the pipeline, used to convey refined products to another's terminal, being indicative of the existence of something akin to Lord Roche's common adventure [in *Greystoke*]; the defendant's knowledge or means of knowledge that the plaintiff was a user of the pipeline and the nature of the damages claimed, being not loss of profits because collateral commercial arrangements were adversely affected, but the quite direct consequence of the detriment suffered, namely the expense directly incurred in employing alternative modes of transport.

Based on foreseeability

On the facts of *Caltex*, this looks very similar to the known plaintiff test in a different guise, and therefore must suffer from the same weaknesses and criticisms as that test. Another problem in applying a proximity test to relational economic loss cases is that, with the plaintiff being only a secondary loss sufferer and usually not being physically present when the defendant damages the third party's property, the only facet of proximity between the defendant and the plaintiff that might exist is that it must have been foreseeable to the defendant that, if he damaged the third party's property, a person in the position of the plaintiff would suffer relational economic loss. This is not sufficient to satisfy the test of proximity. This weakness was recognised by the three concurring majority judges in *Norsk*, even though they were in favour of proximity being the appropriate test. McLachlin J said (at p 375): "The plaintiff's right to recover depends on: (1) whether it can establish sufficient proximity or 'closeness', and (2) whether extension of recovery to this type of loss is desirable from a practical point of view".

McLachlin J in CNR v Norsk

In the search for evidence to establish proximity, McLachlin J said (at p 375): "One might fasten on the fact that damaging the bridge raised the danger of physical injury to CNR's property, namely its trains, which were frequently on the bridge and stood to be damaged by an accident involving the bridge. However, to found the decision on this criterion would be to affirm the minority position in [the Supreme Court of Canada in] *Rivtow Marine Ltd v Washington Iron Works* (1973) 40 DLR (3d) 530 (see para 7.7) that danger of physical loss is sufficient to found liability". McLachlin J said that she did not need to consider this question further because there were other factors present in this case which were related to the plaintiff's connection with the property damaged (as opposed to the plaintiff's 'relationship' with the defendant), which satisfied the test of proximity. These factors have been considered *above*, where it has been noted that they are only relevant if and to the extent that they can suffice to bring the situation into the 'common adventure' exception. It has also been noted *above* that McLachlin J was able to achieve this feat only by considerably enlarging the scope of this exception.

5.6.6 *Relational economic Loss*

Rejection by Stevenson J in CNR v Norsk

The other majority judge, Stevenson J, rejected proximity as a test in this type of case. He said (at p 387): "In my view, proximity expresses a conclusion, a judgment, a result, rather than a principle. If a loss is not proximate, it may be said to be too remote. The concept of proximity is incapable of providing a principled basis for drawing the line on the issue of liability". The three minority judges agreed with this.

Comment

It seems strange to suggest that proximity has no role in this type of case, because it clearly has a significant role in other types of accident cases as well as non-accident cases such as negligent misstatement, albeit that in each category the content, and the degree of proximity required to satisfy the test, or 'to balance the equation' (see paras 2.3.1 and 5.5.4) is different. Perhaps the real answer is that in cases of relational economic loss the exclusionary rule, for sound pragmatic reasons, as discussed *above*, dictates that the plaintiff will only have sufficient proximity to the defendant for his relational economic losses if he had a proprietary or a possessory interest in the third party's property which the defendant negligently damaged. Ironically, this was acknowledged by McLachlin J herself in *Norsk* when she said (at p 370): "The absolute exclusionary rule adopted in *Cattle v Stockton* can itself be seen as an indicator of proximity. Where there is physical injury or damage, one posits proximity on the ground that if one is close enough to someone or something to do physical damage to it, one is close enough to be held legally responsible for the consequences".

5.6.6 Physical propinquity

Description of the concept

In *Caltex* Jacobs J (at p 597) devised a test for the recovery of what he called injury to person or property "which consists not of physical injury, but of the physical effect thereon short of physical injury". He said that an example of this would be an act or omission which prevents physical movement of a person or which prevents physical movement or operation of property.

Jacobs J in Caltex

Such losses are not the same as the losses which would ordinarily be suffered by a plaintiff whose contract with a third party is rendered less beneficial when the defendant negligently damages the third party's property. To be recoverable, the plaintiff's person or property must have suffered 'a physical effect' and for this to occur, Jacobs J said (at p 597) the plaintiff or his property must have been "in such physical propinquity to the place where the defendant's act or omission had its physical effect that a physical effect on the person or property of the plaintiff was foreseeable as the result of the defendant's act or omission".

Satisfaction in Caltex

Jacobs J held that all of these conditions were satisfied because the crude oil which the plaintiff delivered to the third party for processing, and its refined products, were at all times the property of the plaintiff. The property of the third party which the defendant damaged was the third party's pipeline which ran from its refinery on one side of a bay to the plaintiff's terminal on the other side. Jacobs J said that the physical effect of the defendant's negligent act extended to the third party's refinery, where some of the plaintiff's oil was held. Thus, the plaintiff satisfied his test of having property "in physical propinquity to the place where the act or omission of the defendant had its physical effect", and this was foreseeable as the result of the defendant's negligent act. Accordingly, he held that the defendant owed the plaintiff a duty of care in respect of the losses suffered by the plaintiff from the 'physical effect' on the plaintiff's oil at the third party's refinery. This consisted of the cost of arranging alternative means of obtaining delivery of the refined oil products from the third party's refinery while its pipeline was being repaired. Jacobs J, together with all of the other judges in this case (albeit each for different reasons), held that these damages were recoverable by the plaintiff.

Comparison with exclusionary rule

This test is similar to the exclusionary rule, to the extent that it requires that the plaintiff's property (or, presumably, property in which the plaintiff had a proprietary or a possessory interest) was affected by the defendant's negligent act. However, it differs in two important respects: first, the property in which the plaintiff will be held to have a sufficient interest need not be actually physically damaged (it only needs to be immobilised); secondly, the connection between the plaintiff and the property which the defendant actually damaged need not be contractual: it will suffice that the plaintiff had property nearby which was physically affected without being damaged (ie it was immobilised) and that this was foreseeable. It is thus quite a sensible test and could alleviate some of the hardship which can result from a strict application of the exclusionary rule.

Approval in Privy Council

Jacobs J's test was approved by the Privy Council (at p 24) in *Candlewood Navigation Corporation Ltd v Mitsui OSK Lines Ltd (The Mineral Transporter)* [1986] 1 AC (PC). *Caltex* was not referred to by the House of Lords in *Leigh and Sillivan v Aliakmon Ltd (The Aliakmon)* [1986] AC 785 (HL), but in the Court of Appeal [1985] 1 QB 350 Robert Goff LJ (at p 395–96) referred to Jacobs J's test and said that he found it difficult to understand why this type of economic loss, which transcends damage to the property itself, should be recoverable rather than any other.

Partial acceptance in CNR v Norsk

In *Norsk* the plaintiff relied on Jacobs J's test by virtue of its ownership of land and railway track on both sides of the river and the fact that the bridge formed an integral part of its railway network. Only the minority judges dealt with this submission. They seem to have accepted the validity of this test but (at p 343) they rejected it on the facts, because they said that no property of the plaintiff suffered a "physical effect" in the sense of being immobilised as a result of the accident. For this to occur, they said that one or more of the plaintiff's trains would have had to be "in physical propinquity" to the bridge when the barge hit it, and the plaintiff's recoverable losses would then have been limited to the cost of rerouting those actual trains, and not also others which were not that close to the bridge at the time.

5.6.7   Loss-bearing ability

Relaxation of exclusionary rule

In *Norsk* the minority judges wholeheartedly embraced the exclusionary rule, but said (at p 356) that the policy factors which might justify relaxing it are "(1) the ability of the plaintiff to protect itself and (2) the quantum of property damage caused by the tortfeasor, with its attendant impact on the issue of deterrence". No such relaxation was justified on the facts, because the plaintiff was clearly able to protect itself (by obtaining insurance) and the property damage caused to the bridge was sufficient to afford deterrence.

La Forest J in CNR v Norsk

La Forest J said (at p 345) that: "given the eminently pragmatic policy basis of decisions about liability in this area, the situation of both the defendant and the plaintiff needs to be examined. In particular, the plaintiff's ability to foresee and provide for the particular damage is a key factor in the proximity analysis. In my view, analysis of loss-bearing ability is particularly relevant in determining whether proximity exists in the context of contractual relational economic loss cases".

Plaintiff's perspective

It is the very fact that the plaintiff's losses are 'relational' that makes it legitimate to consider this factor. The plaintiff is voluntarily making use of a third party's property and knows that he will suffer financial loss if that property is damaged. It is therefore legitimate to expect the plaintiff to have considered the viability of obtaining insurance against that loss. Also, because of the continuing liability of the defendant to compensate the third party for damage to his property, it cannot be said that defendants will thereby be encouraged to lower their standards of care if they know that they are not going to be held liable for losses suffered by a party in the position of the plaintiff in this type of case.

No application in CNR v Norsk

On the facts, the minority had no doubt that the plaintiff in this case was not a party in whose favour the exclusionary rule should be relaxed on this account. La Forest J said (at p 349): "It is hard to imagine a more sophisticated group of plaintiffs than the users of railway bridges. These parties have access to the full range of protective options: first party commercial insurance or self-insurance, or contracts with the bridge owner or the railway's customers". Furthermore, the defendant did cause substantial physical damage to the bridge, for which it had to compensate the bridge owner, and this, held the minority, served to satisfy the requirement that rules of law in tort must have a deterrent effect.

An open question

It is interesting to note that La Forest J specifically left open, without expressing any opinion, what the position would be if the defendant had caused minimal, or no, property damage, and if the plaintiff had not been able to protect itself. He said (at p 357): "Whether such factors would, in fact, provide workable criteria sufficient to provide for recovery despite the strong arguments in favour of the long-standing exclusionary rule, based on certainty and other factors, is an open question. What I have decided is that in the absence of these factors, there is no reason to disturb the rule".

5.6.8 Reconciliation of approaches

D'Amato v Badger

In *D'Amato v Badger* (1996) 137 DLR (4th) 129, the facts of which are set out in para 5.3.1, *above*, the Supreme Court of Canada attempted to reconcile the two main approaches in *Norsk*. Major J, speaking for the full complement of nine judges, said (at p 137):

> While the tests of La Forest and McLachlin JJ in *Norsk* are different, they will usually achieve the same result. This is because in the identified categories outlined by La Forest J permitting pure economic recovery [see para 5.8.2, *below*], McLachlin J's tests of proximity and foreseeability [see para 5.8.2] will usually also be met. For the reasons which follow [these are set out in para 5.3.2, *above*], this case is not one in which the plaintiff would succeed on one test, but not on the other. A choice between the two will have to await the appropriate case.

Comment

While it may well be true that in most cases the result will be the same whichever of these tests is applied, it is a pity that, given that the panel in this case included all of the judges of the Supreme Court of Canada, there was no attempt to clarify which approach is to be preferred in cases like *Norsk*, where the two approaches *do* in fact lead to different results.

Bow Valley Husky v Saint John Shipbuilding

In *Bow Valley Husky (Bermuda) Ltd v Saint John Shipbuilding Ltd* (1998) 153 DLR (4th) 385, a further attempt was made in the Supreme Court of Canada to reconcile the approaches of McLachlin J and La Forest J in *Norsk*. The plaintiffs, Husky Oil Operations Ltd ('HOOL') and Bow Valley Industries Ltd ('BVI'), were two oil exploration companies who had contracted with the first defendant, Saint John Shipbuilding Ltd ('SJSL'), a shipbuilder, to construct an oil drilling rig for them. The plaintiffs subsequently incorporated an off-shore company, Bow Valley Husky (Bermuda) Ltd ('BVHB'), and transferred the ownership of the rig and the benefit of the construction contract to it.

The plaintiffs then entered into contracts with BVHB to hire the rig back from BVHB to conduct their drilling operations. Under the terms of those contracts, the plaintiffs were obligated to continue to pay day rates to BVHB in the event of the rig being out of service for any reason. Subsequently, the rig was out of service for several months due to a fire caused by the negligence of SJSL and Raychem Canada Ltd ('Raychem'), the second defendant, who had manufactured and supplied a (defective) heat tracing system to keep the rig's pipes from freezing.

In the present action the plaintiffs sought to recover from SJSL and Raychem the day rates which they had been contractually obligated to pay to BVHB while the rig was out of service. The Supreme Court of Canada (in a panel consisting of six judges) rejected their claim. McLachlin J, in a joint judgment delivered on behalf of herself and La Forest J, said (at p 405):

> The plaintiff HOOL and BVI seek to recover the economic loss they suffered as a result of damage to the property of a third party. This sort of loss is often called 'contractual relational economic loss'. The common law Provinces of Canada, while treating recovery in tort of contractual relational economic loss as exceptional, accept that there may be cases where it may be recovered.
>
> There is a need for a rule to distinguish between cases where contractual relational economic loss can be recovered and cases where it cannot be recovered. Such a rule, as I wrote in *Canadian National Railway Co v Norsk Pacific Steamship Co* (1992) 91 DLR (4th) 289, should be morally and economically defensible and provide a logical basis upon which individuals can predicate their conduct and courts can decide future cases. Although this court attempted to formulate such a rule in *Norsk*, a split decision prevented the emergence of a clear rule. Given the commercial importance of the issue, it is important that the rule be settled. It is therefore necessary for this court to revisit the issue.

McLachlin J then set out the differences between the two main approaches in *Norsk* as follows:

> The differences between the reasons of La Forest J and myself in *Norsk* are of two orders: difference in result and difference in methodology. The difference in result, taken at its narrowest, is a difference in the definition of what constitutes a 'joint venture' for the purposes of determining whether recovery for contractual relational economic loss should be allowed. We both agreed that if the plaintiff is in a joint venture with the person whose property is damaged, the plaintiff may claim consequential economic loss related to that property. We parted company because La Forest J took a stricter view of what constituted a joint venture than I did.
>
> The difference in methodology is not, on close analysis, as great as might be supposed. Broadly put, La Forest J started from a general exclusionary rule and proceeded to articulate exceptions to that rule where recovery would be permitted. I, by contrast, stressed the two-step test for when recovery would be

available, based on the general principles of recovery in tort as set out in *Anns v Merton London Borough Council* [1978] AC 728, and *Kamloops (City of) v Nielsen* (1984) 10 DLR (4th) 641: (1) whether the relationship between the plaintiff and defendant was sufficiently proximate to give rise to a *prima facie* duty of care; and (2) whether, if such a *prima facie* duty existed, it was negated for policy reasons and recovery should be denied.

McLachlin J then identified the common elements of both approaches as follows:

> Despite this difference in approach, La Forest J and I agreed on several important propositions: (1) relational economic loss is recoverable only in special circumstances where the appropriate conditions are met; (2) these circumstances can be defined by reference to categories, which will make the law generally predictable; (3) the categories are not closed. La Forest J identified the categories of recovery of relational economic loss defined to date as (i) cases where the claimant has a possessory or proprietary interest in the damaged property; (ii) general average cases; and (iii) cases where the relationship between the claimant and the property owner constitutes a joint venture.

In applying these principles to the facts of the present case, McLachlin J said (at p 406):

> The case at bar does not fall into any of the above three categories. The plaintiffs here had no possessory or proprietary interest in the rig and the case is not one of general averaging. While related contractually, the plaintiff and the property owner cannot, on any view of the term, be viewed as joint venturers.

McLachlin J held, however, that this conclusion was not the end of the inquiry into whether a contractual relational economic loss plaintiff should succeed. She said:

> ... The categories of recoverable contractual relational economic loss in tort are not closed. Where a case does not fall within a recognised category the court may go on to consider whether the situation is one where the right to recover contractual relational economic loss should nevertheless be recognised. This is in accordance with *Norsk*, *per* La Forest J, at p 1134:
>
>> Thus I do not say that the right to recovery in all cases of contractual relational economic loss depends exclusively on the terms of the contract. Rather, I note that such is the tenor of the exclusionary rule and that *departures from that rule should be justified on defensible policy grounds*. [Emphasis added.]
>
> More particularly, La Forest J suggested that the general rule against recovery for policy-based reasons might be relaxed where the deterrent effect of potential liability to the property owner is low, or, despite a degree of indeterminate liability, where the claimant's opportunity to allocate the risk by contract is slight, either because of the type of transaction or an inequality of bargaining power. I agreed with La Forest J that policy considerations relating to increased costs of processing claims and contractual allocation of the risk are important. I concluded that the test for recovery 'should be flexible enough to meet the complexities of commercial reality and to permit the recognition of new situations in which liability ought, in justice, to lie as such situations arise'. It thus appears

that new categories of recoverable contractual relational economic loss may be recognised where justified by policy considerations and required by justice. At the same time, courts should not assiduously seek new categories; what is required is a clear rule predicting when recovery is available.

McLachlin J then embarked on a discussion of the principles that were applied by the Supreme Court of Canada in a recent case which had nothing to do with relational economic loss, namely, *Hercules Managements Ltd v Ernst & Young* (1997) 146 DLR (4th) 577 ('*Hercules*'), the facts of which are set out in Chapter 9, para 9.9.3. McLachlin J said (at p 407):

> Although styled as an action for negligent misrepresentation, the plaintiffs' claim [in *Hercules*] was treated as a case of relational economic loss owing to the fact that the services were performed pursuant to a contract with the company. The primary loser was the company, which had contracted with the auditors. The plaintiffs' loss was derivative of, or relational to, the company's loss. The defendant auditors asserted that their only duty was to the company with which they had contracted. They argued that no relational tort duty to third parties lay in the circumstances. To affirm such a duty, they maintained, would be contrary to the policy considerations that had led courts in the past to deny recovery for relational economic loss. The Court, *per* La Forest J, unanimously held that the shareholders had no cause of action against the auditors.

McLachlin J then described the court's process of reasoning in *Hercules*, when she said (at p 408):

> La Forest J concluded that the first branch of the *Anns* test was satisfied and the defendant auditors owed a *prima facie* duty of care to the plaintiffs. First, the possibility that the plaintiffs would rely on the audited statements prepared for the company was reasonably foreseeable. Second, the relationship between the parties and nature of the statements made the plaintiffs' reliance reasonable.
>
> Policy considerations under the second branch of the test, however, negatived a duty of care. La Forest J began by noting that while policy concerns surrounding indeterminate liability will serve to negate a *prima facie* duty of care in many auditors' negligence cases, there may be particular situations where such concerns do not inhere. The specific factual matrix of a given case may bring it within a category which, for policy reasons, is identified as an exception to the exclusionary rule; considerations of proximity may militate in favour of finding a *prima facie* duty of care at the first stage, and the policy considerations which usually negate it may be absent. In such cases, liability would appropriately lie.
>
> The main policy consideration at stake in *Hercules* was the spectre of indeterminate liability. Not everyone who picks up a financial statement and relies on it can sue for financial loss incurred as a result of reliance on the statement. Only persons that the makers of the statement can reasonably be expected to have foreseen relying on the statements can sue, and then only for uses that the auditors could reasonably have foreseen. The question thus became whether the plaintiffs had used the statements for the purpose for which they had been prepared. The Court held they had not. The statements had been prepared for the purpose of permitting the shareholders to collectively oversee the management of the company, not for the purpose of assisting individual shareholders in

investment decisions. The policy considerations surrounding indeterminate liability accordingly inhered, negating the *prima facie* duty of care.

McLachlin J linked the court's analysis in *Hercules* to the present case by saying (at p 409):

> The same approach may be applied to the contractual relational economic loss at stake in the case at bar. The first step is to inquire whether the relationship of neighbourhood or proximity necessary to found a *prima facie* duty of care is present. If so, one moves to the second step of inquiring whether the policy concerns that usually preclude recovery of contractual relational economic loss, such as indeterminacy, are overridden.

In applying the '*Hercules* test' to the present case, McLachlin J said (at p 410):

> As in *Hercules, supra*, the decision as to whether a *prima facie* duty of care exists requires an investigation into whether the defendant and the plaintiff can be said to be in a relationship of proximity or neighbourhood. Proximity exists on a given set of facts if the defendant may be said to be under an obligation to be mindful of the plaintiff's legitimate interests in conducting his or her affairs: *Hercules, supra*, at p 190. On the facts of this case, a *prima facie* duty of care arises. Indeed, the duty to warn raised against the defendants is the correlative of the duty to disclose financial facts raised against the auditors in *Hercules*.

McLachlin J then considered the second part of the two-stage test by saying (at p 411):

> The next question is whether this *prima facie* duty of care is negatived by policy considerations. In my view, it is. The most serious problem is the problem of indeterminate liability. If the defendants owed a duty to warn the plaintiffs, it is difficult to see why they would not owe a similar duty to a host of other persons who would foreseeably lose money if the rig was shut down as a result of being damaged. Other investors in the project are the most obvious persons who would also be owed a duty, although the list could arguably be extended to additional classes of persons. What has been referred to as the ripple effect is present in this case. A number of investment companies which contracted with HOOL are making claims against it, as has BVI.
>
> No sound reason to permit the plaintiffs to recover while denying recovery to these other persons emerges. To hold otherwise would pose problems for defendants, who would face liability in an indeterminate amount for an indeterminate time to an indeterminate class. It also would pose problems for potential plaintiffs. Which of all the potential plaintiffs can expect and anticipate they will succeed? Why should one type of contractual relationship, that of HOOL, be treated as more worthy than another, eg, that of the employees on the rig? In this state, what contractual and insurance arrangements should potential plaintiffs make against future loss?

Having reached the conclusion that the plaintiffs' claims in the present case could not succeed, McLachlin J went on to make some general remarks about the type of situations in which the court might decide to relax the exclusionary rule. She said (at p 413):

> The problem of indeterminate liability constitutes a policy consideration tending to negative a duty of care for contractual relational economic loss.

However, the courts have recognised positive policy considerations tending to support the imposition of such a duty of care. One of these, discussed by La Forest J in *Norsk*, is the need to provide additional deterrence against negligence. The potential liability to the owner of the damaged property usually satisfies the goal of encouraging persons to exercise due care not to damage the property. However, situations may arise where this is not the case. In such a case, the additional deterrent of liability to others might be justified. The facts in the case at bar do not support liability to the plaintiffs on this basis. BVHB, the owner of the drilling rig, suffered property damage in excess of five million dollars. This is a significant sum. It is not apparent that increasing the defendants' potential liability would have led to different behaviour and avoidance of the loss.

Another situation which may support imposition of liability for contractual relational economic loss, recognised by La Forest J in *Norsk*, is the case where the plaintiff's ability to allocate the risk to the property owner by contract is slight, either because of the type of the transaction or inequality of bargaining power. Again, this does not assist the plaintiffs in this case. BVI and HOOL not only had the ability to allocate their risks; they did just that. It cannot be said that BVI and HOOL suffered from inequality of bargaining power with BVHB, the very company they created. Moreover, the record shows they exercised that power. The risk of loss caused by down-time of the rig was specifically allocated under the Drilling Contracts between BVI, HOOL and BHB. The contracts provided for day rate payments to BVHB and/or termination rights in the event of lost or diminished use of the rig. The parties also set out in the contracts their liability to each other and made provision for their third party claims arising out of rig operations. Finally, the contracts contained provisions related to the purchase and maintenance of insurance.

The only other judgment was delivered by Iacobucci J, with whom the other four judges in the case concurred. After saying that he wished to commend McLachlin J for her treatment of the approaches taken by her and La Forest J in *Norsk*, Iacobucci J said (at p 428): "I understand my colleague's discussion of this matter to mean that she has adopted the general exclusionary rule and categorical exceptions approach set forth by La Forest J in *Norsk*".

Comment

To the extent that Iacobucci J is correct in stating that McLachlin J has adopted the general exclusionary rule and categorical exceptions approach set forth by La Forest J in *Norsk*, the law has been clarified. However, it does seem questionable whether McLachlin J did in fact adopt this approach, because the approach which she purported to follow, namely the approach of the Supreme Court of Canada in *Hercules*, was not this approach, but rather was the traditional two-stage test whereby, far from starting off by accepting the existence of an exclusionary rule in a particular category of cases (as La Forest J did in *Norsk*), the court applies an open-ended approach to every case. The aim of the two-stage test is to determine, first, whether there is a sufficiently close relationship of proximity to give rise to the imposition of a *prima facie* duty of care; and if so, whether other indefinable policy and pragmatic considerations exist which have the effect of negativing the existence of that *prima facie* duty.

Furthermore, it is submitted that it would not be surprising to conclude that an analysis of McLachlin J's judgment shows that she did not adopt "the general exclusionary rule and categorical exceptions approach" because the case on which she purported to base her analysis of the true approach, namely the *Hercules* case, had nothing to do with relational economic loss. It was a case in an entirely different category, namely economic loss suffered by a plaintiff through having relied on a statement made (or information provided or a service rendered) by the defendant.

In a relational economic loss case, the plaintiff's loss arises because its relationship with a third party has been harmed by a wrong done by the defendant to the third party. The plaintiff's claim is parasitic on the plaintiff's relationship with the third party. The defendant's contractual arrangements with the third party or with anyone else are irrelevant. This point was recognised by La Forest J himself in *London Drugs Ltd v Kuehne and Nagel International Ltd* (1992) 97 DLR (4th) 261, when he said (at p 277):

> In *Norsk* the principal relevant contract was between the plaintiff and the property owner [whose property (the bridge) was damaged by the defendant tortfeasor]. Not only was there no privity of contract between the plaintiff and the defendant, but the defendant's contractual arrangements were largely irrelevant.

On the other hand, in a negligent misstatement case, the plaintiff's loss arises because the plaintiff has placed reliance on a statement made (or on information or a service provided) by the defendant in circumstances where the plaintiff did not have a contract with the defendant or, if he did, he cannot for one reason or another pursue his contractual claim or his right to recover in tort is more favourable than his contractual right. A third party might be involved (ie the statement, advice or service might have been rendered by the defendant to the third party), but not necessarily, as in the case of a relational economic loss claim.

These differences are important in shaping the analysis that needs to be made in considering cases in these very different categories of economic loss claims (see Chapter 1, para 1.3, this chapter, and Chapters 7, 8 and 9). Another important difference, which La Forest J highlighted in *Norsk* (see para 5.8.2, *below*), is that relational economic loss cases usually arise out of an accident, whereas negligent misstatement cases and product liability cases usually involve planned transactions.

Furthermore, it is submitted that McLachlin J's above-cited statement that "although styled as an action for negligent misrepresentation, the plaintiffs' claim [in *Hercules*] was treated as a case of relational economic loss" is without foundation. There is no suggestion in the report of the *Hercules* decision that it was being treated as a case of relational economic loss. La Forest J made it clear that he was characterising the plaintiffs' claims in the category of negligent misstatements when he said (at p 597): "The foregoing analysis should render the following points clear. A *prima facie* duty of care will arise on the part of a defendant in a negligent misrepresentation action when it can be said (a) that the defendant ought reasonably

225

to have foreseen that the plaintiff would rely on his representation and (b) that reliance by the plaintiff, in the circumstances, would be reasonable"; and when, in applying these principles to the facts of *Hercules*, he referred exclusively to negligent misstatement cases, such as *Hedley Byrne and Co Ltd v Heller and Partners Ltd* [1964] AC 465, *Haig v Bamford* (1976) 72 DLR (3d) 68 and *Caparo Industries plc v Dickman* [1990] 2 AC 605, all of which are considered in Chapter 9 (negligent misstatements and services).

Of greater concern is McLachlin J's reason for believing that *Hercules* was a case of relational economic loss. She said: "Although styled as an action for negligent misrepresentation, the plaintiffs' claim [in *Hercules*] was treated as a case of relational economic loss *owing to the fact that the services were performed pursuant to a contract with the company*". In other words, McLachlin J believed that the contract between the defendant (the auditors) and a third party (the company whose accounts the defendant audited) served to make *Hercules* a case of relational economic loss. This is not correct: as La Forest J said in the passage cited *above* from his judgment in *London Drugs Ltd v Kuehne and Nagel International Ltd* (1992) 97 DLR (4th) 261, the principal relevant contract in a relational economic loss case is the contract between the plaintiff and the third party, and the defendant's contractual arrangements are largely irrelevant. Indeed, given that relational economic loss cases usually arise out of accidents, it is rare for the defendant in such cases to have had any contractual arrangements with the third party.

For these reasons it is doubted whether the joint judgment of McLachlin J and La Forest J in *Bow Valley* has achieved its aim of clarifying the law on relational economic loss.

5.7 Conclusion

While it is easy to criticise the exclusionary rule as excluding recovery by innocent plaintiffs who have suffered losses as a result of a defendant's negligence, it must be appreciated that, whichever other alternative theory, or test, is applied, recovery will still be denied to the vast majority of relational economic loss sufferers.

5.8 Relevant cases

5.8.1 Cases which affirm the exclusionary rule

Cattle v The Stockton Waterworks Co (1875) LR 10 QB 453: The plaintiff had entered into a lump sum contract with a Mr Knight to construct a tunnel on K's land. Due to the negligence of the defendant the tunnelling works became flooded. The plaintiff eventually completed his contract, but he was delayed and put to extra expense. The plaintiff sued the defendant for these losses. The court, however, held that the plaintiff did not have a cause of action.

Blackburn J said (at p 457):

> In the present case the objection is technical and against the merits, and we should be glad to avoid giving it effect. But if we did so, we should establish an authority for saying that, in such a case as *Fletcher v Rylands* (Law Rep 3 HL 330), the defendant would be liable, not only to an action by the owner of the drowned mine, and by such of his workmen as had their tools or clothes destroyed, but also to an action by every workman and person employed in the mine who, in consequence of its stoppage, made less wages than he would otherwise have done. And many similar cases to which this would apply might be suggested. It may be said that it is just that all such persons should have compensation for such a loss and that, if the law does not give them redress, it is imperfect. Perhaps it may be so. But, as was pointed out by Coleridge J, in *Lumley v Gye* (22 LJ (QB) 463) courts of justice should not 'allow themselves, in the pursuit of perfectly complete remedies for all wrongful acts, to transgress the bounds which our law, in a wise consciousness of its limited powers, has imposed on itself, of redressing only the proximate and direct consequences of wrongful acts'. In this we quite agree. No authority in favour of the plaintiff's right to sue was cited, and, as far as our knowledge goes, there was none that could have been cited.

Simpson & Co v Thomson (1877) 3 App Cas 279, HL (Sc): A Mr Burrell ('B') was the owner of two ships, 'D' and 'F', which collided at sea, resulting in the total loss of D and its cargo. The collision was due entirely to the negligence of those in charge of F. The plaintiff was the insurer of D and paid its full value to B as the owner of the lost ship, D. The plaintiff then sought to recover this sum from B in his capacity as owner of the negligent ship, F. The House of Lords rejected this claim. The plaintiff clearly could not found this alleged right on subrogation of the rights of the owner of D because that would have amounted to B suing himself.

The plaintiff therefore argued that it had an independent right of action which did not depend on its being subrogated to the rights of the owner of the ship (D) which it had insured, in as much as any injury or loss sustained by the ship would indirectly fall upon it as a consequence of its contract; and that this interest was such as would support an action by the plaintiff in its own name against a wrongdoer. This argument was rejected. Lord Penzance said (at p 289):

> The principle involved seems to me to be this—that where damage is done by a wrongdoer to a chattel not only the owner of that chattel, but all those who by contract with the owner have bound themselves to obligations which are rendered more onerous, or have secured to themselves advantages which are rendered less beneficial by the damage done to the chattel, have a right of action against the wrongdoer although they have no immediate or reversionary property in the chattel, and no possessory right by reason of any contract attaching to the chattel itself, such as by lien or hypothecation.
>
> This is the principle involved in the respondents' [ie the underwriters'] contention. If it be a sound one, it would seem to follow that if, by the negligence of a wrongdoer, goods are destroyed which the owner of them had bound himself by contract to supply to a third person, this person as well as the owner has a right of action for any loss inflicted on him by their destruction.

But if this be true as to injuries done to chattels, it would seem to be equally so as to injuries to the person. An individual injured by a negligently driven carriage has an action against the owner of it. Would a doctor, it may be asked, who had contracted to attend him and provide medicines for a fixed sum by the year also have a right of action in respect of the additional cost of attendance and medicine cast upon him by that accident? And yet it cannot be denied that the doctor had an interest in his patient's safety. Such instances might be indefinitely multiplied, giving rise to rights of action which in modern communities, where every complexity of mutual relation is daily created by contract, might be both numerous and novel. I have given these illustrations because I fail to see any distinction in principle between them and the right asserted by the underwriters in the present case.

The first of these examples corresponds with the facts of *The Wear Breeze* [1969] 1 QB 219 and *The Aliakmon* [1986] 1 AC 785, discussed *below*. The facts of the second example correspond with the Supreme Court of California decision in *Fifield Manor v Finston* (1960) 354 P (2d) 1073, discussed *above* in the main text.

La Société Anonyme de Remorquage à Hélice v Bennetts [1911] 1 KB 243: A tug boat belonging to the plaintiff was engaged under a towage contract in towing a ship ('the tow'), when a ship belonging to the defendant negligently collided with, and sank, the tow. No damage was caused to the tug, but the plaintiff suffered a financial loss by not being able to complete the towage contract. This was not a lump sum contract, and the plaintiff was thus deprived of the amount of towage remuneration which it would have earned if it had been allowed to complete the contract. The plaintiff sought to recover this sum from the defendant as damages. The court held that the plaintiff had no cause of action.

Hamilton J (who subsequently became Lord Sumner) said (at p 248): "All that has occurred is that, in the course of performing a profitable contract, an event happened which rendered the contract not further performable, and therefore less profitable to the plaintiff. That appears to me to bring the case within the authority of *Cattle v Stockton Waterworks Co* and within the general statement of the law by Lord Penzance in his judgment in *Simpson v Thomson*".

Elliott Steam Tug Co Ltd v Shipping Controller [1922] 1 KB 127: The plaintiff, a towage and salvage company, had a tug in its possession under the terms of a charterparty. The Admiralty requisitioned the tug from the plaintiff under its statutory powers. The plaintiff had been operating the tug profitably up to that time. In these proceedings the plaintiff sought to recover the estimated average net earnings which it would have made from the tug during the period of the requisition. The plaintiff was successful, but only because it fell within the terms of the relevant statute. If not for this, the plaintiff's claim would have failed.

Scrutton LJ said (at p 139): "At common law there is no doubt about the position. In case of a wrong done to a chattel the common law does not recognise a person whose only rights are a contractual right to have the use or services of the chattel for purposes of making profits or gains without possession of or property in the chattel. Such a person cannot claim for injury done to his contractual right: see *Stockton Waterworks* and *Simpson v Thomson*".

Scrutton LJ also made it clear that the reason for excluding recovery in these cases is not that the damage suffered by the charterer is considered to be too remote, but that the policy of the law so dictates. He said (at p 140): "The charterer in collision cases does not recover profits, not because the loss of profits during repairs is not the direct consequence of the wrong, but because the common law rightly or wrongly does not recognise him as able to sue for such an injury to his merely contractual rights".

Robins Dry Dock and Repair Co v Flint (1927) 275 US 303: The plaintiff was the time charterer of a vessel which was undergoing repair in the defendant's dockyard. The plaintiff was not obliged to pay charter hire to the owner during this period. The defendant negligently damaged the ship's propeller. The plaintiff suffered economic loss through not being able to use the vessel during the period of the delay which thus ensued. The US Supreme Court held that the plaintiff had no cause of action against the defendant for this loss.

Holmes J said (at p 308): "The injury to the propeller was no wrong to the plaintiff, but only to those to whom it belonged. The plaintiff's loss arose only through its contract with the owners. While intentionally to bring about a breach of contract may give rise to a cause of action, no authority need be cited to show that, as a general rule, a tort to the person or property of one man does not make the tortfeasor liable to another merely because the injured person was under a contract with that other, unknown to the doer of the wrong. A good statement, applicable here, will be found in *Elliott Steam Tug Co v The Shipping Controller*".

Konstantinidis v World Tankers Corporation (The World Harmony) [1967] P 341: The plaintiff was a time charterer of a passenger cruise ship. As this was not a charter by demise, the plaintiff did not have a property right in, or possession of, the ship. The plaintiff only had a contractual right to use the ship. In consequence of a collision which was wholly the fault of the operators of *The World Harmony*, the ship which the plaintiff had chartered was totally destroyed. The plaintiff instituted proceedings for its losses, consisting of the profits which it would have earned in the following year by continuing to use the chartered ship.

The plaintiff did not question the validity of the cases mentioned *above*, but contended that they were all decided before, and were affected by *Donoghue v Stevenson* [1932] AC 562. Hewson J answered this by saying (at p 362): "*Donoghue v Stevenson* and the cases on duty towards one's neighbour which have followed it are quite different on their facts, and they have not touched upon the question posed here. The *Donoghue v Stevenson* line of cases in general appears to restrict the duty to your neighbour to avoid injuring him either in his person or in his property".

The plaintiff also contended that the position had been altered by the fact that, in *Hedley Byrne & Co Ltd v Heller & Partners Ltd* [1964] AC 465, the House of Lords had approved in principle the recovery of pure economic loss suffered by a plaintiff because of a wrongdoer's negligence. Hewson J also rejected this argument, saying (at p 362): "That case was very much nearer contract than tort. The facts are so entirely different from the present case, and, as the line of cases to which I have been referred in this action was not quoted in the House of Lords in the *Hedley Byrne* case, I would hesitate long before I would apply anything that was said by their Lordships in that case to this one".

Hewson J was quite correct to reject these contentions. As his above-quoted words make clear, those cases were in different categories from the present case, and therefore different considerations apply.

Weller & Co v Foot and Mouth Disease Research Institute [1966] 1 QB 569: The defendant was an organisation which carried out experimental work in connection with foot and mouth disease. Some cattle in the vicinity of its premises became infected with the disease. The Minister of Agriculture closed two markets in the area. In consequence, the plaintiff, an auctioneer, was unable to auction cattle at those markets. The plaintiff sued the defendant for its lost profits during the period of closure. The court held that the plaintiff did not have a cause of action. The plaintiff was not an owner of cattle, and did not have a proprietary interest in anything which could be damaged by the escape of the virus. The court thus applied the principle set out in the cases mentioned *above* and rejected the plaintiff's claim.

Widgery J explained the rationale, or policy consideration, which underlies the restriction of the scope of the duty of care in this type of case by saying (at p 585): "The world of commerce would come to a halt and ordinary life would become intolerable if the law imposed a duty on all persons at all times to refrain from any conduct which might foreseeably cause detriment to another".

Magarine Union GmbH v Cambay Prince Steamship Co Ltd (The Wear Breeze) [1969] 1 QB 219: The plaintiff was the purchaser of a quantity of copra which was shipped in the defendant's vessel. Title was to pass to the plaintiff on delivery. On out-turn at the port of delivery, it was found that this copra was seriously damaged by giant American cockroaches, because the defendant had failed to fumigate the vessel. The defendant admitted negligence, but pleaded that it was not liable to the plaintiff for this damage because the plaintiff did not have legal title to (or a possessory interest in) the copra at the time of the defendant's act of negligence. The court, applying the principle of the cases mentioned *above*, agreed with the defendant.

The plaintiff sought to distinguish those cases by virtue of the fact that, in the present case, the plaintiff's goods had suffered actual physical damage. Roskill J rejected this, and said (at p 254): "English law does not recognise and never has recognised a duty of care upon a shipowner to anyone who was not the owner of the goods at the time when the tort was committed".

State of Louisiana, ex rel Guste v M/V Testbank (1985) 752 F (2d) 1019 (US CA 5th Cir): Two ships collided in the Mississippi River gulf outlet. Some containers aboard one of them were damaged and lost overboard. The contents were a very toxic chemical. In consequence, all residents within a ten-mile radius had to be evacuated and the Coast Guard closed the outlet to navigation and suspended all fishing and associated activities within 400 square miles of surrounding waterways and marshes, and imposed an embargo on seafood caught in the area. Forty-one law suits were filed against the owners of the ships by such diverse plaintiffs as commercial fishermen, shipowners suffering losses from delays or rerouting, marina and boat operators, wholesale and retail seafood enterprises not actually engaged in fishing, seafood restaurants, tackle and bait shops and recreational fishermen.

The court rejected all except the claims of the commercial fishermen. In doing so, the court affirmed and applied the principle established in *Robins Dry Dock v Flint* and the exception to it established in *Union Oil v Oppen*.

As regards *Robins*, Higginbotham J, one of the majority judges (in a majority of ten to five), said (at p 1021): "Our re-examination of the history and central purpose of this pragmatic restriction on the doctrine of foreseeability heightens our commitment to it". As regards *Union Oil*, Sneed J noted (at fn 10, p 1027): "A substantial argument can be made that commercial fishermen possess a proprietary interest in fish in waters they normally harvest sufficient to allow recovery for their loss".

Candlewood Navigation Corporation Ltd v Mitsui OSK Lines Ltd (The Mineral Transporter) [1986] AC 1 (PC): The plaintiff was the owner, and was in possession of a ship, 'IM', which was damaged by the negligence of the operators of another ship, 'MT'. Some time before this accident the plaintiff had let 'IM' to a third party by a bareboat charter, which was a charter by demise. The third party then let 'IM' back to the plaintiff by a time charter which was not a charter by demise. While 'IM' was being repaired the plaintiff's daily hire charge payable to the third party under the time charter was reduced to one quarter of the normal rate. The third party (the bareboat charterer) recovered from the defendant the cost of the repairs to 'IM' and the amount by which the hire charge payable to it by the plaintiff under the time charter was reduced while the ship was not operational.

In this action the plaintiff sought to recover from the defendant the economic losses which it had suffered by virtue of the collision, namely the one quarter daily hire charge which it still had to pay to the bareboat charterer, and its loss of profits during the period while 'IM' was not operational. The Privy Council, applying the principle of the above-mentioned cases, held that the plaintiff had no cause of action. The plaintiff argued that this principle did not apply because, being also the owner of 'IM', it had a reversionary interest which was enough to give it title to sue for damages arising out of physical injury to the ship. The Privy Council rejected this because the plaintiff's claim was made exclusively in respect of losses which it had suffered as time charterer. It had suffered no loss as owner. The Privy Council also held that the plaintiff did not have a sufficient possessory interest because the plaintiff was in possession of the ship, not as owner, but under a charterparty agreement not by demise.

Secondly, the plaintiff argued that it would be unreasonable to apply the exclusionary rule in this case because, if the plaintiff had been operating 'IM' in its capacity as owner, it would clearly have been entitled to recover the whole cost of repairing the collision damage and its whole loss of profits while the ship was non-operational. Because the ship was subject to the bareboat charter and the time charter, the loss of profits was divided between the bareboat charterer and the time charterer (ie the plaintiff, who owned the ship), but the loss was the same.

Lord Fraser, speaking for the Privy Council, said (at p 19) that this argument "is not without its appeal", especially where, as in this case, the whole loss falls on only two parties. Nevertheless he said that this was no reason for making an exception to the general principle. He referred to the quotation set out *above* from *Cattle v The Stockton Waterworks Co* and said (at p 16): "It is apparent from that citation that the court regarded the rule as a pragmatic one dictated by necessity". He then referred to the quotation set out *above* from *Simpson & Co v Thomson*, and said (at p 17): "These two cases show that the justification for denying a right of action to a person who has suffered economic damage through injury to the property of another is that, for reasons of practical policy, it is considered to be inexpedient to admit his claim".

The policy consideration which Lord Fraser had in mind is variously known as the 'floodgates' argument, or the 'spectre of indeterminate liability' argument. He said (at p 19):

> The plaintiff's argument, if accepted, would have far-reaching consequences, which would run counter to the accepted policy of the law. If claims for economic loss by sub-charterers are to be admitted, why not also claims by any person with a contractual interest in any goods being carried in the damaged vessel, and by any passenger in her, who suffers economic loss by reason of the delay attributable to the collision? An exceedingly wide, new range of liability would be opened up. The Lordships accordingly reject this submission.

Leigh and Sillivan Ltd v Aliakmon Ltd (The Aliakmon) [1986] AC 785 (HL): The plaintiff was a buyer of goods which had been transported on the defendant's vessel. Due to the defendant's negligence the goods were damaged in transit. At that time the plaintiff had the risk, but not yet the legal property in the goods. The contractual arrangements between the plaintiff and the seller were such that, unusually, the property in the goods did not pass to the buyer (ie the plaintiff) under the bill of lading. Therefore the plaintiff had to bring its claim against the shipowners in the tort of negligence. The House of Lords, applying the principle of the cases mentioned *above*, rejected the plaintiff's claim.

The plaintiff accepted that principle in general, but argued that *The Wear Breeze*, which was very similar to the present case, was wrong. The plaintiff's counsel (at p 816) pointed to the fact that the policy reason for excluding a duty of care in cases like this is "to avoid the opening of the floodgates, so as to expose a person guilty of want of care to unlimited liability to an indefinite number of other persons whose contractual rights have been adversely affected by such want of care". He argued that recognition by the law of a duty of care by shipowners to a buyer to whom the risk, but not yet the property in the goods carried in the shipowner's ship had passed, would not of itself open any floodgates of the kind described.

Lord Brandon, delivering the unanimous judgment of the House of Lords, rejected that argument and said (at p 816):

> If an exception to the general rule were to be made in the field of carriage by sea, it would no doubt have to be extended to the field of carriage by land, and I do not think that it is possible to say that no undue increase in the scope of a person's liability for want of care would follow. In any event, where a general rule, which is simple to understand and easy to apply, has been established by a long line of authority over many years, I do not think that the law should allow special pleading in a particular case within the general rule to detract from its application. If such detraction were to be permitted in one particular case, it would lead to attempts to have it permitted in a variety of cases, and the result would be that the certainty which the application of the general rule presently provides would be seriously undermined. Yet certainty of the law is of the utmost importance, especially, but by no means only, in commercial matters. I therefore think that the general rule, re-affirmed as it has been so recently by the Privy Council in *The Mineral Transporter*, ought to apply to a case like the present one.

5.8.2 Cases which challenge the exclusionary rule

The Sucarseco (1935) 51 Ll.L Rep 238 (US SC), ***Aktieselskabet Cuzo v The Sucarseco*** (1935) 294 US 394: Two ships, 'S' and 'T', collided. The plaintiff was the owner of cargo which was being carried on 'T'. This cargo was not damaged, but the plaintiff suffered a loss, by virtue of having to comply with a clause in the bill of lading which required it to contribute with the owner of 'T' in general average for the cost of repairs to 'T'. The plaintiff then sought to recover these expenses from the owners of 'S'. The US Supreme Court upheld the plaintiff's claim.

Hughes CJ referred to *Elliott Steam Tug* and to *Robins Dry Dock* and said (at p 241):

> This is not a case of an attempt to make the tortfeasor liable to another merely because the injured person was under a contract with that other. Here, cargo as well as ship was placed in jeopardy. The claim of the cargo owner [ie the plaintiff] for its general average contribution is not in any sense a derivative claim. It accrues to the cargo owner in its own right because of the cargo owner's participation in the common adventure and the action taken on behalf of the

cargo owner to avert a peril with which that adventure was threatened. The fact that the owners of the vessel ['T'] and the cargo owners under the bill of lading bear their proportionate shares of the expenses gives the owners of Sucarseco no ground for a contention that the cargo owner's share of the expenses was not occasioned directly by the tort.

Morrison Steamship Co Ltd v Greystoke Castle (Cargo Owners) [1947] AC 265 (HL): The facts of this case were almost identical to those of *The Sucarseco*. The House of Lords, by a majority of three to two, upheld the plaintiff cargo owner's claim against the owners of the colliding ship for the general average contribution which the plaintiff had made towards the repairs of the damaged ship. In doing so the majority specifically followed *The Sucarseco* and adopted the above-quoted words of Hughes CJ.

All of the early cases referred to *above* on the exclusionary rule were referred to the court. Lord Roche, one of the members of the majority, said (at p 280): "If the cargo owner's expense is occasioned by the collision, then no authority was cited to support the proposition that, whether by land or by sea, physical or material damage is necessary to support a cause of action in a case like this". Lord Roche did not say specifically what he meant by "in a case like this", but the example which he then proceeded to give makes it clear that he did not simply have in mind a loss incurred by a plaintiff in the way of a general average contribution. He said (at p 280):

> If two lorries A and B meet one another on the road, I cannot bring myself to doubt that the driver of lorry A owes a duty to both the owner of lorry B and to the owner of goods then carried in lorry B. Those owners are engaged in a common adventure with or by means of lorry B, and if lorry A is negligently driven and damages lorry B so severely that whilst no damage is done to the goods in it, the goods have to be unloaded for the repair of the lorry and then reloaded or carried forward in some other way and the consequent expense is by reason of his contract or otherwise the expense of the goods owner, then in my judgment the goods owner has a direct cause of action to recover such expense.

Lord Porter, in response to the defendant's counsel's submission that damage arising from a contract with a third party gives no ground for a claim in negligence against a wrongdoer unless the damage arises from property owned by or in possession of the plaintiff, said (at p 296): "For this contention there may be much to be said where the person or thing injured was not engaged, as is cargo when being carried in a ship, on a joint adventure. I do not, however, think it applies to such carriage".

Lord Simonds, dissenting, on the other hand, said that this case falls squarely within the ambit of the exclusionary rule. He said that he shared the apprehension expressed by Lord Penzance in *Simpson v Thomson* that a decision in favour of the plaintiff in this case might have far-reaching and unforeseen consequences. He said (at p 307):

> This [ie the exclusionary rule] I take to be unquestionably the law of the land and I cannot assent to the view that the law of the sea is otherwise. I do not ignore that the law of the sea has many special characteristics, but I do not get any help from the use of such expressions as 'joint venture', 'common adventure' or 'com-

munity of interest', which are not terms of art unless they import some notion of partnership or co-ownership. The primary fact is that the cargo owner has made a contract of affreightment with the shipowner. It is convenient and not inapt to say that ship and cargo are engaged in a joint adventure, but to do so leads to no conclusion.

Caltex Oil (Australia) Pty Ltd v The Dredge Willemstad (1976) 136 CLR 529: The defendant fractured a pipeline laid in the bed of a bay. The pipeline was owned by Australian Oil Refining Pty Ltd ('AOR'), and was used by it to transport refined oil products from its refinery to the plaintiff's terminal on the other side of the bay. While the pipeline was being repaired the plaintiff incurred additional expenses in providing alternative means of transporting refined oil from AOR's refinery to its terminal. The plaintiff sought to recover those expenses from the defendant. The High Court of Australia upheld the plaintiff's claim.

This decision was unanimous, but the case was decided on four separate bases, which are discussed *above* in the main text of this chapter. Gibbs and Mason JJ decided the case on the 'individual plaintiff test', Stephens J decided it on the basis of proximity, Jacobs J on the basis of 'physical propinquity' and Murphy J on the basis that all foreseeable loss, physical or economic, is recoverable. This case is discussed further in the main text of this chapter (particularly in para 5.6).

Amoco Transport Co v S/S Mason Lykes (1986) 768 F (2d) 659 (US CA 5th Cir): The plaintiff's goods were being carried on the 'ML', when it was negligently damaged by another ship, the 'AC', in consequence of which 'ML' returned to port and unloaded the plaintiff's cargo. The bill of lading nevertheless obliged the plaintiff to pay the full freight charge. The court held that the plaintiff was entitled to recover this cost from the owners of the 'AC', notwithstanding that the plaintiff's goods had not been physically damaged.

The court said that the voyage in this case was a common adventure between the vessel and the cargo owners similar to that in *The Sucarseco*. Politz J said (at p 667): "The common adventure concept is a venerable one and is firmly established as an exception to the rule in *Robins Dry Dock v Flint*".

Canadian National Railway Co v Norsk Pacific Steamship Co (1992) 91 DLR (4th) 489: A barge owned by the defendant negligently collided with a railway bridge, over which the plaintiff carried freight. The plaintiff incurred economic loss in rerouting its traffic while the bridge was being repaired. The defendant knew that the plaintiff was the principal user of the bridge, accounting for 85 per cent of its traffic. The defendant's barge captain mistakenly thought that the plaintiff owned the bridge. The plaintiff owned the track leading to each end of the bridge, and provided certain maintenance services for the bridge, but the bridge was owned by Public Works Canada ('PWC'). The plaintiff's right to use the bridge stemmed from an agreement with PWC, which PWC could terminate on three years' notice. The plaintiff paid a small toll to PWC, which was calculated in such a way as only to cover PWC's costs, and not to leave PWC with a profit.

The agreement between PWC and the plaintiff (and the other three users of the bridge) did not provide for any indemnification by PWC in the event of interruption of the use of the bridge. Unable to claim under its contract, the plaintiff brought this action in tort against the defendant, claiming the actual costs incurred by it by reason of the bridge's closure. The Supreme Court of Canada upheld the plaintiff's claim. The court was split four to three, but, of the four judges who were in the majority, three gave one reason (a common adventure between the plaintiff and the bridge owner based on the proximity between them), the other gave another reason (foreseeability of the actual plaintiff) and rejected proximity as the test. The three minority judges affirmed the exclusionary rule subject to certain exceptions which did not apply here. Furthermore, both of the groups of judges and the single judge rejected the approaches of all of the other judges.

The judgment of the three concurring judges who ruled in favour of the plaintiff was given by McLachlin J. With reference to the long line of cases which have denied recovery of relational losses consequent upon the negligent infliction of damage to the property of another person, McLachlin J said:

> While the criterion of physical damage successfully avoided the spectre of unlimited damages, it suffered from the defect that it arbitrarily and, in some cases, arguably unjustly, deprived deserving plaintiffs of recovery. Why, it was asked, should the right to recover economic loss be dependent on whether physical damage, however minuscule, had been inflicted on the plaintiff's property?

After comparing the position in other jurisdictions, McLachlin J said:

> Even in the United States, where fear of the floodgates of unlimited liability has held the strongest sway, courts have been forced to make exceptions in the interests of justice. The fact is that situations arise, other than those falling within the old exclusionary rule, where it is manifestly fair and just that recovery of economic loss be permitted. Faced with these situations, courts will strain to allow recovery, provided they are satisfied that the case will not open the door to a plethora of undeserving claims. They will refuse to accept injustice merely for the sake of doctrinal tidiness. The search should be not for a universal rule, but for the elaboration of categories where recovery of economic loss is justifiable on a case-by-case basis. In the United States it is recognised that pure economic loss can be recoverable in certain 'joint venture' situations.

After making some general pronouncements about the concept of proximity, McLachlin J said:

> Before the law will impose liability, there must be a connection between the defendant's conduct and the plaintiff's loss which makes it just for the defendant to indemnify the plaintiff. In contract, the contractual relationship provides this link. In trust, it is the fiduciary obligation which establishes the necessary connection. In tort, the equivalent notion is proximity. Proximity may consist of

various forms of closeness—physical, circumstantial, causal or assumed—which serve to identify the categories of cases in which liability lies. The concept of proximity may be seen as an umbrella, covering a number of disparate circumstances in which the relationship between the parties is so close that it is just and reasonable to permit recovery in tort. The complexity and diversity of the circumstances in which tort liability may arise defy identification of a single criterion capable of serving as the universal hallmark of liability. The meaning of proximity is to be found rather in viewing the circumstances in which it has been found to exist, and determining whether the case at issue is similar enough to justify a similar finding. In my view, pure economic loss is *prima facie* recoverable where, in addition to negligence and foreseeable loss, there is sufficient proximity between the negligent act and the loss. Proximity is the controlling concept which avoids the spectre of unlimited liability. Proximity may be established by a variety of factors, depending on the nature of the case. In determining whether liability should be extended to a new situation, courts will have regard to the factors traditionally relevant to proximity such as the relationship between the parties, physical propinquity, assumed or imposed obligations and close causal connection. And they will insist on sufficient special factors to avoid the imposition of indeterminate and unreasonable liability. The result will be a principled yet flexible approach to tort liability for pure economic loss. It will allow recovery where recovery is justified, while excluding indeterminate and inappropriate liability.

On the connection between proximity and the traditional exclusionary rule in relational economic loss cases, McLachlin J said:

> The absolute exclusionary rule adopted in *Cattle v The Stockton Waterworks Co* (1875) LR 10 QB 453 [see *above*] can itself be seen as an indicator of proximity. Where there is physical injury or damage, one posits proximity on the ground that if one is close enough to someone or something to do physical damage to it, one is close enough to be held legally responsible for the consequences. Physical injury has the advantage of being a clear and simple indicator of proximity. The problem arises when it is taken as the *only* indicator of proximity. The judgments below [in this case] focused on the relationship between the tortfeasor, Norsk, and the plaintiff, CN, both within and outside their discussion of proximity. A more comprehensive, and I submit objective, consideration of proximity requires that the court review all of the factors connecting the negligent act with the loss. This includes not only the relationship between the parties, but all forms of proximity—physical, circumstantial, causal or assumed indicators of closeness.

In considering whether, and to what extent, other factors are also relevant, McLachlin J said:

> While proximity is critical to establishing the right to recover pure economic loss in tort, it does not always indicate liability. It is a necessary but not necessarily sufficient condition of liability. Recognising that proximity is itself concerned with policy requires the court to consider the purposes served by permitting recovery as well as whether there are any residual policy considerations which call for a limitation on liability. This permits courts to reject liability for pure economic loss where indicated by policy reasons not taken into account in the proximity analysis.

5.8.2 *Relational economic Loss*

Under the heading "Pragmatic considerations", McLachlin J asked:

Are there practical reasons why the recovery of economic loss should be confined to cases where the plaintiff has sustained physical damage or injury or relied on a negligent misrepresentation? Will extension of recovery of economic loss to other situations open the floodgates of liability, prove so uncertain as to be unworkable or have an adverse economic impact?

The comparative historical perspective provides little support for the need for a rule which confines recovery of economic loss to cases where the plaintiff has suffered physical loss or has relied on a negligent misstatement. The civil law in Canada and abroad appears to function adequately without recourse to such a rule. In the common law jurisdictions of Canada, where the availability of damages for pure economic loss has been accepted for a decade and a half, the twin spectres of unlimited liability and unworkable uncertainty have not materialised; and to the extent that recovery for pure economic loss has been allowed in the United States, it seems not to have provoked adverse consequences, but rather to have satisfied the public demand for justice so essential to maintaining the vitality of the law of negligence.

Under the heading "Economic theory", McLachlin J said:

The arguments advanced under this head proceed from the premise that a certain type of loss should not be seen in terms of fault, but rather as the more or less inevitable by-product of desirable but inherently dangerous (or 'risky') activity. Three arguments are put forward (see below). None of them, in my view, establishes that the extension of recovery granted by the courts in this case is unfair or inefficient.

The insurance argument says that the plaintiff is in a better position to predict economic loss consequent on an accident and hence better able to obtain cheap insurance against the contingency. From a macro-economic point of view, this will result in an overall saving. The argument, however, depends on a number of questionable assumptions. The common law restriction of financial loss recovery reduces incentives to tortfeasors to take care, and results in more accidents. If the insurance argument is to be sustained, the victim must be not only the better insurer, but better by some margin so great that it justifies the losses from more frequent and more severe injury.

The second argument, the loss-spreading argument, asserts that it is better for the economic well-being of society to spread the risk among many parties rather than place it on the shoulders of the tortfeasor. Again, this argument is based on questionable assumptions. It is a variant of the insurance argument. Where losses are spread by relieving the tortfeasor of liability, we can expect more accidents to occur. In any case, the loss-spreading rationale cannot justify the numerous cases where there is only one victim.

A third argument focuses on the ability of persons who stand to suffer economic loss due to the property of another to allocate the risk within their contracts effectively with property owners. It is argued that the law of negligence has no business compensating such person because it makes better economic sense for them to provide for the possibility of damage to the bridge by negotiating a term that, in the event of failure, the owner of the bridge would compensate them. In this way, relational economic loss cases are 'channelled' rather than denied. The proponents of this position argue that judicial affirmation of a rule that recovery of economic loss is confined to cases where the plaintiff has suffered physical damage to its person or property or has relied in the sense of *Hedley Byrne* [see Chapter 9] will send a clear message to the business community to plan its affairs accordingly. Following this argument, the court can presume in the present case that if CN failed to contract for this indemnification: (a) CN paid less for its lease; (b) CN did not consider the risk of unavailability to be significant enough to negotiate for such indemnification or alternatively to insure itself; or (c) CN did not act reasonably and was itself negligent in organising its business affairs. As such, the preclusion of CN from recovery is justified.

The contractual allocation of risk argument rests on a number of questionable assumptions. First, it assumes that all persons or business entities organise their affairs in accordance with the laws of economic efficiency, assigning liability to the least-cost risk avoider. Secondly, it assumes that all parties to a transaction share an equality of bargaining power which will result in the effective allocation of risk. Thirdly, it overlooks the historical centrality of personal fault to our concept of negligence and the role this may have in curbing negligent conduct and thus limiting the harm done to innocent parties, not all of whom are large enterprises capable of maximising their economic situation.

Based on these observations, McLachlin J said:

There is no practical reasons evident at this stage for the courts to retreat to the inflexibility of a rule that never continuances recovery of economic loss except where the plaintiff has suffered physical damage or injury or has relied on a negligent misrepresentation.

Under the heading "Application to this case", McLachlin J said:

The plaintiff CN suffered economic loss as a result of being deprived of its contractual right to use the bridge damaged by the defendant's negligence. Applying the *Kamloops* approach [ie the two-stage test enunciated by Lord Wilberforce in *Anns v Merton London Borough Council* [1978] AC 728 and adopted by the Supreme Court of Canada in *City of Kamloops* (1984) 10 DLR (4th) 641, see Chapter 3, para 3.6.2], CN's right to recover depends on: (1) whether it can establish sufficient proximity or 'closeness', and (2) whether extension of recovery to this type of loss is desirable from a practical point of view.

A number of factors have been suggested in support of a finding of the necessary proximity. One might fasten on the fact that damaging the bridge raised the danger of physical injury to CN's property, namely, its trains, which were frequently on the bridge and stood to be damaged by an accident involving the bridge. Whether they were in fact damaged is immaterial to the question of proximity. What is important is that this danger indicates a measure of closeness which has traditionally been held to establish the proximity necessary to found liability in tort for pure economic loss. However, to found the decision on this criterion would be to affirm the minority position of Laskin and Hall JJ in *Rivtow Marine Ltd v Washington Iron Works* (1973) 40 DLR (3d) 530 that danger of physical loss is sufficient to found liability [see Chapter 7, para 7.7]. However, it is not necessary to address that issue in this case since other factors clearly indicate the necessary proximity.

In addition to focusing on the relationship between Norsk and CN—a significant indicator of proximity in and of itself, there was sufficient proximity based on a number of factors related to CN's connection with the property damaged, namely, the bridge. These include the fact that CN's property was in close proximity to the bridge, that CN's property could not be enjoyed without the link of the bridge, which was an integral part of its railway system, and that CN supplied materials, inspection and consulting services for the bridge, was its predominant user and was recognised in the periodic negotiations surrounding the closing of the bridge.

Such a characterisation brings the situation into the 'joint' or 'common venture' category under which recovery for pure economic loss has heretofore been recognised in maritime law cases from the United Kingdom (*Morrison Steamship Co Ltd v Greystoke Castle (Cargo Owners)* [1947] [see *above*]) and the United States (*Amoco Transport Co v S/S Mason Lykes* (1986) 768 F (2d) 659 [see *above*]). The reasoning, as I apprehend it, is that where the plaintiff's operations are so closely allied to the operations of the party suffering physical damage and to its property (which—as damaged—caused the plaintiff's loss) that it can be considered a joint venturer with the owner of the property, the plaintiff can recover its economic loss even though the plaintiff has suffered no physical damage to its own property. To deny recovery in such circumstances would be to deny it to a person who for practical purposes is in the same position as if he owned the property physically damaged.

Having reached this point in her reasoning, McLachlin J then went on to consider the second part of the test which she said is applicable. Thus, she said:

The second question is whether extension of recovery to this type of loss is desirable from a practical point of view. Recovery serves the purpose of permitting a plaintiff whose position for practical purposes *vis-à-vis* the tortfeasor is indistinguishable from that of the owner of the damaged property, to recover what the actual owner could have recovered. This is fair and avoids an anomalous result. Nor does the recovery of economic loss in this case open the floodgates to unlimited liability. The category is a limited one. It has been applied in England [??] and the United States without apparent difficulty. It does not embrace casual users of the property or those secondarily and incidentally affected by the damage done to the property. Potential tortfeasors can gauge in advance the scope of their liability. Businesses are not precluded from self-insurance or from contracting for indemnity, nor are they 'penalised' for not so doing. Finally, frivolous claims are not encouraged.

I conclude that here the necessary duty and proximity are established; that valid purposes are served by permitting recovery; and that recovery will not open the floodgates to unlimited liability. In such circumstances, recovery should be permitted.

Finally, McLachlin J commented on the other two judgments in this case. She said:

With respect to the reasons of Stevenson J, I, like La Forest J, would not accept the known plaintiff test or the ascertained class test which, to borrow La Forest J's phrase, places a premium on notoriety.

With respect to the reasons of La Forest J, we are in agreement that the broad and flexible approach set out in *Anns* governs the right to recover for economic loss in tort. We also agree that the law of tort does not permit recovery for all economic loss. We further agree that where the plaintiff establishes a joint venture with the owner of the damaged property, it should be able to recover economic loss. Where we differ, in the final analysis, is on the test for determining a joint venture.

La Forest J says that the right to recovery in cases such as this depends exclusively on the terms of the formal contract between the plaintiff and the property owner. If the contract creates a possessory interest or a joint venture, or if it provides for indemnification by the property owner, the plaintiff may recover against a tortfeasor who damages the property and causes economic loss. I do not read the authorities which have considered the implications of a joint venture between the plaintiff and the owner of the damaged property as confining themselves to the formal terms of the contract. I prefer a more flexible test which permits the trial judge to consider all factors relevant to their relationship. The terms of the contract are an important consideration in determining whether economic loss is recoverable. But the contract may tell only part of the story between the parties. If the evidence establishes that, having regard to the entire relationship between the owner of the damaged property and the plaintiff, the plaintiff must be regarded as standing in the relation of joint or common venturer (or a concept akin thereto) with the property owner, with the result that in justice his rights against third parties should be the same as the owner's, then I would not interfere.

From the point of view of policy, I share La Forest J's concern with avoiding recovery which increases the cost of dealing with a given loss and I agree with the importance of the considerations he raises as to the contractual allocation of the risk. While important, I do not find these considerations to be exclusively determinative of the issue. For the reasons given earlier, the policy arguments against recovery are not conclusive, particularly where the individual case is considered.

I agree too that generally people should be able to predict when they can recover economic loss from third parties, so they can determine in advance how to arrange their affairs, ie, whether to purchase casualty (or accident) insurance or not. I suggest that the test I propose permits this in substantial measure, while leaving open the door to future developments in the law. At a minimum, if there is no special connection, physical or circumstantial, between the plaintiff's operations and the property damaged, recovery cannot be assumed and casualty insurance should be purchased. I doubt whether greater predictability in practical terms can be achieved.

McLachlin J concluded her judgment by saying:

In the end, I conclude that a test for recovery of economic loss outside situations akin to *Hedley Byrne*—whether contractual relational economic loss or otherwise—should be flexible enough to meet the complexities of commercial reality and to permit the recognition of new situations in which liability ought, in justice, to lie as such situations arise. With the greatest respect, it seems to me that a test which is confined to the terms of the formal contract between the owner of the property damaged and the person who suffers economic loss as a consequence of that damage may not fill these objectives.

The concurring judgment of the three judges who held that the plaintiff was not entitled to recover was delivered by La Forest J. He started off by noting that different policy concerns arise in the different categories of economic loss. He said:

Cases of contractual relational loss have a number of specific characteristics that differentiate them from other economic loss cases. The first is that the right of action of the property owner already puts pressure on the defendant to act with care. The deterrent effect of tort law is already present. In this case PWC collected substantial damages. Consequently Norsk was already under a substantial incentive to take care with respect to the bridge since its liability to the bridge owner would and did require the payment of substantial damages. In most cases of this type, imposing further liability cannot reasonably be justified on the grounds of deterrence.

Secondly, a firm exclusionary rule in this area does not have the effect of necessarily excluding compensation to the plaintiff for his loss. Rather, it simply channels to the property owner both potential liability to the plaintiff and the right of recovery against the tortfeasor. The property owner is both entitled to recover from the tortfeasor and potentially liable under contract to the plaintiff. Here, the licence agreement explicitly rejected any liability, so the plaintiff cannot recover under it against PWC. In contracts between sophisticated parties such as those in the case at bar, who are well-advised by counsel, such exclusions of liability often result from determinations regarding who is in the best position to insure the risk at the lowest cost.

A third distinction is that perfect compensation of all contractual relational economic loss is almost always impossible because of the ripple effects which are of the very essence of contractual relational economic loss. This aspect has been recognised as critical from the very beginning. It is in this sense that the solution to cases of this type is necessarily pragmatic and involves drawing a line that will exclude at least some people who have been undeniably injured owing to the tortfeasor's admitted failure to meet the requisite standard of care.

Finally, contractual relational economic loss cases typically involve accidents. This distinguishes them from both products liability economic loss cases and negligent misrepresentation cases. This aspect is of fundamental importance with regard to tests of liability founded on the foreseeability of an individual plaintiff or an ascertained class of plaintiffs.

In light of these substantial differences between contractual relational economic loss cases and other pure economic loss cases, it assists little, if at all, to generalise on the basis of proximity from other types of economic loss cases to the relational loss cases.

In rejecting the plaintiff's 'common adventure' argument (which the other three concurring judges accepted), La Forest J said:

There was no common adventure in this case. The parties agreed that the bridge was owned, operated and maintained by PWC. PWC was, by contract with the railways, obligated to operate and maintain the bridge. CN's preponderant usage of the bridge and participation in negotiations over bridge closure do not justify a finding of common adventure. I can see no reason to allow recovery based simply on the plaintiff's status as a principal client.

In my view, the provision of materials for repairs is also not sufficient to constitute a 'common adventure' between CN and PWC. While the licence agreement does provide that CN will make emergency repairs to the bridge, it provides both for prior approval and reasonable reimbursement by PWC. These provisions merely provide for the establishment of further contractual relations between CN and PWC. None of these clauses provides for any joint responsibility for property losses. It would be curious if a bridge user could found a contractual loss claim on the fortuitous circumstance that it was also the company hired to fix the bridge on occasion.

There is no case for a common adventure that equates to the relationship between ship and cargo in a general average case. In cases of common adventure, A, the ship, has suffered damage which is recoverable against the wrongdoer, C. B is bound to contribute to A's loss and seeks to recover the amount of its contribution from the wrongdoer: see *The Greystoke Castle* [see para 5.4.1, *above*]. In my view, the general average cases are not applicable to the facts of this case. There was no common imminent peril. CN was not required to contribute to PWC's loss. The loss fell exactly where the contract between CN and PWC attributed it. It cannot suffice that losses were incurred by both parties, for that is always the case in this type of situation.

It remains unclear to me how the court is to proceed to establish the existence of a joint venture other than by looking at the contractual relationship between the plaintiff and the property owner. McLachlin J considers that the evidence in this case is sufficient to establish the existence of a joint venture. With respect, I am unable to agree. None of the traditional *indicia* of a joint venture are present either through contract or extracontractually. There was no legal entity in the nature of a partnership. There was no joint undertaking of any commercial enterprise. There was no duty to share both profits and losses. In my view, where the contractual or extracontractual relationship between the parties excludes any form of possible joint liability or contribution in cases of loss of this type, a finding of the existence of a joint venture in this context is excluded.

In conclusion, I do not find CN's arguments to the effect that it had more than a mere contractual interest to be convincing. CN's entitlement to use the bridge finds its sole source in the contract. The contract sets out the full extent of CN's rights: without the contract, CN would be trespassing. It has wisely not argued the existence of any possessory interest. This case does not involve a common adventure such as exists in the cases dealing with general average contributions. As a result, I cannot accept the rationale for recovery set forth by McLachlin J to the effect that the purpose of allowing recovery in this case is to permit 'a plaintiff whose position for practical purposes, *vis-à-vis* the tortfeasor, is indistinguishable from that of the owner of the damaged property, to recover what the actual owner could have recovered'.

In attacking McLachlin J's view that the imposition of liability on Norsk in this case did not raise concerns about indeterminate liability, La Forest J said:

The first critical question is whether the liability needs to be determinate before or after the accident. It is important to underline that, since most claims of this nature occur in the commercial area, the requisite certainty should exist *before* the accident occurs. A company like CN should be able to consult legal counsel and receive reasonably clear advice with respect to potential liability in the case of an accident that is as common as a ship hitting a bridge. Even more importantly, when the shoe is on the other foot, CN should also be able to get some reasonably clear guidance from counsel with respect to its potential liabilities in a case where a train derails and damages a factory. Estimating such liability is, of course, a key aspect to the pricing of insurance for potential tortfeasors. Under the exclusionary rule, liability is determinate *before* the accident. Unless the contract is such as to create a joint venture or a possessory interest, all parties are aware that no recovery will lie for damage to those contractual interests.

The problem with this case from the perspective of indeterminacy is that it involves a type of accident that will very likely lead to a great number of claims. It so happens that on the facts of this case the number of injured parties is small.

5.8.2 *Relational economic Loss*

The fact that Norsk was fortunate enough to hit a bridge with few users does not make its potential liability for contractual relational economic loss any less indeterminate. Its liability after the accident is, of course, determinate; but beforehand, when potential tortfeasors are looking for insurance, they and their insurance company do not know which bridge will be hit. It seems hard to establish one set of rules for negligent tortfeasors who hit busy bridges—liability for economic loss is excused because of indeterminacy—and a different set for those who hit bridges used by few users.

After rejecting the proximity approach applied by McLachlin J, La Forest proposed "a refined proximity analysis in contractual relational economic loss cases". He said:

The crucial problem with the various formulations of the proximity test examined so far is that they look at the problem strictly from the perspective of the defendant. The defendant's negligence places it in a position of liability *vis-à-vis* the entire world. However, if it can show that its liability would be indeterminate, it can be excused. In my opinion, given the eminently pragmatic and policy basis of decisions about liability in this area, the situation of both the defendant and the plaintiff needs to be examined in cases of this kind. In particular, the plaintiff's ability to foresee and provide for the particular damage in question is a key factor in the proximity analysis.

In my view, it is legitimate to consider which party is the better loss-bearer in this type of case. This involves asking which party is in a better position to predict the frequency and severity of CN's economic loss when bridges are damaged, and to plan accordingly. Analysis of loss-bearing ability emphasises how the parties deal with accidents that tort law has not succeeded in preventing, rather than with preventing accidents. In my view, analysis of loss-bearing ability is particularly relevant in determining whether proximity exists in the context of contractual relational economic loss cases.

Consideration of loss-bearing ability is by no means entirely absent from the cases. For example, in *Leigh and Sillivan Ltd v Aliakmon Shipping Ltd* [1986] AC 785 Lord Brandon, in refusing to impose liability, relied on the fact that the plaintiff had open to it an adequate avenue of protection in contract [see Chapter 10, para 10.2.1]. In this case a determination of which party is the better loss-bearer is relatively straightforward. CN is undoubtedly in a better position to bear the loss than Norsk. First, in light of the significant information available regarding bridge failure and CN's long use of the bridge, CN was probably at least equally competent in terms of estimating the potential risks of bridge failure. Secondly, CN would clearly be in a better position than PWC to estimate the potential costs of bridge failure to CN's operations. CN knows exactly how much use it gets out of the various bridges crossed by its trains. It also knows what the alternatives are in cases of bridge failure. Norsk, of course, is very poorly placed to estimate the value of the use that various people and companies get out of the bridges that cross the rivers which its tugs sail on. It is also poorly placed to estimate the potential costs to those users of an interruption in bridge service. Thirdly, CN was better placed to protect itself from the consequences of those losses. It is hard to imagine a more sophisticated group of plaintiffs than the users of railway bridges. These parties have access to the full range of protective options, namely, first party commercial insurance or self-insurance and contracts with both the bridge owner and with the railway's customers.

In expressing his conclusions, La Forest J said:

> In my view, to justify recovery in cases of this nature, the plaintiff would, at the very least, have to respond effectively not only to the concern about indeterminacy, but also show that no adequate alternative means of protection was available. Other concerns may also need to be met. At the very least, the requirement that the plaintiff not have had any commercially reasonable method of protecting itself is an important addition to what remains a conceptually difficult *ex post facto* inquiry into the 'determinate nature' of the particular victim and damage from the perspective of the defendant.
>
> The question of whether recovery should be allowed in the residual cases in which these two barriers are overcome does not require an answer in the context of this case. Individuals and small businesses may be incapable of effectively protecting themselves in any meaningful fashion. In some cases, contractual relational economic loss cases may occur in a different form, such as loss of salary. The failure to protect against it by first party insurance cannot be said to lead to an inference of social unimportance. In such cases, however, the indeterminacy problem is often very acute. If the number of potential individual plaintiffs is great, recovery will be denied on grounds of indeterminacy, even though the plaintiffs may not have had any real ability to protect themselves. Where the plaintiff passes the indeterminacy test, it will often be sophisticated. The argument that recovery should be denied to those who could have protected themselves does not support a bright line in and of itself. Rather, it complements the indeterminacy analysis.
>
> The exclusionary rule is not in itself attractive. It excludes recovery by people who have undeniably suffered losses as a result of an accident. It also leads to some arbitrary but generally predictable results in cases at the margin. The results with respect to time charters may be 'capricious', but time charterers know their rights and obligations from the start and can act accordingly. The rule only becomes defensible when it is realised that full recovery is impossible, that recovery is, in fact, going to be refused in the vast majority of such claims regardless of the rule that we adopt, and when the exclusionary rule is compared to the alternatives. In my view, it should not be disturbed on the facts of this case.

In responding to McLachlin J's criticisms of La Forest J's reasons, La Forest J said:

> I should add a few words about McLachlin J's suggestion that the essential difference between her approach and mine lies in the flexibility allowed by her approach. She characterises my approach as providing for recovery depending exclusively on the terms of the formal contract between the plaintiff and the property owner.
>
> I do not see the essential difference between our two approaches as that between certainty and flexibility. In my view, the key difference is between a principled flexibility, which adheres to a general rule in the absence of policy reasons for excluding its application and arbitrariness. Among the policy factors considered in the course of this opinion that might justify relaxing the rule are the ability of the plaintiff to protect itself and the quantum of property damage caused by the tortfeasor with its attendant impact on the issue of deterrence.
>
> I have not found it necessary to consider the precise role of these factors in this case since CN was clearly able to protect itself, and the property damage sustained was sufficient to afford deterrence. Whether such factors would, in fact,

provide workable criteria sufficient to provide for recovery despite the strong arguments in favour of the long-standing exclusionary rule, based on certainty and other factors, is an open question. What I have decided is that in the absence of all of these factors, there is no reason to disturb the rule.

Thus, I do not say that the right to recovery in all cases of contractual economic loss depends exclusively on the terms of the contract. Rather, I note that such is the tenor of the exclusionary rule and that departures from that rule should be justified on defensible policy grounds. The court should do more than simply establish a rule that allows judges to resolve cases as they see fit. That, as I see it, is the effect of the approach proposed by McLachlin J.

Chapter 6

Product liability—physical injury and property damage

It will be an advantage to make it clear that the law in this matter, as in most others, is in accordance with sound common sense. (**Lord Atkin in *Donoghue v Stevenson* [1932] AC 562**)

In the law of negligence the concept of proximity is inconsistent with the contemplation or expectation of an intermediate check. (**Hobhouse LJ in *McCullagh v Lane Fox & Partners Ltd* (1996) 49 Con LR 124**)

To find a duty of care it is necessary that Mr Bishop should have known that ADT would place reliance on his information or advice without independent inquiry. In this case, the very fact that the meeting was seen as 'the final hurdle', added to the fact that it was never open to ADT to have an independent accountants' investigation into the affairs of BSG, meant that it was obvious that further detailed investigation after the meeting into BSG's accounts would not take place. (**May J in *ADT Ltd v BDO Binder Hamlyn* (6 December 1995, unreported)**)

Both vendors and purchasers had their own advisers, including solicitors and accountants, and Mrs Land was herself both professionally qualified and an experienced businesswoman. The maxim caveat emptor remains as applicable in such a transaction as ever; one party does not just rely on what he is told by the opposite party or his adviser. (**Morritt LJ in *Peach Publishing Ltd v Slater and Co* (13 February 1997, unreported)**)

6.1   Context

Although this chapter is headed *Product Liability*, it is not confined to 'products'. It covers all situations where the defendant puts into circulation something which is defective and the plaintiff, who did not acquire it directly from the defendant, suffers personal injury or property damage in consequence. This type of situation differs from that dealt with in Chapter 9, where the 'thing' which the defendant puts into circulation is a misleading statement or incorrect advice. It also differs from the type of situation considered in Chapter 5, para 5.2 (and, to a certain extent, in Chapter 4, para 4.3), where the plaintiff's injury is relational, in the sense that it arises only because of (and is dependent upon) the defendant's having damaged the property of a third person. By way of contrast, in the cases considered in this chapter (and in Chapter 7, para 7.1) the plaintiff's injury is direct. The loss suffered by the plaintiff in the cases considered in this chapter (unlike Chapter 7, para 7.3) is not pure economic loss. However, it is necessary to consider the non-economic loss cases in order to appreciate fully the tenor of the economic loss decisions.

6.2 Importance of *Donoghue v Stevenson*

6.2.1 The actual decision

General

The headnote to the report of this case at [1932] AC 562 states: "By Scots and English law alike, the manufacturer of an article of food, medicine, or the like, sold by him to a distributor in circumstances which prevent the distributor or the ultimate purchaser or consumer from discovering by inspection any defect, is under a legal duty to the ultimate purchaser or consumer to take reasonable care to ensure that the article is free from *any* defect likely to cause injury to health". The facts are well known and were very ordinary. The plaintiff's action was for damages for personal injuries (consisting of shock and gastro-enteritis) which she had suffered as a result of consuming part of the contents of a bottle of ginger beer which had been manufactured by the defendant, and which contained the decomposed remains of a snail. The House of Lords upheld the plaintiff's claim; at least in principle, because the actual decision was concerned only with a preliminary question of law on the assumption that the plaintiff's allegations of fact were true.

Split decision

To any lawyer trained in the latter part of the twentieth century, the principle encapsulated in the headnote might seem obvious. Lord Atkin said (at p 599) that it was a proposition which no one who was not a lawyer would for one moment doubt. Yet, at that time—1932—there was a long line of authority opposed to the plaintiff's contentions. In the House of Lords, the decision was split 3:2, and the two dissenting Law Lords (Buckmaster and Tomlin) were vehement in their opposition. Lord Atkin said (at p 579) that he did not think that a more important problem had ever occupied the House of Lords in its judicial capacity.

Claim in tort

Why was this so? The purchase of the bottle of ginger beer was made not by the plaintiff herself, but by a friend of hers. This meant that the plaintiff was not able to exercise the rights of a purchaser of goods of unmerchantable quality under s 14 of the Sale of Goods Act 1893 (now s 14 of the Sale of Goods Act 1979). Also, the purchase by the plaintiff's friend had not been from the manufacturer, but from a café. This meant that the plaintiff's claim against the manufacturer had, of necessity, to be in tort, as she had no contract with the manufacturer. The only contracts which had come into existence were between the manufacturer and the café owner on the one hand, and between the café owner and the plaintiff's friend on the other hand.

6.2.2   The general exclusionary rule

The proposition which the plaintiff wished the court to uphold was thus in conflict with the well-established and seemingly competing principle of privity of contract, whereby if A and B make a contract between themselves, then C, who is not a party to that contract, cannot have any rights under it. On this basis, the theory preventing recovery in a case like *Donoghue* was that a breach by a manufacturer (A) of his contract with the distributor (B), to whom he had sold the article in question, did not give any cause of action to C, being a sub-purchaser from B, if C was injured by virtue of the article proving to be defective, notwithstanding that this was totally A's fault and A was in breach of the terms of his contract with B.

6.2.3   Two important exceptions

The general rule was applied rigorously except in two circumstances, both of which are discussed *below*:

Knowledge of a danger

Langridge v Levy: Where the seller of an article of a type which was not ordinarily dangerous knew that the particular article which he was selling was dangerous, and either concealed that knowledge from the buyer, or made a fraudulent misrepresentation as to its safety which induced the buyer to buy it, he could be held liable for injuries suffered by a third party. *Langridge v Levy* (1838) 3 M & W 337 was decided on this basis. The defendant had sold a gun to the plaintiff's father who, in due course, allowed the plaintiff to use it. Through no fault of the plaintiff or his father, the gun exploded while the plaintiff was using it, thereby causing physical injury to him. Although the only contract had been between the plaintiff's father and the defendant, it was held that the plaintiff had a good cause of action against the defendant for his injuries. Parke B, delivering the judgment of the court, expressly disclaimed any wider implications of this decision, and said that it was based on the ground that the defendant had falsely and fraudulently warranted to the plaintiff's father that the gun was made by a certain reputable manufacturer and was in a good and safe condition, with the intention that the gun should be used by the plaintiff (apparently the plaintiff's father had told the defendant that the gun was going to be used by the plaintiff).

Comment

The reasoning of the court in this case is difficult to follow. The court did not require that the defendant intended the false representation to be communicated to the plaintiff, yet did apparently deem it to be a necessary ingredient of liability that the defendant made his misrepresentation to a third person (the plaintiff's father) with the intention that the gun should be used by the plaintiff. It is difficult to understand why the defendant should have had such an intention when his immediate object must have been to induce the father to buy the gun, and it must have been immaterial to him by whom the gun was thereafter to be used. However, it is worth noting that this factor (intention that the defective product should be used by a particular person), which was important to the court in 1837 in relation to a case of physical injury, was also important to the House of Lords in 1983 in *Junior Books Limited v Veitchi Co* [1983] AC 520, in imposing liability in tort for pure economic loss suffered by a plaintiff in consequence of the defendant's negligence in laying a defective floor in the plaintiff's factory (see para 7.3.6).

A modern relic: Rivtow Marine: A relic of this exception formed the basis of the decision of the Supreme Court of Canada in *Rivtow Marine Ltd v Washington Iron Works* (1973) 40 DLR (3d) 530 (which is discussed in Chapter 7, para 7.4.2). Although the court endorsed the view that the cost of remedying defects in a product was irrecoverable since it was pure economic loss, it was held that, where the defendant was aware of such defects and failed to warn the plaintiff of them, the plaintiff could recover its loss of profits (but not the cost of remedying the defects) which resulted from the barges having to be repaired at their busiest time of use, as this loss of profits could have been avoided if the defendant had notified the plaintiff of the defects promptly.

Dangerous articles

Thomas v Winchester: Where the defendant was a supplier of articles which were dangerous in themselves, such as loaded firearms, poisons or explosives, he could also be held liable for a third party's injuries. Here there was no requirement that the defendant must have known of the danger when he supplied the article in question. In *Thomas v Winchester* (1852) 6 NY 397, the defendant, who was a wholesale dealer in medicines, had sold a quantity of the poison belladonna to a druggist (pharmacist) having negligently labelled the bottle as being an extract of dandelion. The druggist then innocently re-sold this potion to the plaintiff, who had asked for a quantity of extract of dandelion. The plaintiff suffered personal injuries in consuming this mixture. The court held that the plaintiff was entitled to recover damages from the defendant, notwithstanding that there was no contract between them. The court affirmed the general rule, saying: "If *A* builds a wagon and sells it to *B*, who sells it to *C*, and *C* hires it to *D*, who in consequence of the negligence of *A* in building the wagon, is injured, *D* cannot recover damages against *A*. *A*'s obligation to build the wagon faithfully arises solely out of his contract with *B*. The public have nothing to do with it". However, it was held that an exception existed to this rule where, as in this case, the defendant's act of negligence was "imminently dangerous to the lives of others".

Dixon v Bell (1816) 5 M & S 198: This old English case falls within the dangerous articles exception. The defendant, who owned a gun, was held liable to the plaintiff, whose son had accidentally been shot with it by the defendant's servant. The defendant had in fact taken the precaution of removing the priming (the substance used to ignite the explosive charge in the gun), but not the gunpowder. The court held that as a gun is an instrument of danger, the defendant ought to have gone further in the precautions which he took and he was therefore liable to the plaintiff, notwithstanding the absence of any contract between the plaintiff and the defendant. Another interesting feature of this case is that the court might inadvertently have been awarding damages for pure economic loss, because the plaintiff's case averred that the plaintiff's son was his servant, and that in consequence of the injury the plaintiff was deprived of the son's services, and was put to great expense in looking after him.

Dominion Natural Gas: These decisions were instrumental in the Privy Council (on appeal from the Court of Appeal for Ontario—a procedure abolished in 1949) imposing liability on the defendant in *Dominion Natural Gas Co Ltd v Collins & Perkins* [1909] AC 640. The defendant had installed, under agreement with a railway company, a gas supplying apparatus on the railway company's premises. Due to the defendant's negligence, an explosion occurred, which caused physical injury to certain railway workmen, the plaintiffs. The defendant was held liable, notwithstanding the absence of a contract between it and the plaintiffs. Lord Dunedin, in delivering the opinion of the Judicial Committee of the Privy Council, affirmed the general privity of contract rule, but said that, in the case of articles dangerous in themselves, which included the apparatus in this case, "... there is a peculiar duty to take precaution upon those who send forth or install such articles when it is necessarily the case that other parties will come within their proximity".

Comment

In the light of the decision in *Donoghue v Stevenson*, the decision in each of the above-mentioned exceptional cases was correct, albeit that the process of reasoning adopted was sometimes quite artificial. This type of reasoning need no longer be followed, because the House of Lords in *Donoghue* did away with the general 'privity of contract recovery prohibition doctrine' which had previously been so slavishly adhered to. However, as several subsequent cases have shown, including the very important House of Lords' decision in *Murphy v Brentwood District Council* [1991] 1 AC 398 (see para 7.3.2), this rejection of the general rule applies only where the plaintiff has suffered physical injury or damage to property other than the actual defective article or building which the defendant manufactured, supplied or constructed. A relic of the general rule is thus alive and well in this type of case (ie the negligent manufacture, supply or construction of a defective article or building) in those cases where the plaintiff's loss is purely economic—which, for this purpose, has been held by the courts to include damage to the actual defective article or building itself. Therefore it is instructive to examine the reasoning in some of the old cases which applied the general rule in circumstances where the plaintiff had suffered only physical injury. It is also useful to consider how these cases, or fact-situations analogous to them, would be decided today.

The Orjula: a post-Murphy revival

In *Murphy v Brentwood District Council* [1991] 1 AC 398, the House of Lords stated that as a matter of fact it was concerned with defects in property which, once detected, could no longer cause damage and were to be categorised as pure economic loss, because the purchaser could then either repair the property or discard it as useless. Thus, Lord Bridge said (at p 475):

> If a dangerous defect in a chattel is discovered before it causes any personal injury or damage to property, because the danger is now known and the chattel cannot safely be used unless the defect is repaired, the defect becomes merely a defect in quality. The chattel is either capable of repair at economic cost or it is worthless and must be scrapped. In either case, the loss sustained by the owner or hirer of the chattel is purely economic. It is recoverable against any party who owes the loser a relevant contractual duty, but it is not recoverable in tort in the absence of a special relationship of proximity imposing on the tortfeasor a duty of care to safeguard the plaintiff from economic loss. There is no such special relationship between the manufacturer of a chattel and remote owner or hirer.

In *Losinjska Plovidba v Transco Overseas Ltd ('The Orjula')* [1995] 2 Lloyd's Rep 395, the facts of which are set out in para 7.1.4, the plaintiff's counsel argued that the above-cited rationale of *Murphy* was not applicable and that the case fell into a different category, namely the 'dangerous articles' exception referred to here. He focused on the fact that the two containers with their leaking drums were positively dangerous and could not remain on the ship, nor could they be abandoned at sea or in Rotterdam. The plaintiff, who had brought the containers and the drums into Holland, was not able to leave without undertaking expensive steps to neutralise the active danger that existed not only to the plaintiff's own property but also to third parties. The judge, Mance J, agreed with the plaintiff's counsel's submission. He said:

> In the present case, the property put into circulation constituted a continuing active danger to anyone on whose vessel or land it was, as well as to any others in the vicinity, so long as measures were not taken to neutralise and contain it. In these circumstances, it is in my view still at least arguable in law that, if property is put into circulation which remains positively dangerous unless preventive measures are taken to neutralise the danger, a person who is obliged to take such steps and does not have the option simply to abandon the property may have a claim in tort against a person who negligently put the article into circulation.

6.2.4   The early cases: the 'floodgates' fear

Winterbottom v Wright

The most important 'general rule' case was *Winterbottom v Wright* (1842) 10 M & W 109. Here, the defendant had constructed a horse-drawn mailcoach for the Postmaster General, who in turn entered into a contract with another party to drive the coach and deliver the mail. The plaintiff was a mailcoachman, employed by that other party, and was injured when the mailcoach collapsed and broke, due to certain latent defects in it which were attributable to the defendant's negligent construction of it. The Court of Exchequer rejected the plaintiff's claim and made some very strong statements in favour of the general rule of exclusion. Lord Abinger CB said: "We must not allow a doubt to rest upon this subject, since our doing so might be the means of letting in upon us a world of actions". He went on to point out that there was no privity of contract between the plaintiff and the defendant and said that, if the plaintiff could sue, then every passenger, or even a person passing along the road, who was injured by the upsetting of the coach might bring an action.

Lord Abinger's answer to this possible scenario was: "Unless we confine the operation of such contracts as this to the parties who enter into them, the most absurd consequences, to which I can see no limit, would ensue". He laid further emphasis on the sanctity of the initial contract, which was between only the defendant and the Postmaster General, by saying that, if the plaintiff was allowed to succeed in this case, then "The court would be working this injustice, namely, that after the defendant had done everything to the satisfaction of his employer [the Postmaster General], after all matters between them had been adjusted, and all accounts had been settled, we would subject them to be ripped open by this action of tort being brought against the defendant".

The other members of the court were of the same mind. Alderson B said: "If we were to hold that the plaintiff could sue, then there is no point at which we could stop. The only safe rule is to confine the right to those who enter into the contract. If we go one step beyond that, there is no reason why we should not go fifty". He said that the only argument in favour of the plaintiff was hardship, but he said that that could have been obviated if the plaintiff had made himself a party to the contract. This is wholly unconvincing, because in practice the plaintiff, or any other person in his position, would probably have had almost no chance of becoming a party to the original contract between the coachmaker and the Postmaster General.

The court, by its decision, impliedly gave approval to a submission by the defendant's counsel that, if privity to the contract was not an essential element of liability in this case, then there would be no limit to actions, when he said: "If the plaintiff may run through three contracts, as here, he may run through any number, and enormous and frightful consequences would ensue; for instance, in the recent accident on the Versailles Railway, every person injured might sue the manufacturer of the defective axle". After *Donoghue v Stevenson*, this proposition, which was so unacceptable in 1842, became a perfectly acceptable legal answer, but only in respect of the passengers' personal injuries or damage to their property and any economic losses flowing directly therefrom, but not in relation to any pure economic losses suffered as a result of such an accident.

Comment

It is worth noting that the analysis of the court in this case, and of the defendant's counsel, whilst no longer applicable in relation to personal injuries or damage to the plaintiff's property, is still used today as a rationale for depriving plaintiffs of a remedy against the negligent manufacturer of a defective product or the negligent constructor of a defective building where the plaintiff is not the original purchaser of it from the defendant (and therefore does not have a contractual relationship with the defendant), in the case where the plaintiff's only loss is that the article or the building is defective and has to be replaced or repaired. See, for example, the decision of the Supreme Court of Canada in *Rivtow Marine Ltd v Washington Iron Works* (1973) 40 DLR (3d) 530 and the House of Lords' decision in *Murphy v Brentwood District Council* [1991] 1 AC 398, which are discussed in Chapter 7, paras 7.5.7 and 7.7.

The decision in *Winterbottom* (1842) held sway for 90 years, and contributed considerably towards the two powerful dissenting judgments (of Lords Buckmaster and Tomlin) in *Donoghue*. There is little doubt that *Winterbottom* would be decided differently today, even though Lord Atkin in *Donoghue* said (at p 589) that he thought that it was correctly decided. This is surprising in the light of Lord Atkin's views about when a duty of care arises in tort, but understandable in view of the fact that the decision in *Donoghue* was so revolutionary in its time; and perhaps for that very reason, Lord Atkin (at p 583) stressed that the principle which he was thereby endorsing was confined to manufacturers of food and other articles of common household use "where everyone, including the manufacturer, knows that the articles will be used by persons other than the actual ultimate purchaser".

Longmeid v Holliday

Another important early case was *Longmeid v Holliday* (1851) 6 Ex 761, in which the plaintiff, Mrs Longmeid, had been injured by an explosion in a defective lamp which the defendant had made and sold to the plaintiff's husband. The court held that the plaintiff had no cause of action. Surprisingly, *Winterbottom v Wright* was not referred to. Instead, the court saw this case as being a variant of *Dixon v Bell* (1816) 5 M & S 198 (see *above*, para 6.2.3), which it approved, and then went on to say (through Parke B): "But it would be going much too far to say that so much care is required in the ordinary intercourse of life between one individual and another, that, if a machine not in its nature dangerous, a carriage, for instance [this could be seen as an indirect reference to *Winterbottom v Wright*] which might become so by a latent defect entirely unknown . . . should be lent or given by one person, even by the person who manufactured it, to another, the former should be answerable to the latter for subsequent damage accruing by the use of it". Although these words were influential in subsequent cases, there is no doubt that this case would be decided differently today.

Earl v Lubbock

So, too, would the Court of Appeal decision in *Earl v Lubbock* [1905] 1 KB 253. The defendant was a master wheelwright and had entered into a contract with a particular firm to keep its vans in good repair. The plaintiff was a driver employed by that firm. While he was driving one of the vans a wheel came off, and he sustained injuries by falling from the van. His cause of action against the defendant was based on the negligence of the defendant's employees in failing properly to inspect and repair the van, which had been in their hands earlier on the day of the accident. The Court of Appeal, applying *Winterbottom v Wright*, held that the defendant was under no duty to the plaintiff. The judgment of Matthew LJ contains an interesting comment. He observed that the plaintiff's argument in this case was that the defendant's servants had been negligent in the performance of the contract which the defendant had with the owners of the van, and that it should follow as a matter of law that anyone who sustained an injury traceable to that negligence should have a cause of action against the defendant; and then said: "It is impossible to accept such a wide proposition, and, indeed, it is difficult to see how, if it were the law, trade could be carried on".

Lord Atkin, in *Donoghue* (at p 592), thought that *Earl v Lubbock* was correctly decided, but again, this is understandable in view of the restrictive view of the ambit of liability which he was compelled to take.

Blacker v Lake and Elliot

Another case which was strongly supportive of the general rule, but which would be decided differently today, is *Blacker v Lake and Elliot Ltd* (1912) 106 LT 533, in which the plaintiff had been injured by the explosion of a brazing lamp which he had bought from a retail dealer, who had in turn bought it from the defendant manufacturer. The factual context was thus very similar to that which existed in *Donoghue*. The Divisional Court of the King's Bench, although satisfied that the explosion had been caused by the defendant's negligent manufacture of the lamp, nevertheless held that the plaintiff had no cause of action against the defendant. Hamilton J (who subsequently became Lord Sumner) recognised the exceptions to the general exclusionary rule referred to *above*, but said that, where these do not apply, the position is that "The breach of the defendant's contract with *A* to use due care and skill in the manufacture or repair of an article does not of itself give any cause of action to *B*, when *B* is injured by reason of the article proving to be defective in breach of that contract".

Other 'ginger beer cases'

It is also worth noting that, before *Donoghue*, there were three reported cases involving ginger beer.

Bates v Batey & Co Ltd [1913] 3 KB 351: It was actually the bottle, rather than the ginger beer in it, which was defective. The defendant manufactured ginger beer, which it placed in bottles it had bought from another company. It sold some of the bottled ginger beer to a shopkeeper, from whom the plaintiff bought one bottle. Due to a defect in the bottle, it burst when the plaintiff was opening it and injured him. The defendant did not know of the defect, but could have discovered it by the exercise of reasonable care. The court held that the defendant was not liable. Surprisingly, the judge (Horridge J) held that this bottle of ginger beer, in its defective state, was a dangerous thing. This meant that the general exclusionary rule did not apply, but one of the exceptions to it (referred to *above*) did. Nevertheless, he held that the defendant was not liable because it did not know that the bottle was defective, and, in his view, the defendant could not be made liable simply because it had the means of knowledge. After *Donoghue* this would no longer be correct.

Mullen v Barr and M'Gowan v Barr: The other two cases were decisions of the Court of Session in Scotland, and they are reported together as *Mullen v AG Barr & Co Ltd* and *M'Gowan v Barr & Company* [1929] SC 461. In both cases the plaintiff had bought from a retailer a bottle of ginger beer which had been manufactured by the defendant, who had sold it to the retailer. In both cases, unknown to the defendant and the retailer, there was the decayed body of a mouse in each bottle. This was discovered only after the plaintiffs had drunk some of the ginger beer and had become ill in consequence. The bottles were made of very dark glass, which meant that the contents could be seen only if the bottles were held up to a strong light. Thus the facts were indistinguishable from *Donoghue*. Nevertheless, the court held that the defendants owed no duty to the plaintiffs, because they had not contracted directly with them. Lord Anderson said: "In a case like the present, where the goods of the defenders are widely distributed throughout Scotland, it would seem little short of outrageous to make them responsible to members of the public for the condition of the contents of every bottle which issues from their works. It is obvious that, if such responsibility attached to the defenders, they might be called on to meet claims of damages which they could not possibly investigate or answer".

Comment

The rationale for this early general exclusionary rule was the fear of opening the floodgates to a mass of claims, some of which might be spurious. However, this rule worked such a great hardship on innocent plaintiffs that eventually, with changing times and attitudes, its downfall seemed inevitable; as one would hope will also happen to the current rule which prevents an innocent purchaser of a defective article or building from recovering his losses from a negligent manufacturer or builder with whom he did not have a contractual relationship, where no personal injury has been suffered, and the only thing damaged is the defective article or building itself. However, the extremely strong support for this rule of exclusion which was expressed by the House of Lords in *Murphy v Brentwood District Council* [1991] 1 AC 398, and in some other leading Commonwealth authorities, discussed in Chapter 7, renders this a faint hope at the moment.

6.2.5   The pedigree of *Donoghue v Stevenson*

Distinguishing earlier cases

Faced with such strong support for the general exclusionary rule, one might wonder how the majority of the House in *Donoghue* were able to base their decision on authority. First, they said that the cases mentioned *above* which endorsed the general rule in strong terms were distinguishable, because they dealt with different fact situations or were not true cases of negligence. For example, in reference to *Longmeid v Holliday* (1851) 6 Ex 761 (see *above*, para 6.2.4), Lord Atkin said (at p 591): "I do not for a moment believe that Parke B had in his mind such a case as a loaf negligently mixed with poison by the baker which poisoned a purchaser's family. He is, in my opinion, confining his remarks primarily to cases where a person is seeking to rely on a duty of care which arises out of a contract with a third party, and has never even discussed the case of a manufacturer negligently causing an article to be dangerous and selling it in that condition"; and, in relation to *Winterbottom v Wright* (1842) 10 M & W 109 (see *above*, para 6.2.4), Lord Macmillan said (at p 608):

> In view of the deference paid to English precedents, it is a singular fact that the case of *Winterbottom v Wright* is one in which no negligence in the sense of breach of a duty owed by the defendant to the plaintiff was alleged on the part of the plaintiff. The truth, as I hope to show, is that there is in the English reports no such 'unbroken and consistent current of decisions' as would justify the aspersion that the law of England has committed itself irrevocably to what is neither reasonable nor equitable, or require a Scottish judge in following them to do violence to his conscience.

Justice and reasonableness

The reasoning of Lords Atkin and Macmillan in distinguishing the earlier cases is not wholly convincing. However, they seemed quite unashamedly to be basing their decision more on their sense of what was just and reasonable than on anything else. This is borne out by the last-quoted words of Lord Macmillan and also by the fact that he immediately follows those words by quoting from Lord Esher in *Emmens v Pottle* (1885) 16 QBD 354 (at p 357): "In my opinion any proposition the result of which would be to show that the common law of England is wholly unreasonable and unjust cannot be part of the common law of England". In similar vein, Lord Atkin said (at p 583): "I do not think so ill of our jurisprudence as to suppose that its principles are so remote from the ordinary needs of civilised society as to deny a legal remedy where there is obviously a social wrong"; and (at p 599) in relation to the proposition which he said the House's decision established (which is slightly wider than that stated in the headnote, in that he said that it would include injury to the consumer's property): "It is a proposition which I venture to say no one in Scotland or England who was not a lawyer would for one moment doubt. It will be an advantage to make it clear that the law in this matter, as in most others, is in accordance with sound common sense".

Supporting cases

George v Skivington: There was *some* authority in favour of 'the *Donoghue* proposition' and it was enthusiastically embraced by the majority in the House of Lords. The only case directly in point was *George and Wife v Skivington* (1869) LR 5 Ex 1, in which the second plaintiff had suffered a personal injury through having used a chemical compound which had been sold by the defendant to her husband (the first plaintiff) as a hair wash for her use. The court held the defendant liable for these injuries, notwithstanding that there was no contract between the second plaintiff and the defendant, and therefore no warranty from him to her. The court said that these questions were irrelevant because (*per* Kelly CB) ". . . the contract of sale is only alleged by way of inducement, the cause of action being not upon that contract, but for an injury caused to the wife of the purchaser by reason of an article being sold to him for the use of his wife turning out to be unfit for the purpose for which it was bought. Quite apart from any question of warranty, there was a duty on the defendant to use ordinary care in compounding this wash for the hair. Unquestionably there was such a duty towards the purchaser, and it extends, in my judgment, to the person for whose use the vendor knew the compound was purchased".

MacPherson v Buick Motor Co (1916) 217 NY 382: The defendant car manufacturer had sold a car to a retail dealer who had resold it to the plaintiff. While the plaintiff was driving the car it suddenly collapsed due to one of its wheels being defective, and he was injured. The New York Court of Appeals held that he was entitled to recover damages from the manufacturer. Cardozo J said (at p 389): "We are dealing with the liability of the manufacturer of a finished product who puts it on the market to be used without inspection by his customers. If he is negligent, where danger is to be foreseen, liability will follow. There is here no break in the chain of cause and effect. The maker of this car supplied it for the use of purchasers from the dealer. The dealer was indeed the one person of whom it might be said with some certainty that the car would not be used. Yet the defendant would have us say that the dealer was the only person whom the defendant was under a legal duty to protect. The law does not lead us to so inconsequent a conclusion".

This case was cited with approval by Lord Atkin and Lord Macmillan in *Donoghue*. Lord Atkin said (at p 598): "Cardozo J in *MacPherson v Buick Motor Co* states the principles of the law as I should desire to state them".

Reconciliation of approaches: Judges in subsequent cases criticised and distinguished *George v Skivington* wherever possible and preferred, instead, to follow the '*Winterbottom* line of reasoning' (see para 6.2.4, *above*). In *Donoghue* Lord Buckmaster (dissenting) said (at p 570): "Few cases can have lived so dangerously and so long as *George v Skivington*". On one level, it is true that there was a conflict between the '*Winterbottom* approach' and the '*George* approach'. On another level, however, as pointed out by Lord Macmillan, this conflict can be seen to be illusory. He said (at p 610): "There is no reason why the same set of facts should not give one person a right of action in contract and another person a right of action in tort". He thought that it was wrong to focus on the contract of sale between the manufacturer and the retailer, and to exclude the plaintiff's claim because she was not a party to that contract. He said (at p 611): "If you disregard the fact that the circumstances of the case at one stage included the existence of a contract of sale between the manufacturer and the retailer, and approach the question by asking whether there is evidence of carelessness on the part of the manufacturer, and whether he owed a duty to be careful to the party who has been injured in consequence of his want of care, the circumstance that the injured party was not a party to the incidental contract of sale becomes irrelevant, and his title to sue the manufacturer is unaffected by that circumstance".

Heaven v Pender: This was also the approach of Brett MR (who subsequently became Lord Esher) in *Heaven v Pender* (1883) 11 QBD 503, in which the defendant, a dock owner, had installed a platform supported by ropes on the outside of a ship in his dock under a contract with the shipowner. The plaintiff was a workman in the employ of a ship painter who had contracted with the shipowner to paint the outside of the ship. For this purpose the plaintiff went onto the platform. He suffered personal injuries when one of the ropes by which it was slung broke due to its having been defective when supplied by the defendant. The court upheld the plaintiff's claim.

Two of the judges (Cotton and Bowen LJJ) said (at p 515) that all persons who painted or repaired ships ". . . must be considered as invited by the dock owner to use the dock and all appliances provided by him. To these persons the dock owner was under an obligation to take reasonable care that the appliances provided were in a fit state, so as not to expose those who might use them to any danger". Brett MR went further and said (at p 509): "Whenever one person is by circumstances placed in such a position with regard to another that everyone of ordinary sense who did think, would at once recognise that if he did not use ordinary care and skill in his conduct with regard to those circumstances, he would cause danger of injury to the person or property of the other, a duty arises to use ordinary care and skill to avoid such danger". In *Le Lievre v Gould* [1893] 1 QB 491, as Lord Esher MR, he narrowed down this statement slightly by saying (at p 497): "If one man is near to another or is near to the property of another, a duty lies on him not to do that which may cause a personal injury to that other, or may injure his property".

Influence of Heaven v Pender: These *dicta* of Lord Esher (and the sale of goods example given by him—see *below*, para 6.3.1), and the following *dictum* of A L Smith LJ in *Le Lievre v Gould* [1893] 1 QB 491, to a large extent shaped the decision of the majority in *Donoghue*. A L Smith LJ said (at p 581):

> The decision of *Heaven v Pender* was founded upon the principle that a duty to take due care did arise when the person or property of one was in such proximity to the person or property of another that, if due care was not taken, damage might be done by the one to the other.

By way of contrast, the dissenting Lords in *Donoghue* said that *Heaven v Pender* had no bearing on the question before them because the plaintiff in *Donoghue* was not 'near to' the defendant or his property. Lord Buckmaster felt so strongly that the position should be as laid down in *Winterbottom* that he said (at p 576): "So far as the case of *George v Skivington* and the *dicta* in *Heaven v Pender* are concerned, it is in my opinion better that they should be buried so securely that their perturbed spirits shall no longer vex the law".

Comment

This examination of the antecedents of *Donoghue v Stevenson* [1932] AC 562 has not been conducted for the purpose of questioning the soundness of its foundation. Rather, the purpose has been to demonstrate the creative and expansionist judicial approach adopted by their Lordships, so as to be able to compare this with the narrow and restrictive approach adopted by their latter-day brethren in *Murphy v Brentwood District Council* [1991] 1 AC 398, which is discussed in Chapter 7. From the point of view of moral and social justice, it was clear that, by 1932, the sort of liability which the plaintiff in *Donoghue* wished the court to impose on the defendant was an idea whose time had come. As Lord Atkin said (at p 599): "It is a proposition which I venture to say no one in Scotland or England who was not a lawyer would for one moment doubt". It is regrettable that the seven Law Lords who formed the unanimous panel in *Murphy* emphatically turned themselves (and, in the process, the development of the common law) away from this reasoning in relation to the question whether a manufacturer or a builder of a defective product or building should be liable in tort to an ultimate consumer or purchaser for economic loss suffered by him in consequence of the product or building being defective (but not causing injury to the plaintiff or damage to any other property of the plaintiff) through the sole fault of the manufacturer or builder.

6.3   Intermediate inspection

6.3.1   Lord Esher's example

In *Heaven v Pender* (1883) 11 QBD 503 Brett MR (who subsequently became Lord Esher) said (at p 510):

This [ie the principle which he had just formulated—see *above*] includes the case of goods supplied to be used immediately by a particular person or persons or one of a class of persons, where it would be obvious to the person supplying, if he thought, that the goods would in all probability be used at once by such persons before a reasonable opportunity for discovering any defect which might exist, and where the thing supplied would be of such a nature that a neglect of ordinary care or skill as to its condition or the manner of supplying it would probably cause danger to the person or property of the person for whose use it was supplied, and who was about to use it.

6.3.2 Application in *Donoghue v Stevenson*

As is well known, and as discussed in Chapter 3, para 3.2.1, Lord Atkin in *Donoghue* formulated a test of liability for negligence which (at p 580) he called "a general conception of relations giving rise to a duty of care". He said that this would be satisfied where there existed between the defendant and the plaintiff such a high degree of 'closeness of relationship' or 'neighbourliness' or 'proximity' that the defendant ought reasonably to have had the plaintiff in his contemplation as being likely to be injured when directing his mind to acts or omissions of his which he could reasonably foresee would be likely to cause injury to other persons. Lord Thankerton expressed the same view when he said (at p 603): "Unless the consumer can establish a special relationship with the manufacturer it is clear, in my opinion, that neither the law of Scotland nor the law of England will hold that the manufacturer has any duty towards the consumer to exercise diligence".

In view of the fact that the manufacturer had fully divested itself of all dealings with the bottle of ginger beer when it sold it to the distributor, and had no knowledge of, nor any interest in, what might happen to the bottle of ginger beer after that, it might well be asked how the House was able to conclude that there did exist 'a special relationship' or a sufficiently high degree of proximity between the manufacturer/defendant and the plaintiff, so as to make the defendant liable for the plaintiff's injuries when she consumed the defective ginger beer. The answer lies in the fact that the bottle was made of opaque glass, so that no one could have seen the snail even if the bottle had been held up to the light. There was thus no opportunity of an intermediate examination between the time that the defendant put the defective product into circulation and the time that the plaintiff began to consume it. The fact that the defendant knew, or ought to have realised, that there would not be an intermediate inspection of the ginger beer before it came to be consumed by an unknown third party (the plaintiff) served to bring him into 'a special relationship' or served to create a sufficiently high degree of 'proximity' as to make it just and reasonable to impose a duty of care on him for the plaintiff's injuries. In *Farr v Butters Brothers & Co* [1932] 2 KB 606 (which is discussed further in para 6.3.4, *below*) Scrutton LJ expressed this point succinctly when he said (at p 615): "The impossibility of intermediate examination makes the relation so proximate that there is a liability".

6.3.3   *Product liability—physical injury and property damage*

In a more recent case, *McCullagh v Lane Fox and Partners Ltd* (1996) 49 Con LR 124 (CA), Hobhouse LJ articulated this point pithily when he said: "In the law of negligence, the concept of proximity is inconsistent with the contemplation or expectation of an intermediate check". Then, with specific reference to *Donoghue v Stevenson*, Hobhouse LJ continued:

> In *Donoghue v Stevenson* [1932] AC 562, Lord Atkin referred to 'the proximate relationship which may be too remote where inspection, even of the person using the article, certainly of an intermediate person, may be interposed' [see *below*]. Thus, in product liability cases, the likelihood that there will be an intermediate inspection or check negatives the existence of the duty of care (see *Herschtal v Stewart and Arden Ltd* [1940] 1 KB 155 [see para 6.3.4] and *Haseldine v CA Daw and Son Ltd* [1941] 2 KB 343 [see para 6.4.4]).

6.3.3   Fundamental importance

Introduction

The point made *above* is of such fundamental importance in understanding the creation of duties of care in all cases where the defendant negligently puts something into circulation, whether it be a product, a building or a statement, and whether the loss be physical or purely economic, that it is worthwhile examining how each of the majority Lords dealt with this question in *Donoghue*.

Lord Thankerton

Having said that the plaintiff must be able to establish 'a special relationship' with the defendant in order to succeed, Lord Thankerton then said (at p 603):

> The special circumstances from which the appellant claims that such a relationship of duty should be inferred may, I think, be stated thus—namely, that the respondent, in placing his manufactured article of drink upon the market, has intentionally so excluded interference with, or examination of, the article by any intermediate handler of the goods between himself and the consumer that he has, of his own accord, brought himself into direct relationship with the consumer, with the result that the consumer is entitled to rely upon the exercise of diligence by the manufacturer to secure that the article shall not be harmful to the consumer.

Comment

It is interesting to note that Lord Thankerton has linked the absence of an opportunity for an intermediate examination of the product before it is used by the plaintiff with the plaintiff's right to 'rely' on the exercise of due diligence by the defendant. It is sometimes said that reliance has no part to play in this type of case, but this must be questioned. Indeed, it is submitted that in all negligence cases, in addition to looking at the conduct of the defendant, it is legitimate, if not desirable, to question whether the plaintiff was entitled to assume that a certain state of affairs presented to him was in order before his injuries occurred. In accident cases, including relational economic loss cases, this question translates into asking whether the plaintiff should have taken some precautionary measures to safeguard his own safety, and whether he can be held contributorily negligent for failing to do so. In cases like *Donoghue* and all other cases where the defendant has negligently put something into circulation, this question translates into asking whether it was reasonable for the plaintiff to rely on the apparent soundness of the 'thing' which the defendant put into circulation without conducting his own inspection or making his own inquiries. Sometimes, as in the product liability sphere, this will depend on whether the defendant has intentionally excluded the possibility of such an inspection by, for example, distributing food in a sealed tin or constructing a house with concealed foundations; or the situation created by the defendant (for example, providing trains for public transport) might be such that it would plainly be ridiculous to excuse the defendant from liability on the ground that the injured plaintiff had the opportunity to examine 'the situation' before accepting it. In *Gallagher v N McDowell Ltd* [1961] NI 26, Lord MacDermott LCJ expressed this point when he said (at p 42): "At almost every turn in the modern workaday world people have to depend for their safety on the care and skill of others in circumstances which make an immediate investigation, however possible in theory, quite impractical in fact".

At other times, the conclusion that it would be unreasonable for the defendant to have expected the plaintiff to make an intermediate inspection might depend on empirical evidence as to what other persons in the position of the plaintiff might or might not do in similar circumstances. In *Smith v Eric S Bush* [1990] 1 AC 831 (which is also discussed in para 9.7.3), the House of Lords, in holding that a surveyor owed a duty of care in tort to a purchaser of a house who had relied on his report, which had been commissioned by the building society, was influenced by the fact that the expert evidence established that 90 per cent of house purchasers in the position of the plaintiff would also have done so and would not have commissioned an independent report of their own. Their Lordships therefore held that the plaintiff was entitled to rely on the defendant's report, but they made it clear that purchasers at the "upper end of the market" (the plaintiff's house was "modest") and purchasers of commercial property would not be able to do so.

Similarly, in *McCullagh v Lane Fox and Partners Ltd* (1996) 49 Con LR 124 (CA), the Court of Appeal took judicial notice of the fact that prospective house purchasers normally obtain pre-contract inspections. After making the general statement that "in the law of negligence, the concept of proximity is inconsistent with the contemplation or expectation of an intermediate check", Hobhouse LJ said:

> In a transaction for the sale of land, it will normally be contemplated that there will be pre-contract inquiries which will be used by the prospective purchaser to obtain specific representations verifying important facts. Similarly, parties will very frequently instruct a surveyor to carry out a structural survey before deciding to make an offer or to exchange contracts. Thus, it does not follow that a

representation, although intended to influence the representee, will be relied upon in the relevant way without an intermediate check. It is therefore necessary to examine further the significance of the representation in the transaction.

Lord Atkin

Throughout his judgment in *Donoghue*, Lord Atkin makes the defendant's liability turn on the question of a proximate relationship, and he rests this proximate relationship on the fact that there could not have been any inter-vention between the manufacturer and the consumer because the way in which the ginger beer was put up prevented intermediate inspection. Thus, after setting out Lord Esher's example in *Heaven v Pender* (see para 6.3.1, *above*), Lord Atkin said (at p 582): "I draw particular attention to the fact that Lord Esher emphasises the necessity of goods having to be 'used immediately' and 'used at once' before a reasonable opportunity of inspec-tion. This is obviously to exclude the possibility of goods having their condition altered by lapse of time, and to call attention to the proximate relationship which may be too remote where inspection, even of the person using, certainly of an intermediate person, may reasonably be interposed".

Lord Atkin continued:

> There will no doubt arise cases where it will be difficult to determine whether the contemplated relationship is so close that the duty arises. But in the class of case now before the Court I cannot conceive any difficulty to arise. A manufacturer puts up an article of food in a container which he knows will be opened by the actual consumer. There can be no inspection by any purchaser and no reason-able preliminary inspection by the consumer. Negligently, in the course of preparation, he allows the contents to be mixed with poison. It is said that the law of England and Scotland is that the poisoned consumer has no remedy against the negligent manufacturer. If this were the result of the authorities, I should consider the result a grave defect in the law, and so contrary to principle that I should hesitate long before following any decision to that effect which had not the authority of this House.

Lord Macmillan

Like Lord Atkin, Lord Macmillan recognised that the principle which the House was laying down had to be confined within its natural boundaries. He said (at p 622):

> I can readily conceive that where a manufacturer has parted with his product and it has passed into other hands, it may well be exposed to vicissitudes which may render it defective or noxious for which the manufacturer could not in any view be held to be to blame. It may be a good general rule to regard responsibility as ceasing when control ceases. So, also, where between the manufacturer and the user there is interposed a party who has the means and opportunity of examin-ing the manufacturer's product before he reissues it to the actual user. But where, as in the present case, the article of consumption is so prepared as to be intended to reach the consumer in the condition in which it leaves the manufacturer, and the manufacturer takes steps to ensure this by sealing or otherwise closing the container so that the contents cannot be tampered with, I regard his control as remaining effective until the article reaches the consumer and the container is

opened by him. The intervention of any exterior agency is intended to be excluded, and was in fact in the present case excluded.

6.3.4 Applications of the principle

Farr v Butters

In *Farr v Butters Brothers & Co* [1932] 2 KB 606, decided less than one month after *Donoghue*, the defendant crane manufacturers sold a crane in parts to a firm of builders who were going to assemble it themselves. The plaintiff's deceased husband was an experienced crane erector who worked for the builders. In the course of assembling the crane, he found that certain cogwheels did not fit accurately. He marked in chalk the places where there was inaccurate fitting, saying that he would report the matter to his employers. Nevertheless, before these defects had been remedied he began working the crane, in the course of which a part of it fell off due to the above-mentioned defect. The court held that the defendant owed no duty of care to the deceased man because the defect in question was patent and discoverable on reasonable inspection, there was ample opportunity for intermediate inspection before the crane was assembled and used, and the defect had in fact been discovered by the deceased man before he put the crane into operation.

Grant v Australian Knitting Mills

In *Grant v Australian Knitting Mills Ltd* [1936] AC 85 (PC), the plaintiff sued the defendant manufacturer in tort for damages for personal injuries in the form of severe dermatitis he had contracted as a result of wearing woollen underwear manufactured by them (which he had purchased from a retailer), which was in a defective condition due to the presence of excess sulphites that had been negligently left in the wool in the process of manufacture. The court upheld the plaintiff's claim. Lord Wright said (at p 105): "The principle of *Donoghue*'s case can only be applied where the defect is hidden and unknown to the consumer. The presence of the deleterious chemical in the pants, due to negligence in manufacture, was a hidden and latent defect, just as much as were the remains of the snail in the opaque bottle: it could not be detected by any examination that could reasonably be made. Nothing happened between the making of the garments and their being worn to change their condition. The garments were made by the manufacturers for the purpose of being worn exactly as they were worn in fact by the appellant: it was not contemplated that they should be first washed".

Otto v Bolton

In *Otto v Bolton and Norris* [1936] 2 KB 46 the plaintiff had been injured when some ceiling plaster fell on her in a house which had been negligently constructed by the defendants. This was a new house. The plaintiff was not the purchaser, but she was living in it with the purchaser. The court rejected the plaintiff's claims for compensation for her personal injuries. First, it was held that the principle of liability established in *Donoghue* did not apply to land. This is discussed *below*, para 6.6. Secondly, however, Atkinson J said (at p 58): "Even if this principle does apply to buildings which are sold by the man who has built them, it would be impossible to hold that there was the necessary proximity between the defendants and Mrs Otto. There was nothing to prevent examination of the house on the intermediate purchase. The defect was not hidden or latent. The blobs were there plainly to be seen and would have put anybody making a proper inspection on his guard".

McCullagh v Lane Fox

In *McCullagh v Lane Fox and Partners Ltd* (1996) 49 Con LR 124 (CA), the facts of which are set out in Chapter 10, para 10.3.3 and Chapter 9, para 9.7.3, the defendant was a firm of estate agents which had been retained by the vendor of a house to sell it. The plaintiff was the eventual purchaser. During the plaintiff's first visit to the house, the defendant's director, Mr Scott, made a misrepresentation to the plaintiff about the size of the plot.

One of the questions in the Court of Appeal was whether a duty of care came into existence between the defendant and the plaintiff at the above-mentioned first meeting by virtue of Mr Scott's direct incorrect statement to the plaintiff about the acreage of the property. Two of the judges held that it did not, for the simple reason that, at that stage, it was reasonable for the defendant to expect that the plaintiff would not purchase the property without carrying out an intermediate inspection to verify for himself any information provided to him by the defendant. Thus, Sir Christopher Slade, with whom Nourse LJ agreed, said:

> In my judgment, Mr Scott did not owe the plaintiff a duty of care on the Saturday morning when Mr Scott made the relevant statement, if only because at that time he would have been entitled reasonably to take the view that his statement would be independently checked and would not be relied on.

The third judge, Hobhouse LJ, was of the view that a duty of care did come into existence at the first meeting between the plaintiff and Mr Scott; not because he (Hobhouse LJ) did not agree with the principle enunciated by Sir Christopher Slade (on the contrary, he endorsed it strongly), but because he believed that that principle was not applicable as the plaintiff had told Mr Scott that he intended to demolish the house, thereby conveying the inference that he was not going to have it surveyed before he bought it. Thus, Hobhouse LJ said:

> In the law of negligence, the concept of proximity is inconsistent with the contemplation or expectation of an intermediate check. [He then referred to *Donoghue v Stevenson* and stated that, in product liability cases, the likelihood that there will be an intermediate inspection or check negatives the existence of the duty of care (see para 6.3.2), and he then continued:]
> In a transaction for the sale of land, it will normally be contemplated that there will be pre-contract inquiries which will be used by the prospective purchaser to obtain specific representations verifying important facts. Similarly,

parties will very frequently instruct a surveyor to carry out a structural survey before deciding to make an offer or to exchange contracts. Although intended to influence the representee, a representation will be relied upon in the relevant way without an intermediate check. It is therefore necessary to examine further the significance of the representation in the transaction. This is not something which is peculiar to estate agents, nor does it amount to some special principle of qualified liability for estate agents. The application of this principle must depend on the facts of the case before the Court.

In examining the facts, Hobhouse LJ noted that, at the first meeting between the plaintiff and Mr Scott, where Mr Scott made the misrepresentation about the size of the plot, the plaintiff also told Mr Scott that he intended to demolish the house. Hobhouse LJ observed that, from this, it would be reasonable to infer that the plaintiff was not going to obtain an intermediate inspection of the house, thereby negating the usual effect of an opportunity for conducting such an inspection in a normal house purchase transaction.

6.3.5 'Opportunity' not always sufficient

The mere fact that the plaintiff had an opportunity to inspect the article or building before using it, and the fact that such inspection would have revealed the defect in question, will not defeat the plaintiff's claim. Sometimes, too, the plaintiff will still have a claim even if he did carry out an examination of the article or building before he used it and, in so doing, discovered the defect. The following cases illustrate these points.

Herschtal v Stewart

In *Herschtal v Stewart and Arden Ltd* [1940] 1 KB 155, the defendant motor car engineers and distributors supplied a reconditioned car to a company of which the plaintiff was a director. The day after the car had been delivered, the rear wheel came off while the plaintiff was driving it. The cause of this was that the nuts had not been properly tightened by the defendant's employees. The court upheld the plaintiff's claim, rejecting the defendant's defence that it owed no duty of care to the plaintiff as he had had an opportunity to inspect and adjust the wheel before using the car. Tucker J said (at p 159): "The real issue in this case is this: is the proper test here whether there was an opportunity for an intermediate examination, or is the test whether any intermediate examination could reasonably be anticipated by the defendants?". He answered this question by saying (at p 170): "The mere existence of the opportunity for examination is not sufficient to break the chain or destroy the proximate relationship". On the facts, he held that although there did exist an opportunity to make such an examination, the defendant was nevertheless liable for the plaintiff's injuries, because "the last thing they contemplated was that there was going to be any such intermediate examination by the plaintiff or by anyone else as would be likely to reveal a defect of this kind" before the car was used.

Denny v Supplies and Transport

In *Denny v Supplies and Transport Co Ltd* [1950] 2 KB 374, the plaintiff had been injured while unloading timber from a barge which had been negligently loaded by stevedores employed by the defendant. At the start of the unloading, the plaintiff drew his employer's attention to the bad loading and suggested that it was a case for payment of danger money. His employer agreed. The plaintiff continued unloading the timber, in the course of which he was injured as a result of the negligent way in which it had been stacked by the defendant's employees. The court held that, even though the bad loading had been ascertained by inspection at the start of the unloading, there was "no practical alternative to going on" with the unloading. Therefore, neither knowledge of the bad loading, nor inspection, operated to break the chain of causation which began with the unskilful loading by the stevedores, so as to relieve them from their liability to the plaintiff.

Greene v Chelsea Borough Council

In *Greene v Chelsea Borough Council* [1954] 2 QB 127 the plaintiff, together with her husband and their three children, lived in accommodation provided by the defendant for people in need. The plaintiff had noticed a large crack and a bulge in the ceiling of the kitchen. She reported this to the defendant, who sent men to inspect it. They said that they would repair it, but never did so. Subsequently the ceiling collapsed on the plaintiff's head and injured her. As the only formal agreement was between the defendant and the plaintiff's husband, the plaintiff had to sue the defendant in tort. The court upheld her claim, thereby rejecting the defendant's defence that it was not liable because the plaintiff had notice of the defect. Denning LJ said (at p 139): "Knowledge or notice of the danger is only a defence when the plaintiff is free to act upon that knowledge or notice so as to avoid the danger". The court held that the plaintiff was not in a position to act on her knowledge of the defective ceiling so as to avoid the danger of it since she and her family had been housed in that accommodation by the defendant because they were homeless. Denning LJ said (at p 140): "Can anyone reasonably say that she was free to give up the use of the kitchen in this house simply because the ceiling had a crack in it and was bulged? In my judgment, she was not free to avoid the danger. She had to stay there and live in her kitchen. Although she had notice of the danger, it does not disentitle her from recovering for the negligence of the local authority".

Gallagher v McDowell

In *Gallagher v N McDowell Ltd* [1961] NI 26, the plaintiff had been injured when a plug of wood in a hole in the floor of the house of which the plaintiff's husband was the tenant gave way under the weight of the plaintiff 's high-heeled shoe. The house had been constructed by the defendant contractor, whose workmen had plugged the hole negligently, in that the plug was not tapered and therefore would give way if someone walked over it with a high-heeled shoe. The court upheld the plaintiff's claim, notwithstanding that the house had been carefully inspected before the plaintiff and her husband went into occupation. The court said that, although the defendant could reasonably have anticipated an inspection before the house was used, the defendant could not reasonably have anticipated an inspection that would expose this particular danger—a defect which was concealed and which could only have been discovered by taking the plug out of the floor for examination.

Sharpe v Sweeting

The principle established by the Northern Ireland Court of Appeal in *Gallagher* was adopted into English law in *Sharpe v E T Sweeting & Son Ltd* [1963] 1 WLR 665 in a case which raised the same issues.

Rimmer v Liverpool City Council

In *Rimmer v Liverpool City Council* [1985] QB 1, the plaintiff was the tenant of a flat in a block designed and built by the defendant. Part of an internal wall consisted of a thin glass panel. When the plaintiff took the tenancy he complained to the defendant that the glass panel was a danger to his young son because of its thinness, but he was told that it was standard and that nothing could be done about it. Subsequently the plaintiff tripped over some of his son's toys, fell through the glass panel and sustained severe injuries. The court upheld the plaintiff's claim, rejecting the defence that the plaintiff's knowledge that the glass was dangerous negatived any duty of care which would otherwise arise. Stephenson LJ said (at p 14): "An opportunity for inspection of a dangerous defect, even if exercised by the plaintiff who is injured by it, will not destroy the proximity which existed between the plaintiff and the defendant who created the danger, unless the plaintiff was free to remove or avoid the danger, in the sense that it was reasonable to expect him to do so, and unreasonable for him to run the risk of being injured by the danger. It was not reasonable or practical for the plaintiff to leave the flat or to alter the glass panel. He remained in law the council's neighbour, although he had complained that the glass was too thin".

Targett v Torfaen Borough Council

In *Targett v Torfaen Borough Council* [1992] 3 All ER 27 (CA), the plaintiff was the tenant of a council house which had been designed and built by the defendant. Access to the house was down two flights of stone steps. There was no handrail for the lower steps and no lighting in the immediate vicinity. Before moving into the house the plaintiff complained to the defendant, but nothing was done. One night the plaintiff fell down the steps and was injured. The Court of Appeal held that the defendant owed the plaintiff a duty of care to provide a handrail or lighting for the steps, notwithstanding the plaintiff's knowledge of the dangerous defect which had caused his injuries, because it was not reasonable or practical for the plaintiff to move out of the house or to provide a handrail or lighting himself, and it was not unreasonable for him to run the risk of injury. However, the court reduced the plaintiff's damages by 25 per cent for contributory negligence on his part, on the ground that it was practical for him to take greater care for his own safety by carrying a torch.

The importance of this decision is that it post-dated *Murphy v Brentwood District Council* [1991] 1 AC 398, and it considered squarely the continuing correctness of the principle of *Rimmer* set out *above* in the light of certain *dicta* in *Murphy* which suggest that knowledge of a defect will always prevent the plaintiff from claiming damages for a loss sustained subsequently, notwithstanding the defendant's admitted or proven negligence. This aspect of the decision in *Targett* is discussed in para 6.3.6, *below*.

6.3.6 Relationship with *Murphy*

In Chapter 7, para 7.5.3, the discussion of the House of Lords' decision in *Murphy v Brentwood District Council* [1991] 1 AC 398 questions the soundness of the conclusions drawn by the House of Lords from the fact that, once a defect in a product or a building has been discovered, it is no longer latent, so that any damage to that thing itself—as opposed to personal injury or damage to other property—is pure economic loss. For the moment, consideration is given as to whether their *dicta* to this effect undermine the principles stated *above*.

Lord Keith

The words of Lord Keith in *Murphy* which might cause some concern in the context of the present discussion are (at p 464):

> . . . an essential feature of the species of liability in negligence established by *Donoghue v Stevenson* was that the carelessly manufactured product should be intended to reach the injured consumer in the same state as that in which it was put up, with no reasonable prospect of intermediate examination. It is the latency of the defect which constitutes the mischief. . . . there can be no doubt that, whatever the rationale, a person who is injured through consuming or using a product, the defective nature of which he is well aware, has no remedy against the manufacturer. In the case of a building, it is right to accept that a careless builder is liable, on the principle of *Donoghue v Stevenson*, where a latent defect results in physical injury to anyone, whether owner, occupier, visitor or passerby, or to the property of any such person. But that principle is not apt to bring home liability towards an occupier who knows the full extent of the defect yet continues to occupy the building.

Lord Bridge

Lord Bridge made similar comments, but he widened the discussion so as to relate his comments to the type of loss with which the House was concerned, namely pure economic loss. He said (at p 475):

> If a dangerous defect in a chattel is discovered before it causes any personal injury or damage to property, because the danger is now known and the chattel cannot safely be used unless the defect is repaired, the defect becomes merely a defect in quality. The chattel is either capable of repair at economic cost or it is worthless and must be scrapped. In either case the loss sustained by the owner

or hirer of the chattel is purely economic. It is recoverable against any party who owes the loser a relevant contractual duty. But it is not recoverable in tort in the absence of a special relationship of proximity imposing on the tortfeasor a duty of care to safeguard the plaintiff from economic loss. There is no such special relationship between the manufacturer of a chattel and a remote owner or hirer. I believe that these principles are equally applicable to buildings.

Comment

It is submitted that these *dicta* (and the decision of the House in *Murphy*) do not affect the principle discussed *above* in such cases as *Rimmer*. In those cases the injury for which compensation was awarded notwithstanding the plaintiff's knowledge of the defect was personal injury to the plaintiff or damage to the property of the plaintiff other than the very item which was itself defective. Whatever the rationale (which is discussed in Chapter 7, para 7.5) this distinction is crucial, as the passage quoted from Lord Bridge's speech makes clear.

In *Targett v Torfaen Borough Council* [1992] 3 All ER 27 (CA) (see para 6.3.5, *above*) the defendant argued that the plaintiff's long-standing knowledge of the potential danger precluded the existence of a duty of care in tort by the defendant for the plaintiff's injuries. The defendant argued that the plaintiff's true remedy was to put right the defects himself and to charge the local authority with the expense involved. The Court of Appeal rejected these submissions. Russell LJ said (at p 32): "I do not read the speeches in *Murphy*'s case as supporting the defendant's counsel's propositions. A weekly tenant is in an entirely different position from an owner of a house defectively constructed who discovers the defect, thereby rendering it no longer a latent defect. In my judgment, the scope of *Murphy*'s case was defined by Lord Keith when he said (at p 463): 'The question is whether the defendant council owed the plaintiff a duty to take reasonable care to safeguard him against the particular kind of damage which he has in fact suffered, which was not injury to person or health, nor damage to anything other than the defective house itself'".

With reference to the principle cited *above* (in para 6.3.5) from *Rimmer v Liverpool City Council* [1985] QB 1 (CA), Russell LJ said (at p 33): "*Rimmer*'s case was not even cited in *Murphy*'s case, for in my view it had nothing whatever to do with the problem posed in *Murphy*'s case. Likewise I am satisfied that their Lordships did not refer to *Rimmer*'s case because it had no relevance. I am firmly of the opinion that the House of Lords in *Murphy*'s case did not overrule *Rimmer*'s case by implication or otherwise; and in my view, *Rimmer*'s case remains an authority binding upon this Court".

The other two Lord Justices of Appeal concurred. Sir Donald Nicholls VC said (at p 37):

> . . . it was argued, in accordance with the observations of Lord Keith and Lord Bridge [in *Murphy*], the claim by the plaintiff in *Rimmer*'s case, and the claim in the present action, must fail.
>
> I cannot accept this. In *Murphy v Brentwood DC*, the House of Lords was

concerned to consider the principles applicable to a claim to recover the cost of making good a defective product, there a building, which had not yet caused any physical injury to persons or damage to other property. Their Lordships explained why the *Donoghue v Stevenson* principle did not embrace such a claim. When the defect was discovered, the goods or building ceased to be dangerous, although they remained defective. The loss sustained by the owner, eg in making good the defect, was economic loss. Thus, their Lordships were concerned with examining the interrelation between the *Donoghue v Stevenson* principle and a claim by the owner of goods or a building to recover purely economic loss. That examination did not call for a consideration of whether there were any circumstances in which, under *Donoghue v Stevenson*, there might be liability for injuries sustained even though the plaintiff was aware of the existence of the hazard. In *Murphy*'s case, a statement of the broad principle was sufficient.

That is the context of the passages relied on in the speeches of Lord Keith and Lord Bridge. Given that context, I cannot read those speeches as an expression of the view that, in no circumstances, can a person recover compensation for personal injuries sustained by using defective goods or a defective building once he has become aware of the existence of the defect. The general principle is, indeed, that such a person cannot recover compensation, because in the ordinary way his knowledge of the existence of the dangerous defect will suffice to enable him to avoid the danger. If he finds there is a decomposed snail in his ginger beer, he will not drink it. He does not use underwear which he knows contains a mischievous chemical.

[Nicholls VC then referred to *Grant v Australian Knitting Mills Ltd* [1936] AC 85 (the defective underpants case—see Chapter 6, para 6.3.5, *above*) and continued:]

... But knowledge of the existence of a danger does not always enable a person to avoid the danger. In simple cases it does. In other cases, especially where buildings are concerned, it would be absurdly unrealistic to suggest that a person can always take steps to avoid a danger once he knows of its existence, and that if he does not do so, he is the author of his own misfortune. Here, as elsewhere, the law seeks to be realistic. Hence, the established principle, referred to by this Court in *Rimmer*'s case . . . [see para 6.3.5, *above*] that knowledge or opportunity for inspection per se, and without regard to any consequences it may have in the circumstances, cannot be conclusive against the plaintiff. Knowledge, or opportunity for inspection, does not by itself always negative the duty of care or break the chain of causation. Whether it does so depends on all the circumstances. It will only do so when it is reasonable to expect the plaintiff to remove or avoid the danger, and unreasonable for him to run the risk of being injured by the danger.

The Court of Appeal's decision in *Targett v Torfaen* contains mixed messages. While on the one hand it was open to their Lordships to hold that the previous Court of Appeal decision in *Rimmer* had been impliedly overruled by the House of Lords' decision in *Murphy*, they chose not to do so and instead went out of their way to try to distinguish the underlying fact situation in *Targett* from that which pertained in *Murphy* in relation to the plaintiff's opportunity to conduct an intermediate inspection of the premises and his continued use of them after acquiring knowledge of the defect. On the other hand, the manner in which their Lordships tried to distinguish the situation in *Murphy*, without being critical of the House of Lords' decision therein, seems only to highlight the impossibility of making such a distinction and the illogicality of the House's decision in *Murphy* on this aspect of the case. *Murphy* was binding on the Court of Appeal in *Targett*. Therefore the Court of Appeal had to find ways of distinguishing *Murphy*. It is submitted that the way in which they tried to do so is not satisfactory because there is in truth no distinction between the Court of Appeal's statement of the principle of intermediate inspection in *Targett* and the application of that principle in a case like *Murphy*, where the foundations were covered over and a pre-purchase inspection by the plaintiff would have been futile. It is submitted that the logic of the Court of Appeal in *Targett* is compelling and that the type of artificial distinction that the Court of Appeal drew between *Targett* and *Murphy* further bears out the fragility of the House of Lords' reasoning in *Murphy*.

This last-made point comes out most clearly in the judgment of Nicholls VC, particularly in the passage cited *above* where his Lordship said that, where buildings are concerned, it would be absurdly unrealistic to suggest that a person can always take steps to avoid a danger once he knows of its existence, and that if he does not do so he is the author of his own misfortune. If this principle was applicable to the facts of *Rimmer* and *Targett*, why should it not also be applicable to the facts of *Murphy*, where the plaintiff not only had no knowledge of the existence of the defective foundation until it was too late to do anything about it, but also the defect was of such a nature that it would not have been revealed upon an intermediate inspection; and even if it had been so revealed, the plaintiff was not in a position to bear the cost of the necessary repairs without seeking recovery from anyone else, or to move out of the house and abandon it, as Lord Bridge and Lord Keith in *Murphy* suggested he should have done (see Chapter 7, paras 7.3.4, 7.5.3 and 7.7). That suggestion, and Lord Oliver's statement in *Murphy* that the principle of *Donoghue v Stevenson* "is not apt to bring home liability towards an occupier who knows the full extent of the defect yet continues to occupy the building" (see Chapter 7, para 7.5.3), leave one with an uneasy feeling of injustice about the House of Lords' decision in *Murphy*. There, the defect was just as latent as in *Donoghue v Stevenson*, in that it could not reasonably have been discovered by Mr Murphy before he bought his house, because the foundations had been covered up in the course of construction and the defects in them would not have been revealed on a pre-purchase survey. This point is discussed further in para 7.5.3.

Criticism in Canada

In *Winnipeg Condominium Corporation No 36 v Bird Construction Co* (1995) 121 DLR (4th) 193, the Supreme Court of Canada strongly deprecated Lord Keith's above-mentioned view in *Murphy*, that the cost of repair cannot be characterised as a recoverable loss because the owner of the defective article may simply discard it and thereby remove the danger. La Forest J, speaking for all seven judges of the panel, said (at p 214):

While Lord Keith's argument has some appeal on the basis of abstract logic, I do not believe it is sufficient to preclude imposing liability on contractors for the cost of repairing dangerous defects. The weakness of the argument is that it is based upon an unrealistic view of the choice faced by homeowners in deciding whether to repair a dangerous defect in their home. In fact, a choice to 'discard' a home instead of repairing the dangerous defect is no choice at all; most homeowners buy a home as a long-term investment, and few homeowners, upon discovering a dangerous defect in the home, will choose to abandon or sell the building rather than to repair the defect. Indeed, in most cases, the cost of fixing a defect in a household building, within the reasonable life of that house or building, will be far outweighed by the cost of replacing the house or buying a new one.

6.4   Wider application of 'the neighbour principle'

6.4.1   Narrow ratio

The specific point which was decided by the House of Lords in *Donoghue* is encapsulated in the headnote, which is set out at the beginning of this chapter (para 6.2.1). Lord Atkin said (at p 583): "I confine myself to articles of common household use, where everyone, including the manufacturer, knows that the articles will be used by other persons than the actual ultimate purchaser, namely by members of his family and his servants and in some cases, his guests". He added that, in addition to articles of food and drink, he had in mind "medicine, an ointment, a soap, a cleaning fluid or cleaning powder".

Thus confined, in some cases following soon after *Donoghue* there was still uncertainty as to whether the 'neighbour doctrine' which the House had invoked, and which Lord Atkin defined in the form of a general test, applied to other types of goods (such as motor vehicles) and to other situations (such as repairing or hiring), or whether those situations were still governed by the competing doctrine of *Winterbottom v Wright* (1842) 10 M & W 109 and *Earl v Lubbock* [1905] 1 KB 253, discussed *above* (para 6.2.4). As will be seen *below* (para 6.4.4), these doubts were resolved in favour of 'the neighbour principle' being the appropriate test, at least where the plaintiff's loss consisted of personal injury or damage to his property, other than the actual defective piece of property which the defendant had created or put into circulation. As will be seen in Chapter 7, para 7.1, damage to that property is categorised as pure economic loss and is dealt with in accordance with a principle which, to all intents and purposes, is the same as that which was applied in *Winterbottom* and *Earl*.

6.4.2   Wider application of the principle

An almost infinite variety of circumstances could be imagined in which it would be appropriate, applying Lord Atkin's words, to say that the defendant owed a duty to take reasonable care to avoid an act or omission which he could reasonably foresee would be likely to injure a person so closely and directly affected by his act or omission that he ought reasonably to have had such a person (who is thus, in law, his 'neighbour') in his contemplation as being so affected. This principle has been so widely applied, and is so well known, that apart from the few early cases referred to *below*, it is not proposed to cite examples of its application. There are also some statutes, which will be considered *below*, which have improved the plaintiff's position.

6.4.3   Limited ambit

It is also worth noting in passing that in *Hedley Byrne & Co Ltd v Heller & Partners Ltd* [1964] AC 465 (discussed in detail in Chapter 9, para 9.4) the House of Lords held that this principle has no application in negligent misstatement cases (see para 9.2.3). Also, as seen in Chapter 5, para 5.6.5, it has no application (at least in English law) in relational economic loss cases; and, as will be seen in Chapter 7, para 7.3.6, its application in cases of pure economic loss suffered by the plaintiff as a result of a 'thing' created or distributed by the defendant proving to be defective is extremely limited.

6.4.4   Some early cases

Today, it would be taken for granted that 'the neighbour principle' applies in the following circumstances, but at the time this was contested (unsuccessfully) in each of the following cases, some of which have already been considered in the context of the discussion of the effect on the defendant's position of the possibility of an intermediate inspection by the plaintiff or a third party before use of the defective product by the plaintiff.

These cases are *Farr v Butters Brothers & Co* [1932] 2 KB 606 (see *above*, para 6.3.4), in which it was held that the principle applies to a machine (here a crane) manufactured by the defendant; *Malfroot v Noxal Ltd* (1935) 51 TLR 551, in which it was held that the principle applies to motor vehicles—here, a motor cycle to which the defendant had negligently fitted a side-car; *Grant v Australian Knitting Mills Ltd* [1936] AC 85 (PC) (see *above*, para 6.3.4)—defectively manufactured clothing; *Stennett v Hancock & Peters* [1939] 2 All ER 578—repairer of a part (a tyre) of a motor vehicle; *Herschtal v Stewart & Arden Ltd* [1940] 1 KB 155 (see *above*), where it was held that the principle applies not only to manufacturers, but also to suppliers or repairers of goods—here, a reconditioned motor car; *Haseldine v C A Daw & Son Ltd* [1941] 2 KB 343, where the principle was held to be applicable to a repairer (of a lift in a block of flats) and *Buckland v Guildford Gas Light & Coke Co* [1949] 1 KB 410, where it was held to be applicable to an electricity supply company in relation to the death of a young girl who had climbed a tree through whose foliage the defendant's electricity wires passed.

6.5   The Consumer Protection Act 1987

Part I of this Act contains certain provisions which can sometimes improve the position of the plaintiff quite dramatically.

6.5.1 Liability for defective products

Section 2(1) of the Act provides: "Subject to the following provisions of this Part, where any damage is caused wholly or partly by a defect in a product, every person to whom sub-section (2) below applies shall be liable for the damage".

Subsection (2) states that the persons included in subs (1) are the producer of the product or any person who has held himself out to be the producer (ie an 'own brander') or any person who has imported the product into a member state of the EEC from a place outside the EEC in order to supply it to anyone else.

Furthermore, subs (3) provides that any person who supplied the product, whether to the person who suffered the damage or to anyone else, shall be liable for the damage if he fails to identify the person who supplied the product to him.

This section imposes strict liability. The plaintiff does not have to prove any negligence or the existence of a duty of care on the part of the defendant. On the other hand, the plaintiff must prove (on a balance of probabilities):

(1) that a 'product' contained a 'defect';
(2) that the plaintiff suffered 'damage';
(3) that the damage 'was caused' by the defect; and
(4) that the defendant was the 'producer' or someone else falling within subs (2).

6.5.2 Food

Section 2(4) provides that neither subs (2) nor subs (3) *above* shall apply to a person in respect of any defect in any game or agricultural produce if the only supply of it by that person was at a time when it had not undergone any industrial process. Thus liability is excluded for defects in agricultural products and game except where they have been subjected to processing of an industrial nature.

6.5.3 Definitions

'Caused'

All of the terms highlighted *above* except for 'caused' are defined in the Act and therefore need to be satisfied strictly. Before looking at these, it is worth noting that the requirement that the plaintiff has to prove that the damage was 'caused' by the defect means that the principles relating to the opportunity for an intermediate inspection of the product before its use, discussed *above* (para 6.3), are still applicable.

'Product'

'Product' is defined in s 1 as any goods or electricity. 'Goods' are defined in s 45(1) to include growing crops and things comprised in land by virtue of being attached to it and any ship, aircraft or vehicle.

'Defect'

'Defect' is defined in s 3(1), which states: "Subject to the following provisions of this section, there is a defect in a product if the safety of the product is not such as persons generally are entitled to expect". In subs (2) it is stated that this is to be determined by taking into account all the circumstances, including the manner in which, and the purposes for which, the product has been marketed, its get-up and any instructions or warnings with respect to doing anything with the product.

'Safety'

'Safety' is not specifically defined, but it is stated in s 3(1) that 'safety' in relation to a product shall include safety with respect to products comprised in that product and safety in the context of risks of damage to property, death or personal injury.

It will be noted that, in accordance with these definitions, products will not be defective simply because they might wear out quickly or not function properly: defectiveness is determined purely in terms of safety. In other words, a product will not be defective unless it poses a risk of personal injury or damage to property.

6.5.4 Defences

If a product does pose such a risk, then, subject to certain defences set out in s 4 (and subject to the possibility of the intermediate inspection point, mentioned *above*), the producer will be strictly liable for the plaintiff's personal injuries or property damage. The plaintiff will not have to establish that the producer owed him a duty of care or was negligent.

Of these statutory defences, the two that are likely to cause the most trouble for plaintiffs in practice are:

(1) s 4(1)(*d*), which provides that it will be a defence for the defendant to show that the defect did not exist in the product at the time when he supplied it to another. The burden of proof will be on the defendant. Where he manufactures or sells goods in sealed containers, he will be unlikely to succeed in discharging this onus; and

(2) s 4(1)(*e*), which provides that it will be a defence for the defendant to show that the state of scientific and technical knowledge at the relevant time was not such that a producer of products of the same description as the product in question might be expected to have discovered the defect if it had existed in his products while they were under his control. This is known as the 'development risks' defence and is likely to be attractive to manufacturers of innovative medical drugs and new electronic devices designed for mass consumption. An example here could be the controversy which is raging at the time of writing over allegations that prolonged playing of certain new games has caused epileptic fits in children by virtue of the children reacting adversely to the intermittent flashes of light generated by those games.

The manufacturers and distributors have voluntarily agreed to include a written health warning with every new item sold, but it is possible that, if sued for damages for personal injuries which have already occurred, they might be able to rely on s 4(1)(*e*) as their defence.

6.5.5   Land and buildings excluded

It has been noted *above* that 'goods' are defined as including ". . . things comprised in land by virtue of being attached to it". This means that, whilst the Act will apply where a 'thing' attached to land is defective (as defined in s 3(1)), it will not apply where the defect is merely in the land itself.

This raises the question whether a house, or any other building, is 'land', or whether it is 'a thing attached to land'. It is submitted that buildings are not 'things attached to land' for the purposes of the Act. This answer is not to be found directly in the Act, but, rather, in the Directive of the Council of the European Communities dated 25 July 1985 concerning liability for defective products (the 'Directive'). Section 1(1) of the Act states: "This Part shall have effect for the purpose of making such provision as is necessary in order to comply with the Product Liability Directive and shall be construed accordingly".

Article 2 of the Directive states that 'product' means all moveables except for primary agricultural products and game, even though incorporated into another moveable or an immoveable. Thus a house or any other building, being an immoveable, will not itself be a 'product'. Therefore, if a house collapses and injures someone because of a defect in construction, the builder will not be liable under the Act. His liability, if any, will be determined under the applicable common law rules of contract or tort or under the Defective Premises Act 1972, the latter of which is discussed *below* (paras 6.6.3–4). On the other hand, if a moveable item which had been incorporated into the construction of the house, such as a boiler, proves to be unsafe, then the manufacturer of the boiler and, possibly, also the builder of the house as the supplier of the boiler would be liable if he is not able to identify the original manufacturer of it.

6.5.6   Consequential loss excluded

Section 5(1) defines 'damage' in terms which indicate that consequential economic loss is excluded. It states: "In this Part 'damage' means death or personal injury or damage to any property (including land)".

It is also worth noting at this point that the only property which is covered by this Part of the Act is (s 5(3)) property which is ordinarily intended for private use, occupation or consumption and that (s 5(4)) the plaintiff's damages have to be at least £275 before an award can be made against a defendant.

For example, if the tube in a television set which the plaintiff has bought and is using in his private house explodes and causes a fire, and the plaintiff's damages amount to more than £275, the manufacturer of the defective television set will be liable for the cost of the damage caused by the fire, but not for the cost of any alternative accommodation which the plaintiff might have had to incur in consequence of the fire. This is because such damages would not be "damage to any property" within the meaning of s 5. This loss might, however, be recoverable in accordance with the principles covering consequential economic loss laid down in cases like *Spartan Steel & Alloys Ltd v Martin & Co (Contractors) Ltd* [1973] QB 27, which are considered in Chapter 4, para 4.3.2.

6.5.7 Economic loss excluded

It has been noted *above* in Chapter 1, para 1.2.2 (and Chapter 7 considers the proposition in detail) that damage to or destruction of a defective item itself is categorised as pure economic loss. In the example given *above* the damage sustained by the television set itself as a result of its tube having exploded would fall into this category. Section 5(2) makes it clear that this loss is not recoverable under the Act. It states: "A person shall not be liable under s 2 [the section which imposes strict liability for defective products] in respect of any defect in a product for the loss of or any damage to the product itself".

Chapter 7, para 7.3 considers whether, and to what extent, the position at common law is different.

6.6 Defective buildings

6.6.1 Early obstacles

Introduction

For a long time it was thought that where the plaintiff was injured as a result of a defect in a building, or in something attached to a building, he had no claim. This meant that many claims which were meritorious, and which would succeed today, were shut out. An example is *Otto v Bolton & Norris* [1936] 2 KB 46, which has been considered *above* (para 6.3.2) in relation to the plaintiff's intermediate inspection and knowledge of the defect in question. However, that was only the secondary reason for rejection of the plaintiff's claim. The main reason was the so-called rule in *Bottomley v Bannister* [1932] 1 KB 458, in which it was held that a builder who builds a house for sale is under no duty to a future purchaser or to persons who might come to live in it to take care that it is well constructed and safe. The House of Lords' decision in *Cavalier v Pope* [1906] AC 428 was said to lay down a similar rule where the defendant was the lessor of defective premises.

Cavalier v Pope

In *Cavalier v Pope* [1906] AC 428 the plaintiff's husband was the tenant of a house which the defendant had let to him in a dilapidated state. The defendant promised the plaintiff's husband that he would carry out certain repairs, in particular to the kitchen floor, but failed to do so. The plaintiff was injured when she fell through the defective floor in the kitchen. Her claim failed. Lord Loreburn LC simply said (at p 429): "I can find no right of action in the wife of the tenant against the landlord either for letting the premises in a dangerous state or for failing to repair them according to his promise. The husband has sued successfully for breach of contract, but the wife was not party to any contract"; and Lord MacNaghten said (at p 430): "The law laid down by the Court of Common Pleas in the passage quoted by the Master of the Rolls from the judgment of Erle CJ in *Robbins v Jones* (1863) 15 CB (NS) 221 is beyond question: 'A landlord who lets a house in a dangerous state is not liable to the tenant's customers or guests for accidents happening during the term: for, fraud apart, there is no law against letting a tumbledown house; and the tenant's remedy is upon his contract, if any'".

Bottomley v Bannister

In *Bottomley v Bannister* [1932] 1 KB 458 the defendant had built and sold a house to the deceased parents (Mr and Mrs Bottomley) of the 18-month-old child on whose behalf the plaintiff administrators brought this action. A boiler had been installed in the kitchen, which was heated by a gas burner. A pipe from the boiler led into an enclosed cupboard in the kitchen. From this cupboard a linen chute led upwards to another cupboard in the bathroom. There was no flue to carry gas or fumes from the burner to the outside air. A month after going into occupation, Mr and Mrs Bottomley were found dead in the bathroom, having been poisoned by carbon monoxide gas.

The court rejected the claims of the administrators, primarily because the evidence failed to establish that the defendant was negligent in having installed the boiler without a flue, but two of the judges, in particular Scrutton LJ, made statements which had a profound effect in later cases. Thus, Scrutton LJ said (at p 468) (emphasis added): "In the absence of express contract, a landlord of an unfurnished house is not liable to his tenant, or a vendor of real estate to his purchaser, for defects in the house or land rendering it dangerous or unfit for occupation, *even if he has constructed the defects himself* or is aware of their existence"; and Greer LJ said (at p 477): "No case was cited to us in which a tenant or purchaser has ever recovered against a lessor or vendor, either by implied contract or in tort, by establishing the liability of the vendor or landlord for injuries sustained through the house or its fixtures being unsafe at the date of the sale or of the lease".

Conflict with Donoghue v Stevenson

The decisions in *Cavalier* and *Bottomley* were left untouched by the House of Lords' decision in *Donoghue*. Of the three majority Law Lords, Lord Thankerton did not mention these cases at all, Lord Macmillan mentioned only *Cavalier*, and said (at p 609) that it and cases like it "are in a different chapter of the law", and Lord Atkin (at p 597) approved *Cavalier* and did not make any adverse comments on *Bottomley*. Indeed, by saying (at p 598) that "The case was determined on the ground that the apparatus was part of the realty", it seems that he was prepared to accept that the defendant was in a different position where the defective item which he had created was a building or something attached to a building as a fixture.

Subsequent decisions

The decision of the court in *Otto v Bolton & Norris* [1936] 2 KB 46 has already been mentioned (para 6.3.2). Its facts were similar to *Bottomley* and it was justified on the judge's view that the law as stated in *Bottomley* had not been altered by the House of Lords in *Donoghue*.

In *Davis v Foots* [1940] 1 KB 116 the plaintiff became very ill and her husband died by asphyxiation from gas flowing into the bedroom of the flat which they had just rented. The landlord had recently removed a gas fire from the bedroom, but had not shut off the pipe leading to it. The court rejected the plaintiff's claim. MacKinnon LJ cited Scrutton LJ's above-quoted *dictum* in *Bottomley* and then said (at p 121): "The defendants let this house to the plaintiff with a disconnected pipe from which gas could escape when the gas was turned on at the meter. That, of course, may be said to be a dangerous defect. But, the principle being what I have stated and being one which has been recognised over and over again, the defendants are not liable for that defect".

6.6.2 The first signs of change

Gallagher v McDowell

In *Gallagher v N McDowell Ltd* [1961] NI 26, the facts of which are set out *above* (para 6.3.5), one of the defendant's arguments was that it was not liable because the defect in question, which had caused the plaintiff's injury, was in realty. The Northern Ireland Court of Appeal rejected this argument and held that the principles of *Cavalier* and *Bottomley* do not apply where the defendant has done work on the land which has had the effect of 'creating' the defect or the dangerous situation which caused the plaintiff's injury. Subject to this, and subject to any statutory obligations imposed on the defendant (see *below*, paras 6.6.2–4), the court held that where the defendant is sued merely as a landowner, the law as stated in those two cases remained intact. As mentioned *above* (para 6.3.5), this decision was followed in England in *Sharpe v ET Sweeting & Son Ltd* [1963] 1 WLR 665.

Dutton v Bognor Regis UDC

In *Dutton v Bognor Regis Urban District Council* [1972] 1 QB 373, which is considered in Chapter 7, para 7.2, one of the defendant's arguments was that, by virtue of *Cavalier* and *Bottomley*, the 'neighbour principle' does not apply to realty. This was rejected by two of the judges and the third (Stamp LJ) said that it was not necessary to decide the point. Sachs LJ said that *Bottomley* and other cases which had applied it (see para 6.6.1, *above*) were all at first instance and were not binding on the Court of Appeal, and that *Cavalier* was not comparable because the defendant there had not actually created the dangerous state of affairs, nor was the defect hidden. He went on to say (at p 402):

> In the result there is thus nowhere to be found any authority binding this court to hold that the principles enunciated in *Donoghue v Stevenson* cannot apply to an owner of realty. It is obvious that a builder who by his negligence creates a hidden defect is liable to anyone suffering damage from it just as a manufacturer is liable when a hidden defect in the goods he makes injures a workman using it and as a producer of consumable goods is liable when a hidden defect injures a consumer. I can find nothing in principle which absolves from liability a builder who creates a hidden defect because he happens to be or to become the owner of the premises built.

Lord Denning MR went a bit further and was more outspoken. He said (at p 393–4): "The distinction between chattels and real property is quite unsustainable. If the manufacturer of an article is liable to a person injured by his negligence, so should the builder of a house be liable. In my opinion *Bottomley v Bannister* is no longer authority. Nor is *Otto v Bolton and Norris*. They are both overruled. *Cavalier v Pope* has gone too. It was reversed by the Occupiers' Liability Act 1957, s 4(1)". These words are considered further in the discussion of *Rimmer, below*.

Anns v Merton LBC

In *Anns v Merton London Borough Council* [1978] AC 728, which is also considered in Chapter 7, Lord Wilberforce, with whose speech Lords Diplock, Simon and Russell agreed, said (at p 758): "If there was at one time a supposed rule that the doctrine of *Donoghue v Stevenson* did not apply to realty, there is no doubt under modern authority that a builder of defective premises may be liable in negligence to persons who thereby suffer injury".

The fifth judge, Lord Salmon, referred to the above-quoted *dictum* of Scrutton LJ in *Bottomley* and said (at p 768):

> I do not agree with the words in that passage '. . . even if he has constructed the defects himself'. The immunity of a landlord who sells or lets his house which is dangerous or unfit for habitation is deeply entrenched in our law. I cannot, however, accept the proposition that a contractor who negligently built a dangerous house can escape liability to pay damages to anyone who, for example, falls through a shoddily constructed floor and is seriously injured. To the extent that *Bottomley v Bannister* differs from this proposition it should, in my view, be overruled. *Cavalier v Pope* is so far away from the present case that I express no opinion about it.

In *Murphy v Brentwood District Council* [1991] 1 AC 398 the House of Lords overruled both *Dutton* and *Anns*. However, this does not affect the comments made in those cases about the principles under discussion here.

Rimmer v Liverpool City Council

This case ([1985] 1 QB 1) has been considered *above* (para 6.3.5) in relation to the opportunity of an intermediate inspection. However, the defendant also contended that the authority of *Cavalier* rendered it immune from liability to the plaintiff. The Court of Appeal rejected this argument and held that the principle of *Cavalier* does not apply to a 'bare' landlord, namely a landlord who simply let out property but did not design or construct the defects which rendered the property dangerous. The court also disagreed with Denning MR's comment in *Dutton* that *Cavalier* was overruled by the Occupiers' Liability Act 1957, s 4(1).

6.6.3 Section 4 of the Defective Premises Act 1972

Section 4(1) of the Occupiers' Liability Act 1957 has been replaced by the Defective Premises Act 1972, s 4(1), which provides: "Where premises are let under a tenancy which puts on the landlord an obligation to the tenant for the maintenance or repair of the premises, the landlord owes to all persons who might reasonably be expected to be affected by defects in the state of the premises a duty to take such care as is reasonable in all the circumstances to see that they are reasonably safe from personal injury or from damage to their property caused by a relevant defect".

A 'relevant defect' is defined in subs (3) as a defect in the state of the premises arising from or continuing because of an act or omission by the landlord which constitutes a failure by him to carry out his obligation to the tenant for the maintenance or repair of the premises.

Thus, unless the landlord had agreed to put the premises into a certain condition before he let them, this section does not impose on him any duty in respect of the state of the premises at the date of letting. There are some statutory provisions which, however, do improve the position of some tenants against some landlords by the statutory imposition of covenants to keep certain premises (namely 'houses') in repair. Thus, s 11 of the Landlord and Tenant Act 1985 imposes on a lessor of a 'dwelling-house', in a lease of less than seven years, an obligation to put (before the lease takes effect) and keep (throughout its terms) the structure and the exterior in repair and the water, gas and electricity installations in the dwelling-house in proper working order.

These provisions are limited to residential accommodation and do not cover all defects, only those which are specifically mentioned. In all other respects, the rule in *Cavalier* is left intact. Also, these provisions only assist the tenant, and not third parties who might be sharing the accommodation or visiting him. Section 4 of the Defective Premises Act 1972 does cover such other persons (and premises other than residential accommodation), but, as seen *above*, it applies only where the landlord has agreed to be responsible for the maintenance or repair of the premises and where the defect is specifically covered by the obligation which the landlord has undertaken to the tenant.

6.6.4 Section 1 of the Defective Premises Act 1972

Section 1 of the Defective Premises Act 1972 provides:

> A person taking on work for or in connection with the provision of a dwelling owes a duty to every person who acquires an interest in the dwelling to see that the work is done in a workmanlike or, as the case may be, professional manner, so that the dwelling will be fit for habitation when completed.

This section clearly impinges on the principle of *Bottomley* and *Cavalier* to the extent that that principle applied to a landlord or a vendor who (in the words of Scrutton LJ in *Bottomley*) "had constructed the defects himself". These words were disapproved of, and *Bottomley* was overruled to this extent by the House of Lords in *Anns* in 1977 (but the original writ was issued in February 1972 and the Act did not come into force until 1974). This section applies only to 'dwellings', but the House of Lords' partial overruling of *Bottomley* by the deletion of these words means that the principle embodied in this section effectively applies to all buildings where the plaintiff has suffered a personal injury or 'damage to other property'. What the position is where only the building itself is damaged is considered in Chapter 7, para 7.4.5. Also, the duty imposed by this section is limited to persons who might acquire an interest in the dwelling, whereas the common law duty extends to all persons (including visitors, and sometimes trespassers) whom the defendant could reasonably expect to be affected by his want of care.

For a long time s 1 was not available to most houseowners because s 2(1) states:

> No action shall be brought under the Act by any person having or acquiring an interest in a dwelling in regard to which, at the time of its first sale or letting, any rights in respect of it are conferred by an 'approved scheme'.

Most new dwellings are covered by the NHBC Scheme. Until 31 March 1979 it was an approved scheme, but since then it has ceased to be approved, which means that s 1 has assumed much greater practical significance.

Lastly, this section applies only where the defect renders the dwelling 'unfit for habitation'. Therefore if, for example, a house exhibits cracks in the internal walls which are not so serious as to affect the habitability of the house, and are not likely to deteriorate, it is possible that this section will not apply. The plaintiff would have to bring his claim at common law. Chapter 7, para 7.3 considers whether such a claim would succeed.

6.6.5   Conclusions

From this discussion of cases and statutory provisions, it is possible to draw the following conclusions:

Letting premises

Where a landlord lets out premises which are in a dangerous or dilapidated condition, he will not be liable for injuries which may be sustained by the tenant or anyone else on the premises unless:

(1)   he has actually created the defect which causes the danger (s 1 of the Defective Premises Act, or at common law); or

(2) he has not created the defect, but he is aware of it and has fraudulently concealed it from the prospective tenant (common law); or

(3) he has agreed with the tenant to be responsible for the maintenance of the premises and the defect falls within the ambit of the obligations which he has undertaken to the tenant (s 4 of the Defective Premises Act); or

(4) he has not contractually agreed to carry out any repairs, but the premises consist of a dwelling and he has failed to carry out certain limited repairing obligations or to keep the premises fit for human habitation (s 11 of the Landlord and Tenant Act 1985); but here his liability is limited to the tenant (and not, as under s 4 of the 1972 Act, to all persons who might reasonably be expected to be affected by defects in the state of the premises).

Selling premises

A vendor of a building will not be liable to his purchaser or to anyone else for injuries sustained in consequence of a defect in the building rendering it dangerous or unfit for occupation, unless:

(1) he created the defect; or

(2) he did not create the defect, but he was aware of it and fraudulently concealed it from his purchaser.

6.6.6 Comment

The points raised in this section have been discussed in some detail, partly because of the immense amount of trouble which they have caused in practice and partly because of their importance in the pure economic loss, product and building liability cases discussed in Chapter 7, para 7.3. In particular, it is worth emphasising that, while s 1 of the Defective Premises Act 1972 does create a warranty in tort of the quality of a dwelling in respect of which the defendant 'took on work', this is, as observed *above*, of limited effect. The question whether this, by implication, excludes damage to the defective property itself in other contexts is considered in Chapter 7, para 7.5.7.

Chapter 7

Product liability—pure economic loss

It is difficult to see why, as a matter of principle, policy or common sense, a negligent builder should be liable for ordinary physical injury caused to any person or to other property by reason of the collapse of a building by reason of the inadequacy of the foundations but not be liable to the owners for the cost of the remedial work necessary to remedy that inadequacy and to avert such damage. **(Mason CJ in *Bryan v Maloney* (1995) 69 ALJR 375)**

The foundations of a house are in a class by themselves. Once covered up, they will not be seen again until the damage appears. **(Lord Denning MR in *Dutton v Bognor Regis Urban District Council* [1972] 1 QB 373)**

Whatever may be the position in the United Kingdom, homeowners in New Zealand do traditionally rely on local authorities to exercise reasonable care not to allow unstable houses to be built in breach of byelaws. **(Cooke P in the Court of Appeal of New Zealand in *Invercargill City Council v Hamlin* [1974] 3 NZLR 513)**

. . . in the present case the Judges in the New Zealand Court of Appeal were consciously departing from English case law on the ground that conditions in New Zealand are different. Were they entitled to do so? The answer must surely be 'Yes'. The ability of the common law to adapt itself to the different circumstances of the countries in which it has taken root is not a weakness, but one of its great strengths. **(Lord Lloyd in the Privy Council in *Invercargill City Council v Hamlin* [1996] AC 624)**

7.1   Context

7.1.1   General

This chapter is concerned with the situation where a defendant negligently manufactures and/or puts into circulation a defective product or constructs a defective building and the plaintiff, who did not have a contractual relationship with him, suffers economic loss by virtue of the product or building proving to be defective. This economic loss is not economic loss of the type which is considered in Chapter 4, para 4.3.3, namely consequential economic loss in the form of lost profits when the plaintiff's property has been damaged by the defendant's negligent act or omission. Rather, it is economic loss through the decrease in value of the defective product or building itself, by virtue of the plaintiff not being able to use it at all, or at least not for its intended purpose.

7.1.2 Example

By way of an example, if the plaintiff owned a factory in which he used a machine which he had not bought directly from the defendant manufacturer, and the machine exploded due to a defect in manufacture for which the defendant was responsible in negligence, then:

(1) the plaintiff's claims against the defendant for the physical damage to his property other than the defective machine itself, and for any personal injuries suffered by the plaintiff (or by anyone else), would be dealt with in accordance with the principles discussed in Chapter 6, para 6.4;

(2) the plaintiff's claims against the defendant for economic loss in the form of lost profits due to the machine being unusable and the factory being closed down for a period of time would be dealt with in accordance with the principles discussed in this chapter. The recovery of consequential economic losses considered in Chapter 4, para 4.3.3, arises only if the defendant has accidentally damaged property which he did not manufacture;

(3) claims against the defendant by third parties who did business with the plaintiff and who will now suffer economic loss in consequence of the plaintiff not being able to continue supplying goods to them would be dealt with in accordance with the principles discussed in Chapter 5, para 5.2;

(4) the plaintiff's claim against the defendant for the replacement cost of the defective machine will be dealt with in accordance with the principles considered in this chapter.

7.1.3 The problem stated

In accordance with the principles discussed in Chapter 6, para 6.3, if the plaintiff in the above example could not reasonably have been expected to have discovered the defect by means of an intermediate examination of the machine before the damage materialised, then it is likely that the defendant would be liable for his personal injuries and for damage to his property *other than* the defective machine itself. This much was established in *Donoghue v Stevenson* [1932] AC 572 and has been the law ever since. What is not so clear, however, is whether, in addition, the defendant should be made to compensate the plaintiff in tort for the cost of *replacing* the defective machine. To put this question into *Donoghue v Stevenson* terminology, one might ask what would have happened in *Donoghue* if the plaintiff had claimed compensation not only for the physical injuries which she alleged she had suffered as a result of consuming the defective ginger beer, but also for the replacement cost of the contaminated (ie defective) bottle of ginger beer itself, which obviously had to be discarded.

This question is considered in this chapter in relation to the negligent manufacturer, distributor, builder, architect or engineer of the product or building in question. Sometimes, in these cases, the question has also been whether liability can be fixed on another party who did not actually physically create the defective product or building, but who negligently approved the defective design or construction of it at an early stage in the process of its creation. The typical defendant here will be a local authority whose building inspectors are alleged to have negligently approved plans for the construction of part of a building (often the foundations) which subsequently proves to be defective. That aspect of these cases is considered in Chapter 8, para 8.2, which deals with what one might loosely call acts of 'nonfeasance', as opposed to actual positive acts of 'misfeasance'.

7.1.4 Determining the type of loss

General

In view of the general exclusionary rule that the English courts have devised in this category of cases, it is sometimes crucial, as a starting point in these cases, to determine whether the plaintiff's loss is to be classified as damage to property or as pure economic loss. In this context, damage to a building or an article is categorised as economic loss when the person who suffered the loss did not have a contractual relationship with the builder or manufacturer to whom he is looking to make good the loss. The English courts see it as their duty to protect builders and manufacturers against claims in tort from plaintiffs with whom they did not have a contractual relationship for defects in the quality of the building or article which they constructed or manufactured negligently. The courts feel that such claims properly lie in contract between the plaintiff and the plaintiff's immediate vendor (see para 7.3, *below*).

Although judges invented the term 'economic loss' to describe the damage sustained by a defectively constructed building or a defectively manufactured article where the plaintiff and the defendant did not have a contractual relationship with each other, some judges have doubted whether this terminology is in fact apt. For example, Lord Lloyd, in *Invercargill City Council v Hamlin* [1996] AC 624 (speaking for the full panel of the Privy Council in that case), after noting certain New Zealand decisions in this category of cases, said (at p 636):

> Whether it is right to describe such cases as instances of 'pure' economic loss may not matter very much. They do not depend on pure economic loss in the sense of *White v Jones* [1995] 2 AC 207 [see Chapter 9, para 9.7.5] or *Henderson v Merrett Syndicates Ltd* [1995] 2 AC 145 [see para 9.7.6]. For in the building cases, the economic loss is suffered by reason of a defect in a physical object.

Another example is the following statement from the main majority judgment in the High Court of Australia in *Bryan v Maloney* (1995) 69 ALJR 375, which is considered fully in para 7.6.4, *below*. After noting that a relationship of proximity with respect to physical injury differs from such a relationship with respect to pure economic loss "according to the particular kind of economic loss which is involved in the relevant category of case" (see Chapter 1, para 1.3.3), Mason CJ said (at p 380):

Here, the distinction is between ordinary physical damage to a house by some external cause and mere economic loss in the form of diminution in value of a house when the inadequacy of its footings first becomes manifest by consequent damage to its fabric. Obviously, that distinction is an essentially technical one. Indeed, it is arguably inapplicable in circumstances where a latent defect in the work of one builder or contractor causes damage to a part of the building constructed by a different builder or contractor.

Thus, the term 'economic loss' is probably a bit of a misnomer in this type of case. However, it continues to be used and, as the decisions mentioned *below* demonstrate, the classification of a loss as economic or as physical damage can sometimes make all the difference.

The Junior Books conundrum

In *Junior Books Ltd v Veitchi Co Ltd* [1983] 1 AC 520, the House of Lords upheld the plaintiff's claim for the cost of repairing a defective floor that had been supplied and laid by the defendant pursuant to a contract between the defendant and a third party (see paras 7.3.6 and 7.7). One of the majority Lords, Lord Roskill, was not troubled by the fact that the plaintiff's loss was pure economic loss in accordance with the courts' definition of economic loss in this category of cases. He said (at p 546):

> . . . in the present case, the only suggested reason for limiting the damage (ex hypothesi economic or financial only) recoverable for the breach of the duty of care just enunciated [ie a duty of care based on foreseeability of reliance in accordance with the principles enunciated in *Hedley Byrne & Co Ltd v Heller & Partners Ltd* [1964] AC 465 (see Chapter 9)] is that hitherto the law has not allowed such recovery and therefore ought not in the future to do so. My Lords, with all respect to those who find this a sufficient answer, I do not. This is the next logical step forward in the development of this branch of the law. I see no reason why what was called during the argument 'damage to the pocket' simpliciter should be disallowed when 'damage to the pocket' coupled with physical damage has hitherto always been allowed. I do not think that this development, if development it be, will lead to untoward consequences.

On the other hand, one of the other majority Lords, Lord Fraser, was concerned by this development, and he thought that he saw a way around it on the facts of the case. He said (at p 535):

> It is the averments of loss which cause me some trouble. On the face of it, their averments might be read as meaning no more than that the respondents [the plaintiffs] have got a bad floor instead of a good one and that their loss is represented by the cost of replacing the floor. But they also do aver that the cost of maintaining the floor which they have got is heavy, and that it would be cheaper to take up the floor surface and lay a new one. If the cost of maintaining the defective floor is substantially greater than it would have been in respect of a sound one, it must necessarily follow that their manufacturing operations are being carried on at a less profitable level than would otherwise have been the case, and that they are therefore suffering economic loss. That is the sort of loss which the appellants [the defendants], standing in the relationship to the respondents which they did, ought reasonably to have anticipated as likely to occur if

their workmanship was faulty. They must have been aware of the nature of the respondents' business, the purpose for which the floor was required, and the part it was to play in their operations. The appellants accordingly owed the respondents a duty to take reasonable care to see that their workmanship was not faulty, and are liable for the foreseeable consequences sounding in economic loss of their failure to do so. These consequences may properly be held to include less profitable operation due to the heavy cost of maintenance. In so far as the respondents, in order to avert or mitigate such loss, incur expenditure on relaying the floor surface, that expenditure becomes the measure of the appellants' liability. Upon that analysis of the situation, I am of the opinion that the respondents have stated a proper case for inquiry into the facts. . . .

It is submitted that Lord Fraser's above-cited exposition amounts to a distinction without a difference and that, in truth, the plaintiff's loss in *Junior Books* was just as much pure economic loss as was the plaintiff's loss in *Murphy v Brentwood District Council* [1991] 1 AC 398. Indeed, in *Murphy* the House of Lords, in refusing to follow *Junior Books*, did not try to reclassify the plaintiff's loss as property damage, but rather said that *Junior Books* must be regarded as an exceptional case in which the relationship of proximity between the plaintiff and the defendants was "sufficiently akin to contract to introduce the element of reliance" which is necessary for the scope of a duty of care in this type of situation to be wide enough to embrace pure economic loss (*per* Lord Bridge at p 481—see para 7.3.6, *below*).

In some of the decisions that were made by the English courts in the period between the House of Lords' decision in *Junior Books* (in July 1982) and its ruling in *Murphy* (in July 1990), there were pronouncements that *Junior Books* was a case where the plaintiff's damage consisted of damage to property rather than pure economic loss. An example is *Tate and Lyle Industries Ltd v GLC* [1983] 2 AC 509, in which Lord Templeman, delivering the unanimous decision of the panel (which, ironically, included Lord Roskill), said (at p 530):

> In *Junior Books Ltd v Veitchi Co Ltd* [1983] 1 AC 520, a subcontractor was held liable to the owner of premises for damaging those premises by installing a defective floor. . . . My Lords, in the cited relevant cases from *Donoghue v Stevenson* to *Junior Books*, the plaintiff suffered personal injury or damage to his property.

Another example is *London Congregational Union Inc v Harriss and Harriss* [1988] 1 All ER 15 (CA), in which Ralph Gibson LJ, in rejecting the application of the principle of *Junior Books* to the facts in *Harriss*, said (at p 25):

> In *Junior Books*, it was the defect resulting from the negligent work which was seen as being the cause of the need to spend money on putting right physical defects in the floor; it was not the mere existence of the faulty elements in design or construction which would lead to the coming into existence of the physical defects.

Again, it is submitted that this is a rather sophisticated distinction without a difference, and is not helpful in trying to discern whether loss is pure economic loss or damage to property. Nevertheless, in certain other pre-*Murphy* cases, *dicta* like these led other English courts to treat *Junior Books* as being a physical damage case, and to use it as a point of departure for determining the nature of the plaintiff's damage in other particular circumstances. Thus, in *Simaan General Contracting Co v Pilkington Glass Ltd (No 2)* [1988] QB 758 (see para 7.3.6), Bingham LJ, in holding that the glass panels which were defective by reason of discrepancies in their colouring were not physically damaged in the sense required in the law of negligence, said (at p 781):

> The *Junior Books* case has been interpreted as a case arising from physical damage. I doubt if that interpretation accords with Lord Roskill's intention but it [ie that interpretation] is binding upon us. There is in my view no physical damage in this case. The units are as good as ever they were and will not deteriorate. I bridle somewhat at the assumption of defects which we are asked to make because what we have here are not, in my view, defects, but failures to comply with Sale of Goods Act conditions of correspondence with description or sample, merchantability or (perhaps) fitness for purpose. It would, I think, be an abuse of language to describe these units as damaged. The contrast with the floor in the *Junior Books* case is obvious.

Post-Murphy decisions

Even if, since *Murphy*, it is to be accepted that *Junior Books* was indeed a case of pure economic loss and that it is to be put on one side as being an exception to the general exclusionary rule enunciated by the House of Lords in cases where the defendant's negligence in the construction, manufacture or design of a building or an article has resulted in that building or article being defective in one way or another, and where the plaintiff is a person who did not have a contractual relationship with the defendant, the difficulty still sometimes arises of determining whether the plaintiff's loss in any particular case is to be classified as damage to property or as pure economic loss.

The Orjula

An example is *Losinjska Plovidba v Transco Overseas Ltd ('The Orjula')* [1995] 2 Lloyd's Rep 395, in which the plaintiff was a bareboat charterer of the vessel *The Orjula* which had been loaded in Felixstowe with two containers in which there were respectively 72 drums of hydrochloric acid and 72 drums of sodium hypochloride. The first defendant appeared as the named shipper in the bill of lading. The second defendant had supplied the drums of chemicals to the first defendant at the first defendant's inland premises. After an encounter with heavy weather en route from Felixstowe to Rotterdam, leakage was noted from the container carrying hydrochloric acid. In Rotterdam, both of the containers were discharged and the ship's deck and hatch covers had to be decontaminated by an outside contractor using soda to neutralise the acid and then washing the surfaces down with fresh water.

When the plaintiff sued the second defendant for the plaintiff's losses arising from the second defendant's alleged failure to lash, stow and/or secure the drums of chemicals within the containers in such a manner as to enable them to withstand the ordinary risks of transport by sea, the second defendant applied to strike out the plaintiff's claim on the basis that the second defendant did not owe the plaintiff a duty of care because the plaintiff had suffered only pure economic loss and not physical damage, because the contamination that the chemicals caused to the vessel's surfaces could be and was cleaned off fully and did not leave any lasting physical damage. The judge, Mance J, rejected this argument. After referring to the initial decision in *Hunter v London Docklands Development Corp* (see *below*), in which the deposit of dust by building works on the plaintiffs' property was held to constitute physical damage, he said:

> Here, specialist contractors were engaged in undertaking the decontamination work using soda to neutralise the acid before washing the deck and hatch covers down with fresh water. Further, the vessel was required to be decontaminated of the hydrochloric acid before she could sail from the special berth to which she had been directed after discovery of the leakage. On these alleged facts, I would have no hesitation in concluding that the vessel should be regarded as having suffered 'physical' damage by reason of her contamination.

Hunter v London Docklands

Another example is *Hunter v London Docklands Development Corp* [1996] 2 WLR 348 (which went to the House of Lords on another point), in which one of the issues was whether the plaintiffs, who were homeowners living in the vicinity of major construction works being carried out under the control of the defendant, could bring an action in negligence against the defendant for damages arising from the deposit of dust on the plaintiffs' houses and possessions during the construction works.

It was common ground that the plaintiffs' action in negligence depended on the dust having caused actual physical damage to the plaintiffs' property. The plaintiffs' counsel submitted that the deposit of dust, subject to the *de minimis* principle, amounted to damage in the ordinary sense of the word because it impaired the utility of the objects onto which the dust was deposited; and that impairment of utility should be equated with damage. The Court of Appeal rejected this submission, but nevertheless held that the plaintiffs' damage in this case did consist of damage to property. Pill LJ, speaking for all three Lord Justices, said (at p 366) (emphasis added):

> In my judgment, the deposit of dust is capable of giving rise to an action in negligence. Whether it does depends on proof of physical damage and that depends on the evidence and the circumstances. Dust is an inevitable incident of urban life, and the claim arises on the assumption that the defendants have caused 'excessive' deposits. Reasonable conduct and a reasonable amount of cleaning to limit the ill effects of dust can be expected of householders. Subject to that, if, for example, in ordinary use the excessive deposit is trodden into the fabric of a carpet by householders in such a way as to lessen the value of the fabric, an action would lie.
>
> Similarly, if it follows from the effects of excessive dust on the fabric that professional cleaning of the fabric is reasonably required, the cost is actionable and

if the fabric is diminished by the cleaning, that too would constitute damage. Excessive dust might also be shown to have damaged electric apparatus, and there could no doubt be many other examples.

The damage is in *the physical change which renders the article less useful or less valuable. . . .* that, *rather than any general concept of loss of utility*, is the appropriate test.

Blue Circle v Ministry of Defence

In *Blue Circle Industries plc v Ministry of Defence* (HCJ, 26 November 1996, unreported) this *dictum* was adopted as a statement of principle. The issue here was whether water contaminated with radioactive matter, which had spilled over onto the plaintiff's property from a pond on the defendant's adjoining atomic weapons establishment site, constituted "damage to any property" so as to invoke the application of the strict liability provisions of the Nuclear Installations Act 1965. The content of the radioactive matter in the water did not pose a threat to health, but it was above regulatory levels, and the discovery of it on the plaintiff's land caused a potential purchaser of the plaintiff's land to pull out of the purchase, and the plaintiff was thereafter unable to find another buyer.

At the hearing it seems to have been accepted that, if there had been any damage to the plaintiff's property so as to make the defendant strictly liable under the Act, the defendant would also be liable for compensating the plaintiff for such losses as were "truly consequential" upon the physical damage caused by the contamination, in accordance with the principle formulated in *Spartan Steel and Alloys Ltd v Martin and Co (Contractors Ltd)* [1973] QB 27 (CA) and other similar cases (see Chapter 4, para 4.3). This would include the measure of the detrimental effect on the saleability or the value of the plaintiff's property (which was in excess of £5m).

Thus, the all-important question was whether the plaintiff's loss was property damage or pure economic loss. The judge, Carnwath J, held that it was property damage. He said (at para 17):

I have no doubt that the present case falls on the physical damage 'side of the line'. As Pill LJ said [in *Hunter v London Docklands Development Corp*—see *above*], the damage is in the physical change which renders the property less useful or less valuable. It is unnecessary in my view to go into any detailed scientific analysis to conclude that the contamination caused a physical change to the area affected, which rendered it less valuable. The physical change is evident from the fact that decontamination required a major engineering operation involving the removal of large quantities of earth from the site. That the contamination rendered the property less useful or less valuable is again to my mind self-evident.

The matter can be looked at narrowly, simply on the basis that, from the time that the contamination was made known until it had been dealt with by removing the earth, that part of the estate could not be used as freely as it had been. Indeed, during the course of the works it could not be used at all. Nor on the evidence is there any dispute that, at least in the short term, while the contamination was being evaluated and dealt with, it rendered the estate less saleable, and therefore less valuable.

Relation to Murphy

In this case (ie *Blue Circle*), the defendant's counsel, in submitting that the damage suffered by the plaintiff should be treated as being pure economic loss, placed reliance on the principle established by the House of Lords in *Murphy v Brentwood District Council* [1991] 1 AC 398 (see para 7.3.4) and endorsed by the Privy Council in *Invercargill City Council v Hamlin* [1996] AC 624 (see para 7.6.2), that if a defect in a building is discovered before there is any injury to health or damage to property, the cost incurred by a subsequent purchaser (or any person who did not have a contractual relationship with the builder) in putting the defect right is pure economic loss. Carnwath J rejected this submission. He said (at para 28):

> I do not accept the parallel. In those cases [ie *Murphy* and *Invercargill*] the defendant's action did not cause the physical defect. It simply led the plaintiff to act to his economic disadvantage by buying a defective house. In this case, it is the escape from the defendant's land which has caused the physical damage. I would accept, by analogy with *Invercargill* [where one of the issues was when the limitation period commenced—see para 7.3.9, *below*], that the cause of action is not complete until the contamination is discovered, since until then there is no loss, but [in the present case] there is still a direct link between that loss and the physical impact caused by the escape.

7.1.5 Case summaries

Some of the leading cases are summarised at the end of this chapter. However, unlike the summary of cases at the end of Chapter 5, para 5.8, this summary is purely chronological, rather than being a division between those cases which have affirmed the exclusionary rule which exists in this category of cases and those which have denied it. This is because nearly all of the cases which have denied the existence of this exclusionary rule have since been overruled and therefore, unlike the cases in the second part of the summaries at the end of Chapter 5, para 5.8.2, do not still stand as exceptions to the general rule. They are nevertheless included in the list so as to allow for a full understanding of the issues involved, and because this exclusionary rule is not universally accepted.

7.2 'An impossible distinction'

7.2.1 Submission in *Dutton*

In *Dutton v Bognor Regis Urban District Council* [1972] 1 QB 373 (which is summarised in para 7.7, *below*) the defendant inspector submitted that if the council was liable, its liability was limited to those who had suffered bodily harm, and did not extend to those who had suffered only economic loss. He suggested, therefore, that although the council might be liable if, for example, the ceiling fell down and injured a visitor, they would not be liable simply because the house was diminished in value.

7.2.2 Distinction rejected

In response to this submission, Denning MR said (at p 396): "I cannot accept this submission. The damage done here was not solely economic loss. It was physical damage to the house. If [the defendant's counsel's] submission were right, it would mean that if the inspector negligently passes the house as properly built and it collapses and injures a person, the Council are liable; but if the owner discovers the defect in time to repair it—and he does repair it—the Council are not liable. That is an impossible distinction. They are liable in either case".

Although the defendant's submission and Denning MR's reply were directed to the position of the council's inspection, they would have been equally apposite in relation to the plaintiff's claim against the builder, which she had settled out of court because she thought that the rule in *Bottomley v Bannister* [1932] 1 KB 458 (para 6.6.1) ruled it out.

7.2.3 Chattels

Lord Denning also related his remarks to defective chattels and said at p 396: "I would say the same about the manufacturer of an article. If he makes it negligently, with a latent defect (so that it breaks into pieces and injures someone), he is undoubtedly liable. Suppose that the defect is discovered in time to prevent the injury. Surely he is liable for the cost of repair".

7.2.4 'An unhappily odd state of the law'

Sachs LJ expressed the same sentiment as Denning MR when he said (at pp 403–404):

> In the instant case there is ample evidence of physical damage having occurred to the property. But it has been argued that this damage is on analysis the equivalent of a diminution of the value of the premises and does not rank for consideration as physical injury. Mr Tapp [the defendant's counsel] found himself submitting that if, for instance, the relevant defect had been in the ceiling of a room, and if it fell on somebody's head or on to the occupier's chattels and thus caused physical damage, then there could be a cause of action in negligence, but not if it fell on to a bare floor and caused no further damage. Apparently in the former case damages would be limited so as to exclude repairs to the ceiling: in the latter case there would be no cause of action at all. That subtle line of argument failed to attract me and would lead to an unhappily odd state of the law.

7.3 The current law

7.3.1 Rejection of *Dutton*

The current law in England represents a complete rejection of the sentiments expressed *above* by Denning MR and Sachs LJ in *Dutton* and a complete vindication and reinstatement of the submissions of the defendant's counsel in that case. In *Murphy v Brentwood District Council* [1991] 1 AC 398 the House of Lords overruled *Dutton* as well as its own previous decision in *Anns v Merton London Borough Council* [1978] AC 728, which had approved and applied *Dutton*, and also all other decisions which had applied the principles of these two cases, such as *Batty v Metropolitan Property Realisations Ltd* [1978] QB 554, *Acrecrest Ltd v WS Hattrell & Partners* [1983] 1 QB 260 and *Dennis v Charnwood Borough Council* [1983] 1 QB 409.

In consequence, it is no longer necessary to be concerned with those cases in which the '*Anns* principle' was distinguished, such as *Peabody Donation Fund (Governors of) v Sir Lindsay Parkinson & Co Ltd* [1985] AC 210, *Investors in Industry Commercial Properties Ltd v South Bedfordshire District Council* [1986] QB 1034, *Curran v Northern Ireland Co-Ownership Housing Association Ltd* [1987] AC 718 and *Richardson v West Lindsey District Council* [1990] 1 WLR 522.

7.3.2 Three propositions

The current law in England (the position is different in varying degrees in New Zealand, Australia, Canada and some parts of the United States—see *below*) derives from the decisions of the House of Lords in *D & F Estates Ltd v Church Commissioners for England* [1989] AC 177 and *Murphy*, both of which are summarised at the end of this chapter. The current law can be summed up in the following three propositions:

(1) the loss suffered by the owner of, or by a person with a proprietary or a possessory interest in (see Chapter 5, para 5.2), a chattel or a building by reason of it being defective is pure economic loss;

(2) such loss is not recoverable in tort in the absence of 'a special relationship of proximity' which serves to impose on the negligent manufacturer or builder a duty of care to safeguard the plaintiff from economic loss; and

(3) apart from very exceptional circumstances, no such special relationship exists between a manufacturer of a chattel or a builder of a building and a person who did not directly contract with him for the manufacture or construction of the chattel or the building. It is in this last respect that the law is different in varying degrees in the other jurisdictions mentioned *above*.

7.3.3 Example

Thus, in the example cited at the beginning of this chapter, the plaintiff would be entitled to recover all of his losses except the cost of repairing or replacing the actual defective machine itself and any consequential loss of profits. The same rule would apply in the consumer field if, for example, a person's refrigerator, television set or motor car were to cease working, or even to explode and destroy itself due to a manufacturing defect. Unless (which is highly unusual) the item had been bought directly from the manufacturer, that person would have no claim against the manufacturer for the cost of repairing or replacing the item in question, even if, as is not so unusual these days, he could not make any claim against the retailer from whom he had bought the item because of that party's insolvency. He would, however, nevertheless be entitled to sue the manufacturer for any personal injuries suffered by virtue of the defect or for damage to any other property of his. The same rule of exclusion would apply to any expenditure incurred by a person to avert the materialisation of an imminent danger to himself and other persons living with him in a defective building constructed by a builder with whom he did not have a direct contractual relationship.

7.3.4 Lord Bridge's exposition

The following statement from the speech of Lord Bridge in *Murphy* (p 475) contains a complete exposition of the current law in England:

> If a manufacturer negligently puts into circulation a chattel containing a latent defect which renders it dangerous to persons or property, the manufacturer, on the well-known principles established by *Donoghue v Stevenson*, will be liable in tort for injury to persons or damage to property which the chattel causes. But if a manufacturer produces and sells a chattel which is merely defective in quality, even to the extent that it is valueless for the purpose for which it is intended, the manufacturer's liability at common law arises only under and by reference to the terms of any contract to which he is a party in relation to the chattel; the common law does not impose on him any liability in tort to persons to whom he owes no duty in contract but who, having acquired the chattel, suffer economic loss because the chattel is defective in quality. If a dangerous defect in a chattel is discovered before it causes any personal injury or damage to property, because the danger is now known and the chattel cannot safely be used unless the defect is repaired, the defect becomes merely a defect in quality. The chattel is either capable of repair at economic cost or it is worthless and must be scrapped. In either case the loss sustained by the owner or hirer of the chattel is purely economic. It is recoverable against any party who owes the loser a relevant contractual duty. But it is not recoverable in tort in the absence of a special relationship of proximity imposing on the tortfeasor a duty of care to safeguard the plaintiff from economic loss. There is no such special relationship between the manufacturer of a chattel and a remote owner or hirer.

Lord Bridge continued by saying:

> I believe that these principles are equally applicable to buildings. If a builder erects a structure containing a latent defect which renders it dangerous to persons or property, he will be liable in tort for injury to persons or damage to property resulting from that dangerous defect. But if the defect becomes apparent before any injury or damage has been caused, the loss sustained by the building owner is purely economic. If the defect can be repaired at economic cost, that is the measure of the loss. If the building cannot be repaired, it may have to be abandoned as unfit for occupation and therefore valueless. These economic losses are recoverable if they flow from breach of a relevant contractual duty, but, here again, in the absence of a special relationship of proximity they are not recoverable in tort.

This is similar to his formulation of principle in *D & F* and to Lord Keith's formulation in *Murphy*, both of which are included in the case summaries at the end of this chapter (para 7.7).

7.3.5   Consequential loss

If the plaintiff is unable to recover the cost of repairing or replacing the defective item from the negligent manufacturer or builder, then the plaintiff also cannot recover any consequential economic losses which he might suffer through not being able to use the article or building. This might seem obvious, but it is worth contrasting this with the type of situation considered in Chapter 4, para 4.3.3. There, it will be noted, the plaintiff is indeed entitled to recover from the defendant in tort both the cost of repairing the damaged machine and part of his consequential economic loss through not being able to use it. The difference is that, in that situation, the defendant is not the manufacturer of the machine, and the defect is not inherent in the machine itself, but the defendant has simply damaged it accidentally. So long as the plaintiff was someone whom the defendant ought reasonably to have had in his contemplation when directing his mind to the act or omission of his which caused the plaintiff's machine to be damaged, then the defendant owed a duty of care to the plaintiff. As noted *above*, however, the position is completely different where the defendant actually manufactured the item in question.

Sometimes the plaintiff's consequential loss flowing from his inability to use a defective product manufactured by the defendant will consist of physical damage to other property than the actual defective item manufactured by the defendant. Where this occurs, the defendant's liability for that other property damage will be decided in accordance with 'the neighbour principle' of *Donoghue v Stevenson*, as discussed in Chapter 6, para 6.4.2, and the question whether the defendant will be liable for any loss of profits suffered by the plaintiff through not being able to use that other property will be decided in accordance with the principles discussed in Chapter 4, para 4.3.3. Recovery of these two types of loss is perfectly possible despite the absence of any duty of care by the defendant in respect of the cost of repairing or replacing the damaged item itself and not being liable to compensate the plaintiff for his loss of profits consequent thereon. A case which illustrates the operation of these principles is *Muirhead v Industrial Tank Specialities Ltd* [1986] 1 QB 507, which is discussed *below*, para 7.3.6.

7.3.6   'A special relationship of proximity'

Introduction

It will be noted that the above exposition of the general exclusionary rule laid down by the House of Lords in *D & F* and *Murphy* nevertheless leaves the door open to a potentially successful claim in tort by the purchaser of a defective chattel or building where (*per* Lord Bridge in *Murphy*) there is "a special relationship of proximity imposing on the tortfeasor a duty of care to safeguard the plaintiff from economic loss". The situations in which such a special relationship will exist in these circumstances are very heavily circumscribed. This is demonstrated by the cases discussed *below*.

Junior Books v Veitchi

Junior Books Ltd v Veitchi Co Ltd [1983] AC 520, which is summarised at the end of this chapter, is the only case in which it has been held specifically (in *Pirelli General Cable Works Ltd v Oscar Faber & Partners* [1983] 2 AC 1 it was so held by implication) that there was a sufficiently close relationship of proximity to justify the imposition of a duty of care in tort on the manufacturer of a defective item in respect of the plaintiff's economic loss incurred through not being able to obtain the full benefit of the item in question. This was decided by a 4:1 majority. As noted in the summary, even the majority Law Lords recognised that the relief that they were granting to the plaintiff was exceptional. They all stressed the importance to their decision of the following factors:

(1) that the defendant, though not in a direct contractual relationship with the plaintiff, was, as a nominated sub-contractor, in almost as close a commercial relationship with the plaintiff as it is possible to envisage short of privity of contract;

(2) that the plaintiff relied on the defendant's skill and experience;

(3) that the defendant, as a nominated sub-contractor, must have known that the plaintiff was doing so;

(4) that the sufficiently close relationship of proximity which they held to exist by virtue of factors (1) and (2), *above*, "would not easily be found to exist between a purchaser and a manufacturer in the ordinary everyday transaction of purchasing chattels, when it is obvious that in truth the real reliance was upon the immediate vendor and not upon the manufacturer" (*per* Lord Roskill) at p 547; and Lord Fraser said (at p 533): "I would decide this appeal strictly on its own facts. I rely particularly on the very close proximity between the parties which in my view distinguishes this case from the case of purchasers of goods to be offered for sale to the public".

A limited exception

This case has not been overruled. The principle which it enunciates stands as a limited exception to the general exclusionary rule in this category of case. In *D & F* Lord Bridge said (at p 202): "The consensus of judicial opinion, with which I concur, seems to be that the decision of the majority in *Junior Books v Veitchi* is so dependent upon the unique, albeit non-contractual, relationship between the pursuer and the defender that the decision cannot be regarded as laying down any principle of general application"; and in *Murphy* he said (at p 481) that *Junior Books* can only be understood on the basis that the relationship of proximity between the plaintiff and the defendant was "sufficiently akin to contract to introduce the element of reliance" which he said is necessary for the scope of a duty of care in this type of situation to be wide enough to embrace pure economic loss.

Similarly, Lord Keith said (at p 466) that he regarded *Junior Books* (and *Pirelli* too) as falling within the 'reliance principle' of *Hedley Byrne*, which is discussed in Chapter 9.

Muirhead v Industrial Tank

In *Muirhead v Industrial Tank Specialities Ltd* [1986] 1 QB 507, the plaintiff was a wholesale fish merchant who devised a plan for expanding his trade in lobsters by buying them in summer, when the price was low, keeping them alive in a large tank of circulating sea water, and then reselling them towards Christmas time when the price was high. The tank and the pumps which he needed for this purpose were installed by the first defendant, who had bought the pumps from the distributor (the second defendant) who, in turn, had bought them from the manufacturer (the third defendant). Due to a manufacturing defect the pumps cut out, the recirculation and oxygenation of the water in the tank stopped and all of the lobsters in it died within an hour and a half. The plaintiff instituted proceedings against all three defendants for the cost of replacing the pumps, for the cost price of the lobsters which had died and for his estimated loss of profit on intended sales.

The plaintiff obtained judgment against the first defendant but it subsequently went into liquidation and that judgment was not satisfied. The plaintiff therefore proceeded against the second and the third defendants. As he did not have a contractual relationship with either of them his claims were founded in the tort of negligence. The court rejected the plaintiff's claim for the cost of replacing the defective pumps on the ground that this was a claim for pure economic loss in circumstances which were distinguishable from the principles enunciated in *Junior Books*. Nourse LJ said (at p 534): "In the present case there was no very close proximity between the third defendant and the plaintiff. Contractually they were several stages removed from each other. More important, there was no reliance by the plaintiff on the defendant in the sense in which that concept was applied in *Junior Books v Veitchi*. The people on whom the plaintiff relied to install the system and get the right equipment, including pumps with electric motors which worked, were the first defendant".

On the other hand, the court held that the third defendant did owe a duty of care to the plaintiff in respect of the lobsters which had died and such financial loss suffered by the plaintiff in consequence of that damage as fell within the principle of *Spartan Steel and Alloys Ltd v Martin & Co (Contractors) Ltd* [1973] QB 27, which is discussed in Chapter 4, para 4.3.2. In practice this meant that the plaintiff did not recover the total loss of profits which he had claimed, which was based on not being able to restock the tank with lobsters several times over before Christmas, but only such loss of profit as was attributable to the lobsters which were actually in the tank and which died when the pumps failed.

Simaan v Pilkington

In *Simaan General Contracting Co v Pilkington Glass Ltd (No 2)* [1988] 1 QB 758, the Sheikh of Abu Dhabi, who was not a party to the action, had appointed the plaintiff building contractors to construct a new building which was to be clad in green glass. The plaintiff sub-contracted the supply and installation of this glass to a company called Feal which was also not a party to the action. Feal obtained the glass units from the defendant. Due to defects in manufacture the glass, when installed, was observed not to be of a uniform shade of green, as ordered, but of variable shades of green and, in places, red. This was contrary to the contractual specification in the building contract and was unacceptable to the Sheikh, who refused to pay the plaintiff. Instead of suing Feal in contract, the plaintiff sued the defendant manufacturer in tort for its economic loss in the form of the monies which the Sheikh was withholding from it under the building contract. (If the Sheikh himself had sued, his claim too would have been for pure economic loss by virtue of the article manufactured by the defendant proving to be defective in the sense of being of inferior quality.)

The court rejected the plaintiff's claim. On the facts, this case was distinguished from *Junior Books* on the ground that there the floor which the defendant had supplied was unfit for use as such, whereas here the glass was serviceable as such but was unacceptable visually; and also on the ground that the defendant in that case was a sub-contractor nominated by the plaintiff, which was not the case here. These differences, especially the second one, were important in the context of the narrow scope of the *Junior Books* principle. Bingham LJ said (at p 781): "There is no meaningful sense in which the plaintiff can be said to have relied on the defendant. No doubt the plaintiff hoped and expected that the defendant would supply good quality goods conforming with the contract specification. But the plaintiff required Feal to buy these units from the defendant. There was no technical discussion of the product between the plaintiff and the defendant".

Greater Nottingham Co-op v Cementation

In *Greater Nottingham Co-operative Society Ltd v Cementation Piling and Foundations Ltd* [1989] 1 QB 71, the plaintiff was the main contractor under a building contract between itself and a construction company. The defendant was a nominated sub-contractor which specialised in the piling of foundations. The plaintiff also entered into a direct collateral agreement which contained warranties by the defendant to exercise all reasonable skill and care in the design of the sub-contract works and in the selection of materials. This contract did not, however, say anything about the manner in which the sub-contract work was to be executed. During the course of piling operations, and due to the negligent operation of drilling equipment by the defendant's workman, physical damage was caused to an adjoining restaurant. Work on site was suspended for some time while the damage caused to the substratum of the site itself was assessed and an alternative drilling scheme was devised.

In consequence the plaintiff suffered economic loss consisting of the additional sums which it had to pay to the main contractor under the building contract. The plaintiff sued the defendant in contract and in tort for this loss. It was conceded that the contractual claim would not succeed because the collateral warranty agreement did not extend to the defendant's standard of workmanship, and therefore had not been breached by the defendant's negligent operation of the drilling equipment. The Court of Appeal was therefore only concerned with the plaintiff's claim in tort. This claim failed, notwithstanding the obvious similarities with *Junior Books*, including the fact that the defendant knew that the plaintiff was relying on it for its specialist skill.

The only real difference between this case and *Junior Books* is that, whereas in that case the relationship between the parties was "as close as it could be short of actual privity", here there was an actual contract between the parties. One might have expected that this would improve the plaintiff's position, but that was not how the court saw it. Purchas LJ said (at p 99): "I do not believe that it would be in accordance with present policy to extend *Junior Books v Veitchi*"; and Woolf LJ said (at p 106): "The critical issue in this case is whether the sub-contractors assumed a direct responsibility to the employers for economic loss. Where, as here, the sub-contractor has entered into a direct contract and has expressly undertaken a direct but limited contractual responsibility to the building owner, I regard the direct contract as being inconsistent with an assumption of responsibility beyond that which has been expressly undertaken".

It should be noted that this restrictive view expressed by the court would not have applied to any personal injuries caused to any of the plaintiff's employees or to damage to any property (say, an adjoining building) belonging to the plaintiff. This is borne out by what Woolf LJ said next, namely: "This does not affect the sub-contractor's normal liability in tort, but only negatives the existence of the exceptional circumstances needed for liability for economic loss".

University of Regina v Pettick

In *University of Regina v Pettick* (1991) 6 CCLT (2d) 1, 77 DLR (4th) 615 (Saskatchewan Court of Appeal), the plaintiff suffered economic loss when the design of a space frame which was meant to be able to hold up the roof of its gymnasium safely proved to be inadequate to this task. It instituted proceedings against the architect whom it had engaged to design the building, the construction contractor whom the architect had appointed to build it, the patentee of the roof truss space frame which was to be used to support the roof and F Ltd as the fabricators of the defective components which were used in the construction of the space frame by another company whom the plaintiff did not sue.

The court found that the only party who had been negligent was F Ltd, with whom the plaintiff did not have a contractual relationship. The plaintiff's claim was for pure economic loss because the inadequacy of the roof frame was discovered before it had done damage to any other property or injured any person. Nevertheless, the court held that the defendant was liable for the plaintiff's loss, consisting in the cost of replacing the roof. Faced with the exclusionary rule laid down by the Supreme Court of Canada in *Rivtow Marine Ltd v Washington Iron Works* (1973) 40 DLR (3d)

530 (summarised at the end of this chapter, para 7.7), which is the same as the rule laid down by the House of Lords in *D & F* and *Murphy* unless the defects have made the structure 'dangerous' (see para 7.6.3), the plaintiff had to bring itself within the exceptional circumstances of *Junior Books* which the court referred to as "the reliance principle in *Hedley Byrne*" if it was to succeed.

The court held that the plaintiff did overcome this hurdle. Sherstobitoff JA said (at p 38):

> The relationship between Fentiman [ie F Ltd] and the university is mischaracterised as that of manufacturer and purchaser. If Fentiman is to be treated as manufacturer only, *Rivtow* [which is summarised at the end of this chapter] would probably operate to preclude liability for negligence. However, Fentiman was also responsible for the design of the space frame. This required special skills, namely expertise in design of space frames and of the hubs, a key component, in respect of which it held the patent. If Fentiman is to be liable, it will have to be on the basis of a provider of special skills upon which the university relied, so as to bring the principle of *Hedley Byrne* into play and thereby make the provider of special skills liable for economic loss caused by negligence in the provision of those skills.

The plaintiff did not have any direct contact with F Ltd. The various arrangements, contractual and otherwise, between the plaintiff's architect and the other parties involved in the chain, such as the structural engineer and the building contractor appointed by the architect and the sub-contractor who was to supply the roof frame and the patentee of it and F Ltd, were such that F Ltd was to supply all design services for the roof frame and to manufacture all of its components. Nevertheless, the court held (at p 46) that a position of sufficient proximity under the principle in *Hedley Byrne* existed between the plaintiff and F Ltd by virtue of the fact that the plaintiff "was made privy to this arrangement by the architect, accepted it, and placed reliance on the expertise and professional services to be provided by Fentiman".

Comment

This decision is a good example of the type of judicial inventiveness which is bound to arise in lower courts to circumvent the strictures of a higher court decision which leads to injustice. Given the much more restrictive view of reliance taken by the Court of Appeal in *Muirhead* and *Simaan*, it is unlikely that any higher court in England would adopt similar reasoning at the moment. This is shown by the decision in *Nitrigen Eireann*, discussed *below*. However, it is submitted that there is no legal principle preventing this. It is simply a question of the general trend, or 'mood', or prevalent policy which exists at any particular time. Purchas LJ's above-quoted remark in *Greater Nottingham Co-op*, "I do not believe that it would be in accordance with present policy to extend *Junior Books v Veitchi*", is very telling in this regard. As more and more decisions are given which are clearly unjust to plaintiffs, the time might arrive when the court's 'policy' swings the other way and the current conservative judicial mould is broken once more, as it was 60 years ago by *Donoghue v Stevenson* [1932] AC 562 in comparable circumstances (see Chapter 6, para 6.2.2).

Nitrigen Eireann v Inco

In *Nitrigen Eireann Teoranta v Inco Alloys Ltd* [1992] 1 WLR 498, the plaintiff was a chemical manufacturer whose plant included a furnace containing ten rows of tubing. Pursuant to a contract between the defendant and the plaintiff, the defendant manufactured and supplied the plaintiff with the necessary tubing for the plaintiff's furnace. The plaintiff's claim against the defendant in contract for loss suffered by virtue of defects in the tubing was statute-barred, and the plaintiff therefore had to found its action in tort.

May J rejected this claim. He said that a plaintiff claiming in negligence cannot normally recover pure economic loss unless there is a special relationship with the defendant amounting to reliance, and here there was no such relationship. Ironically, it was the defendant who was trying to establish this relationship, because this would have meant that the plaintiff's claim was also statute-barred in tort. This is discussed *below* (para 7.3.9). For the moment, the point to note is that May J rejected the contention that the relationship between the plaintiff and the defendant in this case could be equated with that between the plaintiff and the defendant in *Pirelli* (see *below* (para 7.3.9)). He said (at p 503): "In the *Pirelli* case, the defendants were a firm of professional consulting engineers engaged to advise and design. Here Mr Harris [the defendant's counsel] can glean no more from the pleadings than that the defendants are alleged to be specialist manufacturers who knew or ought to have known the purpose for which their specialist pipes were needed. In my judgment that is neither a professional relationship in the sense in which the law treats professional negligence nor a *Hedley Byrne* relationship".

Comment

This approach contrasts sharply with the approach of the Canadian Court in *University of Regina v Pettick*, discussed *above*. It demonstrates the restrictive approach of the English courts to this question because, on the facts of this case, the judge was not precluded from holding that there was sufficient reliance by the plaintiff and sufficient imputed knowledge of such reliance by the defendant to found a relationship of proximity. Perhaps this is explicable by virtue of the fact that the facts of this case were never ventilated before the court. The case was concerned simply with a preliminary issue of law by reference to the pleadings alone, although the above-quoted passage from May J's judgment does perhaps indicate that he would have required a great deal of persuading to have come to a different conclusion to the one he reached.

Hiron v Pynford

In *Hiron v Pynford South Ltd* (1992) 28 EG 112, the first plaintiffs were owners of a house whose floors began to crack. They engaged a building surveyor (the fourth defendant) to advise them. They also made a claim on their household insurance policy with the second plaintiff insurance company, who retained structural engineers (the third defendant) to advise them as to the cause of, and the remedy for, the damage. Subsequently the second plaintiffs entered into a contract with the first defendant, a specialist in the remedying of foundation failures, to carry out the necessary remedial works to the house under the supervision of the third defendants. Some time after the work was completed further physical damage developed in the house.

One of the issues for the court to decide was whether the structural engineers owed a duty of care in tort to the first plaintiff. The court held that it did not. Judge John Newey QC, sitting as an Official Referee, said (at p 115):

> [The structural engineers] were engaged under contract by [the insurance company] whose interests were not precisely the same as those of the first plaintiffs, who wanted their house to be made secure against subsidence and who doubtless were not troubled as to the cost of doing so, so long as the second plaintiffs were going to bear it. There presumably was no direct communication between the first plaintiffs and the [engineers]. The first plaintiffs had [the building surveyors] to advise them. Although the [surveyors] were not engineers, as building surveyors they would have considerable knowledge and probably practical experience of subsidence. On balance I do not think that there was sufficient proximity between the first plaintiffs and [the structural engineers]. *A fortiori* I do not think that the first plaintiffs relied upon the [engineers] or that the [engineers] had reason to believe that they did so.

Comment

This is another example of a post-*Murphy* case in which it is submitted that the judge adopted a restrictive approach which he was not compelled to take. Unlike in *Nitrigen Eireann, above*, the judge did hear evidence, but this was probably not as full as it should have been in view of the fact that two important findings were made by the judge on the basis of presumptions by him (see *above*). These presumptions enabled the judge to conclude that he did not think that there was sufficient proximity between the first plaintiffs and the structural engineers. It is not clear what he would have said if he had been presented with evidence which established that there had in fact been direct communication between the first plaintiffs and the engineers, but it is submitted that the tenor of the passage quoted *above* is that he would have reached the same decision.

Another point to note here is that the judge treated proximity and reliance as separate tests, whereas, as discussed in Chapter 2, para 2.3.3, reliance is *one* of the ways in which proximity can be established, but it is not a separate test on its own. This point is borne out by the fact that in *Donoghue v Stevenson* [1932] AC 562 itself the defendant's imputed knowledge of the absence of an opportunity for intermediate inspection, which really amounts to no more than saying that the defendant ought to have realised that the plaintiff was relying on the defendant to put out a non-defective product, was treated by the House of Lords as being the factor which actually established the existence of a sufficiently close relationship of proximity between the parties. As discussed in Chapter 6, para 6.3.2, this was not viewed as a separate and additional requirement, as the judge viewed it here.

Lancashire and Cheshire Association v Howard and Seddon

Another restrictive post-*Murphy* decision is *Lancashire and Cheshire Association of Baptist Churches Inc v Howard and Seddon Partnership* [1993] 3 All ER 467. Here, the plaintiff church association wanted a new sanctuary for one of its churches. It was not able to afford to proceed in the usual manner of retaining an architect to prepare drawings, obtain tenders from contractors and provide advice thereon, and thereafter to enter into a contract with a building contractor under the terms of which the architect would have certain powers to control the contractor's work. The only way that the plaintiff was able to achieve its aim of having a new sanctuary was to take advantage of a special employment programme that was operated by the Manpower Services Commission ('the MSC'), pursuant to which the MSC would enter into an agreement with 'a sponsor', who would employ workers who were otherwise unemployed, and the MSC would pay their wages.

The defendants were a firm of architects who became the sponsor under an agreement between themselves and the MSC in respect of the design and construction of the plaintiff's new sanctuary. It appears from the report of the decision that the defendants also had a contractual relationship with the plaintiff, but it is not clear how it arose or what its terms were. In furtherance of this agreement, the defendants prepared designs and drawings and submitted them to the plaintiff. In due course, after the sanctuary had been built, the plaintiff noticed certain defects which related to the design of the building, namely condensation within the roof voids and an insufficiency of ventilation in the building.

The plaintiff's claim against the architects was statute-barred. Therefore, the question was whether, in the circumstances of this case, the architects owed the plaintiff a duty of care in tort with regard to the plaintiff's economic loss consisting of the diminution in value of the sanctuary by virtue of the above-mentioned defects in its design arising from the architects' negligence. Judge Kershaw QC, sitting as an Official Referee, answered this question in the negative. First, he rejected the submission that, if a duty of care was owed by the flooring sub-contractor in *Junior Books Ltd v Veitchi Co Ltd* [1983] 1 AC 520 (see para 7.7), it should also be owed by the architects in the present case. He said (at p 479):

> I see nothing in the relationship between the plaintiff and the defendants in relation to design which could possibly be described as 'unique' or 'exceptional', such that if the *Junior Books* case was rightly decided, and the basis of that decision was as suggested by Lord Bridge in the *D&F Estates* and *Murphy* cases [see *above*] the present case can be classified as an exception so as to impose on the defendants a duty of care in tort not to cause economic loss by lack of care in design.

The plaintiff's counsel also submitted that a duty of care arose between the architects and the plaintiff by virtue of an application of the *Hedley Byrne* foreseeability of reliance principle, which the House of Lords said in *Murphy v Brentwood District Council* [1991] 1 AC 398 is the basis on which a duty of care could be founded in this category of cases. Lord Oliver expressed this point succinctly in *Murphy* when he said (at p 485): "That the requisite degree of proximity may be established in circumstances in which the plaintiff's injury results from his reliance upon a statement or advice upon which he was entitled to rely, and upon which it was contemplated that he would be likely to rely, is clear from *Hedley Byrne* and subsequent cases, but *Anns* was not such a case, and neither is the instant case [ie *Murphy*]".

Therefore, the question for Judge Kershaw QC was whether the present case was a 'reliance upon a statement or advice' case as contemplated by Lord Oliver in *Murphy*. Judge Kershaw QC held that it was not. He said (at p 477):

> The basis of the *Hedley Byrne* case is that there can be liability in tort (and, moreover, liability for economic loss) where the defendant says something in the knowledge that the plaintiff will rely upon what he says and the plaintiff does so rely and suffers loss. In this case, the plaintiff relied upon the defendants to produce designs which were technically sound, but the plaintiffs decided to place that reliance upon the defendants when deciding to retain the defendants as their architects. . . . When the defendants submitted designs, it was so that the plaintiff could consider them in the light of the accommodation which the proposed building would offer and its appearance. . . . Upon the evidence put before me I find as a fact that when submitting designs the defendants did not make any express statement about the technical qualities of the proposed building. . . . It would, in my judgment, be artificial to treat the submission of drawings and designs by an architect to his client as some form of implied statement as to the technical adequacy of the proposed building. Further, I find as a fact that when the plaintiffs approved the defendants' design, the plaintiffs were not at that stage relying upon the design in the context of technical adequacy because the reliance upon the defendants to prepare designs which were technically sound had been established at an earlier stage.

Continuing with this theme, Judge Kershaw QC concluded by saying (at p 480):

> I do not consider that the *Hedley Byrne* case is authority for more than the proposition that there can be a duty on A to take care not to cause economic loss when making a statement to B if A should foresee that B is likely to rely on the accuracy of the statement and to suffer economic loss if the statement is inaccurate. In my judgment, the inadequate plans in the present case did not amount to negligent misstatements within the *Hedley Byrne* case.

Comment

It is submitted that this case was indeed a case in which the limited 'foreseeability of reliance on a statement or advice' test that the House of Lords left intact in *Murphy* was satisfied. The judge seems to have gone out of his way to try to find reasons for avoiding the imposition of a duty of care on the architects to the plaintiff for the plaintiff's economic loss caused by the architects' negligence in designing the sanctuary. It is submitted that the distinctions that the judge drew in order to arrive at this conclusion (eg as to the *time* at which the plaintiff placed reliance on the defendants to produce accurate drawings—see *above*) are not convincing.

In *Storey v Charles Church Developments Ltd* [1996] 12 Const LJ 206, Judge Hicks QC, sitting as an Official Referee, criticised this decision and declined to follow it (see para 7.4.6).

Preston v Torfaen Borough Council

In *Preston v Torfaen Borough Council and Another* (1993) 36 Con LR 48 (CA), the plaintiff's counsel sought to get around the rigours of *Murphy* by arguing that this case (ie *Torfaen*) was not a reliance case at all. Here, the Torfaen Borough Council ('the Council') had commissioned the second defendant, a soil and foundations expert, to investigate the soil conditions and the foundations of a site on which the Council was proposing to build a housing estate. In due course, after the houses had been built, the plaintiff bought one of the houses from the Council. Shortly afterwards, cracks began to appear in the walls of the house, caused by its defective foundations.

The plaintiff brought proceedings against the Council and the second defendant, but discontinued the action against the Council when the House of Lords' decision in *Murphy v Brentwood District Council* [1991] 1 AC 398 was released. The plaintiff nevertheless continued with the action against the second defendant. The plaintiff's counsel disclaimed an approach based on the *Hedley Byrne* reliance principle that the Court had rejected in *Lancashire and Cheshire Association of Baptist Churches Inc v Howard and Seddon Partnership* [1993] 3 All ER 467 (see *above*). The plaintiff's counsel made this concession because the plaintiff had not, as a matter of fact, relied on the second defendant's report when he purchased the house from the Council. The plaintiff's counsel submitted that the present case fell into a different category, where reliance by the plaintiff on the defendant was not required, and it sufficed if the defendant had provided his advice to a third party in the knowledge that the actual beneficiary of the advice would be someone other than that third party (such as the plaintiff in the present case). For this proposition, the plaintiff's counsel relied on the following statement of Lord Oliver in *Murphy v Brentwood District Council* [1991] 1 AC 398 (at p 485): "It is not, however, necessarily to be assumed that the reliance cases form the only possible category of cases in which a duty to take care to avoid or prevent pecuniary loss can arise. *Morrison Steamship Co Ltd v Greystoke (Cargo Owners)* [1947] AC 652 [see Chapter 5, para 5.4.1], for instance, clearly was not a reliance case. Nor indeed was *Ross v Caunters* [1980] Ch 297 [see Chapter 9, para 9.7.5] so far as the disappointed beneficiary was concerned. Another example may be *Ministry of Housing and Local Government v Sharp* [1980] 2 QB 223 [see para 9.7.4], although this may, on analysis, properly be categorised as a reliance case".

The Court of Appeal accepted that this trilogy of cases (and also *White v Jones* (see para 9.7.5), which the Court of Appeal had recently decided) did justify the plaintiff's counsel's contention that there are cases where economic loss can be recovered which is outside the *Hedley Byrne* line of authorities. The Court dismissed the *Greystoke* case as having any relevance, and dealt with the other cases. Farquharson LJ said:

> While it is arguable that the features of foreseeability, proximity and fairness are present, the plaintiff still has to establish *in law* that it is entitled to recover its economic or pecuniary loss before it can say that the second defendant's alleged duty of care had the scope contended for. To do so the plaintiff has to show that its claim is in the same category or group of cases as *Sharp, Ross v Caunters* and *White v Jones*.

Farquharson LJ then analysed those cases and concluded that they were different from the present case. He said:

> Can the plaintiff in the present case show comparable features with those relied upon by the courts in the above cases? First and primarily, the proximity is in no way comparable. At the time of the negligent act, there was no complainant who could be identified otherwise than as a member of a class of potential purchasers. The report was submitted to the Council. The plaintiff never saw it, nor, one would suppose, has any other householder. When purchasing the house it is unthinkable that the plaintiff would have asked to inspect the report of the soil engineer or that of any other expert. There is no reason of policy which requires a claim of this nature to be available to the purchasers of houses. Normally they would have a claim against the vendor of the property.

The Court also rejected the plaintiff's counsel's alternative submission that if this case could not be brought within the same 'category' of non-reliance cases as the trilogy mentioned *above*, and if it could not be brought "within the principle of *Hedley Byrne*", the plaintiff's claim in this case should nevertheless be upheld by an incremental approach to existing principles of law. Farquharson LJ dismissed this submission tersely by saying: "I would have difficulty in accepting as an increment a case that lacks the central feature of *Hedley Byrne*, namely the reliance of the injured party on the negligent statement".

Comment

It is submitted that, contrary to what Farquharson LJ said in *Preston*, there is indeed a good reason of policy which requires a claim of the nature in that case to be available to purchasers of houses; namely that the defect in question, caused by the second defendant's negligence, was a defect that was covered up in the course of construction and therefore could not reasonably be expected to have been discovered upon a pre-purchase inspection by the prospective purchaser. This point is discussed more fully in para 7.5.2.

It is also submitted that it is not a sufficient answer to say, as Farquharson LJ did in *Preston*, that normally a purchaser of a house would have a claim against his immediate vendor, because most houses are sold subject to the operation of the *caveat emptor* principle, pursuant to which the risk of the quality or condition of the house resides with the purchaser unless there has been deliberate concealment of the defect by the vendor. The question whether the application of the *caveat emptor* doctrine as between the plaintiff and his immediate vendor in a case like *Preston* should be able to be relied upon as a defence by a person in the position of the second defendant (the foundations and soil expert) is considered in Chapter 10, para 10.2.1.

Henderson v Merrett

Henderson v Merrett Syndicates Ltd [1995] 2 AC 145 was not a building case. It was a case involving, *inter alia*, the liability in tort of managing agents at Lloyd's to Indirect Names (see Chapter 9, para 9.7.6). The possible similarity with cases involving buildings is that the services that the managing agents provided (eg underwriting and reinsuring contracts of insurance and paying claims under those contracts) were clearly intended to be carried out for the benefit of the Indirect Names, but the managing agents did not have any contracts with the Indirect Names. Instead, the managing agents had contracts with the members' agents only, and the members' agents in turn had contracts with the Indirect Names.

The House of Lords nevertheless held that in these circumstances the managing agents owed a duty of care in tort to the Indirect Names for their economic losses sustained through the negligence of the managing agents in performing the above-mentioned services. The basis of their Lordships' reasoning was that the managing agents, in performing these services in the knowledge that the Indirect Names were placing reliance on their expertise, must be taken in law to have assumed a responsibility to the Indirect Names to perform those services competently. At the same time, however, their Lordships went out of their way to stress that, in their view, the present case was exceptional. Lord Goff, with whose speech all of the other Law Lords concurred, said (at p 195):

> . . . I strongly suspect that the situation which arises in the present case is most unusual; and that in many cases in which a contractual chain comparable to that in the present case is constructed it may well prove to be inconsistent with an assumption of responsibility which has the effect of . . . short-circuiting the contractual structure so put in place by the parties. It cannot therefore be inferred from the present case that other sub-agents will be held directly liable to the agent's principal in tort.

Lord Goff continued in this passage by tailoring his remarks specifically to the type of contractual structure that typically exists in a building case and said (at p 195):

> Let me take the analogy of the common case of an ordinary building contract, under which main contractors contract with the building owner for the construction of the relevant building, and the main contractor sub-contracts with subcontractors or suppliers (often nominated by the building owner) for the performance of work or the supply of materials in accordance with the stan-

dards, and subject to the terms established in the sub-contract. . . . if the sub-contracted work or materials do not conform to the required standard, it will not ordinarily be open to the building owner to sue the sub-contractor or supplier direct under the *Hedley Byrne* principle, . . . [f]or there is generally no assumption of responsibility by the sub-contractor or supplier direct to the building owner, the parties having so structured their relationship that it is inconsistent with any such assumption of responsibility.

Their Lordships were thus clearly troubled by the fact that if they were to impose liability on the managing agents to the Indirect Names, the case for imposing duties of care in tort on sub-contractors in building cases would become stronger. However, it is submitted that the way that their Lordships sought to distinguish the two types of situation is confusing. It is not clear whether their rationale for making this distinction is based on the mere *existence* of the tripartite contractual structure in the building sphere or on the inconsistency in the actual *content* of the contracts entered into by the sub-contractor and the main contractor on the one hand, and between the employer/developer and the main contractor on the other hand.

After making the bald assertion of no liability set out *above*, Lord Goff then referred to the fact that in *Simaan General Contracting Co v Pilkington Glass Ltd (No 2)* [1988] QB 758 (see Chapter 7, para 7.3.6), the Court of Appeal, through Bingham LJ, concluded (at p 781):

I do not, however, see any basis on which the defendants could be said to have assumed a direct responsibility for the quality of the goods [manufactured by them] to the plaintiffs: such a responsibility is, I think, inconsistent with the structure of the contract that the parties have chosen to make.

After observing that "some difficulty has been created" by the House of Lords' decision in *Junior Books Ltd v Veitchi Co Ltd* [1983] 1 AC 520 (see Chapter 7, para 7.3.6), Lord Goff opined (at p 196):

Here, however, I can see no inconsistency between the assumption of responsibility by the managing agents to the Indirect Names, and that which arises under the sub-agency agreement between the managing agents and the members' agents. For these reasons, I can see no reason why the Indirect Names should not be free to pursue their remedy against the managing agents in tort under the *Hedley Byrne* principle.

Bingham LJ's point in *Simaan* was that the mere *existence* of the tripartite contractual *structure* in and of itself prevented the creation of a duty of care in tort by the defendant (a manufacturer of glass) towards the plaintiff for the economic loss suffered by the plaintiff when the glass became discoloured after being installed in the plaintiff's palace, notwithstanding that such discoloration occurred through the defendant's negligence. Lord Goff, on the other hand, focused on the *content* of the contract that existed between the defendants (the managing agents) and the third party (the members' agents) and concluded that the contractual structure erected between the Indirect Names and the members' agents on the one hand, and the members' agents and the managing agents on the other, did not inhibit the Indirect Names from pursuing their economic loss claims directly against the managing agents because the content of the managing agents' contractual duty to the members' agents was not inconsistent with the scope of the duty that the managing agents had assumed to the Indirect Names in tort.

It is submitted that Lord Goff's approach is more satisfactory. However, we are left without any explanation as to why, even on Lord Goff's approach, an inconsistency existed in *Simaan* and other similar cases considered in this chapter between the duty of care assumed in contract by the defendant (a manufacturer of a product or a builder of a building) to the third party who engaged the defendant to create that object or building, on the one hand, and the responsibilities assumed by such manufacturer or builder in tort to the person whom the manufacturer or builder knows will acquire the chattel or building from the third party without making an intermediate inspection.

A good example is the purchase by a consumer of a new car from a dealer. If the car is defective and needs to be repaired or discarded, the consumer cannot recover this economic cost from the manufacturer (see Chapter 7, para 7.5.3). In Lord Goff's terms, the reason for this is that the manufacturer will not have assumed responsibility to the consumer for such defects. It is submitted that this reasoning is difficult to comprehend in the typical case of the purchase of a car, where almost all of the information conveyed to the consumer about the quality, performance and reliability of the car is provided by the manufacturer, in the form of advertising and publicity materials, with the intent that it should be relied upon by the consumer in purchasing the car. Why is it that, in these circumstances, the manufacturer will be treated as having assumed a responsibility for the quality of its cars only to the dealers to whom it sells those cars directly, but not also to the ultimate consumers who purchase those same cars in reliance on the information that the manufacturer has provided to them about the quality of those cars with the intent that they should so rely?

It is worth noting that the Court of Appeal of New Zealand, in *Invercargill City Council v Hamlin* [1994] 3 NZLR 513, approved of Lord Goff's above-cited *dictum* relating to the possible liability in tort of a sub-contractor or supplier to the building owner for economic loss occasioned through their negligence (see para 7.6.2).

Cliffe v Parkman: architect different from sub-contractor

In *Cliffe (Holdings) Limited v Parkman Buck Limited and others* (6 August 1996, unreported) the plaintiff was a general contractor who had undertaken to a developer to erect a number of buildings in a business park for light industrial, storage and office use. The plaintiff engaged the first defendant, a firm of consulting and civil engineers, to carry out engineering and architectural services. With the plaintiff's consent, the first defendant sub-contracted the architectural element to the second defendant, a firm of architects.

In due course after the buildings had been completed, certain defects materialised which were believed to have resulted from defects in design caused by the negligence of the architects (the second defendant). The second defendant did not have a contract with the plaintiff. The second defendant's only contract was with the first defendant. Therefore the question was whether the second defendant owed the plaintiff a duty of care in tort with regard to the plaintiff's economic loss consisting in the diminution in value of the buildings caused by the second defendant's negligence.

The second defendant, in denying that such a duty of care existed, placed reliance on Lord Goff's above-mentioned *dictum* in *Henderson v Merrett Syndicates Ltd* [1995] 2 AC 145, and contended that the position of the second defendant, as "a professional", ought not to be different from ordinary cases where sub-contractors did not owe such duties in tort to the party employing the main contractor.

Wilcox J, sitting as an Official Referee, rejected the second defendant's submission and held that, in the circumstances of this case, the second defendant did owe a duty of care in tort to the plaintiff for the plaintiff's economic losses resulting from the second defendant's negligence in designing the buildings. He said (emphasis added):

> Where the sub-contractor is an architect hired for his professional expertise, there is no reason why the *Hedley Byrne* principle should not apply. The proper test to be applied here is whether the architect has assumed a responsibility for giving advice to the contractor (ie, the plaintiff) in circumstances where he knew that it was likely to be relied upon, and where it was reasonably foreseeable that, if it is relied upon, and if it was carelessly given, economic damage would or might result to the contractor (the plaintiff). In this case I have no difficulty in concluding that the architect owed a duty of care in tort to the contractor (the plaintiff). *The position of the professional thus differs from that of an ordinary trade sub-contractor.*

Tesco v Norman Hitchcox

The claims in *Tesco Stores Ltd v The Norman Hitchcox Partnership* (8 October 1997, unreported) arose out of a devastating fire in a large shopping centre which had been started by some vandals. Three separate actions were consolidated in the present proceedings. In the first action the plaintiff, Tesco Stores Ltd ('Tesco'), was the lessee of a supermarket in the shopping centre, suing for damage to the structure of the supermarket and for damage to stock-in-trade and equipment in the supermarket. These claims were levelled at the architects who had designed the shopping centre, namely, The Norman Hitchcox Partnership ('NHP'). Tesco did not have a contract with NHP in relation to the design of the structure ('the shell works') of the shopping centre. Tesco did, however, have a contract with NHP in relation to the fitting out of the supermarket.

In the second action, the plaintiffs were the Clark Care Group, the owners of a retail shoe store in the shopping centre, and a number of other entities who were also tenants of shops in the centre ('the Clark Care plaintiffs'). Their claims against NHP were the same as Tesco's, but they did not have any contracts at all with NHP.

In the third action, the plaintiffs were Maidstone Grove Ltd, the free-hold owners of the shopping centre at the time of the fire. However, they were a subsequent purchaser from the original developer ('Investments') and did not have any direct contracts with NHP. Their claim was for the cost of rebuilding the shopping centre and for loss of rent.

The substance of all of the plaintiffs' allegations against NHP was that their design of the building as found in their drawings was defective, in that the drawings did not make adequate provision to contain the spread of fire, and that they failed properly to perform their duties of inspecting the shopping centre during and after its construction and during and after the fitting out of the interior of the supermarket so as to detect any defects of design or construction relating to the need to contain the spread of any fire.

The judge, Esyr Lewis QC, sitting as an Official Referee, rejected the part of Tesco's claim which related to damage to the supermarket structure, the whole of Maidstone Grove's claim and the part of the Clark Care plaintiffs' claim which related to the physical damage to their shop units. This damage was pure economic loss of the sort which the House of Lords held to be irrecoverable in tort in *Murphy v Brentwood District Council* [1991] 1 AC 398. In this regard his Honour cited the following *dictum* of Lord Bridge in *Murphy* (at p 479):

> ... damage to a house ... which is attributable to a defect in the structure of a house is not recoverable in tort but represents pure economic loss which is only recoverable in contract or in tort by reason of some special relationship of proximity which imposes on the tortfeasor a duty of care to protect against economic loss.

The judge said that, as he could not find any such relationship of proximity between NHP and any of the plaintiffs in relation to NHP's design responsibilities under its contract with Investments, the plaintiffs' claims for losses suffered by them as a result of physical damage to the structure of the shopping centre, or the parts of it which each of them occupied, had to fail.

This conclusion applied also to Tesco notwithstanding the judge's finding that, during the period when NHP was engaged by Tesco for the fitting-out of the supermarket, a close relationship was formed between NHP and Tesco pursuant to which NHP owed Tesco a duty "on *Donoghue v Stevenson* principles" to use reasonable skill and care in the design of the shell works for the supermarket and, in particular, in relation to the provision of structures to inhibit the spread of fire. His Honour held that, even though such a duty of care existed, its scope did not extend to loss caused to Tesco as a result of physical damage to the structure of the supermarket because that was economic loss of the sort which the House of Lords in *Murphy* has held to be irrecoverable in tort. The judge did, however, hold (and NHP's counsel conceded) that the claims of Tesco and the Clark Care plaintiffs for damage to their stock-in-trade and certain other equipment in their units were recoverable from NHP on the basis that it was property other than the structure which NHP had negligently designed (see para 7.4.4).

7.3.7 Manufacturers' warranties

General

It is very common for manufacturers of consumer goods voluntarily to offer a limited warranty about the quality and/or fitness for purpose of their products. A manufacturer who gives such a warranty is effectively agreeing to compensate the consumer for the pure economic loss which he may suffer by virtue of the product being defective and needing to be repaired or replaced.

It must be noted, however:

(1) that, in English law, it is doubtful whether such a warranty would actually be enforceable in contract if the manufacturer were to decline to honour it. This would be because of a lack of consideration passing from the consumer to the manufacturer when the consumer bought the product from the retailer. The point has not been tested in court, probably because in practice manufacturers do regard themselves as being bound by their guarantees and because their reputations would suffer seriously if they were to renege on such offers. In any event, a manufacturer who has provided such a warranty might be liable in tort to the purchaser for economic loss under the 'knowledge of reliance exception' established by *Junior Books v Veitchi*; and

(2) such warranties are always only offered for a relatively short period (usually one year) and, especially with regard to motor vehicles, often cover only some of the components used in the manufacture of the article—typically the standard items which very rarely go wrong in the first year.

Consumer Protection Order

In view of the limited nature of manufacturers' warranties, the Consumer Protection (Restrictions on Statements) Order 1976 (SI No 1817) was made. It exposes manufacturers and wholesalers to criminal prosecution if they supply goods intended or expected to be the subject of a consumer transaction which bear, or are in a container bearing, a statement about the obligations accepted by the manufacturer or wholesaler about the quality, fitness or description of the goods in question unless that statement also notifies the consumer that his statutory rights are unaffected. In practice it is common for the actual wording to be: "This guarantee does not affect your statutory or other rights".

The Unfair Contract Terms Act

In England and Wales, s 5(1) of the Unfair Contract Terms Act 1977 (and, in Scotland, s 19, in very similar terms) provides:

> In the case of goods of a type ordinarily supplied for private use or consumption, where loss or damage—
> (a) arises from the goods proving defective while in consumer use; and
> (b) results from the negligence of a person concerned in the manufacture or distribution of the goods,

315

liability for the loss or damage cannot be excluded or restricted by reference to any contract term or notice contained in or operating by reference to a guarantee of the goods.

This is not a section which imposes liability, but only one which says that, if liability would otherwise arise, then it cannot be taken away by a limited guarantee clause. Thus, it does not alter the common law rules set out *above* (para 7.3.4) of a manufacturer's immunity against claims by consumers for defects in the products which he has manufactured. The benefit of this section is in those cases where the defective product has caused physical injury to the consumer or damage to other property of his. The manufacturer's attempt to restrict his liability for such damage by way of a limited guarantee is thwarted by this section. Section 2 of this Act effectively does the same thing, with the difference that, under s 2, an exclusion clause relating to damage to other property will be valid if it satisfies the "requirement of reasonableness" specified in the Act, whereas a limited guarantee offered by a manufacturer of a consumer product is rendered void by s 5, irrespective of whether or not it might satisfy the "requirement of reasonableness".

Non-consumers

One might ask what the position would have been in *Junior Books* if the defendant had given a one-year guarantee to the plaintiff about the fitness for purpose of the floor, as the cracks in it which started the plaintiff's claim did not appear until two years later. (The same question would arise where the plaintiff's loss was physical and the product or building in respect of which the defendant had given its limited warranty was not "goods in consumer use" within s 5 of the 1977 Act.) The question arose in the Canadian case of *University of Regina v Pettick* (1991) 6 CCLT 2d 1 (considered *above*, para 7.3.6), where the manufacturer of the space frame had given a one-year warranty in respect of its design integrity, the failure of which caused the plaintiff substantial economic loss as a result of having to replace it.

The plaintiff's discovery that the roof frame was coming apart was made well outside the warranty period. Nevertheless, the court held that this was not an obstacle to the plaintiff's claim. The court said (at p 55): "There was no evidence of any exclusion of liability. There is nothing in a warranty by itself that suggests that further liability should be excluded. The warranty is a bargain that holds the contractor liable irrespective of negligence for a period of time. A tort claim requires proof of negligence. That it should continue beyond the warranty period does not interfere with the legitimate expectations of the parties as to their contractual relationship".

This approach should be contrasted with the approach of the Court of Appeal in *Greater Nottingham Co-operative Society Ltd v Cementation Piling and Foundations Ltd* [1989] 1 QB 71, considered *above* (para 7.3.6). The difference between the factual matrices of these cases, which an English court might well say is a distinction without a difference, is that in the *Co-op* case the warranty question was considered at the stage of deciding whether a duty of care should be imposed at all, whereas in *Pettick* the court had already decided that the defendant was liable for the plaintiff's economic loss and then went on to consider whether that finding was negated by the terms of the limited warranty which the defendant had given to the plaintiff.

7.3.8   The Consumer Protection Act 1987

General

The strict liability aspects of the Consumer Protection Act 1987 are considered in Chapter 6 (para 6.5). Section 2(1), which provides:

> . . . where any damage is caused wholly or partly by a defect in a product, every person to whom subsection (2) below applies shall be liable for the damage.

is considered in some detail in Chapter 6 (para 6.5), but the question is there left open as to whether 'damage' in this section includes damage to the product itself.

Product damage

The answer is contained in the first part of s 5(2), which states:

> A person shall not be liable under section 2 above in respect of any defect in a product for the loss or any damage to the product itself . . .

This provision might sound as though it is the death knell to proponents of liability in tort of manufacturers for manufacturing defects in their products. Far from improving the position of, say, the purchaser of a television set whose tube explodes, and who is unable to sue his seller under the Sale of Goods Act 1979 because that seller is insolvent or because he personally did not buy it directly from that seller (like the plaintiff in *Donoghue v Stevenson*, whose friend had bought the bottle of ginger beer for her) and who is therefore only left with a claim in tort against the negligent manufacturer, the Consumer Protection Act 1987 at first sight would appear to make this person's position worse. However, it must be noted:

(1) that the effect of s 5(2) is restricted to s 2, which imposes strict liability for a "defect"; this is defined in s 3 in terms of the safety of a product (this is discussed in more detail in Chapter 6 (para 6.5.1));

(2) that s 2(6) states: "This section shall be without prejudice to any liability arising otherwise than by virtue of this Part".

Limited effect

Thus, all that this Part of the Act does is relieve the plaintiff of the burden of proving negligence on the part of the defendant: it only alters the method of proving liability in cases that fall strictly within its definitions, but otherwise it does not affect the common law rules as stated *above*. It would not, therefore, prevent a court from holding a negligent manufacturer liable for the cost of repair or replacement of the defective item. The only difference is that, because of s 5(2), the plaintiff would have to *prove* that the defendant had been negligent, whereas if the plaintiff had been injured or if other property of his had been damaged, the defendant would be *presumed* to have been negligent and would only have a limited range of defences available to him (see Chapter 6, para 6.5.4).

No doctrinal inconsistency

It might nevertheless still be asked whether this type of distinction is no more than an exercise in legal semantics, so that the courts should conclude that, if Parliament has seen fit to preclude liability for this type of loss in this Act, then they too should do so at common law. This line of reasoning was adopted by the House of Lords in *Murphy* in relation to the Defective Premises Act 1972. This is discussed *below*, para 7.4.5. For the moment, the point to be made is that it is open to a judge to hold, if he so wishes, that there would be no doctrinal inconsistency between the exclusionary principle of s 5(2) and imposing liability at common law for the same damage if negligence can be proved. This is because, first, the definition of 'defect' in terms of the safety of a product (see *above*) makes it logical to exclude defects which might have nothing to do with the product's safety, which might otherwise be included if damage to the product itself was included; and, secondly, and more importantly, because it is right that there should be an inquiry into the appropriate *standard* of care to be expected from the defendant where the question is one of compensating the plaintiff for the unfitness for purpose or unsatisfactory quality of the product in question.

The 'standard of quality argument'

Such an inquiry is, of course, conducted in relation to the seller's implied warranty of 'satisfactory quality' under s 14 of the Sale of Goods Act 1979, as amended in 1994. The Act provides that goods are of satisfactory quality if they meet the standard that a reasonable person would regard as satisfactory, taking account of any description of the goods, the price (if relevant) and all other relevant circumstances. The Act also states that the quality of goods includes their state and condition and that, in appropriate cases, relevant aspects of the quality of goods can include whether they are as fit for all the purposes for which goods of the kind in question are commonly supplied, and their appearance, finish, freedom from minor defects, safety and durability.

In *Junior Books Ltd v Veitchi Co Ltd* [1983] AC 520, Lord Brandon, dissenting, whose judgment has been embraced by the House of Lords in *D & F Estates Ltd v Church Commissioners for England* [1989] 1 AC 177 and in *Murphy v Brentwood District Council* [1991] 1 AC 398, said that if the plaintiff's case had succeeded, insuperable difficulties would arise in other cases in deciding upon the standard of quality to determine the question of defectiveness. This question is considered further in para 7.5.7. For the moment, the point to note is that it is believed that the need to consider the standard of care when one is considering liability for defects in the quality or fitness for purpose of a product is a valid reason for excluding such liability from the strict liability provisions of Part I of the Consumer

Protection Act 1987, and for not using that exclusion as a justification for saying that such liability should therefore be excluded in all other cases too.

7.3.9   Limitation ramifications

General

Limitation periods are entirely the creature of statute. Thus, for example, the Limitation Act 1980, s 14A(4) provides that, in respect of a claim in tort for latent damage not involving personal injuries, the limitation period is six years from the date on which "the cause of action accrued" or three years from the date on which the plaintiff had the knowledge required to bring an action, whichever is the later, subject to a long-stop date of 15 years from the defendant's negligent act or omission. However, what the Act does not define is when a cause of action 'accrues'.

Pirelli v Oscar Faber

In *Pirelli General Cable Works Ltd v Oscar Faber & Partners* [1983] 2 AC 1, the House of Lords held that a cause of action based on damage to property accrues only when physical damage occurs to that property, even if the plaintiff could not reasonably have been expected to have discovered that damage at the time when it occurred or reasonably soon afterwards. In this case, the facts were that in 1969 the plaintiff had engaged the defendant, a firm of consulting engineers, to advise on and design an addition to its factory premises, including the provision of a 160 ft high chimney. It was built shortly afterwards by a nominated sub-contractor (who subsequently went into liquidation).

The concrete used for the inner lining of the chimney was unsuitable for its purpose. In early 1970 cracks developed at the top of the chimney. The plaintiff did not discover these until November 1977, and the court found as a fact that the plaintiff could not with reasonable diligence have discovered the cracks before October 1972. The writ was issued more than six years after the date when the cracks had developed, but less than six years after the date when the plaintiff could with reasonable diligence have discovered the cracks. At that time s 14A of the Limitation Act 1980 had not yet been enacted. The only relevant section was s 2, which provides for a six-year limitation period from the date on which the cause of action accrued. It was therefore crucial for the plaintiff to establish that the true date when an action accrues is when the plaintiff could with reasonable diligence have discovered the defect. The plaintiff failed to do this. The court held that, except in the case of a building which is "doomed from the start", a cause of action in tort accrues when physical damage first appears. Therefore the plaintiff's claim was statute-barred.

Comment

This decision was clearly unsatisfactory for plaintiffs, because it meant that many actions might become statute-barred before the plaintiff became aware that he had a cause of action. It was also unsatisfactory for defendants, because, without a long-stop date in s 2, it meant that they could be exposed to potential liability for an inordinate number of years, since a latent defect might not cause actual physical damage to the fabric of the building or other item in question until, say, 10, 20 or more years after it had been erected. To alleviate these potential injustices, s 14A was inserted into the Limitation Act 1980.

As mentioned *above*, s 14A does not, however, say when a cause of action accrues. The position is still as stated by the House of Lords in *Pirelli*, but the comments made by the Privy Council on *Pirelli* in *Invercargill City Council v Hamlin* [1996] AC 624 (see *below*) suggest that the *Pirelli* approach will not survive when the matter comes up for reconsideration by the House of Lords. The plaintiff's claim in *Pirelli* was essentially a claim for pure economic loss, representing the diminution in the value of the chimney stack by virtue of the cracks which had appeared in it. Thus, in cases of damage to property, including cases where such damage is categorised as pure economic loss, the plaintiff's cause of action in tort accrues when the damage occurs. This is the position in English law at the moment, but, as mentioned *above*, it is expected that this position will soon change (see *below*).

On the other hand, if the plaintiff's case for this same damage is founded on a contractual relationship between himself and the defendant, time runs from the date of the defendant's breach of that contract. Section 5 of the 1980 Act provides that the limitation period for an action founded on a contract is six years from the date on which the cause of action accrued. In *Pirelli* the defendant's breach of contract occurred (and the cause of action accrued) when the chimney was erected. Therefore the plaintiff's claim against the defendant in contract was statute-barred. This was why the plaintiff founded its action against the defendant in tort. This type of scenario commonly arises, and can lead to some interesting consequences, as is demonstrated by the two cases mentioned *below*.

Nitrigen Eireann v Inco

In *Nitrigen Eireann Teoranta v Inco Alloys Ltd* [1992] 1 WLR 498, the above-mentioned 'accrual of action rule' created the bizarre situation of the defendant being the party who was arguing that the relationship between itself and the plaintiff was sufficiently proximate to justify the imposition of a duty of care on the defendant in respect of the plaintiff's economic loss caused by the diminution in the value of the defective steel alloy tubing which the defendant had supplied to the plaintiff. Part of the facts of this case are set out *above* (para 7.3.6). In addition, it should be noted that the tubing had been supplied in 1981. In 1983 the plaintiff found that a pipe had cracked. The plaintiff was unable to discover the cause of the cracking, but repaired the pipe. On 27 June 1984 the pipe cracked again, but this time it burst and caused an explosion which damaged the structure of the plant around the pipe, causing the plant to be shut down. The plaintiff issued a writ against the defendant on 21 June 1990 claiming damages for the cost of replacing the burst pipe, the cost of repairing the plant and loss of profits.

The plaintiff's cause of action in contract was statute-barred, having accrued when the pipes were supplied in 1981. The plaintiff's cause of action in tort would have been statute-barred if it accrued in 1983 when the first cracks appeared, but not if it accrued on 27 June 1984 when the second cracks, the explosion and the damage to the plaintiff's other property occurred. The defendant therefore argued that the plaintiff's cause of action accrued in 1983. That damage was damage to the defective pipe alone, without also being damage to any other property. On the authority of *D & F* and *Murphy*, that damage was pure economic loss. In order to succeed on the limitation point, the defendant argued that the plaintiff would have had a good cause of action for that damage. As mentioned *above*, the judge held against the defendant on this point because he was not satisfied that the relationship between the plaintiff and the defendant could be equated with that between the parties in *Pirelli* so as to give rise to a relationship of reliance in accordance with the principle of *Hedley Byrne & Co Ltd v Heller & Partners Ltd* [1964] AC 465, which is discussed in Chapter 9. (As mentioned *above*, para 7.3.6, the House of Lords in *Murphy* said that *Pirelli* was decided on this basis.)

Thus the plaintiff's cause of action could not have accrued in 1983 because, although actual physical damage occurred at that time, it consisted of irrecoverable pure economic loss. The same could not, however, be said of the damage which occurred in 1984, as it consisted of damage to "other property" which was actionable on *Donoghue v Stevenson* principles (see *below*, para 7.4.4).

Hiron v Pynford

Part of the facts of this case (*Hiron v Pynford South Ltd* (1992) 28 EG 112) are set out *above* (para 7.3.6) in relation to the first plaintiff's claim against the third defendant structural engineer. The court held that the third defendant did not owe a duty of care to the plaintiff. The court also rejected the plaintiff's claim on the ground that, even if a duty of care had been owed, the plaintiff's claim in respect of it was statute-barred. The underpinning work was done by the first defendant in 1981. The defective work was done by the first defendant in 1981. The writ was issued on 4 May 1989, just one day within six years from the date when the actual physical damage occurred. Nevertheless, the judge held that the plaintiffs' causes of action were statute-barred. He said (at p 116): "In this case, if the 1980–81 underpinning was, as I have to assume, completely useless and did not even help to support part of the house, then I think that the plaintiffs' causes of action against the individual defendants must at the very least have arisen when the second plaintiffs provided the first plaintiffs with the money to pay for the works and the first plaintiffs paid the first defendants for them. That was well before 4 May 1983, so that the plaintiffs' claims are statute-barred".

7.3.9 *Product liability—pure economic Loss*

Comment

It is not clear why the judge (Judge John Newey QC, sitting as an Official Referee) felt obliged to assume that the underpinning was completely useless. However, this had the effect of causing the plaintiffs' causes of action to have accrued at a time before any physical damage occurred. This, therefore, is an example of the 'doomed from the start' exception which the House of Lords countenanced in *Pirelli*.

Ketteman and Invercargill

In *Pirelli*, some of their Lordships acknowledged the injustice that their decision could cause by barring a plaintiff's right to sue before he had even had a reasonable opportunity to become aware of his cause of action, and they openly called for Parliament to change the Limitation Act. This was done in 1986, resulting in the above-mentioned s 14A of the Limitation Act 1980. However, that section solves only half the problem because it is still left to the courts to determine when the plaintiff's cause of action accrued. Is this to be the date when the actual physical damage to the building first occurred, even though it remained hidden from view and did not become apparent until after the limitation period had expired, as in *Pirelli*; or is it when the defect became apparent or ought reasonably to have become apparent to a plaintiff who did not shut his eyes to the obvious, as the Court of Appeal held in *Sparham-Souter v Town and Country Developments (Essex) Ltd* [1976] QB 858 (which the House of Lords overruled in *Pirelli*)?

In *Ketteman v Hansel Properties Ltd* [1987] AC 189, these questions did not arise squarely for the House of Lords' determination, but their Lordships nevertheless applied their earlier decision in *Pirelli* without any criticism of it in a case that was in the same category as *Pirelli*, namely economic loss in tort consisting of the diminution in value of a defectively constructed building.

The focus of the limitation issue in *Ketteman* was actually on whether the defects that the plaintiffs' houses developed within a year and a half of their completion were such as to categorise them as being "doomed from the start", so as to move the commencement of the limitation period back even further to the time of commencement of construction. The House of Lords held that the mere fact that the houses had been constructed in such a way that damage was bound to occur eventually was not sufficient to render the houses "doomed from the start". Instead their Lordships held that, in accordance with *Pirelli*, time ran from the date of the damage occurring which, in contrast to the facts that occurred in *Pirelli*, was within the limitation period.

One of the contentions advanced by the defendants in *Ketteman* was that, even if it could be said (in line with *Pirelli*) that a cause of action for physical damage accrued when the actual damage occurred, if the damage was economic loss consisting of the diminution in the value of the building, the cause of action for that loss accrued at the date when the houses were built because the inherency of the defects would always have had the effect of depressing the market value of the houses. The House of Lords rejected this argument, saying that there was no difference from a limitation point of view between actual physical damage and damage consisting of economic loss in the form of the diminution in value of a house by virtue of it containing a latent defect. In *Invercargill City Council v Hamlin* [1996] AC 624 (see *below*), the Privy Council did see such a distinction, and used it as a way of overcoming the problem of the limitation period having expired before the plaintiff was even aware or should, by not shutting his eyes to the obvious, have been aware of the damage in question.

In *Invercargill City Council v Hamlin* [1996] AC 624, which was an appeal to the Privy Council from the Court of Appeal of New Zealand, the negligent act or omission of the building inspector in approving the foundations of the house occurred in 1972. The first cracks in the masonry veneer and in the north wall of the kitchen appeared in 1974. By 1979, a crack in the eastern wall had developed to such an extent that a brick was loose. In the early 1980s, the plaintiff noticed some cracks in the foundation wall. Proceedings were not issued until November 1990.

The limitation period applicable to the plaintiff's claim was six years from the date on which the cause of action accrued. If the principle of *Pirelli* was applicable, the plaintiff's claim would have been out of time. However, this would not have been the case if the *Sparham-Souter* approach was followed, because the Privy Council was bound by a finding of the trial judge that, despite the history of minor defects, a reasonable, ordinary, prudent homeowner in New Zealand would not have discovered that the true cause was the subsidence of the foundations until expert advice was received from a master builder, and that the plaintiff acted reasonably in not seeking that advice until 1989.

The Privy Council solved this problem by effectively opting for the *Sparham-Souter* approach, but they did so in a way that treats *Pirelli* as being a case that has not been properly understood rather than a case that has been wrongly decided, at least where the plaintiff's claim is for economic loss in tort for the diminution in value of a defectively constructed building. Thus, Lord Lloyd, speaking for the whole panel, said (at p 648):

> Once it is appreciated that the loss in respect of which the plaintiff in the present case is suing is loss to his pocket, and not for physical damage to the house or foundations, then most, if not all, of the difficulties surrounding the limitation question fall away. The plaintiff's loss occurs when the market value of the house is depreciated by reason of the defective foundations, and not before. If he resells the house at full value before the defect is discovered, he has suffered no loss. Thus, in the common case, the occurrence of the loss and the discovery of the loss will coincide.
>
> But the plaintiff cannot postpone the start of the limitation period by shutting his eyes to the obvious.
>
> In other words, the cause of action accrues when the cracks become so bad, or the defects so obvious, that any reasonable homeowner would call in an expert. Since the defects would then be obvious to a potential buyer, or his expert, that marks the moment when the market value of the building is depreciated and therefore the moment when the economic loss occurs.
>
> This approach avoids almost all of the practical and theoretical difficulties

[. . .] of the *Pirelli* decision. . . . The approach is consistent with the underlying principle that a cause of action accrues when, but not before, all of the elements necessary to support the plaintiff's claim are in existence. For in the case of a latent defect in a building, the element of loss or damage which is necessary to support a claim for economic loss in tort does not exist so long as the market value of the house is unaffected. Whether or not it is right to describe an undiscoverable crack as damage, it clearly cannot affect the value of the building on the market. The existence of such a crack is thus irrelevant to the cause of action. It follows that the judge applied the right test in law.

Lastly, Lord Lloyd went out of his way to state that these remarks are confined to "the problem created by latent defects in building"; and he attached a further qualification on his speech by concluding (at p 649): "Whether the *Pirelli* case should still be regarded as good law in England is not for their Lordships [in the Privy Council] to say".

It is submitted that, in the light of these remarks, future cases of this nature in England will be decided by interpreting *Pirelli* in the way that the Privy Council did in *Invercargill*. It will thus not be necessary to say that *Pirelli* was wrongly decided: the decision will remain intact, but the interpretation to be placed on it will resolve the problems that hitherto have made it unpalatable.

7.4   Emerging areas of the law

7.4.1   'Close to the edge'

In *Murphy* Lord Bridge did make one qualification, or exception, to his all-embracing enunciation of the current law as set out *above* (para 7.3.4). He said (at p 475):

> The only qualification I would make to this is that, if a building stands so close to the boundary of the building owner's land that, after discovery of the danger-ous defect, it remains a potential source of injury to persons or property on neighbouring land or on the highway, the building owner ought, in principle, to be entitled to recover in tort from the negligent builder the cost of obviating the danger, whether by repair or by demolition, so far as that cost is necessarily incurred in order to protect himself from potential liability to third parties.

This remark was clearly *obiter*. The only other Law Lord to mention this point was Lord Oliver and he said (at p 489): "This is a question upon which I prefer to reserve my opinion until the case arises, although I am not at the moment convinced of the basis for making such a distinction".

Clearly, what Lord Bridge said here cannot be regarded as representing the current law, but it is worth mentioning it if only to ask what 'principle' Lord Bridge had in mind here. The answer is not known but it is submitted that neither the rule in *Rylands v Fletcher* (1868) LR 3 HL 330 (which imposes strict liability on a person who, by making a non-natural use of his land, keeps anything there which is likely to cause damage to his neighbours if it escapes) nor the common law of nuisance would provide the answer, because these principles depend on damage having been caused before liability can arise. More importantly, though, one might ask why this qualification should also not apply to the building owner's economic losses in obviating the same danger to persons or property on his own land, such as his tenants and/or members of his family (including himself) and their possessions. The nature of the loss and the source of it (ie the builder's negligence) is the same in both instances.

Furthermore, if there is merit in Lord Bridge's proposed principle, then it could be argued that it applies even more strongly where the landowner incurs expense in averting a potential source of injury to persons or property on his own land than on neighbouring land because the Occupiers' Liability Act 1957, s 2(2) imposes on an occupier of premises a duty

> . . . to take such care as in all the circumstances of the case is reasonable to see that the visitor will be reasonably safe in using the premises for the purposes for which he is invited or permitted by the occupier to be there.

and the Occupiers' Liability Act 1984, s 1(4) imposes a duty on an occupier to persons other than his visitors "to take such care as is reasonable in all the circumstances to see that such persons do not suffer injury on the premises by reason of the danger concerned".

In Losinjska Plovidba v Transco Overseas Ltd ('The Orjula') [1995] 2 Lloyd's Rep 395, the facts of which are set out in para 7.1.4 *above*, the judge referred to Lord Bridge's above-cited 'close to the edge' *dictum*, but did not try to explain what it meant. He did, however, say that he was satisfied that it did not envisage a case whose facts were as radical as the case before him. He resolved the case before him by reference to another exception to the *Murphy* doctrine, namely the 'dangerous articles' exception that is discussed in Chapter 6, para 6.2.3.

7.4.2   A duty to warn

Rivtow v Washington

Included in the case summaries at the end of this chapter (see para 7.7) is the Supreme Court of Canada decision in *Rivtow Marine Limited v Washington Iron Works* (1973) 40 DLR (3d) 530. Despite holding that a manufacturer of a defective article is not liable in tort for the cost of repairing damage arising in the article itself (see para 7.7), the court held that the defendant was liable for part of the plaintiff's consequential economic losses, consisting of the amount of the plaintiff's lost profits while the cranes were being repaired which could have been avoided if the defendant, knowing of the defect, had warned the plaintiff of it at the time, so as to have enabled the repairs to be made at a slack season, rather than, as happened, at the busiest time of the year. This is clearly a very limited exception, and may not often arise.

In holding that the defendant's knowledge of the danger involved in the continued use of the cranes for the purpose for which they were designed carried with it a duty to warn those to whom the cranes had been supplied, the court was influenced by *Langridge v Levy* (1838) 3 M & W 337 (see

Chapter 6, para 6.2.3). In that case the plaintiff had suffered a physical injury as a result of the defendant's failure to warn him of the danger of which the defendant was aware, whereas in *Rivtow* the plaintiff's loss was categorised as purely economic, in that the inherent defects in the cranes had not yet caused any physical damage. The Supreme Court of Canada held that the defendant manufacturer was nevertheless liable for part of this loss; namely such part of it as was attributable solely to the defendant's failure to warn the plaintiff promptly of the danger, saying that the duty to warn arose at the moment that the defendant learned of the danger.

It must be noted that the relief thus granted to the plaintiff was extremely limited because the court was unanimous in holding that the manufacturer was not under a duty of care to compensate the plaintiff for the cost of repairing non-dangerous defects in the crane itself. This is still the law in Canada even after the Supreme Court's recent decision in *Winnipeg Condominium Corporation No 36 v Bird Construction Co* (1995) 121 DLR (4th) 193. The only change that *Winnipeg Condominium* has brought about in this field is that if the defendant's negligence in constructing a building has resulted in the building containing defects that pose a danger to the health or safety of persons or to the safety of other property, then, and to that extent only, the defendant will be under a duty of care to compensate the plaintiff for the cost of alleviating that danger. In so holding, the Supreme Court adopted the views of two of the judges in *Rivtow* (Laskin and Hall JJ), who would have held the defendant in that case under a duty of care to the plaintiff for the cost of repairing the defective crane to the extent that such defect posed a danger to the safety of persons and other property. This aspect of the legacy of *Rivtow* is discussed further in para 7.6.3.

Comment

It is submitted that the reasoning of the Supreme Court of Canada on the defendant's liability for its failure to warn the plaintiff of a danger of which the defendant was aware makes sound sense. In the parallel exclusionary rule which existed before *Donoghue v Stevenson* [1932] AC 562 with regard to physical injury and damage to other property, there always was an exception in cases where the defendant was aware of a danger in goods which he manufactured or sold, and failed to share that knowledge with his purchaser (see Chapter 6, para 6.2.3).

Hobbs v Baxenden

The comment made *above* is strengthened by the fact that in *E Hobbs (Farms) Ltd v The Baxenden Chemical Co Ltd* [1992] 1 Lloyd's Rep 54 the court held that a manufacturer had a duty to warn its past customers of defects in its products of which it became aware even if he was not negligent at the time the goods were manufactured and sold. Here, the plaintiff's barn and a neighbouring barn had burned down in a fire which spread out of control when it came into contact with the insulating foam manufactured by the defendant which had been applied to the walls of the barn. On the question of fire resistance, this product had been said by the manufacturers and their agents to be "self extinguishing". In the state of scientific knowledge available at the time when the defendant first started to make and sell this product, this was a fair description. However, in later years, the British Standards Institution published research which showed this claim to be misleading.

The defendant was aware of this, but failed to do anything about it. The court held the defendant liable for the damage caused by the fire on the plaintiff's farm. Sir Michael Ogden QC, sitting as a deputy judge, said (at p 65):

> In my view, a manufacturer's duty of care does not end when the goods are sold. A manufacturer who realises that omitting to warn past customers about something which might result in injury to them must take reasonable steps to attempt to warn them, however lacking in negligence he may have been at the time the goods were sold. Announcements should have been made in the media. Many manufacturers take similar steps, for example, recalling motor cars in order to remedy a design fault.

Comment

The judge did not say that he was limiting his remarks to damage caused to 'other property', and excluding from the plaintiff's damages the cost of the defective foam manufactured by the defendant which had caused the fire to spread. The point simply did not arise, so it is not possible to surmise as to what he might have said; although one could venture the comment that it would seem churlish to make a deduction from the plaintiff's damages for the cost of the defective product in a case like this where devastating and extensive damage far in excess of the replacement cost of the defective product has been caused. To do so would be the same as saying that, in *Donoghue v Stevenson*, the replacement cost of the defective ginger beer would have had to be excluded from the plaintiff's injuries if she had claimed for it. However, the current state of English law compels one to this conclusion.

7.4.3 The complex structures theory

Origins in D & F Estates

It has been noted *above* that, whilst damage to a defective article itself is not recoverable in tort unless, exceptionally, there was a very close relationship of proximity between the plaintiff and the defendant, damage to 'other property' might be recoverable if it is caused by the damage to the defective article itself. Examples of the operation of this principle have been given earlier in this chapter. In cases where a building or particular chattel consists of several distinct components, the question arises whether damage to one part (say, cracking in the walls) caused by an original inherent defect in another part (say, the foundations) can be regarded as damage to 'other property' so as to enable the plaintiff to recover damages for at least part of his loss (ie the cracking in the walls).

Such a structure is known as a 'complex structure'. In *D & F*, Lords

7.4.3 Product liability—pure economic Loss

Bridge and Oliver suggested that, in such a case, the plaintiff might be able to recover damages for the cost of repairing both the cracked walls and the defective foundations because there would be no point in repairing the one without the other. They said that this was the only basis on which they could justify the decision in *Anns*, which they thought was otherwise contrary to principle. Thus, Lord Oliver said (at p 214):

> In the case of a complex structure such as a building, individual parts of the building fall to be treated as separate and distinct items of property. On that footing, damage caused to other parts of the building from, for instance, defective foundations or defective steelwork would ground an action, but not damage to the defective part itself except in so far as that part caused other damage, when the damages would include the cost of repair to that part so far as necessary to remedy damage caused to other parts. Thus, to remedy cracking in the walls and ceilings caused by defective foundations necessarily involves repairing or replacing the foundations themselves.

Partial demise in Murphy

Two years later Lord Bridge and Lord Oliver retreated from this theory, at least in so far as concerns the above-mentioned example, which matched the facts of *Anns* and *Murphy*. Lord Bridge said (at p 478):

> The reality is that the structural elements in any building form a single indivisible unit of which the different parts are essentially interdependent. To the extent that there is a defect in one part of the structure it must to a greater or lesser degree necessarily affect all other parts of the structure. Therefore any defect in the structure is a defect in the quality of the whole. It is quite artificial, in order to impose a legal liability which the law would not otherwise impose, to treat a defect in an integral structure, so far as it weakens the structure, as a dangerous defect liable to cause damage to 'other property'.

On the other hand, Lord Bridge was prepared to continue to endorse the complex structures theory in relation to a part of a structure which was not 'interdependent' with the other parts of the structure, but which was effectively 'a stand alone' part which was attached to the structure. He said (p 478):

> A critical distinction must be drawn here between some part of a complex structure which is said to be a 'danger' only because it does not perform its proper function in sustaining the other parts and some distinct item incorporated in the structure which positively malfunctions so as to inflict positive damage on the structure in which it is incorporated. Thus, if a defective central heating boiler explodes and damages a house or a defective electrical installation malfunctions and sets the house on fire, I see no reason to doubt that the owner of the house, if he can prove that the damage was due to the negligence of the boiler manufacturer in the one case or the electrical contractor on the other, can recover damages in tort on *Donoghue v Stevenson* principles. But the position in law is entirely different where, by reason of the inadequacy of the foundations of the building to support the weight of the superstructure, differential settlement and consequent cracking occurs. Here, once the first cracks appear, the structure as a whole is seen to be defective.

Lord Jauncey expressed himself in similar terms, but also added another dimension when he said (at p 497):

> It seems to me that the only context for the complex structure theory in the case of a building would be where one integral component of the structure was built by a separate contractor and where a defect in such a component had caused damage to other parts of the structure, eg a steel frame erected by a specialist contractor which failed to give adequate support to floors or walls. Defects in such ancillary equipment as central heating boilers or electrical installations would be subject to the normal *Donoghue v Stevenson* principle if such defects gave rise to damage to other parts of the building.

Lord Keith endorsed this view when he said (at p 470) that he thought that it would be unrealistic to apply the complex structures theory to a building which had been erected and equipped by the same contractor. He went on to say:

> On the other hand where, for example, the electric wiring has been installed by a subcontractor and due to a defect caused by lack of care a fire occurred which destroyed the building, it might not be stretching ordinary principles too far to hold the electrical subcontractor liable for the damage. If, in the *East River* case [which is discussed *below* in para 7.6.1] the defective turbine had caused the loss of the ship, the manufacturer of it could consistently with normal principles, I would think, properly have been held liable for that loss.

Comment

Thus, the complex structures theory still survives, albeit in a limited and somewhat convoluted form. It seems that the less work that one does on a complex structure, the greater the degree of one's exposure for damage caused to the structure by a defect in the work which one has done. These *dicta* mean that if a builder has constructed a whole building which collapses due to his having constructed the foundations negligently, he will not be liable at all in tort for this damage (and will be liable under the Defective Premises Act 1972 only if the case falls within its narrow confines, see para 7.4.5), but a sub-contractor who merely did one item of the work, such as the wiring, will be liable for all of the damage caused if that wiring, through his negligence in installing it, causes a fire which destroys the building. It would seem fair to comment that a fertile source of some very interesting future litigation has thus been spawned.

In *Winnipeg Condominium Corporation No 36 v Bird Construction Co* (1995) 121 DLR (4th) 193, La Forest J, speaking for the unanimous panel of the Supreme Court of Canada, referred to Lord Bridge's above-cited comments in *Murphy* and said (at p 201):

> I am in full agreement with Lord Bridge's criticism of the complex structure theory. In cases involving the recoverability of economic loss in tort, it is preferable for the court to weigh the relevant policy issues openly. Since the use of this theory serves mainly to circumvent and obscure the underlying policy questions, I reject the use of the complex structure theory in cases involving the liability of contractors for the cost of repairing defective buildings;

and in *Lancashire and Cheshire Association of Baptist Churches Inc v Howard and Seddon Partnership* [1993] 3 All ER 467 (see para 7.3.6), Judge Kershaw said (at p 479): "It may be that the 'unique relationship' [in *Junior Books Ltd v Veitchi Co Ltd* [1983] 1 AC 520—see para 7.3.6] was put forward as little more than a theoretical possibility and that it will in practice avail a plaintiff as seldom as the 'complex structure' argument".

In *Tesco Stores Ltd v The Norman Hitchcox Partnership* (8 October 1997, unreported), the facts of which are set out in para 7.4.6, Tesco's counsel submitted that the part of the complex structures theory which still survives (see *above*) applied in the present case on the basis that the parts of the structure which were designed to inhibit the spread of fire in the building were a 'stand alone' part of the building distinct from the building as a whole, and that if there was a defect in that part which caused damage to the rest of the building such damage was recoverable as being damage to other property. He placed specific reliance on Lord Bridge's above-cited *dictum* in *Murphy v Brentwood District Council* [1991] 1 AC 398 at p 478 that:

> A critical distinction must be drawn between some part of a complex structure which is said to be a 'danger' only because it does not perform its proper function in sustaining the other parts and some distinct item incorporated in the structure which positively malfunctions so as to inflict positive damage on the structure in which it is incorporated.

Judge Esyr Lewis QC, sitting as an Official Referee, responded to this submission by saying:

> Tesco's counsel relies on this passage primarily in relation to NHP's design of the structures in the shell intended to inhibit the spread of fire. He submits that the parts of the structures designed to inhibit the spread of fire in the building fall into the second of the two categories distinguished by Lord Bridge. However, it seems to be clear that any defects in the structures which were intended to inhibit the spread of fire fall into the first of the two categories which Lord Bridge distinguished, and that this is not a case where a distinct item malfunctioned 'so as to inflict positive damage on the structure in which it is incorporated'.

The Consumer Protection Act

The second part of s 5(2) of the Consumer Protection Act 1987 excludes the complex structures theory from the ambit of Part I ('Product Liability') of the Act. It states:

> A person shall not be liable under section 2 above . . . for the loss of or any damage to the whole or any part of any product which has been supplied with the product in question comprised in it.

This is clearly different from the solution proposed by their Lordships in *Murphy*; so we must ask which one is correct. In fact, they are both as correct, or as incorrect, as the case may be, as each other. The difference lies in the fact that the only effect of the Act is to relieve the plaintiff from the burden of proving negligence by the defendant (see para 7.3.8). The fact that s 5(2) precludes the complex structures theory applying to those chattels and those suppliers which it covers does not mean that the plaintiff's case is barred, but merely that it might be more difficult to prove. In other words, where the article is a complex structure within the definition of s 5(2), the plaintiff will have to sue the defendant in tort at common law and will have to prove that the defendant had been negligent in doing the act which caused damage to the other parts of it; whereas, if the general provisions of the Act applied, negligence on the part of the defendant would be presumed.

7.4.4 Damage to other property

General

Closely allied to the complex structures theory is the idea that a plaintiff might be able to evade the *D & F* and *Murphy* exclusionary rule if he can establish that an item of property which has been damaged is 'other property' than the defective item itself created by the defendant. An example might be if a seat in an aeroplane were to come loose in flight due to a manufacturing defect in the bolts which held it in place, thereby starting off a chain of events which led to the aeroplane crashing. The question would be whether the owners of the aeroplane would be prevented from recovering damages in tort from the manufacturers of the seat and/or of the bolts and/or of the aeroplane on '*Murphy* principles' or whether it could be said that damage to the aeroplane was damage to 'other property' than the single defective item (the bolts or the seat) which sparked off the chain of events that led to much more substantial damage. Another example, taken from one of the cases mentioned *above* (para 7.3.6), *Muirhead v Industrial Tank Specialities Ltd* [1986] QB 507, is that the physical damage to the lobsters in that case was physical damage to 'other property' of the plaintiff which was suffered when the electric motors manufactured by the defendant failed.

Aswan v Lupdine

In *M/S Aswan Engineering Establishment Co v Lupdine Ltd* [1987] 1 WLR 1, the plaintiff had bought from the first defendant, now in liquidation, a large consignment of liquid waterproofing compound in sealed plastic pails for shipment to Kuwait. On arrival there the containers were left standing on the quayside in full sunshine. The temperature inside the containers became so high that it was as if the liquid was being heated in a very hot oven. In consequence the plastic pails burst and the entire consignment of waterproofing compound was lost.

As the seller had gone into liquidation, the plaintiff sued the manufacturer of the pails (the second defendant) in tort for its loss. If the pails and the liquid in them were treated as a single defective product which had been manufactured by the second defendant, the plaintiff's claim would have been for pure economic loss in the form of the diminution in the value of that product by virtue of the defects in it. Such a claim was advanced in the trial court, but was rejected. The judge said: "I am satisfied that a sufficient degree of proximity has not been shown. Aswan relied on Lupdine [the seller] to provide proper packaging and proper stowage. They did not rely on Thurgar Bolle [the manufacturer of the pails] and had no contact with them". This decision was not appealed. Instead, in the Court of Appeal, the plaintiff argued that the damage sustained by the waterproofing agent as a result of the allegedly defective pails manufactured by the second defendant was damage to 'other property' of the plaintiff and was therefore recoverable on '*Donoghue v Stevenson* principles'.

The Court of Appeal rejected this argument, but only just. Lloyd LJ said (at p 21):

> If Aswan had bought empty pails from a third party and then used the pails for exporting the Lupguard, clearly there would have been damage to other property of the plaintiffs. But in the present case the property in the Lupguard and in the pails passed to the plaintiffs simultaneously. Indeed, it is rather artificial to think of the property in the pails passing at all. Aswan were buying Lupguard in pails. They were not buying Lupguard and pails. One can think of other cases by way of illustration without difficulty. If I buy a defective tyre for my car and it bursts, I can sue the manufacturer of the tyre for damage to the car as well as injury to my person. But what if the tyre was part of the original equipment? Presumably the car is other property of the plaintiff, even though the tyre was a component part of the car, and property in the tyre and property in the car passes simultaneously. Another example, perhaps even closer to the present case, would be if I buy a bottle of wine and find that the wine is undrinkable owing to a defect in the cork. Is the wine other property, so as to enable me to bring an action against the manufacturer of the cork in tort?

Lloyd LJ went on to say that his "provisional view" was that in all these cases there is in fact damage to other property of the plaintiff, so as to make the defendant liable for that damage. Nicholls LJ (at p 28) agreed that "in strict legal analysis" it must be correct to say that the waterproofing solution and the pails were different items of property, so that the failure of the pails caused physical damage to the plaintiff's other property. However, he, too, said that this argument did not work in the present case because, when the plaintiff acquired ownership, the waterproofing compound was already in the pails.

Failure of packaging generally

Nicholls LJ went on to say that he would, in any event, have rejected the plaintiff's claim for damage to 'other property' even if the container and its contents had been supplied by different parties. He made some general comments which certainly give food for thought. He said (at p 29):

> But quite apart from this [ie the fact that the plaintiff had bought the liquid in the pails], I have found the submission surprising and unattractive, having regard to the nature of the goods, the nature of the defect, and the nature of the damage sustained. The goods consisted of strong, but simple, plastic pails with lids, the defect was that they were not sufficiently robust, and the damage sustained consisted of the loss of the value of the contents of the pails when the lids and sides gave way. If Aswan's argument is correct, it seems to follow that with the simplest

containers, such as bags and cartons and buckets, the duty of care owed by a manufacturer under the principle of *Donoghue v Stevenson* would give rise to liability if, through carelessness in manufacture, those containers (not otherwise harmful) failed when used as intended, and the contents (whatever they might be) were lost. To my mind that, as a general proposition, would be to press the extent of the duty of care under *Donoghue v Stevenson* unacceptably far. If a customer buys a light and fragile piece of jewellery in a jeweller's shop, and the assistant hands the jewellery to the customer inside an elegant carrier bag, is the carrier bag manufacturer liable to the customer if, through carelessness in manufacture, the bag tears open outside the shop and the expensive piece of jewellery falls out and is broken? A similar question can be asked with regard to plastic bags provided in a supermarket and filled with household shopping. Although normally the value of the lost contents in this type of case will be small, that will not always be so. I can see no material difference between the ultimate user of a household carrier bag or bucket and the ultimate user of an industrial plastic pail.

Nitrigen Eireann v Inco

In *Nitrigen Eireann Teoranta v Inco Alloys Ltd* [1992] 1 WLR 498, the facts of which are set out *above* (paras 7.3.6 and 7.3.9), when the pipe cracked for the second time it caused an explosion which damaged the structure of the plaintiff's plant around the pipe. The plaintiff succeeded in recovering damages for this loss. The defendant did not even contest this aspect of the case. As May J said (at p 501): "It was accepted by the first defendants that the explosion in 1984 caused damage to property of the plaintiffs other than the pipe itself and that I was not concerned with possible problems of a 'complex structure'".

The Orjula

In *Losinjska Plovidba v Transco Overseas Ltd ('The Orjula')* [1995] 2 Lloyd's Rep 395, the facts of which are set out in para 7.1.4 *above*, the plaintiff was successful in arguing that the damage sustained by the containers was physical damage to 'other property' of the plaintiff, thereby evading the principle established in *Murphy* that a person putting a defective article into circulation is not normally responsible in tort for a defect which renders it valueless in the hands of a subsequent purchaser or possessor. This result was achieved, however, only because, while the second defendant had supplied the storage drums and the chemicals in them, the plaintiff had supplied the containers. Thus Mance J said:

> The plaintiff's counsel points out that the containers are shown in the photographs attached to the survey report to bear the plaintiff's name, and he informs me that they are in fact under long-term lease to the plaintiff, a Panamanian company. The plaintiff's interest in the containers is not therefore a subsequent interest deriving from the fact that the second defendant put them into circulation. It is a prior interest, and it would in fact appear to have been the plaintiff who, directly or indirectly, supplied the containers to the second defendant for loading. So far as any damage to the containers is concerned, this would seem to me to give the plaintiff a legitimate basis for distinguishing *Murphy*, and for claiming in tort against the second defendant if it caused damage by its alleged negligent stowage affecting the plaintiff as a long-term lessee of the containers.

The judge was not, however, prepared to arrive at the same conclusion in respect of damage to the drums. He said:

> I do not, however, accept the plaintiff's further submission that the individual drums and/or the allegedly negligent stow should be differentiated from each other and treated as separate for present purposes. The plaintiff's basic complaint concerns the poor quality of the stow and its consequences for the drums which were poorly stowed. It may or may not be true that some of the drums were damaged by being hit by other negligently stowed drums which remained undamaged. Even if that were the case, it seems to me to be contrary to the spirit and reasoning of *Murphy* to suggest that the plaintiff as bailee of the damaged drums can claim against the second defendant in tort for negligently putting into circulation another undamaged drum or an inadequate stow of drums.

In *Tesco Stores Ltd v The Norman Hitchcox Partnership* (8 October 1997, unreported), the facts of which are set out in para 7.4.6, although the judge rejected the claims of all of the plaintiffs for their economic losses consisting of the cost of reinstating the structure of the shopping centre or the units occupied by each of the plaintiffs respectively, he upheld the claims of Tesco and of the Clark Care plaintiffs against the architects whose negligent design had contributed to the rapid spread of the fire to the extent that those claims were for damage to their stock-in-trade and certain equipment in their units on the basis that this was property other than the structure of the units themselves.

7.4.5   The Defective Premises Act 1972

Context

Given that the Defective Premises Act came into force on 1 January 1974, it might seem strange to include it in a section dealing with emerging areas of the law. However, prior to the House of Lords' decisions in *D & F* and *Murphy*, a plaintiff whose property was rendered less valuable by virtue of a defect in its construction might have had more extensive rights at common law, because:

(1) the Act applies only to work done in connection with the provision of "a dwelling" (s 1(1));

(2) the Act applies only if the defendant's negligence has rendered the dwelling "unfit for habitation" (s 1(1));

(3) liability under the Act is subject to a limitation period of six years (s 1(5));

(4) for a long time the Act was not in any event available to most house-owners because s 2(1) states that no action shall be brought under the Act by any person having or acquiring an interest in a dwelling in regard to which, at the time of its first sale or letting, any rights in respect of defects in the state of it are conferred by an "approved scheme". Most new dwellings are covered by the NHBC Scheme, which was officially approved until 31 March 1979. (This is also discussed in Chapter 6, para 6.6.4.)

Furthermore, a person with an interest in a dwelling was not restricted to his rights under the Act, because s 6(2) expressly so provides. Consequently the Act came to be largely ignored in practice. However, now that the House of Lords in *D & F* and *Murphy* has effectively ruled out all common law tortious claims for damage to, or even for the total destruction of, a defectively built building (or a defectively manufactured chattel), plaintiffs will now need to try to bring themselves within the provisions of this Act if they are to be able to recover damages for these losses.

Damage to the dwelling itself: Andrews v Schooling

In *Andrews v Schooling* [1991] 1 WLR 783, the plaintiff had purchased from the defendants a long lease of a ground-floor flat including a cellar. The defendants, through sub-contractors, had carried out extensive works to the flat, but the only work carried out to the cellar was the painting of the walls. The flat suffered from penetrating dampness which emanated from the cellar. The plaintiff claimed damages from the defendants under s 1 of the Act, which provides: "A person taking on work for or in connection with the provision of a dwelling owes a duty to every person who acquires an interest in the dwelling to see that the work which he takes on is done in a workmanlike or, as the case may be, professional manner, with proper materials and so that as regards that work the dwelling will be fit for habitation when completed".

The defendants argued, first, that they were not liable because they had not "taken on work" with regard to the cellar, because they had not done any relevant work to it, and, secondly, that, even if they had, this particular defect did not render the flat unfit for habitation. The Court of Appeal rejected both of these defences (see *below*) and upheld the plaintiff's claim. In so doing the court effectively awarded the plaintiff damages for pure economic loss consisting in the diminution in value of her flat by reason of the defect in construction created by the defendants.

Taking on work

As mentioned *above*, in *Andrews v Schooling* the defendant argued that it could not be liable under s 1 for the penetrating damp emanating from the plaintiff's cellar because it had not done any work to the cellar apart from painting the walls. The defendant contended that the Act applies only to acts of misfeasance, and does not impose liability for nonfeasance. The court rejected this argument. Balcombe LJ said (at p 789): "Supposing that the owner of a plot of land instructs a builder to erect a dwelling house on it. The builder erects the house but fails to include a damp course. Without the damp course the house, when completed, is not fit for human habitation because of rising damp. I cannot conceive that Parliament could have intended that in those circumstances the builder would be free from any duty under s 1(1)".

Fitness for habitation

In *Andrews v Schooling* the court held that, on the evidence presented in the experts' reports submitted by both sides, the dampness emanating from the cellar in the plaintiff's flat did render it unfit for human habitation. In each case it will be a question of the degree of the defect, as revealed by the evidence, which will determine this question. Principles established in cases on landlord and tenant law will no doubt prove to be useful guides in formulating the appropriate acceptable dividing line between fitness and unfitness for habitation.

Alexander v Mercouris

In *Alexander v Mercouris* [1979] 1 WLR 1270, the Court of Appeal held that the Act did not apply to work which had been commenced before the Act came into force but which was completed after it came into force. In view of the limitation period of six years from the date of completion (see *above*), this point is not likely to arise again.

In the course of his judgment, Buckley LJ nevertheless made the following comment about the scope of s 1(1) (at p 1274): "The reference to the dwelling being fit for habitation indicates the intended consequence of the proper performance of the duty and provides a *measure* of the standard of the requisite work and materials. *It is not*, I think, *part of the duty itself* ".

Goff LJ expressed a similar sentiment when he said (at p 1275): "The concluding words of the section do not state the duty, but the *measure* of the duty imposed by the earlier words, namely, to do the work in a workmanlike or professional manner and to do it with proper materials, so that the *result* may be produced that the dwelling will be fit for habitation when completed".

The third Lord Justice, Waller LJ, agreed with Buckley and Goff LJJ. Thus, in their Lordships' view the Defective Premises Act does not confer an independent right of action on a plaintiff homeowner who did not have a contractual relationship with the defendant builder for defects in the building itself caused by the builder's poor workmanship or use of improper materials. Such a right of action will vest only if, and to the extent that, the defects in question have resulted in the dwelling being unfit for habitation. Clearly, not all defects will satisfy this test. For those that do not, the plaintiff will be left without a remedy. These views were expressed as *obiter dicta* by the Court of Appeal in *Alexander v Mercouris*, but they found favour with the judge in *Thompson v Alexander*, discussed *below*.

Thompson v Alexander

In *Miles Charles Thompson v Clive Alexander and Partners* (1992) CILL 753, three house owners brought proceedings against the architects and engineers who had designed and supervised the construction of their houses. Their claim was founded exclusively on s 1(1) of the Act. In respect of many of the defects complained of, the plaintiffs did not contend that those defects had made their dwellings unfit for habitation.

The defendants argued that they were not liable under s 1(1) to compensate the plaintiffs for their losses resulting from those specific defects. The plaintiffs' counter-argument was that s 1(1) conferred on them a separate warranty from the defendants in respect of the habitability of their dwellings without their having to prove that each defect was of a type which rendered the premises unfit for habitation. The court rejected this argument and held for the defendants. Judge Esyer Lewis QC, sitting as an Official Referee, adopted what was said by the Court of Appeal on this topic in *Alexander v Mercouris* (see *above*) and said (at p 757) (emphasis added):

> I am of the opinion that the provision regarding fitness for habitation is a measure of the *standard* required in performance of the duty imposed by s 1(1). It does not seem to me to be reasonable to construe this section in a way which would make the builders or designers of a dwelling liable to a person who was not even the original purchaser for trivial defects in its design, construction or in the materials used which did not render it unfit for habitation. In my judgment the section is intended to ensure that persons concerned in the design and construction of buildings carry out their work in a manner which will *result* in the building being fit for habitation when completed. The duty imposed by section 1(1) of the Defective Premises Act is limited to the kind of defect in the work done and the materials used which makes the dwelling unfit for habitation on completion.

Comment

Thus, the right of action provided by the Defective Premises Act to a home-owner against the builder for defects in construction, in cases where the plaintiff did not have a contractual relationship with the builder, is very limited. Only defects which render the dwelling "unfit for habitation" will be actionable; and the homeowner will be left without any remedy for defects which do not satisfy this test.

7.4.6 Concurrent contractual duty

Sometimes the plaintiff suing for economic loss consisting of the diminution in value of a building which he owns will have been the original contracting party with the builder or other professional person whose negligence resulted in the creation of the defect which has caused the plaintiff's loss. If the plaintiff's claim is not statute-barred under the contractual limitation period, the plaintiff will be entitled to sue the defendant in contract for that economic loss. If, however, the limitation period has expired and the plaintiff is confined to an action in tort, the question arises whether the plaintiff's claim is prevented from being actionable because it is a claim for pure economic loss in tort of the type which the House of Lords rejected emphatically in *D & F Estates Ltd v Church Commissioners for England* [1989] AC 177 and in *Murphy v Brentwood District Council* [1991] 1 AC 398.

The answer to this question is in the negative; ie in these circumstances the plaintiff will be entitled to bring his claim in tort notwithstanding that he would thereby be succeeding in a tortious claim for economic loss consisting of the diminution in value of a building by virtue of defects created by the negligence of the builder or other professional people involved in its construction or design. That this is the case first became apparent in *Pirelli*

General Cable Works Ltd v Oscar Faber and Partners [1983] 2 AC 1. As noted in para 7.3.9, in the House of Lords the focus was on whether the plaintiff's cause of action was statute-barred, and the duty of care question was not addressed. The plaintiff's claim in contract, which was statute-barred, arose out of a contract between the plaintiff and the defendant, a firm of consulting engineers, to advise on and design an addition to the plaintiff's factory premises, including the provision of a tall chimney. Due to the defendant's negligence, cracks developed in the chimney itself, necessitating extensive remedial work, thereby causing the plaintiff to suffer pure economic loss of the type dealt with in this chapter.

The plaintiff sued the defendant for damages for breach of contract and for tort, but in due course the plaintiff accepted that its claim for breach of contract was time-barred and confined its claim to tort. The trial judge upheld the plaintiff's claim in tort, and his decision in that respect was not challenged in the Court of Appeal or in the House of Lords, where the question related to the time when the plaintiff's cause of action in tort arose. No doubt was cast in the Court of Appeal or in the House of Lords on the correctness of the trial judge's decision upholding the plaintiff's claim in tort.

Furthermore, the plaintiff's successful claim in tort in *Pirelli* was endorsed by the House of Lords in *Murphy v Brentwood District Council* [1991] 1 AC 398. In this regard, Lord Keith said (at p 466):

> In *Pirelli General Cable Works Ltd v Oscar Faber & Partners* [1983] AC 1 it was held that the cause of action in tort against consulting engineers who had negligently approved a defective design for a chimney arose when damage to the chimney caused by the defective design first occurred, not when the damage was discovered or with reasonable diligence might have been discovered. The defendants there had in relation to the design been in contractual relations with the plaintiffs, but it was common ground that a claim in contract was time-barred. If the plaintiffs had happened to discover the defect before any damage had occurred there would seem to be no good reason for holding that they would not have had a cause of action in tort at that stage, without having to wait until some damage had occurred. They would have suffered *economic loss* through having a defective chimney upon which they required to expend money for the purpose of removing the defect. It would seem that in a case such as *Pirelli*, where the tortious liability arose out of a contractual relationship with professional people, the duty extended to take reasonable care not to cause economic loss to the client by the advice given. The plaintiffs built the chimney as they did in reliance on that advice. The case would accordingly fall within the principle of *Hedley Byrne & Co Ltd v Heller & Partners Ltd* [1964] AC 465. I regard *Junior Books Ltd v Veitchi Co Ltd* [1983] 1 AC 520 as being an application of that principle.

These *dicta* have led to the submission being made in concurrent liability cases where the plaintiff's contractual claim is statute-barred that the existence of the defendant's contractual duty not to cause economic loss to the plaintiff by virtue of the creation of latent defects in the building itself should provide the foundation for a like duty in tort. This submission failed in *Lancashire and Cheshire Association of Baptist Churches Inc v Howard and Seddon Partnership* [1993] 3 All ER 467, the facts of which are set out in para 7.3.6. Having reached the conclusion that there could be a duty of care in tort despite the existence of a contract for professional services, Judge Kershaw QC, sitting as an Official Referee, referred to Lord Keith's above-cited *dictum* in *Murphy* and said (at p 480):

> In the *Pirelli* case there was physical damage. It is true that the damage was to the very thing which the defendants had designed, but the issue was not over economic loss but over the date when the cause of action accrued.
>
> ... In my judgment I am entitled to treat the *Junior Books* case as a decision on fact only and to treat what was said about it in later cases as providing an explanation for the result in the *Junior Books* case, rather than as stating doctrines of law to be derived from or supported by the *Junior Books* case.
>
> I do not consider that the *Hedley Byrne* case is authority for more than the proposition that there can be a duty on A to take care not to cause economic loss when making a statement to B if A should foresee that B is likely to rely on the accuracy of the statement and to suffer economic loss if the statement is inaccurate. In my judgment the inadequate plans in the present case did not amount to negligent misstatements within the *Hedley Byrne* case.

For these reasons his Honour refused to uphold the plaintiff's claim in tort, notwithstanding that the duties which it would have imposed on the defendant would have been the same as those which the defendant undertook to the plaintiff in their contract. This decision has been heavily criticised by another Official Referee in *Storey v Charles Church Developments Ltd* (see *below*).

In *Storey v Charles Church Developments Ltd* [1996] 12 Const LJ 206, in 1982 the defendant had built a house for the plaintiffs, Mr and Mrs Storey, pursuant to a 'design and build' contract in which the defendant undertook full responsibility for the design and construction of the house. In the early 1990s structural faults appeared in the house, which were attributable to the negligence of the defendant in constructing it.

Although there had been a contract between the plaintiffs and the defendant, there was no claim for breach of contract because it would have been statute-barred under the Limitation Acts. The plaintiffs' action was for damages in tort for negligence. In view of the House of Lords' decision in *Henderson v Merrett Syndicates Ltd* [1995] 2 AC 145 (see Chapter 10, para 10.4.2), the defendant's counsel did not argue that the existence of a contract between the parties was a bar to concurrent liability in tort. Instead, he submitted that the plaintiffs' action, being an action for diminution in the value of a building by virtue of defects in it created by the defendant's negligence, was ruled out by the House of Lords' decision in *Murphy* and by Judge Kershaw QC's decision in the *Lancashire and Cheshire* case. The plaintiffs' counsel, on the other hand, submitted that if the plaintiff's claim in tort could succeed in *Pirelli* then there was no reason why it should not also succeed in the present case.

Judge Hicks QC, sitting as an Official Referee, preferred the plaintiffs' counsel's submission. He said that the difficulty which he had about Judge Kershaw's reasoning in *Lancashire and Cheshire* is that it treats the contractual relationship between the parties as irrelevant to the scope of the tort duty. He said that this should not be done in situations where a duty in tort to take reasonable care not to cause economic loss arises out of a contractual relationship. He concluded (at p 212):

> I do not, therefore, find myself able to follow the *Lancashire and Cheshire Association* case on this point. On the basis of the considerations and authorities canvassed in paragraphs 21 and 22 above [ie *Pirelli* and Lord Keith's above-cited *dicta* in *Murphy*], I consider that, where there are concurrent duties in contract and tort to use due care and skill, the scope of the duty in tort is normally coterminous with that in contract. Whether or not I am right in believing that there is such a general principle, I conclude in particular that a designer's concurrent duty in tort to use due care and skill extends to taking care not to cause economic loss [in tort] unless the contractual duty is more limited.

In *Tesco Stores Ltd v The Norman Hitchcox Partnership Ltd* (8 October 1997, unreported), Judge Esyr Lewis QC, sitting as an Official Referee, preferred the approach of Judge Hicks in *Storey v Charles Church* to the approach of Judge Kershaw in *Lancashire and Cheshire*. One of the issues in the *Tesco* case was the liability in tort of the defendant architects ('NHP') to the developers of the shopping centre ('Investments') for Investments' economic loss consisting of the rebuilding costs of the shopping centre after it had been destroyed by fire. NHP had designed the shopping centre. Investments (and the other plaintiffs—see *below*) alleged that NHP's design of the building was defective in that it did not make adequate provision to contain the spread of fire. Investments and NHP had a contract under which NHP owed a duty of care to Investments in relation to the design of the building. However, any claims under that contract were statute-barred. Therefore, Investments' claim had to be brought in tort. In upholding this claim, Judge Esyr Lewis QC said:

> As to the design of the shell, I have found that NHP owed an implied contractual duty of care to Investments in relation to the shell design works. I consider that they also owed a concurrent duty of care in tort to the same effect. In my view, a breach of this duty would entitle Investments to recover losses stemming from the physical damage to the building for the reasons given in the opinion of Lord Keith in *Murphy v Brentwood District Council* in the passage which I have set out above [ie the same passage set out *above* in this section] and by Judge Hicks in *Storey v Charles Church*.

The application of this principle also led his Honour to hold that NHP did not owe a duty of care in tort to Tesco Stores Ltd ('Tesco'). Tesco was the lessee of a supermarket in the shopping centre and did not have a contract with NHP in relation to the design of the shopping centre. Thus, Judge Esyr Lewis said:

> I do not consider that the circumstances of the present case bring the Tesco claim within the *Hedley Byrne* principles as described both by Lord Goff [in *Henderson v Merrett*] and Lord Keith [in *Murphy*]. As NHP never had any obligation to inspect the shell works under their contract with Investments and had no obligation to do so under their fit-out contract with Tesco, I do not consider that NHP

ever assumed an obligation towards Tesco to carry out detailed inspections of the shell for the express purpose of seeing that the shell works had been properly constructed or to detect any possible deficiencies in their design. It follows from this conclusion that the decision of Judge Hicks in *Storey v Charles Church* is not relevant to the circumstances of the relationship between Tesco and NHP, although it is relevant to the relationship between Investments and NHP [see para 7.3.6 *above*].

7.5   Critical comment on the current law

7.5.1   Introduction

In *Murphy* the House of Lords recognised that the exclusionary rule which they were endorsing so strongly could be regarded as unjust, but they felt that they had no alternative but to hold as they did. Thus, Lord Keith said (at p 472):

> The decision in *Anns* is capable of being regarded as affording a measure of justice, but, as against that, the impossibility of finding any coherent and logically based doctrine behind it is calculated to put the law of negligence into a state of confusion defying rational analysis. There is much to be said for the view that in what is essentially a consumer protection field, as was observed by Lord Bridge in *D & F Estates* [1989] AC 177 at 207, the precise extent and limits of the liabilities which in the public interest should be imposed on builders and local authorities are best left to the legislature.

With these comments in mind, it will be instructive to examine more closely the reasons given for the decisions in *Murphy* and *D & F* to see whether their Lordships were indeed bound to hold in these cases that a negligent builder or a negligent manufacturer owes no duty of care in tort for damage caused to the building or the article constructed or manufactured by him. The additional local authority, or nonfeasance, aspects, which only arose in *Murphy*, are considered in Chapter 8, para 8.2.

7.5.2   Proximity based on reliance

Difficulties in Murphy

Of the several reasons given by their Lordships in *Murphy* for rejecting the plaintiff's claims in tort against the builder and the local authority, the most important one is the fact that they were not able to discern a sufficient relationship of proximity to justify the imposition of a duty of care. Thus, Lord Oliver said (at p 485):

> The critical question is not the nature of the damage in itself, whether physical or pecuniary, but whether the scope of the duty of care in the circumstances of the case is such as to embrace damage of the kind which the plaintiff claims to have sustained. The essential question which has to be asked in every case, given that damage which is the essential ingredient of the action has occurred, is whether the relationship between the plaintiff and the defendant is such—or, to use the favoured expression, whether it is of sufficient 'proximity'—that it

imposes upon the latter a duty to take care to avoid or prevent that loss which has in fact been sustained. That the requisite degree of proximity may be established in circumstances in which the plaintiff's injury results from his reliance upon a statement or advice upon which he was entitled to rely and upon which it was contemplated that he would be likely to rely is clear from *Hedley Byrne* and subsequent cases, but *Anns* was not such a case and neither is the instant case.

Lord Oliver continued (at pp 486–489):

In the straightforward case of the direct infliction of physical injury by the act of the plaintiff there is no need to look beyond the foreseeability by the defendant of the result in order to establish that he is in a 'proximate' relationship with the plaintiff. The infliction of physical injury to the person or property of another universally requires to be justified. The causing of economic loss does not. If it is to be categorised as wrongful it is necessary to find some factor beyond the mere occurrence of the loss and the fact that its occurrence could be foreseen. Thus the categorisation of damage as economic serves at least the useful purpose of indicating that something more is required. It is one of the unfortunate features of *Anns* [where the damage was categorised as physical, not economic] that it resulted initially in this essential distinction being lost sight of. ... Anyone who builds a semi-permanent structure must be taken to contemplate that at some time in the future it will come to be occupied by another person and that if it is defectively built it may fall down and injure that person or his property or may put him in a position in which, if he wishes to occupy it safely or comfortably, he will have to expend money on rectifying the defect. The case of physical injury to the owner or his licensees or his or their property presents no difficulty. He who was responsible for the defect is, by the reasonable foreseeability of that injury, in a proximate 'neighbour' relationship with the injured person on ordinary *Donoghue v Stevenson* principles. But when no such injury has occurred and when the defect has been discovered and is therefore no longer latent, whence arises that relationship of proximity required to fix him with responsibility for putting right the defect? Foresight alone is not enough but from what else can the relationship be derived?

Lord Oliver rounded off on this topic by saying: "I am able to see no circumstances from which there can be deduced a relationship of proximity such as to render the builder liable in tort for pure pecuniary damage sustained by a derivative owner with whom he has no contractual or other relationship".

The answer

The answer to Lord Oliver's questions is that the necessary relationship of proximity, founded on reliance, "required to fix the builder with responsibility for putting right the defect" arises from the fact that the imposition of such responsibility is justified where the defect created by the defendant is hidden and would not, to the knowledge or expectation of the defendant, have been discovered by an intermediate inspection before it became patent. In *Donoghue v Stevenson* this was the single factor which established proximity, rather than simply the fact that the plaintiff suffered a foreseeable physical injury. As pointed out in Chapter 6, para 6.3.2, the speeches in *Donoghue* make it clear that if it had not been for this factor (for example, if the ginger beer had been sold in a clear bottle, rather than in a dark, opaque bottle) the decision would have been different. Contrary to what Lord Oliver and his fellow Law Lords have suggested, it is submitted that the 'reliance principle' is not confined to negligent misstatements or advice, but can apply in appropriate circumstances in cases like *Donoghue* and *Murphy*. This point was fully appreciated by the British Columbia Court of Appeal in *Kama Lap Enterprises Ltd v Chu's Central Market Ltd* (1989) 64 DLR (4th) 167, when Taylor JA said (at p 170): "It was, of course, the impossibility of intermediate examination of the product which resulted in reliance by the consumer on the manufacturer in *Donoghue v Stevenson*". It is neither logical nor in accordance with authority (see para 7.5.4, *below*) to say that proximity can be founded on reliance but then to say that such reliance has to be on a statement or advice and on nothing else.

In *Murphy* Lord Keith recognised the importance of the absence of an opportunity for intermediate inspection when he said (at p 464): "An essential feature of the species of liability in negligence established by *Donoghue v Stevenson* was that the carelessly manufactured product should be intended to reach the injured consumer in the same state as that in which it was put up with no reasonable prospect of intermediate examination. It is the latency of the defect which constitutes the mischief".

It is a pity that Lord Keith did not, however, appreciate the importance of the absence of an opportunity for intermediate inspection in a case like *Donoghue* in the context of the concept of reliance. The House of Lords certainly did do so in *Hedley Byrne & Co Ltd v Heller & Partners Ltd* [1964] AC 465. One of the defendant's submissions in *Hedley Byrne* was that, in contradistinction to the position which pertained with regard to injury caused by the defendant's negligent act, there could be no liability where a careless misstatement was in question unless there was a contractual or a fiduciary relationship between the plaintiff and the defendant. In rejecting this contention, Lord Morris referred to the decisions in *Heaven v Pender* (1883), *George v Skivington* (1869) and *Donoghue v Stevenson* (1932), all of which are considered in Chapter 6, para 6.2.5, and then said (at p 496): "In logic I can see no essential reason for distinguishing injury which is caused by a reliance upon words [as in *Hedley Byrne*] from injury which is caused by a reliance upon the safety of the staging of a ship [as in *Heaven v Pender*] or by a reliance upon the safety for use of the contents of a bottle of hair wash [as in *George*] or a bottle of some consumable liquid [as in *Donoghue*]".

It would seem that the supreme irony of *Murphy* is the fact that their Lordships said that there could be no reliance "in the *Hedley Byrne* sense" in the type of situation which arose in *D & F* and *Murphy*, but they failed to realise that the very foundation of, and the justification for, that principle in *Hedley Byrne* was that the House in *Hedley* recognised that this principle already existed in relation to cases like *Donoghue*. It is true, of course, that the actual loss suffered by the plaintiff in *Donoghue* was physical injury, but if, as Lord Oliver said in *Murphy* (at pp 485–6), "the critical question is not the nature of the damage", but whether there was sufficient proximity based on reliance between the plaintiff and the defendant, then, where such reliance did exist, as it did in *Donoghue*, and as it might have in *Murphy* (the case report does not reveal whether there was such reliance in fact), it should not matter whether what the plaintiff relied on was a statement or some other inference which arose from a physical state of being (such as the bottle of ginger beer in *Donoghue* or the foundations in *Murphy*). Their Lordships in *Murphy* seemed to think that the reliance principle established in *Hedley Byrne* is confined to negligent statements or advice (Lord Oliver, for example, said this expressly), but they failed to notice that the House of Lords before them in *Hedley Byrne* had already (correctly) recognised that *Donoghue*, which did not involve a negligent statement or advice, was in fact a 'reliance case' within the scope of the principle enunciated by the House in *Hedley Byrne*.

It is crucial to appreciate that the defendant's knowledge or expectation, actual or imputed, that there will most likely not be an intermediate examination of the product or building which he has created (or that, if such an examination could be expected, it would not be likely to reveal the hidden defect in question) before its intended use by the ultimate purchaser or user, is no more than a reformulation of the principle endorsed by the House of Lords in *Junior Books*, *D & F* and *Murphy* that the defendant cannot be under a duty of care in this type of case unless the plaintiff relied on the defendant's skill and experience and the defendant knew, or ought in the circumstances to have known, that the plaintiff was doing so.

In other words, if, as the House of Lords has said, the key factor in establishing proximity is reliance, or, more accurately, knowledge, actual or imputed, by the defendant that the plaintiff would be relying on his (defendant's) skill and experience, it is submitted that this test will be capable of being satisfied where the defendant knew, or ought to have known, that the plaintiff, or a person within the same class as the plaintiff, would be likely to use the defendant's product without making an independent intermediate examination of his own which would be likely to reveal the hidden defect. The plaintiff's reliance, and the defendant's foresight of such reliance, does not, in these circumstances, have to be only on 'a statement or advice', as Lord Oliver suggested in one of the passages quoted *above*. Whether this test will actually be satisfied in any particular case will depend on what the parties actually said or did, or ought, in the circumstances, to have said or done, as can be seen from the discussion of the 'intermediate inspection cases' in Chapter 6, para 6.3.

Application in Anns

As noted *above*, Lord Oliver in *Murphy* said that the categorisation of the damage to the maisonette itself as physical damage, rather than as pure economic loss, led to the court in *Anns* losing sight of the 'essential distinction' between physical loss and pure economic loss, namely that, in the former case, foreseeability of damage alone will suffice to establish a proximate relationship, whereas in the latter "something more" is required. Two important observations can be made on this. First, as mentioned *above* in demonstrating how proximity was actually founded in *Donoghue*, it is not believed that this distinction actually exists: a duty of care arose in *Donoghue* not simply because physical injury was foreseeable if the product was defective, but because the defendant knew, or was taken as having known, that there would be no intermediate inspection of the product before its consumption which would reveal the hidden defect.

Secondly, even if this distinction does exist, it is submitted that the House of Lords in *Anns* (which is summarised in para 7.7) did not "lose sight of it". Thus, Lord Wilberforce, who spoke for himself, Lord Diplock, Lord Simon and Lord Russell, said (at p 753):

> One of the particular matters within the area of local authority supervision is the foundations of buildings—clearly a matter of vital importance, particularly because this part of the building comes to be covered up as building proceeds. Thus any weakness or inadequacy will create a hidden defect which whoever acquires the building has no means of discovering: in legal parlance there is no opportunity for intermediate inspection. It must be in the reasonable contemplation, not only of the builder but also of the local authority, that failure to comply with the byelaws' requirement as to foundations may give rise to a hidden defect which in the future may cause damage to the building affecting the safety and health of owners and occupiers.

The fifth judge, Lord Salmon, expressed similar sentiments when he said (at p 763):

> The seven maisonettes which comprise the building were to be let on 999-year leases at nominal rents and acquired for substantial capital sums. The building inspector and the council who sent him to inspect the foundations must have realised that the inspection was of great importance for the protection of future occupants of the maisonettes who indeed might suffer serious damage if the inspection was carried out negligently. Nor was there any likelihood that any survey on behalf of the original tenants or their assignees would include an inspection of the foundations since they would be concealed by the building. The whole purpose of the inspection on behalf of the council before the foundations were covered up was to discover whether the foundations were secure and to ensure that if they were not, they should be made so before the building was erected for the protection of future tenants. It is impossible to think of anyone more closely and directly affected by the inspection than the original tenants of the maisonettes and their assignees. I have therefore come to the clear conclusion that the council, acting through their building inspector if and when he inspected the foundations, owed a duty to the plaintiffs to carry out the inspection with reasonable care and skill.

Application in Dutton

Likewise, it is submitted that the Court of Appeal in *Dutton* (which is summarised in para 7.7) did not simply say that because the damage was physical, rather than purely economic, mere foresight of harm was sufficient to establish the requisite relationship of proximity. Lord Denning MR said (at p 396) under the heading, "Proximity":

[The defendant] submitted that in any case the duty ought to be limited to those immediately concerned and not to purchaser after purchaser down the line. There is a good deal in this, but I think the reason is because a subsequent purchaser often has the house surveyed. This intermediate inspection, or opportunity of inspection, may break the proximity. It would certainly do so when it ought to disclose the damage. But the foundations of a house are in a class by themselves. Once covered up, they will not be seen again until the damage appears. The inspector must know this, or, at any rate, he ought to know it. Applying the test laid down by Lord Atkin in *Donoghue v Stevenson* I should have thought that the inspector ought to have had subsequent purchasers in mind when he was inspecting the foundations. He ought to have realised that, if he was negligent, they might suffer damage.

The other two judges also recognised the importance of this point in their decision. Sachs LJ said (at p 407): "It must be kept in mind that the instant case is concerned with negligence against which normal intermediate examination would not generally afford protection"; and Stamp LJ said (at p 411):

It is common ground that the defects in the foundations in the instant case were, as they would be bound to be, concealed. No reasonable inspection of the property by any purchaser would disclose the defects, which could only become manifest as the foundations started to settle. Unless the local authority was carrying out an academic exercise, for what other purpose, except primarily to protect future owners of the house, was the exercise performed?

Comment

Thus, it is submitted that:
(1) contrary to what the House of Lords said in *Murphy*, the categorisation of the plaintiff's loss as purely economic does not mean that a proximate relationship based on reliance cannot arise between the plaintiff and the defendant in cases like *Anns* and *Murphy* where the plaintiff's reliance, if it occurs at all, will not be on a negligent statement or advice emanating from the defendant, but on a state of affairs created by the defendant (eg a consumer product in a sealed non-translucent container or covered up foundations) which is such that the defendant therefore ought to have known that the plaintiff would rely on the defendant's skill and judgment without making an investigation of his own;
(2) contrary to what the House of Lords said in *Murphy*, the categorisation of the plaintiff's loss as physical damage in *Dutton* and in *Anns* did not mean that the courts in those two cases treated foreseeability of damage as being sufficiently determinative of the existence of a proximate relationship. In fact in both *Dutton* and *Anns* the Court of Appeal and the House of Lords respectively concluded that there was sufficient proximity between the defendant and the plaintiff in each case only because, in the particular circumstances, each defendant knew or ought reasonably to have known that the plaintiff would not have discovered the defect if the plaintiff had

carried out an intermediate inspection. Thus in *Anns*, Lord Wilberforce (who spoke for himself and Lords Diplock, Simon and Russell), after observing that the foundations of a building come to be covered up as the building proceeds, said (at p 735): "Thus any weakness or inadequacy will create a hidden defect which whoever acquires the building has no means of discovering: in legal parlance there is no opportunity for intermediate inspection"; and Lord Danning in *Dutton*, after noting that normally an intermediate inspection (or the opportunity of such an inspection) might break the chain of proximity, said (at p 396): "But the foundations of a house are in a class by themselves. Once covered up, they will not be seen again until the damage appears. The inspector must know this or, at any rate, he ought to know it.";

(3) contrary to the House of Lords in *Murphy*, whether the damage suffered is physical or purely economic, foreseeability of harm is never sufficient on its own to establish the requisite special relationship. (Lord Oliver said that foreseeability is sufficient where the damage is physical.) This is discussed further in Chapter 2, para 2.2.3;

(4) in partial agreement with the House of Lords in *Murphy*, whether the damage sustained by the plaintiff is physical injury to himself or damage to other property or pure economic loss, consisting of the diminution in the value of the item in question by virtue of the defects contained in it for which the defendant is responsible in negligence, it can be argued that the requisite proximate relationship can only be established if the plaintiff actually relied on the defendant's skill and experience; and the defendant knew, or ought in the circumstances to have known, that the plaintiff would do so (the House of Lords in *Murphy* imposed this requirement only in respect of economic loss but not in respect of physical injury);

(5) in this type of case, reliance can take the form of the defendant's knowing, or being imputed to have known, that the plaintiff or a person in the same class as the plaintiff, or anyone else higher up in the chain of distribution than the plaintiff, would not carry out an intermediate inspection of the article which would reveal the hidden defect in it before its use by the plaintiff, or would carry out an intermediate inspection but it would not reveal the defect in question because it was covered up, eg the defective foundations in *Dutton*, *Anns* and *Murphy*; and

(6) in so far as the courts in *Dutton* and *Anns* applied these principles, those cases were in fact correctly decided and should not have been overruled on this ground. Whether they should have been overruled on the ground that they held that the duty of care applied not only to the builder, but also to the local authority, is considered in Chapter 8, para 8.2.

Whether the House of Lords in *Murphy* and in *D & F* were right to reject the plaintiffs' claims on other grounds is considered *below*. However, the point to note here is that it is submitted that the House of Lords was wrong to reject out of hand (as Lord Oliver did in the passages quoted *above*) the possibility of there being a sufficient relationship of proximity between the plaintiff and the defendant simply because, if there had been reliance by the plaintiff, it was not on a negligent misstatement or advice.

7.5.3 Knowledge of the defect

Difficulties in Murphy

In the long quotation set out *above* (para 7.3.4) from Lord Bridge's speech in *Murphy*, Lord Bridge said (at p 475) *inter alia*:

> If a dangerous defect in a chattel is discovered before it causes any personal injury or damage to property, because the danger is now known and the chattel cannot safely be used unless the defect is repaired, the defect becomes merely a defect in quality. The chattel is either capable of repair at economic cost or it is worthless and must be scrapped. In either case the loss sustained by the owner or hirer of the chattel is purely economic. It is recoverable against any party who owes the loser a relevant contractual duty. But it is not recoverable in tort in the absence of a special relationship of proximity imposing on the tortfeasor a duty of care to safeguard the plaintiff from economic loss. There is no such special relationship between the manufacturer of a chattel and a remote owner or hirer.

Lord Bridge extended this statement of principle to buildings by continuing:

> I believe that these principles are equally applicable to buildings. If a builder erects a structure containing a latent defect, which renders it dangerous to persons or property, he will be liable in tort for injury to persons or damage to property resulting from that dangerous defect. But if the defect becomes apparent before any injury or damage has been caused, the loss sustained by the building owner is purely economic. If the defect can be repaired at economic cost, that is the measure of the loss. If the building cannot be repaired, it may have to be abandoned as unfit for occupation and therefore valueless. These economic losses are recoverable if they flow from the breach of a relevant contractual duty, but, here again, in the absence of a special relationship of proximity they are not recoverable in tort.

This is similar to Lord Oliver's exposition set out *above* (para 7.5.2). Lord Bridge, too, did not say that it is the economic nature of the loss as such that will preclude the plaintiff's claim. He accepted that such a claim will succeed in these circumstances if there is a "special relationship of proximity", but then said that no such special relationship exists between the manufacturer of a chattel and a remote owner. Looked at in these terms, Lord Bridge's formulation of principle is the same as Lord Oliver's and is therefore subject to the same criticism as set out *above* in para 7.5.2.

However, Lord Bridge also gives the impression that knowledge of the defect before it causes any personal injury or damage to other property has the effect of converting the plaintiff's loss from being recoverable physical damage to irrecoverable economic loss. In fact, this is not correct. The plaintiff's loss by virtue of the chattel itself proving to be defective (even if the chattel is destroyed completely by virtue of the defects in it that resulted from the manufacturer's negligence) is always pure economic loss, whether he discovers it before it causes physical injury to himself or damage to his other property, or afterwards. Mere knowledge of the defect does not affect the plaintiff's right to be compensated for his loss, consisting of the diminution in the value of the chattel by virtue of the defect. Whether the plaintiff will have such a right or not will depend on whether there is 'a special relationship of proximity', as discussed *above*.

Relationship with Dutton

Certain important passages from the judgments of Lord Denning MR and Sachs LJ in *Dutton* are set out at the beginning of this chapter (paras 7.2.2 and 7.2.4). Lord Bridge in *Murphy* continued in the passage just referred to by saying (at p 475): "The fallacy which, in my opinion, vitiates the judgments of Lord Denning MR and Sachs LJ in *Dutton* is that they brush these distinctions [ie the distinction between the conditions required for a claim for economic loss in contract and in tort] aside as of no consequence". As mentioned *above* (para 7.5.2), however, Lord Denning MR and Sachs LJ were in fact very much alive to the necessity to find a special relationship of proximity before they were prepared to impose a duty of care, which they said (as the House of Lords had said before them in *Donoghue v Stevenson*) depended on the opportunity for an intermediate inspection: "This intermediate inspection, or opportunity of inspection, may break the proximity" (*per* Lord Denning MR in *Dutton* at p 396).

Continued use of the defective item

In *Murphy*, Lord Keith made the sweeping statement that a person who continues to use a defective product or to occupy a defective building after becoming aware of the defect will have no remedy against the manufacturer or the builder. He said (at p 464):

> . . . an essential feature of the species of liability in negligence established by *Donoghue v Stevenson* was that the carelessly manufactured product should be intended to reach the injured consumer in the same state as that in which it was put up, with no reasonable prospect of intermediate examination. . . . It is the latency of the defect which constitutes the mischief.
>
> . . . there can be no doubt that, whatever the rationale, a person who is injured through consuming or using a product of the defective nature of which he is well aware has no remedy against the manufacturer. In the case of a building, it is right to accept that a careless builder is liable, on the principle of *Donoghue v Stevenson*, where a latent defect results in physical injury to anyone, whether owner, occupier, visitor or passerby, or to the property of any such person. But that principle is not apt to bring home liability towards an occupier who knows the full extent of the defect, yet continues to occupy the building.

In Chapter 6, para 6.3.6, it is pointed out that the seemingly wide-spreading significance of this quotation is not what it seems. There are cases in which the plaintiff has been entitled to recover for his physical injuries notwithstanding that he was aware of the nature of the defect in the building or product, yet continued to use it. It all depends on whether it was practicable and within the plaintiff's means to require him to cease using the defective item after he became aware of the defect. This is discussed in Chapter 6, para 6.3.5 in relation to defects which caused physical injury to the plaintiff. It is submitted that the same principle should apply where the plaintiff's loss is purely economic, consisting in the diminution of the value of the defective article itself. So long as the plaintiff accepts that he has a duty to mitigate his loss, and does not make it worse by continuing to use the article, or occupy the building, then that use alone should not make any difference to a claim which he would otherwise have if he has been able to establish a sufficient relationship of proximity on the basis discussed *above*. See also the discussion *below* on *Targett v Torfaen Borough Council* [1992] 3 All ER 27, a post-*Murphy* decision.

Comment

If, as Lord Keith said, it was the latency of the defect which was the essential feature of the species of liability in negligence established by *Donoghue*, then it is submitted that it is the essential fallacy of *Murphy* to hold that, because the plaintiff had knowledge of the defect, he is outside the ambit of that species of liability. The defect was just as latent in *Murphy* as in *Donoghue*, in that it could not reasonably have been discovered by Mr Murphy before he bought his house because the foundations had been covered up in the course of construction and the defect in them would not have been revealed on a pre-purchase survey.

The point made by Lord Keith in the last sentence of the quotation set out *above* would be applicable only where a purchaser has carried out a survey which did reveal the defect, but nevertheless continued with the purchase, or where a purchaser failed to carry out a survey which would have revealed the defect. This was manifestly not the case in *Murphy*. Furthermore, at the time when the defective nature of the foundations was discovered, the damage had already been caused. Therefore this was not, to use Lord Keith's words, a case of "a person who is injured through consuming or using a product of the defective nature of which he is well aware". Rather, it was the case of a person who had already suffered loss, albeit pure economic loss, at the time when he became aware of the defect. If that loss would not be affected (ie made worse) by his continued use of the defective item (in this case, by his continued occupation of his house), then there can surely be no reason why his continued use should defeat a claim which he would otherwise have.

Whether the plaintiff would otherwise have a claim in these circumstances will depend, as Lord Oliver said in *Murphy*, not on whether the plaintiff's damages were physical or purely economic, but on whether the loss which the plaintiff actually suffered was within the scope of the defendant's duty of care; and this, in turn, will depend on whether there was a sufficient relationship of proximity between the plaintiff and the defendant such that the plaintiff's loss resulted from his reliance on the defendant's skill and experience in circumstances in which the defendant knew or ought to have known that the plaintiff would do so. Such reliance, as submitted *above*, can be established by the defendant's knowledge, actual or imputed, that the defect would not be discovered before the use of the product.

Further illogicality: Targett v Torfaen

In *Targett v Torfaen Borough Council* [1992] 3 All ER 27 (the facts of which are set out in para 6.3.5), a post-*Murphy* decision, the Court of Appeal tried to make some sense of the above-cited passages from the speeches of Lord Bridge and Lord Keith in *Murphy*; but it is submitted that, in so doing, their Lordships merely heaped further illogicality upon Lord Bridge's and Lord Keith's *dicta*.

In this case, when the plaintiff moved into the council house that was owned by the defendant, the plaintiff complained to the defendant that there was no handrail on the flight of steps going down to the house and no lighting in the immediate vicinity. Nothing was done to alleviate this obvious danger, but the plaintiff continued to live in the house. One night the plaintiff fell down the steps and was injured. He sued the defendant for his losses.

Notwithstanding the plaintiff's knowledge of the dangerous defect which caused his injuries, and notwithstanding his continued habitation of the house in the light of that knowledge, the Court of Appeal held that the defendant owed the plaintiff a duty of care to provide a handrail or lighting for the steps because—despite Lord Bridge's and Lord Keith's above-cited *dicta* in *Murphy*—the Court felt that it was not reasonable or practical to require that the plaintiff should have moved out of the house or should have provided a handrail or lighting himself. Nicholls VC (in a passage that is more fully set out in para 6.3.6) said (at p 37):

> ... knowledge of the existence of a danger does not always enable a person to avoid the danger. In simple cases it does. In other cases, especially where buildings are concerned, it would be absurdly unrealistic to suggest that a person can always take steps to avoid a danger once he knows of its existence, and that if he does not do so he is the author of his own misfortune.

If this principle was applicable to the facts of *Targett* (and also to the facts of *Rimmer v Liverpool City Council* [1985] QB 1—see para 6.3.5), one can question why it should not also have been applicable to the facts of *Murphy*. There the plaintiff not only had no knowledge of the existence of the defective foundation until it was too late to do anything about it, but also the defect was of such a nature that it would not have been revealed upon an intermediate inspection; and even if it had been so revealed, the plaintiff was not in a position to bear the cost of the necessary repairs without seeking recovery from someone else, or to move out of the house and abandon it, as Lord Bridge and Lord Keith suggested in their speeches in *Murphy*.

In *Targett*, their Lordships in the Court of Appeal went out of their way to avoid concluding that the position in *Targett* and *Murphy* was the same on this point, but it is submitted that their efforts were futile. Thus, Russell

LJ, in trying to distinguish the fact-situation of *Targett* from that of *Murphy*, said (at p 32): "A weekly tenant is in an entirely different position from an owner of a house defectively constructed who discovers the defect, thereby rendering it no longer a latent defect"; and Nicholls VC said (at p 37): "In *Murphy*, the House of Lords was concerned to consider the principles applicable to a claim to recover the cost of making good a defective product, there a building, which had not yet caused any physical injury to persons or damage to other property. When the defect was discovered, the goods or building ceased to be dangerous, although they remained defective. The loss sustained by the owner, eg in making good the defect, was economic loss".

It is submitted that these suggested differences between the considerations that needed to be addressed on this point in *Murphy* and in cases like *Targett* and *Rimmer* are patently illusory and serve only to highlight further the illogicality of the House of Lords' decision in *Murphy* on this aspect of the case.

Criticism in Canada

In *Winnipeg Condominium Corporation No 36 v Bird Construction Co* (1995) 121 DLR (4th) 193, the Supreme Court of Canada strongly deprecated the above-cited views of Lord Bridge and Lord Keith in *Murphy*, that the cost of repair of a defective product cannot be characterised as a recoverable loss because the owner of the defective article can simply discard it and thereby remove the danger. After referring in particular to Lord Keith's *dictum*, La Forest J, speaking for all seven members of the panel, said (at p 214):

> While Lord Keith's argument has some appeal on the basis of abstract logic, I do not believe it is sufficient to preclude imposing liability on contractors for the cost of repairing dangerous defects. The weakness of the argument is that it is based upon an unrealistic view of the choice faced by homeowners in deciding whether to repair a dangerous defect in their home. In fact, a choice to 'discard' a home instead of repairing the dangerous defect is no choice at all; most homeowners buy a home as a long-term investment, and few homeowners, upon discovering a dangerous defect in the home, will choose to abandon or sell the building rather than to repair the defect. Indeed, in most cases, the cost of fixing a defect in a household building, within the reasonable life of that house or building, will be far outweighed by the cost of replacing the house or buying a new one.

7.5.4 Contrary to *Donoghue v Stevenson*

Various Law Lords, including Lord Brandon in *Junior Books* and Lord Jauncey in *Murphy*, have said that it emerges clearly from Lord Atkin's speech in *Donoghue* and from subsequent cases which have applied it that damage to the offending or defective article itself was not within the scope of the duty which the House of Lords enunciated in *Donoghue* and that it was limited to cases where there was physical injury to a person or damage to 'other property'.

In fact, a close examination of Lord Atkin's speech will reveal that there was not even a hint of any such restriction in anything that he said. The point was not raised by the plaintiff's counsel, nor was it mentioned at all by Lord Atkin or by any of the other Law Lords. It must be remembered (see Chapter 6, para 6.2.1) that the decision in *Donoghue* was completely revolutionary in terms of the firmly established exclusionary rule which had existed up until then. It is therefore quite understandable that the three majority Law Lords restricted their comments to the type of injury, namely physical injury consisting of severe shock and gastro-enteritis, in respect of which the plaintiff was asking them to rule that the defendant owed a duty of care to her, and to the type of goods, namely food or other household consumables, actually involved in the case. The essential feature which they specifically stressed was that the necessary relationship of proximity to make the defendant liable was established, and would have been absent but for the fact that (*per* Lord Atkin at p 599) the defendant manufacturer had sold products "in such a form as to show that he intends them to reach the ultimate consumer in the form in which they left him with no reasonable possibility of intermediate examination".

Lord Atkin finished his speech by saying (at p 599) that the proposition which he and the other two majority Law Lords had just enunciated was "a proposition which I venture to say no one in Scotland or England who was not a lawyer would for one moment doubt. It will be an advantage to make it clear that the law in this matter, as in most others, is in accordance with sound common sense". It is impossible to conceive that, in the same breath, Lord Atkin would have said that, while the duty of care thus imposed extended to the plaintiff's physical injuries, it did not also include the replacement price of the defective bottle of ginger beer from which those injuries flowed. In 1932 that would have been, as it is in 1998, a proposition which no one could accept as a matter of sound common sense.

In *Murphy* Lord Jauncey (at p 492) cited two cases, namely *Grant v Australia Knitting Mills Ltd* [1936] AC 85 and *Farr v Butters Bros & Co* [1932] 2 KB 606, in support of his view that damage to the defective article is outside the scope of the principles enunciated by Lord Atkin in *Donoghue*. Those cases are considered in Chapter 6, para 6.3.4. Again, there is no hint in any of the judgments in those cases that the principles enunciated by Lord Atkin in *Donoghue* are limited in the manner contended. Indeed, if one is looking for signals, one could say that the Privy Council in *Grant* in fact indicated that the replacement cost of the defective underpants which had caused the plaintiff's dermatitis was recoverable in tort. In addition to suing the manufacturer in tort, the plaintiff had sued the retailers under s 14 of the South Australia Sale of Goods Act 1895 for breach of implied warranty as to the fitness for purpose of the goods supplied. Lord Wright said (at p 97) (emphasis added): "The liability of each respondent [*defendant*] depends on a different cause of action, though it is *for the same damage*". He said that the only restriction was the obvious one, namely that the plaintiff could not recover his damage twice over. The formulation of principle by the House of Lords in cases like *D & F* and

Murphy would, however, have required Lord Wright to have said that the damages which the plaintiff was seeking to recover from the manufacturer in tort should have excluded the replacement cost of the underpants which was included as part of the plaintiff's claim against the retailer under the Sale of Goods Act.

7.5.5   Legislative intent

General

In both *D & F* and *Murphy*, the House of Lords justified its decisions by reference to what the Law Lords believed was the policy of Parliament behind the Defective Premises Act 1972. Thus, in *D & F* Lord Bridge said (at p 207):

> I am glad to reach the conclusion that this [ie exclusion of liability on the builder for the cost of replacing the defective plaster] is not the law, if only for the reason that a conclusion to the opposite effect would mean that the courts, in developing the common law, had gone much farther than the legislature were prepared to go in 1972, after comprehensive examination of the subject by the Law Commission, in making builders liable for defects in the quality of their work to all who subsequently acquire interests in buildings they have erected. The statutory duty imposed by the Act of 1972 is confined to dwelling houses and limited to defects appearing within six years. The common law duty, if it exists, could not be so confined or so limited.

In *Murphy* Lord Keith continued with this theme by saying (at p 472): "It is also material that *Anns* has the effect of imposing upon builders generally a liability going far beyond that which Parliament thought fit to impose upon house builders alone by the Defective Premises Act 1972, a statute very material to the policy of the decision [in *Anns*] but not adverted to in it"; and Lord Oliver said (at p 491): "At the date when *Anns* was decided the Defective Premises Act 1972, enacted after most careful consideration by the Law Commission, had shown clearly the limits within which Parliament had thought it right to superimpose additional liabilities upon those previously existing at common law. It is one of the curious features of *Anns* that no mention was made of this important measure, in particular the provision regarding the accrual of the cause of action".

The Law Commission Report

No effect on economic loss: It is submitted that, despite what their Lordships said, as quoted *above,* the Law Commission did not in fact make a "comprehensive examination of the subject" (ie the liability in tort of a builder in the tort of negligence for his defective work) or "show clearly the limits within which Parliament thought it right to superimpose additional liabilities upon those previously existing at common law".

In fact the Law Commission Report (Law Com No 40, dated 15 December 1970) did not even mention or affect in any way the liability of a builder in tort for loss suffered by virtue of his building proving to be defective. The Commission's report dealt with four independent areas of deficiency in the then existing law. Of these, only the first two, headed, respectively: *Liability in Contract—Defects of Quality* and *Dangerous Defects created by the Vendor or Lessor*, could have had any bearing on the questions raised in *Anns, D & F* and *Murphy*.

Discussion of contractual issues: The Commission's deliberations on the first of these topics were confined to questions of contract, and did not include any discussion of the position in tort. Thus the Commission stated (at p 4):

> In a contract for the sale or letting of premises to be constructed or completed by the vendor or the lessor there is *prima facie* an implied term that the work will be done in an efficient and workmanlike manner, that the builder will supply and use proper materials and, in some circumstances, that the building will be fit for the particular purpose for which, to the knowledge of the builder, it is to be constructed. These implied terms may, however, be varied or excluded by the terms of the contract. We are not aware of any substantial criticism of the present law as it applies to commercial or industrial premises. In such cases the parties are normally in a position to protect their own interests with the help of their professional advisers. The appropriate terms for inclusion in the contract in such cases are the subject of negotiation. Considerable disquiet has, however, been expressed in recent years as to the operation of the law in relation to the purchase of dwellings.

Disquiet with builders: The 'disquiet' referred to was the practice which was then rife with builders of houses to exclude the above-mentioned implied terms from their sale contracts with homeowners who, because of the housing shortage, did not have sufficient bargaining power to resist this. The Commission felt that this was unsatisfactory and therefore proposed the imposition of a statutory duty on builders and others who take on work in connection with the construction of dwellings from which there would not be able to be any contracting-out.

Different point considered: This recommendation resulted in the enactment of s 1 of the Act (see para 7.4.5, *above*). As noted *above*, this section does confer rights on persons other than the original purchaser, and to that extent it is, of course, a provision which deals with the liability in tort of a builder for economic loss suffered by the owner in the form of the diminution in the value of the house arising from a defect in construction. However, this provision did not come about as a result of a "comprehensive examination of 'the subject'" by the Law Commission: as pointed out *above*, it arose as part of the Commission's discussion of the unsatisfactory situation which had arisen in contracts for sales of new houses, where builders were excluding one or more of the implied terms which would otherwise have been applicable. This is not to say that the Commission's report was not thorough: it is simply to point out that the points which the

Commission did consider in detail were different from the main point in *Dutton, Anns, Junior Books, D & F* and *Murphy*, namely the liability in tort of a builder or a manufacturer for economic loss suffered by the owner of the building or chattel by virtue of it being defective. It is not surprising that the Commission did not consider this point, because, before *Dutton*, it had never arisen for decision in any court in the Commonwealth. The Commission's report was tabled in the House of Commons on 15 December 1970, which was four months before argument in *Dutton* commenced in the High Court.

Restricted scope: More importantly, the right of action that s 1 of the Defective Premises Act confers on a person who was not the original purchaser of the dwelling arises only if, and to the extent that, the defects in question have resulted in the dwelling being unfit for habitation (see para 7.4.5, *above*). Clearly, not all defects will satisfy this test. An example is the defects in the foundations of Mr Murphy's house in *Murphy v Brentwood District Council* [1991] 1 AC 398. For defects like these, that do not render the dwelling unfit for habitation, the Act does not provide a remedy. Such a plaintiff would then be left to sue the negligent builder in tort, and would have to establish negligence and causation (the Act relieves the plaintiff of this burden if the defect has rendered the dwelling unfit for habitation—see *below*). However, even though the Act preserves the common law and confers additional rights only in situations where the defendant builder's negligence has made the dwelling unfit for habitation, an action at common law by a person who cannot bring his case within the confines of the Act has been ruled out by the House of Lords' decision in *Murphy*. Ironically, their Lordships thought that in so holding they were merely complying with the tenor of the Act, but, as this discussion demonstrates, they were quite far off course.

Another point worth noting is that the Act applies only to 'dwellings', whereas the doctrine enunciated by the House of Lords in *Murphy* applies to all buildings, as was made clear in the House of Lords' decision in *Department of the Environment v Thomas Bates and Son Ltd* [1991] 1 AC 499 (see para 7.7). Therefore, in relation to other buildings, a subsequent purchaser has no avenue of redress at all in tort for the cost of rectifying latent defects which would not have been revealed on an intermediate inspection, despite the negligence of the builder, architect or engineer in creating those defects during the course of construction. (*Cf.* the position in Canada in *Winnipeg Condominium Corporation No 36 v Bird Construction Co*, which is discussed in para 7.6.3.)

Common law preserved: It is also important to note that the Law Commission recommended, and s 6(2) of the Defective Premises Act 1972 provides, that any duty imposed by any provision of the Act is in addition to any duty which a person might owe apart from that provision. Thus, common law rights are preserved. It is this provision that has enabled houseowners to bring claims in tort which would be time-barred under the limitation period in the Act (six years from the time when the dwelling was completed—s 1(5)); and this has never been criticised by the courts.

Strict liability difference: It is this preservation of the house owner's common law rights which belies the House of Lords' view that the type of liability imposed by the courts in *Dutton* and *Anns* "went much further than the legislature was prepared to go in 1972". The real difference is that the Act imposes strict liability, whereas the common law position which is preserved by the Act is dependent on the plaintiff's being able to establish negligence and causation. There is nothing to prevent an owner of a dwelling from suing the builder in tort, rather than under the Act, even if he is within the Act's limitation period, but then he would have to show that it was reasonable for him not to carry out an intermediate examination of the dwelling, or that, if he did so, the defect was one which was not likely to be revealed by such inspection, and that the circumstances were such that the builder knew, or by reason of the nature of the defect ought to have known, that this would be the case. If he is unable to do this, then he will not establish a common law duty of care.

For these reasons it is not correct simply to assert that the common law duty of care supported by *Dutton* and *Anns* is far more extensive than that imposed under s 1 of the Act, and therefore could not have been contemplated by the legislature. The conditions required for the existence of the common law duty are far more stringent and will be able to be satisfied only in those cases where the plaintiff can demonstrate that he did actually rely on the defendant's skill and experience and that the defendant knew, or in the circumstances ought to have known, that he was doing so (see *above*).

Different question considered: As regards the second topic mentioned *above* (ie dangerous defects), in considering what changes were needed to the law to deal with the unsatisfactory aspects of the immunity which was then enjoyed by a vendor or lessor of land from liability for his own negligent acts, the Commission also did not consider the question which arose in *Anns*, *D & F* and *Murphy*. Instead, the Commission concentrated on such cases as *Cavalier v Pope* [1906] AC 428, *Bottomley v Bannister* [1932] 1 KB 458, *Otto v Bolton and Norris* [1936] 2 KB 46 and *Davis v Foots* [1936] 2 KB 46, all of which are considered in Chapter 6 (para 6.6).

Parliamentary debates: Pepper v Hart

At the time of the decisions in *D & F* and *Murphy* it was not permissible for the courts to refer to debates in Parliament to ascertain the intention of Parliament as an aid to the construction of any particular Act. It was only permissible to refer to White Papers and to reports of the Law Commission, and then only for the purpose of ascertaining the mischief which the statute was intended to cure, but not for the purpose of discovering the meaning of the words used by Parliament to effect such cure.

However, on 26 November 1992 the House of Lords, in *Pepper*

(Inspector of Taxes) v Hart [1993] AC 593, held that in future, subject to questions of the privileges of the House of Commons, reference to parliamentary material should be permitted as an aid to the construction of legislation

(1) which is ambiguous or obscure or the literal meaning of which leads to an absurdity;

(2) where the material relied upon consists of one or more statements by a minister or other promoter of the bill, together, if necessary, with such other parliamentary material as is necessary to understand such statements and their effect;

(3) where the statements relied upon are clear.

Relation to D & F and Murphy

Mention in Parliament: As there is nothing ambiguous about s 1 of the Defective Premises Act 1972, the above new principles would probably not apply to allow a court to refer to the debates which took place in Parliament before it was enacted, for the purpose of ascertaining Parliament's true intention with regard to the common law position which was intended to be left in place after the Act was passed. Nevertheless, it might be instructive to note that the Defective Premises Bill was mentioned in the House of Commons on 11 February 1972 and in the House of Lords on 5 June 1972. The Court of Appeal had given its judgment in *Dutton* on 17 December 1971. If that decision extended further than, or was substantially different from, the intention of Parliament in enacting the Defective Premises Act, one would have expected to see some criticism of that decision in Parliament. This did not occur. The only reference to it was by the then Solicitor-General, Sir Geoffrey Howe, who said (at column 1824 of Hansard):

> In so far as they [the provisions of the Bill] deal with the matter covered by the case of *Dutton v Bognor Regis Urban District Council*, the judgment in which was given just before Christmas, they will set at rest a doubt which still exists; there was a disagreement between the Master of the Rolls and one of the other members of the Court of Appeal.

Endorsement of Dutton: This is a reference to Stamp LJ's approval in principle of the distinction drawn by the defendant's counsel between the consequences of constructing a dangerous article and one which is defective or of inferior quality. It has been noted *above* (para 7.2) that Lord Denning rejected this distinction as "impossible" and that Sachs LJ said that it would lead to "an unhappily odd state of the law". The solution adopted by s 1 of the Defective Premises Act accords with the views of Lord Denning and Sachs LJ and rejects Stamp LJ's view on this point. The above-quoted words of the Solicitor-General also stand as an endorsement of the decision in *Dutton*. It might, of course, be said that this is not surprising, given that *Dutton* was a case involving a "dwelling", and therefore would fall within the Act. On the other hand, if the Solicitor-General had thought that the principle laid down in *Dutton* should not apply to other buildings, this was surely the time when he should have said so.

Parliament's true intention: Accordingly, it is submitted that, contrary to what the House of Lords has suggested in *D & F* and *Murphy*, the intention of the legislature in passing the Defective Premises Act 1972 was not thereby to express disapproval of the same principle expressed in *Dutton* and, subsequently, in *Anns* in relation to those situations which do not fall within s 1 of the Act. One might then ask, what is the purpose of the Act? The answer is given *above*, namely that at common law the test of liability is much more stringent than under the Act.

Further approval of Dutton and Anns: It is also worth noting that *Dutton* and *Anns* were approved of in debate in the House of Lords during its discussion of the Latent Damage Bill, which led to the enactment of the Latent Damage Act 1986, the relevant section of which has been inserted as s 14A of the Limitation Act 1980, which is considered *above* (para 7.3.9). On 8 April 1986 at Committee stage Lord Denning moved an amendment to include financial loss in the definition of damages which was to be incorporated in the proposed statute. The then Lord Chancellor (Lord Hailsham) said (at column 88 of Hansard):

> The Bill as drafted deals with all damages for negligence and it thus applies to claims for damages in respect of damage caused, for instance, by cracked foundations in the building industry. For instance, I think that it would apply to a case like *Dutton v Bognor Regis Urban District Council* and the case of *Anns v Merton London Borough Council*, where the decision was followed by your Lordships' House. It is quite clear that the negligent breach by local authorities in the performance of their duties under the building regulations is not excluded by the Bill as drafted. Therefore, I would respectfully suggest that the proposed amendment is superfluous.

7.5.6 Judicial legislation

In *Murphy* Lord Keith said (at p 471) that the decision in *Anns* did not proceed on any basis of principle at all, but "constituted a remarkable example of judicial legislation". Other Law Lords made similar remarks. First, as pointed out *above* (para 7.5.2), *Anns* did in fact proceed on the basis of principle, namely the principle that a special relationship of proximity can be established where the defendant had created a defect in a building which he knew would not be discovered on an intermediate inspection.

Secondly, the House of Lords' decision in *Donoghue v Stevenson* itself was an example par excellence of judicial legislation (see Chapter 6, para 6.2.5), yet no one has attacked it on that basis. The common sense qualities of the decision in *Donoghue* have given it its popular and enduring appeal.

Why is it that, despite the acknowledged injustice by their Lordships of their decision in *Murphy* (see the quote from Lord Keith at the beginning of this section, para 7.5.1), they nevertheless rejected the plaintiff's claim and held that this type of matter is best left to the legislature? As pointed out *above*, the answer cannot be founded on the fact that no sufficient relationship of proximity could arise in these circumstances, nor on the basis that knowledge of the defect by itself makes a crucial difference, nor on the basis that such relief was ruled out by *Donoghue v Stevenson* and cases which have followed it, nor by Parliament's intention in passing the Defective Premises Act 1972. What emerges, as will be seen in the next subsection, is a strange form of a retrogressive judicial conservatism which was rejected by the House of Lords in *Donoghue v Stevenson* in 1932 in parallel circumstances.

7.5.7 Transmissible warranties of quality

Concern in the House of Lords

It will be recalled that in *Junior Books* (para 7.3.6) the plaintiff did succeed in establishing a duty of care in tort for its economic loss consisting of the diminution in the value of the defective floor which the defendant had laid on the instructions of and by way of a contract with a third party. Lord Brandon, dissenting, said (at p 551):

> The effect of accepting the plaintiff's contention with regard to the scope of the duty of care involved would be, in substance, to create, as between two persons who are not in any contractual relationship with each other, obligations of one of those two persons to the other which are only really appropriate as between persons who do have such a relationship between them. In the case of a manufacturer or distributor of goods, the position would be that he warranted to the ultimate user or consumer of such goods that they were as well designed, as merchantable and as fit for their contemplated purpose as the exercise of reasonable care could make them. In my view, the imposition of warranties of this kind on one person in favour of another, when there is no contractual relationship between them, is contrary to any sound policy requirement.

In *D & F* Lord Bridge endorsed this view when he said (at p 207):

> To make the defendant liable for the cost of replacing the defective plaster would be to impose upon him for the benefit of those with whom he had no contractual relationship the obligation of one who warrants the quality of the plaster as regards materials, workmanship and fitness for purpose. I am glad to reach the conclusion that this is not the law, if only for the reason that a conclusion to the opposite effect would mean that the courts, in developing the common law, had gone much farther than the legislature were prepared to go in 1972 . . . [see para 7.5.5, *above*];

and Lord Oliver (who was the only other Law Lord to deliver a speech) said (at p 212):

> That would be, in effect, to attach to goods a non-contractual warranty of fitness which would follow the goods into whosoever's hands they came. Such a concept was suggested, *obiter*, by Lord Denning MR in *Dutton*'s case, at p 396 [see para 7.2, *above*], but it was entirely unsupported by any authority and is, in my opinion, contrary to principle.

The same theme was taken up by their Lordships in *Murphy*. Thus, Lord Keith said (at p 469) that if a local authority, or a builder or a manufacturer, were to be subject to the type of duty which the House of Lords had upheld in *Anns*,

> that would open up an exceedingly wide field of claims, involving the introduction of something in the nature of a transmissible warranty of quality. The purchaser of an article who discovered that it suffered from a dangerous defect before that defect had caused any damage would be entitled to recover from the manufacturer the cost of rectifying the defect, and presumably, if the article was not capable of economic repair, the amount of loss sustained through discarding it. Then it would be open to question whether there should not also be a right of recovery where the defect renders the article not dangerous, but merely useless. The economic loss in either case would be the same.

Outmoded approach

The distinctions drawn by their Lordships in the quotations set out *above* are reminiscent of the distinction which, prior to the House of Lords' decision in *Donoghue*, operated as a block against the recovery by a purchaser of a defective article of any damages, physical or economic. In *Junior Books* Lord Roskill said (at p 545):

> It was powerfully urged on behalf of the defendant that, were your Lordships so to extend the law (ie to include damage to the defective item itself), a pursuer in the position of the pursuer in *Donoghue v Stevenson* [1932] AC 562 could, in addition to recovering for any personal injuries suffered, have also recovered for the diminished value of the offending bottle of gingerbeer. Any remedy of that kind, it was argued, must lie in contract and not in tort. My Lords, I seem to detect in that able argument reflections of the previous judicial approach in comparable problems before *Donoghue v Stevenson* was decided. That approach usually resulted in the conclusion that in principle the proper remedy lay in contract and not outside it. But that approach and its concomitant philosophy ended in 1932 and for my part I should be reluctant to countenance its re-emergence some 50 years later in the instant case.

The 'floodgates' fear

The 'administrative nightmare': The 'floodgates' fear is often invoked as the reason for excluding claims for pure economic loss. This argument takes two forms. First, it is argued that, from an administrative point of view, the courts would become flooded with an overwhelming number of similar claims, many of which would be dubious. As mentioned in Chapter 4, para 4.5.5, this was one of the reasons given by Lord Denning MR for rejecting the plaintiff's claim for pure economic loss in *Spartan Steel and Alloys Ltd v Martin & Co (Contractors) Ltd* [1973] QB 27. However, the difference is that *Spartan Steel* was in a different category from the present type of case. Here, the requirement of sufficient relationship of proximity, based on reliance, serves to stem the flood. Lord Roskill recognised this in *Junior Books* when he said (at p 545): "My Lords, it is I think in the application of these two principles [ie the two-stage test of liability formulated by Lord Wilberforce in *Anns*, which has been supplanted by the proximate relationship test just mentioned] that the ability to control the extent of liability in negligence lies. The history of the development of the law in the last 50 years shows that fears aroused by the floodgates argument have been unfounded"; and in *Dutton* Sachs LJ said (at p 407): "Practical experience points against any flood of such [ie similar] claims".

Indeterminate liability: The second manifestation of the floodgates argument is the more familiar one, namely that the imposition of a duty of care on a defendant for the plaintiff's pure economic loss would expose the defendant to "liability in an indeterminate amount for an indeterminate time to an indeterminate class". As mentioned in Chapter 1, para 1.4.3, this principle derives from a *dictum* in the judgment of Cardozo CJ in the decision of the Court of Appeals of New York in *Ultramares Corporation v Touche* (1931) 255 NY 170. It is not suggested that this is not a legitimate concern, but it must be remembered that *Ultramares* was a case of a negligent misstatement by an accountant, where there was a very real fear that the imposition of liability on the accountant to all third parties who might have relied on the accounts in making business decisions of their own would have exposed the accountant to indeterminate, and therefore unreasonable, liability, as regards the amount of such liability and the class of persons to whom the duty might have been owed.

Non-existent fear: However, these concerns do not exist in the category of case considered in this chapter. As mentioned in Chapter 2 (para 2.4.3), 'determinate' in this context does not mean 'large': it means being able to determine in advance the range, or identifiable class, of possible plaintiff and the extent of the defendant's liability to such persons. If a manufacturer of chattels is to be liable for the cost of making good defects in those chattels, then the size of the class of potential claimants will be equal to the number of articles which the defendant has manufactured, and the amount of money to which the defendant could potentially be exposed will be equal to the replacement cost of all of those items. These numbers might be large, but that is not relevant: the function of the law is to guard against the creation of rules which could expose the defendant to 'indeterminate' liability, as opposed to 'extensive' liability.

It is interesting to note that in *Council of the Shire of Sutherland v Heyman* (1985) 157 CLR 424, which was the case on which the House of Lords placed most reliance in *Murphy* (see Chapter 8, para 8.2.2), Mason J expressed similar sentiments to the above, when he said (at p 465): "The proposition that in general damages are not recoverable for economic loss unless it is consequential upon injury to the plaintiff's personal property is by no means absolute or inflexible; it is a reflection of the law's concern about endless indeterminate liability. In the absence of any such concern in a particular class of case, there is no necessity to give effect to the proposition". He then cited with approval the partially dissenting judgment of Laskin J in the Supreme Court of Canada in *Rivtow Marine Ltd v Washington Iron Works* (1973) 40 DLR (3d) 530 (see para 7.7), which the

House of Lords disapproved of in *Murphy* and then said (at p 466): "In this case it matters not whether the damage sustained by the plaintiff is characterised as being economic loss or physical damage. It is how the affair stands, viewed from the defendant's perspective, that is important in relation to a duty of care".

As pointed out in Chapter 8, para 8.2.2, the only reason that Mason J did not actually hold in the plaintiff's favour was that there was no evidence that the plaintiff had actually relied on the defendant council. Subject to this, he would have held that the council was under a duty of care to the plaintiff in respect of the plaintiff's economic loss, which was of the same type as the plaintiff's loss in *Murphy*. In so doing, Mason J would not have been deterred by the 'floodgates' fear.

The point made here was also articulated by the High Court of Australia in *Bryan v Maloney* (1995) 69 ALJR 375. Mason CJ, delivering the main majority judgment, said (at p 381):

> The policy considerations underlying the reluctance of the Courts to recognise a relationship of proximity and a consequential duty of care in cases of mere economic loss are largely inapplicable to the relationship between a builder and a subsequent owner as regards that particular kind of economic loss. In circumstances where the particular kind of economic loss is that sustained by an owner of a house on the occasion when the inadequacy of the footings first becomes manifest, there is no basis for thinking that recognition of a relevant relationship of proximity between the builder and that owner would be more likely to give rise to liability 'in an indeterminate amount . . . to an indeterminate class' than does recognition of such an element of proximity in the relationship between the builder and the first owner.
>
> It is true that, in so far as an 'indeterminate time' is concerned, the time span in which liability to a subsequent owner might arise could be greater than if liability were restricted to the first owner. Nonetheless, the extent of that time span would be limited by the element of reasonableness, both in the requirement that damage be foreseeable and in the content of the duty of care. Moreover, any difference in duration between liability to the first owner and liability to a subsequent owner is likely to do no more than reflect the chance element of whether and when the first owner disposes of the house.

Similar sentiments were expressed by the Supreme Court of Canada in *Winnipeg Condominium Corporation No 36 v Bird Construction Co* (1995) 121 DLR (4th) 193, when La Forest said (at p 218):

> No serious risk of indeterminate liability arises with respect to the tortious duty to construct a building safely. In the first place, there is no risk of liability to an indeterminate class because the potential class of claimants is limited to the very person for whom the building is constructed: the inhabitants of the building. The fact that the class of claimants may include successors in title who have no contractual relationship with the contractors does not, in my view, render the class of potential claimants indeterminate. As noted by the New Jersey Supreme Court in *Aronsohn v Mandara* (1984) 484 A 2d 675 at p 680: 'The contractor should not be relieved of liability for unworkmanlike construction simply because of the fortuity that the property on which he did the construction has changed hands.' [see also *Lempke v Dagenais* (1988) 547 A 2d 290, discussed in para 7.6.1].

Secondly, there is no risk of liability in an indeterminate amount because the amount of liability will always be limited by the reasonable cost of repairing the dangerous defect in the building and restoring the building to a non-dangerous state. Counsel for Bird advanced the argument that the cost of repairs for averting a danger caused by a defect in construction could, in some cases, be disproportionate to the actual damage to person or property that might be caused if that defect were not repaired. However, in my view, any danger of indeterminacy in damages is averted by the requirement that the defect for which the costs of repair are claimed must constitute a real and substantial danger to the inhabitants of the building, and by the fact that the inhabitants of the building can only claim the reasonable cost of repairing the defect and mitigate the danger.

Finally, there is little risk of liability for an indeterminate time because the contractor will only be liable for the cost of repair of dangerous defects during the useful life of the building. Practically speaking, I believe that the period in which the contractor may be exposed to liability for negligence will be much shorter than the full useful life of the building. With the passage of time, it will become increasingly difficult for owners of a building to prove at trial that any deterioration in the building is attributable to the initial negligence of the contractor, and not simply to the inevitable wear and tear suffered by every building.

Ironic inconsistency: In the light of the courts' expressed concern to guard against indeterminate liability in this area, it is ironic that, under the doctrine of cases like *Murphy*, the defendant manufacturer can be held liable for all of the damage to the plaintiff's 'other property' (see para 7.4.4, *above*) and for such of the plaintiff's pure economic losses as are 'truly consequential' on that property damage (see Chapter 4, para 4.3.3), because this really is uncontrolled exposure to indeterminate liability for pure economic loss. The only 'control' is that this economic loss must be 'truly consequential' upon the physical damage to the plaintiff's other property; but this is really not a control on the indeterminacy of the defendant's exposure to such liability, because the actual extent of such exposure will not be able to be determined in any case until after the loss has been incurred and all of the facts have been investigated.

This point was also expressed by the High Court of Australia in *Bryan v Maloney* (1995) 69 ALJR 375, when Mason CJ, delivering the main majority judgment, said (at p 381):

The only factor which arguably precludes the recognition of a relevant relationship of proximity between a builder and a subsequent owner for the purposes of the present case is the kind of damage involved, namely, mere economic loss. As has been seen, a relevant relationship of proximity would have existed between the builder and Mrs Maloney [the plaintiff] with respect to ordinary physical injury to her person or other property caused by a partial collapse of the house due to its inadequate footings, even if she had not been the owner. Here again, it is important to bear in mind the particular kind of economic loss involved. The distinction between that kind of economic loss and ordinary physical damage to property is an essentially technical one.

Indeed, the economic loss sustained by the owner of a house by reason of the diminution of its value when the inadequacy of the footings first becomes manifest by consequent damage to the fabric of the house is, at least arguably, less remote and more readily foreseeable than ordinary physical damage to other property of the owner which might be caused by an actual collapse of part of the house as a result of the inadequacy of those footings.

The 'standards' difficulty

In *Junior Books* Lord Brandon, dissenting, whose judgment has been embraced by the House of Lords in *D & F* and *Murphy*, said (at p 551):

> It is worthwhile to consider the difficulties which would arise if the wider scope of the duty of care put forward by the plaintiff were accepted. In any case where complaint was made by an ultimate consumer that a product made by some person with whom he himself had no contract was defective, by what standard or standards of quality would the question of defectiveness fall to be decided? In the case of goods bought from a retailer, it could hardly be the standard prescribed by the contract between the retailer and the wholesaler, or between the wholesaler and the distributor, or between the distributor and the manufacturer, for the terms of such contracts would not even be known to the ultimate buyer. It follows that the question by what standard or standards alleged defects in a product complained of by its ultimate user or consumer are to be judged remains entirely at large and cannot be given any just or satisfactory answer.

The answer

The answer to Lord Brandon's difficulty lies in the fact that the considerations which led to liability being imposed in contract and in tort are different, even though the damage might be the same. While Lord Brandon is correct in stating that the standard of quality in a contract of sale between two parties higher up in the chain of distribution cannot be expected to determine the standard to be applied in a claim in tort by the buyer or ultimate consumer against the manufacturer, it does not follow from this that it is impossible to determine the standard of quality to be applied in tort. If this were so, then there could never be a successful tortious claim in these circumstances, yet the House of Lords in *Junior Books*, *D & F* and *Murphy* has said that there can be such a claim, so long as there exists a "sufficient relationship of proximity based on reliance" between the plaintiff and the defendant.

In all negligence cases the court has to determine the acceptable standard of the defendant's conduct, because it is only if his act or omission in the case in question has fallen below that standard that he can be held to have been negligent. If the defendant is a professional person or someone who has held himself out as possessing special skills and experience, the standard of care is that which is to be expected of a reasonable professional person with special skills in that field. As the Saskatchewan Court of Appeal stated in *University of Regina v Pettick* (1991) 6 CCLT (2d) 1 (see para 7.3.8) (at p 33): "This standard of care is therefore determined by one's status, not by the specifics of the contract".

If this principle is applicable to services rendered by professional people and others holding themselves out as possessing special skills, then there seems to be no reason why it could not be equally applicable to the manufacturer of a product in those cases where the court has determined that a sufficient relationship of proximity based on reliance did exist between the plaintiff consumer and the defendant manufacturer. As mentioned *above*, such a relationship will exist only where the manufacturer of the product intended it to be used without inspection by the ultimate consumer. The standard to be applied in any such case will depend, first, on any express representations made by the manufacturer to the consumer, either verbally in advertising or in other pre-sale literature, such as a promotional display at the point of sale or information written on the packaging and, secondly, on reasonable inferences to be drawn from the characteristics of the goods themselves (as opposed to anything which the retailer might have said about them), including the price, as compared with other goods of the same type.

It is difficult to comprehend why this should appear to be such an impossible task in this type of case, when the courts are, in any event, already involved in carrying out this exercise in determining the question of satisfactory quality under s 14 of the Sale of Goods Act 1979, as amended in 1994, which provides that goods are of satisfactory quality if they meet the standard that a reasonable person would regard as satisfactory, taking account of any description of the goods, the price (if relevant) and all other relevant circumstances. The Act also states that the quality of goods includes their state and condition and that, in appropriate cases, relevant aspects of the quality of goods can include whether they are fit for all the purposes for which goods of the kind in question are commonly supplied, and their appearance, finish, freedom from minor defects, safety and durability.

In applying s 14 of the Sale of Goods Act the courts effectively have to determine by what standard alleged defects in a product are to be judged, and, in carrying out this exercise, they are not confined to the terms of the contract between the plaintiff and the retailer.

Rogers v Parish

An example of the above-suggested principle being applied in practice is the Court of Appeal's decision in *Rogers v Parish (Scarborough) Ltd* [1987] 1 QB 933, in which the question was whether a Range Rover motor car with several defects was of merchantable quality. Mustill LJ said (at p 944):

> What is the appropriate degree and what relative weight is to be attached to one characteristic of the car rather than another will depend on the market at which the car is aimed. To identify the relevant expectation one must look at the factors listed in the subsection. The first is the description applied to the goods. In the present case the vehicle was sold as new. Deficiencies which might be acceptable in a secondhand vehicle are not to be expected in one purchased as new. Next, the description 'Range Rover' would conjure up a particular set of expectations, not the same as those relating to an ordinary saloon car, as to the balance between performance, handling, comfort and resilience. The factor of price was also significant. At more than £14,000 this vehicle was, if not at the top end of the scale, well above the level of the ordinary family saloon. The buyer was entitled to value for his money.

The correct approach: Grant v Australian Knitting Mills

It has been pointed out *above* in para 7.5.4 that in *Grant v Australian Knitting Mills Ltd* [1935] AC 85 the Privy Council probably compensated the plaintiff for his pure economic loss consisting of the diminution in the value of the defective underpants which the defendant had manufactured, because the court upheld that claim as well as the plaintiff's claim "for the same damage" under the relevant Sale of Goods Act. Lord Wright said (at p 105): "It is immaterial that the plaintiff has a claim in contract against the retailers, because that is a quite independent cause of action, based on different considerations, even though the damage may be the same. Equally irrelevant is any question of liability between the retailers and the manufacturers on the contract of sale between them. The tort liability is independent of any question of contract".

The court determined the retailer's liability by reference to s 14 of the South Australia Sale of Goods Act 1893 and said (at p 100): "The retailers are liable in contract. So far as they are concerned, no question of negligence is relevant to the liability in contract. But when the question of the manufacturers is considered, different questions arise: there is no privity of contract between the plaintiff and the manufacturers: between them the liability, if any, must be in tort, and the gist of the cause of action is negligence".

In considering the plaintiff's claim in negligence, it was not simply the fact of the defendant's negligence and the fact of the plaintiff's consequential injury that sufficed. Rather, as Lord Wright said (at p 105): "The principle of *Donoghue*'s case can only be applied where the defect is hidden and unknown to the consumer. The presence of the deleterious chemical in the pants, due to negligence in manufacture, was a hidden and latent defect, just as much as were the remains of the snail in the opaque bottle: it could not be detected by any examination that could reasonably be made. The garments were made by the manufacturers for the purpose of being worn exactly as they were worn in fact by the plaintiff: it was not contemplated that they should be first washed".

Thus the plaintiff succeeded in contract and in tort for 'the same loss' which, it seems, included the replacement cost of the defective goods; and the court, without difficulty, applied the appropriate contract test to determine the retailer's liability, and the appropriate tort test to determine the manufacturer's liability. Each test is subject to its own criteria and may or may not be satisfied, depending on what actually happened, but the fact that the satisfaction of the tort test leads to the plaintiff recovering damages for the defective quality of the goods should not of itself be an obstacle.

A false hypothesis

The reasoning of the House of Lords in *D & F* and *Murphy* seems to be based on a belief that the plaintiff will always have a claim in contract against his immediate vendor for his economic loss consisting of the diminution in the value of the defective goods, and therefore there should be no need for him to want to sue anyone else for that loss. However, in real property cases, the purchaser will not have this right, because it is excluded by the automatic application of the *caveat emptor* rule, which has not been modified by the Defective Premises Act 1972, except in relation to defects which the vendor himself created (see Chapter 6, para 6.6.5); and in sales of chattels the purchaser will not have this right or it will be worthless if the seller has become insolvent, as was the case in *Muirhead*, considered *above* (para 7.3.6). (Another aspect of the existence of the *caveat emptor* rule in this type of case is considered in Chapter 10, para 10.2.2.)

If, as the House of Lords has said in *Junior Books*, *D & F* and *Murphy*, reliance is the key to the establishment of a sufficient relationship of proximity to justify the imposition of a duty of care in respect of the plaintiff's economic loss (see para 7.3.6), one is left wondering why it should make such a great difference that, where this test is satisfied, the defendant is thereby effectively providing the ultimate purchaser or consumer with a non-contractual warranty of the product's merchantability. Surely this is no more than the inevitable conclusion of saying, as the House of Lords has done, that the plaintiff's right of recovery in this type of case depends, not on whether his loss is physical or purely economic, but on whether he is able to establish a sufficient relationship of proximity with the defendant, based on reliance?

Lord Roskill recognised this connection in *Junior Books* when he said (at p 546):

> The concept of proximity must always involve, at least in most cases, some degree of reliance—I have already mentioned the words 'skill' and 'judgment' in the speech of Lord Morris in *Hedley Byrne* [see Chapter 9, para 9.4.3]. These words seem to me to be an echo of the language of s 14(1) of the Sale of Goods Act 1893 [which imposed a condition of merchantability in a commercial sale of goods and which has now been replaced by a requirement of 'satisfactory quality']. Though the analogy is not exact, I do not find it unhelpful, for I think that the concept of proximity of which I have spoken and the reasoning of Lord Devlin in *Hedley Byrne* involve factual considerations not unlike those involved in a claim under s 14(1).

In other words, Lord Roskill was here recognising that the imposition of a duty of care in tort on the basis of a special relationship of proximity based on reliance would be the equivalent of the establishment of an implied warranty of merchantability in tort; and far from being troubled by this realisation, he saw it as being of assistance in determining the standard of care to be imposed in tort. As will be seen *below*, such a doctrine is quite well developed in the United States, and the House of Lords in *D & F* and *Murphy* were misled in the implications to be drawn from the two American cases which were cited to them.

As noted *above* (in the main discussion of *Junior Books* in para 7.3.6), Lord Roskill qualified the principle which he enunciated by saying (at p 547) that this principle "would not easily be found to exist in the ordinary everyday transaction of purchasing chattels, when it is obvious that in truth the real reliance was upon the immediate vendor and not upon the manufacturer". It would seem that Lord Roskill was here taking judicial notice of something which should in fact be left to expert evidence, as was done in *Smith v Eric S Bush* [1990] 1 AC 831 (see Chapter 9, para 9.7.3) in relation to the crucial finding that 90 per cent of purchasers of 'modest homes' do not obtain surveys of their own, but rely instead on their mortgagee's valuation report. In any event, without producing any expert evidence, it is submitted, on the basis of common experience, that in practice the position *vis-à-vis* reliance is exactly the opposite of what Lord Roskill has suggested in the vast majority of ordinary everyday transactions of purchasing chattels: it is the manufacturer, rather than the retailer, who, through advertising and by means of displays at the point of sale and through wording on the packaging of its products, disseminates the information upon which the purchaser relies in making his purchase. This point is explored further in considering the American cases which have allowed recovery on the basis of an implied warranty between the manufacturer and the ultimate purchaser or consumer.

7.5.8 The *Linden Gardens* solution

In *Linden Gardens Ltd v Lenesta Sludge Disposals Ltd* [1994] 1 AC 85, the House of Lords fashioned a remedy whereby, albeit indirectly, a transferee of a building in which defects created by the negligence of the builder emerged after the transfer was enabled to recover compensation from the builder for the transferee's economic loss consisting of the diminution in value of the building by virtue of those defects.

Before referring to the facts of *Linden Gardens* and the House of Lords' pronouncements therein, it is necessary to refer briefly to a principle which is often referred to as 'the rule in *The Albazero*', which derives from the House of Lords' decision in *Albacruz (Cargo Owners) v Albazero (Owners)* (*'The Albazero'*) [1977] AC 774, the facts of which are set out in Chapter 5, para 5.5.1. The plaintiff in *The Albazero* was a charterparty suing the shipowner under the bill of lading for the cost of cargo that had been lost at sea. The plaintiff's claim suffered from the defect that, at the time the goods were lost, the plaintiff was no longer the owner of the cargo, and therefore suffered no loss itself by reason of the non-delivery of the cargo at its destination. Therefore, although the plaintiff technically had a right of action against the defendant under the bill of lading, the practical effect of that right was worthless because, having suffered no loss, the plaintiff was not entitled to recover damages from the defendant for the defendant's breach of the contract.

Ultimately, the plaintiff's claim failed for technical reasons concerned with bills of lading. However, the House of Lords went out of its way to endorse the fact that, in appropriate circumstances, English law recognises exceptions to the general rule that a plaintiff suing a defendant in an action for breach of contract can recover only the actual loss that he has himself sustained. One of these exceptions is the so-called rule in *Dunlop v Lambert* (1839) 6 Cl & F 600 (see Chapter 5, para 5.5.1). In holding in *The Albazero* that the exceptions to the general rule are not confined to the circumstances of *Dunlop v Lambert*, Lord Diplock, delivering the unanimous decision of the House, said (at p 847):

> ... the rule [in *Dunlop v Lambert*] extends to all forms of carriage, including carriage by sea itself where no bill of lading has been issued; and there may still be occasional cases in which the rule would provide a remedy where no other remedy would be available to a person sustaining loss which, under a rational legal system, ought to be compensated by the person who caused it.

The House of Lords' decision in *Linden Gardens Trust Ltd v Lenesta Sludge Disposals Ltd* [1994] 1 AC 85 was concerned with two separate appeals. In the second of these, *St Martins Property Corporation Ltd v Sir Robert McAlpine Ltd*, the first plaintiff, St Martins Property Corporation Ltd ('Corporation'), was the developer of a large multi-use commercial and residential property complex. It entered into a building contract with the defendant building contractors (McAlpine) which contained a clause prohibiting the employer (the first plaintiff) from assigning the (benefit of) the building contract without the contractor's (the defendant's) consent. During the course of construction the plaintiff assigned the benefit of the building contract to a sister company, St Martins Holdings Limited, the second plaintiff ('Investment').

A few years later, after the building works had been completed, part of the development was found to be leaking. It was repaired at great cost. This cost was borne entirely by Investment. In the present action, both Corporation and Investment sued McAlpine, alleging that the leaks in the building were caused by breaches of contract by McAlpine occurring after the date of assignment of the contract to Investment. The loss claimed was the cost of the repair work.

The House of Lords held, first, that Investment had no cause of action against the defendant because the assignment to Investment had taken place in contravention of the prohibition against assignment without the consent of McAlpine. It was common ground that if the attempted assignment by Corporation of its rights under the contract to Investment was ineffective, Corporation retained those rights and was entitled to judgment against McAlpine for McAlpine's breach of the contract. The problem here was that the breaches of contract took place after the date of the assignment, when Corporation had no interest in the property, and therefore suffered no loss as a result of McAlpine's breach of the contract.

Their Lordships said that, while they appreciated the logic of this argument, they were not going to let it render Corporation's claim nugatory. Thus, Lord Browne-Wilkinson said (at p 112): "On any view, the facts of this case bring it within the class of exceptions to the general rule which Lord Diplock referred to in *The Albazero*".

Lord Browne-Wilkinson then referred extensively to Lord Diplock's speech in *The Albazero*. Lord Browne-Wilkinson then continued by saying (on p 114):

> In my judgment, the present case falls within the rationale of the exceptions to the general rule that a plaintiff can only recover damages for his own loss. The con-

tract was for a large development of property which, to the knowledge of both Corporation and McAlpine [the defendant], was going to be occupied, and possibly purchased, by third parties and not by Corporation itself. Therefore it could be foreseen that damage caused by a breach of the contract would cause loss to a later owner, and not merely to the original contracting party, Corporation.

McAlpine specifically contracted that the rights of action under the building contract could not, without McAlpine's consent, be transferred to third parties who became owners or occupiers and might suffer loss. In such a case, it seems to me proper, as in the case of the carriage of goods by land, to treat the parties as having entered into the contract on the footing that Corporation would be entitled to enforce contractual rights for the benefit of those who suffered from defective performance but who, under the terms of the contract, could not acquire any right to hold McAlpine liable for breach. This is truly a case in which the rule provides 'a remedy where no other would be available to a person sustaining loss which, under a rational legal system, ought to be compensated by the person who has caused it' [*per* Lord Diplock in *The Albazero*].

In *Linden Gardens*, the damage caused by the building contractor's negligence in carrying out the terms of its contract with Corporation consisted of damage to the structure itself. In accordance with the definition of economic loss in this category of cases, this loss is treated as pure economic loss, consisting of the diminution in value of the defectively constructed building (see Chapter 1, para 1.2.2 and para 7.1.2, *above*). The effect and, more importantly, the intention of the House of Lords' decision in *Linden Gardens* was that the person who suffered this loss (Investment—see *above*) would be compensated for it by the negligent builder. Although the House of Lords' decisions in *D & F Estates Ltd v Church Commissioners for England* [1989] 1 AC 177 and *Murphy v Brentwood District Council* [1991] 1 AC 398 (see para 7.7, *below*) were not referred to, the economic loss for which Investment was compensated in *Linden Gardens* was precisely the type of economic loss that the House of Lords held in *D & F* and *Murphy* is not recoverable by a plaintiff in the position of Investment suing in tort.

In *Linden Gardens*, the plaintiff, who was not the party who had sustained the loss, sued the negligent builder in contract for its breaches of the building contract. Notwithstanding that the plaintiff had not suffered the loss because it occurred after the plaintiff had parted with possession of the building, the defendant was ordered to pay damages to the plaintiff, consisting of the cost of remedying the defects in the building (ie the economic loss caused by the defendant), on condition that the plaintiff would thereafter account for that loss to the person who had suffered the loss.

In *D & F* and *Murphy*, the plaintiff was the person who had actually suffered the loss, and his claim against the negligent builder was brought in tort. The question is whether these differences are sufficient to justify holding the defendant liable for the economic loss occasioned through his negligence in the one type of situation, but not in the other. It is submitted that the answer depends on the courts' rationale for holding that the builder is not liable for that loss in the one type of case, as contrasted with their rationale for holding the builder liable in the other type of case.

In the *D & F/Murphy* type of situation, the rationale provided by the

House of Lords for holding that a negligent builder did not owe a duty of care in tort for the consequence of defects created by the builder's negligence in the structure of the building itself to a person with whom the builder did not have a contractual relationship was, first, that the scope of any such potential duty of care was adequately provided for by the provisions of the Defective Premises Act 1972; and, secondly, and more importantly, that if a duty of care was imposed on the defendant for the plaintiff's loss consisting of the diminution in value of the building, the defendant would be providing a warranty in tort to a person with whom he did not have a contract, that the building was as fit for its contemplated purpose as the exercise of reasonable care could make it (see para 7.5.7, *above*).

In *D & F* and *Murphy*, not only did their Lordships regard the possibility of the imposition of such a non-contractual warranty of quality as being contrary to principle, but they also envisaged serious problems in determining the standards by which the defectiveness of the building would fall to be decided. Their view was that the scope of transmissible warranties of quality is properly limited to contractual claims, with the consequence that the scope of any duty of care to be imposed in tort should correspondingly exclude such claims.

In *Linden Gardens*, the plaintiff was indeed suing for breach of a contract, and therefore, at least *prima facie*, this would provide a reason for distinguishing the decision to impose liability on the builder for the economic loss caused by his negligence, when this situation is contrasted with the *D & F/Murphy* type of situation. It is submitted, however, that the passage cited *above* from the speech of Lord Browne-Wilkinson in *Linden Gardens*, with which all of the other Law Lords concurred, suggests that this factor did not feature in their Lordships' decision. It is submitted that the rationale of that decision is contained in the following excerpt from Lord Browne-Wilkinson's speech (at p 114):

> In my judgment, the present case falls within the rationale of the exceptions to the general rule that a plaintiff can only recover damages for his own loss. The contract was for a large development of property which, to the knowledge of both Corporation and McAlpine [the defendant], was going to be occupied, and possibly purchased, by third parties and not by Corporation itself. Therefore it could be foreseen that damage caused by a breach of the contract would cause loss to a later owner, and not merely to the original contracting party, Corporation.
>
> McAlpine specifically contracted that the rights of action under the building contract could not, without McAlpine's consent, be transferred to third parties who became owners or occupiers and might suffer loss. In such a case, it seems to me proper, as in the case of the carriage of goods by land, to treat the parties as having entered into the contract on the footing that Corporation would be entitled to enforce contractual rights for the benefit of those who suffered from defective performance but who, under the terms of the contract, could not acquire any right to hold McAlpine liable for breach. This is truly a case in which the rule provides 'a remedy where no other would be available to a person sustaining loss which, under a rational legal system, ought to be compensated by the person who has caused it' [*per* Lord Diplock in *The Albazero*].

It is submitted that this rationale can be explained only on the basis of the imposition of a transmissible warranty of quality on the builder to an entity (Investment) with whom the builder did not have a contract. The concept expressed by Lord Browne-Wilkinson is very similar to the policy and practical considerations in favour of imposing a duty of care in tort on a builder for latent defects that were expressed by the Supreme Court of New Hampshire in *Lempke v Dagenais* (1988) 547 A (2d) 290 (see para 7.6.1, *above*); particularly the following *dicta* (emphasis added):

> First, common experience teaches that latent defects in a house will not manifest themselves for a considerable period of time after the original purchaser has sold the property to a subsequent unsuspecting buyer.
>
> Secondly, our society is rapidly changing. We are an increasingly mobile people. A builder-vendor should know that a house he builds might be resold within a relatively short period of time, and should not expect that his *warranty* will be limited by the number of days that the original owner holds onto the property.

It is submitted that the sentiments expressed in these *dicta* are no different from those expressed by Lord Browne-Wilkinson in *Linden Gardens*, with the consequence that the rationale which motivated the House of Lords to give effect to a transmissible warranty of quality in *Linden Gardens* effectively nullifies the House of Lords' reason for being opposed to the creation of such a warranty in *D & F* and *Murphy*.

It is worth noting that the rationale of *Lempke v Dagenais* was adopted by both the High Court of Australia in *Bryan v Maloney* (1995) 69 ALJR 375 (see para 7.6.4) and the Supreme Court of Canada in *Winnipeg Condominium Corporation No 36 v Bird Construction Co* (1995) 121 DLR (4th) 193 (see para 7.6.3), in holding that a builder can be held liable in tort to a remote purchaser or occupier for economic loss of the type sustained by the plaintiff in *D & F* and *Murphy*.

In *Linden Gardens*, the plaintiff was not the person who had suffered the loss, but the remedy granted by the House of Lords, whereunder the person who had suffered the loss was compensated by the defendant, creates an inconsistency with the other cases in which the House of Lords has refused to grant such a remedy directly to the person who has suffered the loss (eg Mr Murphy in the *Murphy* case), especially as the rationale for granting the remedy in *Linden Gardens* (ie that a contractual warranty given by a builder to his original purchaser ought to enure to a transferee from that purchaser) seems to conflict directly with the rationale for having refused the remedy in the other cases (ie that a contractual warranty given by a builder to his original purchaser must not be allowed to enure to a transferee from that purchaser). The House of Lords' decision in *Linden Gardens* suggests that, in future cases like *D & F* and *Murphy*, if the original contracting party is prepared to sue the builder for breach of the building contract for defects in the building that manifested themselves only after the plaintiff had sold the building to a third party, and the costs of repair of which were borne by that third party, the original contracting party should nevertheless be able to recover the cost of those repairs from the builder and should be made to account to the third party for any damages so recovered.

If this is the situation that will now pertain in this type of case as a result of the House of Lords' decision in *Linden Gardens*—and why shouldn't it, if it pertained in *Linden Gardens*—then it is submitted that the courts should be just as willing (like the High Court of Australia in *Bryan v Maloney* and the Supreme Court of Canada in *Winnipeg Condominium*) to allow the party who sustained the loss to bring a direct action in his own name against the negligent builder to recover that loss.

7.6   Other jurisdictions

7.6.1   The United States

Two relatively early decisions of the Supreme Court of New York are summarised at the end of this chapter, para 7.7. They are *Quackenbush v Ford Motor Co* (1915) 153 NYS 131 and *Trans World Airlines v Curtiss-Wright Corp* (1955) 148 NYS (2d) 284. Both were claims for damages 'to the thing itself'. In the first case the plaintiff succeeded, in the second case it did not. The reconciliation of these opposite results was stated by the court in *Trans World* to be the fact that in *Quackenbush* the accident had actually occurred before the defect was discovered. Eder J said (at p 290): "Until there is an accident, there can be no loss arising from breach of this duty, ie as a result of negligence as distinguished from warranty". He said that if the plaintiff had a warranty claim to have the defective brakes replaced, that claim could only be against the seller.

East River and Aloe

In *East River Steamship Corp v Trans America Delaval Inc* (1986) 476 US 865, an engine turbine on a supertanker malfunctioned due to design and manufacturing defects. No other property was damaged, but the charterer suffered economic loss consisting of the cost of repairing the turbine and lost profits while the ship was out of service. It sought to recover these losses from the manufacturer of the turbine. The Supreme Court rejected this claim, saying (at p 877):

> The tort concern with safety is reduced when an injury is only to the product itself. Even when the harm to the product itself occurs through an abrupt, accident-like event, the resulting loss due to repair costs, decreased value, and lost profits is essentially the failure of the purchaser to receive the benefit of its bargain—traditionally the core concern of contract law. Obviously, damage to a product itself has certain attributes of a products liability claim; but the injury suffered—the failure of the product to function properly—is the essence of a warranty claim, through which a contracting party can seek to recoup the benefit of its bargain.

The court noted that different states have adopted different approaches. The majority approach is typified by *Trans World Airlines*, referred to *above*, and by *Seely v White Motor Co* (1965) 403 P (2d) 145, in which the Supreme

Court of California held that a purchaser of a truck from a dealer did not have a strict liability/products liability claim against the manufacturer in tort for his commercial losses when the truck did not perform properly in his business. The minority approach is typified by *Quackenbush* and by *Santor v A and M Karagheusian* (1965) 207 A (2d) 305, in which the Supreme Court of New Jersey held that the purchaser of defective carpeting from a retailer (who had gone out of business) was entitled to sue the manufacturer in tort, on the basis of the manufacturer's strict liability flowing from the manufacturer's responsibility for its own actions when it creates defective products and puts them out into the stream of commerce. In *East River* the US Supreme Court rejected the minority view, saying: "The minority view fails to account for the need to keep products liability and contract law in separate spheres and to maintain a realistic limitation on damages".

In *Aloe Coal Co v Clark Equipment Co* (1987) 816 F (2d) 110 the Court of Appeals for the Third Circuit (Pennsylvania) followed *East River* even though it was not bound to do so, as that case was concerned solely with an interpretation of federal admiralty law. Accordingly, the court held that the plaintiff did not have a claim in negligence against the manufacturer for damage sustained by the plaintiff's tractor shovel through suddenly catching fire.

Relation to English cases

In *D & F* Lord Bridge (at p 204) referred to *East River* with approval, as did Lord Keith in *Murphy* (at p 469), as well as to *Aloe Coal*. Lord Keith said (at p 469): "These American cases would appear to destroy the authority of the earlier decision in *Quackenbush v Ford Motor Co*, founded on by the New Zealand Court of Appeal in *Bowen v Paramount Builders (Hamilton) Ltd* [see para 7.6.2, *below*], from which Lord Wilberforce in *Anns* said he derived assistance".

Comment

To the extent that the courts' decisions in *Quackenbush* and *Santor* were based on theories of strict liability for negligence, the House of Lords was right to conclude that those decisions have been undermined by *East River*. However, this does not mean that a person in the position of the plaintiff in either of those cases would therefore not have a successful claim in the United States for his economic loss consisting of damage to the defective product itself. This is because, in addition to strict liability/products liability and negligence law, a separate and quite well-developed doctrine, namely implied warranty, is available for the plaintiff to plead in this type of case. It is similar to, and can be viewed as, a practical application of the principle of 'proximity based on reliance' which the House of Lords has sanctioned in cases of this type. It has been held to be particularly appropriate to consumer cases in the United States and it was endorsed as an acceptable principle in *East River* when the Supreme Court said (at p 878): "Contract law, and the law of warranty [by which, in this context, the court meant 'express' warranty] in particular, is well suited to 'commercial' controversies of the sort involved in this case because the parties may set the terms of their own agreements. We recognise, of course, that warranty and products liability may overlap. In certain situations the privity requirement of warranty has been discarded, eg, *Henningsen v Bloomfield Motors* [see *below*]".

Implied warranty

The implied warranty theory is founded on the thesis that if the manufacturer of a product, or the builder of a building, represents it as having certain qualities which it does not in fact possess, and which would not be discoverable in the course of an intermediate inspection of the product or building before its use, and if the consumer relied on that representation in purchasing the product or building, the manufacturer or builder cannot escape responsibility for the consumer's consequent losses simply because there was no privity of contract between himself and the consumer. In an early case, *Baxter v Ford Motor Co* (1932) 12 P (2d) 409, the Supreme Court of Washington expressed this principle in the following terms (emphasis added):

> Since the rule of *caveat emptor* was first formulated, vast changes have taken place in the economic structures of the English speaking peoples. Methods of business have undergone a great transition. Radio, billboards, and the products of the printing press have become the means of creating a large part of the demand that causes goods to depart from factories to the ultimate consumer. It would be unjust to *recognise a rule* that would permit *manufacturers* of goods to create a demand for their products by representing that they possess qualities which they, in fact, do not possess, and then, because there is no privity of contract, deny the consumer the right to recover if damages result from the absence of those qualities, when such absence is not readily noticeable.

Henningsen v Bloomfield

In *Henningsen v Bloomfield Motors Inc and Chrysler Corp* (1960) 161 A (2d) 69 (which was approved by the US Supreme Court in *East River*—see *above*) the Supreme Court of New Jersey took up this theme by saying (at p 83):

> Under modern conditions the ordinary layman, on responding to the importunity of colourful advertising, has neither the opportunity nor the capacity to inspect or to determine the fitness of an automobile for use. He must rely on the manufacturer who has control of its construction and, to some degree, on the dealer who, to the limited extent called for by the manufacturer's instructions, inspects and services it before delivery. In such a marketing milieu the obligation of the manufacturer should not be based alone on privity of contract. Accordingly, we hold that under modern marketing conditions, when a manufacturer puts a new automobile in the stream of trade and promotes its purchase to the public, an implied warranty that it is reasonably suitable for use as such accompanies it into the hands of the ultimate purchaser.

Randy Knitwear

In *Baxter* and *Henningsen* the plaintiffs' injuries were physical, but the principle which they established was applied in *Randy Knitwear v American*

Cyanamid (1961) 181 NE (2d) 399 to justify the Court of Appeals of New York in upholding the plaintiff's claim for pure economic loss where the plaintiff had relied on the defendant manufacturer's advertising in purchasing the defendant's product from a middleman. The court said (at pp 402–403) (emphasis added):

> It may once have been true that the warranty which really induced the sale was an actual term of the contract of sale. Today, however, the significant warranty, the one which effectively *induces* the purchase, is frequently that given by the manufacturer through mass advertising and labelling to ultimate consumers with whom he has no direct contractual relationship. The world of merchandising is in brief, no longer a world of direct contract: it is, rather, a world of advertising. When representations expressed in the mass communications media prove false and the user is damaged by reason of his *reliance on those representations* it is difficult to justify the manufacturer's denial of liability on the sole ground of the absence of technical privity. Manufacturers make extensive use of the media to call attention, in glowing terms, to the qualities of their products and this advertising is directed at the ultimate consumer who is not in privity with them. Equally sanguine *representations* on packages and labels frequently accompany the article throughout its journey to the ultimate consumer and, *as intended*, are *relied* upon by remote purchasers. Under these circumstances it is highly unrealistic to limit a purchaser's protection to warranties made directly to him by his immediate seller. The protection he really needs is against the manufacturer whose published *representations* caused him to make the purchase. . . . The manufacturer places his product upon the market and, by advertising and labelling, *represents* its quality to the public in such a way as to *induce reliance* upon his representations. He unquestionably *intends* and *expects* that the product will be purchased and used *in reliance* upon his *express assurance of its quality* and, in fact, it is so purchased and used. Having *invited* and *solicited* the use, the manufacturer should not be permitted to avoid responsibility when the *expected use leads to* injury and loss by claiming that he made no contract directly with the user.

Inglis v American Motors

In *Inglis v American Motors Corp* (1965) 209 NE (2d) 583 the Supreme Court of Ohio rejected the plaintiff's claim for pure economic loss consisting of the cost of repairing his defective motor car to the extent that it was founded in negligence, but upheld it to the extent that it was founded in, and could be shown to be referable to, implied warranties made by the manufacturer extolling the virtues of its products in advertising, upon which the plaintiff had relied in making his decision to purchase that particular car. The court said (emphasis added) at p 586:

> Today, many manufacturers make extensive use of newspapers, periodicals, signboards, radio and television to advertise their products. The worth, quality and benefits of these products are described in glowing terms and in considerable detail and the appeal is almost universally directed to the ultimate consumer. Many of these manufactured articles are shipped out in *sealed containers* by the manufacturers, and the *retailers* who dispense them to the ultimate consumer are but *conduits* or outlets through which the manufacturer distributes his goods. The consuming public ordinarily relies exclusively on the representations of the

manufacturer in his advertisements. . . . The warranties made by the manufacturer in his advertisements and by the labels on his products are *inducements* to the ultimate consumer, and the manufacturer ought to be held to strict accountability to any consumer who buys the product in *reliance* on such representations and later suffers injury because the product proves to be defective or deleterious.

Comment

These principles have been set out in some detail because it is submitted that their application would provide a sound basis for the satisfaction in English law of the 'sufficient relationship of proximity based on reliance', which is required for the establishment of a duty of care where the plaintiff has suffered pure economic loss by virtue of a product manufactured by the defendant proving to be defective. Obviously, the plaintiff would still have to prove that the manufacturer's representation in question did in fact induce him to purchase the defendant's product (as opposed to having relied on something that the intermediate seller had told him), that the defect could not have been discovered by himself or someone else higher up in the chain of distribution before he used it, that the defect in question arose in a feature of the product which the manufacturer had specifically stressed in its advertising and that the manufacturer was in fact responsible for the defect (as opposed to it having arisen through fair wear and tear). However, these are all matters of evidence, and should not be used as arguments to debar the plaintiff's claim in principle in an appropriate case.

Real property cases

It is also significant that the House of Lords in *D & F* and *Murphy* were not referred to in any of the American real property cases in which it has been held that an implied warranty of habitability exists at common law between the builder of a house and a subsequent purchaser in respect of latent defects which would not be discoverable on a reasonable pre-purchase inspection of the property.

Redarowicz v Ohlendorf

An example is *Redarowicz v Ohlendorf* (1982) 441 NE (2d) 324. The court noted that the damage to the house itself was pure economic loss which was not recoverable "under a negligence theory". Nevertheless, the court held the defendant builder liable to the plaintiff (who was not the original purchaser) in tort on the basis of a non-contractual (transmissible) implied warranty of habitability of the house which the defendant had built. The court noted that the implied warranty of habitability as between the builder and the original purchaser was first recognised in the English case of *Miller v Cannon Hill Estates Ltd* [1931] 2 KB 113, where the court said that, in the purchase of an unfinished house, the builder was aware that his buyer intended to live in the house and therefore impliedly warranted that it would be suitable for that purpose.

The Supreme Court of Illinois in the present case said that logic compelled the extension of this warranty to subsequent purchasers (at p 330):

Like the initial purchaser, the subsequent purchaser has little opportunity to inspect the construction methods used in building the home. Like the initial purchaser, the subsequent purchaser is usually not knowledgeable in construction practices and must, to a substantial degree, rely upon the expertise of the person who built the home. . . . The compelling public policies underlying the implied warranty of habitability should not be frustrated because of the short intervening ownership of the first purchaser. . . . 'The fact that the subsequent purchaser did not know the builder, as did the original purchaser, does not negate the reality of the holding out of the builder's expertise and reliance which occurs in the marketplace'.

The court did, however, temper the potentially far reaching effect of its decision by saying: "Our holding today in extending the implied warranty of habitability to subsequent purchasers is limited to latent defects which manifest themselves within a reasonable time after the purchase of the house". The court also noted that, at the time of its decision, four other states applied the same principle.

Lempke v Dagenais

In *Lempke v Dagenais* (1988) 547 A (2d) 290, the Supreme Court of New Hampshire also decided to abandon its previous rulings and to adopt this principle. The court noted that, since 1982, six more states had decided to do so too. Thayer J said (at p 294):

In keeping with judicial trends and the spirit of the law in New Hampshire, we now hold that the privity requirement should be abandoned in suits by subsequent purchasers against a builder for breach of an implied warranty of good workmanship for latent defects. . . .[; and (at p 297):] Our extension is limited to latent defects which 'become manifest after the subsequent owner's purchase and which were not discoverable had a reasonable inspection of the structure been made prior to the purchase. . . . The plaintiff still has the burden to show that the defect was caused by the defendant's workmanship. The builder will have a defence if he can demonstrate that the defects were not attributable to him, that they were the result of age or ordinary wear and tear or that previous owners had made substantial alterations.

In addition, the court articulated the following policy and practical considerations in favour of imposing a duty of care on a builder for latent defects:

First, common experience teaches that latent defects in a house will not manifest themselves for a considerable period of time after the original purchaser has sold the property to a subsequent unsuspecting buyer.

Secondly, our society is rapidly changing. We are an increasingly mobile people. A builder-vendor should know that a house he builds might be resold within a relatively short period of time, and should not expect that his warranty will be limited by the number of days that the original owner holds onto the property.

Thirdly, like an initial buyer, the subsequent purchaser has little opportunity to inspect, and little experience and knowledge about construction. Consumer protection demands that those who buy homes are entitled to rely on the skill of a builder and that the house is constructed so as to be reasonably fit for its intended use.

Fourthly, the builder/contractor will not be unduly taken unaware by the extension of the warranty to a subsequent purchaser. The builder already owes a duty to construct the home in a workmanlike manner, and the extension of that duty to a subsequent purchaser, within a reasonable time, will not change this basic obligation.

Fifthly, the builder should not be relieved of liability for unworkmanlike construction simply because of the fortuity that the property on which he did the construction has changed hands. Arbitrarily imposing an intermediate purchaser as a bar to recovery might encourage sham first sales to insulate builders from liability.

Having enumerated these important factors, Thayer J continued with this theme by saying:

Economic policies influence our decision as well. By virtue of superior knowledge, skill and experience in the construction of houses, a builder-vendor is generally better positioned than the purchaser to evaluate and guard against the financial risk posed by a latent defect.

This court, as well, does not find it logical to limit protection arbitrarily to the first purchaser. Most purchasers do not have the expertise to discover latent defects, and they need to rely on the skill and experience of the builder. After all, the effect of a latent defect will be equally debilitating to a subsequent purchaser as to a first owner, and the builder will be just as unable to justify his improper or substandard work.

For these reasons, the court was prepared to impose a duty of care on the builder to the plaintiff, who was a subsequent purchaser of a garage which the defendant had built for the plaintiff's predecessor and had sold to the plaintiff six months later, in circumstances where the plaintiff's loss consisted of structural problems with the garage itself, which manifested themselves only after the plaintiff had bought the garage. Lest it might be thought that the court's decision was opening a wider vista of liability than policy might require, Thayer J ended off the court's decision by attaching the following qualifications:

Our extension is limited to latent defects which become manifest after the subsequent owner's purchase, and which were not discoverable had a reasonable inspection of the structure been made prior to the purchase. [Secondly] the implied warranty of workmanlike quality for latent defects is limited to a reasonable period of time. Furthermore, the plaintiff still has the burden to show that the defect was caused by the defendant's workmanship, as opposed to being the result of age or ordinary wear and tear. Finally, we want to clarify that the duty inherent in an implied warranty of workmanlike quality is to perform in a workmanlike manner and in accordance with accepted standards.

Comment

It is not known what the House of Lords would have said if these cases had been cited to it in *D & F* and *Murphy*, but the fact that they were not certainly undermines the conclusions which they drew about American law by reference only to *East River* and *Aloe*.

The House of Lords was also not referred to in any of the American cases in which a local authority has been held liable for economic loss which could have been prevented if the local authority had carried out an inspection properly. These are considered in Chapter 8, para 8.2.

The above-mentioned policy considerations in favour of liability that were enunciated by Thayer J in the Supreme Court of New Hampshire in *Lempke v Dagenais* were referred to with approval, and influenced the courts' decisions, in the Supreme Court of Canada in *Winnipeg Condominium Corporation No 36 v Bird Construction Co* (1995) 121 DLR (4th) 193 (see para 7.6.3) and in the High Court of Australia in *Bryan v Maloney* (1995) 69 ALJR 375 (see para 7.6.4).

7.6.2 New Zealand cases

General

It has been noted *above* in para 7.6.1 that Lord Keith in *Murphy* dismissed the New Zealand Court of Appeal decision in *Bowen v Paramount Builders (Hamilton) Ltd* [1977] 1 NZLR 394, because it had followed the New York decision in *Quackenbush*, which has been undermined by the Supreme Court decision in *East River Steamship*. However, *Bowen* was more than a simple adoption of *Quackenbush*, and *dicta* in subsequent New Zealand decisions, some of which were cited in argument in *Murphy*, have made some important points in this area of the law. Significantly, the New Zealand courts approve of the House of Lords' decision in *Anns* and disagree with its approach in *D & F* and *Murphy*.

Bowen v Paramount

In *Bowen v Paramount Builders (Hamilton) Ltd* [1977] 1 NZLR 394, which was decided before *Anns*, the court held that a builder is liable in negligence to a subsequent purchaser for damage which then occurs in the building by reason of his carelessness in construction. The court regarded the plaintiff 's loss as physical damage, and not as pure economic loss. However, it is clear from some of the *dicta* that the court would have reached the same conclusion if it had characterised the damage as purely economic. Thus, Cooke J said (at p 422): "The issue is whether it makes a difference that the damage has been limited to the structure of the building itself. As a simple matter of fairness, there seems to be no reason why that should be so. . . . I do not see why the law of tort should necessarily stop short of recognising a duty not to put out carelessly a defective thing, nor any reason compelling the courts to withhold relief in tort from a plaintiff misled by the appearance of the thing into paying too much for it".

Other decisions

In subsequent cases, the New Zealand Court of Appeal has accepted that the plaintiff's loss in this type of situation is purely economic, but it has nevertheless held that the plaintiff is entitled to recover damages in tort for this loss from the negligent builder who created the defective building, or from the local authority who negligently failed to detect these defects. Examples follow.

Mount Albert Borough Council v Johnson [1979] 2 NZLR 234: The New Zealand Court of Appeal, in holding the local authority liable for the plaintiff house-purchaser's economic loss suffered by virtue of the house's defective foundations, which could have been prevented if the local authority had inspected the works properly, went further than the House of Lords had gone in *Anns* and held that there did not need to be any danger to the health or safety of the plaintiff or members of her family before the defendant could be made liable for her loss. At that time *Anns* had not yet been subjected to any criticism.

Stieller v Porirua City Council [1986] 1 NZLR 84: The New Zealand Court of Appeal, although aware of the criticisms which had been made of *Anns* in *Peabody* and *Sutherland* (see Chapter 3, para 3.3.3 and Chapter 8, para 8.2.2), nevertheless held the defendant council liable for the plaintiff house-purchaser's economic loss occasioned through defects in exterior cladding to his house, even though questions of safety and health did not arise. Interestingly, the court applied the very test propounded by Lord Keith in *Peabody* (ie "In determining whether or not a duty of care of a particular scope was incumbent on a defendant, it is material to take into consideration whether it is just and reasonable that it should be so"—see Chapter 2, para 2.4.2) but it reached the completely opposite conclusion to the House of Lords in *Peabody*.

Craig v East Coast Bays City Council [1986] 1 NZLR 99: The court held that the defendant council owed a duty of care to and was liable to the plaintiff in damages for the economic loss which he suffered when the council negligently exercised its planning powers and allowed someone to build a house in front of the plaintiff's house, thereby obscuring his view of the sea.

Brown v Heathcote County Council [1986] 1 NZLR 76: This case was subsequently upheld by the Privy Council—see Chapter 8. The New Zealand Court of Appeal's decision was delivered on the same day as its decisions in the last two cases mentioned above. Cooke P, after referring to a series of New Zealand cases on economic loss, said (at p 79): "When a New Zealand court is urged not to hold that a duty of care existed in a kind of factual situation not precisely covered by existing authority, the whole matter should be weighed against a background, and in the spirit of what is now a not inconsiderable body of indigenous New Zealand case law. One of its features is perhaps a certain simplicity".

With reference to the restriction which then existed in English law that liability would only attach if the defect in the building constituted a danger to the health or safety of occupants (the House of Lords' overruling of *Anns* in *Murphy* means that, in English law, the presence of such a danger will no longer assist a plaintiff), Cooke P said (at p 80): "In New Zealand, local authorities are concerned with matters going well beyond the range of personal health and safety: the preservation of community building and living standards, property values and amenities is part of their proper sphere. In this respect, the New Zealand position appears to be similar to the Canadian one. In the *Kamloops* case [see Chapter 8, para 8.4.3], the Supreme Court of Canada held that it would be too narrow an approach, in formulating a duty on a city respecting foundations under municipal bye-laws, to hold that it was limited to avoiding injury to the occupants or damage from the house sliding down the hill. I would respectfully follow that case in this country. One other general comment is that, while there is a great deal of valuable discussion in the Australian High Court *Caltex* [see Chapter 5, para 5.6] and *Sutherland* [see Chapter 8, para 8.2.2] cases, the variations between the ten individual judgments [in those two cases] limit the guidance that can be derived. In the end, I cannot avoid the conclusion that, in the negligence field, we in New Zealand will have to continue to hew our own way".

Askin v Knox [1989] 1 NZLR 248: Although, as the above-mentioned cases demonstrate, the New Zealand courts are prepared to hold that a builder or a local authority can be liable in tort to a remote purchaser or owner of a building for the economic loss suffered by that person in the form of the diminution in value of the building occasioned through the negligence of the builder or the local authority during the course of construction, it must not be thought that the New Zealand courts have jettisoned other established notions of the law of tort. As the decision in this case shows, the plaintiff still has to prove all of the elements of his case before the court will sanction a remedy for his economic loss.

In this case, the first defendant, Knox, was a builder who constructed a house for the plaintiffs, Mr and Mrs Askin, on land that they owned. In the course of digging the foundations, the defendant discovered that there had been a hollow which had apparently been filled with top soil. Consequently, he dug deeper than was usual. He dug down to a hard pan of light-coloured clay, which, in his view, was sufficient as a base for the house's foundations. The diggings were inspected by the local authority, which expressed satisfaction with the foundations, subject to the inclusion of a concrete slab in one corner of the house.

In later years, serious defects developed in the structure. A consulting engineer reported that the principal cause of the damage was the failure to backfill the creek correctly. Nevertheless, the plaintiffs' claim against the builder and the local authority failed. The Court of Appeal affirmed its right in principle to hold a builder or a local authority liable for this type of economic loss, but stated that proof of negligence is required before a builder or a local authority can be found liable in damages. The plaintiffs failed to discharge their onus of establishing negligence on the part of the defendants because, on the evidence, the court was satisfied that a reasonable builder or a reasonable local authority could have thought that the bottom of the trenches, together with the extra precaution of the slab in the one corner, provided reasonable solidity for the house's foundations.

Invercargill City Council v Hamlin [1994] 3 NZLR 513: The facts of this case were fairly typical. The plaintiff had, many years before this proceeding, purchased a section of land from a building company which also contracted to build a comparatively modest suburban house for the plaintiff. The land had been low-lying and wet. The relevant byelaws required the foundations to rest on a solid bottom at least twelve inches below the adjacent ground. During the course of construction the local authority's inspector inspected the foundations and approved them. In later years, when cracks and other defects appeared in the structure, a close inspection revealed that not only were the foundations defective, but also the inspector had been negligent in approving them.

As the builder was no longer in business by this time, the plaintiff commenced an action against the local authority for the recovery of the plaintiff's economic loss consisting of the diminution in the value of his house as a result of the inspector's negligence. In light of the established New Zealand law mentioned *above* on this topic, it is doubtful that the plaintiff's claim would have been contested—at least not up to the level of the New Zealand Court of Appeal, let alone in the Privy Council (see Chapter 8, para 8.4.2)—were it not for the fact that, in the intervening period, the House of Lords had rendered its decision in *Murphy v Brentwood District Council* [1991] 1 AC 398. Therefore, the local authority's argument before the New Zealand Court of Appeal was that that Court should alter the established New Zealand approach in cases of this sort in the light of the House of Lords' decision in *Murphy*.

Despite the almost indistinguishable facts of the two cases, the full bench of the New Zealand Court of Appeal unanimously refused to follow the House of Lords' decision in *Murphy*, and affirmed its own previous decisions in this field. Thus, Cooke P said (at p 519): "Whatever may be the position in the United Kingdom, homeowners in New Zealand do traditionally rely on local authorities to exercise reasonable care not to allow unstable houses to be built in breach of byelaws. The linked concepts of reliance and control have underlain New Zealand case law in this field from *Bowen* [see *above*] onwards".

Richardson J, in his judgment, emphasised certain factors that he believed distinguished the position in New Zealand from the position in England. Included in this list are the high proportion of occupier-owned housing in New Zealand, significant government support for private home building and home ownership, governmental regulation of the building industry through building byelaws and the fact that it is not common for house buyers, including those contracted with builders for the construction of houses, to commission engineering or architectural examinations or surveys. He said (at p 424): "The common law of New Zealand should reflect the kind of society we are and meet the needs of our society". In light of the above-mentioned factors that, in Richardson J's view, made the case special to New Zealand, he held that it was just and equitable for the defendant local authority to be under a duty of care to the plaintiff in discharging its responsibilities in relation to the inspection of houses under construction.

As this decision, strictly speaking, dealt with the exposure to liability of local authorities rather than builders, it is discussed more fully in Chapter 8, in considering whether local authorities should be liable to purchasers of buildings for the diminution in value resulting from latent defects that could have been prevented if the local authorities had not acted negligently in performing their building supervisory functions. It is not difficult to predict that the New Zealand courts would reach the same decision as they did in this case in a future case if the defendant was a builder or someone else who was involved in the construction or design of the house that was ultimately purchased by the plaintiff.

Commercial buildings

It is less predictable, however, whether a New Zealand court would reach the same conclusion if the building in question was a commercial building rather than a house. In *Invercargill City Council v Hamlin* [1994] 3 NZLR 513, Cooke P, after referring to the House of Lords' decision in *Junior Books Ltd v Veitchi Co Ltd* [1983] 1 AC 520 (see para 7.7), said (at p 520):

> I would interpolate that in this court we have not had to consider a similar case. Following the general New Zealand approach to duty of care questions, restated in *South Pacific Manufacturing Co Ltd v New Zealand Security Consultants and Investigations Ltd* [1992] 2 NZLR 282, it would be open to us to hold that in such a case of industrial construction, the network of contractual relationships normally provides sufficient avenues of redress to make the imposition of supervening tort duties not demanded. It might be said, in the words of Lord Goff in *Henderson v Merrett Syndicates Ltd* [1995] 2 AC 145 [see para 9.7.6] that there is no assumption of responsibility by the sub-contractor or supplier direct to the building owner, the parties having so structured their relationship that it is inconsistent with any assumption of responsibility.

In *South Pacific Manufacturing Co Ltd v New Zealand Security Consultants and Investigations Ltd* [1992] 2 NZLR 282, the court was concerned with two separate but similar appeals, namely the *South Pacific* case itself and *Mortensen v Laing*. In both cases the insured's liability under an insurance policy had been rejected by the insurer because the defendant, a private investigator engaged by the insurer, had reported to the insurer that his investigation revealed that the fire had been started deliberately by the insured. In due course it was established that the insured had not started the fire and that the investigator had been negligent in carrying out his investigation and making his report to the insurer.

The plaintiffs sued the investigators for the economic losses that they had sustained through their insurance coverage being denied. The New Zealand Court of Appeal rejected the plaintiffs' claims in the *South Pacific* appeal because they offended the relational economic loss exclusionary rule (see Chapter 5, para 5.5.3). In the *Mortensen v Laing* appeal, the court rejected the plaintiff's claim for a variety of other reasons (see Chapter 9, para 9.7.7), including the reason that, in cases where there has been a chain of commercial contracts, the plaintiff should pursue his contractual remedy against the person with whom he had a contract and should not be entitled to look to the law of tort to provide redress. Thus, Cooke P said (at p 303): "The insured has his ordinary remedy against the insurer if liability is wrongly declined as a result of a report by investigators. The proper vehicle for determining responsibility for the fire is a proceeding between insured and insurer. Such a proceeding provides the insured with a reasonable, if not an entirely comprehensive, remedy"; and Richardson J said (at p 308):

> If the insured have a remedy in contract against the insurer, they should exercise that remedy. If they do not have an adequate remedy, that is because they only paid a premium which gave them that lesser protection. In that situation I cannot see any justification for allowing them greater recovery through tort than they were prepared to pay for in contract.
>
> The second contract is between the insurer and the investigator. There too, the parties have their expressly or impliedly agreed remedies for any negligence in the performance of the contract. Those were the respective bargains that the parties made. Tort theory should remain consistent with contract policies. In public policy terms, I consider that where, as here, contracts cover the two relationships, those contracts should ordinarily control the allocation of risk unless special reasons are established to warrant a direct suit in tort. That accords, too, with *Simaan General Contracting Co v Pilkington Glass Ltd (No 2)* [1988] QB 758 [see para 7.3.6] where, for policy reasons, the English Court of Appeal concluded that any claims by (A) (Simaan) against (B) (Feal) and by (B) against (C) (Pilkington) could and should be pursued down the contractual chain and that there was no warrant for extending the law of negligence to impose direct liability in tort on (C) in favour of (A). No special factors such as those discussed in *Smith v Eric S Bush* [1990] 1 AC 831 [see para 9.7.3] have been advanced in this case.

These remarks, coupled with Cooke P's above-cited *dictum* in *Invercargill*, suggest that New Zealand courts would not readily impose a duty of care on a builder of a commercial building in favour of a remote purchaser for the purchaser's economic loss consisting of the diminution in value of the building by virtue of the emergence of latent defects, notwithstanding that those defects had been caused by the builder's negligence.

7.6.3 Canada

The starting point: Rivtow

The Supreme Court of Canada's decision in *Rivtow Marine Ltd v Washington Ironworks* (1973) 40 DLR (3d) 530 is summarised at the end of this chapter (para 7.7). The full bench of the Court, consisting of nine judges, was unanimous in holding that a manufacturer of a *non-dangerous* defective article is not liable in tort to the ultimate consumer or user for his economic loss consisting of the diminution in value of the product due to a defect created by the manufacturer's negligence. In this regard, the law of Canada was stated in terms that are the same as those that exist in England in relation to defective products or buildings as expressed by the House of Lords in *D & F Estates Ltd v Church Commissioner for England* [1989] 1 AC 177 and *Murphy v Brentwood District Council* [1991] 1 AC 398; and the law in Canada is still to this effect in relation to *non-dangerous* defects (see *below*).

An exception was suggested in *Rivtow* by two of the judges (Laskin and Hall JJ) in relation to *dangerous defects*. In their view, economic loss incurred by a subsequent owner or user of a defective product in taking steps to avert the physical harm that might materialise if no such steps were taken should be recoverable in tort as an exception to the general rule that they endorsed with the other judges. Thus, Laskin J said (at p 552):

> The case [ie *Rivtow*] is not one where a manufactured product proves to be merely defective, but rather one where, by reason of the defect, there is a foreseeable risk of physical harm from its use, and where the alert avoidance of such harm gives rise to economic loss. Prevention of threatened harm resulting directly in economic loss should not be treated differently from post-injury cure.

This partially dissenting view of Laskin and Hall JJ was approved by the House of Lords in *Anns* in 1977, but it was emphatically rejected in 1990 by the House of Lords in *Murphy*. In Canada, there have been some comments over the years suggesting that the minority view in *Rivtow* is commendable. For example, in *Canadian National Railway Co v Norsk Pacific Steamship Co Ltd* (1992) 91 DLR (4th) 289 (which is discussed extensively in Chapter 5), La Forest J said (at p 310): "In Laskin J's view [in *Rivtow*], the courts must be careful to avoid giving redress in tort for safe but shoddy products. Where the products are unsafe, however, tort may have a role; prevention of threatened harm resulting directly in economic loss should not be treated differently from post-injury treatment".

Prior to this, there had been other *dicta* that questioned the majority view in *Rivtow* (ie the view of seven of the judges that, even where a defendant has created a dangerous defect in a chattel or a building, he is not liable for the diminution in value of it suffered by someone with whom he did not have a contract). No doubts had, however, been expressed on the Court's unanimous view that no such liability should attach in respect of non-dangerous defects. Thus, in *City of Kamloops v Nielson* (1984) 10 DLR (4th) 641 (which is discussed further in Chapter 8), Wilson J said (at p 679): "The majority judgment of this court in *Rivtow* stands until such time as it may be reconsidered by a full panel of the court"; and in *Attorney General for Ontario v Fatehi* (1984) 15 DLR (4th) 132, Estey J said (at p 139): "The decision of the majority in *Rivtow* has been variously applied or rejected by the courts of this country. It is not possible to say whether the law of Canada, as reflected in the authorities to date, contemplates recovery for a pure economic loss in the sense of *Junior Books*" (which is also summarised at the end of this chapter). The opportunity to answer these questions came in late 1994 when the Supreme Court of Canada considered the building owners' claim in *Winnipeg Condominium Corporation No 36 v Bird Construction Co* (1995) 121 DLR (4th) 193.

7.6.3 Product liability—pure economic Loss

The current position: Winnipeg Condominium

In *Winnipeg Condominium Corporation No 36 v Bird Construction Co* (1995) 121 DLR (4th) 193, an apartment building had been constructed in 1972 and the plaintiff became the owner of it in 1978. In 1982, the plaintiff retained the original architects and a firm of structural engineers to inspect the building. They recommended some minor remedial work but advised that the stonework of the building was structurally sound. In 1989, a storey-high section of the exterior stone cladding, weighing a few tons, fell from the ninth-storey level of the building to the ground below. No one was injured. Following an inspection by an engineering consultant, the owner had the entire cladding removed and replaced at a cost in excess of $1.5 million.

In this proceeding, the owner/plaintiff sought to recover this cost from the builder, the cladding sub-contractor and the architect. The Supreme Court of Canada upheld the plaintiff's claim, but did so only because the defect in question was 'dangerous', and the plaintiff's economic loss consisted solely of expenditure to avert the risk of that danger materialising into actual physical harm. Thus, La Forest J, speaking for all seven judges of the panel, said (at p 199):

> The negligently supplied structure in this case was not merely shoddy; it was dangerous. In my view, this is important because the degree of danger to persons and other property created by the negligent construction of a building is a cornerstone of the policy analysis that must take place in determining whether the cost of repair of the building is recoverable in tort. A distinction can be drawn on a policy level between dangerous defects in buildings and merely shoddy construction in buildings. With respect to dangerous defects, compelling policy reasons exist for the imposition on contractors of tortious liability for the cost of repair of these defects.

La Forest J reinforced this approach by concluding (at p 203):

> Where a contractor (or any other person) is negligent in planning or constructing a building, and where that building is found to contain defects resulting from that negligence which pose a real and substantial danger to the occupants of the building, the reasonable costs of repairing the defects and putting the building back into a non-dangerous state are recoverable in tort by the occupants. The underlying rationale for this conclusion is that a person who participates in the construction of a large and permanent structure which, if negligently constructed, has the capacity to cause serious damage to other persons and property in the community should be held to a reasonable standard of care.

La Forest J reiterated this conclusion by saying (at p 216):

> I conclude that the law in Canada has now progressed to the point where it can be said that contractors (as well as sub-contractors, architects and engineers) who take part in the design and construction of a building will owe a duty in tort to subsequent purchasers of the building if it can be shown that it was foreseeable that a failure to take reasonable care in constructing the building would create defects that pose a substantial danger to the health and safety of the occupants. Where negligence is established and such defects manifest themselves

before any damage to persons or property occur, they should be liable for the reasonable cost of repairing the defects and putting the building back into a non-dangerous state.

Comment

The minority view of Laskin and Hall JJ in *Rivtow* has thus been vindicated. The focus in future cases involving 'dangerous' defects will be on the degree and type of danger that needs to exist before liability will attach.

Another area that is fertile for development is whether there has been any change in the unanimous decision of the Supreme Court in *Rivtow* in relation to defective but safe products. It seems clear that, at the moment, the law in Canada on this topic is as stated in *Rivtow*, and is therefore the same as the law in England as stated in *D & F* and *Murphy*. This comes through clearly in the emphasis that was laid in *Winnipeg Condominium* on the dangerousness of the defects as a precondition to founding liability, and on the slant that was placed on the *obiter dicta* in the judgment on this topic. Thus, La Forest J said (at p 199): "A distinction can be drawn on a policy level between dangerous defects in buildings and merely shoddy construction in buildings. With respect to dangerous defects, compelling policy reasons exist for the imposition on contractors of tortious liability for the cost of repair of these defects"; and at p 205 he said:

A contractor who enters into a contract with the original homeowner for the use of high-grade materials in the construction of the building will not be held liable to subsequent purchasers if the building does not meet these special contractual standards. However, such a contract cannot absolve the contractor from the duty in tort to subsequent owners to construct the building according to reasonable standards. [It is clear from other passages in La Forest's judgment that by 'reasonable standards' he meant the standard of creating a building that is not dangerous.]

La Forest J continued (at p 215):

Without entering into the question whether contractors should also in principle be held to owe a duty to subsequent purchasers for the cost of repairing non-dangerous defects in buildings, I note that the present case is distinguishable on a policy level from cases where the workmanship is merely shoddy or sub-standard, but not dangerously defective. In the latter class of cases, tort law serves to encourage the repair of dangerous defects and thereby to protect the bodily integrity of inhabitants of buildings. By contrast, the former class of cases brings into play the questions of quality of workmanship and fitness for purpose.

It is submitted that these *dicta*, coupled with the absence of any criticism of the unanimous decision of the Supreme Court in *Rivtow*, lead to the conclusion that that unanimous decision is still the law in Canada. That decision is to the effect that a person who manufactures and puts into circulation a defective (but not a dangerous) product will have no liability in tort to a purchaser or user who did not acquire the product under a contract with the manufacturer for the purchaser/user's economic loss consisting of the diminution in value of the defective product, notwithstanding that the defect was caused by the manufacturer's negligence. After the Supreme Court of Canada's decision in *Winnipeg Condominium*, there is little doubt that this principle applies also to 'non-dangerous' defects in buildings.

To this extent, the law in Canada is the same as the law in England, as expressed in *D & F* and in *Murphy*, despite the Supreme Court of Canada's criticism of those decisions. Ironically, in both *D & F* and *Murphy* the defects were not dangerous, which means that if either or both of the fact situations in those cases were to come up for decision in Canada, the court would be compelled, in accordance with the current Canadian law on this topic, to reach the same decision as the House of Lords reached in those cases; and, by the same token, it would have to reach a different conclusion to that reached by the High Court of Australia in *Bryan v Maloney* (1985) 182 CLR 109 (see para 7.6.4) because in that case the defect was not regarded as dangerous.

Although it is felt that the Supreme Court of Canada reached the right decision in *Winnipeg Condominium*, it is submitted that the court's judgment is both confused and confusing. First, La Forest J sought to distinguish the House of Lords' decision in *D & F Estates Ltd v Church Commissioners for England* [1989] 1 AC 177 on the ground that "it is inconsistent with recent Canadian decisions recognizing the possibility of concurrent contractual and tortious duties" (at p 204). With respect, this is a false hypothesis and an irrelevant consideration, because neither *D & F* nor *Winnipeg Condominium* had anything to do with concurrent liability. This point is discussed more fully in Chapter 10, para 10.2.

Secondly, La Forest J said that the House of Lords' decision in *D & F* was inconsistent with the Supreme Court of Canada's "continued application of the principles established in *Anns*". In making this statement, and in elaborating on it, La Forest J demonstrated a confusion between *rules, principles* or *concepts* and the *approach* or *test* that should be applied to ascertain those *rules, principles* or *concepts*. With reference to the 'two-stage *test*' that Lord Wilberforce enunciated in *Anns* [see Chapter 3, para 3.2.2], La Forest J said (at p 207): "Lord Wilberforce rejected the traditional broad exclusionary *rule* and instead proposed the following general *approach* to cases involving economic loss in tort".

After setting out a passage in *D & F* in which Lord Oliver disagreed with the *concept* (or *principle*) on which the House's decision in *Anns* had been founded, and after referring to the fact that Lord Bridge in *D & F* also expressed doubts about the *Anns* decision, La Forest J said (at p 209) (emphasis added):

> The reasons given by Lord Oliver and Lord Bridge in *D & F* were a signal that the days of the *Anns test* in England were numbered. This became apparent in *Murphy*, where the Law Lords explicitly rejected the two-part *test* suggested by Lord Wilberforce in *Anns* and restored the traditional broad exclusionary *rule* against recovery for pure economic loss in tort in the absence of a special relationship of reliance;

and on p 210 La Forest J described what he saw as the difference between the position in England and the position in Canada, as follows (emphasis added):

> In *Murphy*, Lord Bridge noted that the reasoning of the speeches in *D & F* has gone far to question the *principles* on which the *Anns* doctrine rests. By contrast, this court has not followed the House of Lords in repudiating the two-part *test* established by Lord Wilberforce in *Anns*. The *approach* proposed by Lord Wilberforce in *Anns* was adopted by this court in the *City of Kamloops v Nielsen* (1984) 10 DLR (4th) 641 where Wilson J suggested the following slightly modified version of the *Anns test*:
>> (1) is there a sufficiently close relationship between the parties, so that, in the reasonable contemplation of the defendant, carelessness on its part might cause damage to the plaintiff?
>> (2) if so, are there any considerations which ought to negative or limit the scope of the duty, the class of persons to whom it is owed or the damages to which a breach of it may give rise?

La Forest J has thus drawn conclusions from a comparison in which he was not comparing like with like. The criticisms that the House of Lords made in *D & F* and *Murphy* of its earlier decision in *Anns* were directed to the decision itself and to the *principles* or *concepts* on which it was founded, rather than to the *test* or *approach* that was applied (ie Lord Wilberforce's 'two-stage test'). Their Lordships' rejection of those principles had nothing to do with whether or not they approved of the *test* or *approach* that Lord Wilberforce had formulated in *Anns*. Therefore, the above-cited *dicta* of La Forest J in *Winnipeg Condominium* are inaccurate and are prone to be misleading because they suggest that the *test* that is applied dictates the result.

Thirdly, having stated the test that the Supreme Court of Canada favoured, La Forest J went on to apply that test in a manner that could be misleading in future cases. In asking whether there was a sufficiently close relationship between the parties so as to give rise to a *prima facie* duty of care in accordance with the first part of the test, La Forest J used foreseeability as the sole criterion. After setting out the question that needs to be asked under the first stage of the test, La Forest J said (at p 212) (emphasis added):

> In my view, it is reasonably *foreseeable* to contractors that, if they design or construct a building negligently, and if that building contains latent defects as a result of that negligence, subsequent purchasers of the building may suffer personal injury or damage to other property when those defects manifest themselves. A lack of contractual privity between the contractor and the inhabitants at the time the defect becomes manifest does not make the potential for injury any less *foreseeable*. By constructing the building negligently, contractors (or any other person responsible for the design and construction of a building) create a *foreseeable* danger that will threaten not only the original owner, but every inhabitant during the useful life of the building.
>
> In my view, the reasonable *likelihood* that a defect in a building will cause injury to its inhabitants is also sufficient to ground a contractor's duty in tort to subsequent purchasers of the building for the cost of repairing the defect if that defect is discovered prior to any injury and if it poses a real and substantial danger to the inhabitants of the building;

and at p 216 he concluded by saying:

> I conclude that the law in Canada has now progressed to the point where it can be said that contractors (as well as sub-contractors, architects and engineers) who take part in the design and construction of a building will owe a duty in tort to subsequent purchasers of the building if it can be shown that it was *foreseeable* that a failure to take reasonable care in constructing the building would create defects that pose a substantial danger to the health and safety of the occupants. . . .

The fault with this reasoning is that, to base the finding of even a *prima facie* duty of care under the first stage of the two-stage test purely on *foreseeability* of harm is contrary to established principle (see Chapter 2, para 2.2). It is also disconcerting and a departure from established principle that the concept of proximity was not included in La Forest J's analysis. Indeed, the word 'proximity' was not even mentioned. It is worthwhile contrasting this part of La Forest J's judgment with the main majority judgment of the High Court of Australia in *Bryan v Maloney* (see para 7.6.4).

Fourthly, La Forest J also made a false comparison with the position in English law when he said (at p 213):

> Under the law as developed in *D & F* and *Murphy*, a plaintiff who moves quickly and responsibly to fix a defect before it causes injury to persons or damage to property must do so at his or her own expense. By contrast, a plaintiff who, intentionally or through neglect, allows a defect to develop into an accident may benefit at law from the costly and potentially tragic consequences. In my view, this legal doctrine is difficult to justify because it serves to encourage, rather than discourage, reckless and hazardous behaviour.

La Forest J is thus saying that the House of Lords would have granted recovery to a plaintiff who, with knowledge of a latent defect, stood by and waited for actual damage to materialise. It must be pointed out, however, that the House of Lords did not say that such a plaintiff would be entitled to compensation. The view that their Lordships did express—namely, that neither such a plaintiff nor a plaintiff who, upon discovering a latent defect, incurs expenditure to avert the threatened harm is entitled to compensation—is indeed indefensible, except where the defect was of such a nature that it could reasonably have been expected to have been discovered upon an intermediate inspection (see Chapter 7). However, the above-cited observation of La Forest J is not to be found in the judgments of the House in *D & F* and *Murphy*.

Fifthly, in discussing the policy considerations that might negate the existence of a *prima facie* duty of care in accordance with the second part of the two-stage test, La Forest J's judgment demonstrates a confusion between certain important concepts. He said (at p 216):

> There are two primary and interrelated concerns raised by the recognition of a contractor's duty in tort to subsequent purchasers of buildings for the cost of repairing dangerous defects. The first is that warranties respecting quality of construction are primarily contractual in nature and cannot be easily defined or limited in tort. The second concern is that the recognition of such a duty interferes with the doctrine of *caveat emptor*.

In my view, these concerns are both merely versions of the more general and traditional concern that allowing recovery for economic loss in tort will subject a defendant to liability in an indeterminate amount for an indeterminate time to an indeterminate class.

It is submitted that the last-cited statement of La Forest J is incorrect. The indeterminacy concern is the by-product of the reluctance of countenancing the existence of legal rules under which there is an inability to determine in advance the existence of the number of possible claims, the size of the class of possible claimants to whom the defendant might be liable, the possible amount of money which the defendant might have to pay to those claimants or the length of time for which the defendant might be exposed to their claims (see further, Chapter 2, para 2.4.3).

These concerns are variously met by rules of law devised by the courts to determine proximity in the relationship between the defendant and the plaintiff (with regard to the indeterminate class concern); by certain (albeit very few) statutes that limit the amount of recoverable damages (in the case of the indeterminate amount concern); and by limitation acts (in the case of the indeterminate time concern).

The warranty of quality concern does not raise the same considerations as any of the components of the indeterminacy concern. The warranty of quality concern is based on the difficulty of deciding on the acceptable standard of quality of a particular product or building in a tort context, as La Forest J himself seemed to acknowledge in the passage cited *above*. In *Junior Books Ltd v Veitchi Co Ltd* [1983] AC 520 (see para 7.5.7), Lord Brandon (dissenting) expressed the concern clearly when he said (at p 551):

> In any case where a complaint was made by an ultimate consumer that a product made by some person with whom he himself had no contract was defective, by what standard of quality would the question of defectiveness fall to be decided? In the case of goods bought from a retailer, it could hardly be the standard prescribed by the contract between the retailer and the wholesaler, or between the wholesaler and the distributor, or between the distributor and the manufacturer, for the terms of such contracts would not even be known to the ultimate buyer. It follows that the question by what standard alleged defects in a product complained of by its ultimate user or consumer are to be judged remains entirely at large and cannot be given any just or satisfactory answer.

Thus it is submitted that, contrary to what La Forest J said in *Winnipeg Condominium*, the indeterminate liability concern is not the same as the warranty of quality concern, and that La Forest J's analysis of the situation is flawed. La Forest J said (at p 217):

> The duty to construct a building according to reasonable standards and without dangerous defects arises independently of the contractual stipulations between the original owner and the contractor because it arises from a duty to create the building safely and not merely according to contractual standards of quality.
>
> The tort duty to construct a building safely is thus a duty that is not parasitic upon any contractual duties between the contractor and the original owner. Seen in this way, no serious risk of indeterminate liability arises to an indeterminate

class because the potential class of claimants is limited to the very persons for whom the building is constructed, namely, the inhabitants of the building.

It is submitted that La Forest J is correct in saying that there is no risk of exposing the defendant to liability for the economic losses of an indeterminate class of claimants in this category of case, but he is wrong in saying that the reason for this conclusion is that the builder's duty in tort not to construct an unsafe building is not affected by his contract with the original owner. The real reason is that the range or identifiable class of possible plaintiffs and, hence, the extent of the defendant's potential liability to such persons for economic loss consisting of the diminution in value of the defective product or building, is determinable in advance, with the result that the indeterminate class spectre is either illusory or non-existent in this category of case (see para 7.5.7).

This still leaves open the question whether La Forest J dealt adequately with the warranty of quality concern. It is submitted that, on the one hand, he did do so by virtue of his not shying away from the task of determining an appropriate standard in tort, as Lord Brandon did in *Junior Books* (see *above*); but, on the other hand, it is unsatisfactory that he and the other judges in the Supreme Court seem to be willing to undertake this task only in respect of defects that they deem to be dangerous, but not in respect of 'non-dangerous' defects.

Lastly, it is submitted that La Forest J's pronouncements on the interrelationship between the indeterminacy concern and the *caveat emptor* rule are also misguided. Despite what La Forest J said, it is submitted that it is clear that the *caveat emptor* doctrine does not raise the same considerations as the indeterminacy concern. The *caveat emptor* doctrine is merely an example of the existence of a contract between the plaintiff and a third party under which the plaintiff has agreed not to sue the third party for certain losses (see further, Chapter 10, para 10.2.1). The question in a tort context in a case like *Winnipeg Condominium* is whether, and to what extent, the defendant builder should be entitled to the benefit of that contract in relation to his duty of care in tort to the plaintiff.

The answer to this question has nothing to do with devising rules to limit the possibility of the defendant being exposed to claims from an indeterminate class of claimants because, in this category of case, this concern is illusory or non-existent (see *above* and para 7.5.7). The answer depends on whether, in the circumstances of any particular case, the defect in question was of such a nature that it could reasonably have been expected to have been discovered by the plaintiff upon an intermediate inspection of the property carried out by the plaintiff. If so, and if it would have been reasonable in the circumstances to expect the plaintiff to carry out such an inspection, the defendant should not be held liable.

If, however, the defect was of such a nature that it could not reasonably have been expected to have been discovered on such an inspection (for example, the hidden defects in the foundations in *Murphy*), then the defendant should be held liable even if it was reasonable to expect the plaintiff to have made such an inspection. This principle was in fact recognised and applied by La Forest J in *Winnipeg Condominium*, when he said (at p 220):

> My conclusion that a subsequent purchaser is not the best placed to bear the risk of the emergence of latent defects is borne out by the facts of this case. It is significant that, when cracking first appeared in the mortar of the building in 1982, the Condominium Corporation actually hired the original architect of the building, along with a firm of structural engineers, to assess the condition of the mortar work and the exterior cladding. These experts failed to detect the latent defects that appear to have caused the cladding to fall in 1989.

For this reason, La Forest J held that the operation of the doctrine of *caveat emptor* between the plaintiff and the plaintiff's vendor (who was not the defendant) did not have the effect of negating the defendant's duty of care in tort in this case.

Conclusion

It is submitted that the Supreme Court of Canada reached the right decision in *Winnipeg Condominium* on the facts of the case, despite some questionable reasoning along the way. The unanimous decision of the Supreme Court of Canada in *Rivtow* relating to 'non-dangerous' defects has been left intact, and the minority view in that case relating to 'dangerous' defects has been endorsed. It remains to be seen what the Supreme Court of Canada will do when confronted with a case involving non-dangerous latent defects such as occurred in *D & F* and *Murphy* in England, or in *Bryan v Maloney* in Australia.

7.6.4 Australia

Introduction

The High Court of Australia in *Bryan v Maloney* (see *below*) has taken the bold step of adopting the approach of the New Zealand Court of Appeal (see *above*) in relation to a claim by a subsequent purchaser of a house against the original builder for the diminution in value caused by the builder's negligence in building the house. Unlike the Supreme Court of Canada (see *above*), this new head of liability is not restricted to compensation for the repair of defects that pose "a real and substantial danger" to the health and safety of the inhabitants of the building in question.

Bryan v Maloney

In *Bryan v Maloney* (1995) 69 ALJR 375, the defendant (Mr Bryan) built a house for a Mrs Manion in 1979. She subsequently sold it to a Mr and Mrs Quittenden who, in 1986, sold it to the plaintiff, Mrs Maloney. The plaintiff inspected the house three times before she bought it. She noticed no cracks or other defects. She concluded that it was "a good solid house" and she assumed that it had been built properly. She neither knew nor inquired about the identity of the builder.

About six months after the plaintiff had purchased the house, cracks began to appear in the walls. The reason for the cracks and the consequent damage was that the house had been built with footings that were inadequate to withstand the seasonal changes in the clay soil. The plaintiff sued the defendant for the cost of making good the defects. It was common ground that the defendant had been negligent in his construction of the house, that the damage sustained was a foreseeable consequence of his negligence, and that the damage sustained by the plaintiff was properly classified as pure economic loss consisting of the diminution in value of the house when the latent and previously unknown defects in its footings and structure first became manifest.

The sole remaining question, therefore, was whether the defendant builder owed the plaintiff, as a subsequent purchaser of the house, a relevant duty of care in the law of negligence. The High Court of Australia, by 4:1, answered this question in the affirmative. The main majority judgment was delivered by Mason CJ on behalf of himself, Deane and Gaudron JJ. No other case at the High Court level in Australia was directly on point. Their Honours approached the issue by way of analogy with the duty of care that existed between the defendant and the original owner in contract and in tort, and by considering whether there was sufficient proximity between the defendant and the plaintiff based on assumption of responsibility, causation, foreseeability of reliance and the opportunity for an intermediate inspection that would be likely to reveal the defects in question. They also considered whether the policy considerations which are usually put forward to limit duties of care in relation to economic loss are applicable in this category of cases. Mason CJ said (at p 380):

> The policy considerations underlying the reluctance of the courts to recognise a relationship of proximity and a consequent duty of care in cases of mere economic loss are inapplicable to a relationship of the kind which existed between Mr Bryan [the defendant] and Mrs Manion [the original owner] with regard to the kind of economic loss sustained by Mrs Maloney [the plaintiff]. Thus, there is no basis for thinking that recognition of a relationship of proximity between a builder and the first owner, with respect to that particular kind of economic loss, would give rise to the type of liability in an indeterminate amount for an indeterminate time to an indeterminate class which the courts are reluctant to recognise. Again, in circumstances where the builder is under a duty of care to the first owner to avoid physical injury to that owner's person or property by reason of the inadequacy of the footings, there can be no real question of inconsistency between the existence of a relationship of proximity with respect to that particular kind of economic loss and the legitimate pursuit by the builder of his own financial interests. [See further, Chapter 1, para 1.4.3.]

Mason CJ continued with this analysis by stating that *prima facie* a relationship of proximity also existed between the defendant and persons other than the original owner, including the plaintiff, who might sustain *physical injury* to person or property as a consequence of a collapse of part of the house as a result of inadequate footings constructed by the defendant. He then continued (at p 381):

It is in the context of the above-mentioned relationship of proximity that one must determine whether the relationship which exists between a professional builder of a house and a subsequent owner possesses the requisite degree of proximity to give rise to a duty to take reasonable care on the part of the builder to avoid the kind of economic loss sustained by Mrs Maloney in the present case.

In considering whether sufficient proximity can exist in this type of situation, Mason CJ said (at p 381):

> It is likely that the only connection between such a builder and such a subsequent owner will be the house itself. Nonetheless, the relationship between them is marked by proximity in a number of important respects. The connecting link of the house is itself a substantial one. It is a permanent structure to be used indefinitely and, in this country, is likely to represent one of the most significant investments which the subsequent owner will make during his lifetime. It is obviously foreseeable by a builder that the negligent construction of the house with inadequate footings is likely to cause economic loss of the kind sustained by Mrs Maloney when the inadequacy of the footings first becomes manifest. When there is no intervening negligence or other causative event, the causal proximity between the loss and the builder's lack of reasonable care is unextinguished by either lapse of time or change of ownership.

Mason CJ then considered what difference, if any, it would make if the plaintiff's loss was purely economic. He said (at p 381):

> The only factor which arguably precludes the recognition of a relevant relationship of proximity between builder and subsequent owner for the purpose of the present case is the kind of damage involved, namely, mere economic loss. It is important to bear in mind the particular kind of economic loss involved. The distinction between that kind of economic loss and ordinary physical damage to property is an essentially technical one. The policy considerations underlying the reluctance of the courts to recognise a relationship of proximity and a consequential duty of care in cases of mere economic loss are largely inapplicable to the relationship between builder and subsequent owner with regard to that particular kind of economic loss.

Mason CJ elaborated on the policy issues arising in this type of case by saying (at p 381):

> There can be no question of inconsistency with the builder's legitimate pursuit of his own financial interests, since the builder owed a duty of care to the first owner with respect to such loss. In circumstances where the particular kind of economic loss is that sustained by an owner of a house on the occasion when the inadequacy of the footings first becomes manifest, there is no basis for thinking that recognition of a relevant relationship of proximity between the builder and that owner would be more likely to give rise to liability in an indeterminate amount to an indeterminate class than does recognition of such an element of proximity in the relationship between the builder and the first owner.

Mason CJ also took into account the other factors that are relevant to the question whether a duty of care should be held to exist in this type of case, namely, foreseeability of reliance and whether an intermediate inspection would be likely to reveal the defects. He said (at p 382):

397

Upon analysis, the relationship between a builder and a subsequent owner with respect to this particular kind of economic loss is, like that between the builder and the first owner, marked by the kind of assumption of responsibility and known reliance which is commonly present in the categories of case in which a relationship of proximity exists with respect to pure economic loss. A builder of a house undertakes the responsibility of erecting a structure on the basis that its footings are adequate to support it for a period during which it is likely that there will be one or more subsequent owners. Such a subsequent owner will ordinarily have less opportunity to inspect and test the footings than the first owner. Any builder should be aware that such a subsequent owner will be likely to assume that the house has been competently built and that the footings are in fact adequate.

Mason CJ thus reached the conclusion that there was no reason to rule out the existence of a duty of care by the defendant to the plaintiff in this case for the plaintiff's economic loss. He said (at p 382):

Ultimately, it seems to us that, from the point of view of proximity, the similarities in the relationship between the builder and the first owner, and the relationship between the builder and a subsequent owner with regard to the particular kind of economic loss sustained by the plaintiff in this case, are of much greater significance than the differences to which attention has been drawn, namely the absence of direct contact and the possibly extended time in which liability might arise. Both relationships are characterised to a comparable extent by assumption of responsibility on the part of the builder and likely reliance on the part of the owner. No distinction can be drawn between the two relationships in so far as foreseeability of the particular kind of economic loss is concerned, and, in the absence of intervening negligence, the causal proximity is the same regardless of whether the owner in question is the first owner or a subsequent owner. In the case of both relationships, the policy considerations which ordinarily militate against the recognition of a relationship of proximity and a consequent duty of care with respect to pure economic loss are insignificant. Moreover, there are persuasive policy reasons supporting the recognition of a relationship of proximity between the builder and a subsequent owner of an ordinary dwelling-house with respect to this particular kind of economic loss.

In relation to the last-mentioned point (ie policy considerations in favour of liability), Mason CJ referred with approval to the Supreme Court of New Hampshire's decision in *Lempke v Dagenais* (1988) 547 A (2d) 290, which is considered in para 7.6.1, *above*. Lastly, their Honours endorsed Lord Denning MR's "impossible distinction" aphorism in *Dutton v Bognor Regis Urban District Council* [1972] 1 QB 373 (see para 7.2, *above*) and added the following observation (at p 383):

It is difficult to see why, as a matter of principle, policy or common sense, a negligent builder should be liable for ordinary physical injury caused to any person or to other property by reason of the collapse of a building by reason of the inadequacy of the foundations, but not be liable to the owner of the building for the cost of remedial work necessary to remedy that inadequacy and to avert such damage.

Comment

This decision is to be applauded for its common sense and pragmatic approach. Clearly, the full scope of the doctrine will have to be worked out in later cases when different variants present themselves for decision. For example, what, if any, effect would an exclusion clause in the contract between the builder and the first owner have on the builder's liability in tort to a subsequent owner, or what would the position be if the building was a commercial building rather than a dwelling-house? Mason CJ seemed to be at pains to try to limit the *ratio* of the decision to houses, and both his and the other majority judgment dwelt on the fact that the contract between the builders/defendant and the original purchasers did not contain any limitations on the defendant's liability.

Their Honours were just as pragmatic in their treatment of the second aspect of the indeterminacy mantra (exposure to liability for an indeterminate time), which could not simply be dismissed as being inapplicable to this category of case. Mason CJ said (at p 381):

> It is true that, in so far as 'an indeterminate time' is concerned, the time span in which liability to a subsequent owner might arise could be greater than if liability were restricted to the first owner. Nonetheless, the extent of that time span would be limited by the element of reasonableness both in the requirement that damage be foreseeable and in the content of the duty of care. Moreover, any difference in duration between liability to the first owner and liability to a subsequent owner is likely to do no more than reflect the chance element of whether and when the first owner disposes of the house.

Their Honours were also very conscious of the fact that their decision was completely contrary to the views of the members of the House of Lords in *D & F Estates Ltd v Church Commissioners* [1989] 1 AC 177 and *Murphy v Brentwood District Council* [1991] 1 AC 398. Mason CJ dispensed with those decisions by saying (at p 382): "Their Lordships' view in that regard seems to us to have rested upon a narrower view of the scope of the modern law of negligence and a more rigid compartmentalisation of contract and tort than is acceptable under the law of this country".

It is difficult to predict whether this swingeing comment will have any effect on the members of the House of Lords if a similar case should come before them again. On the one hand, one would hope that this would be the case, given some of the recent progressive decisions of the House of Lords in cases like *Henderson v Merrett Syndicates Ltd* [1995] 2 AC 145 (see Chapter 9, para 9.7.6) and *White v Jones* [1995] 2 AC 207 (see Chapter 9, para 9.7.5) and given the state of the law in Australia, New Zealand, Canada and the USA, and the Privy Council's decision in *Invercargill City Council v Hamlin* [1996] AC 624. On the other hand, however, Lord Goff made some unhelpful and uncalled-for comments in this regard in *Henderson v Merrett Syndicates Ltd* [1995] 2 AC 145 (see para 7.3.6, *above*).

Lastly, it must be noted that, despite the expansive language used in the main majority judgment (in *Bryan v Maloney*), their Honours not only went out of their way to try to restrict their reasoning to dwelling-houses (see *above*), but they also stated expressly that their reasoning did not apply to defects in chattels. Thus, Mason CJ said (at p 383):

It should be apparent from what has been written above that the decision in this case turns, to no small extent, on the particular kind of economic loss involved, namely, the diminution in value of a house when the inadequacy of its footings first becomes manifest by reason of consequent damage to the fabric of the house. That being so, the decision in this case is not directly decisive of the question whether a relevant relationship of proximity exists in other categories of case or as regards other kinds of damage. In particular, the decision in this case should not be seen as determinative of the question whether a relationship of proximity can, in some circumstances, exist between the manufacturer and the purchaser or subsequent owner of a chattel in respect of the diminution in the value of the chattel which is sustained when a latent defect in it first becomes manifest.

Subsequent decisions

Since the High Court of Australia's decision in *Bryan v Maloney*, there have been comments by certain judges in state courts questioning the basis of the High Court's reasoning.

Woollahra Council v Sved

An example is *Woollahra Municipal Council v Sved & Others* (1996) 40 NSWLR 101, in the New South Wales Court of Appeal. Here, the plaintiffs, Mr and Mrs Sved, discovered certain defects in their house soon after they had bought it. These defects related to the design of the house's drainage system, and resulted in the house becoming severely flooded after heavy rainstorms.

The Court found as a fact that, in contrast to the defects in *Bryan v Maloney*, these defects would have been discoverable on a pre-purchase inspection. The Court also found as a fact that the plaintiffs deliberately elected not to have an independent inspection and decided instead to make completion of the contract dependent on the issue of a particular certificate from the local council (a 's 317A Certificate'). The effect of such a certificate is to convey a representation by the local council that in all respects a building complies with the Local Government Act, the ordinances made under it and the plans and specifications, if any, that had been approved by the council.

In these circumstances, the plaintiffs' case against the builder did not succeed (by 2:1). One of the majority judges, Clarke JA, after referring extensively to the decision of the High Court in *Bryan v Maloney*, said (at p 133):

> The authority of the decision does not extend to the case of damage, which, although discoverable on a reasonable inspection, was not in fact discovered until after the plaintiff had purchased the property. There is no evidence that the Sveds relied on the Di Balasios [the builders]. Indeed, the evidence is to the contrary. The Sveds were aware that they could protect themselves against the risk that they would suffer financial loss if the building had been constructed defectively. They knew that they could arrange for an inspection of the premises by a building contractor or they could seek to protect themselves by the inclusion of

a term in the contract of purchase. They deliberately elected not to have an independent inspection and decided that they would protect themselves by making completion of the contract dependent on the issuance of a s 317A Certificate. This may not have been entirely wise, but that is presently of little moment. What matters is that the Sveds knew of the availability of steps which would protect them from the risk of financial loss and they only took one of them, namely, their insistence on the inclusion of a clause in the contract of purchase which entitled them to rescind it if a s 317A Certificate did not issue.

Bryan deals with a latent defect, a fact which appeared to be of significance in the reasoning of the majority. In this case, in contrast, many of the defects would have been discoverable upon a reasonably comprehensive inspection. In the light of these differences, *Bryan* does not govern the present case. Indeed, I am bound to say that the narrow ambit of the proximity relationship found in *Bryan* seems to me, with respect, to be more reflective of a determination based upon the particular facts rather than one applicable to a broad category of cases.

It is submitted that the above-mentioned reasons that the Court stated for distinguishing its decision in *Sved* from the High Court's decision in *Bryan v Maloney* are sound. In fact, far from undermining the reasoning in *Bryan*, these differences bolster it because, in this category of cases, the key determinant of the question whether a duty of care should be imposed on a builder, architect, engineer or local authority for the economic loss suffered by a remote purchaser through the building containing defects in construction or design is whether the defect in question was of such a nature that it could not reasonably have been expected to have been revealed by an intermediate inspection of the property before the plaintiff purchased it (see paras 7.5.1, 7.5.2 and 7.5.3). Nevertheless, in *Sved*, Clarke JA thought fit to criticise the reasoning of the majority in *Bryan v Maloney*. This can be seen, first, in the last sentence of the passage cited *above* from Clarke JA's judgment. He continued with this theme later on in his judgment by saying (at p 137):

> Because *Bryan* concerned a claim bearing general characteristics similar to the one under consideration, it is to that authority which I should turn for guidance. While the majority does not expressly base liability solely on reliance and assumption of responsibility, they undoubtedly accorded those factors fundamental importance. In essence, they adopted the premise that a builder should be taken to know that a subsequent owner will assume that the house was competently built, in the absence of clear evidence of defects, and therefore assumes a responsibility to that subsequent owner. For his or her part, the subsequent owner should be taken to have relied on the builder to construct the building properly.
>
> These conclusions involve a significant development of the concepts of known reliance and assumption of responsibility. Further, they were not based upon evidence, but on a number of perceptions. One, at least, of these perceptions troubles me. When their Honours said that 'such a subsequent owner is likely to be unskilled in building matters and inexperienced in the niceties of real property investment', they were clearly not adverting to evidence in the case. Nonetheless, they regarded these factors as important considerations. I do not know whether the perceptions there expressed are correct or not. Frankly, I doubt that they are. Most purchasers in New South Wales have, until recently,

retained solicitors. Now, some may use conveyancers. Both would, I venture to suggest, advise their clients about the desirability of an independent inspection of the home to be purchased. It may be that I am overstating the position, but what I would seek to emphasise is that no assumption should be made as to the knowledge, or the incidence, of the use of solicitors or building inspectors by potential home purchasers in the absence of evidence.

Later, Clarke JA continued with this theme by saying (at p 138):

There is a danger in courts assuming, without evidence, that something does, or may, exist or not exist, particularly when the subject matter of the assumption is not strictly within judicial knowledge. That danger is magnified where the judicial perception guides a court to a decision laying down a principle to be applied generally or even in a restricted category of case.

He then added the following further, but related, criticism (at p 138):

It is to be observed that neither express, known reliance nor assumption of responsibility were proved in *Bryan*. It is true that Mrs Maloney [the plaintiff] assumed that the home had been properly constructed, but that is a concept quite different from the known reliance spoken of in *Hedley Byrne*. Again, the assumption of responsibility by the builder bears little relationship to the assumption of responsibility discussed in the context of claims in tort against professional advisors. What the majority say [in *Bryan v Maloney*] could, for convenience, be characterised as presumed assumption of responsibility and general (as opposed to specific) reliance. These are concepts which appear to be relatively well understood in New Zealand (see *Invercargill City Council v Hamlin* [see para 7.6.2]). These have not, to my knowledge, received the same attention in Australia. It is true that, in the context of claims for economic loss, the importance of reliance and the assumption of responsibility (usually by a course of conduct) by public authorities was discussed at length by Mason J in *Council of the Shire of Sutherland v Heyman* [see para 8.2.2], but what was said by the majority on these two subjects in *Bryan* represents a significant advance on that discussion.

Although I have found it difficult to understand by reference to what evidence the court (in *Bryan*) was able to reach its conclusions on reliance and assumption of responsibility, these two elements seem to be at the heart of the decision of the majority. It follows that I must recognise, for the purposes of deciding this case, that in circumstances such as arose in *Bryan*, a builder will be taken to have assumed responsibility to a subsequent purchaser who, for his or her part, will be taken to have relied on the builder. So much is straightforward. What is not so simple is whether the presumption of reliance and assumption of responsibility may be displaced and, if so, to determine what facts should lead a court to conclude that there was neither the relevant reliance nor assumption of responsibility.

These comments represent a bit of an overreaction to the change in the law that was brought about in Australia by the High Court's decision in *Bryan v Maloney*. It is submitted that the answer to the possible weaknesses in that decision which Clarke JA identified in *Sved* lies in the point made *above*, namely, that the principle of *Bryan* applies only in cases where the defect is latent and is of such a nature that it could not reasonably be expected to be revealed on an intermediate inspection of the property by the purchaser before buying it. Only in those cases will it be proper to attribute an assumption of responsibility to the builder for the diminution in value of the property in the hands of a subsequent purchaser when the defect becomes patent, and only in those cases will it be reasonable for the subsequent purchaser to be able to place general reliance on the builder and to be entitled to be compensated by the builder for that economic loss even though the subsequent purchaser did not carry out an intermediate inspection of the property before buying it. It is submitted that this principle, although perhaps not as clearly spelt out as one might have liked, clearly did underlie the reasoning of the majority in *Bryan v Maloney*, and that their decision would have been different if the defects would have been such that they would have been discoverable on an intermediate inspection, like the defects in *Sved*. Therefore, it is submitted that the decisions of the courts in *Bryan* and *Sved* respectively are consistent with each other and that Clarke JA's above-noted criticisms of the majority reasoning in *Bryan* are misplaced.

Zumpano v Montagnese

Another case in which criticism has been levelled at the High Court's decision in *Bryan v Maloney* is *Zumpano v Montagnese* (1997) Aust Torts Reports 81-406, in the Victoria Court of Appeal. Here, the defendants, Mr and Mrs Zumpano, were professional builders who built a house for themselves as their family home and lived in it for a time before selling it to the plaintiffs, Mr and Mrs Montagnese. About four years later, the plaintiffs discovered that a boundary trap had not been installed in the house's sewerage works by the plumber whom the defendants had engaged to do the plumbing work when the house was built.

The plaintiffs' claim against the defendants for their economic loss, consisting of the diminution in value of the house by virtue of the absence of a boundary trap in the sewerage system when the house was built, was rejected by the Court. First, all three of the judges concurred in holding that there was no claim against the builders because, on ordinary principles, they were not to be held answerable for the default of their independent contractor in circumstances where, as here, they were obliged by law to engage a plumber to carry out the sewerage works and where, as here, there was no suggestion that the defendants had been negligent in their choice of plumber: he was fully licensed and appeared to be competent.

One of the judges, Brooking JA, went further and held that the defendants did not in any event owe a duty of care in tort to the plaintiffs for the plaintiffs' economic loss because, in his view, the decision of the High Court in *Bryan v Maloney* is confined to cases where the defendant builder erected the house under a contract for the then owner of the land, and excludes cases of a builder who erected a house initially for his own occupation. He said (at p 63-712):

> In my opinion, both the joint judgment of Mason CJ, Dean and Gaudron JJ and the Judgment of Toohey J treat the circumstance that the builder erected the house under a contract as one of the circumstances founding the duty of care.

403

All four judges seem to me to proceed from the duty of care to guard against physical injury and the duty of care to guard against economic loss owed by the builder to the [original] building owner, to the corresponding duties of care owed by the builder to a purchaser from the [original] building owner, or a subsequent purchaser. Although it is not possible to be certain on the point, it seems to me that their Honours treated the duty held to exist in *Bryan v Maloney* as a legitimate extension of the duty or duties of care to which the builder was already subjected in consequence of his relationship with the [original] building owner, and that the decision would not have been the same had this element been absent.

A different view has been taken in New Zealand in the case of *Chase v De Groot* [1994] 1 NZLR 613. For an Australian judge, the question must be determined by careful consideration of the majority judgment in *Bryan v Maloney*; and, as I have said, such consideration shows in my opinion that a builder who erects a house otherwise than under a contract does not come under the duty of care recognised in *Bryan v Maloney*. I do not regard what was said, or not said, in *Woollahra v Sved* [see *above*] as standing in the way of the view that *Bryan v Maloney* is confined to builders who built under contract. The question is not discussed in *Sved*.

It is submitted that this *dictum* involves an unduly restrictive interpretation of the High Court's reasoning in *Bryan v Maloney*. In any event, it is contrary to the established principle that, as between contracting parties, a duty of care in tort can arise concurrently with a duty of care in contract if the preconditions for the existence of such a duty in tort are present, and the plaintiff will be prevented from pursuing the remedy in tort only if, and to the extent that, it has been excluded by the terms of the contract.

This was only one of Brooking JA's criticisms of *Bryan v Maloney*. He felt that it is a decision that raises more questions than it answers and should be reconsidered in the future. He said (at p 63-703): "A large number of questions arise about the scope of *Bryan v Maloney*. They include questions which may be grouped under the following twelve headings". Brooking JA then proceeded to identify a large number of questions which were not specifically answered in *Bryan v Maloney*, such as the kinds of buildings covered by it, the type of defects and the significance of the terms of the contract between the builder and the first owner. Brooking JA also referred to the fact that some academics have criticised the possible breadth of the doctrine formulated in *Bryan v Maloney*, and he said, with apparent approval: "Some learned commentators evidently believe that, with its decision, the High Court has opened Pandora's Box, visiting on builders all the evils of the world, although the commentaries suggest that there is no more agreement about the limits of the decision than there is about what the lidded vase carried by Pandora really contained".

It is submitted that, whilst Brooking JA is correct in stating that the High Court's decision in *Bryan v Maloney* does not provide the answers to the questions that he has identified, this is not a valid reason for suggesting that the decision ought to be reconsidered by the High Court. As noted *above* in the commentary on the *Sved* case, it is submitted that the doctrine of *Bryan v Maloney* is, and was intended by the High Court to be, restricted to those cases in which the defect created by the builder, architect, engineer or local authority was latent and would not reasonably have been discovered on an intermediate inspection; and, indeed, the decision of the New South Wales Court of Appeal in *Sved* testifies to this. Thus confined, it is submitted that the other variations on a theme identified by Brooking JA in *Zumpano* will be able to be resolved quite easily by judges in due course when appropriate fact-situations present themselves for decision. In this regard, it is submitted that it is worthwhile to bear in mind the following words of Stephen J in *Caltex Oil (Australia) Pty Ltd v The Dredge Willemstad* (1975) 136 CLR 529 (see Chapter 2, para 2.3.2): "The articulation, through the cases, of situations which denote sufficient proximity will provide a body of precedent productive of the necessary certainty".

7.7   Relevant cases

Quackenbush v Ford Motor Co (1915) 153 NYS 131: The plaintiff had purchased from a third party a car which had been manufactured by the defendant. While she was driving it, it went out of control and ran over an embankment. The car was badly damaged, but the plaintiff was not injured. She alleged that the brakes were defective and sued the defendant manufacturer for the cost of repairing the car. Ford conceded that if the plaintiff had been injured, it would have been liable to compensate her for such injuries and for the damage to her car, but not if only the car was damaged. The court rejected this distinction by saying: "We are asked to hold that the manufacturer's duty is made to depend, not upon the question of the inherent danger of the enginery which he places in the public highways, but upon the result of the accident which grows out of his faults in construction. We think that this is not the rule. We think that the manufacturer's duty depends, not upon the result of the accident, but upon the fact that his failure properly to construct the car resulted in the accident". The court therefore held that the defendant was liable to compensate the plaintiff for the cost of repairing the car.

With regard to the interrelationship between this liability and any contractual warranties, the court said: "The suggestion that this doctrine enlarges the liability of the manufacturer beyond what he assumes in warranting the machine is, in our opinion, without force. The contract of warranty simply provides for the quality of workmanship and materials. The plaintiff would have been entitled to have the defective brakes replaced if she had discovered the defect and no accident had resulted; but there was a relationship created by reason of the inherent danger to the public in sending out a defective machine without taking proper precautions to determine its safety. The plaintiff is entitled to recover the damages sustained under this new relation entirely independent of the contractual relation between the manufacturer and the original purchaser. The two are not inconsistent rights. The one provides for securing what was contemplated in the transaction of purchase and sale. The other takes care of the damages sustained because of the failure of the manufacturer to perform a duty which he owed to the original purchaser in common with the public generally".

Trans World Airlines v Curtiss-Wright Corp and Others (1955) 148 NYS (2d) 284: The plaintiff had purchased a number of aeroplanes from their manufacturer, Lockheed Aircraft Corporation. All of them were fitted with engines which had been manufactured by the defendant, Curtiss-Wright. When one such aeroplane crashed the plaintiff took the rest of them out of service for checking. It was found that all of the engines were defective and required repairs. The plaintiff sought to recover the cost of such repairs from the defendant manufacturer of the engines.

The New York Supreme Court rejected the plaintiff's claim. Eder J said (at p 287): "It has always been the general rule that the only person liable for damages caused by defects in goods sold is the immediate seller by virtue of express or implied warranty to the immediate buyer. Any other rule would hamper the enterprising manufacturer whose ingenuity was the chief factor in causing the economy to expand. It would make it difficult to measure the extent of his responsibility, and no prudent man would engage in such occupations upon such conditions. It is safer and wiser to confine such liabilities to the parties immediately concerned. This general rule is the doctrine of privity of contract".

The plaintiff placed reliance on *Quackenbush*, but the court held that it was distinguishable because there an accident actually did occur, whereas in the present case, so far as the other defective engines were concerned, this was not the case. Eder J said (at p 290): "Until there is an accident there can be no loss arising from breach of this duty, ie negligence, as distinguished from warranty. Though negligence may endanger the person or property of another, no actionable wrong is committed if the danger is averted. The damage asserted by TWA is for the replacement cost of allegedly inferior engines—a matter of qualitative inadequacy in a product purchased from Lockheed, a proper subject for a claim of breach of warranty, pure and simple. It is true that when the engines 'failed to operate', the planes became 'imminently dangerous'; but the danger was 'averted'. There was no accident".

Eder J summed up his views by saying: "If the ultimate user were allowed to sue the manufacturer in negligence merely because an article with latent defects turned out to be bad when used in 'regular service' without any accident occurring, there would be nothing left of the citadel of privity and not much scope for the law of warranty. There seems to me to be good reason for maintaining that, short of an accident, the citadel should be preserved. Manufacturers would be subject to indiscriminate lawsuits by persons having no contractual relations with them, persons who could thereby escape the limitations, if any, agreed upon in their contract of purchase. Damages for inferior quality, *per se*, should better be left to suits between vendors and purchasers since they depend on the terms of the bargain between them".

Dutton v Bognor Regis Urban District Council [1972] 1 KB 372: The plaintiff was the second purchaser of a house which was less than two years old. Soon after the plaintiff moved in, serious cracks developed in the walls and the ceiling, the staircase slipped and the doors and windows would not close. An investigation showed that this was due to subsidence of an internal wall which, in turn, was due to the fact that that wall had inadequate foundations. At an early stage in the building works one of the council's building inspectors inspected the excavations for the foundations and approved them. However, he did so negligently in that he failed to detect, as he would have done if he had made a careful inspection, that the foundations were constructed upon the remains of an old rubbish tip, so that the foundations should have had extra reinforcements. The builder was aware of this, but had not told the inspector.

The plaintiff sued both the builder and the council's inspector for the cost of the repairs and depreciation in the value of the house. The builder claimed that he was exempted from liability by the decisions of *Bottomley v Bannister* [1932] 1 KB 458 and *Otto v Bolton and Morris* [1936] 2 KB 46, which are considered in Chapter 6, para 6.6.1. For this reason the plaintiff settled her claim against the builder. However, she continued with her claim against the council. The court held in her favour.

The plaintiff's claim against the council was novel. The 'nonfeasance' aspects of the council's negligence are considered in Chapter 8, para 8.2, where it is also noted that this case has been overruled by the House of Lords in *Murphy v Brentwood District Council* [1991] 1 AC 398. That overruling applies both to the decision itself and to the characterisation by the court of the damage to the plaintiff's house as being not economic loss. In particular, the distinction which Denning MR labelled as 'impossible' in the passage which is set out at the beginning of this chapter in para 7.2 has been totally rejected. It should also be noted that the concession which the plaintiff made to the builder, based on his reliance on 'the *Bottomley* principle', need no longer be made, in accordance with the discussion in Chapter 6, para 6.6.1.

Rivtow Marine Ltd v Washington Iron Works (1973) 40 DLR (3d) 530: The plaintiff was the charterer by demise of a log barge which was fitted with two pintel type cranes for the loading and unloading of logs. The barge builder had bought the cranes from the second defendant, Walkem Machinery & Equipment Ltd, who had, in turn, bought them from their manufacturer, the first defendant. Other cranes of the same design had been installed on barges belonging to other logging companies. One of these cranes developed cracks. Both defendants were informed, but they failed to share this information with the plaintiff. Those cracks were repaired, but a few months later that crane collapsed, killing its operator. The plaintiff heard about this and immediately had its cranes surveyed. Cracks were discovered. This led to a complete dismantling of the cranes, modifications, repairs and re-assembly. This took a month, during which time the plaintiff's barge stood idle in harbour.

The plaintiff sued the first defendant as manufacturer and the second defendant as distributor for damages for the cost of repairs to the cranes on its barge and for loss of use of the barge during the repair period, which happened to coincide with the most profitable period of logging operations throughout the whole year. The Supreme Court of Canada, by a majority of 7:2, rejected the first of these claims, but was unanimous in upholding the second of them.

On the first of these issues, the Court's split decision somewhat belies the fact that all of the judges, being influenced particularly by the New York Supreme Court's reasoning in *Trans World Airlines v Curtiss-Wright* (see *above*), were unanimous in holding that a manufacturer of a defective article is not liable in tort to the ultimate consumer or user for the cost of repairing non-dangerous defects in the article itself, because this liability would be akin to liability under the terms of an express or implied warranty of fitness which, being contractual in origin, could not be enforced against the manufacturer by a stranger to the contract.

The division between the judges related to whether this principle should also apply in cases where the defect not only renders the product less valuable, but also renders it dangerous. Seven of the judges held that a manufacturer's immunity from liability for the cost of repairs of a defective article applies even where that cost was incurred to avert a threat of physical harm to persons or property. On the other hand, two of the judges, Laskin and Hall JJ, said that the cost of repairing a defective article should be recoverable in tort if, as here, it represents the cost of averting a threat of physical harm. Laskin J referred to *Spartan Steel and Alloys Ltd v Martin & Co (Contractors) Ltd* [1973] QB 27 (see Chapter 4) as authority for the recovery of pure economic loss where actual physical injury to person or property has occurred and said (at p 552):

> If recovery for economic loss is allowed when such injury is suffered, I see no reason to deny it when the threatened injury is forestalled. [The manufacturer] can be no better off in the latter case than in the former. Here was a piece of equipment whose use was fraught with danger to person and property because of negligence in its design and manufacture. One death had already resulted from the use of a similar piece of equipment. I see nothing untoward in holding [the manufacturer] liable in such circumstances for economic loss resulting from the down time necessary to effect repairs to the crane.
>
> The case is not one where a manufactured product proves to be merely defective (in short, where it has not met promised expectations), but, rather, one where, by reason of the defect, there is a foreseeable risk of physical harm from its use and where the alert avoidance of such harm gives rise to economic loss. Prevention of threatened harm resulting directly in economic loss should not be treated differently from post-injury cure.

On the second issue the Court unanimously held that the defendant's knowledge of the danger involved in the continued use of the cranes for the purpose for which they were designed carried with it a duty to warn those to whom the cranes had been supplied of such danger. The Court was influenced by *Langridge v Levy* (1838) 3 M & W 337 (which is discussed in

Chapter 6, para 6.2.3). In that case the plaintiff suffered a physical injury as a result of the defendant's failure to warn him of the danger of which the defendant was aware, whereas in the present case the plaintiff's loss could be said to be purely economic, in that the inherent defects in the cranes had not yet caused any damage. The Court held, however, that the defendants were nevertheless liable for part of this loss, namely such part of it as was attributable solely to the defendants' failure to warn the plaintiff promptly of the danger, saying that the duty to warn arose at the moment that the defendants learned of the danger. If they had warned the plaintiff at that time, they would not have been liable for the plaintiff's lost earnings during the period of repair. Thus the plaintiff's damages under this head consisted of its gross loss of earnings during the actual period of repair of the cranes (during the busiest period of the year) less the earnings which would have been lost in any event during the one-month period required by the plaintiff to make repairs had it been properly warned by the defendants.

Anns v Merton London Borough Council [1978] AC 728: The facts of this case are very similar to those in *Dutton*. Here, the seven plaintiffs were long lessees of maisonettes in a block of flats which had been constructed by a certain building company. Some years later cracks appeared in the wall, some of the floors started to slope and doors would not close. The cause of these defects was the fact that the block had been erected on inadequate foundations. Unless remedied, these defects could have become worse and the flats would have become uninhabitable.

The plaintiffs sued the builder and the local authority for the cost of remedying these defects. The builders did not submit a defence and did not take part in the proceedings. All of the argument in the case was concerned with whether the council owed a duty of care in tort to the plaintiffs on the assumption that the plaintiffs' allegations of negligence against the council were true, such alleged negligence consisting of a failure by the council to have inspected the foundations sufficiently, or at all, before they were covered up. The House of Lords held that the council did owe a duty of care in these circumstances. This aspect of the case is considered in Chapter 8, para 8.2. The court disposed very briskly with the liability of the builder by referring, with approval, to *Gallagher v N McDowell Ltd* [1961] NI 26 and to the comments made on this point by the court in *Dutton*, both of which are considered in Chapter 6, paras 6.3.5 and 6.6.2.

The court also held that the plaintiffs' damages could include damage to the maisonettes themselves. However, their Lordships did not classify this damage as pure economic loss. Lord Wilberforce said (at p 759): "If classification is required, the relevant damage is in my opinion material physical damage, and what is recoverable is the amount of expenditure necessary to restore the dwelling to a condition in which it is no longer a danger to the health or safety of persons occupying. On the question of damages generally I have derived much assistance from the judgment (dissenting on this point, but of strong persuasive force) of Laskin J in the Canadian Supreme Court case of *Rivtow Marine Ltd v Washington Iron Works* and from the judgments of the New Zealand Court of Appeal in *Bowen v Paramount Builders (Hamilton) Ltd and McKay*".

This decision has been overruled by the House of Lords in *Murphy v Brentwood District Council* [1991] 1 AC 398. In particular, criticism was made of the characterisation of the classification of the plaintiffs' losses as physical damage. The House of Lords in *Murphy* was most emphatic in saying that this type of loss must be regarded as pure economic loss.

Junior Books Ltd v Veitchi Co Ltd [1983] AC 520: The plaintiff entered into a contract with a building contractor for the construction of a new factory. The contractor in turn entered into a contract with the defendant as a nominated sub-contractor under the main building contract, to lay the flooring of the production area of the plaintiff's factory. The defendant was a company which specialised in the laying of floors. There was no privity of contract between the plaintiff and the defendant. Some time after the completion of this work the flooring showed defects, allegedly due to bad workmanship and/or bad materials.

There was no allegation that the flooring was in a dangerous state or that repairs were urgently required to avoid any such danger or that the flooring was likely to cause damage to any property other than the floor itself. The plaintiff's claim was for the cost of replacing the floor, which they said was necessary to avoid continual maintenance that would have been more expensive in the long run. The question for the House of Lords was whether the defendant, having negligently laid a floor which was defective, but which had not caused danger to the health or safety of any person nor risk of damage to any other property belonging to the owner of the floor, may be liable for the economic loss caused to the owner by having to replace the floor.

The House of Lords, by a majority of 4:1, answered this question in the affirmative. They applied the 'two-stage test' formulated by Lord Wilberforce in *Anns* (which is discussed in Chapter 3). First, they said that the "requisite" degree of proximity existed between the defendant and the plaintiff by virtue of a number of factors, including the defendant's knowledge of the plaintiff's requirements, the plaintiff's reliance on the defendant's expertise, the fact that the defendant, as a nominated sub-contractor, must have known that the plaintiff relied upon its skill and experience and the fact that the relationship between the parties "was as close as it could be short of actual privity of contract".

Secondly, they said that they could see no reason why, in these circumstances, a duty of care should not exist. Lord Roskill said (at p 546): "I see no reason why what was called during the argument 'damage to the pocket' simpliciter should be disallowed when 'damage to the pocket' coupled with physical damage has hitherto always been allowed".

Despite these general-sounding words, it must be noted that the majority made it clear that they would probably have decided this case differently if it had been an ordinary consumer purchase case. Lord Fraser said (at p 533): "I would decide this appeal strictly on its own facts. I rely particularly on the very close proximity between the parties which, in my view, distinguishes this case from the case of producers of goods to be offered for sale to the public"; and Lord Roskill said (at p 547): "The concept of proximity of which I have spoken would not easily be found to exist in the ordinary everyday transaction of purchasing chattels when it is obvious that in truth the real reliance was upon the immediate vendor and not upon the manufacturer".

Lord Brandon dissented. He too applied Lord Wilberforce's 'two-stage test'. First, he said (at p 551), in agreement with the majority: "It is difficult to imagine a greater degree of proximity, in the absence of a direct contractual relationship, than that which exists between a building owner and a sub-contractor nominated by him or his architect". However, he answered the second question in this test differently from the majority. First, he said that it has always been taken for granted that in *Donoghue v Stevenson* the relevant property which the defendant was under a duty not to damage was property other than the very property which gave rise to the danger of physical damage concerned. In his view, to hold otherwise would involve a radical departure from long established authority. Secondly, he said that to hold in the plaintiff's favour would be to impose on a manufacturer or distributor of goods a warranty to the ultimate consumer that they were as well-designed, merchantable and fit for their contemplated purpose as the exercise of reasonable care could make them. He said (at p 551): "In my view, the imposition of warranties of this kind on one person in favour of another, when there is no contractual relationship between them, is contrary to any sound policy requirement".

Lord Brandon said that if the plaintiff's case succeeded, insuperable difficulties would arise in other cases in deciding upon the standard of quality to determine the question of defectiveness. He said (at p 552): "In the case of goods bought from a retailer, it could hardly be the standard prescribed by the contract between the retailer and the wholesaler, or between the wholesaler and the distributor, or between the distributor and the manufacturer, for the terms of such contracts would not be known to the ultimate buyer. In a case like the present, although the building owner would probably be aware of the terms of the sub-contract, he could not, since he was not a party to it, rely on any standards prescribed in it. It follows that the question by what standard alleged defects in a product complained of by its ultimate consumer are to be judged would remain entirely at large and could not be given any just or satisfactory answer".

D & F Estates Ltd v Church Commissioners for England [1989] 1 AC 177:
The first plaintiff was the long lessee from the first defendant of a flat which had been constructed by the third defendant, Wates Ltd. The second and third plaintiffs were the occupiers of the flat. Some years after completion it was discovered that some of the plaster on the ceilings and the internal walls was loose. Some of it fell down, causing minor damage to the plaintiffs' carpets and other possessions. An investigation showed that all of the first plaintiff's work was defective because the sub-contractors had

failed to follow the plaster manufacturers' instructions. The plaintiffs' claim against Wates was for the estimated cost of re-plastering the ceiling and walls of the flat and for the cost of cleaning carpets and other possessions which had been damaged or dirtied by falling plaster.

The House of Lords unanimously rejected the first of these claims, but upheld the second. Lord Bridge said (at p 206): "If a hidden defect in a chattel is the cause of personal injury or of damage to property other than the chattel itself, the manufacturer is liable. But if the hidden defect is discovered before any such damage is caused, there is no longer any room for the application of the *Donoghue v Stevenson* principle. The chattel is now defective in quality, but is no longer dangerous. It may be valueless or it may be capable of economic repair. In either case the economic loss is recoverable in contract by a buyer or hirer of the chattel entitled to the benefit of a relevant warranty of quality, but is not recoverable in tort by a remote buyer or hirer of the chattel. If the same principle applies in the field of real property to the liability of the builder of a permanent structure which is dangerously defective, that liability can only arise if the defect remains hidden until the defective structure causes personal injury or damage to property other than the structure itself. If the defect is discovered before any damage is done, the loss sustained by the owner of the structure, who has to repair or demolish it to avoid a potential source of danger to third parties, would seem to be purely economic".

Lord Bridge also said (at p 207): "It seems to me clear that the cost of replacing the defective plaster itself is not an item of damage for which the builder could possibly be made liable in negligence under the principle of *Donoghue v Stevenson* or any legitimate development of it. To make him so liable would be to impose upon him for the benefit of those with whom he had no contractual relationship the obligation of one who warranted the quality of the plaster as regards material, workmanship and fitness for purpose".

Murphy v Brentwood District Council [1991] 1 AC 398: In 1970 the plaintiff bought a house which they had built in 1969 from a firm of builders. Because the site was sloping and had a ditch running through it, careful consideration was required in the design of the foundations. In order to prevent damage from differential settlement if conventional foundations were used, the house was constructed on a single concrete raft foundation which covered the whole surface area of the house. Nevertheless, it proved to be inadequate. Differential settlement of the ground caused the raft to distort and this led to cracks appearing in the walls of the house. An investigation showed that the design of the raft was defective in that, relative to the soil conditions which existed at the site and the weight which the superstructure of the house would impose on the raft, the strength of steel reinforcement required in the raft had been underestimated by about 30 per cent.

The raft foundation had been designed by a firm of civil engineers who had submitted their calculations to the defendant council's building control department for approval. This approval was given, but only after the defendant, in turn, had submitted the civil engineers' foundation plans and calculations to an outside consultant who, in approving the design of the foundation, failed to discover the civil engineers' calculation errors.

The estimated cost of repairing the damage caused to the house was £45,000. The plaintiff could not afford this. Instead, he sold the house, in the process suffering a £35,000 loss on the estimated market value of the house in an undamaged condition. He sought to recover this sum from the defendant in tort on the ground that the defendant had negligently passed the plans for the foundations. The House of Lords unanimously rejected his claim. Although there are 11 Law Lords, most cases are usually heard by only five of them. However, on this occasion (and research seems to indicate that this had not been done before, at least in modern times) seven Law Lords heard the appeal. Five separate speeches were delivered, but they are in conformity with each other.

Chapter 9 is concerned with the nonfeasance and local authority aspects of the decision. This summary is concerned only with the products liability aspects. Although the building company was not a party to these proceedings (having gone into liquidation at some time in the past) the court considered what the position of the builder would have been if it had been sued in tort in these circumstances because (like the House of Lords before it in *Anns*) it took the view that it would be unreasonable to impose liability for defective foundations on the council if the builder "whose primary fault it was" should be immune from liability. The correctness of this premise is considered in Chapter 8, para 8.2.

Their Lordships' comments on the position of the builder and of manufacturers of products are similar to those which were made by the House of Lords in *D & F*. Lord Keith (at p 465) referred to Lord Denning MR's "impossible distinction" in *Dutton*, which is set out at the beginning of this chapter, and said: "The jump which is here made from liability under the *Donoghue v Stevenson* principle for damage to person or property caused by a latent defect in a carelessly manufactured article to liability for the cost of rectifying a defect in such an article which is *ex hypothesi* no longer latent is difficult to accept. There is no liability in tort upon a manufacturer towards the purchaser from a retailer of an article which turns out to be useless or valueless through defects due to careless manufacture. The loss is economic. It is difficult to draw a distinction in principle between an article which is useless or valueless and one which suffers from a defect which would render it dangerous in use but which is discovered by the purchaser in time to avert any possibility of injury. The purchaser may incur expense in putting right the defect, or, more probably, discard the article. In either case the loss is purely economic".

Based on the above, Lord Keith went on to say (at p 466): "In my opinion it must now be recognised that, although the damage in *Anns* was characterised as physical damage by Lord Wilberforce, it was purely economic loss". Lord Keith was most concerned about the implications of imposing a duty of care on the person responsible for causing the plaintiff's loss in these circumstances. He said (at p 469): "That would open up an exceedingly wide field of claims, involving the introduction of something in the nature of transmissible warranty of quality. The purchaser of an article who discovered that it suffered from a dangerous defect before that defect had caused any damage would be entitled to recover from the manufacturer the cost of rectifying the defect, and presumably, if the article was not capable of economic repair, the amount of loss sustained through discarding it. Then it would be open to question whether there should not also be a right to recovery where the defect renders the article not dangerous but merely useless. The economic loss in either case would be the same".

Lord Bridge's speech is very similar to that which he delivered in *D & F*, which is set out *above*. His speech in this case is set out in the main text of this chapter (para 7.3.4), as it contains a complete statement of the current position in English law.

In the light of these views their Lordships had no hesitation in overruling *Dutton* and their own previous ruling in *Anns* as well as all other cases which had followed those two decisions.

Department of the Environment v Thomas Bates & Son Ltd [1991] 1 AC 499:
This case was argued in the House of Lords before *Murphy*, but judgment was delayed until after the judgment in *Murphy*. The plaintiff was the undertenant of part of an office block in which some of the pillars were not strong enough to support safely the potential design load of the building. This did not cause a danger to health or safety of the plaintiff's employees or to the public, nor did this defect impair the plaintiff's use of the building in the manner in which the plaintiff was using it. Nevertheless, the plaintiff wished to carry out the necessary works to strengthen the pillars so as to make the building fit to carry its potential design load.

The plaintiff sought to recover the cost of carrying out these works from the defendant building contractor. The court rejected the plaintiff's claim. Lord Keith said (at p 519): "It was the unanimous view of this House in *Murphy v Brentwood District Council* that, while the builder would be liable under the principle of *Donoghue v Stevenson* in the event of the defect, before it had been discovered, causing physical injury to persons or damage to property other than the building itself, there was no sound basis in principle for holding him liable for the pure economic loss suffered by a purchaser who discovered the defect and required to expend money in order to make the building safe and suitable for its intended purpose. In the present case it is clear that the loss suffered by the plaintiffs is pure economic loss. For the reason stated in *Murphy v Brentwood District Council* that conclusion must inevitably lead to the result that the plaintiff's claim fails".

Chapter 8

Nonfeasance

It is one matter to require a person to take care if he embarks on a course of conduct which may harm others. It is another matter to require a person who is doing nothing to take positive action to protect others from harm for which he was not responsible, and to hold him liable in damages if he fails to do so. **(Lord Nicholls in *Stovin v Wise* [1996] AC 923)**

Where Parliament confers a discretion there may, and almost certainly will, be errors of judgment in exercising such a discretion and Parliament cannot have intended that members of the public should be entitled to sue in respect of such errors. **(Lord Reid in *Dorset Yacht Co Ltd v The Home Office* [1970] AC 1004)**

How wide the sphere of the duty of care in negligence is to be laid depends ultimately on the courts' assessment of the demands of society for protection from the carelessness of others. **(Lord Pearce in *Hedley Byrne & Co Ltd v Heller & Partners Ltd* [1964] AC 465 at 536)**

The decision of a court as to whether a duty of care exists is in reality a policy decision. **(Lord Morris in *Dorset Yacht Co Ltd v The Home Office* [1970] AC 1004)**

The judicial function can, I believe, be epitomised as an educated reflex to facts. **(Lord Goff in *Smith v Littlewoods Organisation Ltd* [1987] 1 AC 241)**

8.1 Introduction

8.1.1 Context

This chapter deals with those situations in which it is alleged that the plaintiff's loss has been caused by the defendant's inaction in circumstances where, if the defendant had acted, the plaintiff's loss most probably would have been avoided. This must be distinguished from the type of omission which falls within the category of cases discussed in Chapters 6 and 7 (paras 6.4 and 7.3 respectively). When Lord Atkin in *Donoghue v Stevenson* [1932] AC 562 said (at p 580) that one's neighbour in law is a person whom one ought reasonably to have in contemplation as being directly affected when one is directing one's mind to the "acts or omissions" which are called into question (see Chapter 3, para 3.2.1), the type of omission for that purpose is different from the type of omission in the present context. An omission within Lord Atkin's formulation is an omission which occurs as part of doing a positive act. For example, in that case, it could either be said that the manufacturer's duty arose as a result of the manufacturer having

actively put into circulation a defective product or as a result of the manufacturer having negligently omitted to inspect that product before putting
it into circulation.

This must be contrasted with what may be called, somewhat inaccu-
rately, an 'act' of nonfeasance or, more correctly, a 'pure omission'. This
would arise where the defendant has done nothing to create or make worse
the situation from which the plaintiff's loss arose. An obvious example
would be where the defendant had seen a stranger in distress in a river, and
did nothing to try to rescue that person. More pertinent would be the
example of an employer who failed to advise his employee to take out personal accident insurance for third party risks before going abroad, a school
principal who failed to advise parents to take out personal accident insurance against their children being injured on the sports field or an insurance
broker who failed to inform a bank that another insurance broker whom
the bank was dealing with was fraudulently concealing vital information
from it. In all of these cases the defendant might well have been under a
moral duty to do or say something, but this does not, of course, mean that
he will have thereby also been under a legal duty to do so. Indeed, in all of
the cases from which the last three examples have been taken (see para
8.3.3, *below*) it was held that, despite the closeness of the relationship
between the parties, the defendant was not under a duty of care in law to
pass the information in question on to the plaintiff.

8.1.2 Different considerations

Different considerations are involved in determining whether a duty of care
should be imposed on a defendant in respect of loss (economic or physical)
sustained by a plaintiff in circumstances where the defendant negligently
omitted to do or say something which, if said or done, would have prevented the plaintiff's loss from occurring. As will be seen in this chapter, the
law is reluctant to impose a duty of care on a defendant in this type of situation, especially where the defendant's alleged negligent omission consisted
of his inaction to prevent a third party from causing loss or damage to the
plaintiff. Lord Diplock expressed this point vividly in *Dorset Yacht Co Ltd
v Home Office* [1970] AC 1004, when he said (at p 1060):

> The very parable of the good Samaritan (Luke 10, *v*30) which was evoked by
> Lord Atkin [in formulating his neighbour test] in *Donoghue v Stevenson* [1932]
> AC 562 illustrates, in the conduct of the priest and of the Levite who passed by
> on the other side, an omission which was likely to have as its reasonable and
> probable consequence damage to the health of the victim of the thieves, but for
> which the priest and the Levite would have incurred no civil liability in English
> law. Examples could be multiplied. You may cause loss to a tradesman by with-
> drawing your custom though the goods which he supplies are entirely satisfac-
> tory; you may damage your neighbour's land by intercepting the flow of
> percolating water to it even though the interception is of no advantage to your-
> self; you need not warn him of a risk of physical danger to which he is about to
> expose himself unless there is some special relationship between the two of you

such as that of occupier of land and visitor; you may watch your neighbour's goods being ruined by a thunderstorm though the slightest effort on your part could protect them from the rain and you may do so with impunity unless there is some special relationship between you such as that of bailor and bailee.

This point also arose in *Stovin v Wise* [1996] AC 923, where the issue was whether the Norfolk County Council owed a duty of care at common law to the plaintiff for injuries sustained by him which could have been avoided if the council had not failed to take action to remove a mound of earth on the side of a road which blocked the vision of motorists turning into that road from another road. The case is discussed in more detail *below*, but, on the importance of the distinction between acts and omissions, Lord Hoffmann, speaking for the majority of 4:1, said (at p 943):

> ... the complaint against the council was not about anything which it had done to make the highway dangerous but about its omission to make it safer. Omissions, like economic loss, are notoriously a category of conduct in which Lord Atkin's generalisation in *Donoghue v Stevenson* offers limited help. ... There are sound reasons why omissions require different treatment from positive conduct. It is one thing for the law to say that a person who undertakes some activity shall take reasonable care not to cause damage to others. It is another thing for the law to require that a person who is doing nothing in particular shall take steps to prevent another from suffering harm from the acts of third parties (like Mrs Wise) [the motorist who collided with the plaintiff] or natural causes.

Lord Hoffmann then expanded in philosophical terms on the reason for the distinction in the law of negligence between omissions and acts by saying (at p 943):

> One can put the matter in political, moral or economic terms. In political terms it is less of an invasion of an individual's freedom for the law to require him to consider the safety of others in his actions than to impose upon him a duty to rescue or protect. ... In economic terms, the efficient allocation of resources usually requires an activity should bear its own costs. If it benefits from being able to impose some of its costs on other people (what economists call 'externalities'), the market is distorted because the activity appears cheaper than it really is. So liability to pay compensation for loss caused by negligent conduct acts as a deterrent against increasing the cost of the activity to the community and reduces externalities. But there is no similar justification for requiring a person who is not doing anything to spend money on behalf of someone else. Except in special cases (such as marine salvage) English law does not reward someone who voluntarily confers a benefit on another. So there must be some special reason why he should have to put his hand in his pocket. ... There may be a duty to act if one has undertaken to do so or induced a person to rely upon one doing so.

Lord Hoffmann also highlighted the difference between a pure omission and an omission which occurs in the course of carrying out a positive act. First, he set out the following statement of Kennedy LJ in the Court of Appeal in this case ([1994] 1 WLR 1124 at p 1138):

> Here the highway authority did not simply fail to act. It decided positively to proceed by seeking agreement from British Rail [the owner of the land on which

the obstructing mound of earth stood], and its failure to pursue that course is not an omission on which it can rely to escape liability, any more than a car driver could escape liability simply because his breach of duty consisted in a failure to apply the brakes.

Lord Hoffmann disagreed with this exposition. He said (at p 945):

I do not find this analogy convincing. Of course it is true that the conditions necessary to bring about an event always consist of a combination of acts and omissions. Mr Stovin's accident was caused by the fact that Mrs Wise drove out into Station Road and omitted to keep a proper look-out. But this does not mean that the distinction between acts and omissions is meaningless or illogical. One must have regard to the purpose of the distinction as it is used in the law of negligence, which is to distinguish between regulating the way in which an activity may be conducted and imposing a duty to act upon a person who is not carrying on any relevant activity.

To hold the defendant liable for an act, rather than an omission, it is therefore necessary to be able to say, according to common sense principles of causation, that the damage was caused by something which the defendant did. If I am driving at 50 miles an hour and fail to apply the brakes, the motorist with whom I collide can plausibly say that the damage was caused by my driving into him at 50 miles an hour. But Mr Stovin's injuries were not caused by . . . anything . . . which the council did.

Lord Nicholls, although dissenting, expressed similar views to Lord Hoffmann on this point when he said (at p 930):

The distinction between liability for acts and liability for omissions is well known. It is not free from controversy. In some cases the distinction is not clear cut. The categorisation may depend upon how broadly one looks when deciding whether the omission is a 'pure' omission or is part of a larger course of activity set in motion by the defendant. Failure to apply the handbrake when parking a vehicle is the classic illustration of the latter. Then the omission is the element which makes the activity negligent. *Dorset Yacht Co Ltd v Home Office* [1970] AC 1004 is an instance where the distinction was not so easy to apply.

Despite the difficulties, the distinction is fundamentally sound in this area of the law. The distinction is based on a recognition that it is one matter to require a person to take care if he embarks on a course of conduct which may harm others. He must take care not to create a risk of danger. It is another matter to require a person, who is doing nothing, to take positive action to protect others from harm for which he was not responsible, and to hold him liable in damages if he fails to do so.

The law has long recognised that liability can arise more readily in the first situation than the second. This is reasonable. In the second situation a person is being compelled to act, and to act for the benefit of another. There must be some special justification for imposing an obligation of this character. Compulsory altruism needs more justification than an obligation not to create dangers to others when acting for one's own purposes.

There is no difficulty over categorisation in the present case. The council did not bring about the dangerous configuration and poor visibility at the road junction. The question is whether it was in breach of a common law duty by carelessly failing to remove this source of danger.

Lastly, Lord Nicholls stated one further reason for the law's reluctance to impose duties of care in pure omission situations. He said (at p 933):

> I must mention one further feature of common law liability for omissions. . . . Liability for omissions gives rise to a problem not present with liability for careless acts. He who wishes to act must act carefully or not at all. A producer of ginger beer must adopt a safe manufacturing process. If this would be uneconomic, he ought not to carry on the business. With liability for omissions, however, a person is not offered a choice. The law compels him to act, when left to himself he might do nothing.

8.2 Statutory authorities

8.2.1 Special features

A statutory authority is a governmental or quasi-governmental body which derives its authority entirely from statute. In the context of actions by individuals for compensation for loss or damage suffered by them through the negligent performance or exercise by a statutory authority of the duties or powers conferred on it, or in consequence of the statutory authority having omitted to perform such duties or exercise such powers, the fact that a statutory authority's duties and powers derive entirely from statute can be important in three ways.

First, the reasons set out *above* for the law's reluctance to impose duties of care in pure omission situations are, in many instances, not as compelling, because judges are generally more willing to conclude that the statutory authority did have a legal duty of one sort or another to act than they are in the case of private individuals. In *Stovin v Wise* [1996] AC 923, Lord Hoffmann expressed this point pithily when he said (at p 946): "Some of the arguments against liability for omissions do not apply to public bodies like a highway authority. There is no 'why pick on me?' argument: the highway authority alone had the financial and physical resources, as well as the legal powers, to eliminate the hazard". Lord Hoffmann hastened to add, however, that this does not mean that there are not other arguments peculiar to public bodies which serve to negative the existence of a duty of care.

Secondly (and this is one of those other peculiar features), even if in all other respects the statutory authority would be subject to a duty of care under the statute or at common law for the loss or damage sustained by the plaintiff through the negligent performance or non-performance by the statutory authority of its statutory duties or powers, the plaintiff's claim will fail if the empowering statute expressly or impliedly rules out a claim for compensation by an individual claimant. This is often the reason why claims in this category of cases fail, because the courts interpret the purpose of the empowering legislation to be only to confer benefits on the public as a whole or on a defined group of citizens as a whole, rather than on individual plaintiffs.

Thirdly, even if under the statute or at common law the court is satisfied that in all other respects the statutory authority would be subject to a duty of care to individual claimants, claims in this type of case often fail because the courts have concluded that general public policy considerations exist which override individual rights. An example which frequently occurs is the conclusion that the imposition of a duty of care in a particular type of case, eg cases involving the police, would inhibit the statutory authority in the future in the way that it performs its statutory duties or exercises its statutory powers and responds to the needs of the public in general or of the limited class of persons for whose benefit the statutory duties or powers in question are designed to be performed. Where such a conclusion is reached, the plaintiff's action will ultimately fail.

8.2.2 General principles

Introduction

Claims for damages by private individuals against statutory authorities are generally framed in either or both of the following ways. The first of these (which is sometimes referred to as 'breach of statutory duty simpliciter'— see para 8.2.3) involves claims where the plaintiff does not allege negligence by the statutory authority in the performance of its duties or in the exercise of its powers, but simply that the statutory authority owed a particular, precisely delineated duty under the express terms of a statute to the plaintiff which it breached, and that the plaintiff suffered economic loss and/or physical injury or property damage in consequence. The resolution of this type of claim involves a direct question of construction of the provisions of the governing statute, in much the same way as would be done in a breach of contract claim. If the plaintiff succeeds in establishing that its claim based on breach of statutory duty is sustainable, it will not be necessary for the plaintiff to proceed with its common law claim as well.

Sometimes a statutory authority will have the power to carry out an activity but no duty to do so, or the duty will be expressed too generally to found an action for breach of duty simpliciter, eg "a duty to repair the highway". In this type of situation a person who has suffered loss by virtue of the statutory authority's act or omission will have to bring his action at common law (see para 8.2.4). Where it is necessary for the plaintiff to proceed in this fashion, the plaintiff usually alleges that, in the course of carrying out, or failing to carry out or exercise, its statutory duties or powers, the statutory authority formed a 'special relationship' with the plaintiff such as to enable a court to impose a duty of care in negligence on the statutory authority for the plaintiff's consequential loss or damage.

The resolution of this type of claim involves a multitude of considerations. First, the court has to consider whether the act or omission of the statutory authority about which the plaintiff has complained is *justiciable* by a court of law. This will depend on whether the decision was a 'policy' decision. If it was a policy decision, it will not be justiciable by a court, and that will be the end of the inquiry.

Secondly, if the decision is justiciable, it will not be *actionable* if the act or omission complained of was within the limits of the discretion conferred on the statutory authority in relation to acts or omissions of that nature. To be actionable the statutory authority's act or omission must have been so unreasonable or 'irrational' that no reasonable statutory authority could have acted in the same way.

Thirdly, if the statutory authority's act or omission is actionable, the court must consider whether, by the application of ordinary common law principles, and leaving aside the statutory framework pursuant to which the statutory authority acted or failed to act, the circumstances of the case are such that the court feels justified in imposing a duty of care on the statutory authority for the plaintiff's loss.

Fourthly, if the answer to this question is in the affirmative, the court must consider whether there are any overriding reasons, deriving from the governing legislation itself (eg that it impliedly excludes actions for loss by individuals) or from its milieu (eg that the local authority's officers might become overly defensive in their enforcement of legislation if they know they can face claims by individuals), which outweigh the conferring of rights of action on individual members of the public even if they belong to a defined class for whose benefit the legislation was passed, such as children at risk in the community.

Exposition

The general principles mentioned *above* will now be expanded upon. The formulation that follows is based on a distillation of *dicta* in such cases as *Geddis v Bann Reservoir Proprietors* (1878) 3 App Cas 430 (HL), *East Suffolk Rivers Catchment Board v Kent* [1941] AC 74, *Dutton v Bognor Regis Urban District Council* [1972] 1 QB 373, *Anns v Merton London Borough Council* [1978] AC 728, *Council of the Shire of Sutherland v Heyman* (1985) 157 CLR 424 (Australia), *X (Minors) v Bedfordshire County Council* [1995] 2 AC 633, and *Stovin v Wise* [1996] AC 923. Nevertheless, it must be noted that this formulation is only a guide, because as Lord Browne-Wilkinson pointed out in the *X* case, statutory duties now exist over such a wide range of diverse activities, and take so many different forms, that no single principle is capable of being formulated which is applicable to all cases.

8.2.3   Breach of statutory duty simpliciter

As mentioned *above*, this is the first of the two ways in which claims by private individuals against statutory authorities are formulated. Here, the plaintiff will not allege negligence by the statutory authority in the performance of its duties, but will simply allege that the statutory authority owed a particular duty to the plaintiff which it breached, and that the plaintiff suffered economic loss and/or physical injury or property damage in consequence. It is almost as if the plaintiff is alleging that a contract existed between the statutory authority and the plaintiff, the terms of which the statutory authority breached, thereby entitling the plaintiff to damages.

In order for a plaintiff to succeed in such a claim, the plaintiff will have to establish that:
(1) the statute confers a private law cause of action on individuals. This, in turn, will depend on the plaintiff being able to establish as a matter of construction of the statute as a whole, including the history of prior legislation on the same topic, that:
   (a) the statutory duty was imposed for the protection of a limited class of the public; and
   (b) Parliament intended to confer on members of that class a private right of action for breach of the duty (this point is considered further *below*);
(2) the plaintiff was a member of the limited class for whose protection or benefit the statute was passed;
(3) the statute was breached by the statutory authority;
(4) the plaintiff suffered loss or damage in consequence of such breach; and
(5) Parliament intended that the scope of compensation payable by the statutory authority for breach of the statute in question included loss of the type suffered by the plaintiff, ie pure economic loss, physical injury or damage to the plaintiff's property.

There is no general rule of construction by which it can be decided whether Parliament did indeed intend to confer a private right of action on individual members of the class of the public for whose protection or benefit any particular statute was passed (ie criterion (1)(b), *above*). However, the following general indicators are worth noting:
(1) If the statute provides no other remedy for its breach, this will often be taken as an indication that Parliament intended to confer a private right of action, because otherwise members of the limited class would have no way of securing the protection which the statute was intended to confer on them.
(2) If the statute does provide some other means of enforcing the duty, this will often be taken to indicate that the statutory right was intended to be enforceable by those other means alone, and not by way of a private right of action.
(3) The mere existence of some other statutory remedy will not necessarily be decisive. It will still be open to the plaintiff to demonstrate that, on the true construction of the statute, the protected class was intended by Parliament to have a private remedy.
(4) Where the statutory provisions establish a regulatory system or a scheme of social welfare for the benefit of the public at large, this will often be taken as an indication that Parliament did not intend to confer private rights of action on individuals who have been adversely affected by a failure in the regulatory system or the overall scheme which the statute created. In this context, legislation which covers a particular area of activity (such as child welfare)—and which therefore *prima facie* benefits only a limited class of individuals (ie children)—will generally not be treated as having been passed

specifically for the benefit of those individuals so as to confer private rights of action on them, but for the benefit of society in general.

(5) A private right of action is more likely to be inferred where the statutory duty is very limited and specific, as opposed to involving general administrative functions and discretions.

8.2.4   Common law duty of care

This is the second of the two ways in which claims by private individuals are formulated. It arises only where there was no statutory duty simpliciter. Many statutes, however, confer on statutory authorities the power to carry on an activity but no duty to do so, or confer a duty in a general sense (eg "to maintain the highway") coupled with a power or a discretion (these words are used interchangeably in this context) as to the extent to which, and the methods by which, such duty is to be performed. Here, the plaintiff's case will be based on an allegation that, in the course of carrying out (or failing to carry out or exercise) its statutory powers, the statutory authority formed a 'special relationship' with the plaintiff, ie a relationship of sufficient proximity to enable a court to impose a common law duty of care in negligence on the statutory authority for the plaintiff's consequential loss or damage.

In order to succeed in such a claim, the plaintiff will have to establish:

(1) that the statutory authority's act or omission about which the plaintiff is complaining is *justiciable* by a court. This will depend on whether the statutory authority's decision was based on policy grounds. If it was based on policy grounds it will not be justiciable and that will be the end of the inquiry. It is not possible to define with precision when this condition will be satisfied, but examples of policy decisions are decisions which are dictated by financial, economic, social and/or political factors or constraints, including the wider social policy behind the governing legislation, decisions based on the balance between pursuing desirable social aims and the risk to the public inherent of so doing (as in the *Dorset Yacht* case—see *below*) and decisions based on budgetary restraints involving the allocation of finite financial resources between the numerous services provided by the statutory authority.

Sometimes the analysis is assisted by contrasting the decision that was taken with 'operational' decisions. These are generally accepted as being decisions concerned with the practical implementation of the statutory authority's formulated policies. Operational decisions will usually be made on the basis of administrative direction, expert or professional opinion, technical standards or general standards of reasonableness.

It must not be thought that policy decisions can be made only by the statutory authority's 'policy-makers' at the highest level of the statutory authority's decision-making processes. In fact, policy decisions can be made by persons at all levels of authority, and can even be made in the 'operational arena'. In determining whether a decision is one of policy, it is the *nature* of the decision itself that must be scrutinised, rather than the position of the person who makes it. For example, a decision as to the manner and extent of a particular power—such as the power to fight fires—conferred on local authorities could be treated as a policy decision if what was being questioned was the number of fire engines deployed to a fire on budgetary grounds by the station-master; or it could be seen as an operational decision if what was being questioned was the chief fire officer's decision at the scene of a fire to direct the hoses at the upstairs part of the building first, when in fact he should have directed them at the ground floor instead. This point (the policy–operational dichotomy) is discussed further *below*.

If the conclusion is reached that the decision was based on policy grounds, it is not justiciable by a court and that is the end of the inquiry. If the decision is justiciable, the next step is to prove that it was *actionable*.

(2) That the statutory authority's act or omission about which the plaintiff is complaining is actionable. If the statutory authority's alleged negligent act related purely to the practical manner in which that act was performed (eg directing a fire-hose at the upstairs part of a building instead of at the ground floor), the act will be actionable without further inquiry and the plaintiff's case can proceed to the next stage/s described in (3)–(9) *below*. If, however, the plaintiff's complaint alleges carelessness by the statutory authority in the taking of a discretionary decision to do an act (which decision was not based on policy grounds—see *above*), the decision will not be actionable if it was within the limits of the statutory authority's discretion, even if an error of judgment was involved. Such an act will be actionable only if it can be established (on a balance of probabilities—the onus being on the plaintiff) that it was outside the ambit of the discretion altogether.

In order to establish that the statutory authority's decision was outside the ambit of its discretion, the plaintiff has to establish that the statutory authority's decision to exercise its statutory power or discretion in a particular way, or its decision not to exercise the power or authority at all, was so irrational in all of the circumstances of the case that the statutory authority exceeded the ambit or limits of the power or discretion in making that decision. This process involves a scrupulous examination of all of the facts, and the application of common sense, judicial experience and reasoning by analogy to other similar, decided cases.

The process is similar to a decision as to whether any person's conduct on any particular occasion was negligent in the sense that it fell below the standard that could reasonably be expected of a reasonable person with the same qualifications and experience as the defendant, with the added complication that here the defendant is a statutory authority; and therefore it is proper that certain other considerations might legitimately be taken into account by it in deciding whether to do or not to do a particular act on a particular occasion, with the result that the standard of care required of the statutory authority may be lower than that which would be owed by an individual. For example, an individual might be expected to clear snow and ice from his pavement more promptly and more thoroughly than a governmental agency which is responsible for the maintenance of hundreds of miles of highway.

In essence, the plaintiff has to satisfy the court, on a balance of probabilities, that the decision of the statutory authority to exercise its statutory discretion in a particular way, or not to exercise it at all, was so unreasonable that no reasonable statutory authority acting rationally could have reached it. If the plaintiff cannot establish this, the court will have to accept that the statutory authority's decision was within the ambit or limits of its relevant power or discretion, and the plaintiff's case will fail.

If, however, the plaintiff does succeed in establishing that the statutory authority's decision was so irrational that it exceeded the limits of the power or discretion in question, then negligence will have been established for the purposes of considering whether a common law duty of care should be imposed, and the plaintiff's case can proceed to the next stage/s described *below*.

(3) That the defendants act or omission complained of was negligent. (This test will be 'subsumed in the ambit of the discretion' test in these cases where it is necessary for the act or omission to pass that test before it is actionable—see *above*).

(4) That the plaintiff's loss was a foreseeable consequence of that negligence.

(5) That the plaintiff's loss was caused by the statutory authority's negligence.

(6) That it was reasonable for the plaintiff to place reliance in a general sense on the statutory authority to look out for the plaintiff's interests and to safeguard him against the type of loss that he sustained. This point is also discussed further *below*.

(7) That a sufficiently close relationship of proximity existed between the statutory authority and the plaintiff so as to make it fair, just and reasonable for the court to impose a duty of care on the statutory authority in respect of the plaintiff's loss.

(8) That in cases where the plaintiff's loss was actually and directly caused by the act or omission of a third party then, in addition to all of the above:

(a) the third party himself owed the plaintiff a duty in law (this could be a tortious, contractual, criminal or fiduciary duty) not to cause the plaintiff's loss;

(b) there existed a 'special relationship of control' between the statutory authority and the third party.

(9) that there are no overriding reasons deriving from the governing

legislation itself which outweigh the conferring of a right of action on the plaintiff, as an individual member of the public, for compensation for the loss sustained by the plaintiff in consequence of the statutory authority's negligence in performing or failing to perform the particular duty or power/discretion which has caused the plaintiff's loss. This point is also discussed further *below*.

8.2.5   Quotable quotations

The following quotations from some of the judgments in some of the leading cases might assist in understanding and applying the above-stated principles.

Breach of statutory duty simpliciter

In *X (Minors) v Bedfordshire County Council* [1995] 2 AC 633, Lord Browne-Wilkinson said (at p 731):

> ... a breach of statutory duty does not, by itself, give rise to any private law cause of action. However a private law cause of action will arise if it can be shown, as a matter of construction of the statute, that the statutory duty was imposed for the protection of a limited class of the public and that Parliament intended to confer on members of that class a private right of action for breach of the duty. There is no general rule by reference to which it can be decided whether a statute does create such a right of action but there are a number of indicators. If the statute provides no other remedy for its breach and the Parliamentary intention to protect a limited class is shown, this indicates that there may be a private right of action since otherwise there is no method of securing the protection the statute was intended to confer. If the statute does provide some other means of enforcing the duty that will normally indicate that the statutory right was intended to be enforceable by those means and not by private right of action. ... However, the mere existence of some other statutory remedy is not necessarily decisive. It is still possible to show that on the true construction of the statute the protected class was intended by Parliament to have a private remedy. ...
>
> Although the question is one of statutory construction and therefore each case turns on the provisions in the relevant statute, it is significant that your Lordships were not referred to any case where it had been held that statutory provisions establishing a regulatory system or a scheme of social welfare for the benefit of the public at large have been held to give rise to a private right of action for damages for breach of statutory duty. Although regulatory or welfare legislation affecting a particular area of activity does in fact provide protection to those individuals particularly affected by that activity, the legislation is not to be treated as being passed for the benefit of those individuals but for the benefit of society in general. ... The cases where a private right of action for breach of statutory duty has been held to arise are all cases in which the statutory duty has been very limited and specific as opposed to general administrative functions imposed on public bodies and involving the exercise of administrative discretions.

In *Stovin v Wise* [1996] AC 923, Lord Hoffman said (at p 952):

> Whether a statutory duty gives rise to a private cause of action is a question of construction. ... It requires an examination of the policy of the statute to decide whether it was intended to confer a right to compensation for breach.

Common law duty of care

In *Anns v Merton London Borough Council* [1978] AC 728, Lord Wilberforce said (at p 755):

> A plaintiff complaining of negligence must prove, the burden being on him, that action taken was not within the limits of a discretion *bona fide* exercised, before he can begin to rely upon a common law duty of care. But if he can do this, he should, in principle, be able to sue.

In *Dorset Yacht v The Home Office* [1970] AC 1004, Lord Reid said (at p 1031):

> Where Parliament confers a discretion . . . there may, and almost certainly will, be errors of judgment in exercising such a discretion and Parliament cannot have intended that members of the public should be entitled to sue in respect of such errors. But there must come a stage when the discretion is exercised so carelessly or unreasonably that there has been no reasonable exercise of the discretion which Parliament has conferred. The person purporting to exercise his discretion has acted in abuse or excess of his power. Parliament cannot be supposed to have granted immunity to persons who do that.

In *X (Minors) v Bedfordshire County Council* [1995] 2 AC 633, Lord Browne-Wilkinson said at (p 735):

> . . . statutory duties now exist over such a wide range of diverse activities and take so many different forms that no one principle is capable of being formulated applicable to all cases. However, in my view it is possible . . . to identify certain points which are of significance.

1 Co-existence of statutory duty and common law duty of care
It is clear that a common law duty of care may arise in the performance of statutory functions. But a broad distinction has to be drawn between:

(a) cases in which it is alleged that the authority owes a duty of care in the manner in which it exercises a statutory discretion; and
(b) cases in which a duty of care is alleged to arise from the manner in which the statutory duty has been implemented in practice.

An example of (a) in the educational field would be a decision whether or not to exercise a statutory discretion to close a school, being a decision which necessarily involves the exercise of a discretion. An example of (b) would be the actual running of a school pursuant to the statutory duties. In such latter case a common law duty to take reasonable care for the physical safety of the pupils will arise. The fact that the school is being run pursuant to a statutory duty is not necessarily incompatible with a common law duty of care arising from the proximate relationship between a school and the pupils it has agreed to accept. The distinction is between (a) taking care in exercising a statutory discretion whether or not to do an act and (b) having decided to do that act, taking care in the manner in which you do it.

2 Discretion: justiciability and the policy/operational test

(a) Discretion
Most statutes which impose a statutory duty on local authorities confer on the authority a discretion as to the extent to which, and the methods by which, such statutory duty is to be performed. It is clear both in principle and from the

decided cases that the local authority cannot be liable in damages for doing that which Parliament has authorised. Therefore, if the decisions complained of fall within the ambit of such statutory discretion, they cannot be actionable in common law. However, if the decision complained of is so unreasonable that it falls outside of the ambit of the discretion conferred on the local authority, there is no a priori reason for excluding all common law liability.

[Lord Browne-Wilkinson then quoted the *dictum* of Lord Reid in *Dorset Yacht Co Ltd v Home Office* [1970] AC 1004 at 1031, set out *above* . . .]

Exactly the same approach was adopted by Lord Wilberforce in *Anns v Merton London Borough Council* [1978] AC 728 who, speaking of the duty of a local authority which had in fact inspected a building under construction, said, at p 755:

> But this duty, heavily operational though it may be, is still a duty arising under the statute. There may be a discretionary element in its exercise—discretionary as to the time and manner of inspection, and the techniques to be used. A plaintiff complaining of negligence must prove, the burden being on him, that action taken was not within the limits of a discretion bona fide exercised, before he can begin to rely upon a common law duty of care.

It follows that in seeking to establish that a local authority is liable at common law for negligence in the exercise of a discretion conferred by statute, the first requirement is to show that the decision was outside the ambit of the discretion altogether: if it was not, a local authority cannot itself be in breach of any duty of care owed to the plaintiff.

In deciding whether or not this requirement is satisfied, the court has to assess the relevant factors taken into account by the authority in exercising the discretion. Since what are under consideration are discretionary powers conferred on public bodies for public purposes, the relevant factors will often include policy matters, for example social policy, the allocation of finite financial resources between the different calls made upon them or (as in *Dorset Yacht*) the balance between pursuing desirable social aims as against the risk to the public inherent in so doing. It is established that the courts cannot enter upon the assessment of such 'policy' matters. The difficulty is to identify in any particular case whether or not the decision in question is a 'policy' decision.

(b) Justiciability and the policy/operational dichotomy

In English law, the first attempt to lay down the principles applicable in deciding whether or not a decision was one of policy was made by Lord Wilberforce in *Anns v Merton London Borough Council* [1978] AC 728. [Lord Browne-Wilkinson then set out Lord Wilberforce's *dictum* on this point, which is to be found in para 8.2.7, *below*, as well as Lord Keith's *dictum* in *Rowling v Takaro Properties Ltd* [1988] AC 473, and then continued:]

From these authorities I understand the applicable principles to be as follows. Where Parliament has conferred a statutory discretion on a public authority, it is for that authority, not for the courts, to exercise the discretion: nothing which the authority does within the ambit of the discretion can be actionable at common law. If the decision complained of falls outside the statutory discretion it *can* (but not necessarily will) give rise to common law liability. However, if the factors relevant to the exercise of the discretion include matters of policy, the court cannot adjudicate on such policy matters and therefore cannot reach the conclusion that the decision was outside the ambit of the statutory discretion. Therefore a common law duty of care in relation to the taking of decisions involving policy matters cannot exist.

3 If justiciable, the ordinary principles of negligence apply

If the plaintiff's complaint alleges carelessness, not in the taking of a discretionary decision to do some act, but in the practical manner in which that act has been performed (eg the running of a school) the question whether or not there is a common law duty of care falls to be decided by applying the usual principles, ie those laid down in *Caparo Industries plc v Dickman* [1990] 2 AC 605. Was the damage to the plaintiff reasonably foreseeable? Was the relationship between the plaintiff and the defendant sufficiently proximate? Is it just and reasonable to impose a duty of care?

However, the question whether there is such a common law duty [of care] and, if so, its ambit, must be profoundly influenced by the statutory framework within which the acts complained of were done. . . . A common law duty of care cannot be imposed on a statutory duty if the observance of such common law duty of care would be inconsistent with, or have a tendency to discourage, the due performance by the local authority of its statutory duties.

In *Stovin v Wise* [1996] AC 923, Lord Hoffmann said (at p 952):

Whether [a statutory duty] can be relied upon to support the existence of a common law duty of care is not exactly a question of construction, because the cause of action does not arise out of the statute itself. But the policy of the statute is nevertheless a crucial factor in the decision [Lord Hoffmann then continued with the passage that is set out in para 8.2.6, *below*, in which he said that he doubted whether a common law duty of care can ever exist for the breach of a statutory discretion, and he concluded (at p 953):]

In summary, therefore, I think that the minimum preconditions for basing a duty of care upon the existence of a statutory power, if it can be done at all, are, first, that it would in the circumstances have been irrational not to have exercised the power, so that there was in effect a public law duty to act; and secondly, that there are exceptional grounds for holding that the policy of the statute requires compensation to be paid to persons who suffer loss because the power was not exercised.

Policy decisions

In *Just v British Columbia* (1989) 64 DLR (4th) 689, Cory J, in the Supreme Court of Canada, said (at p 705):

Policy decisions should be exempt from tortious claims so that governments are not restricted in making decisions based on social, political or economic factors. However, the implementation of those decisions may well be subject to claims in tort. What constitutes a policy decision may vary infinitely and may be made at different levels, although usually at a high level.

In determining what constitutes a policy decision, it should be borne in mind that such decisions are generally made by persons of a high level of authority in the agency, but may also properly be made by persons of a lower level of authority. The characterisation of such a decision rests on the nature of the decision and not on the identity of the actors. As a general rule, decisions concerning budgetary allotments for departments or government agencies will be classified as policy decisions.

8.2.6 Lord Hoffmann's *caveat*

In *Stovin v Wise* [1996] AC 923, Lord Hoffmann, with whose speech the three other majority Law Lords concurred, expressed doubt as to whether a wrongful exercise by a statutory authority of a statutory power or discretion can ever give rise to a private law cause of action to an individual plaintiff who has suffered loss through the exercise or non-exercise of the power or discretion in question.

Lord Hoffmann pointed out that, until the House of Lords' decision in *Anns v Merton London Borough Council* [1978] AC 728, there was no authority for treating a statutory power as giving rise to a common law duty of care. He said that two cases in particular were thought to be against it. The first of these is *Sheppard v Glossop Corporation* [1921] 3 KB 132, in which the defendant City Council had the power to light the streets of Glossop. Pursuant to this power they installed street lamps, but their policy was to turn these off at 9 pm. The plaintiff was injured when he fell over a retaining wall in the dark after the lamps had been extinguished. He sued the council for negligence. The Court of Appeal held that the council owed him no duty of care. Atkin LJ (subsequently Lord Atkin) said (at p 150):

> [The local authority] . . . is under no legal duty to act reasonably in deciding whether it shall exercise its statutory powers or not, or in deciding to what extent, over what particular area, or for what particular time, it shall exercise its powers. . . . The real complaint of the plaintiff is not that they caused the danger, but that, the danger being there, if they had lighted it up, he would have seen and avoided it.

In the second of these cases, *East Suffolk Rivers Catchment Board v Kent* [1941] AC 74, Lord Romer, basing himself on *Sheppard v Glossop Corporation*, said (at p 102): "Where a statutory authority is entrusted with a mere power it cannot be made liable for any damage sustained by a member of the public by reason of a failure to exercise that power".

Thirty-six years later, in *Anns v Merton London Borough Council* [1978] AC 728, Lord Wilberforce, speaking for himself and for Lords Diplock, Simon and Russell, dismissed the above-stated principle enunciated by Lord Romer in the *East Suffolk* case by saying (at p 755):

> I think that this [ie Lord Romer's above-cited principle] is too crude an argument. It overlooks the fact that local authorities are public bodies operating under statute with a clear responsibility for public health in their area. They must, and in fact do, make their discretionary decisions responsibly and for reasons which accord with the statutory purpose. . . . If they do not exercise their discretion in this way they can be challenged in the courts. Thus, to say that councils are under no duty to inspect is not a sufficient statement of the position. They are under a duty to give proper consideration to the question whether they should inspect or not. Their immunity from attack, in the event of failure to inspect, . . . though great, is not absolute. And because it is not absolute, the necessary premise for the proposition 'if no duty to inspect, then no duty to take care in inspection' vanishes.

In *Stovin v Wise*, Lord Nicholls, dissenting, applauded this development in *Anns*, when he said (at p 931): "Before 1978 a simple failure to exercise a statutory power did not give rise to a common law claim for damages: see [the *East Suffolk* case]. The decision in *Anns v Merton London Borough Council* [1978] AC 728 liberated the law from this unacceptable yoke. This was the great contribution that the *Anns* case made to the development of the common law".

The other four Law Lords in *Stovin v Wise* did not, however, share this feeling. After mentioning the point made *above*, that the policy of the empowering legislation pursuant to which the statutory authority has acted or decided not to act is an important factor in deciding whether an individual plaintiff should be entitled to recover damages from the statutory authority, Lord Hoffmann said (at p 952):

> The same is true of omission to perform a statutory duty [ie if the statute is important where the plaintiff has complained about an act of the statutory authority, then the statute is also important where the complaint relates to an omission]. If such a duty does not give rise to a private right to sue for breach, it would be unusual if it nevertheless gave rise to a duty of care at common law which made the public authority liable to pay compensation for foreseeable loss caused by the duty not being performed. It will often be foreseeable that loss will result if a benefit or service is not provided. If the policy of the Act is not to create a statutory liability to pay compensation, the same policy should ordinarily exclude the existence of a common law duty of care.
>
> In the case of a mere statutory power, there is the further point that the legislature has chosen to confer a discretion rather than create a duty. Of course, there may be cases in which Parliament has chosen to confer a power because the subject matter did not permit a duty to be stated with sufficient precision. It may nevertheless have contemplated that in circumstances in which it would be irrational not to exercise the power, a person who suffered loss because it had not been exercised, or not properly exercised, would be entitled to compensation. I therefore do not say that a statutory 'may' can never give rise to a common law duty of care. I prefer to leave open the question of whether the *Anns* case was wrong to create any exception to Lord Romer's statement of principle in the *East Suffolk* case. . . .

Lastly, Lord Hoffmann made clear his scepticism about plaintiffs in this type of case succeeding with their claims when he said (at p 953):

> . . . I think that the minimum preconditions for basing a duty of care upon the existence of a statutory power, if it can be done at all, are, first, that it would in the circumstances have been irrational not to have exercised the power, so that there was in effect a public law duty to act; and, secondly, that there are exceptional grounds for holding that the policy of the statute requires compensation to be paid to persons who suffer loss because the power was not exercised.

8.2.7 The policy–operational dichotomy

Until recently, the established wisdom in the cases was that if a statutory authority's exercise of a power or discretion, or its decision not to exercise a power or discretion, was based on 'policy' grounds, the courts were prohibited from pronouncing on the propriety or rationality of that decision, so that any claim by a plaintiff based on the exercise or non-exercise of such a power could not proceed because it was not justiciable by a court; but that if the exercise of the discretion (or the decision not to exercise) was based on 'operational' grounds, the courts could pronounce on the propriety or rationality of the decision.

To a large extent this principle still applies, at least where the decision was based on 'pure' policy grounds, but it is now recognised more openly that, even on a more mundane level, when considering the implementation of a statutory power or discretion on a day-to-day basis (ie at the 'operational' level), questions of policy can be involved which will effectively confer immunity from suit on the statutory authority.

In the context of this discussion, a policy decision has generally been accepted to be a decision which was based on broad considerations of social policy, or on the allocation of the statutory authority's finite financial resources between the different calls that were being made on such resources, or which was made by considering the balance between pursuing desirable social aims and the risk to the public inherent in so doing (as in the *Dorset Yacht* case—see *below*).

The other part of the established position, until recently, was that if the statutory authority's decision was based on operational factors, namely, factors involved in the practical implementation of a decision already reached (whether on policy grounds or otherwise), the court was empowered to adjudicate on the propriety or rationality of the decision even if such decision involved policy considerations.

The problem, of course, is that, while it is right and proper that policy decisions should generally be made by the statutory authority's highest forum, on a day-to-day basis the statutory authority's employees who have been charged with the task of implementing decisions made in the higher forum might also have to make decisions which involve some of these policy considerations, especially in relation to the allocation of the statutory authority's finite financial resources. The question then becomes whether, because such decisions have been made at the operational level, the statutory authority is not entitled to the same level of protection as it would have been if the same decisions had been made at a higher level.

This problem is not new. Even Lord Wilberforce, who introduced these concepts into the common law in *Anns v Merton London Borough Council* [1978] AC 728, advised against making any rigid distinctions between decisions made in the 'policy area' and in the 'operational area' of a statutory authority's activities. Thus, he said (at p 754):

> Most, indeed probably all, statutes relating to public authorities or public bodies contain in them a large area of policy. The courts call this 'discretion', meaning that the decision is one for the authority or body to make, and not for the courts. Many statutes also prescribe or at least presuppose the practical execution of policy decisions: a convenient description of this is to say that in addition to the area of policy or discretion, there is an operational area. Although this distinction between the policy area and the operational area is convenient, and illumi-

nating, it is probably a distinction of degree; many 'operational' powers or duties have in them some element of 'discretion'. It can safely be said that the more 'operational' a power or duty may be, the easier it is to superimpose upon it a common law duty of care.

This difficulty was also recognised by the Privy Council in *Rowling v Takaro Properties Ltd* [1988] AC 473, when Lord Keith said (at p 501):

> . . . this distinction does not provide a touchstone of liability, but rather is expressive of the need to exclude altogether those cases in which the decision under attack is of such a kind that a question whether it has been made negligently is unsuitable for judicial resolution, of which notable examples are discretionary decisions on the allocation of scarce resources or the distribution of risks. . . . If this is right, classification of the relevant decision as a policy or planning decision in this sense may exclude liability; but a conclusion that it does not fall within that category does not, in their Lordships' opinion, mean that a duty of care will *necessarily* exist.

In *Stovin v Wise* [1996] AC 923, Lord Hoffmann took this point one step further when he said (at p 951):

> . . . the distinction between policy and operations is an inadequate tool with which to discover whether it is appropriate to impose a duty of care or not. . . .
>
> There are at least two reasons why the distinction is inadequate. The first is that, as Lord Wilberforce himself pointed out, the distinction is often elusive. This is particularly true of powers to provide public benefits which involve the expenditure of money. Practically every decision about the provision of such benefits, no matter how trivial it may seem, affects the budget of the public authority in either timing or amount. . . . But another reason is that even if the distinction is clear cut, leaving no element of discretion in the sense that it would be irrational (in the public law meaning of that word) for the public authority not to exercise its power, it does not follow that the law should superimpose a common law duty of care. This can be seen if one looks at cases in which a public authority has been under a statutory or common law *duty* to provide a service or other benefit for the public or a section of the public. In such cases there is no discretion but the courts have nevertheless not been willing to hold that a member of the public who has suffered loss because the service was not provided to him should necessarily have a cause of action, either for breach of statutory duty or for negligence at common law.

Lord Hoffmann then referred to two decisions of the Supreme Court of Canada, namely, *Just v British Columbia* (1989) 64 DLR (4th) 689, in which a decision by a local authority on the frequency of boulder inspections was held to be operational, and *Brown v British Columbia (Minister of Transportation and Highways)* (1994) 112 DLR (4th) 1, in which the Department of Highways' decision to continue its infrequent summer schedule of road maintenance into November was held to be a matter of policy. Lord Hoffmann criticised these decisions (which are considered further in para 8.4.3, *below*) by saying: "These cases seem to me to illustrate the inadequacy of the concepts of policy and operations to provide a convincing criterion for deciding when a duty of care should exist. The distinctions which they draw are hardly visible to the naked eye".

Turning to the facts of the present case, Lord Hoffmann said that the fact that two of the county council's employees (Mr Longhurst and Mr Deller) had decided to do the work did not show that it would have been unreasonable or irrational for the council not to have done it. He said (at p 956):

> The Court of Appeal seems to have reasoned that the 'decision' to do the work disposed of any question of policy or discretion and left only the operational question of when the work should have been done. But this seems to me fallacious. The timing of the work and the budgetary year in which the money is spent is surely as much a matter of discretion as the decision in principle to do it. And why should the council be in a worse position than if Mr Longhurst had left Mr Deller's report at the bottom of his in-tray and forgotten about it? In that case, it is said, the council would have been in breach of its duty in public law to give consideration to the exercise of its powers. Perhaps it would, but that does not advance the case far enough. It would still be necessary to say that if the council had considered the matter, it would have been bound to decide to do the work. One comes back, therefore, to the question of whether it would have been irrational to decide not to do it.

Lord Hoffmann then noted that Mr Longhurst (the supervisor) had not committed himself to any particular time within which the work would be done, nor had any firm decision been taken on expenditure, and concluded (at p 957):

> It seems to me therefore that the question of whether anything should be done about the junction was at all times firmly within the area of the council's discretion. As they were therefore not under a public law duty to do the work, the first condition for the imposition of a duty of care [ie that the statutory authority had exceeded the limits of its power or discretion] was not satisfied.

8.2.8 General reliance

Often in cases involving statutory authorities, the plaintiff will not have specifically relied on the statutory authority to have exercised its power in a particular way, or to have acted rationally in deciding not to exercise that power. Indeed, the plaintiff might not have even known that the particular power existed. At the same time, however, the plaintiff might well have had a general expectation, in common with most other people in the community, that because a particular area of activity—such as the inspection of buildings in the course of their construction—was under the regulation of the statutory authority, the plaintiff was reasonably entitled to rely on the statutory authority to carry out its inspection functions without acting negligently.

This is known as the concept of 'general reliance'. In *Council of the Shire of Sutherland v Heyman* (1985) 157 CLR 424, Mason J in the High Court of Australia defined the concept of general reliance in the following terms. He said (at p 464):

> There will be cases in which the plaintiff's reasonable reliance will arise out of a general dependence on an authority's performance of its functions with due

care, without the need for action on the part of the plaintiff. Reliance or dependence in this sense is in general the product of the grant (and exercise) of powers designed to prevent or minimise a risk of personal injury or disability, recognised by the legislature as being of such magnitude or complexity that individuals cannot, or may not, take adequate steps for their own protection.

This situation generates on one side (the individual) a general expectation that the power will be exercised, and on the other side (the authority) a realisation that there is a general reliance or dependence on its exercise of the power. The control of air traffic, the safety inspection of aircraft and the fighting of a fire in a building by a fire authority may well be examples of this type of function.

The principle of general reliance is well established in New Zealand as a facet of the possible imposition of liability on statutory authorities for economic loss sustained by purchasers of houses through the statutory authority having acted negligently in inspecting the houses' foundations during the course of their construction. This can be seen in the following *dictum* of Casey J in *Williams v Mount Eden Borough Council* [1986] 1 NZBLC 102, 544:

> Having had these powers in relation to the construction of buildings conferred on it, the reasonable local authority would no doubt have accepted that they were intended to be exercised for the protection of those members of the public concerned with those buildings, whether as owners, occupiers or users. No doubt it would also have appeared to such an authority that many of them would have had no opportunity or expectation of checking or controlling *hidden* details in its construction to ensure that appropriate standards had been complied with.
>
> Conversely, those members of the public would have been aware that local bodies exercise this control over buildings constructed in their districts. This has been a known fact of New Zealand urban life for several generations. The statement by Mrs Williams that her knowledge of the Mount Eden Borough Council as 'the toughest' [council] and her assumption that everything would be all right reflects what I am sure most of the community at large would have felt.
>
> Work essential to the structural integrity of a building is almost invariably covered up, and in the usual house-buying situation, purchasers have to rely on the council doing its job properly under the building controls conferred on it. I am also satisfied that the latter and its officers would have been well aware that such reliance was placed upon it by the community at large, especially in this case where they must have realised that the builder was likely to sell the units and that there was no feasible way that any purchaser could have discovered hidden structural defects.

In two appeals from the Court of Appeal of New Zealand, *Brown v Heathcote County Council* [1987] 1 NZLR 720 and *Invercargill City Council v Hamlin* [1996] AC 624 (see para 8.4.2, *below*), the Privy Council recognised and gave effect to the principle of general reliance in the terms stated by Casey J *above*, in upholding the New Zealand Court of Appeal's decisions to impose liability on statutory authorities for their negligence in inspecting the foundations of buildings in the course of their construction.

As noted in Casey J's above-cited *dictum*, an important feature in these cases was the fact that the statutory authority knew, or ought reasonably to have known, that the consequence of its negligent performance of its inspection powers (ie defective foundations) would not be able to be discovered by subsequent purchasers of the houses, even if they commissioned independent pre-purchase inspections, because the foundations, by their very nature, would become covered up during the course of construction. In these circumstances both foreseeability of reliance on the part of the defendant (the local authority) and reasonable reliance on the part of the plaintiff (the subsequent house purchaser) were established.

It is submitted that this principle provides a full rebuttal to the following *dictum* of Lord Bridge in *Murphy v Brentwood District Council* [1991] 1 AC 398:

> A duty of care of a scope sufficient to make the authority liable for damage of the kind suffered can only be based on the principle of reliance. There is nothing in the ordinary relationship of a local authority, as statutory supervisor of building operations, and the purchaser of a defective building, capable of giving rise to such a duty;

and to the following question of Lord Oliver in the same case:

> What is it, apart from the foreseeability that the builder's failure to observe the regulations might create a situation in which expenditure by a remote owner will be required, that creates the relationship of proximity between the local authority and a remote purchaser?

The answer, it is submitted, lies in the application of the principle of general reliance in these circumstances. Interestingly, the New Zealand authorities on general reliance were not cited to their Lordships in *Murphy*, although Lord Keith was a member of the panel in both *Murphy* and *Brown v Heathcote County Council*.

In *Stovin v Wise* [1996] AC 923, Lord Hoffmann made the following comments about the doctrine of general reliance (at p 954):

> It appears to be essential to the doctrine of general reliance that the benefit or service provided under statutory powers should be of a uniform and routine nature, so that one can describe exactly what the public authority was supposed to do. Powers of inspection for defects clearly fall into this category. Another way of looking at the matter is to say that if a particular service is provided as a matter of routine, it would be irrational for a public authority to provide it in one case and arbitrarily to withhold it in another. This was obviously the main ground upon which this House in the *Anns* case considered that the power of the local authority to inspect foundations should give rise to a duty of care.

Lord Hoffmann said that he did not propose to explore the doctrine of general reliance any further because he concluded that there were no grounds upon which the present case could be brought within it. In this latter regard he said (at p 957):

> There is no question here of reliance on the council having improved the junction. Everyone could see that it was still the same. Mr Stovin was not arbitrarily denied a benefit which was routinely provided to others. In respect of the junction, he was treated in exactly the same way as any other road user. The founda-

tion for the doctrine of general reliance is missing in this case, because we are not concerned with provision of a uniform identifiable benefit or service. Every hazardous junction, intersection or stretch of road is different and requires a separate decision as to whether anything should be done to improve it. It is not without significance that the Canadian cases in which a duty of care has been held to exist have all involved routine inspection and maintenance, rather than improvements.

In *Capital and Counties Plc v Hampshire County Council* [1997] QB 1004, the Court of Appeal rejected the application of the principle of general reliance to the question whether, in the absence of a statutory duty, a statutory power to act could be converted into a common law duty to exercise the power. Counsel for the plaintiffs in one of the appeals in this case, the *London Fire Brigade* case (see para 8.2.10, *below*), submitted that the plaintiffs were entitled to rely on the doctrine of general reliance as giving rise to a duty of care on the fire brigade to respond to the public's call for help, when all that the governing legislation did was create a power to fight fires. In rejecting this submission, Stuart-Smith LJ, delivering the judgment of the court, said that the doctrine has received little if any support in English law and that there appears to be no case, except the *Anns* case itself, which could be said to be an example of its application.

8.2.9   The statutory framework

It has been noted *above* that, even if otherwise all of the reasons for imposing a duty of care at common law exist, a plaintiff's claim against a local authority for breach of a common law duty of care will often fail because the court has concluded that certain compelling overriding reasons of policy and pragmatism exist, flowing from the governing legislation pursuant to which the statutory authority derived its authority to make the decision which affected the plaintiff, and out of which the 'special relationship' between the plaintiff and the statutory authority arose, which outweigh the conferring of a right of action on the plaintiff as an individual member of the public. In other words, even though a common law duty of care owed by a statutory authority to an individual plaintiff will not exactly be a question of construction of the statute, because the cause of action does not arise out of the statute itself, the policy of the statute will nevertheless be a factor to be taken into account in the court's decision whether a duty of care should be imposed on the statutory authority for the plaintiff's loss. In *X (Minors) v Bedfordshire County Council* [1995] 2 AC 633, Lord Browne-Wilkinson expressed this point succinctly when he said (at p 739): ". . . the question whether there is such a common law duty and if so its ambit [or scope] must be profoundly influenced by the statutory framework within which the acts complained of were done".

It is not possible to lay down any general principles as to the factors which will or will not influence the court's decision either way in particular cases. However, the following general indicators are worth noting:

(1) If the court finds it impossible to discern a policy which confers a

right on individual claimants to financial compensation if the statutory power has not been exercised, this will undermine (and probably rule out) the plaintiff's claim. In *Stovin v Wise* [1996] AC 923, this was one of the reasons for the majority's rejection of the plaintiff's claim. In reaching such a conclusion, the court did not consider only the particular section relied on by the plaintiff, but also the history of the legislation. Thus, Lord Hoffmann said (at p 957): "The power in section 79 of the Highways Act 1980, upon which the plaintiff principally relies to generate a duty of care, was first enacted as section 4 of the Roads Improvement Act 1925. It seems to me impossible to discern a legislative intent that there should be a duty of care in respect of the use of that power, giving rise to a liability to compensate persons injured by a failure to use it. It is one thing to provide a service at the public expense. It is another to require the public to pay compensation when a failure to provide the service has resulted in loss".

(2) If the common law duty would impose on the statutory authority an obligation that is more onerous, so far as its behaviour is concerned, than its public law obligations, the plaintiff's common law claim will usually fail. A good example is the Privy Council's decision in *Deloitte Haskins and Sells v National Mutual Life Nominees Ltd* [1993] AC 774, which is considered *below*.

(3) If the common law duty would cut across the whole statutory system set up for the protection of the particular limited class for whose benefit the statute was passed, this too will operate against the imposition of a duty of care to an individual. This was one of the factors for the rejection of the claim by the five children in the *Bedfordshire* appeal in the *X* case in relation to their allegation that the Bedfordshire County Council, as the local authority responsible for social services, had exceeded its powers in deciding not to place the children on the child protection register and to remove them from the dangers which they faced in their parents' home. Lord Browne-Wilkinson explained this reasoning when he said (at p 749): "The task of the local authority and its servants in dealing with children at risk is extraordinarily delicate. Legislation requires the local authority to have regard not only to the physical wellbeing of the child, but also to the advantages of not disrupting the child's family environment".

(4) If the court feels that the statutory authority would adopt a more cautious and defensive approach to the implementation of its decisions if it knew that it was exposed to the possible imposition of liability to pay damages to individual claimants, this could have a negative impact on the plaintiff's claim, especially if the nature of the statutory authority's particular powers is such as to require it sometimes to make speedy decisions in the interests of protecting the limited class of person for whose benefit the statute was passed, such as children at risk.

(5) A court will be unlikely to uphold an individual plaintiff's claim for compensation against a statutory authority if the court concludes that, if a common law duty of care is held to exist, there will be a very real risk that many hopeless, and possibly vexatious, cases will be brought, thereby exposing the statutory authority to great expenditure of time and money in its defence.

8.2.10 Illustrations from cases

Introduction

The cases mentioned *below* illustrate the general principles discussed *above*. To the extent possible, similar cases have been grouped together, but this grouping must not be taken to mean that different principles are applicable to cases falling under the different groupings. On the contrary, the same principles apply across the board to all of these cases.

Construction cases

Dutton v Bognor Regis Urban District Council [1972] 1 QB 373: This case is mentioned only in passing because it was overruled by the House of Lords in *Murphy v Brentwood District Council* [1991] 1 AC 398. The facts of *Dutton* are set out in Chapter 7, para 7.7, and the case is mentioned at various other points in this book in relation to the other points that arose in it.

Anns v Merton London Borough Council [1978] AC 728: This case, too, was overruled by the House of Lords in *Murphy*. The facts are also set out in Chapter 7, para 7.7, and the 'nonfeasance' aspects of the council's decision are considered *above* in this chapter.

Peabody Donation Fund (Governors of) v Sir Lindsay Parkinson & Co Ltd and Others [1985] 1 AC 210: The relevant section of the Local Government Act 1963 stated: "It shall not be lawful to erect any building unless there are provided, to the satisfaction of the borough council, drains conforming with the requirements of this paragraph, and all such drains are constructed to the satisfaction of the council. If any works in connection with such a drain are carried out in contravention of these provisions the borough council at its option may serve on the owner of the drain a notice requiring him to cause the drain to be altered".

The plaintiff was the developer of a large housing scheme. Its architects had obtained approval to a particular type of drainage system. During the course of construction they unilaterally varied this design. The council became aware of this but took no action. When the drains were tested two years later they were found to be unsatisfactory and had to be reconstructed, causing the development to be delayed, with consequent and substantial economic loss to the plaintiff.

The court held that the council did not owe a duty of care to the plaintiff in respect of this loss; on two grounds, both of which relate to the 'scope' of the defendant's duty of care. First, the court held that, even if all the other requirements were satisfied, including the existence of a sufficient relationship of proximity, it was not "just and reasonable" to impose a duty of care in favour of this particular plaintiff, who was the original building developer, and who therefore, through its architects and contractors, was itself responsible for the defective construction of the drains. Secondly, the type of loss suffered by the plaintiff was not within the ambit of the purposes of the enabling legislation. Lord Keith said (at p 241): "The purpose for which the powers contained in paragraph 15 of Part III of Schedule 9 have been conferred on Lambeth [the defendant] is not to safeguard building developers against economic loss resulting from their failure to comply with approved plans. It is, in my opinion, to safeguard the occupiers of houses built in the local authority's area and also members of the public generally against dangers to their health which may arise from defective drainage installations. The provisions are public health measures".

Curran v Northern Ireland Co-ownership Housing Association Ltd [1987] AC 718: The plaintiff bought a house in respect of which a predecessor in title had constructed an extension with the benefit of an improvement grant from the Northern Ireland Housing Executive, whose enabling legislation stated: "The executive shall not approve an application for an improvement grant unless it is satisfied that, on completion of the relevant works, the dwelling will attain the required standard. The payment of a grant shall be conditional on the works being executed to the satisfaction of the executive". Some time after its purchase of the house the plaintiff discovered that the extension was severely defective and needed to be rebuilt at substantial cost. The plaintiff sought to recover this loss from the defendant housing association on the ground that it had been negligent in permitting the extension works to be carried out in a defective manner.

The House of Lords rejected the plaintiff's claim because the defendant did not have any control over the third party (ie the builder) who had caused the plaintiff's loss. Lord Bridge said (at p 728):

> . . . the Order which must be considered not only confers on the Executive no powers of control of building operations analogous to those on which the decision in the *Anns* case depended, it confers no powers of such control at all. Once approval has been given to an application for an improvement grant, the Executive have no powers under the Order to control the building owner, still less the builder whom he chooses to employ. . . . Their only power is to withhold payment of the grant . . . if the works . . . have not been executed to their satisfaction. . . . To hold that the Executive owe a duty of care to a building owner which they can only perform by refusing to pay him the grant they have approved seems to me an almost bizarre conclusion. In so far as article 60(5) of the Order imposes any duty on the Executive to satisfy themselves that the grant-aided works have been properly executed, as opposed to conferring a power to withhold payment if not so satisfied, it seems to me clear that the purpose of imposing any such duty is for the protection of the public revenue, not of the recipients of the grant of their successors in title.

Murphy v Brentwood District Council [1991] 1 AC 398: The facts of this case are set out in Chapter 7, para 7.7. As mentioned in this chapter, the main ground for rejecting the plaintiff's claim was that the House of Lords concluded that there was not a sufficient relationship of proximity between the plaintiff purchaser of the house with the defectively designed foundations and the local authority which had negligently approved that design.

The court also held that, in any event, the purposes of the Public Health Act 1936 (pursuant to which the defendant had, as it was obliged to do, referred the plans to consulting engineers) did not extend to protection of house owners against pure economic loss by virtue of the negligent approval of any such plans. Thus, Lord Keith said (at p 468): "Though the purposes of the Act of 1936 as regards securing compliance with building bye-laws covered the avoidance of injury to the safety or health of inhabitants of houses and of members of the public generally, the purposes did not cover the avoidance of pure economic loss to owners of buildings", and Lord Oliver said (at p 490): "There is nothing in the statutory provisions [ie the Public Health Acts] which even suggests that the purpose of the statute was to protect owners of buildings from economic loss". This aspect of the case is discussed further in para 8.2.9.

Financial regulation cases

Minories Finance Ltd v Arthur Young (Bank of England, third party) [1989] 2 All ER 105 (also sometimes referred to as *Johnson Matthey plc v Arthur Young (Bank of England, third party)*: Following the insolvency of Johnson Matthey Bankers Ltd's ('JMB') commercial banking business and its financial rescue by the Bank of England ('the Bank'), Minories Finance Ltd ('MF') claimed damages in negligence against JMB's auditors (Arthur Young), alleging that they should have discovered and reported on the state of JMB's loan portfolio and that, had they done so, much of the loss sustained by JMB would have been avoided. The auditors denied liability but joined the Bank as a third party from whom they claimed an indemnity on the basis that the Bank, as the body responsible for the supervision of banks, owed a duty of care to JMB to carry out its investigations and checks of JMB with reasonable care and had failed to do so.

The present action was concerned with the Bank's application to strike out the auditors' third party notice on the ground that the Bank did not owe a duty of care to an individual commercial bank to exercise reasonable skill and care in carrying out its function of supervising the operations of individual commercial banks. The judge, Saville J, agreed with this contention and struck out the third party notice. He said (at p 110):

> ... the negligence alleged against the Bank of England is not that wrong or misleading advice or instructions were given in the course of supervision. What is alleged is that the Bank of England negligently failed to discover or comment on or take any appropriate action in relation to the imprudent and careless manner in which JMB was conducting its commercial loan portfolio.
> ... therefore, the proposition is that the Bank of England was under a legal obligation to JMB to exercise reasonable care and skill in its supervision of this

bank, so as to avoid financial loss accruing to JMB from its own imprudent or careless conduct.

In my judgment principles of common sense and reason do not indicate that such an obligation should exist. On the contrary, it seems to offend these principles to suggest that a commercial concern such as JMB can look to the Bank of England to make good its losses arising from its own imprudence or carelessness, on the basis that the Bank of England should have discovered and dealt with those shortcomings. It was suggested in argument on behalf of JMB that a true analogy with the relationship between the Bank of England and JMB was one of nurse and mental patient. That cannot be right. . . . Unlike the mental patient, whose responsibility for himself is diminished to such an extent that others must assume that responsibility, there is nothing in the alleged relationship between the Bank of England and private banks . . . to suggest that the latter should be protected from themselves by the former.

Yuen Kun Yeu and Others v Attorney General of Hong Kong [1988] 1 AC 175: The plaintiffs were four individuals resident in Hong Kong who had made substantial deposits with a registered deposit-taking company which subsequently went into insolvent liquidation, thereby causing the plaintiffs to lose all their money. The relevant legislation appointed a commissioner of deposit-taking companies and established a system of compulsory registration. The commissioner was obliged to refuse to register or to cancel the registration of any company which appeared to him to be not a fit and proper body to be so registered. All registered deposit-taking companies were obliged to lodge their annual accounts with the commissioner, to submit monthly returns to him showing their assets and liabilities, to maintain certain reserves, to limit the number of loans made to directors and employees, etc.

The plaintiffs alleged that the commissioner was negligent in not discovering that the affairs of the company with whom they had placed their deposits were being conducted fraudulently and to the detriment of depositors, so that he should have revoked its registration. The plaintiffs would then not have deposited their money with that company. They claimed that the commissioner owed them a duty of care in respect of their losses because they said that they made their deposits in reliance on the fact that the company was registered by the commissioner, because this indicated to them that it was a fit and proper body to be registered and that it was the subject of continued prudential supervision by the commissioner.

The Privy Council rejected their claim. First, the court rejected the plaintiffs' reliance argument on the ground that the cases which have upheld it have turned on the voluntary assumption of responsibility towards a particular party, giving rise to a special relationship. Lord Bridge said (at p 196): "In the present case there was clearly no voluntary assumption by the commissioner of any responsibility towards the plaintiffs, in relation to the affairs of the company. It was argued, however, that the effect of the Ordinance was to place such a responsibility upon him. Their Lordships consider that the Ordinance placed a duty on the commissioner to supervise deposit-taking companies in the general public interest, but no special responsibility towards individual members of the public. His position is analogous to that of a police force [see the case of *Hill*, para 8.3.3, *below*]".

Secondly, the court held that there was not a special relationship between the commissioner and the third party who had actually caused the plaintiff's loss (ie the fraudulent deposit-taking company) "of the nature described by Dixon J in *Smith v Leurs* [see para 8.3.3, *below*] and such as was held to exist between the prison officers and the borstal boys in *Dorset Yacht Co v Home Office* [see para 8.3.3, *below*]". Lord Keith said (at p 196): "In contradistinction to the position in *Dorset Yacht*, the commissioner had no power to control the day-to-day activities of those who caused the loss. The commissioner only had power to stop the company carrying on business. The circumstance that the commissioner had, on the plaintiff's averments, cogent reason to suspect that the company's business was being carried on fraudulently did not create a special relationship between the commissioner and the company of the nature described in the authorities".

Rowling v Takaro Properties Ltd [1988] AC 473: The plaintiff was a property developer in New Zealand, who applied to Mr Rowling, the Minister of Finance (the defendant), for consent under the relevant regulations to issue shares in the plaintiff company to a Japanese prospective investor in relation to the development of a holiday resort in New Zealand. The Minister, in consultation with the Cabinet Economic Committee, rejected the plaintiff's application. The plaintiff applied for and obtained judicial review, which was to the effect that the Minister's decision was wrong. The Minister appealed, but was not successful. In the meantime the Japanese investor lost interest and withdrew from the scheme, which then collapsed completely, causing the plaintiff to suffer substantial losses, which the plaintiff sought to recover from the defendant on the ground that he owed the plaintiff a duty of care in tort because he knew that the plaintiff would suffer serious financial loss if he refused to give his consent.

The Privy Council rejected the plaintiff's claim because, although the defendant had wrongly estimated the extent of his powers, the defendant had not acted negligently, as he and his colleagues had acted in good faith, albeit mistakenly. The court therefore did not need to consider whether the Minister owed the plaintiff a duty of care. Nevertheless, the court expressed the opinion that where, as here, the allegation is that the Minister of another governmental agency mistook the extent of its powers, it does not seem right, even if the Minister acted negligently, to say that he owed a duty of care in tort to the person affected thereby. That person's primary remedy is to obtain judicial review, as the plaintiff did in this case. The Minister would then have to consider his decision afresh.

Having succeeded in getting the Minister's decision quashed, the plaintiff was in the same position as if it had never applied to the Minister for consent to issue shares to an overseas investor, except for the losses which it had suffered by virtue of the delay. The court said that it would be highly unusual to find that an individual member of the public could make a minister or other governmental body responsible for the economic losses which it had suffered by virtue of a delay in the exercise of a discretion, especially where, as here, the Minister was not under any duty to exercise his discretion within any particular time.

Davis v Radcliffe [1990] 1 WLR 821: This was a claim by two plaintiffs who had deposited money with a bank in the Isle of Man which subsequently went into insolvent liquidation. Their claim was against the Isle's Finance Board members on the ground of their negligence in exercising their supervisory duties over the failed bank. The Privy Council rejected their claim and said that it was indistinguishable from its decision in *Yuen Kun Yeu*.

Nevertheless, it is interesting to note the court's specific reasons. First, the court said that it is clear from the relevant enabling legislation that the functions of the Finance Board are to be exercised in the general public interest, and not for the benefit of any particular individual. In exercising its licensing powers, it would have been involved in matters of judgment (at p 827):

> ... of a delicate nature affecting the whole future of the relevant bank in the Isle of Man, and the impact of any consequent cessation of the bank's business in the Isle of Man, not merely upon the customers and creditors of the bank, but indeed upon the future of financial services in the island. In circumstances such as these, competing considerations have to be carefully weighed and balanced in the public interest, [so that it might] be more in the public interest to attempt to nurse an ailing bank to health than to hasten its collapse. The making of decisions such as these is a characteristic task of modern regulatory agencies; and the very nature of the task, with its emphasis on the broader public interest, is one which militates strongly against the imposition of a duty of care ... in favour of any particular section of the public.

Secondly, the court dealt with the difficulty created by the fact that the plaintiffs' loss had actually been caused by a third party (the fraudulent bank) and not by the defendant regulatory authority. Lord Goff said (at p 827):

> In the case of physical damage caused by the deliberate wrongdoing of a third party, such liability will only be imposed in limited classes of case... Here it is suggested that such liability should be imposed for purely financial loss flowing from the negligence of a third party. It must be rare that any such liability will be imposed; but in any event it is difficult to see that, in the present case, the defendants possessed sufficient control over the management of [the bank] to warrant the imposition of any such liability.

Lonrho plc v Tebbit [1992] 4 All ER 280: In 1981 the plaintiffs announced a takeover bid for a company which owned the Harrods department store. This resulted in a reference to the Monopolies and Mergers Commission (MMC), which ruled that this merger situation might be expected to operate against the public interest. The plaintiff was therefore invited to give, and gave, an undertaking to the Secretary of State for Trade and Industry (represented by the defendant) that it would not seek to increase its shareholding to 30 per cent or more. Subsequently, after certain board changes, there was another reference to the MMC, which, on 14 February 1985, reported that the plaintiff's proposed acquisition would not operate contrary to the public interest. Shortly before this report came out the plaintiff had been pressing the defendant to release it from its undertaking, so that it could make an offer for the whole share capital of the company. When the report came out, the defendant failed to give this release. The plaintiff continued to press the defendant for this release, but it was not given until 14 March 1985, by which time a rival bidder had acquired control of the company, and it was too late for the plaintiff to make a bid.

The plaintiff instituted proceedings against the defendant for the losses which it suffered by not being able to make the bid which it would have done if the defendant had released it from its undertaking immediately after 14 February 1985, when the whole basis of that undertaking had gone, in view of the MMC's conclusion that the takeover would not operate contrary to the public interest. The defendant applied to have the plaintiff's claim struck out on the grounds that it disclosed no reasonable cause of action or was an abuse of the process of the court on the grounds

(1) that, being a claim based on negligence by the defendant in the exercise of his discretionary powers under statute, it was not justiciable because it raised matters of state policy and the defendant owed no duty of care to the plaintiff regarding the exercise of those powers;

(2) that there did not exist between the plaintiff and the defendant a sufficient relationship of proximity necessary to found a claim in negligence for pure economic loss;

(3) that the plaintiff's claims related to public law duties and should therefore have been brought by way of judicial review.

Thus, this case was similar to *Rowling v Takara*, considered *above*. Nevertheless, the court refused to accede to the defendant's application. This does not, of course, mean that it has been established that the defendant owed a duty of care to the plaintiff in these circumstances but simply that the court was not prepared to conclude that the plaintiff's claim was "obviously doomed to fail". Dillon LJ took note of the fact that a person in the position of the plaintiff has never succeeded in a case like this (see *above*) but said (at p 286): "But the fields of law with which we are concerned in this case are difficult and developing". He noted in particular the difficulties in the plaintiff's case highlighted by the Privy Council in *Rowling v Takara*, but also pointed to the fact that Lord Keith in that case had said (at p 501): "The question whether a duty of care should be imposed is a question of an intensely pragmatic character, well-suited for gradual development but requiring most careful analysis". The facts of the present case were not sufficiently the same as those in *Rowling* to say that that case was decisive in this case. (Also, as noted *above*, the court's comments on this point in *Rowling* were *obiter*.)

Deloitte Haskins and Sells v National Mutual Life Nominees Ltd [1993] AC 774: Australasia Investment Co Securities Ltd's ('AICS') business included the receipt of deposits from the public on an unsecured basis. This brought

AICS within the ambit of certain securities legislation, pursuant to which AICS had to appoint a trustee in respect of the securities and an auditor, whose duties were prescribed by the Act. Section 50(2) of the Act stated: "Whenever, in the performance of his duties as auditor, the auditor of an issuer of debt securities becomes aware of any matter that in his opinion is relevant to the exercise of the performance of the powers or duties of the trustee, he shall, within seven days of becoming so aware, send a report in writing on the matter to the issuer and to the trustee".

In early 1986, Deloitte Haskins and Sells (the defendant), as the appointed auditor in relation to AICS's deposit-taking business, while preparing AICS's audit for the year ending 31 December 1985, became concerned about the collectibility of certain loans. After further inquiries, the defendant made a report under s 50(2) of the Act on 15 May 1986, but it did not state therein that, in its opinion, AICS was insolvent or on the brink of insolvency, either or both of which assertions would probably have been true at that time.

After receiving this report, AICS continued to trade as normal. On 11 August 1986, the defendant, as auditor of AIC Merchant Finance, an associated company of AICS, issued a further (and sterner) report under s 50(2), which resulted in the trustee putting AIC Merchant Finance into receivership, and this led directly to the liquidation of AICS itself on 30 August 1996. The liquidation of AICS left the trustee of AICS with a liability of $6.75m to AIC depositors, which the trustee settled in due course.

In the present action, the trustee sought to recover the $6.75m from the defendant (the auditor) on the basis of an alleged breach of a common law duty in relation to the defendant's reporting obligation under s 50(2) of the Act, claiming that the defendant was negligent in failing to report AICS's probable insolvency by mid-March 1986 when it was preparing its 1985 audit report and s 50(2) report on AICS. The Court of Appeal of New Zealand upheld the trustee's claim, but this was overruled by the Privy Council because the common law duty of care contended for (and accepted by the New Zealand Court of Appeal) would have been more extensive than the duty imposed on the defendant under the Act. Thus, Lord Jauncey, delivering the unanimous opinion of the Privy Council, said (at p 786):

> There is no doubt that, by reason of the provisions of section 50(2) of the Act of 1978, there was created a relationship of proximity between the auditor and the trustee. If the auditor sent a report to AICS and the trustee under section 50(2), it was under a duty to exercise reasonable care in the preparation thereof, knowing that it would be received and relied upon by the trustee. . . The issue in this appeal, however, is not whether there was such a relationship of proximity but how far any duties arising out of that relationship extended.
>
> . . . s 50(2) creates no statutory duty to form an opinion. . . the inclusion of the words 'in his opinion' [in section 50(2)] suggests that it is a subjective rather than an objective test which has to be applied. Had the intention been to apply the test of the reasonably careful auditor these words would have been out of

place. This analysis affords no support for the view that the legislature intended the subsection to impose any duty on an auditor other than to report when he had formed the relevant opinion.

Given that the duty under s 50(2) only arose when the auditor had formed an opinion, the effect of the decisions in the courts below was to impose upon the auditor a common law duty more extensive than that imposed by the Act.

For this reason the Privy Council held that the defendant did not owe a duty of care to the plaintiff at common law for the plaintiff's loss. This aspect of the decision is considered further in Chapter 2, para 2.1.5.

West Wiltshire District Council v Garland [1993] Ch 409: The plaintiff district council sued two of its senior officers ('the officers') for breach of contract and for breach of fiduciary duties owed by them to the council arising out of certain payments of the council's funds which they procured to be made without proper authority. The present action was concerned with the officers' third party claim for an indemnity from the council's statutory auditor ('the auditor') based on the officers' allegation that at all times they performed their duties as servant or agent of the council in the manner prescribed or recommended by the auditor.

The auditor applied to strike out the officers' third party claim on the ground that, when the auditor exercises its statutory functions under the Local Government Finance Act 1982, it cannot be liable in damages for breach of statutory duty, nor does it owe a duty of care in common law to the local authority whose accounts it audits or to the officers of that authority. At first instance, Morritt J accepted this submission in relation to the officers, but not in relation to the council. He said (at p 418):

> This issue depends on the proper construction of the Local Government Finance Act 1982 and the answer to two questions: . . .
> (1) whether the provision in question is intended to protect the interests of a class of which the council or the officer is a member, and
> (2) did Parliament intend to confer on the council or the officer a cause of action for a breach of such duty.
>
> The first question may be elaborated by considering what was the primary object which Parliament intended thereby to achieve. . .
>
> It is manifest that the functions of the auditor go a long way beyond that of the auditor of the accounts of a limited company pursuant to the Companies Acts. . .
>
> But it seems to me to be clear beyond doubt that it is not the primary object of [the Local Government Finance Act] to protect the officers. It is not the function of any audit to protect the servants or agents of the body whose accounts are being examined; rather, it is the actions of those servants or agents which are to be scrutinised. . . . It seems to me to be clear beyond argument that there can be no cause of action against the auditor for damages for breach of statutory duty at the suit of the officers.

However, Morritt J did conclude that it was arguable that the auditor did owe a statutory duty to the council itself, and he therefore refused to strike out that part of the third party claim. Having so concluded, Morritt J said that he did not find it necessary to consider the alternative claim that the auditor owed a common law duty of care to the council, thereby leaving this part of the third party notice intact. The auditor appealed against both of these parts of Morritt J's decision. The officers did not appeal against the decision mentioned *above*, that their third party notice be struck out as disclosing no cause of action against the auditor.

West Wiltshire District Council v Garland [1995] Ch 297 (CA): This case was concerned with the appeal of the auditor against Morritt J's refusal to strike out the part of the third party claim against it in which it was alleged that it owed a statutory duty and a duty of care at common law to the council.

First, the Court of Appeal agreed with Morritt J that it is arguable that the auditor did owe a statutory duty to the council because the primary purpose of the legislation was to protect the local authority as a body.

Secondly, although Morritt J had felt it unnecessary to deal with the council's alternative common law claim in view of his finding that it was arguable that the auditor owed the council a statutory duty, the Court of Appeal did deal with this question, and held that this part of the third party notice could not be struck out. The Court of Appeal's reasoning on this point is, however, very brief and does not contain any analysis. Thus, Balcombe LJ said (at p 310): ". . . I do not find it necessary to consider the many cases to which we were referred on the substantive question whether there exists a common law duty of care on the part of the district auditors towards the council. It is sufficient to say that in my judgment the existence of such a duty enforceable by action for negligence is clearly arguable and a pleading making such a claim should not be struck out *in limine*".

Three Rivers District Council v Bank of England (No 3) [1997] 3 All ER 558: The plaintiffs were depositors with a deposit-taker (BCCI) licensed by the Bank of England ('the Bank'), who lost the amount deposited when BCCI went into insolvent liquidation. The plaintiffs contended that the Bank was liable to make good their losses. The present action proceeded by way of a trial of certain preliminary issues, including the question whether the plaintiffs could base their personal claim for a duty of care by the Bank to them on Council Directive (EEC) 77/780 ('the 1977 directive'). The plaintiffs recognised that, in the light of the Privy Council's decisions in *Yuen Kun Yeu v Attorney General of Hong Kong* and *Davis v Radcliffe* (see *above*), they could not simply allege that the Bank was in breach of its statutory duty under the Banking Acts 1979 and 1987 by failing properly and carefully to supervise BCCI. Instead, the plaintiffs argued that the 1977 directive has direct effect in the United Kingdom and that, as parties intended to benefit from it, they were entitled to rely on its terms in an English court in order to obtain damages.

The judge, Clarke J, rejected the plaintiffs' claim, and in so doing accepted the Bank's submission that the 1977 directive was not intended to confer rights upon depositors of commercial banks like BCCI, even if such depositors were intended to benefit from the supervision system contemplated by the directive. Clarke J said (at p 600):

> The two Privy Council cases [ie *Yuen* and *Davis*] are important for three reasons. The first is that in each case it was held that the supervisor had no day-to-day control of the supervised institution. The same is true here. The second important factor to be derived from the Privy Council cases is closely related to the first. It is that the immediate cause of the loss was the fraud of the managers of the supervised institution. The supervisor neither had the power to control the day-to-day operation of the supervised institution and thus to prevent fraud, nor did it in fact have that control, unlike the prison officers in *Dorset Yacht* [see *below*]. The third important factor is that the exercise of the powers and duties of a supervisor in this field involves the balancing of many different factors in the interests both of the public generally and of both existing and future depositors. The interests of these and other different groups may conflict, so that it makes no real sense to hold that a [common law] duty of care or a statutory duty is owed to only one or some of those groups. Those [Privy Council] cases make it clear that it does not follow from the fact that one of the underlying purposes of the supervisory scheme was to give protection to existing and future savers, that the statutes setting up the scheme either did or were intended to confer rights upon such savers exercisable against the supervisor. Whether any particular statute does so depends on its true construction having regard to all the circumstances of the case including its purpose. The same is true of the directive.

Clarke J then construed the operative provisions of the directive in detail. He concluded that the directive did not confer rights on individual savers, because it was clear from a reading of the directive that, even though the underlying purpose of the supervision of credit institutions is to protect savers, the purpose of the directive was to harmonise banking systems in the European Community, not to confer legal rights on savers and depositors enforceable against national supervising bodies.

Tee v Lautro Ltd (16 July 1996, unreported): The defendant, The Life and Unit Trust Regulatory Organisation ('Lautro'), is a self-regulating organisation under the Financial Services Act 1986. One of its functions is the regulation of its members, who are companies engaged in the provision of financial, insurance or investment services in the life and unit trusts industries. The plaintiff, Mr Tee, was the holder of 51 per cent of the shares in a company named The Winchester Group plc ('WG'), which was established for the purpose of providing insurance services as the representative of one or more insurance companies. In due course it became an appointed representative of Norwich Union Life Insurance Society ('Norwich Union'), which was a member of Lautro.

Subsequently, Lautro became concerned about certain matters connected with WG's business. Lautro had no power over WG itself because WG was not one of its members. Lautro did, however, have power over Norwich Union, as a Lautro member. Lautro therefore served an 'Intervention Notice' on Norwich Union, barring it from accepting new business from WG. Lautro stated that its reason for proceeding in this fashion was its concern that Mr Tee was associating with certain known criminals.

After issuing the Intervention Notice, Lautro continued its investigations, in the course of which Mr Tee and other representatives of WG were given the opportunity to make representations to Lautro. Mr Tee brought an application in the High Court for judicial review of Lautro's decision to issue the Intervention Notice. This application was refused. Mr Tee appealed to the Court of Appeal. While the appeal was pending, Lautro received a report which cleared Mr Tee of the criminal association case, but Lautro nevertheless decided not to revoke the Intervention Notice because it concluded that WG was responsible for a significant number of breaches of the Lautro code of conduct. In due course, Mr Tee's judicial review appeal was heard by the Court of Appeal. Its decision was that Lautro had breached the duty that it owed to Mr Tee to act fairly when issuing and serving an Intervention Notice, but the Court of Appeal was not prepared to quash the Intervention Notice because Lautro had acted within the limits of its discretion in not revoking the Notice due to WG's breaches of the Lautro code of conduct.

In the present action, Mr Tee claimed damages from Lautro on the ground that Lautro owed him a duty of care, which it breached by its alleged negligence in issuing the Intervention Notice in the first place because, at that time, Lautro ought to have known that there was no connection between Mr Tee and the known criminals with whom Lautro alleged he had associated. Mr Tee's counsel submitted that he was in a very different position *vis-à-vis* Lautro from the position of depositors *vis-à-vis* the authorities in *Yuen Kun Yeu* and *Davis v Radcliffe*, because his career in the financial services field was likely to be devastated by the criminal association allegations that Lautro had negligently made against him, by way of an analogy with the employee/plaintiff in *Spring v Guardian Assurance plc* [1995] 2 AC 296 who was unable to find other employment in the financial services sector because of the bad reference on him which Guardian had given to a prospective employer (see Chapter 9, para 9.7.7).

Lautro denied that any such duty of care existed, and applied to strike out Mr Tee's Statement of Claim. The judge, Ferris J, agreed with Lautro. He said (at para 52):

> Although I can follow the reasoning which led Lord Goff [in *Spring v Guardian*] to the conclusion that, on the facts of that case, there was an element of assumption of responsibility on the part of the defendant and of reliance on the part of the plaintiff, I am unable to discover in the pleaded facts of the case before me anything which is sufficient to support an equivalent line of reasoning. Mr Tee was not an employee, even in the widest possible sense of the term, of Lautro or of any company with which Lautro was associated or which Lautro regulated. He was merely a shareholder in, and perhaps an employee of, WG, whose business was already affected by a step taken by Lautro in the regulation of one of its members, Norwich Union. Even though it was foreseeable that the step which Lautro took in relation to Norwich Union would cause loss and damage to WG and so be likely to cause detriment to the shareholders and employees of WG, foreseeability by itself is not sufficient. I see nothing in the facts which is capable

of bringing Mr Tee's claim within the principles of assumption of responsibility and reliance in the way in which Lord Goff thought the facts of Mr Spring's case did.

Ferris J also rejected Mr Tee's counsel's submission that, if Lautro owed Mr Tee a public law duty of procedural fairness (see *above*), why should it not also owe Mr Tee a private law duty of care? Thus, Ferris J said (at para 55):

> Mr Tee's counsel's superficially attractive argument to the effect of 'Granted that Lautro owed Mr Tee a duty of fairness, why should it not also owe him a duty of care?' is, I think, dangerous in its simplicity. The true view, in my judgment, is that in exercising its regulatory functions under its rules, Lautro owes to Mr Tee, and to others in a similar position, a public law duty to exercise procedural fairness in the way which was established on Mr Tee's application for judicial review. While the movement involved in passing from procedural fairness to a duty of care may seem to be slight, it is in fact very substantial. The public law duty and the supposed private law duty are based on very different principles. In my judgment the duty of care which is suggested in this case cannot be derived from the relevant private law principles.

Social services cases

T (a minor) v Surrey County Council [1994] 4 All ER 577: The mother of the plaintiff, a six-month-old baby boy, wished to find a full-time child-minder for him. She contacted the defendant's social services department in this regard because she wanted to engage a registered child-minder only. She spoke to the defendant's nursery and child-minding adviser, Mr Bodycomb, but he was unable to provide her with the name of anyone suitable or available at that time. Subsequently, the plaintiff's mother saw an advertisement that had been placed by a Mrs Walton, who said that she was available for child-minding.

The plaintiff's mother then telephoned Mr Bodycomb again. She told him that she had seen Mrs Walton's advertisement and that she had spoken to Mrs Walton over the telephone. She asked Mr Bodycomb for his confirmation that Mrs Walton was registered, and he said that she was. The plaintiff's mother then asked Mr Bodycomb if he was happy for the plaintiff to be placed in Mrs Walton's care, and he replied "Yes".

What Mr Bodycomb did not tell the plaintiff's mother was that, less than three months earlier, another baby in the care of Mrs Walton had been seriously injured, probably through violent shaking, and that this incident had been discussed at two case conferences convened by the defendant, at which Mr Bodycomb was present. Those present at the case conferences were unable to resolve whether Mrs Walton had caused the other child's injury, with the result that the defendant took no action to deregister Mrs Walton, although Mr Bodycomb advised her informally that in the future she should look after children between the ages of two and five only. Mr Bodycomb did not pass any of this information on to the plaintiff's mother during the above-mentioned conversation.

Soon after the plaintiff had been placed with Mrs Walton, he suffered a non-accidental injury involving serious brain damage similar to the injury suffered by the previous infant. In the present action, the plaintiff's action against the local authority was based on breach of statutory duty for failure to cancel Mrs Walton's registration pursuant to s 5 of the Nurseries and Child-minders Regulation Act 1948, for breach of a common law duty of care for failure to cancel the registration and for negligent misstatement by Mr Bodycomb. The first two of these causes of action failed, but the third succeeded.

In dealing with the plaintiff's first claim, the judge, Scott Baker J, first set out s 5 of the Act, which states: "Where it appears to the local health authority as respects any premises or person registered under the Act that circumstances exist which would justify a refusal to register, the local health authority may cancel the registration"; and then said (at p 595):

> The way the Act works is that section 5 gives the local authority a discretion to cancel a registration where circumstances exist that would justify a refusal to register. It was clearly the intention of Parliament that only those who are fit to look after children under five should be registered as child-minders. In my judgment, a person cannot be so fit for the purposes of this legislation where there is, as here, an unresolved question about a non-accidental injury.
>
> In evidence Mr Bodycomb agreed that there was a real and not fanciful risk to [the plaintiff] in placing him with Mrs Walton and that the risk was of non-accidental injury by an adult. I am not confident that Mr Bodycomb, or anybody else at the local authority, ever really addressed his mind properly to the question of cancellation of registration.
>
> . . . I am in no doubt that the local authority failed to meet their obligations under the Act. They should either have cancelled Mrs Walton's registration or at the very least have suspended it whilst they made vigorous further inquiries.

Despite this finding, Scott Baker J rejected this part of the plaintiff's claim. He said (at p 596):

> It by no means follows that, because the local authority failed to meet its obligations under the Act, an action lies against it for breach of statutory duty. It is a question of the true construction of the Act whether an action lies with a private individual for breach of its provisions.
>
> . . . I agree with [the defendant's counsel's] analysis . . . that the intention of Parliament was that the local authority should provide information by means of a register and take precautions to ensure appropriate persons and premises were registered and deregistered. The Act was passed for the benefit of the public as a whole and only, in the very broadest sense, for the benefit of children under the age of five (the age to which the legislation then related).

Scott Baker J then referred to the following *dictum* of Lord Jauncey in *Hague v Deputy Governor of Parkhurst Prison, Weldon v Home Office* [1992] 1 AC 58 (at p 170): "The fact that a particular provision was intended to protect certain individuals is not of itself sufficient to confer private law rights of action upon them, something more is required to show that the legislation intended such conferment"; and concluded by saying (at p 597):

> I can find nothing in the present Act to indicate such an intention. I detect a considerable reluctance on the part of the courts to impose upon local author-

ities any liability for breach of statutory duty other than that expressly imposed in the statute. In my judgment, the claim for breach of statutory duty fails.

In rejecting the plaintiff's claim that the defendant breached a common law duty of care to the plaintiff, based on its failure to cancel Mrs Walton's registration, Scott Baker J said (at p 599):

> Whilst it is true that the courts are more ready to find a duty of care owed where the consequence of a breach is personal injury rather than damage to property and still less mere economic loss, to hold that a duty was owed in the present case would be breaking entirely new ground.
> ... What we have here is the local authority required by statute to act as a licensing authority. It is going a long way, without more, to hold a licensing authority liable for the misfeasance of a third party [Mrs Walton] when it negligently grants or refuses to cancel a licence. As Lord Goff said in *Smith v Littlewoods Organisation Ltd* [1997] AC 241 (see *below*), 'there is no *general* duty of care to prevent third parties from [causing damage to the plaintiff or his property by the third party's own deliberate wrongdoing].
> [Although] the local authority's powers [in this case] . . . are specifically defined by statute, . . . the word 'may' rather than 'shall' is used in defining the local authority's obligations.
> In my judgment, the issues of breach of statutory duty and common law negligence in respect of the exercise by the local authority of its power under this Act run very much hand in glove. In my judgment, there is no common law duty owed of the nature contended for by the plaintiff. . . .

However, as noted *above*, Scott Baker J did grant the plaintiff's claim based on negligent misrepresentation. He said (at p 600):

> In my judgment, the criteria for founding liability for negligent misstatement are met. . . . this case falls four square within the principle laid down in *Hedley Byrne and Co Ltd v Heller and Partners Ltd* [1964] AC 465, but the plaintiff's position is stronger in the present case because he suffered physical injury rather than mere economic loss.

In so holding, Scott Baker J rejected the defendant's counsel's submission that, even if a duty of care did exist, and even if it was breached, that breach was not the cause of the plaintiff's injury because that injury was inflicted solely by Mrs Walton. In rejecting this submission, Scott Baker J said (at p 601):

> In the present case, Mr Bodycomb knew that [the plaintiff's mother] was considering placing [the plaintiff] with Mrs Walton. He knew, too, or would have done had he stopped to think about it, that had she known the information that was imparted to him at the two case conferences, she would not have placed [the plaintiff] with Mrs Walton. He knew that there was a significant risk to any small baby in Mrs Walton's care. In these circumstances I find the local authority liable in negligence to the plaintiff. There will therefore be judgment for the plaintiff against the local authority with damages to be assessed.

X (Minors) v Bedfordshire County Council [1995] 2 AC 633: This case was concerned with five separate appeals, which raised issues relating to two separate strands of legislation, but all of the appeals were concerned with striking out applications by the defendant statutory authorities. For the purpose of such applications the facts alleged by the plaintiff/s in each case had to be assumed to be correct.

In the *Bedfordshire* case (ie *X (Minors) v Bedfordshire County Council*) and the *Newham* case (ie *M (a minor) v Newham London Borough Council*) the relevant legislation related to the protection of children at risk in the community. In the other three cases, namely, the *Dorset* case (ie *E (a minor) v Dorset County Council*), the *Hampshire* case (ie *Christmas v Hampshire County Council*) and the *Bromley* case (ie *Keating v Bromley London Borough Council*), the legislation related to the educational needs of children in state schools.

In the *Bedfordshire* case, the plaintiffs were five children between one and eight years old in the same family, who claimed damages for personal injury from the defendant council for the breach of its statutory duties under the Children and Young Persons Act 1969 and the Child Care Act 1980, and at common law on the basis of a duty of care owed by the defendant to them arising out of the defendant's investigation of reports made to the defendant by third parties that the plaintiffs had suffered parental abuse and neglect and the defendant's failure to remove the plaintiffs from their parents' custody.

In the *Newham* case, the plaintiffs, a four-year-old girl and her mother, claimed damages for personal injuries against the local authority and the area health authority and a consultant psychiatrist employed by the latter authority, based on breach of statutory duty and common law negligence arising out of the defendants' inept investigation of their suspicions that the plaintiff's mother's cohabitee had sexually abused the minor plaintiff, with the consequence that she was removed from her mother's care and suffered damage in consequence.

In both of these cases the plaintiffs' claims based on breach of statutory duty were struck out as disclosing no cause of action, because their Lordships held that the statutes in question were all concerned with the establishment of a system to promote social welfare, where difficult decisions often have to be taken on the basis of inadequate and disputed facts. In such a context, exceptionally clear statutory language is required to indicate a parliamentary intention to create a private law remedy, because the actual words used in the primary legislation are clearly inconsistent with any such intention.

In these two cases the plaintiffs' claims based on a common law duty of care owed to them by the statutory authorities also failed because, even if otherwise all the conditions existed for the imposition of a common law duty of care, the House of Lords refused to impose such a duty on the statutory authorities because it would cut across the statutory system for the protection of children and might, in a delicate situation, make local authorities adopt a more cautious approach in exercising their duties and powers under the legislation, to the prejudice of children; and because there was no justification, by analogy with decided categories of established cases in the law of negligence, for extending a common law duty of care to those charged with the protection of weaker members of society from the wrong-doing of others.

The House of Lords also held that the psychiatrist in the *Newham* case did not owe a separate duty of care to the plaintiffs because the psychiatrist had been retained by the local authority to advise it, and not the plaintiffs. The fact that the carrying out of this retainer involved contact with a person for whose benefit the legislation had been passed (ie a child) did not alter the extent of the psychiatrist's duty owed (to the local authority) under its retainer.

In the *Dorset* case, the plaintiff, a 14-year-old boy, claimed damages from the defendant council for breach of statutory duty under the Education Act 1944 and the Education Act 1981, and at common law on the ground that the defendant negligently failed to diagnose that the plaintiff suffered from a special learning disorder and should therefore have been moved to a school which catered for his special educational needs, rather than keeping him in a local primary school thereby causing harm to him.

In the *Hampshire* case, the plaintiff, aged 19, alleged that the defendant council, in its capacity as the employer of the headmaster of the local primary school which the plaintiff attended, and as the supervisor of the teachers' advisory centre, owed the plaintiff a duty of care at common law, which the defendant breached in failing to use reasonable skill and care in the assessment of the plaintiff's special educational needs, thereby failing to treat his condition of dyslexia which would have improved if it had been correctly diagnosed and treated. This failure caused the plaintiff to be disadvantaged in realising his potential and thereby significantly restricted his vocational prospects.

In the *Bromley* case, the plaintiff, aged 22, claimed damages from the local authority for breach of statutory duty under the Education Acts and the Education (Special Educational Needs) Regulations Act 1983, and for breach of a common law duty of care owed to him, on the ground that, having failed to identify him as a child with special needs, the defendant failed to provide placements for him at any reasonably appropriate school, thereby keeping him out of the school system for several extended periods of time, with the consequence that he suffered impairment of his development and disadvantage in seeking employment in later life.

The claims based on breach of statutory duty in the *Dorset* case and the *Bromley* case were struck out because the Education Acts did not confer any right of action on anyone for their breach. Nor could any such right of action be inferred, because there was nothing in the relevant sections of the Acts which demonstrated a parliamentary intention to confer a statutory right of action for damages, even on the limited class of persons for whose protection the Acts were passed (ie children).

In the *Dorset* case the plaintiff's common law duty of care claim failed because, even if all of the requirements for such a claim were otherwise established, they were outweighed by the fact that the aim of the Education Acts was to provide, for the benefit of society as a whole, an administrative system to help one disadvantaged section of society, and the Education Act 1981 itself provided its own detailed machinery for securing that the statutory purpose was performed.

However, the House of Lords did hold in the *Dorset* case that the statutory authority could have come under a common law duty of care in relation to the psychological service that the authority offered to the public, even though the power to offer that service emanated from a statute. The educational psychologists who operated that service held themselves out as having special skills, and therefore, like any other professional persons, were bound to exercise those skills carefully. As it was possible that it might be demonstrated at trial that the defendant council was directly or vicariously liable for the acts and omissions of the persons who operated the psychological service, this part of the Statement of Claim in the *Dorset* case was not struck out.

The plaintiff's common law claim in the *Hampshire* case was also not struck out. This was an independent common law claim in which the question was whether the headmaster of a school, or a person operating the teachers' advisory service, is under a duty of care at common law to the pupils of that school to exercise skill and care in advising on their educational needs. In refusing to strike out such a claim, the House of Lords rejected the defendant authority's counsel's submission that, because Parliament had established a statutory regime for the protection of children with special educational needs, a parallel common law duty of care owed to children with special educational needs could not also exist. In rejecting this submission, Lord Browne-Wilkinson said (at p 765):

> Although . . . it is impossible to impose a common law duty of care which is inconsistent with, or fetters, a statutory duty, I can see no legal or common sense principle which requires one to deny a common law duty of care which would otherwise exist just because there is a statutory scheme which addresses the same problem. There is no inconsistency or incompatibility between the statutory scheme for children with special educational needs and any duty owed by headmasters and teaching advisers to give careful advice as to the educational needs of their pupils. If the child were to be educated at a private fee paying school or consulted a private teaching adviser, the existence of the statutory scheme . . . would be irrelevant. Why should it be relevant simply because the school and teaching advice is provided by a local education authority?

In rejecting the defendant's submission that no such duty of care should be imposed on it because there has never been a case where a school or a teacher has been held liable for negligent advice relating to the educational needs of a pupil, Lord Browne-Wilkinson said (at p 766):

> In my judgment a school which accepts a pupil assumes responsibility not only for his physical well-being, but also for his educational needs. The education of the pupil is the very purpose for which the child goes to the school. The head teacher, being responsible for the school, himself comes under a duty of care to exercise the reasonable skills of a headmaster in relation to such educational needs. If it comes to the attention of the headmaster that a pupil is under-performing, he does owe a duty to take such steps as a reasonable teacher would

consider appropriate to try to deal with such under-performance. To hold that, in such circumstances, the head teacher could properly ignore the matter and make no attempt to deal with it would fly in the face . . . of society's expectations of what a school will provide. . . . If such head teacher gives advice to the parents, then in my judgment he must exercise the skills and care of a reasonable teacher in giving such advice.

[The same applies to an] advisory teacher brought in to advise on the educational needs of a specific pupil, if he knows that his advice will be communicated to the pupil's parents. . . .

Once it is established that a head teacher or advisory teacher is under some duty of care to the pupil in relation to his educational well-being, it is impossible to strike out the claim in this case.

Lastly, the plaintiff's common law claim in the *Bromley* case was struck out because it was badly pleaded, in the sense that it failed to identify what was done, by whom, or the manner in which the defendant acted negligently in exercising its statutory duty of assessing the plaintiff's disability and its decision-making powers to educate him in special schools.

Barrett v Enfield London Borough Council [1998] 3 QB 367: The plaintiff, aged 24, had been placed in the care of the defendant local authority pursuant to a care order when he was 10 months old, and remained there until the age of 17. He claimed damages for personal injury based on an alleged common law duty of care owed by the authority to him for its alleged negligence in failing to protect him from physical, emotional, psychiatric and/or psychological injury, failing to provide him with education and a home where his safety would be secured and monitored, failing to promote his development or to secure his rights to family life and failing to provide competent social workers to monitor his welfare. The defendant had been moved nine times during his years in care. The defendant council applied to strike out the plaintiff's claim on the basis that it failed to disclose a sustainable cause of action. The Court of Appeal granted this application and struck out the plaintiff's claim. Lord Woolf MR said (at p 375):

The complaints which go to the heart of the plaintiff's claim are all ones which involve the type of decisions which an authority has to take in order to perform its statutory role in relation to children in its care. They all involve the exercise of discretion in the performance of the differing statutory responsibilities of the local authority. As to the exercise of this class of discretion, Lord Browne-Wilkinson in the *Bedfordshire* case made it clear that if the decisions complained of fall within the ambit of the authority's statutory discretion, they cannot be actionable in law. However, if the decision complained of is so unreasonable that it falls outside the ambit of the discretion conferred upon the local authority then, as Lord Browne-Wilkinson said, there is no *a priori* reason for excluding all common law liability.

Unreasonableness in this sense is difficult to establish. It requires the plaintiff to show that the defendant's decisions were outside the ambit of the discretion granted to the local authority by the legislation. If this very substantial hurdle could be surmounted, then, whether or not there is a common law duty of care is to be decided by applying the usual principles laid down in *Caparo Industries*

Plc v Dickman [1990] 2 AC 605 [see Chapter 9, para 9.6.2]. There has been no previous decision establishing a common law duty of care in the circumstances of this case, so it is necessary to consider whether it is just and reasonable to extend the common law duty of care by analogy to a local authority when it is performing its duties to protect and promote the welfare of children in care.

Lord Woolf MR then referred to the *Bedfordshire* case and continued (at p 377):

> In relation to the decisions of the local authority of which complaint is made which it is alleged could have contributed to the psychiatric and psychological difficulties of which the plaintiff complains (ie his damages), it would be contrary to the public interest and therefore not just or reasonable to impose a duty of care. The very fact that the defendant is stated to have been in the position of a parent to the plaintiff brings home the public policy aspects of this situation. Parents are daily making decisions with regard to their children's future, and it seems to me that it would be wholly inappropriate that those decisions, even if they could be shown to be wrong, should be ones which give rise to a liability for damages. If the decisions are taken by the local authority in place of the parents, the position should be the same.
>
> In the situation disclosed by the present appeal, there would be decisions which were of an interdisciplinary nature. Sometimes the decisions will involve seeking to determine which of two imperfect solutions is preferable. It would be unfortunate if the possibility of litigation years afterwards could cause a more defensive and cautious approach to taking positive decisions as to a child's future than would otherwise be the case. Social workers are all too often open to criticism for intervening, but intervening is often what is necessary and, when it is, they should not be discouraged from doing so by the possibility of litigation. It would be intolerable if social workers adopted a safety first approach.

Lord Woolf MR did, however, concede that the defendant in the present case could nevertheless owe a duty of care to the plaintiff at common law in respect of negligent acts or omissions committed by the defendant in the 'operational' area. Thus, he said (at p 378):

> Social workers and other members of staff could however be negligent in an operational manner. They could, for example, be careless in looking after property belonging to the child or in reporting what they had observed for the purposes of an interdisciplinary assessment of what action should be taken in relation to a child. They could also be negligent in failing to carry out instructions properly. If, in implementing their decisions or the decisions of the authority itself, a social worker was careless, I accept that there would be a case for the defendant being vicariously liable if the necessary causation of injury or other damage could be established. However, in this case, although complaints as to this type of conduct are made, there would be no prospect of the plaintiff's succeeding on those complaints alone. He would be quite unable to attribute any part of his condition to that sort of incident. This potential liability does not therefore assist the plaintiff here.

O'Rourke v Camden London Borough Council [1997] 3 WLR 86: The plaintiff had presented himself as a homeless person to the defendant council, which placed him in temporary accommodation pursuant to s 63(1) of the Housing

Act 1985, which states: "If the council has reason to believe that an applicant may be homeless and has a priority need, it shall secure accommodation for his occupation pending a decision as a result of its inquiries under section 62". Before a decision was reached under s 62, the plaintiff was evicted from his accommodation, and no further temporary accommodation was secured for him pending the final determination of his application.

The plaintiff brought the present action for damages against the council, claiming breach of statutory duty under s 63(1) in respect of its alleged failure to provide such further accommodation. The council applied to strike out the plaintiff's claim as disclosing no reasonable cause of action. The House of Lords upheld this application and struck out the plaintiff's Statement of Claim. Lord Hoffmann, with whose speech all of the other Law Lords concurred, said (at p 89):

> Whether section 63(1) gives rise to a cause of action sounding in damages depends on whether the Act shows a legislative intention to create such a remedy. There are certain contra-indications which make it unlikely that Parliament intended to create private law rights of action. The first is that the Act is a scheme of social welfare, intended to confer benefits at the public expense on grounds of public policy. Public money is being spent on housing the homeless, not merely for the private benefit of people who find themselves homeless, but on grounds of general public interest, because, for example, proper housing means that people will be less likely to suffer illness, turn to crime or require the attention of other social services. The expenditure interacts with expenditure on other public services such as education, the National Health Service and even the police. It is not simply a private matter between the claimant and the housing authority. Accordingly, the fact that Parliament has provided for the expenditure of public money on benefits in kind, such as housing the homeless, does not necessarily mean that it intended cash payments to be made by way of damages to persons who, in breach of the housing authority's statutory duty, have unfortunately not received the benefits which they should have done.
>
> A second contra-indication is that the Act makes the existence of the duty to provide accommodation dependent upon a good deal of judgment on the part of the housing authority. The duty to inquire under section 62 arises if the housing authority 'has reason to believe' that the applicant may be homeless, and the inquiries must be such as are 'necessary to satisfy themselves' [*per* s 62(1)] as to whether he is homeless, whether he has a priority need and whether he became homeless intentionally. If a duty does arise, the authority has a wide discretion in deciding how to provide accommodation and what kind of accommodation it will provide.

For these reasons, Lord Hoffmann said that it was unlikely that Parliament intended errors of judgment to give rise to an obligation to make financial reparation to any individual person adversely affected by the council's failure to exercise its powers or duties under the Act.

W and Others v Essex County Council ((1997) *The Times*, 16 July): The plaintiffs, Mr and Mrs W, became full-time adolescent foster parents for the defendant council in 1991. Before accepting their first placement, they sought, and were given, assurances by the council that the council would not place with them any child who was a known or a suspected sexual abuser. In 1992 they signed a Specialist Foster Carer Agreement with the council. In 1993 they fostered a boy aged 15 named G, who allegedly abused each of their children during his stay. The plaintiffs claimed that the council and the second defendant, the council's social worker, knew that G was an active sexual abuser, and that the second defendant had lied to them about that.

The defendants, relying on some of the cases referred to *above*, argued that it was not just and reasonable to impose a common law duty of care on them. The judge, Hooper J, rejected this submission. He said that although decisions concerning foster placements could be very delicate, he could not see, in fairness to the foster parents who played an important role in looking after children, that they should be denied information with which they should reasonably be provided. The imposition of a duty to provide information would not be against public policy.

Hooper J said that a social worker placing a child with foster parents had a duty of care to provide to the foster parents, before and during the placement, such information about the child as a reasonable social worker would provide in all of the circumstances; and a local authority was vicariously liable for the conduct of its social worker in that respect. Accordingly, his Lordship declined to strike out the portions of the Statement of Claim which relied on that duty, as well as the claim for negligent misstatement.

Non-repair of the highway

Wentworth v Wiltshire County Council [1993] QB 654: The plaintiff was a dairy farmer. Access to his farm was by way of a road which fell into disrepair and became dangerous. As a result, in January 1980 the Milk Marketing Board stopped collecting milk from the plaintiff's farm, and this led to the collapse of the plaintiff's dairy farming business. In Crown Court proceedings initiated by the plaintiff under the Highways Act 1959, the plaintiff established that the road was a highway maintainable at public expense and the defendant highway authority was in breach of its duty of repair under the Act. The defendant duly repaired the road in August 1981.

In the present action the plaintiff claimed damages from the defendant for breach of its statutory duty in failing to repair the road. The plaintiff's damages consisted of pure economic loss, because no person had been injured and no property belonging to the plaintiff had been damaged by virtue of the defendant's breach of duty. The plaintiff's claim was rejected by the Court of Appeal. Parker LJ said (at p 658):

> The sole question is whether the plaintiff can claim for the economic loss which admittedly flowed from the [defendant's] breach [of its statutory duty]. This depends upon the construction of certain provisions of the Highways Act 1959 and of the Highways (Miscellaneous) Provisions Act 1961. . .
>
> Section 59 of the 1959 Act enabled any person who alleges that a way . . . is a highway maintainable at the public expense and is out of repair to establish those matters . . . by application to [the Crown Court] and obtain an order that it be put in proper repair by the highway authority. . . If the order is not com-

plied with within the time specified, the complainant must be authorised by the court to carry out such works as may be necessary to put the highway in proper repair and to recover any expenses reasonably incurred in carrying out the works so authorised from the highway authority as a civil debt. The Act of 1959 thus provides a specific and very detailed means of enforcing the statutory duty which it has placed on the highway authority.

This, in my judgment, indicates that no other means of enforcement was intended by Parliament.

This conclusion would have been enough to dispose of the plaintiff's claim. However, Parker LJ noted that the 1961 Act had added some further complications for persons in the position of the plaintiff suing to obtain damages for the highway authority's breach of its statutory duty. Thus, Parker LJ said (emphasis added) (at p 660):

If, however, the Act of 1959 stood alone I would have no hesitation in conclud-ing that, as a matter of construction, no other method of enforcement was avail-able. It does not however stand alone, and it is necessary to see what is the effect of construing it as one with the Act of 1961.

. . . section 1(2) of the 1961 Act provided a defence to *any* action against a highway authority in respect of damage resulting from [its] failure to maintain [a highway]. That defence consists in proof [by the highway authority] 'that the authority has taken such care as in all the circumstances was reasonably required to secure that the part of the highway to which the action relates was not danger-ous for traffic'.

. . . [Section 1(3) sheds further light on the nature of the action contemplated by prescribing] the matters to which the court is to have particular regard when considering a defence under section 1(2). . . [These include consideration of] 'whether the highway authority knew, or could reasonably have been expected to know, that the condition of the part of the highway to which the action relates was likely to cause danger to users of the highway . . . [and whether] warning notices of the condition [of the highway] had been displayed'.

. . . [These] provisions indicate that the contemplated action is one for damage to a road user or his property [ie not for economic loss] from a condition of the highway making it dangerous to road users. . .

. . . the matter is . . . one of statutory construction, and in my judgment the intention of Parliament, to be gathered from the wording of the two Acts, is . . . to replace the previous exemption from civil liability for damage resulting from non-repair by an action for damage to the person or property of a road user from the dangerous condition of a highway, subject only to the statutory defence under section 1(2) of the 1961 Act.

Stovin v Wise [1996] AC 923: This case is dealt with extensively in the main body of this chapter, where it is noted that the plaintiff's action failed prin-cipally because he was not able to demonstrate that the council's failure to exercise its statutory power was irrational in the sense that no reasonable council could have come to the same conclusion. However, the majority of 4:1 in the House of Lords also concluded that the policy of the Highways Act 1980 did not require compensation to be paid to persons who suffered loss, even in the form of physical injury, because the highway authority's power to remove an obstruction alongside a road had not been exercised.

Thus, Lord Hoffmann said (at p 957):

> Assuming that the highway authority ought, as a matter of public law, to have done the work, I do not think that there are any grounds upon which it can be said that the public law duty should give rise to an obligation to compensate persons who have suffered loss because it was not performed. . .
>
> The power in section 79 of the Highways Act 1980, upon which the plaintiff principally relies to generate a duty of care, was first enacted as section 4 of the Roads Improvement Act 1925. It seems to me impossible to discern a legislative intent that there should be a duty of care in respect of the use of that power, giving rise to a liability to compensate persons injured by a failure to use it. . .

It is one thing to provide a service at the public expense. It is another to require the public to pay compensation when a failure to provide the service has resulted in loss.

Planning decisions

Tidman v Reading Borough Council [1994] 3 PLR 72: The facts of this case are set out in Chapter 9, para 9.7.8, and the issues there considered relate to whether a duty of care at common law came into existence between the planning authority and the plaintiff by virtue of alleged negligent misrepresentations that were made to the plaintiff by the planning authority's representative over the telephone and by the planning authority itself in a leaflet that it issued, encouraging people to seek advice on planning from the planning authority.

In so far as the planning authority was also a statutory authority, so that the plaintiff's claim at common law depended on the plaintiff being able to establish that the planning authority exceeded the limits of its discretion, the judge, Buxton J, said:

> The plaintiff's case is carefully and rightly not based on the planning decision or on the considerations that led to it. It is based solely on the advice given or omitted to have been given on or about 18 December 1989 [the date of the above-mentioned telephone conversation]. In respect of that part of their activities, it is argued that the local authority stepped outside their statutory planning function. They volunteered advice, as shown by the booklet, which they did not need to do. So it is argued that they are, potentially at least, caught by the general *Hedley Byrne* rule, like any other adviser. Nevertheless, even granted that analysis of the facts, the local authority, unlike an ordinary professional adviser, owes a public duty to apply the planning law, and also a public duty to exercise their judgment and discretion in the general public interest. It would be inconsistent with those duties to recognise an overriding obligation to give advice in the interests of particular individuals who are engaged in the planning process. The private interest of that particular individual cannot be allowed to override the interests of the public at large in the proper performance of the planning process.

Chung Tak Lam v Borough of Torbay (30 July 1997, unreported): The plaintiff owned a restaurant which was in the vicinity of commercial premises owned by the first defendant in which the first defendant carried on a business of making and finishing toys. That activity involved spraying the toys with chemicals and paint sprays. The plaintiff alleged that the noxious fumes generated by that activity caused a very sharp drop in the number of people coming to eat in the plaintiff's restaurant. The second defendant was the local planning authority which had granted the planning permission which led to the noxious processes being carried out on the first defendant's premises.

In the present action the plaintiff claimed damages of more than £500,000 from the defendants. The plaintiff effectively discontinued his action against the first defendant because he was a man of straw. However, he vigorously pursued his action against the planning authority, whom he claimed owed him a common law duty of care based on the planning authority's alleged negligence in failing, in response to complaints from the plaintiff and other members of the community, to take enforcement proceedings under the Planning Acts or the Environmental Protection Acts to ensure that the first defendant's activities were controlled, so as to safeguard the plaintiff's restaurant from the economic loss which he sustained when the first defendant continued with its spraying activities.

The planning authority applied to strike out the plaintiff's claim as disclosing no reasonable cause of action. The Court of Appeal granted this application and struck out the plaintiff's claim. Potter LJ said:

> The question is always whether, looking at the whole statute and at all the circumstances, including the history of the legislation, the relevant Act was passed primarily for the benefit of the individual or for the public in general. In our view it is quite plain that the regime of the Town and County Planning Acts is a regulatory system for the benefit of the public at large involving general administrative functions imposed on the planning authorities and involving the exercise of administrative discretion. Such a system is one in respect of which the reported decisions reveal no example of a private right of action for breach of statutory duty ever having been recognised by the court.

It was for this reason that the plaintiff's counsel abandoned reliance upon any averment of breach of statutory duty as giving rise to a cause of action by the plaintiff in the present case, and he also did not press his argument that the defendant was in breach of a parallel duty of care at common law in granting planning permission to the first defendant without proper inquiry. The Court of Appeal said that he was right to do so because the planning system is designed to regulate the development and use of land in the public interest. In this regard the Court of Appeal approved the following *dictum* of the trial judge (Collins J):

> The local authority's duty under the Planning Acts is to control and regulate development in the interests of the inhabitants of the area. It is of course inevitable that some people are going to be adversely affected. There may be more noise as a result. There may be other adverse effects. Nuisances may even be created in some situations. Of course the local authority has to consider the effect on the environment and the adverse effect on neighbouring occupiers. Those are all proper planning considerations. However, it would be wholly detrimental to the proper process of considering planning applications if the local authority, in addition, had to have regard to the private law interests of any

person who might be affected by the grant of permission, and to ask itself in each case whether it had properly had regard to the individual rights of those concerned. If it were potentially liable to actions in negligence in those circumstances, the carrying out of its important functions in the public interest would be likely to be adversely affected.

Instead, the plaintiff's counsel focused on the planning authority's enforcement function and argued that, upon receiving complaints from the plaintiff, among others, the planning authority, by its actions in partially responding to those complaints, assumed responsibility for dealing with the complaints and remedying the nuisance, and that the plaintiff relied upon the planning authority to do so. In rejecting this submission, Potter LJ said:

> We cannot think that the position is any different in respect of the enforcement functions of the local authority in respect of statutory nuisances. [After referring to the various statutory provisions dealing with the control of nuisances, Potter LJ said:] These are plainly provisions for the benefit of the public at large living within the area of the local authority and, albeit under section 80 of the Environmental Protection Act 1990, service of an abatement notice is obligatory if the local authority is satisfied that a statutory nuisance exists, it is not mandatory for the local authority to take proceedings for an offence under section 80. Indeed, should it not see fit to do so, section 82(1) anticipates the right of any person aggrieved thereby to make complaint to a Magistrate's Court himself. In these circumstances, it seems to us plain that there is neither reason nor necessity, in relation to a landowner aggrieved by the failure of a local authority to take action in respect of a nuisance, to create a right of action in damages based on such failure.
>
> Nor does it seem to us that the plaintiff's position can be improved by some alternative formulation of his cause of action on the basis of 'assumption of responsibility'. Where an allegation of 'assumption of responsibility' is made against a person or body carrying out a statutory function, there must be something more than the performance (negligent or otherwise) of the statutory function to establish such assumption of responsibility: see, for instance, *Welton v North Cornwall District Council* [1997] 1 WLR 570 [see *below*], in which the servant of the defendant authority acted far outside the ambit of his statutory powers and duties. The analysis of the position in the judgments of the members of this court in that case can give no comfort to the plaintiff in this context. It is clear to us that the facts pleaded in the present case fall well short of establishing any such assumption of responsibility. All of them relate to matters which arose in the course and scope of the planning authority's planning and enforcement functions. The matters relied upon are essentially no more than the fact that the planning authority, on the complaint and at the prompting of the plaintiff or his solicitors, set about seeking to remedy the situation, but took inadequate steps to do so.

The Court then considered the plaintiff's counsel's submission that the planning authority's breach of duty was qualitatively not one of simple carelessness in the course of the planning authority's exercise of its statutory functions, but that it consisted of acts or omissions "well outside the ambit of the planning authority's discretion". If this was the case, the plaintiff's complaints did not relate to "policy matters" but to "operating decisions" taken by the planning authority. In holding that this submission did not advance the plaintiff's case any further, Potter LJ said:

> Even assuming that the actions of the planning authority were so negligent and unreasonable as to amount to irrationality, that does not in itself suffice to create a private right of action in negligence, as opposed to founding the basis of some public law challenge to the exercise of the planning authority's powers. The cause of action, if it exists, remains one for breach of duty in the tort of negligence. To allege that the effect of the negligence complained of is to produce an irrational result adds nothing in terms of the cause of action.

The Crown Prosecution Service

Welsh v Chief Constable of the Merseyside Police [1993] 1 All ER 692: On 24 July 1987, the plaintiff appeared before a magistrates' court charged with two offences of theft. He was remanded on bail to appear before that court on 19 August. On 7 August the plaintiff was due to appear in the Crown Court to be dealt with for numerous criminal matters. Before the case was called on in the Crown Court, the plaintiff's counsel reached an agreement with the Crown Prosecution Service ('the CPS') for the two magistrates' court offences to be taken into consideration by the Crown Court, and this was in fact done when the plaintiff appeared before the judge in the Crown Court.

As part of this arrangement the CPS undertook to inform the magistrates' court that the plaintiff's offences had been taken into consideration by the Crown Court. The CPS, however, failed to inform the magistrates' court of this fact. The plaintiff, believing that this had been done and that therefore the charges against him in the magistrates' court no longer existed, failed to appear before the magistrates' court on 19 August to answer to his bail. The magistrates' court, being unaware of the arrangement that the plaintiff had made with the CPS, issued a warrant for the plaintiff's arrest, not backed by bail. In due course the plaintiff was arrested and was held in custody for two days until he was able to secure his release.

In the present action the plaintiff claimed damages against the police and the CPS as a result of the CPS's negligent failure to ensure that the magistrates' court was informed that the offences for which he had been bailed had subsequently been taken into consideration by the Crown Court. The CPS applied to strike out the plaintiff's case on the ground that it failed to disclose a reasonable cause of action. The judge, Tudor Evans J, rejected this application on the ground that, in his view, there was a close relationship based on proximity between the CPS and the plaintiff and that it was fair, just and reasonable to hold that a duty of care existed on the assumed facts of this case and because, in his view, no grounds of public policy existed for excluding such a duty.

Elgozouli-Daf v Commissioner of Police of the Metropolis [1995] QB 335: The Court of Appeal's decision in this case deals with two appeals (the other being *McBrearty v Ministry of Defence*). The plaintiffs in both cases had been arrested, charged and remanded in custody for serious offences; but after periods of detention of 22 and 85 days respectively, the CPS discontinued proceedings against them. In actions against the CPS the plaintiff in the first case claimed that the CPS was negligent in failing to act with reasonable diligence in obtaining, processing and communicating the results of forensic scientific evidence which showed him to be innocent; and the plaintiff in the second case claimed that it should not have taken the CPS 85 days to conclude that the prosecution was bound to fail.

In both cases the High Court judge struck out the plaintiffs' cases as disclosing no reasonable cause of action. The Court of Appeal agreed with the High Court judge. In response to the plaintiffs' counsel's submission that the *Welsh* case entitled the plaintiffs to damages in the present case, Steyn LJ said (at p 348):

> *Welsh's* case must be put in perspective. The judge in *Welsh* approached the matter on the basis that the CPS assumed by conduct a responsibility to keep the Magistrates' Court informed as to the fact that the offences had been taken into consideration. The judge repeatedly emphasised this feature of the case. By contrast, the cases before us do not involve any suggestion of an assumption of responsibility by the CPS. Ultimately, it seems to me that the decision in *Welsh's* case is not of assistance on the central point before us. Contrary to the views of the judge in the case before us, I do not regard *Welsh's* case as being wrongly decided. But it turned on its own special facts and in particular on the issue of assumption of responsibility by the CPS.
>
> That brings me to the policy factors which, in my view, argue against the recognition of a duty of care owed by the CPS to those it prosecutes. While it is always tempting to yield to an argument based on the protection of civil liberties, I have come to the conclusion that the interests of the whole community are better served by not imposing a duty of care on the CPS. In my view, such a duty of care would tend to have an inhibiting effect on the discharge by the CPS of its central function of prosecuting crime. It would in some cases lead to a defensive approach by prosecutors to their multifarious duties. It would introduce a risk that prosecutors would act so as to protect themselves from claims of negligence. The CPS would have to spend valuable time and use scarce resources in order to prevent lawsuits in negligence against the CPS. It would generate a great deal of paper to guard against the risks of lawsuits. The time and energy of CPS lawyers would be diverted from concentrating on their prime function of prosecuting offenders. That would be likely to happen, not only during the prosecution process, but also when the CPS is sued in negligence by aggrieved defendants. The CPS would be constantly enmeshed in an avalanche of interlocutory civil proceedings and civil trials. That is a spectre that would bode ill for the efficiency of the CPS and the quality of our criminal justice system. I conclude that there are compelling reasons, rooted in the welfare of the whole community, which outweigh the dictates of individual justice.
>
> Subject to one qualification, my conclusion that there is no duty of care owed by the CPS to those it prosecutes is intended to be of general application. The qualification is that there may be cases, of which *Welsh v Chief Constable of the Merseyside Police* was an example, where the CPS assumes by conduct a responsibility to a particular defendant; and it is trite law that such an assump-

tion of responsibility may generate legal duties. But that qualification has no relevance to the cases before us.

Kumar v Commissioner of Police for the Metropolis (31 January 1995, unreported): On 26 August 1990, Una O'Brien falsely alleged that the plaintiff had raped her in her house. The plaintiff was arrested on the following day and charged with raping her. When interviewed by the police, the plaintiff explained that he had had a sexual relationship with Una O'Brien for two months, in the course of which consensual sexual intercourse had taken place many times. The plaintiff was detained in custody continuously until March 1991, after a hearing at which the CPS did not offer any evidence because the CPS had, in the meantime, learned that Una O'Brien was unlikely to be a reliable witness due to the fact that she had previously made false allegations of rape against other men.

In the present action the plaintiff claimed damages from the CPS on the basis that the CPS owed the plaintiff a duty of care when instituting or continuing his prosecution to take reasonable steps to ascertain whether Una O'Brien would be a reliable witness, and that the CPS and the police officers assisting the CPS had acted negligently in carrying out that duty. The High Court judge granted the CPS's application to strike out the plaintiff's claim as disclosing no reasonable cause of action. The plaintiff appealed, but the Court of Appeal agreed with the High Court judge, for essentially the same reasons as were given by the Court of Appeal in the *Elgozouli* case, *above.* After setting out the long passage cited *above* from Steyn LJ's judgment in that case, Sir Ralph Gibson said:

> In my judgment, for similar reasons, the interests of the whole community are better served by not imposing a duty of care upon the police officers in their decisions whether or not to place sufficient reliance upon the account of a complainant to justify the making of a charge against an accused. In this case, also, other protections and remedies are available when a citizen is aggrieved by the decision of police officers in that context. The victim has the private law remedy of malicious prosecution which has, for many years, been regarded as the only remedy at common law available to a plaintiff who complains that a decision to start or continue a prosecution has been made on inadequate evidence.

Miscellaneous

Wood v The Law Society (28 July 1993, unreported; and (1995) *The Times*, 1 March (CA)): In 1974, the private individual to whom the plaintiff had mortgaged her home called in his loan. The amount outstanding was £7,000. The plaintiff consulted her solicitors, Hubbard and Co, in order to find money to replace the existing mortgage. One of the partners, Mrs Hubbard, told the plaintiff that the firm was able to obtain a replacement loan of £7,000 for her for a period of "at least three months" at an interest rate of 16 per cent per annum. The plaintiff accepted this. The loan was arranged by Mrs Hubbard with Mobile Homes Limited ('Mobile Homes') to whom the plaintiff duly gave a first mortgage over her house.

Mrs Hubbard did not tell the plaintiff that her husband, Mr Hubbard, the senior partner of Hubbard and Co, was also a director and part-owner of Mobile Homes. The plaintiff only discovered this more than a year later when Hubbard and Co served on the plaintiff a writ on behalf of Mobile Homes for the repayment of the loan of £7,000 or possession of her house. The plaintiff did nothing with this information at that time. Through her new solicitors she reached a compromise with Mobile Homes whereby they undertook not to take any steps to enforce their loan for two years.

At the end of that two-year period the plaintiff made a complaint about Hubbard and Co to the Law Society. About six months later Mobile Homes brought possession proceedings to enforce the compromise agreement, and in due course they obtained possession of the plaintiff's house. Two years later the plaintiff brought an action against Hubbard and Co, which she subsequently settled for £2,500.

In the meantime, the Law Society was still considering the plaintiff's complaint against Hubbard and Co. Eventually it issued its decision in which it agreed with the plaintiff that it was professionally improper for Mrs Hubbard to fail to disclose to the plaintiff that her husband had a financial interest in Mobile Homes and thereafter to continue to act for both parties in the transaction. The Law Society issued a rebuke to Mrs Hubbard for her conduct in that respect.

The plaintiff then commenced the present action against the Law Society, in which she claimed that the Law Society had owed her a duty of care in respect of her loss, which it breached by its delay in dealing with her complaint about Mrs Hubbard. She alleged that if the Law Society had acted more quickly, and issued its rebuke to Mrs Hubbard many years previously, Mobile Homes, because of its connection with Mr Hubbard, might have stayed its hand in the eviction process. The trial judge, Otton J, held that the Law Society did not owe the plaintiff a duty of care. He said:

> The Law Society, although not a statutory body in origin, is subject to statutory duties and, through its Counsel, exercises statutory powers including those under the Solicitors' Act 1974. The primary consideration is whether there exists between the Law Society and complainants such close and direct relations as to place the Law Society, in the exercise of its powers and functions, under a duty of care towards complainants. I have come to the conclusion that such proximity did not exist between the plaintiff and the Law Society. She was a member of an unascertained class which is wide and diffuse and includes for example those complaining about their own solicitors, unsuccessful defendants and victims of injustice in civil and criminal proceedings, and those who complain about solicitors acting for third parties.
>
> Furthermore, the investigative functions of the Law Society in dealing with the complaints against the plaintiff's former solicitors were discretionary and quasi-judicial acts in exercise of a statutory power and called for the exercise of discretion and judgment on the part of the official concerned. The fact that the plaintiff's complaints were inefficiently handled without due diligence could not alter the quasi-judicial character of the function.
>
> In addition, the duty owed by the Law Society was not to safeguard the plaintiff against loss, but rather to sanction conduct unbecoming a solicitor. The powers conferred on the Law Society are not to prevent or avoid loss to individuals such as the plaintiff. Also, the Law Society had no power to control the day-

to-day activities of solicitors who, by their activities, caused the loss. This is in contra-distinction to the borstal officers in the *Dorset Yacht* case [see *below*]. Finally, it is not unreasonable to require a plaintiff who has suffered loss to look for redress to the person who caused the loss, ie, the solicitors about whose conduct the complaint is made. The plaintiff sued Hubbard and Co for negligence and conspiracy. She compromised the action for £2,500. It is unreasonable for her now to be able to sue the regulatory body of the solicitors' profession.

The plaintiff's appeal to the Court of Appeal was unsuccessful; but the Court of Appeal did not make any comments on the duty of care point because it was satisfied that the plaintiff's loss, occasioned by the repossession of her house by Mobile Homes, was not caused by the Law Society's delay in dealing with her complaint. First, the Law Society's disciplinary powers over solicitors did not extend to stopping a client (Mobile Homes) of one of those solicitors (Hubbard and Co) from exercising its legal right to possess a property over which it had a secured loan. Secondly, the Court of Appeal was satisfied on the facts that any rebuke by the Law Society to Mrs Hubbard would have had no effect on Mr Hubbard's or Mobile Homes's decision to repossess the plaintiff's house.

In September 1997, the European Commission of Human Rights rejected the plaintiff's application to it and upheld the above-mentioned decisions of the High Court and the Court of Appeal.

Philcox v The Civil Aviation Authority ((1995) *The Times*, 8 June): The plaintiff was the owner of a light aeroplane. In June 1985, the Civil Aviation Authority ('the CAA') issued a Certificate of Airworthiness pursuant to the Air Navigation Order 1980, which provides: "An aircraft shall not fly unless there is in force in respect thereof a Certificate of Airworthiness duly issued in respect thereof and any conditions subject to which the Certificate was issued are complied with".

A month later the aeroplane crashed as a result of mechanical failures which the plaintiff alleged the CAA should have detected when it inspected the aeroplane prior to issuing the Certificate of Airworthiness. On this basis the plaintiff claimed damages from the CAA in the present action. The Court of Appeal, agreeing with the High Court judge, dismissed the plaintiff's action. Staughton LJ said:

> What seems to me to be critical in this case is whether it is fair, just and reasonable to impose a duty of care on a body which is entrusted by Parliament with the duty of supervising the activities of others, particularly when it is said that that duty is owed to the person who is to be supervised. There is no universal rule that a supervising authority cannot owe a duty of care to anybody. Can it be owed to the very person whom the supervising authority is supposed to supervise?
>
> There are examples in legislation where Parliament has aimed at protecting people from their own folly. For example, the law about seat belts or crash helmets. Do we find in this case that Parliament intended the CAA to be responsible for protecting the owners of aircraft from failure to maintain them properly? [Staughton LJ then referred to the *Yuen Kun* case and to *Minories Finance Ltd v Arthur Young*, both of which are considered *above*, and said:] It is the task

of the owner of an aircraft to maintain it properly. He can do it himself or engage others to do so. The Air Navigation Order itself provides for a class of licensed maintenance engineers. It is the owner's job to engage one of those engineers and to see that the task is properly carried out. The CAA supervises in order to make sure that the owner has done what he, the owner, ought to have done and what it is his responsibility to do. The CAA is there to protect the public against the owner's failures, and not to protect the owner against his own errors. I would not regard it as fair, just or reasonable that the owner of an aircraft should be owed a duty of care by the CAA to inform him if it were the case that he had not carried out his primary duty of maintaining his own aircraft properly.

Morrit LJ, concurring, said:

> I ask myself two questions: (1) What is the risk for the prevention of which the supervisory scheme has been established?; (2) What is the class of persons intended to be protected? The legislative scheme is to make it an offence for the owner or operator of an aircraft to fly an aircraft unless a Certificate of Airworthiness is in force. The issue of a Certificate does not guarantee the airworthiness of the aircraft. It merely ensures that the owner or operator of the aircraft takes steps to have the aircraft maintained in a state of airworthiness. It is clear, to my mind, that the risk which the scheme of the legislation is designed to prevent is the risk that the owner or operator of an aircraft will fly the aircraft even when it is unfit to fly; and that the persons for whose protection the scheme has been established are the passengers, cargo-owners and other members of the public likely to be harmed if an unfit aircraft is allowed to fly. The owners and operators of the aircraft are not within the class of persons for whose protection the scheme has been established. They are the persons against whose imprudent activities the scheme is designed to protect the public. They are not entitled to rely on the issue of a Certificate to exonerate them from their own responsibility to ensure that their aircraft are fit to fly. It follows that the test of proximity is not satisfied. The relationship which the statutory scheme brings into existence does not satisfy the proximity test for the purposes of the law of negligence.

Mulcahy v Ministry of Defence [1996] QB 732: The plaintiff, while on active service with the British Army in Saudi Arabia during the Gulf War, was injured by the negligence of his own gun commander. His claim for damages was struck out primarily on the ground that his injuries were sustained when he was in a war zone taking part in warlike operations, thereby entitling the defendant to claim Crown Immunity. The Court of Appeal made it clear, however, that it would have struck out the plaintiff's claim even if Crown Immunity had not been available to the defendant. Thus, Neill LJ said (at p 749):

> In the present case it is accepted on behalf of the defendant that two of the components of a duty of care—proximity and foreseeability of damage—are present. The issue to be determined is whether it is fair, just and reasonable that a duty of care should be imposed on one soldier in his conduct towards another when engaging the enemy during hostilities. In order to decide whether it is fair, just and reasonable to impose a duty of care, one must consider all the circumstances including the position and role of the alleged tortfeasor and any relevant

policy considerations. In my opinion there is no basis for extending the scope of the duty of care in the present case. To hold that there is no civil liability for injury caused by the negligence of a person in the course of an actual engagement with the enemy seems to me to accord with common sense and sound policy.

Welton v North Cornwall District Council [1997] 1 WLR 570: The plaintiffs owned a guest house which constituted food premises for the purpose of the Food Act 1984 and the Food Safety Act 1990. In October 1990, Mr Evans, who was employed by the defendant council as an environmental health officer under the Acts, entered the plaintiffs' premises to inspect them. In the course of the inspection he told the plaintiffs to execute substantial building works, purportedly to comply with regulations ('the Regulations') made under the Acts, and threatened to close the plaintiffs' premises down if they failed to meet his requirements.

Despite repeated requests, and in contravention of the council's established policy, Mr Evans never confirmed his requirements in writing, but over the following months he visited the plaintiffs' premises several times to inspect and approve the works which were being carried out. Upon discovering in due course that Mr Evans's requirements were vastly in excess of those which could properly have been required under the Regulations, the plaintiffs brought the present action against the council, claiming damages for the unnecessary expenditure incurred as a result of the negligent misstatements of Mr Evans as to the extent of the alterations required to comply with the law. The court accepted the plaintiffs' evidence that they had undertaken the work as a result of Mr Evans's threat of closure and that 90 per cent of the work which Mr Evans had required to be undertaken was unnecessary to comply with the Regulations. The judge also concluded that Mr Evans knew, or ought reasonably to have known, that what he told the plaintiffs would be relied upon by them without independent inquiry.

In these circumstances the question was whether a 'special relationship' existed between the defendant, acting through Mr Evans, and the plaintiffs which entitled the court to impose a duty of care at common law on the defendant for the plaintiffs' losses. The Court of Appeal answered this question in the affirmative. Rose LJ said (at p 580):

> Leaving aside for the moment the existence of the defendants' statutory powers and duties which provided the backcloth and reason for the relationship between Mr Evans and the plaintiffs, it seems to me that the judge's conclusion that the relationship gave rise to a duty of care within the ambit of the *Hedley Byrne* principle is unassailable. His unchallenged findings of fact include reliance by the plaintiffs on Mr Evans and knowledge of such reliance on Mr Evans's part. Accordingly, there was, within *Hedley Byrne* as subsequently analysed, an assumption of responsibility by Mr Evans and hence a duty of care owed by him.
>
> There was, however, no statutory duty involved in the *Hedley Byrne* case. Accordingly, the last question which arises in the present case is whether the existence of a statutory duty provides any ground for excluding from the ambit of a *Hedley Byrne* duty a relationship derived from the exercise of statutory powers and duties.

In answering this question in the negative, Rose LJ said (at p 580):

There are at least three categories of conduct to which the existence of the defendants' statutory enforcement duties might have given rise. First, there might be conduct specifically directed to statutory enforcement, such as the institution of proceedings before the justices, the service of an improvement notice and the obtaining of a closure order. Such conduct, even if careless, would only give rise to common law liability if the circumstances were such as to raise a duty of care at common law; and such a duty will not be raised if it would be inconsistent with, or would have a tendency to discourage, the performance of the statutory duty.

Secondly, there is the offering of an advisory service. In so far as this is merely part and parcel of the defendants' system for discharging its statutory duties, liability will be excluded so as not to impede the due performance of those duties. But, in so far as it goes beyond this, the advisory service is capable of giving rise to a duty of care, and the fact that the service is offered by reason of the statutory duty is immaterial.

Thirdly, there is conduct of the sort which is at the heart of this case, namely, the imposition by Mr Evans, outwith the legislation, of detailed requirements enforced by threat of closure and close supervision. In my judgment, the existence of the defendants' statutory powers and duties affords no reason why the defendants should not be liable at common law for this third type of conduct by their servant, which is otherwise well within the *Hedley Byrne* principle.

Ward LJ, concurring, commented (at p 584):

Mr Evans was acting both outside the powers of the Acts and also outside the informal enforcement practice of the defendants. In the scale and detail of the directions he gave, and the degree of control he exerted, he was conducting himself in a manner which was exceptional. These circumstances make this case special to its own facts, and I would not wish my conclusions to be thought certain to govern, for example, a negligent assessment of defects in premises which are then made the grounds of a prosecution, or even those which are then asserted in a letter of the kind the local authority do send. A duty of care may still arise, but on the other hand, it may not. I am, however, quite satisfied that on the facts before us, the local authority was under a duty to take reasonable care.

With reference to the particular legislation pursuant to which Mr Evans was empowered to act, Ward LJ said (at p 585):

The purpose of the Act is for our collective welfare. There is, therefore, a public interest in not imposing a common law duty of care if it would render the correct operation of the statutory duty disproportionately onerous by, for example, deterring inspections and recommendations for fear of having to defend and meet claims for negligence which further deplete precious human and financial resources. In such cases the interests of the individual (Mrs Welton) may have to be sacrificed for the greater common good. The defendants have not made out such a case.

W v The Home Office (19 February 1997, unreported): On 11 March 1994, the plaintiff, a Liberian citizen, presented himself to the immigration officers at Heathrow Airport in England and claimed asylum for the second time (he had previously made this claim, but the immigration officers rejected it and returned him to Germany, which was his last transit stop). The Home Office agreed to consider the plaintiff's claim for asylum, but said that the plaintiff would be held in detention until a decision was made. On 18 and 19 March 1994, the plaintiff was interviewed at length by the Home Office. His solicitor was told that unless and until the plaintiff had established his identity as a citizen of Liberia, the question of his being released from detention and granted temporary admission would not arise.

The plaintiff's solicitor made further representations to obtain the plaintiff's temporary release from detention. The Home Office agreed to a meeting with the plaintiff and his solicitor. This took place on 11 April 1994, during which the Immigration Officer, Mr Carmichael, said that the Home Office did not accept that the plaintiff was a Liberian citizen in view of his poor performance at an interview on 28 March 1994. It was explained that the plaintiff had scored three out of a possible 15 points, and that true Liberians would have found it easy to answer all of the questions. The plaintiff denied that he had taken a test on 28 March, and asked if he could take a further test there and then. Having given the further test to the plaintiff, who passed it with ease, Mr Carmichael left the interview room. When he returned a short while later, he explained that, having rechecked the plaintiff's file, he had discovered that, by mistake, a test given to someone else other than the plaintiff had been placed on the plaintiff's file, thus causing the Home Office to have doubts about the plaintiff's true identity. He apologised for the error. The Chief Immigration Officer then entered the room and stated that, in the light of the plaintiff's performance in the test, his claim for temporary admission would be reassessed. He also apologised for the mistake in placing the wrong test in the plaintiff's file. After further representations from the plaintiff's solicitor, the plaintiff was immediately released from detention and granted temporary admission.

In the present action, the plaintiff claimed damages from the Home Office based on an allegation that the Home Office owed the plaintiff a duty of care in respect of the length of time for which the plaintiff was detained, which the Home Office breached by its negligence in putting another person's questionnaire in the plaintiff's file. The Home Office applied to strike out the plaintiff's claim as disclosing no reasonable cause of action. The Court of Appeal agreed with the Home Office and struck out the plaintiff's claim, principally because the Immigration Acts, pursuant to which the immigration officers had acted, did confer other remedies, such as judicial review and *mandamus*, and because, in the court's view, it was not possible to say that the immigration officers, although negligent, had exceeded the limits of their powers. Thus, their Lordships said:

> The essence of the allegation made is that the decision-making body has negligently taken into account matters that it should not have taken into account by having regard to some irrelevant and misleading information, namely, that contained in the first questionnaire. But this cannot constitute the tort of negligence. The process whereby the decision-making body gathers information and comes to its decision cannot be the subject of an action in negligence. In gathering

information and taking it into account, the defendants were acting pursuant to their statutory powers and within that area of their discretion where only deliberate abuse would provide a private remedy. For them to owe a duty of care to immigrants would be inconsistent with the proper performance of their responsibilities as immigration officers.

Reeman v Department of Transport (26 March 1997, unreported): The plaintiffs, Mr and Mrs Reeman, had bought a fishing vessel, which they proposed to use to make a living. No British-registered fishing vessel can put out to sea unless it carries a certificate issued by the Department of Transport ('the Department') which certifies that it complies with various statutory regulations designed to ensure that it is seaworthy. When the plaintiffs bought the vessel it carried such a certificate. They relied on this as demonstrating that the vessel's design and construction rendered it fit for service as a fishing vessel. However, the Department surveyor responsible for the issue of that certificate had failed to carry out his duties in relation to it with due skill and care. He had made an arithmetical error in calculating the vessel's stability. This led him to issue a certificate indicating that its stability was satisfactory when, in fact, it was unstable. The error came to light in the year after the purchase of the vessel by the plaintiffs when the Department carried out stability tests and found that the vessel did not meet the minimum requirement. The result was a financial disaster for the plaintiffs, because the vessel's certificate was withdrawn and it could no longer put out to sea. Attempts to make satisfactory modifications to meet the Department's requirements were beyond the plaintiffs' means.

In the present action, the plaintiffs claimed damages from the Department for breach of a common law duty of care which they alleged the Department owed to them in the issue of the vessel's Certificate of Seaworthiness. The Court of Appeal rejected the plaintiffs' claim. Phillips LJ said:

> The facts of this case raise the question of the liability that attaches to the performance of statutory duties in a type of situation that has distinguishing features that are readily identifiable and commonplace. The duties relate to the regulation of the performance of obligations of owners of property designed to be used for commercial purposes that involved potential risks to third parties. The properties involved in the present case are fishing vessels. The duties of the owners of those vessels, that are regulated by the Department, are designed to ensure that those vessels are seaworthy for the protection of those who put out to sea in them. Similar regulatory functions are carried out by designated authorities in relation to the safety of premises frequented by the public, such as hotels, theatres and dance halls. Vehicles are required to be regularly tested to ensure that they are roadworthy. In most of these cases, potential purchasers of the property in question are likely to be influenced, when deciding whether, and for how much to purchase the property, by the certificate which appears to demonstrate compliance with the relevant regulations, indicating that the property is in a condition in which it can lawfully be used for its commercial purpose. Equally, those advancing finance on the security of such property, or agreeing to insure it, are likely to be influenced by the existence of such a certificate.

Phillips LJ responded to the plaintiffs' counsel's submission that if the vessel had capsized and those on board had been drowned, the Department would have been liable to satisfy their dependants' claims, by saying:

> I do not find this proposition axiomatic [unlike the plaintiffs' counsel]. In *Murphy v Brentwood District Council* [1991] 1 AC 398, the House of Lords expressly left open the question of whether a local authority, which had failed to take reasonable care to ensure compliance with building bye-laws, would be legally liable in respect of injury to persons resulting from such failure. In *Philcox v Civil Aviation Authority* (*The Times*, 8 June 1995), the Court of Appeal held that the CAA's statutory duty to issue Certificates of Airworthiness involved no duty to the owner of the aircraft to exercise reasonable care to prevent him or his aircraft suffering injury as a result of taking off in an unairworthy condition. These decisions raise a serious question as to whether the Department owed any duty to Mr Reeman or his crew in respect of the risk of death or injury flowing from the unseaworthiness of the vessel.

Phillips LJ then considered whether the Department owed a duty of care to owners of vessels surveyed by it to exercise reasonable care not to cause economic loss to them. In considering the test of proximity he said:

> The statutory framework in the present case is designed to promote safety at sea. The scheme adopted to achieve this is to impose duties as to seaworthiness on the owners of vessels and then to provide for the Department to check and certify that these duties have been complied with. The purpose of issuing certificates is not really to encourage skippers or others to rely upon them by putting out to sea, or in any other matter. Somewhat paradoxically, the purpose of issuing certificates is to help to prevent fishing vessels which are uncertified, and which may be unseaworthy, from putting out to sea. More broadly, one can say that the purpose of issuing certificates is the promotion of safety at sea. I accept that there may be more than one purpose for which an advice is given. What I cannot accept is the plaintiffs' counsel's submission that, in the case of Fishing Vessel Certificates, a subsidiary purpose for which the certificate is issued is to inform those who may, in the future, consider entering into commercial transactions, such as purchase or charter, in relation to the certified vessels. No trace of such a purpose is to be found in the statute under which the Rules are issued, which is entitled 'Fishing Vessels (Safety Provision) Act' and which bears the preamble 'an Act to make further provision for the safety of Fishing Vessels'. The protection of those whose commercial interests may foreseeably be affected by the unseaworthiness of vessels forms no part of the purpose of the legislation and no part of the purpose for which Fishing Vessel Certificates are issued. So far as the purpose of the advice is concerned, the facts of this case are far more inimical to the finding of a relationship of proximity than the facts in *Caparo* [see Chapter 9, para 9.7.2].

In response to the plaintiffs' counsel's submission that in the present case the advice had been given to an identifiable class because there could be only a handful of potential purchasers and there was no difficulty in identifying them, Phillips LJ said:

> When Lord Bridge and Lord Oliver in *Caparo* spoke of the need for the advice to be given in the knowledge that it would be communicated to an ascertainable or identifiable class of persons [see Chapter 9, para 9.6.2], I believe that they were

probably speaking of a class of persons the membership of which was capable of ascertainment at the time that the advice was given, eg, shareholders who could be identified by consultation of the share register. I am sure that they were speaking of a class, in existence at the time of giving the advice, whose identifiable characteristics necessarily limited the number of its members. When a British Fishing Vessel Certificate is issued, those who may in the future place reliance on that certificate when deciding whether to purchase the vessel do not form part of a class that is capable of definition and delimitation by identifiable characteristics. The vessel may be sold during the currency of the certificate to a buyer from anywhere in the United Kingdom or an even wider geographical area. Not only did potential future purchasers not form an identifiable class when the certificate was issued, but the certificate was not issued for the purpose of providing information to assist them in deciding whether or not to purchase the vessel. It was issued as part of a scheme designed to prevent fishing vessels putting out to sea when unseaworthy.

In considering the question whether it would be fair, just and reasonable to impose a duty of care on the Department, Phillips LJ said:

There is no obvious reason why the Department of Transport's duty to regulate the seaworthiness of British vessels should impose a greater duty of care than that borne by those who build the vessels. Were such a duty to exist, the cost of it would have to be borne by the public in the form of increased survey fees, rather than by those concerned in the relevant commercial transactions.

In response to the plaintiffs' counsel's submission that justice required the existence of a duty of care in the present case because no alternative avenue of redress was open to the plaintiffs, Phillips LJ said:

In a case such as the present, it will always be open to a party entering into a commercial transaction in relation to a certified vessel to take steps, such as surveying the vessel or stipulating for contractual warranties that will provide protection against the risk that the certificate does not reflect the true condition of the vessel.

8.2.11   The Public Health Act

As noted *above* in para 8.2.10, one of the reasons for the House of Lords in *Murphy* holding that the defendant council did not owe a duty of care to the plaintiff house owner for his economic loss suffered by virtue of the defendant having negligently exercised its duties under the Public Health Act 1936 was (*per* Lord Keith at p 468) that the purposes of the Act as regards securing compliance with building bye-laws did not cover the avoidance of economic loss to owners of buildings, and (*per* Lord Oliver at p 490) that there was nothing in the Act which even suggests that its purpose was to protect owners of buildings from economic loss.

The impression given by their Lordships is that the Public Health Act 1936 contains a statement of its purposes. In fact it does not. While it is true that the emphasis of its provisions is on health and safety, this does not mean that the court was compelled to hold that it therefore excluded economic loss. The view taken by the Court of Appeal in *Murphy* (also reported at [1991] 1 AC 398) is just as tenable and is more in line with common sense. Nicholls LJ said (at p 432):

... the concept of injury to the safety or health of occupants requires a little elaboration. The Public Health Acts are concerned to avoid actual injury. They seek to achieve that end by reducing the risk of such injury. Accordingly houses are to be built to standards which are not hazardous to health or safety. Hence the logic ... in identifying the onset of present or imminent danger to the health or safety of occupants, as being in itself a type of damage which a duty of care imposed on a local authority regarding the building regulations is intended to avoid, as well as actual physical injury.

... it must surely follow that *prima facie* on a breach of that duty, the local authority's liability extends to the cost of carrying out the remedial works reasonably necessary to remove the danger. If the premise is correct, that must be a sound conclusion. If the wrong lies in the creation of a health or safety hazard, *prima facie* the remedy is an award of damages covering the cost of removing the hazard. To seek to label the damage as economic loss on the one hand or material, physical damage on the other hand does not, with all respect to the submissions made to us, really advance the argument either way.

8.2.12 The Building Act

The provisions in the Public Health Act 1936 relating to building regulations are now contained in the Building Act 1984. This Act does contain a statement about the purposes of any regulations which might be made pursuant to it. Section 1(1)(*a*) states: "The Secretary of State may, for any of the purposes of securing the health, safety, welfare and convenience of persons in or about buildings, make regulations with respect to the design and construction of buildings and the provision of services, fittings and equipment". This section is identical to s 61 of the Health and Safety at Work Act 1974, which superseded the relevant sections of the Public Health Act 1936 with effect from 17 March 1977.

One wonders whether, if the facts of a case like *Murphy* were to recur, the court would be prepared to hold that the words 'welfare' and 'convenience' in the statement of the purposes of these Acts, and the regulations made pursuant to them (the current building regulations are called the 1991 Building Regulations and came into force on 1 June 1992), are wide enough to encompass economic loss suffered by an owner of a building if such loss is suffered by virtue of the local authority's negligence in complying with its statutory obligations under the building regulations. These words appear in addition to the words "health and safety". If they are to have any meaning, it is submitted that they must include the economic interests of the owner of a building. Of course, this would not solve the problem completely, because the plaintiff would still have to establish a sufficient relationship of proximity based on reliance between himself and the local authority. However, as noted *above*, this should be possible where the particular function performed by the local authority (such as inspection of foundations which will then be covered up and which will not be able to be inspected by a subsequent purchaser) is such that the local authority can expect that subsequent purchasers will rely on it to have performed its functions without negligence, and where the plaintiff has indeed so relied.

8.3 Other relationships

8.3.1 Introduction

In the cases considered so far in this chapter the defendant has been a statutory authority whose powers and duties derive entirely from statute. As noted *above*, although this fact detracts from the 'why pick on me?' argument relating to duties of care for pure omissions, it also means that the wider social purposes of the legislation can sometimes negate the existence of a duty of care which would otherwise be justified in all of the circumstances of the case. Also, in some of the statutory authority cases considered *above*, the plaintiff's loss was caused directly by the inaction of the statutory authority; and in others the plaintiff's loss was caused directly by a third party's act or omission, but it was sought to make the statutory authority liable for that loss on the ground that the statutory authority could have prevented it by taking positive action.

All of the cases which are discussed *below* are of the second type, namely, where the plaintiff's loss was directly caused by a third party's act or omission, but it is sought to make the defendant liable for that loss on the ground that the defendant could have prevented it by taking positive action or by not being negligent in the action which he actually took. In some of the cases considered the defendant is a statutory authority, or a body which ultimately derives its authority from a statute or which performs its services in the public domain, an example being the police. These cases are, however, considered in this part of this chapter because the main focus has been on whether a duty of care is appropriate in circumstances where the defendant's negligence consisted of an omission to take steps to prevent a third party from causing harm to the plaintiff. To the extent that the courts in these cases have gone on to consider whether the position should be any different because the defendant's authority derived from statute, the principles that the courts have applied are the same as those considered *above*.

The range of situations in which the question whether the defendant can be made liable for his failure to prevent a third party from inflicting loss on the plaintiff is not easily definable. New situations are capable of arising all the time, and the various categories of situations which have been identified sometimes overlap with each other. Practitioners must therefore be prepared to cast their nets wider than the cases which fall strictly within only one of the following limited categories if they are searching for an answer in any previously identified fact situation.

8.3.2 Overview

Subject to the warning made *above* about rigid classification of cases, it is nevertheless useful to consider the relevant decisions in this area under the following groupings:

    (1) where the defendant is vicariously liable in law for the negligent act or omission of the third party who has caused the plaintiff's loss.

These are not really cases of pure omission at all, because, by virtue of the vicarious relationship between the defendant and the third party, the third party's negligence is automatically attributed to the defendant. An example is the negligent act or omission of an employee committed during the course of and within the scope of his employment by the defendant;

(2) where there was no vicarious relationship between the defendant and the third party, but the defendant had a prior relationship with the third party under which the defendant was able to exercise a degree of control over the third party's conduct, which would probably have had the effect of avoiding the plaintiff's loss being caused. An example is *Dorset Yacht* (the escaping borstal boys), considered in para 8.3.3, *below*;

(3) where the defendant has himself negligently created a dangerous situation which, in turn, has caused the plaintiff's loss. An example is *Haynes v Harwood* (the runaway horse), considered in para 8.3.3, *below*;

(4) where the plaintiff has invited people onto his land, and they have caused damage to neighbouring land. An example is *Scott's Trustees v Moss* (a balloon landing in neighbouring field), considered in para 8.3.3, *below*;

(5) where the defendant has not had any relationship at all with the third party who caused the plaintiff's loss, but that loss could have been avoided if the defendant had acted, or had acted differently. An example is *Perl v Camden* (burglars entering through defendant's property), considered in para 8.3.3, *below*;

(6) where the defendant had a contractual relationship with the plaintiff, whose loss, caused by a third party, could probably have been prevented if the defendant had acted, or had acted differently. An example is *Reid v Rush & Tompkins plc* (employer failing to advise employee to obtain insurance), considered in para 8.3.3, *below*;

(7) where the situation is the same as in (6) *above*, except that the prior relationship between the defendant and the plaintiff was not fully contractual. An example is *Banque Keyser Ullmann v Skandia* (insurer failing to tell bank about bank's broker's misconduct), considered in para 8.3.3, *below*.

8.3.3   The individual groupings

Vicarious liability

In accordance with the general comment made *above*, this category does not need to be considered further, save to mention that an example of its operation as an incidental factor in *Dorset Yacht* is the fact that the Home Office was the defendant, and not the actual borstal officers who had acted negligently in allowing the boys in their charge to escape, because the Home Office was vicariously liable for the negligent acts and omissions of the officers if (as happened in that case) they fell within the scope of their employment.

Control of the third party

The cases which have arisen in this group, and many of the cases in groups (3)–(6), have involved physical injury to the plaintiff or damage to the plaintiff's property. Therefore the analysis of the relationship between the defendant and the plaintiff has sometimes tended to be a bit simplistic: foreseeability of the plaintiff's loss has sufficed to establish the duty of care.

Smith v Leurs (1945) 70 CLR 256 (High Court of Australia): In this case the question was whether the parents of a boy who had injured another boy with a stone fired from a catapult should be held liable for want of care in allowing their son to use the catapult. On the facts, the court concluded that the parents had not been negligent in allowing their son to use the catapult. Dixon J expressed the following *dictum*, which has been adopted in subsequent English cases. He said (at p 262):

> It is exceptional to find in the law a duty to control another's actions to prevent harm to strangers. The general rule is that one man is under no duty of controlling another man to prevent his doing damage to a third. There are, however, special relations [between the defendant and the third party who caused the damage] which are the source of a duty of this nature. It is incumbent upon a parent who maintains control over a young child to take reasonable care so to exercise that control as to avoid conduct on his part exposing the person or property of others to unreasonable danger.

Carmarthenshire County Council v Lewis [1955] AC 549: A four-year-old boy attending a nursery school under the management of the defendant council strayed from those premises onto the adjoining road. The plaintiff's husband, who was driving a lorry, struck a telegraph pole in avoiding him and was killed. The court held that the council was liable to the plaintiff in damages. Lord Reid said (at p 563): "The actions of a child of this age are unpredictable. I think that it ought to have been anticipated by the appellants [ie the council] or their responsible officers that in such a case a child might well try to get out on to the street and that if it did, a traffic accident was far from improbable".

Home Office v Dorset Yacht Co Ltd [1970] AC 1004: A group of boys who were sentenced to borstal training were taken by their wardens to do some work on an island in Poole harbour. As part of this exercise the boys and the three officers in charge of them slept overnight in an empty house on the island. During the night seven of the boys absconded and boarded a yacht which was moored off the island and caused it to collide with, and thereby to damage, another yacht, which belonged to the plaintiff. The court held (by 4:1) that the Home Office, as the employer of the officers, owed a duty of care to the plaintiff in respect of the acts of the borstal trainees who had caused the damage.

The first step in the court's reasoning was that the officers did not simply have a discretion to take steps to guard against the boys escaping: they were under a positive duty to do so. As Lord Reid said (at p 1031): "The present case does not raise this issue because no discretion was given to these borstal officers. They were given orders which they negligently failed to carry out". The second step was that the plaintiff's loss was foreseeable. As Lord Reid said (at p 1026):

> All the escaping trainees had criminal records and five of them had a record of previous escapes from Borstal institutions. The three officers knew or ought to have known that these trainees would probably try to escape during the night, would take some vessel to make good their escape and would probably cause damage to it or some other vessel. There were numerous vessels moored in the harbour, and the trainees could readily board one of them. So it was a likely consequence of [the officers'] neglect of duty that the [plaintiff's] yacht would suffer damage.

The third step was the fact that, by virtue of the control which the borstal officers exercised over the boys in their charge, there existed "a special relation" of the type described by Dixon J in *Smith v Leurs* (see *above*) sufficient to enable the court to hold that in law the officers had a duty to control the boys' actions, so as to prevent harm to strangers.

The fourth step was to decide whether the plaintiff and its yacht which the boys had damaged were within the ambit, or the scope, of the officers' duty of care. Only three of the four majority Lords specifically dealt with this point. For the purposes of comparison with subsequent cases where the plaintiff's loss has been purely economic, it is interesting to see how each of their Lordships dealt with this point. Thus, Lord Morris said (at p 1034):

> The possibilities of damage being done to one of the nearby yachts (assuming that they were nearby) were many and apparent. In . . . those circumstances I consider that a duty of care was owed by the officers to the owners of the nearby yachts. The principle expressed in Lord Atkin's classic words in *Donoghue v Stevenson* would seem to be directly applicable . . . it was incumbent on the officers to avoid acts or omissions which they could reasonably foresee would be likely to injure the owners of yachts. They were persons so closely and directly affected by what the officers did or failed to do that they ought reasonably to have been in the contemplation of the officers.

Lord Pearson said (at p 1054):

> It seems to me that *prima facie*, in the situation which arose in this case according to the allegations, the plaintiffs as boatowners were in law 'neighbours' of the defendants and so there was a duty of care owing by the defendants to the plaintiffs.
> . . . It seems clear that there was sufficient proximity: there was geographical proximity and it was foreseeable that the damage was likely to occur unless some care was taken to prevent it. In other cases a difficult problem may arise as to how widely the 'neighbourhood' extends, but no such problem faces the plaintiffs in this case.

Lastly, Lord Diplock, after concluding that a duty of care should be imposed on the borstal officers, said (at p 1070):

> I should therefore hold that any duty of a Borstal officer to use reasonable care to prevent a Borstal trainee from escaping from his custody was owed only to persons whom he could reasonably foresee had property situate in the vicinity of the place of detention of the detainee which the detainee was likely to steal or to appropriate and damage in the course of eluding immediate pursuit and recapture.

It is interesting to note that Lord Diplock included property which could foreseeably be stolen within his formulation, because it is arguable that the loss of property by stealing is pure economic loss. The court in *Reid v Rush and Tompkins Group plc* (see *below*) so regarded it. However, it would be wrong to draw any conclusions from what Lord Diplock said, because it seems that he was not specifically directing his mind to the separate question of pure economic loss when he formulated this principle.

Creating a dangerous situation

Where the defendant has negligently created or permitted to be created a source of danger and it is reasonably foreseeable that a stranger (ie the plaintiff) might be injured by that situation, the defendant might be held to owe a duty of care to the plaintiff in respect of his losses. A typical example here would be the case of a defendant who had left a bonfire in a field unattended and some young boys who came upon it made use of its flames to start another fire, which caused damage to the plaintiff's property. Closely allied to this type of case are the 'rescue cases'. A case which embodies both of these aspects is *Haynes v Harwood*.

Haynes v Harwood [1935] 1 KB 146: The plaintiff, a policeman on duty, was injured when he stopped two runaway horses with a van attached. The court held that the defendant delivery-man, who had left these horses unattended in a busy street, owed a duty of care to the plaintiff for his injuries. In doing so the court rejected the defendant's defence of *novus actus interveniens*, ie that the defendant was not the 'proximate cause' of the plaintiff's injury. Greer LJ said (at p 156):

> If what is relied upon as *novus actus interveniens* is the very kind of thing which is likely to happen if the want of care which is alleged takes place, the principle embodied in the maxim is no defence. The whole question is whether or not . . . the accident can be said to be the 'natural and probable result' of the breach of duty. If it is the very thing which ought to be anticipated by a man leaving his horses, or one of the things likely to arise as a consequence of his wrongful act, it is no defence. . .
>
> It is not necessary to show that this particular accident and this particular damage were probable; it is sufficient if the accident is of a class that might well be anticipated as one of the reasonable and probable results of the wrongful act.

The court also rejected the defendant's contention that the plaintiff had acted as a volunteer. Maugham LJ said (at p 161): "In my opinion the police constable was not in any true sense a volunteer. It is true that he was under no positive legal duty to run out into the street and, at risk of his life, to stop two galloping horses. It is also true that the primary duty of the police is the prevention of crime and the arrest of criminals. But that is only a part of the duties of the police in London". He went on to say that, in the circumstances of this case, namely a police officer on duty in a busy street, the plaintiff did not act unreasonably in the risks that he took. He stressed that this does not mean that any member of the public who might voluntarily run out to stop a runaway horse would be entitled to sue the person whose negligence caused the horse to run away.

Damage caused by invitees

Sometimes a crowd of people who have gathered on one's land might become unruly and cause damage to neighbouring property. This occurred in *Scott's Trustees v Moss* (1899) 17 R (Ct of Sess) 32. The defendant was a promotor of entertainment who had advertised that a balloon would descend at a certain time into certain recreation grounds. For a small fee he admitted people into those grounds to await the balloon's arrival. Unfortunately the wind carried it into a nearby field. The crowd who had assembled in the recreation ground burst into that field and caused considerable damage. The court held that the defendant was liable for that damage. Lord Shand said (at p 37): "In the ordinary case the mere bringing of a crowd together does not lead to the inference that the person who has been instrumental in assembling the crowd is answerable for its actions. I think that the principle which ought to receive effect is that if the collection of the crowd, and the actions of the crowd, are the natural and probable consequence of the action of the defender—a consequence which the defender ought to have foreseen—then the case is relevant".

No relationship with the third party

In all of the cases considered *above*, the defendant had a prior relationship with the third party who caused the plaintiff's loss. In the cases considered in this group, the defendant did not have a prior relationship with the third party.

Lamb v Camden Borough Council [1981] 1 QB 625: The defendant local council and its contractors had broken a water main while they were replacing a sewer in a public road. A vast quantity of water flowed out and washed out soil from the foundations of the plaintiff's neighbouring house. This caused subsidence and the walls cracked. The house became unsafe to live in and had to be vacated by the tenant to whom the plaintiff had let the house while she was overseas for an extended period. While the house was empty some squatters moved in. The plaintiff instituted proceedings and managed to get them removed. She then boarded up the house (although not very securely). A few months later some more squatters moved in. They caused substantial damage to the fixtures and fittings in the house. Eventually they too were removed, but that was nearly three years after the bursting of the water pipe by the defendant.

The council did not resist the plaintiff's claims for the cost of making good the subsidence damage but did resist paying the plaintiff for the cost of repairing the malicious damage done by the squatters. The court held that the council was not liable for this damage. The court viewed this case as a simple question of remoteness of damage, namely whether a reasonable man in the position of the defendant could reasonably have been expected to have foreseen the type of damage suffered by the plaintiff. Oliver LJ said (at p 643): "I find it inconceivable that the reasonable man wielding his pick in the road in 1973 could be said reasonably to foresee that his puncturing of a water main would fill the plaintiff's house with uninvited guests in 1974".

It should be noted that, once it had been decided that the plaintiff's loss was too remote (ie was not of a kind which was foreseeable), it was not necessary to consider whether there was a sufficient relationship of proximity between the plaintiff and the defendant to warrant the imposition of a duty of care with regard to the losses sustained by the plaintiff at the hands of the squatters. By way of analogy with the intermediate inspection cases, it might be said that such proximity did not exist because of the plaintiff's opportunity to have made the house secure against squatters when she moved her furniture out of it after the initial flooding.

P Perl (Exporters) Ltd v Camden London Borough Council [1984] 1 QB 342: The defendant was the owner of certain unoccupied and unsecured premises. The defendant also owned the adjoining premises, which were occupied by the plaintiff for the purpose of its business as a retailer of knitwear. With the knowledge of the defendant (the plaintiff was the defendant's tenant), the plaintiff used the basement for the storage of garments. One weekend intruders broke into the defendant's neighbouring premises and knocked a hole through the common wall in the basement and stole the plaintiff's garments. The court held that the defendant was not liable to the plaintiff for its loss, notwithstanding that the defendant had received complaints about the lack of security at the neighbouring premises and had done nothing about it.

Unlike in *Lamb*, the court's reasoning is not based on the foreseeability of the plaintiff's loss but, rather, on the fact that there was no special relationship, similar to control, between the defendant and the third party, which would make the defendant responsible for the third party's negligent acts or omissions. Robert Goff LJ said (at p 359):

> It is . . . true that . . . the plaintiffs do not allege that the defendants should have controlled the thieves who broke into their storeroom. But they do allege that the defendants should have exercised reasonable care to prevent them from gaining access through their own premises; and in my judgment the statement of principle by Dixon J [in *Smith v Leurs*, see *above*] is equally apposite in such a case. I know of no case where it has been held in the absence of a special relationship [between the defendant and the third party who caused the plaintiff's damage], that the defendant was liable in negligence for having failed to prevent a third party from wrongfully causing damage to the plaintiff.

King v Liverpool City Council [1986] 1 WLR 890: The facts were similar to those of *Perl*, in that the plaintiff's flat had been damaged by water escaping from vandalised pipes in the vacant flat immediately above the plaintiff's flat. The defendant, who owned the whole block of flats, had failed to secure the vacant flat against intruders, despite having been asked to do so by the plaintiff.

Following *Perl*, the court rejected the plaintiff's claim, saying that, although there was no principle of law excluding liability in negligence for damage caused by the deliberate wrongdoing of a third party, liability would attach only where there was some special relationship between the defendant and the third party; or, possibly, where the injury to the plaintiff by the third party was the inevitable and foreseeable result of the defendant's act or omission. This second possibility was ruled out by the fact that the defendant was unable to take effective steps to defeat the activities of vandals.

Smith v Littlewoods Organisation Ltd [1987] 1 AC 241: The defendant had purchased a cinema building with the intention of demolishing it and replacing it with a supermarket. After the defendant's contractors had done some work, the cinema remained empty and unattended. It was securely locked up, but that security was overcome from time to time by vandals who destroyed some fittings and tried to light a fire in the cinema. The defendant was totally unaware of these activities. The defendant's name, address and telephone number were prominently displayed on the door of the cinema, but no one reported these activities to the defendant. Soon afterwards a fire was deliberately started in the cinema by intruders. The cinema burned down completely and several buildings in the vicinity were damaged by the spreading fire. The owners of those buildings sued the defendant for damages on the ground that the defendant owed them a duty of care to prevent this damage occurring.

The court rejected the plaintiff's claims. Building on the principle of *Haynes v Harwood*, discussed *above*, Lord Goff said that, while an owner or occupier of land is not under a general duty of care to prevent third parties from causing damage to premises in the neighbourhood, such a duty is capable of arising:

(1) where the defendant has negligently caused or permitted the creation of a source of danger on his land, and where it is foreseeable that third parties might trespass on his land and spark it off, thereby causing damage to the person or property of those in the vicinity; or

(2) where the defendant has knowledge or the means of knowledge that a third party has created or is creating a risk of fire on his premises and fails to take such steps as are reasonably open to him to prevent any such fire from damaging neighbouring property.

Lord Goff said that the first of these principles could not be satisfied here because the empty cinema could not properly be described as an unusual danger in the nature of a fire hazard. There was nothing about the building to suggest that it could easily be set alight. The second principle was not applicable because, if third parties had created a fire risk on the defendant's property, the defendant had no means of knowing that it existed.

Hill v Chief Constable of West Yorkshire [1989] 1 AC 53: The plaintiff was the mother of a young woman who had been attacked and killed by a man known as the Yorkshire Ripper who had committed 12 similar murders and eight attempted murders before being caught. The plaintiff claimed that the West Yorkshire police force had been negligent in its conduct of the investigation of the perpetrator's other crimes, so that, if they had exercised proper skill and care, he would have been apprehended before the date upon which her daughter was murdered. The plaintiff's claim, on behalf of her daughter's estate, was for damages for loss of expectation of life and for pain and suffering. However, the House of Lords' judgment would also cover a plaintiff who had only suffered pure economic loss in consequence of the activities of an unapprehended criminal.

The House of Lords struck out the plaintiff's claim as disclosing no reasonable cause of action. Lord Keith said (at p 60):

> The foundation of the duty of care [contended for by the plaintiff] was said to be reasonable foreseeability of harm to potential future victims if Sutcliffe were not promptly apprehended.
>
> . . . It has been said almost too frequently to require repetition that foreseeability of likely harm is not in itself a sufficient test of liability in negligence. Some further ingredient is invariably needed to establish the requisite proximity of relationship between plaintiff and defendant, and all the circumstances of the case must be carefully considered and analysed in order to ascertain whether such an ingredient is present.

Lord Keith stressed that there is no question that a police officer, like anyone else, may be liable in tort to a person who has been injured as a direct result of his acts or omissions. However, by comparing the present case with *Dorset Yacht* he concluded that the "requisite proximity of relationship" between the plaintiff and the defendant did not exist in this case. Although the plaintiff yacht owner succeeded in *Dorset Yacht*, the court there made it clear that the class of persons to whom a duty of care might be owed was limited to those persons whom the defendant could reasonably foresee had property situate in the vicinity of the place from which the detainees had escaped (see *above*), and would not have been owed to persons or property who were further afield. Based on this distinction in *Dorset Yacht*, Lord Keith said (at p 62):

> . . . if there is no general duty of care owed to individual members of the public by the responsible authorities to prevent the escape of a known criminal or to recapture him, there cannot reasonably be imposed upon any police force a duty of care similarly owed to identify and apprehend an unknown one . . .

and that

> Miss Hill was one of a vast number of the female general public who might be at risk from [Sutcliffe's] activities, but she was at no special distinctive risk in relation to them, unlike the owners of yachts moored off Brownsea Island in relation to the foreseeable conduct of the Borstal boys.

By a similar process of comparison with *Dorset Yacht*, Lord Keith also concluded that the necessary special relationship to found liability in this type of case between the defendant and the third party who had caused the plaintiff's loss was also lacking. As Sutcliffe had never been in the custody of the police force, the element of control, which served to satisfy this requirement in *Dorset Yacht*, could not be satisfied here.

Although these factors were sufficient to dispose of the plaintiff's case, the House of Lords held that the plaintiff's case should be struck out on the ground that, as a matter of public policy, the police should be immune from actions for negligence in respect of their activities in the investigation and suppression of crime. Thus, Lord Keith said (at p 63):

> ... in my opinion there is another reason why an action for damages in negligence should not lie against the police in circumstances such as those of the present case, and that is public policy. ... Potential existence of ... liability may in many instances be in the general public interest, as tending towards the observance of a higher standard of care in the carrying on of various different types of activity. I do not, however, consider that this can be said of police activities. The general sense of public duty which motivates police forces is unlikely to be appreciably reinforced by the imposition of such liability so far as concerns their functions in the investigation and suppression of crime. From time to time they make mistakes in the exercise of that function, but it is not to be doubted that they apply their best endeavours to the performance of it. In some instances the imposition of liability may lead to the exercise of a function being carried out in a detrimentally defensive frame of mind. The possibility of this happening in relation to the investigative operations of the police cannot be excluded. Further, it would not be reasonable to expect that if potential liability were to be imposed, it would not be uncommon for actions to be raised against police forces on the ground that they had failed to catch some criminal as soon as they might have done, with the result that he went on to commit further crimes. While some such actions might involve allegations of a simple and straightforward type of failure—for example that a police officer negligently tripped and fell while pursuing a burglar—others would be likely to enter deeply into the general nature of a police investigation, as indeed the present action would seek to do. The manner of conduct of such an investigation must necessarily involve a variety of decisions to be made on matters of policy and discretion, for example as to which particular line of inquiry is most advantageously to be pursued and what is the most advantageous way to deploy the available resources. Many such decisions would not be regarded by the courts as appropriate to be called in question, yet elaborate investigation of the facts might be necessary to ascertain whether or not this was so. A great deal of police time, trouble and expense might be expected to have to be put into the preparation of the defence to the action and the attendance of witnesses at the trial. The result would be a significant diversion of police manpower and attention from their most important function, that of the suppression of crime.

Lord Templeman expressed similar sentiments when he said (at p 65):

> ... if this action lies, every citizen will be able to require the court to investigate the performance of every policeman. If the policeman concentrates on one crime, he may be accused of neglecting others. If the policeman does not arrest

on suspicion a suspect with previous convictions, the police force may be held liable for subsequent crimes. The threat of litigation against a police force would not make a policeman more efficient. The necessity for defending proceedings, successfully or unsuccessfully, would distract the policeman from his duties.

Clough v Bussan (West Yorkshire Police Authority, third party) [1990] 1 All ER 431: The court, following *Hill*, held that the fact that a police station had received information that the traffic lights at a particular junction were malfunctioning could not be sufficient to impose on the police a duty of care to every motorist (and to the plaintiff in particular) who might thereafter use the junction and be injured in consequence of the traffic lights not functioning.

Kirkham v Chief Constable of the Greater Manchester Police [1990] 2 QB 283: The plaintiff's husband had been charged with criminal damage and was remanded in custody by magistrates on 9 January 1980. The police knew that he was a suicide risk and that he had made recent attempts to commit suicide. The police did not communicate that information to the prison authorities when handing the plaintiff's husband over to them. In particular, the police failed to complete and hand over a police form (POL 1) intended for use in respect of prisoners regarded as exceptional risks, which category included prisoners with known suicidal tendencies. The following day, while in prison, the plaintiff's husband committed suicide. The trial judge found as a fact that, had the prison authorities known of his suicidal tendencies, they would probably have taken steps which would have prevented, or at least lessened, the risk of his suicide.

In the present action, the plaintiff, as administratrix of her husband's estate, brought an action in negligence for damages against the Chief Constable of Police. The Court of Appeal upheld the plaintiff's action. Lloyd LJ said (at p 289):

> The question depends in each case on whether, having regard to the particular relationship between the parties, the defendant has assumed a responsibility towards the plaintiff, and whether the plaintiff has relied on that assumption of responsibility.
>
> In the present case I have no difficulty in holding that the police assumed certain responsibilities towards Mr Kirkham when they took him into custody, and in particular assumed a responsibility to pass on information which might affect his well-being when he was transferred from their custody to the custody of the prison authorities. Nor have I any difficulty in inferring reliance. That is sufficient to impose on the police a duty to speak.

Alexandrou v Oxford [1993] 4 All ER 328 (the decision in this case was delivered on 16 February 1990, but was not reported until 1993): The plaintiff's clothing shop was burgled on a Sunday evening. The burglars' entry activated the shop's burglar alarm and also a recorded telephone message to the local police station, stating that the alarm had been activated. Two police officers promptly attended the scene, but failed to inspect the rear of the shop where the burglars had forced entry. Some hours later a substantial quantity of goods was removed from the shop. The plaintiff sued the Chief Constable (Kenneth Oxford) for the value of the goods stolen, alleging that the police had been negligent in the way that they inspected the plaintiff's premises and concluded that it was a false alarm.

Despite the trial judge's finding of fact that the theft would have been prevented if the police officers had properly inspected the rear of the plaintiff's premises, the Court of Appeal held that the police did not owe a duty of care to the plaintiff in respect of his loss. Glidewell LJ said (at p 334):

> The difficulty in answering the question [whether the police did owe the plaintiff a duty of care] arises from the fact that the plaintiff's loss was not caused directly by any act or failure on the part of the police, but by the activities of the burglars. The police, on the judge's findings of fact, were indirectly responsible for the plaintiff's loss because of PC Smith's failure properly to inspect the rear of the shop. . . .
>
> It is not sufficient for a plaintiff who seeks to establish that a defendant owed him a duty to take reasonable care to prevent loss being caused to the plaintiff by the activities of another person simply to prove that if the defendant did not exercise reasonable care it was foreseeable that the plaintiff would suffer the loss. It is necessary for the plaintiff also to show that in the circumstances of the particular case he stands in a special relationship to the defendant, from which the duty of care arose.

In response to the plaintiff's counsel's submission that the present case was distinguishable from *Hill* because the owners of intruder alarms connected to the police station constitute a much more limited group than the category of "young or fairly young women" to whom it was alleged that the police owed a duty of care in *Hill*, Glidewell LJ said (at p 338):

> It is possible to envisage an agreement between an occupier of a property protected by a burglar alarm and the police which would impose a contractual liability on the police. This is not, however, the situation in this case. The communication with the police in this case was by a 999 telephone call, followed by a recorded message. If as a result of that communication the police came under a duty of care to the plaintiff, it must follow that they would be under a similar duty to any person who informs them, whether by a 999 call or in some other way, that a burglary, or indeed any crime, against himself or his property is being committed or is about to be committed. So in my view if there is a duty of care, it is owed to . . . all members of the public who give information of a suspected crime against themselves or their property. It follows, therefore, that on the facts of this case . . . there was no such special relationship between the plaintiff and the police as was present in the *Dorset Yacht* case.

Osman v Ferguson [1993] 4 All ER 344 (the judgment in this case was delivered on 7 October 1992, but it was not reported until the end of 1993): P, a school teacher, had formed an unhealthy attachment to a 15-year-old male pupil and started to harass him and accuse him of deviant sexual practices and followed him to his home. In May 1987, P changed his surname to that of the boy and threw a brick through a window of the boy's home and caused other acts of vandalism to property connected with the boy. In mid-1987, P was dismissed from the school, but continued to harass the boy. The police were aware of these facts and, in the latter part of 1987, P himself told a police officer that the loss of his job was distressing and that there was a danger that he would do something criminally insane. In December 1987, P deliberately rammed a vehicle in which the boy was a passenger. The police laid an information against P in January 1988, but it was not served. In March 1988, P followed the boy and his family to their flat and shot and severely injured the boy and killed his father.

In the present action the boy and his mother, as administratrix of the father's estate, brought an action against the Commissioner of Police ('the Commissioner') for damages based on an alleged duty of care owed by the police to the plaintiff to safeguard them against the criminal acts of P. The Commissioner applied to strike out the plaintiffs' claim as disclosing no reasonable cause of action. The Court of Appeal granted this application, notwithstanding that their Lordships were satisfied that, as between the boy and his family on the one hand, and the investigating officers on the other, there existed a very close degree of proximity amounting to a special relationship. The Court of Appeal nevertheless felt that there were overriding reasons of public policy which led to the conclusion that the plaintiffs' case was bound to fail by virtue of the public policy factors mentioned by the House of Lords in *Hill*. Thus, McCowan LJ said (emphasis added) (at p 353):

> [The plaintiffs' counsel] submits that the *ratio* of *Hill's* case is that policy decisions are protected by public policy immunity but operational decisions are not and that, whereas the failures in *Hill's* case were of a policy nature, those in the present case were of an operational nature. In my judgment, such a distinction is not to be supported by the speeches in *Hill's* case. Indeed, I consider such a dividing line to be utterly artificial and impossible to draw in the present case.
>
> In giving judgment in the present case, Sir Peter Pain [the High Court Judge to whom the application to strike out was made in the first instance] said:
>
> > '[that in his] view the plaintiffs are going to have a distinctly uphill task . . . but [he] did not think there [was] so obviously no case that it would be right to strike the action out on those grounds.'
>
> I do not take that view. In my view the House of Lords decision on public policy in *Hill's* case dooms this action to failure as against the [Commissioner].

Topp v London County Bus (South West) Ltd [1993] 3 All ER 448; [1993] 1 WLR 976 (CA): Late one night the plaintiff's wife, Mrs Jacqueline Topp, was cycling home from work when she was run over by one of the defendant's buses which had been hijacked from a bus stop in a lay-by up the road a few minutes earlier. The driver did not stop. The bus was later found abandoned. The driver was never identified. The bus stop from which the bus was hijacked was outside the White Horse public house and directly opposite the District Hospital. It was the changeover point for drivers. The defendant's system was for a driver who ended his shift to leave the bus parked at the bus stop unlocked with the ignition keys in it. If the schedule ran to time, there was an eight-minute interval between shifts during which the bus was unattended.

On this particular day, the bus in question stood unattended in the lay-by for approximately nine hours because the changeover driver failed to report to work. Another driver who was working the same route during the afternoon with a different bus saw the bus standing in the lay-by. He telephoned the defendant's controller and told him that the bus was there. The defendant, however, took no steps to recover the bus before it was stolen.

In the present action the plaintiff, the deceased's husband, sought to recover damages from the defendant on the basis of the defendant's alleged negligence in leaving its unlocked bus with its ignition key in the switch for nine hours in a lay-by outside a public house so that it was an allurement constituting a source of danger on the highway which foreseeably resulted in Mrs Topp's death. At the trial the defendant accepted that it had been negligent in leaving the bus in the lay-by for nine hours without attempting to retrieve it. The judge, May J, considered that the label 'proximity' could be attached to the relationship between Mrs Topp and the defendant, but he nevertheless concluded that it would not be fair, just and reasonable to impose a duty of care on the defendant for the plaintiff's losses in all of the circumstances of the case.

The Court of Appeal did not agree with May J's view about proximity in this case, but did agree with his ultimate conclusion that no duty of care was owed by the defendant to the plaintiff, because the parked bus did not fall within a special category of risk as a source of danger on the highway since the acts of the wrongdoer constituted a *novus actus interveniens* which broke the chain of causation.

Ancell v McDermott [1993] 4 All ER 355: The fuel tank of the car of the first defendant had become ruptured while he was driving along a highway. He was unaware of this and drove on until his car stopped because it had run out of fuel. In the process of continuing to drive in this state, the first defendant had left a long trail of slippery diesel fuel on the road. Shortly afterwards a police car driven by an officer in the service of the second defendant noticed the diesel fuel on the road and followed the trail until he came to the first defendant's stationary car. By radio the officers notified their headquarters that diesel fuel had been spilt on the road. Some time later another police officer drove past the spillage and reported the matter to the local highways department. He then continued on his way.

About ten minutes later the plaintiff's wife, driving her car along that stretch of road, skidded on the diesel fuel, lost control and collided head-on with an oncoming truck. She suffered serious injuries from which she died the following day. The plaintiff (being the deceased's husband) sued the police for his loss. They applied to have the Statement of Claim struck out as disclosing no reasonable cause of action. The trial judge refused to grant that application, but the Court of Appeal overruled the trial judge. After referring to *Dorset Yacht* and *Hill*, Beldam LJ said (at p 365):

. . . it is exceptional to find in the law a duty to control another's actions to prevent harm to strangers and where they are found they arise from special relationships. When it is contended that such special relationship arises out of duties carried out in the performance of a public office, the court must have regard to the purpose and scope of the public duties, whether they are intended to benefit a particular section of the public, eg, investors or depositors, and whether such persons could reasonably place reliance on the fulfilment of the duties.

. . . such a duty of care would impose on a police force potential liabilities of almost unlimited scope. Not only would the class of persons to whom the duty was owed be extensive, but the activities of police officers which might give rise to the existence of such a duty would be widespread. The constable on the beat who failed to notice a danger on the pavement or noticed it but dismissed it as insufficiently serious to warrant his attention, the officer who searched for but failed to find property when he might have done or the officer who misinterpreted a breathalyser reading, might all be said to come under liability to anyone who could show that they suffered injury or loss as a result of his failure. Further, I am not persuaded that there is any sufficient distinction between the reasoning which led the House of Lords to reject the existence of a duty in *Hill*'s case to justify the imposition of a duty to act in the circumstances of the present case. . . .

The diversion of police resources and manpower if such a duty were held to exist would, in my judgment, extensively hamper the performance of ordinary police duties and create a formidable diversion of police manpower.

Skinner v The Secretary of State for Transport ((1994) *The Times*, 3 January): One afternoon a fishing vessel became overwhelmed and swamped by a enormous wave. It capsized and sank. Three of the four men on board lost their lives. The fourth man, the first plaintiff, survived. He gave evidence that, just before the vessel went down, he managed to transmit a message on the emergency radio channel, stating the name of the vessel and the fact that it was sinking. This message was received by an auxiliary Coast Guard officer, Ms Wray, but the message was practically unintelligible and she was not sure what she had heard. Having carefully listened for any repeated message and having inquired of a colleague whether the colleague had heard anything, Ms Wray decided not to report the matter to the senior watch officer. This was a breach of standing instructions which required her to inform the senior watch officer of any dubious call which could have emergency implications.

In the present action the plaintiffs, who were the sole surviving seaman and the dependants of those who did not survive, alleged that, had the senior watch officer been informed, he would have caused a message to be transmitted by radio to all vessels in the vicinity, and that they would then have been on the lookout for signs of a sinking ship, so that the chances of earlier rescue would have been greater. The Coast Guard submitted that it was immune from actions for negligence in respect of the performance of its duties to the same extent as the police force and that, in any event, it did not owe a duty of care to mariners generally or to mariners known to be in danger. Judge Gareth Edwards QC, sitting as a High Court judge, agreed with both of these submissions and rejected the plaintiffs' claims.

On the duty of care question, the plaintiffs' counsel submitted that the present case was different from the police cases on the basis that the police deal with the public at large whereas the Coast Guard deals only with seafarers. The judge said that he did not think that this distinction was sufficient to make a difference of principle. He said that this can be seen if one considers that the police do not owe a duty of care to persons known from an emergency call to be immediately at risk (see *above*). He also rejected the plaintiffs' counsel's submission that the present case was different to the police cases because a seafarer puts himself at risk and places his trust in the Coast Guard, but the same cannot be said of the public and the police. In rejecting this submission the judge said:

> With regard to the other argument, that is that mariners deliberately place their lives at risk in the knowledge that the coastal waters are watched, there is a danger of putting the cart before the horse. Coast Guards watch coastal waters because mariners are out there putting themselves at risk and not *vice versa*. The Coast Guard is a service for which mariners are, I am sure, profoundly grateful, but I would not think that there are many in the seafaring community who would regard themselves, because they go out to sea, as having rights legally enforceable against that agency if it were to make a mistake in its watching and search co-ordinating role.

On the 'immunity from actions for negligence point', his Honour said:

> The same result is achieved, but by a shorter route, upon a consideration of public policy. This was an alternative reason for denying the plaintiff a remedy in *Hill v Chief Constable of West Yorkshire*. The considerations there set out apply even more forcefully to the Coast Guard Service. The Coast Guard has vast responsibilities and slender resources. It can ill afford to have a single one of its permanent staff tied up in court proceedings. Litigation could involve the examination of operational decisions made at a time when an officer had to choose swiftly between several options. It might require a very lengthy unravelling of the facts to ascertain whether he had acted negligently. The litigation might involve counter-allegations against the crew of a rescued vessel or against the masters of other vessels. It could involve disputes with foreign shipowners or foreign Coast Guards. It could bring into the arena of legal conflict the very rescue services upon whose co-operation and goodwill the Coast Guard is reliant. The damage which could be done to the Coast Guard's efficiency and to the trust which exists between it and the seafaring community, foreign Coast Guards and the providers of rescue vessels and aircraft is incalculable.
>
> It is in my view most unlikely that the possibility of legal action would lead to higher standards. It might well, however, lead to the defensive mentality referred to in *Hill*. The consequences of that would be the over-deployment of scarce resources or the overuse of the resources of other rescue agencies. The result would certainly be a diminution in the effectiveness of the Coast Guard Service and a consequent increase in the risk to mariners around our shores. I am entirely satisfied therefore that it is contrary to the public interest that the Coast Guard should be open to actions for negligence in respect of its usual watching, listening and rescue co-ordination functions. Accordingly, quite apart from any other finds, these actions must fail for reasons of public policy.

Barrett v The Ministry of Defence [1995] 1 WLR 1217: A naval airman, Terence Barrett, at a shore-based naval establishment in Norway, allowed himself to become so drunk that he became unconscious. In this state his colleagues at the naval base took him to his cabin and placed him on his bunk in the recovery position. He was in a coma but was tossing and turning. He was visited on about three occasions by the duty ratings. When his cabin mate went to turn in at about 2.30 am, he found that Terence Barrett was dead.

The cause of Terence Barrett's death was suffocation due to inhalation of vomit. In the present action, brought by Mr Barrett's widow, the Court of Appeal held that the Ministry of Defence did not owe the plaintiff a duty of care initially in respect of his over-indulgence of alcohol. However, after he collapsed, the Ministry did assume a responsibility for the deceased's situation such as to give rise to a duty of care to the plaintiff, which duty the Court held the defendant had breached by its inadequate supervision of the deceased after it had assumed control for his safety.

Although the Court concluded that the defendant did owe a duty of care to the plaintiff, it reduced the extent of that duty by two-thirds of the value of the plaintiff's claim because the defendant had effectively been thrust into accepting responsibility for the deceased's safety in circumstances where he had shown little regard himself for his welfare. Thus, Beldam LJ said (at p 1225):

> The deceased involved the defendant in a situation in which it had to assume responsibility for his care and I would not regard it as just and equitable in such circumstances to be unduly critical of the defendant's fault. I consider a greater share of blame should rest upon the deceased than on the defendant, and I would reduce the amount of the damages recoverable by the plaintiff by two-thirds, holding the defendant only one-third to blame.

Swinney v Chief Constable of the Northumbria Police Force [1997] QB 464: The plaintiffs, Mr and Mrs Swinney, were the tenants of a public house. One day a police officer was fatally injured when he was run over by a car which he was trying to stop. The driver got away and was not caught. Mrs Swinney received certain information which could have helped the police to identify the criminal responsible for the officer's death. She passed this information on to a certain police officer who recorded it in a document, which also included Mrs Swinney's name, address and telephone number. The police knew of the violent and ruthless character of the person to whom the information related. They also knew that Mrs Swinney and her husband would be at risk if it became known that she had passed this information on to the police. The police left the document in a parked police vehicle, which, when unattended, was broken into. The document was stolen. It was shown by the thief/thieves to the person whose name had been given to the police by Mrs Swinney, and as a result Mr and Mrs Swinney were threatened with violence and arson.

The plaintiffs brought the present action against the police for compensation, based on an alleged duty of care owed to them by the police to safeguard them from the harm which they suffered at the hands of the criminal whose name Mrs Swinney had passed on to the police. The police brought an application to have the Statement of Claim struck out as disclosing no cause of action. The Court of Appeal rejected that application and refused to strike out the Statement of Claim. First, their Lordships held that in the circumstances of the case a special relationship existed between Mrs Swinney and the police, which relationship was of such a character as to distinguish Mrs Swinney as being particularly at risk in contrast to the public generally or any section of the public. As Hirst LJ put it (at p 478): "At least arguably this case falls into the *Dorset Yacht* category rather than the *Hill* category on proximity".

In response to the defendant's counsel's question "If there was no special relationship with the plaintiff whose burglar alarm went off in the *Alexandrou* case so as to single him out from the general run of the public [see *above*], why should the same not apply to the present plaintiffs on the facts of the present case?", Hirst LJ said that *Alexandrou*'s case is arguably distinguishable because there was no element of confidentiality in that case, whereas that element looms large in the present case.

The Court also rejected the defendant's submission that the police have a blanket immunity which gives them a complete answer in the present case. In this regard Hirst LJ said (at p 484):

> . . . there are here [ie in contrast to *Hill* and the other police cases considered *above*] other considerations of public policy which also have weight, namely, the need to preserve the springs of information, to protect informers and to encourage them to come forward without an undue fear of the risk that their identity will subsequently become known to the suspect or his associates. In my judgment, public policy in this field must be assessed in the round, which in this case means assessing the applicable considerations advanced in the *Hill* case which are, of course, of great importance, together with the considerations just mentioned in relation to informers in order to reach a fair and just decision on public policy.

In a similar vein Peter Gibson LJ said (at p 485):

> On the question of public policy . . ., [the] comments of Lord Keith in the *Hill* case [1989] AC 53 must be read and understood against the background of the case with which he is dealing . . .
>
> The circumstances of the present case seem to me to be plainly distinguishable . . . when one is considering whether the police have an immunity from liability in negligence to which liability otherwise they would be subject, the court must evaluate all the public policy considerations that may apply. In the present case it seems to me plain that the position of an informant does require special consideration from the viewpoint of public policy. It is obvious that information imparted in confidence to the police by informants should normally not be disclosed and that it is in the public interest that confidentiality should be preserved.

and Ward LJ added (at p 487):

> The public interest would be affronted were it to be the law that members of the public should be expected, in the execution of public service, to undertake the risk of harm to themselves without the police, in return, being expected to take

no more than reasonable care to ensure that the confidential information imparted to them is protected.

Capital and Counties plc v Hampshire County Council [1997] QB 1004: This appeal involved four actions. In the first two actions, which are referred to as 'the *Hampshire* case', the plaintiffs were respectively the lessees and underlessees of premises which were destroyed by fire in circumstances where an officer of the fire brigade, on arriving at the scene of the fire, turned off the premises' sprinkler system which, up to that point, had been effective in keeping the fire under control. At the time when the sprinklers were disabled the fire brigade had not yet found the seat of the fire and was not effectively fighting the fire itself. Disabling the sprinklers had an immediate adverse effect on the restraining of the fire and rapidly led to its going out of control and causing the maximum damage.

In the third case, which is referred to as 'the *London Fire Brigade*' case, the second defendant, a company specialising in creating special effects for film and television, had caused a deliberate explosion on waste land near to the plaintiff's industrial premises, which were unoccupied. Burning debris was scattered over a wide area and small fires broke out. Some of the debris was seen to fall onto the plaintiff's premises and smoke was observed coming from a corner of the plaintiff's yard. Members of the public had made emergency calls to the fire brigade, who responded promptly. By the time that the fire brigade arrived the second defendant's staff had extinguished the fires on the waste land, and there was no visible evidence of any continuing conflagration. The firemen at the scene satisfied themselves that all of the fires on the waste land had been extinguished and departed in due course. However, they did not inspect the plaintiff's premises. If they had, they would have found some smouldering debris which, after a few hours, turned into a fire which destroyed the plaintiff's premises.

In the fourth case, 'the *West Yorkshire*' case, late one night a fire was spotted in a classroom attached to the plaintiffs' chapel. The fire brigade arrived promptly, but it was unable to fight the fire efficiently because, of the seven fire hydrants surrounding the chapel, four failed to work and three were either never found or were found too late to be of any use. After a lot of time had been wasted, water was obtained from a mill dam over a half a mile away. By this time the fire in the classroom had spread to the chapel, which was totally destroyed.

The Court of Appeal upheld the plaintiffs' claims in the *Hampshire* case, but not in the *London Fire Brigade* case or the *West Yorkshire* case. As a preliminary point, the Court held that, on the authority of *Alexandrou v Oxford* [1993] 4 All ER 328 (see *above*), the fire brigade does not owe a common law duty of care to answer calls to fires or to take reasonable care to do so. Thus, Stuart-Smith LJ said, delivering the judgment of the Court (at p 1029):

> The *Alexandrou* case is clear authority for the proposition that there is no sufficient proximity simply on the basis that an emergency call is sent to the police, even if there is a direct line from the premises to the police station. That

decision is binding on us, unless it can be distinguished, and in our view on this aspect it cannot.

In our judgment, the fire brigade are not under a common law duty to answer the call for help, and are not under a duty to take care to do so. If, therefore, they fail to turn up or fail to turn up in time because they have carelessly misunderstood the message, got lost on the way or run into a tree, they are not liable.

Part of the plaintiff's claim in the *West Yorkshire* case was that a statutory duty was owed to the plaintiff under s 13 of the Fire Services Act 1947, which states: "A fire authority shall take all reasonable measures for ensuring the provision of an adequate supply of water and for securing that it will be available for use in case of fire." After referring to Lord Browne-Wilkinson's *dictum* in *X (Minors) v Bedfordshire County Council* [1995] 2 AC 633 (see *above*), that the cases where a private right of action for breach of statutory duty has been held to arise are all cases in which the statutory duty had been "very limited and specific as opposed to general administrative functions imposed on public bodies and involving the exercise of administrative discretion", Stuart-Smith LJ said (at p 1050):

> Considered in that light, we do not consider that section 13 is intended to confer a right of private action upon a member of the public injured by a breach. The duty propounded in section 13 is in no way 'limited and specific' in the sense contemplated by Lord Browne-Wilkinson. It is more in the nature of a general administrative function of procurement placed on the fire authority in relation to supply of water for fire-fighting generally. There is no reference to any specific measure contemplated, nor any reference, whether expressly or by implication, to any class of person, short of the public as a whole, being ear-marked for protection under the section.

Their Lordships then considered the common law claims of the plaintiffs in all of the cases. They concluded that sufficient proximity existed only in the *Hampshire* case, for the following reasons (at p 1031):

> The peculiarity of fire brigades together with other rescue services, such as ambulances or coastal rescue and protective services such as the police, is that they do not as a rule create the danger which causes injury to the plaintiff or loss to his property. For the most part they act in the context of a danger already created and damage already caused whether by the forces of nature or the acts of some third party or even of the plaintiff himself, and whether those acts are criminal, negligent or non-culpable. But where [as in the *Hampshire* case] the rescue/protective service itself by negligence creates the danger which caused the plaintiff's injury, there is no doubt in our judgment that the plaintiff can recover.
>
> It is not clear why a rescuer who is not under an obligation to attempt a rescue should assume a duty to be careful in effecting the rescue merely by undertaking the attempt. There *are* a number of cases where the courts have held that a relationship of proximity arises so as to give rise to a duty of care for the plaintiff's physical safety which are based on assumption of responsibility and reliance. [Stuart-Smith LJ then referred to *Kirkham v The Chief Constable of the Greater Manchester Police* [1990] 2 QB 283, *Welsh v The Chief Constable of the Merseyside Police* [1993] 1 All ER 692, *Osman v Ferguson* (1993) 4 All ER 344 and *Barrett v The Ministry of Defence* [1995] 1 WLR 1217, all of which are considered *above*, and said:] These are all examples of where

the court has considered on the special facts of the case that there is a sufficiently close relationship of proximity to give rise to a duty of care. But we do not think that they are anywhere near the circumstances that arise in these appeals.

In our judgment, a fire brigade does not enter into a sufficiently proximate relationship with the owner or occupier of premises to come under a duty of care merely by attending at the fire ground and fighting the fire. This is so even though the senior officer actually assumes control of the fire-fighting operation.

In the light of this conclusion, there was no need for the Court to go on and consider, in the *London Fire Brigade* and the *West Yorkshire* cases, if it was fair, just and reasonable to impose a duty of care on the fire brigade for the plaintiffs' losses. However, this question did need to be addressed in the *Hampshire* case. By placing reliance on the police cases (particularly *Hill*— see *above*) the fire brigade's counsel submitted that there are good reasons of policy why the Hampshire Fire Authority should not owe a duty of care to the plaintiffs for their losses. In rejecting this submission, the Court of Appeal expressed views that would appear to be more liberal than the views on public policy immunity that have been expressed in the other cases considered *above* in this chapter. Thus, Stuart-Smith LJ said (at p 1040):

It seems to us that in those cases where the courts have granted immunity or refused to impose a duty of care, it is usually possible to discern a recognition that such a duty would be inconsistent with some wider object of the law or interest of the particular parties. Thus, if the existence of a duty of care would impede the careful performance of the relevant function, or its investigation of the allegedly negligent conduct would itself be undesirable and open to abuse by those bearing grudges, the law would not impose a duty.

In our judgment there is no doubt on which side of the line a case such as the *Hampshire* case falls. It is one where the defendants, by their action in turning off the sprinklers, created or increased the danger. There is no ground for giving immunity in such a case.

Stuart-Smith LJ then noted that counsel for the plaintiffs in all of the cases had made the following criticisms on the reasons that had been advanced in favour of conferring public policy immunity on fire brigades:

(1) and (2)   No improvement in standard of care; defensive fire-fighting
It seems hardly realistic that a fire officer who has to make a split second decision as to the manner in which fire-fighting operations are to be conducted will be looking over his shoulder at the possibility of his employers being made vicariously liable for his negligence. If there can be liability for negligence, it is better to have a high threshold of negligence established in the *Bolam* test [ie the test emanating from *Bolam v Friern Hospital Management Committee* [1957] 1 WLR 582, that the applicable standard of care is not perfection but only such as would be possessed by another fire brigade with the same resources and training] and for judges to remind themselves that fire officers who make difficult decisions in difficult circumstances should be given considerable latitude before being held guilty of negligence. It is not readily apparent why the imposition of a duty of care should divert the fire brigade's resources from other fire-fighting duties.

(3) Private litigation unsuitable for discovering failures of service
. . . in the *Hampshire* case . . ., although there was a very extensive internal inquiry in that case starting on the day of the fire, it was only the litigation that uncovered the serious shortcomings of the service.

(4) Undesirability of actions against authorities operating for collective welfare
. . . the fact that the defendant is a public authority acting for the collective welfare of the community such as the National Health Service has never been regarded as a ground for immunity; in any event the benefit is also for the individual householder.

(5) Floodgates
Having regard to the extreme paucity of recorded cases against fire brigades in spite of the fact that for over 40 years *Halsbury's Laws of England* have indicated that an action would lie, this argument should be disregarded. Again, the *Bolam* test should afford sufficient protection.

(6) Distraction from fire-fighting
In any action against a public authority, officers and employees will be distracted from their ordinary duties; that should not be regarded as a valid ground for granting immunity.

(7) Massive claims against the taxpayer
This is ultimately an argument for the immunity from suit of government departments and all public authorities.

and commented thereon (at p 1044):

> In our judgment there is considerable force in the criticisms made. If we had found a sufficient relationship of proximity in the *London Fire Brigade* and *West Yorkshire* cases, we do not think that we would have found the arguments for excluding a duty of care on the ground that it would not be just, fair and reasonable convincing. The analogy with the police exercising their functions of investigating and suppressing crime is not close. The floodgates argument is not persuasive. . . . Many of the other arguments are equally applicable to other public services, for example, the National Health Service. We do not think that the principles which underlay those decisions where immunity has been granted can be sufficiently identified in the case of fire brigades.

Having thus reached the conclusion that it would be fair, just and reasonable to impose a duty of care on the fire brigade in the *Hampshire* case, their Lordships went on to consider whether there were any considerations emanating from the governing legislation which would negate the existence of this duty. The defendants' counsel in all of the cases argued that s 30 of the Fire Services Act 1947 had this effect. It states, *inter alia*:

> (1) Any member of a fire brigade maintained in pursuance of this Act who is on duty . . . may enter . . . any premises . . . in which a fire has . . . broken out . . . for the purposes of extinguishing a fire . . . without the consent of the owner or occupier thereof . . .
>
> (3) At any fire the senior fire brigade officer present shall have the sole charge and control of all operations for the extinction of the fire, including the fixing of the positions of fire engines and apparatus, the attaching of hose to any water

pipes or the use of any water supply, and the selection of the parts of the premises . . . or of adjoining premises . . . against which the water is to be directed.

In holding that these provisions did not confer immunity on the fire brigade, Stuart-Smith LJ said (at p 1044):

The argument for the defendant authorities is that section 30 confers immunity or creates a statutory defence against liability for negligence or breach of statutory duty by the fire brigade and firemen involved in extinguishing a fire. If that is correct, the plaintiffs' claims [in all of the cases] would fail.

Liability for activities which caused damage at the scene is said to be limited to cases of deliberate bad faith, which is not in question in any of the present cases. There is a clear distinction to be observed at this stage of the argument between the general question whether the plaintiffs are entitled to maintain an action at common law and the question currently under consideration, which is whether, assuming that the 1947 Act would otherwise be appropriate to sustain an action for negligence at common law or breach of statutory duty, section 30 precludes any such liability.

Liability of a public authority in tort may be restricted or avoided by appropriate statutory language. Section 30 itself provides a clear example of language which authorises what would otherwise be a tortious interference with property. However, it is an elementary principle that a public body is normally expected to use its statutory powers with reasonable care: see *inter alia Dorset Yacht Co Ltd v Home Office* [1970] AC 1004, *X (Minors) v Bedfordshire County Council* [1995] 2 AC 633 and *Stovin v Wise* [1996] AC 923 [all of which are considered *above*].

For the purpose of construing any particular section on which a purported claim for immunity is based, Lord Greene MR in *Fisher v Ruislip-Northwood Urban District Council* [1945] KB 584 explained:

If . . . the legislature authorises the construction and maintenance of a work which will be safe or dangerous to the public according as reasonable care is or is not taken in its construction or maintenance, as the case may be, the fact that no duty to take such care is especially imposed by the statute cannot be relied upon as showing that no such duty exists. It is not to be expected that the legislature will go out of its way to impose express obligations or restrictions in respect of matters which every reasonably-minded citizen would take for granted.

Accordingly, liability for negligence or breach of a statutory duty by a public body in the course of fulfilling its statutory obligations may only be excluded by express language or by necessary implication.

In testing s 30 against this 'principle', Stuart-Smith LJ said (at p 1047):

Although the powers are very wide, there is nothing in section 30 which permits them to be exercised negligently. If it had been intended to exclude liability for negligence, express provision could easily have been made. None was, and the omission in a section which otherwise expressly exonerates firemen from potential liability in tort for trespass is striking.

The language of section 30 is not apt to establish an implied immunity from proceedings in negligence, whether brought by those whose property has been damaged or individuals present who have suffered personal injury as a result of negligence in the course of fire fighting.

For these reasons, the Court of Appeal held that there were no reasons of policy deriving from the governing legislation which overrode the fire brigade's common law duty of care in the *Hampshire* case.

OLL v Secretary of State for Transport [1997] 3 All ER 897: A party of eight children and a teacher had been taken on a canoeing trip with two instructors from the plaintiff's 'challenge centre'. The party set off at 10 am and were due back at noon, but they did not then return. They had run into severe difficulties at sea. The canoes capsized and eventually sank. Some members of the party made attempts to swim ashore. The group became separated. They were all eventually rescued from a number of positions between 5.30 pm and 6.40 pm, but four of the children died afterwards and the other members of the party suffered from severe hypothermia and shock.

The plaintiff, having settled claims made on it by the parents and families of the canoeists, brought the present action against the Secretary of State for Transport as being responsible for HM Coastguard ('the coastguard') on the basis that the coastguard owed the party of canoeists a duty of care in its conduct in the rescue operation, which the plaintiff alleged the coastguard breached by taking an inordinate length of time to mount an effective rescue operation. The judge, May J, granted the coastguard's application to strike out the plaintiff's claim as disclosing no reasonable cause of action. With reference to the *Capital and Counties* decision, he said (at p 905):

> There is no obvious distinction between the fire brigade responding to a fire where lives are at risk and the coastguard responding to an emergency at sea. On this basis, the coastguard would be under no enforceable private law duty to respond to an emergency call, nor, if they do respond, would they be liable if their response was negligent, unless their negligence amounted to a positive act which directly caused greater injury than would have occurred if they had not intervened at all.

In response to the plaintiff's counsel's submission that the coastguard is not directly comparable with the fire services because its powers are not prescribed by statute, May J said (at p 907):

> . . . I do not see that the substantial absence of any such a framework for the coastguard points to any particular answer to the question. The answer must be derived from the nature of the organisation and the nature of the service which it provides. The coastguard is a national, publicly-funded watching and rescue organisation partly staffed by volunteers whose service includes searching for and, where possible, rescuing those who are in distress in sea. The fact that no statute expressly obliges them to do any thing in particular does not in my view suggest that when they do turn out—voluntarily—they ought to be taken to have assumed a greater degree of responsibility than the fire services acting in similar circumstances but under a more explicit statutory framework.

8.3.3 *Nonfeasance*

Contractual relationship

Introduction: A common theme of the cases considered *above* in which the plaintiff has succeeded is that there was a pre-existing relationship of one sort or another, albeit sometimes quite tenuous, between the defendant and the third party who caused the plaintiff's loss. In the cases considered in this grouping and the following one, the focus is on the pre-existing relationship between the defendant and the plaintiff. The question is whether, on account of that relationship, the defendant owed the plaintiff a duty of care to prevent a third party from causing loss to the plaintiff in circumstances where that loss was reasonably foreseeable and where it was within the defendant's power to do something to assist the plaintiff if he so chose.

Where the defendant and the plaintiff had a pre-existing contractual relationship with each other, the first question will be whether a term can be implied in the agreement between them that the defendant would be in breach of contract if he failed to take appropriate action to safeguard the plaintiff's position. If the answer to this question is in the affirmative, then it will not be necessary to consider whether, in the alternative, a similar duty was owed in tort. An example is *Stansbie v Troman*, considered *below*. Of course, one will never be able to say for definite that a court will be prepared to imply such a term into the contract. Therefore practitioners will always have to be prepared to argue such cases in the alternative.

Another unpredictable element in this type of case is that sometimes the court will say that it is wrong to impose a duty of care in tort where the plaintiff and the defendant already have an existing contractual relationship. This is known as the principle against concurrent liability, and is considered in Chapter 10, para 10.4. For the moment, it is worth noting that it is not always easy to predict when a court will apply this principle and when it will not. The relevant rules are still in the course of development by the courts, and no definitive test, one way or the other, has yet been formulated.

Stansbie v Troman [1948] 2 KB 48: The court held that a decorator owed a duty of care to a house owner in respect of the house owner's loss caused by burglars who had entered through the front door which the decorator had left unlocked (because he did not have a key) when he went out of the house (for two hours) to buy wallpaper. The court agreed with the decorator's counsel that, if there was to be a duty, it had to be within the scope of the contractual relationship which existed between the plaintiff and the defendant, but held that that contractual relationship did impose a duty on the decorator to take reasonable care with regard to the state of the premises if he left them during the performance of his work. Having reached this conclusion, it was not necessary for the court to consider any of the problems which can arise in tort where it is sought to make one person responsible to another for damage caused to that other by a third party over whom he has no control.

Deyong v Shenburn [1946] 1 KB 227: The plaintiff was an actor whose personal belongings had been stolen from his dressing room whilst he was on stage. The defendant, a theatrical producer, was his employer. The court held that the defendant was not liable for the plaintiff's loss. First, the court held that it was not possible to imply an obligation into the parties' contractual relationship that the defendant would take care for the safety of the plaintiff's belongings.

The court then went on to consider whether such a duty could be imposed in tort. This, too, was rejected. Du Parcq LJ said (at p 233):

> There has to be a breach of a duty which the law recognises, and to ascertain what the law recognises regard must be had to decisions of the courts. There has never been a decision that a master must, merely because of the relationship which exists between master and servant, take reasonable care for the safety of the servant's belongings in the sense that he must take steps to ensure, so far as he can, that no wicked person shall have an opportunity of stealing the servant's goods. That is the duty contended for here, and there is not a shred of authority to suggest that any such duty exists or ever has existed . . .
>
> The defendant's omission to guard against theft was not, in my opinion, a tort for which an action can be brought.

This decision was approved and applied by the Court of Appeal in *Edwards v West Herts Group Hospital Management Committee* [1957] 1 WLR 415, in which a resident house physician unsuccessfully sued his hospital's management committee for the losses which he had sustained when some of his personal belongings were stolen from his bedroom in the hospital's hostel.

Reid v Rush and Tompkins Group plc [1990] 1 WLR 212: The plaintiff was the defendant's employee. While working for the defendant in Ethiopia the plaintiff was injured in a motor collision which was solely the fault of the other driver, who disappeared and could not be found. This left the plaintiff without a remedy in Ethiopia. Therefore the plaintiff sought compensation from the defendant. The plaintiff's claim was not for compensation for his personal injuries as such, but for breach by the defendant of its (alleged) duty of care as employer in failing either to insure the plaintiff against injury by a third party or to advise the plaintiff to obtain such insurance cover for himself (which he maintained he would have obtained if he had been so advised).

The court considered and rejected the plaintiff's claims on three grounds. First, the court held that, although terms can in principle be implied by law into contracts of employment, it was not possible in the present case to imply terms of the sort which the plaintiff wanted as being terms which the parties must have agreed, but failed to express, because the contract was sufficiently detailed in many other respects which provided for the plaintiff's economic welfare, such as kit allowance, paid accommodation, paid holidays and travel, pension scheme contribution and payment of medical treatment for the plaintiff in Ethiopia.

In reaching this conclusion the court was influenced by the fact that the term which the plaintiff wished to imply was a duty to warn the plaintiff of a risk of economic loss. Ralph Gibson LJ said (at p 221):

... although the duty of a master to his servant may extend to warning him of unavoidable risks of physical injury, it has hitherto not been extended to the taking of reasonable care to protect the servant from economic loss. Apart from *Deyong v Shenburn* and *Edwards v West Herts Group Hospital Management Committee* [see *above*], which were mentioned in argument, we were not referred to any case in which the court has considered and rejected any such claim and no doubt the reason for that is not only the limitation of the duty ... to personal safety but also the fact that it must be rare for any matter of economic loss to have been arguably caused by a breach of duty of the master without it being a breach of contract.

By way of comment it is worth noting that in neither *Deyong* nor *Edwards* was any consideration given to the fact that the plaintiff's loss was in fact pure economic loss. This did not present a problem to the imposition of liability on the decorator in *Stansbie*, which was not cited to the court in this case. It is difficult to see why, from a contractual point of view, it should make any difference that the term sought to be implied relates to protecting the plaintiff against economic loss, rather than physical injury. After all, most of the terms in an employment contract relate to the employee's economic interests, rather than his physical safety.

Secondly, the court held that no general duty of care (ie a duty which did not depend on 'voluntary assumption' of risk by the defendant and reliance by the plaintiff) existed in this case. Following *Banque Keyser Ullmann* (see *below*), the court said that it was prepared to accept that in some cases of pure economic loss a duty of care could be imposed even in the absence of any voluntary assumption by the defendant of such a duty and/or of any reliance on such assumption by the plaintiff. Instead, the court would need to be satisfied that there was a sufficiently close relationship of proximity between the defendant and the plaintiff as to cause the defendant to be under a positive duty to warn the plaintiff of the risks to which the plaintiff would be exposed, and the court would have to be satisfied that it was just and reasonable to impose a duty of care in all the circumstances.

The chain of reasoning by which Ralph Gibson LJ held that this test was not satisfied is interesting. He said that the imposition of such a duty would have to be by way of an extension of the scope of the duty of a master to his servant, which extension would need to be made "incrementally and by analogy with established categories of negligence" (*per* Brennan J in *Council of the Shire of Sutherland v Heyman*, see Chapter 3, para 3.4.4) and then set out a number of factors which might justify such an extension. These included the fact that, while the plaintiff's claim was for financial loss, it was a loss related to and arising out of personal injury suffered in the course of the plaintiff's employment; and (at p 230): "... the capacity of the common law to develop, so as to recognise changes which have taken place in the expectations of people who make up our society". He then reached the interim conclusion (at p 230):

In my judgment, if the question were whether the giving of a warning about the special risk was something which a reasonable employer, with knowledge of the existence of the risk and of his servant's ignorance of it, would think it neces-

sary to give the servant, then I would hold that the plaintiff had alleged a reasonable case for persuading the court on a trial [this case was considered on a
striking out summons] that such an employer would think it necessary.

Having got to the point where he clearly thought that such an incremental
extension of principle was justified, Ralph Gibson LJ took an unexpected
turn in a different direction and concluded that he could not extend the
employer's duty of care in the manner contended for by the plaintiff. He
said (at p 231):

> But that answer [ie the interim conclusion which he had reached at the end of
> the last paragraph] is not sufficient. There is clear authority that it is not open
> to the court to hold that a duty of care exists in negligence at common law . . .
> if the duty is not performed in 'a factual situation in which the existence of such
> a duty has repeatedly been held not to exist' *per* Lord Brandon in *Leigh and
> Sillivan Ltd v Aliakmon Shipping Co Ltd* [1986] AC 785 at 815F. As pointed out
> earlier in this judgment, the absence of a duty upon an employer, under the
> general duty of a master to his servant, to protect his servant from economic
> loss, caused through the wrongdoing of a person for whom the employer is not
> responsible, has not been repeatedly the subject of the decisions of the court; but
> it has been stated on at least two occasions (see the theft of property cases cited
> above [ie *Deyong* and *Edwards*]) and, I am sure, assumed on countless other occa-
> sions that the duty of the master is, in the absence of a contractual term, express
> or implied, limited to the protection of the servant against physical harm or
> disease.

This is a pity. As pointed out in Chapter 5 (para 5.2), *The Aliakmon* was
a case of relational economic loss, where an extremely long line of venerable authority had consistently held, for sound policy reasons, that it would
be wrong to impose a duty of care on a tortfeasor who had damaged one
person's property for the pure economic losses suffered by another person
who was thereby unable to use that property and who did not have a proprietary or a possessory interest in it. This is the context in which Lord
Brandon expressed the above-quoted *dictum*. Obviously that *dictum* is
capable of having wider effects, but the context in which it was made should
provide a strong indication that it should not stand as an absolute bar (as
it did in this case) to the law's development on an incremental basis where
there have been only two previous cases (ie *Deyong* and *Edwards*, neither of
which was in the House of Lords) in which the actual question in point was
not even directly considered.

Thirdly, the court rejected the plaintiff's contention that the defendant
owed him a duty of care in tort by virtue of having voluntarily assumed a
responsibility to the plaintiff to advise him of the special risks to which the
plaintiff was going to be exposed when he went to Ethiopia; because the
court felt that it would be wrong to say that the defendant had assumed
such a responsibility in tort if he had not assumed it within the terms of the
contract between himself and the plaintiff. Ralph Gibson LJ said (at p 229):

> Where there is a contract between the parties, and any 'voluntary assumption
> of responsibility' occurred, if at all, at the time of making and by reason of the
> contract, it seems unreal to me to try to separate a duty of care arising from the

relationship created by the contract from one 'voluntarily assumed' but not specifically assumed by a term of the contract itself. There was at no time any reference by either side to the special risk or to what might be done with reference to it. For these reasons, I conclude that this plaintiff has no reasonable cause of action based upon voluntary assumption of responsibility.

The court's emphasis of 'voluntary assumption of responsibility' requires qualification. This is discussed further in Chapter 9, para 9.5.

Daniel Sweeney v Dennis Duggan [1991] 2 IR 274: The plaintiff was badly injured in an accident at work. He sued his employer, a limited company, and obtained judgment for a large sum and costs. Before that judgment could be satisfied the company went into insolvent liquidation. This meant that the plaintiff, although a preferential creditor, was deprived of 80 per cent of the value of his judgment. The plaintiff sued the defendant, as the owner of the company, alleging that the defendant had a duty of care to take reasonable steps to ensure that the business would be capable of paying compensation to employees such as the plaintiff for their foreseeable physical injuries (the company operated a quarry) by means of an appropriate policy of insurance taken out on the company. Alternatively, the plaintiff alleged that the defendant was personally under a duty to warn the plaintiff that the company did not have employer's liability insurance.

Following the principles established in *Reid*, and *Van Oppen* and *Banque Keyser Ullman* (see *below*, which were applicable here because there was no contractual relationship between the plaintiff and the defendant), the court rejected the plaintiff's claim. The court also commented that to allow the plaintiff's claim here would nullify one of the essential principles of company law, namely that the plaintiff's contract of employment was with the company, which was a separate legal entity from its owner, the defendant. As the plaintiff was suing the defendant in tort, while this factor should probably be taken into account in considering whether it would be just and reasonable to impose a duty of care on the defendant, it should not operate as an absolute bar.

Weir v National Westminster Bank plc (7 August 1992, Court of Session, Outer House): The plaintiff was a solicitor who had a current account in the name of a third party at the same branch of the same bank as his solicitor's practice. He had a power of attorney for the third party, which empowered him to sign cheques on the third party's account. Unknown to the plaintiff, his cashier had, over a period of time, misappropriated funds from his firm. This included the forging of the plaintiff's signature on a cheque drawn on the third party's account. The defendant bank reinstated the amount of that cheque in the third party's account, as it was obliged to do under its banker–customer relationship with the third party.

The plaintiff sued the bank for the economic losses which he personally suffered by virtue of his cashier's fraud after the date when that cheque had gone through on the third party's account. He alleged that the bank owed him a duty of care in the processing of cheques through the third party's account. If the bank had questioned the authenticity of his signature on that cheque (which he averred the bank should have done in the circumstances), he would have discovered what his cashier was doing. He would have dismissed her and no further frauds by her would have taken place. The court rejected the plaintiff's claim. Although the plaintiff's loss might have been foreseeable, the court did not think that there was sufficient proximity between the bank and the plaintiff, or that it would be just and reasonable to impose a duty of care on the bank in these circumstances.

The court accepted that, as part of the bank's duty to its customer (the third party), the bank owed a duty to communicate relevant information about the third party's account to the plaintiff as the customer's agent. However, the court said that this was not sufficient to create an independent duty owed by the bank to the plaintiff in another capacity, notwithstanding that the plaintiff had a personal account at the same branch and was known to the bank. Lord Abernethy said:

> There is physical proximity, of course, but that cannot be the test to determine whether there is an independent duty of care owed by the bank to the agent of a disclosed principal. The agent might be on the other side of the world. As it happens, in this case the agent was here in Edinburgh, had a personal account at the same branch, was known there and at times was physically present in the bank. These factors, however, cannot in my opinion be determinative of the existence of a duty of care owed by a bank to a customer's agent as an individual. If such a duty exists, I do not see why it should exist only when the customer's agent is physically close to the bank. If it exists at all, it must exist for all agents of disclosed principals. Similar considerations lead me to the conclusion that it would not be fair, just and reasonable to hold that the banker's duty of care to a customer should be extended when the customer is a disclosed principal to the customer's agent as an individual. Such a result would in my opinion impose a quite impractical burden on bankers.

Given the fact that the judge held that the bank owed a contractual duty "to communicate relevant information" to the plaintiff as the third party's agent, it is submitted that the tort duty of care exercise which the court carried out in this case was otiose. Having found a breach of contract, the court should have then considered whether the plaintiff's claimed damages for breach of that contractual duty were too remote, in accordance with the applicable contractual test. On the facts, the result might well have been the same, but in another similar case this will not necessarily be so.

Other cases: In three recent cases which fall within this grouping, the court concluded that, because of the contractual relationship which existed between the plaintiff and the defendant, it would be wrong to impose a duty of care in tort on the defendant for having failed to pass certain information on to the plaintiff. In these cases the court first had to consider whether the duty contended for by the plaintiff could be regarded as an implied term of the parties' contractual relationship. Upon finding that it could not, the court was then invited by the plaintiff's counsel to consider whether such a duty could instead be held to exist in tort, according to the relevant established principles (ie assumption of responsibility and reliance, as discussed in this chapter). In each of these cases the court declined to take up this invitation because it held that the parties' pre-existing contractual relationship was determinative of all of the duties which could arise between them. If that contract did not include, expressly or by implication, the duty contended for, then it would be wrong to "fill the contractual gap" by imposing the contended for duty of care in tort alongside the contractual provisions which the parties had mutually agreed. These cases are *Bank of Nova Scotia v Hellenic Mutual War Risks Association (Bermuda) Ltd* [1990] 1 QB 818 (CA), [1992] 1 AC 233 (HL), *National Bank of Greece SA v Pinios Shipping Co (No 1)* [1990] 1 AC 637 (CA and HL) and *Scally v Southern Health and Social Services Board* [1991] 1 AC 294. They are considered in Chapter 10, para 10.4 (in the section dealing with concurrent liability) where it is also noted that Phillips J in *Youell v Bland Welch & Co Ltd (No 2)* [1990] 2 Lloyd's Rep 431 adopted a different view.

Non-contractual relationships

Sometimes the plaintiff and the defendant can be involved with each other, directly or indirectly, in a loose form of arrangement which is not contractual. If, during the course of those dealings, the defendant becomes aware of certain information which might save the plaintiff from suffering a loss if that information were shared with the plaintiff, the question will arise whether the defendant was under a duty of care to the plaintiff to pass that information on to him. This is a developing area of the law. Many (but not all) of the cases have involved complex commercial interrelationships between many parties.

Van Oppen v Clerk to the Bedford Charity Trustees [1990] 1 WLR 234: The plaintiff was injured during a rugby match at a school, the responsibility for the administration and running of which rested with the defendants. The plaintiff's claim was for the economic loss which he suffered by virtue of the school failing to effect personal accident insurance for its pupils in these circumstances and/or in failing to inform or advise his father of the inherent risk of serious injury in the game of rugby, of the consequent need for personal accident insurance and of the fact that the school had not arranged such insurance itself. The court rejected the plaintiff's claim.

The school did not dispute that it was under a duty to take reasonable care for the health and safety of its pupils. Its case was that this duty did not extend to taking reasonable care to guard against the pupils suffering economic loss by not having appropriate insurance to compensate them for any personal injuries which they might suffer at the hands of a third party (ie their opponents in a rugby match) against whom there was no claim for compensation. Following *Reid* and the Court of Appeal's decision in *Banque Keyser Ullmann* (see *below*), the court agreed with the school. Balcombe LJ said (at p 259):

From these two cases I derive the following principles . . .

(1) A pure omission, consisting of a failure to speak or act, by A resulting in economic loss to B, can give rise to a liability in negligence by A to B, provided there has on the facts been a voluntary assumption of responsibility by A, and there has been reliance on that assumption by B.

(2) Exceptionally, in some cases of pure economic loss the court *may* be prepared to find the existence of a duty of care and to treat the defendant in law as having assumed a responsibility or duty to the plaintiff which is capable of giving rise to a claim for damages for such loss. Although the point is not altogether free from doubt, for the purposes of this appeal I am prepared to assume that this duty of care not to cause economic loss can exist in the exceptional case.

(3) An existing relationship between the parties which may give rise to a duty of care by one party for the physical well-being and safety of the other (eg master and servant) does not of itself mean that there is sufficient proximity between the parties to justify finding the existence of a duty of care not to cause economic loss.

(4) Whether a duty of care should be held to exist in a particular case must in the last resort be a question of policy to be decided by the court by reference to the principles to be deduced from the decided cases.

On the question of the imposition of a duty of care not based on an assumption of responsibility by the defendant and reliance by the plaintiff, the court adopted in full the reasoning of the trial judge, Boreham J, in this case ([1989] 1 All ER 273), who said (at p 291):

There are risks of injury inherent in many human activities, even of serious injury in some. Because of this, the school, having the pupils in its care, is under a duty to exercise reasonable care for their health and safety. Provided due care is exercised in this sphere, it seems to me that the school's duty is fulfilled. . . In particular, there is no general duty to insure, not even against negligence. No doubt it is prudent for a school to insure against negligence, but that is in its own interests; it is under no duty to the pupils to do so.

It could hardly be said therefore, that a school is under a duty to insure against personal accident . . .

. . . even the parent has no duty to insure. It has often been said that the standard of care required to discharge the school's duty is that of the reasonably careful parent. While this does not, of course, define the scope of the duty, it does seem somewhat remarkable if the school is to be judged by a standard which the parent is bound neither to adopt nor even to consider. It would be neither fair nor reasonable to place a wider duty on the school . . . than is imposed on the parent.

. . . the plaintiff [in this case] clearly had a right to have his person and his property protected from careless acts or omissions of those for whom the defendants were vicariously liable. He had no right to protection from purely accidental injury or from the consequences of such injury . . .

If . . . the plaintiff had no right to protection from purely accidental injury or its consequences, how can it be said that he had a right to have his father informed of matters which might induce the father to exercise a discretion to insure him against personal accident?

On the question of a duty of care founded on an assumption of responsibility by the defendant and reliance by the plaintiff, the court held that, on the facts, the school had certainly not assumed such a responsibility voluntarily; nor would it be right to say that the school, by its actions, had assumed such a responsibility because of the fact (see *above*) that the school had no duty to provide information to the parents. In any event, the court held that the plaintiff's claim was doomed to fail under this head because of the judge's uncontested finding that neither the plaintiff's father, nor any other parent, relied upon the school to advise them on the question of insurance.

Banque Keyser Ullmann SA v Skandia (UK) Insurance Co Ltd [1990] 1 QB 665; *Banque Financière de la Cité (formerly Banque Keyser Ullmann SA) v Westgate Insurance Co Ltd (formerly Hodge General Mercantile Co Ltd)* [1991] 2 AC 249: A certain individual (Mr Ballestero) had persuaded a number of banks to make very large loans to companies which he owned or controlled. The securities offered in each case were a pledge of gemstones and a credit insurance policy. The purpose of the insurance policies was to provide insurance protection to the lending banks in the event of the borrowing companies failing to repay the loans. Each policy contained a fraud exclusion clause, which would have the effect of voiding the policy if, for example, the value of the gemstones had been fraudulently overstated. In fact, this is exactly what happened. The borrower defaulted on the loans and disappeared. The gemstones proved to be practically valueless by virtue of the borrower's fraud. The insurers accordingly declined liability under the policies.

The banks then focused their attention on the brokers who had placed the insurance, and on the insurers who had accepted it. The brokers' employee, a Mr Lee, had been guilty of dishonest conduct in the issue of the insurance policies, which consisted of primary cover for 25 per cent of the risk (which was taken up by Hodge General and Mercantile Insurance Co Ltd) and three layers of excess cover for 25 per cent each, which Mr Lee was attempting to place with various excess insurers in the insurance market. He told the banks that he had secured 100 per cent cover in the insurance market at a time when he had not in fact done so, and he produced fraudulent cover notes to back up this misrepresentation (which related to part of the excess cover). In relying on this misrepresentation, which the banks had no reason to question, the banks completed their loans to Mr Ballestero's companies, and Mr Lee collected his commission on the premiums paid by the banks in respect of the partially non-existent insurance policies. Thereafter, Mr Lee allowed the banks unwittingly to remain with only partial cover for a period of several months until he was able to find underwriters who were prepared to take up all of the layers of excess cover.

A Mr Dungate, an employee of Hodge (the insurers of the primary layer), subsequently became aware of Mr Lee's misconduct. He did not report this to the banks at that time, nor did he do so subsequently when the banks were considering making a further loan to Mr Ballestero's companies, notwithstanding that the further loan was to be secured by an extension of the limit of the third excess layer of insurance coverage that Mr Lee had placed for the banks, and notwithstanding that Mr Lee was again acting as the banks' agent in effecting this additional insurance coverage.

In due course, after the borrower had defaulted on the loans and after it had been discovered that the gemstones were valueless by virtue of Mr Ballestero's fraud, it also emerged that the cover note that Mr Lee had issued, which certified that the third excess layer of insurance in respect of the further loan had been insured by a particular American insurer, was fraudulent because that insurer was a bogus company. Mr Dungate was not aware of this fraud (but, as the trial judge found, he ought reasonably to have foreseen its occurrence).

In seeking to recover the amount of this additional loan from Hodge, the banks claimed (and the trial judge accepted) that if Mr Lee's earlier dishonesty had been disclosed to them, they would not have lent any further sums to Mr Ballestero's companies, and would therefore not have incurred any further losses after that time. Accordingly, they submitted that Hodge, as Mr Dungate's employer, should be held accountable to them for those losses (ie the amount of the further loan).

Both the Court of Appeal and House of Lords rejected the plaintiff banks' claims against Hodge. The Court of Appeal did so on the basis that Hodge did not owe a duty of care to the banks in respect of this loss. The House of Lords did not find it necessary to consider this point in detail, because even if Hodge did have such a duty, no damage flowed from it because the damage suffered by the banks was the consequence of the fraud of the borrower, and not the consequence of the silence of Mr Dungate. The Court of Appeal's judgment on this point is therefore relevant.

On the question whether a duty of care could arise in respect of Mr Dungate's silence on the basis of 'voluntary' assumption by him and reliance by the banks, Slade LJ said (at p 794):

> Can a mere failure to speak ever give rise to liability in negligence under *Hedley Byrne* principles? [see Chapter 9]. In our view it can, but subject to the all important proviso that there has been on the facts a voluntary assumption of responsibility in the relevant sense and reliance on that assumption. These features may be much more difficult to infer in a case of mere silence than in a case of misrepresentation.

He said that he could see no justification for holding that Mr Dungate, who had made no representations, assumed any responsibility at all in relation to Mr Lee's honesty or dishonesty. Slade LJ said (at p 795):

> The phrase 'voluntary assumption of responsibility' in this context means what it says: conduct by the party signifying that he assumes responsibility for taking due care in respect of the statement or action. No doubt . . . the conduct of the party may be objectively construed. To deal in the ordinary way with an agent [Mr Lee] without any relevant communication to his principal [the banks] cannot, we think, be held to be an assumption of responsibility . . .

511

Furthermore, this head of claim was bound to fail because there was no evidence that the banks did in fact rely on any assumption of responsibility by the insurers in respect of Mr Lee's dishonesty.

On the question as to whether a duty of care is capable of arising in the absence of a voluntary assumption of responsibility coupled with reliance, Slade LJ said (at p 797):

> . . . we are prepared to accept, for the purposes of the judgment, that in some cases (if rare) of pure economic loss the court may be willing to find the existence of a duty of care owed by a defendant to a plaintiff even in the absence of evidence of any actual voluntary assumption by the defendant of such duty and/or of any reliance on such assumption.

He said that where this applies the defendant will be treated in law, even though not in fact, as having assumed a responsibility to the plaintiff which is capable of giving rise to a claim for damages for pure economic loss.

On the facts, this principle could not be satisfied. Slade LJ said (at p 798):

> . . . to hold that these factors [ie the established and continuing business relationship between the banks and the insurers] by themselves gave rise to a duty on the part of Mr Dungate to report Mr Lee's dishonesty to the banks, capable of exposing him or his employers to a liability in tort . . . [for failing to do so], would undermine basic principles of our law of contract.
>
> . . . it has to be borne in mind that the period in . . . which it is said that Mr Dungate's duty to report arose and continued was one during which he was in the course of conducting contractual negotiations with the banks on behalf of his employers.
>
> The general principle that there is no obligation to speak within the context of negotiations for an ordinary commercial contract (. . . qualified by the well known special principles relating to contracts of *uberrimae fidei*, fraud, undue influence, fiduciary duty, etc) is one of the foundations of our law of contract . . . There are countless cases in which one party to a contract has in the course of negotiations failed to disclose a fact known to him which the other party would have regarded as highly material if it had been revealed. However, ordinarily, in the absence of misrepresentation, our law leaves that other party entirely without remedy.

The Court of Appeal also rejected the banks' submission that Hodge should be treated as having in law voluntarily assumed responsibility to tell the banks about Mr Lee's dishonesty because the negotiations between Mr Dungate (as Hodge's employee) and the banks resulted in a contract of insurance; which, being a contract of the utmost good faith, imported obligations of mutual disclosure of all relevant facts into the negotiations. The Court said that, while this was true, the only remedy in law for material non-disclosure was that the contract may be avoided. In those circumstances the Court said that it did not think that it was open to it to assist the banks by providing a supplementary remedy in tort.

Lastly, the Court of Appeal said that it was not satisfied that justice and reasonableness imperatively required the finding of a duty of care owed by the insurers (Hodge) to the banks, because this was not a case in which the denial to the banks of a cause of action in negligence would mean that they were left without any remedy at all. They had remedies against the brokers (Mr Lee's employers) and against the borrower (although he, of course, had disappeared or was not worth suing).

As noted *above*, the House of Lords, in dismissing the banks' appeal, [1991] 2 AC 249 dealt briefly with the duty of care question because, even if Hodge had owed a duty of care to the banks to inform them of Mr Lee's earlier dishonesty, that was not the cause of the loss for which the banks were trying to make Hodge liable, namely, the amount of money that the banks would have recovered from Hodge and the other insurers if the insurers had not denied coverage under the policy (see *below*).

On the question of the duty of care, Lord Templeman, with whose speech all of the other Law Lords concurred, said (at p 273):

> Prior to the insurance contract of June 24, 1980 [ie the increase in the third excess layer effected in connection with the subsequent loan], Mr Dungate became apprised of information from which he deduced that Mr Lee had committed, in January 1980, a breach of duty to his principals [the banks] and had remedied that breach by June 11, 1980. No breach of duty by Mr Lee could by June 1980 have affected the insurances that were made in January 1980. On June 23, 1980 [when the subsequent insurance was placed], Mr Dungate did not do or say anything. Mr Dungate did not, by his silence, assume any responsibility for the trustworthiness *in the future* of Mr Lee, and the banks did not rely on his silence as a representation that Mr Dungate believed Mr Lee to be honest.
>
> It would be strange if, in these circumstances, one party to a contract owed a duty in negligence to the other party to warn the other party of his suspicions of former misconduct by the agent of that other party. It would be stranger still if the party who failed to disclose his suspicions were liable in damages for the misconduct of the agent thereafter. The trial judge held that Hodge was under a legal duty to report the misconduct of Mr Lee to the banks even if that misconduct had been remedied by the completion of the first and second excess layers. I do not agree. A professional should wear a halo, but need not wear a hair shirt.
>
> No authority was cited for the proposition that a negotiating party owes a duty to disclose to the opposite party information that the agent of the opposite party had committed a breach of the duty that he owed to his principal in an earlier transaction. The party possessing the information will no longer himself trust the agent, and may refuse to deal with the agent. The party possessing the information must not himself become involved with any misconduct by the agent, and the courts will naturally consider whether he is, or has become, involved. Subject to these reservations, a duty to disclose, sounding in damages for breach, would give rise to great difficulties. The information may be unreliable, or doubtful, or inconclusive. Disclosure may expose the informer to criticism or litigation.

Lord Templeman disposed of the banks' counsel's further submissions that, at common law, Hodge owed the banks a duty of care by saying, curtly (at p 274):

> Counsel for the banks, in urging that Mr Dungate and Hodge owed a duty of disclosure to the banks, referred to *Governors of Peabody Donation Fund v Sir Lindsay Parkinson and Co Ltd* [1985] AC 210, which dealt with the liability of a

local authority for defective drains, *Smith v Eric S Bush* [1990] 1 AC 831, which dealt with the liability of a valuer to a mortgagor [see Chapter 9, para 9.7.3] and *Caparo Industries plc v Dickman* [1990] 2 AC 605, which dealt with the liability of auditors to shareholders [see para 9.7.2]. These cases are far removed from the suggested liability of a negotiating party to disclose information concerning the conduct of the agent of the opposite party.

The other cases cited by the banks in support of the proposition that Mr Dungate owed a duty to disclose to the banks his knowledge of the earlier misconduct of Mr Lee were the cases dealing with negligent misstatements such as *Hedley Byrne and Co Ltd v Heller and Partners Ltd* [1964] AC 365 and *Esso Petroleum Co Ltd v Mardon* [1976] QB 801 [see Chapter 9]. The person who makes a negligent misstatement which is relied upon by a negotiating or contracting party may be liable in damages. In the present case, there was no negligent misstatement, and the silence of Mr Dungate did not amount to an assertion that Mr Lee was trustworthy, and the banks did not rely on the silence of Mr Dungate.

The primary ground on which the House of Lords dismissed the banks' claim was that Mr Lee's fraud, which they alleged Mr Dungate/Hodge owed a duty to disclose to them, had not caused their loss, which was caused by the insurers invoking the fraud exclusion clause in the insurance policies as a result of the fraud of Mr Ballestero. If Mr Ballestero had not been fraudulent but Mr Lee had, the insurers would nevertheless have had to meet the banks' claims. Lord Ackner expressed the point succinctly when he said (at p 281): "The inability of the insurers to rely on the fraud exclusion clause in relation to Mr Lee's dishonesty is fatal to the banks' *cri de coeur*—if we had known of Mr Lee's fraud, we would not have entered into the Loan Agreement—since that fraud did not cause their loss. That was caused by the fraud of Mr Ballestero and his companies"; and Lord Templeman said (at p 279):

> The banks argue that they would not have advanced SF 10,750 on September 2, 1980 [ie the further advance] if Mr Dungate had disclosed the earlier fraud of Mr Lee, and therefore, they lost SF 10,750 because of the silence of Mr Dungate. My Lords, this argument confuses the cause of the advance and the cause of the loss of the advance. The cause of the advance was the fraud of Mr Lee. The fraud was foreseeable by Mr Dungate who is liable (if at all) for the consequences of that fraud. The consequence of Mr Lee's fraud was that the advance was uninsured. Mr Dungate [ie Hodge] is liable (if at all) for the fact that the advance was uninsured.
>
> The advance would have been lost whether it was insured or not because the banks had accepted and paid a premium for insurance which contained a fraud exemption clause. The fraud of Mr Ballestero caused the loss of the advance, and the rejection of the claims under the insurance policies was, as the judge found, not foreseeable.
>
> The fraud of Mr Lee which caused the advance to be made did not affect the rights of the banks to recover their loss and therefore did not cause the loss of the advance. The policies of insurance did not, or would not have, protected the banks against the fraud of Mr Ballestero, and his fraud was causative of the loss of the advance. Accordingly, the failure by Mr Dungate to inform the banks of the fraud of Mr Lee was not causative of the banks' loss.

This aspect of the House of Lords' decision is discussed further in Chapter 2, para 2.1.5 in relation to the importance of the scope of a duty of care, because what their Lordships were effectively saying in these passages is that, even if Hodge did have a duty of care to inform the banks of Mr Lee's dishonesty, the scope of that duty did not embrace the actual loss for which the banks were seeking to hold Hodge liable as that loss would have occurred anyway even if Mr Lee had not been fraudulent. The principle that was given effect to by their Lordships is that the scope of a duty of care for a negligent misrepresentation, or for the omission to make a statement, does not extend to all of the consequences that have in fact occurred through someone else having relied on that statement, or through the omission to make a statement to that other person. Rather, the scope of such a duty, in the case of a statement, is limited to the consequences of the information being wrong or, in the case of an omission, it is limited to the difference that would have occurred in the risks that the plaintiff undertook anyway if the disclosure had been made. In the present case, Lord Jauncey recognised this point when he said (albeit in relation to an insurer's duty of disclosure, as opposed to a duty of care at common law) (at p 282):

> In the present case, the risk to the insured was the inability, otherwise than by reason of fraud, of Mr Ballestero and his companies to repay the loan to the banks. Mr Lee's dishonesty neither increased nor decreased that risk. It was irrelevant thereto. It follows that the obligation of disclosure incumbent upon Mr Dungate did not extend to telling the banks that their agent, Mr Lee, was dishonest. If the obligation incumbent upon parties to a contract of insurance could ever *per se* create the necessary proximity to give rise to a duty of care, a matter upon which I reserve my opinion, it is clear that the scope of any such duty would not extend to the disclosure of facts which are not material to the risk insured. It follows that the banks' reliance on the duty of disclosure does not assist them to establish negligence on the part of Dungate.

McCullagh v Lane Fox and Partners Ltd (1996) 49 Con LR 124 (CA): One of the issues in this case, the facts of which are set out in Chapter 10, para 10.3.3 and Chapter 9, para 9.7.3, was whether, if a duty of care did not arise initially when the defendant made the misrepresentation about the size of the plot orally to the plaintiff, because at that stage the defendant was entitled reasonably to expect that his statement would be independently checked (*per* Sir Christopher Slade and Nourse LJ), it did nevertheless arise at a subsequent time when the defendant first appreciated that the plaintiff would be exchanging contracts without a survey. In relation to the proposition that a duty of care did come into existence at this later stage, Sir Christopher Slade, with whom Nourse LJ agreed, said:

> This conclusion imports the concept that, at that time, Mr Scott [the defendant's director] became under a duty to correct his previous oral misstatement as to acreage, even though—
> (a) at the time when he made it, he owed no duty to the plaintiff; and
> (b) at the relevant later time, he was still not aware that his previous statement had been mistaken.

I, for my part, find this a difficult concept. The decision in *Davies v London and Provincial Marine Insurance Co* (1878) 8 ChD 469 is authority for the well established principle that if a party to a contract has made a statement to the other party which he believes to be true, but which in the course of the negotiation he discovers to be false, he is bound to correct his erroneous statement. I accept also that a failure to speak can give rise to tortious liability in negligence under *Hedley Byrne* principles, provided that there has been on the facts a voluntary assumption of responsibility in the relevant sense, so as to give rise to a duty to speak, and reliance on that assumption: see *Banque Keyser Ullmann SA v Skandia (UK) Insurance Co Ltd* [1990] 1 QB 665 at p 794 [see *above*].

Special considerations may apply to cases where parties are negotiating a contract *uberrimae fidei*. In other cases, however, I am doubtful whether a mere failure to correct an innocent misrepresentation can give rise to liability in tort, unless either—

(a) the representor assumed liability for its truth at the time when the representation was originally made; or

(b) the representor subsequently became aware that it was untrue and was likely to be acted upon, before in fact it was acted upon by the representee.

No authority has been cited to us which supports a contrary conclusion. Neither condition (a) or (b) is, in my view, satisfied in the present case. I therefore incline to the view that, on the particular facts of this case, no breach of duty by the defendant to the plaintiff would have been established even in the absence of the disclaimers contained in the particulars.

With reference to the last-cited sentence, it should be noted that what Sir Christopher Slade and Nourse LJ really meant is that no duty of care arose, or existed, at the subsequent time when the defendant became aware that the plaintiff was not going to carry out an intermediate inspection of the property, not simply that such a duty existed but was not breached by the defendant. It is also worth noting that Sir Christopher Slade (now retired) is the same person as Lord Justice Slade, whose *dicta* in the *Banque Keyser Ullmann* case are cited *above*.

Woodcock v Kennedy (trading as SW Builders) (17 January 1996, unreported): This was an appeal against the trial judge's refusal to allow a late amendment to be made to the Statement of Claim. In the course of considering this appeal, the Court of Appeal also expressed views as to whether the new alleged cause of action would have succeeded in any event.

The plaintiff was employed as a building labourer by the first defendant, a small building firm, which was a sub-contractor to the main contractor, the second defendant. In the course of carrying out the building works, the plaintiff leant a ladder owned by the second defendant against a plastic guttering in order to do some work on the roof of the building. The guttering broke, the ladder was displaced, and the plaintiff fell to the ground and sustained injuries.

The plaintiff sued both of the defendants for compensation. He effectively discontinued the proceeding against the first defendant, who was uninsured and insolvent. The plaintiff's case against the second defendant was initially that the second defendant had assumed a responsibility to the plaintiff to warn him that the ladder was too short. Both the trial judge and the Court of Appeal rejected this part of the plaintiff's claim because there was no evidence of any transfer of the plaintiff's services to the second defendant and there was no evidence that the second defendant had assumed control of the way in which the plaintiff did his work.

At a late stage during the trial the plaintiff's counsel sought to amend the Statement of Claim to allege that the second defendant owed a duty of care to the plaintiff to ensure that the plaintiff's employer (the first defendant) was adequately insured against injuries sustained by his employees. This proposed cause of action was based on the fact that the main contractor, in its JCT contract with the building owner, had undertaken to ensure that it (the second defendant) and the first defendant would both have sufficient insurance in place to cover all risks on site. Thus, this new cause of action was for economic loss on the basis that the second defendant had assumed a duty to prevent such loss to the plaintiff through the second defendant's failure to ensure that the first defendant was properly insured in the event that the first defendant was not himself worth suing. The Court of Appeal agreed with the trial judge's refusal to allow the Statement of Claim to be amended in the circumstances of this case. However, their Lordships also stated that, in their view, this proposed cause of action would have failed in any event.

In submitting that the new cause of action would have succeeded, the plaintiff's counsel relied on the *dictum* of Lord Goff in *White v Jones* [1995] 2 AC 207, that it is open to the law to fashion a remedy to fill a lacuna in the law and so prevent the injustice which would otherwise occur on the facts of a case like *White v Jones*. In rejecting this submission, Stuart-Smith LJ said:

> Lord Goff I think would be surprised to learn that this passage was relied upon to support a submission that, because the plaintiff has suffered hardship because there is no one to pay him compensation, a remedy must be found. For my part, I can find little or nothing in the principles enunciated in the cases on duty of care to support the plaintiff's proposed re-amended claim.

Roch LJ agreed with Stuart-Smith LJ that a cause of action framed in these terms would fail; but the third Lord Justice of Appeal, Evans LJ, expressed agreement with the trial judge that this proposed cause of action was arguable. Thus, Evans LJ said:

> The second defendant clearly broke its contractual undertaking to ensure that the plaintiff's employer would have sufficient insurance. It is the plaintiff who has suffered from that breach because the first defendant is without means, and that is the essential reason why the insurance was required in the first place. The plaintiff cannot sue the second defendant for its breach of contract because he was not a party to the contract. That is a rule of law which protects the second defendant from such a claim, unless the circumstances of the case are such that some qualification should be made to it by reference to the law of tort or otherwise. The learned judge recognised the difficulty, and also the public policy aspect. I for my part would not differ from his assessment of the merits, which was that such a claim would be fit for argument in a proper case.

8.3.3 *Nonfeasance*

Habibsons Bank Ltd v Naim Anwar t/a Pearl Fashions (19 February 1996, unreported): The plaintiff ('the Bank') had an arrangement with its customer, the first defendant ('Pearl Fashions'), an importer, exporter, wholesaler and distributor of leather garments and textiles, whereby the Bank extended credit to the first defendant in return for the first defendant depositing with the Bank bills of exchange that the first defendant had received from its customers. Each bill of exchange was insured by the first defendant with Trade Indemnity Plc, the second defendant ('TI').

TI was fully aware of this arrangement and, in each case, signed a document headed "Declaration for Assigning Payments in respect of Specific Bills" ('the Assignment Declarations') and sent it to the Bank, which in turn countersigned a copy of this document in each case and returned it to TI together with a copy of the relevant bills of exchange that were covered by the insurance.

In due course the first defendant fell into arrears in the payment of its insurance premiums, but TI, without conveying this information to the Bank, nevertheless continued to complete the Assignment Declarations and to send them to the Bank. Subsequently, when some of the bills were dishonoured and the Bank was unable to obtain recovery from the first defendant, the Bank sought recovery from TI under the insurance policies that had been assigned to it. TI refused to meet those claims because it had voided the insurance policies on the ground of the first defendant's default in paying the premiums.

In the present action the Bank sought to recover its losses from TI, based on TI's breach of a duty of care owed to the Bank by TI not to represent that the insurance coverage taken out by the first defendant was valid when TI knew that this was in fact not true. The judge, Ian Hunter QC, sitting as a deputy judge of the High Court, rejected the plaintiff's claim. He said:

> In considering whether a duty of care in tort falls to be imposed on insurers in the circumstances of the present case, the starting point must be the fact that, not only is the claim for pure economic loss, but it is also founded on an omission on the part of the insurers. The important question in the present case is whether it can properly be said that the insurers assumed the responsibility of warning the Bank in the event of the policyholder failing to pay the premium. In his judgment in *Spring v Guardian Assurance* Lord Goff explained the wide scope of the principle and said that it is broad enough to embrace special knowledge.
>
> I am far from convinced that the insurers' ability to discover whether the policyholder was up to date with the payment of his premium does constitute special knowledge for this purpose, since it was equally open to the Bank to interest itself in the terms of the policy [the Bank's witnesses said that they did not bother to read the terms of the policy because they assumed that, if TI was sending signed Assignment Declarations to them, the policy was in order] by requiring the policyholder to confirm (and perhaps even prove to them) payment of the premium. But the important point is that the Bank is in my judgment unable to bring itself within the relevant principle, which has two limbs, namely, (1) an assumption of responsibility by the insurers towards the Bank coupled (2) with reliance by the Bank on the exercise by the insurers of due care and skill.

In my judgment the Bank failed on both counts. The Assignment Declaration forms contain nothing to suggest that TI was accepting, or could reasonably be taken to have been accepting, a responsibility to warn the Bank in the event of circumstances arising (such as non-payment of the premium) which might provide the insurers with a defence to any claim under the policy. Not only that, but the statement in the policy that payment was subject to due observance of all of the terms and conditions of the policy was calculated to put any assignee of the proceeds on notice that his right of recovery under the policy was at risk if the policyholder failed so to observe the policy's terms and conditions. In addition, the Bank is quite unable to demonstrate that it relied on the insurers to comply with the suggested duty of care. The Bank's witnesses all regarded the terms of the policy with studied indifference and none of them claimed even to have read the Declaration form.

The plain truth about the present case is that the Bank was the author of its own misfortune. Its rights as assignee of the proceeds of the policy were entirely dependent on compliance by the policyholder with the terms and conditions of the policy. Yet it took no interest in the terms of the policy and none of its employees who gave evidence admitted to reading the Declaration form. The Bank merely assumed that it had cover under the policy. When it discovered that the insurers were contending that it had no such cover, the Bank sought to argue that the insurers were under a duty to protect its commercial interests—interests to which the Bank itself paid little regard. I have no hesitation in rejecting the contention that the insurers owe a duty of care to the Bank in such circumstances. To extend the law by finding a duty to exist here would, in my judgment, be a retrograde step, one step too far in the incremental development of the law, and would introduce a degree of paternalism towards the Bank which is not warranted by any policy consideration of which I am aware.

Furthermore, in conformity with the House of Lords' decision in the *Banque Keyser Ullmann* case (see *above*), the deputy judge held that, even if TI was under a duty of care to warn the Bank of the policyholder's failure to pay instalments of premium, such breach constituted the occasion for, but not the cause of, the Bank's loss, because, as in *Banque Keyser Ullmann*, the real and effective cause of the Bank's loss was the failure of the policyholder to pay the premium in accordance with the terms of the policy.

8.3.4 Comment

It is interesting to note that in not even one of the above-mentioned cases has the defendant been held to be under a duty of care in tort by virtue of the defendant having omitted to pass on to the plaintiff some information which probably would have caused the plaintiff to have acted differently, and therefore to have been able to avoid incurring that loss. There is no reason in principle why such a claim should not succeed, but the fact that no such case has yet done so, despite the wide variety of circumstances in which the question has arisen, coupled with the seemingly growing reaction of the English courts against finding parallel duties of care in contract and tort (see Chapter 10, para 10.4), indicates how difficult this can be in practice. As mentioned *above*, it is unfortunate that the Court of Appeal did not seize the opportunity in *Reid v Rush & Tompkins plc* [1990] 1 WLR 212 to extend an employer's duty to take care for the protection of his employee's physical well-being to include protection for the financial well-being of the employee where that financial loss related to and arose out of personal injury suffered in the course of the employee's employment. In the list of factors which supported this extension being made, Ralph Gibson LJ said (at p 230): "Finally, the existence of some capacity of the common law to develop, so as to recognise changes which have taken place in the expectations of the people who make up our society, is not in doubt". Unfortunately (and, it is submitted, incorrectly; see *above*) he held himself constrained by two prior cases in which the point had not been considered at all from making this extension.

It is necessary to appreciate that some of the changes which have indeed taken place in our modern commercial society in recent times have created different expectations and do call for different approaches and different solutions in the tort of negligence from those which might have been appropriate in a less well-developed market society than the one we have at present. Phillips J recognised this in *Youell v Bland Welch & Co Ltd (No 2)* [1990] 2 Lloyd's Rep 431 when, in relation to a submission that he should interpret the Law Reform (Contributory Negligence) Act 1945 in a certain way, he said (at p 460): "I do not consider it a satisfactory approach to the Act to attempt to find a solution by considering the result which a 1990 factual situation would have produced under 1944 law".

In *Smith v Littlewoods Organisation Ltd* [1987] 1 AC 241 Lord Goff said (at p 280): "The judicial function can, I believe, be epitomised as an educated reflex to facts". This is similar to Lord Atkin's statement in *Donoghue v Stevenson* [1932] AC 562 (at p 599): "It will be an advantage to make it clear that the law in this matter, as in most others, is in accordance with sound common sense". In some of the important decisions considered in this chapter, such as *Murphy* and *Reid*, the courts have had the right reflexes, but have shied away from imposing the just solutions which those reflexes require. In neither of these two cases was this because they were constrained by authority to do so, but, rather, it would seem, because of an almost institutionalised fear of extending the boundaries of those situations in which a defendant is to be held liable in the tort of negligence for pure economic loss suffered by the plaintiff in consequence of the defendant's negligent 'pure' omission. To the extent that this fear is founded upon the need to guard against the exposure of a defendant to indeterminate liability, this fear simply does not exist in the categories of case with which both *Murphy* and *Reid* were concerned (see paras 7.5.7 and 8.3.3, *above*).

8.4 Overseas cases

8.4.1 Australia

The approach of the High Court of Australia in *The Council of the Shire of Sutherland v Heyman* (1985) 157 CLR 424 and in *Shaddock & Associates Pty Ltd v Parramatta City Council (No 1)* (1981) 150 CLR 225 has been noted earlier in the chapter (para 8.2.2). *Sutherland* was enthusiastically embraced by the House of Lords in *Murphy* for its rejection of Lord Wilberforce's 'two-stage test' in *Anns* (see Chapter 3, para 3.2.2). The actual decision in *Sutherland* went against the plaintiff on the facts. To this extent, the impression might therefore be created that, in Australia, a person in the position of the plaintiff in *Murphy* would be debarred from recovering his economic loss from a local authority who had negligently inspected the foundations of a building while it was being constructed. This would be an erroneous conclusion: the High Court in *Sutherland* was fully prepared to accept that the principle of reasonable foreseeability of reliance was applicable in this category of case as a basis for imposing a duty of care; and the plaintiff failed only because he did not, in fact, place any such reliance on the defendant council (see para 8.2.2).

8.4.2 New Zealand

As noted in the discussions of overseas cases in Chapter 7, para 7.6, the Court of Appeal of New Zealand has not followed the restrictive attitude of the English courts in this area of the law. On the contrary, it is prepared to impose liability on local authorities in circumstances where there was no specific reliance by the plaintiff on the local authority; reliance was present only in the most generalised sense. An example is its decision in *Brown v Heathcote County Council* [1986] 1 NZLR 76 which (as noted *above* in para 8.2.4) was subsequently upheld by the Privy Council ([1987] 1 NZLR 720) on the same ground. It is a pity that *Brown* was not referred to in *Murphy*, especially as Lord Keith was a member of the panel in both cases, and it was he who said, in *Rowling v Takaro Properties Ltd* [1988] AC 473, delivering the judgment of the Privy Council, on appeal from the Court of Appeal of New Zealand (at p 501), that the question whether a duty of care should be imposed is a question

> upon which all common law jurisdictions can learn much from each other; because, apart from exceptional cases, no sensible distinction can be drawn in this respect between the various countries and the social conditions existing in them. It is incumbent on the courts' in different jurisdictions to be sensitive to each other's reactions, but what they are all searching for in others, and each of them is striving to achieve, is a careful analysis and weighing of the relevant competing considerations.

Another example is *Invercargill City Council v Hamlin* [1994] 3 NZLR 513, the facts of which are set out in Chapter 7, para 7.6.2—a post-*Murphy* decision. The Court, in affirming the exposure of local authorities to claims by homeowners for the diminution in value of their houses due to the negligence of the local authority, went out of its way to highlight what it saw as the differences between the position in England and in New Zealand. Thus, Cooke P said (at p 519): "Whatever may be the position in the United Kingdom, homeowners in New Zealand do traditionally rely on local authorities to exercise reasonable care not to allow unstable houses to be built in breach of byelaws. The linked concepts of reliance and control have underlain New Zealand case law in this field from *Bowen* [see para 7.6.2] onwards"; and Richardson J, after emphasising certain differences between the two countries [see para 7.6.2], said (at p 424): "The common law of New Zealand should reflect the kind of society we are and meet the needs of our society".

Their Honours were also influenced by the fact that a new statute, the Building Act 1991, which would apply prospectively to new claims, had recently been enacted. Under this Act, territorial authorities can be held liable to private individuals until the expiration of a longstop limitation period for damages suffered by them through buildings not complying with building code requirements.

The Court of Appeal of New Zealand's decision in *Invercargill* has been upheld by the Privy Council in *Invercargill City Council v Hamlin* [1996] AC 624 (PC). The Privy Council upheld the New Zealand Court's decision, notwithstanding that it was at odds with the House of Lords' decisions in *D & F* and *Murphy*. Lord Lloyd, speaking for the unanimous panel, said (at p 640):

> In the present case, the judges in the New Zealand Court of Appeal were consciously departing from English case law on the ground that conditions in New Zealand are different. Were they entitled to do so? The answer must surely be 'Yes'. The ability of the common law to adapt itself to the different circumstances of the countries in which it has taken root is not a weakness, but one of its great strengths. The Court of Appeal of New Zealand should not be deflected from developing the common law of New Zealand (nor the Board from affirming their decisions) by the consideration that the House of Lords in *D & F* and *Murphy* has not regarded an identical development as appropriate in the English setting.
>
> The particular branch of the law of negligence with which the present appeal is concerned is especially unsuited for the imposition of a single monolithic solution. The first and most obvious reason is that there is already a marked divergence of view among other common law jurisdictions.

Lord Lloyd then referred without criticism to the position in Australia (as exemplified in *Bryan v Maloney* (see para 7.6.4)) and in Canada (as exemplified in *City of Kamloops v Nielsen* (1984) 10 DLR (4th) 641 (SCC) (see para 8.4.3) and *Winnipeg Condominium Corporation No 36 v Bird Construction Co* (1995) 121 DLR (4th) 193 (SCC) (see para 7.6.3)) and then commented (at p 642):

> Their Lordships cite these judgments in other common law jurisdictions, not to cast any doubt on *Murphy*'s case, but rather to illustrate the point that in this branch of the law, more than one view is possible; there is no single correct answer. In *Bryan v Maloney*, the majority decision was based on the twin concepts of assumption of responsibility and reliance by the subsequent purchaser. If that be a possible and respectable view, it cannot be said that the decision of the Court of Appeal [of New Zealand] in the present case, based as it was on the same or very similar twin concepts, was reached by a process of faulty reasoning.

Lord Lloyd then added:

> In truth, the explanation for divergent views in different common law jurisdictions (or within different jurisdictions of the United States of America) is not far to seek. The decision whether to hold a local authority liable for the negligence of a building inspector is bound to be based at least in part on policy considerations. As Mason J said in *Bryan v Maloney*: 'Inevitably, the policy considerations which are legitimately taken into account in determining whether sufficient proximity exists in a novel category will be influenced by the court's assessment of community standards and demands.'

With particular reference to the position in New Zealand, Lord Lloyd said:

> In a succession of cases in New Zealand over the last twenty years, it has been decided that community standards and expectations demand the imposition of a duty of care on local authorities and builders alike to ensure compliance with local byelaws. New Zealand judges are in a much better position to decide on such matters than the Board. Whether circumstances are in fact so very different in England and New Zealand may not matter greatly. What matters is the perception. The New Zealand judges in their judgments stress that to change New Zealand law so as to make it comply with *Murphy*'s case would have significant community implications and would require a major attitudinal shift. It would be rash for the Board to ignore those views.

Lord Lloyd then considered what he saw as the differences between the legislative framework in England and New Zealand. He said (at p 642):

> In one important respect, circumstances prevailing in England at the time of *Murphy*'s case and those prevailing in New Zealand are indeed very different. Their Lordships have in mind the statutory background. In *Murphy*'s case, the House of Lords attached great weight to the passing of the Defective Premises Act 1972. By contrast, there is no corresponding legislation in New Zealand. The [New Zealand] Building Act 1991 was passed a year and a half after the decision in *Murphy*'s case. There is nothing in that Act to amend the existing common law as developed by New Zealand judges, so as to bring it in line with *Murphy*'s case. On the contrary, a number of provisions in the Act clearly envisage that private law claims for damages against local authorities will continue to be made as before.
>
> It is neither here nor there that the Building Act 1991 was not in force at the time of the inspection of the foundations in the present case. The question is whether New Zealand law should now be changed so as to bring it into line with *Murphy*'s case. If the New Zealand Parliament has not chosen to do so, as a matter of policy it would hardly be appropriate for their Lordships to do so by judicial decision.

Comment

It is interesting to note that, as in *Brown v Heathcote County Council*, the panel of the Privy Council included Lord Keith and that, again, a duty of care was upheld despite the absence of any evidence of actual reliance by the plaintiff on the defendant local authority. Indeed, as Lord Lloyd observed (at p 639), reliance was not even pleaded. Instead, however, general reliance by the community at large on local authorities to carry out their functions without negligence—or, more correctly, foreseeability by the local authorities that such reliance was being placed on them—was held to be sufficient.

If, as Cooke P said, "homeowners in New Zealand do traditionally rely on local authorities to exercise reasonable care not to allow unstable houses to be built in breach of the byelaws", it is submitted that it can seriously be questioned why homeowners in the United Kingdom should have a different expectation. It is expected that the answer that would be given by those who seek to restrict liability in this area of the law is that in the United Kingdom prospective house purchasers (unlike their counterparts in New Zealand) generally do commission survey reports to assess the structural integrity of houses before they purchase them.

The counter to this—and the essence of the criticism of the House of Lords' decision in *Murphy*—is that where the defect in question is of such a nature that it would not reasonably be expected to be discovered on such an inspection (for example, a defect in the digging of the foundations that had been covered up in the course of construction), it is reasonable for a purchaser to rely on the local authority not to act negligently in ensuring compliance with byelaws that regulate standards of construction. The principle suggested for the imposition of liability in this type of situation is not simply that, in a general sense, house purchasers should be entitled to recover all of their losses arising from negligent construction from the local authority: they should be entitled to recover only such losses as result from defects that the local authority's inspectors ought reasonably to have foreseen would not have reasonably been discovered by a purchaser conducting a pre-purchase inspection of the property. This point is discussed further in para 7.5.3, *above*. In this respect (ie with regard to the non-discoverability of the defect by way of an intermediate inspection), it is submitted that the legitimate expectations of Mr Thomas Murphy, the prospective purchaser in *Murphy v Brentwood District Council* [1991] 1 AC 398 of the house that contained the hidden, undiscoverable defects in its foundations, were the same as any similarly placed house purchaser in New Zealand. It seems that the Privy Council recognised this fact in its decision in *Invercargill City Council v Hamlin*, when Lord Lloyd said (at p 642):

> In a succession of cases in New Zealand over the last twenty years, it has been decided that community standards and expectations demand the imposition of a duty of care on local authorities and builders alike to ensure compliance with local byelaws. . . . Whether circumstances are in fact so very different in England and New Zealand may not matter greatly. What matters is the perception. . . .

It is submitted that this response is quite startling. Why should it not matter to the courts if the expectation of a purchaser like Mr Murphy was that Brentwood District Council would not act negligently in complying with the byelaw that required it to approve the foundations of the house that he would purchase in due course? It is hard to imagine that this would not have been his expectation in relation to a defect that became hidden in the course of construction and would not likely have been discovered in his pre-purchase inspection. And why should the perception matter more than the reality; and whose perception is being accepted by the Court? Surely its own, unguided by any empirical evidence (for there was none in *Murphy*) as to whether purchasers of houses in England expect local authorities not to act negligently in ensuring compliance with byelaws relating to areas of construction, like foundations, that cannot easily be inspected by subsequent purchasers. It is submitted that, in relation to such byelaws, the expectations of house purchasers in England are in fact no different than those of house purchasers in New Zealand; and that *this* is the perception—and the reality—that should guide the English courts.

It is also important to note that the supposed distinction that their Lordships purported to draw in the Privy Council between the position in England and the position in New Zealand, based on the Defective Premises Act 1972, is illusory, because that Act does not, and was never intended by Parliament to, circumscribe the liabilities of builders or local authorities in tort for economic loss occasioned by purchasers through their negligence. This point is discussed further in Chapter 7, para 7.5.5.

8.4.3   Canada

In *City of Kamloops v Nielsen* (1984) 10 DLR (4th) 641, a Mr Hughes Jr had decided to build a house on a hillside for his father who was an alderman in the city of Kamloops. To this end he submitted plans to the city's building inspector. The plans were approved, subject to the requirement that the footings were to be taken down to solid bearing, and a building permit was issued. Mr Hughes did not take the footings down to a solid bearing. Instead he set the foundations on piles which were set into loose fill. He then requested an inspection of the foundations. When one of the city's building inspectors arrived to make his inspection, he realised that the foundations were not in accordance with the plans, but he was unable to check whether they were adequate to support the building because the concrete had been poured. The inspector placed a stop work order on the site and said that it would not be lifted until new plans had been submitted showing how the structural defects were going to be remedied. Mr Hughes retained a firm of professional engineers to prepare the new plans. On receipt of these the building inspector lifted the stop work order. Mr Hughes, however, did not co-operate with the engineers on the required changes but continued with the construction of the house on the original plans. The engineers, disavowing all liability, notified the building inspector, who re-imposed the stop work order and told Mr Hughes it would remain in effect until he submitted a report from a structural engineer. Mr Hughes ignored this communication and carried on with the building.

After the house was completed, Mr Hughes sold it to his father and mother. The city solicitor informed them that the stop work order was still in place and would not be lifted until the city was provided with complete structural drawings from an engineer verifying the adequacy of the proposed construction. Mr Hughes Sr protested to his fellow council members that he was being harassed. No further inspections were made and no occupancy permit was ever issued. Nevertheless, Mr and Mrs Hughes Sr moved into the house and remained there for a few years until they sold it to the plaintiff, Mr Nielsen, without telling him anything about the house's checkered history. Before completing the purchase, the plaintiff had the house inspected by a contractor, but he did not see anything to alert him to a potential problem with the foundations. Some time later the plaintiff discovered that the foundations of the house were subsiding. The plaintiff sued both Mr Hughes Sr and the City of Kamloops ('the City').

In the Supreme Court of Canada the question was whether the City owed the plaintiff a duty of care in tort for his economic loss consisting of the diminution in value of his house by virtue of it having been constructed with defective foundations. By a majority of 3:2 their Honours answered this question in the affirmative. The relevant statute pursuant to which the City carried out building inspections conferred only a power or discretion on the City whether to regulate the construction of buildings by byelaw or not. The City decided to exercise this power and passed byelaw No 11-1, which prohibited construction without a building permit, prohibited occupancy without an occupancy permit and imposed on the building inspector the duty to enforce its provisions. It was this last-mentioned fact which led the Court to conclude that the City did owe a duty of care to the plaintiff in this case. Thus, Wilson J, delivering the majority judgment, said (at p 664):

> It seems to me that, applying the principle in *Anns*, it is fair to say that the City of Kamloops had a statutory power to regulate construction by byelaw. It did not have to do so. It was in its discretion whether to do so or not. It was, in other words, a 'policy' decision. However, not only did it make the policy decision in favour of regulating construction by byelaw, it also imposed on the City's building inspector a duty to enforce the provisions of the byelaw. This would be Lord Wilberforce's 'operational duty' [see para 8.2.7, *above*]. Is the City not then in the position where in discharging its operational duty, it must take care not to injure persons such as the plaintiff whose relationship to the City was sufficiently close that the City ought reasonably to have had him in contemplation?
>
> This is not a case of a power which the City decided to exercise, but exercised in a negligent manner. This is the case of a duty owed by the City to the plaintiff, a person who met Lord Wilberforce's test of proximity in *Anns*. The City's responsibility as set out in the byelaw was to vet the work of the builder and protect the plaintiff against the consequences of any negligence in the performance of it. In these circumstances it cannot, in my view, be argued that the City's breach of duty was not causative. The builder's negligence, it is true, was primary. He laid the defective foundations. But the City, whose duty it was to see that they were remedied, permitted the building to be constructed on top of them. The City's negligence in this case was its breach of duty in failing to protect the plaintiff against the builder's negligence.
>
> The courses of conduct open to the building inspector called for 'operational' decisions. The essential question was what steps to take to enforce the provisions of the byelaw in the circumstances that had arisen. The inspector had a duty to

enforce its provisions. He did not have a discretion whether to enforce them or not. He did, however, have a discretion as to how to go about it. This may, therefore, be the kind of situation envisaged by Lord Wilberforce when he said that the distinction between the policy area and the operational area is probably a distinction of degree and that many operational powers or duties have in them some element of discretion.

It may be, for example, that although the building inspector had a duty to enforce the byelaw, the lengths to which he should go in doing so involved policy considerations. The making of inspections, the issuance of stop orders and the withholding of occupancy permits may be one thing; resort to litigation, if this became necessary, may be quite another. Must the City enforce infractions by legal proceedings or does there come a point at which economic considerations, for example, enter into the question? And if so, how do you measure the 'operational' against the 'policy' content of the decision in order to decide whether it is more 'operational' than 'policy' or vice versa? Clearly this is a matter of very fine distinctions.

The Court of Appeal in this case resolved this problem by concluding that the City could have made a policy decision either to prosecute or to seek an injunction. If it had taken either of those steps, it could not be faulted. Moreover, if it had considered taking either of those steps and decided against them, it could likewise not be faulted. But not to consider taking them at all was not open to it. In other words, the City at the very least had to give serious consideration to taking these steps towards enforcement that were open to it. If it decided against taking them, say on economic grounds, then that would be a legitimate policy decision within the operational context and the courts should not interfere with it. It would be a decision made, as Lord Wilberforce put it, within the limits of a discretion *bona fide* exercised.

There is no evidence to support the proposition that the City gave serious consideration to legal proceedings and decided against them on policy grounds. Rather, the evidence gives rise to a stronger inference that the City, with full knowledge that the work was progressing in violation of the byelaw and that the house was being occupied without a permit, dropped the matter because one of its aldermen was involved. Having regard to the fact that we are here concerned with a statutory duty and that the plaintiff was clearly a person who should have been in the contemplation of the City as someone who might be injured by any breach of that duty, I think that this is an appropriate case for the application of the principle in *Anns*.

The minority judges dissented on the basis that in *Anns* the building inspector had been negligent in his inspection, but this was not the position in the present case. Thus, Mcintyre J said (at p 649):

This is a situation fundamentally different from that arising in *Anns*. If liability is to be found against the City in this case, it can have nothing to do with the conduct of the building inspectors. It can only be on the basis of its own conduct in not seeking to enforce the 'stop work' order and to prevent the occupation of the unsafe house by legal proceedings. Since the case sounds in negligence, it must be shown that the City was under a duty to enforce its byelaw by proceeding in the courts and that the duty was one the non-performance of which could give a cause of action in damages to persons injured. The power is permissive, lying within the discretion of the City and one with which the court would not interfere. To recognise a duty on the City to enforce its byelaw by legal proceedings would impose an impossible burden on it, exceeding any burden imposed by the governing statute.

Recognising that the case involved pure economic loss, the majority judges considered the 'floodgates' argument and the Supreme Court's previous decision in *Rivtow Marine Ltd v Washington Iron Works* (1973) 40 DLR (3d) 530, in which they had held that economic loss in the form of the diminution of a defective *product* was not recoverable in tort (see Chapter 7, para 7.7). On the floodgates point, Wilson J, for the majority, said (at p 673):

> The floodgates argument would discourage a finding of private law duties owed by public officials on the ground that such a finding would open the floodgates and create an open season on municipalities. No doubt a similar type of concern was expressed about the vulnerability of manufacturers following the decision in *Donoghue v Stevenson*. While I think this is an argument which cannot be dismissed lightly, I believe that the decision in *Anns* contains its own built-in barriers against the flood. On the assumption that, by and large, municipalities and their officials discharge their responsibilities in a conscientious fashion, I believe that a failure by them to do so will be the exception rather than the rule, and that the scope for application for the principle in *Anns* will be relatively narrow. I do not see it as potentially ruinous financially to municipalities. I do see it as a useful protection to the citizen whose ever-increasing reliance on public officials seems to be a feature of our age.

With regard to the Supreme Court's earlier decision in *Rivtow* (see Chapter 7, para 7.7), excluding liability for economic loss consisting of the diminution in value of a defective product, Wilson J said (at p 679) that *Rivtow* was distinguishable because it was

> a law suit between private litigants. The plaintiff's claim here is against a public authority for breach of a private law duty of care arising under a statute. If economic loss was within the purview of the statute, then it should be recoverable for breach of the private law duty arising under the statute, whether or not it is recoverable for breach of a duty at common law. The private law duty in this case was designed to prevent the expense incurred by the plaintiff in putting proper foundations under his house. I suppose it is arguable that the damage the duty was designed to prevent was injury to the occupants from the collapse of the house or damage caused by the house sliding down the hill, but it seems to me that this is too narrow an approach to the protection the statute was designed to provide. The purpose of the byelaw in this case was to prevent the construction of houses on defective foundations. This is not a case, like *Rivtow*, of failure to warn of the defective foundations: this is a case of failure to give consideration to a course of action which would have prevented the defective foundations. What else was the plaintiff to do to rectify the situation resulting from the city's breach?

and (at p 681):

> Recovery for economic loss on the foregoing basis accomplishes a number of worthy objectives. It gives a remedy where the legislature has impliedly sanctioned it and justice clearly requires it. It imposes enough of a burden on public authorities to act as a check on the arbitrary and negligent discharge of statutory duties.

In *Rothfield v Manolakos* (1989) 63 DLR (4th) 449, the Supreme Court of Canada applied its reasoning in *Kamloops* to a situation in which the plaintiff was the original building owner rather than a subsequent purchaser. Also, the plaintiff was, to a large extent, the author of his own misfortune because he had breached the duty which he knew he had, to inform the building inspector when various stages of construction had been reached so as to enable appropriate inspections to be carried out by the municipality. His failure to do so meant that when the inspector did come to make his inspection, the concrete had already been poured and the defects in the foundations could not be detected. The statutory position of the building inspectors in this case was the same as in *Kamloops*. In these circumstances, the Supreme Court held that the municipality was not absolved from its duties by virtue of the plaintiff's failure to call them to the site at the appropriate time, although the Court did reduce the municipality's fault to 70 per cent on this account. In reaching this conclusion, the Court expressly distinguished Lord Wilberforce's *dictum* in *Anns*, that the duty of care imposed by the House of Lords in *Anns* was not intended to apply to "a negligent building owner, the source of his own loss". Thus, La Forest J said (at p 457):

> I do not think Lord Wilberforce's pronouncement was meant to extend to every failure by an owner-builder or his contractors to comply with the applicable building regulations. It is to be expected that contractors, in the normal course of events, will fail to observe certain aspects of the building byelaws. That is why municipalities employ building inspectors. Their role is to detect such negligent omissions before they translate into dangers to health and safety. If, as I believe, owner-builders are within the ambit of the duty of care owed by the building inspector, it would simply make no sense to proceed on the assumption that every negligent act of an owner-builder relieves the municipality of its duty to show reasonable care in approving building plans and inspecting construction. These considerations suggest that it is only in the narrowest of circumstances that Lord Wilberforce's *dictum* will find application.

In *Just v British Columbia* (1989) 64 DLR (4th) 689, one morning in winter the plaintiff and his daughter set out in their car on Highway 99 in British Columbia for a day of skiing at Whistler Mountain. While their car was stopped in a line of traffic due to a heavy snowfall, a boulder weighing more than a ton rolled down from the wooded slopes abutting the highway and crashed onto the plaintiff's car, killing the plaintiff's daughter. The plaintiff brought this action against the Province of British Columbia, contending that it had negligently failed to maintain the highway properly.

At the time of the accident the Department of Highways ('the Department') had set up a system for inspection and remedial work on rock slopes, particularly along Highway 99. The Department employed a rock work engineer, who was required to inspect rock-cut areas to assess the stability of the slope and to determine whether there was a risk that a rock might fall onto the highway, and a rock scaling crew to perform remedial work on the slopes. When the rock work engineer inspected rock slopes, he would report his findings and recommendations to the district highways manager who, in turn, through the regional geotechnical material manager, would submit requests for the services of the rock scaling crew. The crew itself had no discretion as to when and where it worked. Its schedule was determined by the requests for remedial work made to the rock work section.

The governing legislation gave the Province the power to maintain highways and also stated that the Province had the management, charge and direction of all matters relating to the construction, repair and maintenance of highways. Prior to the accident in the present case the Department's practice had been to make visual inspections of the rock cuts on Highway 99 from the highway unless there was evidence or history of instability in an area, in which case the rock engineer would climb the slope. In addition, highway personnel carried out numerous informal inspections as they drove along the road when they would look for signs of change in the rock cut and for rocks in the ditch.

In the Supreme Court of Canada, the question was whether this manner of carrying out inspections was a 'policy decision'. If it was, the Court would have been prevented from adjudicating on the plaintiff's claim. By a majority of 6:1 the Court held that this was not a policy decision. Cory J, delivering the judgment of the majority, said (at p 708) (emphasis added):

> As a general rule, decisions concerning budgetary allotments for departments for government agencies will be classified as policy decisions. The manner and quality of an inspection system is clearly part of the operational aspect of a governmental activity. In the case at bar, what was challenged was the *manner* in which the inspections were carried out, their *frequency* or infrequency and *how* and *when* trees above the rock cut should have been inspected and the *manner* in which the cutting and scaling operations should have been carried out. In short, the public authority had settled on a plan which called upon it to inspect all slopes visually and then conduct further inspections of those slopes where the taking of additional safety measures was warranted. Those matters are all part and parcel of administrative direction, expert or professional opinion, technical standards or general standards of care. They were not decisions that could be designated as policy decisions. Rather, they were the manifestations of the implementation of the policy decision to inspect and were operational in nature.

In view of the fact that the trial judge had concluded that the number and frequency of inspections, and the Department's decisions as to what other remedial remedies were appropriate, were matters of policy, no findings of fact were made on the standard of care which would have been applicable to determine whether, even if these decisions were 'operational' decisions rather than policy decisions, they were actionable in the tort of negligence. Therefore the Supreme Court ordered a new trial for those findings of fact to be determined.

Sopinka J, dissenting, was of the view that the *system* that the Department had devised for inspecting for loose rocks was not justiciable. He said (at p 696):

> The principal authorities do not support my colleague's [Cory J's] view that the *manner* and *extent* of inspections are operational. Indeed, they confirm that

these are the very substance of policy. My colleague's reasons are based essentially on an attack on the policy of the Department with respect to the extent and manner of the inspection program. In my opinion, absent evidence that a policy was adopted for some ulterior motive and not for a municipal purpose, it is not open to a litigant to attack it, nor is it appropriate for a court to pass judgment on it. If a court assumes the power to review a policy decision which is made in accordance with the statute, this amounts to a usurpation by the court of a power committed by statute to the designated body.

In reaching this conclusion, Sopinka J was heavily influenced by the finding of the trial judge that, although the slope where the accident occurred had been visually inspected from the highway on a number of occasions, there had never been scaling or close inspection of the area above the cut "because the rock scaling crew did not deem that work to be a priority". This indicated that budgetary concerns had entered into the decision, thereby, in Sopinka J's view, compelling the court to classify the decision as a policy decision. It is interesting to note that in *Stovin v Wise* [1996] AC 923, Lord Hoffmann, speaking for the majority of 4:1 in the House of Lords, said that he preferred the dissenting views of Sopinka J in the present case.

In *Brown v British Columbia (Minister of Transportation and Highways)* (1994) 112 DLR (4th) 1, the plaintiff was injured when his truck slid on black ice on a provincial road. Three other accidents had occurred on the same stretch of road earlier that morning. The police had called for a salt and sanding truck to cover that stretch of road after the first of those accidents occurred. At the time of the plaintiff's accident the salt and sanding truck was operating along that stretch of highway and reached the scene of the plaintiff's accident about eight minutes after it had occurred.

The plaintiff brought the present action against the Province of British Columbia, alleging negligence by the Province in carrying out its powers of maintaining the highway, such powers being the same as those referred to in the *Just* case *above*. The plaintiff's accident occurred at the beginning of the second week of November. At that time the Department of Highways ('the Department') was still operating its summer schedule for road maintenance. This meant that fewer men were deployed for fewer shifts in salting and sanding the highway. In previous years the Department had commenced the winter schedule on 1 November, but in this particular year the Department had decided to maintain the summer schedule until the middle of November.

The plaintiff was not able to establish that the Department had been negligent in the way in which it operated the summer schedule in regard to its response to the police officer's call for salt and sand on the morning of the plaintiff's accident. The plaintiff's case against the Province therefore rested on the plaintiff's assertion that the Province should have instituted the winter schedule on 1 November as it had done in previous years and that, if that had been done, the stretch of road on which the plaintiff's truck slid would probably have been salted and sanded and the plaintiff's accident would not have occurred. In the Supreme Court of Canada, the question was whether the Department's decision to implement its winter road maintenance schedule later than in previous years was justiciable. In a unanimous decision the Court answered this question in the negative. Cory J said (at p 16):

> The decision of the Department to maintain a summer schedule, with all that it entailed, was a policy decision. Whether the winter or summer schedule was to be followed involved a consideration of matters of finance and personnel. The decision required the Department to discuss and negotiate the dates for the commencement of the summer and winter schedules with its unions. This was a policy decision involving classic policy considerations of financial resources, personnel and, as well, significant negotiation with government unions. It was truly a governmental decision involving social, political and economic factors.

In *Stovin v Wise* [1996] AC 923, Lord Hoffmann commented on the Supreme Court of Canada's decisions in *Just* and *Brown* by saying (at p 955): "These cases seem to me to illustrate the inadequacy of the concepts of policy and operations to provide a convincing criterion for deciding when a duty of care would exist. The distinctions which they draw are hardly visible to the naked eye".

8.4.4 United States

Despite the impression created in *Murphy*, there are several jurisdictions (ie states) in the USA in which a local authority can be held liable for the pure economic loss sustained by a plaintiff building owner in circumstances similar to those which existed in *Murphy*. Examples are *Brown v Syson* (1983) 663 P (2d) 251 (Court of Appeals of Arizona), *Butler v Bogdanovich* (1986) 705 P (2d) 662 (Supreme Court of Nevada), and *Wood v Milin* (1986) 397 NW (2d) 479 (Supreme Court of Wisconsin). In all of these cases, the building inspector had been obliged to inspect the building in question, which was subsequently purchased by the plaintiff from the original owner, during the course of its construction. The building inspector had negligently failed to detect that the building was being constructed in a defective manner in certain respects, and the court found as a fact that the plaintiff's damages, consisting in the diminution of the value of his property, flowed directly from such defects. Thus, the facts were essentially the same as in *Murphy*. In all of these cases, the courts held that the negligent building inspector and the local authority which employed him owed a duty of care to the plaintiff for the plaintiff's pure economic loss.

Chapter 9

Negligent misstatements and services

In my view the liability of professional advisers, including auditors, can truly be said to be in a state of transition or development. (**Chadwick LJ in** *Coulthard v Neville Russell (a firm)* **(1997)** *The Times,* **27 November)**

Although the expression 'assumption of responsibility' is to be found in some of the recent cases, it does not appear to signify any different approach to the imposition of liability set out in Caparo. It is, as Lord Roskill pointed out in the latter case [Caparo], simply another imprecise phrase used to cover situations in which a duty of care has been held to exist. It does little to define why or the circumstances in which liability arises. (**Laddie J in** *BCCI (Overseas) Ltd v Price Waterhouse and Another* **(1997)** *The Times,* **30 October)**

It does not conduce to the orderly development of the law, or to the certainty which practical convenience demands, if duties are simply conjured up as a matter of positive law, to answer the apparent injustice of an individual case. (**Lord Mustill, dissenting, in** *White v Jones* **[1995] 2 AC 207)**

Classification societies are charitable non-profit making organisations, promoting the collective welfare and fulfilling a public role. But why should this make any difference? Remedies in the law of tort are not discretionary. Hospitals also are charitable non-profit making organisations. But they are subject to the same common duty of care under the Occupiers Liability Act 1957 and 1984 as betting shops or brothels. (**Lord Lloyd, dissenting, in** *Marc Rich & Co v Bishop Rock Marine Co Ltd* **[1996] 1 AC 211)**

The facts of this case are most unusual, and I would not wish the conclusion which I have reached on the pleadings to be used in support of an argument in some other case that the court should be more ready than in the past to impose liability whenever a close relationship between adviser and advisee is established. (**Sir Brian Neill in the Court of Appeal in** *BCCI (Overseas) Ltd v Price Waterhouse and Ernst & Whinney,* **13 February 1998, unreported)**

9.1 Introduction

9.1.1 Context

As with the cases considered in Chapters 6 and 7 (paras 6.4 and 7.3 respectively), the cases in this chapter are concerned with the creation and/or putting into circulation by the defendant of something which did not previously exist, and which has caused a loss to the plaintiff. In Chapters 4 and 5 the defendant's conduct was accidental. In Chapters 6 and 7, although the defendant no doubt did not intend to cause the plaintiff's injury, his conduct was conscious, deliberate and/or voluntary. To that extent, those cases bear an affinity with the cases in this chapter. The difference lies in the fact that in those cases the defendant will have created or put into circulation a tangible item, whereas in the present case the defendant will only have created or put into circulation a statement or will have given advice or have rendered a service; although, as some of the cases in Chapter 7 demonstrate, for example *University of Regina v Pettick* (1991) 77 DLR (4th) 615 (para 7.3.6), the line is not always easy to draw. The cases considered in Chapter 8 fall somewhere in between the cases considered in Chapters 6 and 7 and those considered in this chapter. However, to the extent that the defendant's omission is considered in those cases to have been non-accidental, those cases bear a greater affinity with the cases considered in Chapters 6, 7 and this chapter, than to the accidental cases considered in Chapters 4 and 5.

9.1.2   Unifying principle: foreseeability of reliance

Subject to the *caveat* mentioned at the end of this section, the unifying principle which underlies the justification for the imposition of a duty of care in the cases considered in Chapters 6, 7, 8 (paras 6.3.3, 7.5.2 and 8.2.2, respectively) and this chapter is 'reliance'; or, more particularly, foreseeability by the defendant that the plaintiff would rely on the situation created by the defendant without making any other form of inquiry, or conducting any other type of examination, to verify the otherwise apparent soundness of that situation. As liability in tort is imposed by the law, rather than being voluntarily undertaken by the defendant, as in contract, this necessary element of foreseeability of reliance can be imputed to the defendant against his will if, in all the circumstances, it is just and reasonable to do so. In *Donoghue v Stevenson* [1932] AC 562, the fact that the defendant had manufactured and sold ginger beer in a dark opaque sealed bottle, so that the decomposing snail in it could not be seen, was held to be sufficient to impute knowledge to the defendant manufacturer that the plaintiff consumer would rely on the defendant not to put out a defective product without making an intermediate examination of his own before consuming it (see Chapter 6, para 6.3.2).

Another way of stating the same point is to say that foreseeability of actual reliance establishes the necessary degree of proximity required for a duty of care, so as to enable the court to ask whether, in all the circumstances, it is fair, just and reasonable to impose such a duty on the defendant. As noted in Chapter 7, para 7.5.2, this is the principle upon which the House of Lords in *D & F Estates Limited v Church Commissioners for England* [1989] AC 177 and in *Murphy v Brentwood District Council* [1991] 1 AC 398 held that a duty of care 'could' arise in tort in respect of the plaintiff's pure economic loss consisting of the diminution in value of a defective product or building for whose creation the defendant (who did not have a contractual relationship with the plaintiff) had been responsible. Thus, for example, Lord Oliver said in *Murphy* (at p 486):

The essential question which has to be asked in every case, given that damage which is the essential ingredient of the action has occurred, is whether the relationship between the plaintiff and the defendant is such—or, to use the favoured expression, whether it is of sufficient 'proximity'—that it imposes upon the latter a duty to take care to avoid or prevent that loss which has in fact been sustained. The requisite degree of proximity may be established in circumstances in which the plaintiff's injury results from his reliance upon a statement or advice upon which he was entitled to rely and upon which it was contemplated that he would rely. . .

Certain *dicta* in certain recent cases in the House of Lords make it necessary to attach a *caveat* to the assertion that the governing principle in the cases considered in this chapter (negligent statements, advice or services) is foreseeability of reliance. In particular, Lord Goff has stated that the underlying principle in this category of cases is the voluntary assumption of responsibility by the defendant for the statement, advice or service made, given or performed by the defendant. This is discussed in full in Chapter 3, para 3.5.2 and briefly in para 9.5, *below*.

In reality, however, despite the ascendency of the concept of voluntary assumption of responsibility, the concept of foreseeability of reliance still plays a central role because there can be no claimable loss in tort for a defendant's negligent misstatement unless the plaintiff has relied on it, since the statement itself does not cause damage: the damage, if any, is caused only by the consequences to the plaintiff of having placed reliance on the statement. Furthermore, in any particular case, it will not be proper to treat the defendant as having voluntarily assumed responsibility to the plaintiff for the plaintiff's loss unless the defendant foresaw, or ought reasonably to have foreseen, that the plaintiff would rely on the defendant's statement or act without taking independent steps to verify the accuracy of the defendant's statement or act.

9.2 Historical obstacles

9.2.1 Introduction

It has been noted in Chapter 6, para 6.2.2 that, until *Donoghue v Stevenson* [1932] AC 562, the principle of privity of contract prevented a duty of care from arising in tort between the defendant manufacturer in a case like *Donoghue* and the plaintiff consumer where the defendant had a contract only with an intermediate third party (to whom he had originally sold the defective product) and not with the plaintiff. In the sphere of negligent misstatements, until the House of Lords' decision in *Hedley Byrne & Co Ltd v Heller & Partners Ltd* [1964] AC 465, there existed a similar contractually based restriction against the existence in tort of a duty of care in respect of a negligently made statement. A large part of the speeches in *Hedley Byrne* is devoted to an analysis and refutation of this restriction. In view of the direction which the law has taken since *Hedley Byrne*, as discussed in this chapter, it is no longer necessary to pay much regard to those old cases. Accordingly, only brief reference will be made to them here.

9.2.2 The contractual block

Foundation in Derry v Peek

In *Derry v Peek* (1889) 14 App Cas 337, the defendant directors of a tramway company had issued a prospectus containing a statement that, by the Act of Parliament by which that company had been incorporated, they had the right to use steam power instead of horses. The plaintiff subscribed for shares on the faith of this statement. The Board of Trade subsequently refused their consent to the use of steam power, and the company was wound up. The plaintiff's action of deceit against the directors founded upon the false statement failed because the court found as a fact that the directors' statement as to the availability of steam power was made in the honest belief that it was true. In the course of his judgment, Lord Bramwell said (at p 347): "To found an action for damages there must be a contract and breach, or fraud". It is this statement which caused the courts in subsequent cases to adhere to the restrictive principle outlined *above*, even though this case had dealt only with the fraud aspect of the directors' misstatement, and had not even considered what their position might be in negligence.

Le Lievre v Gould

In *Le Lievre and Dennes v Gould* [1893] 1 QB 491, a surveyor had provided a builder with some certificates as to the progress made at various stages in the building of some houses. The plaintiff, as the builder's mortgagee, advanced money to him from time to time on the faith of these certificates. Due to the surveyor's negligence, the certificates contained untrue statements as to the progress of the buildings, but there was no fraud on his part. Following *Derry v Peek*, the court held that the surveyor owed no duty of care to the plaintiff mortgagee. The decision is correct in view of the fact that the builder showed the surveyor's certificates to the plaintiff without the surveyor's authority, and the surveyor knew nothing about the plaintiff or the terms of the mortgage, but the case was actually decided on the basis that the defendant surveyor owed no liability to the plaintiff mortgagee because there was no contract between them. Bowen LJ said (at p 502): "The law of England does not consider that what a man writes on paper is like a gun or other dangerous instrument, and, unless he intended to deceive, the law does not, in the absence of contract, hold him responsible for drawing his certificate carelessly".

Partial breakthrough in Nocton v Lord Ashburton

In *Nocton v Lord Ashburton* [1914] AC 932, the defendant, who was the plaintiff's solicitor, was sued by the plaintiff for damages arising out of the defendant's alleged fraud in relation to certain lending transactions from which the defendant personally benefited (unbeknown to the plaintiff) through the plaintiff following his advice. The trial judge found as a fact that the defendant had not acted fraudulently, but that his advice to the plaintiff had simply been negligent. The trial judge believed that he was constrained by *Derry v Peek* from giving relief to the plaintiff in these circumstances in the absence of a finding of fraud.

The House of Lords agreed that the defendant had not acted fraudulently, but their Lordships did not believe that *Derry v Peek* prevented them from examining whether, on the facts, the defendant should be held liable to the plaintiff on any other non-contractual ground. Viscount Haldane LC said (at p 947):

> . . . the discussion by the . . . Lords who took part in [*Derry v Peek*] appears to me to exclude the hypothesis that they considered any other question to be before them than what was the necessary foundation of an ordinary action for deceit. . . . But they do not say that where a different sort of relationship ought to be inferred from the circumstances the case is to be concluded by asking whether an action for deceit will lie. . . In reality the judgment covered only a part of the field in which liabilities may arise. There are other obligations besides that of honesty the breach of which may give a right to damages. These obligations depend on principles which the judges have worked out in the fashion that is characteristic of a system where much of the law has always been judge-made and unwritten.

Viscount Haldane LC continued (at p 950):

> In his judgment [in *Derry v Peek*] Lord Herschell carefully excluded [from the principle of *Derry v Peek*]
>
> > 'those cases where a person within whose special province it lay to know a particular fact has given an erroneous answer to an inquiry made with regard to it by a person desirous of ascertaining the fact for the purpose of determining his course'.

Viscount Haldane LC referred to various situations in which liability had been imposed on defendants for their negligent acts or omissions which had injured "the property or persons of others"; and then said with regard to negligent misstatements (at p 948):

> Although liability for negligence in word has in material respects been developed in our law differently from liability for negligence in act, it is nonetheless true that a man may come under a special duty to exercise care in giving information or advice. . . Whether such a duty has been assumed must depend on the relationship of the parties, and it is at least certain that there are a good many cases in which that relationship may be properly treated as giving rise to a special duty of care in statement.

Lord Shaw approached the matter slightly differently, when he said (at p 971):

> Equity will only interfere in the following cases: ... thirdly, where a representation has been made which binds the conscience of the party and estops and obliges him to make it good. In [this] case, the representation in equity is equivalent to a contract and very nearly coincides with a warranty at law; and in order that a person may avail himself of relief founded on it he must show that there was such a proximate relation between himself and the person making the representation as to bring them virtually into the position of parties contracting with each other.

In the present case the defendant, as the plaintiff's solicitor, stood in a fiduciary relation to the plaintiff. That duty, the House held, was breached by the defendant's conduct in relation to the advice that he gave to the plaintiff which benefited the defendant personally.

This decision and the *dicta* mentioned *above* were influential in enabling the House of Lords in *Hedley Byrne & Co Ltd v Heller and Partners Ltd* [1964] AC 465 to hold that a duty of care can exist in tort in respect of a negligently made statement even where the parties do not stand in a contractual or a fiduciary relationship with each other.

Candler v Crane—I

In *Candler v Crane, Christmas & Co* [1951] 2 KB 164, the plaintiff had responded to an advertisement in the newspaper by a tin mining company seeking further capital. He was prepared to invest £2,000, but first asked to see the company's accounts. The company's sole director put him in touch with the company's accountants, who were at that time in the course of preparing up-to-date accounts. He had several meetings with the accountants, who knew that he was considering an investment in the company and was relying on the accounts which they had drafted in making his decision. On the strength of the accounts, he made his investment and in fact began working for the company. Two months later he invested another £200 in it. Subsequently he discovered that the company was in financial difficulties. It was not even able to pay his salary. He presented a petition for the winding up of the company. A winding-up order was made. There were no assets. The sole director became bankrupt. The plaintiff lost all of his money.

The plaintiff therefore brought an action against the accountants because, by that time, he had discovered that the accounts which he had been given provided an altogether false picture of the position of the company. The accountants had, for example, failed to verify the information which the director had given them about the company's supposed assets, which simply did not exist. The accountants admitted that they had entirely failed to use proper care and skill in the preparation of the accounts. The plaintiff claimed that it was due to the accountants' carelessness that he had lost his money, because, if they had put properly prepared accounts before him, the true position of the company's affairs would have been disclosed and he would never have invested his money.

The Court of Appeal rejected by 2:1 the plaintiff's claim. Following *Derry* and *Le Lievre*, the majority judges held that a false statement carelessly, but not fraudulently, made by one person to another, though acted on by that other to his detriment, was not actionable in the absence of any contractual or fiduciary relationship between the parties.

Here, unlike in *Nocton v Lord Ashburton*, there was no fiduciary relationship between the parties. In these circumstances the majority judges were not prepared to impose a duty of care on the defendants for the plaintiff's economic losses. That development had to await the House of Lords' decision in *Hedley Byrne* (see para 9.4.2, *below*).

Denning LJ dissented. His judgment is considered *below* in para 9.6.2, as it has been held by the House of Lords in *Caparo Industries plc v Dickman* [1990] 2 AC 605 to have been correct, and *Candler* has been overruled accordingly.

9.2.3 Not affected by *Donoghue*

Attempts were made in some cases to suggest that the negligent statements restrictive rule had been abolished by the House of Lords' decision in *Donoghue v Stevenson* [1932] AC 562.

Old Gate Estates v Toplis

In *Old Gate Estates Ltd v Toplis & Harding & Russell* [1939] 3 All ER 209, the defendant valuer had provided a valuation on a block of flats to two promoters of a company which was to be formed. The valuation had been negligently prepared. The company sued the valuer for its loss. As the valuation had been made before the company was formed, the company could not sue him in contract. The company sued the valuer in tort, contending that it was his 'neighbour' within the ambit of *Donoghue v Stevenson* because he knew that the valuation was going to be put into the company's prospectus and therefore he owed a duty of care to it by way of an application of the 'neighbour principle'.

The court rejected this claim. Wrottesley J referred to the above-quoted words of Bowen LJ in *Le Lievre* and said (at p 216):

> I think that [these words] are as true today as when they were said by Bowen LJ, and that there is nothing in *Donoghue v Stevenson* which makes them bad law. The exceptions laid down in *Donoghue*—the exceptions to the rule that a man is obliged to be careful only to those to whom he owes a duty by contract—are, as I understand the decision in that case, confined to negligence which results in danger to life, danger to limb or danger to health, and, this being none of those, the plaintiff has no cause of action on the analogy of *Donoghue*.

Candler v Crane—II

In *Candler v Crane, Christmas & Co* (mentioned *above*), Asquith LJ expressed a similar view when he said (at p 186): "The notion that *Donoghue's case* was intended *sub silentio* to sweep away the substratum of *Derry v Peek* seems to me to be quite unconvincing"; and (at p 189): "Although Lord Atkin's definition of a 'neighbour' has been applied outside its limited ambit, it has, however, never been applied where the damage complained of was not physical"; and (at p 195): "In the present state of our law different rules still seem to apply to negligent misstatement on the one hand and to negligent circulation or repair of chattels on the other; and *Donoghue's* case does not seem to me to have abolished these differences. I am not concerned with defending the existing state of the law or contending that it is strictly logical—it clearly is not. I am merely recording what I think it is."

9.2.3 *Negligent misstatements and services*

Hedley Byrne

As already noted, in *Hedley Byrne* the House of Lords departed from the restrictive principle discussed *above*. However, it did not do so by holding that the 'neighbour principle' of *Donoghue* applied to negligent misstatements. On the contrary, it held that this principle was not applicable, and it held that proximity in this type of case was established by other means, namely 'reliance' (see Chapter 7, para 7.5.2). Thus, Lord Reid said (at p 482): "The plaintiff's first argument was based on *Donoghue v Stevenson*. That is a very important decision, but I do not think that it has any bearing on this case"; Lord Hodson, in apparent agreement with Asquith LJ in *Candler*, said (at p 506): "The decision in *Donoghue*, although its effect has been extended . . . has never been applied to cases where damages are claimed in tort for negligent statements producing damage"; and Lord Devlin said (at p 525):

> In my opinion the [plaintiffs] . . . tried to press *Donoghue v Stevenson* too hard. They asked whether the principle of proximity should not apply as well to words as to deeds. I think it should, but as it is only a general conception it does not get them very far. Then they take the specific proposition laid down by *Donoghue* and try to apply it literally to a certificate or a banker's reference. That will not do, for a general conception cannot be applied to pieces of paper in the same way as to articles of commerce or to writers in the same way as to manufacturers.

Comment

None of these judges explained why they felt that Lord Atkin's 'neighbour principle' in *Donoghue* was not applicable to cases of negligent misstatement. In one sense they were right, in another sense they were not. It is in fact true to say that an application of the 'neighbour principle' by itself would have proved nothing in *Hedley Byrne* (or in any other case, see *below*), but to say that it had no application at all is to misunderstand its meaning and intended purpose.

Lord Atkin formulated his 'neighbour principle' (ie his test for determining proximity) by saying (at p 580):

> . . . acts or omissions which any moral code would censure cannot in a practical world be treated so as to give a right to every person injured by them to demand relief. In this way rules of law arise which limit the range of complainants and the extent of their remedy. The rule that you are to love your neighbour becomes in law, you must not injure your neighbour; and the lawyer's question, Who is my neighbour? receives a restricted reply. You must take reasonable care to avoid acts or omissions which you can reasonably foresee would be likely to injure your neighbour. Who, then, in law is my neighbour? The answer seems to be—persons who are so closely and directly affected by my act that I ought reasonably to have them in contemplation as being so affected when I am directing my mind to the acts or omissions which are called in question.

It will be immediately apparent that this is just a test for determining the class of plaintiffs or, as Lord Atkin put it, 'the range of complainants' to whom a duty of care, if it exists, is owed. This test tells us nothing about whether such a duty of care does exist or, in Lord Atkin's words, about "the extent of [the injured person's] remedy". In *Home Office v Dorset Yacht Co Ltd* [1970] AC 1004, Viscount Dilhorne recognised this point when he said (at p 1042): "It should be remembered that the question for decision in *Donoghue v Stevenson* was not so much as to the existence of a duty of care, but as to whom it was owed"; and (at p 1043): "Lord Atkin's answer to the question 'Who, then, in law is my neighbour?', while very relevant to determine to whom a duty of care is owed, cannot determine, in my opinion, the question whether a duty of care exists".

Indeed, this is exactly what Lord Atkin himself intended. As discussed in Chapter 6, para 6.3.2, he held that a duty of care existed in that case, not simply because the defendant had manufactured a defective product which injured the plaintiff and that this was foreseeable, but because, by virtue of the ginger beer being in a dark opaque bottle, there was, to the defendant's knowledge, no reasonable prospect of an intermediate examination of it by the plaintiff or anyone else higher up in the chain of distribution before the plaintiff consumed it and was injured by it. It is this factor which established the duty of care. It is Lord Atkin's neighbour test which established to whom the duty was owed. As pointed out in Chapter 6, para 6.2, the real importance of *Donoghue* was that it rejected decisively the previously existing general exclusionary rule that a person who was injured by a defect in a product could only sue the party with whom he had had a contract (ie his immediate seller) and not the actual manufacturer of it unless he had a direct contract with that manufacturer. It is to this rule that Lord Atkin's 'neighbour principle' is directed. Whether, in any particular case, the manufacturer was to be made liable, or was to owe a duty of care in tort to an individual who fell within Lord Atkin's definition of a 'neighbour', was to be determined by a different rule of law appropriate to that particular type of case. This is what Lord Atkin intended, and it is how he in fact applied these principles in *Donoghue*.

Another way of stating the above is to say that, while Lord Atkin's 'neighbour principle' correctly defines the range of possible plaintiffs with whom the defendant will have a sufficiently proximate relationship for liability to be imposed on him for harm caused to such persons, it does not define the *content* of that relationship. The fault of the judges mentioned *above* who said that Lord Atkin's 'neighbour principle' does not apply to cases of negligent misstatement is that they have wrongly treated that principle as being synonymous with the test for determining whether a duty of care exists in any particular case. The correct answer, it is submitted, is that Lord Atkin's principle is fully applicable, but that its effect is limited only to identifying the class of persons (ie "persons who are so closely and directly affected by [the defendant's act] that [he] ought reasonably to have them in contemplation . . .") to whom a duty of care will be owed, if it exists at all. It is thus a rule of very limited effect and purpose; but at the time of its formulation it was extremely important in the context of overturning the general exclusionary rule, under which the defendant's 'neighbours' in a case like *Donoghue* would have included only the distributor to whom he had actually sold the bottle of ginger beer in question, and no one else (see Chapter 6, para 6.2.2).

9.3   Other conceptual difficulties

9.3.1   Characteristics of words

Introduction

It has been noted *above* in para 9.2.3 that the House of Lords' decision in *Donoghue* broke the mould of the privity of contract general exclusionary rule which had previously prevented recovery in that type of case, and that a similar contract-based restriction, supposedly based on *Derry v Peek*, prevented recovery in cases of negligent misstatement. One of the reasons which the courts gave for rejecting the application of the House's decision in *Donoghue* to cases of negligent misstatement was that it was concerned with a negligent act or deed, whereas these cases are concerned with negligent words. Thus, for example, in *Hedley Byrne* Lord Reid said (at p 482): "Apart altogether from authority, I would think that the law must treat negligent words differently from negligent acts".

Deliberateness of acts

In *Hedley Byrne* Lord Reid said (at p 482):

> The most obvious difference between negligent words and negligent acts is this. Quite careful people often express different opinions on social or informal occasions even when they see that others are likely to be influenced by them; and they often do that without taking that care which they would take if asked for their opinion professionally or in a business connection. The [plaintiff] agrees that there can be no duty of care on such occasions . . . But it is at least unusual casually to put into circulation negligently made articles which are dangerous.

No causative difference

Lord Devlin (at p 516) thought that "it would be absurd" to distinguish between "negligence in word and negligence in deed", at least from a causative point of view. He gave the example of a plaintiff who was injured through the defendant having repaired his car negligently, as contrasted with a plaintiff who was injured through relying on the defendant's negligent statement that the plaintiff's car had been repaired, when in fact it had not. He said: "It would be absurd in any of these cases to argue that the proximate cause of the driver's injury was not what the defendant did or failed to do, but his negligent statement on the faith of which the driver drove the car".

No difference vis-à-vis reliance

In Chapter 7, para 7.5.2, it is submitted that, to the extent that the defendant's knowledge, actual or imputed, of the absence of an opportunity for intermediate inspection in a case like *Donoghue* justified the court in imposing a duty of care on him, that principle is the same as the principle of knowledge, actual or imputed, of reliance, which forms the foundation of the test for the existence of a duty of care for a negligently made statement. In *Hedley Byrne*, Lord Morris recognised this connection when, after discussing the courts' decisions in *Heaven v Pender* (1883), *George v Skivington* (1869) and *Donoghue* (all of which are discussed in Chapter 6, para 6.2.5), he said (at p 496):

> In logic I can see no essential reason for distinguishing injury which is caused by a reliance upon words from injury which is caused by a reliance upon the safety of the staging to a ship [as in *Heaven*] or by a reliance upon the safety for use of the contents of a bottle of hair wash [as in *George*] or a bottle of some consumable liquid [as in *Donoghue*].

Wide range of complainants

The very nature of the way in which words can be disseminated widely and can be heard or read by an extensive range of persons means that it would be difficult to determine in advance the "range of complainants" to whom the defendant should owe a duty of care if his statement was negligent and other persons relied on it to their detriment. Also, as such detriment will usually consist of pure economic loss in this type of case, it is generally felt that such loss will be more difficult to predict, not only because there might be a wide range of possible responses which potential plaintiffs might make on the strength of the negligent statement (for example, where it consists of negligently certified accounts of a company and investors decide to put money into the company on the strength of those accounts), but also because of the temptation by plaintiffs to exaggerate their losses in these circumstances. To counteract these concerns the courts have devised very stringent tests for determining whether a duty of care should be imposed in these circumstances.

In *Hedley Byrne* two of their Lordships expressed these concerns. Lord Reid said (at p 483):

> ... a negligently made article will only cause one accident, and so it is not very difficult to find the necessary degree of proximity or neighbourhood between the negligent manufacturer and the person injured. But words can be broadcast with or without the consent or the foresight of the speaker or writer. It would be one thing to say that the speaker owes a duty to a limited class, but it would be going very far to say that he owes a duty to every ultimate 'consumer' who acts on those words to his detriment.

Lord Pearce said (at p 534):

> Words are more volatile than deeds. They travel fast and far afield. They are used without being expended and take effect in combination with innumerable facts and other words. Yet they are dangerous and can cause vast financial damage. How far they are relied on unchecked (by analogy with there being no probability of intermediate inspection) must in many cases be a matter of doubt and difficulty. If the mere hearing or reading of words were held to create proximity, there might be no limit to the persons to whom the speaker or writer could be liable. Damage by negligent acts to persons or property on the other hand is more visible and obvious; its limits are more easily defined.

9.3.2   Comment

There is truth in the concerns expressed by the judges under the headings *Deliberateness of acts* and *Wide range of complainants, above.* The rules which the courts have devised (as discussed in this chapter) for the imposition of a duty of care in this type of case recognise the legitimacy of these concerns and full allowance is made for them accordingly.

9.3.3   Indeterminate liability: *Ultramares v Touche*

Introduction

One of the most influential and most often quoted *dicta* in the field of economic loss in tort is Cardozo J's statement in the Court of Appeal of New York in *Ultramares Corporation v Touche, Niven & Company* (1931) 255 NY 170, that if a duty of care for negligence existed in that type of case (see *below*), "the defendant would be exposed to a liability in an indeterminate amount for an indeterminate time to an indeterminate class". This factor formed the basis of the Court's decision in refusing to impose a duty of care on the negligent accountants in that case.

The actual decision

A particular company whose business was the importation and sale of rubber required extensive credit to finance its operations. It borrowed large sums of money from banks and other lenders. The defendant was the company's accountants. It knew that this was how the company ran its finances. It knew that the company's balance sheet, when certified by the defendant, would be exhibited by the company to banks, creditors, shareholders, purchasers or sellers, according to the needs of the occasion, as the basis of financial dealings. Indeed, when the balance sheet was made up, the defendants supplied the company with 32 copies certified with serial numbers as counterpart originals.

The plaintiff was a factor, who had been requested by the company to lend it money to finance the sale of rubber. As a condition of making any loans, the plaintiff insisted on receiving a balance sheet certified by public accountants. In response to that request it was given one of the certified copies which the defendant had provided to the company. On the faith of that certification, which showed a very healthy state of affairs, the plaintiff made several loans to the company. Subsequently the company went into insolvent liquidation. It was discovered that the accounts had been fraudulently prepared by the company and that the defendant had been negligent (but not fraudulent) in not detecting that fraud when it audited the company's books and accounts.

Due to the company's insolvency, there was no point in the plaintiff suing the company. The plaintiff therefore sued the defendant auditors. The court rejected this claim. Cardozo J said: "Nothing was said [by the company to the auditors] as to the persons to whom these counterparts would be shown or the extent or number of the transactions in which they would be used. In particular, there was no mention of the plaintiff, which until then had never made advances to the company. The range of the transactions in which a certificate of audit might be expected to play a part was as indefinite and wide as the possibilities of the business that was mirrored in the summary".

Cardozo J continued:

> To creditors and investors to whom the employer [ie the company] exhibited the certificate, the defendants owed a duty to make it without fraud, since they had notice that the employer did not intend to keep it to himself. A different question develops when we ask whether they owed a duty to creditors and investors to make it without negligence. If liability for negligence exists, a thoughtless slip or blunder, the failure to detect a theft or forgery beneath the cover of deceptive entries, may expose accountants to a liability in an indeterminate amount for an indeterminate time to an indeterminate class. The hazards of a business conducted on these terms are so extreme as to enkindle doubt where a flaw may not exist in the implication of a duty that exposes to these consequences.

Cardozo J then referred to, and contrasted, the present case with his own previous decision in *Glanzer v Shepard* (see *below*) and concluded that the only duty of care which the auditors owed in *Ultramares* was a duty in contract to the company which had engaged them. Having reached this conclusion, he said: "We doubt whether the average businessman receiving a certificate without paying for it, and receiving it merely as one among a multitude of possible investors, would look for anything more".

Glanzer v Shepard

In *Glanzer Bros v Levi Shepard* (1922) 233 NY 236, the plaintiff had bought a number of bags of beans from a certain company. The beans were to be paid for in accordance with weight sheets certified by public weighers. The seller requested the defendant, whose business was public weighing, to weigh the beans at the dock pier before they were due to be delivered by the seller to the plaintiff, and to furnish the plaintiff with a copy of the weighing certificate. The plaintiff duly paid for the beans on the faith of the certificate. Subsequently the plaintiff found that the actual weight was substantially less than the weight certified.

The plaintiff sued the weighers for the amount of money which they had thus overpaid. The weighers contended that they were not liable, as they had had no contract with the plaintiff, who, they said, must seek its remedy against the seller. The court held for the plaintiff. Cardozo J said:

> The plaintiff's use of the certificate was not an indirect or collateral consequence of the action of the weighers. It was a consequence which, to the weighers' knowledge, was the end and aim of the transaction. The defendants held themselves out to the public as skilled and careful in their calling. They knew that the beans had been sold and that on the faith of their certificate payment would be made. They sent a copy to the plaintiff for the very purpose of inducing action. In such circumstances, assumption of the task of weighing was the assumption of a duty to weigh carefully for the benefit of all whose conduct was to be governed. We do not need to state the duty in terms of contract or of privity.

9.3.3 *Negligent misstatements and services*

Contrast with Ultramares

In *Ultramares*, Cardozo J referred to *Glanzer* and said:

> The bond [in *Glanzer*] was so close as to approach that of privity. Not so in the case at hand. No one would be likely to urge that there was a relationship even approaching contract at the root of any duty that was owing from the defendants now before us [ie the auditors] to the indeterminate class of persons who, presently or in the future, might deal with the company in reliance on the audit. In a word, the service rendered by the defendant in *Glanzer* was primarily for the information of a third person and only incidentally for that of the formal promisee. In the case at hand, the service was primarily rendered for the benefit of the company in the development of its business, and only incidentally or collaterally for the use of those to whom the company might exhibit it thereafter.

Comment

The analysis of Cardozo J in these two cases has not only contributed to, but also fully accords with, the development and the current position of English law in this type of case. All of the formulations of the principles that the courts have fashioned for the imposition of duties of care in tort in cases of negligent misstatement or the negligent provision of a service or advice, and the limits that the courts have devised on the scope of such duties, have been heavily influenced by Cardozo J's above-mentioned admonition about the need to guard against creating rules whereby defendants would be exposed to indeterminate liability, ie exposure to possible liability to a class of claims, the size of which cannot be determined in advance (see Chapter 2, para 2.4.3). An example of a judge being consciously aware of these factors in fashioning the applicable legal principle in the case before him is the following statement of Lord Bridge in *Caparo Industries Plc v Dickman* [1990] 2 AC 605. Lord Bridge said (at p 621):

> . . . in this category of the tort of negligence "the limit or control mechanism imposed on the liability of a wrongdoer to those who have suffered economic damage in consequence of his negligence rests on the necessity to prove", as an essential ingredient of the 'proximity' between the plaintiff and the defendant, that the defendant knew that his statement would be communicated to the plaintiff, either as an individual or as a member of an identifiable class, specifically in connection with a particular transaction or transactions of a particular kind . . . and that the plaintiff would be very likely to rely on it for the purpose of deciding whether or not to enter upon that transaction or upon a transaction of that kind.

The 'floodgates' fear

Closely allied to, but in fact distinct from, the indeterminacy concern mentioned *above* is the concern expressed in some cases that if the court were to allow recovery to the plaintiff in the particular case before it, the courts would become flooded with an overwhelming number of similar claims, many of which would be dubious. This concern is not often expressed in the category of cases considered in this chapter because the rules that the courts have devised for guarding against the imposition of indeterminate liability in this type of case also serve as a check on the number of similar cases that it would be worth arguing in any particular type of case. For example, the above-mentioned rule that Lord Bridge formulated in *Caparo* serves the purpose of limiting not only the size of the class of plaintiffs to whose claims the defendant would be exposed, but also the number of possible plaintiffs who would find it worthwhile to pursue their claims. There would be no point for plaintiffs whose claims do not fall within, or very close to, the parameters of Lord Bridge's exposition to institute proceedings and take them through trial.

Nevertheless, in *South Pacific Manufacturing Co Ltd v New Zealand Security Consultants and Investigations Ltd* [1992] 2 NZLR 282, the floodgates fear, as distinct from the indeterminacy fear, was invoked by the Court of Appeal of New Zealand as a reason for denying the plaintiff's economic loss claim in tort against an insurance investigator who had made a report to the plaintiff's insurer, in consequence of which the insurer had denied liability under the plaintiff's policy. Thus, Richardson J said (at p 309):

> Finally, the imposition of the duty of care contended for could not reasonably be confined to insurance investigators and other related professionals, and its ambit would be inherently expansive and unacceptably indeterminate. It may be said that the plaintiff [in the present appeals] was the only person other than the insurer likely to be affected by a careless allegation of arson. But there is a vast range of similar everyday situations in which only a few people stand to be adversely affected, and it would be difficult to justify extending the duty category to anyone who, in the course of a contractual engagement, carelessly investigates and reports on the conduct of a third party. Credit reports, media investigations and reports of events are obvious examples. And why limit the duty to those who carry out inquiries and make reports pursuant to contract? The effect on a plaintiff may be just as traumatic if carelessly made comments on the plaintiff's conduct are volunteered to a person in authority or other third party. In short, the proposed duty category would be uncertainly expansive for what I would characterise as unacceptably indeterminate consequences for the public interest.

This is in fact a slight variation on the usual reason for expressing the floodgates fear, namely that the number of possible plaintiffs would multiply exponentially and place an unacceptable burden on the administration of the justice system. Here, instead, the court's concern was that, if it were to impose a duty of care on the fire investigator, other related professionals and other non-professional investigators and reporters could be exposed to liability for the subject of their reports (as opposed to liability merely to the recipient) if their reports were materially inaccurate and compiled negligently.

It is submitted that this reasoning is misplaced because it calls into question such major developments in the modern law of negligence as occurred, for example, in *Hedley Byrne & Co v Heller & Partners Ltd* [1964] AC 465. There, the court was concerned only with the possible liability of a banker to the recipient of a reference that the banker had given about a third party, for economic loss sustained by the recipient through having relied on the reference. However, the wider implications of the case for other similarly placed defendants—like accountants and solicitors, or indeed anyone who makes a statement to a third party knowing that it will be relied on by someone else in making an important decision affecting that other person's financial interests—were clear; yet that did not deter the House of Lords from deciding that in principle the banker in *Hedley* owed a duty of care to the plaintiff in that case.

9.4 The importance of *Hedley Byrne*

9.4.1 Introduction

In the last ten years, commencing with *Junior Books Ltd v Veitchi Co Ltd* [1983] 1 AC 520, there have been numerous cases in which the plaintiff has asked the court to impose a duty of care on the defendant in respect of the plaintiff's pure economic loss caused by the defendant's negligent act or omission. In all of these cases, whether the defendant's negligent act or omission has consisted of words or an act, including the creation of a tangible item, the plaintiff's success or failure has depended upon whether he has been able to bring himself and the particular loss which he suffered within "the *Hedley Byrne* principle of reliance". Thus, for example, Lord Oliver said in *Murphy v Brentwood District Council* [1991] 1 AC 398 (at p 480): "The House has already held in *D & F Estates* that a builder, in the absence of any contractual duty or of a special relationship of proximity introducing the *Hedley Byrne* principle of reliance, owes no duty of care in tort in respect of the quality of his work". As noted in Chapter 7, para 7.3.6, *Junior Books*, which is the sole defective products case in which the plaintiff has succeeded in recovering his pure economic loss, was decided on this basis, and is not an exception to it.

Thus *Hedley Byrne* is emerging as the single most important case in English law in the field of duties of care for economic loss in non-accident cases. In accident cases (see Chapters 4 and 5, paras 4.3.3 and 5.2, respectively) the "*Hedley Byrne* principle of reliance" plays no part. The exclusionary rule which exists in those cases is based on other factors.

In practice the actual test which might be applied in any particular case might not necessarily be taken directly from *Hedley Byrne*. It might, in fact, be taken from one of the more recent cases, in particular *Caparo Industries plc v Dickman* [1990] 2 AC 605 (see para 9.6.2, *below*).

9.4.2 The actual decision

In *Hedley Byrne & Co Ltd v Heller & Partners Ltd* [1964] AC 465, the plaintiff was a firm of advertising agents. The plaintiff asked its bankers to obtain a credit reference on one of the plaintiff's clients, 'E Ltd'. The plaintiff's bankers duly approached the defendants, who were E Ltd's bankers. They asked them whether they would consider E Ltd to be trustworthy to the extent of £100,000 per annum in respect of advertising contracts. The defendants replied that E Ltd was a respectably constituted company, considered good for its ordinary business arrangements, but added: "Your figures are larger than we are accustomed to see". Also, this reference was specifically given "without responsibility on the part of the bank".

The plaintiff's bankers passed this information to the plaintiff. Relying on these statements, the plaintiff extended substantial credit to E Ltd. When E Ltd subsequently went into liquidation the plaintiff lost £17,000. The plaintiff sought to recover this loss from the defendants on the ground that their replies to the plaintiff's bankers' questions were given negligently. On the assumption (but without deciding the point) that the defendants had been negligent, a trial was held as to whether, in these circumstances, the defendants owed a duty of care to the plaintiff. As noted *above*, the primary obstacle in the way of such a duty being imposed was the restriction which emanated from *Derry v Peek*, to the effect that a duty of care in respect of a negligent misstatement was owed only to a person with whom the maker of the statement had a contractual or a fiduciary relationship, but to no one else. As noted *above*, the House of Lords held that *Derry v Peek* was not a sound foundation for this principle. It also held that there was no other sound reason for maintaining it, that there were good reasons for not maintaining (such as Lord Morris's analogy from the application of the reliance principle in cases like *Donoghue*, see *above*) and, accordingly, their Lordships would have held the defendants liable for the plaintiff's loss, if not for the defendants' disclaimer of liability, which they held to be effective.

9.4.3   Individual formulations

Although none of the Law Lords in *Hedley Byrne* formulated a principle which stands out above the others as being readily digestible (which explains why Lord Oliver's four-stage test in *Caparo* is easier to apply, see para 9.6.2, *below*), they all made statements which demonstrate that the basis of the existence of a duty of care in this type of case is knowledge or foreseeability, actual or imputed, by the defendant that a particular person or class of persons would most probably place reliance on the defendant's statement, advice or service rendered without making any further enquiries to verify the accuracy of that statement, advice or service.

Thus, Lord Reid said (at p 483): "There must be something more than the mere misstatement. The most natural requirement would be that, expressly or by implication from the circumstances, the speaker or writer has undertaken some responsibility"; and (at p 486): "I can see no logical stopping place short of all those relationships where it is plain that the party seeking information or advice was trusting the other to exercise such a degree of care as the circumstances required, where it was reasonable for him to do that, and where the other gave the information or advice when he knew or ought to have known that the enquirer was relying on him".

Lord Morris (with whose formulation Lord Hodson agreed) said (at p 502):

> ... if someone possessed of a special skill undertakes, quite irrespective of contract, to apply that skill for the assistance of another person who relies upon such skill, a duty of care will arise. The fact that the service is to be given by means of ... words can make no difference. Furthermore, if in a sphere in which a person is so placed that others who could reasonably rely upon his judgment or skill or upon his ability to make careful enquiry, a person takes it upon himself to give information to, or allows his information to be passed on to, another person who, as he knows or should know, will place reliance upon it, then a duty of care will arise.

These two formulations are quite similar. Lord Pearce expressed himself in slightly more restrictive terms when he said (at p 538):

> ... if persons holding themselves out in a calling or situation or profession take on a task within that calling or situation or profession, they have a duty of skill and care. In terms of proximity one might say that they are in particularly close proximity to those who, as they know, are relying on their skill and care although the proximity is not contractual...
>
> To import ... a duty [of care] the representation must ... concern a business or professional transaction whose nature makes clear the gravity of the enquiry and the importance and influence attached to the answer.

Lord Devlin's formulation was even more restrictive. He said (at p 528):

> ... the categories of special relationships which may give rise to a duty to take care in word as well as in deed are not limited to contractual relationships or relationships of fiduciary duty, but include also relationships which ... are 'equivalent to contract', that is, where there is an assumption of responsibility in circumstances in which, but for the absence of consideration, there would be a contract.

He recognised that the defendant's "assumption of responsibility" need not be express or voluntary, but could be imputed or implied. He said (at p 532): "The question in this case is whether the plaintiff can set up a claim equivalent to contract and rely on an implied undertaking by the defendant to accept responsibility".

9.4.4 Economic loss

It has been noted *above* that the real obstacle towards the success of a plaintiff in a case like *Hedley Byrne* was the contractually based restrictive principle which was believed to have derived from *Derry v Peek* in 1889. It is therefore not surprising that there was not much focus in *Hedley Byrne* on the fact that the plaintiff's loss was purely economic, if that was to make any difference at all. Nevertheless, three of their Lordships, Lords Hodson, Devlin and Pearce, were aware of this point.

Lord Hodson dismissed the 'economic loss point' very shortly by saying (at p 509): "It is difficult to see why liability as such should depend on the nature of the damage", and he then referred to Lord Roche's 'lorry example' in *Morrison Steamship Co Ltd v Greystoke Castle (Cargo Owners)* [1947] AC 265 (ie that the owner of cargo in a lorry which is immobilised by another lorry in an accident can recover his pure economic losses consisting of additional transport expenses from the owner of the second lorry, even though his goods had not been damaged, which is discussed further in Chapter 5, para 5.8.2).

Lord Devlin, after dismissing the supposed distinction between negligence in word and negligence in deed (see para 9.4.3, *above*), and after noting that the defendant's counsel in *Hedley Byrne* had not taken that point, said (at p 517): "This is why the distinction is now said to depend on whether financial loss is caused through physical injury or whether it is caused directly. The interposition of the physical injury is said to make a difference in principle. I find neither logic nor common sense in this". He then gave the example of a doctor who negligently advises a patient that he can safely pursue his occupation and the patient's health suffers by following that advice, as contrasted with a doctor who negligently advises a patient that he cannot safely pursue his occupation, and the patient follows that advice, but suffers only financial loss thereby. In both cases the doctor will have given his advice irrespective of contract. He said that to say that in the first case the plaintiff could recover damages because he had suffered personal injury, but that in the latter case he could not because his loss was purely economic was, in his view, "nonsense". Lord Devlin, too, referred to *Greystoke* and said (at p 518): "Their Lordships did not in that case lay down any general principle about liability for financial loss in the absence of physical damage; but that case makes it impossible to argue that there is any general rule showing that such loss is of its nature irrecoverable".

Lord Pearce did not say whether he thought that the distinction between physical damage and economic loss was valid. He simply noted (at p 536) that the House of Lords' decision in *Greystoke* was authority that "economic loss alone, without some physical or material damage to support it, can afford a cause of action in negligence by act". He also commented: "Economic protection has lagged behind protection in physical matters where there is injury to person or property", and suggested as a reason for this: "It may be that the size and width of the range of possible claims has acted as a deterrent to extension of economic protection".

9.4.5 Comment

The above-quoted 'economic loss *dicta*' demonstrate that there was no meaningful analysis in *Hedley Byrne* as to why economic loss claims should be treated differently from physical injury claims. It would be wrong to regard the case as having laid down any general principles in this regard. On the other hand, it is submitted that it is also wrong to regard the case, as, for example, Lord Oliver did in *Murphy* (see para 7.5.2, *above*), as laying down that economic loss can be recovered in the tort of negligence only where "the *Hedley Byrne* principle of reliance" is established. On the other hand, as pointed out in Chapters 7 and 8, if this is to be the applicable principle, both in relation to negligent misstatements, advice or services rendered, and to defectively manufactured products or buildings, then it is submitted that, contrary to what the House of Lords held in *D & F* and *Murphy*, there should be no reason why this principle should not be able to be satisfied in ordinary cases of defective goods or buildings with hidden defects which the ultimate purchaser could not reasonably be expected to have discovered by way of an intermediate examination.

9.5   Voluntary assumption of responsibility

9.5.1   Introduction

When the first edition of this book was written in 1993, the concept of 'voluntary assumption of responsibility', as used in some of the cases, was not considered to be an especially important element of any of the established criteria for determining whether a duty of care should be imposed in any of the various categories of cases. Indeed, there were some powerful *dicta* in certain important House of Lords' decisions which suggested that the concept was not of much use except, perhaps, as one of a host of factors to be weighed in considering the question of sufficient proximity in any particular case (see, further, Chapter 3, para 3.5.2, where these reasons are set out in detail).

In consequence of certain *dicta*, particularly by Lord Goff, in three important economic loss cases in the mid-1990s—namely, *Spring v Guardian Assurance plc* [1995] 2 AC 296, *Henderson v Merrett Syndicates Ltd* [1995] 2 AC 145 and *White v Jones* [1995] 2 AC 207—the concept of voluntary assumption of responsibility has been elevated, in the eyes of some of the judges, to being in and of itself the primary determinant of liability in cases of negligent misstatement (see Chapter 3, para 3.5.2).

9.5.2   Proper use

In many of the post-1994 cases that are discussed in this chapter, the concept of voluntary assumption of responsibility has featured in one way or another in shaping the court's decision. The relevant *dicta* from some of those cases are set out in Chapter 3, para 3.5.2. As a ready guide to the understanding of the role of the concept in duty of care cases involving economic loss generally, and in particular in relation to cases of negligent misstatement of the type that are considered in this chapter, it is submitted that the following observations and conclusions are apt:

(1) The proper use of the phrase or concept 'voluntary assumption of responsibility' is to regard it as being one component amongst many in the proximity analysis or in the overall general pragmatic test for determining liability, in the application of which all the relevant factors are taken into account and are accorded their appropriate weight according to all of the circumstances of the case. As Lord Oliver said in *Caparo Industries Plc v Dickman* [1990] 2 AC 605 (at p 635): "One must be careful about seeking to find any general principle which will serve as a touchstone for all cases, for, even within

the limited category of negligent misstatement cases, circumstances may differ infinitely and, in a swiftly developing field of law, there can be no necessary assumption that those features which have served in one case to create the relationship between the plaintiff and the defendant on which liability depends will necessarily be determinative of liability in the different circumstances of another case".

(2) The range of cases in which it is proper to say that, because the defendant voluntarily assumed responsibility to the plaintiff in respect of the provision of certain information or services, there is no need to embark upon any further inquiry whether it is "fair, just and reasonable" to impose liability on the defendant for the plaintiff's economic loss, is so narrow (ie it is confined to cases where the parties are already in a contractual relationship or where there has been direct contact between them and their relationship can be regarded as being "equivalent to contract") that the law would be better served if this application of the concept was abandoned, given the potential for confusion that this idea engenders and given that principles already exist which are equally applicable to resolve these cases.

(3) The concept of 'voluntary assumption of responsibility' is useful, but not necessary, as a conclusion or as a goal to be achieved, or as a benchmark against which to measure different situations. In other words, if one wants to use the concept in this fashion, its utility will be found in asking whether, in all of the circumstances of the case— including whether, as a fact, the defendant voluntarily assumed responsibility for the task the negligent performance of which can be regarded as being the origin of the plaintiff's claim—the defendant's acts or omissions were such that it is fair, just and reasonable to regard (or *deem*) the defendant in law to be subject to the same consequences, so far as the plaintiff's actual loss is concerned, as a person who had voluntarily, intentionally or consciously accepted legal liability for such acts or omissions without attaching a valid disclaimer thereto.

(4) When used in the sense described in (3) *above*, voluntary assumption of responsibility is not a different test from the established test of foreseeability, proximity and "fair, just and reasonable", but is an equal alternative to it. Some judges and practitioners might find it easier to reason in terms of the deemed voluntary assumption of responsibility approach because it can be envisaged more vividly and might appear to have a more tangible feel than the other approach.

9.6 Other formulations

9.6.1 General

In addition to the formulation of principle by the Law Lords in *Hedley Byrne*, certain other judges have formulated general principles in this area of the law which are worth noting. All of these are fully consistent with the principles enunciated in *Hedley Byrne* and are just another way of stating the same principles in different words.

9.6.2 *Dicta* in judgments

Denning LJ in Candler

In *Candler v Crane, Christmas & Co* [1951] 2 KB 164 (the facts of which are set out in para 9.2.1 *above*), Denning LJ dissented. However, his views were vindicated by the House of Lords in *Hedley Byrne* when they overruled *Candler* and approved Denning LJ's judgment. In *Caparo Industries plc v Dickman* [1990] 2 AC 605, Lord Bridge said (at p 623): "It seems to me that this masterly analysis [which is summarised *below*] requires little, if any, amplification or modification in the light of later authority".

Thus, Denning LJ in *Candler* (at p 179) analysed the position as follows:

> First, what persons are under such a duty? My answer is those persons such as accountants, surveyors, valuers and analysts whose profession and occupation it is to examine books, accounts, and other things, and to make reports on which people—other than their clients—rely in the ordinary course of business.

Denning LJ continued:

> Secondly, to whom do these professional people owe this duty? I will take accountants, but the same reasoning applies to the others. They owe the duty, of course, to their employer or client; and also I think to any third person to whom they themselves show the accounts or to whom they know their employer is going to show the accounts, so as to induce him to invest money or take some other action on them. But I do not think the duty can be extended still further so as to include strangers of whom they have heard nothing and to whom their employer without their knowledge may choose to show their accounts. Once the accountants have handed their accounts to their employer they are not, as a rule, responsible for what he does with them without their knowledge or consent . . .
>
> The test of proximity in these cases is: did the accountants know that the accounts were required for submission to the plaintiff and use by him?

Denning LJ continued:

> Thirdly, to what transactions does the duty of care extend? It extends, I think, only to those transactions for which the accountants knew their accounts were required. For instance, in the present case it extends to the original investment of £2,000 which the plaintiff made in reliance on the accounts, because the accountants knew that the accounts were required for his guidance in making that investment; but it does not extend to the subsequent £200 which he made after he had been two months with the company. This distinction, that the duty only extends to the very transaction in mind at the time, is implicit in the decided cases.

Lord Bridge in Caparo

In *Caparo Industries plc v Dickman* [1990] 2 AC 605, Lord Bridge said (at p 620) that the salient feature of the relevant cases is:

... that the defendant giving advice or information was fully aware of the nature of the transaction which the plaintiff had in contemplation, knew that the advice or information would be communicated to him directly or indirectly and knew that it was very likely that the plaintiff would rely on that advice or information in deciding whether or not to engage in the transaction in contemplation. In these circumstances the defendant could clearly be expected, subject always to the effect of any disclaimer of responsibility, specifically to anticipate that the plaintiff would rely on the advice or information given by the defendant for the very purpose for which he did in the event rely on it. So also the plaintiff, subject again to the effect of any disclaimer, would in that situation reasonably suppose that he was entitled to rely on the advice or information communicated to him for the very purpose for which he required it. The situation is entirely different where a statement is put into more or less general circulation and may foreseeably be relied on by strangers to the making of the statement for any one of a variety of different purposes which the maker of the statement had no specific reason to anticipate. To hold the maker of the statement to be under a duty of care in respect of the accuracy of the statement to all and sundry for any purpose for which they may choose to rely on it is not only to subject him ... to 'liability in an indeterminate amount ... to an indeterminate class'; it is also to confer on the world at large a quite unwarranted entitlement to appropriate for their own purposes the benefit of the expert knowledge or professional expertise attributed to the maker of the statement.

Lord Bridge continued:

... in this category of the tort of negligence [the limit or control mechanism imposed on the liability of a wrongdoer to those who have suffered economic damage in consequence of his negligence rests] in the necessity to prove, as an essential ingredient of the 'proximity' between the plaintiff and the defendant, that the defendant knew that his statement would be communicated to the plaintiff, either as an individual or as a member of an identifiable class, specifically in connection with a particular transaction or transactions of a particular kind ... and that the plaintiff would be very likely to rely on it for the purpose of deciding whether or not to enter upon that transaction or upon a transaction of that kind.

Lord Oliver in Caparo

In *Caparo*, Lord Oliver summarised the applicable principles by saying (at p 638):

What can be deduced from the *Hedley Byrne* case, therefore, is that the necessary relationship between the maker of a statement or giver of advice ('the adviser') and the recipient who acts in reliance upon it ('the advisee') may typically be held to exist where (1) the advice is required for a purpose, whether particularly specified or generally described, which is made known, either actually or inferentially, to the adviser at the time when the advice is given; (2) the adviser knows, either actually or inferentially, that his advice will be communicated to the advisee either specifically or as a member of an ascertainable class, in order that it should be used by the advisee for that purpose; (3) it is known, either actually or inferentially, that the advice so communicated is likely to be acted upon by the advisee for that purpose without independent inquiry; and (4) it is so acted upon by the advisee to his detriment.

Lord Jauncey in Caparo

In *Caparo*, Lord Jauncey expressed these principles pithily when he said (at p 658):

> ... in each of the cases where a duty of care has been held to exist, the statement in question has, to the knowledge of its maker, been made available to the plaintiff for a particular purpose upon which he has relied. In the present case, the auditors, by accepting office, came under a statutory duty to make their report to members of the company. The crucial issue is the purpose for which the report was made.

To paraphrase the words of Denning LJ in *Candler*, the duty only extends to the 'very transaction' in mind at the time the statement was made.

Lord Bingham in Reeman

In *Reeman v The Department of Transport* (26 March 1997, unreported), Lord Bingham CJ provided a succinct formulation of some of the criteria that need to be considered, when he said:

> The cases show that before a plaintiff can recover compensation for financial loss caused by negligent misstatement his claim must meet a number of conditions. Among these, three are particularly relevant here. The statement (whether in the form of advice, an expression of opinion, a certificate or a factual statement) must be plaintiff-specific: that is, it must be given to the actual plaintiff or to a member of a group, identifiable at the time the statement is made, to which the actual plaintiff belongs. Secondly, the statement must be purpose-specific: the statement must be made for the very purpose for which the actual plaintiff has used it. Thirdly, and perhaps overlapping with the second condition, the statement must be transaction-specific: the statement must be made with reference to the very transaction into which the plaintiff has entered in reliance on it. If these conditions are met, it is necessary to turn to other conditions which the plaintiff must satisfy.

9.7 Illustrations from cases

9.7.1 Introduction

The cases discussed *below* demonstrate the practical application of the relevant principles in cases of negligent misstatement in accordance with the above-mentioned general formulation in certain of the leading cases. Where possible, the cases discussed are divided into categories according to the type of business with which the professional person making the negligent statement is involved. This division is made only for the sake of convenience and for the purpose of being able to distinguish similar cases. It must not be taken as indicating that there is, for example, one rule for accountants and another for surveyors. The general principles formulated *above* are equally applicable to all categories of professional people, and indeed to any person who, by virtue of his circumstances, was so placed with regard to the plaintiff and the loss which the plaintiff suffered that these general principles were brought into operation.

9.7.2 'Financial sphere' cases

General

The cases considered in this grouping are varied, but they share the common characteristic that the plaintiff has suffered economic loss through having invested money in the business of a third party as a result of having relied upon a statement by the defendant about the third party's financial stability, where the plaintiff and the defendant were not involved in a contractual relationship with each other.

Ultramares, Candler and Hedley Byrne

These cases are discussed fully *above* and need not be repeated here. Particular regard should be paid to Denning LJ's three-part test in his judgment in *Candler* (see para 9.6.2) because it has been adopted by the House of Lords (in *Caparo Industries plc v Dickman* [1990] 2 AC 605—see *below*) as accurately stating the applicable principles in this type of case.

Putting aside the question of the disclaimer in *Hedley Byrne*, one might, however, ask whether the result in that case would be the same today, because the defendant's inclusion of the statement "Your figures are larger than we are accustomed to see" in its reply (see para 9.4.2, *above*) should have put the plaintiff on further inquiry with the defendant before it extended substantial credit to E Ltd.

Mutual Life v Evatt

This case, *Mutual Life and Citizens' Assurance Co Ltd v Evatt* [1971] AC 793 (PC), is mentioned only for the sake of completeness, because the great profusion of decisions in a wide variety of different circumstances indicates that the restrictive principle which the Privy Council enunciated no longer holds good. The plaintiff, who was a policyholder in the defendant insurance company, claimed damages for the negligence of the company in giving him gratuitous information and advice on the financial stability of an associated company with the knowledge that he would act on that advice and invest in the associated company. The court dismissed his claim on the ground that the defendant's business did not include giving advice on investments and that it did not claim to have the necessary skill and competence to give such advice.

JEB v Bloom

This case, *JEB Fasteners Ltd v Marks, Bloom & Co* [1981] 3 All ER 289, can also be mentioned in passing. The plaintiff, who had made a successful takeover bid for a company in reliance on audited accounts which had been negligently prepared, sued the accountants for damages. The plaintiff succeeded. The judge, following *Anns v London Borough of Merton* [1978] AC 728, seems to have founded the duty of care on foreseeability alone. As pointed out in Chapter 2 (para 2.2), this is not a sufficient test; and, as noted in Chapter 3 (para 3.3) and 7 (para 7.3.1), *Anns* has been overruled. Nevertheless, in *Caparo Industries plc v Dickman* [1990] 2 AC 605, Lord

Bridge (at p 625), while disapproving of the judge's approach in *JEB*, was not prepared to say that the decision itself was wrong because he said that it might well be that the particular facts of the case "were sufficient to establish a basis on which the necessary ingredient of proximity to found a duty of care could be derived from the actual knowledge on the part of the auditors of the specific purpose for which the plaintiff intended to use the accounts".

Twomax v Dickson

This case, *Twomax Ltd v Dickson McFarlane & Robinson* [1983] SLT 98, can also be mentioned in passing, because on facts very similar to *JEB* the judge applied the same test (ie foreseeability alone) and held that a duty of care arose. Thus the same comments as made *above* in relation to *JEB* apply here.

Huxford v Stoy Hayward

In *Huxford & Others v Stoy Hayward & Co* [1989] 5 BCC 421, the plaintiffs were directors of a company which had gone into receivership on the advice of the defendant chartered accountants. The defendant had been engaged by the company as its financial adviser and, in that capacity, owed the company and the directors, who were its owners, a duty of care in contract to give careful advice and consideration as to whether the company should go into receivership. The plaintiffs were also guarantors of part of the company's indebtedness. When the company went into receivership, they were called upon to meet their obligations under their guarantees as the company was completely insolvent. They sought to recover these sums from the defendant on the ground that the defendant owed them a duty of care in tort to protect them from being called upon to meet their liabilities under the guarantees. The court rejected these claims, first, because, applying the above-stated applicable principles, there was no proximity between the defendant and the plaintiffs in their capacity as directors; and, secondly, because the plaintiffs' interests in their capacity as directors (to put the company into receivership if it would otherwise be trading wrongfully) conflicted with their interest as guarantors (to keep the company afloat). The judge (Popplewell J) thus distinguished *Trustee of the Property of P A F Foster v Crusts* [1986] BCLC 307, in which the interests of the guarantor and the company did not conflict, and said (at p 538): "It seems to me impossible for a defendant to owe a duty to a third party where the interests of that third party and the interest of the immediate object of the advice are not substantially coterminous".

Al Saudi Banque v Clarke Pixley

In *Al Saudi Banque and Others v Clarke Pixley (A firm)* [1990] 1 Ch 313, the plaintiffs consisted of ten banks which had lent money to a certain company to enable it to finance its business. The defendant was the company's auditor, who had certified that the financial statements gave a true and fair view of the company's affairs at the balance sheet date. The company was, however, insolvent at that time, and the advances made by the plaintiffs to it were wholly irrecoverable. The plaintiffs therefore sued the auditors, claiming that they had granted new facilities to the company or renewed existing facilities in reliance on the accuracy of the company's audited accounts and the defendant's reports thereon.

The court rejected the plaintiffs' claims, both in respect of those banks which only lent money to the company after the balance sheet date and those who were existing creditors at that time, and whose identity and exposure was therefore known to the defendant. Millett J said that foreseeability of reliance is not enough to create proximity. He said that, in addition, it has to be shown that the maker of the statement knew or intended that it would be relied upon for the transaction for which the plaintiff in fact did rely upon it; and the plaintiff must be a person or persons to whom the defendant actually made the statement or to whom he intended or knew it was to be communicated. Neither of these tests were satisfied here. Millett J said (at p 336):

> . . . the defendants did not make their reports to the plaintiff banks or to any other person with the intention or in the knowledge that they would be communicated to them. The most that can be said is that it was foreseeable that, if any of the plaintiff banks wish to consider the continuance or renewal of existing facilities or the grant of additional facilities, it might well call for copies of the company's latest audited accounts and rely upon them and the accompanying auditors' report.

Millett J compared the lending banks' position with that of shareholders and said (at p 336):

> [The banks] played no part in appointing the defendants as auditors. The defendants were under no statutory obligation to report to them and they did not do so. They did not supply copies of their reports to them, nor did they send them to the company with the intention or in the knowledge that they would be supplied to them. Clearly, to hold that a duty of care was owed to them would be going further than can be supported by any existing English authority.

This decision was expressly approved of by the House of Lords in *Caparo Industries plc v Dickman* [1990] 2 AC 605 (see *below*).

Bank of Scotland v 3i plc

In *The Governor and Company of the Bank of Scotland v 3i plc* [1990] SC 215, the plaintiff had acted as bankers to a certain company in providing overdraft and banking facilities to afford working capital to that company. The plaintiff did not, however, participate in the equity or venture capital funding of the company. This was done by the defendant. Having become concerned about the company's financial position, the plaintiff told the company that its further support of the company was dependent upon the company obtaining a further injection of capital. The company proposed to do this by issuing a large sum of convertible loan stock. During a telephone conversation between an employee of the plaintiff and a senior employee of the defendant, who was also a director of the company, the latter stated that funds to provide a substantial proportion of the convertible loan stock "were committed" and that any balance would be underwritten by the defendant. In reliance on this statement the plaintiff provided bridging finance to the company by increasing its overdraft. In due course it became apparent that this funding was not to be made available. In consequence the company's financial position became untenable and it went into receivership.

The plaintiff was not able to recover any of the monies which it had advanced to the company. It sought to recover from the defendant the additional monies which it had advanced to the company after the above-mentioned telephone conversation. The court upheld the plaintiff's claim. The judge said that in the recognised vocabulary of venture capital financing, the use of the word 'committed' had the meaning that the funding was available on the basis of legal obligation. There was direct contact between the negligent provider of information and the plaintiff. It was reasonable for the plaintiff to seek that information from the defendant, who had information relating to the arrangements to support the company's convertible loan stock issue which the plaintiff did not have. The knowledge by the plaintiff and the defendant of each other's interest in the company was such as to enable the court to conclude that the defendant knew or ought to have known that the plaintiff was relying on the information which the defendant had provided in deciding whether or not to provide additional temporary bridging finance to the company by way of an increase in its overdraft.

Caparo v Dickman

In *Caparo Industries plc v Dickman* [1990] 2 AC 605, the plaintiff had bought some shares on the stock market in a particular public company after the price had fallen dramatically following the directors' announcement of the results, which revealed that the profits were well below prediction. The accounts had been audited by the defendant and had been approved by the directors on the day before the results were announced. Subsequently the plaintiff received a copy of the audited accounts and, in reliance on the information contained therein, made further purchases of shares in the market, and eventually made a full takeover bid for the company. In due course it emerged that the accounts were inaccurate and misleading, in that the apparent pre-tax profits of £1.3m should have been shown as a loss of more than £400,000. The plaintiff alleged that, had the true facts been known, it would not have made a bid for the company at the price paid or at all.

The plaintiff alleged that the defendant, as the company's auditors, owed a duty of care to investors and potential investors, and in particular to the plaintiff, in respect of the audit and certification of the company's accounts, by virtue of the fact that the defendant knew that the company required financial assistance and was therefore vulnerable to a takeover bid and that persons such as the plaintiff might well rely on the accounts for the purpose of deciding whether to take over the company, and might well suffer loss if the accounts were inaccurate.

The House of Lords rejected the plaintiff's claims, both in regard to its position as a potential investor, and in regard to its position as an actual shareholder when it was sent a copy of the accounts and relied on them specifically. One of the main speeches was delivered by Lord Bridge. After referring extensively to some of the other cases that are considered in this chapter, such as *Hedley Byrne, Candler* and *Smith v Bush*, Lord Bridge said (at p 620) (syntax slightly altered and emphasis added):

> The salient feature of all of these cases is that the defendant giving advice or information—
> (i) was *fully aware* of the nature of the transaction which the plaintiff had in contemplation;
> (ii) knew that the advice or information *would be* communicated to him directly or indirectly; and
> (iii) knew that it was *very likely* that the plaintiff would rely on that advice or information in deciding whether or not to engage in the transaction in contemplation.
>
> In these circumstances, the defendant could *clearly* be expected, subject always to the effect of any disclaimer of responsibility, *specifically* to anticipate that the plaintiff would rely on the advice or information given by the defendant *for the very purpose* for which he did in the event rely on it. So also the plaintiff, subject again to the effect of any disclaimer, would in that situation reasonably suppose that he was entitled to rely on the advice or information communicated to him *for the very purpose* for which he required it. The situation is entirely different where a statement is put into more or less general circulation and may foreseeably be relied on by strangers to the maker of the statement for any one of a *variety of different purposes* which the maker of the statement has no specific reason to anticipate.

Further down in his speech, Lord Bridge reformulated this principle in slightly different language by saying (at p 621):

> ... looking only at the ... decided cases where a duty of care in respect of negligent statements ... has been held to exist, I should expect to find that the 'limit or control mechanism ... imposed upon the liability of a wrongdoer towards those who have suffered economic damage in consequence of his negligence' [see *Candlewood Navigation Corporation Ltd v Mitsui OSK Lines Ltd* [1986] AC 1— see Chapter 1, para 1.4.2] rested in the necessity to prove, in this category of the tort of negligence, as an essential ingredient of the 'proximity' between the plaintiff and the defendant, that the defendant *knew*—
> (i) that his statement would be communicated to the plaintiff, either as an individual or as a member of an identifiable class;
> (ii) *specifically* in connection with a *particular* transaction or transactions of a particular kind (eg, in a prospectus inviting investment); and
> (iii) that the plaintiff would be *very likely* to rely on it for the purpose of deciding whether or not to enter upon *that* transaction or upon a transaction of that kind.
>
> I find this expectation fully supported by the dissenting judgment of Denning LJ in *Candler v Crane, Christmas and Co* [1951] 2 KB 164 in the following passages ...

Lord Bridge then set out in full the three-step analysis of Denning LJ in *Candler*, which is also to be found in para 9.6.2, *above*, and said that he was adopting Denning LJ's analysis because it was particularly apt as a guide in the present case.

Lord Bridge concluded that the above-mentioned considerations amply justify the conclusion that auditors of a public company's accounts owe no duty of care to members of the public at large who rely upon the accounts in deciding to buy shares in the company. That disposed of the first part of the plaintiff's claim that the defendant auditors owed the plaintiff a duty of care with regard to the tranche of shares that the plaintiff bought following the directors' announcement, based on the company's audited accounts, that the company's profits were below expectation.

Lord Bridge then dealt with the second part of the plaintiff's claim, namely, that once the plaintiff had purchased the first tranche of shares and had become a shareholder, the auditors did owe the plaintiff a duty of care because the plaintiff was no longer an unidentified member of the public but was a member of an identifiable class which stood in a relationship of proximity with the company's auditors. Lord Bridge rejected this claim, and he said that his view would be the same if one were to assume, in the plaintiff's favour, that the auditors ought to have foreseen that there was a high probability of a takeover bid being made in reliance on the company's accounts which the auditors had just recently certified as showing a true and fair view of the company's state of affairs. In this regard, Lord Bridge adopted the reasoning of Richmond P, dissenting, in *Scott Group Ltd v MacFarlane* [1978] 1 NZLR 553 (see para 9.9.4, *below*) as follows (emphasis added):

> All of the speeches in *Hedley Byrne* seem to recognise the need for a 'special' relationship: a relationship which can properly be treated as giving rise to a special duty to use care in statement. The question in any given case is whether the nature of the relationship is such that one party can fairly be held to have assumed a responsibility to the other as regards the liability of the advice or information. I do not think that such a relationship should be found to exist unless, at least, the maker of the statement was, or ought to have been, aware that his advice or information would *in fact* be made available to and be relied on by a *particular* person or class of persons for the *purposes* of a *particular* transaction or type of transaction. . . . it does not seem reasonable to attribute an assumption of responsibility unless the maker of the statement ought in all the circumstances . . . to have directed his mind . . . to some *particular* and *specific* purpose for which he was *aware* that his advice or information *would be* relied on. In many situations that purpose will be obvious. But the annual accounts of a company can be relied on in all sorts of ways and *for many purposes*.

Lord Bridge then considered the position of auditors in relation to the shareholders of a public company. He noted that one of the auditor's functions is to report to the shareholders in general meeting whether, in the auditor's opinion, the company's accounts give a true and fair view of the company's financial position, and he noted that this undoubtedly established a relationship between the auditors and the shareholders of a company on which an individual shareholder is entitled to rely for the protection of his interest. However, Lord Bridge said that this did not necessarily mean that a duty of care was owed in law by a public company's auditors to individual shareholders for investment decisions that they might make in reliance on the company's audited accounts. He said (at p 626):

> ... the crucial question concerns the extent [or the 'scope'] of the shareholder's interest which the auditor has a duty to protect. The shareholders of a company have a collective interest in the company's proper management and, in so far as a negligent failure of the auditor to report accurately on the state of the company's finances deprives the shareholders of the opportunity to exercise their powers in general meeting to call the directors to book, and to ensure that errors in management are corrected, the shareholders ought to be entitled to a remedy. But in practice no problem arises in this regard since the interest of the shareholders in the proper management of the company's affairs is indistinguishable from the interest of the company itself and any loss suffered by the shareholders eg, by the negligent failure of the auditor to discover and expose a misappropriation of funds by a director of the company, will be recouped by a claim against the auditors in the name of the company, not by individual shareholders.

Thus, even if there was a 'proximate' relationship between the auditors and the shareholders, resulting in some sort of a *prima facie* duty of care, that supposition was negated by the fact that any loss that the plaintiff, as a shareholder, might have incurred in its capacity as an investor, as opposed to its capacity as a shareholder exerting shareholders' rights in a general meeting, was outside the scope of the duty of care that arises when auditors of a public company certify that, in their opinion, the company's accounts present a true and fair view of the company's financial position. In this connection, Lord Bridge said (at p 627):

> It is never sufficient to ask simply whether A owes B a duty of care. It is always necessary to determine the scope of the duty by reference to the kind of damage from which A must take care to save B harmless [see further, Chapter 2, para 2.1.5]. . . . Assuming for the purpose of argument that the relationship between the auditor of a company and its individual shareholders is of sufficient proximity to give rise to a duty of care, I do not understand how the scope of that duty can possibly extend beyond the protection of any individual shareholder from losses in the value of the shares which he holds. As a purchaser of additional shares in reliance on the auditor's report, he stands in no different position from any other investing member of the public to whom the auditor owes no duty.

The second main speech was delivered by Lord Oliver. He, too, saw that the question of the auditor's possible duty of care towards the plaintiff in respect of the second tranche of shares that the plaintiff had bought (ie as an existing shareholder who had received the auditor's report and had placed specific reliance on it) boiled down to determining the proper scope of the auditor's duty of care. He said (at p 630):

> . . . if and so far as the purpose for which the audit was carried out is a relevant consideration in determining the extent [or the scope] of any general duty in tort owed by [the defendant] to persons other than the company which is their immediate employer, that purpose was simply that of fulfilling the statutory requirements of the Companies Act 1985. That, in turn, raises the question . . . of what is the purpose behind the legislative requirement for the carrying out of an annual audit and the circulation of the accounts. For whose protection were these provisions enacted, and what object were they intended to achieve?

Lord Oliver then analysed the purpose of the statutory requirement for an annual audit and reached the same conclusion as Lord Bridge, namely, to provide shareholders with reliable information for the purpose of enabling them to scrutinise the conduct of the company's affairs by the company's directors and officers, and to exercise their collective powers in a general meeting to reward, control or remove errant directors. Lord Oliver rejected the submission that there is to be discerned in the legislation an additional or wider commercial purpose, namely, that of enabling those to whom the accounts are addressed and circulated to make informed investment decisions. Lord Oliver conceded that it is reasonably foreseeable that the accounts might well be relied on for such purposes, but he said that he found it difficult to believe that the legislature, in enacting provisions clearly aimed primarily at the protection of the company and at its informed control by the body of its proprietors/shareholders, could have been inspired also by consideration for the public at large and investors in the market in particular.

Lord Oliver then considered the speeches in *Hedley Byrne* in some detail and stated the relevant applicable principles in this type of case as follows (at p 638):

> . . . the necessary relationship between the maker of a statement or giver of advice ('the adviser') and the recipient who acts in reliance upon it ('the advisee') may typically be held to exist where—
> (1) the advice is required for a *purpose*, whether particularly specified or generally described, which is made *known*, either actually or inferentially, to the adviser at the time when the advice is given;
> (2) the adviser *knows*, either actually or inferentially, that his advice *will be* communicated to the advisee, either *specifically* or as a member of an ascertainable class, *in order* that it should *be used* by the advisee *for that purpose*;
> (3) it is *known*, either actually or inferentially, that the advice so communicated is *likely* to be *acted upon* by the advisee *for that purpose without independent inquiry*; and
> (4) it is so acted upon by the advisee to his detriment.

Lest he might be accused of purporting to lay down a general formula for use in all cases, Lord Oliver added the following qualification: "That is not, of course, to suggest that these conditions are either conclusive or exclusive, but merely that the actual decision in this case does not warrant any broader propositions".

Not surprisingly, the plaintiff placed heavy reliance on the House of

Lords' decision in *Smith v Eric S Bush* [1990] 1 AC 831 (see para 9.7.3). However, Lord Oliver was easily able to distinguish that case from the present. He said (at p 642):

> No decision of this House has gone further than *Smith v Eric S Bush*, but your Lordships are asked by the plaintiff to widen the area of responsibility and to find a relationship of proximity between the adviser and third parties to whose attention the advice may come in circumstances in which the reliance said to have given rise to the loss is strictly unrelated either to the intended recipient or to the purpose for which the advice was required. My Lords, I discern no pressing reason of policy which would require such an extension, and there seem to me to be powerful reasons against it. It is almost always foreseeable that someone may choose to alter his position upon the faith of the accuracy of a statement or report which comes to his attention, and it is always foreseeable that a report—even a confidential report—may come to be communicated to persons other than the original or intended recipient. To apply as a test of liability only the foreseeability of possible damage without some further control would be to create a liability wholly indefinite in area, duration and amount, and would open up a limitless vista of uninsurable risk for the professional man.

Lord Oliver dismissed the plaintiff's submission that a duty of care existed in the plaintiff's favour as a takeover bidder by virtue of the fact that the auditors ought reasonably to have foreseen that their audit report, attached to the company's disappointing accounts, made the company susceptible to a takeover bid, by saying (at p 649):

> ... I can see nothing in the statutory duties of a company's auditor to suggest that [those duties] were intended by Parliament to protect the interests of investors in the market and I can see no reason in policy or in principle why it should be either desirable or appropriate that the ambit of the special relationship required to give rise to liability in cases such as the present should be extended beyond those limits which are deducible from the cases of *Hedley Byrne* and *Smith v Eric S Bush* [see *above*]. Those limits appear to me to be correctly stated in the judgment of Richmond P in the *Scott Group* case [see *above*]. .... In particular, I can see no reason why any special relationship should be held to arise simply from the circumstance that the affairs of the company are such as to render it susceptible to the attention of predators in the market who may be interested in acquiring all or the majority of the shares, rather than merely a parcel of shares by way of addition to a portfolio.

Lord Oliver then dealt separately with the plaintiff's contention that, after he had purchased his first tranche of shares, his position in relation to subsequent purchases was different to ordinary members of the public. The Court of Appeal in this case upheld this distinction, but the House of Lords rejected it. Lord Oliver said (at p 650):

> It cannot be that this event [ie, becoming a shareholder] created for the plaintiffs any new or greater risk of harm in relation to a certification [by the auditors] which had already taken place. The only difference in their position before registration and their position afterwards was that, as registered shareholders, they now had the statutory right to receive the accounts on which they had already relied in acquiring their original shares, and to receive notice of, and attend the

annual general meeting at which the accounts were to be read and, if thought fit, approved and passed. This change of position is less than momentous.

If a distinction is to be found at all, therefore, it can only be that the nature and purpose of the statutory provisions governing the appointment and duties of auditors and the certification and publication to shareholders and others of the accounts have the effect of creating, between the auditors and individual shareholders, as potential investors in that capacity, that special relationship of proximity which is required to give rise to a duty of care and which does not exist between auditors and the investing public generally. If it be right, as I believe that it is, that no relationship of proximity, and thus no duty of care exists between auditors and the investing public generally in relation to the statutory audit—the attribution of such a duty arising from the receipt of exactly the same information by a person who happens to be the registered holder of a share in the company whose accounts are in question produces entirely capricious results.

Interestingly, Lord Oliver did qualify the last-cited *dictum* by saying that he was not ruling out the possibility of a duty of care arising where the company's accounts have been audited specifically for the purpose of submission to a potential investor.

The plaintiff's counsel submitted that a high degree of proximity does exist between the auditors of a public company and its shareholders, because the auditors' remuneration is paid out of funds which might otherwise be available for distribution to shareholders by way of dividend, the auditors are under a duty to report to the shareholders whether the company's accounts present a true and fair view of the company's financial position, and their report is sent to each shareholder as an identifiable individual. This submission raised, again, the importance of the necessity to determine the scope, ambit, or extent of any claimed duty of care before the defendant can be made liable for the plaintiff's actual loss. Lord Oliver dealt with this submission by saying (at p 651):

> Of course, I see the force of this, but 'proximity' in cases such as this is an expression used, not necessarily as indicating literally 'closeness' in a physical or metaphorical sense, but merely as a convenient label to describe circumstances from which the law will attribute a duty of care. It has to be borne in mind that the duty of care is inseparable from the damage which the plaintiff claims to have suffered from its breach. It is not a duty to take care in the abstract, but a duty to avoid causing to the particular plaintiff damage of the particular kind which he has in fact sustained [see further, Chapter 2, para 2.1.5].
>
> In seeking to ascertain whether there should be imposed on the adviser a duty to avoid the occurrence of the kind of damage which the advisee claims to have suffered, it is not sufficient to ask simply whether there existed a 'closeness' between them in the sense that the advisee had a legal entitlement to receive the information upon the basis of which he has acted, or in the sense that the information was intended to serve his interests or to protect him. One must go further and ask, in what capacity was his interest to be served and from what was he intended to be protected?
>
> A company's annual accounts are capable of being utilised for a number of purposes, and it is entirely foreseeable that they may be so employed. But many of those purposes will have absolutely no connection with the recipient's status

or capacity, whether as a shareholder or as a debenture-holder. Before it can be concluded that the duty is imposed to protect the recipient against harm which he suffers by reason of the particular use that he chooses to make of the information which he receives, one must first ascertain the purpose for which the information is required to be given.

If the conclusion is reached that the very purpose of providing the information is to serve as the basis for making investment decisions or giving investment advice, it is not difficult then to conclude also that the duty imposed upon the adviser extends to protecting the recipient against loss occasioned by an unfortunate investment decision which is based on carelessly inaccurate information.

Lord Oliver then considered once again the purposes of the statutory requirement for an annual audit and for the auditors' report to be provided to shareholders, and continued by saying (at p 653):

I do not believe, and I can see no grounds for belief that, in enacting the statutory provisions, Parliament had in mind the provision of information for the assistance of purchasers of shares or debentures in the market, whether they be already the holders of shares or other securities, or persons having no previous proprietary interest in the company. The statutory duty owed by auditors to shareholders is, I think, a duty owed to them as a body. The purpose for which the auditors' certificate is made and published is that of providing those entitled to receive the report with information to enable them to exercise in conjunction [ie, as a group] those powers which their respective proprietary interests confer on them, and not for the purposes of individual speculation with a view to profit.

To widen the scope of the duty to include loss caused to an individual by reliance upon the accounts for a purpose for which they were not supplied and were not intended, would be to extend it beyond the limits which are so far deducible from the decisions of this House.

Lord Jauncey, in a concurring speech, also highlighted the fact that the real issue to be determined was the scope of the auditors' liability. He said (at p 655):

Once foreseeability of likely harm from a careless statement has been established, it becomes necessary to examine the circumstances in, and the purposes for, which the statement was made in order to determine whether there are also present the further ingredients necessary to establish the requisite proximity of relationship between the maker of the statement and the person who acted upon it. If, in any given circumstances, a relationship of proximity is found to exist, consideration must still be given to the scope of the duty which arises therefrom. In the case of physical proximity, few problems will arise, but where there exists a duty of care in relation to the making of statements, problems may arise if those statements are capable of being used for more than one purpose. It is not disputed in the present case that economic loss to the plaintiff as a shareholder was foreseeable by the auditors as a result of any failure on their part to exercise reasonable care in the conduct of the audit. What is disputed is whether the auditors owed any duty to individual shareholders, and, if so, what was the scope of that duty.

In setting out to answer these questions, Lord Jauncey laid particular emphasis on Denning LJ's judgment in *Candler v Crane, Christmas and Co*

[1951] 2 KB 164 (see para 9.6.2, *above*) and observed (at p 657): "Denning LJ clearly considered that the scope of any duty of care was limited to the precise transaction for which the accountants knew that the accounts were to be used". Lord Jauncey then considered certain *dicta* in *Hedley Byrne* and *Smith v Bush* and then stated (at p 658):

> . . . in each of these cases where a duty of care has been held to exist, the state-ment in question has, to the *knowledge* of its *maker*, been made available to the plaintiff *for a particular purpose* upon which he has relied. In the present case, the auditors, by accepting office, came under a statutory duty to make their report to the members of the company. The crucial issue is the *purpose* for which the report was made. To quote the words of Denning LJ in the *Candler* case, what was the 'very transaction' for which [the report] was provided? To answer this question, it is necessary to look at the relevant provisions of the Companies Act 1985.

Lord Jauncey then set out in detail the relevant provisions of the Act, and reached the same conclusion as Lord Oliver and Lord Bridge (see *above*). He continued by saying (at p 660):

> It is inevitable that auditors will be aware that their reports will be seen and relied upon by the company's members. However, that does not answer the funda-mental question of the purpose, and hence the very transactions, for which the annual accounts of a company are prepared and distributed to its members.
>
> Possibility of reliance on a statement for an unspecified purpose will not impose a duty of care on the maker to the addressee. More is required. In *Smith v Eric S Bush* [1990] 1 AC 831, it was probable, if not highly probable, that the potential purchaser would rely on the valuer's report. This probable reliance was an essential ingredient in establishing proximity. Had it been merely a possibil-ity that the purchaser would rely on the report, I very much doubt that this House would have decided that the valuer owed a duty of care to the purchaser. Furthermore, reliance, even if probable, thereby establishing proximity, does not establish a duty of care of unlimited scope. Regard must be had to the transac-tion or transactions for the *purpose* of which the statement was made.
>
> Part VII of the Companies Act 1985 provides that the accounts of a company for each financial year shall be laid before the company's members in general meeting. Copies of the accounts must be sent to the members at least twenty-one days in advance. It is obvious that the reason for this is to enable the members to prepare themselves for attendance at, and participation in the meeting. The annual general meeting provides the opportunity for members to question the stewardship of the company during the preceding year, to vote for or against election or re-election of members, to approve or disapprove the appointment or re-appointment of auditors and to make other decisions affecting the company as a whole or themselves as members of a particular class of shareholders. There is nothing in Part VII which suggests that the accounts are prepared and sent to members for any purpose other than to enable them to exercise class rights in general meeting. Advice to individual shareholders in rela-tion to present or future investment in the company is no part of the statutory purpose of the preparation and distribution of the accounts.

For these reasons, Lord Jauncey, too, rejected the plaintiff's claim that a duty of care was owed to the plaintiff as a shareholder in connection with the losses that the plaintiff, in that capacity, suffered by making investments in the company based on the company's audited accounts. Lord Jauncey was, however, prepared to countenance the possibility that a duty of care could arise in favour of a shareholder *qua* investor in appropriate circumstances. He said (at p 662):

> If the statutory accounts are prepared and distributed for certain limited purposes, can there nevertheless be imposed upon auditors an additional common law duty to individual shareholders who choose to use them for another purpose without the prior knowledge of the auditors? The answer must be 'No'. Use for that other purpose would no longer be use for the 'very transaction' which Denning LJ in the *Candler* case regarded as determinative of the scope of any duty of care. Only where the auditor was aware that the individual shareholder was likely to rely on the accounts for a particular purpose, such as his present or future investment in, or lending to, the company, would a duty of care arise. Such a situation does not obtain in the present case.

Al-Nakib v Longcroft

In *Al-Nakib Investments (Jersey) Ltd v Longcroft and Others* [1990] 1 WLR 1390, the defendants were directors of a company which had published a prospectus to raise money for the company's business. Various claims were made in the prospectus about the company's activities and interests. In reliance on these statements, the plaintiff, who was already a substantial shareholder, subscribed for the number of shares to which it was entitled under the allotment scheme in the prospectus. The plaintiff also bought further shares on the stock exchange in reliance on the prospectus. In due course it materialised that these statements were untrue and misleading. The plaintiff sued the company and the directors for its loss.

The defendants did not contest the plaintiff's claims in respect of the shares allotted to it as an existing shareholder in accordance with the prospectus formula, because s 67 of the Companies Act 1985 expressly covers this situation. They did, however, contest the remainder of the plaintiff's claims, for the losses which it suffered on the additional shares which it purchased in the market place. The court upheld the defendants' contentions in this regard. The judge, Mervyn Davies J, said that, as the prospectus had been issued specifically to enable shareholders to consider the rights offer, the duty of care owed by the defendants to the plaintiff for that purpose did not extend to a situation where reliance was placed on the prospectus for a different purpose, namely the buying of shares in the market, about which the defendants did not know or could not reasonably have been expected to have known.

In so holding, Mervyn Davies J was clearly influenced by the decision of the House of Lords in *Caparo*, which had been delivered less than three months previously. After referring to the speeches of Lords Bridge and Jauncey in *Caparo*, he said (at p 1397): "Those words show that a duty of care is not fastened onto a situation when a statement has been made for a particular purpose and the statement is used for another purpose".

The plaintiff focused on the part of Lord Bridge's speech in *Caparo* in which Lord Bridge gave the example of a "prospectus inviting investment" as a situation in which sufficient proximity might exist to impose a duty of care on the maker of a statement (see *above*). Mervyn Davies J said that this did not assist the plaintiff in the present case. Having noted that the prospectus in the present case was indeed a prospectus that invited investment, he said (at p 1398):

> However, one still has to consider whether the prospectus which Lord Bridge had in mind invites buying in the market or in the way of taking up a rights issue. I see no encouragement to buy in the market contained in the words of the prospectus [in the present case], which opens: 'Application has been made to the Stock Exchange for the grant of permission to deal in the ordinary shares of Mnemos on the Unlisted Securities Market.' . . .

The plaintiff also submitted that the present case was different from *Caparo* because it dealt with a prospectus, as opposed to an auditor's report. Mervyn Davies J rejected this contention by saying (at p 1398):

> The documents, of course, do differ, but the question whether statements in a document give rise to liability is the same whatever may be the nature of the document; that is, was the document written for a particular purpose and to be communicated to a particular person or class of persons.

The question 'What is a sufficiently proximate relationship?' is to be answered by considering by whom, and to whom, the advice is given.

> In my view, the defendants did not owe to the plaintiff a duty of care in respect of transactions 2 to 6, in that the prospectus . . . having been addressed to the plaintiff for a particular purpose (ie, considering the rights issue), was used by the plaintiff for another purpose (ie, buying shares in the market).

It is worth noting that in *Possfund Custodian Trustee Ltd v Diamond* [1996] 1 WLR 1351 (see *below*), Lightman J doubted the correctness of Mervyn Davies J's decision in the present case.

McNaughton v Hicks Anderson

In *James McNaughton Paper Group Ltd v Hicks Anderson & Co* [1991] 2 QB 113, while negotiations were taking place for the takeover of a certain company by the plaintiff, the company instructed the defendant, its accountants, to prepare accounts. The defendant duly submitted the accounts, as 'final drafts', to the company. The defendant knew that the plaintiff was a likely purchaser of the company, that the accounts would be shown to the plaintiff and that the plaintiff was placing reliance on them as part of its decision-making process in the takeover negotiations. The accounts showed a net loss of £48,000. At a meeting on 7 September 1982 between the plaintiff and the company, attended by the defendant, the defendant, in reply to a question by the plaintiff, said that the company was "breaking even or doing marginally worse".

The plaintiff duly completed the takeover of the company. Subsequently it emerged that the company's position was far worse than shown in the draft accounts. The plaintiff sought to recover its loss from the defendant.

The Court of Appeal rejected the plaintiff's claim. After reviewing some of the important decisions considered in this chapter, such as *Hedley Byrne*, *Smith v Bush* and *Caparo*, Neill LJ said (at p 125):

From this scrutiny, it seems to me to be clear—
  (a) that in contrast to developments in the law in New Zealand, of which the decision in *Scott Group Ltd v McFarlane* [1978] 1 NZLR 553 provides an important illustration [see para 9.9.4], in England a restrictive approach is now adopted to any extension of the scope of the duty of care beyond the person directly intended by the maker of the statement to act upon it; and
  (b) that, in deciding whether a duty of care exists in any particular case, it is necessary to take all of the circumstances into account; but
  (c) that, notwithstanding (b), it is possible to identify certain matters which are likely to be of importance in most cases in reaching a decision as to whether or not a duty exists.

Neill LJ then proceeded, under a series of headings, to set out the matters which he perceived to be likely to be of importance in most cases. In so doing, he acknowledged that the headings involved a substantial measure of overlap. Thus, he said that the matters are:

(1) The purpose for which the statement was made
In some cases, the statement will have been prepared or made by the adviser for the express purpose of being communicated to the advisee. In such a case, it may often be right to conclude that the advisee was within the scope of the duty of care. In many cases, however, the statement will have been prepared or made, or primarily prepared or made, for a different purpose and for the benefit of someone other than the advisee. In such cases, it will be necessary to look carefully at the precise purpose for which the statement was communicated to the advisee.

(2) The purpose for which the statement was communicated
Under this heading, it will be necessary to consider the purpose of, and the circumstances surrounding, the communication. Was the communication made for information only? Was it made for some action to be taken and, if so, what action, and by whom? Who requested the information to be made? These are some of the questions which have to be addressed.

(3) The relationship between the adviser, the advisee and any relevant third party
Where the statement was made or prepared in the first instance to or for the benefit of someone other than the advisee, it will be necessary to consider the relationship between the parties. Thus, it may be that the advisee is likely to look to the third party and, through him, to the adviser for advice or guidance; or the advisee may be wholly independent and in a position to make any necessary judgments himself.

(4) The size of any class to which the advisee belongs
Where there is a single advisee or he is a member of only a small class, it may sometimes be simple to infer that a duty of care was owed to him. Membership of a large class, however, may make such an inference more difficult, particularly where the statement was made in the first instance for someone outside the class.

(5) The state of knowledge of the adviser

The precise state of knowledge of the adviser is one of the most important matters to examine. Thus, it will be necessary to consider his knowledge of the purpose for which the statement was made or required in the first place, and also his knowledge of the purpose for which the statement was communicated to the advisee. In this context, knowledge includes not only actual knowledge, but also such knowledge as would be attributed to a reasonable person in the circumstances in which the adviser was placed. On the other hand, any duty of care will be limited to transactions or types of transactions in which the adviser had knowledge, and will only arise where the adviser knows or ought to know that the statement or advice will be relied upon by a particular person or class of persons in connection with that transaction.

It is also necessary to consider whether the adviser knew that the advisee would rely on the statement without obtaining independent advice.

(6) Reliance by the advisee

In cases where the existence of a duty of care is an issue, it is always useful to examine the matter from the point of view of the plaintiff. The question: 'Who is my neighbour?' prompts the response: 'Consider first those who would consider you to be their neighbour.' One should therefore consider whether, and to what extent, the advisee was entitled to rely on the statement to take the action that he did. It is also necessary to consider whether he did in fact rely on the statement, whether he did use, or should have used, his own judgment and whether he did seek, or should have sought, independent advice. In business transactions conducted at arms' length, it may sometimes be difficult for an advisee to prove that he was entitled to act on a statement without taking any independent advice, or to prove that the adviser knew, actually or inferentially, that he would act without taking such advice.

Neill LJ, with whose judgment the other two Lord Justices of Appeal concurred, held that an application of the above-mentioned test led to the conclusion that it would not be fair, just and reasonable to impose a duty of care on the accountants for the plaintiff's loss. In this regard, he said that he was particularly impressed by the following matters:

(1) the person who requested the accounts to be prepared was the chairman of the target company ('MK') and not the takeover bidder (the plaintiff);

(2) the accounts, when produced, were merely draft accounts. In the context of this case, this was an important point because the term 'draft' showed that further work was required before the accounts became final accounts. Accordingly, Mr McNaughton (the plaintiff's chairman) was not entitled to treat them as though they were final accounts, and Mr Pritchard (the relevant accountant in the defendant firm of accountants) could not be expected to foresee that Mr McNaughton would so treat them;

(3) although Mr Pritchard attended the meeting on 7 September 1982 and wrote a letter on that date to Mr McNaughton, there was no evidence that he took any other part in the negotiations leading to the takeover;

(4) the accounts showed that there was a loss for the year ended 30 June

1982 of about £48,000. MK was plainly in a poor state, and Mr McNaughton should have been in no doubt about that;

(5) this was a transaction between experienced businessmen. It was to be anticipated that Mr McNaughton would have access to, and would consult with, his own accountancy advisers. Mr Pritchard and the defendant were MK's accountants; and

(6) the answer given by Mr Pritchard to Mr McNaughton at the meeting on 7 September 1982 was a very general answer and did not affect any of the specific figures in the draft accounts. Moreover, it was not possible to attribute to Mr Pritchard the knowledge that Mr McNaughton would rely on this answer *without any further inquiry or advice* for the purpose of reaching a concluded agreement with the vendor (emphasis in the reported decision).

Balcombe LJ adopted everything that Neill LJ said in his judgment, and added (at p 129):

> The fact that these were draft accounts and that there was no reason for Mr Pritchard to suppose that Mr McNaughton would not consult his own accountants are most material factors in considering the existence of a duty of care in relation to the accounts. The answer to the question at the meeting of September 7, 1982 must be considered in the light of the fact that Mr Pritchard knew that Mr McNaughton had seen the draft accounts showing a loss of £48,000 for the year ended June 30, 1982. Accordingly, it is impossible to attribute to Mr Pritchard the knowledge that Mr McNaughton would rely on this answer without any further inquiry or advice.

Comment

In *Machin v Adams* (7 May 1997, unreported, CA), the facts of which are set out in para 9.7.8, *below*, Sir Brian Neill (previously Neill LJ, now retired), in delivering the judgment of the majority, said:

> In my judgment in *James McNaughton Paper Group Ltd v Hicks Anderson & Co* [1991] 2 QB 113 I attempted to set out some of the factors to be taken into account in considering whether a duty of care exists [see *above*]. This case [*Machin v Adams*] has demonstrated, however, that my analysis in that case was incomplete, and that the matter requires to be looked at again.

Sir Brian Neill's list of relevant factors in the *McNaughton* case was no more than a reformulation, in slightly different language, of the criteria and the boundaries laid down by the House of Lords in *Caparo*; and Sir Brian Neill himself did not claim otherwise at the time. Therefore, what Sir Brian Neill is effectively saying in *Machin v Adams* is that the *Caparo* criteria (which are set out in para 9.6.2, *above*) need to be looked at again. In carrying through this exercise, Sir Brian Neill in the present case referred to the concept of 'assumption of responsibility' (see *above*) and concluded that, in order to establish liability against the adviser in a case like the present, "the advisee must show *some connecting thread* between the *task* the adviser has undertaken to perform and the *course of action* upon which the advisee can be foreseen to be *likely to embark*".

It is not entirely clear what Sir Brian Neill had in mind, but it is submitted that the concept that he articulated is very similar to the principle that underlies the House of Lords' decision in *Smith v Eric S Bush* [1990] 1 AC 831, namely, that it is permissible to impose a duty of care on a defendant in respect of action taken by the plaintiff in reliance on the defendant's valuation of a property in a valuation report made by the defendant to a third party if, in all the circumstances, the defendant ought to have realised that such reliance, without any further independent inquiry or investigation, was, on the evidence, "very likely" (see para 9.7.3, *above*). Lord Jauncey expressed the point pithily when he said (at p 872): "Knowledge, actual or implied, of the mortgagor's likely reliance on the valuation must be brought home to him [the valuer]".

In the context of the circumstances of *Machin v Adams*, it is submitted that Sir Brian Neill was right to suggest that the established criteria for determining whether a duty of care should exist in negligent misstatement cases appear to be unsatisfactory. Indeed, in *Caparo*, Lord Oliver, in enunciating his four-part test, himself said (at p 638): "That is not, of course, to suggest that these conditions are either conclusive or exclusive, but merely that the actual decision in the case [*Caparo*] does not warrant any broader propositions". However, as noted *above*, it would seem that the additional (or, in fact, alternative) 'connecting thread and likely foreseeability' formulation suggested by Sir Brian Neill in *Machin v Adams* does not in fact take the position any further.

Morgan Crucible v Hill Samuel

In *Morgan Crucible Co plc v Hill Samuel & Co Ltd* [1991] Ch 295, the plaintiff had been involved in a contested bid for a certain public company, which was being advised by the defendant merchant bank. During the course of the bid, when the defendant was, of course, fully aware of the identity of the plaintiff and of the transaction which the plaintiff was trying to complete, the company issued a circular in which it forecast a 38 per cent increase in its profits in the current year. This circular included a letter from the defendant stating that in its opinion the profit forecast had been prepared after due and careful enquiry. In reliance on this circular the plaintiff increased its bid and the company's board recommended to the shareholders that this bid be accepted, which it was.

In this action the plaintiff asserted that the profit forecast in the circular and the financial information contained in the company's defence and recommendation documents were negligently prepared and were misleading and that, had the plaintiff known the true facts, it would never have improved its bid and completed the purchase. The defendant applied to have the plaintiff's claim struck out. The Court rejected the defendant's application. While, in view of the House of Lords' decision in *Caparo*, it was clear that the defendant did not owe a duty of care to the plaintiff before the plaintiff's initial bid was made, the Court held that, on the facts pleaded in the Statement of Claim, it was arguable that the position was different after their bid was made. At that stage, and in particular in the company's circular and its accompanying documents, the defendant intended that the plaintiff would rely on the representations contained therein in deciding whether or not to make an increased bid; and the plaintiff did so rely for that purpose.

It must be noted that this does not mean that the Court held that there was a duty of care in these circumstances, but simply that, assuming the plaintiff's averments to be true, its pleading was not so hopeless as to enable the Court to strike it out as disclosing no reasonable cause of action. Thus, Slade LJ, delivering the judgment of the Court of Appeal, said (at p 314):

> The Court's function on this application . . . is simply to decide whether, on the assumed facts, [Morgan Crucible] would be bound to fail in establishing the existence of a duty of care owed to them by the respective defendants. In the end, we have come to the conclusion that Morgan Crucible would not be bound to fail, and that their amended case should be permitted to go forward to trial.

Slade LJ referred extensively to the speeches in *Caparo*, in particular to the emphasis placed on the purpose for which the relevant communication was made. He noted that the plaintiff's counsel accepted that, in the light of the decision in *Caparo*, in general terms the directors and financial advisers of a target company owe no duty of care to safeguard the interests of a potential bidder in their conduct of a contested takeover. However, on the basis that the situation posited by the plaintiff in the present case was much narrower—namely that, during the conduct of a contested takeover, after an identified bidder has emerged, the directors and financial advisers of the target company voluntarily made express representations to the bidder with a view to influencing the conduct of the bidder—Slade LJ accepted that, if this was the proposition being advanced, and if it was properly pleaded, then the House of Lords' decision in *Caparo* did not require the Court of Appeal to strike out that claim, nor was there any other decision which had this effect. He said (at p 319):

> In these circumstances, we are of the opinion that it is at least arguable that the present case can be distinguished from *Caparo*'s case on its assumed facts. On such facts, each of the directors, in making the relevant representations, was aware that Morgan Crucible [the bidder] would rely on them for the purpose of deciding whether or not to make an increased bid, and intended that they should; this was one of the purposes of the defence documents and the representations contained therein. Morgan Crucible duly did rely on them for this purpose. In these circumstances, subject to questions of justice and reasonableness, we think it plainly arguable that there was a relationship of proximity between the directors and Morgan Crucible sufficient to give rise to a duty of care—particularly bearing in mind that . . . much of the information on which the accounts and profit forecast was based was presumably available to the defendants alone.

It is to be noted that in the above-cited passage, the Court's focus was on the possibility of a duty of care inhering in the directors personally. However, both the Court and the plaintiff's counsel accepted that, at trial, no director would be held personally liable unless the plaintiff was able to establish 'personal negligence' against him.

The Court reached the same conclusion on the possibility of a duty of care against the target company's financial advisers (Hill Samuel), because it was alleged in the Statement of Claim that Hill Samuel had intended that its statement relating to the profit forecast would be included in the target company's defence documents and that the bidder and its advisers would rely on that forecast in deciding whether or not to make an increased bid. Thus, Slade LJ said (at p 322):

> On the assumed facts, we think that it must be arguable that Hill Samuel owed to Morgan Crucible a duty of care in making their representations concerning the profit forecast, for the same reasons (*mutatis mutandis*) as those which we have given concerning the directors. In one respect, the case against Hill Samuel is arguably stronger, in that they were giving their advice as experts.

The Court of Appeal also refused to strike out the Statement of Claim in so far as it alleged a duty of care to the plaintiff by the target company's auditors based on the manner in which they had permitted the company's audited accounts to be relied on by the plaintiff as part of the takeover process, and based on their part in preparing the profit forecast. After noting that the auditors had not been requested by the takeover company (Morgan Crucible) to provide any of the information in question for any purpose and that the statements in question had been directed to the directors and shareholders of the target company, whose interests were in conflict with those of Morgan Crucible, and that Morgan Crucible had not paid for the auditors' services, Slade LJ said (at p 324):

> Once again, it may be of critical importance for the trial judge to consider, in the context of duty of care and proximity, whether Morgan Crucible could reasonably have regarded themselves as persons to whom the relevant representations were directly or indirectly addressed. For present purposes, however, we think it will suffice to say that in our judgment Morgan Crucible, on their proposed pleadings and the assumed facts, have established an arguable case as to duty of care against the auditors for the same reasons as those relating to the directors in the case of the financial statements [of the company], and the same reasons relating to the directors and Hill Samuel in the case of the profit forecast.

Lastly, the Court dealt with a submission that it would be wrong to hold that a duty of care could exist to an original bidder in a case like the present, because if, during the course of the takeover process, another, previously unidentified, bidder (a 'white knight') were to come along with a higher bid, the duty of care owed to the original bidder will also have to extend to the white knight because it would have relied to the same extent on the same information on which the original bidder relied, which gave rise to a duty of care to the original bidder. Slade LJ responded to this submission by saying (at p 321):

> No doubt an argument on these lines will be canvassed at the trial in the context of justice and reasonableness. Its correctness, however, is not sufficiently clear to us to justify the dismissal *in limine* of Morgan Crucible's newly formulated

claims against the directors. It occurs to us that possibly the position of the white knight could be distinguished from that of the actual bidder on the ground that, at the time when the relevant representations are made, the white knight, unlike the original bidder, is merely a member of an indeterminate class, and cannot properly be treated as a person to whom the relevant representations are directly or indirectly addressed.

Berg v Adams

In *Berg Sons & Company Ltd and Others v Adams and Others* [1993] BCLC 1045, the business of a certain company involved advancing credit to overseas customers in return for their acceptance of bills of exchange drawn on them. The company then sold these at a discount to banks. Consequently the banks' primary call would be on the overseas debtors, but if they dishonoured their acceptances, the banks would have recourse to the company as the drawer of the bills. In due course, one of the major debtors of the company defaulted on a bill of exchange. The banks called on the company to meet this obligation, but the company went into insolvent liquidation, without any dividend being available to the banks. It also emerged that the company's auditors had incorrectly and negligently certified the company's balance sheet as giving a true and fair view of the company's state of affairs.

The banks sued the auditors for their losses. The court rejected their claims, first, because it was established in evidence that the banks had not in fact placed reliance on the accounts in discounting further bills of the company. Secondly, however, even if the banks had so relied, the auditors did not owe them a duty of care in respect of their losses notwithstanding that it was reasonably foreseeable by the auditors that the company would make use of the audited accounts in its dealings both with its existing bankers and with other bankers whom it might approach thereafter. Hobhouse J said:

> It was foreseeable, and foreseen, that such banks might place some reliance upon the auditors' certification of the accounts. It was not foreseen, nor was it reasonably foreseeable, that the audited accounts would be the *sole* information upon which a bank would rely in assessing the creditworthiness of Berg.

Hobhouse J continued:

> The statements of principle in *Caparo* show that there must be a specific relationship between the function which the defendant is requested to perform and the transaction in relation to which the plaintiff says he has relied upon the proper performance of that function. It is not enough that there should be a general potential for reliance or that there may be a class of transactions which may foreseeably be entered into. There must be a specific transaction which can be said to be the transaction, or among the transactions, to which the carrying out of the function was directed. The result of applying such a test is that it will only be in very clear and immediate circumstances that it will be possible to say that a statutory auditor owes a duty of care to a banker who may at some later date choose to lend money to a company.

Hobhouse J also made the point that the period of foreseeable reliance, if it exists at all, will be very limited. He said:

Furthermore, there would only be a limited period of time within which it would be reasonably foreseeable that a bank would rely upon a given set of audited accounts. By the time of the completion of the audit, over six months had already elapsed since the end of the year covered by these accounts. It would not be reasonably foreseen that these accounts would still be relied upon by any banker acting in the ordinary course of business as a basis for assessing the then creditworthiness of Berg after the passage of more than about 15 months from the end of the period covered by the accounts. By that time the information contained in the audited accounts would be so out of date that it would not reasonably be foreseen as the basis for a business judgment concerning the extension of credit to Berg or the discounting of bills. Audited accounts are, in any event, only one of the sources of information which a prudent banker takes into account. Within a reasonable period after the end of the year covered by the accounts, they may have a dominant role. With the passage of time thereafter, the role of the audited accounts becomes progressively less important and other more up-to-date information becomes progressively more important.

Galoo v Bright Grahame Murray

In *Galoo Ltd (in liquidation) v Bright Grahame Murray* [1994] 1 WLR 1360 (CA), one of the issues was whether the third plaintiff, Hillsdown Holding plc, had properly pleaded a case for the imposition of a duty of care on the defendant firm of auditors to it for the economic losses sustained when it bought shares in two companies (the first and second plaintiffs) pursuant to the terms of an Acquisition Agreement. Under the Agreement, the purchase price of the shares was a multiple of the net profits of one of the companies as reflected in the audited accounts of both of the companies for the year ending December 1996, such accounts having been prepared by the defendant auditors and having been delivered to the third plaintiff for that specific purpose with the defendant's knowledge and consent.

The Court of Appeal held that in these circumstances the Statement of Claim was not defective on this aspect of the third plaintiff's claim. After reviewing the above-mentioned decisions in *Caparo* and *Morgan Crucible* and *Al Saudi Banque*, Glidewell LJ, with whose reasons Waite LJ agreed, said (at p 1382):

> The distinction between the set of facts which it was held in *Morgan Crucible* would suffice to establish a duty of care owed by auditors from those facts which it was held in *Caparo* would not have this effect is inevitably a fine one. In my judgment, that distinction may be expressed as follows. Mere foreseeability that a potential bidder may rely on the audited accounts does not impose on the auditor a duty of care to the bidder, but if the auditor is expressly made aware that a particular identified bidder will rely on the audited accounts or other statements approved by the auditor, and intends that the bidder should so rely, the auditor will be under a duty of care to the bidder. . .

In applying these principles to the third plaintiff's loss resulting from its above-mentioned purchase of shares in the two companies whose accounts the defendant had audited, Glidewell LJ adopted the following statement of the deputy judge whose decision led to this appeal:

At the time when they audited the accounts for the year ended December 31, 1986, the defendants knew of the existence and the terms of the Acquisition Agreement. They accordingly knew that . . . the amount of the purchase consideration . . . was to be calculated by reference to [those] accounts. . . .

It is therefore plain that the 1986 audited accounts were to be prepared not only for the purposes of the audit, but also for the purpose of fixing the purchase consideration under this agreement. It is common ground that the defendants knew of the terms of this agreement and that the accounts which they were to submit to the purchasers were to be for the purposes of these provisions. In those circumstances, the case is immediately, on its face, taken outside the *Caparo* principles. . .

The defendant argued that this part of the plaintiff's claim should nevertheless be struck out because the Acquisition Agreement also specifically gave the third plaintiff's accountants the right to have full access to the books of the two audited companies and to receive full information, together with the right to review the completion accounts. It also provided a mechanism for resolving any disputes between the third plaintiff's accountants and the defendant. The third plaintiff's counsel thus relied on the third principle enunciated by Lord Oliver in *Caparo* (ie that it is known that the defendant's advice is likely to be acted on by the advisee without independent inquiry (see *above*)), and submitted that the above-mentioned opportunity provided by the Acquisition Agreement for the third plaintiff's accountants to make an independent inquiry of the state of the two audited companies' accounts meant that there could be no duty of care on the defendant in the present case.

Glidewell LJ was not prepared to strike out the Statement of Claim on this basis. He said that evidence was required, and the plaintiffs were entitled to have a trial, to determine whether the review which the third plaintiff's accountants were to carry out was the same as the task which the defendant had carried out. It might well appear that, while the completion accounts had been prepared by the defendant specifically for the purpose of determining the amount of the purchase consideration, the function of the purchaser/third plaintiff's accountants in reviewing the accounts was not necessarily precisely the same.

The third Lord Justice, Evans LJ, agreed with the above-mentioned result, but he expressed some doubts as to whether the third plaintiff's claim would be able to succeed at trial in view of the opportunity for intermediate inspection that was afforded to the third plaintiff's own accountants. He said (at p 1387) (emphasis added):

Whether the claim succeeds or not will depend upon not only the plaintiff proving the facts which it alleged, but also the *extent* to which [the third plaintiff's] right to review the completion accounts negatives the duty of care which they allege. . .

. . . if the evidence shows that this 'right of intermediate examination' excludes any duty of care which might otherwise arise, the claim will fail. This is why evidence is necessary. If it were necessary to decide this issue on the basis of the plaintiffs' pleaded facts, then I would be inclined to the view that Hillsdown [the third plaintiff], who were known to be advised by an international firm of accountants and auditors, and who would have full access to the company's books, would not be likely to rely upon statutory accounts, draft or otherwise, prepared by the defendants, when deciding whether or not to bid for the company, and, if so, at what price.

Evans LJ also made comments designed to reconcile *Caparo* and *Morgan Crucible*. Although he expressed himself differently from Glidewell LJ, he reached the same conclusion. He said:

> A distinction between the *Morgan Crucible* and the *Caparo* situations has to be drawn, and the line of demarcation is unclear. . . .
> It is tempting to distinguish between *Caparo* and *Morgan Crucible* on the basis that in the latter, though not in the former case, the identity of a particular purchaser of shares in the company was known to the defendants when they represented that the company's accounts which they had prepared were fair and true. This excludes individual members of the body of existing shareholders to whom the statutory accounts are published (*Caparo*) whilst including an identified takeover bidder, as in the *Morgan Crucible* case. But there could be intervening situations, for example, where an existing shareholder is known to be a potential purchaser of more shares, with a view to acquiring the whole or a majority of the shares. The identification test would not provide the answer in such a case. No duty of care would be owed to such a person . . . on those facts alone, because the third of the four propositions listed by Lord Oliver in *Caparo* (ie, that it is known that the advice so communicated is likely to be acted on by the advisee without independent inquiry) would not be satisfied . . . and, vitally, it could not be said that the auditors in such a case 'intended that they should act' upon it for that purpose (*per* Slade LJ in *Morgan Crucible* [see *above*]).

The Court of Appeal did, however, strike out another aspect of the third plaintiff's Statement of Claim, namely, the third plaintiff's allegation that the defendant owed the third plaintiff a duty of care for the third plaintiff's losses resulting from certain post-acquisition loans that the third plaintiff had made to the audited companies in reliance on the audited accounts. Again, Glidewell LJ adopted the reasoning of the deputy judge who, in this regard, had said:

> Those matters [ie the third plaintiff's pleading in relation to the subsequent loans] . . . go to foreseeability and only to foreseeability and do not establish the degree of proximity that is, on the authorities, required. . . . It is not pleaded that any particular loan was made in reliance upon a particular set of accounts or that the defendants promulgated any set of accounts for the purposes of any specific loan or indeed for the purpose of loans at all, and the mere fact of the knowledge that loans would or might be made [in reliance on the audited accounts] is not sufficient to create that degree of proximity.

Glidewell LJ added only (at p 1385) (emphasis added):

> On this issue . . . the statement of claim does not plead the facts which in *Morgan Crucible* were held to be those necessary in order to establish a duty of care, namely that the auditor knew that the intending lender *would* rely on the accounts approved by the auditors for the purpose of deciding whether to make the loans or increase loans already made and *intended* that the intending lender should so rely.

Lastly, it is worth noting that the audited companies (the first and second plaintiffs) had separate claims against the defendant which were also struck out. They alleged that, if the defendant had not audited their accounts negligently, they would not have accepted the above-mentioned further loans from the third plaintiff, and would therefore not have ended up with a liability to repay those loans to the third plaintiff. In this regard, the deputy judge had said:

> ... I do not accept that accepting loans involving an obligation simpliciter to repay them can be described as damage. At the moment of accepting the loan, the company which accepts the loan has available that amount of money and the obligation to repay that amount of money, and I simply fail to see how that can amount to damage. If there is damage, it must consist of parting with those monies in certain circumstances.

With reference to this *dictum*, Glidewell LJ said (at p 1369):

> I entirely agree with the deputy judge on this issue. Like him, I do not understand how the acceptance of a loan can, of itself, be described as a loss causing damage. If anything, it is a benefit to the borrower. Of course, a loss may result from the use to which the loan monies are put, but no such resultant loss is pleaded [in this case], and, even if it were, it might very well be difficult to attribute it to [the defendant auditors].

Anthony v Wright

In *Anthony and Others v Wright and Others* [1995] 1 BCLC 236, the plaintiffs were a group of 40 individuals who had placed varying sums of money for investment purposes totalling about £3m with a particular company ('GAA') which carried on business as insurance brokers and investment consultants. These monies were received and held by GAA as trustee for the plaintiffs in segregated trust accounts with various banks. The seventh defendant was a firm of accountants and auditors who prepared, audited and published the accounts of GAA over a number of years. In March 1990, an order was made for the compulsory winding up of GAA, with a deficiency of £4.5m. In the liquidation of GAA, the plaintiffs received nothing on account of their investment. The immediate cause of GAA's deficiency was the fraud of its directors, who, over a number of years, had applied the plaintiffs' trust monies for their personal benefit, to repay some investors whose money had been dissipated and for other improper purposes. These defalcations and breaches of trust had not been uncovered by the seventh defendant in carrying out its annual audits of GAA's accounts.

The Court rejected the plaintiffs' claim that the auditors owed them a duty of care in respect of their losses. Lightman J said (at p 239):

> A special relationship is required for a duty of care to be owed to existing or future creditors who may rely on the audited accounts in leaving debts outstanding or making loans to the company; and, in particular, intention (actual or inferred) is required on the part of the auditors that the third party shall rely, and reliance by the third party on the audit [is required] before a claim in negligence against the auditor can be maintained.

There are two remarkable features about the investors' claim in this case. First, there is no apparent assumption on the part of the auditors of any responsibility towards the investors, and no intention that the investors should rely on them. Secondly, there is no suggestion of any actual reliance by the investors on the audit reports; reliance is specifically disavowed.

Instead of pleading actual reliance, the plaintiffs' counsel submitted that a sufficient special relationship between the auditors and the plaintiffs nevertheless existed in this case by reason of the special status of the investors as beneficiaries under trusts of which GAA was trustee, and of whose existence the auditors were fully aware. The plaintiffs' counsel sought support from the Court of Appeal's decision in *White v Jones*, which was subsequently upheld by the House of Lords (see para 9.7.5), where it was held that (in the circumstances of that case) the absence of reliance by the plaintiff on the defendant was not fatal to the plaintiff's claim. In rejecting this submission, Lightman J said (at p 240):

> It would seem to me remarkable and quite unjust and unreasonable that a company, by the method of conduct of its business, its creation of a trust or acceptance of trust monies, should be able to impose on an auditor a duty to the beneficiaries irrespective of the wishes or acceptance of such a duty by the auditor.

Lightman J also referred to the fact that in *White v Jones* the Court felt that there was a need for a special rule, because otherwise the negligent solicitor would not have been exposed to a claim from anyone. Lightman J noted that the present case was, however, different. He said (at p 241): "A remedy in respect of defalcation lies at the instance of the liquidator for the benefit of all creditors including the investors; and the investors as beneficiaries under a trust have a direct claim against the directors for procuring or participating in the breaches of trust. No special case exists for a claim by the investors against the auditors".

Ferguson v Spicer and Pegler

In *Ferguson and Others v Spicer and Pegler* (29 July 1994, unreported) the first plaintiff, Mr Ferguson, had lost money when he and certain companies that he controlled bought all of the shares of another company in respect of which the defendant was the auditor and accountant and effectively the company's financial adviser. For the purpose of the takeover discussions, the defendant prepared documents headed as "pro forma asset values" and "cash flow forecasts" and provided these to the plaintiffs and their accountants without attaching any form of disclaimer of liability.

Subsequently, after the target company had failed, the plaintiffs brought the present action against the defendant in which they contended that the defendant had made material misrepresentations to them in the above-mentioned documents and orally, upon which they maintained they relied in taking over the target company, and that they would not have taken it over if not for those misstatements. One of the questions for the Court was whether the defendant owed the plaintiffs a duty of care in tort for the losses sustained by the plaintiffs through having relied on the incorrect information provided by the defendant. The Court answered this question in the negative after a 58-day trial.

The judge, R Kidwell QC, sitting as a deputy judge of the High Court, held that, even putting aside the expectation that the defendant might have had of an intermediate examination by virtue of the presence of the plaintiffs' own accountants, the distinguishing feature of this case was that the above-mentioned documents which the defendant had produced, and on which the plaintiffs relied, were not even sufficient to qualify as draft accounts. The judge referred to the fact that in the *McNaughton* case (see *above*) the Court of Appeal, in rejecting the plaintiff's case, was heavily influenced by the fact that the accounts were merely draft accounts. The judge contrasted this with the situation in *Candler v Crane, Christmas and Co* [1951] 2 KB 164 (see para 9.2.2) in which, although the accounts were also only draft accounts, they were accompanied by a certificate ready for signature by the accountant, stating that the accountants had audited the company's balance sheet, having obtained all of the information and explanations that the accountants required, and that in their view the balance sheet exhibited a true and accurate view of the state of the company's affairs. In *Candler*, the accountant himself passed this to the bidder, saying it would be signed with a clear docket, subject to one or two small alterations which he wished to consider for another two or three days; and this in fact happened.

Commenting on these cases, the judge in the present case said:

> It is thus abundantly clear that there was present [in *Candler*] the element of assuming responsibility, by audit and verification, which is absent from the present case. There has never been a successful claim in tort against an accountant unless he has assumed responsibility by being an auditor or (in *Candler's* case) the equivalent, by producing an intended certificate, whilst in *McNaughton's* case, the fact that the accounts were only drafts for the audit weighed heavily against the plaintiffs.

Lest he should be taken as having made the sweeping statement that the plaintiffs' case failed simply because the documents produced by the defendant in the present case were in the nature of draft accounts, the judge qualified his above-cited statement by saying:

> I am far from saying that in law the documents produced must constitute a near audit for there to be liability. Accountants may solemnly vouch for interim documents so as to make themselves liable, but the more remote from the rituals of an audit the situation becomes, the less likely is any such vouching.
>
> As to intention, if the accountants have the subjective intention that the bidder will rely on their figures without inquiry or exercising his own judgment, then this element of deliberation may substitute for the usual objective test of likelihood of reliance, but I find that S&P [the defendant] had no such intention.

For these reasons, the judge held that the defendant did not owe a duty of care to the plaintiffs for any economic losses that the plaintiffs might have suffered through having placed reliance on the above-mentioned documents that the defendant had produced for the plaintiffs' use in the takeover process. The judge did, however, consider the possibility of the defendant nevertheless still being under another, more limited, duty to the plaintiffs. He said:

> That leaves open the possibility of a limited duty, which has not been advanced in this case, or ever, but may be implicit in some of the complaints made. It is difficult to define, but it would be on the lines that the defendants did not show reasonable care in obtaining information from the company. It would be difficult to prevent such a duty escalating into the duty that I have rejected, but I will keep the possibility open.

Without considering this proposition further, the judge concluded his judgment by rejecting it. He said: "I have considered, without finding it to be the case, the possibility of a limited duty. I shall not leave this possibility in the air for the encouragement of future plaintiffs, so I reject it as being an unacceptable *Caparo* increment".

ADT v Binder Hamlyn

In *ADT Ltd v BDO Binder Hamlyn* (6 December 1995, unreported), the defendant was a firm of auditors who, in October 1989, had signed the audit certificates for the 1989 accounts of a public company ('BSG'). Shortly afterwards, the plaintiff reached an agreement in principle with BSG to acquire the entire issued capital of BSG. The defendant was not involved in those negotiations.

On 5 January 1990, a meeting took place between representatives of the plaintiff and one of the defendant's audit partners (Mr Bishop), the purpose of which, to the defendant's knowledge (through Mr Bishop), was for the plaintiff to obtain a statement from the defendant to the effect that BSG's financial position was, and remained, to the defendant's knowledge, accurately reflected in the audit report. This confirmation was, again to the defendant's knowledge, the final hurdle before the plaintiff committed itself to the takeover agreement.

At the meeting, Mr Bishop did provide the confirmation requested, and the plaintiff duly completed its takeover of BSG. Subsequently, it emerged that the 1989 accounts did not in fact show a true and fair view of the state of affairs of BSG, and that the defendant had been negligent in certain respects in relation to the 1989 BSG audit. The plaintiff instituted the present action against the defendant, claiming as damages the difference between the price which the plaintiff paid for BSG and what the plaintiff claimed was the true worth of BSG. The judge, May J, said that the issue that he had to determine was whether the defendant assumed any responsibility to ADT on 5 January 1990, including whether ADT relied on what it was told at that meeting. He answered this question in the affirmative, and gave judgment to the plaintiff for £65m against the defendant. He said (at para 103):

> It is part of the terms of the inquiry which I have formulated that, to find a duty of care, it is necessary that Mr Bishop should have known that ADT would place

reliance upon his information or advice without independent inquiry. In this case, the very fact that the meeting was seen as 'the final hurdle', added to the fact that it was never open to ADT to have an independent accountant's investigation into the affairs of BSG, meant that it was obvious that further detailed investigation after the meeting into BSG's accounts would not take place;

and (at para 107):

> Binders [the defendant] undoubtedly professed accounting and, specifically, auditing skills, and Mr Bishop attended the meeting in his capacity as an accountant and audit partner. He was, in my judgment, fully aware of the nature of the very transaction which ADT had in contemplation, *viz*: the acquisition of BSG, the company whose accounts his firm audited. He took it upon himself to give information or advice directly to ADT, *viz*: that he stood by the accounts, by which he meant that within the limits of Binders' professional competence, the accounts gave a true and fair view of the state of affairs of the company. He knew the purpose for which ADT required this information and advice, *viz*: as an ingredient to help them finally to decide whether to make the contemplated bid or not. He knew that ADT would place reliance on what he said without further inquiry, since he knew that it was 'the final hurdle'. The ingredients of a duty of care are therefore all present in this case, and I have to consider whether objectively and in fairness, Binders, through Mr Bishop, are to be taken to have assumed responsibility to ADT for the reliability of the advice or information which he gave.

With reference to the *McNaughton* case (see *above*), May J said (at para 108):

> Neill LJ obviously regarded the nature of the meeting and the nature of the question and answer as important in that case. In my view, there are material distinctions between that case and this case in that respect. In this case, the meeting was convened for the very purpose of asking the questions which I have found were asked. There was no misunderstanding about its purpose. The question whether Binders stood by their accounts was specific. The facts in this case are plainly distinguishable from those in *Caparo*, and I do not consider that *McNaughton* leads me to find that in this case there was no duty of care.

The defendant's counsel had submitted that it would be unfair to deem the auditors to have assumed responsibility for the plaintiff's losses in this case because Mr Bishop had effectively been "bounced into answering questions for which he had inadequate notice or time for preparation" and because the potential additional liability was enormous; and that it would be wrong in law to deem the auditors to have assumed liability to a person other than their client for the consequences of mistakes in their audit, in view of the fact that the House of Lords in *Caparo* had held that the purpose of an audit of a public company is the making of a report to enable shareholders to exercise their class rights in general meetings, and not to provide them with information to assist them in the making of decisions as to future investment in the company (see *above*). May J rejected both of these submissions. He said (at para 110):

Although Mr Bishop had only a short time to consider his answers, he was plainly not being asked to redo all the audit work in his mind. Rather, he was being asked the simple question whether the BSG accounts were accounts which ADT could rely on. This was by its nature a serious business meeting. Mr Bishop did not have to say yes. He could have declined to answer. He could have given a disclaimer. He could have said that, if ADT were to rely on his answers, he would need to take advice. He could have said words to the effect: 'Yes, I do stand by the accounts, but this was a difficult audit because . . .'. Rather than doing any of these things, he undertook to answer the question posed and gave an unqualified favourable answer.

I am not persuaded that the size of potential liability and commercial problems over insurance are by themselves reasons for saying that responsibility was not in law assumed when, apart from these considerations, it was. It is well-recognised that these matters can be guarded against by a *Hedley Byrne* disclaimer. If, for commercial reasons, those who give advice do not want to give disclaimers or otherwise limit their liability, then I can see no reason why they should not have to live with the consequences.

It is not, in my view, sensible that the law should say that Mr Bishop is not to be taken to have assumed responsibility in this case because the potential liability was enormous, and difficult to insure against, but that he should be taken to have assumed responsibility on otherwise identical facts if BSG were a small company with a value of (say) £50,000.

May J concluded this part of his judgment by saying (in para 112):

In some cases, alluded to as possibilities in *Hedley Byrne*, the extent of the responsibility assumed may be no more than a duty to answer honestly. In this case, however, Mr Bishop stood by the accounts and thereby assumed responsibility to ADT for the professional competence with which they had been prepared.

In my judgment, therefore, upon the facts which I have found, Binders are to be taken to have assumed responsibility to ADT for Mr Bishop's statement, whose effect was understood to be that, within the limits of Binders' professional competence, the 1989 BSG accounts showed a true and fair view of the state of affairs of BSG.

Possfund v Diamond

In *Possfund Custodian Trustee Ltd v Diamond* [1996] 1 WLR 1351, the question was whether, for the purposes of a striking-out application, it was arguable that persons responsible for issuing a prospectus in respect of unlisted securities owe a duty of care at common law to an aftermarket purchaser (ie a purchaser of the securities other than an original subscriber/placee to the prospectus) who purchased shares in the market in reliance on the prospectus.

The plaintiffs were two groups of investors who had respectively either subscribed for shares in a particular company pursuant to the company's prospectus, or had subsequently purchased shares on the Unlisted Securities Market shortly after trading in those shares had commenced, again in reliance on the prospectus. Subsequently, it emerged that the prospectus had materially misrepresented the company's financial position and that the shares were worthless.

The plaintiffs sought to recover their losses from the company's directors and financial advisers, based on their negligence in causing or procuring the publication of the prospectus, and from the company's auditors in respect of their financial report which they had consented to being included in the prospectus.

In the case of listed securities, the Financial Services Act 1986 provides a remedy against all of the above classes of defendants, both in respect of shares purchased pursuant to listing particulars (similar to a prospectus) and in respect of aftermarket purchases. With regard to unlisted securities, however, the 'mirror-image' provisions have never been brought into force. The position is therefore still governed by the common law.

For the purposes of the striking-out application in this case, it was common ground that the plaintiffs' pleadings did disclose a cause of action in respect of the actual placing of the shares on the Unlisted Securities Market. The issue was whether such a cause of action was also disclosed in respect of some of the plaintiffs' aftermarket purchases. The judge, Lightman J, answered this question in the affirmative (ie he refused to strike out the plaintiffs' claim merely because it related to aftermarket purchases), but he by no means held that the plaintiffs had in fact established their claim. He said (at p 1365):

> The starting point in determining the ambit of the duty of care in respect of a prospectus is the statutory purpose of the prospectus. In the same way, the starting point in determining the ambit of the duty of auditors in respect of their audit and audit report is the limited statutory purpose of that statutory requirement, namely, to enable shareholders to exercise their class rights in general meeting in an informed manner: see *Caparo Industries Plc v Dickman* [1990] 2 AC 605. But that is only the beginning: it is not necessarily also the end. It does not necessarily preclude a superadded purpose if a superadded purpose can positively be shown to exist. The burden of establishing such a superadded purpose may be heavy or indeed overwhelming, but, whether the burden can or cannot be discharged, is a matter for the trial.
>
> But, the plaintiffs say, the prospectus must be examined in the light of changed market practice and philosophy current at its date of preparation and circulation. The plaintiffs claim that there has developed and been generally recognised an additional purpose, an additional perceived intention on the part of the issuer and other parties to a prospectus, namely, to inform and encourage aftermarket purchasers.
>
> If this is established, then it does seem to me to be at least arguable that a duty of care is assumed and owed to those investors who, as intended, rely on the contents of the prospectus in making such purposes. No doubt the court should think carefully before recognising a duty in the case of unlisted securities which has been withheld by the legislature. It is significant that the courts have since 1873 (before any legislation) recognised a duty of care in the case of prospectuses when there is a sufficient direct connection between those responsible for the prospectus and the party acting in reliance (see *Peek v Gurney* (1873) LR 6 HL 377), and the plaintiffs' claim may be recognised as merely an application of this established principle in a new factual situation.

In so holding, Lightman J cast doubt (albeit obliquely) on the Court's decision in *Al-Nakib Investment (Jersey) Ltd v Longcroft* [1990] 1 WLR 1390—see *above*.

Barings v Coopers and Lybrand

In *Barings plc (in administration) v Coopers and Lybrand* (22 November 1996, unreported, CA) the plaintiff was the English holding company of a group of companies (now in administration and provisional liquidation) which included an indirect subsidiary, Barings Futures Singapore Pte Ltd ('BFS'), which operated in Singapore and whose accounts were audited by the Singapore office ('C&LS') of the defendant firm of accountants and auditors, Coopers and Lybrand. The collapse of the plaintiff's group of companies was caused in February 1995 by the unauthorised and loss-making trading of BFS's general manager, Nicholas Leeson. At no time during C&LS's audits of BFS's consolidation schedules, prepared for the purposes of the plaintiff's group accounts, did C&LS detect Mr Leeson's unauthorised trading or the losses in which it resulted. On the contrary, the consolidation schedules showed BFS to be not only solvent but profitable. The plaintiff's case was that, had the auditors reported on Mr Leeson's fraudulent activities at any time before February 1995, his positions could have been closed and the plaintiff's insolvency could, and would, have been averted.

The present decision arose out of leave that the plaintiffs had obtained to serve C&LS out of the jurisdiction, such leave having been granted *inter alia* on the ground that the claim was founded on a tort, namely C&LS's negligence and that the plaintiff's damage was sustained within the jurisdiction. The defendants applied to have this leave set aside on the ground that no duty of care was owed by them to the plaintiff as the holding company of BFS, because such duty as they did owe was owed only to BFS and not also to its individual shareholders, including its holding company. In making this submission, C&LS's counsel relied on the proposition established by the Court of Appeal in *Prudential Assurance Co Ltd v Newman Industries Ltd* [1982] Ch 204, that a shareholder cannot recover damages merely because the company in which he is interested has suffered damage, because such a loss is merely a reflection of the loss suffered by the company; and on its endorsement in the House of Lords in *Caparo Industries plc v Dickman* [1990] 2 AC 605, particularly Lord Bridge's statement that he found it difficult to visualise a situation in which an individual shareholder could claim to have sustained a loss in respect of his existing shareholding referable to the negligence of the company's auditor, which could not be recouped by the company (see *above*).

The Court of Appeal rejected these submissions because the plaintiff's pleading made it clear that the plaintiff's claim against C&LS was not parasitic on a breach of duty by C&LS to BFS alone, but was based on an independent, direct relationship between C&LS and the plaintiff itself. Thus, Leggatt LJ, speaking for the Court of Appeal, said:

> The present case differs from the *Prudential Assurance* case because here the person in the position of shareholder, namely Barings, has a right of action independent of the company, BFS. The crucial point is that Barings plead that there was a direct relationship between C&LS and Barings arising from the circumstances in which work was done for, and information was supplied by C&LS to

Barings relating to the preparation of consolidated group accounts. Specific facts are pleaded in support of the claim that there was an independent and relevant duty of care owed by C&LS to Barings, which was separate from any duty owed to BFS as statutory auditors. The determination of the scope of that duty and of the consequences of any breach are matters for evidence and legal argument at trial.

On the question of the consequences that C&LS must have foreseen or intended from the consolidation schedules that they prepared during their audit of BFS's accounts, or as to the duty that they must be deemed to have assumed in the course of that role, Leggatt LJ said:

> In my judgment, the argument about duty of care is concluded by the simple fact that C&LS knew that their audit and report on the consolidation schedules were required so that the directors or Barings [the parent company] could comply with their obligation to provide accounts which showed a true and fair view of the financial affairs of the group. C&LS could not have supposed that the only responsibility they assumed to Barings was to submit BFS's accounts in a form suitable for incorporation into the consolidated accounts.
>
> C&LS cannot have supposed that, so long as some accounts were provided, it mattered not whether they showed a true and fair view of the financial affairs of BFS. The primary responsibility for safeguarding a company's assets and preventing errors and defalcations rests with the directors. But material irregularities and, *a fortiori*, fraud will normally be brought to light by sound audit procedures, one of which is the practice of pointing out weaknesses in internal controls. An auditor's task is so to conduct the audit as to make it probable that material misstatements in financial documents will be detected. Detection did not occur here, and there is therefore a case for C&LS to answer.

BCCI v Price Waterhouse

In *Bank of Credit and Commerce International (Overseas) Limited (in liquidation) and Others v Price Waterhouse and Another* ((1997) *The Times*, 10 February; 13 February 1998, unreported, CA), the liquidators of three companies in the BCCI Group brought proceedings for breach of duty of care against the companies' former auditors, Price Waterhouse ('PW') and Ernst and Whinney ('EW'), alleging negligence in the audits carried out respectively by PW and EW, with the consequence that numerous imprudences were not discovered, thereby enabling the BCCI Banks to continue to trade and incur further losses. The plaintiffs alleged that, had the audits been carried out properly, further losses would have been avoided, further substantial payments (including payments of tax and charitable donations) would not have been made, and further irrecoverable loans would not have been made, and there would have been a greater prospect of recovering some or all of the loans which subsequently became wholly or largely irrecoverable. The damages claimed against the auditors amounted to several billion US dollars.

The present application was brought by EW to strike out those paragraphs of the Statement of Claim which related to claims in tort against EW by one of the three plaintiff companies, BCCI (Overseas) Limited (referred to hereafter as 'Overseas'). EW was not Overseas's auditor. EW was only the auditor for the holding company in the BCCI Group, BCCI Holdings (Luxembourg) SA ('Holdings') and for the other flagship bank in the Group, BCCI International SA ('SA'). Overseas had a separate auditor, namely, PW. Also, EW's appointment as auditor of Holdings and SA was only for two financial years, 1985 and 1986.

The plaintiff alleged that, by agreeing to undertake the audits of Holdings and SA in the knowledge that those companies, together with Overseas, formed a single group that was run by the same or virtually the same directors and management, EW assumed a responsibility to Overseas and therefore owed a duty of care to Overseas. The judge, Laddie J, rejected this submission. He said:

> The fact that Overseas and SA were run in close collaboration with each other does not alter the fact that they were separate companies, with separate places of business and separate Boards of Directors. They have separate Liquidators. They chose to appoint different auditors. The fact that the results of the audit carried out on behalf of Holdings and SA would become known to, and would be of interest to, Overseas and its auditors, PW, does not alter the fact that EW was only carrying out audit functions for and on behalf of Holdings and SA.
>
> The EW defendants' duty of care extended to those for or on whose behalf they were carrying out professional services. It is pleaded that their advice and the results of their services would be considered and relied upon by Overseas and PW and that 'in the premises' the EW defendants intended that to be so. But this is no more than an allegation that it must be presumed that the defendants intended the natural and foreseeable results of their actions. This cannot turn knowledge or expectation that a third party will rely on an adviser's work into a relevant intention that it should so rely. If it were otherwise, a duty of care would arise wherever reliance by a third party was foreseeable. That is not the law.
>
> Adopting the approach of Lord Jauncey in *Caparo* [see *above*], if one asks what was the purpose for which the EW defendants carried out the professional activities referred to in the Statement of Claim, it was for auditing Holdings and SA, not Overseas. There is nothing unreasonable or unfair in this conclusion. Overseas had appointed and relied on the professional competence of its own auditors, PW. These pleadings do not raise a case that the EW defendants owed a duty of care to Overseas.

In so holding, Laddie J rejected two submissions by the plaintiffs' counsel. The first of these was that, because the formulation of the criteria for the creation of a duty of care is not rigid (see Chapter 3, para 3.3), it would be wrong for the court to grant EW's striking-out application because the existence and scope of EW's duty of care to Overseas could be determined only after a detailed inquiry into all of the facts, with the assistance of such expert evidence as might be required to place the respective responsibilities of EW and PW in context. In rejecting this submission, Laddie J said:

> Although the precise circumstances which give rise to a duty of care will vary from case to case, and this area of law is one in which expansion of liability is still possible to meet new and unusual situations (as for instance in *White v Jones* [1995] 2 AC 207 [see para 9.7.5]), the line of cases which includes *Henderson v Merrett Syndicates Ltd* [1995] 2 AC 145 [see para 9.7.6], *Spring v Guardian*

Assurance plc [1995] 2 AC 296 [see para 9.7.7] and *Caparo* [see *above*], still maps out the essential ingredients which must be present before liability is established. In virtually all cases, there can be no liability unless it is shown that the adviser's advice was given to and for the purposes of the advisee.

Secondly, the plaintiffs' counsel submitted that EW would owe a duty of care to Overseas if, although EW's services were not performed by EW for or on behalf of Overseas, EW knew or ought to have known that Overseas would rely on the information or advice provided by EW, and if Overseas could establish that EW had "assumed responsibility for a purpose, whether specific or general, which could be shown to correspond with the type of loss suffered". In rejecting this submission, Laddie J said:

> Although the expression 'assumption of responsibility' is to be found in some of the recent cases, it does not appear to signify any different approach to the imposition of liability set out in *Caparo*. It is, as Lord Roskill pointed out in *Caparo*, simply another imprecise phrase used to cover situations in which a duty of care has been held to exist [see para 9.5.2]. It does little to define why, or the circumstances in which, liability arises.
>
> When the plaintiffs' counsel's argument is analysed, it is apparent that, according to it, the EW defendants would be liable to Overseas if they provided services to Holdings and SA which were of relevance to Overseas in circumstances in which EW knew or ought to have known that Overseas would rely on the due exercise by EW of care and skill in the provision of those services, and Overseas did so rely. However, if this is so, liability would be based essentially on foreseeability and, as is well established, that alone is insufficient to give rise to a duty of care.

In addition to the above-mentioned weaknesses, Laddie J held that the averments made by Overseas against EW were defective in another fundamental respect, namely, that the losses which Overseas sought to recover from EW were not within the scope of any relevant duty of care that EW might have owed to Overseas. In this regard, Laddie J cited the *dicta* relating to the scope of a duty of care which are set out in Chapter 2, para 2.1.5, from the speeches of Lord Bridge and Oliver in *Caparo*, from the judgment of Brennan J in *The Council of the Shire of Sutherland v Hayman* (1985) 157 CLR 424 and from the speech of Lord Hoffmann in *South Australia Asset Management Corporation v York Montague Ltd* [1997] AC 191, and continued:

> Even if there is sufficient proximity between the adviser and the advisee, that does not expose the adviser to liability for all damage which can be shown to flow from the breach of duty. In the Statement of Claim, Overseas has identified the losses which it seeks to recover from the EW defendants for the allegedly negligent way in which they conducted the 1985 and 1986 audits for Holdings and SA. Those losses include advances that Overseas made between 1986 and 1991 which are in whole or in part irrecoverable, taxes paid by Overseas on profits reported for the year ending December 31, 1985 and subsequently, which Overseas would not have paid if EW had not been in breach of duty, and expenditure on grants and charitable donations which Overseas would not have incurred if EW had not been in breach of its duty in carrying out its audits of Holdings and SA's accounts.

Laddie J commented on the extreme width of these allegations, which included charitable donations made by Overseas three years after EW had ceased having any professional involvement with any member of the BCCI Group of companies. This revealed a fundamental flaw in these claims. Laddie J said:

> As was pointed out in *Caparo*, it is not sufficient to ask simply whether EW owed Overseas a duty of care. It is necessary to determine the scope of the duty by reference to the kind of damage from which the defendants had to take care to save Overseas harmless. Nowhere in the Statement of Claim is it alleged that these defendants knew and intended that the 1985 and 1986 audits of Holdings and SA would be used by Overseas as a basis upon which to decide whether to make loans, pay dividends and tax, make charitable donations or carry on a variety of other activities which proved to be loss-making. Furthermore, nowhere is it alleged that Overseas in fact relied on the results of those audits when deciding to do any of those things.
>
> Overseas's case is that, had the audit been carried out correctly, either Overseas would have been closed down or its operation would have been over-hauled and the various frauds and imprudences in operation would not have continued. This is no more than an assertion that Overseas has made losses which it would or might not have made if Holdings' and SA's audit had been carried out properly, and therefore EW is liable. I agree with EW's counsel that this is simply another version of the fallacious equation: negligence by A + loss by B = liability of A to B.

For these reasons, Laddie J granted EW's striking-out application in so far as it related to Overseas's claims in tort. He concluded this part of his judgment by saying:

> In summary, I accept EW's counsel's submission that the plaintiffs have failed to make out a reasonable cause of action on the pleadings that the EW defendants owed a duty of care to Overseas because—
> (i) they were not the auditor of Overseas or in any other way carrying out auditing functions for or on behalf of Overseas; and
> (ii) Overseas do not claim that EW knew or ought to have known that Overseas would rely on their auditor's report on the financial statements of Holdings or SA for the purpose of making the loans, charitable donations and the like for which Overseas claims compensation, or that Overseas did in fact rely on them for that purpose.

The Court of Appeal (13 February 1998, unreported) overruled Laddie J's judgment and refused to strike out the plaintiff's claim against EW. In so holding, their Lordships were particularly influenced by the way in which Overseas and SA were effectively operated together as a single bank. This, coupled with EW's appointment as the auditor of Holdings and SA, led their Lordships to conclude that it would be wrong to hold, on a strik-ing-out application, that there was no reasonable prospect of it being estab-lished at trial that EW owed a duty of care in tort to Overseas. Thus, Sir Brian Neill (formerly Neill LJ), delivering the unanimous judgment of the Court of Appeal, accepted the following submissions of Overseas's counsel:

(1) Although Overseas had its own auditors and although EW had no direct audit responsibilities to Overseas, the unusual feature of the case, however, was the manner in which the business operations of Overseas and SA, the principal subsidiaries of Holdings, were carried on as though the two companies constituted a single bank.

(2) Throughout the relevant period the boards of directors of Holdings, SA and Overseas comprised six individuals who were common to all three companies. SA and Overseas did not have separate central or head office management.

(3) At all material times the Central Support Organisation operated as a unitary group management to which each of the branches and regions operated by SA and Overseas were required to report.

(4) In addition, the following matters demonstrated that a close relationship existed between EW and Overseas:

(a) the fact that Overseas and SA operated in large measure as a single bank made it necessary for there to be close co-ordination between the two companies and between their auditors;

(b) it was not possible for PW to conduct complete or self-contained audits of Overseas: the activities of SA and Overseas were too closely linked; and

(c) there was an established practice under which PW requested EW to inform PW of any matter of which EW was aware which might be of relevance to the audit of Overseas.

Sir Brian Neill then considered the various tests which have been enunciated for determining whether a duty of care should be held to exist (see Chapter 3) and then stated:

The threefold test and the assumption of responsibility test indicate the criteria which have to be satisfied if liability is to attach. But the authorities also provide some guidance as to the factors which are to be taken into account in deciding whether these criteria are met. These factors will include:

(a) the precise relationship between the adviser and the advisee. This may be a general relationship or a special relationship which has come into existence for the purpose of a particular transaction. In my opinion, counsel for Overseas was correct when he submitted that there may be an important difference between the cases where the adviser and the advisee are dealing at arm's length and cases where they are acting 'on the same side of the fence';

(b) the precise circumstances in which the advice or information came into existence. Any contract or other relationship with a third party will be relevant;

(c) the precise circumstances in which the advice or information was communicated to the advisee, and for what purpose or purposes, and whether the communication was made by the adviser or by a third party. It will be necessary to consider the purpose or purposes of the communication both as seen by the adviser and as seen by the advisee, and the degree of reliance which the adviser intended or should reasonably have anticipated would be placed on its accuracy by the advisee, and the reliance in fact placed on it;

(d) the presence or absence of other advisers on whom the advisee would or could rely. This factor is analogous to the likelihood of intermediate examination in product liability cases; and

(e) the opportunity, if any, given to the adviser to issue a disclaimer.

In rejecting EW's counsel's submission that it was necessary for Overseas to plead and prove that EW knew and *intended* that Overseas would rely on its work and on statements made by it, Sir Brian Neill said:

> In support of this submission, counsel referred to the following sentence in Lord Oliver's speech in *Caparo* [see para 9.7.2, *above*], where he said (at p 645D):
>
> > To widen the scope of the duty to include loss caused to an individual by reliance upon the accounts for a purpose for which they were not supplied and were not intended would be to extend it beyond the limits which are so far deducible from the decisions of this House.
>
> But I am quite satisfied that the general trend of the authorities makes it clear that liability will depend, not on intention, but on the actual or presumed knowledge of the adviser and on the circumstances of the particular case. Indeed, elsewhere in his judgment in *Caparo*, Lord Oliver made it clear that an expressed intention that advice shall not be acted upon by anyone other than the immediate recipient 'cannot prevail against actual or presumed knowledge that it is in fact likely to be relied upon in a particular transaction without independent verification' (see p 639A).

In applying these principles to reach the conclusion that it would be wrong in this case to strike out the plaintiff's pleading as disclosing no cause of action by Overseas against EW, Sir Brian Neill said:

> The judge rejected Overseas's pleaded case that EW owed it a duty of care. In an important sentence he said:
>
> > The fact that the results of the audit work carried out on behalf of SA would become known to and would be of interest to Overseas and its auditors, PW, does not alter the fact that the EW defendants were only carrying out audit functions for and on behalf of Holdings and SA (see *above*).
>
> With great respect to the judge, this comment appears to me to understate to a significant degree the close relationship between Overseas and EW which the pleadings seek to assert. The phrase 'would be of interest to' does much less than justice to the whole substratum underlying the argument for Overseas.
>
> As I understand the Consolidated Statement of Claim and the particulars, as further explained by the submissions on behalf of Overseas, the alleged duty of care is founded on the special circumstances of this case. As pleaded, these circumstances include:
>
> (a) the fact that the banking activities of SA and Overseas were conducted as those of a single bank. The precise nature of this relationship will have to be examined at the trial, but the particulars indicate the nature of the intertwining of the two businesses;
>
> (b) the unusual arrangement whereby the accounts of Holdings and SA were audited by EW, whereas the accounts of Overseas (the other principal banking subsidiary) were audited by PW. In these circumstances it seems to me to be quite clear that EW, who had overall responsibilities for the consolidated accounts of Holdings, had to rely on information supplied

to it by PW. But the intermingling of the businesses of the two banks supports (at least) an argument that Overseas and PW in turn had to rely on EW. The pleading includes this sentence:

> By reason of the high degree of interdependence of Overseas and SA, the financial well-being and the true financial position of SA were a particular concern to Overseas and to PW as auditors of Overseas, such that any factor materially affecting the financial position of SA was likely to have a significant impact on that of Overseas; and

(c) the interdependence between the two banks and the two firms of auditors was recognised in some of the pleaded correspondence.

In cases where parties are dealing at arm's length, the court is likely to be slow to extend the orbit of the duty of care to include persons other than the immediate client. There is a barrier which has to be overcome, and this barrier will be strengthened or even duplicated if a third party is in receipt of independent advice. But the more one studies the pleadings in this case, the more it appears that (arguably at least) the barrier between EW on the one hand and Overseas and PW on the other hand was a mere shadow. It was necessary, if the operations were conducted as alleged, for there to be a constant interchange of information between the firms of auditors. EW was in effect the supervising firm with responsibilities extending (at least arguably) not only to the Boards and Regulatory Authorities of Holdings and SA, but also to the Boards and Regulatory Authorities of Overseas as well as to PW as Overseas's auditors.

If one applies the threefold test or the assumption of responsibility test to the facts of this case as pleaded, it seems to me that it would be quite wrong to dismiss the claims by Overseas in *limine*.

Being mindful of the potential for this judgment to constitute a precedent which could widen the scope of auditors' liabilities, Sir Brian Neill attached the following rider to the Court of Appeal's judgment:

> The facts of this case are most unusual, and I would not wish the conclusion which I have reached on the pleadings to be used in support of an argument in some other case that the court should be more ready than in the past to impose liability whenever a close relationship between adviser and advisee is established.

Comment

The Court of Appeal's attempt to confine its decision to "the special circumstances" of this case is interesting. It is submitted that, over a period of time, it will become apparent that this attempt was futile, because the structure of the bank in this case was not particularly unusual. One often finds a group of companies which has a common management and a common treasury department, but runs its different operations through separate subsidiaries. If those subsidiaries each have different auditors, it is submitted that there is little room for distinguishing the Court of Appeal's decision in the present case from the position which should pertain in these other analogous situations.

Peach v Slater

In *Peach Publishing Ltd v Slater and Co* (13 February 1997, unreported, CA), the defendant firm was the accountants and auditors of Anthony

Sheil Associates Ltd ('ASA'), which the plaintiff proposed to purchase. The plaintiff's sole shareholder and director, Mrs Land, was an experienced chartered accountant. She and the plaintiff retained external accountants and a firm of solicitors to advise them in their proposed acquisition of ASA.

Mrs Land wanted to see recent accounts of ASA before committing the plaintiff to the acquisition. In November 1990, she asked ASA's managing director, Mr Sheil, to produce management accounts for the ten months to 3 October 1990. These accounts ('the October Accounts') were prepared by the defendant and were produced to Mrs Land for consideration by her and her professional advisers. On 10 December 1990, there was a meeting at the defendant's solicitor's office between Mrs Land and her advisers and Mr Sheil and his advisers. At this meeting, Mrs Land sought and obtained an assurance from Mr Slater (the responsible accountant of the defendant) as to the accuracy of the October Accounts. Four days later, the plaintiff agreed to conclude its purchase of the entire issued share capital of ASA. Subsequently, it emerged that the October Accounts contained certain errors, and did not accurately reflect the trading performance of ASA during the period covered by them.

In the present action, the plaintiff sought to make the defendant accountants liable for the losses incurred by the plaintiff through having relied on the October Accounts. The trial judge found as a fact that the plaintiff had relied on Mr Slater's misrepresentation at the meeting on 10 December 1990 and that, if Mr Slater had told Mrs Land the true position with regard to the October Accounts, the plaintiff would not have acquired ASA on the terms that it did.

In the Court of Appeal, the issue was whether the defendant owed the plaintiff a duty of care in respect of Mr Slater's statement at the meeting on 10 December 1990 that the October Accounts were reliable (subject to the qualification that they were not audited). The Court of Appeal answered this question in the negative. Morritt LJ, with whose judgment the other two Lord Justices of Appeal agreed, referred to a number of recent decisions, including *James McNaughton Paper Group Ltd v Hicks Anderson and Co* [1991] 2 QB 113 (see *above*), *Henderson v Merrett Syndicates Ltd* [1995] 2 AC 145 (see para 9.7.6), *White v Jones* [1995] 2 AC 207 (see para 9.7.5) and *McCullagh v Lane Fox and Partners* (1996) 49 Con LR 124 (see para 9.7.3) and then continued:

> First, the touchstone of liability formerly described as 'a voluntary assumption of responsibility' found to have been unhelpful by Lord Griffiths in *Smith v Bush* [1990] 1 AC 831 [see para 9.5.2] and by Lord Roskill in *Caparo Industries plc v Dickman* [1990] 2 AC 605 has been restored to favour, but without the adjective 'voluntary'. [Morritt LJ then cited at length from Lord Goff's speech in *Henderson* (see para 9.5.1) and continued:]
>
> Secondly, the relevant question is whether the defendant assumed responsibility for the task, not whether he assumed legal responsibility for the statement. [Morritt LJ then cited extensively from Lord Browne-Wilkinson's speech in *White v Jones* (see para 9.5.1) and continued:]

Accordingly, the question to be answered is whether, having regard to all of the circumstances of the case, and looking at the matter objectively, it can be said that Mr Slater undertook responsibility to Peach [the plaintiff] for the substantial accuracy of the Management Accounts [ie 'the October Accounts'—see *above*]. To answer this question, it is necessary to consider the facts in greater detail.

Morritt LJ then set out and analysed the facts as found by the trial judge, as well as the trial judge's conclusion that the defendant did owe the plaintiff a duty of care, and then continued:

Slaters contend that the judge was wrong. They submit that the only reason why Mrs Land was concerned to obtain a statement from Mr Slater as to the accuracy of the Management Accounts was thereby to obtain a warranty from Mr Sheil. It is submitted that any assumption of responsibility by Mr Slater as to such accuracy was to Mr Sheil, and not to Mrs Land. I accept the submissions for Slaters.

The underlying transaction was a straightforward sale by the holders of all of the shares of ASA to the plaintiff company. Both vendors and purchasers had their own advisers. The maxim *'caveat emptor'* remains as applicable in such a transaction as ever; one party does not just rely on what he is told by the opposite party or his adviser.

It is true that Mrs Land wanted reliable accounts and that her advisers, Ernst and Young, did not have direct access to the books or personnel of ASA. It is also true that the Management Accounts were drawn up by Mr Slater so that they might be produced by Mr Sheil to Mrs Land for her consideration in connection with the purchase by her of the shares in ASA. All of this must have been obvious to Mr Slater. But no purchaser in the position of Mrs Land would rely on such accounts without more. He would want his own advisers to check their accuracy and have them backed by the warranty of the vendors. The less able his advisers are to check the accuracy of the accounts for themselves, the more he will require protection in the form of warranties.

The judge placed great weight on the fact that a direct statement had been voluntarily made. But it does not follow from the fact that a statement was made both voluntarily and directly by A to B, that A is assuming responsibility to B. The circumstances in which the statement was made must also be considered in order to evaluate the significance of the fact that the statement was both voluntary and direct. In my view, the overwhelming preponderance of evidence is that the statement was made for the benefit and information of Mr Slater's clients, the vendors, and not for the benefit and information of the opposite party, the purchaser [ie the plaintiff].

Having noted that the evidence disclosed that Mrs Land did not think much of Mr Slater's professional confidence, Morritt LJ concluded by saying:

It is helpful to return to the list of matters set out in the judgment of Neill LJ in the *James McNaughton* case [see *above*], particularly items numbers 1 and 5. The purpose for which the statement was both made and communicated by Mr Slater to Mrs Land was to indicate to Mr Sheil of the vendors that a warranty might be given. Mr Slater was the adviser of Mr Sheil and the other vendors, not some valuer or expert, independent of any of the parties and exercising some independent judgment on whom those on both sides of the transaction might be expected to rely. All this must have been as apparent to Mr Slater as to the others present at the meeting. Mrs Land's concern was to obtain a warranty from the vendors, not a statement from an accountant in whom she had no confidence.

I do not think that Mr Slater did assume responsibility for the accuracy of the Management Accounts to Mrs Land and Peach [the plaintiff]. In so far as there may be a separate point, I do not think that it would be fair, just or reasonable, in all the circumstances of the case, that a duty of care should be imposed on Mr Slater in respect of the statement relied upon by Peach.

Chapman v Barclays Bank

In *Chapman v Barclays Bank plc* (26 March 1997, unreported), the plaintiff, Mr Chapman, had been a director and shareholder of John S Bass and Co Ltd ('Bass'), which was a company to whom the defendant bank provided overdraft facilities. In due course the bank informed Bass of its intention to cancel all of the facilities. In response, Bass presented the bank with a certain deal pursuant to which the plaintiff had the right to acquire all of the issued shares of Bass. The bank responded in turn by informing the plaintiff that it required an independent assessment to be made of Bass, whereupon the plaintiff signed a letter of instruction to Ernst & Whinney ('EW') to prepare a report on the financial state of Bass.

When the EW report was presented on 30 September 1988, it was apparent that it was inaccurate in a number of material respects. It was agreed that an accurate report free from defects should be produced and considered at a meeting to be held on 7 October 1988. At that subsequent meeting the EW report was presented again without any alterations or amendments to correct the inaccuracies in the first draft. Three days later the defendant made formal demand on Bass for the repayment of all of its outstanding indebtedness, and two days later obtained administration orders. Bass subsequently went into liquidation.

In the present action the plaintiff alleged that the bank owed him a duty of care in respect of the economic losses which he suffered through Bass going into liquidation. He alleged that the bank breached this duty by withdrawing Bass's overdraft facilities without obtaining an accurate report from EW and by relying on the first report, knowing it to be inaccurate. The plaintiff asserted that if an accurate report had been obtained, an administration order would not have been made and he would not have suffered loss and damage.

The Court of Appeal, in agreement with the original judge, struck out the plaintiff's claim as disclosing no reasonable cause of action. The plaintiff's counsel had submitted that a sufficiently proximate relationship existed between the plaintiff and the bank by virtue of the fact that, although the bank's customer was Bass (and not the plaintiff personally), all of the bank's dealings were with the plaintiff, who was known as the person running Bass, and the bank knew that its decision in relation to Bass would have a heavy financial impact on the plaintiff. In rejecting these submissions, Otto LJ said:

I accept the plaintiff's counsel's submission that the categories of negligence are not closed and that the law must move forward, particularly in the sphere of economic loss suffered by a third party, on an incremental case by case basis. However, in my view, the plaintiff does not satisfy the [second] of the *Caparo* conditions. There was in my view no proximity between the parties. The plaintiff was not a customer of the bank and the bank was not in a position where advice was sought or given. There were no circumstances from which it can be inferred that the bank assumed any responsibility towards Mr Chapman. The bank merely undertook to consider the Ernst & Whinney report. There is no authority for the proposition that a bank, by requiring an independent report, puts itself under an obligation to consider the granting of a loan facility with a particular degree of care in order to safeguard the interests of not only the borrower, but also third parties known by the bank to have a financial interest in that facility. In summary, the plaintiff's case is at best one of foreseeability of damage alone. That is no relationship of proximity. It would not be just, fair or reasonable to spell out a duty of care in the particular circumstances of this case.

HIT Finance v Cohen Arnold

In *HIT Finance Ltd v Cohen Arnold and Co* (24 September 1997, unreported), the plaintiff agreed to make a loan to a company called Hatchford Ltd, which was controlled by a Mr Osias Schreiber, if certain conditions were satisfied. Two of these were that Mr Schreiber should personally guarantee Hatchford's loan covenant and that he should provide a personal net worth statement signed by his accountants. On 18 May 1989, the defendant, Mr Schreiber's accountants, wrote a letter to the plaintiff in which it was stated: "We can confirm that, according to the information provided to us, the net asset worth of Mr Schreiber, including properties at valuation, is in excess of £3.3m." In reality, this was a gross over-statement by some £2.9m.

In due course, Hatchford defaulted on the loan. HIT, as first mortgagee, sold the property which had been bought with the loan, but the proceeds of sale were less than the amount owing to the plaintiff by Hatchford. The plaintiff sought to recover the shortfall from Mr Schreiber under his guarantee. Mr Schreiber was made bankrupt by his own petition and the dividends were negligible. The plaintiff then commenced the present action against Mr Schreiber's accountants (the defendant), claiming that the defendant had been negligent in its compilation of Mr Schreiber's net asset statement and that the defendant was liable to make good the plaintiff's residual loss.

One of the questions at the trial was whether the defendant owed the plaintiff a duty of care in writing the letter of 18 May 1989 to the plaintiff. The judge, Mantell J, answered this question in the affirmative. After setting out the passage in Lord Bridge's speech in *Caparo Industries plc v Dickman* [1992] AC 605, in which Lord Bridge articulated the features that should be present before a duty of care can be imposed in this type of case (see *above*), Mantell J dealt with the defendant's counsel's submission that the defendant did not know that the letter was required "specifically in connection with a particular transaction or transactions of a particular kind" because Mr Schwarz, the partner in the defendant responsible for producing the net worth statement, maintained that he had simply been asked by Mr

Schreiber to provide a personal reference, and he had no idea as to the purpose for which it was required. The judge rejected this submission because he found as a fact, on a balance of probabilities, that, in writing the letter, Mr Schwarz did in fact know that it was required either to support a loan from the plaintiff to Mr Schreiber personally or as a guarantee from Mr Schreiber in support of a loan to one of his companies. Based on this finding, the judge concluded that, in writing the letter of 18 May 1989, the defendant did owe a duty of care to the plaintiff. He said (at para 41):

> Having held that the defendant knew that its letter of 18 May 1989 would be communicated to the plaintiff, and knew that the purpose for which the letter was required was in connection with a lending either to Mr Schreiber or Mr Schreiber's company, as to which Mr Schreiber's creditworthiness was an important consideration, it is, in my judgment, a short step to the conclusion that the defendant must have known that HIT [the plaintiff] would be 'very likely to rely on it for the purpose of deciding whether or not to enter upon that transaction or a transaction of that kind' [*per* Lord Bridge in *Caparo*].

Mantell J then considered the scope of the defendant's duty of care. In this regard, he cited Lord Hoffmann's *dictum* in *South Australia Asset Management Corporation v York Montague Ltd* [1997] AC 191, to the effect that a person under a duty to take reasonable care to provide information on which someone else will decide upon a course of action is, if negligent, not generally responsible for all of the consequences of that course of action but only for the consequences of the information being wrong [see Chapter 2, para 2.1.5], and concluded, therefore, that the defendant's liability to the plaintiff was limited to the amount of the over-statement of Mr Schreiber's net worth in the defendant's letter of 18 May 1989, namely, £2.9m (see *above*).

Lastly, the defendant's liability to the plaintiff depended on the defendant having been negligent in its compilation of the net worth statement. Mantell J answered this question in the affirmative. He said (at para 69):

> The defendant voluntarily assumed a responsibility towards the plaintiff. It need not have done so. I take on board all that has been said about the difficulty of verifying the information at short notice, but, having assumed the responsibility, the defendant was bound either to verify the information which it provided or to make it plain to the plaintiff that it was unwilling or unable to do so.

Coulthard v Neville Russell

In *Coulthard v Neville Russell (a firm)* ((1997) *The Times*, 18 December), the question in the Court of Appeal was whether the High Court judge was right in refusing to strike out the plaintiffs' Statement of Claim on the ground that it failed to disclose a reasonable cause of action. The background facts were that the whole of the issued share capital of a particular company, 'D&H', was acquired by Hendal Limited ('Hendal'). The plaintiffs, Mr Dawes, Mr Coulthard and Mr Shuttleworth, were directors of D&H. The defendants, Neville Russell, a firm of accountants, were the auditors of D&H and of Hendal.

The acquisition of D&H's shares by Hendal was funded in part by a loan made to Hendal by a bank. This loan was to be serviced by way of funds provided by D&H to Hendal by way of a loan. Unbeknown to the plaintiffs, this arrangement constituted a breach of s 151 of the Companies Act 1985, which makes it a criminal offence for a company to provide financial assistance for the purchase of its own shares. In due course, after D&H had gone into insolvent liquidation, the Secretary of State for Trade and Industry obtained orders for disqualification of the plaintiffs as company directors on the ground that the loans made by D&H to Hendal constituted a breach of s 151 of the Companies Act.

In the present action the plaintiffs contended that Neville Russell owed them a duty of care as directors of D&H to warn them that the loans to be made by D&H to Hendal would or might be in breach of s 151 of the 1985 Act; and that, as a consequence of the illegality of the loans, the accounts of D&H would not show a true and fair view of its financial position if those loans were included as assets in its balance sheet because a loan which contravenes s 151 is unenforceable against the borrower. Neville Russell applied to have the plaintiffs' claim struck out as disclosing no reasonable cause of action. The judge refused to do so.

In the Court of Appeal, Neville Russell's counsel submitted that the plaintiffs' claim should be struck out because, on the authority of *Caparo*, auditors' statutory duties are owed solely to the company whose accounts they have approved, and not to the directors personally. In rejecting this submission, and in refusing to strike out the plaintiffs' Statement of Claim, Chadwick LJ, delivering the court's judgment, said:

> For my part, I would be inclined to accept the proposition that it is no part of the auditors' statutory duties to protect directors personally from the consequences of their mistakes and wrongdoing. But breach of statutory duty is not alleged in the present case. The plaintiffs put their claim on the basis of a duty of care at common law. Properly understood, the plaintiffs' claim is that in the course of the discussions leading to the approval of the 1989 annual accounts by them as directors, the defendants ought to have told them that the proposed treatment of the payments to Hendal would lead to a qualified audit report and so was not a path down which responsible directors could sensibly go—at least without first obtaining clear and authoritative legal advice as to the position under s 151 of the Companies Act 1985. The duty at common law arose, if at all, because, in advance of the audit report in respect of the 1989 accounts, the defendants had, quite properly, entered into discussions with the directors as to the way in which they, as directors, were to perform their duties in relation to the preparation and approval of the accounts. In the course of those discussions, so it is alleged, the defendants advised that the proposed treatment of the payments to Hendal was unexceptionable; or, at the least, they said nothing to suggest that it would give rise to any difficulty when they, as auditors, came to give their audit report.

Without expressing an opinion either way as to whether the plaintiffs' claim would be likely to succeed at trial, Chadwick LJ explained why it would be wrong to dismiss the plaintiffs' claim on a striking-out application.

First, he referred to the following passages from the judgment of Sir Thomas Bingham MR in *E (a minor) v Dorset County Council* [1995] 2 AC 685 (at p 693):

> It is clear that a statement of claim should not be struck out under RSC, Ord 18 r 19 as disclosing no reasonable cause of action save in clear and obvious cases, where the legal basis of the claim is unarguable or almost incontestably bad. It was argued by the plaintiff's counsel that this procedure was inappropriate in a case such as this, raising issues which were novel and difficult. Relying in particular on *Lonrho Plc v Fayed* [1992] 1 AC 448 he urged the undesirability of courts attempting to formulate legal rules against a background of hypothetical facts and pointed to the potential unfairness to plaintiffs if their cases were finally ruled upon before they were able, with the benefit of discovery, to refine their factual allegations. The defendants answered that their applications do in effect raise an issue of law for decision by the court: if they cannot show the plaintiffs' claims to be plainly bad, then their applications must fail; but if they can show that, then it is preferable in the interests of all concerned that the claims should be dismissed now before the costs of a full trial are incurred.
>
> There is great force in both these arguments. I share the unease many judges have expressed at deciding questions of legal principle without knowing the full facts. But applications of this kind are fought on ground of a plaintiff's choosing, since he may generally be assumed to plead his best case, and there should be no risk of injustice to plaintiffs if orders to strike out are indeed made only in plain and obvious cases. This must mean that where the legal viability of a cause of action is unclear (perhaps because the law is in a state of transition), or in any way sensitive to the facts, an order to strike out should not be made. But if after argument the court can be properly persuaded that no matter what (within the reasonable bounds of pleading) the actual facts the claim is bound to fail for want of a cause of action, I can see no reason why the parties should be required to prolong the proceedings before that decision is reached.

Applying these principles to the present case, Chadwick LJ concluded:

> In my view the liability of professional advisers, including auditors, for failure to provide accurate information or correct advice can, truly, be said to be in a state of transition or development. As the House of Lords has pointed out, repeatedly, this is an area in which the law is developing pragmatically and incrementally. It is pre-eminently an area in which the legal result is sensitive to the facts. I am very far from persuaded that the claim in the present case is bound to fail whatever, within the reasonable confines of the pleaded case, the facts turn out to be. That is not to be taken as an expression of the view that the claim will succeed; only as an expression of my conviction that this is not one of those plain and obvious cases in which it could be right to deny the plaintiffs the opportunity to attempt to establish their claim at a trial.

9.7.3   Surveyors

Cann v Willson

In *Cann v Willson* (1888) 39 ChD 39, the defendant was a firm of surveyors who had been asked by the borrower's solicitors to provide a valuation on a certain property for the purpose of enabling a proposed mortgagee to decide whether, and how much money, to lend to the borrower on the faith of that valuation. The solicitor had specifically drawn the defendant's attention to the purpose for which the valuation was required and to the responsibility which the defendant was undertaking. The plaintiff duly relied on the defendant's valuation and advanced a large sum of money to the borrower. In due course the borrower defaulted and the value of the property proved to be less than the amount which the plaintiff had lent the borrower. It also emerged that the defendant's valuation had been negligent.

The court upheld the plaintiff mortgagee's claim against the defendant valuer. Chitty J said (at p42):

> In this case the . . . valuation was sent by the defendants direct to the agents of the plaintiff for the purpose of inducing the plaintiff . . . to lay out the trust money on mortgage. It seems to me that the defendants knowingly placed themselves in that position, and in point of law incurred a duty towards [the plaintiff] to use reasonable care in the preparation of the valuation. I think it is like the case of the supply of an article—the supply of the hair wash in the case of *George v Skivington* [see Chapter 6, para 6.2.5]. There the hair wash was deleterious—not deleterious for all purposes, but deleterious for the purpose for which it was intended to be used. . . . In this case the document supplied appears to me to stand upon a similar footing . . . as if it had been an actual article that had been handed over for the particular purpose of being so used.

In *Le Lievre v Gould* [1893] 1 QB 491, this case was overruled because it was inconsistent with *Derry v Peek* (see para 9.2.2, *above*). However, in *Hedley Byrne* the House of Lords held that this case had in fact been correctly decided and that it was wrong of the Court of Appeal in *Le Lievre* to have overruled it. The principle of law stated by Chitty J in this case is fully consistent with the principles laid down in *Hedley Byrne* and subsequent cases.

Yianni v Evans

In *Yianni v Edwin Evans & Sons* [1982] 1 QB 438, the plaintiff had purchased a house with the assistance of a building society mortgage. The building society had made its advance to the plaintiff on the strength of a valuation provided to the building society by the defendant valuers. Subsequently it emerged that the house was suffering from severe subsidence, which would cost a substantial sum of money to put right. The surveyor was negligent in not detecting this subsidence when he carried out his inspection valuation for the building society.

The plaintiff, who was the owner of the house, sued the surveyor for his loss. The court upheld the plaintiff's claim, notwithstanding that the plaintiff had never seen the defendant's report and notwithstanding that the mortgage application form which he had signed had suggested that applicants who desired a survey for their own information and protection should consult a surveyor on their own account, and notwithstanding that the plaintiff, having read this warning, had decided not to employ his own surveyor because of the expense involved.

The evidence established that the plaintiff's decision not to obtain his own surveyor's report was not unusual: the evidence established that only 10–15 per cent of intending borrowers do so. As Park J said (at p 445):

> ... the intending mortgagor feels that the building society, whom he trusts, must employ for the valuation and survey competent qualified surveyors; and, if the building society acts upon its surveyor's report, then there can be no good reason why he should not also himself act upon it. ... So, if Mr Yianni had had an independent survey, he would have been exceptional in the experience of building societies and of those employed to carry out surveys and valuations for them.

In these circumstances Park J held that a duty of care arose because the defendant knew that his valuation would be passed to the plaintiff (in fact this was not done because the valuation was inadvertently left out of the envelope) who, notwithstanding the building society's literature, in the defendant's reasonable contemplation, would place reliance upon the valuation's correctness in making his decision to buy the house and mortgage it to the building society. This decision was approved by the House of Lords in *Smith v Eric S Bush*.

Smith v Bush

In *Smith v Eric S Bush* [1990] 1 AC 831, the plaintiff applied to a building society for a mortgage to enable her to purchase a house. The building society was required by statute to obtain a valuation report for itself. The society required the plaintiff to pay for this report and to sign a declaration accepting, first, that although a copy of the report would be supplied to her, neither the society nor the surveyor would be warranting, representing or giving any assurance to her that any statements contained in the report were accurate or valid, and secondly, that the report would be supplied to her without any acceptance of responsibility on the surveyor's part to her.

The surveyor duly inspected and valued the house and a copy of the report was supplied to the plaintiff. In reliance upon it she accepted an advance from the building society and purchased the house. One and a half years later bricks from the chimneys collapsed and fell through the roof into the loft and the main bedroom and caused extensive damage. This occurred because two chimney breasts had been removed from the first floor, leaving the chimney breasts in the loft and the chimneys unsupported. The defendant, who was the surveyor who had inspected the house for the building society, had observed the removal of the first floor chimney breasts, but had not checked to see that the chimneys above were adequately supported. The trial judge was satisfied that the defendant had not exercised reasonable skill and care (ie had acted negligently) in carrying out this task. The question was whether the surveyor owed a duty of care to the plaintiff for the loss which she had suffered by virtue of his negligence and, if so, whether this would be negated by the surveyor's disclaimer of liability. This latter aspect is considered in Chapter 10, para 10.3.3.

The House of Lords upheld the plaintiff's claim. Lord Jauncey said (at p 871):

[The question is whether the facts disclose that the defendants] in inspecting and reporting must, but for the disclaimers, by reason of the proximate relationship between them [and the plaintiff], be deemed to have assumed responsibility towards [the plaintiff] as well as to the building society who instructed them. . .

There can only be an affirmative answer to this question. . . [The defendants] knew from the outset: (1) that the report would be shown to Mrs Smith; (2) that she would probably rely on the valuation contained therein in deciding whether to buy the house without obtaining an independent valuation; (3) that if . . . the valuation was . . . excessive, she would be likely to suffer loss; and (4) that she had paid to the building society a sum to defray the defendants' fee. . .

It is critical to this conclusion that the defendants knew that Mrs Smith would be likely to rely on the valuation without obtaining independent advice.

Lord Jauncey was careful to qualify what he had said above by adding (at p 872):

. . . there is likely to be available to [an intending mortgagor] a wide choice of sources of information, to wit, independent valuers to whom he can resort, in addition to the valuer acting for the mortgagee. I would not therefore conclude that the mere fact that a mortgagee's valuer knows that his valuation will be shown to an intending mortgagor of itself imposes upon him a duty of care to the mortgagor. Knowledge, actual or implied, of the mortgagor's likely reliance upon the valuation must be brought home to him. Such knowledge may be fairly readily implied in relation to a potential mortgagor seeking to enter the lower end of the housing market, but *non constat* that such ready implication would arise in the case of a purchase of an expensive property whether residential or commercial.

Lord Griffiths also made this point when he said (at p 859):

It must, however, be remembered that this is a decision in respect of a dwelling house of modest value in which it is widely recognised by surveyors that purchasers are in fact relying on their care and skill. It will obviously be of general application in broadly similar circumstances. But I expressly reserve my position in respect of valuations of quite different types of property for mortgage purposes, such as industrial property, large blocks of flats or very expensive houses. In such cases . . . with very large sums of money at stake, prudence would seem to demand that the purchaser obtain his own structural survey to guide him in his purchase. . . .

Speaking more generally, Lord Griffiths said (at p 865):

[The law will deem that] a duty of care be owed by an adviser to those who act upon his advice . . . only if it is foreseeable that if the advice is negligent the recipient is likely to suffer damage, that there is a sufficiently proximate relationship between the parties and that it is just and reasonable to impose the liability. In the case of a surveyor valuing a small house for a building society or local authority, the application of these three criteria leads to the conclusion that he owes a duty of care to the purchaser. If the valuation is negligent and is relied upon, damage in the form of economic loss to the purchaser is obviously foreseeable. The necessary proximity arises from the surveyor's knowledge that the overwhelming probability is that the purchaser will rely upon his valuation, the evidence was that surveyors know that approximately 90 per cent of purchasers did so, and the fact that the surveyor only obtains the work because the purchaser is willing to pay his fee. It is just and reasonable that the duty should be imposed for the advice is given in a professional as opposed to a social context and liability for breach of the duty will be limited both as to its extent and amount. The extent of the liability is limited to the purchaser of the house—I would not extend it to subsequent purchasers. The amount of the liability cannot be very great because it relates to a modest house. There is no question here of creating a liability of indeterminate amount to an indeterminate class. I would certainly wish to stress that in cases where the advice has not been given for the specific purpose of the recipient acting upon it, it should only be in cases when the adviser knows that there is a high degree of probability that some other identifiable person will act upon the advice that a duty of care should be imposed. It would impose an intolerable burden upon those who give advice in a professional or commercial context if they were to owe a duty not only to those to whom they give the advice, but to any other person who might choose to act upon it.

Harris v Wyre Forest

In *Harris v Wyre Forest District Council* [1990] 1 AC 831, which was decided at the same time as *Smith v Bush*, the plaintiff applied to the defendant local authority for a loan to assist in the purchase of a house. By statute the defendant was obliged to obtain an independent valuation of the property. The defendant required the plaintiff to pay the valuer's fee and to sign a declaration accepting that no responsibility would be accepted by the defendant for the value or the condition of the property by reason of the valuer's report. The defendant also advised the plaintiff for his own protection to instruct his own surveyor and/or architect to inspect the property.

The defendant's valuer duly inspected and valued the property, the defendant offered to lend a certain sum of money to the plaintiff to be secured by way of a mortgage on the property, and the plaintiff duly completed the purchase. The plaintiff did not see the valuer's report, but assumed from the defendant's offer that the valuer had not found serious defects in the house. Three years later it emerged that the house was defective and needed extensive repair work. The trial judge found that the valuer had not exercised reasonable skill and care in making his inspection and his valuation.

The only material difference between this case and *Smith* was that the valuer's report was not shown to the plaintiff in this case. The House of Lords held that this was not a sufficient difference and, accordingly, held that the defendant did owe a duty of care to the plaintiff for the plaintiff's loss. The *dicta* quoted *above* from some of their Lordships' speeches are equally apposite to this case.

Beaumont v Humberts

In *Beaumont v Humberts* (1990) 49 EG 46, the plaintiff, who was described by the court as "an intelligent and sophisticated businessman and not a humble purchaser of a house of modest value, such as was contemplated by Lord Griffiths in *Smith v Bush*", wished to purchase a certain house. For this purpose he instructed the defendant valuer to carry out a structural survey (but not a valuation) for him. Subsequently he approached a bank for a loan to facilitate this purpose. The bank required the house to be valued, and for the plaintiff to pay for this. In order to avoid the expense of another full survey, the plaintiff suggested that the bank should ask the defendant to provide a valuation, in view of his knowledge of the property.

The bank obtained a valuation from the defendant, first, with vacant possession and, secondly, for insurance reinstatement purposes. The bank duly lent the plaintiff a certain sum of money and the plaintiff insured the house for the reinstatement value which the defendant had provided to the bank.

Subsequently, after the house had been destroyed by fire, it emerged that the defendant's estimated reinstatement value was substantially too low. The plaintiff sought to recover this loss from the defendant. The Court of Appeal, by 2:1, upheld the plaintiff's claim. It is worthwhile considering all of the judgments, because they show how difficult the position can be where the court is asked to infer knowledge of likely reliance (which was the issue here) from the circumstances.

Taylor LJ (one of the majority) said (at p 52):

> This case does not concern a valuation at the lower end of the market. Nor, however, was it in the 'very expensive' category alongside blocks of flats and industrial properties to which Lord Griffiths referred in *Smith v Bush*. It is important, therefore, to look at all the specific circumstances, the probabilities and the expectations of the parties. The defendant knew that he had been brought in by the bank because of his previous professional relationship with the plaintiff. He knew that the plaintiff would become aware of his valuation because he was having to pay for it and because he would be required by the bank to insure for not less than the amount of the defendant's reinsurance valuation. It must have seemed unlikely that the plaintiff would have obtained a valuation from another surveyor. Why should he, when he was paying for one from the surveyor upon whom he had recently placed reliance [in obtaining a structural survey]? In my judgment the test of proximity here is whether, when the defendant gave his valuation, it was clear to him that, because of the close relationship stemming from the history between himself and the plaintiff, the plaintiff was likely to rely and act upon that valuation. In my view, once the plaintiff knew of, and had to pay for, the bank's valuation from his own surveyor, it was (in Lord Griffiths' words in *Smith v Bush*) 'an overwhelming probability' that he would rely upon it.

The other majority judge, Dillon LJ, simply said (at p 53):

> The obvious reason why the plaintiff got the bank to instruct his own surveyor rather than instructing some other surveyor of the bank's choice was that he did not want to pay the bills of two surveyors. The position of proximity which the defendant accepted when he agreed to accept the bank's instructions is thus essentially the same as the position in *Smith v Bush*, and the consequence is that the defendant owed a duty to the plaintiff as well as to the bank in making his valuation.

The dissenting judge, Staughton LJ, said (at p 48):

> There is no direct evidence that the defendant in fact knew that the plaintiff was likely to rely on his reinstatement value. The defendant was never asked. The question then is whether such knowledge can be inferred from other evidence or (which is the same thing) whether he ought to have known.

This is the same question which the majority judges posed, but Staughton LJ differed from them in his answer when he said:

> I am not sure whether it is logically possible for the defendant to have known that the plaintiff was going to rely on his valuation. He did, however, know that the plaintiff had not asked him for any valuation when he gave instructions for the structural survey, he may well have regarded his advice to the bank as essentially ancilliary to the advice he had already given to the plaintiff, and he knew that the plaintiff was a company director, a man of substance capable of taking decisions for himself.

Saddington v Colleys

In *Saddington v Colleys Professional Services* ((1995) *The Times*, 22 June, CA), the plaintiff and her husband, the second defendant, had purchased a house in 1980. In 1989, when the mortgage balance stood at £75,000, the second defendant approached a mortgage financier for a loan, to be charged on the said property. The mortgage financier instructed the first defendants, a firm of estate agents and valuers, to value the property for the purpose of assessing the security for the proposed loan.

The first defendants duly inspected the property and provided a written valuation report in which they valued the property at £350,000. The mortgage financier provided a copy of the report to the second defendant, who showed it to the plaintiff. In reliance on the report, the plaintiff and the second defendant executed a new mortgage on the property, which secured an advance of £175,000. Of that sum, £75,000 discharged the existing mortgage and the remaining £100,000 was advanced to the second defendant, who invested it in his business.

In due course, the £100,000 which had been invested in the second defendant's business was lost by reason of the failure of that business. The plaintiff ascertained that the first defendants had over-valued the property. Its true value at the time of the first defendants' valuation should have been no more than £205,000. The plaintiff alleged that if the first defendants had valued the property at £205,000, the plaintiff would not have consented to a further loan being secured on the property, no loan would have been made, and the plaintiff would not have been left with a £100,000 mortgage on the property from which she derived no benefit.

In the circumstances, the plaintiff alleged that the first defendants owed the plaintiff a duty of care in valuing the property, which duty she alleged they had breached by under-valuing it. Her counsel placed reliance on the House of Lords' decision in *Smith v Bush* [1990] 1 AC 831 (see *above*). The Court of Appeal rejected the plaintiff's claim. Balcombe LJ, with whom the other two Lord Justices of Appeal agreed, said:

In my judgment, *Smith v Bush* represents the high water mark in this field, and it would not be a justifiable development of the law to extend it to the pleaded facts of the instant case. Lord Griffiths [in *Smith v Bush*] clearly took the view that *Smith v Bush* was at the outer limit.

The following propositions are relevant to this Appeal:

  (i) the law should develop novel categories of negligence incrementally and by analogy with established categories;

 (ii) there is no duty to take care in the abstract. The duty is to avoid causing to the plaintiff particular damage of the particular kind which he has in fact sustained (see *Caparo Industries plc v Dickman* [1990] 2 AC 605 [see para 9.6.2]);

(iii) in every case, the court must not only consider the foreseeability of the damage and whether the relationship between the parties is sufficiently proximate. It must also pose and answer the question: in this situation, is it fair, just and reasonable that the law should impose on a defendant a duty of the scope suggested for the benefit of the plaintiff? (see *James McNaughton Paper Group Ltd v Hicks Anderson and Co* [1991] 2 QB 113 [see para 9.7.2]); and

 (iv) the acceptance of a loan cannot, of itself, be described as a loss causing damage (see *Galloo Limited v Bright Grahame Murray* [1994] 1 WLR 1360 [see para 9.7.2]).

Balcombe LJ said that he was satisfied that the application of these principles to the facts of the present case led inevitably to the conclusion that the plaintiff's case would necessarily fail. He said:

> If the damage alleged is merely the creation of a mortgage as security for a loan made to the plaintiff and her husband [the second defendant], that is no damage. If the damage alleged is the subsequent loss of the £100,000, it is not damage of a kind which the first defendants could or should have foreseen. To make the first defendants liable for that loss would be unfair, unjust and unreasonable. I would have arrived at the same result if I had approached the matter as one of causation. If there had been a breach of duty by the first defendants in over-valuing the property, it did not cause the loss of the £100,000. At the most, it gave the opportunity for that loss to occur.

McCullagh v Lane Fox

In *McCullagh v Lane Fox and Partners Ltd* (1996) 49 Con LR 124 (CA), the facts of which are set out in Chapter 10, para 10.3.3, the plaintiff, like the plaintiff in *Beaumont v Humberts* (see *above*), was "a sophisticated and experienced member of the public". The issue here was whether the defendant, a firm of estate agents which had been retained by the vendor of a house, was liable to the plaintiff for the plaintiff's economic loss consisting of the diminution in value of the house, bought in reliance on a negligent misrepresentation by the defendant about the size of the plot in the particulars which the defendant had prepared for the purpose of distribution to prospective purchasers.

Because the written particulars contained a comprehensive disclaimer of liability on the part of the defendant for any inaccuracies in the information contained in the particulars, a large part of the court's focus was directed to the effect of the disclaimers in the particular circumstances of the case (see Chapter 10, paras 10.3.3 and 10.3.4). Furthermore, for reasons that are more properly dealt with in Chapter 8, para 8.3.3, two of the judges in the Court of Appeal held that the defendant did not owe the plaintiff a duty of care irrespective of the existence and the effect of the disclaimers in the particulars.

However, the third judge, Hobhouse LJ, was of the view that the defendant did owe the plaintiff a duty of care in tort, but that this was negated by the disclaimers in the particulars. After referring extensively to the House of Lords' decisions in *Hedley Byrne & Co Ltd v Heller & Partners Ltd* [1964] AC 465, *Caparo Industries plc v Dickman* [1990] 2 AC 605, *Henderson v Merrett Syndicates Ltd* [1995] 2 AC 145 and *White v Jones* [1995] 2 AC 270, Hobhouse LJ said:

> It is thus clear from the more recent authorities that *Hedley Byrne* is still the governing authority in cases such as the present. The elements of reasonable foreseeability and reliance are fundamental, as is the element of assumption of responsibility. The existence of a disclaimer is relevant to answering the relevant questions and thus to the question whether there was a duty of care.
>
> In the present case, there was a direct relationship between Mr Scott [the defendant's director] and the plaintiff. Mr Scott made the representation to the plaintiff: he chose to speak to him and make a factual statement which was designed to influence the decision-making process of the plaintiff. Mr Scott was holding himself out as a person who knew the area of the land being offered for sale, presumably because he had measured it or had supervised its measurement. He had special knowledge which was not available to the plaintiff. The relationship was a business one. Mr Scott had a financial interest in influencing persons to buy the property and to buy it at as high a price as could be negotiated. His remuneration, as everyone knew, was dependent upon someone agreeing to buy the land and upon the price at which that person was willing to purchase.
>
> Mr Scott would be paid by way of a commission payable out of the deposit paid by the purchaser. Indirectly, he would be paid by the purchaser. The absence of a specific consideration moving directly from the representee to the representor is the only thing which prevents the relationship between them from being contractual. Thus far, I see nothing in the structure of the transaction which would negative a duty of care to be owed by the estate agent in relation to any representation that the estate agent chooses to make to the prospective purchaser for the purpose of influencing him to buy.

Hobhouse LJ then considered whether, apart from the disclaimers, there were any reasons for negativing this *prima facie* duty of care. In this regard, Hobhouse LJ gave careful consideration to the way in which the possibility of an intermediate inspection can affect the question whether a duty of care should be held to exist in any particular case (see also Chapter 6, para 6.3). He said:

> In the law of negligence, the concept of proximity is inconsistent with the contemplation or expectation of an intermediate check. In *Donoghue v Stevenson* [1932] AC 562, Lord Atkin referred to 'the proximate relationship which may be too remote where inspection, even of the person using the article, certainly of an intermediate person, may be interposed'. Thus, in product liabil-

ity cases, the likelihood that there will be an intermediate inspection or check negatives the existence of the duty of care: see *Herschtal v Stewart and Arden Ltd* [1940] 1 KB 155 [see para 6.3.5] and *Haseldine v CA Daw and Son Ltd* [1941] 2 KB 343 [see para 6.4.4].

In a transaction for the sale of land, it will normally be contemplated that there will be pre-contract inquiries which will be used by the prospective purchaser to obtain specific representations verifying important facts. Similarly, parties will very frequently instruct a surveyor to carry out a structural survey before deciding to make an offer or to exchange contracts. Thus, it does not follow that a representation, although intended to influence the representee, will be relied upon in the relevant way without an intermediate check. It is therefore necessary to examine further the significance of the representation in the transaction. This is not something which is peculiar to estate agents, nor does it amount to some special principle of qualified liability for estate agents. The application of this principle must depend upon the facts of the case before the court.

Normally, in the type of situation that arose in this case, no duty of care would be imposed because it would be reasonable to expect that the prospective purchaser would commission a pre-contract intermediate inspection of the property. However, Hobhouse LJ felt that this was not the situation in the present case because, when the plaintiff and the defendant met at the property and the defendant orally provided the incorrect information about the size of the plot, the plaintiff told the defendant that he intended to demolish the house and rebuild it. Hobhouse LJ said that this led to the reasonable inference that the plaintiff would not be obtaining an intermediate inspection, with the consequence that the normal effect of the expectation of such an inspection did not apply. The defendant did, therefore, owe the plaintiff a duty of care in tort unless the disclaimers had the effect of negativing that duty—which they did (see Chapter 10, para 10.3.3).

The other two judges in the Court of Appeal, Sir Christopher Slade and Nourse LJ, came to a different conclusion on this aspect of the case. Without considering the effect of the plaintiff's statement that he intended to demolish the house, Sir Christopher Slade said: "Mr Scott did not owe the plaintiff a duty of care on the Saturday morning when Mr Scott made the relevant statement, if only because at that time he would have been entitled reasonably to take the view that his statement would be independently checked and would not be relied on". Nourse LJ agreed with this.

For Sir Christopher Slade and Nourse LJ, the more potent question was whether a duty of care arose at a subsequent time when Mr Scott, in their view, first appreciated that the plaintiff would be exchanging contracts without a survey. This aspect of the case is discussed in Chapter 8, para 8.3.3.

Secured Residential Funding plc v Nationwide Building Society

In *Secured Residential Funding plc v Nationwide Building Society* (21 October 1997, unreported), Allied Dunbar Mortgage Limited ('ADM') and Household Mortgage Corporation plc ('HMC'), who were both in the business of lending money on the security of first mortgages of residential property, decided to enter into a joint venture pursuant to which they would offer potential borrowers a form of loan, to be known as a Special Status Home Loan, which would be based not on the earnings of the applicant (as is more usual), but on the value of the property to be offered up as security. For the purpose of giving effect to this scheme, ADM and HMC purchased an off-the-shelf company and changed its name to Secured Residential Funding Limited (ie the plaintiff).

Thereafter ADM and the plaintiff entered into an agreement whereby ADM was to introduce applicants for Special Status Home Loans to the plaintiff, ADM was to examine the applications for such loans and ensure that the specified criteria were satisfied and, if any particular offer to lend was accepted, the contract of loan would then be concluded between the borrower and the plaintiff. One of the specified criteria was that ADM would obtain a valuation of the prospective borrower's property, with the aim of ensuring that the amount of any loan, which would be less than the valuation, would be well covered. In due course, ADM entered into an agreement with the defendant, a major building society with its own property valuation department, whereunder, for a fee, the defendant's valuers would carry out property valuations for ADM on specific properties when requested by ADM to do so. The parties to this agreement were only ADM and the defendant, but not HMC or the plaintiff. The defendant's only contact was with ADM, and ADM alone paid for valuation reports from the defendant. In fact, neither the plaintiff's existence, nor its involvement in any of the loan transactions made by the plaintiff pursuant to the Special Status Home Loan Scheme, were ever known to the defendant.

In the transaction which led to the present action, the borrowers applied to ADM for a Special Status Home Loan of £340,000 to be secured by a mortgage over a property which they were proposing to purchase. ADM asked the defendant to provide a valuation of the property. The defendant duly valued the property at £640,000 and, in due course, the plaintiff lent £340,000 to the borrowers, who, in turn, executed a charge by way of a first legal mortgage over the property in favour of the plaintiff to secure the repayment of monies due under the loan. Subsequently, when the borrowers defaulted in repaying the loan, the property was repossessed and sold. The amount realised on the sale fell far short of the amount due to the plaintiff under the loan.

The plaintiff brought the present action against the defendant to recover its loss on the basis that the defendant had negligently over-valued the property and that, if the defendant had valued it correctly, the plaintiff would have lent far less to the borrower and would not have suffered a loss when the property was sold. At the trial, one of the issues was whether the defendant owed a duty of care to the plaintiff for the plaintiff's economic loss. The judge, Daniel Brennan QC, sitting as a deputy High Court judge, answered this question in the negative. After referring to Lord Oliver's four-part test in *Caparo Industries plc v Dickman* [1990] 2 AC 605 (see *above*), he said (at para 28):

Thus, there must be knowledge by the adviser that his advice will be passed on to a specific recipient or to someone within an ascertainable class. That knowledge may be actual, or it can arise constructively because of all of the circumstances. Knowledge on the part of the allegedly negligent valuer embraces not only actual knowledge, but such knowledge as will be attributed to a reasonable person placed in the valuer's position.

Under the heading "Assumption of Responsibility", his Honour said: "The issue of knowledge is allied to the question of whether a valuer in the circumstances should be held to have assumed responsibility for his report to particular third parties or a class". He then referred to Lord Griffiths' speech in *Smith v Bush* [1990] 1 AC 831 (see *above*) and then continued (at para 35):

> Thus, proximity only arises where there is 'the overwhelming probability' from the surveyor's knowledge that the third party will rely upon his valuation. So, the adviser will only fall within the proximity concept if he knows that there is 'a high degree of probability' that some other identifiable person will act upon the advice. The robust conclusion of Lord Griffiths that 'it would impose an intolerable burden upon those who give advice in a professional or commercial context, if they were to owe a duty, not only to those to whom they give the advice, but to any other person who might choose to act upon it', sets the appropriate limits, based on common sense and practicality, when determining the issue of proximity in this context.

After referring extensively to the expansive descriptions of the concept of assumption of responsibility in *Henderson v Merrett Syndicates Limited* [1995] 2 AC 145 and *White v Jones* [1995] 2 AC 207 (see *above*), the judge said (at para 38):

> Thus, it is clear that, depending on the circumstances, the assumption of responsibility by the defendant (whether judged objectively or subjectively) may greatly assist the inquiry into proximity. But, significantly, Lord Browne-Wilkinson spoke [in *White v Jones*] of a voluntary assumption of responsibility 'in circumstances where he [the defendant] knows, or ought to know, that an identified plaintiff will rely on his answers or advice'. My emphasis of these words is of crucial significance in determining the main issue in this action. Similarly, in *Caparo*, Lord Oliver also referred to knowledge of the adviser that his advice will be relied upon by 'a particular person or class of persons in connection with that transaction'.

Applying these principles to the facts of the present case, Deputy Judge Brennan felt that it was clear that no duty of care could be imposed on the defendant for the plaintiff's loss. He said (at para 40):

> The defendant did not know, nor ought to have known, that this unidentified plaintiff, or anyone other than ADM, would rely on this valuation report. The mere possibility that someone might do so, eg by syndicated loan, is not enough. I conclude that, in this case, there is no reason in principle, as to proximity or fairness, requiring the imposition of a duty of care by this defendant toward this plaintiff in circumstances such as these.

Under the heading "An Incremental Approach?", the judge referred to the approach taken by Neill LJ in *James McNaughton Paper Group Ltd v*

613

Hicks Anderson and Co [1991] 2 QB 113 (see *above*) and stated, *inter alia* (at para 43, using numbering that corresponds with Neill LJ's numbering in *McNaughton*):

> (3) any relationship here arising was between the defendant and ADM. There was no reason, explicit or implicit, for the defendant to know of the existence of the plaintiff and its involvement in these transactions or any reliance by it on the defendant's report;
>
> (4) the size of the class to whom the report was intended by the defendant was limited to ADM alone. There is no reason arising in these circumstances why the defendant should consider that the loan might be syndicated, or that others might become involved;
>
> (5) here, the defendant had no knowledge, either actual or constructive, of the plaintiff. In the circumstances here prevailing, there is no reason to attribute knowledge of the plaintiff to the defendant on the basis of what a reasonable person in the circumstances of the defendant would have considered; and
>
> (6) any reliance on the report as far as the defendant was concerned would be by ADM and no other.

For these reasons, Deputy Judge Brennan held that there was no basis for any incremental extension of the law in relation to the circumstances of this case. So as to drive the point home even more clearly, he added (at para 44):

> It was open to the plaintiff to declare itself to the defendant, or it could have entered into contractual arrangements with the defendant if it had so wished. There is no evidence to establish any good reason for the plaintiff not declaring itself. In the circumstances, it would be a wholly unjustifiable extension of the professional man's duty of care, that he should be regarded as insurer to all those who might rely on his report even though he has not, and could not be expected to have, any knowledge of their existence or use of his report.

In response to the plaintiff's counsel's submission, based on *White v Jones*, that an injustice would be perpetrated if the court refused to impose a duty of care on the defendant to the plaintiff, being the party who had suffered an actual loss because ADM, although having a potential remedy against the defendant, was not able to sue the defendant because ADM had not suffered an actual loss (as the funds advanced to the borrower belonged to the plaintiff as a distinct entity from ADM), his Honour said (at para 51):

> I reject this argument. Concepts of duty and proximity cannot be distorted to accommodate the commercial difficulties in which the plaintiff finds itself. It was open to the plaintiff to identify itself to the defendant as a party who intended to rely on the defendant's valuation. It chose not to do that. This loss must lie where it falls.

Comment

The result in this case seems to be quite harsh, given the very close identity of interest between the plaintiff and ADM. Perhaps Deputy Judge Brennan himself felt the harshness of his decision when he noted that he had invited the parties' counsel to make submissions to him about the possible relevance of *The Albazero* [1977] AC 774 and subsequent related authorities. He also noted that both counsel had declined this invitation.

The principle enunciated in *The Albazero* is that, in certain exceptional cases, a person may sue in his own name to recover a loss which he has not in fact suffered, but he will be personally accountable for any damages so recovered to the person who has in fact suffered the loss. The rationale is to provide a remedy in a situation where no other remedy would be available to the person who has sustained a loss which was caused by the defendant, thereby stopping the defendant from getting off scot-free.

A more recent application of the principle is the House of Lords' decision in *Linden Gardens Trust Ltd v Lenesta Sludge Disposals Ltd* [1994] 1 AC 85. In this case, their Lordships extended the principle to a situation in which building work had been done by the defendant under a contract with the first plaintiffs who, despite a contractual bar against assignment of their contractual rights without the consent of the defendant, had (without consent) assigned those rights to the second plaintiffs, who suffered damage by reason of defective work carried out by the defendant. This case is considered more fully in Chapter 5, para 5.5.1.

The question whether the present case was also a case where a judge would have been justified in making 'an *Albazero* exception' has to be answered in two ways. First, the structure of the action was wrong for the application of the exception because ADM, as the only entity with the contractual right to sue the defendant, was not the plaintiff in the action. This was only a technical defect that could have been cured by an amendment to the Statement of Claim.

Secondly, if ADM had been the plaintiff (or, more likely, one of two joint plaintiffs, the other being Secured Residential Funding Ltd), it is submitted that the answer to the question whether it would be right in this case to extend the exception to ADM would depend on how much weight judges would attach to the fact that, in *Linden Gardens*, the defendant knew, or ought reasonably to have known, that the building was going to be occupied in due course by third parties and not by the original contracting party itself, so that it was foreseeable that damage caused by the defendant by a breach of its contract with the original contracting party would cause loss to a later owner and not merely to the original contracting party. This was in fact the situation in *Linden Gardens*, and it was mentioned as part of the House's reasons, but it is not clear whether it was a *sine qua non* of the decision. In the context of the present case, this point is important because of the judge's express finding of fact that the defendant did not know, nor were there any circumstances from which it ought to have known, that the plaintiff (Secured Residential Funding Ltd) would rely on the defendant's valuation report.

It is also interesting to note how the deputy judge dealt with the case of *Rothschild and Sons Ltd v Berenson* (22 June 1995, unreported, and CA, 7 February 1997, unreported), the facts of which are set out in para 9.7.5. There is an obvious similarity between the present case and the *Berenson* case, which was relied on by the plaintiff's counsel in the present case. However, Deputy Judge Brennan held that the *Rothschild* case did not assist the plaintiff in the present case because, in his view, knowledge on the part of Berensons of the identity and probable participation of the other banks as joint lenders with Barclays was clearly established; whereas in the present case the defendant had no knowledge of the identity or participation of the plaintiff and no circumstances existed from which the defendant ought to have made that connection. He said (at para 46):

> The essential finding of Knox J, and crucial in the assessment of the case by the Court of Appeal, was that Mr Berenson had been informed that the advances would be made by other lenders as well as Barclays, with whom they were dealing directly. In the circumstances, Berensons ought to have known ('indeed it should have been self-evident' [*per* Saville LJ in the Court of Appeal]) that the other lenders would be relying on the Funds Request Form dealt with by Berensons.

Deputy Judge Brennan was correct in saying that this was the reason that moved the Court of Appeal to hold that Berensons owed a duty of care to all of the banks and not just to Barclays, but it is submitted that he is not correct in stating that this also applied to Knox J, who said on this point (emphasis added):

> In my judgment, Berensons should have known that Barclays were not the only financier lending money on the strength of the Funds Request Form. I say this because Mr Berenson was told of the involvement of other banks besides Barclays *but, in any event*, if there was a duty of care to Barclays as lenders to CFL in relation to each specific transaction, I see no reason for the duty not to extend to parties concurrently involved with Barclays in advancing the relevant funds. The ambit of the duty is sufficiently defined by the amount advanced in the particular transaction. Further lenders are within a clearly identifiable class of persons engaged in the particular transaction. If there is a duty of care to Barclays, it will be applicable in relation to the whole of the sum advanced if Barclays advanced it all. I see no logic in limiting the duty of care to whatever share Barclays ultimately undertakes pursuant to any arrangement of which Berensons knew no details.

It is submitted that this passage from Knox J's judgment implies strongly that he would have held that Berensons were under a duty of care to all of the banks even if Mr Berenson had not been told of the involvement of other banks besides Barclays. To this extent, Knox J's decision in *Berenson* is irreconcilable with Deputy Judge Brennan's decision in the present case; although perhaps the way that the Court of Appeal in *Berenson* dealt with the matter (see para 9.7.5) indicates that, if Mr Berenson had not been provided with this information, the Court of Appeal might have overruled Knox J's judgment on this point.

Lastly, it is interesting to note how Deputy Judge Brennan dealt with Knox J's further comment that "a duty of care owed to a lender as principal can properly extend to a duty of care to the same lender as agent for an undisclosed principal". In relation to this *dictum*, Judge Brennan said (at para 47):

> The comment [by Knox J in *Berenson*] in relation to the potential liability to an undisclosed principal was, in my respectful view, an unnecessary gloss, the finding of knowledge having been so clear. But, in any event, the comment is explicable. First, it refers to there being no good policy reason for not imposing

a duty because the ambit of the duty was sufficiently defined by the amount advanced in the particular transaction. More precisely stated, it appears that the ambit of the duty on Berensons was defined by the nature of the transaction, and the ambit of any potential liability was defined by the amount to be advanced, which was known to Berensons since it was they who had to fill in the figures on the appropriate forms.

As Knox J found that, by reason of Berensons' knowledge, there was a *prima facie* duty of care to the other financial institutions, the duty owed to them was the same as the nature of the duty owed to Barclays and, as in his analysis, any potential liability to them in conjunction with Barclays was no greater than the actual amount to be advanced, there was no reason of policy based upon the nature of the duty for not holding it to have been assumed to the other institutions.

In other words, the *prima facie* duty did not offend the limits of Lord Oliver's first requirement in *Caparo Industries plc v Dickman* [1990] 2 AC 605 [ie that the advice was required for a purpose which was made known to the adviser at the time the advice was given (see para 9.6.2, *above*)]. Further, the finding that the fellow lenders were within a clearly identifiable class of persons must follow from the general finding of knowledge of Berensons. Thus, the duty so found does not offend the limits set by Lord Oliver in requirements (2) and (3) of his framework [ie (2), that the adviser knows, actually or inferentially, that his advice will be communicated to the advisee, either specifically or as a member of an ascertainable class, in order that it should be used by the advisee for that purpose; and (3), that it is known, either actually or inferentially, that the advice so communicated is likely to be acted upon by the advisee for that purpose without independent inquiry].

It is submitted that this analysis is not convincing because, first, as pointed out *above*, the finding of knowledge was not a determining feature for Knox J in reaching his decision; and, secondly, because Deputy Judge Brennan, after stating that Knox J's comment was explicable "in any event", went on to analyse Knox J's comment in terms which depended on the finding of knowledge having been made.

9.7.4 Other certifiers

Introduction

Closely allied to the surveyors' cases is the loose grouping of cases involving other persons who have provided a certification of the condition or a valuation of the worth of a particular item of property to a third party, which the plaintiff has relied upon to his detriment.

Glanzer v Shepard

This case, a decision of the New York Court of Appeals (1922) 233 NY 236, is discussed *above* in para 9.3.3 as part of the discussion of *Ultramares v Touche*. It is illustrative of the principles which are applicable here.

Ministry of Housing v Sharp

In *Ministry of Housing and Local Government v Sharp* [1970] 2 QB 223, a person who owned a piece of vacant land had applied to his local planning authority for permission to develop it. This was refused because it was in the green belt. He claimed and received compensation from the plaintiff ministry for this refusal. The ministry's payment was subject to the proviso that if the local authority subsequently did give permission to develop this land, then the compensation which they had paid to the landowner would have to be repaid to them. Such payment would have to be made by the person who developed the land even though it might not be the landowner to whom the compensation had initially been paid.

In order to secure this repayment, and to give notice of it to a subsequent purchaser, the ministry registered a charge on the register of local land charges. Subsequently the landowner applied for planning permission again. This time it was granted. The landowner then decided to sell the land. The prospective purchaser's solicitor requisitioned an official search from the local authority, whose employee was the defendant, Mr Sharp, the local registrar. Due to the defendant's negligence the search of the register overlooked the plaintiff's charge. A clear charge certificate was issued. The purchaser accepted that official certificate as accurate and paid the full purchase price to the plaintiff. In due course the plaintiff found out that planning permission had been granted and that the land was being developed. The plaintiff asked the landowner to pay back the compensation which he had received from the plaintiff. He refused to do so and, indeed, he was under no obligation to do so as the relevant statute only imposed this obligation on "the developer". The purchaser of the property was the developer, but the plaintiff could not recover the compensation payment from him as he had not had notice of the plaintiff's charge.

Therefore the plaintiff sought to recover the amount of the compensation payment from the defendant local registrar. Lord Denning MR said (at p 268) that this case came "four square within the principles which are stated in *Candler v Crane Christmas and Co*, which were approved by the House of Lords in *Hedley Byrne*", and then said:

> ... the duty to use due care in a statement arises ... from the fact that the person making it knows, or ought to know, that others, being his neighbours in this regard, would act on the faith of the statement being accurate. That is enough to bring the duty into being. It is owed, of course, to the person to whom the certificate is issued and whom he knows is going to act on it, see the judgment of Cardozo J in *Glanzer v Shepard*. But it is also owed to any person whom he knows, or ought to know, will be injuriously affected by a mistake, such as the encumbrancer here.

Salmon LJ agreed with Lord Denning MR, that a duty of care should be imposed on the defendant for the plaintiff's loss in this case, and he founded this duty on an even wider basis. He said (at p 278):

> The present case does not fit precisely into any category of negligence yet considered by the courts. The plaintiff has not been misled by any careless statement made to him by the defendant or made by the defendant to someone else whom the defendant knew would be likely to pass it on to a third party such as the plaintiff, in circumstances in which the third party might reasonably be expected

to rely upon it. . . . I am not, however, troubled by the fact that the present case is, in many respects, unique. I rely on the celebrated *dictum* of Lord Macmillan that 'the categories of negligence are never closed' *Donoghue v Stevenson* [1932] AC 562.

Salmon LJ then focused on the fact that if the purchaser who had obtained the certificate from the defendant had suffered economic loss in consequence of the certificate having been inaccurate, the defendant would have owed a duty of care in tort to the purchaser. He said (at p 279):

> I do not think it matters that the search was made at the request of the purchaser and the certificate issued to him. It would be absurd if a duty of care were owed to a purchaser but not to an incumbrancer [ie the plaintiff in this case]. . . . The purchaser who buys on the faith of a clear certificate might suffer very heavy financial loss if the certificate turns out to be incorrect. Such a loss is reasonably to be foreseen as a result of any carelessness in the search of the registrar or the preparation of the certificate. The proximity between the council and a purchaser is even closer than that between the plaintiff and the defendants in *Candler v Crane, Christmas and Co* [1951] 2 KB 164 [see Chapter 9, paras 9.2.2 and 9.2.3]. . . . Clearly a duty to take care must exist in such a case. Our law would be grievously defective if the council owed a duty of care to the purchaser in the one case but no duty to the incumbrancer in the other. The damage in each case is equally foreseeable. It is in my view irrelevant that in the one case the certificate is issued to the person it injures, and in the other case it is not. . . . In my view the proximity is as close in one case as in the other and is certainly sufficient to impose upon the council . . . a duty to take reasonable care.

Mariola v Lloyd's Register

In *Mariola Marine Corporation v Lloyd's Register of Shipping (The Morning Watch)* [1990] 1 Lloyd's Rep 547, the defendant was a ship classification society which regularly surveyed ships on its register. The owner of a certain yacht, before the next scheduled survey was due, requested the defendant to carry out a special survey because he was intending to sell the yacht. The defendant did this and issued a clear certificate. The owner's agents issued particulars offering the yacht for sale and stated: "Always maintained to 100 A1 condition at Lloyds. Has passed current special survey with no difficulty, so purchaser is spared expense of a survey". The plaintiff duly purchased the yacht. Subsequently it emerged that the yacht was suffering from serious corrosion, which the defendant's surveyor should have detected when he made his inspection.

The plaintiff sued the defendant for its economic loss consisting of the cost of the repairs which it needed to carry out to the yacht. The court rejected the plaintiff's claim. Phillips J held that, although it was reasonably foreseeable by Lloyd's that a purchaser would be influenced by the results of the special survey when considering whether to buy the yacht, and although Lloyd's deliberately maintain a system of classification whereby parties other than the owners of classified vessels are expected to rely as providing an assurance that the vessel is maintained in good condition, no duty of care was owed by Lloyd's to the plaintiff in respect of its economic losses suffered in consequence of Lloyd's negligent survey. He said (at p 559): "The primary purpose of the classification system is to enhance the safety of life and property at sea, rather than to protect the economic interests of those involved, in one role or another, in shipping. The objects of Lloyd's are not primarily directed to the protection of such interests".

Phillips J dismissed the plaintiff's submission that this case was covered by *Smith v Bush*, by saying (at p 561): "There is no question of the plaintiff having paid Lloyd's survey fees. The plaintiff's counsel sought to persuade me that these formed a latent element in the purchase price, but I found this submission unrealistic. Thus a factor emphasised in all of the speeches in *Smith v Bush* is missing in the present case". He pointed to another difference between this case and *Smith* by saying:

> The survey was not carried out for the benefit of a specific individual purchaser. Mariola had not come on the scene when the survey was ordered. They were not intended to act on the result of the survey, they were merely one of an indeterminate class of persons who might do so. While it was possible that whoever decided to purchase *Morning Watch* would do so on the strength of the fact that it had passed its special survey, this was not an 'overwhelming probability' [in the words of Lord Griffiths in *Smith*], and I am not even able to find on the evidence that it was more likely than not. While it was possible that a purchaser would rely on the special survey without independent enquiry, this was not probable or highly probable.

Marc Rich v Bishop Rock

In *Marc Rich & Co AG v Bishop Rock Marine Ltd ('The Nicholas H')* [1996] 1 AC 211, the third defendant, 'NKK', was a ship classification society. On 20 February 1986, the *Nicholas H* was in the course of a loaded voyage from South America to Italy when a crack appeared in its hull. On 22 February, the *Nicholas H* anchored in Puerto Rico where further cracks developed. On 25 February, a surveyor employed by NKK was called in by the ship's master at the instigation of the US Coastguard. The surveyor recommended permanent repairs. The owners of the ship baulked at this because it would have involved dry docking, with consequential discharge and reloading of the cargo, and would have been very expensive.

As the case proceeded on a preliminary issue of law, it is not known what conversations then transpired, but it is fair to surmise, as the House of Lords did, that the surveyor was persuaded to change his mind, because on 2 March 1986 he pronounced that the vessel was fit to proceed on its intended voyage after completing only some temporary repairs to the shell plating. The ship sailed the same day. The following day the temporary welding repairs cracked. Six days later the ship sank. No one was killed, but there was a total loss of the ship and all of the cargo on board.

The plaintiff was the owner of the cargo, the value of which was more than US$6m. The plaintiff sued the shipowners and the classification society. The plaintiff settled its claim against the shipowners for about US$500,000, which was in line with the extent of the shipowners' contractual liability to the plaintiff under the contract between them. That contract was contained in a bill of lading which incorporated the Hague Rules, which in turn limited the amount of the shipowners' liability to the plaintiff in the event of a loss at sea of the plaintiff's cargo.

The plaintiff continued with the balance of its claim against the classification society. The question for the court was whether the classification society owed a duty of care in tort to the plaintiff for the loss of the plaintiff's cargo. This question was tried as a preliminary issue, for which purpose it was assumed that:

(1) the plaintiff, by reason of its proprietary interest in the cargo, had title to sue if the classification society otherwise owed it a duty of care (see further on this point, Chapter 5, para 5.2.1);

(2) it was foreseeable that lack of care by the classification surveyor was likely to expose the cargo to danger of physical damage;

(3) the damage in fact suffered by the plaintiff was physical damage to its goods (ie not pure economic loss);

(4) the loss of the ship and its cargo was the result of the carelessness of the surveyor in reversing his initial recommendation of immediate permanent repairs, in permitting the ship to continue on its voyage when only temporary repairs had been carried out, and in failing to ensure that those repairs were adequate for the remainder of the ship's voyage;

(5) although the surveyor had no legal right to stop the ship sailing, his *de facto* control was absolute, in the sense that, if he had maintained his original recommendation, it is inconceivable that the vessel would have sailed away because a disregard of his recommendation would have nullified the shipowners' insurance; and

(6) there was a sufficient degree of proximity "to fulfil that requirement for the existence of a duty of care".

Nevertheless, the House of Lords, by 4:1, held that the classification society did not owe a duty of care to the plaintiff for the loss of its cargo. The main ground for this decision was that, as the primary responsibility for looking after the cargo lay on the shipowners under the contract of carriage, it would not be fair to impose a like duty in tort on the classification society. Lord Steyn, with whose speech the other majority Law Lords agreed (at p 238), adopted the following *dicta* of Saville LJ in the Court of Appeal in this case:

> The Hague Rules . . . form an internationally recognised code adjusting the rights and duties existing between shipowners and those shipping goods under bills of lading. . . the Rules create an intricate blend of responsibilities and liabilities, rights and immunities and limitations on the amount of damages recoverable . . . in relation to the carriage of goods under bills of lading. The proposition advanced by [the plaintiff's counsel] would add an identical duty owed by the classification society to that owed by the shipowners, but without any of these balancing factors, which are internationally recognised and accepted. I do not regard that as a just, fair or reasonable proposition.

Lord Steyn also emphasised the effects on insurance that he believed would follow if the classification society was held liable in this case. He said (at p 239):

The insurance system is structured on the basis that the potential liability of shipowners to cargo owners is limited under the Hague Rules . . . insurance premiums payable by owners obviously reflect such limitations on the shipowners' exposure.

If a duty of care by classification societies to cargo owners is recognised in this case, it must have a substantial impact on international trade. . . Societies would be forced to buy appropriate liability insurance.

Lord Steyn also referred to the fact that classification societies do in fact already carry liability risks insurance, but dismissed this as irrelevant by saying (at p 239):

[It] is no doubt right [that classification societies already do carry liability risks insurance] since classification societies do not have a blanket immunity from all tortious liability. On the other hand, if a duty of care is held to exist in this case, the potential exposure of classification societies to claims by cargo owners will be large. That greater exposure is likely to lead to an increase in the cost to classification societies of obtaining appropriate liability risks insurance. Given their role in maritime trade [see *below*] classification societies are likely to seek to pass on the higher cost to owners. Moreover, it is readily predictable that classification societies will require owners to give appropriate indemnities. Ultimately, shipowners will pay.

The result of a recognition of a duty of care in this case will be to enable cargo owners, or rather their insurers, to disturb the balance created by the Hague Rules . . . by enabling cargo owners to recover in tort against a peripheral party to the prejudice of the protection of shipowners under the existing system. For these reasons, I would hold that the international trade system tends to militate against the recognition of the claim in tort put forward by the cargo owners against the classification society.

Another factor which Lord Steyn regarded as important was that the role of NKK as an international ship classification society was to promote safety of life and ships at sea in the public interest. He said (at p 240):

The fact that a defendant acts for the collective welfare is a matter to be taken into consideration when considering whether it is fair, just and reasonable to impose a duty of care: *Hill v Chief Constable of West Yorkshire* [1989] AC 53; *Elguzouli-Daf v Commissioner of Police of the Metropolis* [1995] QB 335 [see Chapter 8, para 8.3.3, *above*]. Even if such a body has no general immunity from liability in tort, the question may arise whether it owes a duty of care to aggrieved persons and, if so, in what classes of case, eg, only in cases involving the direct infliction of physical harm or on a wider basis. . .

. . . classification societies . . . act in the public interest. . . . NKK is an independent and non-profit making entity, created and operating for the sole purpose of promoting the collective welfare, namely, the safety of lives and ships at sea. In common with other classification societies, NKK fulfils a role which in its absence would have to be fulfilled by states. And the question is whether NKK, and other classification societies, would be able to carry out their functions as efficiently if they become the ready alternative target of cargo owners, who already have contractual claims against shipowners. In my judgment, there must be some apprehension that the classification societies would adopt, to the detriment of their traditional role, a more defensive position.

Comment

This case is a good illustration of the fact that, even where there is a high degree of proximity between the defendant and the plaintiff in terms of space, time and causation, it is open to a court to hold that no duty of care exists because, in all the circumstances, the court does not regard it as fair, just and reasonable so to hold (see further, Chapter 2, para 2.3 and Chapter 3, para 3.3, *above*).

It is submitted that the dissenting speech of Lord Lloyd is more persuasive than the views of the majority Law Lords in this case. First, Lord Lloyd argued persuasively that the cargo owners' claim should be upheld on the basis that the ship and the cargo were taking part in a joint venture pursuant to which, in accordance with the House of Lords' decision in *Morrison Steamship Co Ltd v Greystoke Castle (Cargo Owners)* [1947] AC 265, a cargo owner who has had to contribute to the cost of repairs of a ship under a general average clause in the bill of lading is entitled to recover its general average contribution from the person who damaged the ship, notwithstanding that the plaintiff's own goods have not been damaged (see Chapter 5, paras 5.4.1 and 5.4.6). Thus, Lord Lloyd said (at p 227):

> The principle established in the *Greystoke Castle* case is . . . directly relevant to the present case. When the master called in Mr Ducat [the surveyor employed by the classification society], and thereafter incurred expenditure for the common safety, he was acting as much in the interests and on behalf of the cargo, as of the ship. It seems almost impossible to say, therefore, that, while Mr Ducat owed a duty of care to the ship, he owed no duty of care to the cargo on the ground that the relationship between the parties was insufficiently close.

This point was not dealt with in the majority judgment, but it is submitted that, if the House of Lords' earlier decision in *Greystoke* still stands for the proposition which it laid down—and there is no reason why it should not—then Lord Lloyd was correct in holding that the cargo owners' claim in the present case fell within that principle (see, further, Chapter 5, paras 5.4.1 and 5.4.6).

Secondly, Lord Lloyd seriously challenged the main thesis of the majority's reasoning. He said (at p 222) (emphasis added):

> . . . I have difficulty in seeing why the balance of rights and liabilities between shipowner and cargo would be upset by holding the defendants liable for the consequence of [the surveyor's] negligence. . . The Hague Rules have nothing to say on the issue of duty of care of parties other than cargo owners and carriers.
> . . .
> . . . the 'intricate regime' of the Hague Rules . . . has nothing to do with whether it is fair, just and reasonable that [the surveyor] and his employers should be liable to cargo for their assumed negligence. The irrelevance of the Hague Rules is underlined by the further consideration that the limitation provisions on which the shipowners relied to limit their liability . . . is not derived from the Hague Rules at all, but from section 503 of the Merchant Shipping Act. . . therefore . . . the Court of Appeal's judgment on this part of the case [and the reasons of the majority Law Lords] can only be supported if the *mere existence* of a contract of carriage under which the shipowners can limit their

liability is inconsistent with, or militates against, the imposition of unlimited liability on a third party in tort.

Lord Lloyd observed that the existence of such a contract as a bar to a successful claim by the plaintiff against the classification society in this case would be a retrogressive step which would set the development of the law back by more than half a century. He continued in the passage just cited by saying (at p 233): "This was surely the very error which was exposed in *Donoghue v Stevenson* [1932] AC 562 and *Grant v Australian Knitting Mills Ltd* [1936] AC 85 [see Chapter 6, paras 6.2.1, 6.2.2 and 6.3.5]".

The classification society's counsel sought to distinguish *Grant* on the ground that there was no internationally recognised code in that case for regulating the rights and duties of the party primarily responsible for taking care, ie the manufacturer of the defective underpants. Lord Lloyd dismissed this submission by saying (at p 223):

> I accept, of course, that there is no internationally recognised code governing the manufacturer of underpants. But, for the reasons already mentioned, I do not regard this as a relevant consideration in the case of shipowners. More important, I am not sure what is meant by saying that the shipowners are 'primarily' responsible for taking care, and that this militates against the need to impose a similar duty on NKK. Of course, the shipowners are primarily—indeed solely—responsible for getting the cargo to its destination; and of course, the shipowners must take proper care of the cargo as bailees, subject to the terms of any contract of carriage between the parties. But I am unable to see why the existence of the contract of carriage should 'militate against' a duty of care being owed by a third party in tort. The function of the law of tort is not limited to filling in gaps left by the law of contract, as this House has recently reaffirmed in *Henderson v Merrett Syndicates Ltd* [1995] 2 AC 145 [see para 9.7.6, *below*]. The House rejected an approach which treats the law of tort as supplementary to the law of contract [ie as providing for a tortious remedy only where there is no contract].

Lord Lloyd also referred to various cases involving ships in which a tortfeasor was held liable for the physical damage or personal injury caused to persons or property by his negligent act, notwithstanding the existence of a separate contract between the plaintiff and the shipowner, under which the plaintiff's right of recovery was limited. In one such case, *Adler v Dickson* [1955] 1 QB 158, the Court of Appeal said (through Jenkins LJ):

> The plaintiff's right of action [for her personal injury caused on board ship by the negligence of the ship's master] against the company [the shipowner] is clearly taken away by the exempting provisions of the contract, but I fail to see how that can have the effect of depriving her also of her separate and distinct right of action against the defendants as the actual tortfeasors.

Lord Lloyd also referred to the House of Lords' decision in *Midland Silicones Ltd v Scruttons Ltd* [1962] AC 446, in which stevedores who had damaged the plaintiff's goods while offloading them from a ship owned by a third party were held to be disentitled from placing reliance on the shipowner's limitation of liability to the plaintiff under the bill of lading.

The principle applied by the House in that case was that a stranger to a contract (ie the stevedores) cannot take advantage of it even where it is clear that some provision in the contract was intended to benefit him.

In the present case, Lord Steyn made it clear that the majority's decision exempting the classification society from liability did not involve a departure from this principle because he said that the question was not whether the classification society was covered by the Hague Rules, but whether, in all the circumstances, it was fair, just and reasonable to require them "to shoulder a duty which by the Rules primarily lies on the shipowners" without at the same time extending to them the concomitant benefits of those rules or other international conventions. Lord Lloyd disposed of this apparent difference between the cases by saying (at p 224): "It would have been hopeless to argue [in *Midland Silicones*] that the stevedores should not be liable on the ground that it would not be fair, just and reasonable to impose on them a duty of care in tort with unlimited liability, having regard to the shipowners' limited liability under the Hague Rules".

Lord Lloyd was also scathing about the majority's view that it made a difference that classification societies "act for the collective welfare". He said (at p 228):

> . . . it was pointed out that classification societies are charitable non-profit making organisations, promoting the collective welfare and fulfilling a public role. But why should this make any difference? Remedies in the law of tort are not discretionary. Hospitals are also charitable non-profit making organisations. But they are subject to the same common duty of care . . . as betting shops or brothels.

He also rejected the insurance considerations that weighed with the majority. After noting that NKK would be able to afford the cost of insurance, he said (at p 228):

> . . . it is said . . . that to impose liability on classification societies would involve an extra layer of insurance, and that this would be wasteful and inconvenient. There was no evidence that classification societies do not already insure [*cf. above*, where Lord Steyn observed that classification societies do in fact carry liability risks insurance]. . . Traditionally the courts have regarded the availability of insurance as irrelevant to the question whether a duty of care should be imposed. Even if this traditional view is gradually being displaced, it cannot be right that the courts should reach conclusions on the availability of insurance, or the impact of imposing a fresh liability on the insurance market generally, without proper material.

It is submitted that the logic of Lord Lloyd's dissenting speech is compelling. The majority reasoning probably rules out just about all future claims against classification societies for economic losses suffered by persons with whom they did not have a direct contract. However, it is submitted that judges should be wary of regarding the House's decision as a precedent against the imposition of a duty of care in tort on all certifiers, or indeed on all tortfeasors in cases where the plaintiff has agreed by contract with a third party to restrict the amount of damages that the plaintiff can recover from the third party in the event of the plaintiff's goods being damaged while in the possession of the third party.

In *The Nicholas H*, Lord Steyn said (at p 236): "The present case can only be decided on the basis of an intense and particular focus on all its distinctive features and then applying established legal principles to it". It is submitted, therefore, that it would be better for the future development of the law to regard the majority's decision in this case as being confined to the particular facts of the case, and to seek guidance from the dissenting speech of Lord Lloyd in future cases that involve the same factual matrix. This point is discussed further in Chapter 10, para 10.2.1.

Lastly, it is interesting to note how the majority's approach differed from the approach of the House of Lords in other recent cases on three issues in common. First, in discussing the effect that liability might have on the way in which classification societies might carry out their functions if they were to owe a duty of care to cargo owners who already have (limited) contractual claims against shipowners, Lord Steyn said (at p 241): "In my judgment, there must be some apprehension that the classification societies would adopt, to the detriment of their traditional role, a more defensive position".

This can be contrasted with the way in which the majority in *Spring v Guardian Assurance Plc* [1995] 2 AC 296 (see para 9.7.7, *below*) dealt with the submission that, if a duty of care in tort was to be imposed on employers towards employees for negligent references, employers would become defensive about providing such references, and this would be detrimental to the well-being of employees in general. Lord Lowry responded by saying (at p 326) that he viewed "the possibility that some referees will be deterred from giving frank references or indeed any references as a spectre conjured up by the defendants to frighten your Lordships into submission"; and Lord Slynn said (at p 336): "Even if it is right that the number of references given will be reduced, the quality and value will be greater". Lord Lloyd expressed a similar sentiment in *The Nicholas H* when he said, in dissent (at p 229): "I suspect that a decision in favour of the cargo owners would be welcomed by members of the shipping community at large, who are increasingly concerned by the proliferation of sub-standard classification societies".

Secondly, in *The Nicholas H*, Lord Steyn and the majority succumbed to the floodgates argument by saying (at p 241):

> Counsel for the cargo owners argued that a decision that a duty of care exists in this case would not involve wide ranging exposure for NKK and other classification societies to claims in tort. That is an unrealistic position. If a duty is recognised in this case there is no reason why it should not extend to annual surveys, docking surveys, intermediate surveys, special surveys, boiler surveys, and so forth.

In *White v Jones* [1995] 2 AC 207 (see para 9.7.5, *below*), the defendants argued that, if a duty of care was to be imposed on them in that case, it would be impossible to place any sensible boundaries on the cases in which such recovery would be allowed. Lord Goff dismissed this objection by saying (at p239): "I am not persuaded that we should decide a fairly straightforward case against the dictates of justice because of foreseeable troubles in more difficult cases. There must be boundaries to the availability of a remedy in such cases, but these will have to be worked out in the future, as practical problems come before the courts".

Thirdly, Lord Steyn dismissed the idea of imposition of liability on the classification society by way of an application of the *doctrine* of voluntary assumption of responsibility (which is discussed in detail in para 9.5, *above*) by saying (at p242):

> Given that the cargo owners were not even aware of NKK's examination of the ship, and that the cargo owners simply relied on the undertakings of the ship-owners, it is in my view impossible to force the present set of facts into even the most expansive view of the doctrine of voluntary assumption of responsibility.

This can be contrasted with *White v Jones* [1995] 2 AC 207 (see paras 9.5, *above* and 9.7.5, *below*) in which, notwithstanding the absence of any reliance by the plaintiffs on the defendant solicitor's skill and care and the fact that it was accepted that the solicitor had not assumed a responsibility to the beneficiaries, Lord Goff was able to conclude (at p268): "Your Lordships' House should in cases such as these extend to the intended beneficiary a remedy under the *Hedley Byrne* principle by holding that the assumption of responsibility by the solicitor towards his client should be held in law to extend to the intended beneficiary".

Reeman v Department of Transport

In *Reeman v The Department of Transport* (26 March 1997, unreported), the facts of which are set out in Chapter 8, para 8.2.10, the plaintiffs claimed damages from the Department of Transport ('the Department') for breach of a common law duty of care which they alleged the Department owed to them in the issue of a Certificate of Seaworthiness which the Department had issued to the third party from whom the plaintiffs purchased the fishing vessel to which the certificate attached. However, the Department's surveyor responsible for the issue of the certificate had failed to carry out his duties in relation to it with due skill and care. He had made an arithmetical error in calculating the vessel's stability. This led him to issue a certificate indicating that its stability was satisfactory when in fact it was unstable. The error came to light in the year after the purchase of the vessel by the plaintiffs when the Department carried out stability tests and found that the vessel did not meet the minimum requirement. The result was a financial disaster for the plaintiffs because the vessel's certificate was withdrawn and it could no longer put out to sea. Attempts to make satisfactory modifications to meet the Department's requirements were beyond the plaintiffs' means.

The Court of Appeal rejected the plaintiffs' claim against the Department for the economic losses suffered by the plaintiffs in the above-described circumstances. The Court's reasoning is mainly concerned with the statutory aspects of the defendant's position (see Chapter 8, para 8.2.10). However, the following comments of Phillips LJ are pertinent to the question whether a duty of care should be imposed on an issuer of a certificate whose authority does not derive from a statute. Thus, in considering the test of proximity Phillips LJ said:

> Broadly, one can say that the purpose of issuing certificates is the promotion of safety at sea. I accept that there may be more than one purpose for which an advice is given. What I cannot accept is the plaintiffs' counsel's submission that, in the case of Fishing Vessel Certificates, a subsidiary purpose for which the certificate is issued is to inform those who may, in the future, consider entering into commercial transactions such as a purchase or charter, in relation to the certified vessels.

In response to the plaintiffs' counsel's submission that in the present case the advice had been given to an identifiable class because there could only be a handful of potential purchasers and there was no difficulty in identifying them, Phillips LJ said:

> When Lord Bridge and Lord Oliver in *Caparo* spoke of the need for the advice to be given in the knowledge that it would be communicated to an ascertainable or identifiable class of persons [see Chapter 9, para 9.6.2], I believe that they were probably speaking of a class of persons the membership of which was capable of ascertainment at the time that the advice was given, eg, shareholders who could be identified by consultation of the share register. I am sure that they were speaking of a class, in existence at the time of giving the advice, whose identifiable characteristics necessarily limited the number of its members. When a British Fishing Vessel Certificate is issued, those who may in the future place reliance on that certificate when deciding whether to purchase the vessel do not form part of a class that is capable of definition and delimitation by identifiable characteristics. The vessel may be sold during the currency of the certificate to a buyer from anywhere in the United Kingdom or an even wider geographical area. Not only did potential future purchasers not form an identifiable class when the certificate was issued, but the certificate was not issued for the purpose of providing information to assist them in deciding whether or not to purchase the vessel. It was issued as part of a scheme designed to prevent fishing vessels putting out to sea when unseaworthy.

In considering the question whether it would be fair, just and reasonable to impose a duty of care on the Department, Phillips LJ said:

> There is no obvious reason why the Department of Transport's duty to regulate the seaworthiness of British vessels should impose a greater duty of care than that borne by those who build the vessels. Were such a duty to exist, the cost of it would have to be borne by the public in the form of increased survey fees, rather than by those concerned in the relevant commercial transactions.

In response to the plaintiffs' counsel's submission that justice required the existence of a duty of care in the present case because no alternative avenue of redress was open to the plaintiffs, Phillips LJ said:

> In a case such as the present, it will always be open to a party entering into a commercial transaction in relation to a certified vessel to take steps, such as sur-

veying the vessel or stipulating for contractual warranties that will provide protection against the risk that the certificate does not reflect the true condition of the vessel.

With reference to *Mariola Marine Corporation v Lloyd's Register of Shipping ('The Morning Watch')* [1990] 1 Lloyd's Rep 547 and *Marc Rich and Co AG v Bishop Rock Marine Ltd ('The Nicholas H')* [1996] 1 AC 211, both of which are discussed *above*, Phillips LJ said:

> In each case the Court held that the duty of care was not established. In each case the Court attached importance to the fact that classification societies are non-profit making organisations which exist for the purpose of furthering safety at sea rather than for the protection of commercial interests. The defendant's counsel submitted that the Department of Transport, when performing its regulatory functions under the Merchant Shipping Acts, performs a very similar role and, indeed, often delegates to classification societies the performance of some of its duties. In my judgment this point has force. It reinforces my conclusion that, for the reasons that I have given, to impose on the Department of Transport the duty for which the plaintiffs' counsel contends would be neither fair, just nor reasonable. It follows that neither of the last two limbs of Lord Bridge's test in *Caparo* [see para 9.6.2] is satisfied.

Peter Gibson LJ, concurring, added:

> I do not accept that the plaintiffs were members of 'an identifiable class' (to use Lord Bridge's words in *Caparo*) to whom the Department knew that its statement in the certificate would be communicated. In my judgment the members of the identifiable class must be capable of identification at the time of the making of the negligent statement. It is not sufficient that the plaintiffs should be members of a generic class capable of description at that time, whether as potential purchasers or successors in title of the owner who asks for the certificate. That would be to create a potential liability to an open-ended class. I observe that in *Smith v Eric S Bush* [1990] 1 AC 831 [see para 9.7.3] Lord Griffiths, in finding that a duty of care was owed by a prospective mortgagee's valuer to the prospective mortgagor, limited to that prospective mortgagor the extent of the liability and was not prepared to extend liability to subsequent purchasers.
>
> For the reasons given by Phillips LJ it is also to my mind plain that the purpose for which the certificate was given and the purpose for which the plaintiffs used it do not coincide.

Lord Bingham, also concurring, added:

> The cases show that before a plaintiff can recover compensation for financial loss caused by negligent misstatement, his claim must meet a number of conditions. Among these, three are particularly relevant here. The statement (whether in the form of advice, an expression of opinion, a certificate or a factual statement) must be plaintiff-specific: that is, it must be given to the actual plaintiff or to a member of a group, identifiable at the time the statement is made, to which the actual plaintiff belongs. Secondly, the plaintiff must be purpose-specific: the statement must be made for the very purpose for which the actual plaintiff has used it. Thirdly, and perhaps overlapping with the second condition, the statement must be transaction-specific: the statement must be made with reference to the very transaction into which the plaintiff has entered in reliance on it. If these

conditions are met, it is necessary to turn to other conditions which the plaintiff must satisfy.

But it seems to me inescapable that Reemans cannot meet these three conditions. When the certificate was issued they were in no way involved, nor did they form part of any then identifiable group to whom the certificate was issued. The purpose of the certificate (and the tests which preceded, or should have preceded, it) was to safeguard the physical safety of the vessel and its crew. It was not directed in any way to the market value of the vessel. When the certificate was issued, no sale to the Reemans was in the offing. The certificate was not issued with reference to that transaction. We cannot regard the Department's certificate as if it were a bill of exchange of which the Reemans became the holders in due course, because we are concerned with the law of tort, which does not regard certificates as negotiable instruments.

Machin v Adams

In *Machin v Adams* (7 May 1997, unreported, CA), the plaintiff (Mrs Machin) was in the business of operating care homes for the elderly. By a contract dated 27 May 1992 she agreed to purchase from Mr and Mrs Adams a large property, which Mr Adams, an experienced builder, was to extend and convert into a home for some 30 residents. The purchase price was £850,000, which was to include the specified works of alteration and extension. In addition, the contract stipulated that completion was to be on 25 November 1992, or the date of issue of a final certificate of completion of works (whichever was the earlier), that an architect would be appointed by the parties to supervise the works, and that the architect would issue a final certificate when the works had been completed to his reasonable satisfaction.

No architect was in fact appointed as such under the contract. Instead, Mr and Mrs Adams retained an architectural technician, a Mr Champion, to obtain the various Building Regulation Consents; and Mr Champion in turn retained an architect, Mr Bannister (the defendant), by way of a letter in which Mr Champion said that he was retaining Mr Bannister to undertake the inspection of the building works "and to provide an Architect's Certificate *for my client*, Mrs Adams". At no stage was Mr Bannister ever informed of the above-mentioned provisions in the contract between the plaintiff and Mr and Mrs Adams. In particular, he had not been engaged to supervise the construction works, and was not 'The Architect' under the contract. Nor did he have any idea that any such term had been agreed between the plaintiff and Mr and Mrs Adams. Indeed, it was only much later that he even came to know that the property was to be sold, rather than to be operated as a care home by Mrs Adams herself.

Mr Bannister duly made a number of inspections during the course of the works, and he was expecting to be called back for a final inspection when the works were completed. At this stage, Mr Adams told Mr Bannister that the property was to be sold and that Mrs Adams needed a letter from him indicating the present state of the works.

In consequence, on 13 January 1993, Mr Bannister wrote a letter to Mrs

Adams in which he said that he had inspected the building site again and that in his view about two weeks' further work was required to complete the works at an estimated cost of £25,000, which included the installation of the lift. He also made the statement: "All works to date are to a satisfactory standard".

Four days later the plaintiff's solicitor inspected the property himself. He estimated that the cost of the works was more than Mr Bannister had said in his letter of 13 January, because Mr Bannister had omitted the cost of a fire alarm and a nurse call system. He conveyed this information to Mr Bannister, who then wrote to Mr Adams on 19 January saying that his figures in his earlier letter needed to be revised. Mr Bannister also said that he understood that completion of the sale was scheduled for 28 January and that most of the works should be completed by that time, and that it would be useful to have another site meeting as soon as possible to resolve any ambiguity.

Mr Bannister did not, however, receive any reply from Mr Adams. In fact, he did not hear from Mr or Mrs Adams or the plaintiff's solicitor again. The next involvement that he had in any way with this project was when, six months later, he was served with Mrs Machin's (the plaintiff's) writ and Statement of Claim. The Statement of Claim complained of defective works and claimed from Mr Bannister and from Mr and Mrs Adams the cost of rectifying those works and £100,000 as the plaintiff's estimated loss of profits due to the delay in the registration of the nursing home on account of additional building work to rectify the defects.

Mr and Mrs Adams settled their claim with the plaintiff. The action therefore continued only against Mr Bannister. One of the issues was whether he owed a duty of care in tort to the plaintiff in respect of his letter of 13 January 1993 to Mrs Adams; and, if so, whether the plaintiff relied on it in agreeing to purchase the property subject to a reduction of only £25,000 in the purchase price. Apparently a copy of the letter had been provided by Mr and Mrs Adams's solicitor to the plaintiff's solicitor and, through him, to the plaintiff, on or about 20 January (ie before completion).

The Court of Appeal dealt, first, with the effect of Mr Bannister's letter of 13 January 1993 on the plaintiff and concluded that the plaintiff did not, in fact, place reliance on that letter in completing the purchase with a £25,000 retention. Their Lordships then went on to consider whether Mr Bannister owed the plaintiff a duty of care in tort in respect of his letter of 13 January 1993. They answered this question in the negative (by 2:1), notwithstanding that they did not interfere with the trial judge's finding of fact that Mr Bannister either knew or must be taken to have realised that, as he had been retained to carry out inspections of the property (by Mrs Adams) and because he was a qualified architect, it was likely that his letter would be acted upon without independent inquiry by someone else, probably the purchaser of the nursing home, or possibly a person providing finance in connection with the purchase. Sir Brian Neill (previously Neill LJ), with whose judgment Morritt LJ agreed, said (at para 74):

I see the force of the argument that Mrs Adams was likely to show the letter to a third person. If she had wanted to know about the progress of the works only for her own information, she could have asked her husband [who was the builder—see *above*]. But, in my judgment, it does not follow, even if one postulates that the classes of person to whom the letter might be shown included the purchaser and the purchaser's advisers, as well as the bank or other institution which was supplying funds to Mrs Adams, that Mr Bannister had 'undertaken a responsibility' towards the purchaser in the sense in which that phrase was used by Lord Goff in *Henderson v Merrett Syndicates Ltd* [1995] 2 AC 145. It is to be remembered that Mr Bannister knew nothing of the reference to himself in the contract [between the plaintiff and Mr and Mrs Adams].

Sir Brian Neill then considered in more detail the application of the 'assumption of responsibility' concept to the facts of the present case. He said (at para 75):

The words 'assumption of responsibility' must be understood in the sense of a conscious assumption of responsibility for the task, rather than a conscious assumption of legal liability to the plaintiff for the careful performance of the task: see Lord Browne-Wilkinson in *White v Jones* [1995] 2 AC 207 [see para 9.5, *above*]. The court must therefore examine all of the circumstances of the case. Thus, in my judgment, in order to establish liability against the adviser in a case such as the present, the advisee must show some connecting thread between the task the adviser has undertaken to perform and the course of action upon which the advisee can be foreseen to be likely to embark.

Of course, in some cases, an adviser will provide information to his client in the knowledge that a third party will learn of, and rely on, that advice, and, in reliance on it, will take an anticipated course of action. The adviser knows the purpose of the advice and the purpose for which it will be used by the third party. That knowledge may be actual or inferential. The mortgage cases fall into this category. But in order for the adviser to be liable to the advisee, it seems to me that, if one applies Lord Oliver's criteria in *Caparo Industries plc v Dickman* [1990] 2 AC 605 [see para 9.6.2, *above*], he must have actual or inferential knowledge, not only that the advice will be communicated to the advisee, but also knowledge of the purpose for which the information is required by the advisee. It is only in such circumstances that there is room for a finding that the adviser has undertaken responsibility to the advisee in respect of some foreseeable loss.

An application of these principles to the facts of the present case led Sir Brian Neill to conclude that Mr Bannister did not owe a duty of care to the plaintiff in respect of the information that he conveyed in his letter of 13 January 1993. He said (at para 77):

In the present case, Mr Bannister was not giving advice as to whether a particular course of action should be taken. [This is a reference to a *dictum* of Lord Hoffmann in *South Australia Asset Management Corporation v York Montague Ltd* [1997] AC 191 (which is also indexed as *Banque Bruxelles v Eagle Star*)— see Chapter 2, para 2.1.5.] At its highest, his duty was to supply information for the purpose of enabling someone else to decide upon a course of action. Accordingly, in order to determine the scope, and, indeed, the existence, of any duty owed by him to Mrs Machin [the plaintiff], it is necessary to look closely at the consequences for which, in the circumstances, Mr Bannister could properly be held responsible if the information provided by him proved to be inaccurate;

and (at para 78):

> By 13 January, Mr Bannister knew that the property was to be sold. Let it be assumed that he also knew, or should have foreseen, that the letter might be shown to the purchaser. But, against what harm was Mr Bannister to be regarded as having undertaken to guard Mrs Machin? Was the letter a signal on which she could rely to go ahead with the purchase without any further inquiry? The fact that Mr Bannister was due to carry out another inspection with a view to providing a final certificate puts the answer to the second question beyond doubt. But, even without the additional and overwhelming factor of the impending final certificate, I would hold that on the facts of this case, Mr Bannister owed no duty of care to Mrs Machin in relation to the letter of 13 January 1993.

Comment

The third member of the panel, Lord Justice Simon Brown, agreed with the result, but differed from Sir Brian Neill and Morritt LJ in that he would have concluded that Mr Bannister owed a duty of care to Mrs Machin but for the fact that Mr Bannister was due to carry out a further inspection of the property with a view to the issue of a final certificate. This differed from the majority view that Mr Bannister would not have owed a duty of care to Mrs Machin even if he had not been due to carry out a further inspection with a view to providing a final certificate.

Simon Brown LJ, in reaching the conclusion mentioned *above*, accepted the plaintiff's counsel's submission that the plaintiff was a member of an ascertainable class in the sense required for a duty of care to arise, because the only people for whose benefit Mr Bannister could have thought that his letter was being obtained were the purchaser herself or those providing finance in connection with the purchase. Having reached this stage he said (at para 55):

> But for one consideration, indeed, I would have found the duty of care to exist. That consideration, however, is to my mind crucial and ultimately fatal to Mrs Machin's case. It is this. Mr Bannister still believed on 13 January that he would be asked to return to the site for a final inspection, and Mrs Machin herself said in evidence that a certificate of completion was what she was looking for on the last and final inspection. Yet, contrary to Mrs Machin's understanding, no such final inspection was made and no such certificate was ever forthcoming.
>
> In these circumstances, it seems to me to be quite impossible to regard the letter of 13 January as a document upon which Mr Bannister should have anticipated that Mrs Machin would rely in taking some irrevocable step, or, indeed, one on which she was properly entitled to rely. But for this consideration—had this letter been the final certificate which Mrs Machin said she believed it to be, and which Mr Bannister expected would eventually be issued—I would have held the duty of care to exist.

The question arises as to which decision is correct: the majority decision of Sir Brian Neill and Morritt LJ or the dissenting decision of Simon

Brown LJ, as to whether it would be right to impose a duty of care on Mr Bannister if one puts aside in considering this question (as the majority judges did) the fact that his letter of 13 January 1993 contemplated a further inspection of the property.

In *Smith v Littlewoods Organisation Ltd* [1987] 1 AC 241, Lord Goff said (at p 280): "The judicial function can, I believe, be epitomised as an educated reflex to facts". It is submitted that it is not unfair to suggest that a large part of the majority judges' decision in this case was influenced by their "educated reflex" to the unfortunate predicament in which Mr Bannister found himself, because Simon Brown LJ's views are not only logical and sensible, but also they show that the facts of this case did very probably satisfy the criteria for liability enunciated by Lord Oliver in *Caparo*. This might explain why Sir Brian Neill (who was Neill LJ before his retirement), in delivering the majority judgment, said (at para 68):

> In my judgment in *James McNaughton Paper Group Ltd v Hicks Anderson & Co* [1991] 2 QB 113 I attempted to set out some of the factors to be taken into account in considering whether a duty of care exists [see para 9.7.2, *above*]. This case [*Machin v Adams*] has demonstrated, however, that my analysis in that case was incomplete, and that the matter requires to be looked at again.

Sir Brian Neill's list of relevant factors in the *McNaughton* case was no more than a reformulation, in slightly different language, of the criteria and the boundaries laid down by the House of Lords in *Caparo*; and Sir Brian Neill himself did not claim otherwise at the time. Therefore, what Sir Brian Neill is effectively saying in the present case is that the *Caparo* criteria (which are set out in para 9.6.2, *above*) need to be looked at again. In carrying through this exercise, Sir Brian Neill in the present case referred to the concept of 'assumption of responsibility' (see *above*) and concluded that, in order to establish liability against the adviser in a case like the present, "the advisee must show *some connecting thread* between the *task* the adviser has undertaken to perform and the *course of action* upon which the advisee can be foreseen to be *likely to embark*".

It is not entirely clear what Sir Brian Neill had in mind, but it is submitted that the concept that he articulated is very similar to the principle that underlies the House of Lords' decision in *Smith v Eric S Bush* [1990] 1 AC 831, namely, that it is permissible to impose a duty of care on a defendant in respect of action taken by the plaintiff in reliance on the defendant's valuation of a property in a valuation report made by the defendant to a third party if, in all the circumstances, the defendant ought to have realised that such reliance, without any further independent inquiry or investigation, was, on the evidence, "very likely" (see para 9.7.3, *above*). Lord Jauncey expressed the point pithily when he said (at p 872): "Knowledge, actual or implied, of the mortgagor's likely reliance on the valuation must be brought home to him [the valuer]".

It is submitted that the House of Lords' decision in *Smith v Bush*, and the principles upon which it was stated to be based, are entirely consistent with the principles stated by the House of Lords in *Caparo* (see para 9.7.2), and that Sir Brian Neill's above-cited 'connecting thread and likely fore-seeability' formulation is nothing more than a re-articulation of the *Smith v Bush* formulation, as refined in *Caparo*. It is interesting to note that Sir Brian Neill, having made this statement of principle, did not analyse it further, but instead proceeded to determine the defendant's duty of care in accordance with Lord Oliver's criteria in *Caparo* (see *above*).

As noted *above*, it seems more arguable than not that Lord Oliver's criteria in *Caparo* were indeed satisfied on the findings of fact in the present case, which, it is submitted, would also lead to the conclusion that Sir Brian Neill's 'connecting thread and likely foreseeability' test was also satisfied. As Sir Brian Neill himself said (at para 78):

> By 13 January Mr Bannister knew that that property was to be sold. Let it be assumed that he also knew, or should have foreseen, that the letter might be shown to the purchaser. Was the letter a signal on which she could rely to go ahead with the purchase without any further inquiry?

It is submitted that, if one leaves aside for the purposes of this exercise, as the majority did, the fact that Mr Bannister expected to carry out another inspection, the letter was indeed a signal on which the plaintiff could rely to go ahead with the purchase without any further inquiry because the defendant was a professional architect who had made periodic inspections of the building works and therefore was uniquely placed to express a view on their standard.

In the context of the circumstances of the present case, it is submitted that Sir Brian Neill was right to suggest that established criteria for determining whether a duty of care should exist in negligent misstatement cases appear to be unsatisfactory. Indeed, in *Caparo*, Lord Oliver, in enunciating his four-part test, himself said (at p 638): "That is not, of course, to suggest that these conditions are either conclusive or exclusive, but merely that the actual decision in the case [*Caparo*] does not warrant any broader propositions". However, as noted *above*, it would seem that the additional, or, in fact, alternative 'connecting thread and likely foreseeability' formulation suggested by Sir Brian Neill in the present case does not take the position any further; and this would suggest that perhaps Simon Brown LJ's decision was the more correct one to be reached on the facts in the light of the existing state of the authorities, including the more stringent test enunciated in *Smith v Bush*. While it is dangerous to draw comparisons between individual decisions in this field, it is nevertheless tempting to compare the result in the present case with the Court of Appeal's imposition of liability on the solicitors in *Rothschild and Sons Ltd v Berenson* (7 February 1997, unreported) (see para 9.7.5), in which Saville LJ, with whom the other two Lord Justices of Appeal agreed, said (at para 14):

> The fact that the Funds Request was not addressed to, or seen by, the other Banks seems to me, in the context of this case, to be entirely beside the point, since to my mind it should have been self-evident to any reasonably competent solicitor (informed that advances would be made by Barclays and other financial institutions) that all those lending would be doing so on the basis that the

solicitors had provided to Barclays a true and accurate Funds Request. In these circumstances, so far as the necessary ingredients for a duty of care are concerned, I can find no valid distinction between Barclays and the other Banks.

It is submitted that, *mutatis mutandis*, it is not difficult to apply this *dictum* to the present case, and hence reach the conclusion, as Simon Brown LJ did, that, apart from Mr Bannister's expectation of a further inspection, in all of the circumstances of the case, his statement in his letter of 13 January 1993, that the standard of all of the building works that had been carried out up to that time was satisfactory, did place him under a duty of care to the plaintiff for the diminution in value of the property that she sustained through those building works not having been carried out to a satisfactory standard.

Lastly, it is submitted that the way in which the majority determined the scope of any duty owed by Mr Bannister to the plaintiff is unsatisfactory. Sir Brian Neill approached this question by saying, quite properly, that it is necessary to look closely at the consequences for which, in the circumstances, Mr Bannister could properly be held responsible if the information provided by him proved to be inaccurate. In answering this question Sir Brian Neill said (at para 78): "By 13 January Mr Bannister knew that the property was to be sold. Let it be assumed that he also knew, or should have foreseen, that the letter might be shown to the purchaser. But against what harm was Mr Bannister to be regarded as having undertaken to guard Mrs Machin?"

Interestingly, Sir Brian Neill did not provide an answer to this question. The rest of the passage just cited from his judgment (at para 78) is set out *above*. Nowhere in that passage is an answer to this question to be found, nor is it mentioned anywhere else in this judgment (the last paragraph of the judgment is para 79, which deals with another issue). It is submitted, however, that the answer to the question is that the scope of any duty of care that Mr Bannister might have owed to Mrs Machin was limited to the diminution in value of the property that was directly attributable to the incorrectness of his statement that, as at 13 January 1993, all of the building works up to that date had been carried out to a satisfactory standard (see Chapter 2, para 2.1.5).

9.7.5   Solicitors

Introduction

Some of the cases of solicitors' negligence involve the situation where the party who has suffered the loss did not place any reliance on the solicitor's negligent advice. Typically, these cases involve a negligently drawn or executed will. To the extent that reliance is a prerequisite of liability in this sphere, it could be said that it is sufficient that the person to whom the advice was given relied on the solicitor to give it without acting negligently; and this would then be an exception to or an extension of the general rule that the plaintiff, being the party who has suffered the loss, must have placed reliance on the defendant's negligent misstatement or, alternatively,

it could simply be said that the public policy arguments in favour of imposing liability in this type of case are so strong as to negate any fine distinctions based on who was the party who actually placed reliance on the
solicitor's negligent advice.

Ross v Caunters

In *Ross v Caunters* [1980] 1 Ch 297, the plaintiff was the beneficiary under
a will which had been prepared by the defendant's solicitors. When sending
it to the testator for execution, they pointed out that the will must not be
witnessed by a beneficiary, but they did not say anything about the beneficiary's spouse. The will was witnessed by the plaintiff's husband. This rendered the gift to the plaintiff void. The solicitors had been negligent in not
warning the testator about this, and in not noticing that the will had been
so witnessed when it was returned to them by the testator.

The court held that the solicitors were liable for the plaintiff's loss,
notwithstanding that he had not placed reliance on their advice. Sir Robert
Megarry VC said (at p 302):

> The solicitors are liable, of course, to the testator's estate for a breach of the duty
> that they owed to him, though as he has suffered no financial loss, it seems that
> his estate could recover no more than nominal damages. Yet it is said that,
> however careless the solicitors were, they owed no duty to the beneficiary. If this
> is right, the result is striking. The only person who has a valid claim has suffered
> no loss, and the only person who has suffered a loss has no valid claim.

On the question of proximity, Megarry VC said (at p 308):

> First . . . this is not a case where the only nexus between the plaintiff and the
> defendants is that the plaintiff was the ultimate recipient of a dangerous chattel
> or negligent misstatement which the defendants had put into circulation. The
> plaintiff was named and identified in the will that the defendants drafted for the
> testator. Their contemplation of the plaintiff was actual, nominate and direct. . .
>
> Second, this proximity of the plaintiff to the defendants was a product of the
> duty of care owed by the defendants to the testator: it was in no way casual, acci-
> dental or unforeseen. The defendants accepted a duty towards the testator to
> take reasonable care that the will would, *inter alia*, carry a share of residue from
> the testator's estate to the plaintiff . . . that duty included a duty to confer a
> benefit on the plaintiff. When a solicitor undertakes to a client to carry through
> a transaction which will confer a benefit on a third party, it seems to me that the
> duty to act with due care which binds the solicitor to his client is one which may
> readily be extended to the third party who is intended to benefit.

Megarry VC continued:

> Third, to hold that the defendants were under a duty of care towards the plaintiff
> would raise no spectre of imposing on the defendants an uncertain and unlim-
> ited liability. The liability would be to one person alone, the plaintiff. The
> amount would be limited to the value of the share of residue intended for the
> plaintiff. There would be no question of widespread or repeated liability, as
> might arise from some published misstatement upon which large numbers might
> rely to their detriment. There would be no possibility of the defendants being
> exposed, in the well-known expression of Cardozo CJ in *Ultramares Corporation*

v Touche, 'to a liability in an indeterminate amount for an indeterminate time to an indeterminate class'. Instead, there would be a finite obligation to a finite number of persons, in this case, one.

On the question of reliance, Megarry VC said (at p 312):

> ... in *Hedley Byrne* the liability of the bankers ... depended on the advertising agents having acted in reliance on the reference given by the bankers, coupled with the fact that the bankers knew or ought to have known of that reliance. Where a testamentary gift fails by reason of the negligence of the solicitor who prepares the will, there will often be no reliance at all, as where the beneficiary knows nothing of the intended gift until after the testator's death. In other cases there will be no more than a passive reliance: the beneficiary knows of the making of the will and the gift to him, and does nothing, relying on the solicitor to have seen to it that the will is effective, or simply assuming this.
>
> [... in the passive reliance cases the plaintiff succeeds, first, because] there was no need for the plaintiff to act on the implied representation in order to attract the loss which befell him. Second, the solicitor could reasonably foresee that his negligence would, by itself, cause the very loss that in fact occurred, without the plaintiff doing any act. The chain of causation was complete without any such act.
>
> It seems to me that these reasons apply with equal force to a case in which there was no reliance at all by the beneficiary... If a solicitor negligently fails to secure the due execution of a will, I can see no rational ground for distinguishing between those who knew that a will in their favour was being made and passively relied on the solicitor's skill or his implicit representation of the due execution of the will, and those who knew nothing of the making of the will and relied on nothing. In each case, once it is held that the solicitor owes a duty of care to the beneficiaries, the loss to them is directly caused by the solicitor's breach of that duty, and reliance by the plaintiff is irrelevant.

Clarke v Bruce Lance

In *Clarke v Bruce Lance & Co (a firm)* [1988] 1 WLR 881, the testator had left certain freehold business premises to the plaintiff in his will. Shortly after making the will the testator had granted a 21-year lease of those premises to a third party. Subsequently the testator instructed the defendant solicitors to draft a deed of variation of the lease under which he granted the third party an option to purchase the premises at a certain fixed price at any time within six months after the death of the last survivor of the testator and his wife.

The testator having died, and the plaintiff having learned of the option granted to the third party, and the value of the premises having risen dramatically above the option price, the plaintiff instituted proceedings against the defendants, claiming that their failure to have advised the testator against granting an option to be exercised at a fixed price constituted a breach of their professional duty to the testator and to the plaintiff as well, by virtue of the fact that they knew, or ought to have known, that the plaintiff's interest as the ultimate intended devisee of the premises under the will would be likely to be adversely affected by the grant and the exercise of that option.

The Court rejected the plaintiff's claim. The Court did not doubt the correctness of *Ross v Caunters*, but held that it was distinguishable. Balcombe LJ said (at p 888):

> (1) There was no close degree of proximity between the plaintiff and the defendants. When, six years after the testator had made his will, the defendants were instructed to prepare the deed of variation which included the option, there is no reason why they should have been expected to contemplate the plaintiff as a person likely to be affected by any lack of care on their part. The testator was free to deal with the property during his lifetime in any way he wished, and the defendants' duty was to carry out his instructions. The testator could have made a gift of the property to someone else or he could have altered his will. In either case the plaintiff's potential interest would have been defeated. In no way can it be said that the defendants' contemplation of the plaintiff, in relation to the grant of the option, was 'actual, nominate and direct'.

Balcombe LJ continued:

> (2) The transaction (the preparation of the deed of variation, including the grant of the option) in which the defendants were retained by the testator did not have as its object the benefit of the plaintiff. Far from the interests of the testator and the plaintiff marching hand in hand, there was an obvious conflict of interest.

Lastly, the Court was persuaded by the fact that, unlike in *Ross v Caunters*, if the plaintiff here were to be denied a remedy, the estate would still be able to sue the solicitors. To allow the plaintiff also to have a cause of action against the solicitors in these circumstances would, the Court reasoned, have exposed the solicitors to the risk of having to pay damages twice over for the same loss. Balcombe LJ said (at p 889):

> This is not a case where, if the plaintiff has no cause of action in negligence, there is no other effective remedy. If the defendants were negligent in failing to advise the testator that the grant of the option was an improvident act, then he during his lifetime had, and his personal representatives after his death have, ... a cause of action against them. (If the personal representatives are unwilling to institute proceedings against the defendants, the plaintiff, as a beneficiary under the will, has his remedy.) If the plaintiff has also a cause of action in tort, then the defendants are at risk of having to pay damages twice over, since any damages awarded to the estate would not enure to the benefit of the plaintiff as a specific devisee, unless he were also the general residuary beneficiary.

Al-Kandari v Brown

In *Al-Kandari v J R Brown & Co* [1988] 1 QB 665, the defendants were the plaintiff's husband's solicitors, acting on his behalf in matrimonial proceedings which the plaintiff had brought against him. The defendants had deposited the husband's passport at the Kuwaiti embassy for the purpose of deleting the children's names from it, pursuant to a court order in the custody proceedings. As there was a real risk of the husband abducting the children from the United Kingdom, the embassy was given strict instructions not to release his passport to him. However, the husband did manage to obtain possession of his passport by representing to the embassy that he needed it for an hour or so in connection with a banking transaction. He then kidnapped the plaintiff and the children and left the plaintiff tied up and injured in the back of a van and abducted the children to Kuwait.

The plaintiff sued the defendants for damages for her injuries (which were physical, not economic). The court upheld the plaintiff's claim. The court agreed that, on the authority of *Business Computers International Ltd v Registrar of Companies* [1987] 3 WLR 1134, a solicitor acting for a party who is engaged in hostile litigation does not normally owe any duty of care in negligence to his client's opponent for the way in which he has conducted the litigation. However, the court held that this case was different because the passport was not only that of the defendants' client (the husband), but it was also that of the two children who were in the custody, care and control of the plaintiff. Lord Donaldson MR said (at p 672): "In voluntarily agreeing to hold the passport to the order of the court, the solicitors had stepped outside their role as solicitors for their client [the husband] and accepted responsibilities towards both their client and the plaintiff".

This cast on the defendants a duty to the plaintiff not to hand the passport to the husband. They did not breach this duty, but the court held that they had been negligent, and in breach of a duty of care to the plaintiff, in failing to inform her or her solicitors that the embassy had retained the passport or that they had arranged for the husband to attend at the embassy, albeit for the legitimate purpose of producing the children's passports and birth certificates to the embassy, in the absence of any representative of the defendants, because it must have been obvious to them that there was a risk of the husband somehow or other managing to obtain possession of the passport on that occasion and thereafter abducting the children.

Gran Gelato v Richcliff

In *Gran Gelato Ltd v Richcliff (Group) Ltd and Others* [1992] Ch 560, during the course of negotiations which led to the grant to the plaintiff by the first defendant of a ten-year underlease of certain property, the plaintiff's solicitors sent inquiries before lease in the usual way to the second defendants, who were the first defendant's solicitors. The answer to one of these inquiries was negligent, in that it failed to inform the plaintiff's solicitors that the headlease contained a redevelopment break clause which, if exercised, would have reduced the term granted to the plaintiff by 50 per cent. If the plaintiff had received this information, it would not have taken the underlease. In consequence of the underlease containing the break clause, the plaintiff was unable to assign it to anyone else, and suffered substantial financial loss thereby.

The plaintiff sued the first defendant (the underlessor) and its solicitors for this loss. There was no doubt that the first defendant itself was liable to the plaintiff, both under the Misrepresentation Act 1967 (see para 9.8, *below*) and at common law, on the authority of *Esso Petroleum Co Ltd v Mardon* (see para 9.7.8, *below*). However, as the first defendant was financially unstable, the plaintiff also sued the first defendant's solicitors. The court rejected the plaintiff's claim against them. Sir Donald Nicholls VC said (at p 569):

> ... there is no problem about foreseeability or a close and direct relationship. [The solicitors] intended, or must be taken to have intended, that [the plaintiff] and its solicitors should rely on the accuracy of the answers to the inquiries and they ... foresaw, or are to be taken to have foreseen, that [the plaintiff] might suffer financial loss if the answers were incorrect. ... Thus far, all the indications point towards it being just and reasonable to impose on [the solicitors] a duty of care in favour of [the plaintiff]. Indeed, all the factors which lead to the conclusion that a duty of care was owed by [the first defendant] exist also in the case of [the solicitors]. The only material difference is that in making the representations [the solicitors] were acting not as principals but as agents on behalf of [the first defendant]. Does this make any difference?

Nicholls VC answered this question by saying:

> By itself, it does not. It is now established that the fact that the person making the representation was acting for a known principal does not necessarily nega-tive the existence of a duty of care owed by him to the representee. The mort-gagee's valuer may owe a duty of care to the mortgagor: *Smith v Eric S Bush* [see para 9.7.3, *above*].
>
> In my view, in normal conveyancing transactions solicitors who are acting for a seller do not in general owe to the would-be buyer a duty of care when answer-ing inquiries before contract... The buyer is formally seeking information from the seller about the land and his title to it. The answers given by the solicitor are given on behalf of the seller. The buyer relies upon those answers as given on behalf of the seller, although the confidence of the buyer and his solicitors in the reliability of the answers may be increased when they see that the answers have been given by a solicitor in the ordinary way. They will expect the seller's solici-tor, as a professional acting on behalf of his client, to have got the answers right ... in these circumstances ... the law provides the buyer with a remedy against the seller personally if the answers were given without due care [by his solicitor, even if the fault was that of the solicitor alone]. I am far from persuaded that the fair and reasonable reaction to these facts is that there ought also to be a remedy against the [seller's] solicitor personally.

Nicholls VC continued (at p 571):

> ... in the field of negligent misrepresentation caution should be exercised before the law takes the step of concluding, in any particular context, that an agent acting within the scope of his authority on behalf of a known principal himself owes to third parties a duty of care independent of the duty of care he owes to his principal. There will be cases where it is fair, just and reasonable that there should be such a duty. But, in general, in a case where the principal himself owes a duty of care to the third party, the existence of a further duty of care, owed by the agent to the third party, is not necessary for the reasonable protection of the latter. Good reason, therefore, should exist before the law imposes a duty when the agent already owes to his principal a duty which covers the same ground and the principal is responsible to the third party for his agent's shortcomings. I do not think there is good reason for such a duty in normal conveyancing transac-tions.

Nicholls VC did, however, qualify what he said *above* by recognising that

> . . . there will be special cases where the general rule does not apply and a duty of care will be owed by solicitors to a buyer. . . [This would occur where], to adapt the language used by Lord Donaldson MR in *Al-Kandari v J R Brown & Co*, . . . the solicitors had stepped outside their role as solicitors for their client and had accepted a direct responsibility to the lender.

By way of an example he cited *Allied Finance & Investments Ltd v Haddow & Co* [1983] NZLR 22, in which the defendant solicitors, acting for a borrower of funds from the plaintiff to be secured on a yacht which the borrower was buying, were held to owe a duty of care to the plaintiff for the economic loss which the plaintiff suffered by virtue of the defendant having negligently informed it that certain documents had been duly executed and were fully binding on the borrower and that there were no other charges on the yacht.

Comment

This decision (*Gran Gelato*) has not been appealed, but its soundness must be questioned, because it amounts to saying that a professional person who negligently provides information to a person other than his client in connection with a business transaction "whose nature made clear the gravity of the inquiry and the importance and influence attached to the answer" (in the words of Lord Pearce in *Hedley Byrne* (at p 539)), knowing and intending that the inquirer would rely on this information for the very purpose for which it was provided, and would suffer financial loss if the information was inaccurate, does not owe a duty of care to that person if that person also has a claim against the professional person's client in respect of that inaccurate information. This is contrary to the relevant principles discussed in this chapter, especially as they have been formulated by the House of Lords in *Hedley Byrne* and *Caparo*. It is true that Nicholls VC's formulation would appear to limit what he said to solicitors providing answers to preliminary inquiries in conveyancing transactions, but it is questionable, first, whether public policy requires that solicitors should be provided with this immunity in any event and, secondly, if this principle is to exist, why should it not extend to other types of transaction (such as the negligent reference given by the solicitor in *Edwards v Lee*) and to other professionals as well.

In the Court of Appeal in *White v Jones* [1993] 3 WLR 730, Nicholls VC sought to tone down the possible far-reaching effect of his above-cited *dicta*. In agreeing with the other Lord Justices of Appeal that the solicitors in *White v Jones* did owe a duty of care to the disappointed beneficiary, who was not their client (see *below*), Nicholls VC said (at p 739) (emphasis added):

> In general, and always leaving reliance cases on one side, a solicitor owes a professional duty of care to his client and no one else. He is subject to professional rules and standards, and he owes duties to the court as one of its officers. But within that framework, it is to his client alone that he owes a duty to exercise the standard of skill and care appropriate to his status as a solicitor. Thus, in *general*,

when acting for a seller of land, a solicitor does not himself owe a duty of care to the buyer: see *Gran Gelato Ltd v Richcliff (Group) Ltd.*

In the House of Lords in *White v Jones* [1995] 2 AC 207, Lord Goff, without expressing any criticism of Nicholls VC's judgment in *Gran Gelato*, referred to it (at p 256) as an aspect of the "well-established general rule that, when a solicitor is performing his duties to his client, he will generally owe no duty of care to third parties".

Criticism in the Court of Appeal

Nevertheless, Nicholls VC's judgment in *Gran Gelato* has been criticised by the Court of Appeal in *McCullagh v Lane Fox and Partners Ltd* (1996) 49 Con LR 124 (the facts of which are set out in Chapter 10, para 10.3.3), where the defendant's counsel submitted that the defendant, being only an agent of the vendor, could not be personally liable to the plaintiff in circumstances where the plaintiff had a direct cause of action against the agent's employer (ie the vendor) for the agent's negligence. In making this submission, the defendant's counsel relied on Nicholls VC's above-cited *dicta* in *Gran Gelato*. The Court of Appeal, however, rejected this analogy. Hobhouse LJ, with whose judgment the other two Lord Justices agreed in this respect, first referred to the statement by the Court of Appeal in *Punjab National Bank v DeBoinville* [1992] 1 WLR 1138 (see para 9.7.6, *below*), in which the Court of Appeal said that an employee of a firm or company providing professional services can, in certain circumstances, owe a personal duty of care to the client: "It all depends on what the employee is employed to do. If he was entrusted with the whole or nearly the whole of the task which his employer undertook, a duty of care from him to the client cannot be ruled out" (see Chapter 10, para 10.2.1). Commenting on the Court of Appeal's judgment in *Punjab*, Hobhouse LJ said: "The relevant consideration is the part they [the employees] play in the transaction, not the fact that they are the servant or agent of another; they are responsible for their own conduct". He then referred extensively to Nicholls VC's judgment in *Gran Gelato*, and continued:

> The reasoning of the Vice Chancellor [in *Gran Gelato*], unless it is confined to stating a special rule applicable to solicitors in conveyancing transactions, is, in my judgment, inconsistent with the *ratio decidendi* of *Punjab National Bank*, and with the general principle of tortious liability where the person doing the relevant act is the agent of another, which the Vice Chancellor himself recognised in his citation of *Smith v Bush* [see *above*].
>
> With respect to the Vice Chancellor, when he says that 'where the principal himself owes a duty of care to the third party, the existence of a further duty of care, owed by the agent to the third party, is not necessary', he appears to overlook that, in the relevant context, the duty in tort arises from the act of the solicitor in choosing to answer the inquiry. There is only one duty; it is the duty of the solicitor to take reasonable care in answering. The duty in tort is both created and broken by the solicitor. The tortious liability of the principal is, in this context, not for what he has himself done, but is a vicarious liability for the tort of the solicitor.

Hobhouse LJ then referred to the way in which the *Gran Gelato* decision was dealt with in the Court of Appeal and in the House of Lords in *White v Jones* (see *above*), and then continued:

> It thus appears that there is a rule of policy which gives a solicitor a special immunity even in a non-adversarial context such as conveyancing, where there is no conflict between the duty owed to the client and what might be owed to the third party. Further, this immunity is apparently to coexist with a continuing (vicarious) tortious liability of the principal. In *White v Jones* it was not necessary for the House of Lords to consider the more general question of the liability of agents and, indeed, the actual decision holding the solicitor liable is in no way inconsistent with agents being liable for their *prima facie* tortious acts.

Hobhouse LJ then referred extensively to the House of Lords' decision in *Henderson v Merrett Syndicates Ltd* [1995] 2 AC 145 (see para 9.7.6), and concluded:

> These authorities show that the governing principle is still that in *Hedley Byrne*, and that an agent can be held responsible for a careless misrepresentation as much as his principal. In certain special situations, rules which restrict the liability of the agent may be superimposed. One such situation is, on the basis of *Gran Gelato*, a solicitor in a conveyancing transaction.

Hobhouse LJ then considered whether, in the case before him, it made any difference that the agent was not a solicitor but an estate agent. In the course of considering this point, he made further criticism of Nicholls VC's judgment in *Gran Gelato*. He said:

> The present case [*McCullagh*] concerns a prospective purchase of an estate in land, but the agent involved is an estate agent, not a solicitor. The question therefore becomes whether in this transaction the same special rule should be applied to the estate agent in respect of a misrepresentation. The difficulty in answering this question lies in identifying the reason, consistent with principle, for the solicitor's immunity. For myself, I am unable to make a wholly confident identification, but it is apparently based on the special role of a solicitor and grounds of policy relating to that role. Sir Donald Nicholls VC seems to have put it in this way in what he said in the Court of Appeal in *White v Jones*: It is the professional duty of the solicitor that is owed to his client alone. It is in the activities covered by the rules and standards of his profession and his duties to the Court as one of its officers that the restriction applies. Within that framework, and when exercising the standard of skill and care appropriate to his status as a solicitor, his duty is confined to his client. In other situations, or when it is a reliance (ie, *Hedley Byrne*) case, the special rule does not apply. This conclusion is the minimum which is consistent with deciding *White v Jones* in favour of the plaintiff. There is no need to discuss the further problem whether the activities of a solicitor in a conveyancing transaction, and in answering pre-contract inquiries, will invariably fall into the protected category. What is clear is that these reasons cannot apply to an estate agent or an agent who will not be liable save on a *Hedley Byrne* basis.

This point is discussed further in Chapter 10, para 10.2.1.

Kecskemeti v Rubens

In *Kecskemeti v Rubens Rabin & Co* ((1992) *The Times*, 31 December), a testator had provided in his will that if and when two properties which he owned jointly with his wife were sold, his half share of the proceeds would go to his son (the plaintiff). However, because this was a joint tenancy, the testator's undivided half share passed automatically to his widow on his death, thereby ruling out any possibility of the plaintiff being able to participate in the proceeds of sale of the properties. The defendants were the solicitors who had drafted the testator's will. There was nothing wrong with the drafting of the will nor with its attestation. The plaintiff's complaint was that, despite the testator's obvious intention that the plaintiff should benefit under the will, the defendants had not drawn to the testator's attention the necessity to sever the joint tenancy in order to enable the gift to the plaintiff to be valid.

The court upheld the plaintiff's claim against the solicitors. MacPherson J said: "The present case is a classic example of a situation where the relationship is proximate and where it is fair, just and reasonable that the law should impose a duty of a given scope upon the one party for the benefit of the other". In response to a submission by the defendants' counsel about the dangers of imposing liability in this type of case, MacPherson J said:

> I do not accept the defendants' counsel's broad assertion that if there is a duty in this case, then it must be owed generally to beneficiaries, whatever the circumstances and however far in the future they may be identifiable. *Ross v Caunters* defines a limited area within which a solicitor may be liable to persons who are not his clients. Indefinite cases or cases where there is an indeterminate class of potential beneficiaries, or where there may be conflict [between the testator's wishes as to who should benefit and the wording of the will], are different and must be individually considered.

Lloyd J, in *Carr-Glynn v Frearsons* [1997] 2 All ER 614 (see *below*), has doubted the correctness of this decision.

Hemmens v Wilson Browne

In *Hemmens v Wilson Browne* [1995] Ch 223, the defendants were a firm of solicitors. On 4 June 1990, one of their partners, Mr Saynor, received urgent instructions by telephone from a Mr Panter, who was in hospital with a back injury, to draft a document giving his mistress Mrs Hemmens (the plaintiff) the present right to call at an unspecified time in the future for the sum of £110,000 to enable her to purchase a house for herself and for her daughter. The document was drafted the same day by Mr Saynor and was executed by Mr Panter in the presence of Mrs Hemmens at Mr Panter's bedside in the hospital. Due to the negligence of Mr Saynor, the document did not grant Mrs Hemmens any enforceable rights. It was not a promissory note, nor a contract (because there was no consideration); it was not under seal, and it did not create a trust because there was no identifiable fund which could form the subject matter of the trust.

Subsequently, Mr Panter reneged on his promise and Mrs Hemmens did not receive the £110,000. In the present action, she sought to recover it from

Mr Saynor's firm. It was common ground that, if there was a duty of care, Mr Saynor was in breach of it. The question for decision, therefore, was whether Mr Saynor owed the plaintiff a duty of care in respect of his failure to carry out Mr Panter's instructions with reasonable care and skill.

Relying on *Ross v Caunters* (see *above*) and on the Court of Appeal's decision in *White v Jones* [1993] 3 WLR 730, which endorsed *Ross*, the plaintiff's counsel argued that the principle of those cases should be extended and applied to the gift which Mr Panter had intended to make to the plaintiff, which differed only in the respect that it was a gift *inter vivos*. Judge Moseley QC, sitting as a High Court judge, rejected this submission and held that, in the circumstances of the present case, no duty of care existed by way of an analogy with, or as a justifiable extension of, *Ross v Caunters/White v Jones*. He said that what distinguished those cases from the present was not simply the fact that those cases were concerned with wills, but that, in both of those cases, it was beyond the ability of both the testator and of his personal representatives to put matters right. Judge Moseley QC noted that this type of situation can also arise in the context of *inter vivos* transactions. He said (at p 236):

> I can well understand that if a settlor, acting on the advice of his solicitor, exe-cutes an irrevocable deed of settlement, conferring benefits on X instead of, as intended, on Y, the solicitor may owe a duty of care not only to the settlor, but also to Y. In such circumstances . . . it will be beyond the power of the settlor, though still alive, to put matters right. I can also well understand that a duty of care may be owed by a solicitor to an employee for whose benefit that solicitor is retained by the employer to draft an effective tax avoidance scheme. If the scheme is ineffective, the tax will be payable and it will be beyond the ability of the employer, even if still alive, to put matters right. I accept therefore that there may be circumstances in which a solicitor may owe a duty of care in carrying out an *inter vivos* transaction. That, however, does not lead to the conclusion that a duty of care is owed in the context of all *inter vivos* transactions.

In considering the facts of the present case, the judge concluded that the plaintiff's loss was foreseeable and that there was "a sufficient degree of proximity" between Mr Saynor and the plaintiff. However, Judge Moseley QC nevertheless concluded that the situation in this case was not one where it was fair, just and reasonable that the law should impose a duty of care on Mr Saynor. He said that the factors which led him to this conclusion were:

(a) Mr Panter is still alive and is still able to put matters right. No irremediable situation has occurred which has put it beyond his power to rectify the situa-tion. . . the only reason why the situation has not been rectified is that Mr Panter has changed his mind. In my judgment, it would offend against common sense to grant Mrs Hemmens a remedy against Mr Saynor in those circumstances.

(b) This is not a case in which a negligent solicitor goes scot-free if the law pro-vides no remedy to Mrs Hemmens [see *Ross v Caunters, above*]. . . Mr Panter has an adequate remedy against Mr Saynor . . . [he can] refuse to pay his bill . . . if he has already paid, he can retain another solicitor to draft an appropriate document and recover the additional charges as damages for breach of contract. In neither event is it necessary for the law to give Mrs Hemmens a remedy.

Secondly, the plaintiff's counsel submitted that a duty of care arose on the negligent misrepresentation principles enunciated in *Hedley Byrne and Co Ltd v Heller and Partners Ltd* [1964] AC 465 (see *above*) by virtue of the fact that, during the meeting when the document was signed, Mr Saynor negligently told the plaintiff that the document was "akin to a trust". The judge accepted that the plaintiff had suffered a loss by reason of this misstatement because, if Mr Saynor had told the plaintiff the truth, at that stage the plaintiff could have had an effective document drafted by another solicitor and Mr Panter would have executed it. However, the judge nevertheless held that, in all of the circumstances, no duty of care arose by virtue of the said negligent misstatement because, later on in the same conversation, when the plaintiff asked Mr Saynor for an assurance that the document was effective, he told her that she should consult her own solicitors if she had any doubt on the matter and that his client was only Mr Panter and that he, Mr Saynor, was performing Mr Panter's instructions and that the plaintiff should seek her own advice. Judge Moseley QC said that, although this was not a disclaimer case like *Hedley Byrne*:

> In reality, [Mr Saynor] advised [Mrs Hemmens] not to accept his opinion on the matter, but to seek advice from her own solicitors. . . [It does not] matter in my view that by that stage Mr Saynor had already expressed his opinion concerning the legal effect of the document. That expression of opinion was made on the same occasion as the advice to consult solicitors and was part and parcel of the same advice. What matters is that, by the end of the conversation, Mr Saynor's representation had been qualified by his advice that he was acting for Mr Panter, not for Mrs Hemmens, and that she should seek advice from her own solicitors. In my view, it would not be fair, just or reasonable for the law to impose a duty of care on Mr Saynor in those circumstances.

White v Jones

In *White v Jones* [1995] 2 AC 207, a testator had given instructions to his solicitor (the defendant) to draft a new will for him. Under it, his two daughters, who had been left out of his previous will, were to receive £9,000 each. The defendant was negligent, in that he allowed five weeks to elapse without doing anything about the preparation of the testator's new will. During that period the testator died. The plaintiffs were the testator's two daughters, who sought in these proceedings to have the defendant held liable for the amount of money which they each would have received under the testator's will had the defendant drawn it up in good time.

The House of Lords (by 3:2) upheld the plaintiffs' claim. In so holding, their Lordships approved of the decision, but not the reasoning, in *Ross v Caunters*. Lord Goff said (at p 267): "An ordinary action in tortious negligence on the lines proposed by Sir Robert Megarry VC in *Ross v Caunters* must be regarded as inappropriate because it does not meet any of the conceptual problems which have been raised". Lord Goff identified the following important conceptual difficulties in a case like this:

(1) When a solicitor is performing his duties to his client, he is nearly always acting pursuant to the contract between himself and his client and he will generally owe no duty of care (in tort) to third parties who do not have rights under that contract (see *Gran Gelato Ltd v Richcliff (Group) Ltd* and *Al-Kandari v J R Brown and Co, above*).

(2) No claim will lie in tort for damages in respect of a mere loss of an expectation, as opposed to damages in respect of damage to an existing right or interest of the plaintiff. Such a claim falls within the exclusive zone of contractual liability and it is contrary to principle that the law of tort should be allowed to invade that zone. The present case fell foul of these principles. As Lord Goff explained (at p 257):

> ... the loss suffered by the disappointed beneficiary is not in reality a loss at all; it is, more accurately, a failure to obtain a benefit. All that has happened is that ... a *spes succesionis* has failed to come to fruition. As a result, [the beneficiary] has not become better off; but he is not made worse off. A claim in respect of such a loss of expectation falls clearly within the exclusive zone of contractual liability.

(3) If liability in tort is recognised in cases like this, it would be impossible to place any sensible bounds on cases in which recovery is allowed. The floodgates would be opened and solicitors would be exposed to claims from indeterminate classes of persons, such as unnamed and even unborn beneficiaries who had been adversely affected by the solicitors' negligence.

Lord Goff recognised the validity, in varying degrees, of each of these objections, and of the fact that the *Hedley Byrne* principle of assumption of responsibility and reliance (see para 9.5.1, *above*) does not provide the solution because a solicitor, in performing work for his client, generally assumes a responsibility only to his client, and in most cases there will have been no reliance on the solicitor's skill and care by any intended beneficiaries and they might not even have been aware that the solicitor was engaged on the task in question.

Despite these difficulties Lord Goff felt that the facts of the present case warranted the House of Lords fashioning a remedy to fill a lacuna in the law so as to prevent the injustice which would otherwise occur if the beneficiaries were not able to sue the negligent solicitor. The injustice that Lord Goff had in mind consisted of what he called (at pp 259 and 262) "the extraordinary fact" that, if a duty of care by the testator's solicitor to a disappointed beneficiary is not recognised, the only persons who might have a valid claim (ie the testator and his estate) have suffered no loss, and the only person who has suffered a loss (ie the disappointed beneficiary) has no claim. This point was first made by Sir Robert Megarry VC in *Ross v Caunters*, and Lord Goff in the present case referred to it as "the impulse to do practical justice". Having thus identified this strong need, Lord Goff concluded (at p 268):

In my opinion, therefore, your Lordships' House should in cases such as these extend to the intended beneficiary a remedy under the *Hedley Byrne* principle by holding that the assumption of responsibility by the solicitor towards his client should be held in law to extend to the intended beneficiary who (as the solicitor can reasonably foresee) may, as a result of the solicitor's negligence, be deprived of his intended legacy in circumstances in which neither the testator nor his estate will have a remedy against the solicitor.

Lastly, Lord Goff dismissed the spectre of liability to an indeterminate class by saying (at p 269):

> ... my reaction to this kind of argument is very similar to that of Cooke J in *Gartside v Sheffeld, Young and Ellis* [1983] NZLR 37, 44, when he said that he was 'not persuaded that we should decide a fairly straightforward case against the dictates of justice because of foreseeable troubles in more difficult cases'. We are concerned here with a liability which is imposed by law to do practical justice in a particular type of case. There must be boundaries to the availability of a remedy in such cases; but these will have to be worked out in the future, as practical problems come before the courts. . . the ordinary case is one in which the intended beneficiaries are a small number of identified people. If by any chance a more complicated case should arise to test the precise boundaries of the principle in cases of this kind, that problem can await solution when such a case comes forward for decision.

One of the other concurring Law Lords, Lord Browne-Wilkinson, agreed with Lord Goff that the defendant solicitors were under a duty of care to the plaintiffs "arising from an extension of the principle of assumption of responsibility explored in *Hedley Byrne*". In addition, Lord Browne-Wilkinson opined that there are more general factors which indicate that it is fair, just and reasonable to impose liability on solicitors in this type of case—Lord Goff's view is that it is not necessary to ask this question if the conclusion has been reached that a defendant did assume responsibility for his statement, act, omission or service (see para 9.5.1, *above*)—and said (at p 276):

> Although in any particular case it may not be possible to demonstrate that the intended beneficiary relied upon the solicitor, society as a whole does rely on solicitors to carry out their will-making functions carefully. To my mind it would be unacceptable if, because of some technical rules of law, the wishes and expectations of testators and beneficiaries generally could be defeated by the negligent actions of solicitors without there being any redress. It is only just that the intended beneficiary should be able to recover the benefits which he would otherwise have received.

The third majority Law Lord, Lord Nolan, agreed with Lords Goff and Browne-Wilkinson and added (at p 293):

> The force of [the defendants'] argument [that the decision under appeal extends tortious liability into the exclusive domain of contract] has been substantially diminished by the intervening decision of your Lordships' House in *Henderson v Merrett Syndicates Limited* [1995] 2 AC 145 [see para 9.7.6, *below*], which shows that a contractual duty of care owed by the defendant to A may perfectly well co-exist with an equivalent tortious duty of care to B. Both duties depend

upon an assumption of responsibility by the defendant. In the former case the responsibility is assumed by the making of the contract and is defined by its terms. In the latter, the responsibility is assumed by the defendant embarking upon a potentially harmful activity and is defined by the general law.

Comment

In the Court of Appeal in *White v Jones* [1993] 3 WLR 730, Steyn LJ (now Lord Steyn) aptly expressed the sentiment behind the decision when he said:

> The man on the [London] Underground might regard this [a rejection of the plaintiffs' claims in this case] as a surprising result, and his surprise would not evaporate on the assurance that the solicitor did indeed owe a duty of care to the testator, but that the breach of it will result in an award of nominal damages in the sum of £1. The tortfeasor would go scot-free. That seems contrary to a basic aim of the law of tort. *Prima facie*, therefore, it seems just and reasonable that the law should provide a remedy unless there are doctrinal problems which cannot be overcome or policy considerations which militate against the recognition of a duty of care.

The three majority Law Lords in *White v Jones* did not solve the doctrinal problems that confronted the plaintiffs' case. Their decision, in the plaintiffs' favour, is bold and imaginative and represents a significant victory for the need of common sense and practical justice to respond to the reality of ordinary people's expectations in an area of their lives that is legitimately of great concern to them in modern society. Lord Goff recognised this when he said (at p 260):

> The injustice of denying such a remedy is reinforced if one considers the importance of legacies in a society in which legacies can be of great importance to individual citizens ... providing very often the only opportunity for a citizen to acquire a significant capital sum; or to inherit a house, so providing a secure roof over the heads of himself and his family, or to make special provision for his old age.

Lord Goff then referred to the fact that a number of other claims against solicitors in wills cases were dependent on the outcome of this case, and continued:

> It is striking that, where the amount of the claim [in those other cases] was known, it was, by today's standards, of a comparatively modest size. This perhaps indicates that it is where a testator instructs a small firm of solicitors that mistakes of this kind are most likely to occur, with the result that it tends to be people of modest means, who need the money so badly, who suffer.

Lord Nolan adopted a similarly 'true to life' approach when he said (at p 294):

> ... it would be highly artificial to treat the defendants' responsibility to Mr Barratt [the deceased] in contract as excluding their responsibility to the plaintiffs under the law of tort. The defendants were acting in the role of family solicitors. As is commonly the case the contract was with the head of the family, but it would be astonishing if, as a result, they owed a duty of care to him alone,

to the exclusion of the other members of the family. In the particular circumstances of this case, the degree of proximity to the plaintiffs could hardly have been closer. Carol White, the first plaintiff, had spoken to Mr Jones [the solicitor] about the revised wishes of Mr Barratt, and the letter setting out those wishes was written for Mr Barratt by Mr Heath, the husband of the second plaintiff. It would be absurd to suggest that they placed no reliance on the defendants to carry out the instructions given to them.

Lest he should be taken as unduly restricting the principle of *White v Jones*, Lord Nolan immediately added: "I do not say that other potential legatees, less intimately concerned with the carrying out of the testator's wishes, would necessarily be deprived of a remedy: I simply point to the facts as being relevant to the pragmatic, case-by-case approach which the law now adopts towards negligence claims".

Lords Goff and Nolan did, however, attach the following *caveat*. Lord Goff said (at p 268): "Such liability [as attaches to the solicitor in this case] will not, of course, arise in cases in which the defect in the will comes to light before the death of the testator, and the testator either leaves the will as it is or otherwise continues to exclude the previously intended beneficiary from the relevant benefit", and Lord Nolan said (at p 292):

> There must be many cases of the present kind which would justify [the conclusion that any damage suffered by the beneficiary was too speculative and uncertain to be recoverable] because of, for example, the possibility of a further change of mind by the testator or doubts about the sufficiency of funds to meet his wishes. The plaintiffs are fortunate in having been able to establish that the final intentions of the testator in the present case were firm, clear and attainable.

The decision also reveals a divergence of opinion as to the effect of an exclusion clause in the contract between the solicitor and the testator on the beneficiary's claim against the solicitor. Lord Goff spoke (at p 261) of "the need for the defendant solicitor to be entitled to invoke as against the disappointed beneficiary any terms of the contract with his client which may limit or exclude his liability" and qualified his decision in the case by saying (at p 268): "Such assumption of responsibility [to the disappointed beneficiary] will, of course, be subject to any term of the contract between the solicitor and the testator which may exclude or restrict the solicitor's liability to the testator under the principle in *Hedley Byrne*".

Lord Nolan, on the other hand, seemed to doubt this assertion. He referred to the Australian case of *Voli v Inglewood Shire Council* (1963) 110 CLR 74, in which it was held that the terms of an architect's contract of engagement could not discharge the architect from a duty of care to third parties, and concluded (at p 295):

> *Voli*'s case was a case of physical injury rather than economic loss. I would for my part leave open the question whether, in either type of case, the defendant who engages in the relevant activity pursuant to a contract can exclude or limit his liability to third parties by some provision in the contract. I would prefer to say that the existence and terms of the contract may be *relevant* in determining what the law of tort may reasonably require of the defendant in all the circumstances.

This aspect of the possible exclusion of liability is discussed further in Chapter 10, para 10.3.3.

Rothschild v Berenson

In *Rothschild and Sons Ltd v Berenson* (22 June 1995, unreported; 7 February 1997, unreported, CA), the plaintiffs were four banks who had entered into a complicated loan arrangement ('the Loan Agreement') with Cavendish Funding Ltd ('CFL'), whereby the banks made a £20m rolling credit facility available to CFL for the purpose of CFL's business of providing bridging loans to individuals to fund the purchase of another residence before they had disposed of their existing residences. The lead bank was Barclays Bank Plc ('Barclays'), through whom all payments were to be channelled, even if the funds for any particular transaction were actually provided by one or more of the other banks.

The defendant ('Berensons') was a firm of solicitors whom CFL appointed to perform the necessary conveyancing services to give effect to CFL's bridging finance scheme. At a meeting between CFL's directors and Mr Berenson, the senior partner of Berensons, the directors provided an outline description of how CFL was intended to operate and of the essential feature being the speed with which it was hoped that loan transactions would be processed. They told Mr Berenson that finance was being obtained from Barclays and from Rothschilds (one of the other banks), but they did not go into any details of the arrangement in the Loan Agreement between the banks. There was no specific mention of any reliance that Barclays or any of the other banks would be placing on Berensons' conveyancing skills.

Subsequently, CFL provided Berensons with their Operations Manual, which set out in detail the procedures that the solicitors were to follow, and the criteria that had to be met for any particular loan. These included the requirement that a first legal charge on the property concerned must be given to CFL. Berensons was also provided with a *pro forma* copy of a Funds Request Form which the solicitors had to fill in when they had completed their conveyancing work, and in which they had to confirm to Barclays that they had carried out all of the necessary instructions in the Solicitors' Instruction Pack. Barclays would then process the form and allow CFL to draw down the funds required, and make them available to the individual house purchaser in accordance with CFL's bridging loan finance scheme.

Everything went smoothly until one particular transaction in which the Lending Criteria in the Operations Manual were departed from, in that the purchaser was a corporation rather than an individual and (and more seriously) a first legal charge was not obtained by way of security. In carrying out their conveyancing work in this transaction, Berensons was merely following CFL's instructions. Berensons duly completed the Funds Request Form, which made it clear that the Lending Criteria had been departed from in the above-mentioned manner, and completed the certification on the form, stating that Berensons had carried out all of the necessary instructions in the Solicitors' Instruction Pack. Barclays duly processed the Funds Request Form and allowed CFL to draw down £2.3m, which CFL advanced to the borrower, a limited company. The borrower's business plans fell through and the money that had been lent was absolutely lost, with no chance of recovery from the borrower, which went into receivership. The loan having been unsecured, the plaintiff banks sought to recoup this loss from Berensons. The first question was whether Berensons owed a duty of care to Barclays. If that question was answered in the affirmative, the further question arose as to whether Berensons also owed a duty of care to the other banks.

At first instance, Knox J answered both of these questions in the affirmative. After referring to most of the major decisions considered in this chapter on duties of care in relation to negligent misstatements, he said:

> In the light of the authorities cited above, and on the facts as I have found them, I can state my conclusions as follows. I see no difficulty in concluding that there was foreseeable damage to [all of the] plaintiffs of the sort which in fact ensued if Berensons failed to report that the Lending Criteria were not adhered to and, in particular, if the grant of a first legal mortgage was not obtained by way of security. Similarly, I do not consider that there is any real problem regarding the proximity to Berensons of Barclays, to whom the Funds Request Form was addressed for the purposes of the application of the principles in *Hedley Byrne* and, to the extent that they have been widened thereby, in the later cases in the House of Lords, notably *Henderson v Merrett Syndicates*. There was no argument to the contrary for obvious reasons. Where there was argument, it was in relation to the other plaintiffs ('the Banks'), who were the institutions which actually suffered the loss.

In holding that there was indeed sufficient proximity between Berensons and the banks, Knox J said:

> In my judgment, Berensons should have known that Barclays were not the only financier lending money on the strength of the Funds Request form signed by Berensons. I say this because Mr Berenson was told of the involvement of other Banks besides Barclays, but, in any event, if there was a duty to Barclays as lenders to CFL in relation to each specific transaction, I see no reason for the duty not to extend to parties concurrently involved with Barclays in advancing the relevant funds. The ambit [ie, scope] of the duty is sufficiently defined by the amount advanced in the particular transaction. Fellow lenders are within a clearly identifiable class of persons engaged in the particular transaction. If there is a duty to Barclays, it would be applicable in relation to the whole of the sum advanced if Barclays advanced it all. I see no logic in limiting the duty of care to whatever share Barclays ultimately undertakes pursuant to any arrangement of which Berensons knew no details. A duty owed to a lender as principal can properly extend to a duty of care to the same lender as agent for an undisclosed principal. There is no question of any greater or different liability being imposed by the duty of care if it extends beyond Barclays to concurrent lenders from that which would be owed to Barclays if it lent the whole sum.

With regard to the requirements of actual reliance by the plaintiff and foreseeability of reliance by the defendant, Knox J said: "It is clear that both Barclays and the Banks relied upon the certificate contained in the Funds Request in advancing the requested funds to CFL. Equally, Berensons must be regarded as knowing that Barclays and the Banks would rely on that certificate". Knox J said that he was prepared to reach this conclusion on foreseeability of reliance notwithstanding that the solicitors' duties in the Operations Manual were all couched in terms of obligations to CFL with no mention of lenders to it, and that the Report on Title was addressed to CFL and not to Barclays. Knox J responded to these points by saying: "I have taken all of these features into account but, notwithstanding them, I have reached the conclusion that the Operations Manual, coupled with the explanation of the scheme in outline to Mr Berenson, does warrant the conclusion that Berensons should be taken to have accepted responsibility, not only to CFL, but also to Barclays and the Banks".

Berensons appealed to the Court of Appeal. Again, their counsel submitted that, while Berensons accepted that they owed a duty of care to Barclays to take reasonable care in making statements in the Funds Request Form, no similar duty of care was owed to the other banks. The Court of Appeal agreed with Knox J that Berensons also owed a duty of care to the other banks, but unlike Knox J their Lordships' emphasis was on the fact that Mr Berenson had been informed of the existence of the other banks as participants in the loan scheme. Thus, Saville LJ, with whose judgment the other two Lord Justices of Appeal agreed, said (at para 14):

> The fact that the Funds Request was not addressed to, or seen by, the other Banks seems to me, in the context of this case, to be entirely beside the point, since to my mind it should have been self-evident to any reasonably competent solicitor (informed that advances would be made by Barclays and other financial institutions) that all those lending would be doing so on the basis that the solicitors had provided to Barclays a true and accurate Funds Request. In these circumstances, so far as the necessary ingredients for a duty of care are concerned, I can find no valid distinction between Barclays and the other Banks.

Although Knox J had held that the imposition of a duty of care by Berensons to Barclays and the other banks was warranted, in the end the plaintiffs' action failed before Knox J because he concluded that Berensons had not breached their duty of care, neither to Barclays nor to the banks. He said:

> I have nevertheless reached the conclusion that the plaintiffs' action fails because in the light of what in fact occurred, I do not consider that Barclays, and through them, the other plaintiffs are entitled to rely upon the Funds Request that was sent to Barclays via CFL as a representation that all the requirements of the scheme, and in particular, the Lending Criteria had been complied with. The Funds Request Form on its face conveyed perfectly clearly to anyone with knowledge of the Lending Criteria that the transaction regarding the Wapping Property, and more significantly, Vestry Court [ie the unusual transaction referred to *above*] were outside the Lending Criteria in that they were not for individuals, nor were they for residential purposes. Just as Berensons are not entitled to rely on the fact that the Operations Manual was not studied by any

of their partners, so also the plaintiffs are not in my view entitled to take advantage of the fact that the clerks who received the Funds Request did not know what the Lending Criteria were.

The Court of Appeal held that Knox J erred in concluding that Berensons had not breached their duty of care, and reversed his judgment accordingly. Saville LJ said (at para 16):

> It seems to me that the first question is simply whether the Funds Request contained any inaccurate or untrue statements. If it did, and if those statements had been made negligently, then the solicitors were in breach of duty in providing the Funds Request to the company in the knowledge that it would be presented to Barclays in order to obtain the requested advance. Whether the Funds Request did contain inaccurate or untrue statements cannot depend on the state of knowledge of those to whom the document was presented, but must be ascertained by looking at the words used and comparing them with the factual position. The state of knowledge of those receiving the document is of course relevant to the question whether they knew of its inaccuracy or untruthfulness, but it can play no part in deciding whether or not they were told something inaccurate or untrue.

Young v Clifford Chance

In *Young v Clifford Chance* (21 December 1995, unreported), the plaintiff was the owner of an option to purchase the freehold interest in a particular building. The owners of the building entered into an agreement with a purchaser to sell the building on condition that the plaintiff's option was extinguished. The owners and the plaintiff therefore entered into an agreement, 'the Option Surrender Agreement', whereby the plaintiff would renounce all of his rights in the property when it was sold, in return for the payment of £1.65m by the owners to the plaintiff.

The owners retained the defendant to act for them as their solicitors in relation to the proposed sale to the purchaser and the Option Surrender Agreement with the plaintiff. The plaintiff, in turn, instructed its own solicitors (Simpson Curtis) to deal with the owners' solicitors in connection with the Option Surrender Agreement. The sale agreement was subject to certain preconditions relating to the tenants of the adjoining property. It also contained a clause stipulating that if those preconditions were not satisfied by 26 February 1990, then, unless the purchaser waived the preconditions, the sale contract would cease and determine. If that were to happen, the Option Surrender Agreement would also fall by the wayside.

In due course, due to the negligence of the defendant, the sale agreement was not completed on 26 February 1990, thereby depriving the plaintiff of the £1.65m that it would otherwise have received from the owners. The plaintiff sued the defendant for this loss. One of the issues was whether the defendant owed the plaintiff, not being the defendant's client, a duty of care in tort in respect of the plaintiff's loss. The judge, Popplewell J, answered this question in the negative. First, he dealt with foreseeability, and he noted that it was not in dispute that the defendant foresaw, or ought to have foreseen, damage suffered by the plaintiff as being a likely result of negligence on its part in failing to complete the transaction by the deadline of 26 February 1990; and he then continued (at para 135): "I turn to the second element, which is proximity between the plaintiff and the defendants. This seems to embrace a 'special relationship', 'reliance' and an 'assumption of responsibility'".

Popplewell J then referred to *Simaan General Contracting Co v Pilkington Glass Ltd (No 2)* [1988] 1 QB 758, in which the Court of Appeal held that there was no sufficient relationship of proximity between the plaintiff and the defendant which amounted to reliance by the plaintiff on the defendant, because the plaintiff had not bought the glass directly from the defendant but had bought it from a third party with whom the plaintiff had entered into a contract, so that if the plaintiff relied on anyone, it was on that third party and not on the defendant (see Chapter 7, para 7.3.6); and he commented: "This case [*Simaan*] is also of assistance when it is necessary to consider whether it is fair, just and reasonable that the law should impose a duty where there is a contractual framework". (This point is considered further in Chapter 10, para 10.2.1.)

Popplewell J then went on to consider, as a separate test, the test of voluntarily assuming responsibility. In this regard, he referred extensively to the House of Lords' decisions in *Henderson v Merrett Syndicates Ltd* [1995] 2 AC 145 and *White v Jones* [1995] 2 AC 207. Applying these principles to the facts of the present case, Popplewell J said (at para 181):

> I am wholly unpersuaded that there was any sufficient reliance by the plaintiffs on Clifford Chance or indeed such an assumption of responsibility by Clifford Chance as would entitle the plaintiffs to succeed in this claim. While it is clear that Simpson Curtis were indeed leaving essentially the mechanism of the completion to Clifford Chance, Simpson Curtis were there to protect the plaintiffs' position and had the contractual power to ensure that Clifford Chance complied with the terms of the agreement.

Popplewell J then considered whether it would be fair, just and reasonable for the law to impose a duty of care in all of the circumstances of this case. In this regard, the plaintiff's counsel placed heavy reliance on *White v Jones*, and submitted that if no duty were to be imposed on the defendant, the plaintiff would be deprived of a remedy. He also pointed to the fact that no question of indeterminate liability arose here because the plaintiff was the single known beneficiary of the successful completion of the transaction. Popplewell J rejected this submission. He said (at para 184): "It is clear that *White v Jones* was a very special case in which the court was very much moved by the inability to provide a remedy at all to the beneficiary where the solicitor had been plainly negligent".

After referring again to the *Simaan* case (see *above*) and to *Hemmens v Wilson Browne* [1995] Ch 223 (see *above*), Popplewell J observed that in the present case the owners of the property, in a separate action, had sued the defendant and that that claim had been settled. He also expressed the view that the plaintiff would have a separate right of action against the owners for their failure to have used their reasonable endeavours to procure that the sale agreement became unconditional before 26 February 1990; and held (at para 192):

> I have concluded that this is not a case in which it would be fair, just or reasonable that the law should impose a duty of care on Clifford Chance towards the plaintiff. There is no lacuna in the law. First, this is not a case in which negligent solicitors go scot-free. Secondly, it is not a case in which the plaintiff himself has no remedy. Thirdly, at all times, Simpson Curtis were instructed and were there to protect the plaintiff's interests. Simpson Curtis appear to have done nothing between February 8 and 27, 1990. Whether that would give the plaintiff a direct claim against Simpson Curtis is not a matter I have to decide.
>
> In the end, this aspect of the law is effectively governed by policy, in which the Courts will anxiously and understandably seek to give a remedy where there is a lacuna, and will seek to extend legal principles so as to ensure that a plaintiff is not left without a remedy and that a negligent defendant does not escape scot-free. I find nothing on the facts of the present case which requires me to extend as a matter of policy or as a matter of law, incrementally or otherwise, the law in this area. The plaintiff's counsel accepts that this is a grey area in which it would be necessary to extend the law in order to allow his client a remedy. I find that there are no facts in this case which require me to do so.

Trusted v Clifford Chance

In *Trusted v Clifford Chance* (17 May 1996, unreported), the plaintiff, Dominic Trusted, aged 22, claimed damages against the defendant firm of solicitors for alleged negligence on the part of one of the defendant's partners (Mr Bowyer) in acting for the plaintiff's great-uncle, Eric Hopton, in connection with his will. Mr Hopton died on 10 January 1991, leaving a net estate worth more than £11.7m. By his will dated 11 December 1984, he left the plaintiff a legacy of £50,000. The residuary legatees under the 1984 will and, as such, the beneficiaries of the greater part of Mr Hopton's estate, were his nephews Christopher and Nicholas Hopton (Dominic's uncles).

About nine months before he died, Mr Hopton started speaking to Mr Bowyer about certain changes that he wished to make to the 1984 will. Thereafter, during the remainder of Mr Hopton's life, correspondence and discussions took place between Mr Hopton and Mr Bowyer in relation to the making of a new will. By the time of Mr Hopton's death, a draft of a new will had been provided by Mr Bowyer to Mr Hopton, but no new will had been executed.

Following Mr Hopton's death, and notwithstanding that no new will had been executed, Christopher and Nicholas Hopton (the residuary legatees under the 1984 will) decided to honour Mr Hopton's wishes as to the dispositions of his estate which would have been effected by the proposed new will if it had been executed by Mr Hopton during his lifetime, but only to the extent that he had, as they understood the position, reached a clear, concluded view as to the dispositions which the proposed new will was to contain, and not in respect of those wishes which were much vaguer, and which Mr Hopton had not clarified to the same extent (for example, a certain possible family settlement that had been discussed between Mr Hopton and Mr Bowyer).

Following this decision, a Deed of Family Arrangement was entered into whereby the 1984 will was varied, and Dominic was provided with certain further substantial payments, representing the increased settled legacies that Mr Hopton had decided to make under his proposed new will; and more. In the course of Christopher's and Nicholas's negotiations with Dominic about the provision to be made for Dominic in the Deed of Family Arrangement, the substance of the correspondence and discussions which had taken place prior to Mr Hopton's death about the making of a new will, and as to Mr Hopton's thoughts as to what that new will might contain, became known within the family. This led to Dominic bringing his claim in the present action on the footing that, had the proposed new will been executed, he would have received even greater benefits than he did receive under the 1984 will as varied by the Deed of Family Arrangement, and that the fact that the proposed new will was not executed was due to the negligence of the defendant through the acts or omissions of Mr Bowyer.

One of the issues that had to be determined at the trial was whether the defendant owed Dominic/the plaintiff a duty of care for his alleged loss. The judge (Jonathan Parker J) answered this question in the negative. He said (at para 185):

> The question of the existence of a duty of care has to be addressed by reference to the loss or damage for which Dominic seeks to hold Mr Bowyer liable, *viz.* the loss which Dominic claims to have suffered by reason of the fact that Mr Hopton did not make a new Will giving all or part of his residuary estate to a discretionary settlement (ie, the family settlement) in favour of a class of beneficiaries which included Dominic. As I read the authorities, the question whether or not a duty of care existed cannot be addressed otherwise than in the context of the loss or damage claimed. As Lord Oliver said in *Caparo v Dickman* [1990] 2 AC 605:
>
>> It has to be borne in mind that the duty of care is inseparable from the damage which the plaintiff claims to have suffered from its breach. It is not a duty to take care in the abstract, but a duty to avoid causing to the particular plaintiff damage of the particular kind which he has in fact sustained. [See further, Chapter 2, para 2.1.5.]

Dominic's counsel placed heavy reliance on *White v Jones* [1995] 2 AC 207, in arguing that the defendant owed him a duty of care to avoid or prevent the loss which he claimed to have suffered in consequence of Mr Bowyer's negligence in implementing Mr Hopton's instructions. In dealing with this submission, Parker J referred extensively to the speeches in *White v Jones* and then said (at para 196):

> I would make the following observations about the decision in *White v Jones*:
> (1) It appears clearly from the passages I have just quoted—
>> (a) that the duty owed in tort by the solicitor to the intended beneficiary and the duty owed in contract by the solicitor to his client are, for all practical purposes, one and the same; and
>> (b) that the nature and extent of the duty is determined by the terms of the contract between the solicitor and his client, ie, by the terms of the solicitor's retainer.
> This latter point is graphically illustrated by the fact that the duty of care

towards the intended beneficiary may be restricted or excluded altogether by contract between solicitor and client. [Parker J then referred to Lord Goff's *dictum* to this effect (see *above*), but made no mention of the fact that Lord Nolan doubted this assertion (see *above* and see also Chapter 10, para 10.3.3)];

(2) It follows, not merely—
   (a) that conduct on the part of the solicitor which amounts to a breach of his contractual duty towards his client must also amount to a breach of his tortious duty towards the intended beneficiary; but also
   (b) that, unless the solicitor is in breach of his contractual duty towards his client, he cannot be in breach of his tortious duty towards the intended beneficiary;

(3) *White v Jones* is not authority for the general proposition that a solicitor owes a duty of care in tort to any third party who can prove that, but for the solicitor's breach of his contractual duty of care to his client, the third party would or might have been better off, and that this was reasonably foreseeable by the solicitor. The decision is directed at supplying a remedy for the injustice which would otherwise arise in the particular case where, as Sir Donald Nicholls put it in the Court of Appeal in *White v Jones*, 'The very purpose of the employment of the solicitor is to carry out the client's wish to confer a particular testamentary benefit on the intended beneficiary.'; and

(4) It follows from (3) above that no tortious duty of care will arise in favour of the intended beneficiary unless and until the client has—
   (a) decided to confer on the intended beneficiary a particular testamentary benefit, being the benefit for the loss of which the intended beneficiary seeks to hold the solicitor liable; and
   (b) retained the solicitor for that purpose.

The application of these principles to the present case led Parker J to conclude that no duty of care was owed by the defendant to the plaintiff for the plaintiff's alleged loss because Mr Hopton never did decide to confer on Dominic the particular testamentary benefit for the loss of which Dominic sought in this action to hold Mr Bowyer liable, namely his inclusion as a beneficiary under the family settlement that Mr Hopton was discussing with Mr Bowyer.

It is also worth noting that Parker J held that Mr Bowyer had not been negligent in the way that he had dealt with Mr Hopton's instructions, and that this finding by itself ruled out the plaintiff's claim against Mr Bowyer and his firm in tort. He said (at para 235):

> I am satisfied that Mr Bowyer was not negligent in any respect towards Mr Hopton; in other words, Mr Bowyer did not breach the terms of his retainer in any respect. Mr Hopton could have had no legitimate complaint, let alone any cause of action for breach of contract, in relation to Mr Bowyer's performance of his duties pursuant to his retainer; and neither could his estate, after his death. It follows that Dominic cannot be in any better position in pursuing a claim in tort.

Carr-Glynn v Frearsons

In *Carr-Glynn v Frearsons (a firm)* [1997] 2 All ER 614, the defendant solicitors drafted a will in which the testatrix purported (and intended) to leave her half share in a certain property to the plaintiff. In fact, the testatrix owned the property jointly with a third party under a joint tenancy. This meant that, if the testatrix were to die before the third party, on the testatrix's death the testatrix's share in the property would pass automatically by survivorship to the third party as the remaining joint tenant.

The testatrix did die before the third party and the plaintiff therefore received nothing under the will. Relying on *White v Jones*, she sued the solicitors for her pure economic loss, consisting of the value of the property at the date of the testatrix's death. She alleged that the solicitors had owed her a duty of care as an intended beneficiary, which duty she alleged they had breached by failing to ascertain that the testatrix held the property with the third party on a joint tenancy and by failing to ensure that the joint tenancy was severed, so as to give effect to the testatrix's wishes.

The judge, Lloyd J, rejected the plaintiff's claim. In discussing *White v Jones*, he focused particularly on what Lord Goff (at pp 259 and 262) called "an extraordinary fact, namely that, if a duty owed by the testator's solicitor to the disappointed beneficiary is not recognised, the only persons who might have a valid claim (ie, the testator and his estate) have suffered no loss and the only person who has suffered a loss (ie, the disappointed beneficiary) has no claim". Lloyd J held that this reasoning did not apply here because the non-severance of the joint tenancy meant that the testatrix's estate *had* suffered a loss equal to the value of the testatrix's half share of the property, thereby giving the estate the right to sue the solicitors for that loss if it had been caused by their negligent act or omission. He said (at p 628):

> Thus, this is not a case within the *ratio* of *White v Jones*, which indeed necessarily concerns only the straightforward case of the distribution in one way rather than another of the same gross estate passing on the death of a deceased, because it is only in that case that the estate suffers no loss and therefore has no cause of action.

Comment

The problem with this approach is that it leaves the disappointed beneficiary without a remedy; and it means that if the estate chooses to sue the solicitors in a case like this, any damages that the estate might recover will enure to the benefit of a person other than the disappointed beneficiary (ie the testator's general residuary beneficiary) unless (which is usually unlikely) the disappointed beneficiary, although named as a specific devisee (or legatee), was also the residuary beneficiary.

Lloyd J recognised this difficulty. However, rather than exploring possible ways of overcoming it, he directed his concerns to the theoretical possibility of the solicitors being exposed twice to claims for the same loss. He said (at p 628):

> The present type of case is subject to the double recovery objection advanced in *Clarke v Bruce Lance & Co* [see *above*]. If the plaintiff has a cause of action on the basis that Miss Turner [the solicitor] was negligent in her advice to the testator, so do the personal representatives. The benefit of such a claim would, of

course, not go to the plaintiff, but to the residuary beneficiary. It seems to me to be unacceptable that solicitors should be at risk of two separate claims for identical loss at the suit both of the personal representatives and a beneficiary, when recovery by one would not bar recovery by the other.

Lloyd J referred to and adopted Lord Goff's rejection in *White v Jones* (at p 267) of the idea that the solution lies in conferring on the beneficiary the right to compel the executor to sue the solicitor for the beneficiary's benefit and to hold the executor personally accountable to the beneficiary for any damages so recovered, because this would be contrary to the doctrine of privity of contract.

It is submitted, however, that Lloyd J was wrong to regard this as a sufficient reason for ending the search for a solution. In *White v Jones*, Lord Goff said (at pp 260 and 262) that if the solicitor owed no duty to the intended beneficiaries in that case there was a lacuna in the law that needed to be filled, and that the injustice of denying such a remedy was reinforced if one considers the importance of legacies in a society that recognises the right of citizens to leave their assets to whom they please and in which "legacies can be of great importance to individual citizens, providing very often the only opportunity for a citizen to acquire a significant capital sum or to inherit a house, so providing a secure roof over the heads of himself and his family". Lord Goff said that these considerations created a strong impulse for practical justice, which the law should give effect to if at all possible.

It is submitted that these factors are equally persuasive in the present case, and that the position is not made any better by only recognising the executor's right to sue for the loss to the estate, because, in practically all cases of this nature, any damages thus recovered will end up in the pocket of someone other than the intended beneficiary, thereby, it is submitted, making a mockery of the policy that the House of Lords went out of its way to establish in *White v Jones*. The distinction that Lloyd J has drawn between the factual matrix of *White v Jones* and of the present case is really a distinction without a difference, because in practice the intended beneficiary will end up with nothing in a case like the present, notwithstanding that, in contrast with *White v Jones*, the person who has suffered the loss (the deceased's estate) *does* have a cause of action.

Therefore the lacuna that was identified in *White v Jones*, and the need to fill it with a practical solution, still remains in a case like the present, despite the executor's right to sue for the estate's loss. It is submitted that the courts could easily fashion a suitable procedural device to guard against the double recovery problem that could potentially arise if both the estate and the disappointed beneficiary were entitled to sue the solicitors for the losses occasioned by their negligence. The problem is really procedural, not substantive, and could be solved by a judge without upsetting established doctrines of law.

In *White v Jones*, Lord Browne-Wilkinson said (at p 276) that he would find it unacceptable if, "because of some *technical rules of law*", the wishes and expectations of testators and beneficiaries generally could be defeated by the negligent actions of solicitors without there being any redress, and that it is only just that an intended beneficiary should be able to recover the benefits which he otherwise would have received. To overcome these "technical rules of law", the House of Lords was prepared to fashion a remedy that did ensure that the intended beneficiaries recovered the benefits which the testator had intended. It is submitted that in a case like the present one, the court could just as easily fashion a remedy for this purpose, and that it is no answer to say that the principle of *White v Jones* is not applicable because the executor has a right of action against the solicitor because, as mentioned *above*, any recovery made by the executor will inevitably pass to persons other than the intended beneficiary.

The facts of the present case are clearly very similar to *Kecskemeti v Rubens Rabin & Co* (see *above*). Lloyd J recognised this, but he said quite candidly that he thought that that case can no longer be regarded as having been correctly decided. The decision in *Frearsons* is being appealed.

Woodward v Wolferstans

In *Woodward v Wolferstans* (20 March 1997, unreported), the plaintiff was a student of 22 years of age, living in London, away from her parents. Her father, Mr Smith, came up with the idea of purchasing a flat in London in which the plaintiff and some of her fellow students could lodge. The property would double as a London home for Mr and Mrs Smith, and in the long term would represent a worthwhile family investment. The plaintiff and her friends would pay Mr Smith rent in respect of their occupation of the flat.

In due course, a suitable property was identified and Mr Smith instructed the defendant firm of solicitors to act in the purchase. Initially, their understanding was that Mr Smith would be the purchaser and that he would not need mortgage funding. This position subsequently changed when Mr Smith informed the defendant, first, that he would be providing £20,000 himself and the balance (£110,000) by way of mortgage; and, secondly, when he told the defendant that his daughter, the plaintiff, would be the purchaser and that he would be guaranteeing the mortgage.

In due course, the purchase of the property was completed. Although the plaintiff signed all of the documents that she was asked to sign, she had little understanding of the transaction and had little, if any, say in the matter. She accepted without question her father's explanation that the guarantee that he was providing meant that he was responsible for the mortgage repayments.

Within a short time after completion, Mr Smith defaulted in paying the mortgage and the mortgage financier (the Halifax Building Society) repossessed the property. The plaintiff brought the present proceeding against the defendant, alleging that the defendant (the solicitors) owed her a duty of care, which it breached in allowing her to execute the mortgage without first having advised her as to its legal effect, in particular, her exposure to personal liability in the event that the Halifax might have to resort to its security if the mortgage fell into default and that security proved to be inadequate. This, she alleged, would have afforded her the opportunity, of which she maintained in this action she would have availed herself, either to decline to proceed at all with the purchase, or to proceed only on a basis which would not have exposed her to the risks of a mortgagor.

In view of the fact that only Mr Smith, and not the plaintiff, was the defendant's client, the plaintiff's claim against the defendant was founded solely in tort. One of the issues was whether the defendant owed the plaintiff a duty of care in all of the circumstances of this case; and if so, and more importantly, what was the scope of that duty. The judge, Martin Mann QC, sitting as a deputy judge of the Chancery Division, held that a duty of care did exist, but that the breach of it alleged by the plaintiff (see *above*) was not within the scope of that duty. He said (at para 18):

> Two of the conditions precedent to tortious liability, namely, foreseeability and proximity, are clearly satisfied in this case. A third is that it should be fair, just and reasonable to impose such liability. It is therefore highly relevant that the defendant was simply carrying out the terms of a retainer entered into with someone other than the plaintiff, for it would not, in my judgment, be just and reasonable to confer a greater benefit on the plaintiff through the imposition of a duty of care on the defendant than Mr Smith intended she should receive on completion.

With reference to one of the main motivating factors of the House of Lords' decision in *White v Jones* [1995] 2 AC 207, his Honour said (at para 19):

> In this case, the impulse to do practical justice is strong, since the defendant voluntarily tendered its conveyancing skills in circumstances where it knew, or ought to have known, that the plaintiff would rely on them, and where, irrespective of whether she did or did not rely on them, their work would closely affect her economic well-being. In fact, the plaintiff did not rely on the defendant, so it has to be for the latter reason, if at all, that the defendant owed the plaintiff a duty of care.

His Honour then referred to Lord Browne-Wilkinson's speech in *White v Jones* and continued (at para 21):

> It is settled, therefore, that a solicitor can owe a tortious duty of care to an individual who is not his client if, which in my judgment is this case, a special relationship exists between them. In *White v Jones*, the special relationship lay in the solicitor's assumption of responsibility for the economic well-being of the intended beneficiary. In this case, it lies in the defendant's assumption of a comparable responsibility for the plaintiff.

Having thus concluded that it would be appropriate to impose a duty of care on the defendant in this case to the plaintiff, the deputy judge nevertheless concluded that the plaintiff's case had to fail because the breach of the duty which she alleged caused her loss was not within the scope of the duty that the defendant owed to her. Thus, his Honour said (at para 22):

> But it is not enough for the plaintiff to succeed that she was owed a duty of care. She must show that the content of the duty included explaining the transactional

details and the implications of the mortgage. I have already alluded to the relevance of the contract between Mr Smith and the defendant, and the desirability of restricting the ambit [or scope] of the duty [see *above*]. The defendant's contract with Mr Smith required it to exercise reasonable skill and care in securing a good marketable title to, and the plaintiff's registration as proprietor of, the Flat. It did not entail taking the plaintiff on as a client for the purpose of giving her advice, and the court cannot re-write the contract to bring advising the plaintiff within its ambit. It is *a fortiori*, that it should not do so by the back door. Accordingly, I hold that, while the defendant owed the plaintiff a duty of care, it was restricted to the exercise of reasonable skill and care in carrying the transaction into effect according to Mr Smith's instructions.

9.7.6 Insurance brokers and underwriting agents

MacMillan v Knott

In *MacMillan v A W Knott Becker Scott Ltd and Others* [1990] 1 Lloyd's Rep 98, the plaintiff underwriting syndicate had certain claims against a particular insurance broking company which had gone into liquidation. That company had been required by the rules of its governing body (the Corporation of Lloyd's) to have in place errors and omissions cover to safeguard the claims of persons such as the plaintiff in the event of the company's insolvency. This insurance was placed with E & O insurers on behalf of the company by the defendants, another Lloyd's broker. However, they were negligent in placing the insurance, with the result that the E & O insurers were able to avoid liability under that policy. If that policy had been valid, the plaintiff would have had a direct claim against the E & O insurers under the Third Party (Rights against Insurers) Act 1930.

In the absence of this direct claim under statute, the plaintiff sued the defendant in the tort of negligence for its economic loss. The court rejected the plaintiff's claim. Evans J said that, although the plaintiff's loss was foreseeable, and although, in his view, the plaintiff did establish the necessary degree of proximity, because the plaintiff was the very type of person whom the E & O insurance was designed to protect in the event of the insured broker's insolvency, it would not be "just and reasonable" to impose a duty of care on the defendant for the plaintiff's loss. Evans J's reason for holding against the plaintiff was not the fact that the plaintiff had not relied on the defendant—the plaintiff's only reliance was on the insolvent brokers to obtain proper insurance cover for themselves; nor was it the fact that, at the time when the insurance was placed, the plaintiff could only be identified (if at all) in terms of a general class of potential claimants who might assert any form of civil liability, covered by the E & O insurance, against the insured brokers.

Rather, Evans J said (at p 110):

> It is the contractual aspect of the defendants' position which in my judgment militates against the plaintiffs' contention that the duty is owed to them. From the legal point of view, they have their claims against the insured brokers, now in liquidation, and the liquidator can recover damages commensurate with the

insured brokers' liability from the defendants. If the plaintiffs are correct, then it becomes necessary to decide whether the defendants are liable severally to them and to the liquidator, and whether, if the plaintiffs elect to proceed against the defendants, they are disentitled from pursuing their claims against the liquidator. None of these difficulties is insuperable, but their existence demonstrates the extent to which the plaintiffs' contention would disturb the balance of legal relationships established by the different contracts in this quintessentially commercial context.

Evans J distinguished this situation from *Ross v Caunters*, where the intended beneficiary "would have had no way of securing the lost benefit unless the negligent solicitor was liable to him". Evans J concluded by saying (at p 110):

This legal analysis is consistent with a simpler and more practical approach. In *Smith v Bush* [see para 9.7.3, *above*] Lord Griffiths asked whether the defendant surveyor or accountant in negligence cases would agree that he was voluntarily assuming responsibility to anyone other than his client, and he envisaged that the answer would be: 'Certainly not'. The question, then, is whether the circumstances are such that the law should nevertheless deem the defendant to have assumed such responsibility. That was a case where the defendant was the maker of a statement, but the same approach can usefully be employed here. Insurance brokers, I am sure, would accept professional instructions on the basis that their liability for economic loss arising from negligence in the performance of those instructions was restricted to their clients. If asked about possible insolvency of the clients, they would assume that their liability was towards the liquidator and towards no one else. They would not regard themselves as effectively guaranteeing that third parties, even those whose claims were intended to be covered by the liability insurance, would not suffer some eventual loss should liquidation intervene. Nor would they expect to receive separate and independent claims from each of the third parties as well as from the liquidator.

Although, on the facts, the result in this case is probably correct, Evans J's final comments could be regarded as slightly misguided. Having noted that the question is whether "the circumstances" are such that the law should "deem" the defendant to have assumed responsibility towards anyone other than his client, he then considered factors which do not go towards a deemed, or imposed, liability, which is the correct approach, but to the question of actual voluntary assumption of responsibility. Also, instead of applying these considerations to the circumstances of this case, he applied them to insurance brokers generally, which, again, is the wrong approach in cases where the court is asked to hold whether a duty of care existed between a professional person and a third party who was not his client when the professional person had negligently rendered services to his client.

Punjab v De Boinville

In *Punjab National Bank v De Boinville and Others* [1992] 1 WLR 1138, the plaintiff bank had opened letters of credit on behalf of a certain company, now in liquidation, on condition that the company obtained insurance cover to protect the bank in the event of non-payment of the letters of credit. The arrangement of the necessary insurance policies was entrusted by the company to two brokers. They knew that, in due course, when the policies were in place, the company would assign them to the plaintiff.

The company having gone into liquidation, and the letters of credit not having been paid, the plaintiff made claims under the insurance policies. The insurers declined liability on the grounds of non-disclosure and mis-representation by the brokers when they placed the insurance. The plaintiff then sought to recover this loss from the brokers. The court upheld the plaintiff's claim. Staughton LJ said that the proper approach in deciding whether the brokers owed a duty of care to the plaintiff in tort depended on whether the relationship between them either fell within a recognised category in respect of which it has been held that a duty of care exists or should fall within a recognised category by way of a justifiable increment to an existing category (see Chapter 3, para 3.4.4).

Staughton LJ first noted (at p 1152) that there was no dispute that the principle that a professional man owes to his client a duty to exercise that standard of skill and care appropriate to his professional status "applies as much to insurance brokers as to those who exercise any other professional calling". He then noted that the bank was not a client of the brokers and then said (at p 1153):

> Is it then a justifiable increment to extend the . . . insurance broker . . . category to this case? [The trial judge found as a fact that the brokers knew that finan-cially the bank was at risk and that the bank would be taking an assignment of the policies. This holding was correct on the facts of this case] . . .
>
> In those circumstances it seems to me a justifiable increment to hold that an insurance broker owes a duty of care to the specific person who he knows is to become an assignee of the policy, at all events if (as in this case) that person actively participates in giving instructions for the insurance to the broker's knowledge. In such a case there is a rather greater degree of proximity than that which existed between the solicitor and the beneficiary under the will in *Ross v Caunters*, for the beneficiary may have known nothing of the will . . . and would not have derived any benefit from it if it had later been revoked.

Unfortunately, *MacMillan v Knott* (see para 9.7.6, *above*) was not cited to the court in this case. Nevertheless, these two decisions are consistent, on the basis that in *Punjab* the defendants knew, or ought in the circumstances to have known, that the plaintiff was specifically placing reliance on them, as the intended assignees of the insurance policies, to ensure that they were properly placed.

Interestingly, although the two individual brokers were employees of limited companies, the Court of Appeal held that, in addition to the com-panies, the individual brokers personally owed duties of care to the plaintiff. Thus, after holding that the two brokerage companies owed duties of care to the plaintiff (see *above*), Staughton LJ said (at p 1154):

> That leaves Mr DeBoinville and Mr Deere. It is not every employee of a firm or company providing professional services that owes a personal duty of care to the client; it depends on what he is employed to do. Here, Mr DeBoinville and Mr Deere, whether in their employment with F E Wright (UK) Limited or with Fielding Juggins Money and Stewart Ltd, were entrusted with the whole or

nearly the whole of the task which their employers undertook. Their counsel has argued that they were more remote from the bank [the plaintiff] than their employers. On the contrary, I think that in fact their proximity was greater. Whilst they were employed by Wrights, as professional men, they owed a duty of care to the bank, since the bank was a client of Wrights. Whilst they were employed by Fieldings, they owed a duty of care to the bank by justifiable increment of an existing category until the bank became a client of Fieldings, when their duty came within an existing category.

This point is discussed further in Chapter 10, para 10.2.1.

Verderame v Commercial Union

In *Verderame v Commercial Union Assurance Co plc and Another* [1992] BCLC 793, the plaintiff and his wife were the sole directors and shareholders of a certain company. Insurance brokers advised the plaintiff that insurance of the business should be placed with the defendant insurance company. The brokers effected that insurance in the name of the plaintiff personally, and not in the name of the company. Subsequently most of the company's stock was stolen. The insurance company declined liability on the ground that, as the stock was owned by the company, the plaintiff as an individual had no insurable interest in it.

The plaintiff's claim against the insurance brokers was for the economic loss which he personally suffered by virtue of the insurance company declining liability under the insurance policy. The brokers accepted that the company itself might have claims against them, but sought in these proceedings to have the individual claims by the directors against them struck out as disclosing no reasonable cause of action. The court upheld the brokers' application because to grant the plaintiff's application would involve an unjustifiable piercing of the corporate veil and would have wide-ranging consequences, including giving rise to claims for double recovery.

Henderson v Merrett

In *Henderson v Merrett Syndicates Ltd* [1995] 2 AC 145, one of the issues was whether managing agents of underwriting syndicates at Lloyd's owed duties of care in tort to underwriting members (known as 'Names') in circumstances where there was no contractual relationship between them. These Names were known as Indirect Names. Other Names, who did contract directly with the managing agents, were known as Direct Names. Their position is considered in Chapter 10, para 10.4.2.

The managing agents had the capacity to underwrite contracts of insurance at Lloyd's on behalf of the Names who were members of the syndicates under their management, to reinsure contracts of insurance and to pay claims made under those contracts. The managing agents' contracts of engagement were not with the Indirect Names themselves, but rather with the Indirect Names' agents (known as members' agents). The members' agents' function was to advise Names on their choice of syndicates, place Names on the syndicates chosen by them and give general advice to them.

The question for the court was whether the law of tort imposes a duty of care on managing agents not to cause pure economic loss to Indirect Names in the carrying out of their underwriting, reinsurance and claims settlement functions.

The House of Lords unanimously held that such a duty does exist. Lord Goff, with whose speech all of the other Law Lords concurred, said that the governing principle in this type of case is the principle that underlay the decision of the House of Lords in *Hedley Byrne & Co Ltd v Heller and Partners Ltd* [1964] AC 465. Lord Goff observed (at p 180) that the principle upon which that decision was founded extends beyond the provision of information and advice and includes the performance of other services.

The 'principle of *Hedley Byrne*', according to Lord Goff, is the assumption of responsibility by a person who has provided information or advice or performed a service in circumstances where he knew or ought reasonably to have known that another person was relying on him to exercise due care and skill in the provision of that information or advice, or in the performance of that service (see para 9.5.1, *above*). Lord Goff said that he had no difficulty in holding that in theory the principle was capable of applying to managing agents at Lloyd's *vis-à-vis* Direct and Indirect Names. He said (at p 182):

> . . . the relationship between Name and managing agent appears to provide a classic example of the type of relationship to which the principle in *Hedley Byrne* applies. . . there is in my opinion plainly an assumption of responsibility in the relevant sense by the managing agents towards the Names in their syndicates. The managing agents have accepted the Names as members of a syndicate under their management. They hold themselves out as possessing a special expertise to advise the Names on the suitability of risks to be underwritten; and on the circumstances in which . . . reinsurance should be taken out and claims should be settled. The Names, as the managing agents well knew, placed implicit reliance on that expertise, in that they gave authority to the managing agents to bind them to contracts of insurance and reinsurance and to the settlement of claims. I can see no escape from the conclusion that, in these circumstances, *prima facie* a duty of care is owed in tort by the managing agents to such Names.

Lord Goff referred to a number of decided cases in which 'the *Hedley Byrne* principle' has been applied to different categories of people who perform services of a professional or a quasi-professional nature, such as bankers (in *Hedley Byrne* itself), surveyors and valuers (as in *Smith v Eric S Bush*—see para 9.7.3, *above*), accountants (as in *Caparo Industries Plc v Dickman*—see para 9.7.2, *above*) and insurance brokers (as in *Youell v Bland Welch and Co Ltd*—see *above*), and concluded (at p 182):

> To me, it does not matter if one proceeds by way of analogy from the categories of relationship already recognised as falling within the principle in *Hedley Byrne* or by a straight application of the principle stated in the *Hedley Byrne* case itself. On either basis the conclusion is, in my opinion, clear.

The only remaining question was whether the Indirect Names and the managing agents, as parties to the chain of contracts between the Names and the members' agents on the one hand, and between the members' agents and the managing agents on the other, were to be taken to have thereby structured their relationship so as to exclude any duty of care owed directly by the managing agents to the Indirect Names in tort. As Lord Goff put it (at p 195):

> In essence the argument must be that, because the managing agents have, with the consent of the indirect Names, assumed responsibility in respect of the relevant activities to another party, ie, the members' agents under a sub-agency agreement, it would be inconsistent to hold that they have also assumed responsibility in respect of the same activities to the indirect Names.

Lord Goff dismissed this argument by saying (at p 195): "I, for my part, cannot see why in principle a party should not assume responsibility to more than one person in respect of the same activity"; and, without any further analysis, he held that, on the facts of the present case, the managing agents had in fact assumed responsibility directly to the Indirect Names, notwithstanding the above-described contractual structure that had been erected with the Indirect Names' compliance.

Comment

While the House of Lords' decision on the liability in tort of the managing agents to the Indirect Names accords with principle, its utility as a precedent is undermined by the fact that Lord Goff did not explain why, in this case, the tripartite contractual matrix made no difference. This absence of an explanation is all the more perplexing because Lord Goff was at great pains to stress that, in his view, the present case was exceptional. He said (at p 195):

> ... I strongly suspect that the situation which arises in the present case is most unusual; and that in many cases in which a contractual chain comparable to that in the present case is constructed, it may well prove to be inconsistent with an assumption of responsibility which has the effect of ... short-circuiting the contractual structure so put in place by the parties. It cannot therefore be inferred from the present case that other sub-agents will be held directly liable to the agent's principal in tort.

Lord Goff did not, however, explain why he thought that the situation in the present case was most unusual or why most other sub-agency situations will be treated differently, particularly where the defendant's negligent act or omission falls into the category of the making of a statement, the giving of advice or the provision of a service (ie the type of cases dealt with in this chapter). Instead, Lord Goff veered off into a discussion of what he believes the law should be in a different category of case, where the defendant, pursuant to a contract with a third party, has created a new object—either a building or a product—that is defective, and the plaintiff has acquired it pursuant to another contract with the third party (see para 7.3.6).

9.7.7 Referees

Introduction

This grouping of cases involves the giving of a reference by the defendant (often, an ex-employer) to the plaintiff (often, a prospective employer) about the character and/or reliability of a third party (often, an ex-employee). The reference will have been given negligently, but not fraudulently. This can have implications both for the plaintiff, who, in reliance on the reference, entrusted money or property to the third party, or for the person about whom the reference was given, who, as a result of the reference, suffers economic loss by not being able to enter into a transaction from which he would otherwise have benefited.

Lawton v Transhield

In *Lawton v BOC Transhield Ltd* [1987] ICR 7, the court held that an ex-employer owed a duty of care to a former employee in the compiling and giving of a reference in respect of the economic loss which the employee suffered through being dismissed by his new employer as a result of the reference being unfavourable. This case was correctly decided, but its value as a precedent was downgraded by the House of Lords in *Spring v Guardian Assurance Plc* (see *below*) because the judge failed to give consideration to the impact of the law of defamation on his decision that a duty was owed by the original employer.

Edwards v Lee

In *Edwards v Lee* (1991) *The Times*, 5 November; (1991) 141 NLJ 1517, the plaintiff had placed an advertisement in the newspaper for the sale of an expensive car which he owned. A certain Mr H responded and offered to act as the plaintiff's agent in the sale of the car. The plaintiff handed over the car and the registration documents to Mr H. Subsequently the plaintiff became worried about Mr H's veracity and asked for the car back. Mr H assured him that everything was in order and proffered the defendant, his solicitor, as a referee in respect of his good character.

The plaintiff duly spoke to the defendant, who told him that Mr H had done this type of deal before, that Mr H was very reliable and that if the plaintiff encountered any problems, the defendant would "go round and see Mr Hawkes and sort it out". On this basis the plaintiff allowed Mr H to continue to possess his car. In due course Mr H sold the car, but he did not account to the plaintiff for the proceeds. He disappeared overseas.

The plaintiff then discovered that Mr H had an extensive criminal record, which was known to the defendant, and the defendant had failed to disclose to him that another owner of a car was, at that time, experiencing difficulties with Mr H in receiving payment from him in almost the same circumstances. The plaintiff sought to recover his economic loss from the defendant. The court upheld the plaintiff's claim. Brooke J said:

> It was common ground that the defendant could not be held liable for what he said to the plaintiff unless I could be satisfied that 'a special relationship' existed between them. In my judgment, on the facts of the present case, the necessary special relationship did exist. The defendant knew that the plaintiff was concerned as to whether Mr H was a person with whom it was safe to continue to do business (because the plaintiff told him so), the defendant was fully aware of the nature of the contract between the plaintiff and Mr H and the defendant

knew that it was very likely that the plaintiff would rely on the information he gave to the plaintiff in deciding whether or not he should continue to do business with Mr H or to take immediate steps to try to recover his valuable car. This was not an enquiry made on a casual occasion, but concerned 'a business transaction whose nature made clear the gravity of the enquiry and the importance and influence attached to the answer' (*per* Lord Pearce in *Hedley Byrne*).

Petch v Customs & Excise

In *Petch v Commissioners of Customs & Excise* [1993] ICR 789 (CA), the plaintiff, who had previously worked for the defendant until his retirement on the grounds of ill-health, claimed injury benefit from the defendant under the Civil Service Pension Scheme, which was administered by the Treasury. The issue in this appeal was whether the defendant was liable to the plaintiff in negligence in respect of certain written answers given to the Treasury when the Treasury was considering the plaintiff's claim for injury benefit.

Even on the assumption that those answers had been given negligently, the court, following the Court of Appeal in *Spring v Guardian Assurance plc* [1993] 2 All ER 273, answered this question in the negative. Dillon LJ said that he could see no distinction in principle between giving a reference to an employer from whom the ex-employee was seeking a job, and giving answers to queries about the ex-employee's work record put to the employer by pension scheme trustees from whom the ex-employee was seeking a financial benefit. Therefore there was no duty of care owed by the defendant to the plaintiff.

Although the decision in this case must be treated as having been overruled by the House of Lords' decision in *Spring v Guardian Assurance Plc* (it was cited in argument, but was not mentioned in any of the speeches), it remains interesting as an example of the type of analogous circumstances that can arise where the *Spring v Guardian Plc* principles will be relevant, and where the plaintiff would be remediless if not for those principles.

Spring v Guardian

In *Spring v Guardian Assurance plc* [1995] 2 AC 296, the defendant, as the plaintiff's former employer, gave a very negative reference about the plaintiff to his prospective new employer, who therefore refused to employ the plaintiff. This reference was "so strikingly bad as to amount to 'the kiss of death' to the plaintiff's career in insurance", because no other insurance company would employ the plaintiff on the strength of this reference, and it was obligatory for any new employer in this regulated industry to obtain a reference from the plaintiff's former employer.

The reference had been given negligently, in that, if the defendant had investigated certain alleged facts more carefully, it would not have been justified in making the comments which it did make about the plaintiff. The House of Lords, by 4:1 (Lord Keith dissenting), upheld the plaintiff's claim against the defendant for the economic loss that he suffered by not being able to obtain new employment in the insurance industry as a result of the defendant's negligent reference.

Their Lordships had to decide, first, whether *prima facie* it was right to impose a duty of care on the defendant for the plaintiff's losses. This case differed from *Hedley Byrne* in that there the plaintiff was the recipient of the reference and not the subject of it, whereas here the plaintiff was the subject of the reference but not the recipient of it.

Although their Lordships viewed the imposition of liability in this case as creating a new sub-category in the field of negligence, the four majority Lords had no hesitation in imposing a duty of care on the defendant for the plaintiff's losses. Foreseeability of loss in the circumstances was clear, as was the close proximity of the relationship between the defendant and the plaintiff. To deny the plaintiff the right to recover his economic losses in these circumstances, their Lordships held, would have been unjust, because they would have found it unacceptable if the law were that a prospective or a new employer to whom a reference had been given about an employee could sue for losses suffered by him through having relied on statements provided by the ex-employer about the employee's reliability for the job (by virtue of the decision in *Hedley Byrne*—but see the *Comment* section *below*) but that the employee himself, who had been refused employment because the new employer had relied on a reference negligently given by the old employer, should not be able to do so.

The second (and more difficult) issue for the court was whether, if such a duty were to be recognised in principle, it should be negatived in practice because its existence would undermine the policy underlying the defence of qualified privilege in the law of defamation. The reference given by the defendant was defamatory of the plaintiff. The defendant's counsel argued that the policy that underlies the defence of qualified privilege, namely, "permitting men to communicate frankly and freely with one another about matters which the law recognises they have a duty to perform or an interest to protect", prevented the recognition of a duty of care by the giver of a reference to the subject of the reference.

In making this submission, the defendant's counsel relied on the statement of Hallett J in *Foaminol Laboratories Ltd v British Artid Plastics Ltd* [1941] 2 All ER 393 at p 399, that "a claim for mere loss of reputation is the proper subject of an action for defamation, and cannot ordinarily be sustained by means of any other form of action"; and on the following statement of Cooke P in the Court of Appeal of New Zealand in *Bell-Booth Group Ltd v Attorney-General* [1989] 3 NZLR 148 at pp 156–157:

> The law as to injury to reputation and freedom of speech is a field of its own. To impose the law of negligence upon it by accepting that there may be common law duties of care not to publish the truth would be to introduce a distorting element. The duty in defamation is a duty not to defame without justification or privilege or otherwise by way of fair comment. The plaintiff is attempting to add to these duties a duty in a case like this to take care not to injure the plaintiff's reputation by true [but negligent] statements. In our opinion, to accept it would be to introduce negligence law into a field for which it was not designed and is not appropriate. For these reasons, in our opinion justice does not require or warrant an importation of negligence law into this

class of case. Where remedies are needed, they are already available in the form of actions for defamation, injurious falsehood, breach of contract or breach of confidence.

These sentiments were reiterated by the Court of Appeal of New Zealand in *Balfour v Attorney-General* [1991] 1 NZLR 519 and *South Pacific Manufacturing Co Ltd v New Zealand Security Consultants and Investigations Ltd* [1992] 2 NZLR 282. In *South Pacific Manufacturing*, the facts of which are set out in Chapter 7, para 7.6.2, one of the reasons for the court's rejection of the plaintiff's claim in negligence against the private investigator was that to impose the duty of care asserted would cut across established principles of law in other fields, including defamation. Thus, Cooke P said (at p 301):

> To the extent that the report reflects adversely on the insured by suggesting that he may have been guilty of arson, the insured will *prima facie* have a cause of action in defamation. It will be a defence, however, if the investigators can prove the truth of the imputation; and, more importantly in the present context, the report of the investigators made pursuant to their contractual duty to the insurer will be the subject of qualified privilege.
>
> Qualified privilege can be defeated by proof of malice, but not by proof of mere negligence. The suggested cause of action in negligence would therefore impose a greater restriction on freedom of speech than exists under the law worked out over many years to cover freedom of speech and its limitations. By a side-wind the law of defamation would be overthrown.

The English Court of Appeal in this case (ie *Spring v Guardian Assurance Plc* [1993] 2 All ER 273) was totally convinced by these arguments. Glidewell LJ said (at p 294):

> In our view the decision in *Bell-Booth Group Ltd v Attorney-General* represents the law of England. As a general proposition, in our judgment the giver of a reference owes no duty of care in the tort of negligence to the subject of the reference. His duty to the subject is governed by and lies in the tort of defamation. If it were otherwise, the defence of qualified privilege in an action for defamation where a reference was given, or the necessity for the plaintiff to prove malice in an action for malicious falsehood, would be bypassed. In effect, a substantial section of the law regarding these two associated torts would be emasculated.

In contrast, the House of Lords swept aside these arguments and adopted a far more pragmatic approach. Lord Slynn said (at p 332): "The rule in defamation has been, as the Court of Appeal said, long established. It is, however, no less clear that the rule was established before modern developments in the law of negligence following the decision of your Lordships' House in *Donoghue v Stevenson* [1932] AC 562"; and (at p 334): "A claim that a reference has been given negligently is essentially based on the fact, not so much that reputation has been damaged, as that a job, or an opportunity, has been lost"; and (at p 335): "In many cases an employee will stand no chance of getting another job, let alone a better job, unless he is given a reference".

Lord Woolf, in similar vein, said (at p 346):

> Because of the defence of qualified privilege, before an action for defamation can succeed, it is necessary to establish malice. In my judgment the result of this requirement is that an action for defamation provides a wholly inadequate remedy for an employee who is caused damage by a reference which due to negligence is inaccurate. This is because it places a wholly disproportionate burden on the employee. Malice is extremely difficult to establish.

Their Lordships were also, it seems, influenced by the new mood in the House of Lords on concurrent remedies, as embodied in their decision rendered three weeks later in *Henderson v Merrett Syndicates Ltd* [1995] 2 AC 145 (see Chapter 10, para 10.4.2). Thus, Lord Goff said (at p 324):

> Since . . . it is my opinion that in cases such as the present [ie *Spring v Guardian*], the duty of care arises by reason of an assumption of responsibility by the employer to the employee in respect of the relevant reference, I can see no good reason why the duty to exercise due skill and care which rests upon the employer should be negatived because, if the plaintiff were instead to bring an action for damage to his reputation, he would be met by the defence of qualified privilege, which could only be defeated by proof of malice. It is not to be forgotten that the *Hedley Byrne* duty arises where there is a relationship which is, broadly speaking, either contractual or equivalent to contract. In these circumstances, I cannot see that principles of the law of defamation are of any relevance.

Lord Woolf had the same idea in mind when he said (at p 350):

> This appeal is not concerned with a claim for mere loss of reputation [in contrast to the plaintiff's claim in the *Foaminol Laboratories* decision—see *above*]. What concerns the plaintiff is his loss of an opportunity to obtain employment due to negligence . . . in the preparation of the reference. I do not accept the logic of the argument that to have an action for negligence will undermine the law of defamation. If this appeal is allowed, this will leave the law of defamation in exactly the same state as it was in previously. The plaintiff would not have succeeded in an action for defamation. Negligence has always been an irrelevant consideration . . . in an action for defamation. . . the two causes of action are not primarily directed at the same mischief although they, admittedly, overlap. . . . An action for negligence is concerned with the care exercised in ascertaining the facts and defamation with the truth of the contents of what is published.

Comment

The decision of the House of Lords in *Spring v Guardian Assurance Plc* is important as a precedent on the topic of references and similar situations with regard to the right of the subject of the utterance (as opposed to the recipient of it) to sue for his economic losses if the statement about him was negligently prepared. The decision is particularly important in the light of the strong statements pointing in the opposite direction in the English Court of Appeal and the Court of Appeal of New Zealand and the strong dissent of Lord Keith, the most senior Law Lord at the time, and the architect of the hitherto restrictive approach of the House of Lords in economic loss cases.

Equally important is the manifest willingness of the four majority Lords to expand the law on liability of defendants for economic loss, even though this involved stealing a march on the Court of Appeal of New Zealand, which (*per* Lord Keith at p 313) is "well known to be tender in its approach to claims in negligence involving pure economic loss". In so doing, the four majority Lords were prepared to confront policy head on and to subordinate traditional notions to their strong desire to do practical justice for plaintiffs who would otherwise be remediless in an area which they recognised to be of great social importance.

The traditional view is that the purpose of the defence of qualified privilege is to encourage frankness and that the imposition of liability on negligent referees in cases like this would deter referees from giving frank references, or indeed any references, Lord Lowry dismissed this argument by saying (at p 326): "I am inclined to view this possibility as a spectre conjured up by the defendants to frighten your Lordships into submission". Lord Slynn said (at p 336): "Even . . . if the number of references given will be reduced, the quality and value will be greater, and it is by no means certain that to have more references is more in the public interest than to have more careful references"; and Lord Woolf said (at p 352):

> Freedom of speech has to be balanced against the equally well recognised freedom . . . that an individual should not be deprived of the opportunity of earning his livelihood in his chosen occupation. . .
>
> . . . public policy comes down firmly in favour of not depriving an employee of a remedy to recover the damages to which he would otherwise be entitled as a result of being a victim of a negligent reference.

On the other hand, their Lordships did set some limits on the doctrine that they were espousing. Lord Goff said (at p 316) that if the *Hedley Byrne* principle of an assumption of responsibility by the defendant towards the plaintiff, coupled with reliance by the plaintiff on the exercise by the defendant of due skill and care, could not be invoked on the facts of this case, he would not have held in the plaintiff's favour, "because in those circumstances it would have been a simple case of the defendants having negligently made a statement damaging to the plaintiff's reputation". This is similar to the way that Lord Woolf distinguished the present case from the type of claim referred to in Hallett J's above-cited *dictum* in the *Foaminol* case.

Lord Slynn imposed another restriction when he said (at p 336) that if the statements alleged to have been carelessly given are true, then the considerations adverted to by the New Zealand Court of Appeal would seem plainly to be right. In other words, if the defamatory words in the defendant's report are true, that will be a defence in the defamation action and a barrier to the imposition of a duty of care in tort.

Lord Woolf also imposed a restriction when he said (at p 345): "A distinction must be drawn between cases where the subject of the reference is an employee or an ex-employee and where the relationship is social and has never been contractual". However, he then qualified this by adding that sufficient proximity might nevertheless exist if the reference had been given by a purely social acquaintance at the *request* of the subject of the reference.

Lastly, it is worth noting that although four of their Lordships, including Lord Keith, assumed that it was established law, on the strength of the House's decision in *Hedley Byrne*, that a new employer to whom a reference had been given about an employee should be able to sue the giver of a negligent reference if the new employer suffered loss through having relied on it, Lord Goff was not prepared to make this assumption. He said (at p 320):

> . . . it does not necessarily follow that, because the employer owes such a duty of care to his employee, he also owes a duty of care to the recipient of the reference. The relationship of the employer with the recipient is by no means the same as that with his employee; and whether, in a case such as this, there should be held (as was *prima facie* held to be so on the facts of the *Hedley Byrne* case itself) a duty of care owed by the maker of the reference to the recipient is a point on which I do not propose to express an opinion, and which may depend on the facts of the particular case before the court.

Baker v Kaye

In *Baker v Kaye* (12 June 1996, unreported), a potentially lucrative conditional employment offer had been made to the plaintiff by the television station, NBC (Europe). The condition was that the plaintiff had to undergo a pre-employment medical assessment. The plaintiff duly visited the consulting rooms of Dr Kaye, the defendant, who was a general practitioner in private practice. He was not employed by NBC, but he had been retained by NBC and its associated companies for many years as a medical adviser. In consequence of the results of two blood tests taken by Dr Kaye from the plaintiff on two separate occasions, and in the light of information elicited by Dr Kaye from the plaintiff about the plaintiff's drinking habits, Dr Kaye concluded that he could not recommend the plaintiff for employment by NBC.

The plaintiff was subsequently informed by NBC that he would not be joining the company. The plaintiff brought the present action against Dr Kaye in which he alleged that Dr Kaye's assessment was made negligently and that in consequence the plaintiff suffered substantial economic loss, for which Dr Kaye ought to be made to compensate him. One of the issues at the trial was whether Dr Kaye owed the plaintiff a duty of care. The judge, Mr R Owen QC, sitting as a deputy judge of the High Court, answered this question in the affirmative. First, he said that it was clear that the plaintiff's economic loss was a foreseeable consequence of the breach of the duty for which the plaintiff contended. Secondly, he held that there was a relationship of sufficient proximity to give rise to a duty of care between the defendant and the plaintiff, because the defendant knew that the plaintiff's employment by NBC depended solely upon the defendant's assessment and that if he were to make a non-recommendation it could have serious financial consequences for the plaintiff. Having reached this conclusion, his Honour continued (at para 59):

What is the nature and extent of that duty? In my judgment, the defendant was under a duty to the plaintiff to take reasonable care in carrying out the medical assessment and in making his judgment as to the plaintiff's suitability for employment by NBC by reference to the company's requirements, both general, and specific to the post in question.

In considering what he called "the overriding question" of whether, in all the circumstances, it would be fair, just and reasonable for such a duty to be imposed on the defendant in relation to the loss contended for by the plaintiff, his Honour responded to the defendant's counsel's submission that it would not be fair, just and reasonable to do so because there was a conflict between the discharge of the defendant's primary duty to NBC and any duty to the plaintiff, by saying (at para 61): "Clearly, a conflict between the proper discharge by the defendant of his contractual duties to the company and his putative duty of care to the plaintiff would militate against the imposition of such a duty. Was there such a conflict, actual or potential?" His Honour answered this question in the negative. He said (at para 62):

> The defendant's duty to the company was to take reasonable care in carrying out the assessment, eliciting the material information from the plaintiff, interpreting the test results, and arriving at a judgment as to whether or not to recommend the plaintiff for employment, bearing in mind the company's requirements, both with regard to the employment position in question and as to the company's approach to the consumption of alcohol. The duty to the plaintiff can be couched in identical terms.
>
> I have come to the conclusion that, upon a true analysis of the relationship between the defendant and the company, and between the company and the plaintiff, there is no conflict inconsistent with the imposition of a duty of care. Nor do I consider that there are any other factors that militate against its imposition.

In the event, however, the plaintiff's claim failed ultimately because the deputy judge found that Dr Kaye had not been negligent in interpreting the results of the plaintiff's blood tests and in making his recommendation to NBC; and because Dr Kaye's recommendation, and NBC's decision based on it, were not the cause of the plaintiff's economic loss, because the plaintiff had voluntarily resigned from his previous job before he had heard from NBC whether his conditional offer of employment by NBC was going to be confirmed.

Comment

It is worth noting that, in reaching this decision, Deputy Judge Owen differed from the judge in a county court case, *Kapfunde v Abbey National plc and Dr Diana Daniel*, in which judgment had been given only three days before the trial in *Baker v Kaye* commenced. The facts of both cases were very similar, but the county court judge concluded in the *Kapfunde* case that no relationship of sufficient proximity existed between the plaintiff and the second defendant (the doctor) to give rise to a duty of care. It is submitted that the approach of Judge Owen in the *Baker* case and the result reached by him are in accordance with principle and are to be preferred.

Of particular interest in the *Baker* case is the way in which the deputy judge dealt with the plaintiff's counsel's submission that a very close analogy should be drawn between the *Baker* case and *Spring v Guardian Assurance plc*, on the basis that a doctor carrying out a medical assessment on behalf of prospective employers is in the same position as a former employer providing a reference. Deputy Judge Owen did not, however, accept this submission. He said (at para 42):

> To test the validity of the analogy, it is necessary to consider more closely the basis on which the House of Lords held that there was liability for a reference given by a former employee. It is clear from the speeches of Lords Goff, Slynn and Woolf [see *above*] that the duty of care had its foundation in the relationship of employer and employee. It was an implied term of the contract between the plaintiff and the defendant [his former employers] with whom he was in a contractual relationship that they would ensure that reasonable care was taken in the compiling and giving of the reference, and that they were in breach of that implied term.
>
> There was, of course, no comparable contractual relationship between Mr Baker and Dr Kaye. I do not consider *Spring* to be as closely analogous as the plaintiff's counsel contends.

Nevertheless, as noted *above*, his Honour did hold that it was permissible to impose a duty of care on the defendant in the circumstances of the present case. In so doing he was influenced by the fact that the House of Lords in *Spring* established that a plaintiff's claim for economic loss resulting from the defendant's negligent misstatement to a third party is not necessarily dependent upon the plaintiff having placed reliance on the statement in deciding what action to take. He said (at para 39):

> There is of course a fundamental difference between the situation that gave rise to liability in *Hedley Byrne v Heller* and the facts of the instant case. In *Hedley Byrne*, the advertising agents who had sought the banker's reference relied upon it, as the Bank knew they would, in placing orders with the company, the subject of the reference. In the instant case, the plaintiff was dependent upon the medical assessment made by the defendant; but he did not rely upon it in the sense that it did not lead to any action or inaction on his part. His role was entirely passive. It was for the defendant to make a recommendation or a non-recommendation, and for NBC to act upon it.
>
> However, this distinction was addressed in *Spring v Guardian Assurance plc* [1995] 2 AC 296, and was resolved by an incremental development of the *Hedley Byrne* principle. The [*Guardian*] decision is of central importance because it demonstrates that liability may arise where there has not been reliance in the *Hedley Byrne* sense. As in the instant case, Mr Spring did not act in reliance upon the negligent misrepresentation. Like Mr Baker [the plaintiff in the present case], his role was passive, but that was not fatal to the existence of a duty of care.

9.7.8 Miscellaneous

Clayton v Woodman

In *Clayton v Woodman & Son (Builders) Ltd* [1962] 2 QB 533, an architect (the third defendant) who was involved in a building project gave a negligent instruction to a bricklayer, who suffered physical injury through following it. The court held that the architect owed the bricklayer a duty of care in respect of the bricklayer's physical injuries sustained through relying on the architect's negligent misstatement. Salmon J said (at p 542):

> The architect chose to give the instructions direct to the bricklayer, who had no reason to suspect that any danger was involved. The architect certainly knew that these instructions would be promptly obeyed, and equally certainly should have realised that . . . they would probably lead to the bricklayer's serious injury or death. Having regard to the exceptionally close relationship between the architect and the bricklayer on the particular facts of this case, the law to my mind imposed a duty of care on the architect to take reasonable care for the safety of the bricklayer.

Clay v Crump

In *Clay v A J Crump & Sons Ltd* [1964] 1 QB 533, an architect who had negligently told a demolition contractor that an unsupported wall on a building site could safely be left standing was held liable for the physical injuries which the plaintiff, an employee of the building contractors who subsequently moved onto the site to construct a new building, sustained when the wall collapsed on him. After setting out Lord Atkin's 'neighbour principle' in *Donoghue v Stevenson* [1932] AC 562 (see para 9.2.3), Ormerod LJ said (at p 556):

> Is this a case in which it can be said that the plaintiff was so closely and directly affected by the acts of the architect as to have been reasonably in his contemplation when he was directing his mind to the acts or omissions which are called into question? In my judgment, there must be an affirmative answer to that question.

Esso v Mardon

In *Esso Petroleum Co Ltd v Mardon* [1976] 1 QB 801, the defendant in the counterclaim (ie Esso, hereafter referred to as 'the defendant'), in the course of pre-contractual negotiations with the plaintiff in the counterclaim (ie Mr Mardon, hereafter referred to as 'the plaintiff') for the grant of a lease to the plaintiff of one of its petrol stations, represented to the plaintiff that a certain (large) number of gallons of petrol was likely to be sold every year. The plaintiff queried this, but his doubts were quelled by his trust in the greater experience and expertise of the defendant's employees in this sphere. Subsequently it turned out that the plaintiff's fears were well founded. The sales of petrol at that site were very low. The garage eventually closed down and the plaintiff lost all his savings.

The court held that the defendant owed the plaintiff a duty of care in tort for his losses, notwithstanding that the negligent misstatements of the defendant upon which the plaintiff had relied were made in the context of pre-contractual negotiations, which resulted in an actual contract between the parties. Lord Denning MR said (at p 820):

> It seems to me that *Hedley Byrne*, properly understood, covers this particular proposition: if a man, who has or professes to have special knowledge or skill

makes a representation by virtue thereof to another—be it advice, information or opinion—with the intention of inducing him to enter into a contract with him, he is under a duty to use reasonable care to see that the representation is correct, and that the advice, information or opinion is reliable. If he negligently gives unsound advice or misleading information or expresses an erroneous opinion, and thereby induces the other side to enter into a contract with him, he is liable in damages.

American Express v Hurley

In *American Express International Banking Corp v Hurley* [1985] 3 All ER 564 the plaintiff in the counterclaim (ie Mr Hurley, referred to hereafter as 'the plaintiff') had guaranteed the indebtedness of a certain company with the defendant in the counterclaim (ie American Express, hereafter referred to as 'the bank'). That indebtedness had been secured by way of a floating charge over the company's assets. When the company ran into financial difficulties the bank appointed a receiver (the second defendant in the counterclaim). In due course the receiver sold the company's assets. The court found as a fact that the receiver had not taken reasonable care to obtain the true market value of those assets.

When the bank called on the plaintiff to meet the company's liabilities under his guarantee, the plaintiff counterclaimed against the receiver and the bank for the loss which he, as guarantor, had suffered by virtue of the receiver not having exercised reasonable care in the disposal of the company's assets, in that, if the receiver had done so, more of the company's debt could have been repaid to the bank, and less would have been due from the plaintiff. The court upheld the plaintiff's claim, and rejected the receiver's contention that, while a receiver, like a mortgagee, owes a duty of care to the mortgagor (ie the company) to obtain the best price for the mortgagor's assets, that duty did not extend to a guarantor of the company's indebtedness. The court referred to and relied on *dicta* in *Cuckmere Brick Co Ltd v Mutual Finance Ltd* [1971] Ch 949 and *Standard Chartered Bank Limited v Walker* [1982] 1 WLR 1410, in which Lord Denning MR said (at p 1415):

> If a mortgagee enters into possession and realises a mortgaged property, it is his duty to use reasonable care to obtain the best possible price. . . . He owes this duty not only to himself, to clear off as much of the debt as he can, but also to the mortgagor so as to reduce the balance owing as much as possible, and also to the guarantor so that he is made liable for as little as possible on the guarantee. This duty is only a particular application of the general duty of care to your neighbour which was stated by Lord Atkin in *Donoghue v Stevenson* and applied in many cases since.

The court also held that this duty of care was to be imposed on the bank from the time when the company went into liquidation, at which point the receiver converted from being the mortgagor's agent to the bank/mortgagee's agent. At that time, the bank, as the receiver's principal, assumed liability for the receiver's negligence in not taking reasonable care to obtain the best price for the company's assets.

Tidman v Reading Borough Council

In *Tidman v Reading Borough Council* [1994] 3 PLR 72, the plaintiff was the owner of certain valuable land and buildings in the Reading area, which he was in the process of selling to a Mr Terry who required the property for light engineering purposes. In order to complete the agreement with Mr Terry, the plaintiff had to satisfy Mr Terry as to the planning position of the land. In that connection the plaintiff telephoned the defendant's planning department and briefly outlined his position. He was advised to make an application for planning permission. He disagreed that planning permission was required, but he nevertheless made the application.

When, in due course, the plaintiff's application for planning permission was turned down by the defendant, the defendant suggested that the plaintiff might consider applying for 'a section 53 determination', namely a determination under s 53 of the Town and Country Planning Act 1971, which states that any person who is proposing to make any change in the use of land may apply to the local planning authority to determine whether planning permission is required in respect of such proposed change of use. If a s 53 determination is to the effect that no planning permission is required, it is binding on the local council. If, however, a s 53 determination is to the effect that planning permission is required, then the applicant will have lost the time taken for a s 53 determination to be made (about six weeks) and will have to start afresh with a planning application.

In the present case the plaintiff duly followed the defendant's suggestion that he should make an application for a s 53 determination. This determination, when issued, was to the effect that planning permission was not required for the use of the property within certain limited use classes, which would have accommodated the use that Mr Terry said he was proposing for the land. However, by the time that this s 53 determination was issued, Mr Terry had lost interest in purchasing the land. Thereafter the plaintiff was not able to sell the land elsewhere, or not at the price that he had been discussing with Mr Terry, because during the period of the delay the value of the land had dropped substantially.

The plaintiff therefore brought the present action against the defendant, Reading Borough Council, claiming that his above-described economic losses were caused by the defendant's negligence in failing to advise him, when he first contacted the defendant, to apply for a s 53 determination and/or to obtain independent advice. One of the issues was whether the defendant owed the plaintiff a duty of care in respect of that loss. The judge, Buxton J, answered this question in the negative, notwithstanding that, in seeking the defendant's advice, the plaintiff had been responding to a leaflet put out by the defendant which encouraged persons involved in planning matters to seek advice and guidance from their local authority. Leaving aside considerations as to when it is proper to impose a duty of care on a statutory body exercising its statutory powers or duties (as to which, see Chapter 8, para 8.2.10), Buxton J was nevertheless satisfied that no duty of care on the defendant was appropriate in the present case. He said:

681

The approach here [of the plaintiff to the defendant] was informal, over the telephone, and on the basis of very slight information given by the applicant. It cannot reasonably be thought that in such cases, if the planning officers responded to the inquiry to give such help as they were able, they are immediately placing the local authority under obligations springing from the law of negligence.

I accept that it might be possible that a formal approach to a local authority, which was known by the local authority to have serious implications, which was put on a formal basis, and to which the local authority chose to respond, might conceivably generate a duty of care on their part. I would want to reserve, in a case where that did occur, careful consideration of the implications of such a finding. What I am, however, quite clear about is that the brief telephone inquiries that took place in this case with, as Mr Tidman [the plaintiff] himself says, no serious discussion of the planning implications or the history of the site; no attempt to follow or pursue the matter in writing; and no face-to-face meetings; cannot generate a relationship of reliance in the relevant sense.

On the question of reliance, Buxton J held that it was unreasonable for the plaintiff to rely solely on the defendant's 'advice' because:

It is entirely reasonable to suppose that in any case where the view of the local authority is crucial to the interests of the applicant, and certainly where a matter as grave as a contract for £650,000 is alleged to turn on a planning decision, an applicant would not simply rely on what the local authority said, but would also have the benefit of proper advice of his own.

Buxton J then disposed of the plaintiff's counsel's submission that the defendant ought to have realised that the plaintiff was relying on it by saying:

I then asked the second question, whether there was anything in this particular case that should have made the local authority officers understand that Mr Tidman was in fact relying upon them for advice. The brevity of contact with those officers, and the paucity of information they seemed to have given about the case, renders it impossible to draw any such conclusion.

Goodwill v British Pregnancy Advisory Service

In *Goodwill v British Pregnancy Advisory Service* [1996] 1 WLR 1397 (CA), the defendant was a charitable organisation engaged in the arrangement and provision of sterilisation operations, including vasectomies and associated counselling services. In November 1994, the defendant arranged for a vasectomy to be performed on a Mr MacKinlay. Three months later Mr MacKinlay provided two semen samples to the defendant. On 2 April 1985, the defendant informed Mr MacKinlay by letter that the tests on the samples had proved negative, that the vasectomy had been successful and that Mr MacKinlay no longer needed to use any other method of contraception.

Three years later the plaintiff, Mrs Goodwill, then a 40-year-old teacher, commenced a sexual relationship with Mr MacKinlay. The plaintiff knew of his vasectomy and of its purported success and permanency. This led to the plaintiff ceasing to use a contraceptive coil or any other method of contraception in her ongoing sexual relationship with Mr MacKinlay.

Some time after this, unbeknown to the plaintiff or Mr MacKinlay, his vasectomy underwent a spontaneous reversal, thereby causing him to regain his fertility. In due course the plaintiff became pregnant by Mr MacKinlay. When she realised that this was the case, it was too late for her to have an abortion. In due course she gave birth to a daughter.

In the present action the plaintiff claimed from the defendant the economic loss that she alleged to have sustained in the form of the expenses incurred in her daughter's birth, the cost of bringing her daughter up and her loss of income due to the reduction of her working hours. The defendant applied to strike out the plaintiff's claim on the ground that the defendant did not owe the plaintiff a duty of care in respect of these losses. The court agreed with the defendant, and struck out the plaintiff's claim.

The plaintiff's counsel sought to draw an analogy with *White v Jones* [1995] 2 AC 207 (see para 9.7.5, *above*) on the basis that a woman who had a sexual relationship with Mr MacKinlay was effectively in the same position as the intended beneficiaries under a will because, just as the solicitor was employed to confer a benefit (in the form of bequests) on a particular class of people (the beneficiaries), so a doctor performing a vasectomy on a particular man is employed to confer a benefit (not getting pregnant) on a particular class of people (women who have sexual relationships with that man). In rejecting this submission, Peter Gibson LJ (with whom the other Lord Justice of Appeal on the panel agreed) said (at p 1403):

> It must be recognised that *White v Jones* belonged to an unusual class of cases. A remedy in tort was fashioned to overcome the rank injustice that the only persons who might have a valid claim (the testator and his estate) had suffered no loss, and the only persons who had suffered a loss (the disappointed beneficiaries) had no claim. I do not see any comparable justice in the present case. On the contrary, it might be said that to give a remedy to the plaintiff against the defendant in the circumstances of the present case would *not* be fair, just or reasonable.
>
> A doctor who performs a vasectomy on a man on his instructions cannot realistically be described as having been employed to confer a benefit on the man's sexual partners in the form of avoiding pregnancy. The doctor is concerned only with the man, his patient, and possibly that man's wife or partner if the doctor intends her to receive, and she receives advice from the doctor in relation to the vasectomy and the subsequent tests. Whether the avoidance of pregnancy is a benefit or a disadvantage to a sexual partner of the man will depend on the circumstances.
>
> If the existence of that partner is known to the doctor, and the doctor is aware that she wishes not to become pregnant by the man, and the vasectomy is carried out to meet her wish as well as the man's wish, it may be said that the doctor is employed to confer that benefit on her. But that is not this case. I cannot accept that the present is a *White v Jones* type of case at all.

The Court also rejected the plaintiff's counsel's reliance on *Thake v Maurice* [1986] QB 644 (which is mentioned in Chapter 10, para 10.4.3), in which a successful action in contract and in tort was allowed by a husband

and wife whom the defendant surgeon had failed to warn of the slight risk that the husband's vasectomy might not leave him permanently sterile. Peter Gibson LJ said (at p 1404):

> ... in that case advice on the husband's vasectomy was given directly to him and his wife, and both signed forms consenting to the vasectomy. There could be no doubt therefore but that a duty of care was owed by the surgeon to the wife when the surgeon advised the husband and the wife that they might reasonably take no further contraceptive precautions.

Lastly, Peter Gibson LJ referred to Lord Oliver's four-part formulation in *Caparo Industries plc v Dickman* [1990] 2 AC 605 (see para 9.6.2, *above*) and said (at p 1404):

> Of these conditions, I need only fasten on (3) [ie that it is known, actually or inferentially, that the advice so communicated is likely to be acted on by the advisee for that purpose (ie, a purpose that was known to the adviser at the time that the advice was given) without independent inquiry]. How the defendant knew or should have known that its advice would be communicated to the plaintiff and relied on by her as a warranty of permanent infertility when she did not meet, or commence a sexual relationship with, Mr MacKinlay until three years later is not apparent.

Sumitomo Bank v Banque Bruxelles

In *Sumitomo Bank v Banque Bruxelles* [1997] 1 Lloyd's Rep 487, the defendant (BBL) was a bank which had entered into an agreement with four other banks whereunder all of the banks were going to participate in varying degrees in a large loan to a borrower to enable the borrower to purchase certain commercial property in London. Apart from the property itself, the only other security was to be certain Mortgage Indemnity Guarantee Policies ('MIGs') to be issued by Eagle Star Insurance Company Limited ('Eagle Star').

The only bank that had any direct contact with Eagle Star in arranging the MIGs was BBL, but the policies were issued to BBL as agent for the benefit of the other banks who were participating with BBL in the loans.

In due course the borrowers defaulted on the loans, and all of the banks, including BBL, suffered very substantial losses on their realisation of the properties. Eagle Star, when called upon to indemnify the banks under the MIGs, contended that the MIGs were voidable for non-disclosure by BBL in breach of its duty of disclosure, which required BBL to carry out all such investigations and make all such inquiries in relation to the borrowers and the properties as it would have carried out or made if proposing to enter into the relevant loan agreements without the benefit of the MIGs.

The other banks therefore brought the present action against BBL, alleging that, in so far as Eagle Star's allegation of non-disclosure might be proved to be correct, BBL was liable to them to make good their losses on the basis that BBL, as the arranger of the loans, was responsible to them (and not only to Eagle Star) for the performance of the disclosure obligations under the MIGs, and failed to discharge those obligations. BBL denied that it had breached its disclosure obligations and claimed that, even if it had, it was not liable to the plaintiffs for their losses because it did not owe a duty of care to the plaintiffs in the discharge of its disclosure obligations under the MIGs, which obligations were owed only to Eagle Star.

The judge, Langley J, held that BBL did in fact owe a duty of care to the other banks in the discharge of its disclosure obligations under the MIGs. He said (at para 186):

> BBL was putting together the transactions and had an interest in getting the Banks to participate in them and indeed was being rewarded for that role. Mr Fraser [of BBL] himself readily acknowledged that the MIGs were for each of the Banks a key part of the transaction, and that he knew at the time that, if BBL did not comply with the disclosure obligation in the Policies, Eagle Star could avoid the Policies, which would have the consequence for each of the Banks that they would be unable to enforce them. He agreed that the Banks could not know or verify whether BBL had complied with the disclosure obligation and that each of the Banks in each transaction relied on BBL to perform that obligation, and he knew at the time that they did so. In addition, it was his view, as it was the view of the Banks, that the disclosure obligation was not an exceptional or onerous one and, of course, not only had it been negotiated by BBL, but it was no greater than the 'obligation' that BBL in effect owed to itself in its own interests to establish the efficacy of the Policy. The fact that Mr Fraser or BBL may have believed that the arrangements were 'non-recourse' is, in these circumstances, of no materiality. That was not communicated to the Banks, and the test of duty is objective.
>
> On the other side, the Banks had to rely on BBL performing the disclosure obligation, as it was tailored to BBL's own procedures. Each Bank expected and relied on BBL to perform the obligation, and believed it would do so, and indeed, and understandably, hardly contemplated that it would not do so. That expectation and reliance was, in my judgment, entirely reasonable.
>
> In these circumstances, I think that the relationship between BBL and the plaintiff Banks was, to use the words of Lord Goff in *Henderson v Merrett Syndicates Ltd* [1995] 2 AC 145 [see para 9.7.6], a 'classic example' of a relationship where a duty of care did arise on BBL to the Banks as regards the performance of the disclosure obligations under the MIGs.

Earlier in his judgment, Langley J had said that there are two basic approaches to determining whether a duty of care arises in any particular case: namely, the test of foreseeability, proximity and whether the imposition of a duty of care would be fair, just and reasonable; and, secondly, "voluntary assumption of responsibility". He said that, in this case, he did not think it mattered which approach was taken as the result was the same on either basis. The passages cited *above* from Langley J's judgment relate to the first basis. As regards the second basis, he said (at para 189):

> There was [also] an assumption of responsibility by BBL to the Banks to perform that duty [ie the disclosure obligations under the MIGs]. BBL was the arranger of the facility. It assumed as such the obligation to negotiate and agree the MIGs with Eagle Star. It did so on terms whereby it, and it alone, was the Insured under the Policy, and it, and it alone, had, and could perform, the disclosure obligation provided for, in which it depended on its own expert procedures and skill and

judgment in deciding what should be disclosed to Eagle Star. BBL knew that the validity of the Policies depended on its proper performance of that obligation. It knew that the Policies were vital to the interests both of itself and the Banks, and that the Banks were dependent upon it for the performance of the disclosure obligation which effectively was entrusted to BBL in all of their interests. The Banks relied on BBL accordingly, as BBL knew that they would. Loss to the Banks if the duty was not performed was foreseeable and was indeed foreseen by BBL. The duty arose in the context of the specific purpose of the loan transactions.

Lidl v Clarke Bond

In *Lidl Properties v Clarke Bond Partnership* (6 June 1997, unreported), the plaintiff was a retail food supermarket chain that was very keen on expanding its business in the Midlands area of England. It became aware of a large, vacant site that was also being looked at by the plaintiff's principal competitors. The site was known to the plaintiff to have serious environmental contamination problems. The plaintiff was nevertheless interested in acquiring it, primarily so as to lock out its main competitor.

The defendant was a firm of civil and structural engineers with experience in decontamination works. By September 1993 the defendant had been concerned with investigating the site on behalf of prospective developers for about 16 months. In or about mid-September, the defendant became aware of the plaintiff's interest in the site, but it did not have any contact with the plaintiff at that stage. On or about 27 September, representatives of the plaintiff contacted a representative of the defendant and asked whether he and some of his colleagues would be prepared to attend a site meeting with the plaintiff to discuss the decontamination works that the land might require to make it usable as a supermarket site.

This site meeting duly took place on 30 September 1993. At the meeting the defendant's representatives outlined the measures that the defendant believed were needed to remove the contamination. In particular, the defendant told the plaintiff that the extent of contamination at the site was not as bad as was generally believed, that the contamination problem was not difficult to resolve, and that the proposals previously accepted in principle by the local planning authority were more extensive than was required to solve the problem. The next day the plaintiff, without further communicating with the defendant, agreed with the vendor of the site to an unconditional exchange of contracts without seeking any reduction in price on account of the contamination.

In due course, the plaintiff, without consulting the defendant, concluded that the cost of decontaminating the site was much higher than what the plaintiff had been led to believe by the defendant. The plaintiff therefore brought the present action against the defendant, claiming that the defendant was responsible for the plaintiff's economic loss consisting of the cost of the site, professional fees and construction costs, and the cost of remedying the contamination problem. One of the issues was whether the defendant owed the plaintiff a duty of care in respect of such information as the defendant conveyed to the plaintiff at the meeting on 30 September 1993.

Judge David Wilcox, sitting as an Official Referee, answered this question in the affirmative. He said:

> Clarke Bond were experienced civil and structural engineers with experience in contamination works. They had a hope that they might be appointed as part of the Lidl development team for building Lidl stores in the Midlands area. They had been invited to apply, and wished to be considered as standing engineers to the team. In relation to the meeting of September 30, 1993, they were not paid, and such advice and information as they imparted was gratuitous. Nonetheless, it was not without the hope that, were they helpful and co-operative on this occasion, it might go in their favour.

In response to the defendant's counsel's submission that it would not be fair, just and reasonable to impose a duty on the defendant in view of the fact that, not only had the defendant's advice at the meeting been given gratuitously, but also the meeting was entirely *ad hoc* and had been called without reasonable notice or any agenda, Judge Wilcox said:

> Clarke Bond's Mr Harle and Mr Watton are professional engineers. They were prepared to discuss at a business meeting with experienced developers and other professionals matters affecting the development of the Hinckley building site, relating to the foundations and contamination, to enable abnormal works to be costed by the plaintiff's quantity surveyor, Mr Startin. Clarke Bond may be seen to be 'casting their bread on the waters': I can see nothing unfair or unreasonable in holding that there was a duty situation arising out of their assumption of responsibility.
>
> Lidl knew that there were two schemes to deal with the contamination. Mr Harle expressed the opinion that the Clarke Bond drainage scheme was feasible and that the KPP containment scheme [ie the other proposals referred to above] was not necessary. Mr Harle owed a duty to take reasonable care in imparting the information of the Clarke Bond scheme. Such duty required Clarke Bond to exercise that degree of care and skill which was to be reasonably expected of a consulting civil engineer with experience of dealing with contaminated development sites, in imparting such information in the context of the discussions of September 30, 1993, and in the knowledge that Lidl would place reliance upon Mr Startin's costings as a component in the valuation of the site.

The plaintiff's case ultimately failed because the judge went on to find that the defendant's advice given at the meeting of 30 September 1993 was not negligent, in the sense that nothing that Mr Harle said fell below the above-mentioned standard that was placed on the defendant.

Having reached this conclusion, the judge did not go on to determine the scope of the defendant's duty of care, ie whether Clarke Bond should be held liable for the entire cost of the purchase and development of the site, as alleged by the plaintiff, or for the difference between the price paid by the plaintiff and the true value of the land at that time (which the plaintiff claimed was negative £500,000) or for the cost of the decontamination works or only the estimated additional costs of the decontamination works from that which the plaintiff expected to pay after hearing what the defendant had said at the meeting on 30 September 1993. His Honour did, however, make some comments about the scope of the duty in principle. He said:

The extent of the duty will arise out of the particular circumstances in which the information is required and imparted. In this case, the object of the meeting was to cost the abnormals in the development of the site using the Clarke Bond drainage scheme. Clarke Bond were not asked to give, on an *ad hoc* basis, a complete risk assessment of the site, neither were they asked or instructed to give an exhaustive and comprehensive presentation of the history and investigation of the site. It was no part of their duty to do so.

Comment

It is submitted that these words imply that the judge would have limited the scope of the defendant's duty of care to the cost of the decontamination works incurred by the plaintiff, or even to part of those costs (ie the excess over what the plaintiff reasonably expected to incur after hearing what the defendant said at the meeting on 30 September 1993). It is submitted that this, in particular the latter variation just mentioned, would be the proper approach in a case like the present because, in the absence of evidence (and there was none) that the plaintiff would not have gone ahead with the purchase at all if it had known what the true cost of the decontamination works was likely to be, these are the only damages which, in the words of Lord Hoffman in *South Australia Acid Management Corporation v York Montague Ltd* [1997] AC 191 (see Chapter 2, para 2.1.5), were incurred in consequence of the information being inaccurate.

There is one surprising aspect of Judge Wilcox's judgment which, it is submitted, calls into question the correctness of his imposition of a duty of care on the defendant by virtue of what the defendant's representatives said at the meeting on 30 September 1993. Before reaching this conclusion, his Honour posed the question whether the defendant knew, or ought to have known, that the plaintiff would rely on what was said at the meeting in deciding whether or not to purchase the site on 1 October 1993; and he answered it by saying:

> Mr Smith [of the plaintiff] indicated at the meeting that Lidl were contemplating the submission of an offer on an unconditional basis in the next day or so. I am satisfied that Clarke Bond did not know that Lidl contemplated going as far as to exchange contracts. They did not know that there was to be a contract race. There was outstanding a further site investigation report, and it would be reasonable to expect a prudent bidder to obtain the results of such a report and to carry out such other inquiries before exchanging contracts. [Also] there was no planning permission. The planning permission granted was outline only. It related to the details of another scheme which had not been fully developed, and which involved the disposal of contaminated water in addition to containment.
>
> Clarke Bond could not know what the commercial imperatives or restraints were upon Lidl. They would not know how a proposed purchase might be funded or any of the other commercial considerations that might be brought to bear upon this decision by this company. This was Lidl's first transaction in the United Kingdom. They had no track record as to their approach to acquisitions that professionals such as Clarke Bond and others might know about.
>
> Mr Watton [of the defendant] gave advice in relation to the foundation options. His understanding, and I accept his evidence as being wholly reliable, was that the purpose for which his advice was sought was to enable costings to

be made so that an offer for the site could be considered. He did not know about the time scale of any offer, and he did not expect that this advice would be the 'final hurdle'. Clarke Bond knew that Lidl were likely to rely on what was said for the limited purpose of Mr Startin's costing of the Clarke Bond scheme.

Clarke Bond did not know, and could not reasonably have been expected to know, that Lidl would rely on what was said in deciding whether or not to purchase on October 1, 1993.

It is submitted that this finding militates strongly against the imposition of a duty of care on the defendant; or at least, it motivates strongly in favour of restricting that duty of care very narrowly, as suggested *above*.

9.8   The Misrepresentation Act

9.8.1   Introduction

The Misrepresentation Act 1967 modified the law relating to innocent misrepresentations made after 21 April 1967 between contracting parties. The Act enables a contract to be rescinded on account of an innocent (ie a nonfraudulent) misrepresentation, notwithstanding that it became a term of the contract or that the contract had been performed (s 1). Subject to the provisions of the Act, the person who has been induced to enter into the contract by virtue of such a misrepresentation (ie the plaintiff) is entitled to relief without having to allege fraud on the part of the misrepresentor (ie the defendant).

9.8.2   Section 2(1)

The main operative section of the Act is s 2(1), which provides:

> Where a person has entered into a contract after a misrepresentation has been made to him by another party thereto and as a result thereof he has suffered loss, then, if the person making the misrepresentation would be liable to damages in respect thereof had the misrepresentation been made fraudulently, that person shall be so liable notwithstanding that the misrepresentation was not made fraudulently, unless he proves that he had reasonable ground to believe and did believe up to the time that the contract was made that the facts represented were true.

9.8.3   Limited scope

Section 2(1) applies only where the misrepresentation was made directly by the defendant to the plaintiff; as for example in *Esso v Mardon* or, as in *Gran Gelato v Richcliff*, as between the underlessor and the plaintiff (see paras 9.7.8 and 9.7.5, *above*). It does not apply to cases like *Hedley Byrne*, or to practically any of the other cases considered in this chapter, where the misrepresentation was made by the defendant to a third party, rather than to the plaintiff himself.

Where the Act does apply, the plaintiff is relieved from the burden of having to establish that the defendant owed him a duty of care. All that the plaintiff needs to show is that he and the defendant are parties to a contract which he entered into after a representation had been made to him by the defendant, and as a result thereof he has suffered loss. Then, the onus will be on the defendant to prove that he had reasonable grounds to believe, and did believe, up to the time that the contract was made, that the facts represented by him were true. This is much easier for the plaintiff than having to try to establish a duty of care at common law, as can be seen from some of the difficulties raised in the cases discussed in this chapter.

9.9 Overseas cases

9.9.1 Introduction

In the cases considered in this chapter, there is a large measure of uniformity between the approaches of the courts of the relevant Commonwealth jurisdictions and the English courts. Accordingly, only a brief overview of the overseas decisions is provided here.

9.9.2 Australia

The approach of the High Court of Australia is typified by its decision in *San Sebastian Proprietary Ltd v The Minister* (1986) 162 CLR 340. Here, the Sydney City Council, for whom the defendant was vicariously responsible, adopted a scheme to redevelop a certain part of Sydney in accordance with a plan and documents prepared by the state planning authority. In reliance on alleged representations in the scheme documents, the plaintiff developers bought land in the area in the expectation of being able to redevelop it profitably. Subsequently, the scheme was abandoned unilaterally by the City Council. In consequence, the plaintiff's land lost value. The plaintiff claimed damages from the defendant for the loss which it suffered as a result of its reliance upon representations in the scheme documents, which it alleged had been negligently prepared and published, and for the defendant's failure to warn of the likely abandonment of the scheme.

The plaintiff's claim failed because it was not able to establish that the alleged representation had in fact been made. However, even if the plaintiff would have been able to establish this, the Court would still have rejected its claim, because it would not have been able to establish that the defendant made the representation with the intention of inducing members of the class of developers to act in reliance on it. Gibbs CJ said (at p 357):

> Where a statement is made for the purpose of inducing the plaintiff, or the members of a limited class including the plaintiff, to commit themselves financially on the basis that the statement is true, and the plaintiff acts in reliance on the statement, the law will impose a duty of care on the maker of the statement.

The Court held that this test was not satisfied because the scheme documents did not amount to an invitation to developers to rely on their contents "as a solid and unalterable basis for action by way of acquiring and developing properties in the area". Gibbs CJ said (at p 359):

> In the absence of some such assurance or representation, it is not easy to see why the publication of plans or proposals intended to serve as a guide for future development should be held to impose an obligation on a local authority to take care in making statements in those plans or proposals. In the nature of things, being creatures of an administrative and political process, proposals of this kind are subject to alteration, variation and revocation.

The Court also stressed the role of the concept of reliance (see Chapter 2, para 2.3.3) in this type of case. Gibbs CJ said (at p 355):

> In cases of negligent misstatement, reliance plays an important role, particularly when the defendant directs his statement to a class of persons with the intention of inducing members of the class to act or refrain from acting in reliance on the statement, in circumstances where he should realise that they may thereby suffer economic loss if the statement is not true.

This statement of principle accords with the opinions expressed in the House of Lords in *Caparo* (see para 9.6.2, *above*).

Solicitors

It is also worth noting the High Court's decision in *Hawkins v Clayton* (1988) 164 CLR 539, which was referred to (and impliedly approved) by the House of Lords in *White v Jones* [1995] 2 AC 207 (see para 9.7.5, *above*). Here, a testatrix had made a will appointing the plaintiff as her executor, and leaving him the residue of her estate. The will had been drafted by the defendant solicitors, with whom the testatrix left it for safekeeping. Subsequently the testatrix died. The defendants made no attempt to locate the plaintiff and inform him of the will for more than six years. During that time, the main asset of the estate, a house which the testatrix had owned, and which had initially been let to tenants, fell into disrepair and lay vacant for a period of time. The Court held that the defendants were liable to the plaintiff for the economic loss suffered by him by virtue of the diminution in value of the house, and also for such other damages as he might have suffered by reason of their delay in taking steps to locate him. This case was easier for the Court than *Ross v Caunters* (see para 9.7.5, *above*) or *White v Jones*, because the Court was only concerned with a loss suffered by the plaintiff in his capacity as executor, claiming for loss sustained to the testatrix's estate before the administration had been completed. However, the Court indicated that it would nevertheless have been prepared to find a relationship of sufficient proximity between the defendants and the plaintiff in his capacity as a beneficiary, and impose a duty of care on the defendants to the plaintiff for losses suffered by him personally as a beneficiary. Deane J said (at p 581):

> In such a case, the assumption of responsibility by the solicitor, the unavoidable dependence for information of the beneficiary and the foreseeability of economic loss to the beneficiary in his personal capacity, could well combine to give rise to a relevant duty of care owed directly to the beneficiary.

691

More recently, the High Court of Australia had been faced with a more difficult case in this field, namely, *Hill v Van Erp* (1997) 142 ALR 687. Here, a testatrix wished to change her will so as to make certain substantial gifts to her friend, Mrs Van Erp (the plaintiff). The defendant, Mrs Hill, prepared a new draft will to give effect to this instruction. Mrs Hill brought the new draft will to the testatrix's house, where the testatrix signed it in Mrs Hill's presence. Mrs Hill signed as one attesting witness and then asked Mr Van Erp, who was the only other person present, to sign as the other attesting witness. No advice was sought by Mr Van Erp or given to him by Mrs Hill as to the effect on the gift to his wife (Mrs Van Erp/the plaintiff) of his being an attesting witness.

The consequence of Mr Van Erp's signing the will as an attesting witness was to invalidate the bequests in the will to Mrs Van Erp. In the present case, Mrs Van Erp sued the defendant solicitor for damages representing the value of the property that Mrs Van Erp would have received but for the defendant's negligence in allowing Mr Van Erp to be an attesting witness. The facts of this case were thus almost the same as those in *Ross v Caunters* [1980] 1 Ch 297 (see para 9.7.5, *above*).

The question in the present case was whether Mrs Hill owed Mrs Van Erp a duty of care in tort for Mrs Van Erp's loss. By a majority of 5:1 (McHugh J dissenting) the Court answered this question in the affirmative. In the light of the House of Lords' decision in *White v Jones* [1995] 2 AC 207 this is not surprising. Like the Law Lords in *White v Jones*, their Honours stressed the exceptional nature of this type of case (ie that no other remedy would be available to the plaintiff and the negligent solicitor would get off scot-free) and stated expressly that their decision by no means espoused any general proposition to the effect that if A promises B to perform a service for B which A intends and knows will confer a benefit on C if performed, A owes to C a duty in tort to perform that service with reasonable skill and care.

Comment

Three matters of particular interest stand out in the Court's judgments. First, there was a noticeable retreat from the very strong statements of the High Court in earlier cases on the meaning and the scope of the concept of proximity, and as to its utility in individual cases. This point is considered more fully in Chapter 2, para 2.3.2.

Secondly, the feeling by some of the judges that the proximity analysis would not provide the answer in this case led them to introduce a new concept, namely, 'control'. Thus, Gaudron J said:

> The relationship in this case between Mrs Hill and Mrs Van Erp is not one that is characterised either by the assumption of responsibility or reliance. Rather, what is significant is that Mrs Hill was in a position of control over the testamentary wishes of her client and, thus, in a position to control whether Mrs Van Erp would have the right which the testatrix clearly intended her to have, namely, the right to have her estate properly administered in accordance with the terms of her Will.
>
> The importance of control as a factor in proximity, and also as a factor governing the content of the duty of care, is apparent in *Burnie Port Authority v General Jones Pty Ltd* (1994) 179 CLR 520. And although Deane J rested his

judgment in *Hawkins v Clayton* [see *above*] on the assumption of responsibility and reliance, it seems to me that that case is more easily explained in terms of control. Moreover, control is in some respects a more stringent test than assumption of responsibility. Certainly, neither law nor logic excludes it from consideration as a determinant of proximity in cases of pure economic loss.

I am of the view that, by reason of her position of control, in particular her position to control whether Mrs Van Erp would acquire the right to have the testatrix's estate properly administered in accordance with the terms of her Will, there was a relationship of proximity between Mrs Hill and Mrs Van Erp such that Mrs Hill was under a duty of care to take reasonable steps to ensure that Mrs Van Erp's testamentary intentions were not defeated by s 15 of the Act [ie the Succession Act 1981 of Queensland, pursuant to which the bequest to the plaintiff was rendered invalid by virtue of the plaintiff's husband having been an attesting witness].

The case of *Burnie Port Authority v General Jones Pty Ltd* (1994) 179 LLR 520 which Gaudron J referred to, and the concept of 'control' which she invoked in the present case, are discussed more fully in Chapter 3, para 3.5.3.

Thirdly, there was a conscious effort by some of the judges to reconcile the application of the proximity analysis in new areas of the law with Brennan J's (now Brennan CJ's) view that the law should develop novel categories of negligence incrementally and by analogy with established cases, rather than by trying to apply any type of general formulation, such as proximity. This point is considered more fully in Chapter 3, para 3.4.4.

Accountants

In *Esanda Finance Corporation Ltd v Peat Marwick Hungerfords* (1997) 142 ALR 750, in which the decision was delivered on the same day as in *Hill v Van Erp*, the High Court of Australia had a further opportunity to articulate its thinking on duties of care in economic loss cases involving negligent misstatements. In this case, the plaintiff (Esanda) claimed damages from the defendant firm of accountants (PMH) in respect of its losses incurred through having lent money to a company named Excel Finance Corporation Limited ('Excel'). PMH were the auditors who had certified Excel's accounts for a particular year. For the purposes of this action, it was assumed that such certification was negligent in the sense that the accounts did not provide a true and fair view of the state of affairs of Excel. Esanda was not a shareholder of Excel, but it was common ground that Esanda foresaw that Excel was in a class of persons who might receive Excel's audited accounts and place reliance on them in deciding whether to lend money to Excel.

PMH, as a member of the Institute of Chartered Accountants, was bound by the Australian Accounting Standards. One of those standards related to the materiality of information in financial statements, and required auditors to consider the position of persons who were likely to be the prime users of the financial statements. This group was defined as including present and potential providers of equity or loan capital and creditors. Esanda alleged that it was a member of that class in relation to Excel and that, in consequence, PMH, as the auditors of Excel's accounts, were under a duty to Esanda to take reasonable care to ensure that the accounts complied with the Australian Accounting Standards.

The Court rejected this contention because the standards were not concerned to create a duty, but to develop the concept of materiality for the purpose of indicating what should be included in financial statements. The reference to providers of loan capital and creditors as users of financial statements was made in the context of determining what is material for inclusion in such statements and did not imply any assumption of responsibility to such users.

The case proceeded by way of a striking-out motion. Apart from the accounting standards, the only other plea upon which Esanda's case was based was that it was foreseeable by PMH that its carelessness in making the auditors' report might cause harm to Esanda. The High Court held that this was an unsustainable plea because it amounted to no more than a plea that it was foreseeable that carelessness in making the report might cause harm to Esanda. Thus, Brennan CJ said:

> The uniform course of authority shows that mere foreseeability of the possibility that a statement made or advice given by A to B might be communicated to a class of which C is a member, and that C might enter into some transaction as the result thereof and suffer financial loss in that transaction, is not sufficient to impose on A a duty of care owed to C in the making of the statement or the giving of the advice.
>
> In some situations, a plaintiff who has suffered pure economic loss by entering into a transaction in reliance on a statement made or advice given by a defendant may be entitled to recover without proving that the plaintiff sought the information and advice (eg, *San Sebastian Proprietary Ltd v The Minister* (1986) 162 CLR 341—see *above*).
>
> But, in every case, it is necessary for the plaintiff to allege and prove that the defendant knew, or ought reasonably to have known, that the information or advice would be communicated to the plaintiff, either individually or as a member of an identified class, that the information or advice would be so communicated for a purpose that would be very likely to lead the plaintiff to enter into a transaction of the kind that the plaintiff does enter into, and that it would be very likely that the plaintiff would enter into such a transaction in reliance on the information or advice and thereby risk the incurring of economic loss if the statement should be untrue or the advice should be unsound.
>
> If any of these elements be wanting, the plaintiff fails to establish that the defendant owed the plaintiff a duty to use reasonable care in making the statement or giving the advice.

These criteria are almost identical to the criteria enunciated by the House of Lords in *Caparo Industries Plc v Dickman* [1990] 2 AC 605, which Brennan CJ cited at length.

In addition to these criteria, Toohey and Gaudron JJ, in their joint judgment, said that the person providing the information must have had some special expertise or knowledge or some special means of acquiring information which was not available to the recipient. Thus, they said:

> The decided cases do not identify precisely what it is that results in liability for economic loss suffered in consequence of the voluntary provision of information or advice. However, common sense requires the conclusion that a special relationship of proximity, marked either by reliance or by the assumption of

responsibility, does not arise unless the person providing the information has some special expertise or knowledge, or some special means of acquiring information which is not available to the recipient. Moreover, ordinary principles require that the relationship does not arise unless it is reasonable for the recipient to act on that information or advice without further inquiry. Similarly, ordinary principles require that it be reasonable for the recipient to act upon it for the purpose for which it is used. That is not to say that a special relationship of proximity exists if these conditions are satisfied. Rather, it is to say that the relationship does not arise unless they are.

McHugh and Gummow JJ, in their respective judgments, set out a number of policy and practical considerations which they suggested should be weighed in determining whether an auditor should owe a duty of care in tort to a third party who did not commission the auditor's report. In summary form these factors are:

(1) Extending the liability of auditors for negligent misstatements will probably reduce the supply of their services.

(2) Insurance against extended tort liability in this field may not be as readily obtainable as courts assume.

(3) Extending the liability of auditors for negligent misstatements may also reduce the demand for their services as their fees increase to help them meet the cost of increased insurance premiums.

(4) Absorbing the cost of insurance may force auditors to reduce other overheads such as the time spent for the number of personnel engaged in audits, thereby leading to a reduction in the standard of care, or auditors might respond by reducing audit services to high-risk businesses where there is a greater likelihood of failure and of liability to investors and creditors.

(5) The administration of the court system would suffer because claims against auditors, especially by public company liquidators, tend to take up an inordinate amount of court time, to the detriment of other litigants.

(6) The need for a rule to correct perceived injustice to third party plaintiffs in audit actions is not compelling because such plaintiffs usually consist of a sophisticated group who have the means in most cases to take steps to avoid the risk of loss.

(7) Whichever class bears the loss, it is likely that the public will have to pay, directly or indirectly. The auditor will pass on such costs through increasing its fees, while the third party will do so through increases in the cost of its credit. Without the aid of evidence as to which class is the more efficient absorber of its losses, the court should be extremely cautious before extending auditors' liability to cover cases like this one.

(8) Creditors and shareholders already have an indirect remedy against the company's auditors in many cases in the form of an action by the liquidator or receiver on behalf of the audit client. Situations in which the client will have a cause of action, but will have suffered no loss, are likely to be rare.

(9) The client's conduct is the primary cause of the plaintiff's loss because the accounts are ordinarily prepared by the client and in any event are the client's responsibility. It would have to be an exceptional case for the client and all of its servants and agents to be innocent of fraud or negligence in relation to the publication of accounts that are false or misleading. The auditor's role is secondary.

(10) The result of extending liability will ordinarily be to impose a financial burden on the auditor out of all proportion to his comparative fault.

(11) Determining the issue of reliance is likely to be very difficult. Sophisticated creditors and investors who study audit reports before making decisions are unlikely to regard that study as sufficient due diligence. Consciously or unconsciously, they are likely to be influenced by a myriad of other factors. In the case of creditors, these may include the track record of the debtor in meeting its obligations, industry information as to the state of the debtor's business and of the industry, the level of interest rates and the general outlook for the economy. In the case of investors, they may include the returns on comparable investments, the trends in the industry, the belief in a continuing demand for the company's products, the lack of competitive products, the barriers to entry in the industry and the general economic outlook. It does not follow from the fact that the creditor or investor read the report, and would not have given the credit or made the investment if he had known the true state of the business, that the creditor or investor relied on the report.

(12) Often the likely length and expense of a trial in this type of case will mean that an auditor has to settle a case that, if tried, would be found to be without merit. The prospect of vexatious litigation is a matter to be considered in fashioning a legal rule.

(13) The auditor did not invite or intend the investor or creditor to rely on his report. The investor or the creditor has paid nothing to the auditor for the preparation of his work. They require the auditor to compensate them for the loss that arose from their self-induced reliance, but they were not prepared to pay for the auditor's work.

(14) Because in many cases the corporate client of the auditor will be in receivership, liquidation or under some other form of administration, extending liability to the auditor will enable the third party to elevate itself beyond the status of other creditors by seeking a solvent defendant from which to recoup the consequences of its poor business judgment in financing the company; and the auditing process involves more than the statement of a verifiable fact, such as the zoning of a particular parcel of land. The discharge by the auditor of its statutory functions requires a complex process which may involve differences of professional opinion.

The formulation of these factors was heavily influenced by the decision of the Supreme Court of California in *Bily v Arthur Young and Co* (1992) 834

P 2d 745, which is discussed in para 9.9.5, *below*. Although this list of factors was formulated in the context of cases involving auditors, it can reasonably be expected that some of these factors will be invoked in cases concerning other types of professionals when they are sued by persons other than their own clients.

Lastly, in so far as the future development of the law is concerned, it is interesting to note that Toohey and Gaudron JJ, in their joint judgment, said that they thought that, in the context of liability for negligent misstatements, the question whether the plaintiff reasonably relied on the defendant is better answered in terms of control similar to the use of 'control' in cases involving a non-delegable duty of care (see *above*).

9.9.3 Canada

The approach of the Supreme Court of Canada is also in line with the House of Lords' approach in *Caparo*. In *Haig v Bamford* (1976) 72 DLR (3d) 68, the defendant accountants were held liable to the plaintiff investor in a company for the loss which he suffered through the negligence of the defendants in the certification of the company's accounts. The defendants knew that the accounts would be shown to a potential investor from whom the company was seeking to raise equity capital. They did not know the investor's name, but that did not matter. Dickson J said (at p 75): "Actual knowledge of the limited class is the proper test to apply in this case", and (at p 80): "I can see no good reason for distinguishing between the case in which a defendant accountant delivers information directly to the plaintiff at the request of his employer (as in *Candler*'s case and *Glanzer*'s case [see paras 9.2.2, 9.2.3, 9.6.2 and 9.3.3, *above*]), and the case in which the information is handed to the employer who, to the knowledge of the accountant, passes it to members of a limited class whose identity is unknown to the accountant in furtherance of a transaction, the nature of which is known to the accountant". What is not clear from this decision is whether the defendants knew of the sum of money which the company was proposing to raise on the strength of the accounts. It seems that they did not, in which case this decision extends liability further than the House of Lords did in *Caparo*.

In *VK Mason Construction Ltd v Bank of Nova Scotia* (1985) 16 DLR (4th) 598, the SC applied 'the principle of *Hedley Byrne*' in holding the defendant bank liable for the economic losses suffered by the plaintiff construction company which had signed a contract with a property developer in reliance on an incorrect negligent statement by the defendant in a letter which it had written to the plaintiff to the effect that it had accorded financing to the developer sufficient to cover the contract sum. Wilson J said (at p 603):

> This is not a simple situation in which a bank makes a representation about the creditworthiness of one of its clients to a third party. This is a case in which the bank made a representation to a third party for the specific purpose of inducing

the third party to enter into a contract with one of the bank's own clients, thereby enabling that client to enter into a substantial loan transaction with the bank.

Caparo was referred to and applied in *MacPherson v Schachter* (1989) 1 CCLT (2d) 65 (BC SC), in holding that the defendant chartered accountants did not owe a duty of care to the plaintiff who had bought a share in a residential co-operative company in reliance on an inaccurate financial statement which the defendant had prepared for the company, because the statement had not been made for the benefit of intending purchasers, nor did the defendant have any notion that this particular sale was impending; and in *Dixon v Deacon Morgan McEewen Easson* (1989) 64 DLR (4th) 441 (BC SC), in holding that the defendant auditors did not owe a duty of care to the plaintiff who, having seen a financial statement described as "audited", purchased shares in the company on the stock exchange and suffered a loss when the value of the shares declined after the revelation of irregularities in the management of the company, which the defendant's audit exercise of the plaintiff's accounts had failed to discover.

On the other hand, it is doubtful if the same decision would be reached in England as was reached in *Surrey Credit Union v Willson* (1990) 73 DLR (4th) 207, in which the court held the defendant accountants liable to the plaintiff for the loss which the plaintiff suffered after it had purchased debentures in a bank which shortly afterwards became insolvent. The plaintiff had relied on the accuracy of the audited financial statements of the bank which, to the defendant's knowledge, had been attached to the debenture prospectus which the bank sent to potential debenture purchasers. The court held that, by allowing the accounts to be put to use in this way without qualification, the defendants "provided prospective investors with the very comfort likely to induce them to consider investment in what was otherwise recognised as a very uncertain market", or in *Dixon v Deacon Morgan McEewen Easson* (1990) 70 DLR (4th) 609 (BC SC) (which bears the same name as one of the cases mentioned *above*, but which was a completely separate case), where the court held a company liable for the losses suffered by the plaintiff who had bought shares of the company on the stock exchange in reliance upon an inaccurate statement of the company's financial accounts contained in a press release put out by the company. The court distinguished *Caparo* on the ground that there the defendants were the accountants who had prepared the financial statements for the existing members of the company, whereas in the present case the defendant was the company itself. As such, the defendant had a direct interest in its shares being traded in the market and in persuading potential buyers to buy them. The court said that it did not matter that the defendant did not know the identity of the plaintiff who actually bought its shares. The judge said (at p 618): "There was knowledge of a class who might buy, and interest in them buying and knowledge that such persons might see the published statements and rely upon them for the purposes of deciding to buy. In my opinion, those factors are sufficient to establish proximity from which a duty of care arises in this case".

With regard to the concept of reliance, it is worth noting the Supreme Court's decisions in *BDC Ltd v Hofstrand Farms Ltd* (1986) 26 DLR (4th) 1, in which the defendant courier company had been entrusted with the delivery of an envelope which was marked 'Air Express' and 'Special Delivery'. The contents of the envelope had to be delivered by a certain date in order to meet the plaintiff's obligations under a certain contract. The courier was not told of the envelope's contents, nor the reason why it had to be delivered by that date. Through the carelessness of the courier, the envelope was delivered by truck, not by aeroplane, and did not arrive at its destination on time. In consequence, the plaintiff was not able to complete his contract, and suffered a substantial economic loss. The court held that the defendant was not liable to the plaintiff for this loss. The court made it clear that before it could impose a duty of care on the defendant, the plaintiff had to establish not only that there was reasonable reliance by him on the defendant not to perform the service negligently, but that the defendant was aware of that reliance; and in *Fletcher v Manitoba Public Insurance Co* (1990) 74 DLR (4th) 636, in which the plaintiff suffered substantial economic loss through not being fully insured under a policy of accident insurance which he had bought from the defendant.

This loss arose when the plaintiff was seriously injured in a motor car accident which was the fault of a third party who had inadequate insurance to cover the plaintiff's damages. The plaintiff then attempted to recover the shortfall from its own insurer, the defendant, only to be informed that he did not have "underinsured motorist coverage", a special form of coverage which would have protected him against this type of loss. When the plaintiff had purchased his motor insurance policy from the defendant, the defendant had failed to inform the plaintiff that this option was available. The court accepted the plaintiff's testimony that he would have purchased this additional coverage if the defendant had told him about it. The court held that the defendant did owe the plaintiff a duty of care in respect of the additional loss which the plaintiff suffered by virtue of being underinsured in this fashion. Wilson J said (at p 651):

> In my view, the sale of automobile insurance is a business in the course of which information is routinely provided to prospective customers in the expectation that they will rely on it, and who do in fact reasonably rely on it. It follows, therefore, that the principle in *Hedley Byrne* applies and that the defendant will owe a duty to its customers if: (i) such customers rely on the information; (ii) their reliance is reasonable; and (iii) the defendant knew, or ought to have known that they would rely on the information.

On the facts, the court was able to answer all of these questions in the affirmative, and therefore imposed a duty of care on the defendant for the plaintiff's loss.

In *Queen v Cognos Inc* (1993) 99 DLR (4th) 626, the question was whether the plaintiff could succeed in an action in tort to recover damages caused by the plaintiff's reliance on certain alleged pre-contract misrepresentations made to him in the course of a hiring interview by a prospective employer (the defendant) with respect to the nature and the existence of the employment opportunity. At the interview the defendant's representative told the plaintiff that the company had in mind a special, long-term project for the development of a particular computer software program, which it wished the plaintiff to lead. The defendant's representative did not tell the plaintiff that the company's Board had not yet approved the necessary allocation of funds for this project. Shortly after the plaintiff was hired, the Board rejected the proposal. The plaintiff was initially deployed elsewhere in the company, but eventually his position was terminated because the company did not have a use for his services.

One of the issues in the Supreme Court of Canada was whether a defendant could owe a duty of care to the plaintiff in respect of pre-contract representations in circumstances where the parties subsequently entered into a contract which covered the same subject matter. The court approached the problem as two separate inquiries. In the first inquiry the question was whether the pre-contract misrepresentations on their own gave rise to a duty of care. Iacobucci J, effectively speaking for the whole court on this issue, said that the following five "general requirements" need to be satisfied "for a successful *Hedley Byrne* claim":

(1) there must be a duty of care based on a 'special relationship' between the representor and the representee;

(2) the representation in question must be untrue, inaccurate, or misleading;

(3) the representor must have acted negligently in making the said misrepresentation;

(4) the representee must have relied, in a reasonable manner, on the said negligent misrepresentation; and

(5) the reliance must have been detrimental to the representee in the sense that damage resulted.

The defendant in fact conceded that, at the interview, a 'special relationship' existed between the defendant and the plaintiff "within the meaning of *Hedley Byrne*". The real issue on the appeal was whether the plaintiff's claim for damages in tort was barred by the term in the employment contract which he entered into with the defendant after the interview, pursuant to which the defendant was entitled to terminate the plaintiff's employment at any time without notice and "without cause". This issue is considered in Chapter 10, para 10.4.2.

On the duty of care question, Iacobucci J said that it was sensible of the defendant to make the above-mentioned concession. However, in view of this concession, Iacobucci J did not have to explain the approach that he would have used to find that the defendant was under a duty of care. Nevertheless, he did make the following useful observations on the approach that he felt should be followed in Canada in cases of this nature, when he said (at p 647):

> There is some debate about the proper test that should be applied to determine when a 'special relationship' exists between a representor and a representee which will give rise to a duty of care. Some have suggested that 'foreseeable and reasonable reliance' on the representations is the key element to the analysis,

while others speak of 'voluntary assumption of responsibility' on the part of the representor. Recently, in *Caparo Industries Plc v Dickman* [1990] 2 AC 605, the House of Lords suggested that three criteria determine the imposition of a duty of care: foreseeability of damage, proximity of relationship, and the reasonableness or otherwise of imposing a duty.

For my part, I find it unnecessary to take part in this debate. Regardless of the test applied, the result which the circumstances of this case dictate would be the same. It was foreseeable that the plaintiff would be relying on the information given during the hiring interview in order to make his career decision. It was reasonable for the plaintiff to rely on these representations. There is nothing before this court that suggests that the defendant was not, at the time of the interview or shortly thereafter, assuming responsibility for what was being represented to the defendant by Mr Johnston [the interviewer].

It was foreseeable to the defendant and its representative that the plaintiff would sustain damages should the representations relied on prove to be false and negligently made. There was, undoubtedly, a relationship of proximity between the parties at all material times. Finally, it is not unreasonable to impose a duty of care in all the circumstances of this case; quite the contrary, it would be unreasonable *not* to impose such a duty.

Lastly, Iacobucci J made it clear that the category of persons on whom a duty of care in tort can be imposed for negligent misrepresentations is not confined to 'professionals' who are in the business of providing information and advice. He said that while that factor, if present in any particular case, might provide a good indication as to whether a 'special relationship' existed between the parties, it should not be treated as a threshold requirement; and the present case was a good example of not so treating it.

In *Edgeworth Construction Ltd v ND Lea and Associates Ltd* (1993) 107 DLR (4th) 169, the plaintiff was a construction company engaged in the business of building roads in the Province of British Columbia. It bid on a contract to build a section of highway in a particular area. Its bid was successful and it entered into a contract with the Province to do the work. The plaintiff lost money on the project, allegedly due to errors in the specifications and the construction drawings, which had been prepared by the defendant, a corporation whose business was professional engineering.

The drawings and specifications prepared by the defendant were provided to the plaintiff as part of the tendering process. The contract entered into subsequently between the plaintiff and the Province stipulated that any representations in the tender documents had been furnished merely for the general information of bidders and were not in any way guaranteed by or on behalf of the Minister. In the present action the plaintiff sued the engineering company (the defendant) and the individual engineers who had signed the drawings in tort for damages sustained by the plaintiff through having relied on the defendant's alleged negligent misrepresentations in the design documents. The position of the individual engineers is considered in Chapter 10, para 10.2.1. So far as concerns the engineering corporation itself, the Supreme Court of Canada had no hesitation in holding that it owed a duty of care to the plaintiff for the plaintiff's economic loss, and that this duty was not negated by the above-mentioned provisions in the contract between the plaintiff and the Province. McLachlin J said (at p 173):

> Liability for negligent misrepresentation arises when a person makes a representation knowing that another may rely on it, and the plaintiff in fact relies on the representation to his detriment. The facts in this case meet this test, leaving the contract between the contractor and the Province to one side. The engineers undertook to provide information (the tender package) for use by a definable group of persons with whom it did not have any contractual relationship. The purpose of supplying the information was to allow tenderers to prepare a price to be submitted. The engineers knew this. The plaintiff contractor was one of the tenderers. It relied on the information prepared by the engineers in preparing its bid. Its reliance on the engineers' work was reasonable. It alleges it suffered loss as a consequence. These facts establish a *prima facie* cause of action against the engineering firm. The only question which remains is whether the contract between the contractor and the Province negated the duty of care which would otherwise have arisen on the facts pleaded.

The defendant's counsel's submission that the contract between the plaintiff and the Province negated or subsumed the duty of care owed by the defendant to the plaintiff was put in a number of ways. First, it was said that the contract converted the representation from one made by the engineering firm to one made by the Province. In rejecting this submission, McLachlin J said (at p 173):

> It is true that the engineers' work was incorporated in the tender package and thereafter in the contract. This establishes that the representations in the design became the representations of the Province. But it does not, without more, establish the further proposition that when the representations became the representations of the Province they ceased to be the representations of the engineers. The contractor was relying on the accuracy of the engineers' design just as much after it entered into the contract as before. Neither the Ministry nor the contractor either assumed the risk of errors in the engineers' work. Throughout, the plaintiff was relying on the expertise of the engineers and not of the Province with respect to the accuracy of the design.
>
> The contract, by clause 42, stipulated that any representations in the tender documents were 'furnished merely for the general information of bidders and were not in any way warranted or guaranteed by or on behalf of the Minister'. This exemption extends, on its express words, only to warranties 'by or on behalf of the Minister'. It does not purport to protect the engineers against liability for their representations. [Some of the other contractual implications of the defendant's counsel's submissions are discussed in Chapter 10, para 10.3.2.]

Secondly, the defendant's counsel argued that the plaintiff's claim was unsustainable because it was a claim for pure economic loss. In rejecting this submission, McLachlin J said (at p 175):

> In support of its contention that the factual matrix alleged on the pleadings does not support a relationship of sufficient proximity to found a duty of care, the engineering firm emphasises that the loss claim is purely economic. This argument seems, in my opinion, to overlook the fact that this is a claim for negligent misrepresentation under *Hedley Byrne*. It has long been settled that claims for

pure economic loss may be brought for negligent misrepresentation. The case at bar accordingly does not raise the issue discussed in *Canadian National Railway Co v Norsk Pacific Steamship Co* (1992) 91 DLR (4th) 289 [see Chapter 5] of when new categories of pure economic loss may be recoverable in tort.

Lastly, McLachlin J mentioned an "important policy consideration" which weighs against the engineering firm [the defendant]" when she said (at p 177):

> If the engineering firm is correct, then contractors bidding on construction contracts will be obliged to do their own engineering. In the typically short period allowed for the filing of tenders—in this case about two weeks—the contractor would be obliged, at the very least, to conduct a thorough professional review of the accuracy of the engineering design and information, work which in this case took over two years. The task would be difficult, if not impossible. Moreover, each tendering contractor would be obliged to hire its own engineers and repeat a process already undertaken by the owner. The result would be that the engineering for the job would be done not just once, by the engineers hired by the owner, but a number of times. This duplication of effort would doubtless be reflected in higher bid prices, and ultimately, a greater cost to the public which ultimately bears the cost of road construction. From an economic point of view, it makes more sense for one engineering firm to do the engineering work, which the contractors in turn are entitled to rely on, absent disclaimers or limitations on the part of the firm. In fact, the short tender period suggests that in reality this is the way the process works; contractors who wish to bid have no choice but to rely on the design and documents prepared by the engineering firm. It is on this basis that they submit their bids and on this basis that the successful bidder enters into the contract. The fact that the contractor may agree to exempt the party inviting tenders from liability for the design process does not suggest that it thereby should be taken to have exempted the engineering firm. In the scheme of things, it makes good practical and economic sense to place the responsibility for the adequacy of the design on the shoulders of the designing engineering firm, assuming reasonable reliance and barring disclaimers. The risk of liability to compensate third parties for design error will be reflected in the cost of the engineers' services to the owner inviting tenders. But that is a much better result than requiring the owner to pay not only the engineering firm which it retains, but indirectly, the additional engineers which all tendering parties would otherwise be required to retain.

In *Hercules Managements Ltd v Ernst & Young* (1997) 146 DLR (4th) 577, the plaintiff was the holder of 80 per cent of the shares of Northguard Acceptance Limited, a company whose business was lending and investing money on the security of real property mortgages. The defendant was Northguard's auditor from 1971 until Northguard went into receivership in 1984.

After the receivership the plaintiff brought the present action against the defendant, alleging that the defendant was liable for certain advances that the plaintiff had made to Northguard in 1983 in reliance on Northguard's audited financial statements for the years 1980, 1981 and 1982, which the plaintiff alleged were inaccurate and misleading in a number of material respects. The plaintiff also sought to recover damages from the defendant for the losses it suffered from a decrease in the value of its investment in Northguard as a result of Northguard's receivership.

The Supreme Court of Canada rejected both of these claims. After stating that the established approach in Canadian law to the existence of a duty of care in tort is the two-part test enunciated by Lord Wilberforce in *Anns v Merton London Borough Council* [1978] AC 728 (see Chapter 3, para 3.2.2), La Forest J, speaking for the unanimous court, said (at p 587):

> Whether the defendant owes the plaintiff a duty of care for its allegedly negligent preparation of the 1980-1982 audit reports will depend on (a) whether a *prima facie* duty of care exists; and (b) whether that duty, if it exists, is negatived or limited by policy considerations.
>
> The purpose behind the *Anns* test is simply to ensure that inquiries into the existence of a duty of care in negligence cases are conducted in two parts: the first involves discerning whether, in a given situation, a duty of care would be imposed by law; the second demands an investigation into whether the real duty, if found, ought to be negatived or ousted by policy considerations.
>
> The first branch of the *Anns* test demands an inquiry into whether there is a sufficiently close relationship of proximity between the plaintiff and the defendant such that, in the reasonable contemplation of the latter, carelessness on its part may cause damage to the former. To my mind, proximity can be seen to inhere between a defendant-representor and a plaintiff-representee when two criteria relating to reliance may be said to exist on the facts: (a) the defendant ought reasonably to foresee that the plaintiff will rely on his representation; and (b) reliance by the plaintiff would, in the particular circumstances of the case, be reasonable. To use the term employed by Iacobucci J in *Queen v Cognos* [see *above*], the plaintiff and the defendant can be said to be in a 'special relationship' whenever these two factors inhere.
>
> In negligent misrepresentation actions, the plaintiff's claim stems from his detrimental reliance on the defendant's negligent statement. It is clear that reliance on the statement or representation of another will not, in all circumstances, be reasonable.

La Forest J then formulated the essential criteria that need to be met before a duty of care can be imposed in any particular case. In so doing, he was conscious that this formulation might be seen as being a narrowing of the established doctrine in Canada. Thus, he said (at p 590):

> Where reasonable foreseeability and reasonable reliance inhere, the cases typically require—
>
> (a) that the defendant knew the identity of either the plaintiff or the class of plaintiffs who would rely on the statement; and
> (b) that the reliance losses claimed by the plaintiff stem from the particular transaction in respect of which the statement at issue was made. This narrower approach to defining the duty can be seen in a number of the more prominent English decisions dealing with auditors' liability specifically, or with liability for negligent misstatements generally (See eg, *Candler v Crane, Christmas and Co, Hedley Byrne and Caparo* [see *above*]. It is also evident in the approach taken by this Court in *Haig v Bamford* [see *above*]).
>
> Inquiring into such matters as to whether the defendant had knowledge of the plaintiff or the class of plaintiffs and whether the plaintiff used the statements

at issue for the particular transaction for which they were provided is, in reality, nothing more than a means by which to circumscribe—for reasons of policy— the scope of a representor's potentially infinite liability. In other words, these further requirements serve a policy-based limiting function with respect to the ambit of the duty of care in negligent misrepresentation actions.

In light of this Court's endorsement of the *Anns* test, however, inquiries concerning (a) the defendant's knowledge of the identity of the plaintiff or of the class of plaintiffs and (b) the use to which the statements at issue are put, are quite properly conducted in the second branch of that test when deciding whether or not policy considerations ought to negative or limit a *prima facie* duty that has already been found to exist.

La Forest J then went on to consider the policy considerations that exist in this category of cases. He noted that the fundamental policy consideration in actions based on negligent misrepresentations centres around the undesirable exposure of the defendants to "liability in an indeterminate amount for an indeterminate time to an indeterminate class" (*per* Cardozo CJ in *Ultramares Corp v Touche* (1931) 255 NY 170); and he then continued by saying (at p 592):

This potential problem can be seen quite vividly within the framework of the *Anns* test. Indeed, while the criteria of reasonable foreseeability and reasonable reliance serve to distinguish cases where a *prima facie* duty is owed from those from where it is not, it is nevertheless true that in certain types of situations these criteria can, quite easily, be satisfied; and, absent some means by which to circumscribe the ambit of the duty, the prospect of limitless liability will loom.

The general area of auditors' liability is a case in point. In modern commercial society, the fact that audit reports will be relied on by many different people (eg, shareholders, creditors, potential takeover bidders and investors) for a wide variety of purposes will almost always be reasonably foreseeable to auditors themselves. Similarly, the very nature of audited financial statements will very often mean that any of those people would act wholly reasonably in placing their reliance on such statements in conducting their affairs. In the light of these considerations, the reasonable foreseeability/reasonable reliance test for ascertaining a *prima facie* duty of care may well be satisfied in many negligent misstatement suits against auditors and, consequently, the problem of indeterminate liability will often arise.

Having reached this conclusion in his analysis, La Forest J then explained how the indeterminacy problem in this type of case is to be resolved in Canada. He said (at p 593):

Certain authors have argued that imposing broad duties of care on auditors would give rise to significant economic and social benefits in so far as the spectre of tort liability would act as an incentive to auditors to produce non-negligent reports. I would agree that deterrence of negligent conduct is an important policy consideration with respect to auditors' liability. Nevertheless, I am of the view that, in the final analysis, it is outweighed by the socially undesirable consequences to which the imposition of indeterminate liability on auditors might lead.

In my view, it makes more sense to circumscribe the ambit of the duty of care than to assume that difficulties in proving negligence and reliance will afford sufficient protection to auditors, since this approach avoids both 'indeterminate liability' and 'indeterminate litigation'. In the general run of auditors' cases, concerns over indeterminate liability will serve to negate a *prima facie* duty of care.

Having made this general policy statement, La Forest J immediately went on to qualify it, when he said (at p 595):

> But, while such concerns [ie the indeterminate liability concerns mentioned *above*] may exist in most such cases, there may be particular situations where they do not. In other words, the specific factual matrix of a given case may render it an 'exception' to the general class of cases in that the typical concerns surrounding indeterminate liability do *not* arise. In cases where the defendant knows the identity of the plaintiff or of a class of plaintiffs, and where the defendant's statements are used for the specific purpose or transaction for which they were made, policy considerations surrounding indeterminate liability will not be of any concern since the scope of liability can readily be circumscribed. Consequently, such considerations will not override a positive finding on the first branch of the *Anns* test and a duty of care may quite properly be found to exist.

La Forest J said that this line of reasoning explains the courts' decisions in *Glanzer v Shepard* (1922) 233 NY 236 (see para 9.3.3, *above*), *Hedley Byrne* and *Haig v Bamford*. Furthermore, in applying these principles to the facts of the present case, La Forest J had no hesitation in holding that a *prima facie* duty of care was owed by the defendant to the plaintiff, not only because it was reasonably foreseeable by the defendant that the plaintiff would rely on Northguard's financial statements in conducting its affairs and that the plaintiff might suffer harm if those statements had been negligently prepared, but also because reliance by the plaintiff on Northguard's audited statements was reasonable on the facts of this case. La Forest J then went on to consider whether, in accordance with the application of the second branch of the *Anns* test, any reasons existed in this case for negativing this *prima facie* finding. He said (at p 599):

> At first blush, it may seem that no problems of indeterminate liability are implicated here and that this case can be easily likened to *Glanzer*, *Hedley Byrne* and *Haig*. After all, the defendant knew the very identity of the plaintiff shareholders who claimed to have relied on the audited financial statements prepared by the defendant. However, to arrive at this conclusion without further analysis would be to move too quickly. While knowledge of the plaintiff or of a limited class of plaintiffs is undoubtedly a significant factor serving to obviate concerns over indeterminate liability, it is not, alone, sufficient to do so. In *Glanzer*, *Hedley Byrne* and *Haig*, indeterminate liability did not inhere on the specific facts of those cases because, although the defendant knew the identity of the plaintiff who would rely on the statement at issue, the statement itself was used by the plaintiff *for precisely the purpose or transaction for which it was prepared*. The crucial importance of this additional criterion can clearly be seen when one considers that, even if the specific identity or class of potential plaintiffs is known to a defendant, use of the defendant's statement for a purpose or transaction other than that for which it was prepared could still lead to indeterminate liability.

Applying these principles to the facts of the present case, La Forest J said that the central question was whether or not the plaintiff could be said to have used the 1980–82 audit reports for the specific purpose for which they were prepared. He then referred to, and adopted, the statement by the House of Lords in *Caparo*, that the purpose of an audit report is to provide shareholders with reliable information for the purpose of enabling them, as a group, exercising their rights at the company's annual general meeting, to scrutinise the conduct of the company's affairs and to exercise their collective powers to make decisions as to the manner in which they want the corporation to be managed, rather than to assist individual shareholders in making personal investment decisions. On this basis, the court had no hesitation in rejecting the plaintiff's claim for compensation for the injection of capital that the plaintiff made into Northguard in February 1983 in reliance on the 1982 audit report in which the defendant had said that Northguard's accounts represented a fair and true picture of its financial state.

The issues surrounding the plaintiff's other claim, for compensation for the diminution in value of its equity in Northguard on the ground that the shareholders (ie the plaintiff and others) would have supervised management differently had they known of the alleged inaccuracies in the 1980–82 reports and would thereby have averted the losses which occurred subsequently, were more complicated, but the court rejected this claim too. La Forest J said (at p 604):

> At first glance it might appear that the plaintiff's claim implicates a use of the audit reports which is commensurate with the purpose for which the reports were prepared, ie overseeing or supervising management. One might argue on this basis that a duty of care should be found to inhere because, in view of this compatibility between actual use and intended purpose, no indeterminacy arises. In my view, however, this line of reasoning suffers from a subtle but fundamental flaw.
>
> The purpose for which the audit reports were prepared in this case was the standard statutory purpose of allowing shareholders, *as a group*, to supervise management and to take decisions with respect to matters concerning the proper overall administration *of the corporation*. In other words, the purpose was to permit the shareholders to exercise their role, *as a class*, of overseeing the *corporation*'s affairs at their annual general meetings.
>
> The purpose of providing the auditors' reports to the plaintiff, then, may ultimately be said to have been a 'collective' one; that is, it was aimed, not at protecting the interests of individual shareholders, but at enabling the shareholders, acting as a group, to safeguard the interests of the corporation itself. On the plaintiff's argument, however, the purpose to which the 1980–82 reports was ostensibly put, was not that of allowing the shareholders as a class to take decisions in respect of the overall running of the corporation, but, rather, to allow them, *as individuals*, to monitor management so as to oversee and protect their own personal investments. Indeed, the nature of the plaintiff's claim (ie a personal tort claim) *requires* that the plaintiff asserts reliance on the auditors' reports *qua* an individual shareholder if it is to recover any personal damages. In so far as it must concern the interests of each individual shareholder, then, the plaintiff's claim in this regard is really no different from its other 'investment purposes' discussed above, in respect of which the defendant owes no duty of care to the plaintiff.

9.9.3 *Negligent misstatements and services*

On the other hand, in *Kripps v Touche Ross and Co* (1997) 35 CCLT (2d) 60, the defendant auditors were held liable to the plaintiff debenture holders for losses suffered by the plaintiffs through having lent money to a particular company in reliance on statements in a prospectus to which, to the defendant's knowledge and with its consent, the audit report recently prepared by the defendant was attached. This was a decision of the British Columbia Court of Appeal and it was decided before *Hercules Investments*, but it is included at this point because, after rendering its decision in *Hercules Investments*, the Supreme Court of Canada considered, and rejected, a petition for leave to appeal by the defendant in the present case.

In the British Columbia Court of Appeal, the defendant did not challenge the holding of the trial judge that a sufficiently close relationship of proximity existed between the defendant and the plaintiffs to give rise to a duty of care by virtue of the fact that the defendant knew that the purpose of its audit report was to facilitate the sale of debentures to the public through the distribution of the company's prospectus containing their report. The interest in the case lies in the way in which the court dealt with the auditors' defence that they had not been negligent because their accounts had been prepared in accordance with Generally Accepted Accounting Principles ('GAAP').

The company in respect of whose accounts the audit report was provided was Victoria Mortgage Corporation Ltd ('VMCL'). Its business was providing loans secured by mortgages on real property. These mortgages were its principal asset, and interest from these mortgages was its main source of income. VMCL borrowed money by selling fixed-term debentures which were offered to the public on a continuous basis. The relevant Securities Act prohibited the sale of debentures to the public unless, annually, a prospectus was filed with the Superintendent of Brokers and was provided to prospective purchasers. The Act required that the prospectus include financial statements and an auditor's report. The Act further required that this auditor's report had to state that the company's financial statements presented the financial position of the company fairly according to GAAP.

In the course of carrying out its audit, the defendant observed that 14 loans totalling about $3.5 million, or one quarter of the value of VMCL's portfolio, were in default for more than 90 days ($2.6 million for more than 12 months) and that VMCL's largest loan, the balance of which was $1.4 million, would have been in default if it had not been renegotiated that month with a six-month deferral of interest payments. The defendant's responsible audit partner brought this to the attention of VMCL's management and said that a note to this effect should be included in the financial statements. VMCL's management objected and pointed out, quite correctly, that GAAP did not require such a disclosure. As a result, this suggested note was not included in the accounts or in the audit report.

Less than a year later, in the course of preparing the next year's audit report, the defendant determined that the continued viability of VMCL as a going concern was then in doubt, and told VMCL that the standard form of audit report required by the Securities Act could not be provided. Ultimately, a receiver was appointed over VMCL's business and its loan portfolio was liquidated. The recovery for debenture holders was less than 30¢ in the dollar.

The plaintiffs, who were debenture holders, brought the present action against the defendant for recovery of their losses sustained through having bought debentures in VMCL in reliance on the defendant's audit report. The court agreed with the plaintiffs' counsel's contention that the portion of VMCL's mortgage portfolio that was non-performing was material information that would have affected the plaintiffs' decision to purchase further debentures in VMCL.

The defendant's counsel submitted that the defendant could not be held liable for this omission because the defendant had done all that was required of it, namely, to audit VMCL's accounts in accordance with GAAP, and, as noted *above*, GAAP did not require the disclosure of this information in VMCL's accounts or in the audit report. The Court of Appeal, by 2:1, rejected this submission. Finch JA, speaking for the majority, said (at p 78):

> In my view, the critical issue is the effect of the auditor's report. It is my view that the aim of an auditor's report is to allow auditors to provide their professional opinion which may be relied upon as a guide to business planning and investment. GAAP may be their guide to forming this opinion, but auditors are retained to form an opinion on the fairness of the financial statements, not merely on their conformity to GAAP. A person to whom the auditor owes a duty of care who reads a standard auditor's report and concludes in reliance on it that the financial statements are fair is acting reasonably.
>
> Given the aim in auditing, the understanding of audits that those who rely on them have, and that auditors know of this understanding, auditors cannot hide behind the qualification of their reports (ie, 'prepared according to GAAP') where the financial statements nevertheless misrepresent the financial position of the company.

9.9.4 New Zealand

Accountants

The approach of the Court of Appeal of New Zealand in accountants' negligence cases (and similar cases) is exactly the opposite of the House of Lords' approach in *Caparo*. In *Scott Group Ltd v McFarlane* [1978] 1 NZLR 553, the plaintiff had relied on the accounts of a particular company for the purpose of making a takeover bid. Subsequently it was discovered that those accounts had been negligently audited by the defendants. The court held that the defendants owed a duty of care to the plaintiff for its loss, notwithstanding that, when the defendants carried out their audit and signed their report, they had no knowledge of any intention by the plaintiff or anyone else to formulate a takeover offer for the company. For the majority (of 2:1) Cooke J said that, as the defendants knew that the state of the company's finances were such as to make it vulnerable to a takeover bid, there was a "virtual certainty" that in such an event the accounts would be relied on by an offeror. In other words, the defendants knew that the accounts which they had certified as being correct would be relied on by a takeover bidder. Cooke J continued:

> Another important factor is whether the defendants have held themselves out as having professional skill. No problem arises under that head. Then there is the pervasive fear of imposing indeterminate numbers. Again, this need not cause anxiety. A company purchasing all or the majority of the shares is more directly and closely affected than, for instance, an ordinary purchaser of shares on the stock market. And in all ordinary circumstances, there will in fact be only one offeror who makes a successful takeover offer on the basis of the carelessly certified accounts.

Applying the first stage of the 'two-stage test' in *Anns v Merton London Borough Council* (see Chapter 3, para 3.2.2), Cooke J said:

> I think that on the facts of this case, as between the alleged wrongdoer and the person who has allegedly suffered damage, there is a sufficient relationship of proximity such that, in the reasonable contemplation of the former, carelessness on his part may be likely to cause damage to the latter. So, a *prima facie* duty of care arises. Then it is necessary to consider whether there are any considerations which ought to limit the scope of this duty or the class of person to whom it is owed. The class here is most narrowly limited. It could have been excluded by disclaimer [but it was not]. Seeing no sufficient negativing considerations, I would hold that a duty of care was owed.

In *Caparo Industries plc v Dickman* [1900] 2 AC 605 (see *above*), the House of Lords strongly deprecated this approach and preferred, instead, to adopt the reasoning of the dissenting judge, Richmond P, who held that no duty of care can be imposed on a maker of a statement unless he was, "or ought to have been, aware that his advice or information would be made available to, and would be relied upon, by a particular person or class of persons for the purposes of a particular transaction or type of transaction". In *Caparo* Lord Bridge said that he fully agreed with this reasoning.

In *Jagwar Holdings Ltd v Julian* (1992) 6 NZCLC 68,040, Thorp J, in the High Court, held that both in principle and on authority binding on him in New Zealand, it was appropriate for the High Court to accept and apply Richmond P's minority view in *Scott*. He reached this conclusion by taking note of the fact that in *South Pacific Manufacturing Co Ltd v New Zealand Security Consultants and Investigations Ltd* [1992] 2 NZLR 282 (see *below*), two of the judges referred to *Caparo* "with apparent approval, and no judicial voice was raised against it"; and by virtue of "the acceptance in all recent decisions of our Court of Appeal that foreseeability alone will not establish proximity, which proposition underlay the support in *Caparo* for Richmond P's analysis in *Scott Group v McFarlane*".

Other investigators and reporters

In the accountants' negligence cases considered *above*, the plaintiff was not the person or entity in respect of whom the auditors had made a negligently incorrect report. In each case, the report had been made on the affairs of a third party (ie the company whose accounts the defendant had audited) and the plaintiff was suing for the economic loss that the plaintiff had suffered through having placed reliance on the accountants' report. Sometimes, however, the defendant's investigation and report will have been made about the conduct or state of affairs of the plaintiff himself, and the plaintiff will have suffered loss because a third party has treated the plaintiff differently in consequence of the information contained in the report.

An example of this latter type of situation is the English case of *Spring v Guardian Assurance Plc* [1995] 2 AC 296 (see para 9.7.7). So, too, is the New Zealand case of *South Pacific Manufacturing Co Ltd v New Zealand Security Consultants and Investigations Ltd* [1992] 2 NZLR 282. *Spring* involved a negligently compiled employment reference about the plaintiff; *South Pacific Manufacturing* involved a negligently compiled fire investigation report about the plaintiff's business. In both cases, the plaintiff's claim, based on the incorrect and negligent report made by the defendant, effectively included a claim that the report was defamatory of the plaintiff. The defendants raised the defence that the report, having been made pursuant to a duty (contractual or otherwise), was protected by the defence of qualified privilege. That defence can be defeated only by proof of malice. As there was no allegation of malice in either case, the defendants in both cases argued that the defence of qualified privilege was made out and should also act as a bar to the plaintiff's tortious negligence claim.

In *Spring*, the House of Lords rejected this argument (see para 9.7.7), but in *South Pacific Manufacturing*, the Court of Appeal of New Zealand upheld it. Thus, Cooke P said (at p 302):

> To the extent that the report reflects adversely on the insured by suggesting that he may have been guilty of arson, the insured will *prima facie* have a cause of action in defamation. It will be a defence, however, if the investigators can prove the truth of the imputation. And more importantly in the present context, the report of the investigators made pursuant to their contractual duty to the insurer will be the subject of qualified privilege.
>
> Qualified privilege can be defeated by proof of malice, not by proof of mere negligence. The suggested cause of action in negligence would therefore impose a greater restriction on freedom of speech than exists under the law worked out over many years to cover freedom of speech and its limitations. By a side-wind, the law of defamation would be overthrown.

Richardson J echoed these sentiments when he said (at p 309):

> To allow a duty of care in this class of case would cut across related areas of tort law and would deprive defendants of protection which those laws specifically provide. To allege that the investigator carelessly and incorrectly reported that an insured was responsible for the fire is to say that the investigator carelessly made a defamatory statement about the insured. Redress of harm to reputation is the proper function of the law of defamation which, with the various defences, represents the balancing of competing values in ways considered appropriate in our law in the particular areas with which they are concerned. To

allow an additional remedy in negligence which would not be subject to any such defences would undermine that balance. It is for reasons of this kind that we have held that justice does not require or warrant an importation of negligence law in this class of case (see *Bell Booth Group Ltd v Attorney-General* [1989] 3 NZLR 148 [see para 9.7.7] and *Balfour v Attorney-General* [1991] 1 NZLR 519).

These views are diametrically opposed to those of the House of Lords in *Spring* (see para 9.7.7). In *Spring*, their Lordships did try to reconcile the different decisions by treating them largely as being fact-specific. However, it is submitted that this attempt failed and that, when Lord Woolf said (at p 351) that the approach of the Court of Appeal of New Zealand in this type of case would mean that a plaintiff who would otherwise be entitled to succeed in an action for negligence would go away empty-handed because he could not succeed in an action for defamation (which Lord Woolf said "cannot be a desirable result"), this applies equally to the plaintiff in *South Pacific Manufacturing* as to the plaintiff in *Spring*, despite the attempts that were made to differentiate the two situations.

In *South Pacific Manufacturing*, the Court of Appeal of New Zealand was also inhibited from granting the plaintiff's claim by perceived fears that to do so would open up the floodgates to a host of other claims in an unacceptable way. Thus, Richardson J said (at p 309):

Finally, the imposition of the duty of care contended for could not reasonably be confined to insurance investigators and other related professionals, and its ambit would be inherently expansive and unacceptably indeterminate. It may be said that the plaintiff [in the present appeals] was the only person other than the insurer likely to be affected by a careless allegation of arson. But there is a vast range of similar everyday situations in which only a few people stand to be adversely affected, and it would be difficult to justify extending the duty category to anyone who, in the course of a contractual engagement, carelessly investigates and reports on the conduct of a third party. Credit reports, media investigations and reports of events are obvious examples. And why limit the duty to those who carry out inquiries and make reports pursuant to contract? The effect on a plaintiff may be just as traumatic if carelessly made comments on the plaintiff's conduct are volunteered to a person in authority or other third party. In short, the proposed duty category would be uncertainly expansive for what I would characterise as unacceptably indeterminate consequences for the public interest.

These comments, coupled with the restrictive contract-related reasons given by the court for rejecting the plaintiff's claim in *South Pacific Manufacturing* (see Chapter 7, para 7.6.2) and its echoing of those views in *Invercargill City Council v Hamlin* [1994] 3 NZLR 513 (see also para 7.6.2), lend some irony to Lord Keith's (dissenting) statement in *Spring* (at p 313) that New Zealand is "a jurisdiction which is well known to be tender in its approach to claims in negligence involving pure economic loss".

Richardson J's above-cited remarks are in fact a slight variation on the usual reason for expressing the floodgates fear, namely, that the number of possible plaintiffs would multiply exponentially and place an unacceptable burden on the administration of the justice system. Here, instead, the court's concern was that, if it were to impose a duty of care on the fire investigator, then other related professionals and other non-professional investigators and reporters could be exposed to liability to the subject of their reports (as opposed to liability merely to the recipient) if their reports were materially inaccurate and compiled negligently.

It is submitted that this reasoning is misplaced because it calls into question such major developments in the modern law of negligence as occurred, for example, in *Hedley Byrne & Co v Heller & Partners Ltd* [1964] AC 465. There, the court was concerned only with the possible liability of a banker to the recipient of a reference that the banker had given about a third party, for economic loss sustained by the recipient through having relied on the reference. However, the wider implications of the case for other similarly placed defendants, like accountants and solicitors, or indeed anyone who makes a statement to a third party knowing that it will be relied on by someone else in making an important decision affecting that other person's financial interests, were clear; yet that did not deter the House of Lords from deciding that in principle the banker in *Hedley Byrne* owed a duty of care to the plaintiff in that case.

Solicitors

On the other hand, the New Zealand Court of Appeal's decision in *Gartside v Sheffield, Young and Ellis* [1983] NZLR 37 has not only been approved, but has been specifically adopted and followed by the Court of Appeal and the House of Lords in England in *White v Jones* [1995] 2 AC 207 (see para 9.7.5, *above*). In *Gartside* a testatrix, aged 89, had given instructions to the defendant solicitors to draw up a new will for her, which would have left the residue of her estate to the plaintiff. The testatrix died seven days later, before any will had been presented to her in accordance with her latest instructions. The court held that the defendant owed a duty of care to the plaintiff in respect of her loss, consisting of her failure to inherit the residue of the testatrix's estate. The court followed and applied the English case of *Ross v Caunters* (see para 9.7.5, *above*). Cooke J said (at p 43):

> To deny an effective remedy in a plain case would seem to imply a refusal to acknowledge the solicitor's professional role in the community. In practice, the public relies on solicitors to prepare effective wills. It would be a failure of the legal system not to insist on some practical responsibility. To recognise that the solicitor owed a duty of reasonable care to the intended beneficiary would produce a just result.

In *Connell v Odlum* [1993] 2 NZLR 257, the Court of Appeal held that a solicitor for one party to a matrimonial property agreement owed a duty of care in tort to the other party to the agreement. Prior to their marriage Mr and Mrs Odlum ('O') entered into an agreement whereby they contracted out of the provisions of the Matrimonial Property Act 1976 (NZ) dealing with the division of property on separation or divorce. Mrs O took the draft agreement to her solicitor, Mr Connell, who, as required by s 21 of the Act, certified that the effects and implications of the agreement had been explained to his client in accordance with s 21.

When Mr and Mrs O subsequently separated, Mrs O applied successfully to the Family Court to set the agreement aside on the ground that it had not in fact been properly explained to her by Mr Connell. Mrs O was thus able to make a matrimonial property claim against Mr O. He settled his claim and then brought the present action for negligence against Mr Connell, seeking as damages the amount that he had paid under the settlement.

One of the questions was whether Mr Connell owed Mr O a duty of care in respect of this loss. The Court of Appeal unanimously answered this question in the affirmative. Their Honours held that, although in general a solicitor does not owe a duty of care to the client of another solicitor, in this case the critical factor which established a sufficiently proximate relationship giving rise to a duty of care was the fact that Mr Connell had provided the statutory certificate. It provided an assurance that the prerequisites of a valid agreement had been met and was of critical "procedural" importance to the other spouse (Mr O). The solicitor (Mr Connell) had certified that a certain state of affairs existed, the plaintiff (Mr O) was within the contemplation of the solicitor, and the plaintiff acted reasonably in relying on the assurance which the certificate conveyed.

Furthermore, the Court of Appeal held that its decision to impose a duty of care on the solicitor in this case was readily accommodated within, or was a logical extension of, the reasoning which has led to the imposition of a duty of care on solicitors in other cases; and that considerations of policy favoured the existence of the duty because this would serve to promote professional competence and would enhance public confidence in the efficacy of the provisions of the Act dealing with contracting out and the obtaining of a s 21 certificate.

9.9.5   United States

Two early decisions of the Court of Appeals of New York, *Glanzer v Shepard* in 1922 and *Ultramares Corporation v Touche* in 1931, have been noted *above* (para 9.3.3). These cases have been influential in shaping the rules which have been developed by the English courts in negligent misstatement cases. The more recent decisions of the courts of the different states in the USA are generally in conformity with the approach which has been developed in England in cases like *Caparo*. Space does not permit a full discussion of the American decision, but it is worth noting the following cases.

Biakanja v Irving

In *Biakanja v Irving* (1958) 320 P (2d) 16 (SC of Cal), the defendant, a notary public but not a lawyer, had prepared a will for a testator, which was denied probate for lack of sufficient attestation due to the defendant's negligence in not ensuring that the persons who signed as witnesses were present when the testator signed it. If the will had been valid, the plaintiff, who was the testator's brother, would have inherited the whole of his estate. In consequence of the will's invalidity, the testator died intestate, and the plaintiff inherited only one-eighth of the estate. The court held that the defendant was liable to compensate the plaintiff for the amount of money equivalent to the remaining seven-eighths of the testator's estate.

Gibson CJ said (at p 19):

> The determination whether in a specific case the defendant will be held liable to a third person not in privity with him is a matter of policy, and involves the balancing of various factors, among which are the extent to which the transaction was intended to affect the plaintiff, the foreseeability of harm to him, the degree of certainty that the plaintiff would suffer injury, the closeness of the connection between the defendant's conduct and the injury suffered, the moral blame attached to the defendant's conduct, and the policy of preventing future harm.

The court referred to the *dictum* of Cardozo J in *Glanzer v Shepard* (1922) 233 NY 236 (see para 9.3.3, *above*) that the defendant weigher was liable to the plaintiff purchaser in that case because the purchaser's use of the weighing certificate was, to the weigher's knowledge, "the end and aim of the transaction", and said: "Here, the 'end and aim' of the transaction was to provide for the passing of the testator's estate to the plaintiff. The defendant must have been aware from the terms of the will that, if faulty solemnisation caused the will to be invalid, the plaintiff would suffer the very loss which occurred".

Credit Alliance v Arthur Andersen

In *Credit Alliance Corporation v Arthur Andersen & Co* (1985) 65 NY (2d) 536 (Court of Appeals of New York), the plaintiff had provided working capital finance to a company in reliance upon its accounts, which had been audited by the defendant. When the company subsequently became insolvent, and the plaintiff was not able to recover the amounts which it had advanced to the company, it sued the defendant, claiming that the defendant had been negligent in failing to discover the company's precarious financial condition when it audited the company's accounts. The court accepted that the company might well have been using its accounts to induce the plaintiff and other similar lenders to provide financing for its business, but there was no evidence that the defendant was aware of this. The defendant had carried out its audit and had prepared its report purely for the benefit of the company.

In so holding, the court formulated the following principle (at p 551):

> Before accountants may be held liable in negligence to non-contractual parties who rely to their detriment on inaccurate financial reports, certain prerequisites must be satisfied: (1) the accountants must have been aware that the financial reports were to be used for a particular purpose or purposes; (2) in the furtherance of which a known party or parties was intended to rely; and (3) there must have been some conduct on the part of the accountants linking them to that party or parties, which evinces the accountants' understanding of that party or parties' reliance.

Under this test the relationship of the parties must have been akin to contract.

Pacific Business Credit Inc v Peat Marwick Main & Co

In *Security Pacific Business Credit Inc v Peat Marwick Main & Co* (1992) 79 NY (2d) 695 (Court of Appeals of New York), the plaintiff had advanced substantial sums of money to a particular company in reliance on the company's financial statements and unqualified audit opinion prepared by the defendant chartered accountants. The plaintiff alleged that its case was distinguishable from that of the plaintiff in *Credit Alliance Corporation* because, on receipt from the company of the draft of the company's financial statements and audit opinion, the plaintiff's vice-president had telephoned the defendant's audit partner to discuss the draft audit report. During that conversation, the defendant indicated that it was aware that the company was trying to obtain finance from the plaintiff, the defendant said that there would be no qualifications in its audit opinion when finalised, that the defendant had not uncovered anything that a lender should know that was not reflected in the draft audit report, and the plaintiff informed the defendant that it would be relying on the audit report in advancing credit to the company.

The court held that this did not make any difference. Bellacosa J said:

> The plaintiff cannot unilaterally create such an extraordinary obligation, imposing negligence liability of significant commercial dimension and consequences by merely interposing and announcing its reliance in this fashion. If a lender can secure possible loan recourse against a borrower's auditor by the simple act of calling the auditor before advancing a loan and announcing reliance on the auditor's opinion, then every lender's due diligence list will in the future mandate such a telephone call. For the small price of a phone call, the bank would in effect acquire additional loan protection by placing the auditor in the role of an insurer or guarantor of loans extended to its clients.

Bily v Arthur Young & Co

In *Bily v Arthur Young & Co* (1992) 834 P (2d) 745, the Supreme Court of California criticised the test for liability enunciated in *Credit Alliance Corporation v Arthur Andersen & Co* (see *above*). Lucas CJ said (at p 387):

> From communications with its client, an auditor may acquire full knowledge of third party recipients of the audit report and a specific investment or credit transaction that constitutes the 'end and aim' of the audit. As a consequence, the auditor is placed on notice of a specific risk of liability that accompanies the audit engagement. Yet, under the *Credit Alliance* test [see *above*], the auditor appears to have no liability in this situation in the absence of further, distinct conduct 'linking' the auditor to the third party in a manner that 'evinces the auditor's understanding' of third party reliance. The New York court offers no rationale for the distinct 'linking' element of its rule, nor does it specify what conduct is required to satisfy this element. One might question whether linking conduct should be necessary if the auditor knows his engagement is for the express purpose of benefiting an identifiable class of third parties. The linking conduct element appears to require, not only that the existence of the third party

be known to the auditor, but that the auditor must act in some manner specifically calculated to induce reliance on the report.

The court also noted that this approach, which it called 'the near privity approach', is followed in at least nine states. The court also referred to the extreme opposite approach, whereby liability can be established on the basis of foreseeability by the auditor of the class of persons to whom the audit report would be likely to be distributed, and noted that this approach is almost universally rejected. Instead, the court opted for an intermediate approach, under which liability can be imposed in this type of case if "the supplier of information intends to supply the information for the benefit of one or more third parties in a specific transaction or type of transaction identified to the supplier". The court noted that this approach is followed by at least 17 states.

This approach is not radically different from the New York 'relationship equivalent to contract' approach. The difference lies in the degree of flexibility afforded by the intermediate approach in considering all of the circumstances affecting the decision, including economic and social policy factors in carrying out the balancing exercise of the type described by the Supreme Court of California (in *Biakanja v Irving, above*) which is required to determine whether the relationship between the defendant and the plaintiff, in all the circumstances of the case, was sufficiently proximate to enable the court to conclude that it would be just and reasonable to impose a duty of care on the defendant in tort for the plaintiff's loss. To this extent, the intermediate approach is similar to the approach enunciated by the House of Lords in *Caparo* (see *above*, and see also Chapter 3).

Chapter 10

The contractual connection

Tort theory should remain consistent with contract policies. In public policy terms I consider that where contracts cover the two relationships [ie between the plaintiff and the third party on the one hand and the third party and the defendant on the other], those contracts should ordinarily control the allocation of risk unless special reasons are established to warrant a direct suit in tort. **(Richardson J in South Pacific Manufacturing Co Ltd v NZ Security Consultants & Investigations Ltd [1992] 2 NZLR 282)**

The court must not let tort be used to unjustly and unjustifiably avoid obligations and limitations accepted in contract. **(La Forest J, dissenting, in London Drugs Ltd v Kuehne & Nagel International Ltd (1992) 97 DLR (4th) 261)**

If, for commercial reasons, those who give advice do not want to give disclaimers or otherwise limit their liability, then I see no reason why they should not have to live with the consequences. **(May J in ADT Ltd v BDO Binder Hamlyn (6 December 1995, unreported)**

10.1   Context

In Chapters 4, 5, 7, 8 and 9 different categories of cases are considered in which economic loss can arise (Chapter 6, para 6.4 deals with cases which involve physical injury). In almost all of the situations which have arisen in these categories, with the exception of the cases considered in Chapter 4 (where the plaintiff suffered economic loss consequential upon damage to his property or direct economic loss through an accidental act or omission of the defendant otherwise than by way of a statement or the provision of a service) there will have been, somewhere in the background of the dispute between the plaintiff and the defendant, a contract between two or more of the 'players in the drama', albeit that they might not be participants in the proceedings. Thus, in *Donoghue v Stevenson* [1932] AC 562 (and in the cases which preceded it (see Chapter 6, paras 6.2.4 and 6.2.5)) a contract had existed between the defendant manufacturer and the supplier to whom he had originally sold the defective bottle of ginger beer, and there was a contract between the café owner and the plaintiff's friend who had bought it from him; and in *Smith v Eric S Bush* [1990] 1 AC 831 (see Chapter 9, para 9.7.3) there had been a contract between the defendant surveyor and the building society which had appointed him to survey the house the plaintiff was proposing to buy. In the cases preceding *Donoghue*, the very existence of the contract between the defendant and the third party was a bar to the admissibility of the plaintiff's action against the defendant in tort; and in *Smith* the terms of the contract between the defendant and the third party (specifically the exclusion clause contained in that contract) were a material factor for the court to take into account in considering the plaintiff's claim in tort against the defendant.

In this chapter consideration is given to the situations where the existence of a contract between at least two of the parties in the 'factual matrix' has had, or still has, a bearing on the plaintiff's right to sue the defendant in tort.

10.2   Categories of cases

10.2.1   Contract between plaintiff and third party

Damage to third party's property

In Chapter 5 it is noted that an important category of economic loss cases arises where an existing contract between the plaintiff and a third party has been rendered less valuable to the plaintiff by the defendant injuring that third party or damaging his property. In English law (but not in Australia or Canada—see Chapter 5, para 5.2) there is a strict rule of exclusion in relation to such losses, unless the effect of the contract between the plaintiff and third party was to confer a proprietary right or a possessory interest on the plaintiff in the property which the defendant has damaged.

In most of these cases the reason given for the exclusion of liability is that it is simply not practical to compensate all persons who might suffer economic loss in these circumstances. It is felt that it is better to have an absolute exclusionary rule (subject to a few very limited exceptions) rather than either to grant recovery to all such plaintiffs, thereby opening the floodgates to an indeterminate number of possibly dubious claims, or to grant recovery to a few meritorious plaintiffs, thereby causing injustice to others whose position might not be too dissimilar. Occasionally, however, an additional reason is given, namely that if, in the contractual allocation of risk between the plaintiff and third party, the plaintiff was content to bear the risk of the third party's property being damaged, without obtaining a right of action for himself, by securing a proprietary or a possessory interest in it, then it would be wrong for the court to interfere with this state of affairs and grant the plaintiff a right of action in tort against the defendant when he has damaged the third party's property. Thus, in *Leigh and Sillivan Ltd v Aliakmon Shipping Co Ltd* [1986] 1 AC 785 Lord Brandon said (at p 818):

> . . . the buyers in this case could easily, if properly advised at the time when they agreed to the variation of the original c. and f. contract, have secured to themselves the benefit of such a remedy [ie the right of suit under s 1 of the Bills of Lading Act 1855 which they would otherwise have had];

and in *Canadian National Railway Co v Norsk Pacific Steamship Co* (1992) 91 DLR (4th) 289 La Forest J, speaking for the three dissenting judges, said (at p 296):

In my view, both the surrounding circumstances and the contract itself indicate that the parties either did, or ought to have considered the issue of allocating the risk of the bridge's closing as a result of a ship collision. Indeed, the licence agreement between the plaintiff and the bridge owner did just that [ie it provided for no indemnification by the bridge owner to the plaintiff in the event of the bridge closing for any reason].

Thus, the terms of the contract between the plaintiff and the third party whose property has been damaged by the defendant play an important role in this category of cases. If, under that contract, the plaintiff has secured a proprietary right or a possessory interest in the third party's property, then the exclusionary rule does not apply at all. Alternatively, in those jurisdictions (ie Canada and Australia) where a relaxation of the exclusionary rule is permitted in certain circumstances (see Chapter 5, para 5.6), the terms of the contract between the plaintiff and third party will be material to the question whether the exclusionary rule should be relaxed in any particular case.

Damage to plaintiff's property

Sometimes it might happen that the plaintiff had entered into a contract with a third party under which the plaintiff agreed not to sue the third party for certain types of loss which the third party might cause to the plaintiff in the fulfilment of that contract. The third party might then 'sub-contract' the performance of that contract to the defendant. If the defendant then causes that type of loss to the plaintiff, the question will arise whether the defendant, when sued by the plaintiff in tort, can obtain the benefit of the plaintiff's waiver of rights in his contract with the third party. Some cases in which this type of situation has arisen are discussed *below*.

Norwich City Council v Harvey [1989] 1 WLR 828: The plaintiff building owner had entered into a contract with a third party for the extension of a swimming pool complex. Under that contract the plaintiff agreed to bear the risk of, and not to sue the third party for, any damage which might be caused by a fire negligently started by the third party in carrying out the works. The third party sub-contracted certain roofing work to the defendant, one of whose employees, while using a blow torch, set fire to the plaintiff's existing buildings and the new extension. The plaintiff sued the defendant sub-contractor in tort for the damages it had suffered by virtue of the fire. The defendant claimed that it was not liable by virtue of the plaintiff's acceptance of the risk of fire in the plaintiff's contract with the main contractor. The court upheld the defendant's contention, saying that as the sub-contractor had contracted with the main contractor "on the same terms and conditions as those of the main contract", it would not be just and reasonable to exclude the sub-contractor from the protection of that provision in the main contract when the building was damaged by fire through the negligence of the sub-contractor, even though there was no privity of contract between him and the building owner.

This type of case is similar to the contractual relational economic loss cases considered *above*, in that here too the plaintiff has agreed that, as between himself and the third party, the plaintiff will bear a certain risk. The difference is that, in the relational cases, the plaintiff is bearing the risk of damage to the third party's property, whereas in this type of case, he is bearing the risk of damage to his own property. Although the plaintiff lost in this case, it must be noted that this was not simply because he had agreed by contract with a third party to bear the type of damage which the defendant caused, but because the defendant (as the plaintiff was aware) contracted with the third party on the same basis, to the extent possible, as the third party had contracted with the plaintiff. If the defendant had not done so, he probably would not have been able to take advantage of the plaintiff's waiver of claim against the third party for this type of damage.

Marc Rich and Co AG v Bishop Rock Marine Co Ltd [1994] 1 WLR 1071 (CA): The facts of this case are set out in Chapter 9, para 9.7.4. The House of Lords did not comment on the *Norwich City Council* case but the Court of Appeal expressly endorsed it. In *Marc Rich*, the cargo owners' (the plaintiff ['A']) counsel submitted that if the classification society (the defendant ['C']) were to be entitled to take advantage of the limitation of liability clause in the contract between the cargo owners and the shipowner ('B'), this would fall foul of the House of Lords' decision in *Midland Silicones Ltd v Scruttons Ltd* [1962] AC 446. In that case some stevedores who had damaged the plaintiff's goods while offloading them from a ship owned by a third party were held to be disentitled from placing reliance on the shipowner's limitation of liability to the plaintiff under the bill of lading. The principle applied by the House of Lords in that case was that a stranger to a contract (ie the stevedores) cannot take advantage of the contract even where it is clear that some provision in the contract was intended to benefit him. In *Marc Rich*, in rejecting this submission, and in holding that the classification society did not owe the cargo owners a duty of care in tort for the value of the lost cargo (US$6m) because the cargo owners had agreed, in the contract between themselves and the shipowner, to limit their claim against the shipowner to US$500,000, Mann LJ said (at p 1087):

> [The plaintiff's counsel] submitted that the *Norwich City Council* case ran foul of the well known decision in *Midland Silicones Ltd v Scruttons Ltd* [1962] AC 446, in that [in the *Norwich* case] C was in effect enabled to take advantage of the contract between A and B. He suggested that [the classification society's] argument in this case would also encounter that difficulty. However, I perceive no difficulty. The contract between A and B is simply a material factor in determining whether a duty of care is to be imposed on C and its materiality does not run counter to the rule that C cannot enforce a term of the contract against A or B even though the term was included for his benefit.

Saville LJ, concurring, expressed a similar sentiment when he said (at p 1077):

> . . . whatever the nature of the harm sustained by the plaintiff, it is necessary to consider the matter not only by inquiring about foreseeability but also by con-

sidering the nature of the relationship between the parties; and to be satisfied that in all the circumstances, it is fair, just and reasonable to impose a duty of care. Of course, as Lord Oliver pointed out in *Caparo Industries plc v Dickman* [1990] 2 AC 605 these three matters overlap with each other and are really facets of the same thing. . . Thus the three so-called requirements for a duty of care are not to be treated as wholly separate and distinct requirements, but rather as convenient and helpful approaches to the pragmatic question whether a duty should be imposed in any given case. . . .

Taking this approach resolves all or virtually all that might otherwise be regarded as conflicts among the authorities. In some cases the question whether the relationship is one where the plaintiff has relied upon the defendant to exercise care has been regarded as of paramount importance (as in *Simaan General Contracting Co v Pilkington Glass Ltd (No 2)* [1988] QB 758), whereas in other cases (such as *White v Jones* [1993] 3 WLR 730 [CA]) the absence of reliance has not precluded the existence of a duty. In some cases the existence of contractual rights, obligations and exclusions or limitations of liability have been regarded as militating against the existence of an extra-contractual duty (as in *Pacific Associates Inc v Baxter* [1990] 1 QB 993 and *Norwich City Council v Harvey* [1989] 1 WLR 828), while in other cases such matters have been regarded as irrelevant or immaterial (as in *Grant v Australian Knitting Mills Ltd* [1936] AC 85). In some cases the fact that the claimant would have no other remedy is regarded as an important pointer towards the existence of a duty (as in *White v Jones*), while again in other cases (*Grant*'s case again being a good example) the existence of contractual remedies against others is considered to be of little or no relevance. These cases are not irreconcilable. What they do is to demonstrate that in differing circumstances the same or similar factors may take on a different significance.

Marc Rich and Co AG v Bishop Rock Marine Co Ltd ('The Nicholas H') [1996] 1 AC 211: The House of Lords by 4:1 upheld the Court of Appeal's decision that the classification society did not owe a duty of care in tort to the cargo owners, because the cargo owners had effectively foreclosed their right to pursue such a claim by virtue of their agreement with the shipowner to limit their damages claim against the shipowner to US$500,000. The majority Law Lords were influenced by the fact that that contract was contained in a bill of lading which incorporated the Hague Rules, which in turn limited the amount of the shipowners' liability to the plaintiff in the event of a loss of the plaintiff's cargo at sea. Thus, Lord Steyn, with whose speech the other three majority Law Lords agreed, said (at p 238):

The Hague Rules . . . form an internationally recognised code adjusting the rights and duties existing between shipowners and those shipping goods under bills of lading . . . the Rules create an intricate blend of responsibilities and liabilities, rights and immunities, limitations on the amount of damages recoverable . . . in relation to the carriage of goods under bills of lading. The proposition advanced by [the plaintiff's counsel] would add an identical duty owed by the classification society to that owed by the shipowners, but without any of these balancing factors, which are internationally recognised and accepted. I do not regard that as a just, fair or reasonable proposition. . .

The result of a recognition of a duty of care in this case will be to enable cargo owners, or rather their insurers, to disturb the balance created by the Hague

Rules . . . by enabling cargo owners to recover in tort against a peripheral party to the prejudice of the protection of shipowners under the existing system. For these reasons I would hold that the international trade system tends to militate against the recognition of the claim in tort put forward by the cargo owners against the classification society.

Lord Lloyd, dissenting, argued persuasively that the majority's decision was wrong. He said (at p 222) (emphasis added):

> . . . I have difficulty in seeing why the balance of rights and liabilities between shipowners and cargo would be upset by holding the defendants liable for the consequence of [the surveyor's] negligence. . . 'The Hague Rules have nothing to say on the issue of a duty of care on parties other than cargo owners and carriers'.
> . . . the intricate regime of the Hague Rules . . . has nothing to do with whether it is fair, just and reasonable that [the surveyor] and his employers should be liable to cargo for their assumed negligence. The irrelevance of the Hague Rules is underlined by the further consideration that the limitation provisions on which the shipowners relied to limit their liability . . . is not derived from the Hague Rules at all, but from section 503 of the Merchant Shipping Act.
> . . . therefore . . . the Court of Appeal's judgment on this part of the case [and the reasons of the majority Law Lords] can only be supported if the *mere existence* of a contract of carriage under which the shipowners can limit their liability, is inconsistent with, or militates against, the imposition of unlimited liability on a third party in tort.

Further passages from Lord Lloyd's speech are set out in Chapter 9, para 9.7.4, where the comment is made that the logic of Lord Lloyd's dissenting speech is compelling and that the majority's decision should not be regarded as a precedent against the imposition of a duty of care in tort on all tortfeasors in cases where the plaintiff has agreed by contract with a third party to restrict the amount of damages which the plaintiff can recover from the third party in the event of the plaintiff's goods being damaged while in the possession of the third party or, more generally, in the event of a contract between the plaintiff and the third party becoming less valuable by virtue of the negligence of the defendant. Indeed, it would seem that the majority Law Lords in *The Nicholas H* themselves intended their decision to be treated restrictively when Lord Steyn said (at p 236): "The present case can only be decided on the basis of an intense and particular focus on all its distinctive features and then applying established legal principles to it".

British Telecommunications plc v James Thomson and Sons (Engineers) Ltd (1996) 49 Con LR 163: The facts of this case in the (Scottish) Court of Session (Outer House) were practically indistinguishable from the facts in *Norwich City Council v Harvey*, considered *above*. Here, the pursuer, British Telecommunications plc ('BT'), was the proprietor of a telephone switching station in Glasgow. It invited tenders for works of refurbishment and repair to the building. It accepted a tender from MDW Ltd ('MDW') as the main contractor. The main contract contained a clause whereunder BT agreed to take out and maintain, until the issue of the certificate of Practical Completion, a policy of insurance for the full cost of reinstatement, repair or replacement of loss or damage to the building by one or more of certain specified perils, including 'fire', even if such perils materialised through the negligence of MDW or any of its sub-contractors. MDW sub-contracted part of the works to the defenders. That contract stipulated that the defenders' work would be carried out to the same specification, terms and conditions as those prevailing between MDW and BT.

In the course of carrying out the sub-contract works, the defenders negligently caused a fire. When BT sued the defenders, one of the questions was whether they could take advantage of the fire exclusion clause, so as to be free of all liability to BT for their negligence. The court answered this question in the affirmative and struck out BT's claim as disclosing no reasonable cause of action.

The court noted, first, that the defenders tendered for the sub-contract works in the knowledge that BT were to insure the building and its contents against fire and were to look to that insurance rather than to MDW even if the building and its contents were damaged by a fire caused by the negligence of the defenders. The court then referred to the above-mentioned decisions in *Norwich City Council* and *Marc Rich* and concluded (*per* Lord Rodger):

> Whatever the precise construction of the sub-contract provision may be, there is no dispute that the defenders are to be taken as having concluded the sub-contract in the knowledge and on the basis that BT were undertaking to insure and were in effect accepting that they could not sue the main contractor for fire damage to the building and its contents even if it was caused by the negligence of the defenders or their sub-contractors. For those matters they were to look to their insurance policy alone. If the main contractor was not to be liable in this regard, the defenders [the sub-contractor] would have no reason to expect to face a claim from the main contractor seeking to pass on any such liability to them.
>
> The pursuer does not aver that the defenders were required by the terms of the sub-contract to insure against any such liability. That being so, it would have been proper for the defenders to proceed on the basis that they did not require to insure the existing structures and their contents against the risk of fire due to negligence, and for them to price their tender for the sub-contract works accordingly. It seems to me that in the circumstances averred the court should not impose on the defenders a duty of care to BT since the result of doing so would be to allow BT to sue the defenders in negligence for a loss which BT had in effect agreed to look to their insurers, as the defenders must have known from the terms both of the acceptance of their tender and of the order. Such a claim in delict [tort] would cut across the commercial arrangements embodied in the main contract and the sub-contract by exposing the defenders to a liability which did not accord with those arrangements and against which the defenders would have been entitled not to insure.

Agents, employees and directors

In cases falling within the factual matrix considered in this section, it sometimes happens that the defendant being sued in negligence is an agent, employee or director of the person or entity with whom the plaintiff had a contract for the provision of the services which the plaintiff alleges had been performed negligently. In these circumstances the question arises whether the plaintiff should be confined to an action against the party with whom he contracted, namely, the principal, employer or corporation on whose behalf the defendant performed the relevant services. In the cases mentioned *below*, which have considered this question, the defendant's alleged negligence has occurred in the context of the defendant's performance of the contract between the plaintiff and the principal, employer or corporation. These cases are not concerned with tortious acts which are independent of the performance of the contract. In respect of those torts the law is settled: the agent, employee or director is liable for his own negligent acts or omissions.

Ministry of Housing and Local Government v Sharp [1970] 2 QB 252: The facts of this case are set out in Chapter 9, para 9.7.4, where it is noted that the plaintiff succeeded in its action for damages in tort against the district council for the negligent issue of a clear charge certificate. The plaintiff also sued the individual clerk who had made the mistake. On this point Cross LJ (in the minority of 2:1) reserved his opinion as to whether the clerk, as an employee of the district council, could be held personally liable to the plaintiff for his negligence. He said (at p 291):

> ... I am ... not altogether satisfied that it would be right to hold the searcher liable in this case. Suppose a private organisation were to offer for reward to supply information as to the creditworthiness of persons with whom those who apply for information are thinking of entering into business dealings; suppose, further, that an employee of theirs, by failing to search their records properly, creates an entirely false impression as to the creditworthiness of some person by relying on which the applicant suffers damage; and suppose finally, that the organisation is insolvent and that the applicant sues the employee—who has recently inherited a legacy and so is worth powder and shot—in tort. In such circumstances I think that the defendant might say to the plaintiff with some plausibility:
>
> > 'Of course, I was to blame. My employers may, for all that I know, have some claim against me; but it was they who put this false information into circulation. I did not publish it myself, and you and I ought not to be regarded as "neighbours" for the purpose of the law of tort.'

Fairline Shipping Corporation v Adamson [1975] 1 QB 180: The defendant, Mr Adamson, was a director of a limited company, Game and Meat Products Ltd ('G&M'). Its business was the buying and reselling of game and meat products. This required the storage of such products under refrigeration between their purchase and resale. For this purpose G&M used a cold store which the defendant personally owned.

In the course of time G&M ran into financial difficulties. By January 1972, neither the defendant nor the other directors of G&M expected G&M to survive for more than a few months. Thereafter they were concerned only with the liquidation of that season's business. In March 1972, the plaintiff asked G&M to store some ship's provisions for about six weeks. Initially the plaintiff dealt with one of the other directors of G&M, who arranged for the goods to be placed in the defendant's cold store.

When the defendant heard about this, he queried the fact that there was no written contract. On 23 March 1972 he wrote to the plaintiff confirming the arrangement regarding the storage of the goods in his premises. He said that *his* invoice for the first month's rent would be sent shortly. He signed the letter in his personal name, and it was written on his personal notepaper, rather than on notepaper with G&M's letterhead.

In due course, the refrigeration system in the defendant's cold store failed and the plaintiff's goods in it went off. Shortly after this discovery, the directors of G&M put it into voluntary liquidation. The plaintiff sued the defendant personally for its loss. The defendant contended that he could not be personally liable because the contract had been made with the company (G&M). The judge, Kerr J, rejected this defence. He said (at p 190):

> The fact that [Mr Adamson] was a director of Game & Meat and that the company was the contracting party does not necessarily exclude his personal liability. . .
>
>   . . . the crucial question . . . is whether or not, on the facts, the defendant owed a duty of care to the plaintiffs in respect of their goods which were stored in his cold store, and, if so, whether he was in breach of that duty. In my view, both limbs of this question are to be answered in the affirmative on the special facts of this case. . . . Game & Meat could only perform its duties in relation to these goods through its human servants and agents. At the relevant time the only persons through whom these duties could be performed were the directors. The only one of these who concerned himself with these goods in any way after their delivery was the defendant. The letter of 23 March dictated by him, or on his behalf, in my view, reflected the true position, in that he regarded himself, and not Game & Meat, as concerned with the storage of these goods. On the facts of this case, the defendant in my view assumed and owed a duty of care to the plaintiffs in respect of the storage of their goods in his premises and was in breach of that duty with the result that the plaintiffs' goods were damaged. I therefore give judgment for the plaintiffs against the defendant. . . .

Sealand of the Pacific v Robert C McHaffie Ltd (1974) 51 DLR (3d) 702: The first defendant, Robert C McHaffie Ltd ('McHaffie Ltd'), a company which provided naval architectural services, had been engaged by the plaintiff to provide certain specialist services to the plaintiff in connection with the plaintiff's oceanarium. These services were provided negligently. The plaintiff sued both McHaffie Ltd and Robert McHaffie personally. McHaffie was a director of McHaffie Ltd and the naval architect who personally provided the services which the plaintiff had contracted to receive.

The British Columbia Court of Appeal rejected the plaintiff's claim against Mr McHaffie personally. In this regard Seaton JA said (at p 706):

Now I turn to the claim against Mr McHaffie. For a statement of part of the principle in *Hedley Byrne* I refer to what Lord Morris said:

> If someone possessed of a special skill undertakes, quite irrespective of contract, to apply that skill for the assistance of another person who relies upon such skill, a duty of care will arise.

Here Mr McHaffie did not undertake to apply his skill for the assistance of Sealand. He did exercise, or fail to exercise, his skill as an employee of McHaffie Ltd in the carrying out of its contractual duty to Sealand. Further, while Sealand may have chosen to consult McHaffie Ltd because it had the benefit of Mr McHaffie's services as an employee, it was with McHaffie Ltd that Sealand made a contract and it was upon the skill of McHaffie Ltd that it relied.

An employee's act or omission that constitutes his employer's breach of contract may also impose a liability on the employee in tort. However, this will only be so if there is breach of a duty owed (independently of the contract) by the employee to the other party. Mr McHaffie did not owe the duty to Sealand to make inquiries. That was a company responsibility. It is the failure to carry out the corporate duty imposed by contract that can attract liability to the company. The duty in negligence and the duty in contract may stand side by side but the duty in contract is not imposed upon the employee as a duty in tort.

Punjab National Bank v DeBoinville [1992] 1 WLR 1138: The facts of this case are set out in Chapter 9, para 9.7.6, where it is noted that the plaintiff succeeded in its claim that the defendant's insurance brokers, F E Wright (UK Limited) and Fielding Juggins Money and Stewart Ltd, owed the plaintiff a duty of care in tort for the plaintiff's pure economic loss. In addition, the Court of Appeal held that the two individual brokers, although employees of limited companies, personally owed duties of care to the plaintiff. Thus Staughton LJ said (at p 1154):

> That leaves Mr DeBoinville and Mr Deere. It is not every employee of a firm or company providing professional services that owes a personal duty of care to the client; it depends on what he is employed to do. . . here, Mr DeBoinville and Mr Deere, whether in their employment with F E Wright (UK) Limited or with Fielding Juggins Money and Stewart Ltd, were evidently entrusted with the whole or nearly the whole of the task which their employers undertook. [Their counsel] argued that they were more remote from the bank [the plaintiff] than their employers. On the contrary, I think that in fact their proximity was greater. Whilst they were employed by Wrights . . . as professional men, they owed a duty of care to the bank, since the bank were a client or the client of Wrights. Whilst they were employed by Fieldings they owed a duty of care to the bank by justifiable increment of an existing category until the bank became a client of Fieldings . . . when their duty came within an existing category.

Gran Gelato Ltd v Richcliff (Group) Ltd [1992] Ch 560: The facts of this case are set out in Chapter 9, para 9.7.5, where it is noted that Sir Donald Nicholls VC held that a solicitor acting for a vendor of land, answering inquiries before contract in a normal conveyancing transaction, did not owe a duty of care in tort to the purchaser to exercise reasonable skill and care in answering those inquiries. He said (at p 571):

. . . in the field of negligent misrepresentation caution should be exercised before the law takes the step of concluding, in any particular context, that an agent acting within the scope of his authority on behalf of a known principal himself owes to third parties a duty of care independent of the duty of care he owes to his principal. There will be cases where it is fair, just and reasonable that there should be such a duty. But in general, in a case where the principal himself owes a duty of care to the third party, the existence of a further duty of care, owed by the agent to the third party, is not necessary for the reasonable protection of the latter. Good reason, therefore, should exist before the law imposes a duty when the agent already owes to his principal a duty which covers the same ground and the principal is responsible to the third party for his agent's shortcomings. I do not think there is good reason for such a duty in normal conveyancing transactions.

McCullagh v Lane Fox and Partners Ltd (1996) 49 Con LR 124: The facts of this case are set out in para 10.3.3. One of the defendant's counsel's submissions was that the defendant, being only an agent of the vendor, could not be personally liable to the plaintiff in circumstances where the plaintiff had a direct cause of action against the agent's employer (ie the vendor) for the agent's negligence. In making this submission he relied on Nicholls VC's above-cited *dicta* in *Gran Gelato*. The Court of Appeal, however, rejected this analogy. Hobhouse LJ said:

> The reasoning of the Vice Chancellor [in *Gran Gelato*], unless it is confined to stating a special rule applicable to solicitors in conveyancing transactions, is, in my judgment, inconsistent with the *ratio decidendi* of *Punjab National Bank*, and with the general principle of tortious liability where the person doing the relevant act is the agent of another, which the Vice Chancellor himself recognised in his citation of *Smith v Bush* [see Chapter 9, para 9.7.5].
>
> With respect to the Vice Chancellor, when he says that 'where the principal himself owes a duty of care to the third party, the existence of a further duty of care, owed by the agent to the third party, is not necessary', he appears to overlook that, in the relevant context, the duty in tort arises from the act of the solicitor in choosing to answer the inquiry. There is only one duty; it is the duty of the solicitor to take reasonable care in answering. The duty in tort is both created and broken by the solicitor. The tortious liability of the principal is, in this context, not for what he has himself done, but is a vicarious liability for the tort of the solicitor.

Hobhouse LJ then referred to the way in which the *Gran Gelato* decision was dealt with in the Court of Appeal and in the House of Lords in *White v Jones* [1995] 2 AC 207 (see para 9.7.5), and then continued:

> It thus appears that there is a rule of policy which gives a solicitor a special immunity even in a non-adversarial context such as conveyancing, where there is no conflict between the duty owed to the client and what might be owed to the third party. Further, this immunity is apparently to coexist with a continuing (vicarious) tortious liability of the principal. In *White v Jones* it was not necessary for the House of Lords to consider the more general question of the liability of agents and, indeed, the actual decision holding the solicitor liable is in no way inconsistent with agents being liable for their *prima facie* tortious acts.

Hobhouse LJ then referred extensively to the House of Lords' decision in *Henderson v Merrett Syndicates Ltd* [1995] 2 AC 145 (see para 9.7.6), and concluded:

> These authorities show that the governing principle is still that in *Hedley Byrne*, and that an agent can be held responsible for a careless misrepresentation as much as his principal. In certain special situations, rules which restrict the liability of the agent may be superimposed. One such situation is, on the basis of *Gran Gelato*, a solicitor in a conveyancing transaction.

Trevor Ivory v Anderson [1992] 2 NZLR 517: The plaintiffs owned an orchard which included a raspberry plantation. They contracted as consultant the first defendant, a one-person company carrying on a business as an agricultural and horticultural supplier and an advisory service. The company, through the second defendant, Mr Trevor Ivory, advised the plaintiffs to use 'Roundup', a herbicide, to control the growth of couch grass which the plaintiffs believed was threatening the raspberry crop. Mr Ivory did not instruct the plaintiffs to protect the raspberry plants from the effects of the herbicide, by mowing near and under them or otherwise removing from them any foliage near the ground, before spraying. An employee of the plaintiffs sprayed the herbicide as instructed. The raspberry crop was severely affected and ultimately the plants had to be dug out. The plaintiffs brought their claim in both contract and tort against both the company and Mr Ivory himself. They alleged breaches of an implied term of their contract with the company and of a duty owed by the company and Mr Ivory to exercise all reasonable care, skill, diligence and competence as an adviser on the application of chemical sprays.

The Court of Appeal of New Zealand rejected the plaintiffs' claim against Mr Ivory personally. Cooke P expressed his conclusion as follows (at p 524):

> I commit myself to the opinion that, when he formed his company, Mr Ivory made it plain to all the world that limited liability was intended. Possibly the plaintiffs gave little thought to that in entering into the consultancy contract; but such a limitation is a common fact of business and, in relation to economic loss and duties of care, the consequences should in my view be accepted in the absence of special circumstances. It is not to be doubted that, in relation to an obligation to give careful and skilful advice, the owner of a one-man company may assume personal responsibility. *Fairline* is an analogy. But it seems to me that something special is required to justify putting a case in that class.

Hardie Boys J, concurring, said (at p 526):

> But one cannot from that conclude that whenever a company's liability in tort arises through the act or omission of a director, he, because he must be either an agent or an employee, will be primarily liable, and the company liable only vicariously. In the area of negligence, what must always first be determined is the existence of a duty of care. As is always so in such an inquiry, it is a matter of fact and degree, and a balancing of policy considerations. In the policy area, I find no difficulty in the imposition of personal liability on a director in appropriate

circumstances. The question in the present case is whether, in giving advice pursuant to this company's contract with the plaintiffs, Mr Ivory assumed a personal responsibility. It is not enough that it was a one-man company. Indeed that fact may rather tell against personal responsibility, for use of a company to carry on a one-man business may be seen as itself a personal disclaimer. That this was a one-man company is of course by no means conclusive, but it made it necessary for the plaintiffs to adduce clear evidence that in his dealings with them Mr Ivory was not simply acting as the company performing its contractual obligations towards them. Although I regard the case as approaching the borderline, I am satisfied on balance that the evidence does not demonstrate an assumption of personal responsibility.

Lastly, McGechan J, also concurring, said (at p 532):

When it comes to assumption of responsibility, I do not accept a company director of a one-man company is to be regarded as automatically accepting tort responsibility for advice given on behalf of the company by himself. There may be situations where such liability tends to arise, particularly perhaps where the director as a person is highly prominent and his company is barely visible, resulting in a focus predominantly on the man himself. All will depend upon the facts of individual cases, and the degree of implicit assumption of personal responsibility, with no doubt some policy elements also applying. I do not think this is such a case, although it approaches the line. While the respondents looked to his personal expertise, Mr Ivory made it clear that he traded through a company, which was to be the legal contracting party entitled to charge. That structure was negotiated and known. There was nothing like the personal superimposition so central to the decision in the *Fairline* case. There was no representation, express or implicit, of personal involvement, as distinct from routine involvement for and through his company. There was no singular feature which would justify belief that Mr Ivory was accepting a personal commitment, as opposed to the known company obligation. If anything, the intrinsic high risk nature of spray advice, and his deliberate adoption of an intervening company structure, would have pointed to the contrary likelihood. On the present facts, I see no policy justification for imposing an additional duty of care. In this particular one-man company situation, and against the established trading understandings, I would not view such as just and reasonable.

London Drugs Ltd v Kuehne & Nagel International Ltd (1992) 97 DLR (4th) 261: The plaintiff, London Drugs Ltd, delivered a transformer weighing 7,500 lbs to the first defendant, Kuehne and Nagel International Ltd ('K&N'), for storage pursuant to the terms and conditions of a standard form contract of storage. The transformer had been purchased from its manufacturer and was to be installed in the plaintiff's new warehouse which was under construction. The contract of storage included a limitation of liability clause which stated that K&N's liability on any one package was limited to $40 unless the holder had declared in writing a valuation in excess of $40 and had paid the additional charge specified to cover warehouse liability. With full knowledge and understanding of this clause, the plaintiff chose not to obtain additional insurance from K&N and instead arranged for its own all-risks coverage.

In due course, the transformer was required to be taken out of storage.

Two of K&N's employees received orders to load the transformer onto a truck which would deliver it to the plaintiff's new warehouse. The employees attempted to move the transformer by lifting it with two forklift vehicles, in the course of which it toppled over and fell, causing extensive damage to the transformer. The employees had been negligent because they should have lifted the transformer from above using brackets which were attached to the transformer and which were clearly marked for that purpose.

The plaintiff's action against K&N was limited to $40 because of the limitation clause in the storage contract. The plaintiff sought, however, to make the employees personally liable for the full amount of the damage. In the Supreme Court of Canada the first question was whether the employees personally owed a duty of care to the plaintiff. The second question was, if they did, were they entitled to take advantage of the limitation clause in the contract between the plaintiff and K&N, thereby being liable to the plaintiff for only $40. The Supreme Court of Canada, by 5:1, answered both of these questions in the affirmative.

With regard to the first question, Iacobucci J, speaking for the majority, treated it as self-evident that the employees owed a duty of care to the plaintiff when handling the transformer. He said (at p 335):

> In my opinion the employees unquestionably owed a duty of care to the plaintiff when handling the transformer. I arrive at this conclusion with as little difficulty as the judges in the courts below. I base my conclusion on well-established principles of tort law. In all of the circumstances of this case, it was reasonably foreseeable to the employees that negligence on their part in the handling of the transformer would result in damage to the plaintiff's property. In sum, there was such a close relationship between the parties as to give rise to a duty on the employees to exercise reasonable care.

Iacobucci J's analysis of the second question was more intricate. Also, the other majority judge (McLachlin J) had a different view on the analysis of this question, and the dissenting judge (La Forest J) advanced an entirely different approach to the problem. This whole question is considered in para 10.3.2, *below*.

Edgeworth Construction Ltd v N D Lea and Associates Ltd (1993) 107 DLR (4th) 169: The facts of this case are set out in Chapter 9, para 9.9.3, where it is noted that the defendant engineering corporation was held liable to the plaintiff in tort for the plaintiff's losses sustained through having relied on the specifications and construction drawings which the defendant, under a contract with the province of British Columbia, had prepared for the purpose of contractors like the plaintiff tendering for the job. The plaintiff also sued the individual engineers who had prepared the drawings and the specifications. They were employees of the defendant corporation.

All seven of the judges in the Supreme Court held that the individual engineers were not personally liable for their misrepresentations. McLachlin J, speaking for herself and five of the other judges, dealt with this question very shortly. She said (at p 178):

The position of the individual engineers is different (from that of the engineering firm—their employer). The only basis upon which they are sued is the fact that each of them affixed his seal to the design documents. In my view, this is insufficient to establish a duty of care between the individual engineers and the plaintiff. The seal attests that a qualified engineer prepared the drawing. It is not a guarantee of accuracy. The affixation of a seal, without more, is insufficient to found liability for negligent misrepresentation.

Strangely, no mention was made of the Supreme Court's earlier decision in *London Drugs* (see *above*) in which the individual employees who had dropped the transformer were held liable in tort to their employer's customer. Only the remaining judge, La Forest J, dealt with this point. He said (at p 170):

This case comes hot on the heels of *London Drugs Ltd v Kuehne & Nagel International Ltd* (1992) 97 DLR (4th) 261, where the majority was unwilling to absolve ordinary workers from liability flowing from their negligence in the course of their employment except to the extent that a contractual exemption from liability had been entered into by their employer, whereas in this case the professional employees who, one would have thought, were in a better position to take steps to protect themselves, are absolved from liability resulting from their negligence in the absence of any exonerating contract. It will be evident from my dissent in *London Drugs* that such a distinction, in so far as it favours professional employees, is, at the level of principle, lost on me. And it does not matter that in one case one is dealing with economic loss and in the other with physical damage; as my colleague notes, no issue of indeterminacy arises here.

There are, however, technical distinctions between the ordinary tort of negligence and negligent misrepresentation, in particular, that under the latter the representee must have relied, in a reasonable manner, on the negligent representation. I am quite happy to rely on this technical distinction to absolve the individual engineers from liability because, on balance, it seems to me, there are sound reasons of policy why they should not be subjected to a duty to the plaintiff. The plaintiff here was quite reasonably relying on the skills of the engineering firm and the firm in turn must be taken to have recognised that persons in the position of the plaintiff would rely on their work and act accordingly. I have cast the relationship in terms of reliance but it may also be seen as a matter of voluntary assumption of risk.

The situation of the individual engineers is quite different. While they may, in one sense, have expected that persons in the position of the plaintiff would rely on their work, they would expect that the plaintiff would place reliance on their firm's pocket-book and not theirs for indemnification. Looked at the other way, the plaintiff could not reasonably rely for indemnification on the individual engineers. It would have to show that it was relying on the particular expertise of an individual engineer without regard to the corporate character of the engineering firm. It would seem quite unrealistic, as my colleague observes, to hold that the mere presence of an individual engineer's seal was sufficient indication of personal reliance (or for that matter voluntary assumption of risk).

While it is tempting to criticise the Supreme Court of Canada for holding in *London Drugs* that the employees did owe a duty of care in part to the plaintiff for damaging its transformer, in contrast to their holding in the present case that the individual engineers did not owe a duty to the plaintiff for their negligent drawings and specifications, it must be remembered that the present case proceeded by way of a striking-out motion. Therefore the question was only whether the case *as pleaded* disclosed a cause of action against the employees. This appears clearly from McLachlin J's judgment when she said: "The only basis on which they are sued is the fact that each of them affixed his seal to the design documents. In my view, this is insufficient to establish a duty of care between the individual engineers and the plaintiff". It is submitted that the majority judges' decision must therefore be seen in this light and not as a pronouncement that professional workers enjoy an immunity which manual workers do not, or that a duty of care is owed in tort by employees in respect of physical damage negligently caused by them but not in respect of pure economic loss.

Brostoff v Clark Kenneth Leventhal (a firm) (1996, unreported): In this case the plaintiffs' contract was with the employee himself, and it was sought to hold his employer liable in the tort of negligence for the employee's fraudulent activities. The employee, Nicholas Young, who was employed as the International Executive Officer of Clark Kenneth Leventhal ('CKL'), an international firm of accountants, deceived more than 100 investors by persuading them to deposit money with him for investment in an 'international fund'. The whole scheme was fraudulent, but Mr Young always told the investors that the fund was personal to him. He never represented that it was managed or controlled by CKL.

After Mr Young had been arrested, convicted and made bankrupt, the plaintiffs, who were a group of investors who had entrusted their money to Mr Young, sued CKL. They alleged that CKL, as Mr Young's employer, owed them a duty of care, which it had breached by failing to supervise Mr Young properly. They alleged that proper supervision would have disclosed what was going on, and his activities would have been stopped. In rejecting the plaintiffs' claim, Dyson J said:

> This is a case concerning pure economic loss. It follows, therefore, that the plaintiffs will establish a duty of care only if they can show a special relationship or a voluntary assumption of responsibility of the kind discussed in *Hedley Byrne and Co Ltd v Heller and Partners Ltd* [1964] AC 465, and recently in *Henderson v Merrett Syndicates Ltd* [1995] 2 AC 145 and *White v Jones* [1995] 2 AC 207 [see Chapter 9].

Dyson J then referred extensively to these cases, and concluded:

> It is important to observe about *White v Jones* first that there was an assumption of responsibility by the solicitor in relation to the drawing up of the will (the service provided); and secondly the solicitor was aware of the limited class of persons (namely the intended beneficiaries) who would be affected by a negligent performance of the service for which he had assumed responsibility.
> I turn to the present case. In my view, there was no special relationship between the plaintiffs and CKL, and no assumption of responsibility by CKL in relation to the plaintiffs so as to found a duty on the part of CKL to avoid the economic loss caused by Mr Young's activities. It is important to have in mind

that, for the reasons I have already stated, Mr Young's investment transactions were not carried out by him in the course of his employment or within the scope of any authority vested in him by his employers. They were private activities carried on by him in his personal capacity. I am prepared to assume, for the purpose of deciding whether the suggested duty of care existed, that CKL was aware that he was entering into investment transactions. The reasons why I consider that the suggested duty of care did not exist in the present case are as follows.

First, CKL did not assume any responsibility in relation to the investment activities. They did not give any advice or perform any service in relation to them. The plaintiffs have to say that there was an assumption of responsibility to them, not in relation to the advice given and service performed as to the International Fund, but in relation to their control and supervision of Mr Young. But a *Hedley Byrne* duty is based on the provision of information, advice and the performance of other services, where the relationship between the parties is 'equivalent to contract', or as Lord Devlin put it [in *Hedley Byrne*] 'where there is an assumption of responsibility in circumstances in which, but for the absence of consideration, there would be a contract'. There was no such relationship between the plaintiffs and CKL. In fact, there was no relationship at all between them. The plaintiffs had no dealings with Mr Young in his capacity as employee of CKL. They were not clients of any member firms of CKL when they started investing with Mr Young. CKL was not even aware of the identity of the investors of the Fund.

Secondly, unlike the plaintiffs in *Hedley Byrne v Heller, Henderson v Merrett* and *White v Jones*, the plaintiffs in this case belong to an unlimited class. In this case, the alleged duty was owed not only to those who invested with Mr Young but anyone considering whether to do so. This would include anyone who might come into contact with Mr Young. They would not normally be known to CKL. It is impossible to know how many such persons there were or might be. The present case is analogous to *Goodwill v British Pregnancy Advisory Service* [see Chapter 9, para 9.7.8].

It seems to me that each of the plaintiffs in the present case is a member of an indeterminately large class of persons who might have invested with Mr Young.

Thirdly, as Lord Goff said in *Davis v Radcliffe* [see Chapter 8, para 8.2.10], it will only be in rare cases that liability will be imposed for purely financial loss caused by the deliberate wrongdoing of a third party.

Fourthly, unlike *White v Jones*, in this case there is no lacuna which requires the law exceptionally to fashion a remedy to avoid injustice. The plaintiffs have causes of action against Mr Young in contract and in tort. For the purposes of deciding whether exceptionally a duty of care needs to be fashioned, it is immaterial that, unfortunately from the plaintiffs' point of view, Mr Young is not worth suing.

No case has been cited in which defendant employers have been found liable for loss, let alone purely financial loss, caused by the private activities of an employee. It is possible to think of private activities conducted by an employee with the knowledge and approval of his or her employer. An example is a schoolteacher who gives private tuition out of school hours. Another is an employee of a firm of accountants who gives private tax advice to family and friends. If in the course of these private activities the employee gives negligent advice to this client, the employer is not liable, because there is no special relationship between the employer and the employee's client, and no assumption of responsibility by the employer to that client in relation to the private activities undertaken by the employee.

The plaintiffs did not have a convincing answer to any of these points. Their counsel submitted that it was just and reasonable that the plaintiffs should be owed a duty of care by CKL, who knew or ought to have known that Mr Young was conducting investment business from their premises during ordinary office hours, and was using his position of authority at CKL to lend credibility to what he was doing. I am far from persuaded that on the facts of this case it would be just and reasonable to impose such a duty on the defendants, but I do not have to decide this. This is because as Lord Goff pointed out in *Henderson v Merrett*, in cases concerning pure economic loss, the only question is whether the *Hedley Byrne* requirements have been satisfied, and it is unnecessary to embark on any further enquiry whether it is fair, just and reasonable to impose liability for economic loss.

Williams v Natural Life Health Foods Ltd [1997] 1 BCLC 131: The plaintiffs, Mr Williams and Mrs Reid, who had previously run a post office and general store and who had some short experience of working in a health food shop owned by another company, decided to pool their resources with a view to running a health food shop themselves. They found a potential site for a shop and considered setting up in business there, for which purpose they sought advice and were referred to a Mr Roche, who was experienced in franchising and in the operation of health food shops. He advised them that the site was suitable and that they should approach the first defendant, Natural Life Health Foods Ltd ('the Company'), which was in the business of franchising health food shops. As a result of this introduction, the plaintiffs received the Company's brochure, which described in glowing terms the Company's success in franchising health food shops. Also included was a photograph of the Company's managing director, Mr Mistlin (the second defendant). He was described as having extensive experience and expertise in the franchising of health food shops through his operation of a pilot shop in Salisbury. The brochure also referred to Mr Padwick, franchise director, who was described as being responsible for the development and operation of the Company's 'franchise network'.

Although Mr Padwick had some experience in franchising, he had no experience of health food shops, and both he and Mr Roche were remunerated only by way of commission on the successful introduction of a franchisee. Furthermore, at the relevant time, the Company itself had no relevant previous experience on its own account, since the Salisbury shop was owned and operated by Mr Mistlin independently and not by the Company, and the three franchises that had been granted had each been operating for only a few months. None of this information was known to the plaintiffs when they contacted Mr Mistlin, who put them in touch with Mr Padwick, with whom all discussions about a possible franchise for the plaintiffs took place. He provided financial projections which were also sent to Mr Mistlin. At a further meeting with Mr Padwick, the plaintiffs signed a franchise agreement with the Company for a 10-year term and Mr Padwick produced a further set of financial projections which were significantly more optimistic than the previous ones. Again, a copy was sent to Mr Mistlin.

The plaintiffs duly opened their shop. However, the financial projections had been substantially overstated and, within about eight months, the plaintiffs were in serious financial difficulties despite having done everything that could be expected of them to make the shop a success. The plaintiffs brought an action against the Company for the loss which they had sustained as a result of the negligent financial projections and the negligent advice which they had received from the Company and those associated with it. However, in the meantime, the Company was wound up. The plaintiffs therefore joined Mr Mistlin as a party to the action and, after the Company was dissolved, pursued their claim against him alone. In rejecting Mr Mistlin's defence that he could not be held personally liable because the plaintiffs had contracted with the Company, Hirst LJ, with whose judgment Waite LJ agreed, said (at p 152):

> It is not in dispute that, in order to fix a director with personal liability, it must be shown that he assumed personal responsibility for the negligent misstatement made on behalf of the company. In my judgment, having regard to the importance of the status of limited liability, a company director is only to be held personally liable for the company's negligent misstatements if the plaintiffs can establish some special circumstances setting the case apart from the ordinary; and in the case of a director of a one-man company particular vigilance is needed, lest the protection of incorporation should be virtually nullified. But once such special circumstances are established, the fact of incorporation, even in the case of a one-man company, does not preclude the establishment of personal liability. In each case the decision is one of fact and degree.

Hirst LJ rejected Mr Mistlin's counsel's suggestion that, in addition, there must be some sort of personal dealings between the director and the company's customer. He said that there was "no trace of any such requirement in any of the authorities". Turning to the facts, Hirst LJ said (at p 152):

> Even though the point of contact between the company and the plaintiffs was in the person of Mr Padwick, I am satisfied on the evidence that Mr Mistlin played a very prominent part in the actual production of the projections. Although Mr Mistlin's involvement was indirect, its extent was considerable.
>
> My conclusions so far are very important as part of the factual material leading to the establishment of a *prima facie* case of the assumption by Mr Mistlin of personal responsibility, but they would not in aggregate be quite sufficient to carry the plaintiffs home (any more than were the facts in the *Trevor Ivory* case) since they would be open to the possible interpretation that they showed no more than a very active participation by Mr Mistlin *qua* director only.
>
> The case does not however end there. I see a crucial additional factor which takes the present case out of the ordinary. An intrinsic part of the offer for sale of the franchise contained in the brochure was the skilled advice of a professional team led by Mr Mistlin. As the brochure indicated, the Company's 'exten-

sive trade development experience in the health food industry' was based solely on Mr Mistlin's experience, since he was portrayed as the only member of the team who had been involved in the health food trade, ie, in matters specifically highlighted, such as choice of site and design of shop, training for the proprietor and staff, product knowledge, selection of stock and bulk buying facilities.

From what then was this knowledge and experience derived? Not, be it emphasised, from any company activity, since none of the other franchised shops had accumulated any experience, but rather from Mr Mistlin's personal experience in the Salisbury shop, which was owned and run by him personally and which had nothing whatsoever to do with his position as a director of the company. In other words, the relevant knowledge and experience was entirely his *qua* Mr Mistlin, and not his *qua* director. Indeed, I would go so far as to say that, in reality, Mr Mistlin held himself out as personally responsible for the only available figures to support the projections, as was indeed the fact.

Lastly, with respect to the other authorities in this area, Hirst LJ said (at p 154):

> The case is thus somewhat akin to the *Fairline* case, and is distinguishable from the *Trevor Ivory* case not in principle, but because, as a matter of fact and degree, whereas the former lay (albeit narrowly) on one side of the line, this case falls on the other side. I should emphasise that I have reached this conclusion solely on the particular facts of this case, and I do not think that there is any risk of compromising the general concept of limited liability.

Sir Patrick Russell, dissenting, expressed the following views (at p 155):

> It is axiomatic, in my view, that the court should be very cautious before finding the director of a small limited company personally liable for the negligent misstatements of the company made in the course of its business. Inevitably human agencies have to be at work within the company before the statement can emerge. One or more directors will frequently have had a hand in the production of the statement. To hold that in such circumstances, without more, the directors become personally liable would emasculate the very protection which corporate liability provides. That in my judgment is not in the public interest, nor is it the law.

Sir Patrick Russell then referred to the *Trevor Ivory* case and said:

> That case was *a fortiori* the instant case, but the director nevertheless escaped personal liability because it was not shown that his involvement was anything other than 'routine involvement for and through his company'. It is that phrase which, in my judgment, is the key to the questions raised in this appeal. Did Mr Mistlin do anything other than engage in routine involvement with the activities of the Company? Or was there something involving an assumption of personal responsibility on his behalf which renders the case a special or exceptional one?
>
> Mr Mistlin was portrayed as the experienced expert, but in my view in a company such as the first defendant, the managing director will almost inevitably be the one possessed of qualities essential to the functioning of the company. In fact, in my judgment, Mr Mistlin never stepped outside his function of managing director of the first defendant, nor did he do or say anything save in that capacity. This is to be contrasted with, for example, the director in

10.2.1 *The contractual connection*

the *Fairline* case who personally wrote a letter which indicated that he regarded himself and not Game & Meat as concerned with the storage of the goods which were negligently damaged [see *above*].

See also *Addendum* at p xxv.

Red Sea Tankers Ltd v Papachristidis (30 April 1997, unreported): This action resulted from an ill-fated investment in oil tankers. The first plaintiff ('Red Sea') was a fund incorporated for the purpose of the investment. The second to fifth plaintiffs were the first plaintiff's wholly-owned subsidiaries incorporated to serve as 'one-ship companies' owning the four tankers which were acquired. The second defendant ('PL') and the third defendant ('PSMSL') were limited companies which offered services to persons interested in engaging in the shipping market.

The first defendant, Mr Papachristidis, was the sole shareholder of PL, which in turn owned all of the shares of PSMSL. He was also the chairman of both PL and PSMSL and had 24 years' experience in the shipping industry. He was involved in a number of shipping-related enterprises. The Papachristidis organisation had a reputation as high-class ship managers, maintaining high standards. This was a matter of pride and value to Mr Papachristidis, and one about which prospective clients would be expected to be aware.

The fourth defendant, Mr Anderson, was the managing director of PL and a director of PSMSL. He had 19 years' experience in the shipping industry. He also became chairman of the board of directors of Red Sea when the fund was formed.

The fifth defendant, Mr Dunn, was the managing director of PSMSL and a director of PL. He was a qualified marine engineer and had many years' experience on the technical side of the shipping industry.

In due course, PL entered into a commercial advisory agreement ('CAA') and PSMSL entered into a technical advisory agreement ('TAA') with Red Sea. Thereafter, Red Sea borrowed $70m and used it to purchase second-hand oil tankers in reliance on advice provided to it by PL and PSMSL under the CAA and the TAA, respectively. As a result of higher than anticipated expenses incurred in repairing and upgrading the tankers, and a downturn in the second-hand shipping market, Red Sea recovered very little of its investment when it resold the vessels a couple of years later.

In this action, Red Sea sought to attribute responsibility for its losses to the five defendants. One of the preliminary questions was whether the individual directors could be held responsible for Red Sea's losses. In answering this question in the negative, Mance J said (at p 189):

The plaintiffs draw analogies on the facts with features present in *Henderson v Merrett* [1995] 2 AC 145 [see Chapter 9, para 9.7.6]. They submit that, like the managing agents there, the relevant individuals here accepted the plaintiffs under their 'management' and held themselves out as possessing special expertise on which the plaintiffs relied. They emphasise in this connection the importance of Mr Papachristidis and Mr Anderson to the operations of PL and of Mr Dunn to the operations of PSMSL. They point to the recognition of their importance in references in the Red Sea PPM and prospectus to Mr Papachristidis as the founder and owner and to all three as 'key persons' or 'key management personnel'. It should be noted however that the same documents made very clear that the actual contracts for services were to be with PL and PSMSL.

The plaintiffs point out that at first instance in *Henderson v Merrett* Cresswell J held the active underwriter personally responsible in tort for negligence in effecting the syndicate's reinsurance to close. But the circumstances there were that the effecting of such reinsurance was specifically referred to, in explanatory notes to the relevant Lloyd's Byelaw, as 'the responsibility of the managing agent in consultation with the active underwriter' and was recognised in evidence by the active underwriter himself as his 'most important function'. More generally, great caution is required in extrapolating conclusions from as special a relationship as that between a managing agent or active underwriter and an indirect Lloyd's name into the present entirely different situation. Lord Goff himself voiced strong suspicions that the situation which arose in that case was 'most unusual'.

Mance J then referred to the relevant authorities, which are mentioned *above*, and concluded (at p 201):

> Under the CAA and TAA, Red Sea obtained by contract the undertakings of PL and PSMSL, within their respective spheres. Red Sea never at any time sought express collateral undertakings from the personal defendants in respect of their handling of the matters entrusted to PL and PSMSL. Had they done so, it is improbable to suppose that they would have been forthcoming. In the *Williams* case, as I have pointed out, the representations in question related to personal experience outside the scope of the relevant company's activity. Here, the personal liability in negligence sought to be imposed on the individual defendants as officers of PL and/or PSMSL is in respect of matters falling directly within PL's and PSMSL's responsibility under the CAA and/or TAA. Further, although all three principal officers of PL and PSMSL are criticised as negligent, the roles they played did not cover the whole field of PL's and PSMSL's activity. PL and PSMSL undertook a whole range of responsibilities, commercial and operational, managerial and technical, and had a number of employees as well as engaging outside advisers. Although they had overall responsibility for PL and PSMSL, the actual functions of Mr Papachristidis, Mr Anderson and Mr Dunn cannot be regarded, together or *a fortiori* individually, as coterminous or co-extensive with those undertaken by PL and PSMSL.

Plaintiff's missed contractual opportunity

Sometimes it can happen that a contract that the plaintiff had with a third party has been rendered less valuable by virtue of the breach by the defendant of another contract that existed between the third party and the defendant alone. In an action by the plaintiff directly against the defendant for the plaintiff's economic losses in tort caused by the defendant's breach of the defendant's contract with the third party, the plaintiff's contract with the third party will be a factor in deciding whether the defendant should be under a direct duty of care to the plaintiff in tort.

Sometimes in this type of situation the contract between the plaintiff and the third party will not be a bar to the plaintiff's claim against the defendant in tort. An example is *Smith v Eric S Bush* [1990] 1 AC 831 (see Chapter 9, para 9.7.3). That was a case with certain obvious consumer protection implications, and the House of Lords expressly distinguished the position there from the position that might attain in a commercial context. Thus, in some commercial cases involving a chain of contracts, the judges have rejected the plaintiff's claim against the defendant in tort because they have felt that the plaintiff had the opportunity to obtain adequate protection for itself under its contract with the third party and therefore should not be entitled to look to the law of tort to fill in those gaps. The principle that the courts apply is similar to the *dictum* of Lord Brandon in *Leigh & Sillivan Ltd v Aliakmon Shipping Co Ltd* [1986] 1 AC 785, cited *above*.

Examples of the operation of this principle are the Court of Appeal's decisions in *Muirhead v Industrial Tank Specialities Ltd* [1986] 1 QB 507, *Simaan General Contracting Co v Pilkington Glass Ltd (No 2)* [1988] 1 QB 758 and *Greater Nottingham Cooperative Society Ltd v Cementation Piling & Foundations Ltd* [1989] 1 QB 71 (see para 7.3.6). Thus in *Simaan*, in rejecting the plaintiff's direct claim in tort against the defendants who had manufactured the defective glass that the plaintiff had purchased from their main contractor, Bingham LJ said (at p 782):

> Here, the plaintiffs' real complaint is that the defendants' failure to supply goods in conformity with the specification has rendered their main contract less profitable. This is a type of claim against which, if laid in tort, the law has consistently set its face. I do not think it just and reasonable to impose on the defendants a duty of care towards the plaintiffs of the scope contended for. Just as equity remedied the inadequacies of the common law, so has the law of torts filled gaps left by other causes of action where the interests of justice have so required. I see no such gap here, because there is no reason why claims beginning with the Sheikh should not be pursued down the contractual chain, subject to any short-cut which may be agreed upon, ending up with a contractual claim against the defendants. That is the usual procedure. It must be what the parties contemplated when they made their contracts. I see no reason for departing from it.

Dillon LJ, echoing these sentiments, said (at p 785):

> In the present case I can see nothing whatever to justify a finding that the defendants had voluntarily assumed a direct responsibility to the plaintiffs for the colour and quality of the glass panels. On the contrary, all of the indications are the other way, and show that a chain of contractual relationships was deliberately arranged the way it was without any direct relationship between the plaintiffs and the defendants.
>
> If, by contrast [the plaintiff's claim in tort is rejected], there will be the normal chain of liability, in that the Sheikh can sue the plaintiffs on the main building contract, the plaintiffs can sue Feal on the sub-contract and Feal can sue the defendants. Each liability would be determined in the light of such exemptions as applied contractually at that stage. There is thus no warrant for extending the law of negligence to impose direct liability on the defendants in favour of the plaintiffs.

Another example is *MacMillan v A W Knott Becker Scott Ltd* [1990] 1 Lloyd's Rep 98, the facts of which are set out in Chapter 9, para 9.7.6. In rejecting the plaintiff's claim in tort against the defendant brokers, who were negligent in placing insurance to cover the liabilities of a client (another insurance broker) to the plaintiff under a contract which the plaintiff had with that client, Evans J said (at p 110):

> It is the contractual aspect of the defendants' position which in my judgment militates against the plaintiffs' contention that the duty is owed to them. From the legal point of view, they have their claims against the insured brokers, now in liquidation, and the liquidator can recover damages commensurate with the insured brokers' liability from the defendants. If the plaintiffs are correct, then it becomes necessary to decide whether the defendants are liable severally to them and to the liquidator, and whether, if the plaintiffs elect to proceed against the defendants, they are disentitled from pursuing their claims against the liquidator. None of these difficulties is insuperable, but their existence demonstrates the extent to which the plaintiffs' contention would disturb the balance of legal relationships established by the different contracts in this quintessentially commercial context.

These views were adopted by the Court of Appeal of New Zealand in *South Pacific Manufacturing Co Ltd v New Zealand Security Consultants & Investigations Ltd* [1992] 2 NZLR 282, the facts of which are set out in Chapter 7, para 7.6.2. One of the Court's reasons for rejecting the plaintiff's economic loss claim in tort was that the Court felt that, the plaintiff having made a contract with the insurer, the plaintiff should be confined to his contractual remedy under that contract and should not be entitled to look to the law of tort to provide redress. Thus, Cooke P, after stating (at p 301) that Bingham LJ's above-cited *dictum* in *Simaan* was convincing to him, said (at p 303): "The insured has his ordinary remedy against the insurer if liability is wrongly declined as a result of a report by investigators. The proper vehicle for determining responsibility for the fire is a proceeding between insured and insurer. Such a proceeding provides the insured with a reasonable, if not an entirely comprehensive remedy"; and Richardson J said (at p 308):

> If the insured have a remedy in contract against the insurer, they should exercise that remedy. If they do not have an adequate remedy, that is because they only paid a premium which gave them that lesser protection. In that situation I cannot see any justification for allowing them greater recovery through tort than they were prepared to pay for in contract.
>
> The second contract is between the insurer and the investigator. There too, the parties have their expressly or impliedly agreed remedies for any negligence in the performance of the contract. Those were the respective bargains that the parties made. Tort theory should remain consistent with contract policies. In public policy terms, I consider that where, as here, contracts cover the two relationships, those contracts should ordinarily control the allocation of risk unless special reasons are established to warrant a direct suit in tort. That accords too with *Simaan General Contracting Co v Pilkington Glass Ltd (No 2)* [1988] QB 758 where, for policy reasons, the English Court of Appeal concluded that any claims of A (Simaan) against B (Feal) and by B against C (Pilkington) could and should be pursued down the contractual chain and that there was no warrant extending the law of negligence to impose direct liability in tort on C in favour

of A. No special factors such as those discussed in *Smith v Eric S Bush* [1990] 1 AC 831 have been advanced in this case.

In *Henderson v Merrett Syndicates Ltd* [1995] 2 AC 145, the facts of which are set out in Chapter 9, para 9.7.6 and para 10.4.2, the managing agents' counsel submitted that no duty of care in tort should exist between the Indirect Names and the managing agents because both of them, as parties to the chain of contracts contained in the relevant agency and sub-agency agreements, must be taken to have thereby structured their relationship so as to exclude any duty of care owed directly by the managing agents to the Indirect Names in tort. In rejecting this submission Lord Goff, with whose speech all of the other Law Lords agreed, said (at p 195):

> In essence, the argument must be that, because the managing agents have, with the consent of the indirect Names, assumed responsibility in respect of the relevant activities to another party, ie, the members' agents, under a sub-agency agreement, it would be inconsistent to hold that they have also assumed responsibility in respect of the same activities to the indirect Names. I for my part cannot see why in principle a party should not assume responsibility to more than one person in respect of the same activity. Let it be assumed (unlikely though it may be) that, in the present case, the managing agents were in a contractual relationship not only with the members' agents under a sub-agency agreement but also directly with the relevant Names, under both of which they assumed responsibility for the same activities. I can see no reason in principle why the two duties of care so arising should not be capable of co-existing.
>
> Of course I recognise that the present case presents the unusual feature that claims against the managing agents, whether by the members' agents under the sub-agency agreement or by the indirect Names in tort, will in both cases have the purpose, immediate or ultimate, of obtaining compensation for the indirect Names. In these circumstances, concurrent duties of care could, in theory at least, give rise to problems, for example, in the event of the insolvency of the managing agents or the members' agents. Furthermore . . . questions of contribution might, at least in theory, arise. But your Lordships' task, like that of the courts below, is to answer the questions of principle raised by the issues presented for decision; and in these circumstances it would be quite wrong to embark upon the examination of questions which do not arise on those issues, and indeed may never arise in practice. For myself, I am all the more reluctant to do so since, because the liability (if any) of the managing agents will in each case flow from claims by the indirect Names, it may well be that practical problems such as these will, if they arise, find a practical solution.

Ironically, Lord Goff, after saying that he only wished to answer the questions of principle raised by the issues presented for decision, went on to consider and express a strong opinion about an issue that really did have nothing to do with the *Henderson* case, namely, the liability of a sub-contractor in tort for economic loss caused to the main contractor's employer by the sub-contractor's negligence. He said (at p 195) (emphasis added):

> I wish however to add that I strongly suspect that the situation which arises in the present case is most unusual; and that in many cases in which a contractual

chain comparable to that in the present case is constructed it may well prove to be inconsistent with an assumption of responsibility which has the effect of, so to speak, short circuiting the contractual structure so put in place by the parties. It cannot therefore be inferred from the present case that other sub-agents will be held directly liable to the agent's principal in tort. Let me take the analogy of the common case of an ordinary building contract, under which main contractors contract with the building owner for the construction of the relevant building and the main contractor sub-contracts with sub-contractors or suppliers (often nominated by the building owner) for the performance of work or the supply of materials in accordance with standards and subject to terms established in the sub-contract. I put on one side cases in which the sub-contractor causes physical damage to the property of the building owner, where the claim does not depend on an assumption of responsibility by the sub-contractor to the building owner; though the sub-contractor may be protected from liability by a contractual exemption clause authorised by the building owner. But if the sub-contracted work or materials do not in the result conform to the required standard, it will not ordinarily be open to the building owner to sue the sub-contractor or supplier direct under the *Hedley Byrne* principle, claiming damages from him on the basis that he has been negligent in relation to the performance of his functions. For there is generally no assumption of responsibility by the sub-contractor or supplier direct to the building owner, the parties having so structured their relationship that it is inconsistent with any such assumption of responsibility. This was the conclusion of the Court of Appeal in *Simaan General Contracting Co v Pilkington Glass Ltd (No 2)* [1988] QB 758. As Bingham LJ put it (at p 781):

> I do not, however, see any basis on which [the nominated suppliers] could be said to have assumed a direct responsibility for the quality of the goods to [the building owners]: such a responsibility is, I think, inconsistent with the *structure* of the contract the parties have chosen to make.

It is true that, in this connection, some difficulty has been created by the decision of your Lordships' House in *Junior Books Ltd v Veitchi Co Ltd* [1983] 1 AC 520. In my opinion, however, it is unnecessary for your Lordships to reconsider this decision for the purposes of the present appeal. Here, however, I can see no inconsistency between the assumption of responsibility by the managing agents to the indirect Names, and that which arises under the sub-agency agreement between the managing agents and the members' agents, whether viewed in isolation or as part of the contractual chain stretching back to and so including the indirect Names. For these reasons, I can see no reason why the indirect Names should not be free to pursue their remedy against the managing agents in tort under the *Hedley Byrne* principle.

Their Lordships were thus clearly troubled by the fact that if they were to impose liability on the managing agents to the Indirect Names, the case for imposing duties of care in tort on sub-contractors in building cases would become stronger. However, it is submitted that the way in which their Lordships sought to distinguish the two types of situation is confusing. It is not clear whether their rationale for making this distinction is based on the mere *existence* of the tripartite contractual structure in the building sphere, or on the inconsistency in the actual *content* of the contracts entered into by the sub-contractor and the main contractor on the one hand, and between the employer/developer and the main contractor on the other hand.

Bingham LJ's point in *Simaan* was that the mere *existence* of the tri-partite contractual *structure* in and of itself prevented the creation of a duty of care in tort by the defendant (a manufacturer of glass) towards the plaintiff for the economic loss suffered by the plaintiff when the glass became discoloured after being installed in the plaintiff's palace, notwith-standing that such discoloration occurred through the defendant's negli-gence. Lord Goff, on the other hand, focused on the *content* of the contract that existed between the defendants (the managing agents) and the third party (the members' agents) and concluded that the contractual structure erected between the Indirect Names and the members' agents on the one hand, and the members' agents and the managing agents on the other, did not inhibit the Indirect Names from pursuing their economic loss claims directly against the managing agents because the content of the managing agents' contractual duty to the members' agents was not inconsistent with the scope of the duty which the managing agents had assumed to the Indirect Names in tort.

It is submitted that Lord Goff's approach is more satisfactory. However, we are left without any explanation as to why, even on Lord Goff's approach, an inconsistency existed in *Simaan* and other similar cases con-sidered in Chapter 7 between the duty of care assumed in contract by the defendant (a manufacturer of a product or a builder of a building) to the third party who engaged the defendant to create that object or building, and the responsibilities assumed by such manufacturer or builder in tort to the person whom the manufacturer or builder knows will acquire the chattel or building from the third party without making an intermediate inspection.

A good example is the purchase by a consumer of a new car from a dealer. If the car is defective and needs to be repaired or discarded, the con-sumer cannot recover this economic cost from the manufacturer (para 7.5.3). In Lord Goff's terms, the reason for this is that the manufacturer will not have assumed responsibility to the consumer for such defects. It is sub-mitted that this reasoning is difficult to comprehend in the typical case of the purchase of a car, where almost all of the information conveyed to the consumer about the quality, performance and reliability of the car is pro-vided by the manufacturer, in the form of advertising and publicity materi-als, with the intent that it should be relied upon by the consumer in purchasing the car. Why is it that, in these circumstances, the manufacturer will be treated as having assumed a responsibility for the quality of its cars only to the dealers to whom it sells those cars directly, but not also to the ultimate consumers who purchase those same cars in reliance on the information that the manufacturer has provided to them about the quality of those cars with the intent that they should so rely?

Lord Goff's views in *Henderson v Merrett* were adopted by the Court of Appeal of New Zealand in *Invercargill City Council v Hamlin* [1994] 3 NZLR 513, where Cooke P, after referring to the House of Lords' decision in *Junior Books Ltd v Veitchi Co Ltd* [1983] 1 AC 520 (see Chapter 7, para 7.3.6), said (at p 520):

> I would interpolate that in this court we have not had to consider a similar case. Following the general New Zealand approach to duty of care questions, restated in *South Pacific Manufacturing Co Ltd v New Zealand Security Consultants and Investigations Ltd* [see *above*], it would be open to us to hold that in such a case of industrial construction, the network of contractual relationships normally supplies sufficient avenues of redress to make the imposition of supervening tort duties not demanded. It might be said, in the words of Lord Goff in *Henderson v Merrett Syndicates Ltd* [1995] 2 AC 145 [see *above*], that there is no assumption of responsibility by the sub-contractor or supplier direct to the building owner, the parties having so structured their relationship that it is inconsistent with any assumption of responsibility.

Caveat emptor

It is trite law that the maxim *caveat emptor* describes the legal principle that, in the absence of an express warranty in a contract of sale, and apart from deliberate concealment or the operation of any particular statutory provisions, the risk of the quality or condition of the subject matter of the sale resides with the purchaser. In cases of pure economic loss consisting of the diminution in value of the product or building that the plaintiff has purchased from a third party, the question sometimes arises whether the defendant manufacturer or builder, who was not the person from whom the plaintiff made his purchase, is entitled to escape liability because, by virtue of the applicability of the *caveat emptor* doctrine to the contract of sale between the plaintiff and the third party, the plaintiff assumed the risk of diminution in value of the property through defects that might materialise only after the conclusion of the sale; and the defects were caused by the manufacturer or builder's negligence in manufacturing the product or constructing the building.

This question arose squarely in *Winnipeg Condominium Corporation No 36 v Bird Construction Co* (1995) 121 DLR (4th) 193, the facts of which are set out in Chapter 7, para 7.6.3. Here, the purchaser had bought the building from the original owner without seeking or obtaining any warranty about the condition of the building, with the result that the *caveat emptor* maxim applied as between the purchaser and its vendor.

When the purchaser (the plaintiff) sued the original builder (the defendant) for the cost of making good defects in the building that materialised after the purchase, one of the defendant's arguments was that no liability should attach to the defendant because, although the *caveat emptor* principle strictly operates only between a vendor and his purchaser, the very existence of the principle instructs the potential purchaser to rely on his own investigations, inspections and inquiries; and further instructs the potential purchaser that if he seeks greater protection than would be provided by his own investigations, inspections and inquiries, he should seek appropriate warranties from the vendor or, if those cannot be obtained, he should obtain insurance to cover anticipated future risks.

10.2.1 *The contractual connection*

The Supreme Court of Canada unanimously rejected this defence. La Forest J, speaking for the Court, said (at p 220):

> The assumption underlying the doctrine is that the purchaser of a building is better placed than the seller or builder to inspect the building and to bear the risk that latent defects will emerge, necessitating repair costs. However, in my view this is an assumption which (if ever valid) is simply not responsive to the realities of the modern housing market. In *Lempke v Dagenais* (1988) 547A (2d) 290 [see para 7.6.1] the Supreme Court of New Hampshire made reference to a number of policy factors that strongly militate against the rigid application of the doctrine of *caveat emptor* with regard to tort claims for construction defects, such as:
>
> > Third, like an initial buyer, a subsequent purchaser has little opportunity to inspect and little experience and knowledge about construction. Consumer protection demands that those who buy homes are entitled to rely on the skill of a builder and that the house is constructed so as to be reasonably fit for its intended use;
> > Fourth, the builder/contractor will not be unduly taken unaware by the extension of his warranty [to the original purchaser] to a subsequent purchaser;
> > Fifth, arbitrarily interposing a first purchaser as a bar to recovery might encourage sham first sales to insulate builders from liability.
>
> Furthermore, contractors and builders, because of their knowledge, skill and expertise, are in the best position to ensure the reasonable structural integrity of buildings and their freedom from latent defects. In this respect, the imposition of liability on builders provides an important incentive for care in the construction of buildings and a deterrent against poor workmanship.

For these reasons, the Supreme Court of Canada held that even if, as between the purchaser and its vendor, the purchaser had waived its right to sue its vendor for losses occasioned through defects in the building materialising after the purchase, that waiver could not be set up as a defence by the defendant builder when sued in tort by the purchaser for the purchaser's economic loss consisting of the cost of making good these latent defects.

It is submitted that, on the facts of *Winnipeg Condominium*, the Supreme Court of Canada was correct in so holding. This is because, in this type of case, the defendant's liability should depend on whether, in all the circumstances, the defect in question was of such a nature that it could reasonably have been expected to have been discovered by the plaintiff upon an intermediate inspection of the property carried out by the plaintiff. If the defect was of such a nature that it could not reasonably have been expected to have been discovered on such an inspection (for example, the hidden defects in the foundations in *Murphy v Brentwood District Council* [1991] 1 AC 398: see Chapter 7), the defendant should be held liable even if it was reasonable to expect the plaintiff to have made such an inspection. This principle was in fact recognised and applied by La Forest J in *Winnipeg Condominium*, when he said (at p 220):

> My conclusion that a subsequent purchaser is not the best placed to bear the risk of the emergence of latent defects is borne out by the facts of this case. It is sig-

nificant that, when cracking first appeared in the mortar of the building in 1982, the Condominium Corporation actually hired the original architect of the building, along with a firm of structural engineers, to assess the condition of the mortar work and the exterior cladding. These experts failed to detect the latent defects that appear to have caused the cladding to fall in 1989.

This reasoning accords with the principles set out *above* on which it is submitted liability should be founded in cases in this category.

10.2.2 Contract between defendant and third party

The comments in this section should be read in conjunction with the comments in the sub-section 'Plaintiff's missed contractual opportunity' in para 10.2.1, *above*, because the issues overlap in many instances, such as *Henderson v Merrett Syndicates Ltd* [1995] 2 AC 205. Lord Goff's above-cited comments on the contractual connection apply equally to the factual matrix of the cases considered in this section.

Product liability—physical injury and property damage

In Chapter 6, para 6.2.2 it is noted that, prior to the House of Lords' decision in *Donoghue v Stevenson* [1932] AC 562, there was a general exclusionary rule which prevented a plaintiff from recovering damages from a defendant in tort for injuries sustained by him from a defective chattel which the defendant had manufactured or put into circulation, where the defendant had done so by way of a contract with a third party, and the plaintiff had then acquired the defective chattel either from the third party or from someone else in the chain of distribution. This rule was said to be based on the sanctity of the principle of privity of contract, whereby if A (the manufacturer) and B (the distributor) made a contract between themselves, then C (the plaintiff), who is not a party to it, cannot have any rights under it (see, for example, *Winterbottom v Wright* (1842) 10 M & W 109 and *Blacker v Lake and Elliot Ltd* (1912) 106 LT 533, which are discussed in Chapter 6, para 6.2.4). It was said that this did not work an injustice on the plaintiff, who would have, and should be confined to, his remedy in contract against his immediate seller. Of course, this presumed that the plaintiff would necessarily have had such a contract or that his immediate seller would have been worth suing. *Donoghue* is an example of a case where the plaintiff was not able to sue anyone in contract for her injuries, because the plaintiff's friend and not the plaintiff herself had actually bought the bottle of ginger beer from the café owner.

To have denied the plaintiff in *Donoghue* a cause of action against the negligent manufacturer in these circumstances would obviously have been unjust. The three majority Law Lords fully recognised this and, accordingly, held in the plaintiff's favour. In so doing they abrogated the general exclusionary rule that had powerfully held sway for 90 years since *Winterbottom v Wright* had been decided in 1842. No longer would the existence of a prior contract between the defendant and a third party be a bar to the plaintiff suing the defendant for his damages in these circumstances—at least where the plaintiff's loss consisted of physical injury to himself or damage to his property (see *below*). Lord Atkin, who gave the leading speech, recognised the importance of the decision when he said (at p 579): "I do not think a more important problem has occupied your Lordships in your judicial capacity".

In addition to the doctrinal justification for the existence of the general exclusionary rule, its proponents, such as the judges in *Winterbottom* (see Chapter 6, para 6.2.4), felt that its relaxation would open the floodgates to an uncontrollable number of claims against defendants. The court by its decision approved a submission by the defendant's counsel that "if the plaintiff may run through three contracts, as here, he may run through any number, and enormous and frightful consequences would ensue; for instance, in the recent accident on the Versailles Railway, every person injured might sue the manufacturer of the defective axle". After the House of Lords' decision in *Donoghue* in 1932, this fear, which was so influential in 1842 and in the intervening years, was no longer regarded as a justification for denying relief to plaintiffs in this type of case.

Product liability—pure economic loss

In more recent times the question has arisen whether the relaxation of the general exclusionary rule in *Donoghue* applies only where the plaintiff has suffered a personal injury or damage to his property, or also extends to pure economic loss suffered by the plaintiff in these circumstances. As noted in Chapter 1, para 1.2.2 in this context, the law characterises damage to the defectively manufactured chattel itself as pure economic loss. In other words, the question is whether a plaintiff who suffers pure economic loss consisting in the diminution in value of a defectively manufactured chattel (or a defectively constructed building) can recover damages in tort from the defendant who was responsible for creating the defects.

As noted in Chapter 7, para 7.3.6, the answer to this question will be in the negative, unless the plaintiff is able to establish, on the particular facts of the case, a "special relationship between himself and the defendant, based on the *Hedley Byrne* doctrine of reliance" (*per* the House of Lords in *Murphy v Brentwood District Council* [1991] 1 AC 398—see Chapter 7). In practice, this principle will so rarely be satisfied that it will effectively amount to a reincarnation of the previously existing general exclusionary rule which was abolished by the House of Lords in *Donoghue*. The House of Lords is fully aware of this and is content with the position. Indeed, part of the rationale for this restrictive approach is that their Lordships believe that a plaintiff's claim for his economic loss in these circumstances, being a claim for a defect in the quality of the defective chattel or building, lies more properly in contract against his immediate vendor than against the negligent manufacturer or builder with whom he did not have a contractual relationship.

In *Junior Books Ltd v Veitchi Co Ltd* [1983] AC 520 (see Chapter 7, para 7.3.6), the question was whether a manufacturer's duty of care in tort extended to a duty to avoid defects being present in the defectively created item itself. Lord Roskill noted (at p 454) that it was urged on behalf of the defendant that, were their Lordships to hold the defendant liable (which their Lordships did do—see para 7.3.6), a plaintiff in the position of the plaintiff in *Donoghue v Stevenson*, in addition to recovering for any personal injuries suffered, could also have recovered for the diminished value of the offending bottle of ginger beer. The defendant argued that any remedy of that kind must lie in contract, and not in tort. In rejecting this argument, Lord Roskill said:

> I seem to detect in that argument reflections of the previous judicial approach to comparable problems before *Donoghue* was decided. That approach usually resulted in the conclusion that in principle the proper remedy lay in contract, and not outside it. But that approach and its concomitant philosophy ended in 1932 and, for my part, I should be reluctant to countenance its re-emergence some fifty years later in the instant case.

In *Murphy* the House of Lords (in 1990), by confining the applicable principle in the manner described *above*, has effectively not only countenanced the re-emergence of this principle, but has also strongly endorsed it; as did the Court of Appeal in three earlier important economic loss cases in the same category as *Murphy*, namely, diminution in value of a defectively manufactured product or defectively constructed building. These other cases are *Muirhead v Industrial Tank Specialities Ltd* [1986] 1 QB 507, *Simaan General Contracting Co v Pilkington Glass Ltd (No 2)* [1988] 1 QB 758 and *Greater Nottingham Cooperative Society Ltd v Cementation Piling & Foundations Ltd* [1989] 1 QB 71 (see Chapter 7, para 7.3.6). In these cases, not only was there a contract between the defendant and a third party, but there was also a contract between the plaintiff and the third party. This latter fact seems to have been more influential in the Court's rejection of the plaintiff's claim than the contract between the defendant and the third party. Therefore the effect of the underlying contracts in these cases is more fully discussed in para 10.2.1, *above*.

Again, in addition to the doctrinal objection (ie that, as the plaintiff's claim is effectively a claim for compensation for the defective quality of a chattel or building, it should be brought in contract against his immediate vendor, and not in tort against the manufacturer or builder with whom he did not have a contract), the floodgates argument is also invoked by the proponents of this general exclusionary rule. As noted in Chapters 1, 4 and 7, the floodgates argument has two strands. The first is that administratively the courts would be flooded with an uncontrollable number of claims, some of them dubious (see Chapter 4, para 4.5.5), if relief were to be granted to all those who have suffered pure economic loss in consequence of the defendant's negligent act or omission; and the second, that the granting of such relief would expose a defendant to liability "in an indeterminate amount from an indeterminate class for an indeterminate time".

With regard to the first of these concerns, Lord Roskill said in *Junior Books* (at p 539): "The floodgates argument is very familiar. It still may, on occasion, have its proper place, but if principle suggests that the law should develop along a particular route, and if the adoption of that particular route will accord a remedy where that remedy has hitherto been denied, I see no reason why, if it be just that the law should henceforth accord that remedy, it should be denied simply because it will become available to many rather than to few"; and (at p 545): "The history of the development of the law in the last 50 years shows that fears aroused by the floodgates argument have been unfounded". As pointed out in Chapter 7, para 7.6.1, the 'indeterminate liability strand' of the floodgates fear simply does not exist in this type of case.

Thus, whilst the general denial of relief to a plaintiff in this type of case does not specifically depend on the fact that a prior contract existed between the defendant and a third party, the general exclusionary rule which now exists is nevertheless contract-related, in that the courts have said that as the plaintiff's claim for the diminution in value of a defectively manufactured chattel or a defectively constructed building essentially amounts to a claim for compensation for a defect in quality of the item in question, it lies more properly in contract against the plaintiff's immediate vendor than in tort against the negligent manufacturer or builder with whom the plaintiff did not have a contractual relationship. Unfortunately, this reasoning fails to take account of the fact that, in practice, the plaintiff will very often not be able to bring such a claim against his immediate vendor because of that party's insolvency; and in relation to the sale of buildings, the plaintiff will not have such a claim in any event because of the application of the *caveat emptor* rule.

Negligent misstatement

In many of the cases considered in Chapter 9, para 9.1.1, where the plaintiff suffered pure economic loss through having relied on a negligent statement made by the defendant, that statement would initially have been made by the defendant to a third party under the terms of a contract between the defendant and that third party. Typical examples are the accountants' and the surveyors' negligence cases, in which the accountant or the surveyor will have prepared their reports for the company whose books were being audited or for the building society from whom the plaintiff wished to obtain a mortgage, by way of a contract between those institutions and the accountant or the surveyor. The plaintiff, in placing reliance on the accountant's or the surveyor's report, will normally not have had a contract with anyone in this situation. Therefore, unlike the product liability cases, it would not make any sense to say that the plaintiff must be confined to his remedies in contract. Accordingly, in this type of case, the mere fact that there 'existed' a prior contract between the defendant and a third party for the provision of the information in question is not relevant. Sometimes, however, the 'terms' of such a contract might be relevant in determining whether the defendant owed the plaintiff a duty of care in respect of the losses incurred by the plaintiff by relying on the statement. This point is considered further *below* in para 10.3.

10.2.3 Contract between plaintiff and defendant

Sometimes it might happen that there was a prior existing contract between the plaintiff and the defendant, but the plaintiff's cause of action is founded in tort, perhaps because the defendant's negligent act or omission which caused the plaintiff's loss was not provided for in the contract, or because the plaintiff's action is statute-barred in contract but not in tort, or because the measure of damages in tort might be greater than in contract. The question then arises as to whether the plaintiff is entitled to have the benefit of the tort remedy in these circumstances, or whether he must be confined to the remedies which he agreed to accept in his contract. This is known as the problem of 'concurrent liability'. As it is a large topic in its own right, and as it raises a number of different issues, it is considered separately (see para 10.4).

10.3 Exemption clauses

10.3.1 Introduction

It has been noted *above* that except possibly in the category of cases considered under the heading *Product liability—pure economic loss* (para 10.2.2) the mere 'existence' as such of a contract between the plaintiff and a third party or between the defendant and a third party does not debar the plaintiff from suing the defendant in tort for his losses which resulted from the defendant's negligent act or omission. However, the actual 'terms' of any such contract might be relevant, particularly where those terms purport to limit the extent of the defendant's liability for his negligence. Usually, the defendant will have been a party to the contract containing the exemption clauses (as in *Smith v Eric S Bush*—see para 10.3.4, *below*), but sometimes only the plaintiff and the third party will have been parties to such a contract, as in *Pacific Associates v Baxter* [1990] 1 QB 993 (discussed *below*, para 10.3.3), or as in *Norwich City Council v Harvey* [1989] 1 WLR 828. The difference between these cases is that in *Norwich* the plaintiff waived his rights against the third party, whereas in *Pacific Associates* the plaintiff waived his rights against the defendant.

10.3.2 Waiver of rights by plaintiff against third party in third party contract

Some of the cases which fall under this heading have already been considered in para 10.2.1. These are *Norwich City Council v Harvey* [1989] 1 WLR 828, *Marc Rich & Co AG v Bishop Rock Marine Co Ltd ('The Nicholas H')* [1996] 1 AC 211, and *British Telecommunications plc v James Thomson and Sons (Engineers) Ltd* (1996) 49 Con LR 163.

In all of those cases, the plaintiff had, in its contract with a third party, agreed to bear the risk of a certain event materialising. When the event occurred and the plaintiff was prevented from suing the third party for that loss, the plaintiff sought to recover it from the defendant in tort on the ground that the defendant, whose negligence caused the event to occur, owed a duty of care to the plaintiff in respect of the plaintiff's loss. In all three of these cases, the plaintiff's claim against the defendant failed because the courts felt that, in all of the circumstances of each case, the plaintiff's assumption of the risk in its contract with the third party was an important factor in rendering it not fair, just and reasonable to impose a duty of care on the defendant in tort for the plaintiff's loss.

Some criticism has been made *above* of the House of Lords' decision in *Marc Rich* for the same reasons as were advanced by Lord Lloyd in his dissenting speech. On the other hand, it is felt that the courts' decisions in the *Norwich* and the *British Telecom* cases are correct. The difference, it is submitted, is that in the latter cases the plaintiff expressly knew and intended that part of the works were to be sub-contracted; and the plaintiff contracted expressly on the basis that the plaintiff would obtain insurance to cover the possibility of one or more of the prescribed perils being caused by an act or omission of the sub-contractor. In turn, the sub-contractor was aware of this and reasonably relied on this contractual provision as being a representation that the sub-contractor did not have to obtain its own insurance against the risk of those perils materialising through the sub-contractor's negligence. The situation was thus similar to a 'duty of care in reverse' owed by the plaintiff to the sub-contractor. The plaintiff knew that this representation would be communicated to the sub-contractor specifically in connection with a particular transaction (the sub-contract works) and that the sub-contractor would be very likely to rely on it for the purpose of deciding whether or not to enter upon that transaction (ie whether or not to obtain insurance itself) (using the concepts articulated by Lord Bridge in *Caparo Industries plc v Dickman* [1990] 2 AC 605; see Chapter 9, para 9.6.2).

In these circumstances it is submitted that in the *Norwich* and *British Telecom* cases it was fair, just and reasonable for the defendants to rely on the plaintiffs' representation as to the risk which the plaintiffs accepted. By way of contrast, it is submitted that this conclusion cannot be drawn on the facts of the *Marc Rich* case. There was no indication that the plaintiff's agreement with the shipowner to limit a claim for the loss of its cargo to US$500,000 would be communicated to the classification society in connection with a particular transaction (ie whether or not to obtain insurance to cover the possibility of a claim being made against it by the plaintiff for the plaintiff's losses in excess of US$500,000). The representation flowing to the classification society from that waiver provision was, at best, equivocal; but taken literally, all that it meant was that the plaintiff had agreed to limit its damages claim against *the third party* to US$500,000, so that everyone else, including the classification society, should be on their guard that the plaintiff might look to them for compensation for losses in excess of US$500,000. In these circumstances, it is submitted that it was not fair, just and reasonable to allow the classification society to take advantage of the limitation provision in the contract between the plaintiff and the shipowner.

Other cases in which this type of question has arisen are considered *below*.

London Drugs Ltd v Kuehne and Nagel International Ltd (1992) 97 DLR (4th) 261: The facts of this case are set out in para 10.2.1, where it was noted that in the Supreme Court of Canada the questions were, first, whether the employees who had dropped the plaintiff's transformer owed a duty of care to the plaintiff in tort; and, secondly, if they did, whether they could take advantage of the clause in the contract between the plaintiff and their employer (K&N), whereby the plaintiffs agreed that K&N's liability on any one package was limited to $40 unless the plaintiff declared in writing a valuation in excess of $40 and paid the additional charge specified to cover warehouse liability, which the plaintiff declined to do.

As noted *above*, the court answered the first question in the affirmative, thereby requiring the second question also to be addressed. Three different answers were given by the six-member panel. Writing for four of the judges, Iacobucci J said (at p 340):

> In my opinion, it is unnecessary to embark upon the type of tort analysis suggested by the employees in order to arrive at the result that justice mandates in this case. I believe that a more direct approach is both available and preferable. The employees are seeking the benefit of s 11(b) of the contract of storage between their employer and the plaintiff in order to limit the liability that would otherwise attach to their breach of duty. The main obstacle to the employees' claim is the doctrine of privity of contract. For my part, I prefer to deal head-on with the doctrine of privity and to relax its ambit in the circumstances of this case. Some may argue that the same result can (and should) be reached by using a number of approaches which are seemingly less drastic and/or allegedly more theoretically sound, such as the 'no duty' approach advocated by my colleague, La Forest J (see *below*).
>
> This is both the time and the case for a judicial reconsideration of the rule regarding privity of contract as applied to employers' contractual limitation of liability clauses. In my view, the employees were third party beneficiaries to the limitation of liability clause found in the contract of storage between their employer and the plaintiff and, in view of the circumstances involved, may benefit directly from this clause notwithstanding that they are not a signing party to the contract.

In holding that the employees in this case were entitled to the benefit of the $40 exclusion clause in the contract between K&N and the plaintiff, it is not clear whether Iacobucci J intended to confine his reasoning to employees or intended it to apply in a wider sphere if the criteria which he mentioned were satisfied. He said (at p 360):

> There are very few principled reasons for upholding the doctrine of privity in the circumstances of this case. The most that can be said against the extension of the exceptions to the doctrine of privity in this case is that the employees are mere donees and have provided no consideration for the contractual limitation of liability.
>
> The doctrine of privity fails to appreciate the special considerations which arise from the relationships of employer–employee and employer–customer.

There is clearly an identity of interest between the employer and his or her employees as far as the performance of the employer's contractual obligations is concerned. When a person contracts with an employer for certain services, there can be little doubt in most cases that employees will have the prime responsibilities related to the performance of the obligations which arise under the contract. This was the case in the present appeal, clearly to the knowledge of the plaintiff. While such a similarity or closeness might not be present when an employer performs his or her obligations *through* someone who is not an employee, it is virtually always present when employees are involved. Of course, I am in no way suggesting that employees are a party to their employer's contracts in the traditional sense so that they can bring an action on the contract or be sued for breach of contract. However, when an employer and a customer enter into a contract for services and include a clause limiting the liability of the employer for damages arising from what will normally be conduct contemplated by the contracting parties to be performed by the employer's employees, and in fact so performed, there is simply no valid reason for denying the benefit of the clause to employees who perform the contractual obligations. The nature and scope of the limitation of liability clause in such a case coincides essentially with the nature and scope of the contractual obligations performed by the third party beneficiaries (employees).

In a similar fashion, it would be absurd in the circumstances of this case to let the plaintiff go around the limitation of liability clause by suing the employees in tort. The plaintiff consented to limit the 'warehouseman's' liability to $40 for anything that would happen during the performance of the contract. When the loss occurred, the employees were acting in the course of their employment and performing the very services, albeit negligently, for which the plaintiff had contracted with Kuehne & Nagel. The plaintiff cannot obtain more than $40 from Kuehne & Nagel, whether the action is based in contract or in tort, because of the limitation of liability clause. However, resorting to exactly the same actions, it is trying to obtain the full amount from the individuals ('warehousemen') who were directly responsible for the storing of its goods in accordance with the contract. As stated earlier, there is an identity of interest between the employees and Kuehne & Nagel as far as performance of the latter's contractual obligations is concerned. When these facts are taken into account, and it is recalled that the plaintiff knew the role to be played by employees pursuant to the contract, it is clear to me that this court is witnessing an attempt in effect to circumvent or escape a contractual exclusion or limitation of liability for the act or omission that would constitute the tort. In my view, we should not sanction such an endeavour in the name of privity of contract.

Finally, there are sound policy reasons why the doctrine of privity should be relaxed in the circumstances of this case. A clause such as one in a contract of storage limiting the liability of a 'warehouseman' to $40 in the absence of a declaration by the owner of the goods of their value and the payment of an additional insurance fee makes perfect commercial sense. It enables the contracting parties to allocate the risk of damage to the goods and to procure insurance accordingly. If the owner declares the value of the goods, which he alone knows, and pays the additional premium, the bargain will have placed the entire risk on the shoulders of the 'warehouseman'. On the other hand, if the owner refuses the offer of additional coverage, the bargain will have placed only a limited risk on the 'warehouseman' and the owner will be left with the burden of procuring private insurance if it decides to diminish its own risk. In either scenario, the parties to the contract agree to a certain allocation and then proceed, based on this agreement, to make additional insurance arrangements if required. It stretches commercial credulity to suggest that a customer, acting prudently, will not obtain insurance because he or she is looking to the employees for recovery when generally little or nothing is known about the financial capacity and professional skills of the employees involved. That does not make sense in the modern world.

In addition, employees such as the respondents do not reasonably expect to be subject to unlimited liability for damages that occur in the performance of the contract when the said contract specifically limits the liability of the 'warehouseman' to a fixed amount. According to modern commercial practice, an employer such as Kuehne & Nagel performs its contractual obligations with a party such as the appellant *through* its employees. As far as the contractual obligations are concerned, there is an identity of interest between the employer and the employees. It simply does not make commercial sense to hold that the term 'warehouseman' was not intended to cover the employees and as a result to deny them the benefit of the limitation of liability clause for a loss which occurred during the performance of the very services contracted for.

McLachlin J agreed that the employees' liability to the plaintiff should be limited to \$40, but she disagreed with Iacobucci J's reasoning. She said (at p 320):

> The analysis in this case, as I see it, must start from the self-evident proposition that tort and contract constitute separate legal regimes. The plaintiff's action against the employees in this case is necessarily in tort, since there was no contract between it and the employees. The defendants, however, seek to rely on the terms of the contract between the plaintiff and their employer as a defence. The question is whether they can do this, and if so, on what basis.
>
> Several theories for permitting an employee sued in tort to rely on a term of limitation in his employer's contract have been suggested. The most salient is the assertion that the plaintiff voluntarily accepted the risk of damage over the amount specified in the limitation clause. On this theory, the plaintiff, having agreed to the limitation of liability *vis-à-vis* the employer, must be taken to have done so with respect to the employer's employees.
>
> The first problem in Iacobucci J's approach is whether the defendants, who were not parties to the contract, can rely on the contract at all. In the past, the doctrine of privity of contract has said no. Iacobucci J says this should no longer be a bar; I agree.
>
> But there is a second problem. This arises from the fact that the contract term, even if it can be raised as a defence by the employees, does not *by its content* provide the employees with a defence. The contract exempts only the 'warehouseman'. The term 'warehouseman' is not defined in the contract. But in my respectful view, upon a reading of the contract as a whole, the only reasonable interpretation is that the term 'warehouseman' refers to the employer and does not include the employees.
>
> One way of overcoming this difficulty would be through the doctrine of implied terms. It might be argued that where a customer and an employer contract for a limitation of liability in circumstances where they know that the work will be done by the employer's employees, it is an implied term of that contract

that the plaintiff accepts the risk of the employees' negligence as well, with the consequence that the employees may raise the defence of *volenti* against the plaintiff.

The supposition of an implied term to exempt the employees from liability on this case runs up against the problem that there is nothing to suggest that the parties intended the word 'warehouseman', which defines whose liability is exempted, to include the employees. With all respect to Iacobucci J's apparent finding to the contrary, the conclusion that the parties intended 'warehouseman' to include employees is of doubtful validity, given the absence of evidence on the matter and the fact that elsewhere in the contract a 'warehouseman' can only be read as not extending to employees.

McLachlin J felt that the answer to this problem lay in the fact that the presumed intention of the parties is only one of the grounds on which an implied term may be founded. Another is that a court "where appropriate, may as a matter of policy imply a term in a particular type of contract, even where it is clear that the parties did not intend it". She continued from this point on by saying (at p 322):

> This would seem to me to afford a sufficient foundation for Iacobucci J's conclusion that the contract exemption should afford a defence to the employees. It might be argued that *as a matter of policy* the courts should imply a term in warehousing contracts that 'warehouseman' includes the employees of the warehouse for purposes of contractual limitations of liability. This in turn would permit the conclusion that the plaintiff, by entering into such a contract, waived its right to sue the employees for damage beyond $40. This approach does, however, raise the difficult question of whether the court should, as a matter of policy, imply the term contended for.

McLachlin J also propounded an alternative way of arriving at the same answer when she said (at p 322):

> Quite apart from the particular contract term, it can be argued that the concatenation of circumstances giving rise to the tort duty, of which the contract with its exemption of liability is one, are such that they limit the duty of care the employees owed to the plaintiff. As Purchas LJ said in *Pacific Associates Inc v Baxter* [1990] 1 QB 993, the question of whether there are circumstances qualifying or negating the duty of care 'can only be answered in the context of the factual matrix including especially the contractual structure against which such duty is said to arise'.
>
> The law of tort has long recognised that circumstances may negate or limit the duty of care in tort. Indeed, this is one of the fundamental theories by which scholars have explained the defence of voluntary assumption of the risk. Waivers and exemption clauses, whether contractual or not, have long been accepted as having this effect on the duty in tort. As Fleming puts it: 'The basic idea is that the plaintiff, by agreeing to assume the risk himself, absolves the defendant from all responsibility for it. The latter's duty of care is thus suspended.' Canadian courts, including this one, have applied this principle in determining liability and damages in tort.
>
> I have outlined how the notion of voluntary assumption of the risk, whether on the basis of a contractual waiver via the doctrine of implied terms, or on an analysis based on the scope of the duty of care, permits the conclusion that the

defendant employees are not liable to the plaintiff. It remains to consider briefly the conclusion of my colleague La Forest J that on the matrix of facts relevant to this case, no duty of care whatsoever lies on the employees, that duty lying exclusively on the employer. My concern is whether it is appropriate for this court to take such a step at this time.

The rule proposed by my colleague La Forest J would introduce a change in the common law of tort of major significance. It has always been accepted that a plaintiff has the right to sue the person who was negligent, regardless of whether the employee was working for someone else or not. The employer becomes liable only by the doctrine of vicarious liability, absent independent negligence on its part. The reasons of my colleague would reverse the scheme; the employer, regardless of whether it was itself negligent, would be primarily liable for the negligence of its employees. Only in exceptional cases, as where there is specific reliance on the employee or special 'safety concerns', would there be a right to sue the employee directly.

The remaining judge, La Forest J, held that the employees were not liable in tort to the plaintiff in any event (ie not even for $40). He saw the issue as turning on considerations of the proper allocation of risk, reasonable reliance and on the doctrine of vicarious liability. Apart from the vicarious liability angle, his approach appears to be similar to that of the English courts in cases like *Pacific Associates Inc v Baxter* [1990] 1 QB 993, ie that the duty of care question in a case like the present "can only be answered in the context of the factual matrix including especially the contractual structure against which such duty is said to arise" (see *below*).

In considering whether a duty of care should be imposed on the employees in this case, La Forest J applied the 'two-stage test' from *Anns v Merton London Borough Council* [1978] AC 728 (see Chapter 3, para 3.2.2). He had no difficulty in deciding that the first branch of the test was satisfied. In considering the circumstances in which the second branch of the test will be satisfied in a tortious case with contractual overtones, La Forest J said (at p 270):

> The court must take due account of the contractual context in which the alleged tort duty is said to exist. Courts must be sensitive to the impact that an imposition of tort liability would have on the contractual allocation of risk, whether the damage occurred is economic loss or property damage. Tort liability, however, may be less likely to disrupt contractual arrangements in property damage cases. Property damage cases are generally unproblematic from a policy perspective because they are much less likely than economic loss cases to be associated with planned transactions and contractual expectations. Economic loss, on the other hand, very often occurs in a contractual context.

After referring to the principles of concurrent liability in contract and tort (see para 10.4, *below*), La Forest J said (at p 274): "Today, courts are perhaps readier to extend a limitation of liability for contractual breach to a tort claim arising out of the same circumstances if it is necessary to do so to prevent tort being unjustifiably used to avoid obligations and limitations freely accepted in contract".

La Forest J then referred to the Supreme Court of Canada's decision in

10.3.2 *The contractual connection*

Rivtow Marine Ltd v Washington Iron Works (1973) 40 DLR (3d) 530 (see Chapter 7, para 7.7) and then said (at p 275):

> *Rivtow* was not a true concurrent liability case because of the lack of privity between Rivtow and the defendants: Rivtow had no contractual claim against the defendants. Nonetheless, it was concurrent in the broader sense that I prefer to refer to as tort liability in a contractual context or matrix: see the reasons of Purchas LJ in *Pacific Associates v Baxter* [see *below*]. Many issues raised in concurrent cases must also be considered where there is no privity of contract between the plaintiff and the defendant. The mere lack of privity does not justify the complete disregard of contractual concerns. In fact, since in such circumstances it is more difficult for the parties to contract out of tort liability, tort law may need to be *more* attuned to the contractual allocation of risk than in cases of concurrent liability.
>
> On the other hand, the values protected by tort may predominate in a given context, and the nature of the damage may be a relevant consideration. This is revealed by an examination of cases involving products liability. Since *Donoghue v Stevenson* [1932] AC 562 it is well-established that manufacturers are liable for negligence causing property damage to end users of their products. The safety concerns are obvious. When the question of recovery for economic loss in a products liability case arises, however, the case becomes more difficult. For example, in *Rivtow*, the crux of the disagreement between the majority and the dissent turned on whether the safety concerns underlying the law on products liability for physical damage justified allowing recovery for economic loss. It is not the contractual origin of the manufacturer's liability, but rather the concern with upsetting the contractual bargain struck that lies behind the majority decision in *Rivtow*. Where the concern with safety becomes more tenuous, as in a products liability economic loss case, the contractual aspects begin to predominate. The plaintiff should not be able to use tort law merely to improve its contractual bargain.
>
> Policy concerns about contractual allocation of risk in cases in which tort and contract claims co-exist arise regardless of whether the damage incurred is property damage or economic loss. I emphasise that the recognition that contractual concerns must be considered in tort cases like the present is not to be interpreted as a return to the now discredited reasoning in *Winterbottom v Wright* (1842) 10 M&W 109 [see Chapter 6, para 6.2.4].
>
> The mere fact that this case involves property damage rather than economic loss cannot be sufficient to eliminate inquiry into whether the recognition of a duty of care is justified on policy grounds. In most contractual contexts, all parties are able to plan for potential tort liability for property damage based on foreseeability. I am of the opinion that in general employees are not realistically in a position to so plan.

La Forest J then embarked on an excursus of the principle of vicarious liability and its interrelationship with the allocation of risk in cases like the present. He said (at p 280):

> This case raises the question of the employee's personal liability within the context of the vicarious liability regime. In my opinion, the vicarious liability regime is best seen as a response to a number of policy concerns. In its traditional domain, these are primarily linked to compensation, deterrence and loss internalisation. In addition, in a case like the one at bar, which involves a planned

transaction or a contractual matrix, the issue of tort liability in the context of contractual relations involves a wider range of policy concerns. Alongside those respecting compensation, deterrence and loss internalisation, there are important concerns regarding planning and agreed risk allocation.

The most important policy considerations lying behind the doctrine of vicarious liability are based on the perception that the employer is better placed to incur liability than the employee. First, the vicarious liability regime allows the plaintiff to obtain compensation from someone who is financially capable of satisfying a judgment. Secondly, a person, typically a corporation, who employs others to advance its own economic interest should in fairness be placed under a corresponding liability for losses incurred in the course of the enterprise. Thirdly, the regime promotes a wide distribution of tort losses since the employer is a most suitable channel for passing them on through liability insurance and higher prices. Fourthly, vicarious liability is a coherent doctrine from the perspective of deterrence. K&N is in a much better situation than the employees to adopt policies to prevent accidents of this type. K&N has every incentive to encourage its employees to perform well on the job and to discipline those who are guilty of wrongdoing.

It is apparent that the vicarious liability regime responds to wider policy concerns than simply the desire to protect the plaintiff from the consequences of the possible and indeed likely incapacity of the employee to afford sufficient compensation. Vicarious liability has the broader function of transferring to the enterprise itself the risks created by the activity performed by its agents. The question in this case is whether the elimination of the employee's liability would significantly impact on the policies advanced by vicarious liability. In my view, it would impact favourably on the second and third considerations set out above and have a negligible impact on the fourth. In my view, not only is the elimination of the possibility of the employee bearing the loss logically compatible with the vicarious liability regime, it is practically compelled by the developing logic of that regime. In our modern economy, an employee's capacity to cause loss does not bear any relation to his salary. The employer will almost always be insured against the risk of being liable to third parties by reason of his vicarious liability. The cost of such liability is thus internalised to the profitable activity that gives rise to it. There is no requirement for double insurance, covering both the employee and his employer against the same risk. Shifting the loss to the employee upsets the policy foundation of vicarious liability.

For these reasons La Forest J said that, in cases where the employee's tort was one for which his employer would be vicariously liable (as opposed to an independent tort committed by an employee while he was "on a frolic of his own"), the allocation of the risk of being sued in tort for the employee's negligence should be placed on the employer alone. Relating this principle to the facts of the present case, La Forest J concluded that policy reasons supported a finding of no liability on the employees. He said (at p 291):

> In the context of a commercial vicarious liability claim, placing liability exclusively on the employer places liability on a party who is easily able to modify its liability by contractual stipulations. K&N and the plaintiff took advantage of that possibility in this case. They used the well-accepted application of contractual clauses to limit strictly K&N's tort and contract liability for property damage. As a result the plaintiff had the option of purchasing its own insurance

or purchasing extra insurance from K&N. The plaintiff found it advantageous not to require K&N to insure performance. So long as there are no concerns about unconscionability, this ability of the parties to modify their possible tort and contract liability is an unquestionable advantage. The customer benefits from the ability of the future defendant to contract out of its tort liability. Unlike K&N the employees had no opportunity to decline the risk at all.

Edgeworth Construction Ltd v ND Lea and Associates Ltd (1993) 107 DLR (4th) 169: The facts of this case are set out in Chapter 9, para 9.9.3, where the question of the defendant engineering corporation's liability in tort for its negligent preparation of the design documents is considered. The position of the individual engineers is considered in para 10.2.1, *above*. In this section, consideration is given to the question whether the engineering firm should have been entitled to take advantage of the exemption clause (clause 42) in the contract between the plaintiff and the Province. That clause absolved the Province from any liability for the design drawings. It stipulated that any representations in the tender documents had been furnished "merely for the general information of bidders and were not in anywise warranted or guaranteed by or on behalf of the Minister".

In holding that the engineering firm could not take advantage of this provision, and in distinguishing the present case from *London Drugs*, McLachlin J, speaking on this point for all of the judges on this panel, said (at p 174):

> There is a further problem of whether the engineers, not parties to the contract, could claim the benefit of its exclusion of liability for the representations in the tender documents. This court in *London Drugs Ltd v Kuehne & Nagel International Ltd* (1992) 97 DLR (4th) 261 held that the doctrine of privity of contract did not preclude contractual exclusions for negligence being extended to provide protection for the employees actually charged with doing the work. But before such an argument can succeed, it must be established that the contract clause provides protection, or should by implication be held to provide protection for the persons who, although not parties to the contract, are claiming the benefit of the exclusion. In the case at bar this has not been done. In *London Drugs* the fact that the work for which the exemption was given could only be done by the employees, taken together with other circumstances including the powerlessness of the employees to protect themselves otherwise, suggested that a term should be implied that the clause was intended to benefit them, or alternatively, that the intention of the parties manifested in the contract must be taken to limit the duty of care owed in tort. The facts in this case do not give rise to such an inference; rather, clause 42 is entirely consistent with the conclusion that the protection was intended for the benefit of the Province alone. Moreover, the engineering firm, unlike the employees in *London Drugs*, could have taken measures to protect itself from the liability in question. It could have placed a disclaimer of responsibility on the design documents. Alternatively, it could have refused to agree to provide the design without ongoing supervision duties which would have permitted it to make alterations as the contract was being performed. I raise this point in the context of the engineers' argument that much of the loss might have been avoided had it had ongoing supervisory duties. Finally, the engineering firm might have decided to accept the risk that tenderers would

rely on its design to their detriment, and have insured itself accordingly. In short, the circumstances of the case, combined with the wording of the exclusion clause, negate any inference that the contractor should be taken as having excluded its right to sue the engineers for design deficiencies by its contract with the Province. For these reasons, I conclude that clause 42 of the contract between the contractor and the Province does not assist the engineering firm.

10.3.3 Waiver of rights by plaintiff against defendant in third party contract

Introduction

Sometimes the plaintiff has entered into a contract with a third party which will be partially performed on the third party's behalf by the defendant (who is not a party to this contract), and the plaintiff agrees with the third party not to institute proceedings against the defendant if he negligently performs the services required of him. The question will then arise whether the defendant will be able to take advantage of the exemption clause in the contract between the plaintiff and the third party when the plaintiff sues the defendant in tort for damages sustained through the defendant's negligence. One manifestation of this type of situation has been considered in para 10.2.1 under the heading "*Caveat emptor*".

Pacific Associates v Baxter

An example of this situation is *Pacific Associates Inc v Baxter* [1990] 1 QB 993, in which the plaintiff excavators entered into a contract with a third party ('the employer') to carry out dredging and reclamation works in a lagoon in the Persian Gulf. The contract stipulated that the work was to be supervised, and that any claims by the plaintiff for additional expenses were to be certified by the defendant engineer, who was to carry out this task impartially as between the plaintiff and the employer. If either the employer or the plaintiff were dissatisfied with the defendant's decision, they could refer the matter to arbitration.

The dredging works were hampered by the presence of hard rock in the bed of the channel of the lagoon, which the plaintiff alleged was not foreseeable from the pre-contract data upon which it had based its tender. The plaintiff accordingly made a claim for extra expense. The defendant rejected the bulk of the plaintiff's claim, and the plaintiff submitted the issue to arbitration. The arbitrators awarded the plaintiff some money, but not as much as the plaintiff was claiming. The plaintiff therefore brought an action against the defendant in tort for the difference between the amount of its loss and the amount certified by the arbitrators, claiming that the defendant, by his rejection of the plaintiff's claims for extra expense, had acted negligently and not impartially in administering the contract. The plaintiff claimed that the defendant owed it a duty of care in tort on the ground that (assuming the defendant to have acted negligently) the defendant knew that the plaintiff was relying on him to perform its duties without negligence.

The defendant contended that even if he did owe such a duty of care to the plaintiff, he was entitled to take advantage of, and would have a defence by virtue of, a clause in the contract between the plaintiff and the employer which stated that the defendant was not to be in any way personally liable to the plaintiff for his own acts in performing the obligations imposed on him under the contract. The court upheld the defendant's contention. Purchas LJ said (at p 1011):

> ... there is no simple, unqualified answer to the question: 'Does the engineer [the defendant] owe a duty to the contractor [the plaintiff] in tort to exercise reasonable skill and care?', but this question can only be answered in the context of the factual matrix, including especially the contractual structure against which such duty is said to arise.
>
> The central question which arises here is: against the contractual structure of the contract into which the contractor was prepared to enter with the employer, can it be said that [the contractor] looked to the engineer by way of reliance for the proper execution of the latter's duties under the contract, in extension of the rights which would accrue to [the contractor] under its contract with the employer?

Purchas LJ answered this question in the negative, as did Ralph Gibson LJ, who said (at p 1033): "The fact that the clause is contained in a contract to which the engineer is not a party should not . . . prevent the words having the effect which all the parties to this arrangement, namely contractor, employer and engineer, plainly expected and intended them to have".

Comment

This case must be approached with caution. It is not authority for a general principle that an exemption clause in a contract to which the defendant is not a party will always be available to the defendant if he is subsequently sued in tort by the plaintiff (who was a party to the contract) for his negligent act or omission. The Court of Appeal was strongly influenced in its decision by the fact that the arbitration clause in the contract afforded the plaintiff an avenue for obtaining complete relief if he was dissatisfied with any of the defendant's valuation decisions. Thus, Purchas LJ said (at p 1023): "I emphasise that in coming to this conclusion [ie that no duty of care in tort could be imposed on the defendant] it does depend on the particular circumstances of this case, not the least of which were the contractual provisions in the contract which afforded an avenue enabling the contractor to recover from the employer"; and Russell LJ, after saying (at p 1035) that "the third test which must be satisfied before a duty of care can arise is whether, in the circumstances of the individual case, it is just and reasonable that the duty should be imposed", said (at p 1036): "The circumstances in the instant case were such that the possibility of damage being suffered by this contractor beyond what could be recouped in arbitration has to be regarded as remote, and I believe that this is a factor to be taken into account when one comes to consider the third test". He concluded by saying (at p 1037) that the arbitration clause in the contract between the plaintiff and the employer did "not merely define the ambit of the duty owed [by the defendant to the plaintiff]—it goes to its very existence".

Consideration in Junior Books

This same question arose more generally, and only indirectly, in *Junior Books Ltd v Veitchi Co Ltd* [1983] AC 520 (see Chapter 7), and Lord Roskill (expressing a preference for the type of decision reached in *Pacific Associates*) said (at p 546):

> During the argument, it was asked what the position would be in a case where there was a relevant exclusion clause in the main contract [between the plaintiff and the third party]. . . . that question does not arise for decision in this appeal, but in principle I would venture the view that such a clause according to the manner in which it was worded might in some circumstances limit the duty of care, just as in the *Hedley Byrne* case the plaintiff was ultimately defeated by the defendant's disclaimer of responsibility.

Criticism in Leigh and Sillivan

In *Leigh and Sillivan Ltd v Aliakmon Shipping Co Ltd* [1986] 1 AC 785 (see Chapter 5), Lord Brandon criticised this *dictum* when he said (at p 817): "With great respect to Lord Roskill, there is no analogy between the disclaimer in *Hedley Byrne*, which operated directly between the plaintiff and the defendant, and an exclusion of liability clause in a contract to which the plaintiff is a party but the defendant is not".

The proper approach

In *Pacific Associates* Purchas LJ referred to these conflicting *dicta* and said (at p 1022): "With great respect to Lord Brandon, the absence of a direct contractual nexus between *A* (the defendant) and *B* (the plaintiff) does not necessarily exclude the recognition of a clause limiting liability to be imposed on *A* in a contract between *B* and *C* (a third party), when the existence of that contract is the basis of the creation of a duty of care asserted to be owed by *A* to *B*".

It is submitted that this is the true view, and that it applies both to situations in which the relevant contract containing the exclusion clause is between the plaintiff and a third party, as in *Pacific Associates*, and where it is contained in a contract between the defendant and a third party, as in the cases considered *below*. The question in every case is whether, in all the circumstances, it is just and reasonable to impose a duty of care on the defendant of the scope contended for by the plaintiff (see Chapter 2, para 2.4). In considering this question it is wrong to exclude as a matter of law any fact which might have a material bearing on the inherent justice and reasonableness of the totality of the factual matrix in which the plaintiff is asking the court to impose a duty of care in tort on the defendant for the plaintiff's losses. Saville LJ made a similar observation in *Marc Rich & Co AG v Bishop Rock Marine Co Ltd* [1974] 1 WLR 1071 (see para 10.2.1, *above*).

10.3.4 Exemption clause in contract between defendant and third party

Introduction

A more usual situation than that considered *above* is where the plaintiff is suing the defendant in tort for loss sustained through having acquired a defective product or having relied on a negligently made statement which the defendant initially provided to a third party in a contract which contained a clause exempting the defendant from liability for his negligence or restricting the scope of the defendant's retainer by the third party. The question will then be whether the defendant can rely on this exemption clause or on any other terms of his contract which restrict the scope of his retainer by the third party when he is subsequently sued by the plaintiff in tort for a loss sustained by the plaintiff as a result of the product being defective or the statement being inaccurate.

Specific instances

Grant v Australian Knitting Mills Ltd [1936] AC 85 (see Chapter 6, para 6.3.4): Lord Wright thought that an exemption clause in the contract between the defendant manufacturer and the retailer from whom the plaintiff had bought the defective underwear which caused his injuries would not have availed the defendant when sued by the plaintiff in tort. He said (at p 106): "Equally irrelevant is any question of liability between the retailers and the manufacturers on the contract of sale between them. The tort liability is independent of any question of contract". It is submitted that this statement was correct in the context of the factual matrix of *Grant* because, adapting the above-quoted words of Purchas LJ in *Pacific Associates*, the existence of the contract which contained the exemption clause was not the basis of the creation of a duty of care asserted to be owed by the defendant to the plaintiff.

Herschtal v Stewart and Ardern Ltd [1940] 1 KB 155 (see Chapter 6, para 6.3.4): Tucker J reached the same conclusion when he said (at p 158):

> ... I do not think that the defendants can place any reliance on the form of receipt which was signed by the plaintiff on behalf of Utility Products Ltd [the company whose motor car the defendants had just repaired] when he signed it as being 'in good condition and as seen, tried and approved'. It cannot protect the defendants from a claim founded in negligence by the plaintiff, provided that he can establish that the defendants owed him a duty and that they had been negligent in the performance of that duty.

Voli v Inglewood Shire Council (1963) 110 CLR 74: The plaintiff was one of several people who were injured when a stage on which they were standing at a meeting in a town hall collapsed. The defendant was the architect who had designed the hall and the stage. It was found that he had been negligent because his design and the stage as constructed were capable of bearing a load of about 92 pounds per square foot only, whereas the reasonable standard for a stage of that type should have been a minimum of 150 pounds per square foot. The High Court of Australia had no difficulty in holding that the defendant was liable for the plaintiff's injuries by way of an application of the principles stated in *Donoghue v Stevenson* [1932] AC 562.

On the question of the effect, if any, of the architect's contract with the City Council on his liability to third parties in tort, Windeyer J said:

> Neither the terms of the architect's engagement, nor the terms of the building contract, can operate to discharge the architect from a duty of care to persons who are strangers to those contracts. Nor can they directly determine what he must do to satisfy his duty to such persons. That duty is cast upon him by law, not because he made a contract, but because he entered upon the work. Nevertheless his contract with the building owner is not an irrelevant circumstance. It determines what was the task upon which he entered. If, for example, it was to design a stage to bear only some specified weight, he would not be liable for the consequences of someone thereafter negligently permitting a greater weight to be put upon it.

If this *dictum* is interpreted literally, it appears to be self-contradictory. It is submitted that the proper way to interpret it is to regard the fact that the architect (or any other professional person) was exercising his professional skills pursuant to a contractual duty cannot of itself exclude his responsibility to third parties. The contract may, however, be one of the circumstances to be taken into account in determining the nature and extent of his responsibility to third parties.

Hedley Byrne & Co Ltd v Heller & Partners Ltd [1964] AC 465 (see Chapter 9, para 9.4): The defendant was held to be entitled to rely on wording which exempted it from responsibility for negligence in the reference which it provided to the plaintiff's bankers about the creditworthiness of one of the plaintiff's customers. Although there had not been any direct communication between the plaintiff and the defendant, it was obvious to all parties that the plaintiff's bank was merely a passive conduit through whom the defendant was effectively going to be providing information directly to the plaintiff. The relationship between the plaintiff and the defendant could thus be regarded (*per* Lord Devlin at p 529) as "equivalent to contract, but for the absence of consideration"; in which event, barring any prohibition emanating from the Unfair Contract Terms Act 1977 (see *below*, para 10.3.4), there would be no reason why an answer given to a question of this nature could not be qualified by a denial of responsibility by the maker of the statement. Alternatively, on Purchas LJ's approach in *Pacific Associates*, it could be said that it was right to allow the defendant in *Hedley Byrne* to rely on the exemption clause because the existence of the relationship (which was not a contract) between the defendant and the plaintiff's bank, to whom the communication containing the exemption clause was made, was indeed the basis of the creation of the duty of care asserted to be owed by the defendant to the plaintiff.

Bowen v Paramount Builders (Hamilton) Ltd [1977] 1 NZLR 394 (see Chapter 7, para 7.6.2): In this case the judges in the Court of Appeal of

New Zealand clearly thought that the terms of a builder's or an architect's contract with the original owner could not shield him from a claim by a subsequent owner who was injured as a result of a defect in construction created by the builder's or architect's negligence. Thus Richmond P said (at p 407):

> It is clear that a builder or architect cannot defend a claim in negligence made against him by a third person by saying that he was working under a contract for the owner of the land. He cannot say that the only duty which he owed was his contractual duty to the owner. Likewise he cannot say that the nature of his contractual duties to the owner set a limit to the duty of care which he owes to third parties. As regards the latter point, it is, for example, obvious that a builder who agreed to build a house in a manner which he knows or ought to know will prove a source of danger to third parties cannot say, in answer to a claim by third parties, that he did all that the owner of the land required him to do.

Similarly, Woodhouse J said (at p 419):

> I do not consider that the courts need to be astute to protect those prepared to undertake jerry-building or shoddy work against the reasonable claims of innocent third parties merely because their bad work was done to a deliberate pattern or arrangement. I do not regard a private contractual arrangement for an inefficient design or for an un-workmanlike or inadequate type of construction as any sort of justification or valid explanation for releasing the builder from his duty to those who otherwise could look to him for relief.

Smith v Eric S Bush [1990] 1 AC 831 (see Chapter 9, para 9.7.3): The basis of the plaintiff's claim was very similar to that of the plaintiff in *Hedley Byrne*. As Lord Templeman said (at p 843):

> [This appeal is] based on allegations of negligence in circumstances which are akin to contract. . . . Mrs Smith paid £36.89 to the Abbey National [Building Society] for a report and valuation, and the Abbey National paid the appellants for the report and valuation.
> . . . the valuer knew or ought to have known that the purchaser would only contract to purchase the house if the valuation was satisfactory and that the purchaser might suffer injury or damage . . . if the valuer did not exercise reasonable skill and care. In these circumstances I would expect the law to impose on the valuer a duty owed to the purchaser to exercise reasonable skill and care in carrying out the valuation.

The survey report which the defendant produced for the building society, and which the building society sent to the plaintiff, contained (*per* Lord Griffith at p 855) "in red lettering and in the clearest terms, a disclaimer of liability for the accuracy of the report, covering both the building society and the valuer". Furthermore, the building society's covering letter to the plaintiff drew her attention to the fact that this report was not to be taken as a structural survey and advised her to obtain independent professional advice. However, without obtaining an independent valuation, but instead relying on the defendant's report, the plaintiff purchased the house. Subsequently it proved to be severely structurally defective. The plaintiff sued the defendant surveyor for her economic loss, namely the diminution in value of the house by virtue of the defects which the defendant negligently failed to discover when he inspected the house for the building society. The defendant relied on the exclusion clause in his survey report. The House of Lords rejected this defence, and held the defendant liable for the plaintiff's loss.

The reason for the court's decision in this regard was that the defendant's exclusion clause fell foul of the relevant provisions of the Unfair Contract Terms Act 1977, which had been passed in the intervening years since *Hedley Byrne* was decided in 1964 (see para 10.3.5, *below*).

Ross v Caunters [1980] Ch 297 (see Chapter 9, para 9.7.5): There was no exemption clause in the contract between the defendant solicitor and the deceased testator. However, in the Court of Appeal in *Leigh and Sillivan Ltd v Aliakmon Shipping Co Ltd* [1985] QB 350 (see Chapter 5), Robert Goff LJ considered what the position would have been in *Ross* if such a clause had existed. He said (at p 397):

> [*Ross v Caunters*] is another case in which, like the present [case] [see Chapter 5], a third party, *C* (the disappointed legatee), was claiming (and, indeed, was held to be entitled) to proceed directly against a person, *A* (the solicitor), for damages flowing from *A*'s breach of duty to *B* (the testator). Now let it be supposed that, in such a case, . . . there had been a disclaimer of responsibility by *A* to *B*. . . . I cannot think that, in such a case, a disappointed legatee could sue the solicitor for damages . . . and the answer must, I think, be that it is quite simply because when *C* has a direct right of action in tort against *A* in respect of damages caused by *A*'s breach of his duty to *B*, *C*'s rights against *A* must be regulated by any provisions which controlled or limited *B*'s rights against *A* . . . whether *Ross v Caunters* is rightly decided; but on the assumption that it is, I am satisfied that any claim by a disappointed legatee must be subject to the restriction I have indicated . . .

Simaan General Contracting Co v Pilkington Glass Ltd (No 2) [1988] QB 758 (see Chapter 7, para 7.3.6): One of the reasons that the Court of Appeal gave for rejecting the plaintiff's tortious economic loss claim was the difficulty that the Court perceived might arise if the contract between the defendant and the third party contained an exemption clause. Thus Dillon LJ said (at p 785):

> Moreover, . . . if it were to be established in this case that a main contractor or an owner has a direct claim in tort against the nominated supplier to a sub-contractor for economic loss occasioned by defects in the quality of the goods supplied, the formidable question would arise in future cases if not in this case, as to how far exempting clauses in the contract between the nominated supplier and the sub-contractor were to be imported into the supposed duty in tort owed by the supplier to those higher up in the chain.
>
> If, by contrast [the plaintiff's claim in tort is rejected] . . . [t]here will be the 'normal chain of liability', . . . in that the Sheikh can sue the plaintiffs on the main building contract, the plaintiffs can sue Feal on the sub-contract and Feal can sue the defendants. Each liability would be determined in the light of such

exemptions as applied contractually at that stage. There is thus no warrant for extending the law of negligence to impose direct liability on the defendants in favour of the plaintiffs.

And Bingham LJ said (at p 783):

Although the defendants did not sell subject to exempting conditions, I fully share the difficulty which others have envisaged where there were such conditions. Even as it is, the defendants' sale may well have been subject to terms and conditions imported by the Sale of Goods Act 1979. Some of those are beneficial to the seller. But if the duty [sought to be placed on the seller in tort in a case like the present] is unaffected by the conditions on which the seller supplied the goods, it is in my view unfair to him and makes a mockery of contractual negotiation.

White v Jones [1993] 3 WLR 730 (CA) and [1995] 2 AC 207 (HL) (see Chapter 9, para 9.7.3): The Court of Appeal referred to and approved of Robert Goff LJ's *dictum* in *Leigh and Sillivan, above*. Sir Donald Nicholls VC said:

It was said [by the plaintiff's counsel] that if a duty of care to an intended beneficiary exists, this duty is independent of the solicitor's duty to his client. Accordingly, an agreement of this nature between solicitor and client would not affect the solicitor's duty to the intended beneficiary. This would be an unfair result. I agree [with the defendant's counsel] that, unless the duty to the beneficiary is correspondingly limited, the result would be unfair. I can see no overriding reason why the duty should not be limited in this way;

and Steyn LJ said:

The question was posed of the effect of a disclaimer of liability, or a limitation of liability, as between testator and solicitor. On any view, such cases will rarely occur. But, if they occur, it seems to me unavoidable that the duty will have to be limited in the way suggested by Robert Goff LJ in *Leigh and Sillivan v Aliakmon Shipping Co Ltd*.

These remarks must be approached with caution, because they were made without reference to the Unfair Contract Terms Act 1977 or its application in *Smith v Bush* (see *below*). If the provisions of the Act were sufficient to prevent the defendant in *Smith* from relying on the exemption clause in his contract with the plaintiff in that case, it is difficult to see why a similar exemption clause should be upheld in cases like *Ross v Caunters* and *White v Jones*.

When *White v Jones* reached the House of Lords, Lord Goff (formerly Robert Goff LJ) repeated his above-cited opinion on the way that the disappointed beneficiary's claim in tort against the solicitor could be affected by the terms of the solicitor's contract with the testator. He said (at p 261):

The plaintiffs' claim, if properly analysed, must necessarily have contractual features which cannot ordinarily exist in the case of an ordinary tortious claim. Here I refer not only to the fact that the claim is one for damages for pure economic loss, but also to the need for the defendant solicitor to be entitled to invoke as against the disappointed beneficiary any terms of the contract with his client which may limit or exclude his liability.

Later on in his speech, Lord Goff said that in a case like *White v Jones* the House of Lords should provide the intended beneficiary with a remedy by holding that the assumption of responsibility by the solicitor towards his client should be held in law to extend to the intended beneficiary. However, Lord Goff qualified this statement by saying (at p 268): "Such assumption of responsibility will of course be subject to any terms of the contract between the solicitor and the testator which may exclude or restrict the solicitor's liability to the testator under the principle in *Hedley Byrne*".

Lord Nolan was more cautious. After referring to *Voli v Inglewood Shire Council* (1963) 110 CLR 74 (see *above*), he said (at p 294):

> *Voli's* case was, of course, a case of physical injury rather than economic loss. I would for my part leave open the question whether, in either type of case, the defendant who engages in the relevant activity pursuant to a contract can exclude or limit his liability to third parties by some provision in the contract. I would prefer to say that the exercise and terms of the contract may be relevant in determining what the law of tort may reasonably require of the defendant in all the circumstances.

Winnipeg Condominium Corporation No 36 v Bird Construction Co (1995) 121 DLR (4th) 193 (see Chapter 7, para 7.6.3): In considering a builder's duty of care in tort to third parties in relation to defects which might pose a risk of physical injury to third parties or damage to their property, La Forest J said (at p 217):

> The duty to construct a building according to reasonable standards and without dangerous defects arises independently of the contractual stipulations between the original owner and the contractor because it arises from a duty to create the building safely and not merely according to contractual standards of quality. As this duty arises independently of any contract, there is no logical reason for allowing the contractor to rely upon a contract made with the original owner to shield him from liability to subsequent purchasers arising from a dangerously constructed building. The tort duty to construct a building safely is a circumscribed duty that is not parasitic upon any contractual duties between the contractor and the original owner.

Bryan v Maloney (1995) 69 ALJR 375 (see Chapter 7, para 7.6.4): Mason CJ appeared on the one hand to say that the terms of the contract between the builder and the original owner could negate the existence of a duty of care in tort by the builder to a subsequent purchaser, when he said (at p 379):

> In the circumstances of this case, where the contract between Mr Bryan [the builder] and Mrs Manion [the original owner] contained no exclusion or limitation of liability, neither the existence nor the content of the contract precluded the existence of liability to Mrs Manion or Mrs Maloney [the plaintiff] under the ordinary law of negligence.

On the other hand, Mason CJ seemed to back off from this position later on in his judgment when he said (at p 380):

> The relationship between Mr Bryan and persons other than Mrs Manion [the original owner] corresponded with the relationship between the architect and the injured plaintiff in *Voli v Inglewood Shire Council* (1963) 110 CLR 74. It is unnecessary for the purposes of the present case to consider whether such a relationship of proximity or any consequent duty of care can be excluded or modified by the terms of the contract between the builder and the first owner. As has been mentioned, it is not suggested that there was any special feature of the contract between Mr Bryan and Mrs Manion that had that effect in the present case. There is, however, obvious force in the conclusion expressed by Windeyer J in *Voli* to the effect that, while such a contractual exclusion would be relevant in identifying the task upon which the architect had entered, it could not directly operate to discharge the architect from a duty of care which would otherwise exist to persons who are strangers to the contract.

Brennan J, dissenting, felt that *Voli* could be explained only in terms of the loss there having been physical damage rather than pure economic loss. He said (at p 389):

> It was, of course, no answer to the plaintiff's claim in *Donoghue v Stevenson* [1932] AC 562 that the quality of the ginger beer was the subject of a contract between the defendant and the café proprietor. Nor did the architect's contract with the building owner in *Voli v Inglewood Shire Council* (1963) 110 CLR 74 affect the injured plaintiff's right to recover in that case. But these were cases where the duty imposed by law, in addition to any contractual duty, was a duty to avoid or prevent physical injury. It is another question where the law should impose, in favour of a remote purchaser, a duty on a builder or a manufacturer to build buildings or manufacture chattels of a certain quality when a building or chattel will be sold in an open market in which price reflects, or may be negotiated to reflect, the quality of the thing sold. Absent any risk of damage to person or property, why should the law impose a duty to protect the purchaser's financial interests? The financial interests of a house purchaser are not protected against the immediate vendor except by such terms as are agreed between them in striking their bargain: *caveat emptor*.

McCullagh v Lane Fox and Partners Ltd (1996) 49 Con LR 124 (CA) (see Chapter 9, para 9.7.3): The defendant was a firm of estate agents which, as part of their retainer to sell a house for the owner, prepared certain written particulars about the house for distribution to prospective purchasers. These particulars included the statement that the property was a detached freehold house set in 0.92 of an acre of its own private gardens. This was a misrepresentation because the actual size of the plot was only 0.48 of an acre. This representation arose negligently on the part of one of the defendant's directors who, after taking relevant measurements of the site, inadvertently double-counted the front half of the property when he transcribed his contemporaneous notes at his office.

The above-mentioned particulars also included the following disclaimers: "All statements contained in these particulars as to this property are made without responsibility on the part of Lane Fox or the vendors. None of the statements contained in these particulars as to this property are to be relied on as statements or representations of fact. Any intending purchasers must satisfy themselves by inspection or otherwise as to the correctness of each of the statements contained in these particulars".

The plaintiff was the purchaser of the house and the property on which it stood. He discovered the error in the defendant's description of the size of the property only after concluding the purchase. He did not carry out a pre-contract survey because he had intended to knock down the house and build another one, and because he placed reliance on the professional skill and competence of the defendant in representing to him, both orally during a visit to the property and in the above-mentioned written particulars, that the size of the property was approximately ⁹⁄₁₀ths of an acre.

One of the questions in the Court of Appeal was whether, on the assumption that in all other respects the defendant owed a duty of care to the plaintiff for the plaintiff's loss consisting of the diminution in value of the property by virtue of the defendant's negligent misrepresentation about the size of the plot, the disclaimers in the defendant's particulars negated the existence of that duty. Two of the Lord Justices felt that no duty of care would have existed in any event on the particular facts of the case (see Chapter 9, para 9.7.3 and Chapter 8, para 8.3.3). They did, however, both say that if a duty of care had otherwise been found to exist in this case, it would have been negated by the disclaimers and would not have been saved by the Unfair Contract Terms Act 1977, and they did not discuss these points in any detail. The third judge, Hobhouse LJ, who did believe that a duty of care would have existed if not for the disclaimers, did discuss these points. After referring extensively to the speeches in *Hedley Byrne and Co Ltd v Heller and Partners Ltd* [1964] AC 465 (see Chapter 9), he said:

Thus, the relevance of the disclaimer is to negative one of the essential elements for the existence of the duty of care. It negatives the assumption of responsibility for the statement. It implicitly tells the recipient of the representation that if he chooses to rely upon it, he must realise that the maker is not accepting responsibility for the accuracy of the representation. The disclaimer is part of the factual situation which the court has to take into account in deciding whether or not the defendants owed a duty of care to the plaintiff. Put another way, the question is whether the plaintiff was entitled to treat the representation as one for which the defendants were accepting responsibility. This is primarily a factual question.

Later on in his judgment, Hobhouse LJ continued with this theme by saying:

In my judgment, the disclaimer puts the present case on all fours with the actual decision in *Hedley Byrne*. The right approach, as is made clear in *Hedley Byrne*, is to treat the existence of the disclaimer as one of the facts relevant to answering the question whether there had been an assumption of responsibility by the defendants for the relevant statement. This question must be answered objectively by reference to what a reasonable person in the position of the plaintiff would have understood at the time that he finally relied upon the representation. In this context, it is obvious that the statement that the acreage of the property was not 0.92 of an acre was a statement which was taken from the particulars, and that the defendants were not assuming responsibility for that statement. The mere fact that Mr Scott [the defendant's director], when showing the plaintiff around the property, gave the same information to the plaintiff orally, would not lead a reasonable person to conclude that the defendants were thereby choosing to assume responsibility for the statement which they said in the particulars they were not assuming responsibility for.

Having regard to the disclaimer, the plaintiff was not reasonably entitled to believe that the defendants were assuming responsibility for the relevant statement. Therefore, applying *Hedley Byrne*, they owed him no duty of care in relation to its accuracy, unless the Unfair Contract Terms Act 1977 precludes the defendants from relying on the disclaimer. [This is discussed *below*.]

Trusted v Clifford Chance (17 May 1996, unreported) (see Chapter 9, para 9.7.5): In reliance on Lord Goff's above-cited *dictum* in *White v Jones* (1995) 2 AC 207, Jonathan Parker J said (at para 196):

> The duty owed in tort by the solicitor to the intended beneficiary and the duty owed in contract by the solicitor to the client are for all practical purposes one and the same. The nature and extent of the duty is determined by the terms of the contract between the solicitor and his client, ie, by the terms of the solicitor's retainer. This latter point is graphically illustrated by the fact that the duty of care towards the intended beneficiary may be restricted or excluded altogether by contract between solicitor and client.

Parker J did not, however, refer to Lord Nolan's above-mentioned view, which was less emphatic than Lord Goff's view on this point.

Hill v Van Erp (1997) 142 ALR 687 (see Chapter 9, para 9.9.2): Dawson J was of the view that an exclusion clause in the contract between the defendant (a solicitor) and a third party (the testator) could not be invoked against the plaintiff (a disappointed beneficiary) suing in tort for loss suffered through the defendant's negligence. He said:

> The contract may give rise to an obligation to perform a task but the performance of the task may, in all the circumstances, give rise to a duty of care to perform it so as not to cause damage, whether of a physical or economic kind, to another. Even if one party to a contract can exclude liability to the other for negligence in the performance of the contract but cannot do so with respect to someone who is not a party to the contract, that is no reason to deny the existence of a duty of care to that third party. A party to a contract is able to negotiate with respect to the protection of his interests, whereas a third party is not in a position to do so.

Gaudron J saw the matter in terms of whether the duty of care assumed by the defendant in contract would be inconsistent with the duty imposed by the law in tort. If so, then the contract should prevail. She said:

> A contract between solicitor and client obliging the solicitor to act in the client's interests and contrary to those of a third party excludes any relationship of proximity between the solicitor and the third party. There can be no duty of care owed to a third party if the duty asserted is inconsistent with the

duty owed to the client or if the solicitor is obliged to act exclusively in his client's interests.

Woodward v Wolferstans (20 March 1997, unreported) (see Chapter 9, para 9.7.5): In this case the terms of the solicitors' limited retainer by their client, Mr Smith, served to exclude a duty of care in tort of a particular scope by the solicitors to Mr Smith's daughter (the plaintiff). Thus, Martin Mann QC, sitting as a deputy judge of the High Court, said:

> It is highly relevant that the defendant was simply carrying out the terms of a retainer entered into with someone other than the plaintiff, for it would not, in my judgment, be fair, just and reasonable to confer a greater benefit on the plaintiff through the imposition of a duty of care on the defendant than Mr Smith intended she should receive on completion. It is settled that a solicitor can owe a tortious duty of care to an individual who is not his client if, which, in my judgment, is this case, a special relationship exists between them. But it is not enough for the plaintiff to succeed that she was owed a duty of care. She must show that the content of the duty included explaining the transactional details and the implications of the mortgage.
>
> I have already alluded to the relevance of the contract between Mr Smith and the defendant and the desirability of restricting the ambit of the duty. The defendant's contract with Mr Smith required it to exercise reasonable skill and care in securing a good marketable title to, and the plaintiff's registration as proprietor of, the flat. It did not entail taking the plaintiff on as a client for the purpose of giving her advice, and the court cannot re-write the contract to bring advising the plaintiff within its ambit. It is *a fortiori* that it should not do so by the back door. That, in my judgment, would be particularly unfair, unjust and unreasonable because the advice could, and according to the plaintiff would, have put the plaintiff's interests and those of Mr Smith in conflict. Accordingly, I hold that, while the defendant owed the plaintiff a duty of care, it was one restricted to the exercise of reasonable skill and care in carrying the transaction into effect according to Mr Smith's instruction.

10.3.5 The Unfair Contract Terms Act

Relevant clauses

It has been noted *above* that at common law, when considering whether a duty of care should be imposed on a defendant for a plaintiff's loss, it is legitimate to consider the terms of a clause purporting to limit the defendant's liability for his negligence in a contract between the defendant and a third party when (in the words of Purchas LJ in *Pacific Associates v Baxter*) "the existence of that contract is the basis of the creation of the duty of care asserted to be owed by the defendant to the plaintiff".

The Unfair Contract Terms Act 1977 puts this process on a more formalised basis by providing, in s 2(2), that a person cannot, by reference to any contract term or to a notice, exclude or restrict his liability for loss or damage (otherwise than by way of death or personal injury) resulting from his negligence, "except in so far as the term or notice satisfies the requirement of reasonableness".

As a first step, it is always necessary to decide whether the term or notice in question falls within the ambit of the Act. Section 1(1) defines 'negligence' as the breach:

    (*a*) of any obligation, arising from the express or implied terms of a contract, to take reasonable care or exercise reasonable skill in the performance of the contract;

    (*b*) of any common law duty to take reasonable care or exercise reasonable skill (but not any stricter duty).

In *Smith*, the defendant's report was prepared by him in his capacity as a professional surveyor. As such, the report (which, for this purpose, equates to a *notice* under the Act) constituted a statement to which the common law duty to take care or exercise reasonable skill in its preparation clearly applied.

The 'requirement of reasonableness' referred to in s 2 is defined in s 11(3), which provides: "In relation to a notice (not being a notice having contractual effect), the requirement of reasonableness under this Act is that it should be fair and reasonable to allow reliance on it, having regard to all the circumstances obtaining when the liability arose or (but for the notice) would have arisen".

Applying the Act

It will be noted that the test is not whether the exclusion clause itself is felt to be fair and reasonable, but whether it would be fair and reasonable to allow the defendant to rely on the clause; for this purpose regard is had to all the circumstances obtaining at the time when liability would have arisen between the defendant and the plaintiff apart from the existence of the exclusion clause. The onus is on the defendant to establish that, in all the circumstances, it is fair and reasonable that he should be allowed to rely on his disclaimer of liability. Obviously each case will depend on its own special circumstances, and the slightest nuance between the facts of two similar cases might make all the difference, a fact which was recognised by Lord Griffiths in *Smith v Eric S Bush* [1990] 1 AC 831 (see para 10.3.4) when he said (at p 858): "It is impossible to draw up an exhaustive list of the factors that must be taken into account when a judge is faced with this difficult decision". Nevertheless, he said:

> The following matters should, in my view, always be considered:
>   (1) Were the parties of equal bargaining power. If the court is dealing with a one-off situation between parties of equal bargaining power, the requirement of reasonableness would be more easily discharged than in a case such as the present, where the disclaimer is imposed on the purchaser who has no effective power to object.
>   (2) In the case of advice, would it have been reasonably practical to obtain the advice from an alternative source, taking into account considerations of cost and time. [This is similar to the question as to whether, in products liability cases, it was reasonable for the defendant to expect the plaintiff or someone else higher up in the chain of distribution to make an intermediate inspection of the product before consuming it.]

(3) How difficult is the task being undertaken for which liability is being excluded. When a very difficult or dangerous undertaking is involved there may be a high risk of failure, which would certainly be a pointer towards the reasonableness of excluding liability as a condition of doing the work. A valuation, on the other hand, should present no difficulty if the work is undertaken with reasonable skill and care. . . .

(4) What are the practical consequences of the decision on the question of reasonableness. This must involve the sums of money potentially at stake and the ability of the parties to bear the loss involved which, in its turn, raises the question of insurance. . . . Everyone knows that all prudent professional men carry insurance, and the availability and cost of insurance must be a relevant factor when considering which of two parties should be required to bear the risk of a loss. . . . it can be expected that the surveyor will be insured [against this loss]. [It is unlikely that significant hardship will be caused] if it has to be borne by the surveyor, but it is, on the other hand, quite possible that it will be a financial catastrophe for the purchaser, who may be left with a valueless house and no money to buy another. If the law in these circumstances denies the surveyor the right to exclude his liability, it may result in a few more claims, but I do not think so poorly of the surveyor's profession as to believe that the floodgates will be opened.

Lord Griffiths was careful to add the following qualification to his fourth point. He said (at p 859):

I would not, however, wish it to be thought that I would consider it unreasonable for professional men in all circumstances to seek to exclude or limit their liability for negligence. Sometimes breathtaking sums of money may turn on professional advice, against which it would be impossible for the adviser to obtain adequate insurance cover, and which would ruin him if he were to be held personally liable. In these circumstances, it may indeed be reasonable to give the advice upon a basis of no liability, or possibly of liability limited to the extent of the adviser's insurance cover.

Reconsideration of Hedley Byrne

Lastly, Lord Griffiths said (at p 859):

In addition to the foregoing four factors, which will always have to be considered, there is in this case the additional feature that the surveyor is only employed in the first place because the purchaser wishes to buy the house, and the purchaser in fact provides or contributes to the surveyor's fees. No one has argued that if the purchaser had employed and paid the surveyor himself, it would have been reasonable for the surveyor to exclude liability for negligence, and the present situation is not far removed from that of a direct contract between the surveyor and the purchaser.

This last comment raises the question as to how the disclaimer in *Hedley Byrne* would be viewed by the House of Lords if it were to be reconsidered in the light of the Unfair Contract Terms Act 1977 and its application in *Smith v Bush*. It is submitted that the decision would be exactly the same (ie the disclaimer would be effective), primarily because the plaintiff in a case like *Hedley Byrne* cannot be regarded as being a "helpless consumer" in an inferior bargaining position, in the same way that the purchaser of the "house of modest value" was in *Smith v Bush*, and also because the opinion which a bank is able to provide about the creditworthiness of one of its customers can never be regarded as being an absolute and guaranteed answer to this question: other information from alternative sources would also need to be considered.

McCullagh v Lane Fox

In *McCullagh v Lane Fox and Partners Ltd* (1996) 49 Con LR 124 (CA) (the facts of which are set out in para 10.3.4), one of the questions was whether it would be fair, in all of the circumstances, to allow the defendant to rely on the disclaimers in the particulars of sale prepared by the defendant. The Court of Appeal answered this question in the affirmative. After referring to *Smith v Bush* [1990] 1 AC 831 (see *above*), Hobhouse LJ said:

> It is for the defendants to establish that it is fair and reasonable that they should be allowed to rely upon the disclaimer. This was a transaction which involved a sophisticated and experienced member of the public. The plaintiff had the relevant document in his possession and was aware that it would contain a disclaimer. If [which was a fact] the plaintiff did not even trouble to read the document, he had more than an ample opportunity to do so, and to inform himself fully of what it contained. There is no suggestion that he was in any way misled or was in any material respect unaware of the likely, and the actual, contents of the document. He had ample opportunity to regulate his conduct, having regard to the disclaimer. He could have obtained, had he so chosen, an independent check of the acreage.
>
> Further, the plaintiff had, and would have been assumed to have had, the benefit of legal advice and representation. The normal structure of contracts for the purchase of land is that the intending purchaser, before he exchanges contracts, is able, through his own solicitor, to interrogate the proposed vendor and is entitled to rely upon the answers to such inquiries as representations which have induced the contract, with all the legal consequences that flow from that situation. The use of disclaimers to insulate the estate agent from responsibility for representations made by estate agents is commonplace and is the normal basis upon which house sale transactions are carried out every day across the country. The plaintiff had complete freedom of contract and was in a position to negotiate on an equal footing with the vendor.

In these circumstances, the Court of Appeal had no hesitation in concluding that the defendant in this case was entitled to rely on the disclaimers in the particulars of sale that the defendant had prepared. Thus, Hobhouse LJ said:

> There was no basis for saying, in the context of the present case, that it would be unfair or unreasonable to allow the defendants to rely upon the disclaimer. Indeed, since the plaintiff expected that the particulars would contain a disclaimer, it would, in my judgment, be unreasonable and unfair to the defendants to allow the plaintiff to claim against the defendants as if there had been no such disclaimer.

10.4   Concurrent liability

10.4.1   Introduction

When two parties are in a contractual relationship with each other, one of them, usually the plaintiff, will sometimes allege that, in addition or as an alternative to the rights which the contract expressly or impliedly has conferred on him, he is entitled to the benefit of a duty of care in tort owed to him by the other party (ie the defendant) in respect of the loss which he has suffered. The reason for such an allegation being made in any particular case might be that the limitation period had expired in contract but not in tort, that the plaintiff's damages might be greater if he sues in tort, or that he would be able to obtain leave to serve proceedings out of the jurisdiction or to obtain a right of contribution from a negligent tortfeasor which would not be available against a negligent contract-breaker.

In such cases, the plaintiff will be asking the court to hold the defendant liable concurrently in contract and in tort. A precondition of concurrent tort liability being available is that the circumstances must be such that the duty of care in tort would exist even in the absence of the specific contractual term that created the corresponding contractual obligation.

The basic facts upon which this tortious duty will be alleged to be based will be the same as those which gave rise to the parties' contractual relationship, such as an agreement that the defendant would act as the plaintiff's solicitor and would carry out his instructions with due care and skill but:

(1) the rights which the tortious duty would confer on the plaintiff might be more beneficial to him (such as the later commencement of the limitation period) than if he was confined to his remedies under the contract; or

(2) the plaintiff's damages in tort might be of a different type (ie personal injury or property damage) than those provided for under the contract (ie pure economic loss); or

(3) the scope of the tortious duty might be wider than the contractual duty in terms of the range of activities to which it applies.

There have been numerous reported decisions in which a plaintiff who had a contract with the defendant has sought to pursue concurrent remedies against the defendant in contract and in tort for one or more of the above-mentioned reasons. In such cases the courts have had to decide whether the plaintiff should be confined to his remedies under the contract alone, or whether he should be entitled to choose the remedy which he prefers. Most of the cases in which the question of concurrent liability has arisen have involved claims for pure economic loss. This is not surprising, given that damages for breach of contract are typically claims for pure economic loss.

Two opposing schools of thought have emerged in the cases. In *Donoghue v Stevenson* [1932] AC 562, Lord Macmillan expressed one view when he said (at p 610):

> The fact that there is a contractual relationship between the parties which may give rise to an action for breach of contract does not exclude the co-existence of

a right of action founded on negligence as between the same parties, independently of the contract, though arising out of the relationship in fact brought about by the contract. Of this the best illustration is the right of the injured railway passenger to sue the railway company either for breach of the contract of safe carriage or for negligence in carrying him.

The other view was expressed by Sir Wilfrid Greene MR in *Groom v Crocker* [1939] 1 KB 194, in which the Court of Appeal rejected the plaintiff's claim against his solicitor for damages for mental suffering arising out of the solicitor's negligent conduct of his motor accident claim, because such an action was not covered by the terms of the solicitor's retainer by the plaintiff in relation to the motor accident claim. He said (at p 205): "The relationship of solicitor and client is a contractual one. . . . It was by virtue of that relationship that the duty of the defendants to conduct the case properly arose, and it [ie that duty] had no existence apart from that relationship".

In *Tai Hing Cotton Mill Ltd v Liu Chong Hing Bank Ltd* [1986] AC 80, Lord Scarman, in the Privy Council, expressed the same view when he said (at p 107):

> Their Lordships do not believe that there is anything to the advantage of the law's development in searching for a liability in tort where the parties are in a contractual relationship. This is particularly so in a commercial relationship. . . . their Lordships believe it to be correct in principle and necessary for the avoidance of confusion in the law to adhere to the contractual analysis: In principle, because it is a relationship in which the parties have . . . the right to determine their obligations to each other, and for the avoidance of confusion because different consequences do follow according to whether liability arises from contract or tort, eg, in the limitation of action.

The latter two *dicta* have been particularly influential in leading many judges to hold that, where the parties had a contract with each other, the plaintiff is to be confined to his contractual remedies. Some examples of these decisions are set out in para 10.4.3, *below*. At the same time, certain other judges, who could see neither the logic nor the justice of this exclusionary rule, strove to find ways round it. Examples of their decisions are also provided in para 10.4.3.

The law in England on concurrent liability in contract and in tort was thus in a confused state. In *Wessex Regional Health Authority v HLM Design Ltd* (1994) 40 Con LR 1, Judge Fox-Andrews QC, sitting as an Official Referee, observed this phenomenon when, after referring to more than 40 authorities bearing on the question of concurrent liability, he said: "As the law stands at present, it is not easy for a judge at first instance to rationalise the various decisions to which I have referred". In July 1994, however, the House of Lords in *Henderson v Merrett Syndicates Ltd* [1995] 2 AC 145 clarified the position by ruling very conclusively in favour of the approach expressed by Lord Macmillan in the above-cited passage from his speech in *Donoghue v Stevenson*, subject to certain qualifications.

10.4.2   The new law

Henderson v Merrett

In *Henderson v Merrett Syndicates Ltd* [1995] 2 AC 145, one of the issues was whether managing agents of underwriting syndicates at Lloyd's owed duties of care in tort to underwriting members (known as 'Names') in circumstances where there was a contractual relationship between them. These Names were known as Direct Names. Other Names, who did not contract directly with the managing agents, were known as Indirect Names. Their position is considered in Chapter 9, para 9.7.6.

The managing agents had the capacity to underwrite contracts of insurance at Lloyd's on behalf of the Names who were members of the syndicates under their management, to reinsure contracts of insurance and to pay claims made under those contracts. In the case of Direct Names, there was a contract between them and the managing agents in respect of the underwriting, reinsurance and settlement of claims carried out by the managing agents on behalf of the Direct Names as members of the syndicate under their management.

Despite the existence of these contracts, the Direct Names were concerned to establish the existence of a concurrent duty of care in tort to them by the managing agents so as to enable them to take advantage of the later date for the accrual of their causes of action in tort.

The House of Lords unanimously held that, notwithstanding the existence of the contracts between the Direct Names and the managing agents, the Direct Names were entitled to sue the managing agents in tort, thereby taking advantage of the more favourable tort limitation commencement date. In so holding, their Lordships swept aside all of the previous judgments, which had held that in cases of possible concurrent liability the plaintiff is restricted to his remedy in contract alone. After referring to some of these decisions, including *Groom v Crocker*, cited *above*, Lord Goff said (at p 186):

> I perceive at work in these decisions not only the influence of the dead hand of history, but also the temptation of elegance. We can discern the same impulse behind the much-quoted observation of Lord Scarman when delivering the judgment of the Judicial Committee of the Privy Council in *Tai Hing Cotton Mill Ltd v Liu Chong Hing Bank Ltd* [cited *above*].

Lord Goff placed reliance on many of the cases summarised in para 10.4.3, *below*, that contain *dicta* or conclusions in favour of concurrent liability (in particular, *Edwards v Mallan* [1908] 1 KB 1002, *Donoghue v Stevenson* [1932] AC 562, *Lister v Romford Ice and Cold Storage Co Ltd* [1957] AC 555, *Matthews v Kuwait Bechtel Corporation* [1959] 2 QB 57, *Esso Petroleum Co Ltd v Mardon* [1976] 1 QB 801, *Batty v Metropolitan Property Realisations Ltd* [1978] 1 QB 554 and *Midland Bank Trust Co Ltd v Hett, Stubbs and Kemp (A Firm)* [1979] 1 KB 384).

Lord Goff said that the contrary approach, as exemplified in *Groom v Crocker* (see *above*), "involves regarding the law of tort as supplementary to the law of contract, ie, as providing for a tortious liability [only] in cases where there is no contract". Lord Goff rejected this view, making it clear that the function of the law of tort is not limited to filling in gaps left by the law of contract. He said (at p 193):

> Yet the law of tort is the general law, out of which the parties can, if they wish, contract. . . .
>
> The common law is not antipathetic to concurrent liability and . . . there is no sound basis for a rule which automatically restricts the claimant to either a tortious or a contractual remedy. The result may be untidy: but, given that the tortious duty is imposed by the general law, and the contractual duty is attributable to the will of the parties, I do not find it objectionable that the claimant may be entitled to take advantage of the remedy which is most advantageous to him, subject only to ascertaining whether the tortious duty is so inconsistent with the applicable contract that, in accordance with ordinary principle, the parties must be taken to have agreed that the tortious remedy is to be limited or excluded.
>
> [Consequently], unless his contract precludes him from doing so, the plaintiff, who has available to him concurrent remedies in contract and tort, may choose that remedy which appears to him to be the most advantageous.

The only other Law Lord to deliver a substantive speech, Lord Browne-Wilkinson, expressed his views in similar terms, when he said (at p 206):

> I can see no good reason for holding that the existence of a contractual right is in all circumstances inconsistent with the co-existence of another tortious right, provided that it is understood that the agreement of the parties evidenced by the contract can modify and shape the tortious duties which, in the absence of contract, would be applicable.

Comment

The *new law*, as set out *above*, is not all or nothing. While it is clear that in future it will not be possible to contend that a plaintiff who has or had a contractual relationship with the defendant is *ipso facto* confined to his remedies in contract, he will also not automatically be entitled to pursue his tortious remedy, even if he is able to establish all of the elements of a tortious duty of care. The terms of the contract, express and implied—and, indeed, extrinsic evidence where the contract is ambiguous—will need to be considered to ascertain whether the parties intended to agree to limit the extent of the defendant's liability for losses that might be suffered by the plaintiff in consequence of the defendant's negligent performance of the contract. As Lord Browne-Wilkinson said in *Henderson* (at p 206): "the nature and terms of the contractual relationship between the parties will be determinative of the *scope* of the responsibility assumed and can, in some cases, exclude any assumption of legal responsibility to the plaintiff for whom the defendant has assumed to act".

The relevance of the contract was also well described by Robert Goff LJ (now Lord Goff) in *Coupland v Arabian Gulf Oil Co* [1983] 1 WLR 1136, when he said (at p 1153): "I ask myself: What impact does the existence of the contract have on the claim in tort? In my judgment, on ordinary principles, the contract is only relevant to the claim in tort in so far as it does, *on its true construction*, have the effect of excluding or restricting the tortious claim".

The new law in England, which has been established as the favoured approach in Canada since 1986, was neatly expressed in the following statement of the Supreme Court of Canada in *Central Trust Co v Rafuse* (1986) 31 DLR (4th) 481 (at p 522):

> A concurrent or alternative liability in tort will not be admitted if its effect will be to permit the plaintiff to circumvent or escape a contractual exclusion or limitation of liability for the act or omission that would constitute the tort. Subject to this qualification, where concurrent liability in tort and contract exists, the plaintiff has the right to assert the cause of action that appears to be the most advantageous to him in respect of any particular legal consequence.

In *Henderson v Merrett*, Lord Goff said that he agreed fully with this statement of principle. Accordingly, in future cases involving concurrent liability in contract and in tort, where the plaintiff, for one reason or another, wishes to press the tortious remedy in preference to the contractual remedy, the court's focus will be:

(1) first, to determine whether a duty of care exists in tort and, if so, what is the scope, or the content or extent, of it; and

(2) secondly, whether the contract, on its true construction, envisaged that the scope, or the content or extent, of the defendant's liability under the contract would be less than the scope of the defendant's tortious liability.

When this type of analysis is carried out, it might be found that the result in some of the cases mentioned in para 10.4.3, *below*, that applied the strict contractual analysis, is the same as it was previously, albeit that the result will be reached by a different route. The issue will be decided by asking whether the intention of the parties, on the true construction of their contract, was that the tortious duty should be excluded or limited. While the House of Lords' judgment in *Henderson v Merrett Syndicates Ltd* [1995] 2 AC 145 has certainly clarified the approach for courts to follow in cases of concurrent liability in contract and tort, it has not put an end to litigation in this field because opinions will differ on the interpretation of the parties' contractual intentions.

Post-Henderson decisions

Barclays Bank plc v Fairclough Building Ltd (1995) 44 Con LR 35: The plaintiff, Barclays Bank plc ('Barclays') had engaged the defendant, Fairclough Building Ltd ('Fairclough'), to carry out maintenance work at two large industrial warehouse units which were used for storage. Part of the work involved cleaning the units' corrugated asbestos cement roofs, which had become encrusted with moss, lichen and dirt. The contract required that this aspect of the work should be carried out by a specialist firm of roofing contractors.

The cleaning of the roofs was included in work which Fairclough subcontracted to the third party, Carne (Structural Repair) Co Ltd ('Carne'). Carne, in turn, sub-contracted the cleaning of the asbestos roofs to the fourth party, Trendleway Ltd ('Trendleway'). Within two days of

Trendleway starting to clean the roofs, water leaked through into the storage areas below. Thereafter, steps were taken to try to prevent the problem and to protect the documents stored in the warehouses from damage. At that time, no one suspected that the water contained asbestos. However, when the affected areas dried out, a dust which was left was found to contain asbestos, which created a serious hazard to health. When the Environmental Health Department heard about this, it issued a notice prohibiting further work within the units until the situation had been remedied.

Barclays sued Fairclough for recovery of the cost of the remedial works. Fairclough joined Carne as a third party and Carne joined Trendleway as a fourth party. Fairclough settled with Barclays and Carne settled with Fairclough, but Trendleway refused to pay any money to Carne unless Carne would accept that any damages assessed against Trendleway should be reduced on account of Carne's contributory negligence in performing the work sub-contracted to them by Fairclough.

In accordance with the provisions and the effect of the Law Reform (Contributory Negligence) Act 1945, such an apportionment of damages can be made only if there has been a breach of a tortious duty. The question therefore was whether the fact that there was a contract between Carne and Trendleway prevented the existence of a concurrent duty of care in tort by Trendleway to Carne for the economic loss suffered by Carne through Trendleway's failure to exercise reasonable care and skill in carrying out its sub-sub-contract. The Court of Appeal answered this question in the affirmative.

In accordance with the approach enunciated by the House of Lords in *Henderson*, their Lordships in the Court of Appeal first considered whether, in the circumstances of this case, and leaving aside the terms of the contract between Trendleway and Carne, it was fair, just and reasonable to impose a duty of care on Trendleway for Carne's economic loss consisting of the amount of money that Carne had to pay Fairclough to settle Fairclough's claim against Carne. They had no difficulty in answering this question in the affirmative, because Trendleway was a contractor who had undertaken skilled work for Carne in circumstances in which Trendleway knew that the failure on Trendleway's part to perform that contract adequately would expose Carne to a claim from Fairclough; Trendleway knew that Carne was placing reliance on it to do the work properly and the imposition of such a duty would not expose Trendleway "to the risk of an unrestricted number of claims or to claims greater in extent than those for which it would be liable for breach of the contractual obligations it had undertaken".

Secondly, having reached this conclusion, their Lordships, following *Henderson*, held that this tortious duty could exist concurrently with the duties which Trendleway had undertaken to Carne under the contract between them, because the tortious duty was not inconsistent with any obligations of Trendleway under the contractual relationship which it had with Carne.

White v Jones [1995] 2 AC 207: This case had nothing to do with concurrent liability (see Chapter 9, para 9.7.5), but Lord Nolan thought that the principle of concurrent liability assisted in explaining why there would be nothing wrong in imposing a duty of care in tort on the defendant's solicitors when their only contract was with the deceased testator and they had no contract with the plaintiff beneficiaries. In response to the solicitors' counsel's submission that the imposition of a duty of care on the solicitors would extend tortious liability into what should be the exclusive domain of contract, Lord Nolan said (at p 293):

> The force of this argument has of course been substantially diminished by the intervening decision of your Lordships' House in *Henderson v Merrett Syndicates Ltd* [1995] 2 AC 145 which shows that a contractual duty of care owed by the defendant to A may perfectly well coexist with an equivalent tortious duty of care to B. Both duties depend on the assumption of responsibility by the defendant. In the former case the responsibility is assumed by the making of the contract and is defined by its terms. In the latter the responsibility is assumed by the defendant embarking upon a potentially harmful activity and is defined by the general law. If the defendant drives his car on the highway, he implicitly assumes a responsibility towards other road users and they in turn implicitly rely on him to discharge that responsibility. By taking his car on to the road, he holds himself out as a reasonably careful driver.
>
> In the same way, as it seems to me, a professional man who undertakes to exercise his skill in a manner which, to his knowledge, may cause loss to others if carelessly performed, may thereby implicitly assume a legal responsibility towards them. The fact that he is doing so in pursuance of a contractual duty or a statutory function cannot of itself exclude that responsibility. The most that can be said is that it may be one of the circumstances to be taken into account in determining the nature and extent of the responsibility.

It is submitted that Lord Nolan's comments are misguided in so far as they suggest that the concurrency principle has any relevance in deciding whether a duty of care should be imposed on a defendant who had a contract with a third party but not with the plaintiff. Apart from this, the principles articulated by Lord Nolan are sound, and are discussed elsewhere in this chapter.

Gable House Estates Ltd v The Halpern Partnership (1995) 48 Con LR 1: In this case the defendant, The Halpern Partnership ('Halpern'), was a firm of architects which (in very complicated proceedings) the judge found owed its clients, Gable House Estates ('Gable House') (the plaintiff), a duty of care under the parties' contract. That duty was a duty to use reasonable skill and care in connection with Halpern's provision of schedules of net lettable area to Gable House in relation to the scheme of refurbishment which Gable House was contemplating with regard to a building it was proposing to purchase. Having reached this point, it was necessary for the judge to consider Halpern's alleged tortious liability since it was common ground that the measure of damages was different in contract and in tort.

In the light of the House of Lords' decision in *Henderson*, the defendant's counsel accepted that Halpern owed a duty of care in tort to Gable House co-extensive with its contractual obligation. However, he submitted that the duty of care in tort must stand on its own two feet. Therefore, he submitted, although the contract for professional services will suffice to establish a general assumption of responsibility by the architect for a project design, the plaintiff will not be able to have the benefit of a concurrent tortious duty unless the plaintiff can establish that he in fact relied on a specific act done or on information supplied by the architect. On the other hand, the plaintiff's counsel argued that, where there is a contractual assumption of responsibility by a defendant to a plaintiff to perform services of which the defendant has special knowledge, that will be sufficient to show reliance on the defendant to perform those services with due skill and care.

The judge, Judge Esyr Lewis QC, sitting as an Official Referee, preferred the defendant's argument on this point. After referring extensively to the speeches in *Henderson*, he said:

> I derive the following principles from Lord Goff's speech in *Henderson*:
> 1 A concurrent duty in tort can exist where parties are in a contractual relationship if the terms of the contract do not preclude it.
> 2 That concurrent duty in tort will arise and enable a plaintiff to recover damages for economic loss where, for example, in a contract for services, certainly where the defendant has special knowledge or skills, the defendant assumes responsibility towards the plaintiff. The assumption of responsibility to perform those services with due skill and care will arise from the very nature of the services which the defendant undertakes to provide.
> 3 There must, however, be a 'concomitant reliance' by the plaintiff to enable him to establish his claim.
> 4 'Reliance' may take different forms in different circumstances.
> 5 The assumption of responsibility and the duty to take care is not confined to cases concerned with erroneous information and advice. For example, a solicitor may be liable if he fails to do something which it was his responsibility to do for his client which causes loss. In this kind of situation, the fact that the solicitor has been retained and what he failed to do was within the scope of the duties his retainer required of him will be sufficient to establish 'reliance'.
> 6 However, where the complaint is that there has been negligent advice or negligent misinformation, the plaintiff must show that he specifically relied on that advice or was actually misled. In my view, this distinction appears in the first of the passages which I have quoted from Lord Goff's speech. In the present case it seems to me that it would be odd to attach liability to Halpern if, for example, the evidence showed that Gable House took no notice of the March schedule of areas in making their decision to buy out Clayton [the vendor of the property] or did so for a reason other than the contents of the schedule even though it were proved that the schedule was negligently prepared and gave incorrect information.

Later on his Lordship reinforced the above-cited *dicta* by saying: "Halpern were in breach of their contractual duty to exercise reasonable care in conformity with the normal standards of the architect's profession and also in breach of an identical duty in tort. The claim in tort is not actionable without proof of reliance".

The plaintiff was not able to establish that it did in fact place specific reliance on anything which the defendant had said in deciding to complete its purchase of the building. The judge felt that the plaintiff's decision was motivated more by the fact that demand for property was strong and rents were moving upward than by any actual reliance which it placed on the defendant at that time to provide it with accurate information about the net lettable area which could be achieved on redevelopment. Therefore, this part of the plaintiff's claim for a concurrent tortious duty of care failed.

Citibank NA v Lebihan Contracts Ltd (13 May 1996, unreported): The plaintiff, Citibank, owned and occupied certain premises which were installed with an uninterruptible power supply ('UPS') system, which was maintained partly by the first defendant, Lebihan Contracts Ltd ('Lebihan'), under a contract made in 1983. In 1991, a fault in the UPS system caused an underground cable fire which, in turn, caused considerable damage to a number of cables, the battery room and the equipment in it. The cost to Citibank of repairing this damage was well in excess of £2 million.

Any claim by Citibank against Lebihan was statute-barred; but a tortious claim was not, because the damage necessary to complete a cause of action in tort occurred within the tortious limitation period. Lebihan's counsel submitted that no concurrent tortious duty of care was possible because he said that *Henderson v Merrett* was concerned only with "a *Hedley Byrne* type of duty" (ie a duty of care based on an assumption of responsibility by the defendant with concomitant reliance by the plaintiff). The judge, Langley J, rejected this submission. After noting that there was nothing inconsistent in the terms of Lebihan's contract for the 1983 works with the existence of a concurrent duty of care in tort, he said:

> Citibank's claim is for a failure to take care in the cable installation such as to expose Citibank to the risk of physical damage to its goods and premises. That, in my judgment, is a recognised basis for the existence of a duty of care in tort and I think that Lebihan's were under such a duty in the circumstances of the work they were engaged to carry out in 1983.

Identical duties

Another issue which might need to be decided in the future is whether the plaintiff's right to sue in tort is automatically excluded in cases where the scope, or the content or extent, of the contractual term is identical to the scope of the tortious duty which would be applicable in the absence of its full definition in the contract. The judge in *Hiron v Pynford South Ltd* (1992) 28 EG 112 (see para 10.4.3, *below*) answered this question in the affirmative. He said (at p 115):

> Since the second plaintiffs and the third defendants had entered into an express contract whereby the third defendants were to advise the second plaintiffs in return for payment, and a duty in tort to take care in giving advice would merely

have duplicated an implied term in the contract, I do not think it was just and reasonable that the third defendants should have owed a duty in tort. The only probable result of adding a tortious obligation would have been to have given the second plaintiff a longer period in which to sue the defendant, but if that had been the intention of the parties, they could have provided for it in their contract. The position would probably have been different if the contractual and tortious duties had not precisely coincided.

The two minority judges in the Supreme Court of Canada in *BG Checo International Ltd v British Columbia Hydro and Power Authority* (1993) 99 DLR (4th) 577 (see para 10.4.4, *below*) were also of this belief. One of these minority judges, Iacobucci J, said (at p 612):

> If the duty is defined by an express term of the contract, the plaintiff will be confined to whatever remedies are available in the law of contract. If the parties to a contract choose to define a specific duty as an express term of the contract, the consequences of a breach of that duty ought to be determined by the law of contract, not by tort law;

and he concluded by saying (at p 621):

> It is clear that the fact that the parties are in a contractual relationship is not in itself a bar to an action in tort. However, where a duty arising in tort is co-extensive with a duty created by an express term of the contract, the plaintiff will be limited to whatever remedies are available under the contract.

It is submitted that this approach is fundamentally flawed and that the majority (of 4:2) speaking through La Forest and McLachlin JJ are correct in stating (at p 580): "In our view, our colleague's approach would have the effect of eliminating much of the rationalising thrust behind the movement towards concurrency in tort and contract".

The rationale behind the *new law* is that, given that tortious duties are imposed by the general law, a plaintiff who can establish a relevant tortious duty owed to him by a particular defendant may sue that defendant either in tort or in contract if he has a contract with that defendant, subject only to such limitations as the parties themselves have agreed to place on that right by their contract. As the majority said in *BG Checo* (at p 584):

> The only limit on the right to choose one's action [in contract or in tort] is the principle of primacy of private ordering—the right of individuals to arrange their affairs and assume risks in a different way than would be done by the law of tort. The tort duty, a general duty imputed by the law in all the relevant circumstances, must yield to the parties' superior right to arrange their rights and duties in a different way. In so far as the tort duty is not contradicted by the contract, it remains intact and may be sued upon. The mere fact that the parties have dealt with a matter expressly in their contract does not mean that they intended to exclude the right to sue in tort. It all depends on *how* they have dealt with it.

In *Henderson v Merrett Syndicates Ltd* [1995] 2 AC 145, Lord Goff made the same point when he said (at p 789): "Unless his contract precludes him from doing so, the plaintiff who has available to him concurrent remedies in contract and tort may choose that remedy which appears to him to be the most advantageous".

In *BG Checo*, the plaintiff sued the defendant for damages for negligent misrepresentation in contract and in tort. The alleged misrepresentation had been made in a pre-contractual tender, which (representation) had become a term of the concluded contract. The contract did not contain any terms excluding the defendant's potential liability for misrepresentation. The measure of damages available to the plaintiff in tort was greater than under the contract.

It was clear, therefore, that both the contract and the common law created a duty of care on the defendant not to make negligent misrepresentations to the plaintiff about the extent of the work that the plaintiff would be required to do if the plaintiff were to be awarded the contract. The scope, or the content or extent, of this duty was the same in contract and in tort. For the minority, this fact was sufficient to hold that the plaintiff was to be confined to the remedies available under the contract. Iacobucci J said (at p 605): "No duty of care in tort can be concurrent with a duty of care created by an express term of the contract". The majority, on the other hand, did not regard this fact as being determinative of the issue. Instead, they applied the approach set out *above* and concluded (at p 586) that, notwithstanding that the defendant's duty in contract and its common law duty in tort were co-extensive: "The contract, read as we have proposed, did not negate Hydro's common law duty not to negligently represent that it would have the right of way cleared by others".

It is submitted that the majority's approach is the correct one in cases of this nature because it involves the court in interpreting the contract in accordance with the established rules of interpretation against the backdrop of the supremacy of the tortious remedy being applicable unless the parties have themselves nullified it by clear terms. The flaw in the reasoning of the minority, and of the judge in *Hiron v Pynford South Ltd* (see *above*), is that it disregards this principle.

In *Queen v Cognos Inc* (1993) 99 DLR (4th) 626, Iacobucci J returned to the above-mentioned theme (ie that, in his view, no duty of care in tort can be concurrent with a duty of care created by an express term of the contract), but this time he held that the principle was not applicable because the relevant pre-contract representation had not been incorporated into the contract. The facts of this case are set out fully in Chapter 9, para 9.9.3, but briefly they were as follows. In a job interview the defendant's representative told the plaintiff that if the plaintiff was offered the job he would take charge of a particular project, but the representative did not tell the plaintiff that the project had not yet been approved by the company's Board. In reliance on the defendant's representation as to the scope of the job, the plaintiff accepted the job offer and resigned from his previous secure employment. He also signed an employment contract which entitled the defendant to dismiss him on one month's notice without cause. In due course, the defendant's Board turned down the project and the plaintiff was subsequently given notice of termination.

10.4.2   *The contractual connection*

The plaintiff sued the defendant in tort for damages arising from the defendant's pre-contract representation as to the scope of the job. One of the issues canvassed by Iacobucci J (with whose judgment only one of the other five judges agreed) was whether the scope or content of the plaintiff's concurrent tortious claim was *co-extensive* with his contractual claim. If Iacobucci J had concluded that it was, he would have held that the tortious claim could not be brought for the reasons stated by him in *BG Checo, above*. Thus he said (at p 644):

> As I stated in *BG Checo*, it is now clear that an action in tort for negligent mis-representation may lie even though the relevant parties to the action are in a contractual relationship. The fact that the alleged misrepresentations are made in a pre-contractual setting, such as during negotiations or in the course of an employment interview, and the fact that a contract is subsequently entered into by the parties, do not in themselves bar an action in tort for damages caused by the said misrepresentations. This is not to say that the contract in such a case is irrelevant and that the court should dispose of the plaintiff's tort claim independently of the contractual arrangements. On the contrary, depending on the circumstances, the subsequent contract may play a very important role in determining whether or not, and to what extent, a claim for negligent misrepresentation shall succeed.
>
> Indeed, as evidenced by my conclusion in *BG Checo*, such a contract can have the effect of negating the action in tort and of confining the plaintiff to whatever remedies are available under the law of contract. On the other hand, even if the tort claim is not barred altogether by the contract, the duty or liability of the defendant with respect to negligent misrepresentations may be limited or excluded by a term of the subsequent contract so as to diminish or extinguish the plaintiff's remedy in tort. Equally true, however, is that there are cases where the subsequent contract will have no effect whatsoever on the plaintiff's claim for damages in tort. It is my view that the employment agreement signed by the plaintiff in March 1983 is governed by this last proposition.
>
> When considering the effect of the subsequent contract on the representee's tort action, everything revolves around the nature of the contractual obligations assumed by the parties and the nature of the alleged negligent misrepresentation. The first and foremost question should be whether there is a specific contractual duty created by an express term of the contract which is co-extensive with the common law duty of care which the representee alleges the representor has breached. Put another way, did the pre-contractual representation relied on by the plaintiff become an express term of the subsequent contract? If so, absent any overriding considerations arising from the context in which the transaction occurred, the plaintiff cannot bring a concurrent action in tort for negligent mis-representation and is confined to whatever remedies are available under the law of contract. As alluded to in *BG Checo*, principle is an exception to the general rule of concurrency espoused by this court in *Central Trust v Rafuse* [see *below*].

These *dicta* have been set out in full, not for the purpose of lending any credence to the view that the 'principle of co-extensiveness' is an exception to the 'general rule of concurrency', but to demonstrate the torturous distinctions that would have to be made if this principle were to be accepted. Far more workable is the rule propounded by the House of Lords in *Henderson*, namely, that a plaintiff who has the choice of suing the defendant in contract or in tort may bring his action in tort if that would be to his advantage unless the contract (expressly or impliedly) precludes him from doing so.

Tortious duty more extensive

It has been noted that the *new law* is that a plaintiff who has the choice of suing the defendant in contract or in tort may bring his action in tort if that would be to his advantage unless the contract (expressly or impliedly) precludes him from doing so; and that this principle will apply even if the scope of the defendant's duty in tort is exactly the same as the scope of his contractual duty to the plaintiff. In some cases, however, the question has arisen as to the correct position for the court to take if the scope of the plaintiff's concurrent tortious duty would be *more extensive* than his contractual duty.

Initially there were indications that a concurrent tortious duty would not be able to succeed if (and to the extent that) it was more extensive than the defendant's duty in contract to the plaintiff. For example, in *Burton and Burton v MBC (Builders-Ashingdon) Ltd* and *MBC (Estates-Ashingdon)* (1994) 69 P&CR 496, in considering whether a house purchaser whose contractual claim was statute-barred should be entitled to pursue an action in tort against the vendor of the land, which tortious duty would have cast a heavier burden on the vendor than its duties to the plaintiff under the contract, Mann LJ said: "The infliction of a tortious duty upon the second defendant in excess of its contractual duty might conflict with the rule of *caveat emptor* which typically applies on the sale of a house". In *Conway v Crowe Kelsey and Partners* (1994) 39 Con LR 112, Judge Cyril Newman QC, sitting as an Official Referee, held that the balance of authority favoured the proposition that a concurrent duty in tort could not be wider in scope than the defendant's contractual duties so as to confer a substantive advantage on the plaintiff. The views expressed in these cases are no longer good law in view of the Court of Appeal's decision in *Holt v Payne Skillington* (see *below*).

Holt and Holt v Payne Skillington and De Groot Collis (18 December 1995, unreported): The plaintiffs, David and Bernard Holt, had made a large capital gain on the sale of their business. In order to minimise their capital gains tax liability, they decided to take advantage of the roll-over relief which would result from using the proceeds of sale of their business to purchase a building to be used for the purposes of a trade. Under the relevant legislation the commercial letting of furnished holiday accommodation is to be treated as a trade so long as the property is not in the same occupation for more than 31 days for at least seven months in any year.

The plaintiffs were interested in purchasing such a property. For this purpose the plaintiffs retained the services of the second defendant, De Groot Collis ('DGC'), a prominent firm of estate agents and surveyors. In due course a suitable property was identified and DGC advised the plaintiffs that, if they bought it, they would be able to obtain the roll-over relief which they desired.

The plaintiffs duly went ahead with their purchase of the property, but it subsequently became manifest that the property would not qualify for roll-over relief because, from a planning point of view, no established use of the property for short-term lettings could be proved. The plaintiffs sued DGC and their (the plaintiffs') solicitors, Payne Skillington. The trial judge found the solicitors liable and they did not appeal. Therefore the Court of Appeal was concerned with the case against DGC only.

The Court of Appeal dismissed the plaintiffs' case against DGC in so far as it was based on alleged breaches of contract. The only contract between the plaintiffs and DGC was DGC's retainer agreement. There was no express term in that agreement obliging DGC to investigate the planning position for the plaintiffs or making it a condition that any property introduced to and subsequently purchased by the plaintiffs should have the necessary authorised use; nor was the Court able to imply any such obligation or condition.

The question therefore was whether, if DGC owed the plaintiffs an independent duty of care in tort (which the Court held they did), it was possible for such a duty of care in tort to be concurrent with duties under a contract between the same parties, despite the contractual duties being of a more limited nature than the duty of care in tort. The Court of Appeal answered this question in the affirmative. After noting that Lord Goff in *Henderson v Merrett Syndicates Ltd* [1995] 2 AC 145 said that the basis for the imposition of a duty of care in cases of professional negligence is the assumption of responsibility by the defendant and concomitant reliance by the plaintiff, Hirst LJ, delivering the judgment of the Court, said (at para 48):

> As Lord Goff made clear in *Henderson v Merrett*, it will frequently be the case that the relevant assumption of responsibility occurs within a contractual context. That fact does not mean that it must necessarily do so simply because, at some stage during the relevant course of dealings between the parties, they chose to and did enter into some form of contract. A consideration of the individual facts and circumstances of each case will determine whether any duty of care in tort which the general law may impose is of wider scope than any contract to which the same parties may agree at some stage during the same course of dealing.
>
> It is important to emphasise that the duty of care in tort is, in appropriate circumstances, imposed by the general law, whereas the contractual obligations result from the common intention of the parties. In our opinion there is no reason in principle why a *Hedley Byrne* type duty of care cannot arise in an overall set of circumstances where, by reference to certain limited aspects of those circumstances, the same parties enter into a contractual relationship involving more limited obligations than those imposed by the duty of care in tort.
>
> In such circumstances the duty of care in tort and the duties imposed by the contract will be concurrent but not co-extensive. The difference in scope between the two will reflect the more limited factual basis which gave rise to the contract and the absence of any term in that contract which precludes or restricts the wider duty of care in tort.

For these reasons the Court of Appeal held that, as there were no terms in the plaintiffs' contract with DGC which precluded or restricted DGC's duty of care in tort, the plaintiffs were entitled to pursue their action in tort against DGC, notwithstanding that the duty of care was more extensive than DGC's concurrent duties in contract. It is worth noting that, in the end, the plaintiffs' action in tort against DGC failed because, in deciding to go ahead with the exchange of contracts, the plaintiffs did not in fact rely on DGC, but instead relied on information that had been provided to them by their solicitors.

Sumitomo Bank v Banque Bruxelles [1997] 1 Lloyd's Rep 487: The facts of this case are set out in Chapter 9, para 9.7.8. At this point it is worth noting that the judge, Langley J, applied the principle of *Holt* in relation to the plaintiffs' claims in tort to the extent that they were more extensive than the express or implied obligations to be derived from the terms of the contract which had been made between the parties. After referring to the above-cited *dicta* in *Holt*, Langley J said: "Those words, in my judgment, apply here where the Loan Agreement established and looked forward to the role of BBL as Agent Bank but did not relate to or look back to their role as Arranging Bank prior to the Agreement".

Tesco Stores Ltd v The Norman Hitchcox Partnership (8 October 1997, unreported): The facts of this case are set out in para 7.4.6. At this point it is worth noting that the judge, Judge Esyr Lewis QC, sitting as an Official Referee, would have applied the principle of *Holt* if he had found that the architects had owed an independent duty of care in tort to Tesco in relation to the design of the shell of the supermarket. It would not have mattered that the scope of that duty was more extensive than the scope of the fit-out contract which the architects had with Tesco. Thus, his Honour said:

> It is clear both that a duty of care may arise within the ambit of a contract which is wider than any obligation imposed by the contract itself and that a duty of care under the principles established in *Hedley Byrne and Co Ltd v Heller and Partners Ltd* [1964] AC 465 may arise independently of any contractual relationship. The reason for the first principle was given in Hirst LJ's judgment in the *Skillington* case, namely that the contractual and tortious obligations are independent of each other, although in a contract for services they may be identical in scope, ie, the implied obligation to exercise reasonable skill and care.

Exclusion clauses

Another area of fertile ground for possible future litigation might be cases in which there are arguments as to the *validity* of a relevant contractual exclusion clause. In this regard, the discussion set out in para 10.3.4, *above*, of the Unfair Contract Terms Act is pertinent, as also is the following *dictum* of the majority judgment in the Supreme Court of Canada in *BG Checo International Ltd v British Columbia Hydro and Power Authority* (1993) 99 DLR (4th) 577 (at p 586):

We conclude that actions in contract and tort may be concurrently pursued unless the parties, by a *valid* contractual provision, indicate that they intended otherwise. This excludes, of course, cases where the contractual limitation is invalid, as by fraud, mistake or unconscionability. Similarly, a contractual limitation may not apply where the tort is independent of the contract in the sense of falling outside the scope of the contract, as in the example given in *Elder, Dempster & Co Ltd v Paterson, Zochonis and Co Ltd* [1924] AC 522, of the captain of a vessel falling asleep and starting a fire in relation to a claim for cargo damage.

An example of an invalid contractual exclusion provision for the purpose of limiting or excluding the defendant's liability to the plaintiff in tort can be found in *Gable House Estates Ltd v The Halpern Partnership* (1995) 48 Con LR 1, the facts of which are set out *above*. One of the defendant architects' counsel's submissions was that the plaintiff's concurrent cause of action in tort was ruled out by virtue of the statement in the parties' contract that all of the measurements of areas to be provided by the defendant would be approximate. It was argued that the plaintiff's acceptance of this term constituted a limitation on the plaintiff's right to sue the defendant in tort for breach of an alleged duty to take reasonable care in providing accurate information as to the net lettable area of the building which the plaintiff proposed to purchase and refurbish. In rejecting this submission the judge, Judge Esyr Lewis QC, sitting as an Official Referee, said:

> I have come to the conclusion that, having regard to the fact that the importance of lettable area to Gable House was well understood by Halpern [the architects], the formula 'all areas approximate' was not a sufficient warning to Gable House of the uncertainties which existed in March 1987 and which could affect the figures of lettable area in the March schedule.

On the other hand, in *Woollahra Municipal Council v Sved* (1996) 40 NSW LR 101, the facts of which are set out in Chapter 7, para 7.6.4, the contractual exclusion clause which the plaintiffs had accepted in their contract with one of the defendants did have the effect of ruling out a cause of action in tort against that defendant. In addition to suing the builder and the municipal council, the plaintiffs sued their vendors, Mr and Mrs Goddard. Clause 28 of the contract between the Goddards and the Sveds stated that the purchasers (the Sveds) acknowledged that they had satisfied themselves as to any defects in the house and that they would not make any claims for compensation in relation thereto. In holding that this clause sufficed to rule out a concurrent duty of care in tort, Clarke JA said (at p 141):

> The Goddards and the Sveds were in a contractual relationship. As part of that relationship the Sveds agreed by clause 28 of the contract that they had satisfied themselves as to any defects in the building and that they would not make any objection, requisition or claim in relation thereto. In *Bryan v Maloney* (1995) 182 CLR 609 [see Chapter 7, para 7.6.4], the majority discussed the relevance of the existence of a contract between the parties in terms which indicated approval of the three propositions set out by Le Dain J in *Central Trust Co v Rafuse* (see *below*). One of those directed attention to the relevance of a contractual exclu-

sion or limitation and, of course, the majority [in *Bryan*] themselves recognised that the terms of the contract may militate against the recognition of a relationship of proximity. This is such a case. The Sveds, by clause 28, took the risk of defects in the building upon themselves. In these circumstances there is no basis for a positive finding that the Goddards owed them a duty of care in tort in relation to those defects.

Concurrent statutory duty

The principle of concurrency enunciated by the House of Lords in *Henderson* has been used as the justification for countenancing the existence of a concurrent common law duty of care with a statutory duty if the conditions for the existence of the common law duty can be established in the circumstances of the particular case (see Chapter 8). Thus, in *West Wiltshire District Council v Garland* [1994] Ch 297, the facts of which are set out in Chapter 8, para 8.2.10, Balcombe LJ said (at p 310):

> Because a plaintiff has an action for breach of statutory duty in respect of the negligent performance of a statutory duty, it does not follow that he therefore cannot have an action at common law in respect of the same negligence. Thus in *Henderson v Merrett Syndicates Ltd* [1995] 2 AC 145 it was held that there may legitimately be coexistent remedies for negligence in contract and in tort. In my judgment it is equally true that there may be coexistent remedies for negligence in breach of a statutory duty.

Similarly, in *X (Minors) v Bedfordshire County Council* [1995] 2 AC 633, Lord Browne-Wilkinson said (at p 765):

> [Counsel] for the defendant authority submitted that because Parliament has established the statutory regime for the protection of children with special educational needs, it was inconsistent with that scheme to find a parallel common law duty of care owed to children with special educational needs. I reject this submission. Although, as I have said, it is impossible to impose a common law duty of care which is inconsistent with, or fetters, a statutory duty, I can see no legal or common sense principle which requires one to deny a common law duty of care which would otherwise exist just because there is a statutory scheme which addresses the same problem.

10.4.3 Relevant pre-*Henderson* cases

Cases in favour of concurrent liability

Edwards v Mallan [1908] 1 KB 1002: The plaintiff had contracted with the defendant dentist to have a tooth extracted by the defendant's 'painless process'. The Court of Appeal held that the plaintiff's claim for the illness, pain and suffering which she sustained when, although the tooth had been painlessly extracted, broken portions of it had been left in her jaw, could be brought against the defendant in tort, notwithstanding the existence of the contract between the parties. The court impliedly gave effect to the defendant's counsel's submission that the "relation of the plaintiff and the defendant was such that a duty to take due care arose from that relationship, irrespective of contract".

Donoghue v Stevenson [1932] AC 562: As noted *above*, Lord Macmillan said: "The fact that there is a contractual relationship between the parties which may give rise to an action for breach of contract, does not exclude the co-existence of a right of action founded on negligence as between the same parties, independently of their contract, though arising out of the relationship in fact brought about by the contract". It should be noted that Lord Macmillan was not saying that where there is a contractual relationship between the plaintiff and the defendant, this necessarily means that the plaintiff will also have a right of action in tort if he suffers loss from the defendant's breach of contract, but simply that there is no blanket rule of exclusion of concurrent liability.

Lister v Romford Ice and Cold Storage Co Ltd [1957] AC 555: The plaintiff employer brought an action against the defendant employee to recover the amount of money which the plaintiff had had to pay to a third party who had been injured through the defendant's negligent driving. The defendant argued that there was an implied term in his contract of service that his employer would not seek to recover such monies from him. The House of Lords (by a 3:2 majority) rejected this contention and held that, on the contrary, there was an implied term in the employee's service agreement that he would indemnify the employer for damages paid by the employer to the third party in these circumstances.

The employer's action had also been founded in tort. It was not necessary for the court to decide this question in view of its holding on the contractual question. However, some of their Lordships expressed opinions which indicate that they would have upheld the plaintiff's claim in tort if it had been necessary to do so. Thus, Viscount Simonds said (at p 573): "It is trite law that a single act of negligence may give rise to a claim either in tort or for breach of a term, express or implied, in a contract. Of this, the negligence of a servant in the performance of his duty is a clear example"; and Lord Radcliffe added: "It is a familiar position in our law that the same wrongful act may be made the subject of an action either in contract or in tort at the election of the claimant, and, although the course chosen may produce certain incidental consequences which would not have followed had the other course been adopted, it is a mistake to regard the two kinds of liability as themselves necessarily exclusive of each other".

Matthews v Kuwait Bechtel Corporation [1959] 2 QB 57: The plaintiff, while working for the defendant in Kuwait under a service agreement which was governed by English law, suffered personal injury by falling into a trench. He started proceedings in England, claiming damages for his injuries. As the defendant had no residence in England, the plaintiff had to obtain leave to serve the writ out of the jurisdiction under the relevant Supreme Court rule.

In accordance with this rule, such service was permissible only if the plaintiff's claim was based on a breach of contract by the defendant. The Court of Appeal held that such a claim could indeed be based on an implied term of the contract of employment. In so holding, the Court approved the employee's right to sue the employer concurrently in contract and in tort. Sellers LJ said (at p 67): "The argument of counsel for the defendant was that the common law imposes certain duties upon employers in regard to the safety of workmen in the course of their work, but the obligation so imposed, it was said, is entirely in tort. That the duties arose from the common law, I think is established. The question is whether those duties are [also] contractual duties. The authorities to which I have referred show that there may be implied terms of the contract. It is at the election of the workman in circumstances such as these whether to sue in contract or in tort. In this case, if it suits his purpose, he may sue in contract".

Esso Petroleum Co Ltd v Mardon [1976] 1 QB 801 (the facts of which are set out in para 9.7.8, *above*): The defendant submitted that, as the negotiations between itself and the plaintiff had resulted in a contract between them, its rights and duties were governed by the law of contract and not the law of tort. The purpose of this submission was to prevent the plaintiff being able to place reliance on the principle established by the House of Lords in *Hedley Byrne and Co Ltd v Heller & Partners Ltd* [1964] AC 465 (see Chapter 9, para 9.4), that a defendant can, in certain circumstances, be held liable to a plaintiff in tort for economic loss suffered by the plaintiff through relying on a negligent statement made by the defendant.

The Court of Appeal rejected the defendant's contention, and upheld the plaintiff's claim against the defendant in tort, notwithstanding that there was also a contract between the parties. Lord Denning MR said (at p 819) that the cases relied upon by the defendant's counsel, namely *Groom v Crocker*, *Clark v Kirby-Smith* and *Bagot v Stevens Scanlan* (see *below*) were "in conflict with other decisions of high authority which were not cited in them. These other decisions show that, in the case of a professional man, the duty to use reasonable care arises not only in contract, but is also imposed by the law apart from contract, and is therefore actionable in tort. It is comparable to the duty of reasonable care which is owed by a master to his servant, or *vice versa*. It can be put either in contract or in tort: see *Lister v Romford Ice and Cold Storage* and *Matthews v Kuwait Bechtel Corporation* [see *above*]".

Batty v Metropolitan Property Realisations Ltd [1978] 1 QB 554: The Court of Appeal held that the plaintiff house owner, who suffered loss through the negligence of the defendant builder in constructing the plaintiff's house for him, was entitled to have judgment entered against the defendant in contract and in tort. The Court rejected the defendant's contention that the principle of concurrent liability upheld by the Court of Appeal in *Esso Petroleum* was limited to cases where the common law duty is owed by a person who conducts a 'common calling', and is thus under a special type of legal liability, and to cases where the duty is owed by a professional man in respect of his professional skill. Megaw LJ said (at p 566): "I see no reason in logic or on practical grounds for putting any such limitation on the scope of the right. In my judgment the plaintiff was entitled here to have judgment entered in his favour on the basis of tortious liability as well as on the basis of breach of contract, assuming that the plaintiff had established a breach by the defendant of its common law duty of care owed to him".

Midland Bank Trust Co Ltd v Hett, Stubbs & Kemp (A Firm) [1979] 1 Ch 384: The plaintiff's claim against his solicitor, the defendant, for economic loss suffered through the solicitor's negligent conduct of a certain matter was statute-barred in contract. The plaintiff therefore founded his action in tort. The court held that he was entitled to do so, notwithstanding that the solicitor's negligent acts had been committed in the course of, and were covered by the terms of, the contract which had existed between the parties. Oliver J (now Lord Oliver) held that *Groom v Crocker* (see *below*) had been overruled by *Hedley Byrne*. After quoting the following words of Lord Morris in *Hedley Byrne* (at p 502): "If someone possessed of a special skill undertakes, quite irrespective of contract, to apply that skill for the assistance of another person who relies upon such skill, a duty of care will arise"; he said (at p 411): "This principle was stated by Lord Morris as a perfectly general one, and it is difficult to see why it should be excluded by the fact that the relationship of dependence and reliance between the parties is a contractual one, rather than one gratuitously assumed, in the absence, of course, of contractual terms excluding or restricting the general duties which the law implies. Logically, this [ie only a contractual remedy in these circumstances] could be so only if there is read into every contract a term to the effect that the contract shall be the conclusive and exclusive source of all duties owed by one party to the other to the exclusion of any further or more extensive duties which the general law would otherwise impose".

Oliver J said that *Hedley Byrne* establishes a general principle of liability arising from the relationship created between the defendant and the plaintiff by the assumption of a particular responsibility by the defendant, quite regardless of how the relationship arose. He said (at p 413): "The enquiry upon which the court is to embark is, 'What is the relationship between the plaintiff and the defendant?', not 'How did the relationship, if any, arise?'" Oliver J also rejected the test enunciated by Diplock LJ (sitting as a single High Court judge) in *Bagot v Stevens Scanlan* (see *below*) that a cause of action would necessarily have to be in contract alone if the defendant had "failed to do the very thing which he had contracted to do". With reference to this *dictum*, Oliver J said (at p 416): "The form of the breach cannot affect the nature of the duty, nor does an obligation imposed by law become an obligation different in quality simply because the obligee agrees to accept money for its performance. If an accountant gratuitously undertakes to render a careful and accurate report on a company's affairs to one whom he knows is relying and will act upon it, and he renders a careless and inaccurate report, he has failed to do the very thing that he undertook to do. But that is merely a description of his failure, not an analysis of his duty".

Oliver J pointed to the anomaly of the principle enunciated in *Groom v Crocker* (see *below*) by saying (at p 417): "A solicitor who gratuitously advises a relative, and does it negligently, remains liable to suit at any time within six years of damage occurring. A solicitor who charges a substantial fee to a client who retains his services in the normal way escapes all liability if the damage does not occur, or is not discovered until six years has elapsed from the date on which the negligent advice is given".

Coupland v Arabian Gulf Oil Co [1983] 1 WLR 1136: The plaintiff had been injured while working in Libya for the defendant oil company under a contract governed by Libyan law. The plaintiff sued the defendant in England. The court had no jurisdiction in so far as the plaintiff's claim was based on contract, but would have had jurisdiction if the plaintiff was entitled to sue the defendant in tort for his injuries. The Court of Appeal held that the plaintiff was indeed entitled to sue the defendant in tort for his damages, notwithstanding the existence of the formal contract of employment between the parties. Robert Goff LJ (now Lord Goff) said (at p 1153): "I ask myself: what impact does the existence of the contract have on the claim in tort? In my judgment, on ordinary principles, the contract is only relevant to the claim in tort in so far as it does, on its true construction, have the effect of excluding or restricting the tortious claim".

Thake v Maurice [1986] 1 QB 644: The Court of Appeal held that the defendant surgeon's failure to warn the plaintiffs (a husband and wife) of the slight risk that the husband might again become fertile after the vasectomy operation which the defendant had performed on the husband amounted to a breach of the duty of care that he owed to the plaintiffs, and was sufficient to found an action in negligence, both in contract and in tort. The Privy Council's decision in *Tai Hing* (see *below*), delivered four months earlier, was not referred to. The Court did not question, and in fact endorsed, the fact that the plaintiffs' claim was pleaded both in contract and in tort. On the other hand, this might have been because, in the circumstances of the case, there was no difference between these claims. This appears from Kerr LJ's statement (at p 679): "For present purposes, I do not think that it is necessary to distinguish between them [ie the plaintiffs' claim in contract and in tort]".

Forsikringsaktieselskapet Vesta v Butcher [1989] 1 AC 852: In the Court of Appeal (the case also went to the House of Lords on another point), in the context of the question whether the court had power to apportion liability under the Law Reform (Contributory Negligence) Act 1945, which only applies to tortious claims, O'Connor LJ said (at p 860): "I start by pointing out that Vesta [the plaintiff] pleaded its claim against the brokers in contract and in tort. This is but a recognition of what I regard as a clearly established principle that, where under the general law a person owes a duty to another to exercise reasonable care and skill in some activity, a breach of that duty gives rise to a claim in tort, notwithstanding the fact that the activity is the subject matter of a contract between them. In such a case the breach of duty will also be a breach of contract. The classic example of this situation is the relationship between doctor and patient".

Youell v Bland Welch & Co Ltd (No 2) [1990] 2 Lloyd's Rep 431: The question was whether the defendant insurance brokers could set up a partial defence of contributory negligence against the plaintiff underwriters when sued by them for damages suffered through their failure to tell the plaintiff about certain risks. A defence of contributory negligence under the Law Reform (Contributory Negligence) Act 1945 is only available if the cause of action is in tort. The court held that this defence was available in this case, thereby rejecting the plaintiff's submission that, where a contract creates a relationship of proximity between two parties, the implied obligations arising out of that relationship of proximity should properly be considered only as obligations in contract, and not in tort.

In rejecting this submission, Phillips J said at p458: "When a Lloyd's broker accepts instructions from a client, he implicitly undertakes to exercise reasonable skill and care in relation to his client's interests in accordance with the practice at Lloyd's. That general duty will normally require the broker to perform a number of different activities on behalf of the client, but the performance of those activities constitutes no more than the discharge of the duty to exercise reasonable skill and care. Failure to perform one of the activities will normally constitute a breach of that duty of care, not a breach of absolute obligation [under contract alone]. . . In these circumstances, it is unnecessary to do more than acknowledge that the existence of a cause of action in tort for the careless performance of a contractual duty undoubtedly can exist in appropriate circumstances, and that there are weighty considerations in favour of the view that the tortious liability may extend even to a case where the complaint is that the defendant omitted to do something which the contract required him to do".

Cases against concurrent liability

Notwithstanding that the House of Lords in *Henderson v Merrett Syndicates Ltd* [1995] 2 AC 145 has rejected conclusively the approach that a plaintiff with concurrent claims in contract and tort is confined to his contractual claims, some of the cases that so held are mentioned *below* (the list was much longer in the first edition of this book) because these cases were referred to by Lord Goff in *Henderson* and because these cases illustrate the diverse range of situations in which questions of concurrency can arise.

Jarvis v Moy, Davies, Smith, Vandervell and Company [1936] 1 KB 399: The plaintiff had successfully sued the defendant firm of stockbrokers for the damages which he had sustained through their breaching his instructions as to the purchase of certain shares. The question for the court was whether the plaintiff's costs should be taxed on the scale applicable to a cause of action in contract or on that applicable to a cause of action in tort. The

Court of Appeal held that the plaintiff's action was founded on contract and that this excluded any claim in tort. Greer LJ said (at p 404): "In my judgment it is impossible to regard the plaintiff's action, either in form or in substance, as other than an action for breach of contract. The defendants were employed by the plaintiff under the contract made between the plaintiff as client and the defendants as stockbrokers; their duties were regulated by the contract; and it is only by proving that a term of the contract was broken that any cause of action can be established".

Groom v Crocker [1939] 1 K B 194: The plaintiff alleged that he had suffered mental damage as a result of the defendant solicitors' negligent conduct of his motor accident claim. Such a claim could only succeed in tort, and not in contract. The Court of Appeal held that the plaintiff was not entitled to sue the defendant in tort for this loss because the solicitor's duty to his client lay in contract alone, and, as that duty did not include a duty not to cause mental anguish to the client (even if the case was not conducted properly), the plaintiff had no right to sue the defendant in tort. Sir Wilfrid Greene MR said (at p 205): "In my opinion, the cause of action is in contract and not in tort. The duty of the defendants was to conduct the case properly on behalf of the plaintiff as their client. The relationship of solicitor and client is a contractual one. It was by virtue of that relationship that the duty arose and it had no existence apart from that relationship"; and Scott LJ said (at p 222): "A solicitor, as a professional man, is employed by a client just as much as a doctor, an architect or a stockbroker, and the mutual rights and duties of the two are regulated entirely by the contract of employment".

Clark v Kirby-Smith [1964] 1 Ch 506: This was a solicitor's negligence case in which the plaintiff's counsel contended that the principle enunciated in *Groom v Crocker* (see *above*) had been abolished by the House of Lords' decision in *Hedley Byrne & Co Ltd v Heller and Partners Ltd* [1964] AC 465 (see Chapter 9, para 9.4), which "has made professional negligence a cause of action in tort". The court rejected this submission. Plowman J said (at p 510): "I do not accept the argument that *Hedley Byrne* is an authority for saying that the liability of a solicitor to his client for negligence is a liability in tort. A line of cases going back for nearly 150 years shows, I think, that the client's cause of action is in contract and not in tort".

Bagot v Stevens Scanlan & Co Ltd [1966] 1 QB 197: The plaintiff building owner sued the defendant firm of architects in tort for damages sustained by him through their having negligently performed certain services in relation to his premises. The contractual limitation period had expired, and the plaintiff therefore founded his action in tort. The court rejected it. Basing himself on Greer LJ's above-quoted *dictum* in *Jarvis*, Diplock LJ, sitting as a single High Court judge, said (at p 204): "It seems to me that, in this case, the relationship which created the duty of exercising reasonable skill and care by the architects to their clients arose out of the contract, and not otherwise. The complaint that is made against them is of a failure to do the very thing which they contracted to do. That was the relationship which gave rise to the duty which was broken. It was a contractual relationship, a contractual duty and any action brought for failure to comply with that duty is, in my view, an action founded on contract. It is also, in my view, an action founded upon contract alone".

Cook v Swinfen [1967] 1 WLR 457: The Court of Appeal rejected the plaintiff's claim in tort for damages from her solicitor for the severe anxiety and breakdown in health which she suffered through his negligence in conducting her divorce. Such a claim could only be founded in tort. Lord Denning MR said (at p 461): "The cause of action is one for breach of contract. An action against a solicitor is always one for breach of contract, as was held in *Groom v Crocker* [see *above*]".

It should be noted that this appears to be the exact opposite of what Lord Denning said ten years later in *Esso Petroleum Co Ltd v Mardon* (see *above*).

Tai Hing Cotton Mill Ltd v Liu Chong Hing Bank Ltd [1986] 1 AC 80: The terms of the plaintiff's contract with the defendant bank included a requirement that the plaintiff, as the bank's customer, should notify the defendant within a specified time of any errors in its monthly bank statements, which would otherwise be deemed to be correct. The plaintiff suffered extensive economic loss through the bank's debiting its account over a period of four years in respect of 300 cheques on which the plaintiff's accounts clerk had forged the managing director's signature. The plaintiff had not been in the habit of checking its bank statements, and had not noticed these debits. The plaintiff sought to recover these losses from the defendant in accordance with the established principle that a banker who pays out on a forged cheque of its customer will be liable to reimburse the customer unless the customer has personally been negligent in allowing the cheques to be drawn.

The Privy Council upheld the plaintiff's claims. It held, first, that there was no implied term in the parties' contract that the plaintiff was obliged to check its bank statements. Secondly, the court held that the plaintiff had not, in fact, been negligent in allowing its clerk to draw cheques. Thirdly, the court rejected the defendant's contention that, even if no term could be implied into the contract between the parties that the plaintiff should examine its bank statements within a reasonable time of receiving them, the plaintiff was under a common law duty of care in tort towards the defendant to operate its bank account with reasonable care, and that this included a duty to examine its bank statements within a reasonable time after receiving them.

Lord Scarman said (at p 107): "Their Lordships do not believe that there is anything to the advantage of the law's development in searching for a liability in tort where the parties are in a contractual relationship. This is particularly so in a commercial relationship. Their Lordships believe it to be correct in principle and necessary for the avoidance of confusion to adhere to the contractual analysis: in principle, because it is a relationship in which the parties have, subject to a few exceptions, the right to determine their obligations to each other; and, for the avoidance of confusion, because different consequences follow according to whether liability arises from contract or tort, eg, in the limitation of actions".

Greater Nottingham Co-operative Society Ltd v Cementation Piling & Foundations Ltd [1989] 1 QB 71: The plaintiff building owner, who had appointed a main contractor to erect a building for it, also entered into a direct collateral contract with the defendant sub-contractor in relation to certain piling works which the defendant had contracted with the main contractor to do. In this collateral agreement, the defendant warranted to the plaintiff that it would exercise all reasonable skill and care in the design of the sub-contract works and the selection of materials, but it did not include any warranty about the manner in which the defendant would actually carry out these works. When the defendant did so negligently, and the plaintiff suffered pure economic loss in consequence (see Chapter 7, para 7.3.6), the plaintiff sued the defendant for that loss.

The plaintiff's counsel conceded that no term could be implied into the contract between the parties to the effect that the defendant would exercise reasonable skill and care in the carrying out of the sub-contract works. Therefore, the plaintiff had to found its action on the imposition of such a duty in tort. The Court of Appeal held that this was not possible. Reference has already been made *above* to the 'policy' rationale of the Court's decision (see para 7.3.6), but it is also worth noting here that Purchas LJ said (at p 99): "In considering whether there should be a concurrent but more extensive liability in tort as between the two parties arising out of the execution of the contract, it is relevant to bear in mind—(a) that the parties had an actual opportunity to define their relationship by means of contract, and took it; and (b) that the general contractual structure, as between the employers [the plaintiff], the main contractors and the sub-contractors [the defendant], provided a channel of claim which was open to the employers".

Banque Keyser Ullmann SA v Skandia (UK) Insurance Co Ltd [1990] 1 QB 665 (see Chapter 8, para 8.3.3): In the context of holding that a person (the defendant's employee) did not, during the course of conducting contractual negotiations with the plaintiffs, owe them a duty of care in tort to tell them that a third party was in the process of defrauding them, Slade LJ said (at p 800): "Lord Scarman's opinion [in *Tai Hing*] contains a valuable warning as to the consequences of an ever-expanding field of tort. It should be no part of the general function of the law of tort to fill in contractual gaps".

Bell v Peter Browne & Co [1990] 2 QB 495: This was a solicitor's negligence case in which the plaintiff's claim was statute-barred both in contract and in tort. Mustill LJ nevertheless remarked (at p 511): "I think it is a pity that English law has elected to recognise concurrent rights of action in contract and tort. Other legal systems seem to manage quite well by limiting attention to the contractual obligations which are, after all, the foundation of the relationship between the professional man and his client: as, for example, in the case of French law via the doctrine of *non cumul*. That precisely the same breach of precisely the same obligation should be capable of generating causes of action which arise at different times is, in my judgment, an anomaly which our law could well do without. Nevertheless, the law is clear and we must apply it".

Scally v Southern Health and Social Services Board [1992] 1 AC 294: By virtue of certain regulations employees of some health boards were entitled to purchase additional years of pension entitlement on advantageous terms. This right was exercisable only within 12 months of the coming into force of the regulations. The plaintiffs, four doctors who each required to purchase added years in order to qualify for full pension benefits, had not been informed by their employer (the defendant) of their right to do so. When they found out about this right only after the 12-month period had elapsed, they brought actions against the defendant for damages for breach of contract and/or negligence.

The House of Lords held that a term was properly to be implied into the plaintiffs' contracts of employment to the effect that the employer was under a duty to take reasonable steps to inform the plaintiffs of the regulations. The court, therefore, did not need to consider the plaintiffs' claims in tort, but the House of Lords made it clear that it would not have been prepared to countenance these claims in any event. Thus, Lord Bridge said (at p 302): "It seems to me that the plaintiffs' common law claims can only succeed if the duty allegedly owed to them by their employers arose out of the contract of employment. If a duty of the kind in question was not inherent in the contractual relationship, I do not see how it could possibly be derived from the tort of negligence. The observations of Lord Scarman in *Tai Hing Cotton Mill v Liu Chong Hing Bank* are here very much in point".

Lord Bridge set out Lord Scarman's comments in full and then continued (at p 303): "In the instant case, I believe that an attempt to analyse the issue in terms of the law of tort may be positively misleading. If the question is framed in terms of the law of negligence, it takes the form: 'Did the employers owe a duty of care to employees to save them from economic loss consequent on a failure to purchase added years of pensionable entitlement in due time?' The strong trend of recent authority has been to narrow the range of circumstances which the law of tort will recognise as sufficient to impose on one person a duty of care to protect another from damage which consists of pure economic loss".

Hiron v Pynford South Ltd (1992) 28 EG 112 (see Chapter 7, para 7.3.6): The judge reviewed some of the conflicting decisions on concurrent liability and said (at p 115): "While it may be that the courts are moving towards a more restrictive view of duties of care when there is a contract between the parties, it seems clear that at present the mere existence of a contract does not preclude liability in tort. I think that the correct approach is that when there was a contract between the plaintiff and the defendant, it should be treated as a very important consideration in deciding whether there was sufficient proximity between them and whether it is just and reasonable that the defendant should owe a duty in tort".

The particular issue raising the question of concurrent liability was whether the insurers of the first plaintiff's house (the second plaintiff) could sue the structural engineers (the third defendant) in tort, as its contractual claim was statute-barred. The judge refused to allow this. He said (at p 115): "Since the second plaintiffs and the third defendants had entered into an express contract whereby the third defendants were to advise the second plaintiffs in return for payment, and a duty in tort to take care in giving advice would merely have duplicated an implied term in the contract, I do not think it was just and reasonable that the third defendant should have owed a duty in tort. The only probable result of adding a tortious obligation would have been to have given the second plaintiff a longer period in which to sue the defendant, but if that had been the intention of the parties, they could have provided for it in their contract. The position would probably have been different if contractual and tortious duties had not precisely coincided".

Ashmore v The Corporation of Lloyd's (No 2) [1992] 2 Lloyd's Rep 620: The question was whether the Corporation of Lloyd's owed the Names at Lloyd's an implied duty to alert them of matters which might affect their underwriting interests. The Names' claim had been framed alternatively as an implied term of the membership agreement between Lloyd's and each Name and as a common law duty of care in tort. However, they did not pursue the tortious claim at the hearing. The judge (Gatehouse J) approved of this concession. He said: "The law is now clearly settled following *Tai Hing Cotton Mill v Liu Chong Hing Bank*, and the plaintiffs accept that if they do not succeed in contract, they cannot do so in tort".

10.4.4 Overseas cases

Space does not permit a full discussion of how the question of concurrent liability is approached in other jurisdictions. Reference must, however, be made to certain Canadian authorities which have considered the question.

In *Central Trust Co v Rafuse* (1987) 31 DLR (4th) 481, a solicitor's negligence case, the Supreme Court of Canada reviewed the relevant cases in several jurisdictions and then drew the following conclusions (at p 521):

(1) The common law duty of care that is created by a relationship of sufficient proximity is not confined to relationships that arise apart from contract. Although the relationships in *Donoghue v Stevenson*, *Hedley Byrne* and *Anns* were all of a non-contractual nature, and there was necessarily reference in the judgments to a duty of care that exists independently of contract, I [Le Dane J, delivering the unanimous decision of the court] find nothing in the

statements of general principle in those cases to suggest that the principle was intended to be confined to relationships that arise apart from contract. Indeed, the *dictum* of Lord Macmillan in *Donoghue* concerning concurrent liability [see *above*] would clearly suggest the contrary. I also find this conclusion to be persuasively demonstrated, with particular reference to *Hedley Byrne*, by the judgment of Oliver J in *Midland Bank Trust v Hett, Stubbs & Kemp* [see *above*]. As he suggests, the question is whether there is a relationship of sufficient proximity, not how it arose.

(2) What is undertaken by the contract will indicate the nature of the relationship that gives rise to the common law duty of care, but the nature and scope of the duty of care that is asserted as the foundation of the tortious liability must not depend on specific obligations or duties created by the express terms of the contract. It is in that sense that the common law duty of care must be independent of the contract.

(3) A concurrent or alternative liability in tort will not be admitted if its effect would be to permit the plaintiff to circumvent a contractual exclusion of liability for the act or omission that would constitute the tort. Subject to this qualification, where concurrent liability in tort and contract exists, the plaintiff has the right to assert the cause of action that appears to be most advantageous to him in respect of any particular legal consequence.

In *Canadian Pacific Hotels Ltd v Bank of Montreal* (1987) 40 DLR (4th) 385, whose facts were almost the same as those in *Tai Hing*, the Supreme Court purported to add a *caveat* to its decision in *Central Trust* when Le Dane J said (at p 432): "I am of the opinion that the principle of concurrent or alternate liability in contract and in tort affirmed in *Rafuse* cannot extend to the recognition of a duty of care in tort when that same duty of care has been rejected or excluded by the courts as an implied term of a particular clause of contract". In fact, however, this is not really a qualification of the principles enunciated by the Supreme Court in *Central Trust Co v Rafuse*, but rather is no more than a particular application of the principle mentioned in the first sentence of point (3) quoted *above*.

In *BG Checo International Ltd v British Columbia Hydro and Power Authority* (1993) 99 DLR (4th) 577 (also considered in para 10.4.2, *above*), the defendant had made a negligent misrepresentation in a document calling for tenders to erect electrical power lines. The misrepresentation related to who, as between the tenderers, the employers under the contract (the defendant) and external third parties, would be responsible for the cost of clearing the right of way through which the power lines and their towers would pass. The tender documents stated that the clearing of the right of way would be done by others and would form no part of the work to be performed by the tenderer to whom the contract would be awarded. The plaintiff priced its tender accordingly, and the contract was awarded to the plaintiff.

The parties entered into a written contract which contained the above-mentioned representation, and indeed incorporated all of the terms and conditions of the tender documents. The tender documents and the contract also stated that it was the plaintiff's responsibility to inform itself of all aspects of the work, and that, should any errors appear in the tender documents, or should the plaintiff note any conditions conflicting with the letter or spirit of the tender documents, it was the responsibility of the plaintiff to obtain clarification before submitting its tender.

Before submitting its tender, the plaintiff inspected the right of way by helicopter and found it to be partially cleared. The plaintiff did not discuss this question further with the defendant because it assumed that the defendant would arrange for the right of way to be fully cleared. In fact, no further clearing took place by the defendant or any third parties. The plaintiff had to have this work done at great expense and loss to itself. The plaintiff sued the defendant for these losses on the basis of breach of contract and negligent misrepresentation in tort.

The Supreme Court of Canada unanimously upheld the plaintiff's contractual claim, but it was divided 4:2 on the question whether the plaintiff was entitled, in the alternative, to tortious relief. The majority held that the plaintiff was so entitled, because the terms of the contract, despite the defendant's obvious attempt, did not exclude or limit the defendant's duty of care in tort for negligent misrepresentation. The minority did not feel that it was necessary to consider this question because they were of the view that the plaintiff's claim in tort was automatically barred by virtue of the fact that the defendant's duty in tort was co-extensive with the defendant's duty created by an express term of the contract in relation to the same subject matter, namely, negligent misrepresentations. As discussed in para 10.4.2, *above*, it is submitted that the minority's view on this aspect of the case is wrong.

In *Winnipeg Condominium Corp No 36 v Bird Construction Co* (1995) 121 DLR (4th) 193 (which is considered further in Chapter 7, para 7.6.3), La Forest J, writing for the unanimous bench of the Supreme Court of Canada, offered some observations which could cause confusion about the role of the doctrine of concurrent liability and which could create a misleading impression about the state of English law on the concurrency issue. With reference to the House of Lords' decision in *D & F Estates Ltd v Church Commissioners for England* [1989] AC 177 (which is discussed in detail in Chapter 7), La Forest J said (at p 204):

> I think it is important to clarify why the *D & F Estates* case should not be seen as having strong persuasive authority in Canadian law as that law is currently developing. My reasons for coming to this conclusion are twofold: first, to the extent that the decision of the House of Lords in *D & F Estates* rests upon the assumption that liability in tort for the cost of repair of defective houses represents an unjustifiable intrusion of tort into the contractual sphere, it is inconsistent with recent Canadian decisions recognising the possibility of concurrent contractual and tortious duties.

La Forest J elaborated on this statement by saying: "I observe that it is now well-established in Canada that a duty of care in tort may arise co-extensively with a contractual duty"; and he then referred extensively to the Supreme Court of Canada's decision in *Central Trust Co v Rafuse* (see *above*).

10.4.4 *The contractual connection*

Two criticisms can be made of La Forest J's above-quoted *dictum*. First, no reference was made of the fact that the House of Lords, in its decision in *Henderson v Merrett Syndicates Ltd* [1995] 2 AC 145 (which was rendered on 25 July 1994 and reported in the All England Reports soon afterwards and in the Weekly Law Reports on 19 August 1994, ie some six months before the Supreme Court of Canada's decision in *Winnipeg Condominium*, which was rendered on 26 January 1995), adopted wholeheartedly the concurrency principle in English law and, indeed, specifically agreed with the reasoning of the Supreme Court of Canada in *Central Trust Co v Rafuse* (see para 10.4.2, *above*). Secondly, it is important to note that neither *D & F Estates* nor *Winnipeg Condominium* had anything to do with concurrent liability. Both cases were concerned with the liability in tort of a builder to a third party with whom the builder did not have a contractual relationship (for economic loss consisting of the diminution in value of the building caused by the builder's negligence). Nevertheless, La Forest J remarked (at p 205):

> I emphasise the fact that contractual and tortious duties can arise concurrently in Canadian law because, in my view, the decision in *D & F Estates* was based at least in part upon the assumption that a duty on the part of contractors to take reasonable care in the construction of buildings can only arise in contract. In deciding that the contractor in that case could not be held liable in tort for the cost of repairing the defective plaster, Lord Bridge expressed a concern that the imposition of a tort duty upon a contractor to third parties would be to impose, in effect, a contractual duty in tort. He stated at p 1007:
>
>> To make the contractor so liable would be to impose on him, for the benefit of those with whom he had no contractual relationship, the obligation of one who warranted the quality of the plaster as regards materials, workmanship and fitness for purpose. I am glad to reach the conclusion that this is not the law.
>
> However, in light of this court's decision in *Rafuse*, I do not believe that Lord Bridge's concern should preclude conceptualising Bird's duty in tortious terms.

It is submitted that La Forest J is obfuscating some important distinctions that were made in the Supreme Court of Canada in *Central Trust v Rafuse* and in the House of Lords in *D & F Estates*. In *Central Trust*, the distinction was drawn between cases where the plaintiff and the defendant had a contract with each other, and cases like *Donoghue v Stevenson* [1932] AC 562 (see Chapter 6) where the defendant's possible exposure is to a third party with whom the defendant did not have a contract, but some attention was paid to the fact that the plaintiff and the defendant both had contracts with an intermediate third party.

The importance of this distinction is that in the first of these types of cases, where the plaintiff and the defendant had a contract with each other, the question in a tort context is whether the existence of that contract precludes the imposition by a court of a concurrent tortious duty on the defendant to the plaintiff. In answering this question, the intention of the plaintiff and the defendant, ascertained by the court's construction of their contract, is paramount; and the rule is that, if a tortious duty would exist in the circumstances even if there were no contract, the plaintiff is entitled to pursue the tort remedy as an alternative to the contractual remedy except where, and to the extent that, the plaintiff and the defendant have contractually agreed to limit or exclude it.

This type of analysis takes place only in cases where the plaintiff and the defendant had a contract with each other. If, in cases like *Donoghue v Stevenson* and *D & F Estates*, where the plaintiff and the defendant did not have a contract with each other, the court expresses the view that the *type* of liability sought to be imposed (eg liability in tort for economic loss consisting in the diminution in value of a building caused by the builder's negligence) is more appropriately governed by the law of contract, such comments will not be related to, or dependent on, whether or not the legal system in the jurisdiction in question recognises the doctrine of concurrent liability.

Thus, in *D & F Estates*, where there was no contractual relationship between the defendant and the plaintiff, when Lord Bridge said that he objected to imposing liability on the contractor for the plaintiff's economic loss consisting of the diminution in the value of the building due to the contractor's negligence because that might give rise to a transmissible warranty of quality in tort, he was not influenced in this view by the fact that, at that time, it was arguable that English law did not fully recognise the principle of concurrent liability described *above*. Lord Bridge's concern arose for an entirely different reason, namely, the difficulty that the court perceived it would face in trying to determine the standard of quality that should suffice on the question of defectiveness in any particular case (see Chapter 7, para 7.5.7).

The critical distinction that the House of Lords made in *D & F Estates* was between a difference that the House of Lords perceived in two types of cases in the same *genus*, namely, tort cases where the defendant and the plaintiff did not have a contractual relationship with each other. In the first type of case, the question is whether the defendant should be liable to the plaintiff in tort for the plaintiff's personal injuries or damage to the plaintiff's property other than the defectively manufactured product or the defectively constructed building (see Chapter 6). *Donoghue v Stevenson* is an example of this type of case. In the second type of case, the question is whether the defendant should be held liable in tort for the plaintiff's pure economic loss consisting of the diminution in value of the defectively manufactured product or defectively constructed building. *D & F Estates* is an example of this type of case.

The distinction that the House of Lords drew in *D & F Estates* was between non-contractual cases where the plaintiff suffered a physical injury, like *Donoghue v Stevenson*, and non-contractual cases, like *D & F Estates*, where the plaintiff was suing for pure economic loss. Lord Bridge's above-mentioned concern about the creation of a transmissible warranty of quality in tort was a by-product of this distinction and had nothing to do with whether or not, in cases where the defendant and the plaintiff did have a contractual relationship with each other, the plaintiff should be entitled to assert the existence of a duty of care in tort by the defendant concurrently with the duty that existed between them under their contract.

Ironically, and despite La Forest J's above-cited remarks, the same concern that Lord Bridge expressed in *D & F Estates* about the creation of a transmissible warranty of quality in tort in cases where the defendant and the plaintiff did not have a contractual relationship with each other exists in Canadian law in relation to 'non-dangerous' defects in products and buildings even after the Supreme Court of Canada's decision in *Winnipeg Condominium* (see Chapter 7, para 7.6.3); and it continues to exist despite the fact that Canadian law has, since 1986 (in *Central Trust v Rafuse*), recognised that contractual and tortious duties can arise concurrently.

Index